GO!
with Microsoft®
Office 2016
All in One, Third Edition

**Shelley Gaskin,
Debra Geoghan,
Nancy Graviett, and
Alicia Vargas**

PEARSON

Boston   Columbus   Indianapolis   New York   San Francisco
Amsterdam   Cape Town   Dubai   London   Madrid   Milan   Munich   Paris   Montréal   Toronto
Delhi   Mexico City   São Paulo   Sydney   Hong Kong   Seoul   Singapore   Taipei   Tokyo

Vice President, Career Skills: Andrew Gilfillan
Executive Editor: Jenifer Niles
Project Manager: Holly Haydash
Team Lead, Project Management: Laura Burgess
Development Editor: Nancy Lamm
Editorial Assistant: Michael Campbell
Director of Product Marketing: Maggie Waples
Director of Field Marketing: Leigh Ann Sims
Product Marketing Manager: Kaylee Carlson
Field Marketing Managers: Molly Schmidt and Joanna Conley
Marketing Coordinator: Susan Osterlitz
Operations Specialist: Maura Zaldivar-Garcia
Senior Art Director: Diane Ernsberger
Interior and Cover Design: Cenveo
Project Manager, Permissions: Karen Sanatar

Cover Photos: GaudiLab, Rawpixel.com, Pressmaster, Eugenio Marongiu, Boggy, Gajus, Rocketclips, Inc
Associate Director of Design: Blair Brown
Vice President, Product Strategy: Jason Fournier
Director of Media Development: Blaine Christine
Senior Product Strategy Manager: Eric Hakanson
Product Team Lead, IT: Zachary Alexander
Course Producer, IT: Amanda Losonsky
Digital Project Manager, MyITLab: Becca Lowe
Media Project Manager, Production: John Cassar
Full-Service Project Management: Lumina Datamatics, Inc.
Composition: Lumina Datamatics, Inc.
Printer/Binder: RR Donnelley/Menasha
Cover Printer: Phoenix Color
Text Font: Times LT Pro
Efficacy Curriculum Manager: Jessica Sieminski

Library of Congress Control Number: 2016930975

10 9 8 7 6 5 4 3 2 1

ISBN 10: 0-13-450574-3
ISBN 13: 978-0-13-450574-9

Brief Contents

Excel

Access

PowerPoint

Table of Contents

Introducing Microsoft Excel 2016 **671**

Chapter 15 Creating a Worksheet and Charting Data....................**673**

Introduction to Microsoft Access 2016 **815**

Chapter 17 Using Microsoft Access 2016..................... **817**

xviii   Table of Contents

About the Authors

Shelley Gaskin, Series Editor, is a professor in the Business and Computer Technology Division at Pasadena City College in Pasadena, California. She holds a bachelor's degree in Business Administration from Robert Morris College (Pennsylvania), a master's degree in Business from Northern Illinois University, and a doctorate in Adult and Community Education from Ball State University (Indiana). Before joining Pasadena City College, she spent 12 years in the computer industry, where she was a systems analyst, sales representative, and director of Customer Education with Unisys Corporation. She also worked for Ernst & Young on the development of large systems applications for their clients. She has written and developed training materials for custom systems applications in both the public and private sector, and has also written and edited numerous computer application textbooks.

This book is dedicated to my students, who inspire me every day.

Alicia Vargas is a faculty member in Business Information Technology at Pasadena City College. She holds a master's and a bachelor's degree in business education from California State University, Los Angeles, and has authored several textbooks and training manuals on Microsoft Word, Microsoft Excel, and Microsoft PowerPoint.

This book is dedicated with all my love to my husband Vic, who makes everything possible; and to my children Victor, Phil, and Emmy, who are an unending source of inspiration and who make everything worthwhile.

Nancy Graviett is a professor and department chair in Business Technology at St. Charles Community College in Cottleville, Missouri. She holds a bachelor's degree in marketing and a master's degree in business education from the University of Missouri and has completed a certificate in online education. Nancy has authored textbooks on WordPerfect, Google, Microsoft Outlook and Microsoft Access.

This book is dedicated to my husband, Dave, and my children, Matthew and Andrea. I cannot thank my family enough for the love and support they share everyday.

Debra Geoghan is a Professor of Computer Science in the STEM department at Bucks County Community College, teaching computer classes ranging from basic computer literacy to cybercrime, computer forensics, and networking. She has certifications from Microsoft, CompTIA, and Apple. Deb has taught at the college level since 1996 and also spent 11 years in the high school classroom. She holds a B.S. in Secondary Science Education from Temple University and an M.A. in Computer Science Education from Arcadia University.

Throughout her teaching career Deb has worked with educators to integrate technology across the curriculum. At BCCC she serves on many technology committees, presents technology workshops for BCCC faculty, and heads the Computer Science Area. Deb is an avid user of technology, which has earned her the nickname "gadget lady."

This book is dedicated to my colleagues and students at Bucks County Community College: for your suggestions and encouragement throughout this process. You inspire me every day. And most importantly—my family. My husband and sons for your patience, help, and love—I couldn't have done this without your love and support.

GO! All in One, Third Edition

All in One
ncepts & Applications

HIRD EDITION

S GEOGHAN GRAVIETT

GO! with Office 2016 is the right approach to learning for today's fast-moving, mobile environment. The GO! Series focuses on the *job* and *success* skills students need to succeed in the workforce.

With *GO! All in One*, you can teach Computer Concepts and Applications together—the way it is in the real world! Engage your students right away by focusing on jobs and incorporating cloud computing and collaboration in a logical way. And, put concepts into action using a unique, integrated, jobs-focused, unit approach, or take an IC3 approach to help prepare students to take the IC3 exams. By using job-related projects, students learn Microsoft Office in the context of a real work environment. With these projects, students learn the *how* and *why* at the moment they need to know, and they never get lost because the GO! Series uses Microsoft procedural syntax.

For Office 2016, the hallmark GO! *guided practice-to-skill mastery pathway* is better than ever. Not only do students have multiple opportunities to work live in Microsoft Office to practice and apply the skills they have learned, but also the Microsoft Office

Instructional A and *B* projects are now Grader projects! This enables students to work live in Microsoft Office and receive auto-graded feedback as they learn! By combining these new instructional Grader projects with the variety of existing Grader projects and the high-fidelity simulations that match the text, students have an effective pathway for learning, practicing, and assessing their abilities.

After completing the instructional projects, students are ready to apply the skills by engaging in a wide variety of progressively challenging projects that require them to solve problems, think critically, and create projects on their own. The new *GO! with Google* projects also enable students to apply what they have learned in a different environment. The integrated *IC3* objectives make this the one resource needed to learn Computer Concepts, gain critical productivity skills, and prepare to get IC3 certified!

- **Practical**—Focuses on real-world jobs and the skills and knowledge these jobs require. Each Unit engages students with a Job Focus describing duties for various job titles.
- **Affordable**—Covers the core Computer Concepts and Applications needed all in one book.
- **Current**—Shows students how to create and collaborate by using all the latest Web tools including cloud applications such as Skype, social media, Gmail, LinkedIn, and social media such as Twitter.
- **Interactive**—Includes an interactive eText that enables students to jump right to videos, simulations, and Check Your Knowledge quizzes as they read.
- **Engaging and Flexible**—Offers two approaches to teaching:
  - **Unit-Based** in which Computer Concepts and Applications are integrated together logically with a jobs focus.
  - **IC3-Based** in which the content is covered in order of the three IC3 exams to help prepare students for these exams.

MyITLab—Is designed with the learner in mind. It provides access to all of the resources, including the interactive etext with videos, IT Concepts simulations, and quick check quizzes built in, plus the Grader Projects and Simulations for Microsoft applications.

IC3 Approach to GO! All in One

Computing Fundamentals

Living Online

Key Applications

Jobs-Focused Unit Approach to GO! All in One

What's New

NEW Coverage of new features of Office 2016 Ensures that students are learning the skills they need to work in today's job market.

NEW MyITLab 2016 Grader Projects In addition to the homework and assessment Graders already available, the Microsoft Office A and B *instructional* projects are now Graders, enabling students to *learn by doing* live in the application and receive the instant feedback they need to ensure understanding.

NEW MyITLab HTML 5 Training & Assessment Simulations for Office 2016 These simulations are written by the authors to match the pedagogical approach of the textbook projects and to provide a direct one-to-one learning experience.

NEW Google Projects For each A and B instructional project in Chapters 1–3, students construct a parallel project using Google productivity tools. This gives students the opportunity to think critically and apply what they are learning about Microsoft Office to *other* productivity tools, which is an essential job skill.

NEW IC3 Preparation IC3 objectives are integrated into the text for easy review and reference for students who are preparing for an IC3 certification exam. In MyITLab, there is a short IC3 quiz for each chapter. An IC3 appendix is also included to provide a comprehensive list of the exam objectives.

NEW Lessons on the GO! How do you teach software that is constantly updated and getting new features all the time? This new project type will cover newer Microsoft apps such as Sway and MIX and things yet to come! These lessons are found in MyITLab and the Instructor Resource Center, and come with instructional content, student data files, solutions files, and rubrics for grading.

NEW GO! To Work Page Here, students can review a summary of the chapter items focused on employability, including an IC3 Objective summary, Build Your ePortfolio guidelines, and the GO! For Job Success soft skills videos or discussions.

Application Capstone Projects and Unit Case Projects

Capstone projects for each application provide a variety of opportunities for students to ensure they have reached proficiency, and Unit Case Projects provide a combined project covering concepts and applications.

Expanded Project Summary chart This easy-to-use guide outlines all the instructional and end-of-chapter projects by category, including Instruction, Review, Mastery and Transfer of Learning, and Critical Thinking.

In-text boxed content for easy navigation *Another Way, Notes, More Knowledge, Alerts, Green Computing, On the Job, Fast Forward,* and *By Touch* instructions are included in line with the instruction—not in the margins—so students won't miss this important information and will learn it in context with what is on their screen.

MyITLab 2016 for GO! All in One Let MyITLab do the work by giving students instant feedback and saving hours of grading with GO!'s extensive Grader Project options. And the HTML5 Training and Assessment simulations provide a high-fidelity environment that provide step-by-step summary of student actions and include just-in-time learning aids to assist students: *Read, Watch, Practice.*

All other end-of-chapter projects, C, D, H, I, J, K, L, M, N, and O, have grading rubrics and solution files for easy hand grading. These are all Content-based, Outcomes-based, Problem-Solving, and Critical Thinking projects that enable you to add a variety of assessments—including authentic assessments—to evaluate a student's proficiency with the application.

IT Innovation Station Stay current with Office and Windows updates and important Microsoft and office productivity news and trends with help from your Pearson authors! Now that Microsoft Office is in the cloud, automatic updates occur regularly. These can affect how you to teach your course and the resources you are using. To keep you and your students completely up to date on the changes occurring in Office 2016 and Windows 10, we are launching the *IT Innovation Station*. This website will contain monthly updates from our product team and our author-instructors with tips for understanding updates, utilizing new capabilities, implementing new instructional techniques, and optimizing your Office use.

Why the GO! Approach Helps Students Succeed

GO! Provides Personalized Learning

MyITLab from Pearson is an online homework, training, and assessment system that will improve student results by helping students master skills and concepts through immediate feedback and a robust set of tools that allows instructors to easily gauge and address the performance of individuals and classrooms.

MyITLab learning experiences engage students using both realistic, high-fidelity simulations of Microsoft Office as well as auto-graded, live-in-the-application assignments, so they can understand concepts more thoroughly. With the ability to approach projects and problems as they would in real life—coupled with tutorials that adapt based on performance—students quickly complete skills they know and get help when and where they need it.

For educators, MyITLab establishes a reliable learning environment backed by the Pearson Education 24/7, 99.97 percent uptime service level agreement, and that includes the tools educators need to track and support both individual and class-wide student progress.

GO! Engages Students by Combining a Project-Based Approach with the Teachable Moment

GO!'s project-based approach clusters the learning objectives around the projects rather than around the software features. This tested pedagogical approach teaches students to solve real problems as they practice and learn the features.

GO! instruction is organized around student learning outcomes with numbered objectives and two instructional projects per chapter. Students can engage in a wide variety of end-of-chapter projects where they apply what they have learned in outcomes-based, problem-solving, and critical thinking projects—many of which require students to create the project from scratch.

GO! instruction is based on the teachable moment where students learn important concepts at the exact moment they are practicing the skill. The explanations and concepts are woven into the steps—not presented as paragraphs of text at the beginning of the project before students have even seen the software in action.

Each Project Opening Page clearly outlines Project Activities (what the student will do in this project), Project Files (what starting files are needed and how the student will save the files), and Project Results (what the student's finished project will look like). Additionally, to support this page, the GO! Walk Thru video gives students a 30-second overview of how the project will progress and what they will create.

GO! Demonstrates Excellence in Instructional Design

Student Learning Outcomes and Objectives are clearly defined so students understand what they will learn and what they will be able to do when they finish the chapter.

Clear Instruction provided through project steps written following Microsoft® Procedural Syntax to guide students where to go *and then* what to do, so they never get lost!

Teachable moment approach has students learn important concepts when they need to as they work through the instructional projects. No long paragraphs of text.

Clean Design presents textbook pages that are clean and uncluttered, with screenshots that validate the student's actions and that engage visual learners.

Sequential Pagination displays the pages sequentially numbered, like every other textbook a student uses, instead of using letters or abbreviations. Student don't spend time learning a new numbering approach.

Important information is boxed within the text so that students won't miss or skip the Another Way, By Touch, Note, Alert, or More Knowledge details so there are no distracting and "busy-looking" marginal notes.

Color-Coded Steps guide students through the projects with colors coded by project.

End-of-Project Icon helps students know when they have completed the project, which is especially useful in self-paced or online environments. These icons give students a clearly identifiable end point for each project.

GO! Learn How Videos provide step-by-step visual instruction for the A and B instructional projects— delivered by a real instructor! These videos provide the assistance and personal learning students may need when working on their own.

GO! Delivers Easy Course Implementation

Teach the Course You Want in Less Time

The *GO!* series' one-of-a-kind instructional system provides you with everything you need to prepare for class, teach the material, and assess your students.

Prepare

- **Office 2013 to 2016 Transition Guide** provides an easy-to-use reference for updating your course for Office 2016 using GO!
- **Annotated Instructor Tabs** provide clear guidance on how to implement your course.
- **MyITLab Implementation Guide** is provided for course planning and learning outcome alignment.
- **Syllabus templates** outline various plans for covering the content in an 8-, 12-, or 16-week course.
- **List of Chapter Outcomes and Objectives** is provided for course planning and learning outcome alignment.
- **Student Assignment Tracker** for students to track their own work.
- **Assignment Planning Guide** Description of the *GO!* assignments with recommendations based on class size, delivery method, and student needs.
- **Solution Files** Examples of homework submissions to serve as examples for students.
- **Online Study Guide for Students** Interactive objective-style questions based on chapter content.

Teach

- **Walk Thru Videos** provide a quick 30-second preview of what the student will do and create—from beginning to end—by completing each of the A and B Instructional projects. These videos increase the student's confidence by letting the student see the entire project built quickly.
- **The Annotated Instructors Edition** includes the entire student text, spiral-bound and wrapped with teaching notes and suggestions for how to implement your course.
- **Scripted Lectures** present a detailed guide for delivering live in-class demonstrations of the A and B Instructional Projects.

- **PowerPoint Presentations** provide a visual walk-through of the chapter with suggested lecture notes included.
- **Audio PowerPoint Presentations** provide a visual walk-through of the chapter with the lecture notes read out loud.

Assess

- **A scoring checklist, task-specific rubric, or analytic rubric** accompanies every assignment.
- **Prepared Exams** provide cumulative exams for each project, chapter, and application that are easy to score using the provided scoring checklist and point suggestions for each task.
- **Solution Files** are provided in three formats: native file, PDF, and annotated PDF.
- **Rubrics** provide guidelines for grading open-ended projects.
- **Testbank questions** are available for you to create your own objective-based quizzes for review.

Grader Projects

- **Projects A & B** (Guided Instruction)
- **Project E Homework** (Formative) and Assesment (Summative) (Cover Objectives in Project A)
- **Project F Homework** (Formative) and Assesment (Summative) (Cover Objectives in Project B)
- **Project G Homework** (Formative) and Assesment (Summative) (Cover Objectives in Projects A and B)
- **Application Capstone Homework** (Formative review of core objectives covered in application)
- **Application Capstone Exam** (Summative review of core objectives covered in application—generates badge with 90 percent or higher)

GO! Series Hallmarks

- **Project-Based** – Students learn by creating projects that they will use in the real world.

- **Microsoft Procedural Syntax** – Steps are written to put students in the right place at the right time.

- **Teachable Moment** – Expository text is woven into the steps—at the moment students need to know it—not chunked together in a block of text that will go unread.

- **Sequential Pagination** – Students have actual page numbers instead of confusing letters and abbreviations.

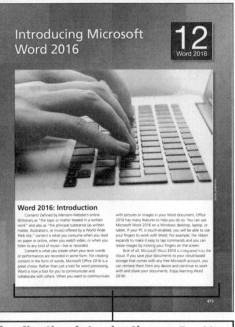

Application Introductions – Provide an overview of the application to prepare students for the upcoming chapters.

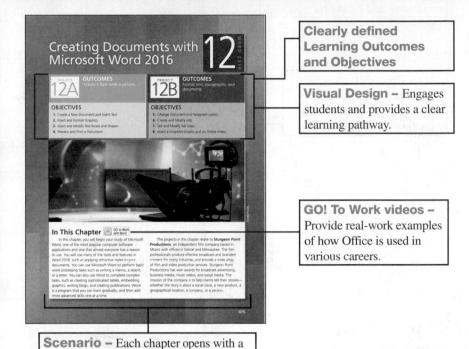

Scenario – Each chapter opens with a job-related scenario that sets the stage for the projects the student will create.

Clearly defined Learning Outcomes and Objectives

Visual Design – Engages students and provides a clear learning pathway.

GO! To Work videos – Provide real-work examples of how Office is used in various careers.

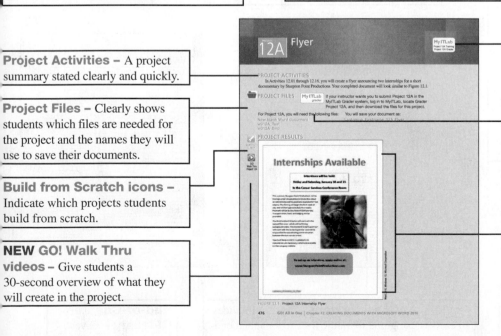

Project Activities – A project summary stated clearly and quickly.

Project Files – Clearly shows students which files are needed for the project and the names they will use to save their documents.

Build from Scratch icons – Indicate which projects students build from scratch.

NEW GO! Walk Thru videos – Give students a 30-second overview of what they will create in the project.

Simulation Training and Assessment – Give your students the most realistic Office 2016 experience with realistic, high-fidelity simulations.

NEW MyITLab Grader projects for Instructional A & B projects – Allow students to work live in the application to learn by doing.

Project Results – Shows students what successful completion looks like.

In-text Features
Another Way, Notes, More Knowledge, Alerts, and By Touch Instructions

Color Coding – Each chapter has two instructional projects, which is less overwhelming for students than one large chapter project. The projects are differentiated by different colored numbering and headings.

MOS Objectives – Are highlighted throughout the text to provide a review and exam prep reference.

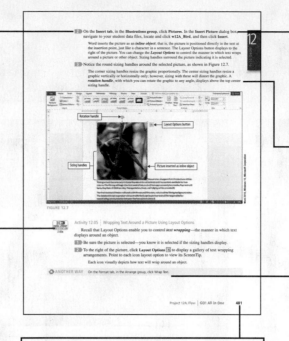

FIGURE 12.7

Microsoft Procedural Syntax – Steps are written to put the student at the right place at the right time.

Teachable Moment – Expository text is woven into the steps—at the moment students need to know it—not chunked together in a block of text that will go unread.

Intext Callouts – Ensure that students will read this important material—Another Way, Notes, More Knowledge, Alerts, and By Touch instructions.

Sequential Pagination – Students are given actual page numbers to navigate through the textbook instead of confusing letters and abbreviations.

End-of-Chapter

MOS Skills Summary – List all the MOS objectives covered in the chapter.

Build Your ePortfolio – Provides guidelines for creating an effective representation of your course work.

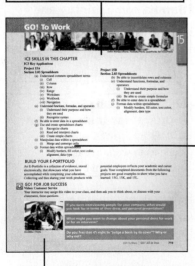

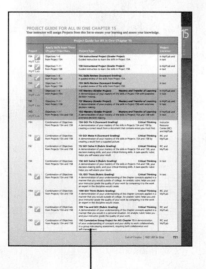

GO! For Job Success – Soft skills, videos, and discussions to prepare students with the soft skills needed for today's work environment.

Review and Assessment Chart – Provides an easy-to-use guide to all the instructional and end-of-chapter projects by category from Mastery and Transfer of Knowledge to Critical Thinking.

End-of-Chapter Glossary – Gives students an easy way to review key terms.

End-of-Chapter

Objective List – Every end-of-chapter project includes a listing of covered Objectives from Projects A and B.

Grader Projects – In addition to the two Grader Projects for the instructional portion of the chapter (Projects A and B), each chapter has six MyITLab Grader projects within the end-of-chapter material— three homework and three assessment—clearly indicated by the MyITLab logo.

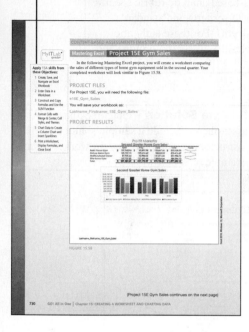

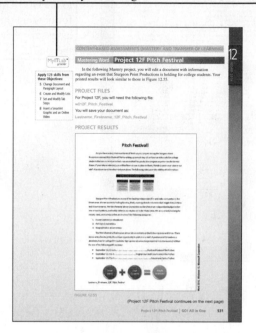

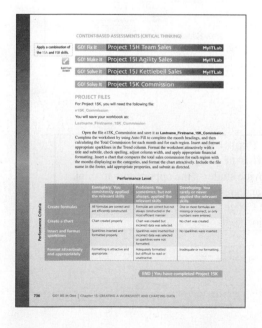

Task-Specific Rubric – A matrix specific to the GO! Solve It projects that states the criteria and standards for grading these defined-solution projects.

End-of-Chapter

Outcomes-Based Assessments – Assessments with open-ended solutions.

Outcomes-Based Assessments – Assessments with open-ended solutions.

Outcomes Rubric – A standards-based analytic rubric specific to the GO! Think projects that states the criteria and standards for grading these open-ended assessments. For these authentic assessments, an analytic rubric enables the instructor to judge and the student to self assess.

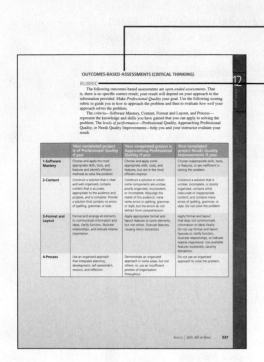

Sample Solution – Outcomes-based assessments include a sample solution so the instructor can compare student work with an example of expert work.

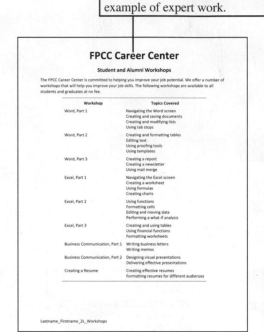

Google Projects for each A & B instructional project in Chapters 1-3– Provide students the opportunity to think critically and apply what they are learning about Microsoft Office to other productivity tools—an essential job skill.

Student Materials

Student Data Files – All student data files are available in MyITLab for Office 2016 or at www.pearsonhighered.com/go

FOUR Types of Videos help students learn and gain skills and insight needed to succeed in the workforce.

- *(NEW) GO! Walk Thru* is a brief overview of the A & B instructional projects to give students the context of what they will be doing in the projects
- *GO! Learn How (formerly Student Training)* instructor-led videos are broken down by Objective for direct guidance; this personal instruction answers the "how-do-I" questions students ask.
- *GO! to Work* videos provide short interviews with workers showing how they use Office in the workplace.
- *GO! for Job Success* videos or discussions relate to the projects in the chapter and cover important career topics such as *Dressing for Success*, *Time Management*, and *Making Ethical Choices*.

Matching and multiple choice questions provide a variety of review options for content in each chapter.

MOS Objective quiz provides a quick assessment of student understanding of the MOS objectives covered in the chapter. Helpful for courses focused on the pathway to MOS certification.

Available in MyITLab for Office 2016.

GO! with MyITLab
Gives you a completely integrated solution

Instruction ▪ Training ▪ Assessment

All of the content in the book and MyITLab is written by the authors, who are instructors, so the instruction works seamlessly with the simulation trainings and grader projects—true 1:1. eText, Training & Assessment Simulations, and Grader Projects.

Instructor Resources

All Instructor Resources found in MyITLab or at pearsonhighered.com/go

Annotated Instructor Edition – This instructor tool includes a full copy of the student textbook and a guide to implementing your course depending on the emphasis you want to place on digital engagement. Also included are teaching tips, discussion topics, and other useful pieces for teaching each chapter.

Assignment Sheets – Lists all the assignments for the chapter. Just add the course information, due dates, and points. Providing these to students ensures they will know what is due and when.

Scripted Lectures – A script to guide your classroom lecture of each instructional project.

Annotated Solution Files – Coupled with the scorecards, these create a grading and scoring system that makes grading easy and efficient.

PowerPoint Lectures – PowerPoint presentations for each chapter.

Audio PowerPoints – Audio versions of the PowerPoint presentations for each chapter.

Scoring Rubrics – Can be used either by students to check their work or by you as a quick check-off for the items that need to be corrected.

Syllabus Templates – For 8-week, 12-week, and 16-week courses.

Test Bank – Includes a variety of test questions for each chapter.

Instruction

Instruction: General

Syllabi templates demonstrate different approaches for covering the content in an 8-, 12-, or 16-week course.

Application Intro Videos provide a quick overview of what the application is and its primary function.

GO! to Work Videos put each chapter into context as related to how people use productivity software in their daily lives and work.

GO! For Success videos and discussions provide real-life scenarios exploring the essential soft skills needed to succeed in the workplace and professional settings.

Instruction: Hands-On *using one or more of the following:*

- **Interactive eText** allows students to read the narrative and instruction and also link directly to the various types of videos included.
- **(NEW) Walk Thru Videos** provide a quick 30-second overview of what students will do in the A & B instructional projects.
- **Scripted Lectures** are a detailed guide through the A & B projects from the book for you to use for in-class demonstration.
- **GO! Learn How** (previously Student Training) videos are instructor-led videos that provide guided instruction through each Objective and the related Activities.
- **PowerPoint Presentations** provide a visual walk-through of the chapter with suggested lecture notes included.
- **Audio PowerPoint Presentations** provide the visual walk-through of chapters with the lecture notes read aloud.
- **(NEW) A & B Instruction Projects** assigned to students. Students can complete the Instructional Projects 1A and 1B and submit for instructor review or manual grading. They can also submit as a MyITLab Grader project, which allows the students to work live in the application starting with files downloaded from MyITLab and then submitted for automatic grading and feedback.
- **(NEW) MOS Objectives** are covered throughout the chapter and are indicated with the **MOS** icon. Instructors use these to point students to content they would encounter on a MOS exam. If a course is focused on MOS preparation, this content would be emphasized in the instruction.

Practice

MyITLab Skill-based Training Simulation provides students with hands-on practice applying the skills they have learned in a simulated environment where they have access to Learning Aids to assist if needed (READ, WATCH, PRACTICE). All of the student's keystrokes are recorded so that instructors can review and provide support to the students. Instructor can set the number of times the students can complete the simulation.

MyITLab Homework Grader Projects (E, F, or G) provide students with live-in-the-application practice with the skills they learned in Projects A and B. These projects provide students with detailed reports showing them where they made errors and also provide "live comments" explaining the details.

Student Assignment Tracker for students to track their work.

Review

GO! Online activities (multiple choice and matching activities) provide objective-based quizzing to allow students to review how they are doing.

Testbank questions are available for instructors to create their own quizzes for review or assessment.

End-of-chapter online projects H–O provide Content-based, Outcome-based, and Critical Thinking projects that you can assign for additional review, practice, or assessments. These are graded manually by the instructor using the provided Solution Files and Grading Scorecards or Rubrics.

MOS Quizzes provide an objective-based quiz to review the MOS objective-related content covered in the chapter. Provides students with review to help if they plan to take a MOS Certification exam.

Assessment

MyITLab Skill-based Exam Simulation provides students with an assessment of their knowledge and ability to apply the skills they have learned. In the Simulated Exams, students do not have access to the Learning Aids. All of the student's keystrokes are recorded so that instructors can review and provide support to the students. Instructors can set the number of times the students can complete the simulation exam.

MyITLab Assessment Grader Projects (E, F, or G) provide students with live-in-the-application testing of the skills they learned in Projects A and B. These projects provide students with detailed reports showing the student where they made errors and also provides "live comments" explaining the details.

Prepared Exams – these are additional projects created specifically for use as exams that the instructor will grade manually. They are available by Project, Chapter, and Unit.

Pre-built Chapter quizzes provide objective-based quizzing to allow students to review how they are doing.

Testbank questions are available for instructors to create their own quizzes for review or assessment.

Reviewers Of The GO! Series

Abul Sheikh	Abraham Baldwin Agricultural College	Kenneth A. Hyatt	Lonestar College - Kingwood
John Percy	Atlantic Cape Community College	Glenn Gray	Lonestar College North Harris
Janette Hicks	Binghamton University	Gene Carbonaro	Long Beach City College
Shannon Ogden	Black River Technical College	Betty Pearman	Los Medanos College
Karen May	Blinn College	Diane Kosharek	Madison College
Susan Fry	Boise State University	Peter Meggison	Massasoit Community College
Chigurupati Rani	Borough of Manhattan Community College / CUNY	George Gabb	Miami Dade College
Ellen Glazer	Broward College	Lennie Alice Cooper	Miami Dade College
Kate LeGrand	Broward College	Richard Mabjish	Miami Dade College
Mike Puopolo	Bunker Hill Community College	Victor Giol	Miami Dade College
Nicole Lytle-Kosola	California State University, San Bernardino	John Meir	Midlands Technical College
Nisheeth Agrawal	Calhoun Community College	Greg Pauley	Moberly Area Community College
Pedro Diaz-Gomez	Cameron	Catherine Glod	Mohawk Valley Community College
Linda Friedel	Central Arizona College	Robert Huyck	Mohawk Valley Community College
Gregg Smith	Central Community College	Kevin Engellant	Montana Western
Norm Cregger	Central Michigan University	Philip Lee	Nashville State Community College
Lisa LaCaria	Central Piedmont Community College	Ruth Neal	Navarro College
Steve Siedschlag	Chaffey College	Sharron Jordan	Navarro College
Terri Helfand	Chaffey College	Richard Dale	New Mexico State University
Susan Mills	Chambersburg	Lori Townsend	Niagara County Community College
Mandy Reininger	Chemeketa Community College	Judson Curry	North Park University
Connie Crossley	Cincinnati State Technical and Community College	Mary Zegarski	Northampton Community College
Marjorie Deutsch	City University of New York - Queensborough Community College	Neal Stenlund	Northern Virginia Community Colege
		Michael Goeken	Northwest Vista College
Mary Ann Zlotow	College of Dupage	Mary Beth Tarver	Northwestern State University
Christine Bohnsak	College of Lake County	Amy Rutledge	Oakland University
Gertrude Brier	College of Staten Island	Marcia Braddock	Okefenokee Technical College
Sharon Brown	College of The Albemarle	Richard Stocke	Oklahoma State University - OKC
Terry Rigsby	Columbia College	Jane Stam	Onondaga Community College
Vicki Brooks	Columbia College	Mike Michaelson	Palomar College
Donald Hames	Delgado Community College	Kungwen (Dave) Chu	Purdue University Calumet
Kristen King	Eastern Kentucky University	Wendy Ford	CUNY - Queensborough CC
Kathie Richer	Edmonds Community College	Lewis Hall	Riverside City College
Gary Smith	Elmhurst College	Karen Acree	San Juan College
Wendi Kappersw	Embry-Riddle Aeronautical University	Tim Ellis	Schoolcraft College
Nancy Woolridge	Fullerton College	Dan Combellick	Scottsdale Community College
Abigail Miller	Gateway Commvunity & Technical College	Pat Serrano	Scottsdale Community College
Deep Ramanayake	Gateway Community & Technical College	Rose Hendrickson	Sheridan College
Gwen White	Gateway Community & Technical College	Kit Carson	South Georgia College
Debbie Glinert	Gloria K School	Rebecca Futch	South Georgia State College
Dana Smith	Golf Academy of America	Brad Hagy	Southern Illinois University Carbondale
Mary Locke	Greenville Technical College	Mimi Spain	Southern Maine Community College
Diane Marie Roselli	Harrisburg Area Community College	David Parker	Southern Oregon University
Linda Arnold	Harrisburg Area Community College - Lebanon	Madeline Baugher	Southwestern Oklahoma State University
Daniel Schoedel	Harrisburg Area Community College - York Campus	Brian Holbert	St. Johns River State College
Ken Mayer	Heald College	Bunny Howard	St. Johns River State College
Xiaodong Qiao	Heald College	Stephanie Cook	State College of Florida
Donna Lamprecht	Hopkinsville Community College	Sharon Wavle	Tompkins Cortland Community College
Kristen Lancaster	Hopkinsville Community College	George Fiori	Tri-County Technical College
Johnny Hurley	Iowa Lakes Community College	Steve St. John	Tulsa Community College
Linda Halverson	Iowa Lakes Community College	Karen Thessing	University of Central Arkansas
Sarah Kilgo	Isothermal Community College	Richard McMahon	University of Houston-Downtown
Chris DeGeare	Jefferson College	Shohreh Hashemi	University of Houston-Downtown
David McNair	Jefferson College	Donna Petty	Wallace Community College
Diane Santurri	Johnson & Wales	Julia Bell	Walters State Community College
Roland Sparks	Johnson & Wales University	Ruby Kowaney	West Los Angeles College
Ram Raghuraman	Joliet Junior College	Casey Thompson	Wiregrass Georgia Technical College
Eduardo Suniga	Lansing Community College	DeAnnia Clements	Wiregrass Georgia Technical College

Computers and Information Processing

OUTCOMES

Identify current and future computer trends and trace the steps of the information processing cycle. Recognize various computing devices and their uses.

OBJECTIVES

1. Recognize Computers
2. Explain the Functions of a Computer
3. Describe How Computers Represent Data Using Binary Codes
4. Describe the Evolution of Computer Systems
5. List the Various Types and Characteristics of Personal Computers
6. Give Examples of Other Personal Computing Devices
7. List the Various Types and Characteristics of Multiuser Computers
8. Explain the Safe and Efficient Use of Technology

Iakobchuk Viacheslav/Shutterstock

In This Chapter

Most people use computers every day, often without even realizing it. Checking out at the grocery store, fueling the car, and watching the weather report on TV are all examples of interactions with computers. In your job as a Guest Relations Officer, you interact with computers and other computing devices on a daily basis. You must not only be familiar with these devices, you must also be comfortable using them to provide the best possible customer service.

In this chapter, you will learn what a computer is, compare different types of devices, and look at the development of computers in the past two centuries.

Job Focus

One of the first people guests meet when they enter an **Oro Jade Hotel** is a **Guest Relations Officer**. As a Guest Relations Officer, you are the face of Oro Jade and your primary role is to provide customer service. You must ensure that customers are happy and that their needs are met. You will need to use the Oro Jade Hotel Group computer system to check guests in and out and to take reservations. You will also need to use mobile technology to communicate and coordinate with other hotel employees. Your professional appearance and excellent technical skills will result in repeat customers to Oro Jade.

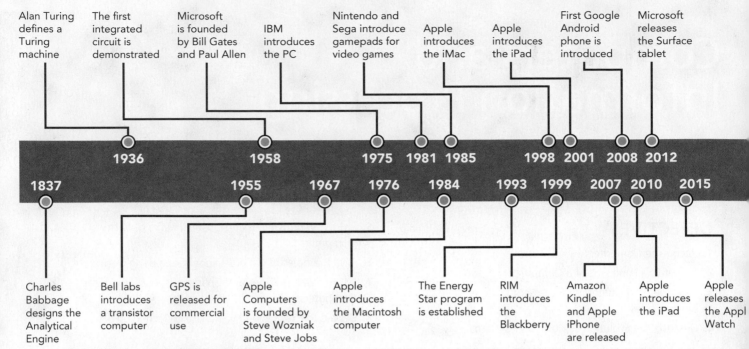

FIGURE 1.1 This timeline highlights important dates in computer history.

Objective 1 | Recognize Computers

As a Guest Relations Officer, you not only work with computers behind the front desk, but you also use other devices such as a smartphone and keycard system on a daily basis. Every department in the hotel relies on computers in some way. A **computer** is a programmable machine that converts raw **data**—numbers, words, pictures, or sounds that represent facts about people, events, things, or ideas—into useful **information**—data converted into a meaningful format. The word *ubiquitous*, according to Merriam-Webster, means existing or being present everywhere. **Ubiquitous computing (ubicomp),** sometimes called invisible computing, refers to technology that recedes into the background. Computers have become so commonplace that often the technology is not identified as being a computer. The technology actually becomes part of the user's environment. Digital signage has replaced traditional billboards, you can pay for gas with the wave of a credit card, and you can upload pictures to Facebook from your mobile phones. **Smart homes**—in which the lights, climate, security, and entertainment are automated—are a glimpse into the future of ubiquitous computing. The **Internet of Things (IoT)** is the connection of the physical world to the Internet. Objects are tagged and can be located, monitored, and controlled using small, embedded electronics. Some examples of IoT devices include fitness and health trackers, smart thermostats, and monitors for babies or the elderly. These devices have existed for some time, but adding the IoT features means they can be monitored and controlled remotely via a web browser or mobile app.

1.01a
1.01b

Concept 1.01 | Understanding Embedded Computers and Convergence

An **embedded computer** is a specialized computer that is part of another device, such as a gasoline pump, home appliance, traffic light, or the self-checkout line at the supermarket (Figure 1.2). Computer chips regulate the flow of gas into a car and the temperature of water inside a dishwasher. This makes modern living easier. These specialized computers have become so commonplace that it would be hard to imagine living without such technology.

Mrgarry/Fotolia

Zelfit/Fotolia

Robert Wilson/Fotolia

FIGURE 1.2 Embedded computers can be found in many objects that you come in contact with every day.

The integration of technology on multifunction devices such as smartphones is referred to as ***convergence***. With this convergence, people have become accustomed to carrying technology at all times (Figure 1.3). Because these devices combine the features of cell phones, personal information management tools, email, web browsing, document editing, MP3 players, cameras, GPS, and games, it is not necessary to carry around several different devices. For many people, smaller, less expensive smartphones have replaced personal computers as the primary computing device. In fact, in some parts of the world, there are more mobile phones than people, and this has resulted in the rapid development of technologies such as ***mobile payment systems***—using a mobile device rather than cash or credit cards to pay for items.

Stockshoppe/Fotolia

FIGURE 1.3 The convergence of technology on a smartphone eliminates the need to carry multiple devices.

Green computing is the efficient and ecologically friendly use of computers and other electronics. Smart homes use automation to control lighting, heating and cooling, security, entertainment, and appliances. Smart homes and smart appliances help save energy and, as a result, are good for both the environment and your budget. You can program a smart home system to turn various components on and off at set times to maximize energy efficiency. So, the heat can turn up, and the house can be warm right before you get home from work while not wasting the energy to keep it warm all day when no one is home. A smart home can be remotely activated by phone or over the Internet (Figure 1.4). ***Smart appliances*** can monitor signals from the power company transmitted over the ***smart grid***—a network for delivering electricity to consumers that includes communication technology to manage electricity distribution efficiently. When the electric grid system is stressed, smart appliances can react by reducing power consumption. Although these advances are called smart home technology, the same technologies can also be found in commercial buildings.

FIGURE 1.4 A smart home can be controlled using a mobile device such as this tablet.

GREEN COMPUTING — A Smart, Green House

In Davis, California, a small town 15 miles west of Sacramento, a collaboration between Honda and UC Davis built a three-bedroom home with smart home technology. The Honda Smart Home (http://www.hondasmarthome.com) includes an electric car and solar panels that collect and convert solar energy into electricity for the home, with zero emissions. The home also includes low tech energy efficient design such insulated window and doors, ground-source heating that captures thermal energy from underground, and low water consumption xeriscaping in the garden. Other low-tech features include using LED lights, which use much less energy than conventional light bulbs. The heating and cooling system, lighting, and other systems in the home are managed by a home energy management system to maximize efficiency.

Objective 2 | Explain the Functions of a Computer

In your job as a Guest Relations Officer, you use computers to make reservations, check customers in and out, and maintain a daily log of activity. A toaster can never be anything more than a toaster—it has one function—but a computer can be a calculator, a media center, and a communications center. The ability to change its programming is what distinguishes a computer from any other machine.

What Is a Computer?

Concept 1.03 | Understanding the Information Processing Cycle

Computers convert data into information using the ***information processing cycle***, also referred to as the ***IPC*** (Figure 1.5). The four steps of the information processing cycle are input, processing, storage, and output. Raw data is entered into the system during the input stage. The data is processed to create useful information. The information is then stored for later retrieval and is returned to the user in the output stage.

The following example illustrates each step of the information processing cycle:

- ***Input***: The raw data is entered into the system. You are writing a research paper for a class. You know it has misspellings and grammatical errors, but you keep typing because you can run your word processing program's spelling checker at any time to help correct the errors. The document that you are typing is the input.

- ***Processing***: The input data is manipulated, calculated, or organized to create useful information. A spelling checker program uses the computer's ability to perform processing operations to construct a list of all of the words in your document. The program compares your words against its own dictionary of correctly spelled words. If you use a word that is not in the computer's dictionary, the program flags the word as a misspelling.

- ***Output***: The processed data is returned to you. The result of the spelling checker processing operation is a document containing words that are flagged as being possibly misspelled. Word processing programs typically flag possible misspellings with a red wavy line under the word.

- ***Storage***: The digital information is saved for archiving for later access. After you correct any misspellings in your document, you save or store the revised document to the hard disk or your flash drive.

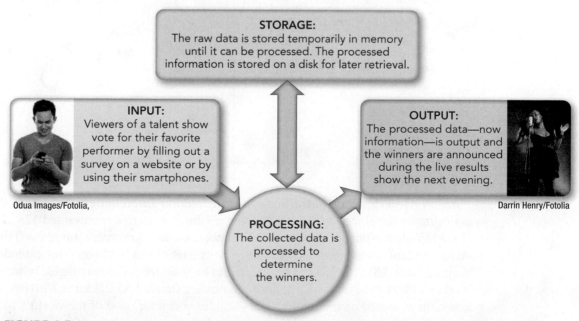

Odua Images/Fotolia,

Darrin Henry/Fotolia

Gaskin, Shelley. GO! All in One, 3E. Pearson Education, 2017.

FIGURE 1.5 The information processing cycle converts raw data collected from viewers of a TV talent show into useful information that determines the winners.

Tech to GO!
Bits and Bytes

As a Guest Relations Officer, you input customer data into the hotel computer systems by typing on the keyboard or swiping a credit card. After the information is entered into the system, it must be converted into something that the computer can understand.

Humans have 10 digits—our fingers!—which is why the most commonly used number system is the decimal, or base 10, number system. Computers have switches, not fingers, and use the *binary number system* also referred to as *base 2*, a number system that has only two digits—0 and 1. All information entered into a computer system must be converted into binary digits.

Concept 1.04 | Understanding Binary Code

Computers do not speak English or Spanish or Chinese or any other human language, so how does a computer interpret what a human inputs? On a typewriter, when you press the A key, you get an A on the page. Computers only understand 0s and 1s, so when you press the A key, it must somehow be converted to 0s and 1s. Digital data is represented using a *binary code*. A binary code represents digital data as a series of 0s and 1s that can be understood by a computer.

Binary code works like a bank of light switches. If there is a single light switch in a room, there are two possible states—the light can either be on or it can be off. This code can be used for situations with only two possibilities, such as yes/no, or true/false, but it fails when there are more than two choices; for example, yes/no/maybe. Adding another switch—or bit—increases the possible combinations by a factor of two (2^2), which equals four possibilities. A third bit or switch results in 2^3, or 8, possibilities, and so on. A *bit*, also called a *binary digit*, is the smallest unit of digital data. Eight bits results in 2^8, or 256, possibilities (Figure 1.6). A *byte* consists of 8 bits and represents a single character in modern computer systems. For example, when you press the A key, the binary code 01000001 is sent to the computer.

A BINARY CODE USING 8 SWITCHES, OR BITS, HAS 256 DIFFERENT POSSIBLE COMBINATIONS		
NUMBER OF BITS (SWITCHES)	**POSSIBILITIES**	**POWER OF TWO**
1	2	2^1
2	4	2^2
3	8	2^3
4	16	2^4
5	32	2^5
6	64	2^6
7	128	2^7
8	256	2^8

Gaskin, Shelley. GO! All in One, 3E. Pearson Education, 2017.

FIGURE 1.6

ASCII (American Standard Code for Information Interchange), pronounced ASK-key, was originally developed in the 1960s using a 7-bit system that represented 128 characters and included English alphabet symbols in both uppercase and lowercase, numbers 0 through 9, punctuation, and a few special characters. It was later expanded to an 8-bit extended set with 256 characters. ASCII needed to be adapted to be used for other languages, however, and many extended sets were developed. The most common extended ASCII set is *Unicode*. Unicode has become the standard on the Internet and includes codes for most of the world's written languages, mathematical systems, and special characters. It has codes for over 100,000 characters. The first 256 characters are the same in both ASCII and Unicode.

Concept 1.05 | Measuring Data

Bits (b) are used to measure data transfer rates, and bytes (B) are used to measure file size and storage capacity. Decimal prefixes such as kilo—10^3, mega—10^6, giga—10^9, and tera—10^{12}, are added to the base unit to indicate larger values (Figure 1.7).

A megabyte (MB) is equal to 1 million bytes—the equivalent of about 500–800 pages of plain text. The size of a single picture taken with a digital camera can be several megabytes. A gigabyte is equal to 1,000 megabytes; most storage is measured in gigabytes. Larger hard drives are measured in terabytes. A terabyte equals 1,000 gigabytes. As the commonly used types of digital files have changed from plain text to images, music, and video, the file sizes have become larger, and the need for storage has grown quite rapidly. Fundamentally, however, all files are still just 0s and 1s.

THE STANDARD DECIMAL PREFIXES TO MEASURE DATA	
UNIT	**NUMBER OF BYTES**
Bit (b)	1/8
Byte (B)	1
Kilobyte (KB)	1,000
Megabyte (MB)	1 million
Gigabyte (GB)	1 billion
Terabyte (TB)	1 trillion
Petabyte (PB)	1,000 TB
Exabyte (EB)	1,000 PB
Zettabyte (ZB)	1,000 EB
Yottabyte (YB)	1,000 ZB

Gaskin, Shelley. GO! All in One, 3E. Pearson Education, 2017.

FIGURE 1.7

Objective 4 | Describe the Evolution of Computer Systems

In your job as a Guest Relations Officer, you will work with a variety of computer systems. Technology systems are updated and replaced at a rapid pace, and you must keep your computer skills up to date to be successful. Try to imagine what your job would be like without computers. As few as 20 years ago, the Internet would not have been part of the hotel's systems.

The original computers were people, not machines, and the mathematical tables they computed tended to be full of errors. The technical and scientific advancements of the Industrial Revolution led to a growing need for this type of hand-calculated information, and the first mechanical computers were developed to automate the tedious work of computing such things as tide charts and ocean navigation tables.

Concept 1.06 | Reviewing a Brief History of Computers

In the early nineteenth century, mathematician Charles Babbage designed a machine called an **Analytical Engine.** This mechanical computer could be programmed using punched cards, which were originally developed by Joseph Marie Jacquard as part of the Jacquard loom to manufacture textiles with complex patterns. Had the Analytical Engine actually been built, it would have been the first mechanical computer, but the technology did not exist at the time to build such a machine.

Mathematician Ada Lovelace, a contemporary of Babbage, wrote a program for the Analytical Engine to calculate a series of Bernoulli numbers— a sequence of rational numbers that is used in number theory. Because of her efforts, she is considered by many to be the first computer programmer. In 1979, the Ada computer language was named in her honor. Lovelace was never able to test the program because there were no machines capable of running it; however, when it is run on a computer today, the program yields the correct mathematical results.

In 1936, mathematician Alan Turing wrote a paper titled *On Computable Numbers*, in which he introduced the concept of machines that could perform mathematical computations. These were later called ***Turing machines***. In 1950, he developed the ***Turing test***, which tests a machine's ability to display intelligent behavior. The first computers to pass the Turing test were built 64 years later, in 2014. Alan Turing is considered by many to be the father of computer science and ***artificial intelligence***—the branch of science concerned with making computers behave like humans. Alan Turing was the subject of the 2014 movie *The Imitation Game*.

As amazing as it may seem, it took nearly a century after Babbage designed his Analytical Engine before the first working mechanical computers were built. From that point, it took only about 40 years to progress from those first-generation machines to the current fourth-generation designs. Since the first working computers became a reality, the computer has become an integral part of our modern lives. Between the mid-nineteenth and mid-twentieth centuries, the Industrial Revolution gave way to the Information Age. Since that time, technology has grown at a startling rate. The pace of technological change is growing exponentially—faster than it ever has before.

During the 1930s and 1940s, several electromechanical and electronic computers were built. These first-generation computers were massive in size and used vacuum tubes and manual switches to process data. ***Vacuum tubes***, which resemble incandescent light bulbs, give off a lot of heat and are notoriously unreliable. ***ENIAC*** or ***Electronic Numerical Integrator and Computer***, built at the University of Pennsylvania between 1943 and 1946, was the first working, digital, general-purpose computer. It used about 18,000 vacuum tubes, weighed almost 30 tons, and occupied about 1,800 square feet. Originally created to calculate artillery firing tables for use during World War II, ENIAC was not actually completed until after the war ended. The computer was reprogrammed to solve a range of other problems, such as atomic energy calculations, weather predictions, and wind-tunnel design. The programming was done by manipulating switches, and took six programmers several days to complete.

Transistors, tiny electronic switches, were invented in 1947 and led to second-generation computers in the 1950s and 1960s. The use of transistors in place of vacuum tubes enabled second-generation computers to be more powerful, smaller, and more reliable. Equally important, these computers could be reprogrammed in far less time.

Developed in the 1960s, ***integrated circuits*** are chips that contain large numbers of tiny transistors fabricated into a semiconducting material called silicon. Third-generation computers used multiple integrated circuits to process data and were even smaller, faster, and more reliable than their predecessors, although there was much overlap between second- and third-generation technologies in the 1960s. The Apollo Guidance Computer, used in the moon landing missions, was originally designed to use transistors, but over time, the design was modified to use integrated circuits. The 2000 Nobel Prize in physics was awarded for the invention of the integrated circuit.

The integrated circuit made the development of the microprocessor possible in the 1970s. A ***microprocessor*** is a complex integrated circuit that contains processing circuitry that enables it to behave as the brain of the computer, control all functions performed by other components, and process all the commands it receives. The microprocessor is also referred to as the ***central processing unit*** or ***CPU*** (Figure 1.8). The first microprocessor was developed in 1971 and was as powerful as ENIAC. Today's personal computers use microprocessors and are considered fourth-generation computers. Microprocessors can be found in everything from alarm clocks to automobiles to refrigerators. The chip inside your smartphone has more processing power than the first microprocessor developed in 1971.

FIGURE 1.8 A microprocessor only a few inches in size contains millions of tiny transistors.

In 1965, Intel co-founder Gordon Moore observed that the number of transistors that could be placed on an integrated circuit had doubled roughly every two years. ***Moore's Law*** predicted that this exponential growth would continue. The law was never intended to be a true measure, but rather an illustration, of the pace of technology advancement. The increase in the capabilities of integrated circuits directly affects the processing speed and storage capacity of modern electronic devices.

☑ **Check Your Knowledge:** In MyITLab, take the quiz covering Objectives 1–4.

Objective 5 List the Various Types and Characteristics of Personal Computers

As a Guest Relations Officer, you use several different computer systems. At the front desk, your system is integrated into the corporate network. In the lobby, there are desktop computers for hotel guests to use for such tasks as printing boarding passes and checking email. Other hotel employees that need to move around the hotel use portable computers.

A ***personal computer*** is a small microprocessor-based computer designed to be used by one person at a time. A personal computer can be a notebook, mobile device, or desktop (Figure 1.9). Although the term personal computer—***PC***—usually refers to a computer running the Microsoft Windows operating system, Apple's Mac computers and computers running Linux operating systems are also personal computers.

FIGURE 1.9 Personal computers include notebooks, mobile devices, and desktops.

Concept 1.07 | Comparing Desktop Computers

Desktop computers sit on a desk, and range in price from under $300 for basic personal systems to thousands of dollars for high-end systems that can be used for video editing, gaming, and complex computations. Desktop computers offer the most speed, power, and upgradability for the lowest cost. In a business environment, a ***workstation*** is a high-end desktop computer or one that is attached to a network.

An ***all-in-one computer*** is a compact desktop computer with the system unit integrated into the monitor. Some systems have a touchscreen monitor or are wall-mountable. All-in-ones save desktop space but may be difficult to upgrade because of their small size. All-in-ones are popular in places where space is limited, such as in emergency rooms, at bank teller windows, and in business cubicles.

Concept 1.08 | Comparing Portable Computers

A ***notebook*** or ***laptop*** computer is a portable personal computer. Notebook computers can rival desktops in power and storage capacity, but can cost significantly more than a comparable desktop system. Recently the cost of all computers has dropped significantly, and notebook computers are more popular as a result. In 2008, sales of notebooks surpassed desktop sales for the first time, and by 2015 notebooks outsold desktops more than 2:1. Modern notebook computers come with built-in wireless networking capabilities, webcams, and bright widescreen displays. High-end notebooks with large screens and powerful processors are referred to as desktop replacements, because many individuals now purchase this type of system instead of a traditional desktop computer.

The smallest notebook computers are called ***netbooks***. Netbooks have screens smaller than 12 inches, built-in wireless capabilities, no CD/DVD drive, and limited computing power and storage. Netbooks have largely been replaced by tablets and ***subnotebooks***—notebook computers that are thin and light, but unlike netbooks, have high-end processing and video capabilities. The screen on a subnotebook is typically larger than on a netbook, in the range of 13–15 inches. ***Ultrabooks*** that run Windows and Apple's Macbook Air are examples of subnotebooks.

A ***convertible notebook*** computer has a screen that can swivel to fold into what resembles a notepad or tablet. These computers include a touch screen or a special digital pen or ***stylus*** that enables you to write directly on the screen, making them useful for taking notes or drawing diagrams and for making information such as sales catalogs portable. The Windows Continuum and Apple iPad Pro are examples of ***two-in-one notebooks***—a portable computer that converts to a tablet by detaching the screen from the keyboard. A ***tablet*** is a handheld mobile device that falls somewhere between a notebook and a smartphone. A tablet has an LCD—liquid-crystal display—screen, a long battery life, and built-in wireless connectivity. A tablet may have a detachable keyboard, making it more notebook-like with the keyboard in place. Tablets come with a variety of pre-installed ***mobile applications***, or ***mobile apps***—programs that extend the functionality of mobile devices. Thousands of apps can be downloaded and installed to make the device even more versatile. With these devices, you can edit documents, take photographs, surf the web, send and receive email, and watch videos. Cellular-enabled tablets use the same network as your smartphone to access the Internet. You need to purchase a data plan from your cellular carrier to use this feature.

Concept 1.09 | Choosing a Personal Computer System

In the personal computer market, there are several types, or platforms, of personal computers to choose from. A platform consists of both the hardware and underlying operating system software. So, the question is: What is the difference between them and which one should you choose?

Mac computers are built by Apple and run the OS X operating system. The current version of OS X is called El Capitan. Using a program called Boot Camp that is included with OS X, you can also install and run the Microsoft Windows operating system on a Mac. Macs have a reputation for being secure, stable, and fun. They come with a variety of useful programs already installed and are very user-friendly. Macs are often used in creative businesses, such as advertising and graphic design.

Although a Mac can be built only by Apple, PCs can be built by any number of companies, including Lenovo, Dell, ASUS, HP, Acer, and Toshiba. PCs that run some version of the Windows or Linux operating systems constitute over 85 percent of the U.S. market share. Because they are produced by a variety of manufacturers, PCs are available in numerous models, configurations, and price ranges. PCs that run Windows have the largest selection of software available.

Chromebooks are less common than Macs or PCs, but are growing in popularity. Chromebooks are subnotebooks that run the Chrome OS—a version of the Linux operating system released by Google. These notebooks are designed to work best when connected to the Internet and rely on web apps and cloud storage rather than traditional software. The Chromebox is a desktop computer running Chrome OS.

The type of computer you choose depends on many factors, including personal preferences, the types of software you need to use, compatibility with school or work computers, and budget (Figure 1.10).

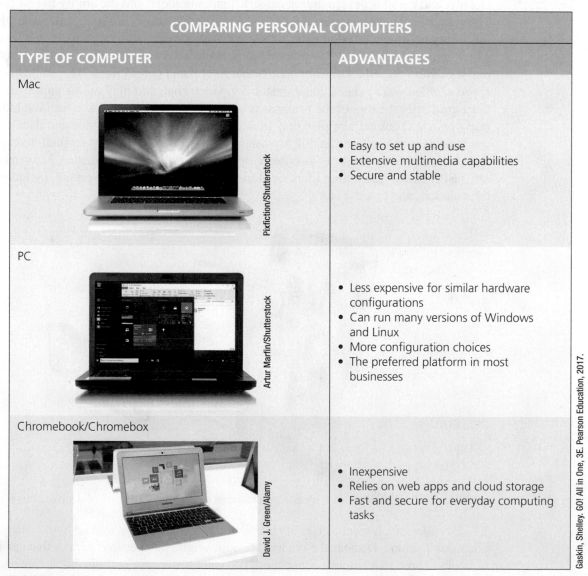

COMPARING PERSONAL COMPUTERS	
TYPE OF COMPUTER	**ADVANTAGES**
Mac	• Easy to set up and use • Extensive multimedia capabilities • Secure and stable
PC	• Less expensive for similar hardware configurations • Can run many versions of Windows and Linux • More configuration choices • The preferred platform in most businesses
Chromebook/Chromebox	• Inexpensive • Relies on web apps and cloud storage • Fast and secure for everyday computing tasks

Pixfiction/Shutterstock

Artur Marfin/Shutterstock

David J. Green/Alamy

Gaskin, Shelley. GO! All in One, 3E. Pearson Education, 2017.

FIGURE 1.10

Before You Buy

Choosing the Right
Mobile Device

As a Guest Relations Officer, you often need to contact other hotel employees to assist guests. Although you are stationed behind the front desk, many other employees move throughout the hotel; therefore, Oro Jade Hotels provide these employees with mobile devices to perform their duties.

Today, the term computer no longer refers only to those desktop devices used for office work. Handheld and *mobile devices* are portable computers for business and entertainment and come in many different shapes and sizes—from smartphones to heart-rate monitors that you wear on your wrist. Some of these devices serve specialized functions, such as medical monitoring or navigation, while others are more general-purpose devices. These devices have more features and capabilities with every new model introduced, and prices continue to drop. Mobile devices are the fastest-growing segment of personal computers.

Concept 1.10 | Looking at Smartphones and E-Readers

1.01a
1.01c
1.03f
1.03f (iv)

Basic mobile phones are limited to making phone calls and perhaps texting and taking photos. *Smartphones* are small computers that combine a cellular phone with such features as Internet and email access, a digital camera, mapping tools, and the ability to edit documents. These mobile devices are useful when carrying a computer is not practical. Smartphones have the ability to download additional mobile applications or mobile apps to extend their capabilities, which makes them true convergence devices (Figure 1.11). The cellular networks offered by major carriers offer data transfer speeds that rival home connections. This improved connection speed enables you to check email, watch TV, video chat, and play online games almost anywhere. Once primarily the tool of the business professional, smartphones have become indispensable to many people. Your cellular plan may include separate charges for voice and data. Using apps that use your data connection can quickly use up the amount of data in your plan, leading to reduced speed or extra cost. Apps can also decrease the battery life of your device. Most mobile phones use a SIM card—Subscriber Identity Module—which identifies the phone, includes account information, and cellular carrier.

Anterovium/Fotolia

FIGURE 1.11 Mobile applications extend the functions of a smartphone.

E-readers are a special class of tablets with a specific design to read books, magazines, and other publications. Dedicated e-readers are lightweight, inexpensive devices that can hold thousands of books. Through a wireless connection, you can browse an electronic bookstore and download a new book in seconds. Some libraries also lend *e-books*—books in digital formats that can be read on a screen, and many textbooks come in e-book form that you can read on a computer or e-reader. A common way to read e-books is by using a mobile app on a tablet or smartphone.

Some e-readers use *e-ink* technology to make screens that are easy to read and extend battery life for as long as two months. E-ink creates a screen that is easy on the eyes and most like the experience of reading a printed book (Figure 1.12). The screen can easily be read even in the brightest conditions—like at the beach—but as with a paper book, you will need a book light to read in bed at night because e-ink readers are not *backlit*—they do not include an internal light source. An e-reader that has an LCD screen is backlit, resulting in a shorter battery life. The glossy surface of an LCD screen is subject to glare and is harder to read in a brightly lit location.

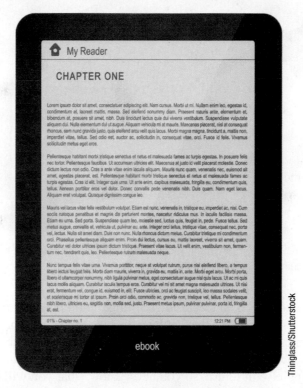

Thinglass/Shutterstock

FIGURE 1.12 A Kindle e-reader can hold hundreds of books.

ON THE JOB Healthcare

The use of technology is commonplace in many careers. Nowhere is this more evident than in healthcare. Many medical schools and nursing programs require students to learn to use handheld devices to gain instant access to enormous amounts of clinical information on one small mobile device. These devices can contain drug and diagnostics manuals, calculators, and other medical reference materials—and they can also track patients, order laboratory tests and prescriptions, and conduct billing. Handheld devices and other computing technology have changed the way healthcare providers practice medicine. The ability to use digital technologies is a critical skill for practitioners to have.

Concept 1.11 | Examining Other Devices

Commonly found on cell phones and in newer cars, another familiar device is a GPS navigation unit. Originally built by the military, the *GPS* or *global positioning system* consists of at least 24 satellites that transmit signals. The signals can be detected by a GPS receiver on the ground and then used to determine its current location, time, and velocity by examining the signals using a mathematical principle called *triangulation* to determine the position of the receiving device in three dimensions (Figure 1.13). There are scientific applications for GPS technology, such as surveying, map making, self-navigating robots, and clock synchronization. GPS is used in automobiles, airplanes, and boats for navigation and tracking. Many mobile apps use GPS for navigation, location services, and for fun. For example, an app might use your location to help you locate nearby restaurants or movie theaters. Since the mid-1990s, GPS devices have been available for civilian use.

FIGURE 1.13 A GPS unit locks in the signal from four satellites and uses triangulation to determine the position of the receiving device.

Geocaching is an electronic scavenger hunt played around the world. Players, called geocachers, hide geocaches—typically a small waterproof container—and post GPS coordinates on the Internet. Other geocachers can then find the geocaches using their own GPS devices. The geocaches have logbooks to sign and often small prizes. Geocachers that find a prize leave something else in return, so you never know what you will find.

A *video game system* is a computer that is designed primarily to play games. The first arcade video games were released in the early 1970s, and video game systems for the home soon followed. Atari released a home version of Pong, an electronic Ping-Pong game, in 1975. It became one of the hottest gifts of the year. Current systems are considered eighth-generation video games and have high-end processing and graphic capabilities, provide the ability to play movies and music, enable online game play, and can enable you to browse the Internet.

A *game console*, such as Microsoft Xbox One or Sony PlayStation 4, is a home entertainment system that connects to a television or monitor to display a game. Consoles may have built-in hard drives for storage and can play DVDs and Blu-ray discs, connect to the Internet, play music and videos, and display high-definition video. Kinect for Xbox has motion and voice sensors, enabling you to play certain games without holding a *game controller*—a device used to interact with a video game. Nintendo's Wii-U is less powerful and less expensive than either the Xbox One or the PlayStation 4. The Wii has unique motion-sensing controllers, giving players new gameplay experiences and interactivity. The Wii has reached out to nontraditional markets, such as senior citizens and young children, by offering such unique games as bowling, tennis, Wii Fit, and Brain Age. Newer systems sometimes incorporate some level of *backward compatibility*—the ability to run some older programs—with older systems from the same company. Handheld video games, such as the Nintendo 3DS and DSi, enable you to take your games wherever you go.

Video game systems are not just for entertainment. By using sophisticated *video game simulation* systems, which replicate realistic environments and scenarios, medical students learn to be better doctors, pilots learn to fly planes (Figure 1.14), and soldiers learn to strategize.

FIGURE 1.14 This F-16 SimuSphere HD flight simulator trains pilots.

Kelley Chinn/Fort Worth Star-Telegram/MCT/Getty Images

FAST FORWARD Unmanned Aircraft Systems

Just a few years ago, aircraft piloted by remote control or onboard computers or **unmanned aircraft systems (UAS)**—also known as **drones**—were used only by the military. Today, commercial applications are being developed. Drones are useful in agriculture, land management, energy, and construction industries; for example, to inspect the underside of bridges and other locations where it is difficult or unsafe for people to go. Amazon plans to develop a drone delivery service. Drones carrying cameras are helpful in search-and-rescue missions, and could replace traffic and news helicopters. As technology improves, many more drone applications are sure to be developed.

There are, however, privacy and safety concerns about the proliferation of UAS in our skies. The Federal Aviation Administration (FAA) has implemented some rules for nonmilitary UAS users (https://www.faa.gov/uas/) "The FAA reviews and approves UAS operations over densely-populated areas on a case-by-case basis." The FAA estimates that as many as 7,500 small commercial UAS may be in use by 2018.

Alexander Kolomietz/Shutterstock

FIGURE 1.15 A UAS records video of icebergs and glaciers.

In your job as a Guest Relations Officer, the computer you use to handle reservations and other transactions is connected to the corporate system. The corporate system is a multiuser system that enables agents from other hotels and travel agencies to access the same information, so that a travel agent can help a client book a room without having to call the hotel to check for availability.

Multiuser computers are systems that allow multiple, simultaneous users to connect to them. The advantages of multiuser systems include centralized resources and security. Multiuser computers are also more powerful than personal computers.

IC3
DIGITAL LITERACY
CERTIFICATION
1.02a (i)

Concept 1.12 | Understanding Servers and Mainframes

A *client* is a computer that connects to, or requests services from, another computer called a *server*. Such services include Internet access, email, or file and print services. Servers range in size and cost from very small systems serving a few workstations in a small office and costing a few hundred dollars to massive enterprise servers costing hundreds of thousands of dollars.

Midrange servers can support hundreds of simultaneous users and are scalable, allowing for growth as a company's needs change. The users connect to the system via client personal computers. Midrange servers can perform complex calculations, store customer information and transactions, or host an email system for an organization.

Mainframes and *enterprise servers* are large computers that can perform millions of transactions in a day (Figure 1.16). These are most commonly found in businesses that have massive amounts of data or transactions to process, such as banks and insurance companies, social networks, and online games. These systems allow thousands of users to utilize the system concurrently.

FIGURE 1.16 Enterprise servers can enable thousands of simultaneous users and perform millions of transactions every day.

IC3
DIGITAL LITERACY
CERTIFICATION
1.02a (i)

1
CONCEPTS

Supercomputers are very expensive computer systems that perform complex mathematical calculations, such as those used in weather forecasting and medical research. A supercomputer can be a single computer with multiple processors or a group of computers that work together. A supercomputer focuses on executing a few sets of instructions as fast as possible, and its performance is measured in *petaflops*—the equivalent of one quadrillion calculations per second, or 150,000 calculations for every human being on the planet per second. The world's top supercomputers can be found at major universities and research institutes around the world (Figure 1.17). For a current list of the top 500 supercomputers, go to http://top500.org/lists.

KEY SUPERCOMPUTERS		
RESEARCH INSTITUTE	**LOCATION**	**USES**
RIKEN Advanced Institute for Computational Science (AICS)	Japan	Simulation research and human resource development programs
Shanghai Supercomputer Center	China	• Weather forecasts • Oil exploration • Biomedical applications • Gene research • Aviation and aeronautics
NASA/Ames Research Center/ NAS	United States	• Critical NASA missions • Scientific discoveries for the benefit of humankind
Amazon Web Services	United States	• High performance computing (HPC)

Gaskin, Shelley. GO! All in One, 3E. Pearson Education, 2017.

FIGURE 1.17

Distributed computing distributes the processing of a task across a group of computers. This can be done on a fairly small scale, using a few computers in one location—known as *grid computing*—or on a much larger scale. Some of these projects rely on volunteer computing, which uses the processing power of hundreds or thousands of personal computers to form an inexpensive version of a supercomputer. A volunteer interested in astronomy might join SETI@home, the Search for Extraterrestrial Life. One of the first volunteer computing projects, SETI@home has had over 6 million participants since it was launched in 1999. A volunteer downloads and installs a program that runs as a *screensaver*, which is a moving image that appears on a computer screen when the computer has been idle for a specified period of time. This allows SETI to utilize the processing abilities of the individual's computer without having to pay for processing time and without compromising the computer owner's ability to complete his or her own projects. The SETI screensaver is actually a complex piece of software that analyzes radio telescope data to search for extraterrestrial intelligence (Figure 1.18). At http://boinc.berkeley.edu, you can choose from a variety of projects to join.

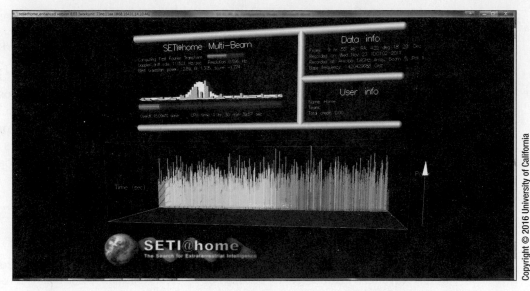

FIGURE 1.18 The SETI@home screen saver displays the results of the processing of signals by a computer.

Multiuser systems enable organizations to leverage the power of computers that far exceed what a PC can do. The ability to centrally manage information and security and to distribute the processing across multiple systems has given the scientific and business communities the power to solve many of our most pressing problems in an extremely short amount of time.

Objective 8 | Explain the Safe and Efficient Use of Technology

As a Guest Relations Officer, you sometimes spend many hours a day working on a computer system. It is important to have a workspace that is comfortable and arranged for safe, healthy work habits.

Concept 1.14 | Creating Healthy and Safe Workspaces

An improperly set up workspace can affect your health, comfort, and productivity. ***Ergonomics*** is the study of the relationship between workers and their workspaces. Ergonomic design creates a work environment that reduces illnesses and musculoskeletal disorders. The furniture you use, the lighting in the room, and the position of your equipment all affect your work environment. Try to follow these basic ergonomic principles:

- Place your computer equipment in a secure position so it will not fall or cause an accident, use a surge protector, and avoid plugging too many devices into the same electrical outlet.

- Leave plenty of space around your computer equipment for sufficient air circulation to prevent overheating.

- Make sure computer cables, cords, and wires are fastened securely and not left where you could trip over them or where they could cause a fire.

- Keep your computer area free of dust, food, and liquids. Moisture, static electricity, and magnetic interference affect your system's performance.

Whether you are working in class at a desktop computer, sitting on the couch playing video games, or reading a book on an e-reader at the beach, your goal should be to keep your body in a neutral body position without twisting or turning to reach or see your screen. You should not need to lean forward, and your feet should be flat on the ground or on a footrest. Your monitor should be at or below eye level so you do not need to tilt your neck to see it, and the lighting should not cause glare on your screen. The keyboard and mouse should be positioned so your arms are in a relaxed position. One important step that many people forget is to take regular breaks to stretch and move around. Following ergonomic design principles will help you work more comfortably and reduce strain on your body (Figure 1.19). Technology can help you be more ergonomic—for example, an app on the Apple watch will remind you to stand up every 50 minutes.

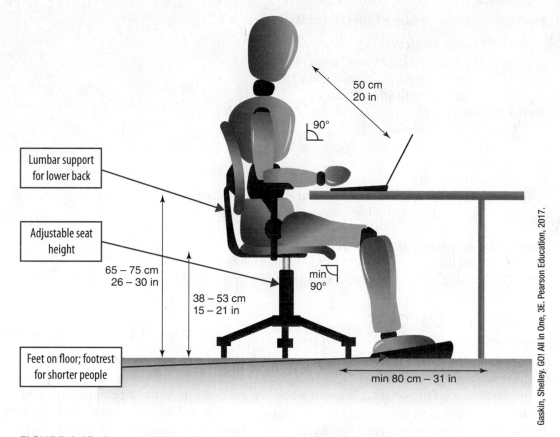

50 cm
20 in

90°

Lumbar support for lower back

Adjustable seat height

65 – 75 cm
26 – 30 in

38 – 53 cm
15 – 21 in

min 90°

Feet on floor; footrest for shorter people

min 80 cm – 31 in

Gaskin, Shelley. GO! All in One, 3E. Pearson Education, 2017.

FIGURE 1.19 Characteristics of an ergonomically correct workstation.

Universal design principles not only help create environments that accommodate people with disabilities, but also benefit those with no special needs. For example, wider doorways allow wheelchairs and walkers through and also make it easier to carry merchandise and move furniture. In technology, applying universal design means designing spaces that are easily accessible. This term also refers to input and output devices that can be used and adjusted by everyone. Devices should be simple and intuitive to use for everyone.

☑ **Check Your Knowledge:**   In MyITLab, take the quiz covering Objectives 5–8.

GO! To Work

Andrew Rodriguez / Fotolia; FotolEdhar/ Fotolia; apops/ Fotolia; Yuri Arcurs/ Fotolia

IC3 SKILLS IN THIS CHAPTER

IC3 —Module 1: Computing Fundamentals

Section 1.01 Mobile Devices
    (a) Understand cellular phone concepts
    (b) Be familiar with cellular-enabled tablets
    (c) Be familiar with smartphones

Section 1.02 Hardware
    (a) Types of devices
        (i) Server
        (ii) Laptop
        (iii) Desktop
    (b) Know the impact of memory and storage on usage
    (h) Know platform implications and considerations
        (i) For Example Mac, PC, Linux, iOS, Android, Firmware

Section 1.03 Computer Software Architecture
    (f) Know file structures and file/folder management
        (i) Managing electronic media [eBooks, songs, videos]

GO! FOR JOB SUCCESS

Topic: Resume Credibility?

Your instructor may assign these questions to your class, and then ask you to think about them or discuss them with your classmates:

    Your resume is an important document when you are building your career, and you want to create the best possible image. However, it is critical to provide only accurate information, particularly in the areas of job history and education. Experts agree, you should resist any temptation to exaggerate or inflate your accomplishments.

FotolEdhar / Fotolia

> **Why is it important to be completely factual when listing accomplishments on your resume?**

> **What are some reasons job applicants might inflate their abilities or experience?**

> **What are some steps you can take to be sure your resume is accurate?**

END OF CHAPTER

SUMMARY

Ubiquitous computing means technology recedes into the background. Convergence is the integration of multiple technologies, such as cell phones, cameras, and MP3 players, on a single device.

A computer converts data into information using the four steps of the information processing cycle: input, processing, output, and storage. Digital data is measured in bits and bytes.

Personal computers include: desktops, workstations, and all-in-ones; portable computers including notebooks, tablets, netbooks, and subnotebooks; and other devices such as smartphones, e-readers, and GPS systems.

Multiuser computers include servers and mainframe computers. Supercomputers perform complex mathematical calculations. Distributed computing is processing a task across a group of computers.

GO! LEARN IT ONLINE

Review the concepts, key terms, and IC3 skills in this chapter by completing these online challenges, which you can find in **MyITLab**.

Matching and Multiple Choice: Answer matching and multiple choice questions to test what you learned in this chapter.

Lessons on the GO!: Learn how to use all the new apps and features as they are introduced by Microsoft.

IC3 Prep Quiz: Answer questions to review the IC3 skills that you practiced in this chapter.

GLOSSARY

GLOSSARY OF CHAPTER KEY TERMS

All-in-one computer A compact desktop computer with the system unit integrated into the monitor.

Analytical Engine A mechanical computer designed, but never built, in the early nineteenth century by mathematician Charles Babbage that could be programmed using punched cards.

Artificial intelligence The branch of science concerned with making computers behave like humans.

ASCII (American Standard Code for Information Interchange) An 8-bit binary code set with 256 characters.

Backlit A device that includes an internal light source.

Backward compatibility The ability to run some older programs on a newer system.

Binary code A system that represents digital data as a series of 0s and 1s that can be understood by a computer.

Binary number system (base 2) A number system that has only two digits—0 and 1.

Bit (binary digit) The smallest unit of digital data.

Byte Consists of 8 bits and is used to represent a single character in modern computer systems.

Central processing unit (CPU) A complex integrated circuit that contains processing circuitry that enables it to behave as the brain of the computer, control all functions performed by other components, and process all the commands it receives. Also referred to as a *microprocessor*.

Chromebook A subnotebook that run the Chrome OS—a version of the Linux operating system released by Google.

Client A computer that connects to, or requests services from, another computer called a server.

Computer A programmable machine that converts raw data into useful information.

Convergence The integration of technology on multifunction devices, such as smartphones.

Convertible notebook A type of notebook computer that has a screen that can swivel to fold into what resembles a notepad or tablet.

Data Numbers, words, pictures, or sounds that represent facts about people, events, things, or ideas.

Desktop computer A personal computer designed to sit on your desk.

Distributed computing The distribution of the processing of a task across a group of computers.

Drone An aircraft piloted by remote control or onboard computers. Also known as an *unmanned aircraft system* (UAS).

Embedded computer A specialized computer found in ordinary devices, such as gasoline pumps, supermarket checkouts, traffic lights, and home appliances.

ENIAC (Electronic Numerical Integrator and Computer) The first working, digital, general-purpose computer; built at the University of Pennsylvania between 1943 and 1946.

Enterprise server A large multiuser computer that can perform millions of transactions in a day.

E-book A book in a digital format that can be read on a screen.

E-ink An e-reader technology that creates a screen that is easy on the eyes and most like the experience of reading a printed book.

E-reader A special class of tablet specifically to read books, magazines, and other publications.

Ergonomics The study of the relationship between workers and their workspaces.

Game console A home entertainment system that connects to a television or monitor to display a game.

Game controller A device used to interact with a video game.

Geocaching An electronic scavenger hunt where players (geocachers) hide geocaches and post GPS coordinates on the Internet for other geocachers to find.

GPS (global positioning system) A system of at least 24 satellites that transmit signals that can be picked up by a receiver on the ground and used to determine the receiver's current location, time, and velocity through triangulation of the signals.

Green computing The efficient and eco-friendly use of computers and other electronics.

Grid computing Distributed computing using a few computers in one location.

Information Data converted into a meaningful format.

Information processing cycle (IPC) The process a computer uses to convert data into information. The four steps of the IPC are input, processing, storage, and output.

Input The process of entering raw data into a system.

Integrated circuit A chip that contains a large number of tiny transistors that are fabricated into a semiconducting material called silicon.

Internet of Things (IoT) The connection of the physical world to the Internet. Objects are tagged and can be located, monitored, and controlled using small embedded electronics.

Laptop A portable personal computer. Also referred to as a *notebook*.

Mac computer A personal computer manufactured by Apple that runs the OS X operating system.

Mainframe A large multiuser computer that can perform millions of transactions in a day.

Microprocessor A complex integrated circuit that contains processing circuitry that enables it to behave as the brain of the computer, control all functions performed by other components, and process all the commands it receives. Also referred to as the *central processing unit*, or *CPU*.

Mobile application (mobile app) A program that extends the functionality of a mobile device.

Mobile device A portable computer for business and entertainment; mobile devices come in many different shapes and sizes such as smartphones, tablets, and other specialized devices.

Mobile payment system Using a mobile device rather than cash or credit cards to pay for items.

Moore's Law An observation made by Gordon Moore in 1965 that the number of transistors that can be placed on an integrated circuit had doubled roughly every two years.

Multiuser computer A system that allows multiple, simultaneous users to connect to it, allowing for centralized resources and security.

Netbook A lightweight, inexpensive notebook computer designed primarily for Internet access, with built-in wireless capabilities, a small screen, and limited computing power and storage.

Notebook A portable personal computer. Also referred to as a *laptop*.

Output The display of processed data.

Personal computer (PC) A small microprocessor-based computer designed to be used by one person at a time.

Petaflops A measure of computer performance obtainable by today's supercomputers.

Processing The manipulation, calculation, or organization of data to create useful information.

Screensaver A moving image that appears on a computer screen when the computer has been idle for a specified period of time.

Server A multiuser computer system that provides services, such as Internet access, email, or file and print services, to client systems.

Smart appliance An appliance that plugs into the smart grid and can monitor signals from the power company. When the electric grid system is stressed, the appliance can react by reducing power consumption.

Smart grid A network for delivering electricity to consumers that includes communication technology to manage electricity distribution efficiently.

Smart home A building that uses automation to control lighting, heating and cooling, security, entertainment, and appliances.

Smartphone A small computer that combines a cellular phone with such features as Internet and email access, a digital camera, GPS and mapping tools, the ability to edit documents, and access to mobile apps.

Storage Saving digital information for archiving or later access.

stylus A special pen-like input tool that enables you to write directly on a touch screen.

subnotebook A notebook computer that is thin and light and that has high-end processing and video capabilities.

Supercomputer A very expensive computer system that is used to perform complex mathematical calculations, such as those used in weather forecasting and medical research.

Tablet A handheld, mobile device somewhere between a computer and a smartphone.

Transistor A tiny electric switch used in second-generation computers.

Triangulation A mathematical principle used by GPS to determine the position of the receiving device in three dimensions.

Turing machine A machine that can perform mathematical computations.

Turing test Measures a machine's ability to display intelligent behavior.

Two-in-one notebook A portable computer that converts to a tablet by detaching the screen from the keyboard.

Ubiquitous computing (ubicomp) Sometimes called invisible computing, technology that recedes into the background and becomes part of the user's environment.

Ultrabook A small Windows notebook computer with high-end processing and video capabilities built into a lightweight system.

Unicode An extended ASCII set that has become the standard on the Internet and includes codes for most of the world's written languages, mathematical systems, and special characters. It has codes for over 100,000 characters.

Universal design Design principles that help create environments that accommodate people with disabilities, but also benefit those without.

Unmanned aircraft system (UAS) An aircraft piloted by remote control or onboard computers. Also known as a *drone*.

Vacuum tube A tube that resembles an incandescent light bulb that was used in first-generation computers.

Video game simulation A system that replicates realistic environments and scenarios.

Video game system A computer system that is designed primarily to play games.

Workstation A high-end desktop computer or one that is attached to a network in a business setting.

GO! Do It

Andrew Rodriguez / Fotolia; FotoIEdhar/ Fotolia; apops/ Fotolia; Yuri Arcurs/ Fotolia

EVALUATE YOUR WORKSTATION ERGONOMICS

The Occupational Safety and Health Administration website has a computer workstation checklist available at http://osha.gov/SLTC/etools/computerworkstations. This checklist is provided with your student data files.

1. From your student data files, open the file **aio01_DOIT_answersheet**. Display the **Save As** dialog box, navigate to the location where you will store your documents for this chapter, and then create a new folder named **AIO Chapter 1** Open the folder, and then save the file as **Lastname_Firstname_01_DOIT_answersheet**

2. Use the checklist to evaluate your computer workstation at home, at work, or on your campus. How did your workstation fare?

3. What are some areas for improvement? How could you improve your score?

4. Print or submit your answer sheet electronically as directed by your instructor.

ON THE WEB

1. **Convergence** Innovation has led to smaller devices that cost less and do more. Today, a tablet or smartphone has the same processing power as a PC from a few years ago. From your student data files, open the file **aio01_OTW1_answersheet**, and then save the file in your **AIO Chapter 1** folder as **Lastname_Firstname_01_OTW1_answersheet** Research three of the newest smartphones or tablets on the market. Create a table comparing the features of each device. Use this research to decide which device would best meet your personal needs.

   Write your decision in a two- to three-paragraph essay. Which device should you buy and why? What other accessories will you need to purchase? Do you need to purchase a data plan to take advantage of all the device's features? Print or submit your answer sheet electronically as directed by your instructor.

2. **Computer History Timeline** There are many important people and events that led to modern computers. From your student data files, open the file **aio01_OTW2_answersheet**, and then save the file in your **AIO Chapter 1** folder as **Lastname_Firstname_01_OTW2_answersheet** In this Activity, you will create a timeline that illustrates the people and events *you* think are the most significant.

   Create a timeline showing five to seven important milestones of the development of computers over the past two centuries. Use a free online timeline generator such as TimeGlider or a presentation tool such as Prezi or PowerPoint to create your timeline. Prepare a summary of your timeline and include the URL where it can be viewed. Print or submit your answer sheet electronically as directed by your instructor.

ETHICS AND SOCIAL MEDIA

1. **Ten Commandments of Computer Ethics** From your student data files, open the file **aio01_ESM1_answersheet**, and then save the file in your **AIO Chapter 1** folder as **Lastname_Firstname_01_ESM1_answersheet** Use a search engine to locate the Ten Commandments of Computer Ethics published by the Computer Ethics Institute.

   Read each one and indicate three commandments with which you agree and three with which you disagree. Give logical and historical reasons for your opinions. Given that they were written in 1992, do you find them still relevant? Cite your references, and present your opinions in a one-page report. Print or submit your answer sheet electronically as directed by your instructor.

2. **Social Media Uses** From your student data files, open the file **aio01_ESM2_answersheet**, and then save the file in your **AIO Chapter 1** folder as **Lastname_Firstname_01_ESM2_answersheet** Create a short survey of eight questions regarding the use of social media and the consequences of using social media—good and bad. Try to construct a question that will enable you to determine why individuals use social media. Construct another question to determine if respondents were ever prevented from obtaining a job because of their inappropriate use of social media.

   Distribute your survey to 25 individuals, and when doing so, attempt to get a range of ages, employment experience, and a mix of male and female respondents. Compile your results and share your results and conclusions with your class. Print or submit your answer sheet electronically as directed by your instructor.

COLLABORATION

1. **Drones** From your student data files, open the file **aio01_Collab1_answersheet**, and then save the file in your **AIO Chapter 1** folder as **Lastname_Firstname_01_Collab1_answersheet** As a team, use a search engine to research the commercial uses of drones.

   Create an infographic using an online tool such as Canva (http://canva.com), Easelly (http://easel.ly), or Piktochart (http://piktochart.com) that illustrates current and future commercial uses of drones. Take a screen shot of your infographic and paste it into your answer sheet, or export it as an image file. Print or submit your infographic or answer sheet electronically as directed by your instructor.

2. **Historical Figure** From your student data files, open the file **aio01_Collab2_answersheet**, and then save the file in your **AIO Chapter 1** folder as

   Lastname_Firstname_01_Collab2_answersheet As a team, research a famous person mentioned in this chapter or one of the following: George Boole, Vannevar Bush, Nikola Tesla, Gottfried Wilhelm Leibniz, Grace Hopper.

   Prepare a dialogue depicting a news reporter interviewing this person. Use at least three references, only one of which may be this textbook. Submit the script and provide documentation that all team members have contributed to the project.

   Perform the interview in a newscast format using the dialogue you have written. The interview should be 3 to 5 minutes long. If possible, videotape the interview, and share the newscast with the rest of the class. Print or submit your answer sheet electronically as directed by your instructor.

Hardware

OUTCOMES

Identify the parts of a computer and their features and functions.
Recognize the advantages and limitations of important peripheral devices.

OBJECTIVES

1. Explain the Function of the Central Processing Unit
2. Identify the Parts of a System Unit and Motherboard
3. Describe Input Devices and Their Uses
4. Describe Output Devices and Their Uses
5. Compare Printer Types
6. Discuss Communication Devices
7. Compare Storage Devices

Dotshock/Shutterstock

In This Chapter

Computers come in a wide range of configurations. There are numerous components that make up and enhance a computer system, and it's useful to understand these elements, their functions, and the many options that are available. Understanding the different parts of a computer system will help you to work more efficiently and effectively.

In this chapter, you will study the hardware components of a computer system and explore how they operate. This information will help you understand the workings and limitations of your system and make you more comfortable talking about technology on a professional level.

Job Focus

At **Oro Jade Hotels**, as a **Site Manager**, you coordinate and supervise the day-to-day operations of the hotel. The job includes managing and supervising departmental managers and staff; carrying out administrative tasks; such as reviewing applications from job candidates; and hiring, firing, and training employees. As Site Manager, you are responsible for customer relations as well as the cleanliness, appearance, maintenance, and all other aspects of the hotel. Creating a warm and welcoming atmosphere encourages guests to return and to recommend Oro Jade to others.

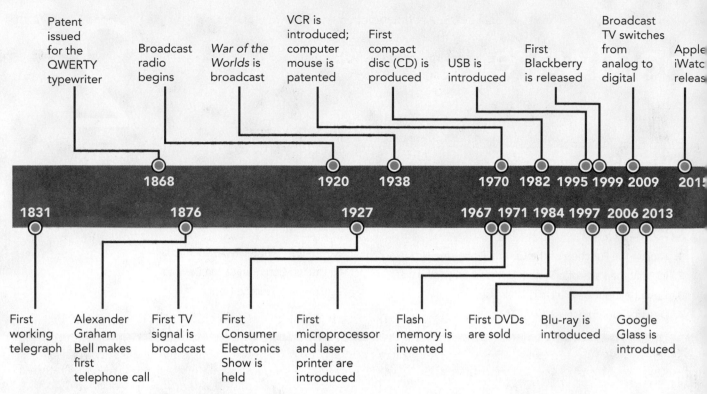

FIGURE 2.1 This timeline highlights important dates in computer history.

Objective 1 | Explain the Function of the Central Processing Unit

As a Site Manager, the computer system that you use is an indispensable tool for your work. You need a dependable system with robust power and reliability. It is useful to know your computer needs and understand how to explain them, so that when you ask your Information Technology department for support, you can explain the problem or situation accurately.

Computers perform four tasks: input, processing, output, and storage. *Hardware* refers to the physical components of a computer. The computer itself consists of the components that process data. The components that serve the input, output, and storage functions are called *peripheral devices*. Peripherals can be external devices or they can be integrated into the system unit.

Concept 2.01 | Examining the Central Processing Unit

The brain of a computer is the *central processing unit (CPU)*, or *processor*, and is housed inside the system unit on the motherboard. The CPU consists of two parts: the *arithmetic logic unit (ALU)* that performs arithmetic and logic calculations and the *control unit* that manages the movement of data through the CPU. Together, these units execute program instructions, including performing calculations and making decisions.

The CPU uses the *instruction cycle*, which is also known as the *machine cycle*, to process each instruction. The four steps of the machine cycle are fetch, decode, execute, and store (Figure 2.2).

- Fetch retrieves the next instruction from the program stored in the computer's random access memory (RAM) located on the motherboard.

- Decode translates the fetched instruction into a form that the control unit understands.

- Execute performs the requested instruction using the arithmetic logic unit—the ALU—to perform arithmetic operations, which include addition, subtraction, multiplication, and division, and logical operations (AND, OR, and NOT) that involve the comparison of two or more data items. Arithmetic operations return a numeric value. Logical operations return a value of *true* or *false*.

- Store holds the results in an internal register—a location on the CPU—for further use by the CPU or in a location in RAM.

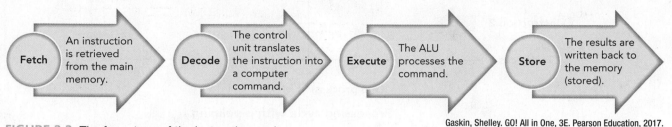

Gaskin, Shelley. GO! All in One, 3E. Pearson Education, 2017.

FIGURE 2.2 The four steps of the instruction cycle.

Concept 2.02 | Improving CPU Performance

The instruction cycle happens so quickly that you are unaware of what is happening. In fact, the processor executes billions of cycles each second. When evaluating processors for performance, one of the variables to consider is **clock speed**, which is the speed at which the processer executes the cycles. Clock speed is measured in billions of cycles per second—referred to as gigahertz and abbreviated GHz. A 3-GHz processor executes 3 billion data cycles per second.

A **multi-core processor** consists of two or more processors that are integrated on a single chip. Multi-core processing increases the processing speed over single-core processors and reduces energy consumption over multiple separate processors. Dual-core, quad-core, and even six- and eight-core processors are found on most personal computers. Multiple processors are typically found in servers, which might have as few as two processors or as many as several hundred. Supercomputers can have thousands of processors.

A video card can have its own processor called a **graphics processing unit (GPU)**, which can contain multiple cores. The GPU reduces the processing required of the system CPU for graphic-intensive processes.

Modern computers are capable of processing multiple instructions simultaneously, which increases the efficiency of the processor and the performance of the computer. **Pipelining** is the method that a processor uses to process multiple instructions simultaneously. As soon as the first instruction has moved from the fetch to the decode stage, the processor fetches the next instruction, as shown in Figure 2.3. The process works much like an assembly line in a factory.

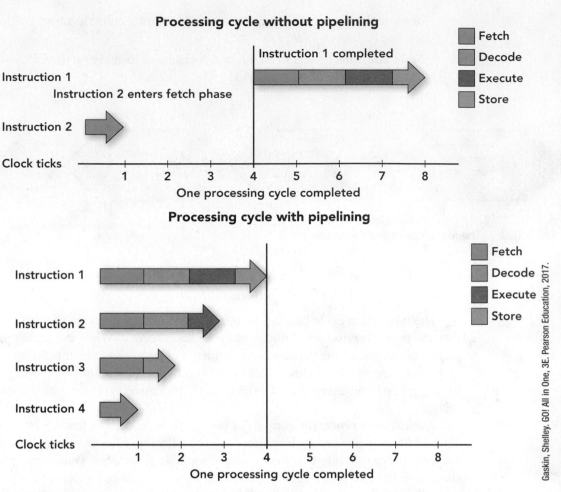

FIGURE 2.3 Without pipelining, one instruction goes through the machine cycle before another one begins the cycle. With pipelining, when an instruction moves from one phase of the cycle to the next, another instruction moves into the vacated phase, greatly reducing processing time.

Parallel processing uses multiple processors or multi-core processors to divide up processing tasks, which can dramatically increase computer performance when running processor-intensive programs, such as system scans or multiple simultaneous programs. Each processor may also use pipelining to boost the processing efficiency of the system further.

Working quickly and using multiple processors or processing paths generates a great deal of heat. Excessive heat can damage a processor or cause it to fail, so computers provide cooling systems for the CPU. To keep the processor from overheating, a *heat sink* and cooling fan are installed above the processor to dissipate the heat the processor produces. The heat sink is composed of metal or ceramic and draws heat away from the processor. The cooling fan then moves the heat away from the CPU (Figure 2.4). A system unit has one or more case fans to keep the entire system cool. Some computers have a liquid cooling system that works like a car radiator by circulating liquid through tubes in the system carrying heat away from the processor.

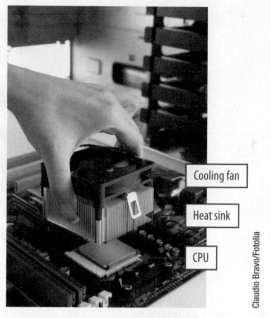

FIGURE 2.4 The cooling fan and heat sink are installed above the CPU.

When using a notebook computer, you should place it on a hard surface, making sure not to block the air vents. You should not use a notebook on your lap, where it can actually cause skin damage and overheat your computer. You can also purchase a USB-powered cooler for notebooks that tend to heat quickly—sometimes referred to as running hot.

Objective 2 | Identify the Parts of a System Unit and Motherboard

Tech to GO!
Setting Up a Computer System

In your job as Site Manager, you rely on your computer system to provide you with the power and reliability to perform your everyday tasks without the frustration of using a slow, outdated system. When your computer needs replacing, you want to be sure that you understand what is inside the box so that you can choose a system that will meet all of your processing needs.

The *system unit* is the case that encloses and protects the power supply, motherboard, processor—the CPU—and memory of a computer. It also has *drive bays* to hold the storage devices and openings for peripheral devices to connect to *expansion cards* on the motherboard. The system unit is what holds everything together (Figure 2.5).

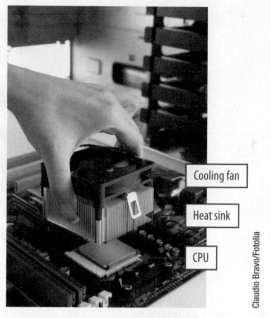

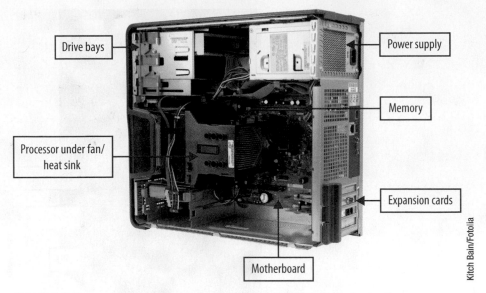

FIGURE 2.5 The system unit is the case that protects and encloses the computer components.

Concept 2.03 | Exploring the Motherboard

The main circuit board of a computer is the ***motherboard***. In addition to housing the CPU, it contains drive controllers and interfaces, expansion slots, data buses, ports and connectors, the BIOS, and memory (Figure 2.6). A motherboard may also include integrated peripherals, such as video, sound, and network adapters. The motherboard provides the way for devices to attach to your computer. Take a moment to study the parts of the motherboard described in Figure 2.7.

FIGURE 2.6 A motherboard with expansion slots, drive controllers, and memory slots.

PARTS OF THE MOTHERBOARD	
COMPONENT	**DESCRIPTION**
Adapter card or Expansion card	A small circuit board that plugs directly into an expansion slot on the motherboard and allows you to connect additional peripheral devices to a computer.
BIOS (basic input output system)	A program, stored on a chip on the motherboard, which is used to start up the computer.
Central processing unit (CPU)	The brain of a computer housed inside the system unit on the motherboard. Also known as the processor.
CMOS (complementary metal oxide semiconductor)	A chip on the motherboard where the BIOS settings are stored. It is volatile memory that uses a small battery to provide it with power to keep the data in memory even when the computer is turned off.
Data bus	Wires on the motherboard over which data flows between the components of the computer.
Drive controller	A component of a motherboard that provides a drive interface, which connects disk drives to the processor.
EIDE (enhanced integrated drive electronics)	Legacy drive interface that may still be found on older computers.
Expansion slot	A component located on the motherboard that enables you to connect an adapter card to a computer.
Port	A connection point that is used to attach peripheral devices to the motherboard.
RAM (random access memory)	A volatile form of memory that stores the operating systems, programs, and data the computer is currently using.
SATA (serial ATA)	The standard internal drive interface used to connect drives to the motherboard.

FIGURE 2.7

Gaskin, Shelley. GO! All in One, 3E. Pearson Education, 2017.

A drive controller on the motherboard provides a drive interface, which connects disk drives to the processor. SATA—Serial Advanced Technology Attachment—is the standard internal drive interface for connecting hard drives into computer systems, but the EIDE—enhanced integrated drive electronics interface—may still be found on older computers. SATA is up to three times faster than EIDE and has smaller, thinner cables that take up less space and allow for better airflow inside the system unit.

Expansion cards (Figure 2.8), also called adapter cards, are small circuit boards that plug directly into expansion slots on the motherboard and enable you to connect additional peripheral devices to a computer. An expansion slot is a receptacle for a card that interfaces with a computer's circuitry. Video cards, network cards, sound cards, and TV tuners are common expansion cards. Most expansion cards plug into a Peripheral Component Interconnect, or PCI, or into the faster PCI express—PCIe—slot on the motherboard. Systems manufactured before 2009 used an accelerated graphics port, or AGP, for video.

FireWire card

Sound card

Video card

Aigarsr/Fotolia

FIGURE 2.8 Expansion cards: FireWire, sound, video.

Data flows between the components of the computer over wires on the motherboard called data buses. Local buses connect the internal devices on the motherboard, and external buses connect the peripheral devices to the CPU and memory of the computer. The speed of the data bus is an important factor in the performance of the system.

Concept 2.04 | Comparing Ports and Connectors

Ports connect peripheral devices to the motherboard. Two common ports found are USB and FireWire. Serial, parallel, and PS/2 ports are older ports and not typically found on modern computers (Figure 2.9).

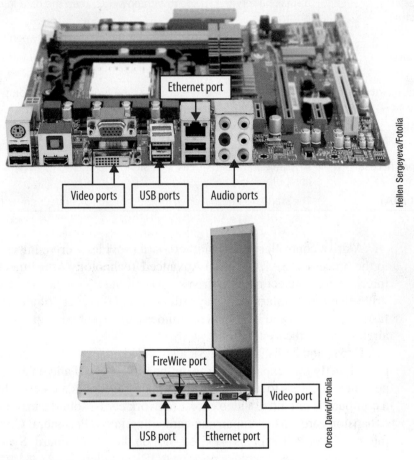

FIGURE 2.9 Some common motherboard ports.

Universal Serial Bus, commonly referred to as *USB*, is a standard port type that connects many kinds of devices, including printers, mice, keyboards, digital cameras, and external drives. Up to 127 devices can share a single USB port. Most computers provide enough connections for all the peripheral devices you might have. USB also provides power to some devices, which enables you to use a USB port to charge a mobile device and power your devices such as webcams. Another advantage of USB devices is that they are hot-swappable, meaning they can be plugged and unplugged without turning off the computer. USB 1.0 was introduced in 1996 and was replaced by USB 2.0 in 2000, which is called Hi-Speed USB and is 40 times faster than its predecessor. The USB 3.0—SuperSpeed—standard, released in 2008, is about 10 times faster than USB 2.0. This additional speed is particularly valuable for hard drives and digital video applications. The standard connection to the computer or hub is called USB-A. USB-B and various mini, micro, and proprietary formats are used to connect to USB devices. The newest version, USB-C, sometimes referred to as USB 3.1, is twice as fast as USB 3.0 and takes up much less space, so it is ideal for the thinnest notebook computers.

FireWire, also known as *IEEE 1394*, was originally released by Apple in 1995. FireWire is hot-swappable and can connect up to 63 devices per port. It also allows for peer-to-peer communication between devices, such as two video cameras, without the use of a computer. The original FireWire 400 is roughly equal to USB 2.0 in speed, and FireWire 800 is twice as fast as FireWire 400. Today, FireWire is primarily used to connect high-end digital camcorders, which benefit from its superior speed. FireWire also can power some devices. FireWire has largely been replaced by USB and the newer *Thunderbolt* technology. Thunderbolt was developed by IBM and Apple and is the standard on most Apple computers. It carries both PCIe and DisplayPort video signals on the same cable, so it can be used to connect many different types of peripherals to a computer. Thunderbolt combines two 10 Gbps channels, making it four times faster than USB 3.0 and 12 times faster than FireWire. You can connect up to six devices using one Thunderbolt connection.

Bluetooth is a short-range wireless technology that's used to connect many types of peripheral devices. It is commonly used to connect mice, keyboards, and printers to personal computers. A computer must have an adapter to communicate with Bluetooth-enabled devices. Bluetooth is also used in game consoles, such as the Nintendo Wii and Sony PlayStation 4, to connect game controllers, and in other applications, such as connecting a smartphone to a vehicle communication system.

Concept 2.05 | Looking at the BIOS

The BIOS, which is the acronym for basic input output system, is a program stored on a chip on the motherboard that starts the computer. The BIOS chip is *read-only memory*, abbreviated as *ROM*, and is a form of *nonvolatile memory*; it does not need power to keep its data. The BIOS uses settings stored on the CMOS chip, which is also on the motherboard. CMOS, which is the acronym for complementary metal oxide semiconductor, is *volatile memory*—any information left in volatile memory is lost when the power is turned off. CMOS uses a small battery to provide it with power to keep the data in memory even when the computer is turned off.

Concept 2.06 | Comparing Types of Memory

Memory is temporary storage that your computer uses to hold instructions and data. The two important types of memory a computer uses are random access memory and cache memory. Your computer stores the operating systems, programs, and data currently in use in random access memory, which is referred to as RAM. You can think of it as your workspace. A computer that does not have enough RAM will be very slow and difficult to use. RAM is volatile memory. For this reason, any work that you have not saved is lost when you close a program or turn off your computer.

Memory boards are small circuit boards that contain memory chips. Most desktop memory uses a *dual in-line memory module*, referred to as *DIMM*. Notebooks use the *small outline dual in-line memory module*, also referred to as *SODIMM*, configuration (Figure 2.10). There are several types of RAM available. Older computers used SDRAM or synchronous dynamic random access memory, and DDR, or double data rate, and DDR2 SDRAM. Newer computers use DDR3. Each type of memory is faster and more efficient than its predecessor. RAM is fairly easy to install, and adding more memory to a computer is an inexpensive way to increase its performance. Installing additional RAM in an older computer can significantly extend its useful life.

Desktop DIMM

Notebook SODIMM

Ksena32/Fotolia

FIGURE 2.10 Desktop DIMMs are about twice the size of a notebook SODIMM.

Most computers have a small amount of very fast memory called *cache memory* that stores frequently accessed information close to the processor. Because it is located close to the processor, it decreases the time it takes to access the data and improves the processor performance. Level 1, or L1, cache is built into the processor; Level 2, or L2, cache is on a separate chip and takes slightly longer to access. Modern processors may have L2 cache built in and have a Level 3, or L3, cache on the motherboard. Each progressive level of cache is farther from the CPU and takes longer to access.

Objective 3 Describe Input Devices and Their Uses

In your job as Site Manager, you must input data into your computer frequently. An *input device* enters data into the computer system so that it can be processed. There are many types of input devices, but the most common are keyboards and mice. Input devices enable you to interact with technology in many different ways, from playing a video game to tapping out an email on a smartphone.

Concept 2.07 | Identifying Keyboards

A *keyboard* uses switches and circuits to translate keystrokes into a signal a computer understands and is the primary input device for entering text into a computer. The most common type of keyboard is the standard *QWERTY* format. *QWERTY* are the first alphabetic keys on the top left of the keyboard. The design was originally developed in 1874 to reduce the number of key jams on a mechanical typewriter. Because computer keyboards are not mechanical, the QWERTY layout is not necessarily required. Keyboards can have alternate layouts or be customized for a particular application. The *Dvorak Simplified Keyboard* places the most commonly used letters where they are more easily accessed to increase efficiency and reduce fatigue. Most modern operating systems include support for the Dvorak layout, but it has not been widely adopted.

In addition to the alphabet and number keys, most standard keyboards have specialized keys (Figure 2.11). Some keys, such as Esc and the Function keys across the top of the keyboard, have specific actions associated with them. Other keys, such as Ctrl, Alt, and Shift, are *modifier keys* and are pressed in conjunction with other keys. *Toggle keys*, such as CapsLock and NumLock, turn a feature on or off when pressed. Full-sized keyboards contain 101 or 104 keys, but notebook computer keyboards are smaller and may not include a separate numeric keypad.

SPECIAL KEYS		
KEY	**TYPE**	**ACTION**
Esc	Normal	Cancel
CapsLock	Toggle	Turns capitalization on/off
Shift	Modifier—pressed with at least one other key	Activates uppercase or alternate-key assignment
Ctrl (Windows)/ Command ⌘ (Mac)	Modifier—pressed with at least one other key	Modifies the behavior of a key press
Alt (Windows)/ Option (Mac)	Modifier—pressed with at least one other key	Modifies the behavior of a key press
⊞	Normal	Displays the Start screen

FIGURE 2.11

Gaskin, Shelley. GO! All in One, 3E. Pearson Education, 2017.

Ergonomic keyboards have a curved shape and keep the wrists in a more natural position to reduce strain. They may look odd, but many people who spend a lot of time on the computer rely on them to prevent injuries.

Another alternative keyboard is a *keypad*, a small keyboard that does not contain all the alphabet keys. People who enter a lot of numbers, such as teachers, accountants, and telemarketers, might find it useful to attach a USB keypad to a notebook computer. Many computer gamers find a dedicated game keypad makes gameplay easier and more fun (Figure 2.12).

Creativa Images/Fotolia　　Kazukazu/Fotolia

FIGURE 2.12 A full-sized ergonomic keyboard and a numeric keypad

IC3
DIGITAL LITERACY CERTIFICATION
1.02n

Concept 2.08 | Comparing a Mouse, Touchscreen, and Other Pointing Devices

Pointing devices are input devices that enable you to interact with objects by moving a pointer on the computer screen. Many different versions of each of these devices are available. They enable you to point and click instead of typing commands (Figure 2.13).

Bloomua/Fotolia　　Natalia Merzlyakova/Fotolia　　Brian Kinney/Fotolia

FIGURE 2.13 Pointing devices: touchscreen, mouse, and stylus.

A *mouse* may include one or more buttons and a scroll wheel and works by moving across a smooth surface to signal movement of the pointer. An *optical mouse* detects motion by bouncing light from a red *LED—light-emitting diode*—off the surface below it. An LED is an electronic component that emits light when an electrical current is passed through it. Most notebook computers include a built-in *touchpad* that you can use instead of a mouse. With this device, motion is detected by moving your finger across the touch-sensitive surface. Touchpads also have buttons that function like mouse buttons and special areas that enable you to scroll quickly through documents, webpages, and images.

Tablets, cell phones, handheld game consoles, and other devices have *touchscreens* that can accept input from a finger or stylus. A *stylus* is a special pen-like input tool. Touchscreens that have a *resistive screen* sense pressure and can be used with a finger or an ordinary stylus. A resistive screen could be used by someone wearing gloves. A *capacitive screen* senses the conductive properties of an object such as a finger or a specially designed conductive stylus. *Interactive whiteboards* are large, interactive touch-sensitive displays found in classrooms and businesses. They enable you to control the computer from the screen and to capture what is written on the screen with special pens. The iPad Pro has an optional stylus called the Apple Pencil, which is pressure and angle sensitive. Using a stylus enables you to draw and write on the screen much more precisely than using your finger.

1.02b
1.02c

Concept 2.09 | Exploring Digital Cameras and Webcams

Digital cameras (Figure 2.14) can capture still images or video. The easiest cameras to use are *point-and-shoot*. They range from very simple and inexpensive cameras with limited features to expensive high-end cameras with sophisticated features. Most point-and-shoot cameras do not have a viewfinder to help you frame your image. They rely instead on the LCD screen. An *LCD* or *liquid crystal display* consists of two layers of glass that are glued together with a layer of liquid crystals between them. When electricity is passed through the individual crystals, it causes them to pass or block light to create an image. Most of the time this is fine, but some people feel that a true viewfinder does a better job of framing the shot. The cameras built in to smartphones and tablets can rival the best point-and-shoots.

FIGURE 2.14 A point-and-shoot, smartphone, and DSLR camera.

Basic point-and-shoot cameras are the simplest, least expensive, and have the fewest features. Basic cameras may not have a flash or viewfinder and may have limited or no optical zoom. These cameras may suffer from noticeable *shutter lag*—the time between pressing the button and the camera snapping the picture. When your subject is smiling and waiting for the flash to go off, several seconds can seem like a long time, and shutter lag can cause you to miss an action shot.

Advanced point-and-shoot cameras are moderate in price, features, and quality. Although still easy to use, they include better zoom, macro functions, viewfinders, and other special effects. Most also include the ability to capture video and may have other features like *image stabilization*, which accounts for camera shake and results in sharper images, and *burst mode*, which allows you to take several pictures in a burst by holding down the shutter button. Although more expensive than basic cameras, advanced point-and-shoots are still relatively inexpensive.

Also known as superzooms, *compact system cameras*, called *CSC*, are advanced point-and-shoot cameras that have interchangeable lenses, some manual controls, 10x to 26x optical zoom lenses, and the ability to capture HD video. CSCs produce better images than basic point-and-shoots. Other features include a hot shoe to attach an external flash and accessory ports to attach a microphone or a viewfinder. CSCs are also known as mirrorless cameras, because unlike *DSLRs* or *digital single lens reflex cameras*, they do not use a mirror to bounce light up from the lens to the viewfinder. This is one of the key differences between CSCs and DSLRs and makes CSCs smaller and lighter than DSLRs. Priced from about $300 to $2,000, CSCs are more expensive than most point-and-shoot cameras, but less expensive than most DSLR cameras. DSLRs are the most versatile and expensive type of digital cameras. With a DSLR, you can change the lens, which can cost hundreds or even thousands of dollars, to get the exact zoom you need. You can attach a hot shoe flash, manually adjust focus and exposure, and look through the viewfinder to frame your shot, all of which enable you to create artistic images that auto-focusing point-and-shoots cannot. There is almost no shutter lag, so DSLRs are the best type of digital camera for shooting action stills. Many DSLRs can shoot HD video. All this comes at a steep cost—from $700 to $5,000, plus hundreds or thousands of dollars for additional lenses.

Webcams are specialized video cameras that provide visual input for online communication. You can use a webcam in live video chat sessions through an instant messaging tool or through more sophisticated video-conferencing software. Webcams enable you to have virtual meetings with people anywhere, connect classrooms on different campuses, collaborate on projects with others in real time, or say goodnight to your family when you are far away. Such two-way interactions require both ends to have webcams and software setups that enable them to communicate with each other. Webcams are relatively inexpensive and come built in to most notebooks.

You can also use webcams to record video, but if you want to record something that is not directly in front of your computer, you will need a video camera. Most digital cameras and cell phones include a video mode. However, for the best quality, you may want a stand-alone video camera. A *digital video camera* enables you to record video that can be easily uploaded to your computer, where you can edit, store, and share the video. The features of video cameras are similar to those of regular digital cameras, and the more money you spend, the more features you get. Some video cameras are small, lightweight, and durable. They enable you to record your activities from your perspective. Rugged video cameras, such as the GoPro, are designed to go anywhere, even under water (Figure 2.15).

FIGURE 2.15 A video camera can record the action anywhere it occurs.

Scanners are input devices that have many uses, such as archiving old documents, checking out customers in grocery stores, organizing libraries, and assisting law enforcement. The use of *scanners* increases the speed and accuracy of data entry and converts information into a digital format that you can save, copy, and manipulate (Figure 2.16).

FIGURE 2.16 A handheld barcode scanner, a QR reader on a smartphone, and a biometric fingerprint scanner.

You can convert a photo or document into a digital file with an *optical scanner*. Flatbed scanners are the most common type of optical scanner found in homes and offices. You place the document or photo you want to scan on a glass screen, and the scanner head moves underneath the glass to convert the image to a digital file. Business card readers and photo scanners typically have a sheet-feed format that moves the page to be scanned and keeps the scanner head stationary. Handheld scanners such as barcode readers are small and portable. You see these in supermarket checkout lines, library circulation desks, and shipping operations.

QR code—Quick Response code—readers and barcode readers on cell phones make shopping in stores an interactive activity. Many retail stores include a QR code on the merchandise tag that you can scan to learn more about the item. Using *barcode scanners*, you can scan an item in a store and quickly determine which store or website has the lowest price. Website analytics can track webpages accessed from QR codes, which provides useful information to the retailer about its shoppers.

Inventory tracking, electronic toll collection, and contactless credit card transactions use a technology called *radio frequency identification* or *RFID*. Passports also use this technology, and there are some security and privacy concerns over the United States' decision to use RFID passports. An *RFID scanner* can read the information coded in an *RFID tag*, which contains a tiny antenna for receiving and sending a radio-frequency signal. *Near field communication* or *NFC* is a method that enables devices to share data with each other by touching them together or bringing them within a few centimeters of each other. Interaction is possible between two NFC-enabled devices or between an NFC device and an NFC tag. A Windows tablet can be configured to use a wireless printer by tapping an NFC tag that has the configuration encoded in it. Apple Pay uses the NFC antenna built into your iPhone to initiate a contactless payment to a merchant. You hold your iPhone near the contactless reader with your finger on Touch ID, and the merchant receives payment automatically. Because your iPhone recognizes you by your fingerprint, if your phone is lost or stolen, it can't be used by someone else.

A *magnetic strip reader*, another common scanner, can read information encoded in the magnetic strip on plastic cards such as drivers' licenses, gift cards, library cards, credit cards, and hotel door keys. *Biometric scanners* measure human characteristics, such as fingerprints and eye retinas, and can be found in banks to identify patrons, in theme parks to assure that tickets are not transferred to other guests, and in corporate security systems. Some notebook computers use a fingerprint scanner to ensure that the person trying to access the computer is an authorized user.

IC3
DIGITAL LITERACY
CERTIFICATION
1.02c (iii)

Concept 2.11 | Using Microphones and Game Controllers

Other common input devices include microphones, game controllers, and joysticks (Figure 2.17). *Microphones* convert sound into digital signals: use a microphone to chat in real time or as part of voice-recognition applications in video games and for dictating text. Microphones are often integrated into notebook computers and headsets or connect via USB to the microphone port on a sound card.

Oleg Kirillov/Fotolia

FIGURE 2.17 A game controller and microphone are input devices for use with video games and simulations.

A *game controller* interacts with a video game. Special game controllers include steering wheels, tennis rackets, musical instruments, and pressure-sensitive mats. These controllers make the gameplay more realistic. A *joystick*, which is mounted on a base, consists of a stick, buttons, and sometimes a trigger. A joystick is typically the game controller in flight-simulator games and is also useful for such tasks as controlling robotic machinery in a factory.

Concept 2.12 | Recognizing Adaptive Input Devices

Alternate input devices include Braille-writing devices, eye-driven keyboards, and keyboards that have locator dots on commonly used keys or large-print key labels. To type on a keyboard displayed on a screen—an on-screen keyboard—you can use a pointing device or touch the screen with your finger or a stylus. Such devices are found in many public locations, such as libraries, schools, and polling places. Trackballs, head wands, mouth sticks, and joysticks are all alternatives to the standard mouse.

Voice-recognition software enables you to verbally control a computer and dictate text. Windows Cortana and Apple's Siri are examples of personal digital assistants that use voice recognition. Software settings, such as Sticky Keys and Mouse Keys on a Windows computer, adapt a standard keyboard for those with limited fine-motor control and enable you to use arrow keys on the keyboard to move the pointer. The Apple OS X operating system includes similar accessibility features to control a Mac computer.

Input devices come in all shapes and sizes and enable you to interact with computer systems in many different ways. The type of input device you use depends on many factors, including the type of data to be input, the type of computer the input device is connected to, and the application you are using. Whether you are narrating a PowerPoint presentation, drawing a picture, or writing an email message, input devices are the way you get the data into the computer system so that it can be processed.

FAST FORWARD | Wearable Tech

At the 2015 Consumer Electronics Show, (**http://cesweb.org**), a big section of the show floor was dedicated to the growing area of **wearable tech**, such as wearable computers, virtual reality headsets, and smartwatches. This annual trade show provides a good glimpse into the future trends in technology.

Wearable computers provide hands-free computing. Headset computers are controlled by voice and head gestures. These devices are not just input devices; rather, they are full computers that can also connect to mobile devices and to the cloud. Virtual reality headsets provide an immersive experience in video games. These headsets replace or enhance a video game controller by enabling you to play the game using head motions and surround your head with goggles that make you feel as if you are in the game. There is no outside distraction as there is when watching the game on a monitor.

Smartwatches range from basic, inexpensive fitness trackers to full-fledged mobile computers that cost thousands of dollars. Manufacturers from Apple, Samsung, Motorola, and LG have developed smartwatches. A partnership between LG and Audi will enable you to unlock your car from your wrist. Voice recognition from Windows Cortana, Apple Siri, or Google enables you to interact with the smartwatch without touching objects on the tiny screen. Ask directions or see how many steps you've walked today. In a meeting, discreetly read an email without looking at your phone. This is a new and rapidly growing technology, and its potential is just beginning to be explored (Figure 2.18).

FIGURE 2.18 A smartwatch linked to a smartphone.

Andrey Popov/Shutterstock

Objective 4 | Describe Output Devices and Their Uses

As a Site Manager, there are times when you must spend hours in front of a computer screen working. It is important that your display is large and bright enough to work for long periods of time. Additionally, you frequently use a large display in meetings.

Information is returned to the user through **output devices**. Some output is tangible, such as photo prints, x-rays, and ID cards. Video and audio output are intangible.

What you see on your computer screen is video output, and there are a variety of video output devices. The most popular types are monitors and projectors, which come in many different sizes, technologies, and price ranges.

Similar to TV screens, monitors work by lighting up *pixels*, which is short for picture elements, on the screen. Each pixel contains three colors—red, green, and blue, commonly referred to as RGB. From that base, all colors can be created by varying the intensities of the three colors. The display *resolution* indicates the number of horizontal pixels by vertical pixels, for example, 1280 × 1024 or 1920 × 1080. The higher the resolution, the sharper the image. The size of a monitor is measured diagonally across the screen.

LCD—liquid crystal display—panels are found on most desktop and notebook computers. LCDs do not give off any light, so they need to be backlit by a light source, typically CCFLs—cold cathode fluorescent lamps. Some LCD monitors are backlit by LEDs. The LED versions are generally thinner and more energy efficient, but they are also more expensive.

Plasma screen monitors are typically found in media center systems or conference rooms because they are available in larger screen sizes. Plasma monitors pass an electric current through gas sealed in thousands of cells inside the screen. The current excites the gas, which in turn excites the phosphors that coat the screen to pass light through an image.

The newest technology in monitors is *OLED* or *organic light-emitting diode*. This type of monitor consists of extremely thin panels of organic molecules sandwiched between two electrodes. The prototypes of these monitors are less than an inch thick and are bendable. OLEDs use very little energy and are expected to be at least ten times more energy efficient than current LCDs. However, OLED monitors are still new to the market and cost many times more than LCDs or plasmas. *AMOLED* or *active matrix OLED screens* can be found in mobile devices. AMOLED screens are sharper and have a wider viewing angle than LCDs and are ideal for watching movies and sports.

If you are making a presentation or sharing media with a group in a classroom, conference room, or home theater, you will find that projectors are more practical than monitors because they produce larger output.

One common projector type is *digital light-processing projectors*, or *DLP*. A DLP has hundreds of thousands of tiny swiveling mirrors that create an image. This projector type produces high-contrast images with deep blacks, but is limited by having weaker reds and yellows. The most portable projectors on the market are DLP projectors, which weigh less than three pounds. DLPs also are very popular as a home theater projector because of the higher contrast and deeper blacks that they produce.

Another common projector type is the *LCD projector*. This projector type passes light through a prism that divides the light into three beams—red, green, and blue. The beams are then passed through an LCD screen. These projectors display richer colors but produce poorer contrast and more washed-out blacks than DLPs. LCDs also tend to have sharper images than DLPs and are better in bright rooms, making them ideal for presentations in conference rooms and classrooms.

The data signal and connection for a monitor or projector are provided by the *display adapter*, also called a *video card* (Figure 2.19). Modern display adapters contain their own *VRAM*, or *video RAM*, and GPU in order to produce the best and fastest images. A **digital visual interface port** or *DVI* is the standard digital video port found on video cards. Some cards also have an *HDMI* port. HDMI—an acronym for High-Definition Multimedia Interface—is a digital port that can transmit both audio and video signals. It is the standard connection for high-definition TVs, video game consoles, and other media devices. A video card may also include input ports to connect a TV tuner or another video device to the system. Some display adapters can support multiple monitors, and a computer can have multiple display adapters.

FIGURE 2.19 A display adapter with HDMI, VGA, and DVI ports.

Concept 2.14 | Exploring Audio Output Devices

Audio output could be your favorite song, sound effects in a video game, or an email alert chime. Any sound that can be heard through speakers or headphones is audio output.

Speakers convert digital signals from a computer or media player into sound. They may be integrated into notebook computers and monitors or connected via USB or to the speaker ports on a sound card. Typical desktop speaker systems include two or three speakers, but speaker systems designed for gaming or home theaters include as many as eight speakers and can cost hundreds of dollars.

Like speakers, *headphones* convert digital signals into sound. They come in several different sizes and styles, ranging from tiny earbuds that fit inside your ear to full-size headphones that completely cover your outer ear. High-quality headphones can cost hundreds of dollars and incorporate up to eight speakers in the design. *Noise-cancelling headphones* reduce the effect of ambient noise and are especially useful in noisy environments, such as airplanes. Headphones can plug into the headphone or speaker port of a computer, the headphone port on a speaker, or USB ports and can connect wirelessly via Bluetooth. Headphones that also include a microphone are called *headsets* (Figure 2.20).

FIGURE 2.20 Earbuds, headphones, wireless headset, and Bluetooth headset.

A *sound card* provides audio connections for both input devices such as microphones and synthesizers, and for output devices such as speakers and headphones. Sound cards can be integrated into the motherboard—referred to as onboard—or connected through expansion cards or USB ports. High-end sound cards have connections for up to eight speakers and include a digital optical port for connecting to a home entertainment system. These cards include support for *surround sound*—a technique used in movies and video games that makes it sound as if the audio surrounds the listener.

Adaptive output devices make it easier for individuals with disabilities to use output. Standard monitors can be adapted by magnifying the screen and adjusting color and contrast settings. Speech synthesis screen reading software and audio alerts aid those with visual and learning disabilities. Closed captions and visual notifications, such as flashing lights, aid those with auditory disabilities. **Braille embossers** are special printers that translate text to Braille. These impact printers create dots in special heavy paper that can be read by touch by those who are visually impaired.

GREEN COMPUTING E-Waste

Every year, millions of tons of *electronic waste*, or *e-waste*, are generated—and only about a quarter of it is recycled (Figure 2.21). Old computers, cell phones, TVs, VCRs, and other electronic devices make up e-waste, some of which is considered hazardous. CRT monitors can contain more than eight pounds of lead, and by Environmental Protection Agency—EPA—regulations cannot be disposed of in landfills. *eCycling*, or recycling electronics, is one way to reduce the amount of e-waste and hazardous materials that end up in landfills, in addition to reducing the cost of having it hauled away. The EPA provides information on its website about eCycling in your community (**http://epa.gov/epawaste/conserve/materials/ecycling**).

Artstudio Pro/Fotolia

FIGURE 2.21 E-waste in the form of old electronics.

You can also dispose of e-waste in an altruistic manner by donating working electronics to worthwhile charities. Your donations of working electronics not only help reduce e-waste, but also benefit the recipients.

✔ **Check Your Knowledge:** In MyITLab, take the quiz covering Objectives 1–4.

Objective 5 Compare Printer Types

Before You Buy
Choosing a Printer

In your job as Site Manager, you often print flyers and documents that you share with employees and hotel guests. It is important that you have high-quality printers available, and they must be cost efficient. The lobby also has a printer for guests to print boarding passes for their flights home.

Hard copies—sometimes referred to as printouts—of documents and photos are produced by printers. There are many types of printers and they produce a wide variety of output; for example, photos, blueprints, and ID cards.

The most common personal printers are ***inkjet printers***. Inkjets work by spraying droplets of ink onto paper. Some printers use one ink cartridge; others may use two, three, four, or more. The standard ink colors are cyan, magenta, yellow, and key, or black, abbreviated as CMYK (Figure 2.22). Printers mix these colors to form all other colors. Inkjets are inexpensive, but the cost of ink can quickly add up. When purchasing a printer, factor in the cost of ink, which is responsible for a large portion of the cost per page.

FIGURE 2.22 Color printers use the four colors CMYK to form all other colors.

Dye-sublimation printers, also called dye-subs, use heat to turn solid dye into a gas that is transferred to special paper. The dye comes on a three- or four-color ribbon that prints a single color at a time. After all colors have been printed, the print is coated with a clear protective layer to produce a high-quality photo that lasts longer than those printed on an inkjet printer. Dye-subs are not general-purpose printers; they are limited to printing photos and some specialty items such as ID badges and medical scans.

A ***photo printer*** is an inkjet or dye-sublimation printer designed to print high-quality photos on special photo paper. Some photo printers allow direct connections to a digital camera or mobile device through USB, FireWire, WiFi, or Bluetooth, or can read data from a memory card so that no computer is needed.

The receipts you receive from gas pumps, ATMs, and many cash registers are printed by ***thermal printers***, which create an image by heating specially coated heat-sensitive paper that changes color where the heat is applied. These receipts will fade over time. If you will need the receipt later, you should scan it for long-term access. Thermal printers can print in one or two colors and can also be used to print barcodes, postage, and labels.

The most common type of printers found in schools and businesses are ***laser printers***, which use a laser beam to draw an image on a drum. The image is electrostatically charged and attracts a dry ink called toner. The drum is then rolled over paper, and the toner is deposited on the paper. Finally, the paper is heated and pressure is applied, bonding the ink to the paper. Laser printers produce the sharpest text at a much lower cost per page than inkjet printers. Although laser printers initially cost more than inkjets, the lower cost per page makes them less expensive for high-volume printing.

All-in-one printers are multifunction devices that have built-in scanners and sometimes have fax capabilities. All-in-one printers can also be used as copy machines and eliminate the need for several different devices, saving both space and money. The disadvantage to using a multifunction device is that if it needs to be repaired, all of its functions are unavailable.

Three-dimensional printers, also called 3-D printers, can create objects such as prototypes and models (Figure 2.23). First, a digital image is created using design software or by scanning an existing object. This image is then sent to the 3-D printer, which creates a model from the image by building layers of material such as paper, polymers, resin, or metal. Three-dimensional printing has many interesting uses such as medical imaging, paleontology, architecture, and creating sculpture and jewelry.

Amer Ghazzal/Alamy

FIGURE 2.23 A 3-D printer can create 3-D objects such as building models, specialized tools, and medical prosthetics.

The type of printer you choose depends on many things, including the type and size of output you need and the cost. Businesses typically have several different types of printers to meet all their needs. For a home user, a multifunction device might be the best choice.

Objective 6 | Discuss Communication Devices

Your job as a Site Manager requires you to connect to the Oro Jade Hotel network and send and receive data on a daily and weekly basis. All hotel computers are connected to the Oro Jade Hotel network through either a wired or wireless connection. *Communication devices* serve as both input and output devices and enable you to connect to other devices on a network or to the Internet. These include network adapters, modems, and fax devices.

1.02d
1.02k (i)

Concept 2.17 | Understanding Ethernet and Wireless Network Adapters and Modems

A *network adapter* establishes a connection with a network; it may be an onboard adapter or USB device and may be wired or wireless. A wired network adapter is also known as an *Ethernet card* and has a port—sometimes called an Ethernet port—that resembles a telephone jack. To connect to a wired network, you plug an Ethernet network cable into the Ethernet port on your computer (Figure 2.24). The cable can be connected to a wall jack or a port on a network connectivity device such as a switch or router. *Wireless network adapters* connect to Wi-Fi networks at home and in hot spots in airports and cafes.

FIGURE 2.24 A network cable connects to the Ethernet port on a notebook computer.

A *modem* connects a computer to a telephone line for dial-up Internet access. Modem is short for *modulator-demodulator*. An analog modem modulates digital data into an analog signal that can be transmitted over a phone line and, on the receiving end, demodulates the analog signal back into digital data. These modems are largely obsolete, as few people use dial-up Internet access. A *cable modem* is a special type of digital modem that connects to the cable system instead of a telephone line to provide fast Internet access.

The difference between analog and digital devices is the way the data is encoded and transmitted. *Analog input devices* convert data signals into continuous electronic waves or pulses. *Analog output devices*, such as telephones, translate electronic pulses into audio and video signals. In *digital devices*, audio or video data is represented by a series of 0s and 1s. Digital signals can carry more data and are less prone to interference than analog signals.

Concept 2.18 | Understanding Fax Devices

A *fax device* or *facsimile* works by scanning a document and converting it into a digital format that can be transmitted over telephone lines to a receiving fax device, which prints or displays the document. A fax device can be a stand-alone fax machine, part of a multifunction device, or be built into a modem. With fax software and a fax modem, you can use a computer as a fax machine.

ON THE JOB Science and Engineering

The scientific applications of digital devices are numerous. Engineers and scientists who work in the field use digital cameras and specialized handheld equipment for collecting data and monitoring conditions. An environmental engineer monitors air conditions, calculates water currents, and measures pH and alkalinity. A civil engineer collects traffic and accident data for an intersection or stretch of highway. Meteorologists gather weather data and geologists monitor for earthquakes.

IT Sims

Hardware

There is a large and varied amount of data that must be stored in an Oro Jade Hotel. The customer data, purchasing requests, employee time cards, and schedules are just some of the data that you must store and access as the Site Manager. Storage comes in many forms, from small portable devices to massive drives accessible across a network or in the cloud.

Concept 2.19 | Comparing Optical Discs

Optical discs are a form of removable storage and include CDs, DVDs, and Blu-ray discs (Figure 2.25). The spelling *disc* refers to optical discs, and *disk* refers to magnetic disks. Data is stored on these discs by using a laser to melt the disc material or to change the color of an embedded dye. A laser can read the variations as binary data.

Ewais/Fotolia

FIGURE 2.25 CDs, DVDs, and Blu-ray discs all have the same physical size.

Optical disc drives are mounted in the system unit in external drive bays, which enables you to access them to insert or eject discs. They can also be peripheral devices connected by a USB or FireWire connection. Optical discs can take several forms: read-only (ROM), recordable (+R/–R), or rewritable (+RW/–RW). The type of disc you should purchase depends on the type of drive you have. This is usually labeled on the front of the drive.

A ***CD*** or ***compact disc*** is the oldest type of optical disc still in use and has a storage capacity of about 700 MB. CDs are still used to distribute software and music and to store photos and data, but have, for the most part, been replaced by larger capacity DVDs to distribute movies and some software.

A digital video disc or digital versatile disc, more commonly known as a ***DVD***, has the same dimensions as a CD but stores more than six times as much data. Single-layer (SL) DVDs can hold about 4.7 GB of information. Double-layer (DL) DVDs have a second layer to store data and can hold about 8.5 GB.

A ***Blu-ray disc*** is an optical disc with about five times the capacity of a DVD. The single-layer disc capacity is 25 GB, and double-layer disc capacity is 50 GB. Blu-ray is primarily used for high-definition video and data storage. BD-R discs are recordable, and BD-RE discs can be erased and re-recorded multiple times. The table in Figure 2.26 compares the storage capacities of the various optical media.

OPTICAL DISC STORAGE CAPACITIES				
OPTICAL DISC	CAPACITY	NUMBER OF 3.5 MB PHOTOS	VIDEO	HIGH-DEFINITION VIDEO
CD-ROM	700 MB	200	35 minutes	—
DVD single layer	4.7 GB	1,343	2 hours	—
DVD dual layer	8.5 GB	2,429	4 hours	—
Blu-ray single layer	25 GB	7,143	—	4.5 hours
Blu-ray dual layer	50 GB	14,286	—	9 hours

FIGURE 2.26

Gaskin, Shelley. GO! All in One, 3E. Pearson Education, 2017.

1.02b

Concept 2.20 | Examining Solid-State Storage

Unlike optical and magnetic storage, ***solid-state storage*** is nonmechanical. The data is stored on ***flash memory*** chips. Flash memory is nonvolatile storage and therefore needs no power to retain information. Because there are no moving parts, solid-state drives—SSDs—are quiet and durable. SSDs are used in small electronic devices, such as media players, and in notebooks and desktop computers. Solid-state drives can use the same controllers as hard drives and can be either internal or external. Because SSDs are significantly more expensive than similar capacity hard drives, they are used primarily where speed, durability, or light weight is important.

Flash drives are small, portable, solid-state drives that can hold up to 1 terabyte (TB) of information. They have become the standard for conveniently transporting small amounts of data such as your schoolwork. Flash drives connect to a computer by a USB port and come in a variety of shapes and sizes, including pens, watches, toys, and Swiss Army knives. Flash drives are also used as the internal storage in tablets and mobile devices.

You can expand the storage of digital cameras, tablets, and other devices with ***memory cards***, which use flash memory to store data in a small, flat design. The type of memory card you use depends on the device. The most common formats include Secure Digital (SD), CompactFlash (CF), Memory Stick (MS), and xD-Picture Card (xD). You can use a ***card reader*** to transfer data, such as photos and music, between a card and a computer or printer. A card reader provides a slot to insert a memory card into a computer so that the data can be read. Figure 2.27 shows SSD drives, flash drives, and various memory cards.

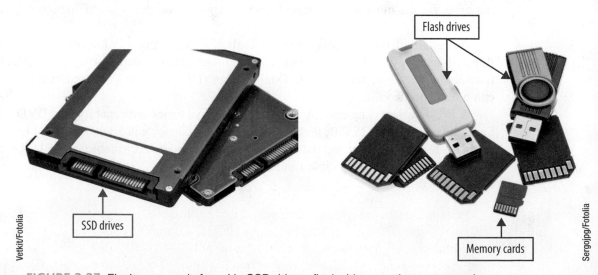

FIGURE 2.27 Flash memory is found in SSD drives, flash drives, and memory cards.

ETHICS | USB Flash Drive Dangers

USB flash drives are very popular, but experts worry that they pose a great security risk because people can carry a lot of critical or personal data on their USB flash drives. Some companies are so concerned about corporate espionage that they disable USB ports to prevent the unauthorized copying of data. What are the implications if the device is lost? Should USB drive manufacturers be required to provide a means of securing these devices or provide some type of registration process? With such processes in place, a lost device could be returned to the manufacturer and matched to the owner. What actions should individuals take to safeguard their data? Is attaching a USB flash drive to your backpack or keychain a very good idea? If you found a USB flash drive and did not know to whom it belonged, what would you do? What should you do?

1.02b

Concept 2.21 | Understanding Hard Drives

Hard drives are the principal mass-storage devices in a computer. They are sometimes called hard disks or hard disk drives. Hard drives are a form of nonvolatile storage; when the computer is powered off, the data is not lost. The primary hard drive stores the operating system, programs, and data files. Hard drives are measured in hundreds of gigabytes or terabytes and can hold hundreds of thousands of files.

Hard drives can be either internal or external. *Internal drives* are inside the system unit in an internal drive bay and are not accessible from the outside. *External drives* may be attached as a peripheral device using a USB or FireWire connection. The advantages of external drives are that they can be installed without opening the system unit and can be easily moved to another computer.

Hard drives store data magnetically on metal platters. The platters are stacked, and read/write heads move across the surface of the platters, reading data and writing it to memory (Figure 2.28). The drives spin at up to 15,000 revolutions per minute, allowing for very fast data transfer.

Naraz/Fotolia

Read-write head

Metal platter

FIGURE 2.28 With the cover removed, the metal platter and read-write head are visible in this hard drive.

Storage capacity has grown dramatically over the past few years, as the operating systems and other software have gotten more sophisticated and the files users save have become larger and more numerous. A decade ago, a floppy disk could hold 1.4 MB of information—roughly 750 pages of text. Today, a 1 TB hard drive can store about 500 million pages of text, 180 hours of high-definition video, or over 280,000 high-quality photos.

✔ Check Your Knowledge: In MyITLab, take the quiz covering Objectives 5–7.

GO! To Work

Andrew Rodriguez / Fotolia; FotolEdhar/ Fotolia; apops/ Fotolia; Yuri Arcurs/ Fotolia

IC3 SKILLS IN THIS CHAPTER

IC3 — Module 1: Computing Fundamentals
Section 1.02 Hardware
- (b) Know the impact of memory and storage on usage
- (c) Know how to connect to different peripherals
  - (i) Camera
  - (ii) Audio
  - (iii) Microphone
  - (iv) Printer
  - (v) USB devices
  - (vi) External display
- (d) Understand the use of Ethernet ports
- (k) Understand concepts regarding connecting to the Internet
  - (i) Modem
- (l) Understand common hardware configurations
- (m) Implications for document usage
- (n) Understand the pros and cons of touch screens vs. non-touch screen devices

Section 1.03 Computer Software Architecture
- (g) Document Management

GO! FOR JOB SUCCESS

Discussion: Bring Your Own Devices

Your instructor may assign these questions to your class, and then ask you to think about them or discuss with your classmates:

A new trend in the workplace is known as Bring Your Own Devices—or BYOD. This poses a challenge to the IT department to both support and secure the system. Although you have a personal smartphone, you should always follow company policy when using such a device for your work.

FotolEdhar / Fotolia

What are two reasons that you might bring your own device to work?

How should you ensure that company information isn't compromised when using your own device to access email or files?

Do you think a company should allow employees to bring their own devices to use at work?

END OF CHAPTER

SUMMARY

The CPU is the brain of a computer. The motherboard is a circuit board that provides a way for devices to attach to a computer. Information flows between the components over data buses. RAM is volatile memory.

The mouse and keyboard are the most common input devices. Digital cameras and webcams input images and video. Scanners convert information into a digital format. Microphones are audio input devices.

Video output devices include monitors and projectors. Speakers and headphones are audio output devices. Printers provide tangible output. Printer types include inkjet, laser, dye-sub, thermal, and 3-D.

Lasers read the data stored on optical discs (CD, DVD, Blu-ray). Hard drives store data magnetically on metal platters. Solid-state storage stores data on a flash memory chip.

GO! LEARN IT ONLINE

Review the concepts, key terms, and IC3 skills in this chapter by completing these online challenges, which you can find at **MyITLab**.

Matching and Multiple Choice: Answer matching and multiple choice questions to test what you learned in this chapter.

Lessons on the GO!: Learn how to use all the new apps and features as they are introduced by Microsoft.

IC3 Prep Quiz: Answer questions to review the IC3 skills that you practiced in this chapter.

GLOSSARY

GLOSSARY OF CHAPTER KEY TERMS

Adapter card A small circuit board that plugs directly into an expansion slot on the motherboard and enables you to connect additional peripheral devices to a computer. Also called expansion card.

All-in-one printer A multifunction device that has a built-in printer and scanner, and that may also have fax capabilities.

AMOLED (active matrix OLED) screen A screen type found in mobile devices that has a sharper display with a wider viewing angle than an LCD and is ideal for watching movies and sports.

Analog input device A device that converts data signals into continuous electronic waves or pulses.

Analog output device An output device such as a telephone, television, or CRT monitor that translates the digital electronic pulses back into audio and video signals.

Arithmetic logic unit (ALU) The part of the CPU that performs arithmetic (addition and subtraction) and logic (AND, OR, and NOT) calculations.

Barcode scanner An input device that scans barcodes such as those found on merchandise and library books.

Biometric scanner An input device that measures human characteristics such as fingerprints and eye retinas.

BIOS (basic input output system) A program, stored on a chip on the motherboard, that starts the computer.

Bluetooth A short-range wireless technology that connects many types of peripheral devices.

Blu-ray disc An optical disc with about five times the capacity of a DVD; the single-layer disc capacity is 25 GB, and double-layer disc capacity is 50 GB.

Braille embosser A special printer that translates text to Braille.

Burst mode A feature found on some digital cameras that enables you to take several pictures in a burst by holding down the shutter button.

Cable modem A special type of digital modem that connects to the cable system instead of a telephone line to provide fast Internet access.

Cache memory Fast memory that stores frequently accessed information close to the processor.

Capacitive screen A touchscreen that senses the conductive properties of an object such as a finger or a specially designed conductive stylus.

Card reader A device that provides a slot to insert a memory card into a computer so that the data on the card can be read. Used to transfer data, such as photos and music, between a card and a computer or printer.

CD (compact disc) The oldest type of optical disc in use today, with a storage capacity of about 700 MB.

Central processing unit (CPU) The brain of a computer housed inside the system unit on the motherboard. Also known as the processor.

Clock speed The speed at which the processor executes the machine cycle, measured in gigahertz (GHz)—billions of cycles per second.

CMOS (complementary metal oxide semiconductor) A chip on the motherboard where the BIOS settings are stored. It is volatile memory that uses a small battery to provide it with power to keep the data in memory even when the computer is turned off.

Communication device A device that serves as both input and output device and enables you to connect to other devices on a network or to the Internet.

Compact system camera (CSC) An advanced point-and-shoot camera that has interchangeable lenses, some manual controls, a 10x to 26x optical zoom lens, and the ability to capture HD video. Also called a mirrorless camera or superzoom.

Control unit The part of the CPU that manages the movement of data through the CPU.

Data bus Wires on the motherboard over which data flows between the components of the computer.

Digital device A device that represents audio or video data as a series of 0s and 1s.

Digital single lens reflex (DSLR) The most expensive and versatile type of digital camera. A high-end digital camera that enables you to change the lens, attach a hot shoe flash, manually adjust focus and exposure, and look through the viewfinder to frame your shot.

Digital video camera A camera designed to record digital video that is easily uploaded to your computer, where it can be edited, stored, and shared.

DIMM (dual in-line memory module) The form of RAM found in most desktop computers.

Display adapter The card that provides the data signal and connection for a monitor or projector. Also called a video card.

DLP (digital light-processing) projector A digital projector that has hundreds of thousands of tiny swiveling mirrors that create an image.

Drive bay Part of the system unit that holds the storage devices.

Drive controller A component located on the motherboard that provides a drive interface that connects disk drives to the processor.

DVD (digital video disc/digital versatile disc) An optical disc that can hold approximately 4.7 GB of information in a single-layer (SL) disc. Double-layer (DL) discs have a second layer to store data and can hold about 8.5 GB.

DVI (digital visual interface) port The standard digital video port found on video cards.

Dvorak Simplified Keyboard An alternate keyboard designed to put the most commonly used letters where they are more easily accessed to increase efficiency and reduce fatigue.

Dye-sublimation printer A printer that uses heat to turn solid dye into a gas that is transferred to special paper.

eCycling Recycling electronics.

EIDE (enhanced integrated drive electronics) An older—legacy—drive interface that may still be found on older computers.

Ergonomic keyboard A full-sized keyboard with a curved shape that positions the wrists in a more natural position to reduce strain.

Ethernet card A wired network adapter with a port that resembles a telephone jack.

E-waste (electronic waste) Old computers, cell phones, TVs, VCRs, and other electronic devices that are discarded.

Expansion card A small circuit board that plugs directly into an expansion slot on the motherboard and that enables you to connect additional peripheral devices to a computer. Also called adapter card.

Expansion slot A component located on the motherboard that enables you to connect an adapter card to a computer.

External drive A drive that may be attached as a peripheral device using a USB or FireWire connection.

Fax device (or facsimile) A communication device that scans a document and converts it into a digital format that can be transmitted over telephone lines to a receiving fax device, which then prints or displays the document.

FireWire A standard port type that is hot-swappable and can connect up to 63 devices per port. It also allows for peer-to-peer communication between devices, such as two video cameras, without the use of a computer. Also known as IEEE 1394.

Flash drive A small, portable, solid-state drive that can hold up to 128 GB of information.

Flash memory Nonvolatile storage used in solid-state storage devices such as solid state drives (SSDs), flash drives, and memory cards.

Game controller An input device used to interact with a video game.

Graphics processing unit (GPU) A processor on a video card that can contain multiple cores.

Hard drive The principal mass-storage device in a computer that stores data magnetically on metal platters.

Hardware The physical components of a computer.

HDMI A digital port that can transmit both audio and video signals. It is the standard connection for high-definition TVs, video game consoles, and other media devices.

Headphones Output devices that convert digital signals into sound; available in several different sizes and styles, ranging from tiny earbuds that fit inside your ear to full-size headphones that completely cover your outer ear.

Headset Headphones that also include a microphone.

Heat sink A part of the cooling system of a computer, mounted above the CPU and composed of metal or ceramic to draw heat away from the processor.

IEEE 1394 A standard port type that is hot-swappable and can connect up to 63 devices per port. It also allows for peer-to-peer communication between devices, such as two video cameras, without the use of a computer. Also known as FireWire.

Image stabilization A feature found on some digital cameras that accounts for camera shake and results in sharper images.

Inkjet printer A printer that sprays droplets of ink onto paper.

Input device A device to enter data into the computer system so that it can be processed.

Instruction cycle The four-part process used by the CPU to process each instruction: fetch, decode, execute, store. Also called a machine cycle.

Interactive whiteboard A large interactive display with a touch-sensitive surface commonly used in classrooms and businesses.

Internal drive A drive located inside the system unit in an internal drive bay that is not accessible from the outside.

Joystick An input device that is mounted on a base and consists of a stick, buttons, and sometimes a trigger. Typically used as a game controller, especially in flight-simulator games, it can also be used for such tasks as controlling robotic machinery in a factory.

Keyboard An input device that uses switches and circuits to translate keystrokes into a signal a computer understands, and the primary input device for entering text into a computer.

Keypad A small alternative keyboard that does not contain all the alphabet keys.

Laser printer A printer that uses a laser beam to draw an image on a drum. The image is electrostatically charged and attracts a dry ink called toner. The drum is then rolled over paper, and the toner is deposited on the paper. Finally, the paper is heated and pressure is applied, bonding the ink to the paper.

LCD (liquid crystal display) Two layers of glass glued together with a layer of liquid crystals between them. Electricity passed through the individual crystals causes them to pass or block light to create an image. Found on most desktop and notebook computers.

LCD projector A digital projector that passes light through a prism, which divides the light into three beams—red, green, and blue—that are then passed through an LCD screen.

LED (light-emitting diode) An electronic component that emits light when an electrical current is passed through it.

Machine cycle The four-part process used by the CPU to process each instruction: fetch, decode, execute, store. Also called the instruction cycle.

Magnetic strip reader An input device that can read information encoded in the magnetic strip on plastic cards, such as drivers' licenses, gift cards, library cards, credit cards, and hotel door keys.

Memory Temporary storage that is used by a computer to hold instructions and data.

Memory board A small circuit board that contains memory chips.

Memory card A storage medium that uses flash memory to store data in a small, flat design.

Microphone An input device that converts sound into digital signals. It is used to chat in real time or as part of voice-recognition applications used in video games and for dictating text.

Modem A communication device that modulates digital data into an analog signal that can be transmitted over a phone line and, on the receiving end, demodulates the analog signal back into digital data.

Modifier key A keyboard key, such as Ctrl, Alt, and Shift, that you press in conjunction with other keys.

Motherboard The main circuit board of a computer that houses the processor (CPU) and contains drive controllers and interfaces, expansion slots, data buses, ports and connectors, the BIOS, and memory. A motherboard may also include integrated peripherals, such as video, sound, and network adapters. It provides the way for devices to attach to your computer.

Mouse An input device that may include one or more buttons and a scroll wheel and works by moving across a smooth surface to signal movement of the pointer.

Multi-core processor A CPU that consists of two or more processors that are integrated on a single chip.

Near field communication (NFC) A method that enables devices to share data with each other by touching them together or bringing them within a few centimeters of each other.

Network adapter A communication device that establishes a connection with a network; may be onboard, an expansion card, or a USB device, and may be wired or wireless.

Noise-cancelling headphones An audio output device that reduces the effect of ambient noise; especially useful in noisy environments, such as airplanes.

Nonvolatile memory A memory chip that needs no power to retain information.

OLED (organic light-emitting diode) A monitor composed of extremely thin panels of organic molecules sandwiched between two electrodes.

Optical disc A form of removable storage that stores digital data by using a laser.

Optical mouse An input device that detects motion by bouncing light from a red LED (light-emitting diode) off the surface below it.

Optical scanner An input device that converts photos or documents into digital files.

Output device A device, for example, a printer or monitor, that returns processed information to the user.

Parallel processing The process of using multiple processors, or multi-core processors, to divide processing tasks.

Peripheral devices The components that serve the input, output, and storage functions of a computer.

Photo printer A printer that prints high-quality photos on special photo paper.

Pipelining A process used by a single processor to process multiple instructions simultaneously; as soon as the first instruction has moved from the fetch to the decode stage, the processor fetches the next instruction.

Pixel The term that is the shortened version of *picture element* and which represents a single point on a display screen. Each pixel contains three colors: red, green, and blue (RGB).

Plasma screen monitor A large display type that works by passing an electric current through gas sealed in thousands of cells inside the screen. The current excites the gas, which in turn excites the phosphors that coat the screen to pass light through an image.

Point-and-shoot The easiest, least expensive type of digital camera.

Pointing device An input device, such as a mouse or touchpad, that enables you to interact with objects by moving a pointer on the computer screen.

Port A connection point that is used to attach peripheral devices to the motherboard.

Processor The brain of a computer housed inside the system unit on the motherboard. Also known as the CPU.

QR code A digital code that can be scanned to learn more information.

QWERTY The first alphabetic keys on the upper left of the keyboard.

RAM (random access memory) A volatile form of memory that stores the operating systems, programs, and data the computer is currently using.

Resistive screen A touchscreen that can sense pressure and can be used with a finger or an ordinary stylus.

Resolution The number of horizontal by vertical pixels on a display screen or image; for example, 1280 × 1024 or 1920 × 1080.

RFID (radio frequency identification) A digital technology that uses RFID tags to provide information and is used in inventory tracking, electronic toll collection, and contactless credit card transactions.

RFID scanner An input device that can read the information in an RFID tag, such as those found on credit cards and passports.

RFID tag A digital tag that contains a tiny antenna for receiving and sending a radio-frequency signal.

ROM (read-only memory) A nonvolatile form of memory that does not need power to keep its data.

SATA (serial ATA) The standard internal drive interface used to connect drives to the motherboard.

Scanner An input device that increases the speed and accuracy of data entry and converts information into a digital format that can be saved, copied, and manipulated.

Shutter lag The time between pressing the shutter button and the camera snapping the picture.

SODIMM (small outline dual in-line memory module) The type of RAM used by most notebook computers.

Solid-state storage A nonmechanical storage format that stores data by using flash memory on a chip.

Sound card Provides audio connections for both input devices—microphones and synthesizers—and output devices—speakers and headphones.

Speakers Output devices that convert digital signals from a computer or media player into sound.

Stylus A special pen-like input tool.

System unit The case that encloses and protects the power supply, motherboard, processor (CPU), and memory of a computer.

Surround sound A technique used in movies and video games that makes it sound as if the audio surrounds the listener.

Thermal printer A printer that creates an image by heating specially coated heat-sensitive paper, which changes color where the heat is applied.

Three-dimensional (3D) printer A printer that can create objects such as prototypes and models.

Thunderbolt A port that carriers both PCIe and DisplayPort video signals on the same cable, so it can be used to connect many different types of peripherals to a computer. Thunderbolt combines two 10 Gbps channels and can connect up to six devices using one connection.

Toggle key A keyboard key, such as CapsLock or NumLock, that turns a feature on or off when pressed.

Touchpad An input device that detects your finger moving across the touch-sensitive surface.

Touchscreen An input device that can accept input from a finger or stylus.

USB (Universal Serial Bus) A standard port type used to connect many kinds of devices, including printers, mice, keyboards, digital cameras, cell phones, and external drives. Up to 127 devices can share a single USB port.

Video card The card that provides the data signal and connection for a monitor or projector. Also called a display adapter.

Voice-recognition software A program that enables you to control a computer verbally and dictate text.

Volatile memory Memory that loses information when the power is turned off.

VRAM (video RAM) The memory found on a display adapter.

Wearable tech Computing devices that are worn on the body, such as wearable computers, virtual reality headsets, and smartwatches.

Webcam A specialized video camera that provides visual input for online communication.

Wireless network adapter A network adapter used to connect to Wi-Fi networks.

GO! Do It

Andrew Rodriguez / Fotolia; FotolEdhar/ Fotolia; apops/ Fotolia; Yuri Arcurs/ Fotolia

ASSESS YOUR COMPUTER HARDWARE

Many things affect a computer's performance. In this Activity, you use the Control Panel and File Explorer to learn about your own computer and how you might improve its performance by upgrading hardware components.

1. From your student data files, open the file **aio06_DOIT_answersheet**. Display the **Save As** dialog box, navigate to the location where you will store your documents for this chapter, and then create a new folder named **AIO Chapter 2** Open the folder, and then save the file as **Lastname_Firstname_02_DOIT_answersheet**

2. From the Windows desktop, on the taskbar, click **File Explorer**. In the **File Explorer Navigation** pane, right-click **This PC**, and then click **Properties**.

🔄 **ANOTHER WAY**   Right-click the Windows Start button, click Control Panel, click System and Security, and then click System.

3. In the middle of the screen, under *System*, you can see information about your processor and memory. What type of processor do you have? What is its clock speed? How much RAM do you have?

4. Close the **System Control Panel** window and return to **File Explorer**. In the **Navigation pane**, click **This PC**. Examine all devices and drives that display. On your answer sheet, record these devices and any additional information, such as size and free space, for each.

5. Print or submit your answer sheet electronically as directed by your instructor.

NOTE	Mac Users

If you are using a Mac, you can view similar information about your computer. Click the Apple menu, and then click About This Mac. This screen displays basic information about the Mac. Click the Storage tab for information about the disks on this system. On the Overview tab, click System Report for a more detailed report.

ON THE WEB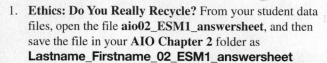

1. **Shopping Green** The EPEAT website provides information to help you "evaluate, compare and select electronic products based on their environmental attributes." From your student data files, open the file **aio02_OTW1_answersheet**. Display the **Save As** dialog box, navigate to the location where you will store your documents for this chapter, and then, if necessary, create a new folder named **AIO Chapter 2** Open the folder, and then save the file as **Lastname_Firstname_02_OTW1_answersheet**

   Visit the site **epeat.net**, and answer the following questions:

   - What types of devices are included in the system? How are they placed into the registry? What testing do they undergo?

   - What are the environmental performance criteria the devices must meet?

   - What manufacturers participate in the program? How is it funded? Is there any conflict of interest?

   Print or submit your answer sheet electronically as directed by your instructor.

2. **Modern Processors** Use the Internet to research current processors. From your student data files, open the file **aio02_OTW2_answersheet**, and then save the file as **Lastname_Firstname_02_OTW2_answersheet**

   What is the fastest processor available today for desktop computers? What about notebooks? Mobile devices? Which two companies are the main manufacturers of processors? Print or submit your answer sheet electronically as directed by your instructor.

ETHICS AND SOCIAL MEDIA ⚖️

1. **Ethics: Do You Really Recycle?** From your student data files, open the file **aio02_ESM1_answersheet**, and then save the file in your **AIO Chapter 2** folder as **Lastname_Firstname_02_ESM1_answersheet**

   Using the Internet, research the recycling and disposal options available in your community for disposing of an aging computing device. Indicate the cost of recycling, if any, and whether the owner of the device, the manufacturer, or the recycling source pays the cost. Then create a brief survey, using an online tool such as SurveyMonkey or Google Forms, which asks questions about the disposal of computing devices; include ink cartridges and cell phones. Be sure you do not request that a name be placed on the survey, because you want honest results. Distribute the survey to at least 10 individuals. Present your disposal/ recycle options and cumulative survey results in a presentation using the tool of your choice, and be sure to cite your references. Print or submit your presentation and answer sheet electronically as directed by your instructor.

2. **Social Media** From your student data files, open the file **aio02_ESM2_answersheet**, and then save the file in your **AIO Chapter 2** folder as **Lastname_Firstname_02_ESM2_answersheet**

   Before purchasing new hardware, many people read product reviews. Open your browser and go to cnet.com. Select a hardware product review from the front page to read. Briefly summarize the results of your search. Can you use this information to help you make a buying decision? How do the editors' reviews and the average user reviews compare? Look at the social networking links. On what social networks can you share this review? How many times has this article been shared? Include the title and URL of the article. Print or submit your answer sheet electronically as directed by your instructor.

COLLABORATION

1. **Shopping for a Computer** From your student data files, open the file **aio02_Collab1_answersheet**, and then save the file in your **AIO Chapter 2** folder as **Lastname_Firstname_02_Collab1_answersheet**

   Look at computer ads on some current retail websites. As a team, create a checklist and use it to compare three desktop or notebook computers that cost approximately the same price. The checklist should include:

   - CPU: Type, clock speed, number of cores
   - RAM: Amount and type
   - Motherboard: Number of expansion slots
   - Primary disk: Capacity, hard drive, or SSD
   - Optical disc drive

   In a poster or report, summarize your findings. Decide which computer is the best value and explain why. Be sure to cite your references. Print or submit your poster or report and your answer sheet electronically as directed by your instructor.

2. **Printers** From your student data files, open the file **aio02_Collab2_answersheet**, and then save the file in your **AIO Chapter 2** folder as **Lastname_Firstname_02_Collab2_answersheet**

   As a team, research one type of printer: inkjet, dye-sublimation, laser, or 3-D. Prepare a multimedia presentation for your printer type. The presentation should explain the features, functions, and uses of the printer. Use at least three references, only one of which may be this textbook. Print or submit your presentation and answer sheet electronically as directed by your instructor.

System Software

OUTCOMES
Identify and describe the features of desktop and specialized computer operating systems.
Describe the importance of file management.

OBJECTIVES

1. Recognize the Purpose and Functions of Operating Systems
2. Use Desktop Operating Systems
3. Compare Specialized Operating Systems
4. Explain the Importance of File Management
5. Recognize and Work with File Types
6. Use Advanced Search Options to Locate Files
7. Share Files

AntonioDiaz/Fotolia

In This Chapter

Computers are complex devices, but most computer users have very little understanding of the technical programs and utilities that help computers run. By having a working knowledge of system software programs, it will be easier for you to avoid and spot trouble and will make using your computer a more enjoyable experience.

In this chapter, you will learn about the system software that makes computers run smoothly and securely.

Job Focus

As the **IT Technical Support Officer**, your responsibilities include supporting users of **Oro Jade Hotel Group's** computer systems, maintaining and securing systems, and managing user access. You must be knowledgeable in the different operating systems that run on various devices and the systems within the hotel and those that you might encounter running on guest devices. The IT department maintains technical and user documentation, system reports, and system repair logs and produces information sheets for Oro Jade staff and guests. As with any position in the hotel, customer service is top priority.

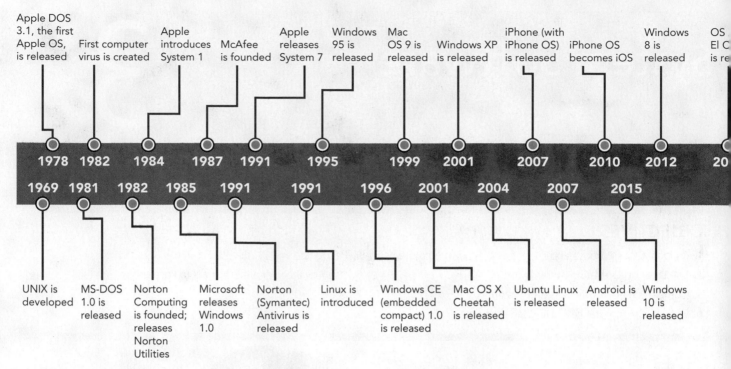

FIGURE 3.1 This timeline highlights some important dates in system software history.

Tech to GO!
Installing Device Drivers

In your job as an IT Technical Support Officer, you often help troubleshoot problems on computers in the hotel. *System software* includes all the programs that provide the infrastructure and hardware control necessary for the computer and its peripheral devices. System software has two major components—the *operating system* and the system utilities. An operating system, commonly referred to as the *OS*, is a computer program that manages all the other programs on your computer, stores files in an organized manner, enables you to use software programs, and coordinates the use of computer hardware such as the keyboard and mouse. The OS is the most important type of system software because it manages system resources and provides you with the interface to communicate with the hardware and other software on the computer. For a computer to run, it must have an OS.

The OS software is usually stored on the computer's hard disk, although it can be stored on and transferred from a USB drive, CD, or DVD. On mobile devices, the OS is held on a memory chip within the system unit.

Utility software helps maintain, repair, and protect the computer. It may be included with the OS or supplied by another company.

Concept 3.01 | Providing the User Interface

The *user interface* is the part of the OS that you see and with which you interact. Modern operating systems such as Microsoft Windows, Linux, and Mac OS X have a *graphical user interface (GUI)* that enables you to interact with your computer and which uses graphics such as an image of a file folder or wastebasket that you click to activate the item represented. Older operating systems used a *command-line interface*, which required you to type all commands. If you look at the interfaces on most personal computers, you will see that they have a lot in common. Figure 3.2 shows how the interface has changed from command line to GUI in Microsoft operating systems. This change made PCs more user-friendly, which helped them increase in popularity. A similar evolution occurred in the Apple systems. In fact, in 1988, Apple unsuccessfully sued Microsoft for copyright infringement of its interface.

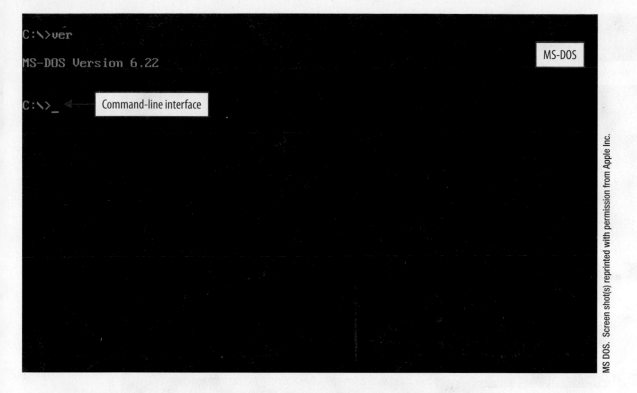

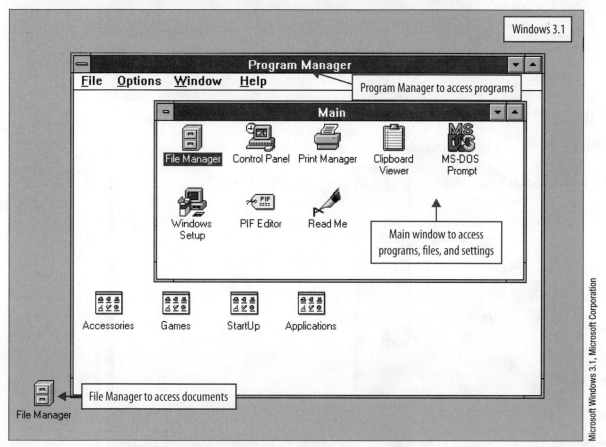

FIGURE 3.2 The evolution of the user interface in Microsoft operating systems.

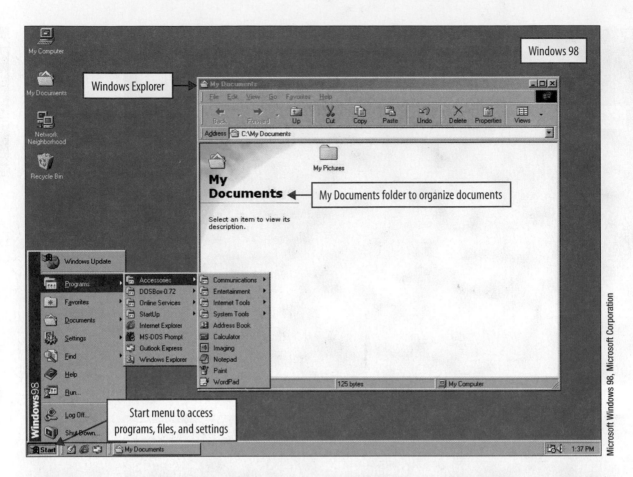

Windows 98

Windows Explorer

My Documents folder to organize documents

Start menu to access programs, files, and settings

Microsoft Windows 98, Microsoft Corporation

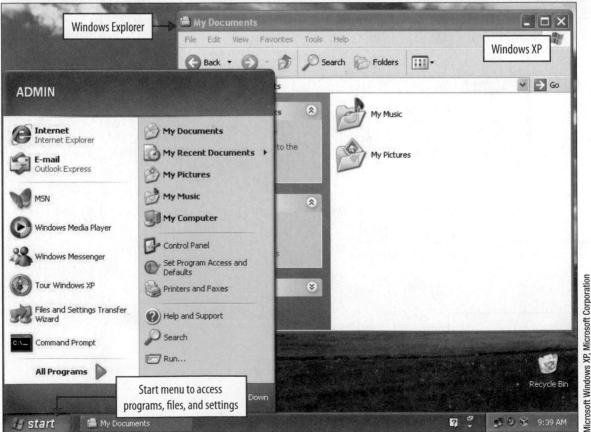

Windows Explorer

Windows XP

ADMIN

Start menu to access programs, files, and settings

Microsoft Windows XP, Microsoft Corporation

FIGURE 3.2 Continued

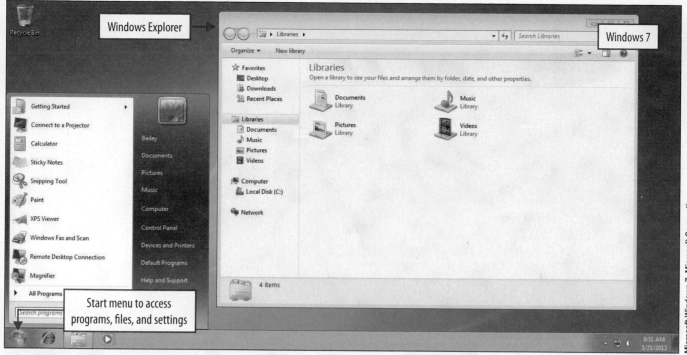

Windows Explorer

Windows 7

Start menu to access programs, files, and settings

Microsoft Windows 7, Microsoft Corporation

Start — Start screen replaces Start menu

Windows 8.1

Tiles to access programs, files, and settings

Desktop

Microsoft Windows 8.1, Microsoft Corporation

FIGURE 3.2 Continued

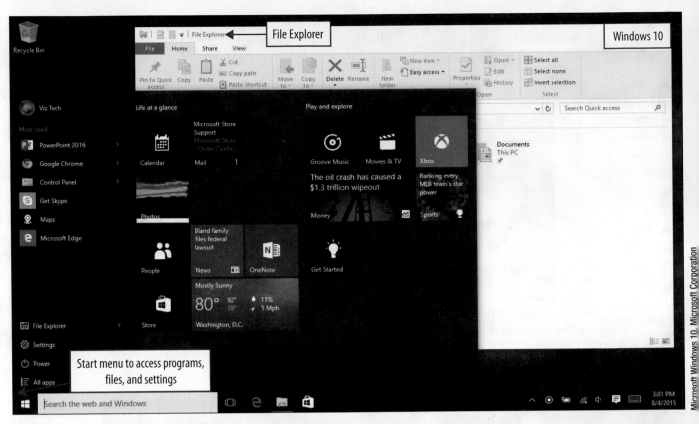

FIGURE 3.2 Continued

All user interfaces serve the same basic function: to enable you to control the computer. For example, if you want to play a game, you navigate to the icon for the game and click it to begin. The clicking tells the computer to open the file—in this instance, to run the game. The procedure to open a Word document is very much the same. These tasks require the OS user interface. GUIs use icons, menus, dialog boxes, and windows; in many instances, there are multiple ways to perform the same task.

FAST FORWARD | User Interface

The Internet of Things enables you to interact with devices that don't necessarily have a traditional screen. This has led to a new generation of user interfaces, including speech/voice recognition, enhanced touch and gestures, and even eye-tracking technologies. UIs in development include mind-control and augmented reality interfaces that project digital displays over top of real environments. Imagine thinking a command or looking at an object to turn it on, or even manipulating a digital object in 3D space with wearable input devices like haptic gloves that create a physical sensation of touch. What once seemed like the stuff of science fiction will be common in the next few years.

Concept 3.02 | Managing System Resources

The **system resources** on your computer include the processor and the memory. The operating system has the very important job of managing how these resources are allocated to both hardware and software. The operating system makes sure that each process is allocated its own memory and manages the instructions that are sent to the processor. Modern operating systems support **multitasking**, which is the ability to do more than one task at a time. A single processor cannot actually do more than one thing at a time, but switches between the tasks so quickly that it seems as if it is. Each running application is assigned its own area of memory and is prevented from accessing the memory area of other programs. This prevents a program that stops responding from affecting other processes running in other areas of memory.

Your computer programs would run very slowly if the operating system had to constantly access the program instructions from their storage location on the hard disk. To ensure that programs run quickly, operating systems use the computer's random access memory (RAM) as a *buffer*—an area that temporarily holds data and instructions. The operating system is responsible for managing this memory area. It gives each running program, and some devices, a portion of RAM, and then keeps the programs from interfering with each other's use of memory.

For example, if you give a command to print three documents one right after another, while the printer is printing the first document, the second and third documents are held in the *print buffer*. The documents wait in the buffer until the *spooling program*—a program that monitors the print requests in the buffer and the busy state of the printer—indicates that the printer is available. Then the second document moves from the buffer to the printer. This process continues until the print buffer is empty. For this reason, turning off the printer to cancel the printing of a document will not work, because turning off the printer does not empty the computer's print buffer. When you turn the printer on again, the documents in the print buffer continue to print. You can see the list of documents waiting to be printed by viewing the *print queue*. In the Windows Search box, type print. In the Search results, click Devices and printers. Click the default printer, and then, on the menu bar, click See what's printing, as shown in Figure 3.3.

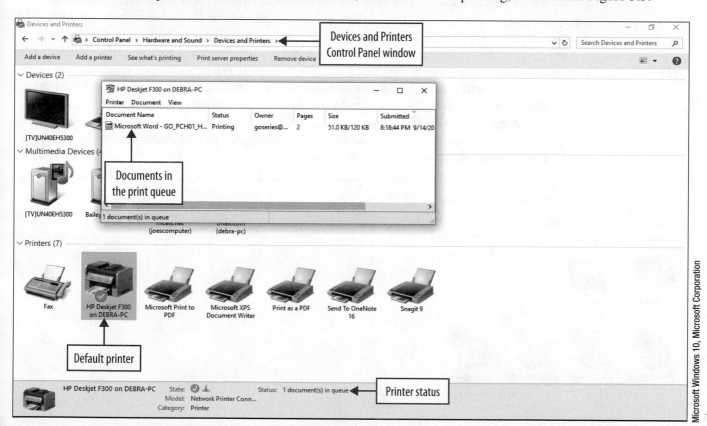

FIGURE 3.3 The print queue displays the list of documents in the print buffer.

NOTE   **No Printer Configured**

A new computer that does not have a printer configured may have a virtual printer, such as Send to OneNote, set as the default. A virtual printer does not have a print queue.

 **ANOTHER WAY**   Right-click the Windows Start button, click Control Panel. Under Hardware and Sound, click View devices and printers.

Modern operating systems can artificially extend the computer's RAM by using *virtual memory*—a technique that uses a portion of the computer's hard disk as an extension of RAM. Program instructions and data are divided into fixed-size units called pages. If memory is full, the operating system starts storing copies of pages in a hard disk file called the *swap file* or *paging file*, creating a temporary storage space for instructions that the operating system can access as you do your work. When the pages are needed, they are copied back into RAM. The process of transferring files from the hard disk to RAM and back is called *paging*.

IC3
DIGITAL LITERACY
CERTIFICATION
1.02f
1.02g (i)
1.02g (ii)
1.02h (i)
1.03b

Concept 3.03 | Managing and Controlling Hardware

The operating system manages and controls the computer's hardware. Early PCs were simple devices that had limited hardware: a keyboard, a monitor, a disk drive, and not much else. Today, computer systems have a wide variety of peripheral devices, including printers, scanners, cameras, media players, video and sound cards, and storage devices. When you turn on, or *boot*, your computer, an important part of the process is the OS detection of the hardware. The OS scans the system and determines how to communicate with the devices connected to it. Windows 95 introduced a feature known as *Plug and Play*. Plug and Play, or *PnP*, enables you to easily add new hardware to a computer system. When you plug in a new piece of hardware, the OS detects it and helps you set it up. An OS communicates with hardware by means of a *device driver*, which acts like a translator between the two. A device driver is software that enhances the capabilities of the operating system, enabling you to expand your computer with new hardware. Without device drivers, there would be no way for you to install new hardware on your system.

When you first connect new hardware to a Windows PC, the OS detects the new hardware and informs you that it is installing the device driver software. If Windows cannot locate the device driver, a message will prompt you for permission to search the web or instruct you to insert the device manufacturer's disc. The message *Device driver software installed successfully* indicates that your new hardware is ready to use.

You can view the devices that are set up on your computer, or add a new device, by using the Devices and Printers Control Panel, as shown in Figure 3.4.

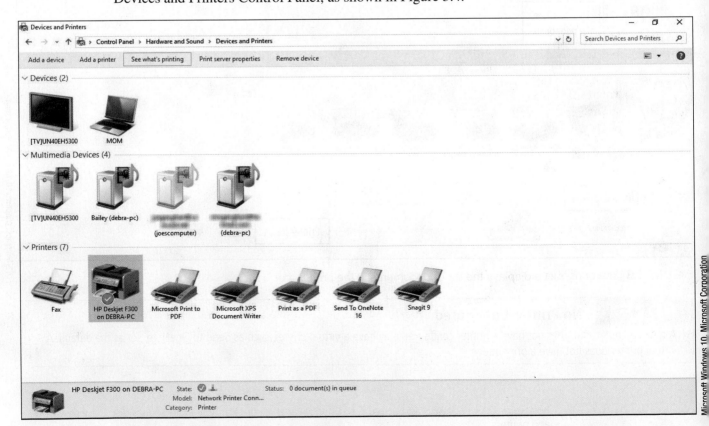

FIGURE 3.4 The Devices and Printers Control Panel window.

Firmware is software stored on a flash ROM (read-only memory) chip in a piece of hardware. Devices such as optical drives, routers, scanners, mobile devices, and digital cameras have firmware that provides instructions for how the device communicates with the other computer hardware. Updating, or flashing, firmware might be necessary for a device to work with a new operating system, read new media or file types, or make it work more efficiently. The Basic Input/Output System (BIOS) on a computer is a form of firmware.

GREEN COMPUTING — Power Management

Did you know that you could cut the energy used by your computer in half, saving between $25 and $75 a year in energy costs, by using its power management features? That would save more than lowering your home thermostat by 2 degrees or replacing 6 regular light bulbs with compact fluorescents—CFLs. Putting your computer into a low power mode can save on home cooling costs and prolong the life of your notebook battery.

Energy Star power management features are standard in both Microsoft Windows and Mac OS X operating systems. Activating these settings is easy and saves both money and resources. The EPA recommends setting computers to sleep or hibernate after 30 to 60 minutes of inactivity. To save more energy, set monitors to sleep after 5 to 20 minutes of inactivity. And do not use screensavers—they actually increase energy use!

On a Windows computer, the Power Options settings are accessed through the Hardware and Sound Control Panel. In the Windows Search box, type **Sleep** and then, in the search results, click Power & sleep settings (Figure 3.5). In OS X, open System Preferences and click Energy Saver.

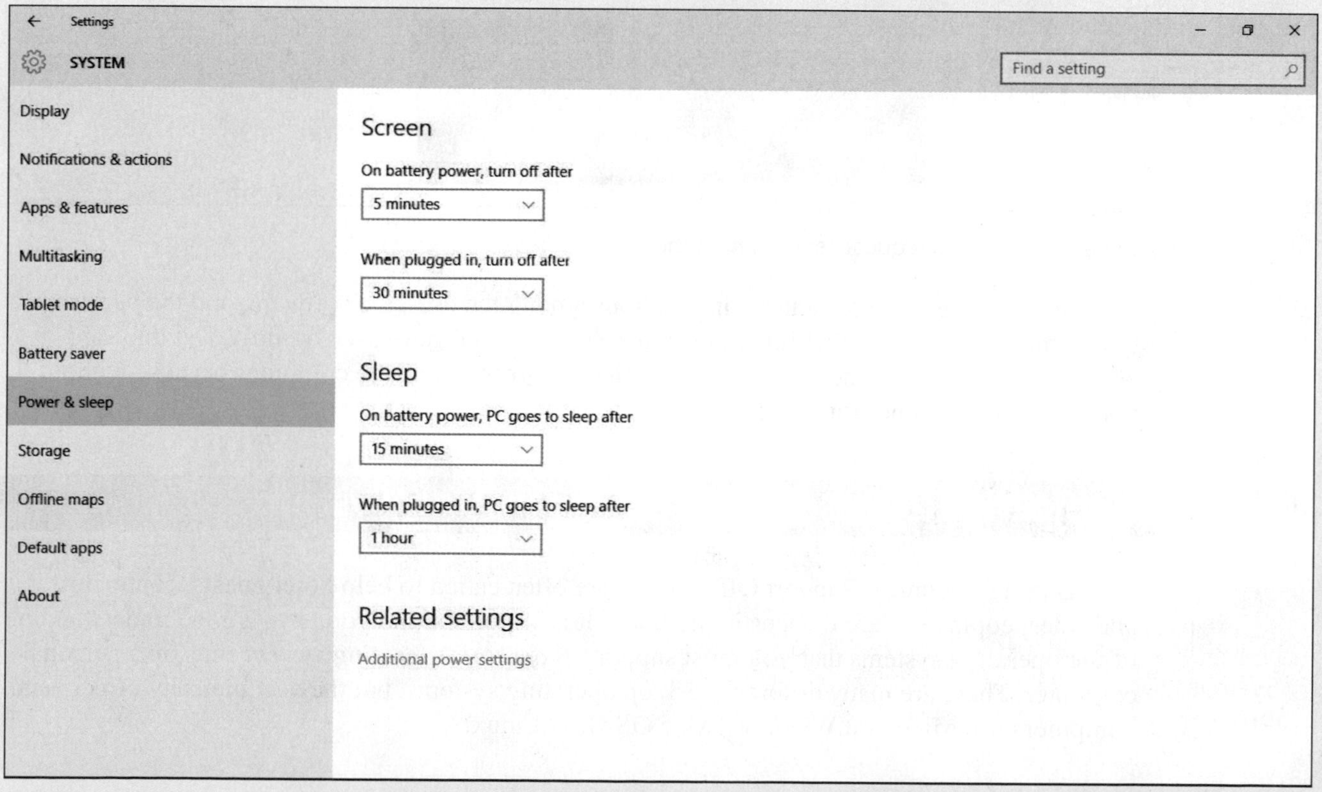

FIGURE 3.5 Windows 10 Power & sleep settings.

Microsoft Windows 10, Microsoft Corporation

Concept 3.04 | Interacting with Software

When you look at the system requirements to install software, you will see a list of supported operating systems. The OS on a computer interacts directly with the software—programs—you install, giving the software access to the resources it needs to run. This happens through the use of an ***application programming interface (API)***, which enables the program to request services from the operating system, such as a request to print or save a file, as shown in Figure 3.6. An API lets a computer programmer write a program that will run on computers with different hardware configurations by sending such service requests to the OS to handle.

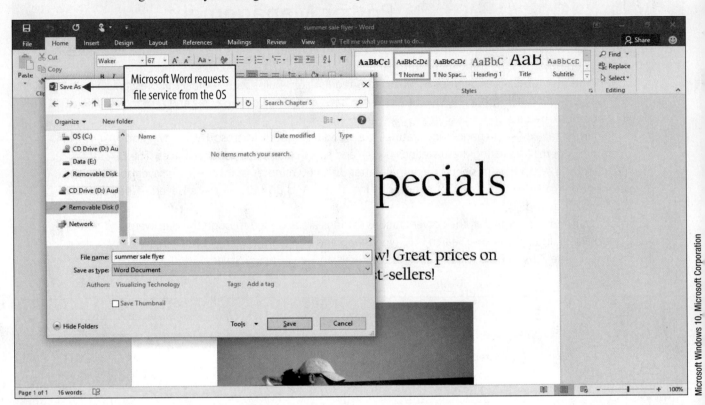

FIGURE 3.6 Programs use an API to request services from the OS.

An operating system manages interactions among the user, the software, and the hardware of a computer. These critical functions make the computer more user-friendly, flexible, and expandable. The OS is the most important piece of software on the computer because without it, your computer will not run at all.

Objective 2 | Use Desktop Operating Systems

System Software

As an IT Technical Support Officer, you are often called to help hotel guests, contractors, and salespeople use their devices in the hotel. It is important that you have a good understanding of the operating systems that you must support. A ***desktop operating system*** runs on a personal computer. There are many different desktop operating systems, but the vast majority of personal computers use Microsoft Windows, Mac OS X, or Linux.

1.03a
1.03b
1.03c

Concept 3.05 | Exploring Windows

The most common desktop operating system is ***Microsoft Windows***. Figure 3.7 shows a timeline of the release of successive versions of the Windows desktop operating systems. The current version is Windows 10, although you will still find computers running previous versions of Windows. It is estimated that over 90 percent of personal computers are running one of these versions of Windows. Each release of Windows added new features and security measures and was easier to use, more secure, and incorporated new technologies:

- Windows 95 introduced Plug and Play, enhanced support for CD-ROMs, and the mouse right-click.
- Windows 98 included Internet Explorer, better PnP support, and more multimedia features.
- Windows XP introduced a new interface, automatic updates, easier networking and Internet connectivity, and increased reliability.
- Windows Vista introduced a new interface, gadgets, enhanced networking, entertainment, and accessibility features.
- Windows 7 included a redesigned taskbar, new ways to manipulate windows, Remote Media Streaming, and Windows Touch multi-touch technology.
- Windows 8 introduced a new interface that uses a Start screen with tiles instead of a Start menu to access applications. Windows 8 also integrates your computer with the cloud.
- Windows 10 replaced the Start screen with a Start menu, added Cortana—an AI search tool and personal assistant—introduced virtual desktops that let you create different desktops for different projects or tasks and easily switch between them, and the Microsoft Edge browser.

Moving from one version of Windows to the next usually requires a fairly small learning curve, and users adapt quickly to the changes.

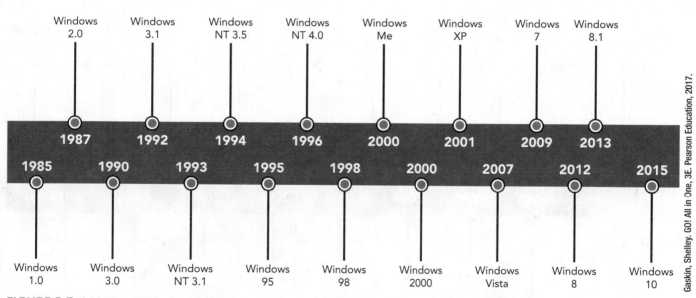

FIGURE 3.7 A history of Windows releases.

1.03a
1.03b
1.03c

Concept 3.06 | Examining Mac OS

In 1984, Apple introduced its first Macintosh computer, which had a GUI interface. The OS at the time was called Mac System Software. Over time, the original Mac System Software was replaced by System 7, Mac OS 8, and Mac OS 9. In 2001, Apple released OS X—an entirely new OS. Figure 3.8 shows a timeline of Mac releases.

Some important features and releases include the following:

- System 7 was released in 1990 with an updated GUI, multitasking support, built-in networking, better hardware and memory management, and new applications. Beginning with version 7.6, the name was changed to Mac OS.
- Mac OS 9 had improved wireless networking support, a better search tool, and the ability to be updated over the Internet. Mac OS 9 is referred to today as Mac Classic.

- *OS X* was first released in 2001 as Mac OS X 10.0, also called Cheetah. This OS was not an updated version of the classic Mac OS; rather, it was an entirely new OS based on Unix. Early versions of OS X included a Mac OS 9 emulation to run older applications. Cheetah introduced iMovie and iTunes; version 10.1, called Puma, added iDVD. Each new version included more integrated applications for email, chat, Internet, and multimedia.

- In OS X version 10.8, also called Mountain Lion, Apple dropped Mac from the name. Mountain Lion was faster, more reliable, and easier to use than the previous version. The interface was updated and included the Time Machine backup utility, better file sharing and networking capabilities, and exceptional multimedia applications. Popular features from the iPad such as a messaging app and iCloud were incorporated.

- OS X Mavericks, version 10.9, features tighter integration among your computer and your iOS mobile devices. Mavericks is streamlined and efficient, and is faster and more responsive than Mountain Lion.

- OS X Yosemite, version 10.10, updated the interface with a sleeker, flatter look, with different fonts and icons. Yosemite's enhanced integration with iOS devices and the cloud makes moving between your devices easier.

- OS X El Capitan, version 10.11, updates the interface, improves some included apps, and enhances overall performance.

OS X is a secure, feature-rich operating system that runs on Mac computers. If you do not have a Mac, then you cannot legally use the Mac OS.

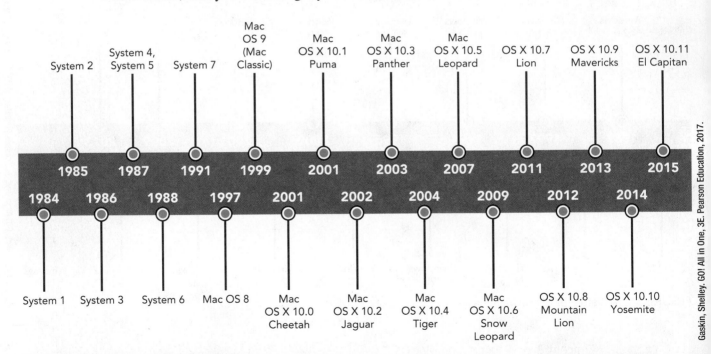

FIGURE 3.8 A history of Mac OS releases.

ETHICS | Hackintosh

Older versions of Mac OS ran only on Mac hardware with PowerPC processors, but modern Macs now use Intel processors just like most PCs. With a bit of tweaking, it is possible to get the OS X to run on a PC. Hackintosh is the name given to a PC that has been modified so OS X can be run on it. Is this legal? Is it ethical? What are the restrictions on the Mac OS X end-user license agreement—also called a EULA? Why do people do it? Would you?

Unix is a pioneering operating system that was developed at AT&T's Bell Laboratories in 1969. Pronounced YOU-nix, Unix defaults to a command-line interface, features multitasking, and is installed primarily on workstations and servers.

Unlike Windows and Mac, *Linux* does not refer to a single OS but rather to many different versions or distributions that use the same kernel OS called Linux. Linux was developed in 1991 by Linus Torvalds, then a graduate student at the University of Helsinki. It was designed to be similar to Unix and is sometimes called Unix-like. Unlike Unix, Windows, and Mac OS X, Linux is *open source*. The code is publically available, and developers all over the world have created hundreds of Linux *distributions* with all kinds of features. Distributions, referred to as *distros*, include the OS, various utilities, and software applications such as browsers, games, entertainment software, and an office suite. One of most popular personal versions of Linux is Fedora, as shown in Figure 3.9. Chrome OS is a Linux distro found on Chromebook notebooks. Most Linux distros come with a GUI that is similar to Windows or OS X, and users can easily navigate through the system. Linux desktops make up a very small percentage of personal computers, but the number is growing. Linux has found a niche in the low-end notebook market—on systems with limited memory and processing power, Linux shines.

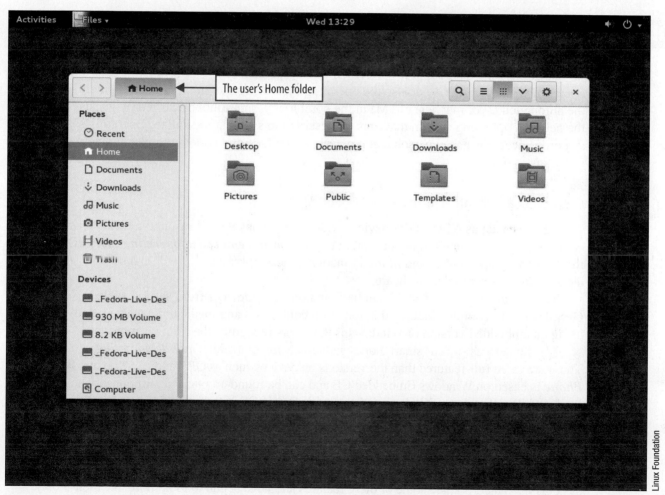

FIGURE 3.9 Fedora Linux

In businesses, Linux has less than a 2 percent market share of desktop computers, but it has a larger share of the server market. Red Hat Enterprise Linux is the world's leading open source application platform.

The operating system that you run largely depends on the hardware you have, but running the most recent version of your OS of choice ensures the best features and security.

ON THE JOB　Administrative Assistant

The job responsibilities of an Administrative Assistant might surprise you. In most positions of this type, the requirements to create and modify documents such as invoices, reports, memos, letters, and financial statements using word processing, spreadsheet, database, and other software such as Microsoft Office, QuickBooks, or other programs are often listed in the required skills. Additional skills required include the ability to conduct efficient research and searches, compile data and prepare papers for consideration and presentation to the Executive Director and Board of Directors, set up and coordinate meetings and conferences including verifying attendance through email or other electronic means, and prepare and electronically distribute agendas for meetings. Recent job postings for this position indicate experience with both Windows and OS X operating systems as a requirement. Are you surprised at the level of familiarity with technology that is expected from a candidate for an Administrative Assistant position? Evaluate your own credentials. Could you apply for such a position? If not, what courses should you take to prepare yourself for jobs that require computer skills?

Objective 3　Compare Specialized Operating Systems

As an IT Technical Support Officer, you are responsible for supporting not only the desktop operating systems on PCs but also the operating systems found on other devices, including the automated teller machine (ATM) in the hotel lobby, smartphones carried by guests, and the network operating system that runs the reservation system. Specialized operating systems run on devices other than personal computers and include embedded, mobile, and network operating systems.

1.01c
1.02h

Concept 3.08　Identifying Embedded Operating Systems

Devices such as ATMs, GPS devices, video game consoles, ultrasound machines, and the communication and entertainment system in your car run *embedded operating systems*. Because they have very specialized and limited functions, these operating systems can be very small and are able to run on simpler hardware.

The Windows Embedded OS can be found on many devices from set-top cable boxes and GPS devices to complex industrial automation controllers and medical devices. The advantage to using an embedded version of Windows is that users recognize the familiar interface.

Mobile devices such as smartphones and tablets run embedded *mobile operating systems*. These are more full-featured than the versions on devices such as GPS and cable boxes. *Windows Phone* is based on Windows Embedded CE and can be found on many smartphones. The iPhone, iPad, and iPod Touch run *iOS*, a scaled-down version of OS X that uses direct manipulation and multi-gesture touch such as swipe, tap, and pinch to control it. *Android*, as shown in Figure 3.10, is an embedded version of Linux that runs on many phones and tablets. *BlackBerry OS* runs on BlackBerry smartphones. These small operating systems have familiar interfaces and features, including touchscreen support, email, and web browsers. The current versions of desktop operating systems have incorporated some of these features and have begun to look more like their mobile counterparts.

As technology becomes more mobile, smaller, faster, and less tethered to the desk, alternative operating systems become an important way to interface with files and applications. Developers know this and strive to create the best interfaces—ones you can learn to use easily and come to depend on quickly.

FIGURE 3.10 The Android screen with icons, notifications, and menus.

Concept 3.09 | Exploring Network Operating Systems

In a business or school environment, a network server centralizes resources, storage, and most important, security in what is known as a ***client-server network***, such as the one shown in Figure 3.11. These servers run a specialized operating system called a ***network operating system (NOS)***, which is a multiuser operating system that controls the software and hardware that run on a network. An NOS enables client devices to communicate with the server and each other, share resources, run applications, and send messages. An NOS centralizes resources and security and provides services such as file and print services, communication services, Internet and email services, and backup and database services to the client computers. The table in Figure 3.12 details the most common network operating systems.

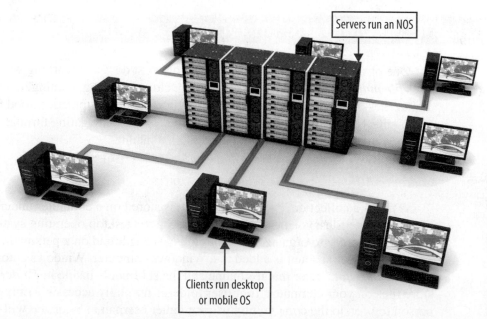

Servers run an NOS

Clients run desktop or mobile OS

FIGURE 3.11 In a client-server network, the servers run an NOS.

NETWORK OPERATING SYSTEMS		
NETWORK NOS	**CURRENT VERSION**	**COMMENTS**
Windows Server: First released as Windows NT in 1993	Windows Server 2012 R2, Windows Server 2016 was in beta testing at the time of this writing	Scalable; found on many corporate networks; available in versions from Small Business edition to Enterprise and Datacenter editions
Linux: Linux kernel is part of many different distros	Some of the most popular server versions used in business are Red Hat Enterprise Linux Server and Novell SUSE Open Enterprise Server.	It is impossible to know how many Linux servers are currently installed because there are so many versions that can be downloaded and installed for free and without registration.
Unix: Developed in 1969; the oldest NOS	Found on servers from HP HP-UX, IBM AIX, and Sun Solaris	Very reliable and secure. Open-source Unix-like versions are based on the Berkeley BSD distribution.

Gaskin, Shelley. GO! All in One, 3E. Pearson Education, 2017.

FIGURE 3.12

Your college network is most likely a client-server network. When you log in to the network, you are given access to certain resources such as printers and file storage. Centralized resources and security make a network operating system indispensable in a business environment.

Most home networks are ***peer-to-peer networks***. A peer-to-peer network does not require an NOS. In a peer-to-peer network, each computer is considered equal. Each device can share its resources with every other device using the networking features built into the desktop or mobile operating system, and there is no centralized authority. An NOS provides important security and resource management in a business environment. Without an NOS, businesses would have to rely on peer-to-peer networks, which are not practical for more than a few computers.

Objective 4 · Explain the Importance of File Management

One of the most important things that you must do when working with computers is referred to as ***file management***. This means opening, closing, saving, naming, deleting, and organizing digital files. As the IT Technical Support Officer, you must practice good file management—organizing your digital files, creating new folders, and navigating through the folder structure of your computer in a systematic and professional manner.

Concept 3.10 | Navigating a Windows Computer

A ***file*** is a collection of information that is stored on a computer under a single name. Before you can create files, you need a place to put them. Desktop operating systems have default file structures in place to organize the thousands of files found on a personal computer.

When a user account is added to a Windows computer, Windows automatically creates a personal ***user folder*** for that username and the subfolders inside it. ***Folders*** are containers that store files on your computer. Your user folder is normally accessible only by you. If another person logs on to the computer by using another username, he or she will not see your files.

The folder structure created by Windows is a hierarchy. There are folders within folders, known as *subfolders* or children, which further organize files. Within your user folder, Windows creates a set of subfolders to help sort your files. The Documents folder is the place to store files such as word processing documents, spreadsheets, presentations, and text files. There are also folders set up for pictures, music, and videos. These specialized folders are the best places to save pictures, music, and videos so that they are easy to find. Without this folder structure, all types of files would be lumped together, making it much harder to keep track of what you have, similar to dumping all your snapshots, bills, and receipts into a shoebox. The sequence of folders that leads to a file or folder is known as its *path*.

File Explorer is a window that displays the contents of the current location and contains helpful parts so that you can navigate within the file organizing structure of Windows, as shown in Figure 3.13. You can open File Explorer by clicking the File Explorer icon on the taskbar. You can use File Explorer to navigate through the folders and drives on your system and to handle most file management tasks.

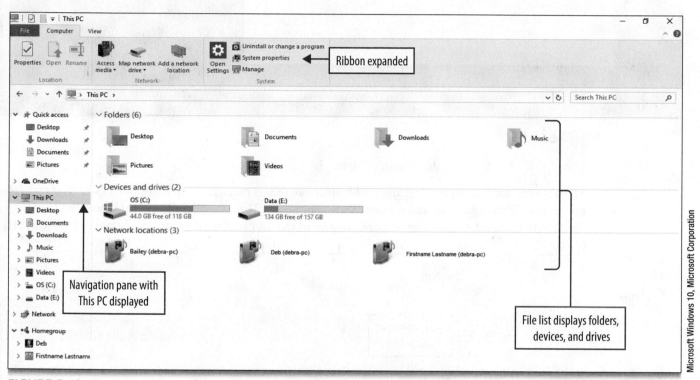

FIGURE 3.13 File Explorer is used for file management tasks on a Windows computer.

Microsoft Windows 10, Microsoft Corporation

Most operating systems include a *search utility*, which you can use to search an entire hard disk or any indexed network storage device for a file. In Microsoft Windows, search is integrated into every File Explorer window in addition to the Start screen. Here you can query for files in a number of ways, including by name, date, and size.

Concept 3.11 | Examining Mac OS X Finder and Folders

The *Finder* in Mac OS X is used to find and organize files, folders, and apps, as shown in Figure 3.14. It is similar to File Explorer. To open the Finder, click the Finder icon on the dock. OS X creates a *Home folder* for each user. The Home folder includes subfolders to store Documents, Downloads, Movies, Music, and Pictures. In OS X, the Spotlight utility performs searches.

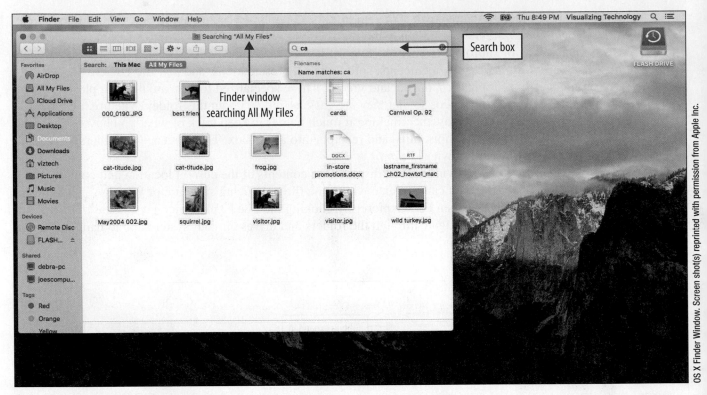

FIGURE 3.14 The OS X Finder window.

IC3
DIGITAL LITERACY
CERTIFICATION
1.03f (i)

Concept 3.12 | Creating and Using Folders

You are not limited to using the folder structure that is created by Windows or OS X. You can create your own organizational scheme to fit your needs. This is especially useful when you use flash drives and other locations that are not part of the user folder hierarchy, as shown in Figure 3.15.

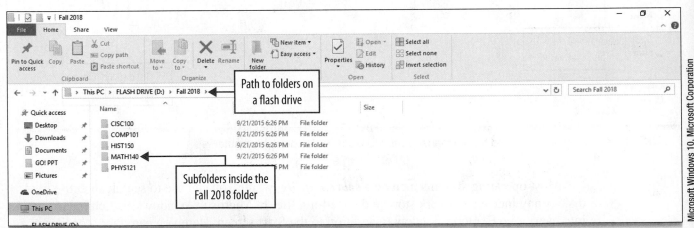

FIGURE 3.15 Creating folders on your flash drive helps organize your files.

You can use File Explorer or Finder, or the Save As dialog box directly from an application, to create new folders. Create folders with meaningful names to organize and make finding files easier. In your music folder, you might have folders for different artists. In the pictures folder, subfolders might be created by date or event name. After the folders have been created, use File Explorer or Finder to organize your files. When you copy a file, you make a duplicate that can be placed in another location, leaving the original file intact. Moving a file changes the location of the file. To select multiple files to copy or move, hold down Ctrl as you click each file name. If the files are adjacent, you can click the first file, hold down Shift, and then click the last file. To select all of the files in a window, press Ctrl + A.

There are two types of files on every computer: the ones that the computer uses to function, such as programs and device drivers, and the ones that are used and created by you—including music, documents, photos, and videos. You should be able to identify the type of file based on the file's location, name, and file extension.

Concept 3.13 | Examining File Names and Extensions

Every file has a file name that consists of a name and an extension. The *file name* is meaningful to the user and describes the contents of the file. When creating your own files, you decide the name. On early PCs, file names were limited to eight characters with a three-letter extension and often seemed cryptic. Today, file names on Windows computers can be up to 260 characters long, including the extension and the path to the file, and can include spaces and special characters. The only illegal characters in a file name are the \ / ? : * " > < | characters. OS X file names can be up to 255 characters, and the only illegal character is the colon (:).

The second part of the file name is the *file extension*—a set of characters at the end of a file name that helps the OS determine what kind of information is in a file and what program should open it. The extension is assigned by the program that creates the file and identifies the type of file. For example, Microsoft Word 2016 files have the extension .docx when you save them. Windows maintains an association between a file extension and a program, so double-clicking a .docx file opens Microsoft Word. The extension helps the operating system determine the type of file. If you change the file extension of a file, you may no longer be able to open it. Figure 3.16 lists some common file types and the programs associated with them. By default, when viewing files in File Explorer, Windows does not display the file extensions for known file types.

COMMON FILE EXTENSIONS AND DEFAULT PROGRAM ASSOCIATIONS		
EXTENSION	**TYPE OF FILE**	**DEFAULT PROGRAM ASSOCIATION—WINDOWS**
.docx/.doc	Word document	Microsoft Word
.rtf	Rich Text Format	WordPad or Word
.xlsx/.xls	Excel file	Excel
.pptx/.ppt	PowerPoint file	PowerPoint
.bmp	Image file	Microsoft Paint
.jpeg/.jpg	Image file	Windows Photo Viewer or Photo Gallery
.mp3	Audio file	Windows Media Player
.wmv	Video file	Windows Media Player
.pdf	Portable Document Format	Microsoft Edge, Adobe Acrobat and Reader
.zip	Compressed file or folder	File Explorer

Gaskin, Shelley. GO! All in One, 3E. Pearson Education, 2017.

FIGURE 3.16

Concept 3.14 | File Properties

Every file includes *file properties*, which provide information about a file such as its author, the date the file was last changed, and any descriptive tags. You can use these properties to organize, sort, and find files more easily. Some file properties, such as type, size, and date, are automatically created with the file. Others, such as title and authors, can be added or edited.

Figure 3.17 shows the properties of a file in the Details pane of File Explorer. The Details pane does not display by default but can be turned on from the View tab. This gives you a preview of the file. You can modify some of these properties, such as Title and Authors, directly in the Details pane.

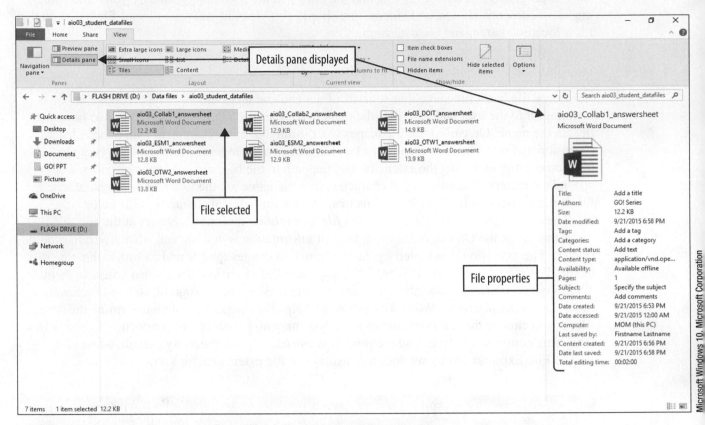

FIGURE 3.17 File Explorer enables you to view and modify some file properties.

You can view more information about a file by right-clicking the file in File Explorer and clicking Properties. This action opens the Properties dialog box for the file. The tabs of the Properties dialog box contain a rich assortment of information. The General tab makes it easy to change the name of a file. The Details tab lists information about the content of the file, such as word count. Figure 3.18 shows the Details tab for a file. Notice that the Details tab contains too much information to display. You must scroll down to see all of it. The type of information that displays depends on the type of file you are viewing. The security tab displays information about the file permissions, which determine the type of access a user has to the file. These include full control, modify, read, and write.

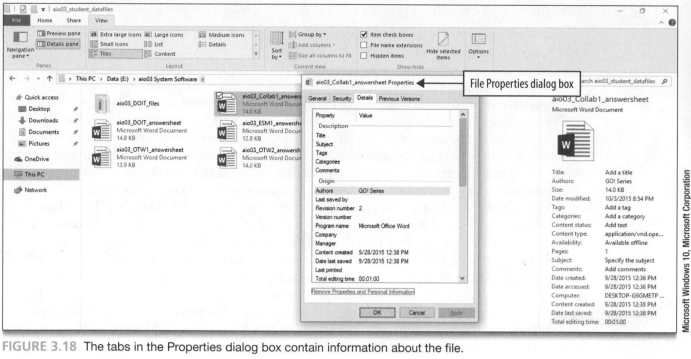

FIGURE 3.18 The tabs in the Properties dialog box contain information about the file.

You can view and modify file properties in OS X, too. In the Finder, select the file and choose Get Info from the File menu. This will open the Info pane for the file, where you can view and change some of the file properties such as the file name, sharing permissions, and Spotlight Comments, as shown in Figure 3.19).

FIGURE 3.19 The Info box in OS X displays file properties.

File names and other properties provide more information about files, which makes locating and managing your files easier.

Concept 3.15 | Compressing Files

Many file types are quite large, especially media files, such as photos, music, and videos. *File compression* is the process of making files smaller to conserve disk space and make the files easier to transfer. There are two types of file compression: lossless and lossy. The type of compression depends on the type of file you are trying to compress.

Lossless compression takes advantage of the fact that files contain a lot of redundant information. This is especially true of files that contain text and numbers. With lossless compression, the compressed file can be decompressed with no loss of data. An *algorithm* is a procedure for solving a problem. A lossless compression algorithm looks for the redundancy in the file and creates an encoded file by using that information to remove the redundant information. When the file is decompressed, all the information from the original file is restored. Lossless compression is used in ZIP files.

A *lossy compression* algorithm is often used on image, audio, and video files. These files contain more information than humans can discern, and that extra information can be removed from the file. An image file taken with a digital camera on its highest setting can yield a file of 5 MB to more than 25 MB in size; however, the normal quality setting yields a file of 1 to 2 MB. If you plan to use the file to create a large high-quality print or a medical image where every detail is critical, then the high-quality information is important. Most people, however, cannot tell the difference between the two when viewing them on a computer screen. Using the high-quality or raw setting on your digital camera results in a larger file. Depending on the camera, the image may be an uncompressed image in BMP or TIFF format. An image taken at the lower quality setting results in a JPEG or JPG file—an image file with lossy compression applied. After an image is saved as a JPG file, you cannot recover the information that was removed from the file. Figure 3.20 shows the same image file in the uncompressed TIFF format and the compressed JPG format.

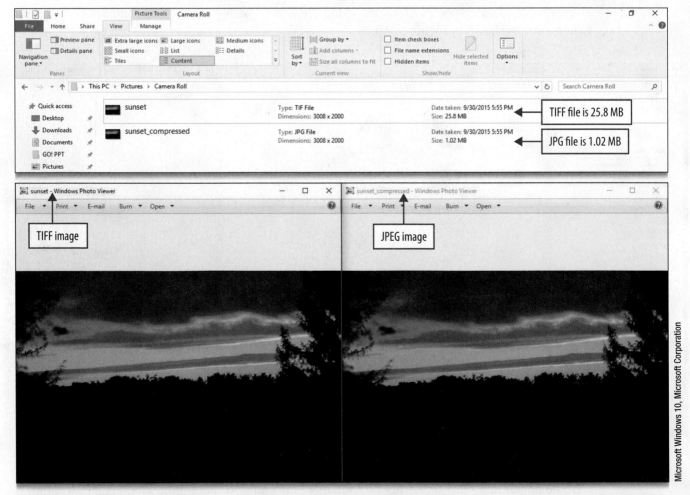

FIGURE 3.20 The compressed image is 25 times smaller than the uncompressed image, but on the screen there is little visible difference.

Another type of file that is commonly compressed is video. Videos files can be very large, making them difficult to transfer or upload to and download from a website. YouTube accepts many video formats for upload, such as MPEG4, 3GPP, MOV, AVI, and WMV, but these files are then processed and converted to other compressed formats, such as Flash, for viewing.

Objective 6   Use Advanced Search Options to Locate Files

A typical computer contains thousands of files, and finding what you need among them can be like looking for the proverbial needle in a haystack. If you follow the principles of good file management, create folders, and save your files in an organized way, then you'll have a much easier time keeping track of your materials.

Concept 3.16 │ Using Windows to Search for Files

Files contain properties that you can use to help organize and find them. Windows includes a search box almost every place you work—on the taskbar, in every Control Panel window, and in the File Explorer window. When you begin to type something in the search box, Windows immediately begins searching (Figure 3.21). Just start typing in the *Search* box on the taskbar to search apps, settings, files, and web images and video. Clicking *My Stuff* at the bottom of the search results launches a search of your files and apps that include that term. Windows maintains an ***index*** that contains information about the files located on your computer. This index makes searching for files very fast. You can include unindexed locations in your search, but it causes the search to be slower.

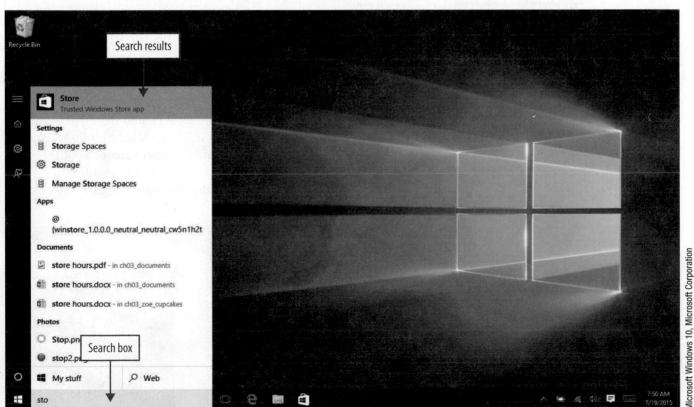

FIGURE 3.21 Windows Search locates programs and settings as well as files.

Beginning a search in File Explorer limits the search to files and folders within that location. The search begins as soon as a letter is typed in the Search box. In the example in Figure 3.22, the letters *fi* are typed in the search box, and the search locates files in the current location and the folders below it in the hierarchy. Search results include files with the letter search text in file names, file properties, and file contents. You can further refine the search results by typing more letters, such as *first*, or by adding a search filter, such as Type or Name. You can also save a search to be repeated later. If you don't find what you're looking for in your initial search, adjust your criteria.

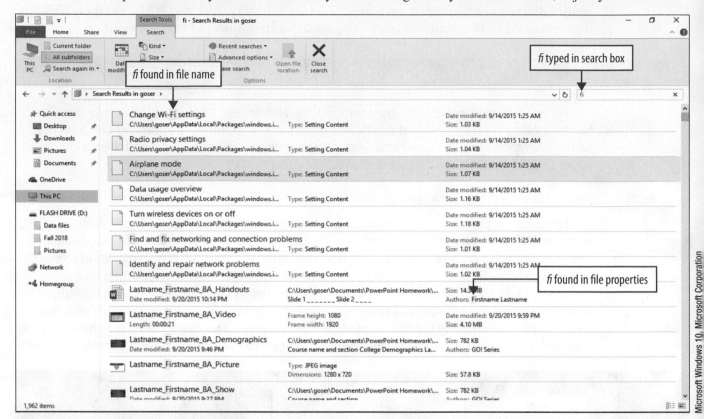

FIGURE 3.22 The search results in File Explorer show the *fi* found in file names, content, and other file properties.

Concept 3.17 | Searching in OS X

You can use the search field in Finder to search for files and folders, and the Help Center also has a built-in search, but the most powerful search tool in OS X is called **Spotlight**. Access Spotlight by clicking the magnifying glass on the upper right side of your screen. Spotlight searches applications, files and folders, contacts, and other objects on your computer. In Figure 3.23, the letters *fi* are typed in the search box in Spotlight. Spotlight can also provide a definition and do simple math calculations.

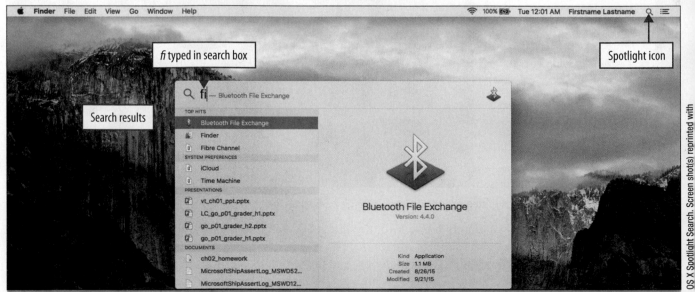

FIGURE 3.23 OS X Spotlight searches for many types of objects on your computer.

Using the Search feature of Windows or OS X can make locating a file or program quick and easy, saving time and minimizing frustration. Good file management and searching techniques are important skills to have.

Objective 7 | Share Files

Before You Buy
Cloud Storage

IC3
DIGITAL LITERACY
CERTIFICATION
1.02i (ii)
1.02j
1.02m
1.03f (iv)
1.03g (ii)
1.06c (iv)
1.06e (i)
1.06e (ii)

In your job as an IT Technical Support Officer, you often share files with other IT staff and hotel employees. Using the easiest and most secure ways to share different types of files enables you to perform these duties in the most efficient manner.

Concept 3.18 | Using Mobile Devices and File Storage

Mobile devices are meant to be fast and light, and they do not have a lot of space to store your files. Some mobile devices enable you to add storage by using an SD card, but in general, rely on using the cloud to organize and store your files. This has the advantage of making your mobile files accessible on all of your devices, not only from the one in your hand. After you have moved your files to the cloud, you can easily share them with others. Some mobile devices include apps that automatically upload photos or videos to websites such as Flickr, Instagram, Vine, or Facebook. Other apps can sync your documents and other important files between all of your devices, so files you create on your mobile device can *sync*—update files that are located in two or more locations—with your personal computers.

IC3
DIGITAL LITERACY
CERTIFICATION
1.02j
1.02m
1.03g (ii)
1.05a (i)
1.05a (ii)
1.05a (iii)
1.06a (i)
1.06a (ii)
1.06b
1.06c (i)
1.06c (ii)
1.06c (iii)
1.06c (iv)
1.06e

Concept 3.19 | Storing and Sharing Files in the Cloud

Cloud storage is a way to store working files in a convenient place so that they are accessible from different places and devices. Apple OS X and iOS devices include a free online storage and sync service known as *iCloud*, which can be set to automatically sync your personal files to the cloud (Figure 3.24), and there is a Windows version, so you can share your files among all of your devices. iCloud also includes free web versions of Pages, Numbers, and Keynote that you can use to create and edit documents.

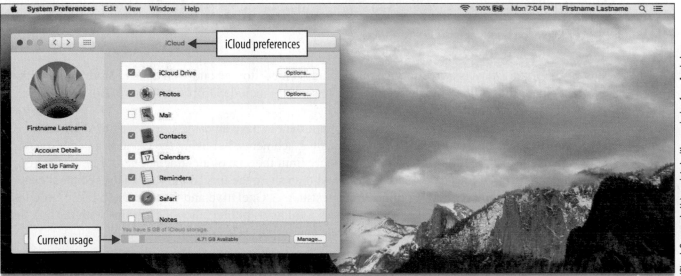

FIGURE 3.24 iCloud provides free online storage for some of your files.

iCloud. Screen shot(s) reprinted with permission from Apple Inc.

When you sign up for a Microsoft account, it includes free online storage, called **OneDrive** (Figure 3.25). If you are logged in to your Windows computer using a Microsoft account, the default save location for Microsoft Office applications is your OneDrive, and you can save to your OneDrive from other programs using the Save As dialog box. Older Windows computers, OS X, Windows Phone, iOS, and Android devices can connect to OneDrive by using a OneDrive app or the OneDrive website, so you can store files, photos, and favorites in the cloud and access and share them from any Internet-connected device. OneDrive also has the advantage of being integrated with Office Online web apps, which enable you to create and edit Microsoft Office documents right in your browser.

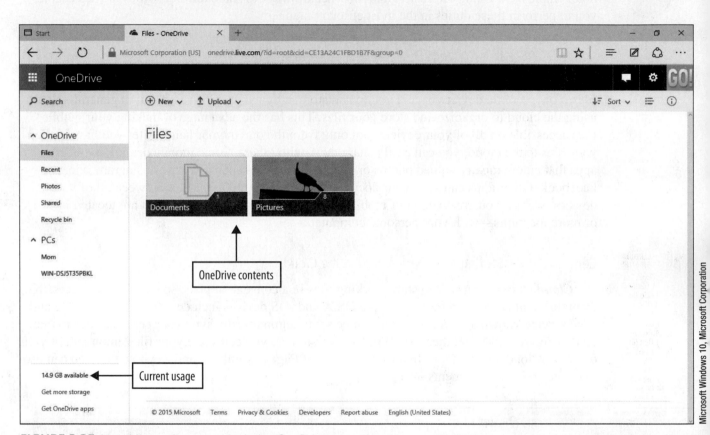

Microsoft Windows 10, Microsoft Corporation

FIGURE 3.25 Your Microsoft account includes OneDrive.

Google Drive is a free service that includes cloud storage and web apps to store, work with, and share files. Other popular cloud storage services include Dropbox, ADrive, Box, MediaFire, and Amazon Cloud.

When collaborating with others, it is important to have an easy, secure way to share and transfer files. Small files can be sent as email attachments, but using the cloud is a better option, especially for large files. Many email services limit the size of an attachment to 1 or 2 MB. You can upload large files to a cloud service, and then share the link to the file, so the recipient can download the file or view it online. Websites such as OneDrive and Google Drive enable you to share and collaborate on files. You can mark a folder as public, allowing anyone with the link to access the folder, or make the folder private and restrict access to specific people.

GO! To Work

Andrew Rodriguez / Fotolia; FotolEdhar/ Fotolia; apops/ Fotolia; Yuri Arcurs/ Fotolia

IC3 SKILLS IN THIS CHAPTER

IC3 — Module 1: Computing Fundamentals

Section 1.01 Mobile Devices

  (c) Be familiar with smartphone

Section 1.02 Hardware

  (f) Understand power management and power settings

  (g) Understand driver concepts as well as their device compatibility

    (i) Know what drivers do

    (ii) Know if specific drivers are compatible with a personal device

  (h) Know platform implications and considerations

    (i) For Example Mac, PC, Linux, iOS, Android, Firmware

  (i) Know platform compatibility

    (ii) Device limitations (a device might only have Wi-Fi or only have wired capabilities)

  (j) Know the difference between cellular, Wi-Fi, and wired networks

  (m) Implications for document usage

Section 1.03 Computer Software Architecture

  (a) Understand operating system versioning and update awareness

  (b) Know concepts surrounding applications vs. operating system vs. global settings

  (c) Have a general understanding of operating systems and software settings

  (f) Know file structures and file/folder management

    (i) Moving/renaming files

    (ii) File permissions

    (iii) File extensions

    (iv) Managing electronic media (eBooks, songs, videos)

    (v) Zipping/compression

  (g) Document Management

    (ii) Taking pictures

  (i) Searching for files

  (j) Rights and permissions (administrative rights)

Section 1.05 File Sharing

  (a) Understand file transfer options and characteristics

    (i) Know how to attach files to email

    (ii) Know how to get links to online
      stored files

    (iii) Understand the difference between publicly shared vs. shared links vs. shared folders

  (b) Understand needs for file compression/zipping in sharing

Section 1.06 Cloud Computing

  (a) Understand "cloud" concepts

    (i) Understand cloud storage vs. cloud access concepts

    (ii) Understand sharing and collaboration via the cloud

  (b) Know the benefits of using cloud storage

  (c) Access and utilization of the cloud

    (i) Understand account management on the cloud

    (ii) Know how to upload content to the cloud

    (iii) Know how to download content from the cloud

    (iv) Know how to sync files between devices using the cloud

  (e) Understand web app types

    (i) Online storage apps (Google Drive, Dropbox, OneDrive, iCloud storage)

    (ii) Online office apps (Google apps, Office 365)

GO! FOR JOB SUCCESS

Why Be Organized?

Your instructor may assign these questions to your class, and then ask you to think about them or discuss with your classmates:

Being organized is a characteristic many employers value. In a recent interview with CNN, Margaret Moore, Director of Coaching at McLean Hospital, describes being organized as, "the ability to 'drive' your attention and keep it focused when you're under pressure or faced with challenging conditions." Keeping your thoughts, your desk, and your work organized can help you make the best use of your time and talents.

FotolEdhar / Fotolia

Question 1: What are some benefits of being organized?

Question 2: What are some challenges to being organized?

Question 3: What are some things you might do to be more organized?

END OF CHAPTER

SUMMARY

An operating system coordinates the interactions of hardware components and the interaction of the hardware with application software. Modern operating systems have a graphical user interface, referred to as a GUI.

A desktop OS runs on a personal computer. Other devices run embedded operating systems, such as mobile operating systems. A network OS runs on a network server. Utility software helps you maintain and back up your computer.

File management means opening, closing, saving, naming, deleting, and organizing digital files. The window you use to look at a library or folder in Windows is called File Explorer and in OS X is called Finder.

The file name describes the contents of the file. The file extension identifies the type of file. File properties provide information about a file. File compression is the process of making files smaller.

GO! LEARN IT ONLINE

Review the concepts, key terms, and IC3 skills in this chapter by completing these online challenges, which you can find in **MyITLab**.

Matching and Multiple Choice: Answer matching and multiple choice questions to test what you learned in this chapter.

Lessons on the GO!: Learn how to use all the new apps and features as they are introduced by Microsoft.

IC3 Prep Quiz: Answer questions to review the IC3 skills that you practiced in this chapter.

GLOSSARY

GLOSSARY OF CHAPTER KEY TERMS

Algorithm A procedure for solving a problem.

Android An embedded version of Linux that runs on many smartphones and tablets.

Application programming interface (API) The feature of an operating system that enables an application to request services from the operating system, such as a request to print or save a file.

BlackBerry OS A mobile operating system that runs on smartphones from BlackBerry.

Boot The process of turning on a computer that has been completely shut down and during which the BIOS program will run.

Buffer An area of memory that temporarily holds data and instructions.

Client-server network A network that has at least one server at its center. Users log in to the network instead of their local computers and are granted access to resources based on that login.

Cloud storage Storage space on an Internet site that may also display as a drive on your computer.

Command-line interface An operating system interface that requires the user to type all commands.

Desktop operating system An operating system that runs on a personal computer.

Device driver Software that acts as a translator, which enhances the capabilities of the operating system by enabling it to communicate with hardware.

Distribution A version of Linux that includes the operating system, various utilities, and software applications such as browsers, games, entertainment software, and an office suite.

Distro Short for *distribution*.

Embedded operating system A specialized operating system that runs on GPS devices, ATMs, smartphones, and other devices.

File A collection of information that is stored on a computer under a single name.

File compression The process of making files smaller to conserve disk space and make them easier to transfer.

File Explorer A window that displays the contents of the current location and contains helpful parts so that you can navigate within the file organizing structure of Windows.

File extension A set of characters at the end of a file name that helps the operating system determine what kind of information is in a file and what program should open it.

File management The process of opening, closing, saving, naming, deleting, and organizing digital files.

File name The property of a file that identifies it and describes the contents of the file.

File properties Information about a file such as its author, the date the file was last changed, and any descriptive tags.

Finder In Mac OS X, the program used to find and organize files, folders, and apps; similar to File Explorer in Windows.

Firmware Software stored on a flash ROM (read-only memory) chip in a piece of hardware that provides instructions for how the device communicates with the other computer hardware.

Folder A container in which you store files.

Google Drive Google's cloud storage.

Graphical user interface (GUI) The system by which you interact with your computer and which uses graphics such as an image of a file folder or wastebasket that you click to activate the item represented.

Home folder In OS X, a folder that is created on a Mac computer for each user and which contains subfolders to store Documents, Downloads, Movies, Music, and Pictures.

iCloud Apple's cloud storage that is integrated into its Mac and iOS operating systems.

Index Contains information about the files located on your computer.

iOS A mobile operating system that is a scaled-down version of OS X and that uses direct manipulation and multi-gesture touch such as swipe, tap, and pinch to control it.

Linux An open source operating system distribution that contains the Linux kernel and bundled utilities and applications.

Lossless compression A compression algorithm that looks for the redundancy in a file and creates an encoded file by removing the redundant information; when the file is decompressed, all the information from the original file is restored.

Lossy compression A compression algorithm on files that contain more information than humans can discern. That extra information is removed from the file.

Microsoft Windows The most common desktop operating system.

Mobile operating system An embedded operating system that runs on mobile devices such as smartphones and tablets and is more full-featured than other embedded operating systems.

Multitasking The ability to do more than one task at a time.

Network operating system (NOS) A multiuser operating system that controls the software and hardware that runs on a network. It enables multiple client devices to communicate with the server and each other, to share resources, to run applications, and to send messages.

OneDrive A free file storage and file sharing service provided by Microsoft when you sign up for a free Microsoft account.

Open source Software that has its source code published and made available to the public, enabling anyone to copy, modify, and redistribute it without paying fees.

Operating system (OS) A computer program that manages all the other programs on your computer, stores files in an organized manner, enables you to use software programs, and coordinates the use of computer hardware such as the keyboard and mouse.

OS X The desktop operating system that runs on Apple Mac computers.

Paging The process of transferring files from the virtual memory file on the hard disk to RAM and back.

Paging file A virtual memory file on the hard disk used as a temporary storage space for instructions that the operating system can access as you do your work. Also known as the swap file.

Path A sequence of folders (directories) that leads to a specific file or folder.

Peer-to-peer network A network that does not require a network operating system, in which each computer is considered equal. Each device can share its resources with every other device, and there is no centralized authority.

Plug and Play (PnP) An operating system feature that you can use to easily add new hardware to a computer system. When you plug in a new piece of hardware, the operating system detects it and helps you set it up.

Print buffer An area of memory that holds documents until they can be sent to the printer.

Print queue The list of documents in the print buffer waiting to be printed.

Search utility A program with which you can search an entire disk or any indexed network storage device for a file.

Spooling program A program that monitors the print requests in the buffer and the busy state of the printer.

Spotlight A search tool in OS X.

Subfolder A folder within another folder.

Swap file A virtual memory file on the hard disk used as a temporary storage space for instructions that the operating system can access as you do your work. Also known as the paging file.

Sync To update files that are located in two or more locations

System resources The processor and memory on your computer.

System software The programs that provide the infrastructure and hardware control necessary for the computer and its peripheral devices.

Unix A pioneering operating system that was developed at AT&T's Bell Laboratories in 1969.

User folder A personal folder with subfolders inside it that Windows creates automatically for each username.

User interface The part of the operating system that you see and with which you interact.

Utility software Software that helps maintain, repair, and protect the computer; it may be included with the operating system or supplied by another organization.

Virtual memory A technique that uses a portion of the computer's hard disk as an extension of RAM.

Windows Phone An embedded version of Windows based on Windows Embedded CE that runs on mobile devices.

GO! Do It

Andrew Rodriguez / Fotolia; FotolEdhar/ Fotolia; apops/ Fotolia; Yuri Arcurs/ Fotolia

CREATE A COMPRESSED (ZIPPED) FOLDER

In this Activity, you'll compress a folder that contains several files to make it easier to email them or to share them with others.

1. From your student data files for this chapter, open the file **aio03_DOIT_ answersheet**. Display the **Save As** dialog box, navigate to the location where you will store your documents for this chapter, and then create a new folder named **AIO Chapter 3** Open the folder, and then save the file as **Lastname_Firstname_03_DOIT_ answersheet**

2. Insert your flash drive into your computer. Use File Explorer to navigate to the student data files for this chapter. Locate the folder **aio03_DOIT_files**. Copy this folder to your flash drive by dragging the folder to your flash drive in the Navigation pane. If you are not using a flash drive, copy the **aio03_DOIT_files** folder to your Documents folder.

3. In the File Explorer Navigation pane, click your flash drive or Documents folder. Right-click the **aio03_DOIT_files** folder, and then click **Properties**. How big is the folder? How many files and folders does it contain? **Close** the **Properties** dialog box.

4. Click the **aio03_DOIT_files** folder, click the **Share** tab, and then click **Zip** to create a zipped archive. Press [Enter] to accept the default file name.

5. Right-click the compressed folder, and then click **Properties**. Compare the size to the original folder. Take a screenshot of the open dialog box and paste it into your answer sheet. Type up your answers, save, and submit as directed by your instructor.

If you are using a Mac:

1. Insert your flash drive into your computer. Open **Finder** and locate the student data files for this chapter. Copy the **aio03_DOIT_files** folder by dragging it to your flash drive. If you are not using a flash drive, copy the **aio03_DOIT_files** folder to your Documents folder.

2. Click the flash drive in the **Sidebar**, and then select the folder in the right pane. From the **File** menu, click **Get Info**. How big is the folder? How many files and folders does it contain?

3. **Close** the Info pane. From the **File** menu, click **Compress "aio03_DOIT_files"** to create a zipped archive.

4. Click the ZIP file, and then from the **File** menu, click **Get Info**. Compare the size to the original folder. Take a screenshot and paste it into your answer sheet. Type your answers, save, and submit as directed by your instructor.

ON THE WEB

1. **Windows Upgrade** Your college is still running Windows 7 in the computer lab, but is investigating an upgrade to Windows 10. As a user of the computer lab, you have been asked to give input into the decision process. From your student data files, open the file **aio03_OTW1_answersheet**, and then save the file in your **AIO Chapter 3** folder as **Lastname_Firstname_03_OTW1_answersheet**

   Use the Internet to research the improvements in Windows 10 over Windows 7. Which improvements do you feel are the most important? Do the improvements that you suggest require any special hardware or software to be installed? Do you recommend that the college upgrade the computer lab? Give two reasons supporting your recommendation. Write a two- to three-paragraph summary that includes the answers to these questions.

   Print or submit your answer sheet electronically as directed by your instructor.

2. **Windows Hardware Requirements** In this Activity, you will compare the hardware requirements for different versions of Windows. From your student data files, open the file **aio03_OTW2_answersheet**, and then save the file in your **AIO Chapter 3** folder as **Lastname_Firstname_03_OTW2_answersheet**

   Use the Internet to research the hardware requirements for each of the following versions of Windows: Windows 3.1, Windows 95, Windows 98, Windows XP, Windows Vista, Windows 7, Windows 8.1, and Windows 10. When there are multiple versions of the OS, choose the original release and the Home or Home Premium version. Complete the table in the answer sheet.

   What is the fastest processor available today for desktop computers? What about notebooks? Mobile devices? What two companies are the main manufacturers of processors today?

   Print or submit your answer sheet electronically as directed by your instructor.

ETHICS AND SOCIAL MEDIA

1. **Ethics** Some operating systems can run directly from an optical disc or flash drive. Booting a computer this way circumvents the OS installed on the hard drive of the system. From your student data files, open the file **aio03_ESM1_answersheet**, and then save the file in your **AIO Chapter 3** folder as **Lastname_Firstname_03_ESM1_answersheet**

   In a school or business environment, this would likely violate an Acceptable Use policy. Is this legal? Is it ethical? Why do people do it? Would you?

   Print or submit your answer sheet electronically as directed by your instructor.

2. **Social Media** Technology companies such as Microsoft and Apple use social media to promote their products. From your student data files, open the file **aio03_ESM2_answersheet**, and then save the file in your **AIO Chapter 3** folder as **Lastname_Firstname_03_ESM2_answersheet**

   Open your browser, go to **www.youtube.com** and search for **Apple** In the search results, below the link for the **Apple channel**, how many videos are posted? Click the **Apple channel** link, and then preview the most recent videos. What type of videos are posted on the official Apple channel? Are there other Apple channels?

   Go to **http://www.youtube.com/channels/tech** and browse the list of technology-themed channels. How many technology channels are listed? Which channels relate to system software?

   In the **YouTube search box** at the top of the screen, search for **Ubuntu** How many results did you get? Browse the list and select a video to watch that gives an overview of Ubuntu. Did you find the video useful? Briefly summarize the video. Provide the URL of the video you chose.

   Print or submit your answer sheet electronically as directed by your instructor.

COLLABORATION

1. **Shopping for an Operating System** As a group, research one of the most recent operating systems: Windows 10, OS X El Capitan, Ubuntu Linux, iOS, or Android. From your student data files, open the file **aio03_Collab1_answersheet**, and then save the file in your **AIO Chapter 3** folder as **Lastname_Firstname_03_Collab1_answersheet**

   As a team, research your selected OS. Prepare a one- to two-minute multimedia commercial for your OS. The presentation should convince a consumer to use the OS. Use at least three references, only one of which may be this textbook. Submit the script and provide documentation that all team members have contributed to the project.

   Perform the commercial using the dialogue you have written. If possible, videotape the commercial, and share with the rest of the class.

   Print or submit your answer sheet electronically as directed by your instructor.

2. **Mobile Platform** As a team, research one popular mobile platform: Android, iOS, Windows, or BlackBerry. Prepare a multimedia presentation or poster for your platform. From your student data files, open the file **aio03_Collab2_answersheet**, and then save the file in your **AIO Chapter 3** folder as **Lastname_Firstname_03_Collab2_answersheet**

   The presentation should explain the features, functions, and uses of the program. Include costs and other license information such as the number of computers on which the program can be installed. Use at least three references, only one of which may be this textbook. Submit the presentation or poster, and provide documentation that all team members have contributed to the project.

   Print or submit your answer sheet electronically as directed by your instructor.

Networks, Security, and Privacy

OUTCOMES

Describe a computer network and identify different types of networks.
Recognize threats to security and privacy and explain how to protect against them.

OBJECTIVES

1. Discuss the Importance of Computer Networks
2. Compare Different Types of LANs and WANs
3. List and Describe the Hardware Used in Both Wired and Wireless Networks
4. List and Describe the Software and Protocols Used in Both Wired and Wireless Networks
5. Explain How to Protect a Network
6. Recognize Various Types of Cybercrime
7. Practice Safe Computing

Rob Marmion/Shutterstock

In This Chapter

The Internet is the largest computer network in the world, but it is actually a network of networks. On a much smaller scale, most of the computers that you use at your college and in the workplace are part of a network, and you possibly also have a network at home.

In this age of universal connectivity, there are numerous threats to security and privacy that you should take steps to protect against. In this chapter, you will learn about different kinds of computer networks. You will also learn about some of the most common security threats and how you can protect yourself in this digital age.

Job Focus

A **Convention Planner** at **Oro Jade Hotels** is responsible for organizing and coordinating all aspects of conventions that are held at each hotel. One of the most important parts of this job is working with the IT department to ensure secure and robust Internet and networking functionality for all convention sessions and participants. The Convention Planner serves as the liaison between the convention leaders and the staff at the hotel. Although the technical work is done by the IT staff, the Convention Planner must understand the way the networks work in order to discuss the technical and security needs of the convention.

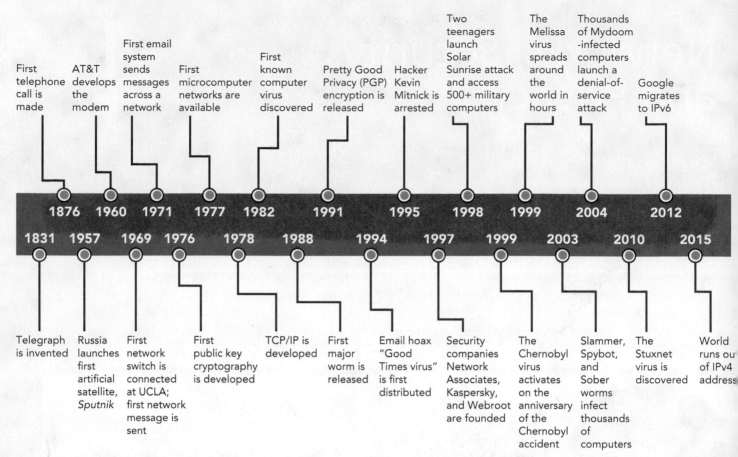

FIGURE 4.1 This timeline highlights some important dates in computer networking and security.

Discuss the Importance of Computer Networks

A *computer network* is two or more computers that share resources. *Network resources* include software, hardware, and files. Computer networks save both time and money and make it easier to work, which increases productivity. Before computers were connected in networks, moving files between them involved physically putting them on a disk and carrying the disk to the new computer. This was sometimes referred to as sneakernet.

Concept 4.01 | Using Peer-To-Peer Networks

Figure 4.2 shows a small *peer-to-peer network—P2P*—in which each computer is considered equal. Each device can share its resources with every other device, and there is no centralized authority. The computers might share music files and hardware such as a printer. They do not necessarily have to connect to the Internet at all. Computers in a P2P network belong to a *workgroup*.

FIGURE 4.2 A peer-to-peer network is common in homes and small offices.

Most P2P networks are found in homes or small businesses. They are easy to set up and configure and offer basic file and print sharing. A P2P network uses the networking functions built into desktop or mobile operating systems, and therefore does not require a network operating system. For example, if you have a printer in your house that is connected to your desktop computer, that printer can easily be shared with your notebook computer through your home network. A major drawback of this type of network is that the computer that is sharing a resource must be turned on and accessible by the other computers in the network. If the desktop computer is turned off or in sleep mode, then printing from the notebook will not be available.

The Windows operating system makes setting up a home network an easy task. When you add a new computer to your home and turn it on, Windows will automatically detect the other devices that are already on your network. Figure 4.3 shows some common network devices found in a home network. Notice that some devices are not personal computers, for example, devices such as a printer, a **router**—a device that connects two or more networks together—a game console, and an Internet-connected TV.

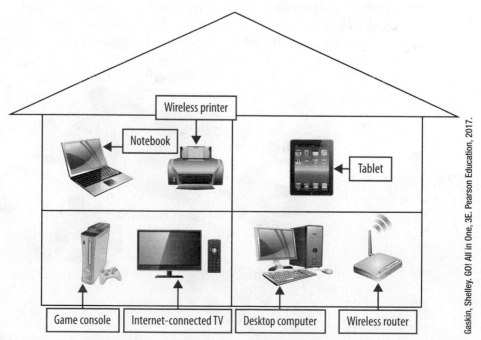

FIGURE 4.3 Home networks include many types of devices.

Windows includes a simple networking feature called a **homegroup**, which consists of the computers on your home network running Windows 7—or a later version of Windows—that are configured with the same homegroup information. Members of a homegroup automatically share their picture, music, and video libraries and printers with each other without any additional configuration. After you create a homegroup, Windows will create a password that can be used to join other Windows computers to the homegroup. In Figure 4.4, you can see a homegroup set up in the File Explorer window. In the navigation pane, DEBRAS-AIR is visible under Network, but DEBRAS-AIR does not display under Homegroup because it is a Mac and computers that are not running Windows 7 or Windows 8 or Windows 10 cannot join a homegroup. To share resources with Macs, Linux, or older Windows computers, you must use a workgroup.

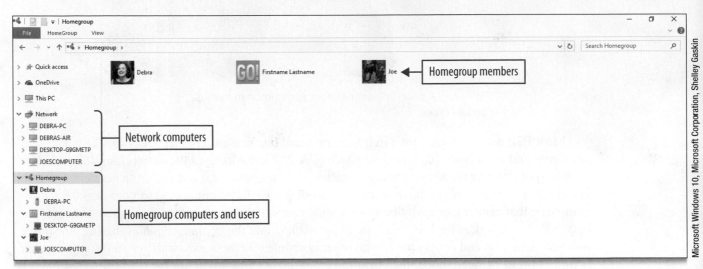

FIGURE 4.4 Computers visible in the network are not necessarily members of the homegroup.

1.02a (i)

Concept 4.02 | Using Client-Server Networks

P2P networks are suitable for homes and very small businesses, but they have two major drawbacks: they are limited to a small number of devices, and they provide no centralization of resources and security. In most business settings, a better choice is a ***client-server network***—a network that has at least one server at its center, as shown in Figure 4.5. The server provides a way to centralize the network management, resources, and security. In a client-server network, users log in to the network instead of their local computers and are granted access to resources based on that login.

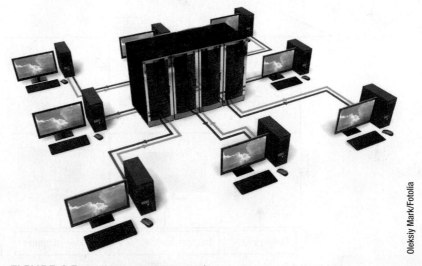

FIGURE 4.5 A client-server network.

A ***server*** is a multiuser computer system that runs a network operating system and provides services—such as Internet access, email, or file and print services—to client systems. The personal computers and other devices that connect to the server are called ***clients***. Servers range from very small to massive enterprise-level systems that serve hundreds of thousands of clients.

GREEN COMPUTING | Server Virtualization

Technically, the term *server* refers to the server software on a computer, not to the hardware it runs on. So a network server computer might actually run mail server, web server, and file and print server software. The advantage to this is that a single physical computer can be several different servers at once. Server computers are high-end, with fast processors and lots of storage. Sometimes, the computer's capabilities are not fully utilized, and its processors are idle much of the time. **Server virtualization**, running multiple versions of server software on the same computer, takes advantage of this unused resource. A good example might be running both an email server and a web server on the same computer. Each virtual server runs in its own space, sharing the hardware but not necessarily interacting with each other in any way. To the client, they appear to be separate servers.

Server virtualization is a big component of cloud computing. A company that offers **Infrastructure as a Service** or **IaaS** provides access to servers through the Internet. An IaaS company can set up virtual servers for many small companies on a large enterprise server. This saves money and reduces the amount of hardware needed and e-waste created for each business. Keeping servers in one location can also save on cooling and electricity costs.

Objective 2 | Compare Different Types of LANs and WANs

Networks come in different shapes and sizes. As a Convention Planner, you will need to understand different types of networks to ensure that the correct setup is implemented at each convention.

1.02a (i)
1.02g (ii)

Concept 4.03 | Comparing Small Networks

A *local area network* or *LAN* is a network that has all connected devices located in the same physical location. On a small scale, a home network is a LAN. In a business, a LAN might consist of a single room as shown in Figure 4.6, a floor, a building, or an entire campus. A home LAN is likely to be a peer-to-peer network, but a business LAN is more likely to be a client-server network and consist of computers, printers, and servers in addition to the network hardware that connects them. Devices on a LAN are connected by using *switches*—network devices that connect multiple devices on a LAN. A switch uses address information to send data packets only to the port to which the appropriate device is connected.

Vladislav Kochelaevs/Fotolia

FIGURE 4.6 A LAN consists of devices in one physical location, such as this classroom.

A small network that consists of devices connected by **Bluetooth**, such as a tablet and a keyboard, is a **personal area network** or **PAN**. Bluetooth has a very limited range of only about 10 to 100 meters, roughly 30 to 300 feet. The most common Bluetooth radio used for personal electronics has a range of 30 feet and a data transfer rate of up to 3 Mbps. Bluetooth is designed to be easy to use, enabling devices to talk to each other securely over short distances. Each device in a PAN can connect to up to seven other devices at a time. Some common devices that use Bluetooth include speakers, mice, keyboards, interactive whiteboards, headsets, cell phones, cameras, media players, video game consoles, and printers. Figure 4.7 shows a PAN connecting a keyboard and tablet using Bluetooth. A **wireless LAN** or **WLAN** is one that uses Wi-Fi to transmit data. Wi-Fi has a much larger range, higher speeds, and better security and supports more devices than Bluetooth, but it is also more expensive and complicated to set up.

Goldyg/Shutterstock

FIGURE 4.7 This Bluetooth personal area network includes a tablet and keyboard.

1.02c
1.02j
3.01a (i)

Concept 4.04 | Recognizing LAN Topologies

A home LAN uses the same network standards and equipment as those used in larger business networks. **Ethernet** standards define the way data is transmitted over a local area network. **Standards** are specifications that have been defined by an industry organization, which ensure that equipment made by different companies will be able to work together. Although there are other network standards, Ethernet is by far the most widely implemented. Ethernet networks transmit signals over copper cable, fiber-optic cable, or Wi-Fi at data transmission speeds of 10 Mbps to 10 Gbps. The maximum speed depends on the type of media and the capability of the network hardware on the LAN. Most home networks use 100 Mbps or 1Gbps Ethernet.

The physical layout of a LAN is called its **topology**. The devices on the LAN can be connected in many different configurations. The most common configurations are bus, ring, or star, as shown in Figure 4.8. In a **bus topology**, the nodes are all connected using a single cable. The data travels back and forth along the cable, which is terminated at both ends. In a **ring topology**, the devices are also connected to a single cable, but the ends of the cable are connected in a circle and the data travels around the circle in one direction. Both buses and rings are simple networks that were popular in the past; however, you are not likely to find a pure bus or ring LAN today. Modern LANs use a physical star topology, a hybrid star-ring, or star-bus topology. In a *star topology*, every node on the network is attached to a central device such as a switch or wireless access point. This connection device enables nodes to be easily added, removed, or moved without disrupting the network.

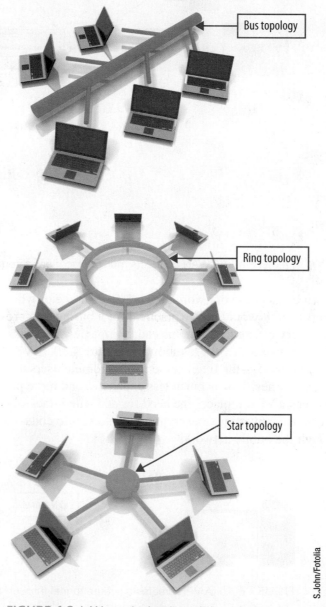

Bus topology

Ring topology

Star topology

S.John/Fotolia

FIGURE 4.8 LAN topologies: bus, ring, and star.

Concept 4.05 | **Examining Large Networks**

1.01a
1.01b
1.01c
1.07i

A *wide area network* or *WAN* is a network that spans multiple locations and connects multiple LANs over dedicated lines by using routers. A college that has multiple campuses would need to use WAN connections between them, such as those shown in Figure 4.9. WAN technologies are slower and more expensive than LAN technologies. At home, the WAN you connect to is the Internet, and the port on your router that connects to the modem is labeled WAN or Internet, distinguishing it from the LAN ports to which other devices connect.

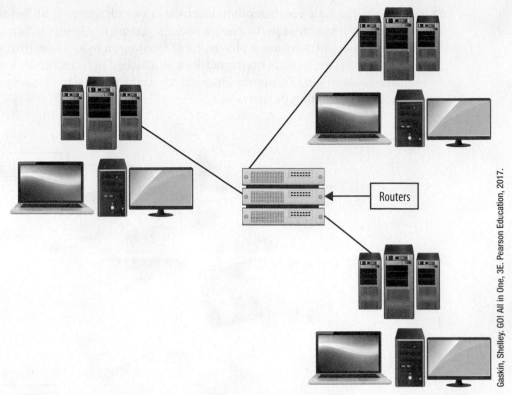

FIGURE 4.9 A WAN connects multiple locations through routers.

To connect to your work network from home or while on the road, you must use a WAN connection. It would not be practical for a business to provide its employees dedicated WAN lines from every offsite location. Instead, companies use a special type of connection called a *virtual private network* or *VPN*, as shown in Figure 4.10. A VPN creates a private network through the public network—the Internet—enabling remote users to access a LAN securely without needing dedicated lines. This is much less expensive and more practical for businesses, and in many instances a VPN replaces the need for dedicated lines completely. VPNs use *encryption*—the process of converting unencrypted plain text into code—to ensure the data is secure as it travels through the public network.

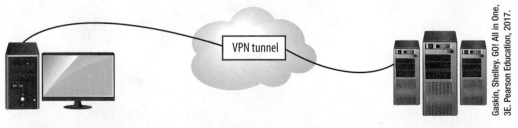

FIGURE 4.10 A VPN creates a secure tunnel through the Internet.

In a business that is too large and has too many computers to manage on a single LAN, there may be multiple LANs in the same location. In this *enterprise network*, the LANs are connected to each other by using routers—technically creating a WAN. A network that covers a single geographic area, such as a part of a city or town, is called a *metropolitan area network* or *MAN*.

Cellular networks use cell towers to transmit voice and data over large distances. Modern cellular 4G—fourth generation—networks have speeds that have made cellular networks a practical way for people on the move to connect to network resources, including the Internet and corporate VPNs, from almost anywhere in the world. Accessing resources using a smartphone or cellular-enabled tablet can quickly use all of your allotted data and increase your cost. When shopping for cellular phone carriers, compare the cost of data and choose a plan that gives you enough data for your normal usage. Some basic plans include only 1 Gb of data a month—enough for casual email users, but if you spend a lot of time on the Internet, play games online, stream videos, or engage in other heavy uses, you should look for plans with at least 5 Gb or more. Unlimited plans often throttle, or slow your speed, after you reach a certain threshold. The data limits are found in the fine print on your cellular contract.

Companies that have massive amounts of information to move and store may have a *storage area network* or *SAN* between the data storage devices and the servers on a network, making the data accessible to all servers in the SAN. Normal users are not part of the SAN, but are able to access the information through the LAN servers.

Computer networks range from two personal computers sharing a printer to large enterprise networks to the Internet. The larger and more complex networks require more hardware, configuration, and expertise to manage, but they all have the same basic purpose: to share resources.

Objective 3 | List and Describe the Hardware Used in Both Wired and Wireless Networks

Tech to GO!
Home Network
Hardware

DIGITAL LITERACY
CERTIFICATION
1.01b
1.02d
1.02e
1.02i (ii)
1.02j
1.02k (ii)
1.02k (iv)
1.02k (v)

Every network has two major components: hardware to create the physical connections between devices and software to configure the resources and security. As a Convention Planner, it is important to understand the types of hardware needed to set up the networks in the hotel.

Concept 4.06 | Understanding Network Adapters

The hardware necessary to set up a peer-to-peer network is much less complicated than what is needed in a client-server network. The simplest P2P network can consist of two devices sharing files by using a wireless connection or a single cable. For example, you can sync data from a smartphone or tablet directly to your computer or beam data to another person's smartphone. Larger home networks with multiple devices need extra hardware to connect them.

Each device that connects to a network must have some type of *network adapter*—a communication device that establishes a connection with a network, as shown in Figure 4.11. Most personal computers come with a built-in *Ethernet adapter*, a wireless adapter, or both. An Ethernet adapter has a port, called an RJ-45, which looks like a large phone jack. The cable used for this type of connection is called Ethernet cable. Cat-5e and Cat-6 are grades of Ethernet cable. Depending on the size of the network you are connecting to, the other end of the cable might plug into a wall jack, a switch, a router, or a modem.

Built-in Ethernet adapter

USB wireless adapter

Ryanking999/Fotolia

Denis Dryashkin/Fotolia

FIGURE 4.11 A network adapter may be wired or wireless.

There are several advantages to using a wired network connection, including speed, location, and security. Network speed is measured in bits per second. Wired Ethernet connections can reach speeds of 1,000 megabits or 1 gigabit per second—also known as Gigabit Ethernet, and some applications can reach 100 gigabits per second. Most current wireless technology cannot reach the 1 Gbps speed. Wired connections are less subject to interference and can travel long distances without slowing. Buildings and other structures can slow or prevent a wireless connection from working. Finally, a wired connection is more secure than a wireless connection, especially if the wireless connection is not configured with strong security settings.

There are several types of *wireless adapters*. A 3G or 4G cellular adapter can be built into a smartphone or notebook computer or can be connected by USB to any computer, providing a connection to the cellular network for network access. The Wi-Fi networks found in homes and public hotspots use the IEEE *802.11 standards*, which ensure that devices developed by different vendors will work with each other.

Notebook computers come with a built-in wireless adapter, and a USB wireless adapter can easily be connected to a desktop or notebook computer that does not have one built in. Wireless printers can be connected directly to a network, eliminating the need to be shared from an individual computer. The table in Figure 4.12 compares the speeds of the most common types of Wi-Fi connections.

A COMPARISON OF WI-FI STANDARDS		
802.11 STANDARD	MAXIMUM SPEED	DATE INTRODUCED
802.11b	11 Mbps	1999
802.11g	54 Mbps	2003
802.11n	300–600 Mbps	2009
802.11ac	1.8–3.6 Gbps	2012

Gaskin, Shelley. GO! All in One, 3E. Pearson Education, 2017.

FIGURE 4.12

When using a device with both cellular data and Wi-Fi access, it is usually less expensive and faster to use a Wi-Fi connection; however, Wi-Fi usage can drain your battery quickly, so you should turn Wi-Fi off when not using it. To view the network adapters that are installed on your computer, open the Network and Sharing Center. To access the Network and Sharing Center, from the Windows desktop, on the right side of the taskbar, right-click the network icon ![icon], and then click Open Network and Sharing Center. In the left pane, click Change adapter settings. This opens the Network Connections window, which lists all the network adapters on the system and the status of each, as shown in Figure 4.13. From here, you can manage your connections. This figure displays a Bluetooth adapter, a wired Ethernet adapter, and a wireless Wi-Fi adapter. Currently, only the Wi-Fi connection is in use, but any or all of them could be used at the same time.

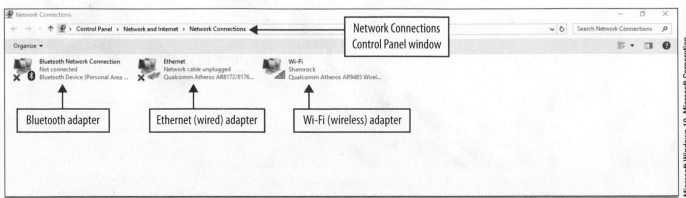

FIGURE 4.13 This computer has three different network adapters.

FAST FORWARD — Mobile 5G

Samsung Electronics and other companies are developing mobile technologies for fifth-generation networks that would provide data transmission up to several hundred times faster than the current 4G technology. The new 5G networks will transmit data up to 1Gbps, which exceeds even wired broadband currently available to most consumers.

The 5G networks will transmit large amounts of data over long distances using a broad band of frequencies. A full-length HD movie could be downloaded in seconds, video streaming will be seamless with no lagging, and online games will be played in real time. Samsung expects to implement 5G by 2020.

Concept 4.07 | Recognizing Network Hardware

Networks with multiple resources and devices require additional hardware. The first device on a network is usually the device that connects to the Internet. This can be an analog modem, a cable or DSL digital modem, or a fiber *optical network terminal* or *ONT*. You can connect a computer directly to a modem or an ONT, but you can share the connection with other devices more easily if you use a router instead.

A router is a device that connects two or more networks together—for example, your home network and the Internet. A router uses address information to route the data packets it receives correctly. In a home network, the router is a convergence device that serves several functions: It shares the Internet connection, provides addresses to the other devices on the network, has a built-in switch, and, if configured correctly, provides security for the network.

In the network displayed in Figure 4.14, under Network Infrastructure, you can see a router with a built-in wired switch and wireless access point called RT-N66U.

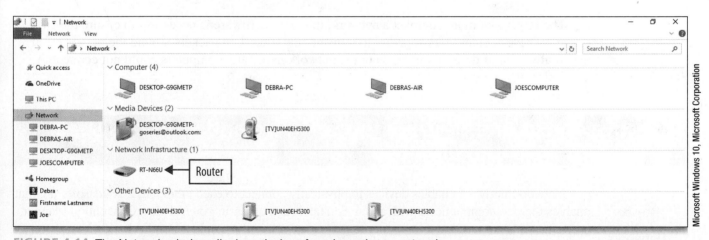

FIGURE 4.14 The Network window displays devices found on a home network.

Routers make up the backbone of the Internet and are responsible for sending the data packets along the correct route to their destination. If you think of the Internet as a map of highways, you will recognize that there are many different ways to get from one place to another. When you plan a trip, you take not only the distances into consideration, but also traffic congestion and construction. You might make a detour if you run into a problem along your way. The shortest route is not always the fastest route. Routers serve the same function, routing data packets around traffic, collisions, and other impediments.

When two wireless devices connect to each other directly, they create an *ad hoc network*. In an *infrastructure wireless network*, devices connect through a *wireless access point* or *WAP*—a device, much like a switch, that enables wireless devices to join a Wi-Fi network. A WAP can be built into a router or it can be a separate device. In a home, one or two are usually enough to provide coverage, but in a larger network, many WAPs may be needed. Figure 4.15 illustrates a home network that includes both wired and wireless devices.

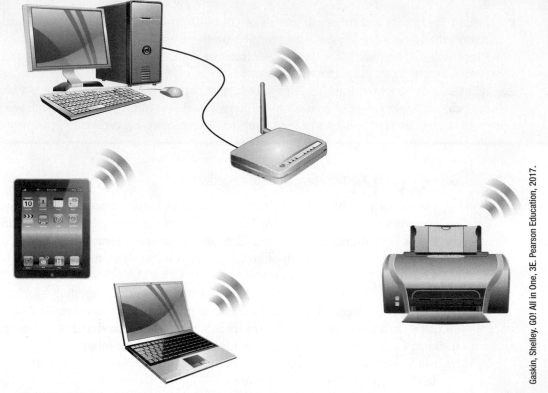

FIGURE 4.15 A network can include both wired and wireless devices.

The larger and more complex a network, the more hardware is necessary to ensure the flow of data. These devices work together to transmit and filter data packets around the network and eventually to their destination. Without the network hardware, computers could not connect to each other.

Objective 4 List and Describe the Software and Protocols Used in Both Wired and Wireless Networks

Network hardware enables devices to physically connect to each other, but it is the software that enables them to communicate with and understand each other. In your job as a Convention Planner, you often must connect your computer to networks both in the hotel and at client sites. You will need to understand network operating systems, communication software, and protocols that make a network work so that you can work efficiently and securely regardless of where you are.

Concept 4.08 | Using Peer-To-Peer Network Software

No special software is required to create a simple peer-to-peer network. Modern desktop operating systems have networking capabilities built into them. When Windows is installed on a computer, it includes a feature called *Client for Microsoft Networks*, which enables it to remotely access files and printers on a Microsoft network. To verify that Client for Microsoft Networks is installed on your computer, you can view the network adapters that are installed on a computer. Open the Network and Sharing Center from the taskbar, and in the left pane, click Change adapter settings. Right-click the active adapter, and then click Properties to open the Properties dialog box for the connection, as shown in Figure 4.16.

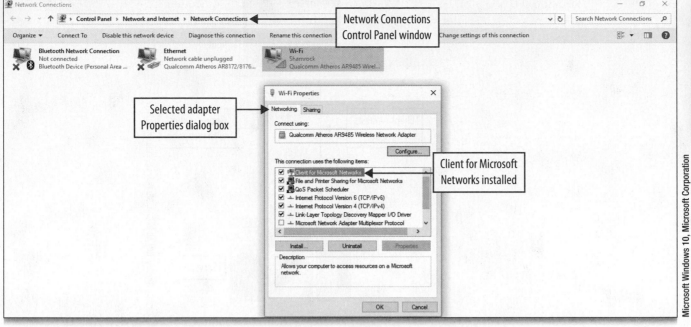

FIGURE 4.16 The Client for Microsoft Networks is installed by default on a Windows computer.

If a network consists of computers running the same operating system (OS), the computers are able to detect and share resources with each other with little or no configuration. In a mixed OS network, some additional configuration is often necessary. To connect computers running Apple OS X to a Microsoft Windows network, you will need to change some configuration settings on the Mac. OS X's network discovery tool should locate Windows computers automatically; as shown in Figure 4.17, however, the Mac must be configured with Windows account information and Windows file sharing in order to share files. It is also possible to include a Linux computer on a Windows network, but each Linux version has a somewhat different method for connecting.

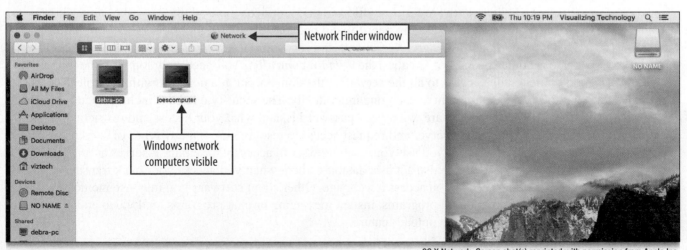

FIGURE 4.17 A Mac can join a Windows network.

OS X Network. Screen shot(s) reprinted with permission from Apple Inc.

Concept 4.09 | Using Client-Server Network Software

As the name implies, both client software and server software are needed on a client-server network. The client software makes requests, and the server software fulfills them, as shown in Figure 4.18.

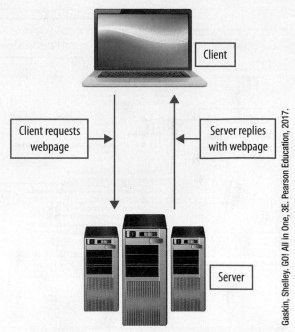

Client

Client requests
webpage

Server replies
with webpage

Server

Gaskin, Shelley. GO! All in One, 3E. Pearson Education, 2017.

FIGURE 4.18 In a client-server network, a client requests services from a server.

Server software or the ***network operating system***, the ***NOS***, is a multiuser operating system that controls the software and hardware that run on a network. It enables multiple client devices to communicate with the server and each other, to share resources, to run applications, and to send messages. An NOS centralizes resources and security and provides services such as file and print services, communication services, Internet and email services, and backup and database services to the client computers. Servers are classified by the type of services they provide. Some common services are file and print services, email, database, web, chat, audio/video, and applications. Whenever you log in to a website such as Facebook or Gmail, you are connecting to a server.

In a network where the servers run the Microsoft Server NOS, Windows clients do not need any special client software for basic file and print services. Instead, they use the same Client for Microsoft Networks used in peer-to-peer networks to connect to the servers. A ***domain*** is a network composed of a group of clients and servers under the control of one central security database on a special server called the ***domain controller***. You need only log in to the domain one time to have access to all the servers in the domain. So in a network with multiple servers, you do not need to log in to each one individually. The security database includes your user information—who you are, what your password is, and what your access and restrictions are.

Clients log in to a server and request access to resources. For many types of servers, a special client is needed. When you use your web browser to access your email, it serves as an email client. The browser can also act as a database client when you access your bank transactions and an HTTP client when you access a webpage. Other client software you may use includes VPN software, desktop email programs, instant messaging or chat programs, and video and photo software that include an upload feature.

1.03m (iv)
3.01a (i)

Concept 4.10 | Understanding Network Protocols

Network hardware is what enables devices to connect to each other, but network protocols enable them to communicate. ***Protocols*** define the rules for communication between devices. These rules determine how data is formatted, transmitted, received, and acknowledged. Without protocols, devices could be physically connected and still unable to communicate.

Think about a meeting between two people. When you walk into the meeting, you greet the other person, perhaps shake hands, and exchange names. There are mutually agreed-on protocols as to how you begin the conversation. Network protocols define how a conversation between devices begins. This ensures that both are ready to communicate and agree on how to proceed. During the meeting, you also follow rules: what to say, how to say it, what language to speak, what is appropriate, and what is not. Protocols also define how devices converse in much the same way. Finally, at the end of your meeting, you likely stand up, shake hands, say goodbye, and depart. Protocols also define the method to end an electronic conversation.

Although there are hundreds of different protocols, the most important ones belong to the *TCP/IP protocol stack*. This is a suite of protocols that define many types of data movement, including the transfer of files and webpages, sending and receiving email, and network configuration. *Transmission Control Protocol—TCP*—is responsible for ensuring that data packets are transmitted reliably. *Internet Protocol—IP*—is responsible for addressing and routing packets to their destination. Devices on a network must have an *IP address*—a set of four numbers, separated by periods, which uniquely identifies devices on a network. Home routers are commonly assigned the IP address 192.168.0.1 or 10.0.0.1 by the manufacturer. You can think of an IP address as similar to a phone number. The first part of the address identifies the network the device belongs to, similar to an area code. The last part of the address is unique to the device on the network. Most devices are set to obtain an IP address automatically from a server or router. Both TCP and IP are needed for data to move between devices. TCP/IP is the protocol stack that runs on the Internet, and because of this, it is also the protocol stack that runs on most LANs. TCP/IP is the default protocol stack installed on Windows, Mac, and Linux computers, and it is what enables them to communicate with each other easily. The table in Figure 4.19 lists some of the important protocols in the TCP/IP stack and their functions.

SOME IMPORTANT NETWORK PROTOCOLS IN THE TCP/IP STACK	
PROTOCOL	**FUNCTION**
TCP—Transmission Control Protocol	Ensuring that data packets are transmitted reliably
IP—Internet Protocol	Addressing and routing packets to their destination
HTTP—Hypertext Transfer Protocol	Requesting/delivering webpages
FTP—File Transfer Protocol	Transferring files between computers
POP—Post Office Protocol	Receiving email
SMTP—Simple Mail Transfer Protocol	Sending email
DHCP—Dynamic Host Configuration Protocol	Requesting/receiving an IP address from a DHCP server
DNS—Domain Name System	Resolving a domain name such as **ebay.com** to an IP address

Gaskin, Shelley. GO! All in One, 3E. Pearson Education, 2017.

FIGURE 4.19

Figure 4.20 shows the adapter properties for an Ethernet connection. You can see that both TCP/IPv6 and TCP/IPv4 are installed. Currently, TCP/IP version 4 is used on the Internet and most LANs. Although many older devices do not currently support TCP/IP version 6, it is slowly being implemented and will eventually replace version 4 altogether. By default, Windows computers are set to *Obtain an IP address automatically* by using DHCP. The computer sends out a DHCP request that is answered by a DHCP server—likely a router at home. Every computer on the network must have a unique IP address. This automatic configuration makes it easy to create a network.

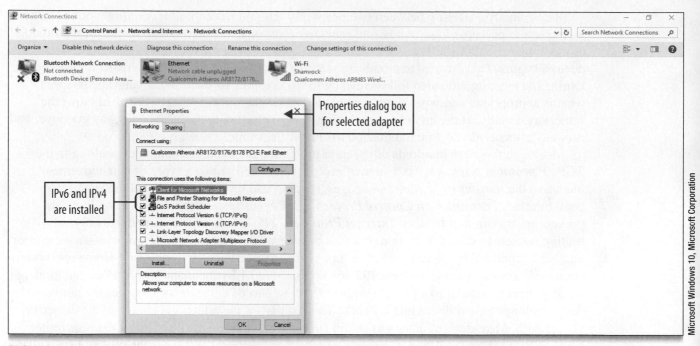

The Ethernet Properties dialog box

- Properties dialog box for selected adapter
- IPv6 and IPv4 are installed

FIGURE 4.20 The Ethernet Properties dialog box—both IPv4 and IPv6 are installed on this computer.

As with any computer system, the hardware of a network is useless without the software to make it work. In a network, that software also includes protocols to define the rules of communication. Together, the hardware, software, and protocols enable devices to share resources securely, efficiently, and easily.

✔ **Check Your Knowledge:** In MyITLab, take the quiz covering Objectives 1–4.

Objective 5 Explain How to Protect a Network

Concept 4.11 | Setting Up Firewalls and Securing Access

Before You Buy
Buying a Router

IC3
DIGITAL LITERACY
CERTIFICATION
1.07g

In a network, the first layer of defense is the hardware at the access point to the network. A *firewall* blocks unauthorized access to a network. There are both software firewalls and hardware firewalls. In a home network, the hardware firewall is part of the router. In a business network, a firewall is a standalone device. The firewall examines the data packets as they enter or leave the network and will deny access to traffic based on rules that the network administrator defines. It also shields the network computers from direct access to the Internet, hiding them from hackers looking for an easy target.

A firewall can be configured with filters to allow or deny various kinds of traffic. Filters can be based on IP address, protocol type, domain names, and other criteria. For example, a firewall might block access to certain websites or deny Internet access to specific computers during certain hours. Incoming packets that try to access restricted data will be denied access to the network.

Concept 4.12 | Securing a System with Hardware

IC3
DIGITAL LITERACY
CERTIFICATION
1.07e (i)
1.07e (ii)

At home, you should use a router between your computers and the Internet. The router provides several important security functions. First, the router acts like a firewall. It can prevent unauthorized access to your network. The default setup of most home routers has this feature enabled, and you can customize it by using the router utility. For example, you might set restrictions on the type of traffic that can access your network, restrict the time of day that a computer can access the Internet, or define which sites can or cannot be accessed. You might need to customize your router to allow certain applications through—especially if you like to play online games. The router faces the public network—the Internet—and has a public IP address that it uses to communicate with the network. Inside your house, the router supplies each device with a private IP address that is only valid on your private network. To the outside world, only the router is visible, so it shields the other devices. The devices inside your network can communicate with each other directly, but any outside communication must go through the router.

A wireless router also provides a wireless access point to your network. This can be a potential security risk if it is not properly secured. Use the router setup utility to change the *service set identifier* or *SSID*, or wireless network name, and enable and configure wireless encryption, as shown in Figure 4.21. *Wireless encryption* adds security to a wireless network by encrypting transmitted data. *Wi-Fi Protected Setup—WPS*—is a way to automatically configure devices to connect to a network by using a button, a personal identification number—PIN—or a USB key. By using this method, you do not need to manually type the network name and wireless security passphrases. You should use the strongest form of wireless encryption that is supported by the devices and operating systems on your network. In addition, you can disable the broadcast of the SSID, preventing the network from being visible to devices not already configured to use it. This requires extra configuration of the devices that connect to the network but adds another layer of security.

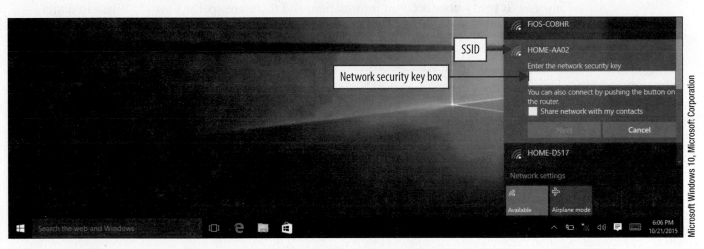

FIGURE 4.21 Enter the security key or press the button on the router to use Wi-Fi Protected Setup to join this network.

Use the highest level of security possible on your network. The harder it is to find and guess the settings on your network, the less likely it will be that someone will access it without your permission. Some things that you can do to secure your network include:

- Change the SSID and disable SSID broadcast so that your network is not visible to others.
- Change the default administrator name and password.
- Use WPA2 encryption and a difficult passphrase. Avoid the older and less secure WEP and EAP encryption options.
- Set up filtering so that only devices in the list are allowed.

Objective 6 Recognize Various Types of Cybercrime

The term *cybercrime* means criminal activity on the Internet. Many of these crimes existed in some form long before computers came along, but technology has made these crimes easier to commit and more widespread. As a Convention Planner at Oro Jade Hotel Group, you come into contact with many people and receive numerous email messages and inquiries from potential clients. You must be aware of the most common forms of cybercrime and be on the lookout for them.

IC3
DIGITAL LITERACY
CERTIFICATION
1.07c
3.05d

Concept 4.13 | Recognizing Personal Cybercrime

Personal cybercrime is perpetrated against individuals as opposed to businesses and other organizations. These are the crimes that affect you directly and for which you should always be on the alert.

Cyberbullying and cyberstalking fall into the category of harassment. The harassers use email, text messages, instant messages (IMs), and social networks to embarrass, threaten, or torment someone—often because of his or her gender, race, religion, nationality, age, or sexual orientation.

Phishing uses email messages or IMs that appear to be from those you do business with, such as your bank, credit card company, social network, auction site, online payment processor, or IT administrator. These messages are designed to trick you into revealing information such as usernames and passwords for your accounts. *Pharming* redirects you to a phony website. The criminal either hijacks the domain name of an organization or poisons the DNS server references to a site, so it points to the wrong website. Both phishing and pharming work because they appear to be messages for legitimate websites. Figure 4.22 shows a phishing email message that appears to be from a credit union. If you look closely, you can see signs that it is fake. The email address of the sender is a **gmail.com** address—not from the bank's domain—a link is provided asking you to verify your account information, and there are spelling errors. When in doubt, always verify with the legitimate organization before responding to any inquiries. Legitimate organizations never ask for personal information or passwords in email messages.

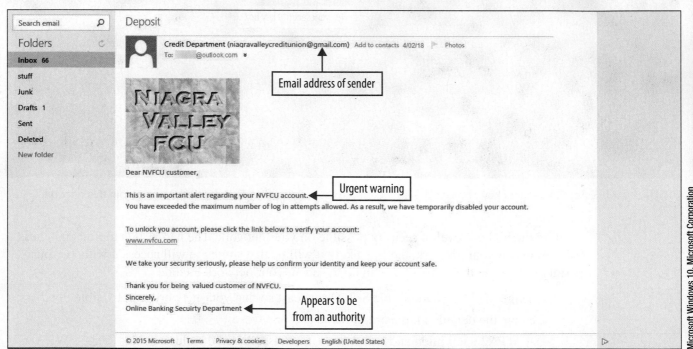

FIGURE 4.22 This phishing email appears to be an urgent message from a credit union.

Social networks are vulnerable to many types of attacks. Because you are *friends* with other users, you tend to trust what they post and send, and it is easy to be fooled into clicking something malicious. You will notice that most of these types of attacks are not specifically social network attacks, but because many people spend so much time on social network sites where they lower their guard, the attacks tend to be more successful. Some common attacks include:

- Suspicious emails and notifications—Appear to be from the social network administrator asking for your password or threatening to suspend your account
- Phishing and "Please send money" scams—Fool you into downloading malware or sending money

- *Clickjacking*—Enables malware to post unwanted links on your page when you click a link
- *Malicious script* scams—Creates pages and events or sends spam out to your friends when you copy and paste some text into your address bar

You can read more on the Facebook Security site at **http://facebook.com/help/security**—it is not necessary to have an account or be logged in.

Successful *computer fraud* schemes convince a victim to voluntarily and knowingly give money or property to a person. Some of the more well-known computer fraud schemes on the Internet involve emails claiming that you have won a lottery or inherited money. Figure 4.23 shows a message promising money for college. Although most people are smart enough to ignore messages as obvious as this one, the messages are often more personal and believable, and many people fall victim to the scams. This scam can also occur on social networks when a cybercriminal hacks into a user's account and sends messages to friends asking for help. Sadly, many victims of computer fraud lose thousands of dollars that can never be recovered.

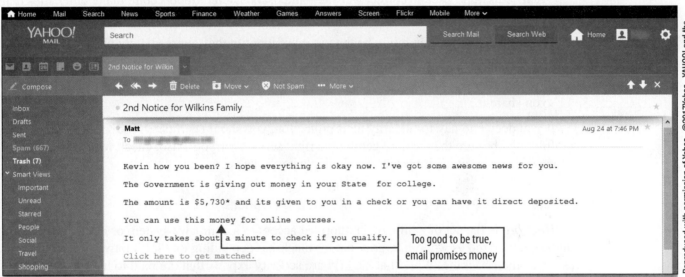

FIGURE 4.23 An example of an obvious fraud message.

ON THE JOB ▶ Network Administrator

You'll find computer networks in every type of business, and knowing how to access network resources is a critical skill for most employees.

A *network administrator* is the person responsible for managing the hardware and software on a network. The job may also include troubleshooting and security. Although not required, a two- or four-year college degree is helpful in this field, as are certifications. According to Salary.com, the average salary for a person in this field with two to five years' experience is about $64,000. As with any technical field, you should expect to continue your training to keep up with the changes in technology. An entry-level person may be called a network technician rather than an administrator.

Because networks and connectivity are critical for most businesses, experts in making networks secure and reliable will always be in demand. The *Occupational Outlook Handbook* at **http://bls.gov/ooh** predicts that network-related jobs will grow faster than the average for all occupations over the next decade, so considering a career in this field might be a good choice for you.

Concept 4.14 | Protecting Yourself from Identity Theft

The form of cybercrime many people fear the most is identity theft. *Identity theft* occurs when someone uses your name, Social Security number, or bank or credit card number fraudulently. The thief may purchase items, open new accounts, steal your income tax refund, or commit a crime using your identity. By using password-stealing software, *keyloggers* that capture what is typed on a keyboard, and phishing and pharming scams, criminals can easily obtain enough personal information to wreak havoc on an individual. Victims of identity theft often spend years and thousands of dollars to clear up the mess. Companies that claim to protect you from identity theft have sprung up, but they do the same things you can and should do yourself, including the following:

1. Monitor your bank and credit card statements, carefully checking each charge every month. Also watch for charges on your phone bills.

2. Monitor your credit report. By law, you are entitled to one free credit report per year from each of the three major credit-reporting companies. Instead of requesting them all at once, space them out every four months to keep an eye out for suspicious activity throughout the year. Be sure to use the correct website—**http://annualcreditreport.com**; many other sites that offer "free" reports actually charge you for expensive credit-monitoring services.

3. If you suspect that you might be the victim of identity theft, immediately place a fraud alert on your credit reports.

4. Protect your personal information. Be smart about the information you share and with whom you share it.

If you decide to pay for identity theft protection, you should compare products and services carefully and be sure that you are getting the right service for you. Also, check with your homeowner's or renter's insurance for available coverage.

Concept 4.15 | Detecting Cybercrime Against Organizations

Hacking is the act of gaining unauthorized access to a computer system or network. Hackers can be categorized as white-hat, gray-hat, or black-hat depending on their motivation and the results of their hacking. White-hat hackers are security experts that are paid to hack systems to find security holes for the purpose of preventing future hacking. They are also called sneakers. Black-hat hackers, also known as crackers, hack into systems for malicious purposes, such as theft or vandalism. Gray-hat hackers hack into systems illegally but not for malicious intent. A gray-hat hacker might break into a system to prove that he or she can or to expose a system's vulnerability. *Hacktivism*, such as that committed by Anonymous (Figure 4.24), is hacking to make a political statement. Although it is possible to hack into an individual's computer, a hacker has more to gain by attacking the computers of large companies and government agencies. A *data breach* occurs when sensitive data is stolen or viewed by someone who is not authorized to do so. Massive data breaches in the past few years, including those at Target, Home Depot, and iCloud, have exposed the personal information of millions of accounts. Internet extortion occurs when a hacker takes control of a database and threatens to release sensitive information unless a ransom is paid.

Dan Race/Fotolia

FIGURE 4.24 The hacktivist group
Anonymous, whose members appear in public
wearing masks, has claimed responsibility for
numerous hacking incidents.

An unlawful attack against computers or networks that is done to intimidate a government
or its people for a political or social agenda is known as *cyberterrorism*. Although many
terrorist groups use technology such as the Internet and email to do business, cyberterrorism
is more than just using computers as a tool. Cyberterrorists actually attack the information
systems to cause harm. According to a report by the Center for Strategic and International
Studies, between 2006 and 2012 there were nearly 100 significant attacks on "government
agencies, defense and high-tech companies, or economic crimes with losses of more than
a million dollars." A June 2014 study by the Center for Strategic and International Studies
estimates that the cybercrime cost to the global economy is at least $400 billion dollars
annually. Though the majority of cyber-terror attacks are unsuccessful and unreported, most
experts believe the threat is growing. Government agencies spend millions of dollars on
protecting themselves. Potential targets include the financial sector; infrastructure, such as
communications, utilities, and transportation; and hospitals. A successful attack on such a target
could cost millions of dollars and cause major problems—even loss of life. In March 2013, a
cyber-attack on the websites of major South Korean banks and TV broadcasters wiped out data
from the hard drives of more than 32,000 computers. The U.S. Cyber Command reported that
the Pentagon systems are attacked 250,000 times an hour—6 million times a day! The attacks
come from ordinary hackers, criminal enterprises, and foreign intelligence agents.

ETHICS — Encryption

When criminals use encryption to hide their illegal activities, law enforcement officials often need to crack the codes. The U.S. government has tried to require encryption companies to provide them with a backdoor key that would enable them to unlock anything that uses the encryption. Thus far, they've been unsuccessful in making this happen and have been forced to use brute-force methods to try to guess criminals' passwords. Over the years, there have been allegations that the National Security Agency (NSA) has embedded a backdoor into various versions of encryption and random number generators used to create encryption algorithms.

In 2010, even after a year of attempts, the U.S. government was unable to crack the password of a Brazilian banker who had been seized by Brazilian authorities. Should the government have the right to require a company to provide the government with the key to unlock such types of evidence? What if such a key also enables the government to decrypt any other information that's encoded with the same key—such as yours? What if the encryption hides suspected terrorism information? Or the hard drive of a suspected pedophile? Does your answer depend on the type of crime?

Objective 7 | Practice Safe Computing

The list of computer threats grows daily in size and danger. The only way to be truly safe is to unplug your computer and never connect it to a network—especially the Internet. Because this is not practical for most people, practicing safe computing is critical to protecting your system and your personal information. As the Convention Planner, part of your job is educating and informing convention guests about safe computing practices.

1.03e
1.03j
1.07a (i)
1.07a (ii)
1.07b

Concept 4.16 | Setting Up and Securing User Accounts

Windows and OS X user accounts have several layers of security built into them. There are three types of accounts:

- *Administrator account*—for making changes, installing software, configuring settings, and completing other tasks; called Admin on a Mac.
- *Standard account*—for everyday computing.
- *Guest account*—for users who need temporary access to a system. This account is off by default.

When you create an account on a Windows computer, you have the option to use an email address linked to a Microsoft account, as shown in Figure 4.25, or to create a local user. Either account type can be set up as an administrator or as a standard user. Using a Microsoft account links the user to cloud resources and syncs settings across systems.

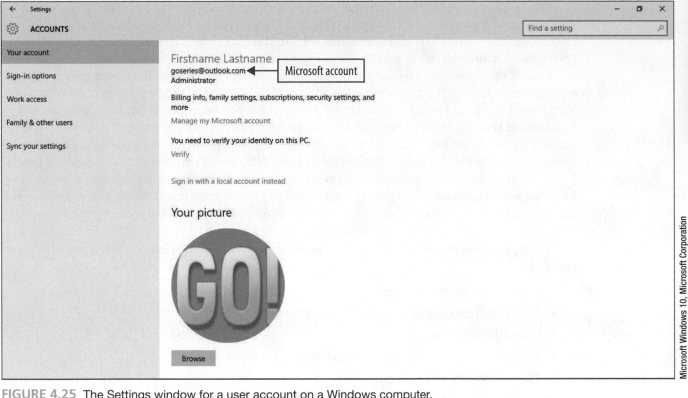

FIGURE 4.25 The Settings window for a user account on a Windows computer.

It is a good idea to create a Standard user account for day-to-day tasks and to use the Administrator account only when necessary for configuration, installation, or troubleshooting. Tasks that require administrator-level permission, such as installing a new program, will prompt for administrator credentials. On a Windows computer, *User Account Control* or *UAC* will notify you before changes are made to your computer, as shown in Figure 4.26. Although this may seem like a nuisance, it prevents malware from making changes to your system without your knowledge. You should not turn it off. It is important to always read the message in the UAC box before clicking *Yes*. Some malware infects computers by tricking users into clicking fake Windows notification boxes. In a business, only the IT staff should have administrator rights to a computer.

FIGURE 4.26 UAC requires administrator credentials to make changes to a computer.

Most people have multiple accounts, both local computer accounts and online accounts, that they access. Although using the same username and password on multiple accounts makes them easier to remember, it also makes them less secure. If a hacker manages to get the password to your email account, he or she may also have just gotten the password to your bank account.

Even if the passwords you use are different, with access to your email account, it is pretty easy for someone to get your password to other accounts. In 2008, the Republican candidate for Vice President of the United States, Sarah Palin, had her personal Yahoo! email account hacked by a college student. He reset her password by correctly answering her security questions. The security questions on most sites are things that are easy to find out about a person: high school mascot, mother's maiden name, favorite color, birth date. In this instance, the victim was a public figure, so the information was common knowledge, but how much of this information could be found on your Facebook profile? Password-cracking software can crack the strongest passwords that are six to eight characters long in a matter of minutes. How well you protect your accounts goes a long way toward protecting the information they contain.

Strong passwords are still the best way to secure your accounts. Here are some rules for good passwords:

- Use at least eight characters
- Use a mixture of uppercase and lowercase letters
- Use at least one number
- If allowed, use at least one special character such as ! or *
- Do not use any words that can be found in a dictionary
- Do not use anything personally identifiable
- Do not write it down
- Answer security questions with unexpected answers—but remember what you answered
- Use different passwords for different accounts
- Use more difficult passwords for accounts such as banks and credit cards
- Always change default passwords
- Change your passwords regularly

Some people use a *password manager* to store passwords rather than trying to remember them all individually. Some of these programs can also generate passwords for you, which are more secure than the passwords people normally create because they are randomly generated. If you choose to use a password manager, do your homework to be sure that the program you choose is very secure and that your passwords are safe. OS X includes a feature, called *Keychain*, which stores various passwords and passphrases in one place and makes them accessible through a master password.

Biometric scanners that measure human characteristics, such as fingerprints, retinas, or voice patterns, can replace the need to enter passwords. Windows Hello is a feature of Windows 10 that uses the built-in fingerprint reader or camera to recognize you. Requiring a magnetic card swipe is another way that businesses control access. You may have seen an example of this when you returned an item to a store. To allow a transaction that takes money out of a cash register, the clerk often will swipe an ID card to complete the transaction. Only someone with the authority to reverse a transaction, such as a manager, will be able to do so.

When you create a new account online (Figure 4.27), you are asked for a lot of information to help identify you. Think about your answers carefully so that they are hard for someone to guess, but also so that you are not giving away too much personal information. Select questions that are hard for other people to answer, and use good passwords following the rules of the site.

Create an account

If you already sign in to a Windows PC, tablet, or phone, Xbox Live, Outlook.com, or OneDrive, use
that email address to sign in. Otherwise, create a new Outlook.com email address.

First name

Firstname

Last name

Lastname

User name

goseries2016   @outlook.com

goseries2016@outlook.com is available.

Password

••••••••

8-character minimum; case sensitive

Reenter password

Country/region

United States

> **Password rules**
>
> Passwords must have at least 8 characters
> and contain at least two of the following:
> uppercase letters, lowercase letters, numbers,
> and symbols.

FIGURE 4.27 Use strong passwords when creating new accounts.

When you create an account on a website that requires registration, such as a discussion board, do not use the same password that you use for other websites that need more security, such as your bank. It also makes sense to have an alternative email account to use only for website registrations. This will help keep the amount of spam down in your regular email account, and if the spam gets too bad, you can always delete the account without losing your personal contacts. Although it is probably fine to have your passwords to such sites saved in your browser, do not have your browser save your passwords to websites such as bank and credit cards companies. Storing secure passwords in a browser leaves them open to potential hackers and other users of your computer.

IC3
DIGITAL LITERACY
CERTIFICATION
1.07h (i)
1.07h (ii)

Concept 4.17 | Encrypting Information

Any time you send information across a network, there is the potential for someone to intercept it. Encryption converts unencrypted, plain text into code called *ciphertext*. To read encrypted information, you must have a key to decrypt it. This prevents the thief from being able to read the information. When you log in to a website, be sure that you are using a secure connection. Verify that the address bar of your browser shows *https*, which indicates that the site is encrypted, as shown in Figure 4.28. This ensures that your information is safe to send. If the connection uses plain HTTP, then your information is sent in plain text.

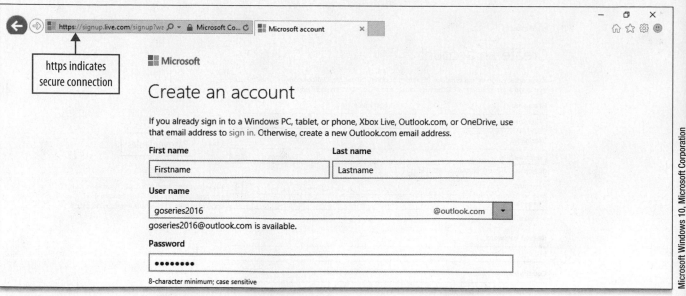

https indicates secure connection

FIGURE 4.28 Look for *https* in the URL to ensure that the data being sent is encrypted.

Microsoft Windows 10, Microsoft Corporation

File and drive encryption secure the data in your files. Windows includes ***Encrypting File System—EFS***, which enables you to encrypt individual files, and ***BitLocker***, which encrypts an entire drive. You can use BitLocker To Go to encrypt removable drives. OS X has a similar feature called ***FileVault***, which when turned on, encrypts the contents of your hard disk.

Concept 4.18 | Implementing Acceptable Use Policies

Many businesses and schools have an ***acceptable use policy*** or ***AUP*** by which computer and network users must abide. Although you might find them restrictive and annoying, from the business perspective, AUPs force you to practice safe computing and consequently help to prevent many potential problems from affecting the systems. The restrictions you have depend on the type of business and the type of information that you need to access. In a highly secure business, the AUP would likely prohibit all personal use of systems, including checking email, shopping online, using social networks, and playing online games. All these activities potentially could lead to malware being introduced into the system.

It is a good idea to have a personal AUP in place, too. It does not need to be a formal document, but all the users of your computers and home network should follow safe computing guidelines. It is a lot easier to prevent damage than it is to fix it.

Here are a few rules commonly found in an AUP:

- Be smart when reading email. Open attachments only if they are expected and you know exactly where they came from, and be sure your antivirus software scans them before you open them.

- Be wary of phishing and fraud scams, and delete any suspicious email right away.

- Be sure your normal user accounts are standard user accounts, and only use administrator accounts when necessary.

- Use good, strong passwords, and change them regularly.

- Be cautious of the information you enter on websites, and look for https-encrypted pages.

✅ **Check Your Knowledge:** In MyITLab, take the quiz covering Objectives 5–7.

GO! To Work

Andrew Rodriguez / Fotolia; FotolEdhar/ Fotolia; apops/ Fotolia; Yuri Arcurs/ Fotolia

IC3 SKILLS IN THIS CHAPTER

IC3 — Module 1: Computing Fundamentals

Section 1.01 Mobile Devices
  - (a) Understand cellular phone concepts
  - (b) Be familiar with cellular-enabled tablets
  - (c) Be familiar with smartphones

Section 1.02 Hardware
  - (a) Types of devices
    - (i) Server
  - (c) Know how to connect to different peripherals
  - (d) Understand the use of Ethernet ports
  - (e) Connect a device to a wireless network (Wi-Fi)
  - (g) Understand driver concepts as well as their device compatibility
    - (ii) Know if specific drivers are compatible with a personal device
  - (i) Know platform compatibility
    - (ii) Device limitations (a device might only have Wi-Fi or only have wired capabilities)
  - (j) Know the difference between cellular, Wi-Fi, and wired networks
  - (k) Understand concepts regarding connecting to the Internet
    - (ii) Bandwidth, speed
    - (iii) Have a basic understanding of what a router is
    - (iv) Wired
    - (v) Wireless

Section 1.03 Computer Software Architecture
  - (e) Users and profiles
  - (j) Rights and permissions (administrative rights)

  - (k) Define an IP address
  - (m) Troubleshooting
    - (iv) Know how to find an IP address on a personal computer

Section 1.07 Security
  - (a) Know credential management best practices
    - (i) Usernames
    - (ii) Passwords
  - (b) Know basic account setting management
  - (c) Know the basic threats to security of computers, data, and identity
    - (iv) Social engineering
  - (e) Connecting to secured vs. unsecured network (wired and wireless)
    - (i) Know the ramifications
    - (ii) Understand the risks
  - (g) Know the use of firewalls and basic settings
  - (h) Know eCommerce interactions and best practices
    - (i) Recognize the use of a secure connection, networks, (https:)
    - (ii) Know how to be a savvy ecommerce consumer
  - (i) Understand what Virtual Private Networks (VPNs) are

IC3—Module 3: Living Online

Section 3.01 Internet (Navigation)
  - (a) Understand what the Internet is
    - (i) Understand how the Internet works

Section 3.05 Social Media
  - (d) Know what cyber bullying is

GO! FOR JOB SUCCESS

Discussion: Network Security Is Everybody's Job

Your instructor may assign these questions to your class, and then ask you to think about them or discuss them with your classmates.

The company computer network is the responsibility of the network administrator and IT people, but protecting the system from outside threats is everyone's job.

What are some steps you can take to help protect the network?

What should you do if you discover someone has learned your password?

What are three ways an employee might inadvertently compromise the security of a company network?

FotolEdhar / Fotolia

END OF CHAPTER

SUMMARY

A network consists of two or more computers that share resources. In a peer-to-peer network, each computer is considered equal. A client-server network is one that has at least one server to which client devices connect.

A local area network—a LAN—has all connected devices or nodes located in the same physical location. A wide area network—a WAN—spans multiple locations and connects multiple LANs over dedicated lines by using routers.

Network hardware includes adapters, firewalls, switches, and routers. Network software includes client and server software and operating systems. Protocols define the rules for communication between devices.

Cybercrime against individuals includes harassment, phishing, pharming, fraud, and identity theft. Hacking and cyberterrorism are attacks against organizations. Malware is designed to be harmful or malicious.

GO! LEARN IT ONLINE

Review the concepts, key terms, and IC3 skills in this chapter by completing these online challenges, which you can find in **MyITLab**.

Matching and Multiple Choice: Answer matching and multiple choice questions to test what you learned in this chapter.

Lessons on the GO!: Learn how to use all the new apps and features as they are introduced by Microsoft.

IC3 Prep Quiz: Answer questions to review the IC3 skills that you practiced in this chapter.

GLOSSARY

GLOSSARY OF CHAPTER KEY TERMS

802.11 standards The standards that define the way data is transmitted over a Wi-Fi network.

Acceptable use policy (AUP) A policy that computer and network users in a business or school must follow that forces users to practice safe computing.

Ad hoc network A network created when two wireless devices connect to each other directly.

Administrator account A user account that should be used only when necessary, for such tasks as configuring and troubleshooting the system, and that should be protected by a strong password.

Biometric scanner An input device that measures human characteristics such as fingerprints and eye retinas.

BitLocker A Windows feature that encrypts an entire drive.

Bluetooth A short-range wireless technology that is used to connect many types of peripheral devices.

Bus topology A local area network topology in which the nodes are all connected using a single cable; the data travels back and forth along the cable, which is terminated at both ends.

Cellular network A network that uses cell towers to transmit voice and data over large distances.

Ciphertext Plain text that has been encrypted.

Clickjacking A social network attack in which clicking a link enables malware to post unwanted links on your page.

Client A personal computer, and other devices, that connect to a server.

Client for Microsoft Networks A Windows feature that enables a computer to remotely access files and printers on a Microsoft network.

Client-server network A network that has at least one server at its center; users log in to the network instead of their local computers and are granted access to resources based on that login.

Computer fraud A scheme perpetrated over the Internet or by email that tricks a victim into voluntarily and knowingly giving money or property to a person.

Computer network Two or more computers that share resources.

Cybercrime Criminal activity on the Internet.

Cyberterrorism An unlawful attack against computers or networks that is done to intimidate a government or its people for a political or social agenda.

Data breach A situation in which sensitive data is stolen or viewed by someone who is not authorized to do so.

Domain A network composed of a group of clients and servers under the control of one central security database on a special server called the domain controller.

Domain controller A special server that contains the central security database of a domain network.

Encrypting File System (EFS) A Windows feature that enables you to encrypt individual files.

Encryption The conversion of unencrypted, plain text into code called ciphertext.

Enterprise network A large network that has multiple local area networks located in the same location.

Ethernet adapter A wired network adapter.

Ethernet Standards that define the way data is transmitted over a local area network.

FileVault An OS X feature, which, when turned on, encrypts the contents of your hard disk.

Firewall A device or software that blocks unauthorized access to a network.

Guest account A user account for users who need temporary access to a system. This account is turned off by default.

Hacking The act of gaining unauthorized access to a computer system or network.

Hacktivism Hacking to make a political statement.

Homegroup The computers on a home network running Windows 7 or later.

Identity theft Theft that occurs when someone uses your name, Social Security number, or bank or credit card number fraudulently.

Infrastructure as a Service (IaaS) Provides access to servers through the Internet.

Infrastructure wireless network A wireless network in which devices connect through a wireless access point.

Internet Protocol (IP) The protocol responsible for addressing and routing packets to their destination.

IP address A set of four numbers, separated by periods, which uniquely identifies devices on a network.

Keychain An OS X feature that stores various passwords and passphrases in one place and makes them accessible through a master password.

Keylogger A program or hardware device that captures what is typed on a keyboard.

Local area network (LAN) A network that has all connected devices or nodes located in the same physical location.

Malicious script A social network attack in which copying and pasting some text into the address bar executes code that creates pages and events or sends spam out to your friends.

Metropolitan area network (MAN) A network that covers a single geographic area.

Network adapter A communication device that establishes a connection with a network; may be onboard, an expansion card, or a USB device, and may be wired or wireless.

Network administrator The person responsible for managing the hardware and software on a network.

Network operating system (NOS) A multiuser operating system that controls the software and hardware that runs on a network. It enables multiple client devices to communicate with the server and each other, share resources, run applications, and send messages.

Network resource Software, hardware, or files shared among computers on a network.

Optical network terminal (ONT) The device that connects a fiber-optic network to the Internet.

Password manager A program used to store passwords; some of these programs can also generate passwords.

Peer-to-peer network (P2P) A network that does not require a network operating system, in which each computer is considered equal; each device can share its resources with every other device, and there is no centralized authority.

Personal area network (PAN) A small network that consists of devices connected by Bluetooth.

Pharming Redirects you to a phony website to trick you into revealing information, such as usernames and passwords for your accounts.

Phishing Email messages and instant messages that appear to be from those you do business with, designed to trick you into revealing information, such as usernames and passwords for your accounts.

Protocols The rules for communication between devices.

Ring topology A local area network topology in which the devices are connected to a single cable; the ends of the cable are connected in a circle and the data travels around the circle in one direction.

Router A device that connects two or more networks together.

Server A multiuser computer system that provides services, such as Internet access, email, or file and print services, to client systems.

Server virtualization Running multiple versions of server software on the same computer.

Service set identifier (SSID) A wireless network name.

Standard account A user account created for normal use, which has limited access to change system and security settings.

Standards Specifications that have been defined by an industry organization, which ensure that equipment that is made by different companies will be able to work together.

Star topology A local area network topology in which every node on the network is attached to a central device such as a switch or wireless access point.

Storage area network (SAN) A network between the data storage devices and the servers on a network that makes the data accessible to all servers in the SAN; normal users are not part of the SAN but are able to access the information through the local area network servers.

Switch Hardware that connects multiple devices on a local area network and uses address information to send data packets only to the port to which the appropriate device is connected.

TCP/IP protocol stack A suite of protocols that define many types of data movement, including the transfer files and webpages, sending and receiving email, and network configuration.

Topology The physical layout of a local area network.

Transmission Control Protocol (TCP) The protocol responsible for assuring that data packets are transmitted reliably.

User Account Control (UAC) A Windows feature that will notify you before changes are made to your computer.

Virtual private network (VPN) Creates a private network through the public network—the Internet—enabling remote users to access a local area network securely without needing dedicated lines.

Wide area network (WAN) A network that spans multiple locations and connects multiple local area networks over dedicated lines by using routers.

Wi-Fi Protected Setup (WPS) A way to set up a secure wireless network by using a button, personal identification number, or USB key to automatically configure devices to connect to a network.

Wireless access point (WAP) A device that enables wireless devices to join a network.

Wireless adapter A network adapter used to connect to Wi-Fi networks.

Wireless encryption A system that adds security to a wireless network by encrypting transmitted data.

Wireless LAN (WLAN) A network that uses Wi-Fi to transmit data.

Workgroup Computers in a peer-to-peer network.

GO! Do It

WEB BROWSER SETTINGS

Web browsers include security features and settings to help protect your computer as you browse the web. In this activity, you will examine and configure these settings for the desktop version of Google Chrome.

1. From your student files, open the file **aio04_DOIT_answersheet**. Display the Save As dialog box, navigate to the location where you will store your documents for this chapter, and then create a new folder named **AIO Chapter 4** Open the folder, and then save the file as **Lastname_Firstname_04_DOIT_answersheet**

2. Open Chrome. To the right of the address bar, click **Customize and control Google Chrome**. Click **Settings**. On the Settings tab, under On startup, what page(s) are configured to display?

3. Scroll down and click **Show advanced settings**. Under Privacy, what web services are enabled? Click **Clear browsing data**. What options are available, and which options are checked? Click **Learn more** and read the Help page. If you were going to delete some of these objects, which would you choose, and why? Close the Help page. Click **Cancel** in the Clear browsing data dialog box.

4. Under Privacy, click **Content settings**. What settings are selected under Cookies, Images, JavaScript, Handlers, Plugins, Pop-ups, and Location? Under Pop-ups, click **Manage exceptions**. Are there any websites in this dialog box? If it's not already listed, in the [*]example.com box, type **pearsoned.com** be sure **Allow** is selected under **Behavior**, take a screenshot of this window, and paste it into your answer sheet. Click **Done**. Use the Internet to answer the following: What is a pop-up? What are two reasons to allow pop-ups? Why should you block them?

5. In the Content settings dialog box, under Plugins, click **Manage individual plugins**. What plugins are installed? Are any disabled? Take a screenshot of this window and paste it into your document. Close any open tabs and dialog boxes.

6. Print or submit your answer sheet electronically as directed by your instructor.

ON THE WEB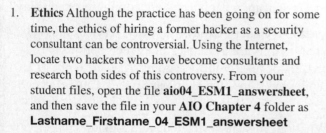

1. **IPv6 vs. IPv4** IPv6 is designed to replace IPv4, but why is this important? From your student files, open the file **aio04_OTW1_answersheet**, and then save the file in your **AIO Chapter 4** folder as **Lastname_Firstname_04_OTW1_answersheet**

   Go to the Internet Society website **http://internetsociety.org** and search for IPv6. What are some advantages of switching to IPv6? What was World IPv6 Day, and what were the results? How does the number of IPv6 addresses compare with the number of IPv4 addresses? Write a two- or three-paragraph summary that includes the answers to these questions.

   Print or submit your answer sheet electronically as directed by your instructor.

2. **Current Data Breaches** There are many high-profile data breaches that have occurred in the past several years. From your student files, open the file **aio04_OTW2_answersheet**, and then save the file in your **AIO Chapter 4** folder as **Lastname_Firstname_04_OTW2_answersheet**

   Search the web for the top data breaches of the current or previous year. How many major data breaches were reported? Are any companies with which you do business? What was the remedy for those whose data may have been compromised? Were there any criminal charges filed? Write a one-page summary of your research, and include your sources.

   Print or submit your answer sheet electronically as directed by your instructor.

ETHICS AND SOCIAL MEDIA

1. **Ethics** Although the practice has been going on for some time, the ethics of hiring a former hacker as a security consultant can be controversial. Using the Internet, locate two hackers who have become consultants and research both sides of this controversy. From your student files, open the file **aio04_ESM1_answersheet**, and then save the file in your **AIO Chapter 4** folder as **Lastname_Firstname_04_ESM1_answersheet**

   Present the pros and cons in a two- to three-paragraph summary; include your references.

   Print or submit your answer sheet electronically as directed by your instructor.

2. **Social Media** The amount of information that someone can find out about you from social media sites can be surprising, even if you have your profile settings secure. From your student files, open the file **aio04_ESM2_answersheet**, and then save the file in your **AIO Chapter 4** folder as **Lastname_Firstname_04_ESM2_answersheet**

   Search for your own name by using Google. Try different variations of your name. Did you find any information about yourself? How many of the results on the first pages are social media accounts? Are there any images of you? Do you have a common name that gave you lots of results, or an uncommon one that netted you fewer? If you had no luck, try searching for a family member who owns a home or business because property owners are likely to yield more results. Now try a few more websites. Choose any two of the following; if you have an account on any of these sites, be sure you are logged out: **http://zabasearch.com**, **http://spokeo.com**, **http://wink.com**, **http://pipl.com**, **http://addresses.com**, **http://anywho.com/whitepages**. Did you find any information about yourself or your family members? Was it correct? Is there a way to have the entry removed from the site? Summarize your results.

   Print or submit your answer sheet electronically as directed by your instructor.

COLLABORATION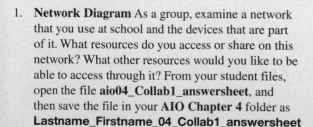

1. **Network Diagram** As a group, examine a network that you use at school and the devices that are part of it. What resources do you access or share on this network? What other resources would you like to be able to access through it? From your student files, open the file **aio04_Collab1_answersheet**, and then save the file in your **AIO Chapter 4** folder as **Lastname_Firstname_04_Collab1_answersheet**

   Create a diagram of the network that you examined. You can use a drawing program such as Microsoft Paint or a website such as **Gliffy.com** or **Creately.com** to create the diagram. Be sure to label the devices, including printers, cell phones, game consoles, and so on. If your network connects to the Internet, label the LAN and WAN parts. Submit the diagram and provide documentation to show that all team members have contributed to the project.

   Print or submit your answer sheet electronically as directed by your instructor.

2. **Acceptable Use Policy** As a team, research your college's acceptable use policy. Prepare a multimedia presentation or poster for your college. From your student files, open the file **aio04_Collab2_answersheet**, and then save the file in your **AIO Chapter 4** folder as **Lastname_Firstname_04_Collab2_answersheet**

   The presentation should explain the policy, to whom it applies, what is considered acceptable, and what the consequences are of violating the policy. Submit the presentation or poster and provide documentation to show that all team members have contributed to the project.

   Print or submit your answer sheet electronically as directed by your instructor.

Troubleshooting and Maintenance

5 CONCEPTS

OUTCOMES
Troubleshoot computer problems and perform routine maintenance to ensure optimum computer performance.
Describe the importance of system utilities and backups.

OBJECTIVES

1. Troubleshoot Common Computer Problems
2. Use System Utilities
3. Compare Methods for Backing Up a System
4. Assess a Computer System for Software Compatibility
5. Install, Uninstall, and Update Software
6. Stay Safe Online

Elnariz/Fotolia

In This Chapter

Frustrations that can come with using a computer include slow performance, error messages, virus infections, and lost files. By having a working knowledge of troubleshooting and system maintenance methods, it will be easier for you to avoid and spot trouble and will make using your computer a more pleasant experience.

In this chapter, you will learn about the programs and procedures you can use to repair and protect your computer systems.

Job Focus

As an **IT Support Technician**, your responsibilities include maintaining and securing **Oro Jade Hotel Group's** computer systems and assisting staff and hotel guests. You must be knowledgeable in the utility software that runs on various devices and the systems within the hotel and those that you might encounter running on guest devices. You must also implement procedures to ensure data is backed up securely. The IT department monitors and protects systems for Oro Jade staff and guests.

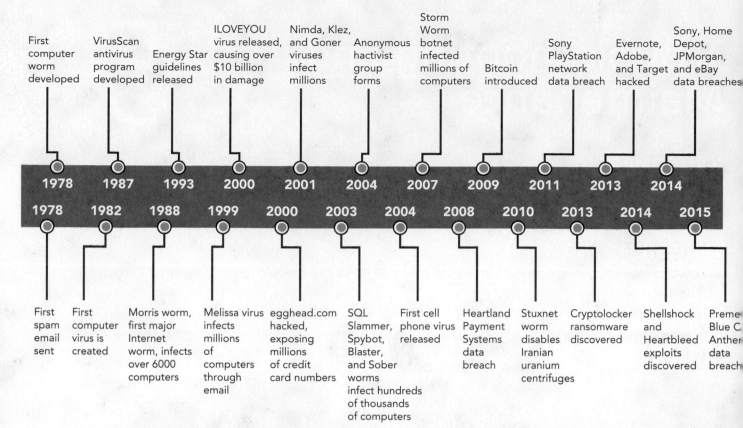

FIGURE 5.1 This timeline highlights some important dates in computer security.

Objective 1 | Troubleshoot Common Computer Problems

In your job as an IT Support Technician, you often help troubleshoot problems on computers in the hotel. Effective troubleshooting involves a systematic approach and attention to detail. Following this approach, from simple to complex, make problem solving effective and efficient.

1.03m (i)
1.03m (ii)
1.03m (iii)

Concept 5.01 | Basic Troubleshooting Methods

Developing a systematic, consistent approach to troubleshooting can solve many problems quickly. More complex problems may still require assistance from tech support, but by performing the first-level troubleshooting tasks first, you can resolve or rule out common problems before seeking help. Most computer users can perform basic troubleshooting by following these steps:

1. **Reboot the system:** This fixes many issues when a program or system is frozen or stuck. Reboot, or restart, the system to clear problems from memory and reload software.

2. **Check connections:** Even if connections appear sound, a loose cable or plug can cause problems. Unplug or disconnect suspicious cables and reconnect them. When possible, try a different cable, outlet, or port.

3. **Ask what has changed:** Has the system been updated recently? A new program installed or additional hardware connected? Rolling back these changes can often fix the problem.

4. **Search online:** Most manufacturers and software companies provide online resources such as forums and knowledge bases where you can find help from other users and company experts.

5. **Run troubleshooters:** Windows includes a number of troubleshooters that you can run to detect and fix problems such as network connectivity or printing issues. Access these from the Troubleshooting Control Panel, as shown in Figure 5.2.

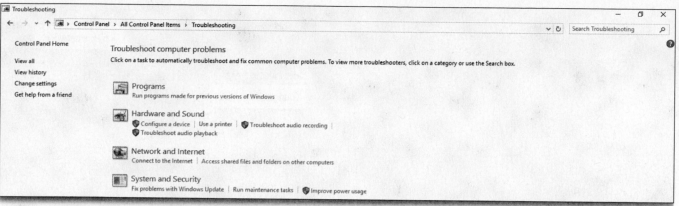

Troubleshooting

← → ∨ ↑ 📁 › Control Panel › All Control Panel Items › Troubleshooting   ∨ ⟳   Search Troubleshooting   🔎

Control Panel Home

Troubleshoot computer problems

View all

View history

Change settings

Get help from a friend

Click on a task to automatically troubleshoot and fix common computer problems. To view more troubleshooters, click on a category or use the Search box.

Programs
Run programs made for previous versions of Windows

Hardware and Sound
🔊 Configure a device | Use a printer | 🔊 Troubleshoot audio recording |
🔊 Troubleshoot audio playback

Network and Internet
Connect to the Internet | Access shared files and folders on other computers

System and Security
Fix problems with Windows Update | Run maintenance tasks | 🛡 Improve power usage

Microsoft Windows 10, Microsoft Corporation

FIGURE 5.2 The Windows Troubleshooting window.

6. **Check the *Task Manager*:** View the processes that are running on a Windows computer. This tool can help you troubleshoot system performance and stop a running process that is causing trouble. To access Task Manager, from the desktop, right-click the taskbar, and then click Task Manager. Only an administrator can use this tool. Along with other troubleshooting utilities, use this tool with caution.

IC3
DIGITAL LITERACY
CERTIFICATION
1.03m (iv)
1.03m (v)

Concept 5.02 │ Troubleshooting Connectivity Problems

Connectivity problems are the most frequent and frustrating type of complaint you are likely to hear as an IT Support Tech. Many hotel guests come to the hotel with their own devices and expect to be able to connect those devices to the hotel's network to access the Internet. The hotel offers both open access and secure network access to its guests, and providing the guests with the correct network information is often all that is required.

Basic network troubleshooting steps include:

1. **Verify that the network adapter is turned on:** For wireless adapters, it is common to put the device into *airplane mode* while traveling, which disables or turns off all network adapters. This can be fixed on a Windows computer by clicking the network icon on the taskbar. On most mobile devices, a pull-down setting at the top of the screen will allow you to turn off flight mode and enable the network adapter. In some cases, there is a physical button or switch on the device.

2. **Verify that the correct network is selected:** As shown in Figure 5.3, many network names can be similar. To view available wireless networks, click the network icon on the Windows taskbar. On a Mac, click the icon on the menu bar at the top of the screen.

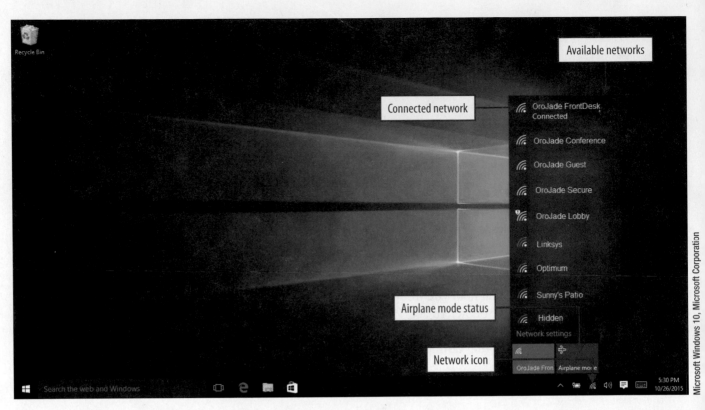

FIGURE 5.3 View available networks.

3. **Enter correct network security information:** Often, to successfully connect to a network, the correct credentials must be entered. This might include the network security key or username and password. If the network is configured with wireless encryption, the device must support the same level of security and be configured to connect using the required encryption and security information.

4. **Check connectivity:** Verify that the device is connected to a network. As shown in Figure 5.4, right-click the network icon in the taskbar, click Open Network and Sharing Center, and under View your active networks, on the right, click the adapter listed next to Connections to open the network adapter status. To determine the IP address of the connection, click the Details button. Here you can view the status of the connection, the connection speed, and the IP addressing information.

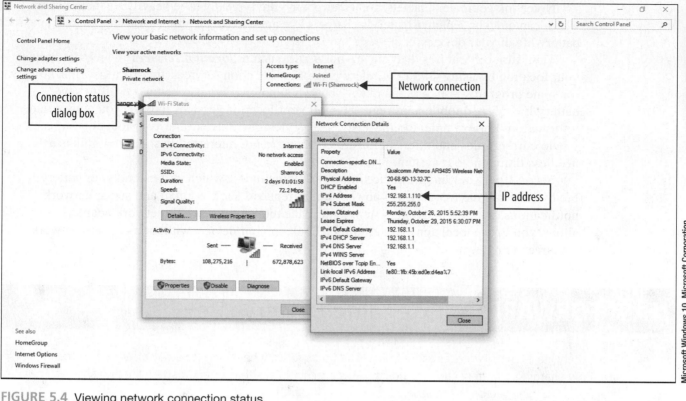

FIGURE 5.4 Viewing network connection status.

ETHICS — Piggybacking and Wardriving

The term *piggybacking* means using an open wireless network to access the Internet without permission. Many times, people intentionally use open wireless access. If an access point is left unsecured, they figure, "Why not?" In some places, it is illegal to use a network without authorization, but many statutes—if they exist at all—are vague. It is difficult to detect someone who is piggybacking. Still, it is unethical to use someone's connection without his or her knowledge.

To make things more confusing, some free hotspots—such as in cafes and hotels—might be accessible beyond the premises. So, a person sitting in a car parked on the street might be able to access the coffee shop hotspot intended for patrons of the shop.

The practice of *wardriving* is closely related. Wardriving means driving around and locating open wireless access points. There are communities on the Internet where wardrivers post maps of the open networks they find, along with free software that makes it easy to locate wireless networks. Wardrivers do not actually access the wireless networks, so the practice is not illegal—but is it ethical? What do you think?

IC3
DIGITAL LITERACY
CERTIFICATION
1.02f

Concept 5.03 | Saving Energy and Extending Battery Life

Energy Star (**energystar.gov**) is a rating system that recognizes devices that use an average of 20 percent to 30 percent less energy than comparable devices. Using less energy saves money and reduces greenhouse gas emissions that contribute to global warming. The Green Electronics Council has a program called the EPEAT (Electronic Product Environmental Assessment Tool; **http://epeat.net**) that can help you choose systems with environmentally friendly designs. The assessment is based on industry standards and ranks the devices as bronze, silver, or gold, depending on the number of environmental performance criteria they meet.

Notebook computers, tablets, and smartphones are typically used heavily by their owners, which can quickly deplete a battery's charge. Here are two simple things you can do to extend the battery life of your devices:

First, turn off features that you are not using, such as *location services*, which determines your location by using GPS or wireless networks. Location services are useful, even necessary, for some programs—such as mapping—but when not needed, can be turned off to save battery life. Many mobile apps regularly poll your location services to offer you appropriate information. For example, RetailMeNot and KeyRing will determine your location and alert you to current sales and offers in the area. If you are not interested in shopping, this is a needless drain on your system.

Second, put your mobile device in power saving mode, which will extend your battery life by reducing the frequency of power-hungry requests such as email and social network notifications. You can put your system in airplane mode to disable all network adapters. This allows you to use local apps, like reading a book on your device, without using any network resources or requests.

FAST FORWARD | Extending Battery Life

The battery life of mobile devices varies from a few hours for very heavy use, to a day or two for lighter use. Fully charging a battery can take hours. Newer technologies that extend battery life and shorten charging to minutes are on the horizon.

Scientists at MIT and Samsung are working on solid-state batteries that are safer, longer lasting, and more powerful than current lithium-ion batteries. Scientists at Stanford University have developed an aluminum-graphite battery that could fully recharge in just a minute.

Other innovations in the works include over-the-air charging and even using the electricity from your skin. Other ideas use water, sound, or solar charging methods.

IC3
DIGITAL LITERACY
CERTIFICATION
1.02g (i)
1.02g (ii)

Concept 5.04 | Configuring Hardware

A common cause of hardware problems is an out-of-date or missing device driver. To update a driver on your system, open the Device Manager Control Panel. To access Device Manager, open File Explorer, right-click This PC, and then click Properties. In the System Control Panel window, on the left, click Device Manager. Double-click a device in the list to open the device Properties dialog box. As a standard user, you can view the settings, but you must be an administrator to make changes. Click the Drivers tab, as shown in Figure 5.5, to view the current installed driver and options to update, roll back, disable, or uninstall the current driver.

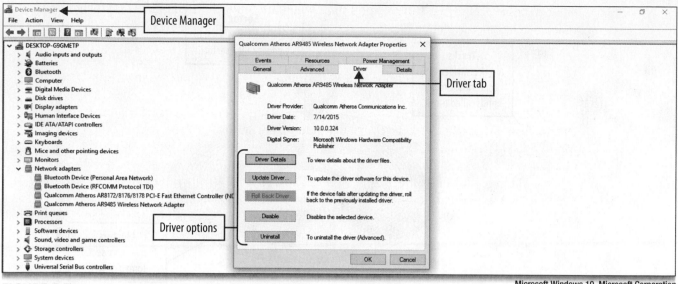

FIGURE 5.5 View the driver for the wireless adapter on this computer.

Microsoft Windows 10, Microsoft Corporation

Occasionally, a device driver causes system problems and must be uninstalled. If the system can boot normally, use the Device Manager to uninstall, or roll back, the driver. If the system cannot boot normally, Windows can be booted into *Safe Mode*—a special diagnostic mode that starts Windows without most device drivers for troubleshooting the system.

Objective 2 | Use System Utilities

Tech to GO!
Using Disk Utilities

IC3
DIGITAL LITERACY
CERTIFICATION
1.04c

Utility software helps you maintain your computer and is also considered system software. As an IT Support Technician, you rely on system utilities to help maintain computer systems.

Concept 5.05 | Formatting Disks

Because hard disk drives can hold large amounts of information, it is important to keep your disks healthy to keep your system running efficiently and to protect the files stored on them. *Disk formatting* prepares a disk to hold files and consists of two steps: low-level formatting and high-level formatting. The physical, low-level disk formatting occurs when the disk is manufactured. A set of concentric circles called *tracks* are created, and the disk is then divided up like a pie into wedge-shaped *sectors*, which are the smallest units of disk storage. The files you save to your disk are stored in groups of sectors called *clusters*, as shown in Figure 5.5. Think of this like a library with rows of empty bookshelves.

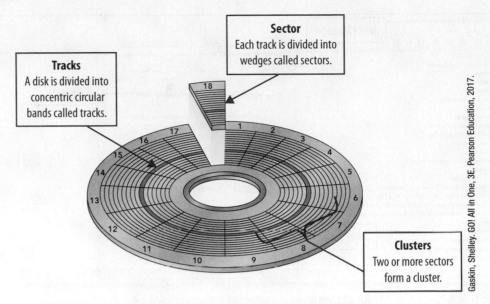

Tracks
A disk is divided into concentric circular bands called tracks.

Sector
Each track is divided into wedges called sectors.

Clusters
Two or more sectors form a cluster.

Gaskin, Shelley. GO! All in One, 3E. Pearson Education, 2017.

FIGURE 5.6 A formatted disk is divided into tracks and sectors.

The second part of formatting a disk is called high-level formatting and is often performed as part of the installation of an operating system. High-level formatting sets up the file system of the disk. You can think of it like a library catalog. Formatting a disk erases everything on it, so you normally would only format a disk to do a clean installation of an operating system or to wipe a disk clean to reuse or dispose of it. When you save files to your disk, the *file system* keeps track of what you saved and where you saved it. To keep track of where specific files are located, the computer's file system records a table of information, like a directory, on the disk. This table contains the name of each file and the file's exact location: the cluster, sector, and track where it is located on the disk. The file system used on hard disks in Windows is *NTFS*. NTFS stands for New Technology File System. External disks or those running older versions of Windows may be formatted with the *FAT file system*. FAT stands for file allocation table. The OS X file system is *HFS Plus or HFS+*, also referred to as the Mac OS Extended file system. HFS stands for hierarchical file system.

IC3
DIGITAL LITERACY
CERTIFICATION
1.03m (ii)
1.03m (iii)

Concept 5.06 | Using Disk Utilities

Windows includes several disk utilities to help you maintain your disks: Check Disk, Optimize Drives, and Disk Cleanup. To open these tools, from the Windows taskbar, open File Explorer, and then with This PC selected in the navigation pane, click the disk you want to work with. On the Computer tab, click Properties to open the Properties dialog box for the disk. You can also access some of these utilities from the Drive Tools Manage tab on the ribbon.

Disk-checking utilities monitor the health of the file system on a disk. To check a disk for errors in Windows, in the disk's Properties dialog box, click the Tools tab, and then, under Error checking, click Check. The Error Checking utility constantly monitors the disk for problems so that you do not have to run it manually. The dialog box message in Figure 5.7 indicates *You don't need to scan this drive*. If you choose to click Scan drive anyway, the scan runs right away and takes only a few minutes. This Windows utility can check both the file system and the physical health of the disk.

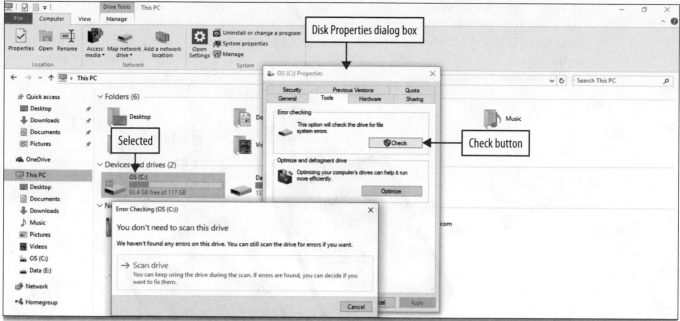

FIGURE 5.7 The Windows Error Checking utility checks disk health.

Microsoft Windows 10, Microsoft Corporation

OS X comes with Disk Utility, as shown in Figure 5.8. You can access it from the Other folder using the Launchpad. Use this utility to get information about the disks on the computer and to verify and repair a disk with which you are having trouble.

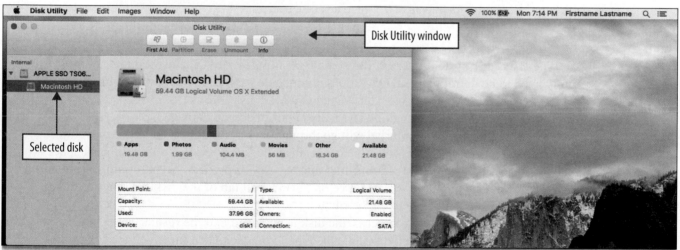

FIGURE 5.8 The OS X Disk Utility.

OS X Disk Utility. Screen shot(s) reprinted with permission from Apple Inc.

Over time, the disk can become disorganized as files are created, edited, saved, and deleted. Staying with the library analogy, as books are checked out, lost, purchased, misplaced, and returned, the shelves can become disorganized and require someone to periodically go through and clean them up. *File fragmentation* occurs as files are broken into small pieces that are stored in nonadjacent or noncontiguous clusters on the disk, as shown in Figure 5.9. A *disk defragmenter* is a utility that rearranges the fragmented files on your disk to improve efficiency. Windows comes with a built-in utility to optimize and defragment drives, and it runs automatically on a weekly basis. You can also run the defragmenter manually if you must do so. The Optimize utility can be accessed from the Tools tab of the disk's Properties dialog box or from the Drive Tools Manage tab on the ribbon. Microsoft recommends that you defragment a drive that is more than 10 percent fragmented. You should not run a defragmenter on a solid-state disk because it will reduce the lifespan of the disk by unnecessarily writing data to it. Windows optimizes the disk regularly, and the automatic settings should be enough to keep your disk healthy without undo wear and tear.

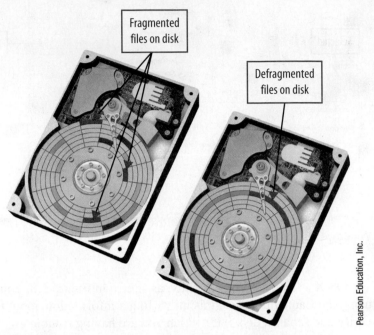

FIGURE 5.9 The defragmentation process repositions the fragments of a file into adjacent sectors.

The HFS+ file system in OS X has some built-in safeguards against fragmentation, so Macs rarely need to be defragmented. OS X does not include a defragmenter utility, although there are third-party tools that you can use to defragment a Mac disk.

Returning to the library analogy, over time, books become damaged, old, outdated, duplicated, and obsolete. A librarian will go through the shelves of books and remove those books. A *disk cleanup utility* looks for files that can be safely deleted to free up disk space so that you have more space to store your files and to help keep your system running efficiently. The Windows Disk Cleanup utility is available on the General tab of the disk's Properties dialog box and the Drive Tools Manage tab on the ribbon.

During the first part of the process, the disk is analyzed and the results can be reviewed by the user. Some file types are selected by default. When you click each file type listed, a description of the file displays, as shown in Figure 5.10. You should read each description carefully to help you decide which files that can be deleted safely. Select the files that you want to delete, and then click OK to complete the Disk Cleanup.

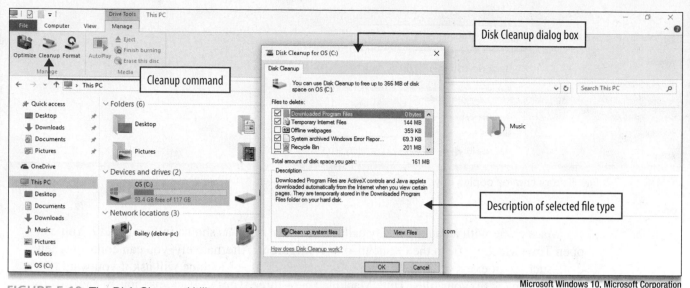

Disk Cleanup dialog box

Cleanup command

Description of selected file type

Microsoft Windows 10, Microsoft Corporation

FIGURE 5.10 The Disk Cleanup Utility searches your computer for files that can be deleted.

Macs have daily, weekly, and monthly maintenance scripts that run automatically overnight, so you do not normally need to do any other disk cleanup of your own. However, it still makes sense to delete unneeded files and empty the Trash to keep your disk free of clutter.

The utilities discussed here are included with Windows and Mac; however, there are also third-party versions available. For these utilities to be beneficial, you must remember to use them. Like changing the oil in your car and checking the tire pressure, regular maintenance of your computer will keep it running more efficiently and help it last longer.

Objective 3 Compare Methods for Backing Up a System

Corporate systems, such as the reservation systems at Oro Jade Hotels, contain **mission-critical information**—information that, if lost, will result in the failure of business operations. A system problem that results in loss of data can be catastrophic, so system backups are required. **Backing up** a system is the process of making copies of important files. Corporate systems are backed up as part of Oro Jade's disaster recovery procedures. In each hotel, the IT Support Technician is responsible for backing up individual hotel systems. A good backup plan ensures that data is not lost and downtime is minimized in the event of a system failure. A full backup includes all of the files that have been designated as part of the backup. This can take a long time to complete if the backup is large. To save time, after the initial full backup of a system, **incremental backups** can be set to back up only those files that have changed. The drawback of this system is that, when restoring a backup, a full restore may consist of several files, and thus, take longer to complete.

IC3
DIGITAL LITERACY
CERTIFICATION
1.04a
1.04b

Concept 5.07 | Backing Up with Windows and OS X

Backing up desktop operating systems can be easy by using built-in or third-party **backup utilities**. Windows includes **File History**, as shown in Figure 5.11, which creates copies of your files on an external or network drive. File History is not turned on by default. To keep backup copies of your files, you should turn it on. To access File History from the desktop, open File Explorer, click Computer, click Control Panel, and then click System and Security Control Panel. To use File History, you must have an external drive or network location accessible where the copies can be stored.

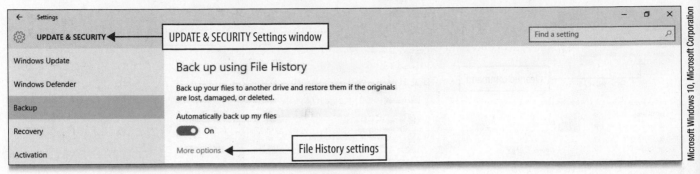

FIGURE 5.11 File History creates copies of your files on a Windows computer.

Macs come with a backup utility called ***Time Machine***, as shown in Figure 5.12. You can open Time Machine from the Launchpad to configure it. Alternatively, you can connect a new disk, such as an external hard drive, to your Mac, and Time Machine will ask if you want to use the disk to back up your files. Time Machine keeps three types of backups: hourly backups for the previous 24 hours, daily backups for the previous month, and weekly backups for all previous months. The oldest backups are deleted as the disk fills up. Time Machine backs up everything on your computer—your personal files, system files, applications, and settings.

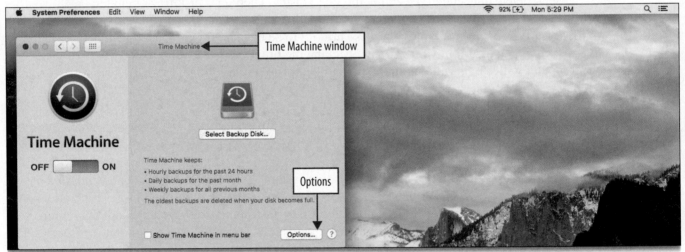

FIGURE 5.12 OS X Time Machine backs up files on a Mac.

External hard drives are an inexpensive place to back up your files. Many drives include a backup utility that you can use for automatic or one-touch backups of your system. You can purchase a large-capacity external hard drive for less than $100.

Another alternative is commercial software. There are many programs on the market, including some that are free or that cost less than $50. DVD-burning software also includes backup features.

1.04a
1.04b

Concept 5.08 │ Using Drive Imaging and System Restore

Drive imaging software goes beyond backups and creates a mirror image of the entire hard disk, including the operating system, applications, and all files. In the event of a hard disk or computer system failure, you can use the drive image to restore the entire system.

Windows includes built-in system protection that consists of options to restore or reset your system. By using *system restore* you can return the system to a previous state saved as a restore point. This is commonly used if the installation of an update, a driver, or an application caused a problem. There are three options when you choose to reset, as shown in Figure 5.13. *Keep my files* removes your apps and settings, but keeps your personal files. *Remove everything* removes all of your personal files, apps, and settings. *Restore factory settings* removes your personal files, apps, and settings, and reinstalls the original version of Windows. You should perform a factory reset on any device that you are finished with, before you trade it in or pass it on to someone else.

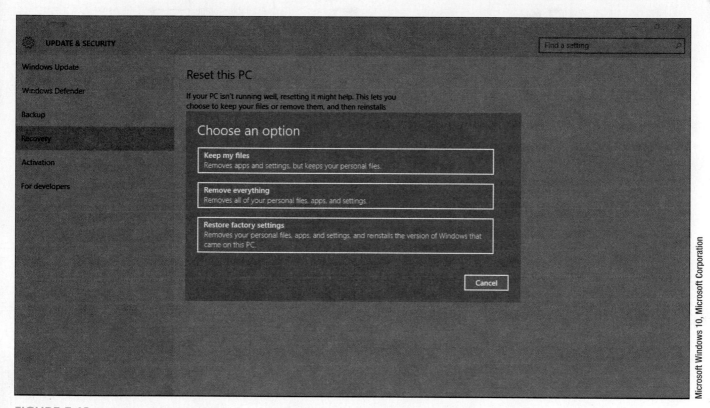

FIGURE 5.13 Windows 10 reset options.

Concept 5.09 | Backing Up to the Cloud

Keeping backups on external drives or other media will help recover files if your computer system fails, but this arrangement offers no protection from natural disasters, fire, or theft if the backups are kept in the same location as the original. The use of Internet or cloud backup services keeps the backups off-site and thereby enables you to recover files from anywhere. Online backup sites such as Carbonite or Mozy offer free personal storage of 1 or 2 GB or unlimited storage for about $5–$10 per month. Business backup solutions can cost thousands of dollars, depending on the amount of storage needed.

Professional backup companies make setup easy, and their services are safe and reliable. After the initial setup is complete, the backup process is automatic, and the backed-up files are then accessible from any Internet-connected device. As with any service, you should do your homework before trusting online backup services with your files.

Concept 5.10 | Backing Up Mobile Devices

Mobile devices tend to have small internal storage, but they contain a lot of important and personal information. You should regularly back up the files and other information, such as contacts and photos. Most mobile platforms include the ability to automate backups to the cloud.

This ensures that should you lose or break your device, or upgrade to a new one, you can restore your system easily. For example, iOS devices use iCloud for cloud backup of your files, as shown in Figure 5.14, and iTunes can restore apps and media purchases to your device.

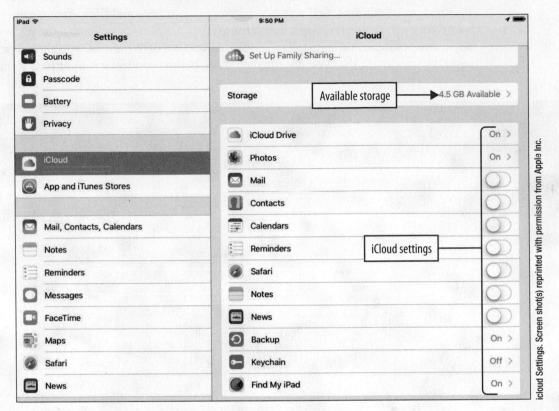

FIGURE 5.14 iCloud settings on an iPad.

✓ **Check Your Knowledge:** In MyITLab, take the quiz covering Objectives 1–3.

Before You Buy
System Specs

Your colleague just told you about a powerful new network diagramming program she bought that you might find useful in your job as an IT Support Technician. Should you run right out and buy it? At $150, the program is an investment that warrants at least some research on your part, as do most software purchases. So, what do you need to know?

IC3
DIGITAL LITERACY
CERTIFICATION
1.02b (i)
1.02b (ii)

Concept 5.11 | Determining System Requirements

Before you purchase new software, you must do some work. First, document your system specifications so you can compare it to the *system requirements*—the minimum hardware and software specifications required to run a software application. That is the only way you will know if your system can run the program. You can get the information you need with just a few mouse clicks.

To see the types of drives you have, and the amount of free space on each, open **File Explorer** and click **This PC** in the navigation pane. In Figure 5.15, this notebook computer does not have a DVD drive, but has two drives listed under Devices and drives. The primary hard disk drive in a computer is usually labeled C:. Additional drives are assigned other letters.

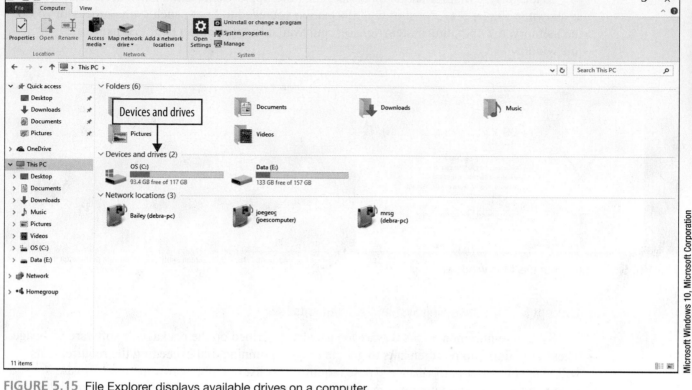

FIGURE 5.15 File Explorer displays available drives on a computer.

On a Windows computer, one of the easiest ways to obtain the other information you need is by using the System Control Panel window, as shown in Figure 5.16. From the Windows desktop, open **File Explorer**, click **This PC**, and then, on the Computer tab, click **System Properties**. Most of the information you need is found on this page, including the operating system version, the processor type and speed, and the amount of memory installed.

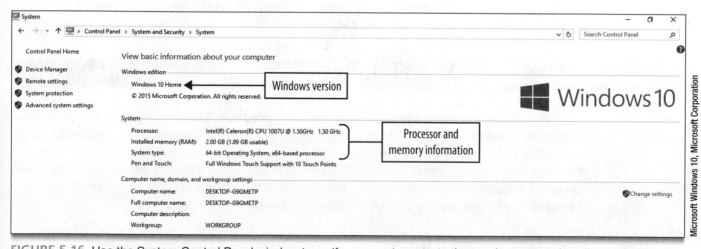

FIGURE 5.16 Use the System Control Panel window to verify your system meets the requirements to install a program.

To locate system information on a Mac, click the Apple menu, and then click About This Mac, as shown in Figure 5.17. Most of the information you need to know, such as the processor speed, the memory, the operating system version, and available storage, can be found using the tabs in this window.

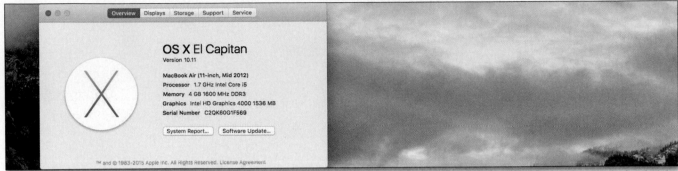

FIGURE 5.17 The About this Mac window.

Concept 5.12 | Reviewing System Requirements

System requirements for software are usually described on the package or software webpage. These are minimum requirements to get the program running, but exceeding the requirements will give you better performance. These requirements list both the hardware and software specifications the computer must meet in order to run the program. Sometimes, you may need to upgrade your system to meet or exceed these requirements. As software becomes more sophisticated, the system requirements go up.

For most software you buy in a store, you will need a DVD drive to perform the installation. If you do not have a DVD drive on your computer, purchase software online that you can download to your system. Although a few programs will run from a DVD or flash drive, most programs are installed on your hard drive. The amount of free drive space required is listed in the system requirements.

It is important to know what the system requirements are for a program before you buy it so you are not stuck with a purchase that you cannot use. Spending a few minutes verifying that your system meets the requirements will help ensure that you can actually use the software you buy or let you know if a system upgrade is necessary.

Objective 5 | Install, Uninstall, and Update Software

Some specialized devices have their instructions coded into the firmware, but most programs must be installed on a computer. Managing the programs on your computer includes installing, uninstalling, and updating the software. As an IT Support Technician, you often test new programs that might be useful in your job. It is important to keep software current and to uninstall unneeded programs to keep your system running efficiently, to free up disk space, and to prevent flawed software from enabling malware or hacker attacks.

1.03I (i)
1.03I (ii)

Concept 5.13 | Installing Software

The software installation process copies files to the computer and may alter system settings and create new folders. The process might require you to enter administrator credentials to proceed. There are three ways to install software on a personal computer: download from an app store, load from a local device using media such as a CD or DVD or USB flash drive, or download from a website.

When you purchase an app from the Windows Store, click the price button or **Free** (Figure 5.18), depending on what type of app you want, and the installation will proceed automatically. If it is a paid app, you will have to complete the purchase before you install the program. From the Apple App Store, for a free app, click **Get** and then click **Install App**. For a paid app, click the price, and then click **Buy App**. You must enter your Apple ID password to complete the purchase and installation.

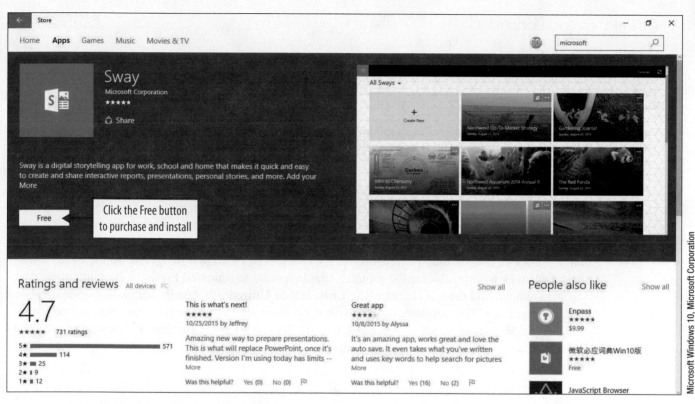

FIGURE 5.18 It is easy to install an app from the Windows Store.

To install from a disc, insert the disc in the drive and follow the instructions on the screen. If the installation does not begin automatically, open File Explorer, click the disc in the navigation pane, and then double-click the setup or installation file. On a Mac, double-click the disc image that appears on the desktop. Installing from a disc will likely require you to enter a product key to validate the software. Because most software is downloaded from the Internet, many notebook computers no longer include an optical drive for installing software in this manner.

To install a program from a website, click the link to download the file. If the file is zipped, you might need to extract it before you can install the program. You may be given the option to run or save the file. The advantage to saving the file is that it can be used to reinstall the program should the need arise. Locate and double-click the installer file, which is usually named Setup.

Concept 5.14 | Updating, Repairing, and Uninstalling Software

Software publishers regularly release updates to their programs. These updates can address security holes or *bugs*—flaws in the programming. An update might add new features, compatibility with new devices or file formats, or in the case of game software, more levels. A *patch* or *hotfix* addresses individual problems as they are discovered. A *service pack* is a larger, planned update that addresses multiple problems or adds multiple features. The previous patches and hotfixes are included in the service pack. Updating software requires an Internet connection. Apps purchased through an app store can be updated through the store, as shown in Figure 5.19. Other programs require files to be downloaded from the Internet. You can configure software to check for updates automatically or search for updates yourself. In a business environment, computers are generally not set to update software automatically, because updates are centrally managed by the IT department.

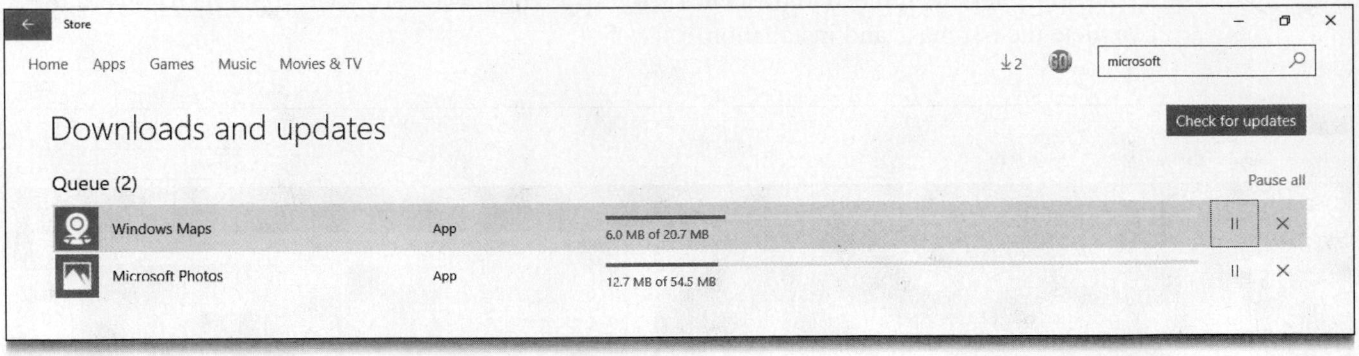

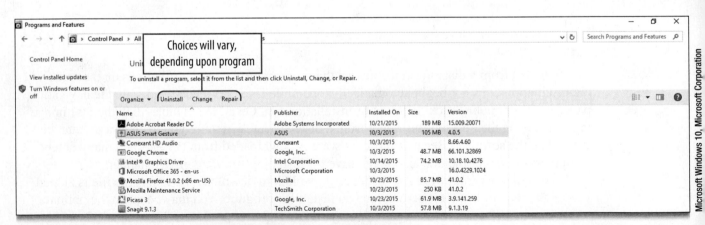

FIGURE 5.19 Update apps through the Windows Store.

When a program is no longer needed on your computer, you should uninstall it using the proper uninstaller to ensure that all files and settings are properly removed. Troubleshooting computer problems sometimes involves uninstalling and reinstalling software or updates. To view or uninstall the programs on a Windows computer, open **File Explorer**, in the navigation pane click **This PC**, and then on the ribbon, click **Uninstall or change a program**. In the **Programs and Features** window, locate the program that you want to uninstall Figure 5.20. Click the program name, and then click either the **Uninstall** or **Uninstall/Change** button that appears above the programs list. The options available will vary depending upon the program. Some programs will have a **Repair** option that you can use to fix the software installation. To uninstall a program on a Mac, if no uninstaller is provided, simply drag the program from the Applications folder to the trash.

FIGURE 5.20 Use Programs and Features to uninstall unneeded software.

The system administrator or home user must be diligent in keeping all systems up to date and secure. Unpatched systems are easy targets for hackers and can enable them to access a network. Windows (Figure 5.21) and OS X can be configured to automatically check for and install updates, but other software applications, especially those that access the Internet such as browsers and plug-ins, can be potential vulnerabilities and must also be kept up to date. Windows 10 updates are enabled by default.

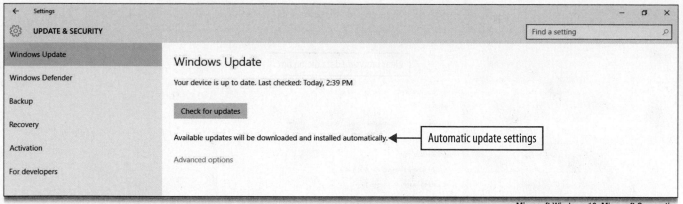

FIGURE 5.21 This Windows system is up to date.

Microsoft Windows 10, Microsoft Corporation

Objective 6 | Stay Safe Online

IT Sims

Security

There are several steps you can take to ensure your privacy online, and you should take these steps when using public computers or networks. You should not expect that anything you type or the name of any website that you visit is private and secure from prying eyes. It is not! Some businesses and organizations use surveillance software to prevent users from visiting unacceptable sites. Employers might look for non-work-related activities.

IC3
DIGITAL LITERACY
CERTIFICATION
1.07c (i)
1.07c (ii)
1.07c (iii)
1.07d
3.01a (iii)

Concept 5.15 | Protecting Your Privacy Online

Many websites put a small text file called a *cookie* on your computer when you visit them. Cookies help the website identify you when you return to a site. Your personal information, such as credit card numbers, is not stored in the cookie. Whenever you visit a site and click the *Remember me* or *Keep me logged in* button, the website puts a cookie on your computer. Do not select this option on public computers, and be sure to log out of any sites that you log in to while browsing. Although cookies are useful, some cookies are also placed on your system without your choosing them and could be used to collect information that you do not want to share. Web browsers include protection against potentially harmful cookies.

Your browsing history, passwords, form data—such as your name and address—and some temporary files are downloaded from the web by your browser to make your experience faster. Files such as images and HTML files are stored on your computer in a temporary storage cache. The Internet cache and other data can be cleared through your browser settings, as shown in Figure 5.22.

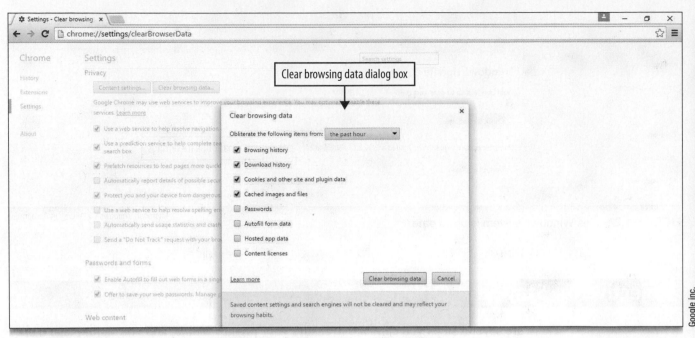

FIGURE 5.22 Chrome enables you to clear cached web items.

1.07e (iii)
3.03b (v)

Concept 5.16 | Recognizing Spyware, Viruses, Worms, Trojans, and Rootkits

The term *malware*, or malicious software, includes different types of programs that are designed to be harmful or malicious. Protecting your computer from malware can be a difficult task. Infected computers can spread an infection across a network and bring down the entire system. As the IT Support Tech at Oro Jade, you must be aware of the complications such malware can cause and must educate employees and guests about the steps they should take to protect their systems.

Sending mass, unsolicited email messages is called *spamming*. It is popular because it is easy and very inexpensive to do: no paper to print, no envelopes to stuff, and no postage to pay. There are other forms of electronic spam, too: IM—instant messaging—spam or spim, fax spam, and text message spam. Although spam may seem to be only a nuisance, in fact, it costs businesses millions of dollars each year. It is estimated that over 80 percent of all email messages are harmful or abusive in some way. That includes ads, phishing messages, and malware. Be wary of unsolicited email and do not click links in messages or open unexpected attachments.

Spyware is a form of malware that secretly gathers personal information about you. The information is sent back to a third party that may use it for anything from targeted advertisements to identity theft. A *browser hijacker* is spyware that changes your home page and redirects you to other websites. Spyware is usually installed inadvertently when you click on a pop-up or install a program that includes tracking features. The information about the tracking feature might be buried in the license agreement, which most people accept without reading or understanding. Sometimes, you can choose not to install these extra features by unchecking them in the installer. Spyware can be very difficult to remove and can cause your security programs to stop running.

A *computer virus* is a program that replicates itself and infects computers. A virus needs a host file to travel on; for example, a game or macro-enabled Word document. The attack, also known as the *payload*, may corrupt or delete files or erase an entire disk. A virus may use the email program on the infected computer to send out copies of itself and infect other systems. *Virus hoaxes* are common in email messages. Although they do not contain a virus, hoaxes can trick you into behavior that can be harmful, such as searching for and deleting files that the computer actually needs. Another danger of hoaxes is that you can get desensitized and ignore the true virus alerts when they do occur. You can check to see if a message is a hoax at **http://lookstoogoodtobetrue.com**, **http://hoax-slayer.com**, or **http://snopes.com** (Figure 5.23).

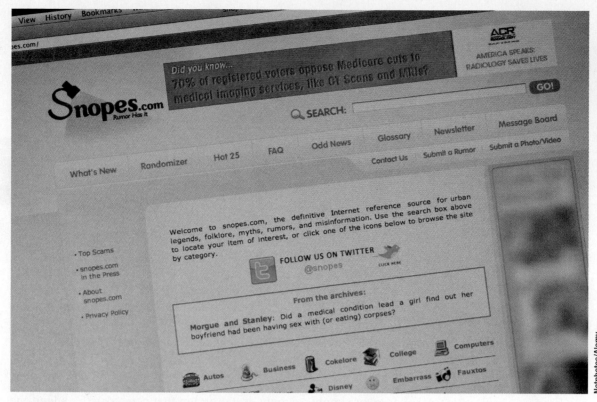

FIGURE 5.23 **Snopes.com** is a reliable place to check for hoaxes.

A *logic bomb* behaves like a virus in that it performs a malicious act such as deleting files. However, unlike a virus, it does not spread to other systems. A logic bomb attacks when certain conditions are met, such as when an employee's name is being removed from a database. Logic bombs are often used by disgruntled IT employees. When a logic bomb trigger is a specific date and time, it is called a *time bomb*. A virus may have logic bomb characteristics in that it can lay dormant on a system until certain conditions are met. There have been viruses and Trojans triggered on April Fool's Day and Friday the 13th.

A *worm*, like a virus, is self-replicating, but it does not need a host to travel. Worms travel over networks, including the Internet. After a system on a network is infected, the worm scans the network for other vulnerable systems to infect and spreads over the network connections without any human intervention. In 1988, the Morris worm was one of the first worms that spread via the Internet. On April 1, 2009, millions of email spam messages were sent out by computers infected with the Conficker worm. These computers were part of a massive *botnet*—a network of *computer zombies* or *bots* controlled by a master, as shown in Figure 5.24. The message was an advertisement for a fake antispyware program that, when installed, infected many more computers. Fake security notifications are one of the most common ways to infect computers. The ability to control millions of computers has the potential to cause real harm. A botnet could be used to send out spam and viruses or to launch a *denial-of-service attack* or *DoS*, which is perpetrated by sending out so much traffic that it cripples a server or network. Denial-of-service attacks have taken down Twitter, Yahoo!, CNN, eBay, Amazon, and numerous other sites.

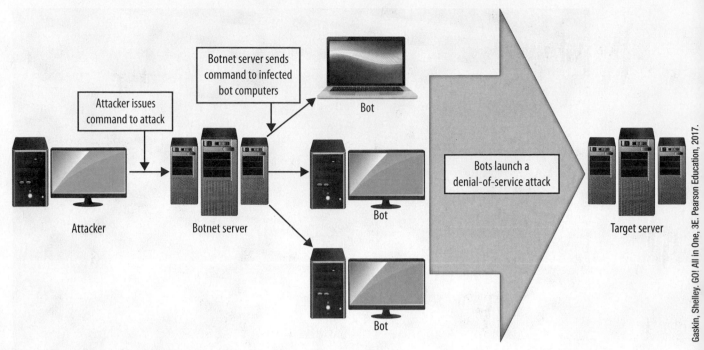

Attacker issues command to attack

Botnet server sends command to infected bot computers

Bot

Bots launch a denial-of-service attack

Bot

Attacker

Botnet server

Bot

Target server

Gaskin, Shelley. GO! All in One, 3E. Pearson Education, 2017.

FIGURE 5.24 A botnet is used to launch an attack.

A *Trojan horse*, or simply a Trojan, is a program that appears to be a legitimate program but is actually malicious. A Trojan might install adware, a toolbar, or a keylogger or open a back door to enable remote access to the system. A keylogger program may be installed as a Trojan and reside unnoticed on an infected computer. When you enter usernames and passwords or credit card numbers, the program gathers that information. There are also hardware keyloggers that plug in between the keyboard and computer. These USB devices are small and barely noticeable, and cannot be detected by security software. Some people install keyloggers on their own computers to monitor the activity of other users.

A *rootkit* is a set of programs that enables someone to gain control over a computer system while hiding the fact that the computer has been compromised. A rootkit can be almost impossible to detect and enables the system to become further infected by masking the behavior of other malware.

Over 1 million computer viruses, Trojans, and worms have been identified, and new infections are discovered every year. Understanding the threats your computer faces is the first step in preventing these programs from infecting your system.

GREEN COMPUTING Botnets

If you leave your computer turned on but idle, you expect it to go into sleep mode. If your computer becomes infected with malware and becomes part of a botnet, then it may be using energy even when you think it's in sleep mode. Imagine the amount of energy that's consumed by the thousands of compromised systems all over the world that are part of botnets. So keep your machine clean and secure, to help ensure that it's not part of a botnet, and when you know you'll be away from it for long periods of time, turn it off.

Concept 5.17 | Securing a System with Software

Because there are so many kinds of malware that can infect a computer, it takes a multilevel approach to safeguard a system from these and other threats. Most of the time, a system becomes infected because of software exploits, lack of security software, or unpatched programs.

A software firewall blocks access to an individual computer. The Windows firewall monitors both outgoing and incoming network requests and protects against local network threats in addition to those from the Internet. The settings block connections to programs that are not on the allowed list of programs. The first time a new program tries to access the network, you are asked whether to allow or deny access. In this way, the firewall program learns which programs should be allowed access and denies access to any unauthorized programs such as a backdoor Trojan. OS X also has a built-in firewall, but it is turned off by default. Use Security and Privacy Preferences to turn it on. Figure 5.25 shows the Windows firewall settings for both private and public networks.

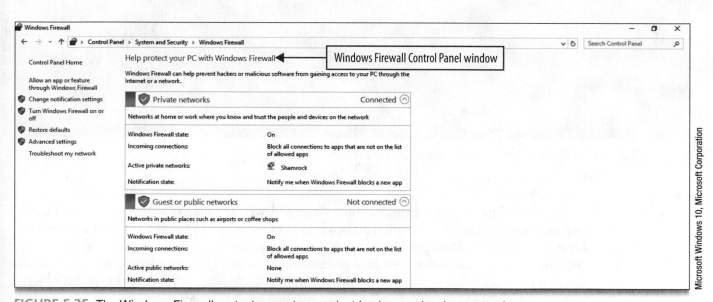

FIGURE 5.25 The Windows Firewall protects a system against hackers and malware attacks.

Antivirus software protects a computer from computer viruses. Such software uses a pattern-matching technique that examines all of the files on a disk, looking for virus code signatures. All antivirus programs use virus definition files to keep track of the newest threats. Outdated definition files leave a system vulnerable to attack. Good antivirus software also uses heuristic methods, such as monitoring your computer for suspicious activity to catch new viruses that are not in the definition files. Windows includes ***Windows Defender*** to protect against viruses and other malware, as shown in Figure 5.26.

Many Internet service providers provide free antivirus and other security software to their customers because infected systems can flood the network with traffic, causing problems not only for the infected system but also for other customers. It is important to have only one antivirus program running on a system because multiple programs will interfere with each other and slow down a computer's performance.

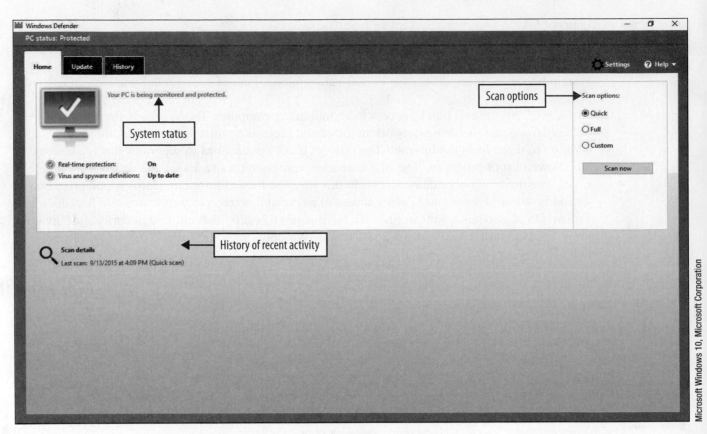

FIGURE 5.26 Windows Defender protects against viruses and other malware.

Most antivirus programs protect against viruses, as well as Trojans, worms, and spyware. If your antivirus program does not offer antispyware protection, then you should install a separate antispyware program. *Antispyware software* prevents adware and spyware software from installing itself on a computer. Real-time protection monitors a system for suspicious behavior such as a program trying to change the browser home page or other Windows settings. Scans can detect and remove any spyware that is already installed on a computer.

Security suites are packages of security software that include a combination of features. The advantage to using a suite is that you get complete protection, but a suite can be expensive and use a lot of system resources. The main complaint many people have is that security software decreases system performance. This may not be a big deal if you have a fast system with lots of RAM, but if you have an older, slower system, the effects could be quite noticeable.

Macs come preconfigured to provide protection against malicious software and security threats, and there are far fewer threats to Macs to begin with, so many Mac users do not install additional security software on their computers. File quarantine, found in OS X applications that download files from the Internet (Safari, Messages, iChat, and Mail), checks for known malware when you try to open a downloaded file. Although less common than attacks on Windows computers, Macs can still be targeted. Between September 2011 and March 2012, over 550,000 Macs were infected with a Trojan that exploited a flaw in Java and downloaded itself when the Mac user visited a website containing the malware. The Trojan stole usernames, passwords, and other data. By using the Security & Privacy preferences, you can lock down a Mac even more by requiring passwords, enabling the firewall, and turning off location services (Figure 5.27). Businesses that have both Mac and Windows computers should consider adding another layer of security to prevent the Macs from becoming hosts that spread viruses to Windows systems. Also, some people run both Mac and Windows on the same computer, which increases the need for security measures.

Security and Privacy Window - OSX. Screen shot(s) reprinted with permission from Apple Inc.

FIGURE 5.27 The Security & Privacy preferences in OS X enable you to secure a Mac.

TECHNOLOGY ON THE JOB

IT Security

IT security is a great field to consider if you have an interest in technology and like to solve problems. According to the *Occupational Outlook Handbook*, "The responsibilities of computer security specialists have increased in recent years as cyberattacks have become more sophisticated." And employment prospects are good, with this and related occupations expected to grow much faster than the average. Upper-level positions require several years of experience, at least a bachelor's degree, and industry certifications, but there are also entry-level positions that have less demanding requirements.

In 2015, CNNMoney ranked forensic PC analyst and computer security specialist among the top 50 Best Jobs in America, with a projected 10-year job growth rate of 37 percent and a median annual salary of $110,000.

✔ **Check Your Knowledge:** In MyITLab, take the quiz covering Objectives 4–6.

GO! To Work

IC3 SKILLS IN THIS CHAPTER

IC3—Module 1: Computing Fundamentals

Section 1.02 Hardware

- (b) Know the impact of memory and storage on usage
- (e) Connect a device wireless network (Wi-Fi)
- (f) Understand power management and power settings
- (g) Understand driver concepts as well as their device compatibility
  - (i) Know what drivers do
  - (ii) Know if specific drivers are compatible with a personal device
- (i) Know platform compatibility
  - (i) Media compatibility issues (Why won't my video play?)

Section 1.03 Computer Software Architecture

- (l) Know how to install, uninstall, update, repair software
  - (i) From the Internet
  - (ii) Using local media (DVD-ROM, etc.)
- (m) Troubleshooting
  - (i) Know basic problem-solving techniques
  - (ii) Know how to determine problems involving hardware vs. software
  - (iii) Know proper terminology to be able to describe the problem
  - (iv) Know how to find an IP address on a personal computer
  - (v) Know how to determine a connection speed

Section 1.04 Backup and Restore

- (a) Understand backing up concepts
- (b) Know how to back up and restore
- (c) Know how to complete a full system restore on a personal device

Section 1.07 Security

- (c) Know the basic threats to security of computers, data, and identity
  - (i) Viruses
  - (ii) Trojans
  - (iii) Malware
- (d) Understand the implications of monitoring software (surveillance)
- (e) Connecting to secured vs. unsecured network (wired and wireless)
  - (iii) Know the difference between public vs. private computing (using a public computer)
    1) Browser histories
    2) Cache/cookies
    3) Logging out of online and OS accounts
- (f) Know the use of and importance of anti-virus software
  - (i) Understand how to prevent virus issues
  - (ii) Understand how to maintain and update anti-virus software
- (g) Know the use of firewalls and basic settings

IC3—Module 3: Living Online

Section 3.01 Internet (Navigation)

- (a) Understand what the Internet is
  - (iii) Understand browser functionality
    2) Cookies
    3) Cache

Section 3.03 Email clients

- (b) Understand email etiquette
  - (v) SPAM

GO! FOR JOB SUCCESS

Discussion: Network Security Is Everybody's Job

Your instructor may assign these questions to your class, and then ask you to think about them or discuss them with your classmates:

The company computer network is the responsibility of the network administrator and IT people, but protecting the system from outside threats is everyone's job.

FotoIEdhar / Fotolia

> **What are some steps you can take to help protect the network?**

> **What should you do if you discover someone has learned your password?**

> **What are three ways an employee might inadvertently compromise the security of a company network?**

END OF CHAPTER

SUMMARY

Troubleshooting common computer problems requires a systematic approach. Built-in tools such as the Control Panel, Task Manager, and troubleshooters, and online knowledge bases can help determine and solve problems.	System utilities help maintain disk health and prevent data loss. File backup protects files, and system backups and restore points protect the entire system. Factory reset can restore a system to its original configuration.	Examine the system requirements to ensure compatibility You can install software from media or by downloading a file from the Internet. Uninstall and update software as needed to save disk space and protect the system.	Stay safe online by using secure passwords, limiting tasks performed on public computers and networks, and using security software and settings. Don't click links in messages or open unexpected attachments.

GO! LEARN IT ONLINE

Review the concepts, key terms, and IC3 skills in this chapter by completing these online challenges, which you can find in **MyITLab**.

Matching and Multiple Choice: Answer matching and multiple choice questions to test what you learned in this chapter.	**Lessons on the GO!:** Learn how to use all the new apps and features as they are introduced by Microsoft.	**IC3 Prep Quiz:** Answer questions to review the IC3 skills that you practiced in this chapter.

GLOSSARY

GLOSSARY OF CHAPTER KEY TERMS

Airplane mode A setting that disables or turns off all network adapters on a device.

Antispyware software A program that prevents adware and spyware software from installing itself on a computer.

Antivirus software A program that protects a computer from computer viruses.

Backing up Making copies of important files.

Backup utility A program that makes copies of important files.

Bot A computer that is part of a botnet, controlled by a master, and used to launch various types of attacks.

Botnet A network of computer zombies or bots that is controlled by a master and that can be used to send out spam and viruses or to launch a denial-of-service attack.

Browser hijacker A form of spyware that changes your home page and redirects you to other websites.

Bug A flaw in software programming.

Cluster A group of sectors where files are stored on a disk.

Computer virus A program that replicates itself and infects computers; a virus needs a host file on which to travel.

Computer zombie A computer that is part of a botnet, controlled by a master, and used to launch various types of attacks.

Cookie A small text file placed on your computer when you visit a website that is used to identify you when you return to the site.

Denial-of-service attack (DoS) An attack that is perpetrated by sending out so much traffic that it cripples a server or network.

Disk cleanup utility A program that looks for files that can be safely deleted to free up disk space, enabling you to have more space to store your files and to help keep your system running efficiently.

Disk defragmenter A utility that rearranges the fragmented files on a disk.

Disk formatting The process that prepares a disk to hold files and which consists of two steps: low-level formatting and high-level formatting.

Disk-checking utility A program that monitors the health of the file system on a disk.

Drive imaging The process of creating a mirror image of an entire hard disk.

Energy Star A rating system that awards devices that use an average of 20 percent to 30 percent less energy than comparable devices.

FAT file system The file system used on some external disks or those running older versions of Windows.

File fragmentation A process that occurs as files are broken into small pieces that are stored in nonadjacent or noncontiguous clusters on the disk.

File History A Windows utility that creates copies of your files on an external or network drive.

File system A system that keeps track of what files are saved and where they are stored on the disk.

HFS+ file system The OS X file system.

Hotfix A software update that addresses individual problems as they are discovered.

Incremental backup A backup that includes only those files that have changed.

Location services Feature of computers and mobile devices that determines your location by using GPS or wireless networks.

Logic bomb An attack by malware that occurs when certain conditions are met.

Malware Malicious software; a program that is designed to be harmful or malicious.

Mission-critical information Information that, if lost, will result in the failure of business operations.

NTFS file system The file system used on hard disks in Windows.

Patch A software update that addresses individual problems as they are discovered.

Payload The action or attack by a computer virus or malware.

Piggybacking Using an open wireless network to access the Internet without permission.

Rootkit A set of programs that enables someone to gain control over a computer system while hiding the fact that the computer has been compromised.

Safe Mode A special diagnostic mode for troubleshooting the system that loads Windows without most device drivers.

Sector A wedge-shaped section of a disk where data is stored.

Security suite A package of security software that includes a combination of security features.

Service pack A large, planned software update that addresses multiple problems, or adds multiple features, and includes previous patches and hotfixes.

Spamming Sending mass, unsolicited email messages.

Spyware A form of malware that secretly gathers personal information about you.

System requirements The minimum hardware and software specifications required to run a software application.

System restore A Windows tool that enables you to return the system to a previous state saved as a restore point.

Task Manager A utility that displays the processes running on a Windows computer.

Time bomb A logic bomb that is triggered by a specific date or time.

Time Machine The backup utility in OS X.

Track A concentric circle created on a disk during low-level disk formatting.

Trojan horse A program that appears to be a legitimate program but that is actually malicious.

Virus hoax An email message that does not contain a virus but that tricks you into behavior that can be harmful, such as searching for and deleting files that the computer actually needs.

Wardriving Driving around and locating open wireless access points.

Windows Defender A Windows utility that protects against viruses and other malware.

Worm A form of self-replicating malware that does not need a host to travel; worms travel over networks and spread over the network connections without any human intervention.

GO! Do It

Andrew Rodriguez/Fotolia; FotoEdhar/Fotolia; apops/Fotolia; Yuri Arcurs/Fotolia

USE DISK CLEANUP

Utility software such as disk defragmenters and cleanup utilities help keep your computer running efficiently. In this Activity, you will use the Windows Disk Cleanup utility to examine some of the files on your computer.

1. From your student data files, open the file **aio05_DOIT_answersheet**. Display the **Save As** dialog box, navigate to the location where you will store your documents for this chapter, and then create a new folder named **AIO Chapter 5** Open the folder, and then save the file as **Lastname_Firstname_05_DOIT_answersheet**

2. On the Windows taskbar, click **File Explorer**. If necessary, in the Navigation pane click This PC. In the **File Explorer** window, what items are listed under **Hard Disk Drives**?

3. Right-click the **C: drive**, and then click **Properties**. What is the capacity of the disk? How much free space is currently available?

4. On the **General tab**, click **Disk Cleanup**. Enable the **Disk Cleanup utility** to analyze your system. When it is finished, use the **Windows Snipping tool** to take a screenshot of the Disk Cleanup dialog box, and then paste it into your answer sheet.

5. Click the text for each of the categories of files listed, and read the descriptions in the bottom of the dialog box. What types of files are included in Downloaded Program Files and Temporary Internet Files? What are Temporary Files, and is it safe to delete them? What other categories of files are listed? Which ones have check marks next to them? How much space could you free up if you cleaned up all of the files found?

6. Print or submit your answer sheet electronically as directed by your instructor.

ON THE WEB

1. **Patch Tuesday** Is your Windows OS up to date? From your student files, open the file **aio05_OTW1_answersheet**, and then save the file in your **AIO Chapter 5** folder as **Lastname_Firstname_05_OTW1_answersheet**

   Microsoft regularly releases updates and patches for its operating systems and other software. Use the Internet to find the meaning of the term *Patch Tuesday*. What is it and why is it important? How does Windows 10 keep itself up to date? How are updates released for older versions of Windows? Write a two- or three-paragraph summary that includes the answers to these questions.

   Print or submit your answer sheet electronically as directed by your instructor.

2. **Current Malware Activity** There are hundreds of known malware threats. From your student files,

   open the file **aio05_OTW2_answersheet**, and then save the file in your **AIO Chapter 5** folder as **Lastname_Firstname_05_OTW2_answersheet**

   Visit the website of two antivirus software vendors, such as McAfee at **http://mcafee.com**, Norton at **http://norton.com**, TrendMicro at **http://trendmicro.com**, Panda at **http://pandasecurity.com**, or CA at **http://ca.com**.

   Which websites did you visit? What is the current threat level? Of the top threats, how many can be classified as viruses? Worms? Trojans? How many of them were discovered today? In the past week? How many are at least one year old? Are the threats and threat level the same on both sites?

   Print or submit your answer sheet electronically as directed by your instructor.

ETHICS AND SOCIAL MEDIA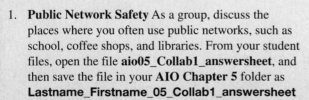

1. **Ethics** Employers may install surveillance software on employees' computers to prevent theft or non-work-related use of resources. As a potential employee, how do you view this surveillance? What if you were the employer? From your student files, open the file **aio05_ESM1_answersheet**, and then save the file in your **AIO Chapter 5** folder as **Lastname_Firstname_05_ESM1_answersheet**

   Present both sides of the argument in a two- to three-paragraph summary; include your references.

   Print or submit your answer sheet electronically as directed by your instructor.

2. **Social Media** Creating a fake social media profile is a common method of social engineering. From your student files, open the file **aio05_ESM2_answersheet**, and then save the file in your **AIO Chapter 5** folder as **Lastname_Firstname_05_ESM2_answersheet**

   How can you tell if someone who sends you a friend request is really who they say they are? Use the Internet and create a list of three to five social media safety tips to share with your online friends to teach them what to look out for.

   Print or submit your answer sheet electronically as directed by your instructor.

COLLABORATION

1. **Public Network Safety** As a group, discuss the places where you often use public networks, such as school, coffee shops, and libraries. From your student files, open the file **aio05_Collab1_answersheet**, and then save the file in your **AIO Chapter 5** folder as **Lastname_Firstname_05_Collab1_answersheet**

   Do any of these networks have security enabled? How difficult are they to access?

   Make a list of the types of tasks it is appropriate to perform on public networks and a second list of those tasks that should be limited to your private, secured network.

   Print or submit your answer sheet electronically as directed by your instructor.

2. **Preventive Computing** As a team, develop a set of eight to ten guidelines to maintain a computer system and prevent potential problems. Prepare a multimedia presentation or poster for your classroom or office. From your student files, open the file **aio05_Collab2_answersheet**, and then save the file in your **AIO Chapter 5** folder as **Lastname_Firstname_05_Collab2_answersheet**

   The presentation should explain list the guidelines in language that is clear, nontechnical, and easy to understand. Submit the presentation or poster and provide documentation to show that all team members have contributed to the project.

   Print or submit your answer sheet electronically as directed by your instructor.

Application Software

OUTCOMES
Evaluate different types of software, licenses, and ways to obtain software.
Use various business communication tools.

OBJECTIVES
1. Identify Types and Uses of Business Productivity Software
2. Categorize Home and Educational Programs
3. Identify Media and Graphic Software
4. Discuss the Importance of Cloud Computing
5. Compare Various Ways of Obtaining Software
6. Respect Software Licenses and Registration Agreements
7. Use Business Communication Tools

Sebra/Fotolia

In This Chapter

A computer is a programmable machine. A program—in particular, an application software program—is what makes a computer a flexible and powerful tool. There are thousands of software programs from which to choose, from simple games played on your smartphone to sophisticated graphics software used in business. In this chapter, you will learn about software applications for both business and personal use. You will learn about sources of software, methods of obtaining software, and licensing models. In addition, you will learn how to assess your system for compatibility with software programs and how to manage the software installed on your computer.

Job Focus

As an **Oro Jade Public Relations Manager**, you plan and manage publicity campaigns and activities for the hotel group. This includes organizing events such as press conferences, exhibitions, and visits; speaking at press conferences and making presentations; and designing, writing, and producing press releases, articles, brochures, reports, website content, and promotional videos. You and your PR team are also responsible for creating internal employee newsletters and stockholders' reports. These tasks require you to be familiar with a variety of software applications to create professional and effective materials.

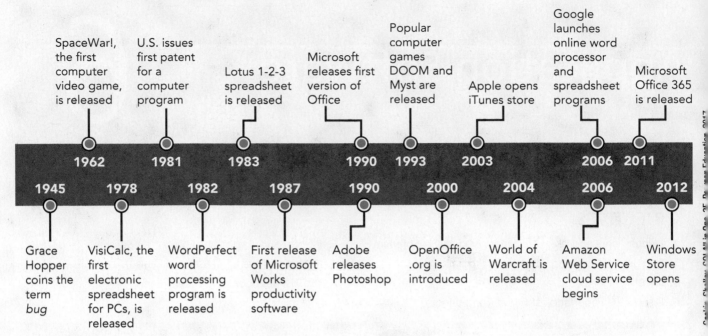

FIGURE 6.1 This timeline highlights some important dates in computer software history.

Identify Types and Uses of Business Productivity Software

Tech to GO!
Connect to an External Monitor or Projector to Display Presentations

Software is a set of instructions that tells the computer how to perform specific tasks. System software runs the computer. *Application software* includes all the programs that direct the computer to carry out specific tasks, such as word processing, playing a game, or computing numbers on a worksheet.

Businesses and other organizations rely on a variety of software applications for almost every aspect of running a business, for example, billing, inventory, payroll, and sales. As a Public Relations Manager, your busy schedule and the many professional reports that you must create require you to use the productivity programs found in an *office application suite*—also referred to as a *productivity suite*—which is a set of programs with a common user interface that individuals use to produce information.

1.01g
1.03b
1.03d
2.06b

Concept 6.01 | Comparing Office Suites

The most popular general-purpose applications are *productivity programs*, which help you work more efficiently and effectively on both personal and business-related documents. Productivity software includes word processors, spreadsheets, databases, and presentation, project management, and personal information management programs. The most commonly used productivity software in business is an *office application suite*, such as Microsoft Office (Figure 6.2), Google for Work, or Apple Productivity Apps (formerly known as iWork). The applications in an office suite work together so that you can create and manage many different types of information. An office suite also includes features that enable you to collaborate with others to share information and build business documents. A suite has the advantage of having a common interface and features. For example, in Office applications, settings to configure how the application behaves or displays, are found by clicking the File tab and clicking Options. In a business environment, Microsoft Office is the standard, but most programs have the ability to save a file in other file types, making them compatible with other products or backward compatible with older software versions. For example, you can save a file created in Google Docs as a Word file.

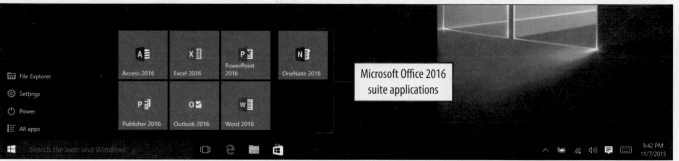

Microsoft Windows 10, Microsoft Corporation

FIGURE 6.2 Microsoft Office 2016 suite applications: Access, Excel, PowerPoint, OneNote, Publisher, Outlook, and Word.

A *word processor* is an application with which you can create, edit, and format text documents; the documents can also contain images. A full-featured word processor, such as Microsoft Word, Apple Pages, or Google Docs, can create everything from simple memos to large complex documents.

Some standard features of word processors include:

- What you see is what you get: The layout on the computer screen shows the document layout as it would appear if printed.

- Formatting styles: Text style, font, color, size, and alignment.

- Spelling and grammar checkers: The ability to search for and replace errors in spelling and grammar, and to create custom dictionaries.

- Graphics: The ability to insert and format images.

- Text organization tools: Tables, bullets, and lists.

- Statistics: Information about the document such as word count.

- Content guides: Footnotes, indexes, and tables of contents.

- Page layout: Headers and footers, page numbers, and margins.

- Mail merge: The ability to generate mail labels or form letters for lists of people.

- Collaboration tools: The ability to merge and track changes made by multiple people.

- Customization: The ability to configure how a program performs or displays, such as how menus display or how often and where a file is saved. These default settings can be changed using the Settings, Preferences, or Options menus in most applications.

A *spreadsheet application*, such as Microsoft Excel (Figure 6.3), Apple Numbers, or Google Sheets, enables you to create electronic worksheets composed of rows and columns. For example, you might use a spreadsheet for a budget, a grade book, or to track inventory. Spreadsheets are quite useful for managing business expenses, payroll, and billing data, although companies may choose tools that are specifically made for such tasks. As a statistical analysis tool, spreadsheets are critical to researchers in both the natural and social sciences. Spreadsheets organize data so it can be sorted, filtered, and rearranged, making a spreadsheet a useful tool for things that do not involve calculations at all—such as address lists and schedules.

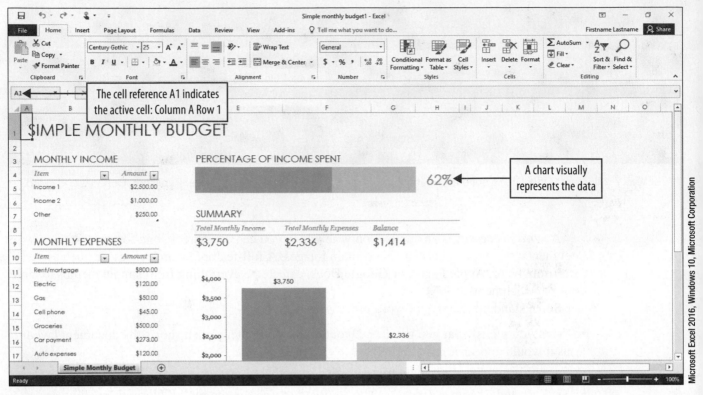

FIGURE 6.3 Excel spreadsheet program.

In a spreadsheet, the intersection of a row and a column is called a *cell*. Cells can contain numbers, text, or formulas. ***Three-dimensional spreadsheets*** can have multiple worksheets that are linked together; for example, a budget spreadsheet might have a worksheet for each quarter plus an annual summary worksheet. A spreadsheet application also enables you to create charts or graphs to visually represent data. Although there are other spreadsheet programs available, in a business environment, Microsoft Excel is used almost exclusively.

One advantage to using a spreadsheet program is that it can be customized. For example, a teacher might use a spreadsheet to create custom formulas and calculations rather than having to adjust grading methods to fit into the format of a commercial grade book program. Another advantage is cost savings. Because most office computers already have a spreadsheet program installed as part of a software suite, there is no need to purchase additional software. Also, most people will have some familiarity with the program interface and need less training to use it.

Use a ***presentation application*** such as Microsoft PowerPoint, Apple Keynote (Figure 6.4), or Google Slides to create electronic slide presentations. If you want to present facts, figures, and ideas while engaging your audience, use the visual tools in your presentation software. Each slide can contain combinations of text, graphics, video, and audio to make your presentation interesting and memorable.

FIGURE 6.4 A Keynote presentation.

Keynote. Screen shot(s) reprinted with permission from Apple Inc., Shelley Gaskin

A good speaker creates a presentation that audiences will be interested in and will remember. Good design principles for presentations include using easy-to-see color schemes, large font sizes, limiting the amount of text on each slide, limiting the use of slide transitions and animations, and using images to enhance your words.

A **database** is an organized collection of facts about people, events, things, or ideas related to a specific topic or purpose. Your telephone book or contact list is a simple database. A library catalog, patient records in a doctor's office, and Internet search engines are all examples of commonly used databases. A desktop **database management system (DBMS)** such as Microsoft Access is software that controls how related collections of data are stored, organized, retrieved, and secured. You can use a desktop database application to create small databases for contact management, inventory management, and employee records.

OneNote is a tool for gathering information and taking notes, structured as notes in a notebook. You can add text, drawings, screenshots, and images, as well as audio clips. There are OneNote apps available for most platforms, so you can work on any of your devices. Using the cloud, OneNote can be used to collaborate with others.

A **personal information manager (PIM)** might be a stand-alone program or be part of an office suite. The most widely used of these programs is Microsoft Outlook (Figure 6.5), which is part of the Microsoft Office suite. A PIM manages your email, calendar, contacts, and tasks all in one place. It includes the ability to share calendars and schedule meetings. Many smartphones incorporate PIM features and can be used in conjunction with desktop systems. Additionally, Microsoft Outlook has a smartphone app for the Android, iOS, and Windows mobile platforms. You can sync your contacts, appointments, and tasks between both systems, taking the information with you wherever you go. You can configure your mobile device with notifications to alert you to appointments and new messages. Notifications can be on-screen alerts, vibrations, sounds, or a combination of these.

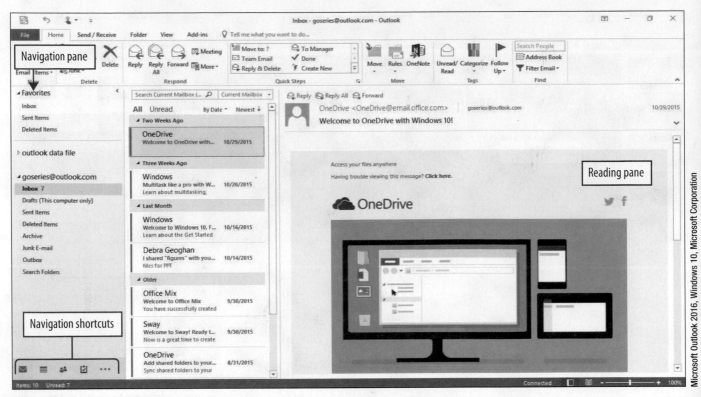

FIGURE 6.5 Outlook manages your email, contacts, calendar, and tasks in one place.

Concept 6.02 | Identifying Other Types of Business Software

Office suites cover the majority of business documents, but organizations typically require additional software for more complex and larger-scale management and projects. Keeping track of finances, projects, and a large number of documents can be a daunting task for any size business. Specialized software can help make these tasks easier and more efficient.

Every business must track expenses and taxes. An Excel spreadsheet system is sufficient for many situations, but some businesses prefer to use basic *accounting software* such as Intuit QuickBooks, Sage 50 (formerly known as Peachtree), or Fresh Books, which is completely cloud-based. Accounting software enables you to track your business finances and generate reports and graphs so that you can make business decisions. You can use accounting software for expense tracking, invoicing, payroll, and inventory management. By organizing all financial information in one place, it is easy to see the big picture and to handle year-end tasks such as income tax returns.

For both practical and legal reasons, even the smallest business needs *document management*—the ability to save, share, search, and audit electronic documents throughout their life cycle. Keeping track of all the documents in a business, ensuring that the right people have access to them, and ensuring that the correct version is available are all part of a *document management system (DMS)* such as Microsoft SharePoint, Alfresco, Dropbox, Citrix ShareFile, and Google Drive for Work. Storage is what defines a DMS. Instead of keeping files on local drives, files are stored on a server or on the web, making them more accessible and secure.

Project management software helps you to organize and complete projects, keep within budget, stay on schedule, and collaborate with team members. The most popular project management program is Microsoft Project (Figure 6.6), and the leading web-based application is Basecamp. Both of these tools excel at helping projects run smoothly. Smartsheet and Jira are also popular.

Project management software features include:

- A timeline that tracks due dates, milestones, and deadlines
- Team-planning capability that, by simply dragging and dropping, creates a team with the right individuals and resources
- A portfolio manager that monitors the allocation of scarce resources and current project costs

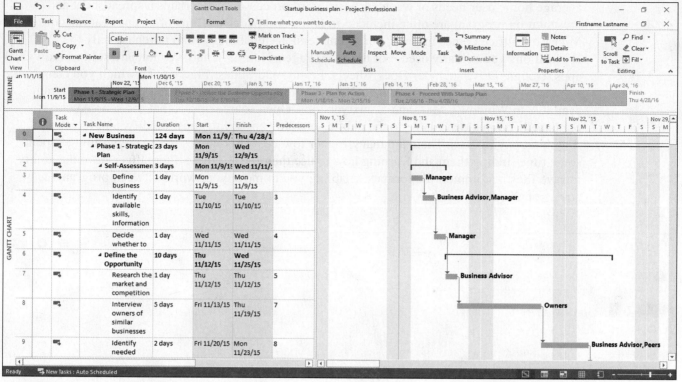

FIGURE 6.6 Microsoft Project software includes many templates to start your project.

Microsoft Project 2016, Windows 10, Microsoft Corporation

ON THE JOB — Software Trainer

Software trainers—sometimes called corporate trainers—are in demand as companies deploy more software programs. This high-paying career may involve some travel and requires good computer skills, organization, and communication skills. Software trainers usually have at least a bachelor's degree and on-the-job training. Some companies offer train-the-trainer courses that can lead to a certification. You might work for a training company, in the training department of a large company, or as a consultant to many companies.

Objective 2 — Categorize Home and Educational Programs

Before You Buy
Video Games

Software is what makes computers useful. A vast variety of software is available, but it only takes a couple of programs to make your computer indispensable—and even fun to use. Your job as a Public Relations Manager can be stressful and involves working long hours. At home, you need to relax and unwind. Perhaps you will take an online class or plan a vacation. Home and educational software turns your personal computer into a useful and enjoyable tool.

IC3
DIGITAL LITERACY
CERTIFICATION
2.06b (i)

Concept 6.03 | Using Office Applications

A full office application suite, which includes word processing, spreadsheet, database, presentation, and personal information management applications, is usually more than the average home user needs or wants. A basic word processor and perhaps a spreadsheet and presentation program are often included in home or student versions of an application suite. Microsoft Office comes in several different versions, enabling you to purchase only the applications you actually need. For the Mac, Pages, Numbers, and Keynote are sold as individual apps. Google Drive includes Docs, Sheets, Forms, and Slides (Figure 6.7), which you can access from any web browser. Apache OpenOffice is a free, *open source* alternative office program available in Windows, Mac, and Linux versions. Open source means that the source code is published and made available to the public, enabling anyone to copy, modify, and redistribute it without paying fees. There are many free or low-cost alternatives if you are willing to spend some time finding them and learning how to use them. All of these alternatives have the ability to save files in common file formats, enabling you to move your work between programs and across platforms.

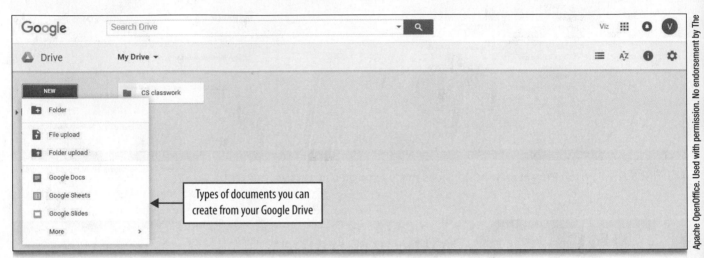

Types of documents you can create from your Google Drive

FIGURE 6.7 Google Drive enables you to choose an application with which to work.

Concept 6.04 | Comparing Finance and Tax Preparation Software

Use personal *finance software* to keep track of your bank accounts, monitor investments, create and stick to a budget, and file income taxes. Similar to office applications, personal finance software ranges from expensive commercial packages to free and online options.

Two of the most popular commercial packages are Intuit Quicken and YNAB—You Need a Budget. Both include features such as online banking, online bill payment, investment portfolio tracking, and budgeting. You can also generate reports, calculate loan interest, and write checks. At tax time, you can easily gather the information you need from these applications. If you prefer to use an online application, Mint.com is a very popular choice (Figure 6.8). After you enter your accounts, use Mint.com to track your spending.

FIGURE 6.8 Software makes managing your money easier.

Tax preparation software enables you to complete your income tax returns by yourself on your computer or online. This reduces the chance of making errors in your calculations and makes it easy to save—and later retrieve—your returns. You can file your return electronically or print and mail it. Previous years' returns can be imported into a new return and generate year-to-year comparisons. Tax preparation programs walk you through the process step by step and provide you with suggestions and help throughout. The three main tax preparation programs are Intuit TurboTax, H&R Block, and TaxACT. For simple tax returns, there are free online options. For more complex returns, you can install the full programs on your computer or use online versions. In general, the more complicated your return is, the more expensive the software you will require. If you start a free return and later discover that you need to upgrade to a full version, you can do so without losing any of the information you have already entered.

IC3
DIGITAL LITERACY
CERTIFICATION
2.06b (i)
2.06b (vii)

Concept 6.05 | Selecting Educational and Reference Software

Educational and reference software is a broad category that includes software to study, plan, design, and create just about anything you are interested in.

In the not too distant past, planning a vacation involved going to a store to buy maps, tour books, and yellow highlighters. You could spend hours mapping out a route, planning stops based on the often outdated information in the tour books, and hoping the food would be decent and the hotel rooms would be clean. Today, you might still spend hours researching and planning your trips using online mapping software such as the Windows Maps app (Figure 6.9) or Google Maps and reading current reviews from other travelers. With trip planning software you can easily reroute your trip if the unexpected happens, such as traffic detours or if you decide to take in an interesting attraction or go exploring off your original route.

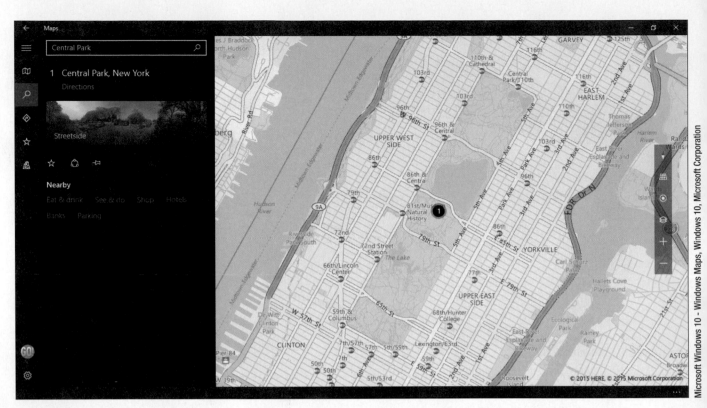

FIGURE 6.9 The Windows Map app.

Use *genealogy programs* to create family trees or slide shows of your family photos, view timelines and maps, and search through millions of historical records on the Internet. Family Tree Maker and the Windows Ancestry app integrate with the **Ancestry.com** website.

Do you want to build a deck? Plant a garden? Remodel your kitchen? Rearrange your furniture? Paint the dining room? Home and landscape design software enables you to design and plan all your home improvement projects. There are several online apps to compare paint colors. Just upload a picture of your room, and experiment with the color choices until you find your favorites. Behr Paint Your Place—**http://behr.com**, Sherwin-Williams Color Visualizer—**http://sherwin-williams.com**, and the Benjamin Moore Personal Color Viewer—**http://benjaminmoore.com** all allow you to upload and color your own photos for free and will help you select the colors from their particular paint lines. Colorjive—**http://colorjive.com** is not affiliated with any brand and includes colors across multiple brands. You should use whatever program has the color codes for the brand of paint you plan to buy.

Health and fitness trackers enable you to monitor your exercise, keep track of your food intake and sleep patterns, and remind you when it is time to take a break from screen time.

Concept 6.06 | Playing and Learning with Games

When you think of someone who plays video games, do you picture a young man on an online quest? What about the grandmother playing puzzle games, or the dad playing online baseball, or the preschooler learning colors and shapes? Games and simulations are more than just first-person shooters in which you play the game from the perspective of the game character and much of the action involves some sort of weapon, and video games are played by all sorts of people. Minecraft (Figure 6.10) is a popular game available across many devices and platforms. The average age of a video game player is 32 to 35 years old, 20 percent are over 50, and about 40 percent are female. Video game sales, which include mobile apps, games for video game systems, and computer games, reached over $15 billion in the United States in 2014.

Georgejmclittle/Fotolia

FIGURE 6.10 Playing Minecraft on a tablet.

Games are one type of software for which you must pay attention to the system requirements for installation. Game software typically requires substantial processing, memory, and video power to run well. Trying to play a game on an inadequate system is a frustrating experience.

ETHICS ❯ Violence in Video Games

Does the video gaming industry have an ethical obligation to produce games that have less violent and addictive content? Gaming has become a method of entertainment, with at least half of the individuals that you meet having tried to play one at least once. But is it really entertainment? Entertainment is an act that should relax people and take their mind off their troubles. Some people who play for hours do not seem to be getting entertainment in the traditional sense of the word. Watching some "gamers," as they are called, you might see signs of frustration and irritation.

Some games have activities that are not legal in the real world, for example, stealing or abuse of another individual. Consider these questions: Is the difference between the ethics in the real world and the gaming world one of the problems with gaming? Is it possible for an individual to transfer the rules of the gaming world into the real world and begin to exhibit these unethical behaviors in his or her real life? Is it possible to become addicted to the gaming world environment and stay there for longer and longer periods of time? How should games be rated so that parents can distinguish violent games from ones that are entertainment? Should the gaming industry change its strategy and develop games that encourage a healthier mind-set—one that promotes the ethics of a nonviolent society?

Concept 6.07 | Using Portable Apps

Portable apps are programs that you can carry with you and run from a flash drive. Portable apps need no installation, so they can run on almost any computer system. Your settings and data are on your flash drive—not the host computer—and when you remove your drive, there is no personal information left behind. One place to find portable apps is at **portableapps.com**. The Portable Apps platform is open source, and the apps are free. Many of the apps you use on your computer—web browsers, email clients, games, utilities, and even operating systems—can run as portable apps.

Objective 3 | Identify Media and Graphic Software

Multimedia is content that integrates text and *media*—graphics, video, animation, and sound. Most media and graphic software applications are referred to as multimedia programs, because they enable you to incorporate more than one of these technologies. These features, which once were considered entertainment or amusement, are now standard components of business, advertising, and educational programs. As a Public Relations Manager, you use multimedia to create engaging and effective presentations, flyers, and other publications for Oro Jade Hotels.

Concept 6.08 | Clarifying Compression and Decompression

Multimedia files, such as photographs, videos, and sounds stored on your computer, require large amounts of storage space. To use the space on your hard drive efficiently and improve file transfer speeds over the Internet, multimedia software reduces file size by using *codecs*, short for compression/decompression. Codecs are compression algorithms that reduce the size of digital media files. Without the use of codecs, downloads would take much longer than they do now because the files would be significantly larger. There are hundreds of codecs. If you download frequently, you probably use a few codecs on a regular basis. Common codecs you might recognize include MP3 and AAC for audio files, and DivX and XviD for video files.

Concept 6.09 | Using Graphic Programs

Use *desktop publishing programs* to create newsletters, product catalogs, advertising brochures—any documents that require unusual design and layout not normally provided by a word processor. By using a desktop publishing program, you can print or save documents in formats that you can send to a professional printer. Microsoft Publisher (Figure 6.11) is a desktop publishing program that has the familiar interface of other Microsoft Office applications.

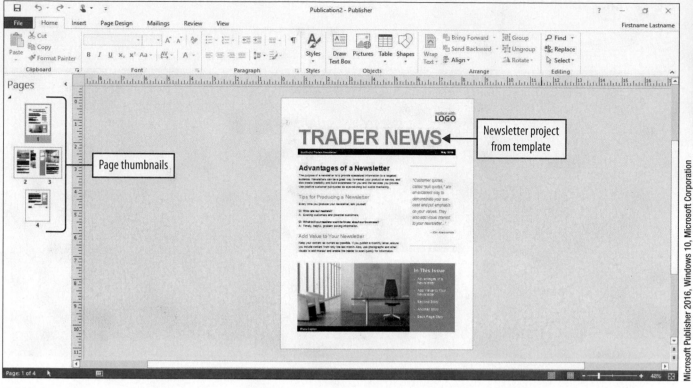

FIGURE 6.11 Microsoft Publisher desktop publishing program includes many templates to start your project.

Use *paint programs* to create *bitmapped graphics*, which are images composed of tiny squares or dots that correspond to one pixel—a single point on a display screen. When editing a bitmapped image, you need to zoom in at a high viewing level. Then the pixels become more apparent and appear to have jagged edges between contrasting colors (Figure 6.12). Windows includes the Paint program with which you can create this type of graphic. Paint is ideal for beginners and provides a tool panel with features to crop images, alter colors, and erase areas you no longer want on the graphic. If you require more advanced features, you can purchase a professional paint program such as Corel Paint to create a wider scope of effects through a more enhanced tool panel.

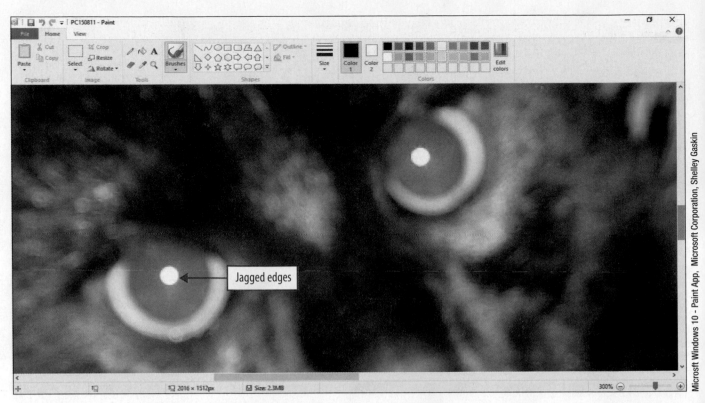

FIGURE 6.12 Jagged edges are visible because this image of a cat's eye is enlarged using Paint.

Use *image editors*—sophisticated versions of graphic programs—to edit and create images. You can add a variety of special effects to photographic images, as well as remove blemishes, crop portions of them, adjust the coloring, and then save them in a variety of file formats. Programs like Adobe Photoshop, powerful image editing software, are used primarily by professionals, but the popularity of digital photography encouraged companies to create simpler photo editing software such as Adobe's Photoshop Elements. These simpler programs enable you to create a professional finished photo or image without the cost and learning curve of complex software. Windows computers (Figure 6.13) and Macs include Photos apps with which you can edit, organize, and share your digital photos.

Microsft Windows 10 - Photos App, Microsoft Corporation, Shelley Gaskin

FIGURE 6.13 Editing an image with the Windows Photos app.

Many online photo services such as Google Photos (Figure 6.14), Shutterfly, and Flickr include basic editing tools like cropping, resizing, red-eye removal, and special effects like making the picture look black-and-white and adding special borders. You can also order photo prints and create personalized gifts like calendars, books, and coffee mugs.

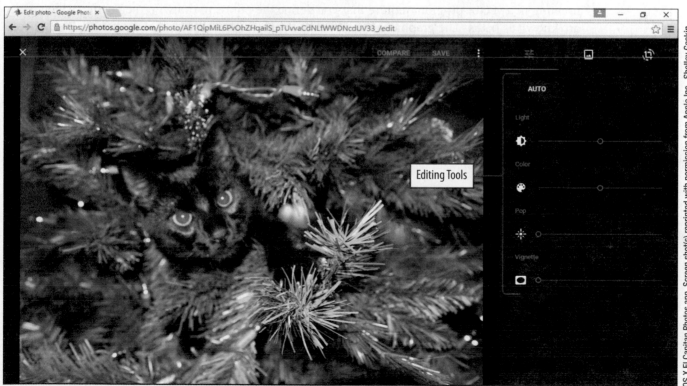

OS X El Capitan Photos app. Screen shot(s) reprinted with permission from Apple Inc., Shelley Gaskin

FIGURE 6.14 Editing an image with Google Photos.

Is it possible to convert an image from one graphic format to another? Yes, some graphic applications enable you to convert a graphic in one format to another format through the Save As command. Figure 6.15 provides a list of the standard formats in which the graphics programs can save your work.

STANDARD GRAPHIC FILE FORMATS		
FORMAT	**FILE EXTENSION**	**DESCRIPTION**
Graphics Interchange Format	*GIF* (pronounced "jiff" or "giff")	A 256-color graphic file format that uses lossless compression and is best for simple images with large areas of solid color. This file format is a web standard for images with a limited number of colors.
Joint Photographic Experts Group	*JPEG* or *JPG* (pronounced "JAY-peg")	A graphic format that can store up to 16.7 million colors, is best for complex images such as photographs, uses lossy compression, and is also a web standard.
Portable Network Graphics	*PNG* (pronounced "ping")	A patent-free graphic format alternative to GIF, this format produces images that use lossless compression and is best suited to web use only.
Windows Bitmap	*BMP*	This standard graphic format was developed for Microsoft Windows. Compression is optional, so BMP files tend to be very large.
Tagged Image File Format	*TIFF* or *TIF*	A lossless graphic format, used in publishing because it allows specific instructions to be embedded within the file to retain image quality. The drawback is the resulting large file size.

FIGURE 6.15

Gaskin, Shelley. GO! All in One, 3E. Pearson Education, 2017.

Vector graphic programs create graphics that are math based. You may remember from your high school math that a line segment is defined as having at least two points. The rules for drawing in a vector program require that you define the points to draw line segments, which are known as paths. The graphic program stores the paths as mathematical equations. When you enlarge or shrink a vector graphic, the program needs only to recalculate the math for the line segments or paths you created. Thus, clarity is perfectly maintained regardless of resized dimensions. For this reason, illustrations such as clip art and logos are often designed in vector graphic programs.

FIGURE 6.16 Adobe Illustrator professional vector graphics software.

Adobe andAdobe Illustrator are registered trademarks of Adobe Systems Incorporated in the United States and/or other countries.Adobe Inc.

2.06b (iv)

Concept 6.10 | Using Video Editing Programs

Use video editing software to enhance your personal videos. You can spend hundreds of dollars for professional programs, but for most people, free or low-cost alternatives have all the features necessary.

Video editors are programs that enable you to modify digitized videos. Video editing software ranges from free online services such as YouTube, to free programs including Windows Movie Maker and Apple iMovie, to very expensive professional-quality programs such as Adobe Premiere and Sony Vegas. Because video editing requires significant system resources, there are few online options available.

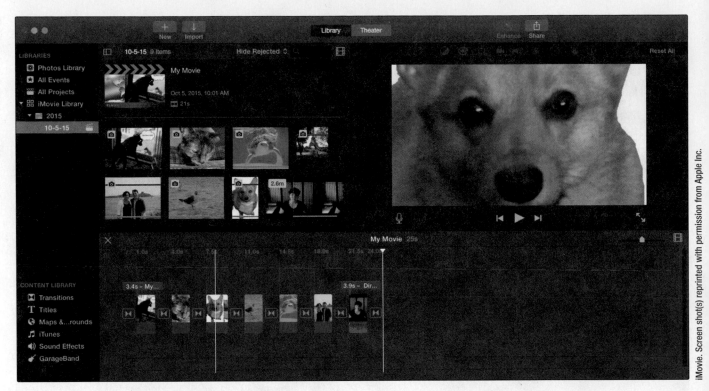

FIGURE 6.17 iMovie is installed on Mac computers.

Streaming video—accessing video clips almost immediately after you click a video link on a webpage without waiting for the entire file to download—is made possible by streaming video formats. These formats rely on compression, low frame rates, and small image size to deliver your video over the Internet, which does not have sufficient bandwidth to disseminate broadcast-quality video. A popular streaming video site is YouTube.

Screen capture software tools enable you to create a video of what happens on your computer screen. This is a simple way to create a how-to video or to capture a video of a problem that you are having. You do not need a camera to do it. Some screen capture programs, like Jing and Screencast-O-Matic, enable you to share the video online. *Machinima*—the art of creating videos using screens captured from video games—is one creative use of screen capture software. Windows 10 includes a built-in tool called the Game Bar, which is part of the Game DVR feature in the Xbox app. The tool records your PC game play, but can also be used to record other screen activities.

Concept 6.11 | Using Audio Editing and Speech Recognition Software

A variety of programs are available for capturing and processing sound for multimedia presentations, including sound mixers, compression software, bass enhancers, synthesized stereo, and even onscreen music composition programs. Most programs include options to create unique music mixes, record podcasts, convert between file formats, filter out background noise and static, and edit content through cut, copy, and paste features.

Sound files contain digitized data in the form of recorded live sounds or music, which are saved in one of several standardized sound formats. These formats specify how sounds should be digitally represented and generally include some type of data compression. A common music file format is *MP3 (MPEG-1 Audio Layer 3)*. The MP3 codec creates files that are compressed, enabling them to maintain excellent quality while being reasonably small. When you rip a CD, you transfer your music files to your computer. The files on an audio CD are very large, which is why there are typically only 10–12 songs per disc. An MP3 file is about one-tenth the size of a

CD file. There is a trade-off between file size and quality; the smaller MP3 files are not the same quality of the original audio files. MP3 files have the file extension *.mp3*.

The default file type used by Apple's iTunes software is **AAC (advanced audio coding)**, which compresses a file in a manner similar to MP3s. The AAC codec creates files that are somewhat higher quality than MP3 files, and support for it is growing on other devices, such as the Sony PlayStation 4, Nintendo WiiU, and many smartphones and media players.

Speech recognition, also known as **voice recognition**, enables you to use a device using voice commands instead of a keyboard. This technology can be used to automatically provide customer service through a call center, dial a cell phone, control features in a car, or dictate a term paper. The Microsoft Windows and Apple OS X operating systems have built-in speech recognition, and there are also other software packages that provide similar services. Figure 6.18 shows the Windows 10 Speech settings window, where you can set up your system to use this feature. Speech recognition is often built into video games, enabling a player to control the action using voice commands. To use speech recognition software, you spend some time training the software to recognize your speech patterns. The more you use it, the better the software becomes at recognizing what you are saying.

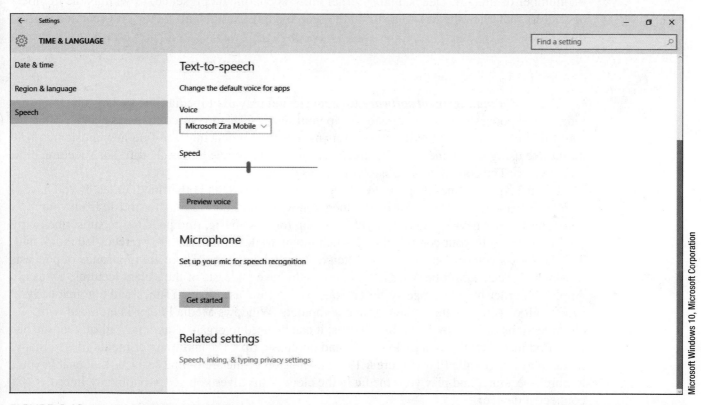

FIGURE 6.18 Windows 10 Speech settings.

Apple iPhones include Siri, an intelligent personal assistant app that enables you to speak using natural language to send messages, make phone calls, and ask questions. Siri uses information from your contacts, music library, calendars, and reminders to make recommendations and perform other actions. It works with built-in apps and some third-party apps, like Facebook and Twitter. Over time, Siri learns your speech patterns and gets even better at understanding you. Android devices have a built-in assistant system called Google Now that can be controlled with voice commands, which is also available as a download for other platforms. Google Now presents information in cards that reflect information from your contacts, searches, and email messages. The personal digital assistant on Windows phones and in Windows 10 is called Cortana. Home entertainment systems, such as the Amazon Echo, can be voice controlled.

2.06b (iii)

Concept 6.12 | Reviewing Webpage Authoring Programs

The Adobe Creative Suite media development kit is a combination of programs that enable you to create multimedia Internet applications. Productivity programs like Word and Excel have options to save your work as a webpage, and this works fine for a beginner. Adobe Creative Suite has two core programs with advanced capabilities for webpage development:

- Dreamweaver: An environment in which you develop webpages both visually and directly in code, and connect to other tools used in web interactivity and design.
- Flash: A platform to create animation and interactivity that can be added to webpages. Flash is being replaced by more modern tools such as HTML5.

Another alternative is to use an online tool, such as Wix.com or Squarespace.com, to both build and host your website.

Search engine optimization (SEO) is a technique to make a website easier to find by both people and software that indexes the web and to increase the webpage ranking in search engine results. SEO is most often associated with using keywords and key phrases in the webpage content and code, but this is only one part of SEO. The quality and quantity of content on a site, the number of images, videos, and external links, social media presence, as well as the number of visitors that click the link to a site in the search engine results, all factor into search engine rankings.

2.06b (iii)
2.06b (vi)

Concept 6.13 | Managing Media

Use **media management software** to organize and play multimedia files such as music, videos, and podcasts. You can transfer or rip your music CDs to your computer; organize your songs into playlists for activities like exercising, driving, or dancing; and find new music that you might like using the online store feature. You can watch a movie trailer, a professor's lecture, or a music video. The content available to you grows daily.

Use the Apple iTunes program to organize music, videos, and other media files. If you have an **iOS device**—iPod, iPhone, or iPad—then you will use iTunes to transfer music from your computer to your device. In iTunes, you can shop for new music, find podcasts to subscribe to, rip your music CDs to your computer, and watch movie trailers. **Podcasts** are prerecorded radio- and TV-like shows you can download and listen to or watch any time. There are thousands of podcasts to which you can subscribe. Your instructors might have podcasts of their class lectures. By using Apple's Internet-based storage system iCloud, items purchased using iTunes will automatically sync to all of your registered devices and computers. Windows Media Player is included with older versions of Windows, and like iTunes, it can be used to organize and play all of your media files, find media on the web to download and purchase, rip CDs, and transfer media files to many media players. Google Play (Figure 6.19) and Amazon Prime are online services that enable you to purchase, store, and play your media in the cloud. This gives you access from any Internet-connected device.

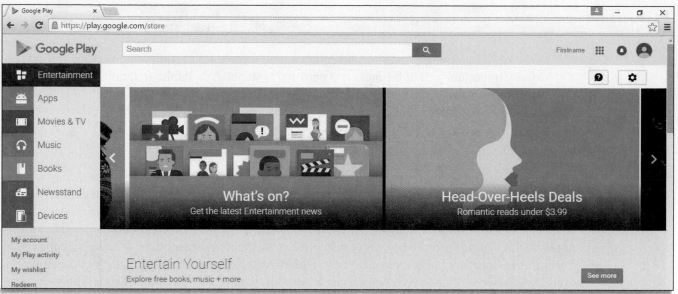

FIGURE 6.19 Google Play organizes your media files.

Microsoft Windows 10, Microsoft Corporation

Cloud computing refers to applications and services that are accessed over the Internet. ***Cloud storage*** is online storage of data that you can access from different places and devices. By connecting your music to the cloud, you can listen to your favorite songs on any device with an Internet connection.

Spotify is a music service that uses both the music on your devices and the millions of tracks stored in the ***cloud***—another term for the Internet. It enables you to share playlists and recommend tracks to your friends. Spotify has a radio feature that will automatically create stations for you based on both your music collection and your most frequently played tracks.

Pandora is a music service with which you can listen to music on an Xbox, Blu-ray player, computer, or mobile device. You create stations by selecting songs or artists that you like. Pandora has a massive collection of music that has been analyzed and classified by what it refers to as *musician-analysts*. You can refine the results you get by giving each track a thumbs up or thumbs down. Pandora also displays the lyrics so you can sing along to your favorite tunes.

Other music services include Amazon Prime, Google Play, and Apple Music. Most services have free, ad-supported plans and premium subscriptions that eliminate ads and add more features. Connections to Facebook, Twitter, and other services make sharing and listening to music a social experience. Using one of these services allows you some control over the songs you listen to—unlike a normal radio broadcast. Some radio stations stream live, over the Internet. In fact, many radio stations broadcast exclusively over the Internet.

Digital rights management (DRM) is a technology applied to digital media files such as music, eBooks, and videos to impose restrictions on the use of these files. DRM may prevent you from transferring a file from one device to another or making a backup copy, or set a time limit on your access to the file. The companies that apply DRM to media files argue that it is necessary to protect the copyright holder. The Digital Millennium Copyright Act (DMCA) made it illegal to remove DRM from protected files. Opponents of DRM argue that although it prevents copyright infringement, it also restricts other lawful uses of the media.

As the need for storage, security, and collaboration grows, cloud computing becomes an increasingly important part of business and personal systems. As a Public Relations Manager at Oro Jade Hotels, you often collaborate with colleagues at other locations. By using cloud computing services, it is easy to share files and applications regardless of the location of the collaborators.

1.06a (i)
1.06a (ii)
1.06b
1.06c
1.06d (i)
1.06d (ii)
1.06e (ii)
1.06e (iv)

Concept 6.14 | Cloud Computing

Technology infrastructure costs for servers and network hardware can be as much as 80 percent of a typical IT budget. *Infrastructure-as-a-Service (IaaS)* means that a company uses servers in the cloud instead of purchasing and maintaining the servers on-site. This reduces the cost of hardware, software, and support personnel. IaaS also enables small companies that may not have the expertise to manage servers to have sophisticated servers to house large databases, to centralize document management, and to add increased security to their data. A commonly used IaaS service is off-site backup services. Although there is some concern about the security of using cloud services for storing sensitive information, large *cloud service providers* or *CSPs*—companies that provide cloud (Internet-based) computing services—offer very secure environments.

Software-as-a-Service (SaaS) is the delivery of applications over the Internet—sometimes referred to as *web apps*. This technology is more visible than an IaaS to a system's users. Any time you open your browser to access your email, upload photos, or share a file, you are using SaaS.

SaaS has several advantages over installing software locally. Because SaaS is delivered on demand, it is available anytime from any computer with Internet access. In addition to the convenience, SaaS also eliminates the need to apply updates to local software installations. You use SaaS whenever you use web mail. A web mail system does not download your email messages to your personal computer. Instead, the messages are stored and accessed from a hosted email server that provides backup and security, gives you access from anywhere, and eliminates the need to install and configure an email program on your computer.

A cloud-based *Learning Management System,* or *LMS*, is an SaaS application used in schools and corporate training environments to deliver educational materials, track student interactions, and assess student performance. Students are able to access the LMS from any Internet-connected device using a web browser. Some LMS systems also provide enhanced mobile access through mobile apps. You may use an LMS at your college, for example, Blackboard, Canvas, or Moodle.

Microsoft Office Online (Figure 6.20), *Office 365*, and Google Drive are all examples of a personal SaaS. These services include productivity tools and online file storage, and they enable you to collaborate and share files with others.

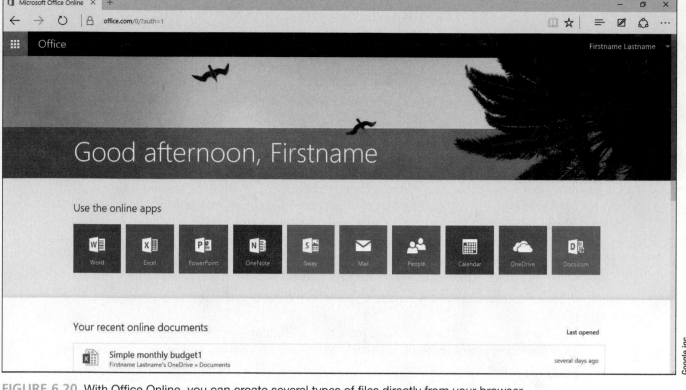

FIGURE 6.20 With Office Online, you can create several types of files directly from your browser.

Applying an update to a software application on each computer can be a costly, time-consuming process. But with an SaaS solution, the updates happen on the remote system and do not impact the local users. Users will instantly have access to new features as soon as they log in to their account on the SaaS site. No local configuration is needed.

For businesses, using the cloud to deliver apps offers several benefits: a simple and quick way of accessing applications from anywhere, a relatively small cost per user, and the elimination of the need to maintain and support the applications on-site. SaaS may not be a term most people use very often, but the services it provides are used every day by individuals and businesses alike. As cloud computing matures, more and more computing is cloud based.

Platform-as-a-Service (PaaS) provides a programming environment to develop, test, and deploy custom web applications. By using such a service, a business gains the ability to build, deploy, and manage SaaS applications. PaaS also makes collaboration easier and requires less programming knowledge. Three popular PaaS programs are AppEngine from Google, Force.com from SalesForce, and Microsoft Azure Services Platform.

Together, IaaS, SaaS, and PaaS can provide a business with an integrated system for delivering applications and content using the cloud. Well-known providers of cloud services include Microsoft, Amazon, Google, Sun Microsystems, and Salesforce.com. Cloud solutions save money in software, hardware, and personnel costs; increase standardization; and increase efficiency and access to technology. The CSPs can build huge datacenters in remote locations near inexpensive and green power supplies such as hydroelectric plants. Building such datacenters is impractical for most businesses.

All the computing power required to maintain large cloud services uses a lot of energy and has a large impact on the environment. A datacenter—sometimes called a server farm—is a facility designed to house a company's servers and other equipment in a secure and controlled environment. The energy costs for a business with large datacenters can be staggering. One of the largest expenses in a datacenter is energy costs.

A green datacenter's mechanical, lighting, electrical, and computer systems are designed for maximum energy efficiency and minimum environmental impact. Green datacenters can be certified by the U.S. Green Building Council (USGBC). Many companies look for datacenter locations with cheaper energy in order to lower power costs. In 2006, Google moved its datacenters to rural Oregon, which has cheap, renewable hydroelectric energy, and according to Google, each of its datacenters uses about half the energy required in a typical datacenter. Locations near wind farms, hydroelectric plants, and geothermal plants are good places to build new datacenters. Building green also involves other steps, such as low-emission building materials, sustainable landscaping, recycling, and the use of alternative energy technologies, such as heat pumps and evaporative cooling.

A number of steps can make existing datacenters greener:

- Redesign cooling system. Channel heat away from servers, seal leaks, and use high-efficiency cooling units.
- Scale back equipment. Use smaller and more energy-efficient systems.
- Consolidate and virtualize. Move equipment to one central location, and consolidate equipment to fewer, more efficient machines.
- Use Energy Star–rated appliances, computers, and servers.

✔ Check Your Knowledge: In MyITLab, take the quiz covering Objectives 1–4.

Objective 5 | Compare Various Ways of Obtaining Software

Application Software

There are many different ways to obtain software. In the past you might have gone to a store to purchase software or ordered software online and had it shipped to you. Increasingly, you obtain software by downloading it from a website or app store. As a Public Relations Manager, you use and purchase many different software programs, so it is important for you to understand both the purchasing and licensing processes for the software you buy.

2.06a

Concept 6.15 | Purchasing: Is It Free or Fee?

Not all proprietary software has a fee, and not all open source software is free. The cost of software is determined by the publisher. There are four basic models for software distribution:

- *Retail software*: The purchaser pays a fee to use the software for an unlimited period of time. Microsoft Office, Adobe Photoshop, and TurboTax are all examples of retail software.

- *Subscription*: Some retail software, such as Microsoft Office and Adobe Creative Cloud, can be purchased through a subscription service. A monthly or yearly fee provides access to the software for a limited time. The advantage to subscriptions is that updates and newer versions of the software are included as long as the subscription is valid.

- *Freeware*: Can be used at no cost for an unlimited period of time. Some popular freeware includes Apple iTunes, Evernote, and 7-Zip.

- *Shareware*: Software offered in trial form or for a limited period that enables you to try it out before purchasing a license. It is sometimes referred to as trialware. This marketing model of selling software has become so popular that you can purchase most retail software this way. You can download a 30- or 60-day free trial of products from Microsoft, Adobe, and many other publishers. New computers often come preloaded with a lot of trialware.

- *Donationware*: A form of freeware in which the developers accept donations, either for themselves or for a nonprofit organization. VLC Media Player and FileZilla are two popular examples of donationware.

- *Freemium*: A common way to monetize—earn money from—a mobile app is via *in-app purchases*. The app itself is free to download and install, but additional features, game levels, or other content can be purchased for small, one-time payments or via subscriptions.

Concepts 6.16 | Locating Sources of Software

Software is available from a variety of sources. Where you choose to obtain it will depend on the type of software you are looking for and how soon you need it. You can purchase software in specialized computer and electronics stores, office supply stores, and mass merchandise stores. The price and variety of programs available in these places will vary widely. If you are looking for a popular piece of software, such as game or tax preparation software, then you will likely find it for a competitive price. But if you are looking for something less popular, you may have a hard time finding it on the shelf.

Online retailers often have a larger selection of software than do retail stores, and prices are comparable. These sites sell software in a box and ship it to you. Some software may also be available for immediate download. When you purchase software directly from the software publisher's website, you can immediately download it. The cost can be competitive with retailers, but you should shop around to compare prices. Websites such as **http://cnet.com**, **http://tucows.com**, and **http://zdnet.com** have large libraries of freeware and shareware to download. For open source software, go to **http://sourceforge.net**. An advantage of using sites like these is that they include editor and user reviews to help you choose the program that is right for you. Also, reputable websites test the programs for malicious intent.

The term *desktop application* refers to a computer program that is installed on your PC and requires a computer operating system such as Microsoft Windows. A desktop app typically has hundreds of features and takes time to learn. An *app* is a self-contained program usually designed for a single purpose and that runs on smartphones and other mobile devices—for example, looking at sports scores or booking a flight on a particular airline. Microsoft's Windows 10 and Apple OS X support both desktop apps and apps that run on all device families—including computers, phones, and tablets.

The Windows Store is included with Windows (Figure 6.21), and the Apple App Store is part of OS X and iOS. These stores give you access to thousands of programs, both free and paid, directly from your device. You can also update previous purchases through the store interface.

FIGURE 6.21 The Windows store has thousands of apps to install on your Windows computer.

*Mobile applications—apps—*that extend the functionality of mobile devices should be downloaded only from trusted sources. It is safest if you use the recommended app store for your device. Apps for Android devices can be found in the Google Play store (Figure 6.22). The apps must pass through rigorous testing to be placed in the market, thus reducing the risk of malicious or harmful code running on your device. There are many mobile apps that improve the connection or interface to a web application or social media site from a mobile device. For example, the Facebook and Twitter apps optimize the way the sites display on your device.

FIGURE 6.22 The Google Play store has thousands of apps for your Android devices.

When you download software from a website, it is good practice to back up the downloaded file and license should you ever need to reinstall the program.

FAST FORWARD — Mobile App Development

Apple and Google opened the first mobile app stores in 2008. By 2015, an estimated two to six million developers were building apps for these stores. A **software developer** designs and writes computer programs. Making an app is the easy part. There are websites where a novice can use pre-made elements to create an app and publish it with ease. A professional developer uses more sophisticated tools and computer programming skills. But building a good app—one that works well, has market appeal, and generates income—is the hard part.

Revenue from mobile apps built for smartphones and tablets is expected to reach $92 billion by 2018, so there is a lot of potential to earn income, but there are over 1,500,000 apps in the Google Play store and almost as many in the Apple App Store, so the competition is steep.

There are four ways to monetize—profit from—a mobile app:

- Pay-per-download: Charge an up-front fee for the app.
- Subscription: Charge a regularly recurring fee for use.
- In-app purchases: Charge for additional content, levels, or other features from within the app.
- In-app advertising: Charge a fee for displaying ads within the app. This is the most common way to monetize a free app.

Objective 6 — Respect Software Licenses and Registration Agreements

As a Public Relations Manager at Oro Jade Hotel Group, you must investigate the license and registration agreements necessary to deploy any new software purchased by your department. Where do you start?

IC3
DIGITAL LITERACY
CERTIFICATION
3.01a (v)

Concept 6.17 | Reviewing Licenses and Registration

A **software license** is a contract distributed with a program that gives you the right to install and use the program on one or more computers. Usually, to install a program on more than one computer, you must purchase additional licenses. However, some programs permit home users to install software on one or two additional computers. This information can be found in the **end user license agreement** or **EULA**—the contract between the software user and the software publisher. A **product key** is a code supplied with the license that you must enter when you install the software (Figure 6.23). The code helps a software publisher verify that the software was purchased legally.

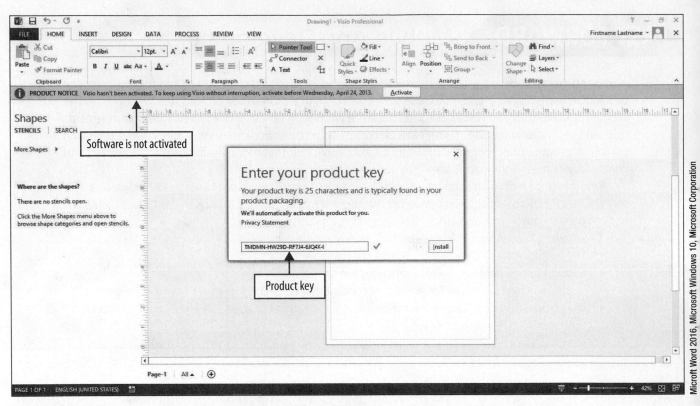

FIGURE 6.23 Enter a product key during installation to validate or activate your purchase.

The two most common software licenses are:

- **Proprietary software license**: Grants a license to use one or more copies of the software, but ownership of those copies remains with the software publisher. This is the type of license found on most commercial software and is the most restrictive in terms of your right to distribute and install the software.

- **Open source software license**: Grants ownership of the copy to the end user. The end user has the right to modify and redistribute the software under the same license.

In both cases, there may or may not be a fee for the use of the software. The cost of software is a big factor in choosing which programs to install.

Organizations such as colleges and universities often purchase *site licenses*, a contract with the software publisher that enables the organization to install copies of a program on a specified number of computers. Site licenses offer large organizations multiple software licenses at a reduced price. Other licensing models for organizations include *volume licensing*, which allows multiple installations of software using the same product key, and *per-seat licensing*, which assigns a product key to individual users.

Objective 7 | Use Business Communication Tools

The Internet and social media have changed how companies and organizations engage consumers and how consumers connect and influence each other. Understanding these technologies and using them effectively are valuable job skills. In your job as a Public Relations Manager, you must communicate the Oro Jade message using modern business tools and techniques.

Concept 6.18 | Connecting with Client Software

1.06e (iii)

A ***Customer Relations Management system***, or ***CRM***, such as Salesforce.com and Microsoft Dynamics CRM, is a system for maintaining customer information and connections. CRM systems can be cloud-based or locally hosted. A CRM is a database system that tracks interactions with a customer and is a valuable to gain information about marketing, sales, and customer service. ***Analytics***—detecting patterns in data—from the CRM can help a business make decisions to improve customer service or raise profits. A specialized example of a CRM is a Student Relations Management (SRM) system, which has admissions and enrollment management features. SRM is used as both a recruitment tool and to provide service to existing students—to improve retention and graduation rates. As part of a student success effort, tracking with an SRM system can alert educators to students who may need intervention to ensure success.

Concept 6.19 | Communicating with Business Phones Systems and Electronic Tools

1.01d
1.01e
1.01f
1.01g
3.06a
3.06b

There is nothing like the personal touch to keep customers happy. When customers have a question or problem, they expect a real live person to be available to assist them. When setting up a phone system, it is important to think about customer perception. For example, there has been a trend to provide automated menus instead of having a person answer each call. The caller is directed to ask a question, or press a number, so the system can either help or correctly direct the caller. This should be configured to provide streamlined service without frustrating and annoying customers.

When a live person answers the call, he or she should be trained in the use of the phone system, so as to easily and correctly transfer calls to another person if needed. When a person isn't available, the voicemail system should be set up with a voicemail message that is clear, short, and gives easy-to-follow directions for the caller; for example, the message should clearly state the name of the company, person, or department, thank the caller for calling, provide information about availability, and request that the caller leave specific information such as name, number, and best time to call back. Voicemail boxes should be checked regularly and calls returned quickly. A full voicemail box equals a missed call and missed opportunity.

Other tools for communicating with customers include live chat or instant messaging tools on the web that enable you to provide live customer service. Using the ***Short Message Service (SMS)***, you can send brief electronic text messages to mobile devices as shown in Figure 6.24. Messages that include multimedia such as images or videos use the ***Multimedia Messaging Service (MMS)***. Most mobile devices include a built-in messaging app, but always ask customers to opt in to ***text messaging***—depending on their cellular plan, they may pay for text and multimedia messages. Text messages are best for notifications such as when a bill is due, a package has shipped, or a table is available in a restaurant.

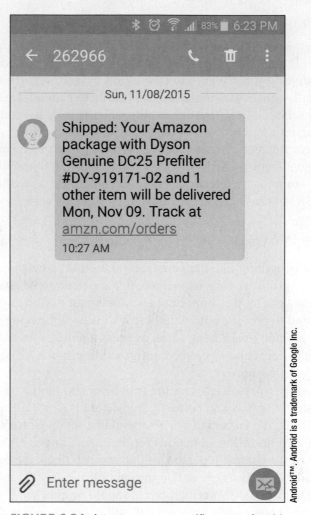

FIGURE 6.24 A text message notifies you of a shipment.

Concept 6.20 | Engaging with Social Media

When customers are looking for a company or service, they typically turn to the web. A successful organization in today's digital world needs to have an online presence that includes both a traditional website and *social media*—tools that enable users to create content, connect, network, and share on the web. The key to successful use of any social media tool is to keep it up to date and relevant to your customers. Use social media to interact with and engage your customers and use it to post interesting updates, specials, and links to relevant information. Share positive messages and include links, images, and videos. Use a *hashtag*—a word or phrase preceded by a # symbol—to organize and make your posts searchable, and respond to customers when they reach out to you or share your messages. You can use social media, such as Facebook, Instagram, and Twitter, to advertise specials, reward loyal customers with discounts, and share your mission and achievements.

For customers to find you, they need to know where to look. Creating social media profiles and websites using your brand is an important step, but most people start by using a search engine to find you. You want your site to appear on the first page of the search results. You should create a local business page on each of the three largest search engines: Google, Bing, and Yahoo!. Doing this is free and enables you to post basic information such as your hours, contact information, location, and website. In fact, the page might already exist, and you simply need to claim it as yours. Make sure that your business is correctly categorized and that everything is correct. Google allows users to review businesses, but Bing and Yahoo! rely on Yelp reviews—so you might also want to list your business on Yelp.

✔ **Check Your Knowledge:** In MyITLab, take the quiz covering Objectives 5–7.

GO! To Work

IC3 SKILLS IN THIS CHAPTER

IC3 — Module 1: Computing Fundamentals

Section 1.01 Mobile Devices
- (d) Understand the use of hard wired phones
- (e) Know how to configure and use voice mail
- (f) Use of instant messaging
- (g) Know how to configure notifications

Section 1.03 Computer Software Architecture
- (b) Know concepts surrounding applications vs. operating system vs global settings
- (d) Set software preferences

Section 1.05 File Sharing
- (b) Understand needs for file compression/ zipping in sharing

Section 1.06 Cloud Computing
- (a) Understand "cloud" concepts
  - (i) Understand cloud storage vs. cloud access concepts
  - (ii) Understand sharing and collaboration via the cloud
- (b) Know the benefits of using cloud storage
- (c) Access and utilization of the cloud
- (d) Web apps vs. local apps
  - (i) Understand Software as a Service (SAAS) concepts
  - (ii) Know what Learning Management Systems (LMS) do
- (e) Understand web app types
  - (ii) Online office apps [Google apps, Office 365]
  - (iii) Database Driven CRM apps [Salesforce, Oracle, Attask]
  - (iv) Browser vs. tablet vs. smartphone vs. desktop apps

IC3 — Module 2: Key Applications

Section 2.06 App Culture
- (a) Understand how to obtain apps
  - (i) Web apps
  - (ii) App stores
- (b) Identify different app genres
  - (i) Productivity
  - (ii) Reference
  - (iii) Content
  - (iv) Creation
  - (v) Social media
  - (vi) Music
  - (vii) Health
- (c) Understand strengths and limits of apps and applications
  - (i) Applications may only run on certain devices

IC3 — Module 3: Living Online

Section 3.01 Internet (Navigation)
- (a) Understand what the Internet is
  - (v) Know about licensing rules/laws

Section 3.06 Communications
- (a) Know the best tool for the various situations and scenarios
  - (ii) SMS
- (b) Know how to use SMS texting
  - (i) Etiquette
  - (ii) Know what it is and how it can be used as a tool
  - (iii) Know when to use and not use
  - (iv) Determine when it is appropriate to use it

GO! FOR JOB SUCCESS

Discussion: Personal Software Use

Your instructor may assign these questions to your class, and then ask you to think about them or discuss with your classmates:

Businesses spend millions of dollars a year on software costs and updates. As an employee of a company, you may be issued a company notebook computer to travel with.

FotolEdhar / Fotolia

> If you are issued the computer to take outside of work, does that give you the right to use it for nonbusiness tasks?

> What types of restrictions might a company put on personal software use?

> If the company computer has software on it that you don't have on your computer, is it OK to use the software outside of work hours and save your files on your own flash drive?

END OF CHAPTER

SUMMARY

Software is a set of instructions that tells the hardware how to perform a certain task. System software runs the computer. Application software directs the computer to carry out specific tasks.

Categories of software include general-purpose productivity programs, specialized business software, video games, finance and accounting, education and reference, and media and graphic software.

System requirements are the minimum hardware and software specifications required to run a program. You can buy software from a store, order online, or download it from a website or app store.

Cloud computing refers to applications and services accessed over the Internet. These services include Infrastructure-as-a-Service—IaaS, Software-as-a-Service—SaaS, and Platform-as-a-Service—PaaS.

GO! LEARN IT ONLINE

Review the concepts, key terms, and IC3 skills in this chapter by completing these online challenges, which you can find at **MyITLab**.

Matching and Multiple Choice: Answer matching and multiple choice questions to test what you learned in this chapter.

Lessons on the GO!: Learn how to use all the new apps and features as they are introduced by Microsoft.

IC3 Prep Quiz: Answer questions to review the IC3 skills that you practiced in this chapter.

GLOSSARY

GLOSSARY OF CHAPTER KEY TERMS

AAC (advanced audio coding) A codec used to compress audio files that creates files that are somewhat higher quality than MP3 files.

Accounting software Business software that tracks business finances such as expenses, invoicing, payroll, and inventory management, and generates reports and graphs to help you make business decisions.

Analytics The process of detecting patterns in data.

App A self-contained program usually designed for a single purpose and that runs on smartphones and other mobile devices.

Application software Programs that direct the computer to carry out specific tasks, for example, word processing, playing a game, or computing numbers on a worksheet.

Bitmapped graphics Images composed of tiny squares or dots that correspond to one pixel.

Cell The intersection of a row and a column in a spreadsheet.

Cloud Another term for the Internet.

Cloud computing Refers to applications and services that are accessed over the Internet, rather than to applications that are installed on your local computer.

Cloud service provider (CSP) A company that provides cloud (Internet-based) computing services.

Cloud storage Online storage of data that you can access from different places and devices.

Codec Short for compression/decompression; an algorithm used to reduce the size of media files.

Customer Relations Management system (CRM) A database system for maintaining customer information and connections.

Database An organized collection of facts about people, events, things, or ideas related to a specific topic or purpose.

Database management system (DBMS) Software that controls how related collections of data are stored, organized, retrieved, and secured.

Desktop application A computer program that is installed on your PC and requires a computer operating system such as Microsoft Windows; also known as a desktop app.

Desktop publishing program Software used to create newsletters, product catalogs, advertising brochures, and other documents that require unusual design and layout not normally provided by a word processor.

Digital rights management (DRM) A technology that is applied to digital media files such as music, eBooks, and videos to impose restrictions on the use of these files.

Document management The ability to save, share, search, and audit electronic documents throughout their life cycle.

Document management system (DMS) Software that businesses use to save, share, search, and audit electronic documents throughout their life cycle.

Donationware A form of freeware where the developers accept donations, either for themselves or for a nonprofit organization.

End-user license agreement (EULA) The contract between the software user and the software publisher.

Finance software A program that tracks your personal bank accounts, monitors your investments, helps you create and stick to a budget, and files your income taxes.

Freemium Software offered for free that requires in-app purchases for additional content.

Freeware Software you can use at no cost for an unlimited period of time.

Genealogy program Software to create family trees and slideshows of your photos, view timelines and maps, and search through millions of historical records on the Internet.

Hashtag A word or phrase preceded by a # symbol that is used to organize and make tweets searchable.

Image editor A sophisticated graphic program to edit and create images and save them in a variety of file formats.

In-app purchases A common way to monetize a mobile app. The app itself is free to download and install, but additional features, levels, or other content can be purchased for small, one-time payments or via subscriptions.

Infrastructure-as-a-Service (IaaS) Part of cloud computing; the use of Internet-based servers.

iOS device An iPod, iPhone, or iPad.

Learning Management System (LMS) An application used in both schools and corporate training environments to deliver educational materials, track student interactions, and assess student performance.

Machinima The art of creating videos using screens captured from video games.

Media Graphics, video, animation, and sound.

Media management software Programs that organize and play multimedia files such as music, videos, and podcasts.

Mobile application (mobile app) A program that extends the functionality of a mobile device.

MP3 (MPEG-1 Audio Layer 3) A codec to compress audio files, allowing them to maintain excellent quality while being reasonably small.

Multimedia Content that integrates text and media—graphics, video, animation, and sound.

Multimedia Messaging Service (MMS) A service used to send electronic messages that include multimedia such as images or videos to mobile devices.

Office application suite A group of applications that work together to manage and create different types of documents and include features that allow multiple users to collaborate.

Office 365 A version of Microsoft Office to which you subscribe for an annual fee.

Open source Software that has its source code published and made available to the public, enabling anyone to copy, modify, and redistribute it without paying fees.

Open source software license A license that grants ownership of the copy to the end user. The end user has the right to modify and redistribute the software under the same license.

Paint program Software to create bitmapped graphics, which are images composed of tiny squares or dots that correspond to one pixel.

Per-seat license A license that assigns a product key to individual users in an organization.

Personal information manager (PIM) A program to manage email, calendar, and tasks that is often part of an office suite.

Photo editing software A program that enables you to create a professional finished photo or image.

Platform-as-a-Service (PaaS) In cloud computing, an online programming environment in which to develop, deploy, and manage custom web applications.

Podcast A prerecorded radio- or TV-like show you can download and listen to or watch any time.

Portable apps Programs that can run from a flash drive.

Presentation application A program to create electronic presentations made up of slides that contain text, graphics, video, audio, or any combination of these.

Product key A code supplied with a software license that you must enter when you install the software that helps a software publisher verify that the software was legally purchased.

Productivity program General-purpose application software that helps you work more efficiently and effectively on both personal and business-related documents.

Project management software An application to help you to complete projects, keep within your budget, stay on schedule, and collaborate with others.

Proprietary software license Grants a license to use one or more copies of software, but ownership of those copies remains with the software publisher.

Retail software A type of software for which the user pays a fee to use the software for an unlimited period of time.

Screen capture software Tools that enable you to create a video of what happens on your computer screen.

Search engine optimization (SEO) The methods used to make a website easier to find by both people and software that indexes the web and to increase the webpage ranking in search engine results.

Shareware Software offered in trial form or for a limited period that enables you to try it out before purchasing a license.

Short Message Service (SMS) A service used to send brief electronic text messages to mobile devices.

Site license A contract with a software publisher that enables an organization to install copies of a program on a specified number of computers.

Social media Websites that enable you to create user-generated content, connect, network, and share.

Software A set of instructions that tells the hardware how to perform a certain task.

Software developer A person who designs and writes computer programs.

Software license A contract distributed with a program that gives you the right to install and use the program on one or more computers.

Software-as-a-Service (SaaS) A form of cloud computing that delivers applications over the Internet.

Sound file Digitized data in the form of recorded live sounds or music, which are saved in one of several standardized sound formats.

Speech recognition Technology that enables you to control a device without a keyboard by using voice commands.

Spreadsheet application A program that creates electronic worksheets composed of rows and columns.

Streaming video Accessing video clips almost immediately after you click a video link on a webpage without waiting for the entire file to download.

Tax preparation software A program that enables you to complete your income tax returns on your computer or online.

Text messaging Sending brief electronic messages between mobile devices using Short Message Service (SMS).

Three-dimensional spreadsheet A spreadsheet that has multiple worksheets that are linked together.

Vector graphic program An application used to create math-based vector graphics.

Video editor A program that enables you to modify digitized videos.

Voice recognition Technology that enables you to use a device without a keyboard by using voice commands.

Volume license A software license that allows multiple installations of software in an organization using the same product key.

Web apps Applications that run in a browser.

Word processor An application to create, edit, and format text documents. The documents can also contain images.

Andrew Rodriguez / Fotolia; FotolEdhar/ Fotolia; apops/ Fotolia; Yuri Arcurs/ Fotolia

System requirements for new software often require a computer system with significant processing power, storage space, and memory. In this Activity, you will assess your own computer to help you make smart software purchases.

1. From your student files, open the file **aio06_DOIT_answersheet**. Display the **Save As** dialog box, navigate to the location where you will store your documents for this chapter, and then create a new folder named **AIO Chapter 06** Open the folder, and then save the file as **Lastname_Firstname_06_DOIT_answersheet**

2. Open **File Explorer**, and in the **Navigation pane**, click **This PC**. In the right pane, under **Devices and drives**, locate the listing of all the drives available on your computer. If necessary, click the View tab and change the Layout to Tiles. Create a table like the one below to record details about your system—include the name, type, capacity, and free space for each drive or device.

DRIVE OR DEVICE NAME	TYPE OF DRIVE OR DEVICE	TOTAL CAPACITY	FREE SPACE

3. In the **Navigation pane**, right-click **This PC** and click **Properties** to open the System Control Panel. List the following information:

Processor	
Installed memory (RAM)	
System type	

4. Print or submit your answer sheet electronically as directed by your instructor.

ON THE WEB

1. **Free Software** One place to learn about free software alternatives is **MakeUseOf.com**. This website is a daily blog that includes a directory of hundreds of useful websites and apps. From your student files, open the file **aio06_OTW1_answersheet**, and then save the file in your **AIO Chapter 6** folder as **Lastname_Firstname_06_OTW1_answersheet**

   Go to **http://makeuseof.com/**, select two articles to read, and then write a one- to two-paragraph summary of each article. Did you decide to try the application described? Why or why not? If so, did you find it useful? Would you recommend it to a friend?

   Print or submit your answer sheet electronically as directed by your instructor.

2. **Computer Games** To run properly, many computer games have robust system requirements. From your student files, open the file **aio06_OTW2_answersheet**, and then save the file in your **AIO Chapter 6** folder as **Lastname_Firstname_06_OTW2_answersheet**

   Use the Internet to locate a current list of the top PC video games for your preferred computing platform. Research a game that you would like to run on your computer. What are the system requirements for the game?

   Open the System Control Panel or About this Mac window and view your system information. Does your computer meet the minimum requirements to run the game? In what ways does it exceed them?

   Print or submit your answer sheet electronically as directed by your instructor.

ETHICS AND SOCIAL MEDIA

1. **Ethics** You decided to buy an expensive video editing program and look online for a good deal. You find a listing from a seller that has good ratings, so you buy the software. From your student files, open the file **aio06_ESM1_answersheet**, and then save the file in your **AIO Chapter 6** folder as **Lastname_Firstname_06_ESM1_answersheet**

   When the software arrives, you discover that it is a copy and includes a program to generate a fake product key to unlock the program. You bought the software in good faith and really need it to complete a class assignment. What do you do? Would you install the software? Why or why not? Is it acceptable to install the software for the assignment and uninstall it when you are finished?

   Print or submit your answer sheet electronically as directed by your instructor.

2. **Social Media** Many social media sites have apps that you can use to add features to the experience. From your student files, open the file **aio06_ESM2_answersheet**, and then save the file in your **AIO Chapter 6** folder as **Lastname_Firstname_06_ESM2_answersheet**

3. Visit **http://facebook.com/help** and then click **Apps, Games & Payments**. Use the links on this page to research Facebook apps. You do not need to be logged in to Facebook to view this page.

   What are Facebook apps? How can you manage app privacy settings? What are three steps you should take to ensure your security when using apps? Do you currently use any social media apps? If so, which ones and why?

   Print or submit your answer sheet electronically as directed by your instructor.

COLLABORATION

1. **Top Five** As a group, discuss which software you use the most. From your student files, open the file **aio06_Collab1_answersheet**, and then save the file in your **AIO Chapter 6** folder as **Lastname_Firstname_06_Collab1_answersheet**

   As a group, select five software programs that you consider to be indispensable. Which programs did you pick, and why? If you could only afford to buy one program, which would it be? Which would you likely use a cloud-based tool for?

   Prepare a multimedia presentation or poster that explains your decisions. Submit the presentation or poster and provide documentation that all team members have contributed to the project.

   Print or submit your answer sheet electronically as directed by your instructor.

2. **Software Licenses** As a team, research the difference between the site licenses available for Microsoft Office for Business and Google for Work. From your student files, open the file **aio06_Collab2_answersheet**, and then save the file in your **AIO Chapter 6** folder as **Lastname_Firstname_06_Collab2_answersheet**

   Prepare a report that outlines the differences between the licenses. What are the advantages and disadvantages of each? Submit the report and provide documentation that all team members have contributed to the project.

   Print or submit your answer sheet electronically as directed by your instructor.

The Internet

OUTCOMES

Explain why the web is so important in today's society and why you need to be fluent in the tools and language of the Internet to be an educated consumer, a better student, an informed citizen, and a valuable employee.

OBJECTIVES

1. Recognize the Importance of the Internet
2. Compare Types of Internet Connections
3. View Content on the Web
4. Demonstrate How to Navigate the Web
5. Compare Different Forms of Synchronous Online Communication
6. Compare Different Forms of Asynchronous Online Communication
7. Discuss the Roles of Social Media in Today's Society

Rawpixel/Shutterstock

In This Chapter

Depending on your age, you either grew up with the Internet or you had to discover it through your work or other interests. Regardless, it is likely that the Internet is a part of your everyday life and that you may already know a lot about it. But there is so much to know that most people only scratch the surface.

In this chapter, you will investigate the wide variety of tools and information that is literally at your fingertips. When you have finished this chapter, you will have a broad understanding of the Internet as a whole as well as a good idea of the parts of the Internet that you find particularly useful, both personally and professionally.

Job Focus

A **Brand Manager** leads the marketing team in promoting the **Oro Jade** brand. Brand Managers work closely with other teams, including Product Developers, Researchers, and Advertising and Marketing personnel. You are responsible for creating a unique and memorable image of Oro Jade—one that guests will recognize and trust.

Two major components of your job are promoting the Oro Jade brand and conducting market research. The Internet is a critical part of both tasks. To be successful, a Brand Manager must have excellent communication, analytic, and technical skills.

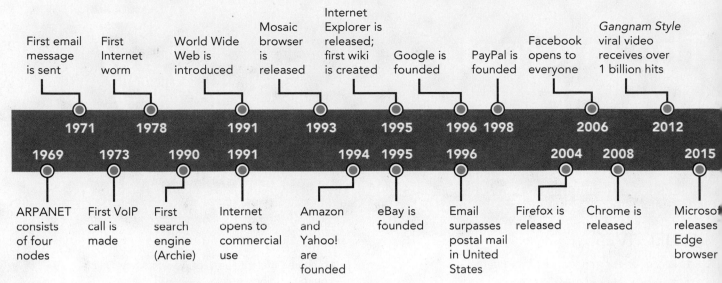

FIGURE 7.1 This timeline highlights important dates in Internet history.

Objective 1 | Recognize the Importance of the Internet

As a Brand Manager, many of your daily tasks involve the Internet. You use email and chat to communicate with the Marketing team, social media to reach out to guests, and the web to find important information about trends in the hospitality industry. Without the exposure of the Internet, it would be nearly impossible for the Oro Jade hotels to remain competitive.

There are very few businesses today that do not have an online presence. Consumers look to the web first to research, shop, and plan everything from tonight's dinner to travel plans to selecting a book to read.

3.01a

Concept 7.01 | Looking Back: How the Internet Got Started

In 1957, the Soviet Union launched the first space satellite: *Sputnik*. The United States and the Soviet Union were, at the time, engaged in a political conflict—called the Cold War—and the launch of Sputnik led to fears that the United States was falling behind in the technology race. In 1958, President Eisenhower created the Advanced Research Projects Agency (ARPA) to jump-start U.S. technology for the military. One of ARPA's early projects was to create a Galactic Network that would connect smaller networks around the world. The Internet started as a U.S. Department of Defense ARPA project called **ARPANET** in the 1960s to design a communications system that had multiple pathways through which information could travel so that losing one part of the system—for example, in a nuclear strike—would not cripple the whole system. It took about 10 years to develop the technology. The original ARPANET had only four locations, called nodes. The four nodes were at the University of California in Los Angeles (UCLA), the Stanford Research Institute (SRI), the University of Utah in Salt Lake City, and University of California, Santa Barbara (UCSB) (Figure 7.2).

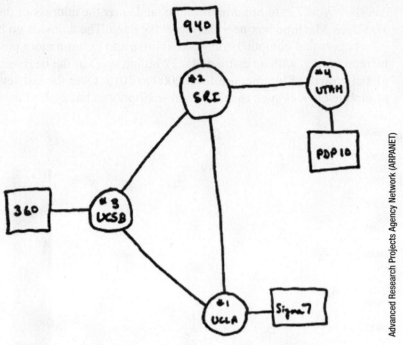

Advanced Research Projects Agency Network (ARPANET)

FIGURE 7.2 This original ARPANET sketch shows the first four nodes.

In 1979, the National Science Foundation (NSF) created CSNET to connect the university computer science departments using the ARPANET technology. In the mid-1980s, the NSF created NSFNET, giving other academic disciplines access to supercomputing centers and connecting smaller networks together. By the late 1980s, NSFNET was the primary *Internet backbone*—the high-speed connection points between networks. In 1995, the NSF decommissioned the NSF backbone, the Internet backbone was privatized, and the first five large network access points, referred to as NAPs, that made up the new backbone were established in Chicago, New Jersey, San Francisco, San Jose, and Washington, DC. Today, the backbone of the Internet is composed of Internet exchange points around the world.

IC3
DIGITAL LITERACY
CERTIFICATION
3.01a (i)

Concept 7.02 | Examining the World Wide Web

Most people use the terms *Internet* and *World Wide Web* interchangeably, but they are, in fact, two different things. The *Internet*, or *net*, is the physical entity—a network of computer networks. The Internet is a public network, but the networks it connects can be public or closed, private networks. The *World Wide Web*, or *web*, is the hypertext system of information on the Internet. The web is only one way that information moves on the Internet. Email, instant messaging, P2P (peer-to-peer) file sharing, and VoIP (Voice over Internet Protocol) are other ways that you might use the Internet. The term *intranet* refers to a private network that runs on web technologies. An intranet is a restricted or closed environment.

In 1991, Tim Berners-Lee and CERN, which is the European Organization for Nuclear Research, released the hypertext system we know as the World Wide Web. In a *hypertext* system, text and other objects are linked in a nonlinear fashion. You can navigate among the objects by using the links, or *hyperlinks*, that connect them. The milestone of having a million Internet hosts—networks or web servers—was reached in 1992, and at that time, commercial websites, such as **PizzaHut.com**, began to appear. The first White House website was launched in 1994. A *website* consists of one or more webpages that all are located in the same place. In 1993, a group of graduate students led by Marc Andreessen released the Mosaic point-and-click graphical browser for the web, which later became Netscape. These events led to a user-friendly Internet. Wondering what your favorite website used to look like? The Internet Archive WayBack Machine can show you. Go to **http://archive.org**, and enter the address of the website you want to see in the WayBack Machine box near the top of the page. The archives go back to 1996.

As personal computers dropped in price and became more powerful, the Internet grew at an incredible rate, with an estimated 2.27 billion users at the beginning of 2012. Figure 7.3 shows the global growth of Internet use from 2000 to 2015. Over the last several years, the widespread use of mobile devices such as tablets and smartphones has given Internet access to even more people.

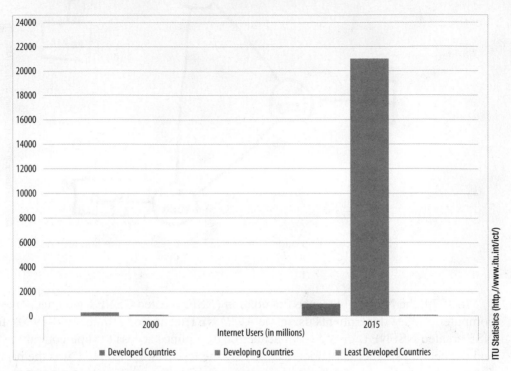

FIGURE 7.3 Individuals using the Internet 2000 and 2015.

From its earliest inception, the Internet was a place for collaboration and information sharing. Today, it is an integral part of education, business, and communication. Even if you do not spend a lot of time surfing the web, it is hard to deny the impact it has on your life.

Objective 2 | Compare Types of Internet Connections

Before You Buy
Choosing the
Right Internet
Service

As a Brand Manager, you spend a significant amount of time using the Internet for communication, research, and brand promotion. Having a fast and reliable Internet connection is vital to your job. Oro Jade must also provide Internet connections for its guests in common areas, event rooms, and guest rooms.

There are many different ways to access the Internet. *Internet service providers (ISPs)* are companies that provide Internet access and offer many different access plans. A large business such as an Oro Jade hotel will have different needs and a different budget than a home or small business.

3.01a (i)

Concept 7.03 | Establishing a Connection

A good place to find local ISPs is by searching the web. The options available to you depend on where you live and how much you have to spend. If you do not have access at home, most schools and libraries offer free access. Search for a list of ISPs that offer service in your area; there are many websites that compare services and prices for you. Before you begin your search, ask yourself what you need based on how you use the net. Do you just check email and look up recipes? If so, a slower connection might work for you. But if you work from home, play games, share photos, or watch videos, then you will need a faster connection. **Bandwidth** is the speed or data transfer rate of a network and is measured in kilobits per second (Kbps), megabits per second (Mbps), or gigabits per second (Gbps). For this measurement, the higher the number, the better. Figure 7.4 compares the bandwidths of various types of Internet connections. The table lists download speeds, but some of these connection types are asynchronous—meaning the download speeds and upload speeds differ. Most people download far more content than they upload, and so the download speed is the more important factor.

COMPARING BANDWIDTH OF INTERNET CONNECTIONS	
TYPE	DOWNLOAD SPEEDS
Dial-up	56 Kbps
DSL	384 Kbps to 20 Mbps
Cable	1 Mbps to 150 Mbps
Fiber	15 Mbps to 10 Gbps
Satellite	512 Kbps to 15 Mbps

FIGURE 7.4

Gaskin, Shelley. GO! All in One, 3E. Pearson Education, 2017.

Data is measured in **bits**—the smallest unit of digital data, and **bytes**, which consist of 8 bits and represents a single character in modern computer systems. Prefixes are added to the base units to represent larger numbers. Bits are normally used to measure data transfer speeds, while bytes arc used to express file sizes. Both use the same prefixes as shown in Figure 7.5.

THE STANDARD DECIMAL PREFIXES TO MEASURE DATA	
UNIT	PREFIX VALUE
Kilo	1,000
Mega	1 million
Giga	1 billion
Tera	1 trillion
Peta	1,000 tera
Exa	1,000 peta
Zetta	1,000 exa
Yotta	1,000 zetta

FIGURE 7.5

Gaskin, Shelley. GO! All in One, 3E. Pearson Education, 2017.

The least expensive type of connection is usually dial-up. With a dial-up connection, you use your regular telephone lines to connect to the network. There are some companies that will give you free access for up to 10 hours per month. This might be a good backup plan to have in case your normal connection should become unavailable. For some people, a dial-up connection may be the only option available. Dial-up is very slow, especially if you are trying to download a file or watch a video. Traditional telephone lines were not designed to carry data, and so they do a poor job of it.

To get more speed than with dial-up, you have several options. The Federal Communications Commission (FCC) defines **broadband** as anything over 10 Mbps, and in 2015 raised its benchmarks for measuring advanced broadband to 25 Mbps. Availability, speed, and costs vary depending on where you live. You'll have to do some research to get the best price and service. You can use the National Broadband Map at **http://broadbandmap.gov** to find out what types of broadband options are available where you live (Figure 7.6).

FIGURE 7.6 The National Broadband Map.

The National Broadband Map. Created and maintained by the NTIA, in collaboration with the FCC, and in partnership with 50 states, five territories and the District of Columbia. . http,//www.broadbandmap.gov/technology

Cable Internet access is offered by a cable TV provider and uses the same wires to carry both signals. Some cable companies also offer digital phone service. This requires older cable systems to be upgraded, so it is not universally available. Cable speeds range from 1 Mbps (megabit per second) to 150 Mbps but are typically 16 to 50 Mbps. Business-class connections can reach 400 Mbps. One drawback to using cable Internet access is that you share the cable, and therefore bandwidth, with your neighbors. This could potentially negatively impact your Internet speed if many neighbors are online at the same time.

Unlike your normal telephone line that is designed to carry analog signals—sound—**DSL (digital subscriber line)** telephone lines are designed to carry digital signals and therefore are much faster than ordinary telephone lines. DSL averages speeds of 384 Kbps to 20 Mbps, which is slower than cable; however, it is generally less expensive. One of the biggest problems with DSL is distance limitations. You must be within three miles of the DSL service provider's facilities. The farther away you are, the slower your connection will be.

Fiber-to-the-home (FTTH), also known as fiber-to-the-premises, carries signals on fiber-optic cable and is the fastest type of broadband, with top speeds of 300 to 500 Mbps—although most companies offer rates only up to 150 Mbps. It can carry Internet, TV, and phone calls to your home over fiber-optic cable and is available in limited areas—those where the fiber-optic cable has been installed. In the United States, the primary FTTH service is Verizon FiOS (Fiber Optic Service). Google Fiber, which is currently available in limited markets, offers speeds of 1 Gbps (1,000 Mbps). FTTH may require a contractor to lay a fiber-optic conduit directly to the home, which can be costly and may involve digging up your lawn.

Satellite Internet access is a more global and more expensive option. Satellite service speeds are comparable to those for DSL. You need a clear view of the southern sky, where the communications satellites are positioned in geosynchronous orbit—traveling around the Earth at a speed that matches the Earth's rotation, which enables the satellite to remain over the same location on Earth. You would probably only consider satellite if there were no other options available where you live. Several new communication satellites are scheduled to be launched, increasing the availability and speed of satellite Internet.

Mobile Internet access enables you to connect to the Internet using cellular 3G—third generation—and 4G—fourth generation—network standards. The signals are transmitted by a series of cellular towers; consequently, coverage is not universal. Coverage maps are available on the providers' websites, allowing you to verify if coverage exists where you need it before making a commitment. Although you may think about 3G/4G in terms of mobile devices, mobile Internet can be used on personal computers with a special network adapter. Special modems make 4G available at home, too. Depending on your cellular data plan and smartphone, a smartphone can serve as a wireless access point to share the connection with other devices via wireless or USB tethering. Several automobile makers have incorporated 4G into their entertainment and navigation systems. Top mobile Internet speeds are considered broadband and rival wired broadband service.

Wi-Fi uses radio waves to provide wireless high-speed network connections. It is the type of wireless networking you may have set up in your home or office. *Municipal Wi-Fi* is free Wi-Fi service offered in some cities and towns, such as CBS Mobile Zone available in central Manhattan. *Wi-Fi hotspots* are wireless access points that are available in many public locations, such as airports, schools, hotels, and restaurants—either free or for a fee.

The device that connects your network to the Internet will be an analog or digital modem, or a fiber optical network terminal. If you are having trouble with your Internet connection, resetting your modem will often fix the problem. If you also have a Wi-Fi router in your network, reset it as well.

According to the Pew Research Center, in 2015, 85 percent of adults in the United States were Internet users, and 70 percent of adults had home broadband access. For those who don't have broadband at home, cost and inaccessibility are often cited as the reasons. The 2015 Broadband Progress Report concluded that 17 percent of the U.S. population lack access to advanced broadband—broadband exceeding 25 Mbps download service. Of course, there are some people who just are not interested—they do not find any reason to have Internet access at home. But for most people, a good Internet connection is very important.

Objective 3 | View Content on the Web

As a Brand Manager, you use the web to market, promote, research, and communicate. Your job requires you to be fluent in the many ways the web can be used as a business and communication tool.

Some people use the Internet strictly for email, others for watching videos, and others for work. Some people have specific websites that they visit regularly, while others like to surf and explore. Regardless of how you use the web, you need the right tools to access it and enjoy the content.

3.01a (ii)

Concept 7.04 | Comparing Browsers

Most information on the web is in the form of basic *webpages*, which are written in *HTML* or *Hypertext Markup Language*, the authoring language that defines the structure of a webpage. Webpage developers can use CSS—cascading style sheets—to define the styles of content in the HTML documents. *Web browsers*, such as Microsoft Internet Explorer, Microsoft Edge, Mozilla Firefox, Google Chrome, and Apple Safari, are programs that interpret the HTML to display webpages and navigate the Internet. Although these are the most widely used browsers for personal computers, there are many alternatives. Many people simply use the browser that comes preinstalled on their device, but using an alternate browser, or even multiple browsers, enables you to use the best browser for each application. Some websites, tools, and technologies are optimized or better supported by specific browsers, so you may find it helpful to have more than one browser installed on your system.

Some important features of browsers:

- **Navigation buttons:** Provide a means to navigate backward and forward through browsed webpages.

- **Address bar:** The area—typically at the top of the browser window—in which you can type a URL to visit a website.

- **Bookmarks:** The term used to describe saved links to commonly visited web pages to allow for efficient web browsing. Bookmarks are sometimes called Favorites.

- **Tabbed browsing:** Enables you to have multiple webpages open in tabs.

- **Settings:** Provide easy access to most settings and features of the browser.

- **Refresh:** Reload webpage content. Use this when a page is not responding, or content is not displaying correctly.

First released in 1995, Internet Explorer (IE) is included with Windows, so there's no special download needed. Windows 8.1 includes two versions of IE: a full-screen app and a desktop version. Windows 10 includes the desktop version of IE 11, and a new browser—***Microsoft Edge***—which has replaced IE as the default browser. Figure 7.7 shows the NASA website displayed in Edge.

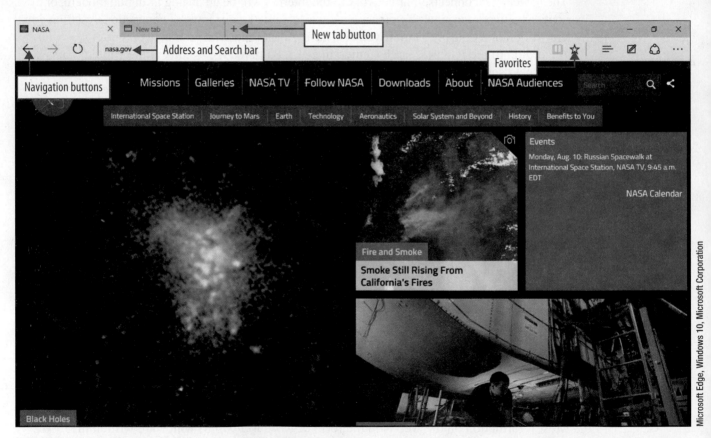

FIGURE 7.7 The NASA website viewed in Microsoft Edge.

Microsoft Edge, Windows 10, Microsoft Corporation

Google ***Chrome*** was released in 2008 with a focus on speed—it loads webpages faster than other browsers. Chrome is free and available for Windows, OS X, and Linux, as well as most mobile platforms. Figure 7.8 shows the National Park Service website in Chrome. You can create an account and log in to Chrome from different devices, accessing and sharing your settings and bookmarks across devices.

Address bar · New tab button · Navigation · Bookmarks and Chrome menu

FIGURE 7.8 The NPS website displayed in Chrome.

Firefox, first released in 2004, is a free browser available across platforms that enables you to sync your bookmarks and settings across your computers automatically. It is a popular choice for those looking for an alternative to the browsers included with Windows, but Firefox retains a small percentage of the overall browser market. Opera is another alternative, but less popular, browser.

Safari is the most popular web browser for Macs. It comes bundled with Mac OS X. Figure 7.9 shows the National Science Foundation (NSF) website in Safari.

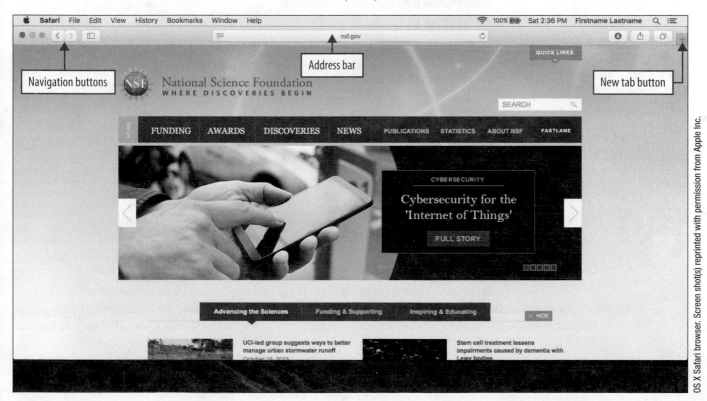

Navigation buttons · Address bar · New tab button

FIGURE 7.9 The NSF website in Safari.

Small-screen devices, such as tablets, e-readers, and smartphones, use ***mobile browsers***, which are sometimes called microbrowsers. Mobile browsers are optimized for small screens. All of the major desktop browsers also come in mobile versions. Other mobile browsers are proprietary—such as the Kindle and Android browsers. Most websites today can be accessed with a mobile browser, and many websites offer alternative pages that are optimized to be viewed with a mobile browser. Figure 7.10 shows the Library of Congress website displayed in the iPad version of Safari.

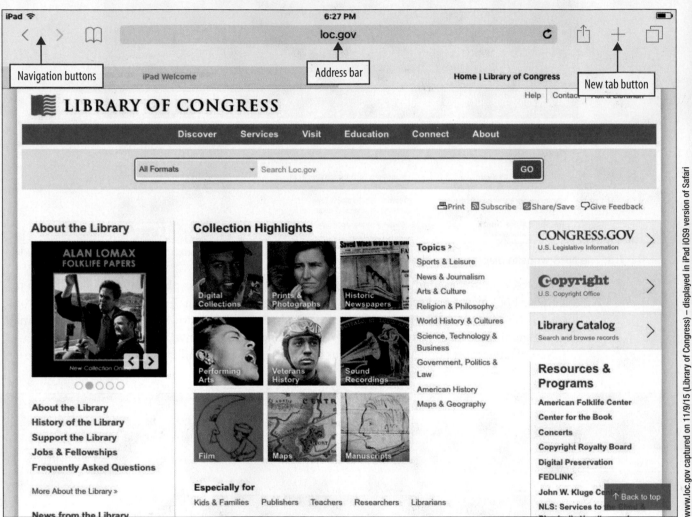

FIGURE 7.10 The iPad version of Safari is a mobile browser.

Concept 7.05 | Configuring a Web Browser

3.01a (ii)

The first time you open any browser, it will have default settings, such as the home page, search provider, default download folder, and default browser, but you can and should customize them for your own use. The location of these settings varies depending on your browser, and may be referred to as options, preferences, or settings.

The term ***home page*** has several meanings. It can mean the first page of a website or the webpage that displays when you first open your browser. The default home page for your browser is determined by your operating system, computer manufacturer, or ISP, but you can set any page you want as your home page. In fact, because most browsers support tabbed browsing, you can set multiple home pages. Chrome distinguishes between the home page—the page that displays when you click the Home button, by default this is **Google.com**—and Startup pages that display when you open Chrome. (Figure 7.11) shows Chrome configured to open two pages on startup. Think about the things that you do as soon as you open your browser. Do you check sports scores? Facebook? Web mail? Weather? Stock prices? Traffic? These are the things that will help you choose your home page(s).

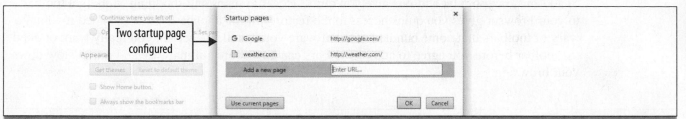

FIGURE 7.11 Google Chrome configured with two startup page tabs.

When you type a search term in the address bar or search box of your browser, what *search provider*—website that provides search capabilities on the web—is used? By default, the search provider will probably be either Microsoft Bing or Google, but as with your home page, you can modify this to your own favorite. In Chrome, the default search is Google, but you can easily change to another. Figure 7.12 shows the Search settings for Chrome, where you can change the default search engine.

FIGURE 7.12 You can easily modify the search engine in most browsers.

You can change the location of the default download folder—the folder where files you download from the Internet are saved. This is the logged-in user's Downloads folder in most browsers. You can also specify which browser should be set as your default browser—the browser that opens links you click from locations such as your desktop, email messages, and links in documents. Also configure the security and privacy settings, history settings, stored passwords, and how *cookies*—small text files placed on your computer by websites that you visit—are handled. A *pop-up blocker* prevents webpages from opening a new window. Pop-ups can be used for advertising, but also for other useful purposes, such as opening a quiz or external video from your classroom learning management system—LMS. You can configure a pop-up blocker to allow pop-ups from specific sites—such as your school or business—while blocking pop-ups for all other sites.

Concept 7.06 | Installing Add-Ons, Plug-Ins, and Toolbars

You can extend the functionality of your web browser by installing add-ons, plug-ins, extensions, and toolbars. The term *extension* is often used to refer to all of them. The distinction between the terms varies by browser. A *plug-in* is a third-party program, such as Adobe Reader.

An *add-on* is created for a specific browser to add features to it. Figure 7.13 shows the Chrome Extensions settings. The extensions installed in this example include Google Docs, Sheets, and Slides. Firefox is well known for having add-ons—there are hundreds of them available. Some popular add-ons allow you to capture video from the web and block ads. IE has a smaller number of add-ons, but popular add-ons give you quick access to maps and shopping. Adding a toolbar to your browser gives you quick access to the features of the application that installed it—but be wary of toolbars that come bundled with software you install. Be certain you really want or need the toolbar before you agree to add it. Toolbars can be a source of malware and might slow down your browsing.

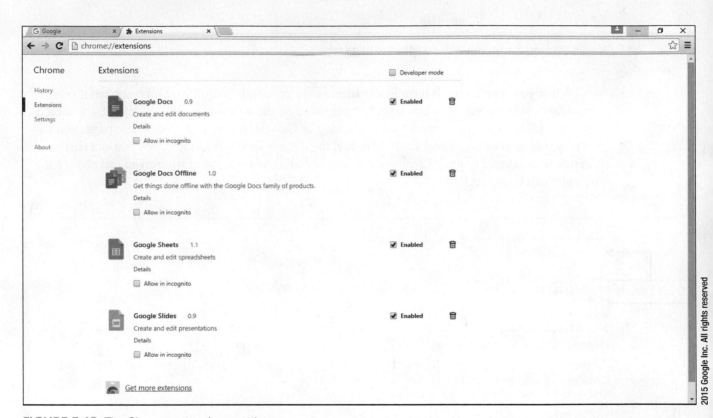

FIGURE 7.13 The Chrome extensions settings.

Plug-in software, such as Adobe Flash Player, Microsoft Silverlight, and Sun Java, helps your browser display the multimedia-rich, interactive, dynamic content that's increasingly common on the Internet. A web *widget* is a small program in a webpage that can be run by the person viewing the page: for example, a stock ticker or weather app. Widgets are *client-side programs*—in which the coding is within a webpage, downloaded to the client computer, and compiled and executed by a browser or plug-in. Many common plug-ins are becoming replaced with newer, safer options such as HTML5. You don't need a plug-in to view a static webpage of text, such as a Wikipedia page, but dynamic content, videos, games, and even flashy ads all rely on plug-ins. If your school uses an online learning management system or other tools, you might need to install specific plug-ins on your computer. You can quickly install plug-ins for free. Modern browsers may restrict some plug-ins from running, and you may find you can't access certain websites with your browser of choice. Chrome refers to plug-ins as Chrome apps.

As a Brand Manager, you must search the web for marketing information, to locate vendors and other clients to work with, and to reach out to customers. Navigating the web efficiently saves you time and frustration.

The amount of information available to you can be overwhelming. It is easy to get lost or sidetracked as you surf the web. How do you know where to start? How do you find what you are looking for? How can you avoid information overload and use the web effectively?

Concept 7.07 | Using Web Addresses

To visit a website, you can type in the address or **URL (uniform resource locator)** of the website you want to visit such as the one shown in Figure 7.14. A URL uniquely identifies a location on the Internet. The home page of a website is the main or starting page. It is the page you see when you type in the web address for a site.

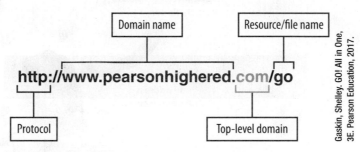

FIGURE 7.14 This is the URL for the GO! Series.

Looking at Figure 7.14, *http* indicates the protocol that tells your computer what type of page you are looking at. A **protocol** is a set of rules for communication between devices that determine how data is formatted, transmitted, received, and acknowledged. The most common protocol is **http**, which stands for **HyperText Transfer Protocol**—the set of communication rules used by your computer to connect to servers on the web. Other protocols are *https*, which is a secure webpage, or *ftp*, which stands for File Transfer Protocol. Because so many sites use the *http* protocol, you need not type it as part of the address in modern browsers.

Following the protocol is the **domain name**, which is sometimes called the second-level domain. In this example, www.pearsonhighered.com is the domain name. It is an organization's unique name on the Internet, which consists of a chosen name combined with a top-level domain such as *.com*, *.org*, or *.gov*. The *www* represents the computer on the *pearsonhighered* domain. It is common to name the computer *www*, so this part of the URL is also often omitted.

At the end of the domain name is the *.com* suffix, which is known as the **top-level domain (TLD)**. The TLD indicates the type of website you are visiting. Common TLDs are *.com* for commercial, *.edu* for U.S. educational, and *.gov* for U.S. government. Websites outside the United States often have a country code TLD, such as *.ca* for Canada or *.uk* for United Kingdom.

When you visit other pages on a website, the URL will have an additional part after the TLD, which may include the path—location—and name of the page. For example, in Figure 7.14, *go* is the name of a folder on the *pearsonhighered.com* website.

ICANN or **Internet Corporation for Assigned Names and Numbers** is the organization that coordinates the Internet naming system. Computers speak in numbers, so computers on the Internet are assigned numeric **IP addresses** or **Internet protocol addresses**. Like telephone numbers, these IP addresses must be unique.

IP addresses are composed of numbers, which can be hard for a person to remember, so the DNS system was developed. The **DNS (Domain Name System)** enables you to use a friendly name like **google.com** instead of an IP address like 173.194.43.2 to contact a website. DNS works like a telephone directory. When you enter a URL in your browser, your computer requests the IP address of the computer belonging to the URL. Your DNS server, which is probably provided by your ISP, locates the IP address information and sends it back to your computer, which then uses it to address your request (Figure 7.15).

FIGURE 7.15 A computer requests the IP address of a website from the DNS system.

Websites use navigation menus to guide you through the multiple pages of content. This is usually at the top or on the left side of the page. A *sitemap* is a page that displays all of the pages in a website in one place. When navigating through a website, you may notice at the top of each webpage, a list of links that you have followed through the structure of the website. This *breadcrumb trail* enables you to see the path you have taken and to quickly go back in that path by clicking the appropriate page name.

Objective 5	Compare Different Forms of Synchronous Online Communication

IT SIM
The Internet

Your job as a Brand Manager often requires you to participate in virtual meetings with marketing and advertising teams in other locations, or with sales reps who are on the road. These meetings take place in real time and allow you to work with people located all over the country.

Synchronous online communication refers to communication that happens in real time, with two or more people online at the same time. Face-to-face conversations or telephone calls are examples of synchronous communication. Online synchronous communication tools enable you to communicate in real time on the web.

Concept 7.08 | Using Chat and IM

Online *chat* enables you to talk to multiple people at the same time. *Instant messaging* or *IM* is real-time communication between two or more participants over the Internet. The terms *chat* and *IM* are often used interchangeably.

Social media sites such as Facebook and Google also enable you to chat with others. With Google *Hangouts*—a private space where you can post status updates, chat, or initiate a video call using your Google account—you can easily create a group video chat for collaboration. You can start a Hangout by inviting people in your circles. It is useful for holding a study group or for getting family members together to talk. There are mobile versions of these tools, so you can start a chat while you are in front of your computer and then continue the conversation from your smartphone or tablet when you are not. Many organizations find IM and chat to be useful tools for holding meetings and providing customer support.

Concept 7.09 | Making Calls with Voice over IP

VoIP or *Voice over Internet Protocol* enables calls to be transmitted over the Internet instead of over traditional telephone lines or cellular towers. If you have broadband Internet access, your ISP may also offer VoIP telephone service to replace your traditional landline telephone. A service like *Skype*—a software application that you can download to create an account to make voice calls over the Internet as well as participate in web conferencing from any location in the world— enables you to place calls to other Skype users for free or to regular telephones for a small fee. By using Skype to talk to friends and family in other countries, you can save a lot of money as compared to traditional telephone calls. Apple's *FaceTime*, which is built into OS X and iOS, enables you to make video calls to other FaceTime users. Using VoIP enables you to make calls from your computer or mobile device anywhere you have Internet access, even if you do not have telephone service. If your device has a camera, you can conduct a video chat (Figure 7.16).

FIGURE 7.16 Using VoIP to conduct a meeting with colleagues in another location.

Millions of Americans telecommute at least part of the time. There are arguments for and against telecommuting, but it definitely has a positive effect on the environment, because it saves gas and decreases the number of cars on the road. It also saves you money by not having to buy gas!

Not every job lends itself to telecommuting, but according to one site created to provide resources to telecommuters, businesses, and individuals, if just 50 percent of the people who could work from home did so just half of the time, the United States would:

- Save over $650 billion a year
- Reduce greenhouse gases by the equivalent of taking 9 million cars off the road
- Reduce oil imports by 37 percent

Businesses that encourage telecommuting can also save on real estate expenses. Fewer employees onsite means smaller office space requirements and lower utility bills. Sun Microsystems has a large telecommuting program that saves over 5,000 kilowatt hours per year for each person who works from home just two days a week.

Objective 6 | Compare Different Forms of Asynchronous Online Communication

As a Brand Manager, you rely on email to communicate with your team members and vendors. Email is an indispensable business tool. *Asynchronous communication* such as email does not require the participants to be online at the same time. Like leaving a voicemail or sending a letter, asynchronous online communication technology lets you send a message that the receiver can access later.

Concept 7.10 | Reading and Sending Email

3.03a (i)
3.03a (ii)
3.03b (i)
3.03b (ii)
3.03b (iii)
3.03b (v)
3.03b (vi)
3.03c (i)
3.03c (ii)
3.03c (iii)
3.03c (iv)
3.03d (i)
3.03e (i)
3.06a (i)

The Internet was originally built for the purpose of communicating and sharing. One of the first applications of the Internet was email, which quickly became the most widely used Internet application. Using email to communicate has become an essential business skill.

Email is a method of exchanging messages via the Internet in which the message resides in the recipient's mailbox until he or she signs in to read it. Email uses *store-and-forward technology*: an email server holds your messages until you request them, and so someone can send you an email message even if you are not online at the time. There are two ways to access email: using an email client on your computer or tablet, smartphone, or some other device, or by reading it online through a webmail interface. When you use an email client, such as Outlook or Mail, the email server sends a copy of the message to you. This makes it available to read offline, after you disconnect from the Internet. If you configure your client to leave a copy of the message on the email server, then you will still be able to access the messages from a webmail interface. The advantage to using a webmail interface, such as the Gmail or Yahoo! Mail website, is that your email is available to you from anywhere whenever you are online; for example, at home, at school, on vacation, or at work.

Whether you use an email client or webmail interface, you can configure it to filter out spam or junk mail, create folders and filters to sort and save messages, and archive old messages in case you should ever need to retrieve them. When you delete an email message, most email clients will move the message to a trash or deleted folder, where you can retrieve it or empty the trash to permanently delete it.

When you need to send an email attachment—a file such as a Word document or picture—make sure the file size does not exceed the email system's limitations. Each email provider sets this limit, but typically files larger than a few megabytes should be shared using online or network drive space, rather than sent as an email attachment.

Email clients or webmail systems enable you to maintain a list of your contacts, sometimes called an address book, which can be used to send email without having to type out email addresses. You can create distribution lists of groups—such as a team of coworkers, family members, or classmates, and you can create email filters to forward, delete, label, or file messages using contact information, determining how the messages are handled when they are received.

Email is not secure. As it travels from your computer over the Internet, an email message can be read by hackers along the way. Copies of the message exist on the servers and routers the message crosses on its journey, and those copies can be retrieved long after you have deleted the message from your Inbox. Your email provider might scan your messages to deliver you targeted advertising, and your employer or school network administrator might also read your email. A good analogy is to think of email as a postcard that can be read by anyone who handles it, not as a letter in a sealed envelope.

Your ISP may provide you with one or more email accounts. Your employer or college may provide you with another. There are also many places where you can sign up for a free email account, such as Yahoo!, Google, and **Outlook.com**. The advantage to using an email account not tied to your ISP is that, should you change your ISP, you will not lose your email account in the process. Figure 7.17 shows the process to create a free Gmail account.

When creating a new account, you might be required to use a *CAPTCHA (Completely Automated Public Turing Test to Tell Computers and Humans Apart)*—a series of letters and numbers that are distorted in some way. This makes them difficult for automated software to read but relatively easy for humans to read.

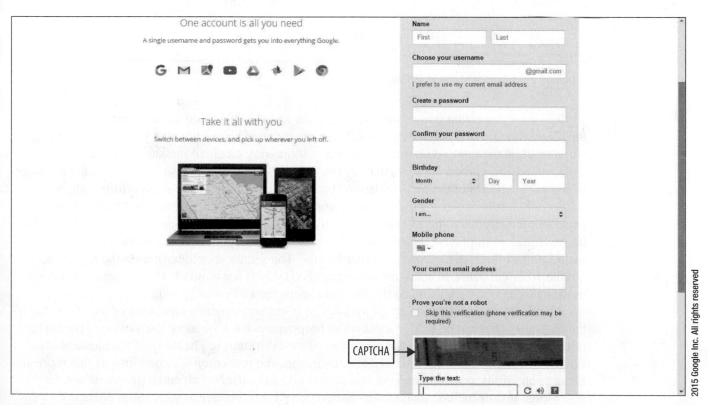

FIGURE 7.17 Creating a free Gmail account.

To access your new Google account, log in to the Google website and click the Mail link. New email messages are in your Inbox. You can read a message by double-clicking it. An email message has some distinct parts that you should be familiar with. Figure 7.18 labels some of the important parts of a new email message that has not yet been sent.

FIGURE 7.18 Composing an email message in Gmail.

The most important part of the message is the address. If you do not address it correctly, the message will not reach its recipient. There are three address fields that you can use: *To*, *Cc*, and *Bcc*. *To* is the field you normally use when addressing an email message to someone. *Cc*, which stands for carbon copy or courtesy copy, is the field you use to send a copy of the message to someone who is not the main addressee but who needs to know about the information or conversation. It is like an FYI (*for your information*), and generally means that a reply is not expected. Functionally, there is no real difference in the way the message is sent or received. *Bcc*, however, has an important difference. Did you ever have an email message forwarded to you that includes the addresses of dozens of other people? The sender should have used the *Bcc* field, not the *To* or *Cc* fields, to send that message. The *B* stands for blind. When you send an email message to several people, using the *Bcc* field keeps the addresses private.

Use the **Subject line** of an email message to give the recipient a clear idea of the content of the message. This can be read in most email programs without opening the message. The body of the message should contain the remainder of the information. The body of the message in Figure 7.18 includes some formatted text, an image, and two **emoji**s—small images that represent facial expressions, common objects, and people and animals. Not all email programs will let you format text or include images, and not everybody will be able to view those elements. You must use an email program that is configured to read HTML email messages in order for those elements to be visible. An email program that is configured to view only text email messages will only see the text in this message.

A **signature line** is a block of text that can be included automatically at the end of the messages that you compose. It can be a very simple message that just includes your name, but in business, it will usually contain more contact information and perhaps a privacy statement of some type. You need to create the signature and activate it in order for it to appear in your email messages.

When you receive an email message, you have the ability to reply to the message or forward it (Figure 7.19). When you choose **Reply**, your response is sent back to the original sender. If you choose **Reply All**—or *Reply to All*, depending on the email program—the response is sent to all the addressees of the original message and the original sender. Think carefully before you use this option. Do you really want everyone to receive your reply? The subject line for a Reply will include Re: before the original subject. If you want to send the message to someone else, you would use the **Forward** option, which enables you to select new addresses and will put Fw: before the subject.

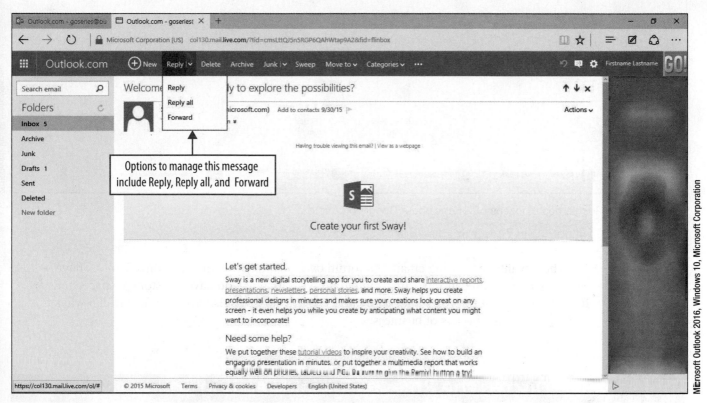

FIGURE 7.19 There are a number of ways you can pass on an email message you have received.

Concept 7.11 | Using Forums and Discussion Boards

Forums, also known as discussion boards or message boards, were one of the first forms of social media. They are conversations much like chat but are not in real time. There are forums for people with common interests, such as sports, pets, travel, or video games. Many technology and product websites include forums, which may be used as a technical support system. Some websites refer to a forum as a *community*.

Participants post comments and questions, usually about a particular topic or problem, and other participants respond. Each conversation is called a **thread**, and the responses are posts. Forums are a great place to get help with problems, ask for advice, or communicate with others with similar interests. Threads can be searched and read long after the initial conversation has ended. Most forums are moderated—comments must be approved by the moderator before they are posted to the group—and require you to create an account before you are allowed to post. Figure 7.20 shows the home page of Google Product Forums, which includes forums for many Google products.

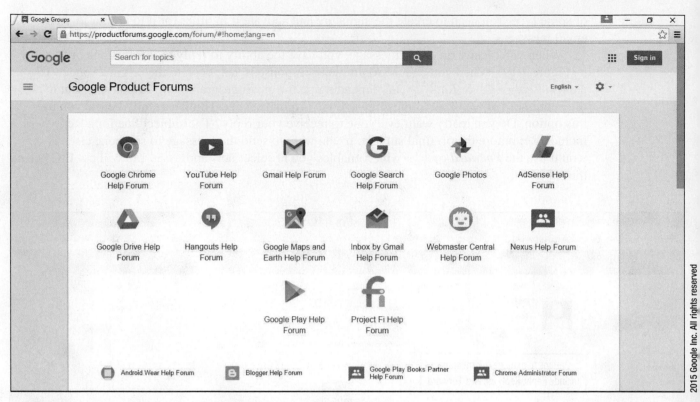

FIGURE 7.20 Google hosts dozens of forums about Google products.

The advantage to using email or a forum over chat or IM is that the conversations have a longer lifespan. You can save emails indefinitely so long as you have the storage space, and forums can persist for years after a thread is started. These tools have become critical ways to communicate in all types of businesses.

Objective 7 | Discuss the Roles of Social Media in Today's Society

Tech to GO!
Microblogging
with Twitter

As a Brand Manager, you use social media to connect with hotel guests and to market the Oro Jade brand. Social media marketing is a vital part of Oro Jade's overall marketing plan. It is important for Oro Jade to create connections with its guests to keep them coming back. Offering incentives and posting updates and photos keeps the brand in the guests' minds long after they have checked out of the hotel.

Forums and email are old technologies, having been around almost as long as the Internet itself. Recently, newer technologies have emerged. In the first few years of the web most people were consumers of information, but now much of the content on the web is user generated. The tools that allow users to create content are sometimes called *Web 2.0 tools* and have changed the way people communicate and collaborate on the web. What is important, interesting, or relevant is no longer decided by a few people sitting around a table but by the crowd of participants. Collectively, these tools—which enable you to create content, connect, network, and share—are called *social media*. *User-generated content*—content that has been written by everyday users—includes the videos and photos you take and post online, and it also includes what you write and say. Every award season, major sporting event, election, and breaking news story sets the social media world abuzz.

Concept 7.12 | Using Social Network Sites

Social networks such as Facebook and LinkedIn are online communities that combine many of the features of the other online tools. Social networks enable you to chat in real time and to post messages for all to see or to send a personal message similar to an email. There are hundreds of social networking sites. Some focus on business, and others are language-specific or location-specific. Social networking enables you to keep in touch with old friends and make new ones.

The Whole Earth 'Lectronic Link, or The WELL, is an online community that launched in 1985. The first social network sites began in the late 1990s; now there are hundreds of social networking sites. Currently, the largest site is ***Facebook***. Facebook was launched in 2004 for Harvard students and in 2006 for everyone else. On Facebook, you can create a profile that includes some personal information, pictures, and interests, and then you can connect with other Facebook users or friends (Figure 7.21). You can also join groups within the network that interest you. For some people, the most important part of using a social network is the number of "friends" they have, but for others, it is a way to stay in touch with people. Many companies use Facebook to connect with customers and to offer special discounts and other perks for those that click the *Like* button associated with the company. Neo is a popular, internal social network used by schools and businesses. Internal social networks provide a common location to store information, discuss ideas, collaborate, and share insights.

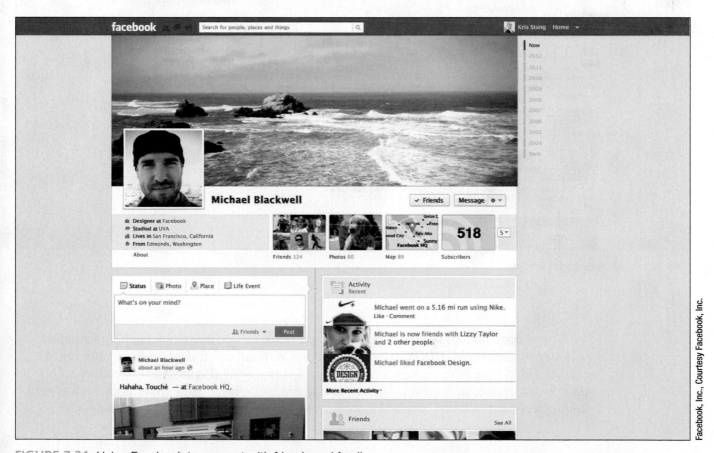

FIGURE 7.21 Using Facebook to connect with friends and family.

If you have friends who tag you in their photos, even if your profile is private, you may be sharing more than you want to. Be sure to use the security and privacy settings to keep your private life private, and consider creating a second public profile on a professional social network. Many employers will expect you to be technically literate and to use social networking tools, so not having a professional online presence could be a disadvantage.

LinkedIn is a professional social networking site where you can find past and present colleagues and classmates, connect with appropriate people when seeking a new job or business opportunity, or get answers from industry experts. Figure 7.22 shows a LinkedIn profile. There are no games or silly applications, no place to post photos except on the standard profile image, and there is no chat. People to whom you are linked are referred to as connections rather than friends. LinkedIn—or other business social networks that relate to your field of interest—should be part of your personal brand.

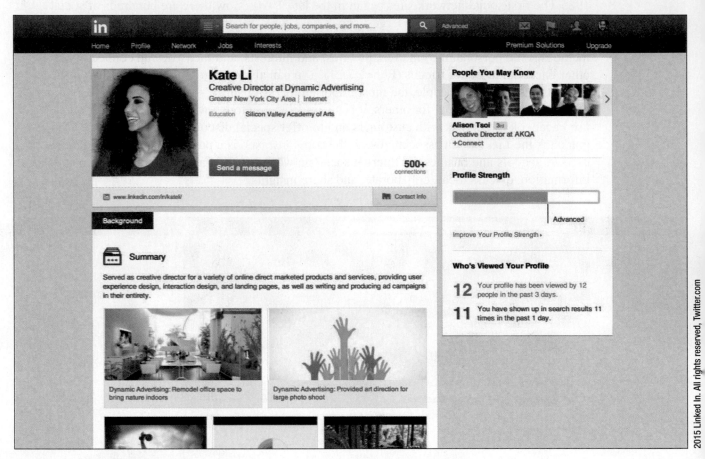

FIGURE 7.22 A LinkedIn Profile.

Concept 7.13 | Exploring Virtual Worlds

Virtual communities such as Second Life and Webkinz, and **massively multiplayer online role-playing games (MMORPG)**, such as World of Warcraft and Elder Scrolls, enable you to interact with people in real time using an **avatar**—virtual body (Figure 7.23). Some schools teach virtual classes in Second Life. Second Life and multiplayer games have fairly high system requirements and require newer and more powerful computers than the average computer.

FIGURE 7.23 Interacting with others using an avatar.

IC3
DIGITAL LITERACY
CERTIFICATION
3.05a (ii)
3.08a (i)
3.08a (ii)
3.08a (iii)

Concept 7.14 | Sharing with Social Video, Image, and Music Sites

Social media sharing sites, such as YouTube, Flickr, and Last.fm, enable anyone to create and share media. These sites are outside social networks like Facebook, although you can often share content across networks. One of the key features of these sites is the ability to tag items. *Tagging* makes sharing a very social experience, because users begin to tag not just their own creations, but also the creations of others. *Streaming media* means accessing video or audio clips almost immediately after you click a video link on a webpage without waiting for the entire file to download. Live streaming events, such as sports or debates can enable people from multiple locations to participate in the event. Live streams can be public or made private to restrict access.

YouTube is the largest online video hosting site in the world. It is also social in the sense that you can subscribe to other users' channels, send messages, and recommend videos. A *viral video* is one that becomes extremely popular because of recommendations and social sharing. Figure 7.24 shows a viral video from YouTube. Once something has gone viral, there is no way to remove it from the Internet. There are other video sharing sites, including CollegeHumor, Vimeo, TeacherTube, and even Facebook and Flickr. Sites like Hulu do not host user-created content, but they are still social because they keep track of the popularity of videos and enable users to review and discuss the videos. Sites such as UStream enable users to stream live content, and many traditional media companies stream live content over the web.

FIGURE 7.24 A viral video may have millions of views.

Flickr is the largest image-sharing site (Figure 7.25). With a free account, you can post up to 1 terabyte of images—that's more than 500,000 images. You can mark your pictures as private or make them public. You can adjust the copyright to allow others to use your images legally, and tag them so that people can search for things that interest them. Other popular photo-sharing sites include Facebook and Google Photos. Instagram and other mobile apps allow you to take and edit photos on your mobile device and upload them to the web automatically. You can also comment on and share images that you like and add location information to your images.

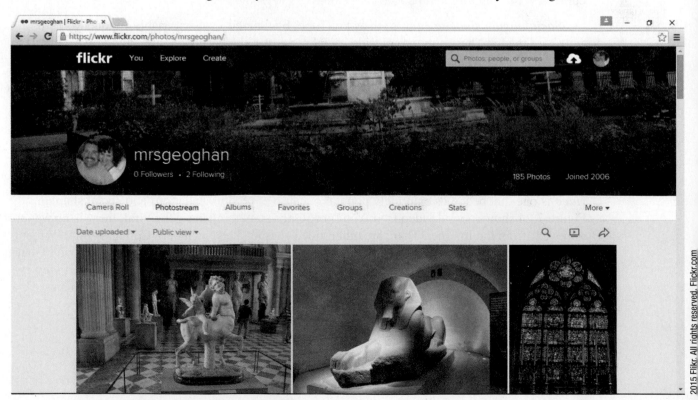

FIGURE 7.25 Using Flickr to share photos.

What is more social than music? There are lots of places on the web to find music, but if you want a social experience, you can create an account on a site such as Pandora. These sites recommend music to you based on what you listen to and what your friends are listening to. You can add tags and comments and mark tracks you like, which will help you get recommendations. The more you listen to and mark tracks, the more recommendations you will get. Apple Music and Google Play are two of the largest music sites. There are also apps such as Spotify for music and Audible for audio books.

If you like to make and share your own music, you can use a website like SoundCloud. Using a browser or mobile app, you can upload sound files that you have created and share them with the community. Users can follow their favorites, comment, and share new finds. Artists can communicate directly with their fans, and musicians can collaborate with each other, even if they are many miles apart.

FAST FORWARD | Detecting Illegal Copies of Videos

NEC Japan released an identification technology capable of detecting, in a matter of seconds, copies of videos illegally uploaded to the Internet. The problem of video copyright infringement has traditionally been addressed by manual inspection. However, with the ever-growing quantity of pirated movies and TV programs, manual detection is impossible. According to NEC, its new technology has a detection rate of 96 percent and an error rate of 5 in 1 million. The technology uses a video's fingerprint or signature generated from each frame of the video based on the difference in luminescence between sub-regions on that frame. The signature of the suspected video is compared to the original, and an unauthorized duplicate is identified.

Concept 7.15 | Blogging and Microblogging

A **blog (weblog)** is an online journal that anyone can set up using simple blog tools and write about whatever they like. Vlogs, or video blogs, are video journals. Blogs are a running commentary—with posts coming frequently (or not so frequently). The difference between just creating a webpage and writing a blog is that a blog can be interactive—your readers can post comments about your blog posts.

There are many prolific bloggers, and some even earn a living by blogging. Some organizations have multi-author blogs, in which multiple authors blog at a common site, rather than have each blogger use his or her own address. Many bloggers link to other related blogs. There are millions of blogs in the **blogosphere**—all the blogs on the web and the connections among them. Two of the most popular blog sites are WordPress (Figure 7.26) and Blogger. Both of these sites allow you to create an account and blog for free.

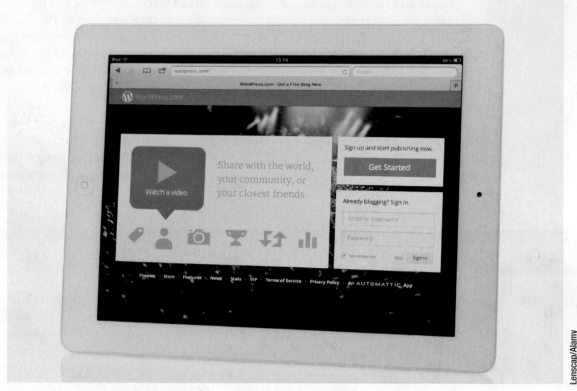

FIGURE 7.26 WordPress enables you to create a blog for free.

Microblogging sites like ***Twitter*** and ***Tumblr*** are a more social form of blogging where posts are typically limited to a relatively small number of characters and users post updates frequently. Posts can be public or restricted to a group of users; sent from computers, mobile apps, and text messages; and received the same ways.

Twitter posts are called ***Tweets*** and are limited to 140 characters (Figure 7.27). Instead of friends, Twitter users have followers. You can link your Twitter account to your Facebook account, so that your Tweets will also appear in your Facebook feed. Unlike most social networks, you do not have to ask for permission to follow someone on Twitter or Tumblr, although they can block you. Twitter describes itself with the words *Twitter is your window to the world*. Here you can post photos, text, links, videos, and music. You can link your Tumblr account to your Twitter account, so that your posts appear on both sites.

Hashtag

Tweet text

Tweet actions

FIGURE 7.27 Tweets contain up to 140 characters, hashtags, and images.

Concept 7.16 | Podcasting and RSS

A *podcast* is a digital media file of a prerecorded radio- or TV-like show that's distributed over the web to be downloaded and played on a computer or portable media player. Podcasts allow both time shifting (listening on your own schedule) and location shifting (taking it with you).

You can find and play podcasts by using a *podcast client* or media player program, such as iTunes, and download single episodes or subscribe to a podcast that's part of a series. There are hundreds of thousands of podcasts available. A few places to search for podcasts are YouTube, iTunes, **podcasts.com**, and **stitcher.com**. Many U.S. government agencies, such as the National Oceanic and Atmospheric Administration (NOAA), produce regular podcasts that you can listen to using a podcast client or directly from their websites, using your browser (Figure 7.28).

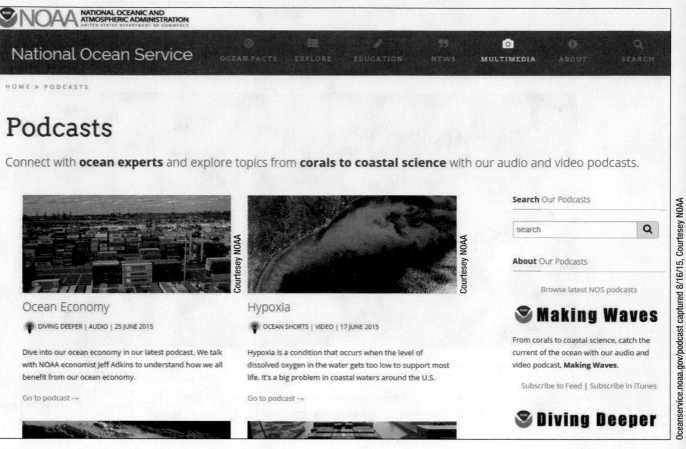

FIGURE 7.28 National Ocean Service Podcasts

How do you keep up with all your favorite websites, blogs, and podcasts? *RSS* or *Really Simple Syndication* is a format used for distributing web feeds that change frequently. RSS saves you time by sending you the updates on the sites you subscribe to. Subscribing to the RSS feeds of your favorite blogs, podcasts, and other websites will bring the information directly to you. You need a feed reader or aggregator, such as Flipboard or Feedly. To add a subscription, you usually click the orange RSS icon at the top of the page.

An interesting aspect of the social uses of the web is the idea of the wisdom of the crowd, or *crowdsourcing*—the idea of trusting the collective opinion of a crowd of people rather than that of an expert. Sites such as Digg, reddit, and Slashdot enable you to share content and webpages you find interesting. *Wikis* are websites that enable users to edit content, even if it was written by someone else. Review sites such as Yelp and TripAdvisor give you a voice and a place to get advice and recommendations from other people.

A social way to get investors for your start-up project or to fund social and charitable projects is *crowdfunding*, which raises money from multiple small investors rather than a few large investors. It also replaces the need to take out a traditional loan. On websites such as **gofundme.com**, **kickstarter.com**, and **indiegogo.com**, you can set up campaigns to seek out investors for your project. Or, you can search for interesting projects to support. Often, the investors receive something in return, such as early access to a game or movie, a discounted price for a product, or a t-shirt.

3.05c

Concept 7.17 | Using Wikis

A wiki differs from a blog or a podcast because its purpose is collaboration—not only posting responses to another post, but actually editing the content. The most well-known wiki is *Wikipedia*, which is a massive free encyclopedia that is written by anyone. How can you trust something that anyone can edit? Well, that is part of the design. The concept is that if many people are involved in a wiki, then the person who knows the right information will eventually be the one to write or edit it. In less than 15 years, Wikipedia grew to over 5 million articles in English alone. Wikipedia is a great place to start looking for information, but is generally frowned upon for use as a source in academic research.

Wikipedia is the most well-known wiki, but it is not the only one. Wikis abound and are often used as a way for a community to develop instructions. For example, wikiHow (Figure 7.29) is a website that contains how-to wikis on thousands of topics. You can read, write, or edit an existing wikiHow article or request that someone else write one if you cannot find what you are looking for.

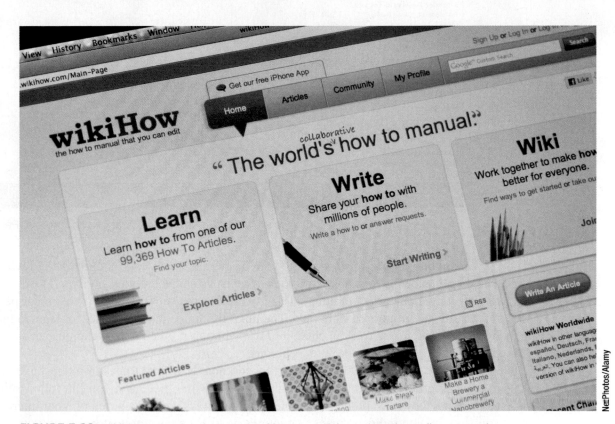

FIGURE 7.29 wikiHow contains thousands of how-to articles written by ordinary people.

Concept 7.18 | Sharing with Social Review, Bookmarking, and News Sites

Social review sites such as TripAdvisor and epinions enable you to read and write reviews of hotels, movies, games, books, and other products and services. Yelp enables you to review local businesses and places with a physical address such as parks. Figure 7.30 shows a Yelp map of Times Square restaurants on the iPad app. The reviews can help you decide where to eat. You can use the Yelp mobile app on a mobile device, so you get the information you need at the time you are in the location.

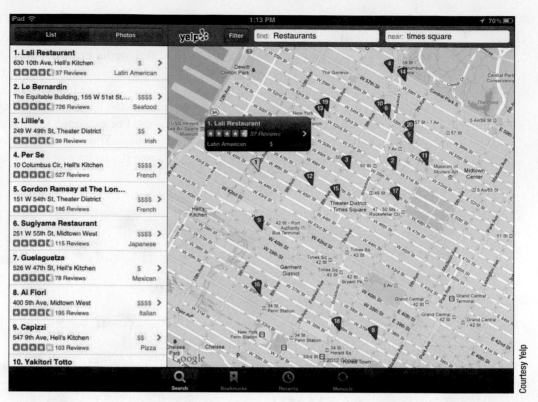

FIGURE 7.30 Searching for a place to eat in Times Square is easy using the Yelp iPad app.

Social bookmarking sites enable you to save and share your bookmarks or favorites online. The **delicious.com** site enables you to not only save and share your bookmarks online, but also to search the bookmarks of others. It is a great way to quickly find out what other people find interesting and important right now. The links are organized into topics, or tags, to make it easier for you to find links. You can click the *Follow* button if you have a Delicious account, but you don't need an account to browse Delicious.

Pinterest enables you to create virtual corkboards around topics of interest and pin webpages to them (Figure 7.31). You can share your boards with others, and you can follow other people to see what they have pinned. StumbleUpon discovers websites based on your interests. When you sign up, you indicate topics that interest you. Then, as you visit websites, you can click the *StumbleUpon* button to be taken to a similar site. You can click *I like this* to improve the selection of pages you stumble onto.

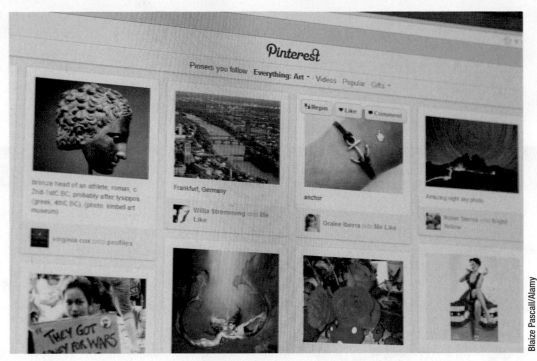

FIGURE 7.31 Pinterest is a place to pin and organize your favorite online content.

Social news sites are different from traditional mass media news sites in that at least some of the content is submitted by users. Social news is interactive in a way that traditional media isn't. It's like having millions of friends sharing their finds with you. Content that's submitted more frequently or gets the most votes is promoted to the front page.

Three of the most popular social news sites are reddit, Digg, and Slashdot. Digg doesn't publish content but allows the community to submit content they discover on the web and puts it in one place for everyone to see and to discuss. reddit (Figure 7.32) allows community members to submit content and to vote that content up or down, as well as discuss it. reddit is organized into categories called subreddits. Celebrities often participate in AMA—ask me anything—interviews on reddit. Slashdot, which focuses primarily on technology topics, produces some content but also accepts submissions from its readers. Whatever your interests, there is probably a social news site for you.

FIGURE 7.32 reddit

Relying on the wisdom of the crowd is much like asking your friends, family, and coworkers for advice. Did you enjoy the movie? What shop serves the best ice cream? How do you change the oil in your car? Everybody is an expert in something, and the web makes it easier for you to find and share that expertise. You should, however, use caution, because like anything else you read on the web, you must be critical in your evaluation of the credibility and reliability of its author.

ETHICS | Artificial Promotion on Social Sites

Some people create multiple accounts on social bookmarking and news sites so that they can promote their own content. For example, a blogger might create several accounts on Digg and use each one to Digg a blog post, artificially raising its popularity on Digg and driving more traffic to it. This violates the Digg terms of use. But what if the blogger had all his or her friends and family members create accounts and Digg his or her post? Is that ethical? Does it violate the terms of use? Is it fair to other bloggers?

ON THE JOB | Marketing Assistant

A Marketing Assistant in the field of entertainment needs both marketing skills and technology skills. Because companies are striving to understand their customers and respond to customer needs quickly, you also need Internet skills and social networking skills. Review the list of technology skills recently posted for a position of Marketing Assistant. Are you surprised at the level of technology required? Do you already possess any of these skills? Individuals in this type of position often travel, so knowledge of portable devices, backup procedures, and network attached storage (NAS) or Internet storage is critical in order to maintain communication with team members and guarantee the availability of data. Try to gain as much experience in these areas as possible.

Technology skills recently posted for a Marketing Assistant position include:
- Developing media packs and organizing conferences and trade shows
- Serving as liaison between advertising agencies and the company, print suppliers, freelance talent, and various marketing services
- Preparing press releases, company newsletters, and event announcements
- Updating company headlines and news in the corporate website
- Assisting in promotional strategies

GO! To Work

Andrew Rodriguez / Fotolia; FotolEdhar / Fotolia; apops / Fotolia; Yuri Arcurs / Fotolia

IC3 SKILLS IN THIS CHAPTER

IC3 — Module 3 Living Online

Section 3.01 Internet (Navigation)
- (a) Understand what the Internet is
    - (i) Understand how the Internet works
    - (ii) Understand browser functionality

Section 3.03 Email clients
- (a) Identify email applications
    - (i) Desktop application platform [ie. Outlook]
    - (ii) Web-based platform [Gmail, Yahoo!]
- (b) Understand email etiquette
    - (i) Reply vs. reply all, forward
    - (ii) Cc vs. Bcc
    - (iii) Signature
    - (v) SPAM
    - (vi) Junk mail
- (c) Understand email history and management
    - (i) Spam / junk email
    - (ii) Archiving
    - (iii) Trash
    - (iv) Folders
- (d) Understand email attachments
    - (i) Size limits
- (e) Understand contact management
    - (i) Address books

Section 3.05 Social Media
- (a) Understand what a digital identity is (identity on social media)

- (i) Know what social networks are and how they are used [FB, LinkedIn, etc.]
    - (ii) Know other types of networks [YouTube, Instagram, etc.]
- (b) Recognize the differences of internal (school/business) vs. open media sites
    - (i) Neo vs. Facebook
- (c) Know what blogs, wikis, and forums are and how they are used

Section 3.06 Communications
- (a) Know the best tool for the various situations and scenarios
    - (i) Email
    - (iii) Instant message
    - (iv) VoIP
- (c) Know how to use chat platforms

Section 3.07 Online Conferencing
- (a) Understand and identify online conference offerings
    - (i) VoIP conferencing [Skype]
    - (ii) Video conferencing [Google hangouts, Skype, FaceTime]

Section 3.08 Streaming
- (a) Understand what streaming is and how it works with devices
    - (i) Video streaming
    - (ii) Live streaming
    - (iii) Audio streaming

GO! FOR JOB SUCCESS

Discussion: What is Plagiarism?

Your instructor may assign these questions to your class, and then ask you to think about them or discuss with your classmates:

The Council of Writing Program Administrators (2013) defines plagiarism as: *In instructional settings, plagiarism occurs when a writer deliberately uses someone else's language, idea, or other original (not common-knowledge) material without acknowledging its source.*

FotolEdhar / Fotolia

Why is it important to acknowledge someone else's work in your own work?

What are some reasons students may plagiarize?

What are some ways to avoid plagiarism in your own work?

END OF CHAPTER

SUMMARY

The Internet is a network of computer networks. The World Wide Web is the hypertext system of information on the Internet. Hypertext enables you to navigate among the linked objects by using hyperlinks.

A website consists of one or more webpages located in the same place. Basic webpages are written in HTML. CSS documents define the way the HTML elements are formatted. Browsers interpret HTML to display webpages.

The URL—uniform resource locator—is the web address and includes a protocol, domain name, and TLD. Common TLDs—top-level domains—include .com, .net, .org, gov, .edu, and country codes such as .ca (Canada).

Synchronous communication such as chat, IM, and VoIP happens in real time. Asynchronous communication does not require the participants to be online at the same time. Social media enables you to create and share content.

GO! LEARN IT ONLINE

Review the concepts, key terms, and IC3 skills in this chapter by completing these online challenges, which you can find at MyITLab.

Matching and Multiple Choice: Answer matching and multiple choice questions to test what you learned in this chapter.

Lessons on the GO!: Learn how to use all the new apps and features as they are introduced by Microsoft.

IC3 Prep Quiz: Answer questions to review the IC3 skills that you practiced in this chapter.

GLOSSARY

GLOSSARY OF CHAPTER KEY TERMS

Add-on A browser extension created for a specific browser to add features to it.

Address bar The area, at the top of the browser window, in which you can type a URL to visit a website.

ARPANET A U.S. Department of Defense ARPA project that later became the Internet. A communications system designed to have multiple pathways through which information could travel so that losing one part of the system—for example, in a nuclear strike—would not cripple the whole system.

Asynchronous communication Communication that does not require the participants to be online at the same time.

Avatar A virtual body used to interact with others in virtual worlds and games.

Bandwidth The speed or data transfer rate of a network.

Bit (binary digit) The smallest unit of digital data.

Blog (weblog) An online journal.

Blogosphere All the blogs on the web and the connections among them.

Bookmarks The term used to describe saved links to commonly visited webpages that allow for efficient web browsing.

Breadcrumb trail A list of links that you have followed through the structure of the website, which enables you to see the path you have taken and to quickly go back in that path by clicking the appropriate page name.

Broadband Internet access that exceeds 10 Mbps as defined by the FCC.

Byte Consists of 8 bits and is used to represent a single character in modern computer systems.

Cable Internet access A broadband Internet service offered by a cable TV provider that uses the same wires to carry both TV and Internet signals.

CAPTCHA (Completely Automated Public Turing Test to Tell Computers and Humans Apart) A series of letters and numbers that are distorted in some way.

Chat A synchronous form of online communication among multiple people at the same time in a chat room.

Chrome A free web browser application developed by Google.

Client-side program A program in which the coding is within a webpage, downloaded to the client computer, and compiled and executed by a browser or plug-in.

Cookie A small text file placed on your computer when you visit a website that is used to identify you when you return.

Crowdfunding Project funding from multiple small investors rather than few large investors.

Crowdsourcing Trusting collective opinion of a crowd of people—referred to as *the wisdom of the crowd*—rather than that of an expert.

DNS (Domain Name System) The directory system on the Internet that allows you to use a friendly name like **google.com** instead of an IP address like 173.194.43.2 to contact a website.

Domain name An organization's unique name on the Internet, which consists of a chosen name combined with a top-level domain such as **.com**, **.org**, or **.gov**.

DSL (digital subscriber line) Telephone lines designed to carry digital signals and therefore are much faster than ordinary telephone lines; a broadband Internet service.

Email A method of exchanging messages via the Internet in which the message resides in the recipient's mailbox until he or she signs in to read it.

Emoji A small image that represents facial expressions, common objects, and people and animals.

Extension Software that extends the functionality of a web browser.

Facebook The largest social network site on the web.

FaceTime An application built into OS X and iOS that enables you to make video calls to other FaceTime users.

Fiber-to-the-home (FTTH) A broadband Internet service that carries signals on fiber-optic cable and is the fastest type of broadband Internet connection.

Flickr The largest image-sharing site on the web.

Forward An email response used to send an email message to someone else.

Forum A conversation much like chat but not in real time. Also known as a discussion board or message board.

Hangouts A hangout is a private space where contacts can post status updates, chat, or initiate a video call using their Google accounts.

Home page On your own computer, the webpage you have selected—or that is set by default—to display on your computer when you start your browser. When visiting a website, the starting point for the remainder of the pages on that site.

HTML (Hypertext Markup Language) The authoring language that defines the structure of a webpage.

http The protocol prefix for HyperText Transfer Protocol.

HyperText Transfer Protocol The set of communication rules used by your computer to connect to servers on the Web.

Hyperlinks Links that connect pieces of information on the Internet.

Hypertext Text that contains links to other text and allows you to navigate through pieces of information by using the links, known as hyperlinks, that connect them.

ICANN (Internet Corporation for Assigned Names and Numbers) The organization that coordinates the Internet naming system.

Instant messaging (IM) The real-time communication between two or more participants over the Internet.

Internet A global network of computer networks.

Internet backbone The high-speed connection points between networks that make up the Internet.

Internet service providers (ISPs) Companies that offer Internet access.

Intranet A private network that runs on web technologies.

IP (Internet protocol) address A unique numeric address assigned to each node on a network.

LinkedIn A professional social networking site where you can find past and present colleagues and classmates, connect with appropriate people when seeking a new job or business opportunity, or get answers from industry experts.

Massively multiplayer online role-playing games (MMORPG) An online game that allows you to interact with people in real time using an avatar—a virtual body.

Microblogging A social form of blogging in which posts are typically limited to a relatively small number of characters and users post updates frequently.

Microsoft Edge The default web browser included with Windows 10.

Mobile browser A web browser used on small-screen devices, such as tablets, e-readers, and smartphones.

Mobile Internet access A broadband Internet service that uses cellular 3G (third generation) and 4G (fourth generation) network standards. The signals are transmitted by a series of cellular towers.

Municipal Wi-Fi Free wireless Internet service offered in some cities and towns.

Plug-in A third-party browser extension, such as Adobe Reader.

Podcast A digital media file of a prerecorded radio- or TV-like show that is distributed over the web to be downloaded and listened to or watched on a computer or portable media player.

Podcast client A Program used to search for and play podcasts.

Pop-up blocker A browser feature that prevents webpages from opening a new window.

Protocol A set of rules for communication between devices that determines how data is formatted, transmitted, received, and acknowledged.

Reply An email response that is sent back to the original sender.

Reply All An email response that is sent to all the addressees of the original message and the original sender.

RSS (Really Simple Syndication) A format used for distributing web feeds that change frequently.

Satellite Internet access A broadband Internet service that uses communications satellites positioned in the southern sky.

Search provider A website that provides search capabilities on the web.

Signature line A block of text that is automatically put at the end of an email message.

Sitemap A page that displays all of the pages in a website in one place.

Skype A software application that users can download to create an account so they can make voice calls over the Internet as well as participate in web conferencing from any location in the world.

Social bookmarking site A website that enables you to save and share your bookmarks or favorites online.

Social media Collectively, the tools that enable users to create content, connect, network, and share on the web.

Social media sharing site A website that enables anyone to create and share media.

Social networks Online communities that combine many of the features of other online tools.

Social news site Different from traditional media news sites in that at least some of the content is submitted by users.

Social review site A website that enables you to review hotels, movies, games, books, and other products and services.

Store-and-forward technology An email server holds messages until the client requests them.

Streaming media Accessing video or audio clips almost immediately after you click a link on a webpage without waiting for the entire file to download.

Subject line Part of an email message used to give the recipient some idea of the content of the email.

Synchronous online communication Communication that happens in real time, with two or more people online at the same time.

Tagging Labeling images or files with keywords to make them easier to organize, search for, and share.

Thread A conversation in a discussion board or forum.

Top-level domain (TLD) The suffix that follows the domain name in a URL that indicates the type of website you are visiting.

Tumblr A microblogging site where posts are limited to a relatively small number of characters and users post updates frequently.

Tweet A short message posted in Twitter, limited to 140 characters and spaces.

Twitter A microblogging platform used for social networking, which allows registered users to post and send messages to other registered users.

URL (uniform resource locator) The address of a website.

User-generated content Web content created by ordinary users.

Viral video An online video that becomes extremely popular because of recommendations and social sharing.

VoIP (voice over IP) Calls transmitted over the Internet instead of over traditional telephone lines or cellular towers.

Web 2.0 tools The tools that allow users to create content.

Web browser A program that interprets HTML to display webpages as you browse the Internet.

Webpage Information on the web, written in HTML, and viewable in a web browser.

Website One or more webpages that all are located in the same place.

Wi-Fi hotspot A wireless access point available in many public locations, such as airports, schools, hotels, and restaurants, either free or for a fee.

Widget A small program in a webpage that can be run by the person viewing the page.

Wiki A website that enables you to edit content, even if it was written by someone else.

Wikipedia The most well-known wiki, a massive free encyclopedia that can be written by anyone.

World Wide Web The hypertext system of information on the Internet that enables you to navigate through pieces of information by using hyperlinks that connect them.

YouTube The largest online video hosting site in the world.

GO! Do It CREATE A BLOG WITH BLOGGER

Andrew Rodriguez / Fotolia; FotolEdhar/ Fotolia; apops/ Fotolia; Yuri Arcurs/ Fotolia

A blog is an online journal that you can easily set up using simple blog tools. In it, you can talk about whatever you like. Blogs can be interactive, allowing readers to post comments about blog posts. One website for creating free blogs is **Blogger.com**. To use Blogger, you need to have a Google account.

If you do not already have a Google account, you will need to create one before you begin this Activity. Go to **http://google.com** and in the upper right corner, click Sign In. On the Sign In screen, click Create Account. On the Create your Google Account page, complete the form, read and agree to the Terms of Service and Privacy Policy, and then click Next step. On the Welcome screen, click Get Started.

1. From your student files, open the file **aio07_DOIT_answersheet**. Display the **Save As** dialog box, navigate to the location where you will store your assignments for this chapter, and then create a new folder named **AIO Chapter 7** Open the folder, and then save the file as **Lastname_Firstname_07_DOIT_answersheet**

2. Go to **http://blogger.com**. Use your Google account to log in to Blogger. If necessary, confirm your profile and then click Continue to Blogger. Click **New Blog**.

3. On the Create a new blog screen, enter a blog title and address and choose a template. Try to select something that is easy to remember (and spell). You want it to be easy for people to find your blog. Choose a template that visually complements the style and content of your blog—you can change or customize it later. Take a screenshot of this window and paste it into your answer sheet. Click **Create blog!** If necessary, on the Google Domains dialog box, click No thanks.

4. Click the orange **New post** button to begin. The Post screen is where you compose and format your blog postings. Use the formatting toolbar to format your text. Include a title using the Heading Style, align center, and insert an image or video clip in your post.

5. Under Post settings, click **Labels** and type at least one label (tag) to help your readers find posts that are related, and then click **Done**. Click **Options** and allow Reader's comments (the default), and then click **Done**.

6. Click **Preview** to view your blog post. Close the Preview tab. Make any edits, and then when you are satisfied with your post, click **Publish**. Share on Google+ if you so choose.

7. Click the **View blog** button to view your finished product. Explain the steps you took to create your blog and include the URL of your blog and a screenshot of the finished blog in your answer sheet. Save the file and submit it as directed by your instructor.

ON THE WEB

1. **Alternative Browsers** The major alternative browsers release new versions frequently with new and updated features. From your student files, open the file **aio07_OTW1_answersheet**, and then save the file in your **AIO Chapter 7** folder as **Lastname_Firstname_07_OTW1_answersheet** Visit **https://www.mozilla.org/en-US/firefox/desktop** and **https://www.google.com/chrome/browser/features. html**. Read the information about each browser and write a two- to three-paragraph summary of each. In your opinion, which browser is the better choice for you, and why? Print or submit your answer sheet electronically as directed by your instructor.

2. **Social News Sites** A great way to find out what other people think is important is using social news sites. From your student files, open the file **aio07_OTW2_answersheet**, and then save the file in your **AIO Chapter 7** folder as **Lastname_Firstname_07_OTW2_answersheet** Visit **Slashdot.org** or **Digg.com**, and look on the *Popular* page. What are some of the trending stories? How do these compare to the headlines today in traditional mass media? Select two stories that you think are interesting or important, and write a short summary of each. Why did you select these stories? Print or submit your answer sheet electronically as directed by your instructor.

ETHICS AND SOCIAL MEDIA

1. **Internet Ethics** In the early days of the web, it was common practice to buy up domain names to resell them. Speculators would buy domain names that they anticipated would be worth a lot of money. This practice is known as cybersquatting. From your student files, open the file **aio07_ESM1_answersheet**, and then save the file in your **AIO Chapter 7** folder as **Lastname_Firstname_07_ESM1_answersheet**

   Intentionally buying a domain name that is the same as a trademark another company owns—for example, Avon or Hertz, which were both victims—for the purpose of selling it to the trademark owner at a profit is a trademark infringement. But what about something that is not trademarked but still recognizable—like a catchphrase or a person's name? Is it legal to purchase these domains? Is it ethical? What about changing the TLD; for example, buying **nasa.com**, which could be confused with **nasa.gov**?

   Suppose you purchase a domain name for your own use, and it turns out that a company wants to buy it from you. Is it legal to sell it to them? At a profit? Print or submit your answer sheet electronically as directed by your instructor.

2. **Social Media Uses** Social networks are often criticized in the media for their privacy settings. In this exercise, you will examine the privacy policy of Facebook to determine the appropriate settings to use for your own profile. You do not need to have a Facebook account to do this exercise. From your student files, open the file **aio07_ESM2_answersheet**, and then save the file in your **AIO Chapter 7** folder as **Lastname_Firstname_07_ESM2_answersheet**

   Go to **http://facebook.com** and click **Privacy** at the bottom of the page. Click the link for **Sharing and finding you on Facebook**. Read through the various topics on this page. How does Facebook protect your privacy? What are the default privacy settings, and do you think they do a good job protecting you? If you have a Facebook account, have you set your privacy settings to keep your personal information protected? When was the last time you checked and updated them? Have the terms of service changed since you first joined this network? Print or submit your answer sheet electronically as directed by your instructor.

COLLABORATION

1. **History of Social Networks** With a group of three to five of your classmates, research the history of social networks. From your student files, open the file **aio07_Collab1_answersheet**, and then save the file in your **AIO Chapter 7** folder as **Lastname_Firstname_07_Collab1_answersheet** Create a timeline showing five to seven important milestones in their development. Use a free online timeline generator, a drawing program, a word processor, or a presentation tool to create your timeline. As directed by your instructor, present your findings to the class and submit your answer sheet.

2. **Web Browsers** As a team, research one browser—Internet Explorer, Edge, Firefox, Chrome, Safari, or Opera. From your

student files, open the file **aio07_Collab2_answersheet**, and then save the file in your **AIO Chapter 7** folder as **Lastname_Firstname_07_Collab2_answersheet** Prepare a one- to two-minute multimedia commercial for your browser. The presentation should convince a consumer to use the browser. Use at least three references, only one of which may be this textbook. Submit the script and provide documentation that all team members have contributed to the project. Perform the commercial using the dialogue you have written. If possible, videotape the commercial, and then as directed by your instructor, share with your class. Print or submit your answer sheet directed by your instructor.

Digital Ethics and Awareness

OUTCOMES
Search for and evaluate information on the web, manage your digital footprint, and use digital communication tools. Select the appropriate tool—desktop, web, or mobile app—for business applications.

OBJECTIVES

1. Demonstrate How to Navigate the Web
2. Discuss How to Evaluate the Credibility of Information Found on the Web
3. Manage Your Online Presence
4. Recognize Different Types of E-commerce
5. Use Digital Communication Tools for Business
6. Recognize the App Culture

Olly/Fotolia

In This Chapter

There is a vast amount of information available on the Internet, and finding, evaluating, and using that information are important skills.

In this chapter, you will learn how to search for, and then critically evaluate, information on the Internet. In addition, you will learn to present yourself online, both personally and professionally, by developing a personal brand and to use digital tools for business communication.

Job Focus

The **Oro Jade Hotel Group** Growth and Development Department is responsible for researching and planning for growth in new markets. Growth may include designing and building new hotels in a new service area, or it may come from repurposing or remodeling an existing hotel property. Most new hotels are owned directly by the company; however, the department is also examining the feasibility of franchise locations. The **Development Director** for the Oro Jade Hotel Group focuses on the development of hotel properties in his or her region.

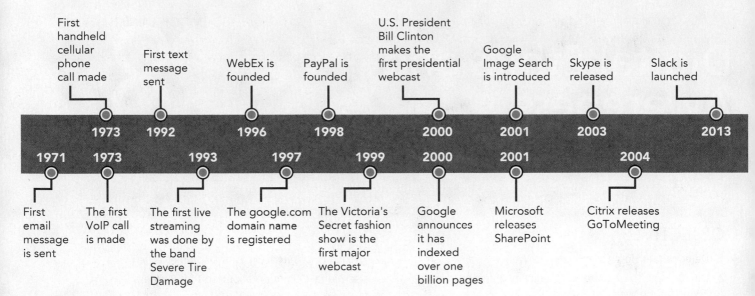

FIGURE 8.1 This timeline highlights important dates in digital communication.

Objective 1 Demonstrate How to Navigate the Web

Tech to GO!
Smart Searching

As a Development Director, you frequently search the web for planning information, to locate potential properties to redevelop, and to research new markets. Navigating the web efficiently saves you time and frustration.

The amount of information available to you can be overwhelming. It is easy to get lost or sidetracked as you conduct research on the Internet. How do you know where to start? How do you find what you are looking for? How do you know the information you find is valid and reliable? How can you avoid information overload and use the web effectively?

3.01a (ii)

Concept 8.01 | Searching the Web

With billions of webpages on the Internet, how do you begin to find what you are looking for, and when you do find it, how can you trust it? Searching for information on the Internet is a critical skill. Although it may seem that everything you want to know can be found by searching Google, the fact is that not every webpage can be found by searching Google. Also, when you type the words *dog care* in a search page such as Google, you will get millions of results—commonly referred to as *hits*. So the first step to conducting a good web search is knowing how to ask the right question.

A *search engine* is a program that searches a database for specific words and returns a list of webpages or documents in which the search term was found. Search engines send out programs called *spiders* to crawl the web and gather information. Because the web is dynamic and constantly changing, this method helps the search engine database stay up to date. Some search engines also accept submissions, and others use both methods to gather information. There are also *metasearch engines* that search other search engines and aggregate results. Dogpile is a metasearch that pulls results from Google, Yahoo!, and several other search engines. Kayak is a content-specific metasearch that pulls results from travel websites. There may also be differences in the way the information is classified and categorized.

Suppose you want to learn about the eagle you saw nesting in a building on the news. You go to google.com and type the word *eagles* in the search box. Performing that search on Google displayed 130 million hits on the day of this writing. Because the web is constantly changing, if you perform the same search today, your numbers will be different. Also, if your browser or device is using location services, your results might be location specific. Because the search was performed from a computer in Philadelphia, the Philadelphia Eagles football team is near the top of the results. If you live in Denver, the results might be different—unless it happens to be football season.

So where do you start? A good approach is to look at the first few hits and see if what you want is there. If not, think about a better way to ask the question. To narrow down the results, you can add some more keywords to the search. The first few hits using the word *eagles* got the football team and the rock band. You need to be more specific in your query if you're really interested in the kind of eagles that fly! You can do this by adding more terms to your search, such as *birds*, *raptors*, or *bald*. Use quotes to search for an exact phrase, and use an asterisk to specify unknown or variable words. To get narrower search results, you can use the advanced search tool to filter the results. You can add or exclude terms as well as specify a language and date, among other things. The advanced search options are fairly common among search sites.

In most search engines, you can conduct ***Boolean searches***, which use logical operators— AND, OR, and NOT—to link the words you are searching for. These operators should be typed in uppercase letters. By using Boolean operators, you can add precision to your search results. A Boolean operator defines the relationship between words or groups of words and is used to create a search filter. Using AND to join two words results in pages that include both words—so the number of hits is lower. Joining two words with an OR means that either word can be present—so the number of hits is much larger. Using NOT is exclusive, which means the results must include the first word but cannot include the second word. You can also use a minus sign in front of the word to exclude. Figure 8.2 shows the eagles search using various Boolean operators.

SEARCHING WITH BOOLEAN OPERATORS		
SEARCH TERM	**SEARCH FILTER/BOOLEAN OPERATOR**	**NUMBER OF RESULTS**
Eagles		130,000,000
eagles AND birds	AND	21,200,000
eagles OR birds	OR	628,000,000
eagles NOT football	NOT	57,500,000
eagles –football	-	57,500,000

FIGURE 8.2

Gaskin, Shelley. GO! All in One, 3E. Pearson Education, 2017.

3.01a (ii)

Concept 8.02 | Using Google

Google is more than just a place to type a simple search string. Here are some tips to get the most out of searching Google:

- To search a particular website, add *site:* before the domain you want to search, followed by your search term. For example, the search **site:nasa.gov solar flare** will display pages on NASA's website that contain the words *solar flare* (Figure 8.3)

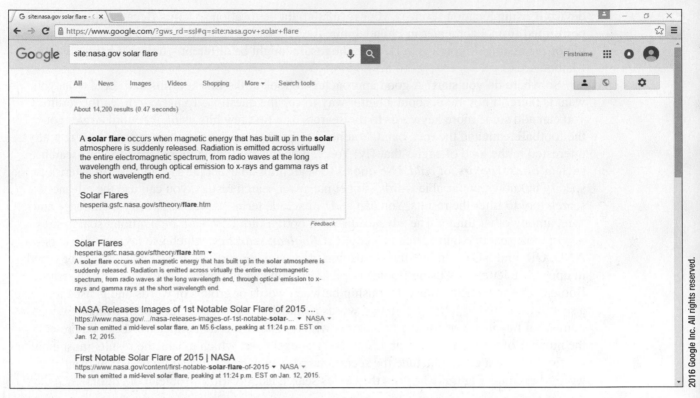

FIGURE 8.3 Searching Google for the term *solar flare* on the NASA website.

- By using *filetype:* you can search for files and images in specific formats. For example, to search for JPG images of a solar flare, type **solar flare filetype:jpg** in the search box.

- Use *define* to look up the definition of a word or phrase. For example, to find the definition of the word *Boolean*, type **define Boolean** in the search bar.

- Enter a stock ticker symbol in the search box to display the stock information and current status.

- To solve a math formula, simply type the formula into the search bar. Enter a function into the search bar to graph the function, as shown in Figure 8.4. You can also perform conversions. For example, to find out how many pounds are in 24 kg, just type **24kg= pounds** to specify the conversion unit desired. Google will display results in a table with a drop-down list you can use to change units. Type **calculator** in the search bar to display the Google calculator & unit converter.

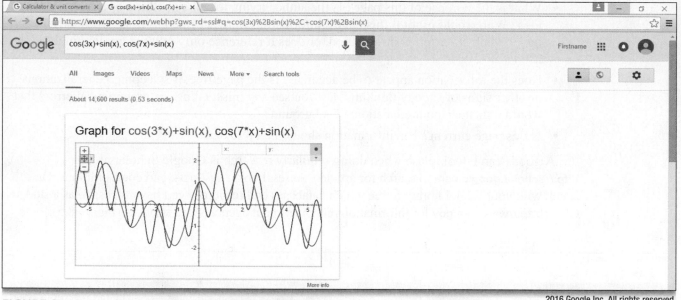

FIGURE 8.4 Graphing a function using the Google calculator.

Objective 2 | Discuss How to Evaluate the Credibility of Information Found on the Web

Your job as a Development Director involves hours of Internet research to new locations and venues. As a result, you must be able to critically evaluate the information you find.

If you conduct a search that results in 130 million hits, how do you know what to believe? The Internet is full of user-generated content—content that has been written by everyday users. Although there is a lot of wonderful content out there, keep in mind that anyone can say anything. You must be able to evaluate the information you find. There are many clues to look for when deciding whether a website is one that you can trust.

3.01a (ii)

Concept 8.03 | Critically Evaluating Web Pages

Do you believe everything you hear? Or everything you read? Do you evaluate the credentials of the people from whom you take advice? How do con artists scam so many people into investing their money with them? They are convincing, and nobody questions the results until it is too late—even if what is promised is too good to be true. Always be a skeptic when evaluating information you find on the Internet.

As you are evaluating a webpage for possible use or reference, read with a critical eye and ask yourself these questions:

- Who is the author of this page? Is the author affiliated with a recognized institution, such as a university or a well-known company? Is there any evidence that the author is qualified and possesses credentials with respect to this topic?

- Does the author reference his or her sources? If so, do they appear to be from recognized and respected publications?

- Who is the webpage affiliated with? Who pays for this page? The association between the page server, sponsor, and author should be credible.

- Is the language objective and dispassionate, or is it strident and argumentative? Is it written in a form and at a level that suits the target population?

- What is the purpose of this page? Is the author trying to sell something or promote a biased idea? Who would profit if this page's information were accepted as true? Does the site include links to external information, or does it reference only other pages within the site itself?

- Does the information appear to be accurate? Is the page free of sweeping generalizations or other signs of shoddy thinking? Do you see any misspellings or grammatical errors that would indicate a poor educational background?

- Is this page current? The information should be up to date.

A good search tool to use when doing scholarly research is Google Scholar at **http://scholar.google.com** to search for articles, theses, books, abstracts, and court opinions. Or, check with your school library to see which databases and resources you have access to as a student. Go to **http://www.usa.gov** for information on government agencies and services (Figure 8.5).

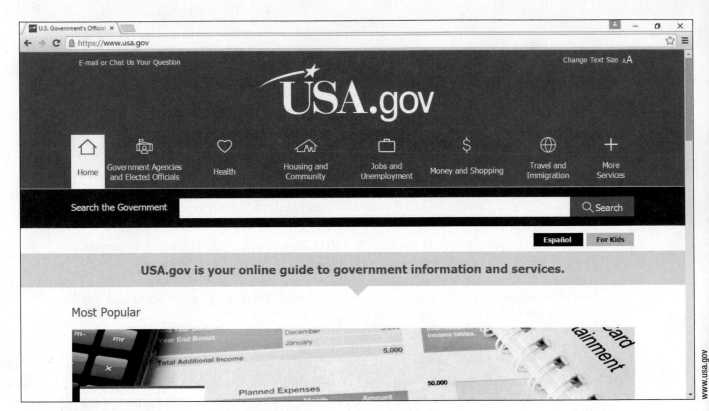

FIGURE 8.5 For accurate government references and information, try www.usa.gov.

3.01a (iv)
3.01a (v)

Concept 8.04 | Recognizing Intellectual Property Rights

According to WIPO—World Intellectual Property Organization at **http://www.wipo.int**, "*Intellectual property (IP)* refers to creations of the mind, such as inventions; literary and artistic works; designs; and symbols, names and images used in commerce."

IP is protected by national and international laws such as *patents* for inventions, *trademarks*—logos or symbols that represent a brand—and *copyright* for literary and artistic works.

Works that are protected by copyright include: written words, photographs, videos, songs, drawings, performances, and anything that you create or post online. Copyright is automatic once a work is in tangible form—ideas can't be copyrighted. You do not need to apply for copyright, nor do you need to put the copyright symbol on the work, but it doesn't hurt to remind people by doing so. *Public domain* works are not restricted by copyright. Public domain works are owned by the public and can be freely used. Public domain works include those works whose copyrights have expired, works that the author has voluntarily placed in the public domain, and works created by U.S federal agencies and employees. In the United States, most works published before 1923 are in the public domain.

The song "Happy Birthday to You" was determined to be in the public domain in 2015. The music was published in 1893 and is in the public domain because it was published before 1923, but the dispute was with the song's words. The copyright dated back to 1935, and the company that owned the rights charged royalties on any public performance of the song until a judge ruled in 2015 that the copyright was no longer valid because the origin of the rights holder could not be determined.

When searching for images using Bing, you can restrict the search to public domain images by clicking *License* below the search results as shown in Figure 8.6. When searching images in Google, you can restrict the license type by using the Advanced Image Search. In the "Usage rights" section, use the drop-down to choose what kind of license you want the content to have. Wikimedia Commons is a vast collection of freely licensed media files, many of which are public domain.

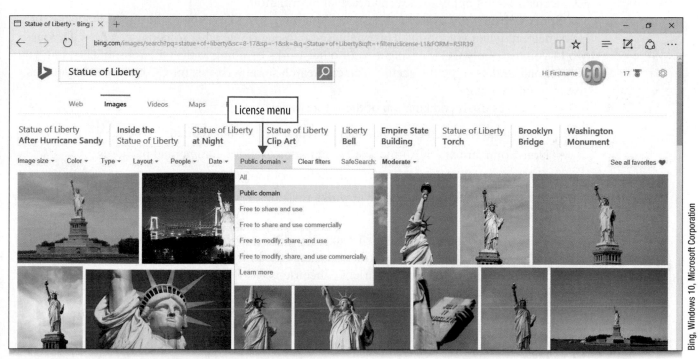

FIGURE 8.6 Searching for public domain images using Bing.

Concept 8.05 | Determining Copyright and Fair Use Applications of Content

3.01a (vi)
3.01a (viii)
3.01a (ix)

Plagiarism is the use of someone else's work without permission or credit, passing it off as your own work. This extends to material found on the web. You must credit the author whenever you use any material that is not common knowledge, whether directly quoting or paraphrasing. Most schools include plagiarism sanctions in their codes of conduct, which may include expulsion, suspension, failure, or fines. Online tools such as TurnItIn or Viper make detecting plagiarism easier for teachers and institutions. As a writer, you can also use these tools to help ensure that your work is free from plagiarism before submitting or posting it. Tools such as these automate the process of content checking by comparing submitted material with vast databases of documents and web content.

Fair use allows, without the permission of the rights holder, the use of brief selections of copyright material for purposes such as commentary and criticism, news reporting, teaching, and research. To determine if an intended use is considered fair use, the courts use a four-factor analysis:

1 Purpose and character of the use

2 Nature of the copyrighted work

3 Amount and substantiality

4 Effect upon work's value

Creative Commons, **http://creativecommons.org/**, is a nonprofit organization that provides free legal tools to change the creator copyright terms from "All Rights Reserved" to "Some Rights Reserved." CC licenses apply to works that are protected by copyright such as books, scripts, websites, lesson plans, blogs, photographs, films, video games, musical compositions, and so on. CC licenses do not apply to ideas and factual information.

Some websites, for example, Flickr and YouTube, will allow you to set up CC licensing on your material when you post it. This enables you to determine what someone can do with your work. You can apply CC licensing to your other works by going to the CC website, choosing your restrictions, and creating the license. You can search some websites for CC content that you can use in your own work.

CC licenses use a combination of these four terms:

- Attribution (BY)—the original author/creator MUST be credited
- Non-Commercial (NC)—the work may not be used for commercial purposes
- No Derivatives (ND)—the work cannot be modified
- Share-alike (SA)—any derivative works must be licensed under the same Creative Commons license

All CC licenses include BY, which requires attribution of the original author. Adding NC, ND, and SA adds more restrictions to what others can do with your work.

The most common, and least restrictive, license is *CC BY*—which requires attribution of the original author, but allows the content to be used in just about any way. The material can be reused, changed, and used in commercial and non-commercial applications, so long as the original author is credited.

CC BY-NC-ND (Attribution—Non-Commercial—No Derivatives) is the most restrictive CC license—the work can be shared but cannot be changed or used in commercial applications.

When you want to use CC Material, click the link on the license to view the license deed—which is a simple summary of the legal terms. When you want to use material that has CC licensing, you must abide by the restrictions that are applied. To learn more about CC licenses, visit **https://creativecommons.org/licenses** (Figure 8.7).

FIGURE 8.7 Watch the video at the Creative Commons website to learn more about CC licenses.

IC3
DIGITAL LITERACY
CERTIFICATION
3.01a (vii)

Concept 8.06 | Comparing Censorship and Filtering of Digital Content

Filtering digital content and ***censorship*** include blocking access to content on the Internet or restricting what can be posted or published. Parents, libraries, and schools may filter Internet content to educate and protect children. This would be considered filtering by most people—not censorship. In some cases, schools and libraries are required by law to filter content. Employers may filter content to increase employee productivity or to prevent malware and potential malicious attacks on the organization's computer systems. Organizations providing Internet for business purposes—not for personal use—have the right to restrict its usage. Acceptable Use Policies—policies that computer and network users in a business or school must abide by that forces users to practice safe computing—reinforce these restrictions.

Most people define government blocking of Internet content as censorship. This extends to blocking the posting of specific types of content. Government censorship is common during periods of political uprising and in countries that are repressive. In extreme examples, the use of the entire Internet may be prohibited or blocked.

Tools for filtering include content-control software, hardware, and operating system settings. Filtering software and hardware-based filtering can overblock and filter out legitimate sites or underblock and allow sites to display that should be blocked. For example, a student researching breast cancer might find important resources blocked because the word *breast* is used. Software can use several different ways to determine if a site should be blocked. These include blacklists of known problem sites, searching the site for specific keywords, or a combination of both methods. The blacklists need to be updated regularly to be effective.

Some websites will remove content that violates the terms of service or offends its intended audience. For example, Facebook will delete posts that it deems inappropriate or that are reported by other users, such as nudity, images of violence, hate speech, and threats.

Parental Controls in the OS can help restrict Internet access. Windows Family Safety settings enable a parent to turn on web filtering on Child accounts as shown in Figure 8.8. The default filtering setting allows social networking and other online forms of communication as well as most websites—except those that display adult content. You can select more restrictive settings that limit the websites that can be accessed, including social networking sites.

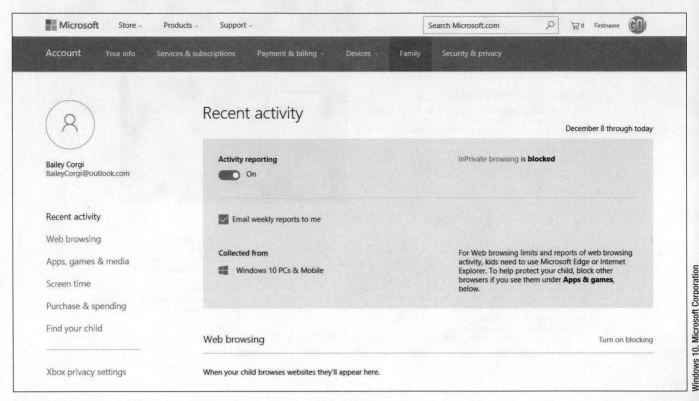

FIGURE 8.8 Windows Family Safety report for a child account.

Objective 3 | Manage Your Online Presence

Concept 8.07 | Practicing Netiquette

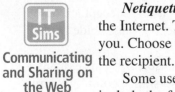

Communicating and Sharing on the Web

Netiquette, short for *Internet etiquette*, is the rules for acceptable behavior and manners on the Internet. The basic idea is this: Talk to others the same way you would want them to talk to you. Choose the appropriate tool for the nature of the communication and your relationship with the recipient.

Some useful rules of netiquette for email, chat rooms, instant messaging, and message boards include the following:

- Keep the message short, although email messages can be longer.
- Avoid sarcasm or the use of phrases or words that could offend the reader.
- Read the message before sending or posting it, correcting spelling and grammar mistakes.
- Do not type in all capital letters, because that is interpreted as shouting.
- Do not assume that everyone knows what acronyms such as BRB (be right back) and LOL (laughing out loud) mean.
- Avoid sending a ***flame***—a message that expresses an opinion without holding back any emotion and that may be seen as being confrontational and argumentative.
- Consider the recipient. Sending a quick text to a friend or classmate can be more informal than sending a message to a teacher or boss.

Take a moment to consider the best tool and the words you use before sending a message. When you follow the rules of netiquette, you make a good impression.

Concept 8.08 | Maintaining Healthy Workspaces

Ergonomics—the study of the relationship between workers and their workspaces—defines how to set up workspaces for optimal productivity and reduce the occurrence of illnesses and musculoskeletal disorders. Any time you are in front a screen, keep your body in a neutral body position without twisting, leaning forward, or turning to reach or see your screen. Keep your feet flat on the ground or on a footrest. Place your screen at or below eye level so you do not need to tilt your neck to see it, and the lighting should not cause glare on your screen. If using a keyboard and mouse, position them so your arms are in a relaxed position as shown in Figure 8.9. Take regular breaks to stretch and move around, and stretch your eyes by focusing on distant objects for a few minutes.

FIGURE 8.9 Proper ergonomic form.

Concept 8.09 | Presenting Yourself Online

First, think about your online identity or ***digital footprint***—all the information that someone can find out about you by searching the web, including social networking sites and online gaming. This includes both content that you post and content posted by others. A cyberbully, disgruntled employee, unhappy customer, or former partner might post negative, untrue, or unflattering information about you. While you have little control over what others post, you can and should carefully curate what you post. Remember that after something has been posted on the web, it is almost impossible to completely get rid of it. Suppose you were a prospective employer. Would you hire someone who has compromising pictures on Facebook?

Separating your personal online identity and professional online identity enables you to share and enjoy yourself while still presenting a professional appearance to employers, clients, and others in your professional network. You can use an alias for your personal identity to keep it independent from your professional one. Keep your privacy settings high on your personal accounts and choose your friends and followers carefully.

You need to develop your own brand and be sure that anything that is publically viewable fits into that brand. Your brand is something you should create and manage to make the best impression. The information that appears at the top of the search results when someone Googles your name should highlight your skills and achievements. The content you share, Tweets you post, and social media connections you make are all part of your brand.

One of the best ways to improve search results for your name is to build a website or set up a blog using Blogger or WordPress. You can create your own website where you post your resume, list your achievements, highlight awards, and write a short bio. Add new content to your site regularly so that it does not become out of date. You can buy a domain from Hover.com or GoDaddy. Try to buy your own name or something closely related, such as your last name and field. Everyone knows Bill Nye the Science Guy!

Your public social media profiles should be complete and present you in the best light possible. Use high-quality professional photography for your profile pictures. Regularly interacting with others and sharing their content will increase your visibility. The more active you are on social media, the better.

Finally, Google yourself regularly to see how others see you, and what they say about you.

ETHICS — Fired Over Social Media Posts

There are numerous stories about people losing jobs because of their social media posts. In Colorado, a young teacher was fired for Tweets showing her intoxicated and in revealing photos. She used an alias, and claimed the account was a parody account, but was fired anyway. Another teacher was fired for posting vacation photos of her holding a glass of wine. Even though her privacy settings were high, a parent saw the posts and reported them to the school board. Search the web and you will find many instances of people losing jobs over inflammatory posts. Is it fair or reasonable for employers to fire employees for their personal posts? How can you protect your online identity while still sharing on social media?

There are many examples of employees being fired for posting negative comments about customers or employers. A teenager who was about to start a new job at a pizza place was fired when her new boss saw her negative posts about the job. Newspaper and television reporters have been fired for posting comments that were considered inappropriate. Waiters have been fired for complaining about customers who do not leave a tip. Is it reasonable for an employer to fire someone over this type of post? Does it make a difference if the posts are on private profiles versus public or professional profiles?

Objective 4 — Recognize Different Types of E-commerce

Businesses and organizations use social media sites to provide support and interaction to customers. *Social media marketing* or *SMM* is the practice of using social media sites to sell products and services.

Concept 8.10 | Comparing Types of E-commerce

E-commerce refers to buying and selling products or services on the Internet. Three main categories of e-commerce include business-to-business or B2B, business-to-consumer or B2C, and consumer-to-consumer or C2C. PayPal, Braintree, and website hosting are examples of B2B, where one business provides products or services for another. B2B services enable smaller companies to have a web presence or store without needing to have the in-house expertise and without great expense. A small business is able to have a professional-looking website and sophisticated shopping cart system because they can purchase B2B services from other companies (Figure 8.10).

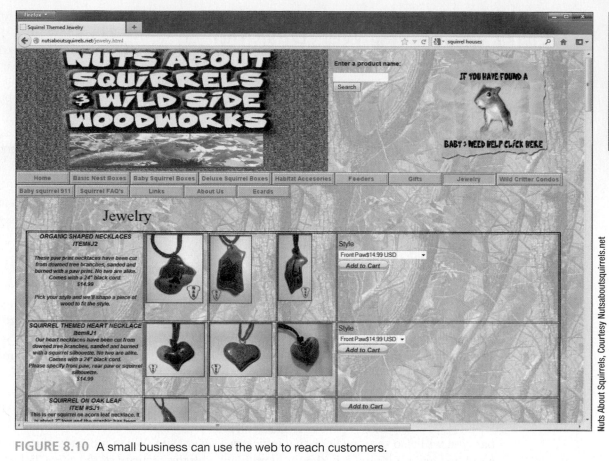

FIGURE 8.10 A small business can use the web to reach customers.

B2C, or business-to-consumer, is the form of e-commerce with which you are probably most familiar. Amazon.com, Overstock.com, and many retail stores, such as Best Buy and Target, sell their goods and services online. This form of e-commerce has grown dramatically since Pizza Hut offered pizza ordering on its website in 1994. B2C companies leverage social media to help customers find out about their products.

Facebook displays ads in your News Feed based on your page likes and those of your friends. There is a complicated algorithm used by Facebook to determine which ads to display and when. Companies pay Facebook to display their ads on the pages of their target audiences. Getting you to Like their page is an even better way for companies to interact with you. This means you are already a customer or fan of the product. Once you Like a page, you opt into receiving information from the page. Marketing to these customers may include special discounts or other incentives. Insider, early-access to content or sales, contests, useful information, and recipes are some of the ways that companies can use social media to interact with and build loyal customers. Businesses that successfully leverage the power of social media are able to create customers that, in turn, create new customers.

The third form of e-commerce is C2C, or consumer-to-consumer. Websites such as eBay and Craigslist have created a global yard sale where you can find, sell, or trade virtually anything. eBay has a seller rating system that helps ensure honest transactions and a community that includes discussion boards, groups, and chats. An unscrupulous seller will quickly get a bad reputation, and a top-rated seller will see more sales as a result.

A person who decides how a website will look is called a web designer. For a simple website, the web designer may also be the person who creates the website. If you have ever created your own webpage, then you were the designer.

There are software programs, templates, and websites such as Squarespace and Wix that can help you make a webpage quickly and easily. A professional web designer, however, goes beyond the basics and creates designs that are customized and branded for a business. A web designer needs to have a good understanding of the capabilities of the web to design an interesting, dynamic, and professional site. Some web designers are self-taught; others have degrees in graphic arts, computer science, e-business, or marketing.

Concept 8.11 | Shopping Online Safely

When you engage in e-commerce on the web—for example, making a purchase from Best Buy's online store—you must provide sensitive information about yourself such as your address and credit card information. So, is it okay to shop online? Of course it is, and record numbers of individuals do so every day. But just as you would not leave your doors unlocked, you need to be sure that you are shopping wisely. Shop at well-known sites or use third-party payment methods such as Google Wallet, Apple Pay, and PayPal (Figure 8.11) to protect credit card information. Make sure you are on a secure website when completing transactions. Look at your browser's address bar. If the URL begins with *https*, then the site is using **SSL** or ***Secure Sockets Layer*** security, which is a protocol that encrypts data before it is sent across the Internet. In the address bar, you will also see a padlock that indicates a secure site. When the https portion of the URL has a red line or an X through it, there is a problem with the security of the site. Clicking the padlock will open a security report about the website.

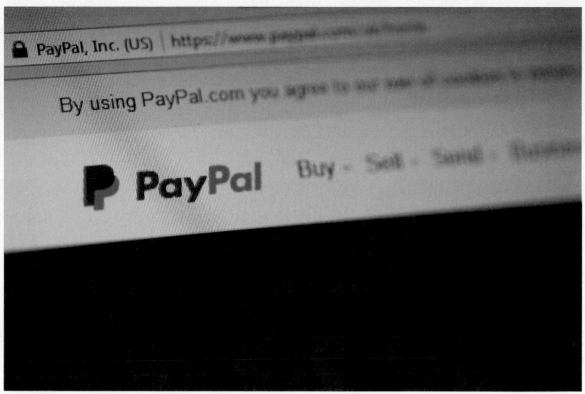

FIGURE 8.11 PayPal is a third-party payment site that protects you from online fraud.

Objective 5 | Use Digital Communication Tools for Business

IC3
DIGITAL LITERACY
CERTIFICATION
3.06a (i)
3.06a (ii)
3.06a (iii)
3.06a (iv)
3.06a (v)
3.06b (i)
3.06b (ii)
3.06b (iii)
3.06b (iv)

Concept 8.12 | Comparing Digital Communication Tools

The immediacy of our digital communications has in some ways changed our expectations and behavior. In the past, it was uncommon to contact someone outside of normal business hours. Today, it is common to expect answers to email and text messages in the evenings and on the weekends. An employer that provides a smartphone to an employee might expect that employee to be available outside of work. These expectations and responsibilities should be clear to both parties. The nature of the business might require someone to be on call at all times. A company with global connections needs to consider the business hours of other locations. A web conference with someone located half way around the world will require at least one party to be online during odd hours. When it is noon in Tokyo, it is 10:00 p.m. the previous day in New York. It is still good manners and business practice to limit these interruptions whenever possible.

Choose the right digital communication tool for the type of message. For urgent messages that require a quick response, use a tool such as **Short Message Service (SMS)**—a service used to send brief electronic text messages to mobile devices—or IM. Keep these types of messages brief. Use email for more complicated and lengthy messages, and for more formal communication such as a follow-up to a meeting or phone call or a thank you for an interview. In combination, a text or IM can alert the recipient of an important email message. SMS is less intrusive than a phone call, which could interrupt a meeting or event. Because written communication does not always convey tone and intention the way a real conversation can, a phone call or video call is sometimes a better way to communicate. Also consider the urgency of the message. Something that requires immediate attention may warrant a text or phone call, while something that is not as pressing could be handled by email. Most organizations use a combination of various communication and collaboration tools. It is important to be aware of the tools your recipient uses. It doesn't make sense to send a text or an email to someone who prefers phone calls.

FAST FORWARD — Virtual Meetings

According to *Merriam-Webster*, **virtual reality** is "an artificial world that consists of images and sounds created by a computer and that is affected by the actions of a person who is experiencing it." In the movie, *The Kingsman: The Secret Service*, there were only two people physically in the room, but when they put on special glasses, they could see the other participants. Virtual reality meetings are not just science fiction. By placing multiple people in the same virtual reality setting, a virtual meeting room can be created. You will be able to interact with other people's avatars, which can be made to look as close to realistic as you want them to. The technology is still fairly new, but it won't be long before a web conference can be replaced with a VR meeting room.

Concept 8.13 | Using Online Collaboration Technologies

Collaboration can go beyond simply exchanging email messages or chatting on the phone. When the collaborators are not in the same location, online tools can enhance this collaboration. Google Apps for Work is a suite of tools to communicate, store, and collaborate. **SharePoint** is a Microsoft technology that enables employees in an organization to access information across organizational and geographic boundaries. Organizations use Microsoft SharePoint to create websites to use as a secure place to store, organize, share, and access information from almost any device. A team site (Figure 8.12) is used by a group of collaborators, such as a department or committee. You can access your SharePoint sites when you sign in to Office 365 or your organization's corporate intranet site. With a SharePoint site, you can share a common document library, and work with others on the same document and at the same time. You can share documents with people inside your organization, and share documents and sites with people outside your organization.

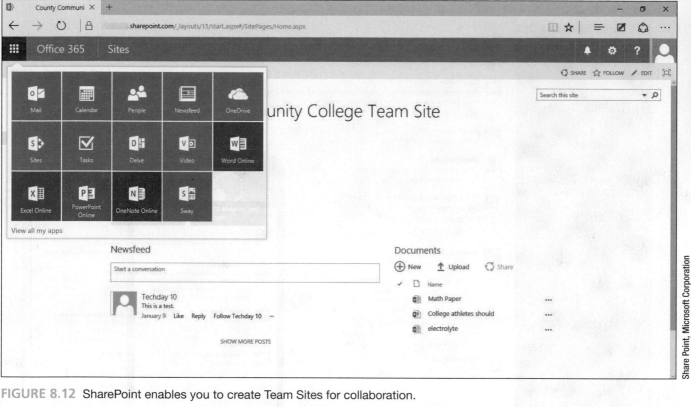

FIGURE 8.12 SharePoint enables you to create Team Sites for collaboration.

Slack is a team communication and collaboration tool. Teams organize conversations and projects into channels, which can be public and accessible by all team members, or private and accessible only by invited members. You might use Slack to collaborate with a team of classmates working on a group project. With Slack you can share files by dragging and dropping them into the app or connecting to Dropbox, Box, or Google Drive. Everything you do in Slack is archived and searchable. Figure 8.13 shows Slack on a desktop and on two mobile devices. Because Slack integrates with your other apps, it provides a single place to work and communicate. Even if you are not online, you can configure Slack to send you notifications.

FIGURE 8.13 Slack is available for multiple devices.

IC3
DIGITAL LITERACY
CERTIFICATION
3.06a (vi)
3.06a (vii)
3.06c
3.07a (i)
3.07a (ii)
3.07a (iii)
3.07a (iv)
3.09a (i)

Concept 8.14 | Conferencing with Digital Tools

Collaborating and conferencing in real-time using digital tools enable teams to work together, even when in different locations. Choose the right tool for the task. For example, save the cost of travel by interviewing potential employees via Skype or FaceTime. Provide client support and offer online presentations or webinars with web conferencing software such as WebEx or GoToMeeting to present to a group, ensuring everyone is on the same virtual page. For simple discussions, a phone call may be all that is needed. Add video by using a tool such as Skype, FaceTime, or Google Hangouts. These tools enable collaborators to log in from anywhere and view the same screen. As the leader of a presentation or conference, you can share your own screen or pass control over to another participant to share theirs. Using a screen-sharing program, you can display your computer screen and make it visible to others. This is a common way to collaborate on a project, enabling everyone to be looking at the same thing at the same time. Figure 8.14 shows screen sharing using Skype. In this example, a teacher is sharing a presentation with her students.

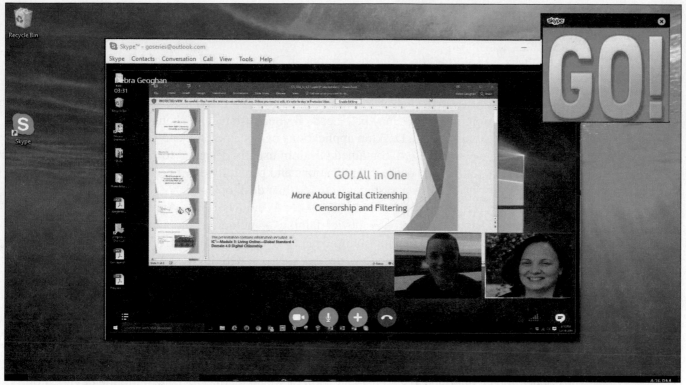

FIGURE 8.14 Sharing a screen with Skype.

Skype 2016, Windows 10, Microsoft Corporation, Debra Geoghan, Courtesy Debra Geoghan

Be aware of your intended audience and collaborators. Verify that everyone has the necessary technology and skills to use it, and do a practice run-through ahead of time to be sure everything works correctly.

GREEN COMPUTING The Paperless Office

The promise of the paperless office hasn't quite become a reality. According to the U.S. Environmental Protection Agency (EPA), in 2013 (the most recent figures available), paper made up 27 percent of our municipal solid waste. The process of making paper uses water and energy in addition to trees, and it results in greenhouse gas emissions and air and water pollution. Reduce your paper usage to help the environment.

The prospect of going paperless has advantages for the environment and for your bottom line. So, how do you achieve it? The reality is that you probably cannot go totally paperless, but here are a few ways to reduce your paper usage:

- At your work, send email and make phone calls instead of sending paper memos.
- Pay your bills online and opt for paperless billing from your billers and banks.
- Do not print out electronic documents unless absolutely necessary.
- Read magazines and books in electronic formats.
- Opt out of receiving junk mail at the DMA website **(http://www.dmachoice.org)** and catalogs at Catalog Choice **(http://www.catalogchoice.org)**.

Concept 8.15 | Exploring the Differences between Desktop, Web, and Mobile Apps

Before You Buy
Choosing an App or
Desktop Program

A ***desktop application*** is a computer program that is installed on your PC and requires a computer operating system such as Microsoft Windows or Apple OS X. When you install a desktop application, many files may be placed on your system, and changes might be made to the operating system settings. Desktop applications can be complex and designed to do many different things. An ***app*** is a self-contained program usually designed for a single purpose. Apps are much smaller than desktop applications and generally don't require any complicated installation. Apps use far fewer system resources than desktop applications and thus can run on lower-end systems and mobile devices. Microsoft's Windows 10 and Apple OS X support both desktop apps and apps that run on all device families—including computers, phones, and tablets. Most popular apps are available for multiple platforms. For example, Evernote is a popular note-taking app that is available for Windows desktops, Macs, iOS devices, Android devices, and Windows phone devices. When you install the corresponding version of the app on each of your devices and platforms, you can access your content from all of them.

Mobile applications—apps—that extend the functionality of mobile devices should be downloaded only from trusted sources. It is safest if you use the recommended app store for your device. The apps must pass through rigorous testing to be placed in the market, reducing the risk of malicious or harmful code running on your device. There are many mobile apps that improve the connection or interface to a web application or social media site from a mobile device. For example, the Facebook and Twitter apps optimize the way the sites display on your device. Because the storage on mobile devices is limited, most mobile apps rely on the cloud for storage of content.

Web apps run in browsers, and therefore are ***platform-neutral***—they will run on any device with a supported browser and Internet access. Web apps typically don't require any installation, and using web apps ensures that you are always using the most current version of the program. The disadvantage to relying on web apps is the requirement to have Internet access.

When choosing the type of app to use, consider the length of the project, the location of any collaborators, the system resources available, and the technical expertise.

GO! To Work

IC3 SKILLS IN THIS CHAPTER

IC3 — Module 3 Living Online

Section 3.01 Internet (Navigation)
- (a) Understand what the Internet is
  - (ii) Be familiar with media literacy
  - (iv) Know about IP rights/usage
  - (v) Know about licensing rules/laws
  - (vi) Know about copyrights
  - (vii) Know about censorship and filtering
  - (viii) Know plagiarism rules/laws
  - (ix) Fair use

Section 3.06 Communications
- (a) Know the best tool for the various situations and scenarios
  - (i) Email
  - (ii) SMS
  - (iii) Instant message
  - (iv) VoIP
  - (v) Phone calls
  - (vi) Web ex
  - (vii) Conference calls
- (b) Know how to use SMS texting
  - (i) Etiquette
  - (ii) Know what it is and how it can be used as a tool
  - (iii) Know when to use and not use
  - (iv) Determine when it is appropriate to use it

- (d) Understand options for and how to use distant/remote/individual learning technologies
  - (i) Know basic remote workforce tools

Section 3.07 Online Conferencing
- (a) Understand and identify online conference offerings
  - (i) VoIP conferencing [Skype]
  - (ii) Video conferencing [Google hangouts, Skype, FaceTime]
  - (iii) Phone conferencing
  - (iv) Screen sharing

Section 3.09 Digital Principles/Ethics/Skills/ Citizenship
- (a) Understand the necessity of coping with change in technology
  - (i) Audience awareness
- (b) Understand Digital Wellness basics
  - (i) Screen time
  - (ii) Ergonomic best practices
- (c) Understand an online identity management
  - (ii) Managing profiles
- (d) Know the difference between personal vs. professional identity

GO! FOR JOB SUCCESS

Discussion: Sustainable Business Practices

Your instructor may assign these questions to your class, and then ask you to think about them or discuss with your classmates:

As public awareness of and concern over environmental and social issues grows, many businesses are finding they must do an just make a profit to be successful. Companies today often strive to be a sustainable business by having a positive, or at least minimally negative, effect on the local and global environment and community.

Traditional management responsibilities have been to focus on the bottom line: making a profit and increasing shareholder value. Managers of sustainable businesses believe they have a broader responsibility, called the Triple Bottom Line: people, planet, and profit. Triple Bottom Line is a strategy and measurement method that benefits the environment and society by encouraging greener business practices and that allows a company to fully account for all of the costs of doing business.

Sustainability is so important that many businesses dedicate websites and social media accounts to publicizing their "green" efforts and community outreach, and they incorporate these messages into their general advertising. Starbucks, for example, prominently displays information about their "responsibility" to coffee farmers and local communities in their stores and advertising.

FotolEdhar / Fotolia

What are some effects that Triple Bottom Line business practices could have on your community?

Are there businesses in your area that communicate their interest in people and planet as well as profit?

What ads or social media postings have you seen that focus more on a company's environmental practices than on its products?

END OF CHAPTER

SUMMARY

Search engines search for specific words and return a list of hits. Use the advanced search tool to filter the results. When evaluating a webpage for possible use or reference, read with a critical eye.

Intellectual property (IP) refers to creations of the mind, such as inventions; literary and artistic works; designs; and symbols, names, and images used in commerce. Public domain works are not restricted by copyright.

Your digital footprint is all the information that someone can find out about you by searching the web, including social network sites and online gaming. Netiquette is the rules for acceptable behavior and manners on the Internet.

Digital tools for business communication include texting, email, online collaboration and storage sites, and digital conferencing tools. Consider the technical skill and availability of technology of collaborators when choosing the tool.

GO! LEARN IT ONLINE

Review the concepts, key terms, and IC3 skills in this chapter by completing these online challenges, which you can find at MyITLab.

Matching and Multiple Choice: Answer matching and multiple choice questions to test what you learned in this chapter.

Lessons on the GO!: Learn how to use all the new apps and features as they are introduced by Microsoft.

IC3 Prep Quiz: Answer questions to review the IC3 skills that you practiced in this chapter.

GLOSSARY

GLOSSARY OF CHAPTER KEY TERMS

App A self-contained program usually designed for a single purpose and that runs on smartphones and other mobile devices.

Boolean search A search that uses logical operators—AND, OR, and NOT—to link the words you are searching for.

Censorship Blocking access to content on the Internet or restricting what can be posted or published.

Copyright Legal protection for literary and artistic works.

Creative Commons A nonprofit organization that provides free legal tools to change the creator copyright terms from "All Rights Reserved" to "Some Rights Reserved".

Desktop application A computer program that is installed on your PC and requires a computer operating system such as Microsoft Windows; also known as a desktop app.

Digital footprint All the information that someone could find out about you by searching the web, including social network sites.

E-commerce Conducting business on the web.

Ergonomics The study of the relationship between workers and their workspaces.

Fair use The use, without the permission of the rights holder, of brief selections of copyright material for purposes such as commentary and criticism, news reporting, teaching, and research.

Flame A message that expresses an opinion without holding back any emotion and that may be seen as being confrontational and argumentative.

Hits Another term for search results.

Intellectual property (IP) Creations of the mind, such as inventions; literary and artistic works; designs; and symbols, names, and images used in commerce.

Metasearch engine A search engine that searches other search engines.

Mobile application (mobile app) A program that extends the functionality of a mobile device.

Netiquette Short for *Internet etiquette*, the code for acceptable behavior and manners while on the Internet.

Patent Legal protection for inventions.

Platform-neutral An application that can run on all modern personal computing systems.

Public domain Works not restricted by copyright.

Search engine A huge database that indexes webpages.

Secure Sockets Layer (SSL) A protocol that encrypts information before it is sent across the Internet.

SharePoint A Microsoft technology that enables employees in an organization to access information across organizational and geographic boundaries.

Short Message Service (SMS) A service used to send brief electronic text messages to mobile devices.

Social media marketing (SMM) The practice of using social media sites to sell products and services.

Spider A program sent out by a search engine to crawl the web and gather information.

Trademark Logos or symbols that represent a brand.

Virtual reality An artificial world that consists of images and sounds created by a computer and that is affected by the actions of a person who is experiencing it.

Web apps Applications that run in a browser.

GO! Do It

Andrew Rodriguez / Fotolia; FotolEdhar / Fotolia; apops / Fotolia; Yuri Arcurs / Fotolia

PERFORM AN ADVANCED SEARCH WITH GOOGLE

In this Activity, you will perform a search using Google and then refine your search by using advanced options.

1. From your student data files, open the file **aio08_DOIT_answersheet**. Display the **Save As** dialog box, navigate to the location where you will store your assignments for this chapter, and then create a new folder named **AIO Chapter 8** Open the folder, and then save the file as **Lastname_Firstname_08_DOIT_answersheet**

2. Open your browser and go to **http://google.com**. In the search box, type **rose** and press Enter. Take a screenshot of this page and paste it into your answer sheet. How many results did you get? What type of information is displayed in the first page of results?

3. Add the word **red** before *rose* and press Enter. How does this affect the results?

4. Click the **Options** icon at the top right of the screen, and then click **Advanced search**. In the *none of these words* box, type **king** to exclude it from the search. Press Enter. How are the results affected? Take a screenshot of the results, and paste it into your answer sheet.

5. Type **filetype:jpg** at the end of the search string, and then press Enter. How are the results affected? Take a screenshot of the results, and paste it into your answer sheet.

6. Type your answers, save the file, and submit it as directed by your instructor.

ON THE WEB

1. **Searching Your School Website** In this Activity, you will perform a search of your school website, using Google, to locate your school's acceptable use policy. From your student data files, open the file **aio08_OTW1_answersheet**, and then save the file in your **AIO Chapter 8** folder as **Lastname_Firstname_08_OTW1_answersheet**

   Go to **http://google.com**. In the search bar, type **acceptable use policy** and then press [Enter]. How many hits did you get? At the end of the search, using your own school's domain, type **site:schooldomain.edu** and then press [Enter]. Take a screenshot of these results and paste it into your answer sheet. From the results, locate your school's acceptable use policy. Write a two- to three-paragraph summary of the policy. Print or submit your answer sheet electronically as directed by your instructor.

2. **IM for Customers** Instant messaging and chatting are important tools that businesses use to provide services to customers. Some schools also offer virtual advisors and librarians with whom you can chat live online. From your student data files, open the file **aio08_OTW2_answersheet**, and then save the file in your **AIO Chapter 8** folder as **Lastname_Firstname_08_OTW2_answersheet**

   If your school or local library offers this service, use it to ask about the success of this service. Take a screenshot of your conversation and paste it into your answer sheet. If you do not have a local library that uses chat or IM, use the Internet to find another library that does. Have you ever used this type of service in researching a topic? What type of help can this particular library chat service provide? What are the hours the service is available? What other online resources does the library offer? Print or submit your answer sheet electronically as directed by your instructor.

ETHICS AND SOCIAL MEDIA

1. **Domain Parking** Use the Internet to research laws regarding parking and selling unused URLs. From your student files, open the file **aio08_ESM1_answersheet**, and then save the file in your **AIO Chapter 8** folder as **Lastname_Firstname_08_ESM1_answersheet** Is it legal to grab up domains and park them? Is it ethical? What about changing the TLD of a well-known website (nasa.com, for example)? With new TLDs being implemented, such as .biz, and .bargain, should all related domain names be protected? Suppose you purchase a domain name for your own use, and it turns out that a company wants to buy it from you? Is it legal to sell it to them? At a profit? Print or submit your answer sheet electronically as directed by your instructor.

2. **The Internet and China** Government censorship is blocking or filtering of the Internet at the national level. From your student files, open the file **aio08_ESM2_answersheet**, and then save the file in your **AIO Chapter 8** folder as **Lastname_Firstname_08_ESM2_answersheet**

   Go to Google or Bing and search for **Great Firewall of China** What is it and how does it work? What types of content is blocked? What happens if someone searches for a prohibited word or tries to access a blocked webpage? Are there ways around the restrictions? Print or submit your answer sheet electronically as directed by your instructor.

COLLABORATION

1. **Creative Commons** With a group of three to five of your classmates, research the types of CC licensing available. From your student files, open the file **aio08_Collab1_answersheet**, and then save the file in your **AIO Chapter 8** folder as **Lastname_Firstname_08_Collab1_answersheet** Create a presentation that explains the types of licenses and appropriate usage for each. Explain how to select and assign CC licensing to your own work. As directed by your instructor, present your findings to the class and submit your answer sheet.

2. **Apps** As a team, prepare a Venn diagram that compares the features of desktop applications, web apps, and mobile apps. From your student files, open the file **aio08_Collab2_answersheet**, and then save the file in your **AIO Chapter 8** folder as **Lastname_Firstname_08_Collab2_answersheet** Prepare a Venn diagram using a computer drawing program or presentation program. The diagram must have at least four items in each area of the diagram. Present your findings to the class. Be sure to include a listing of all team members. Print or submit your answer sheet directed by your instructor.

Cloud Computing

APPLICATIONS

PROJECT 9A

OUTCOMES
Use Google tools online.

OBJECTIVES

1. Navigate the Web Using the Google Chrome Web Browser
2. Search the Internet Using the Google Chrome Web Browser
3. Send and Receive Email Messages Using Gmail
4. Chat Online Using Google Hangouts
5. Manage a Google Calendar

PROJECT 9B

OUTCOMES
Use Microsoft cloud tools and One Note.

OBJECTIVES

6. Use Your Microsoft Account's OneDrive for Storing and Sharing Files
7. Communicate Using Skype
8. Use OneNote to Create a Notebook

PROJECT 9C

OUTCOMES
Use professional social networks.

OBJECTIVES

9. Create a LinkedIn Account
10. Use Twitter

Rawpixel.com/Shutterstock

In This Chapter

Cloud computing enables you to use the Internet—instead of a local server—to utilize software, to store information, to manage and process data, and to collaborate on projects. By using a web browser, you can search the Internet; access free email providers like Gmail, Yahoo! mail, and Outlook.com mail and share information like calendars and files. You can communicate with others online in a live environment by using free tools like Google Hangouts or Skype. OneNote is a desktop application with which you can gather, store, and share information stored locally or online.

The **Oro Jade Hotel Group** is proud to host special events at its corporate locations. Each site has a **Special Events department** responsible for assisting customers as they plan business or social events. The staff is trained in event planning and is very familiar with their local areas. The assistance they provide varies depending on the event requirements, but frequently involves reserving hotel rooms, arranging for meeting space and equipment, providing catering, organizing off-site activities, and booking guest speakers or performers. Recent events have included corporate retreats, training workshops, corporate annual meetings, class and family reunions, and weddings.

Google Productivity

PROJECT ACTIVITIES

In Activities 9.01 through 9.09, you will work with Ellen Mouser, an event planner at Oro Jade New Orleans, as she explores how to browse and navigate the web using Google Chrome. Ellen will use the web to research sites and activities in New Orleans, Louisiana, and other information to assist guests. You will capture screens that will look similar to Figure 9.1.

PROJECT FILES

For Project 9A, you will need the following file:

w09A_Email_Info

You will save your file as:

Lastname_Firstname_9A_Google_Screens (The PowerPoint file will include 9 screenshots that you will create while completing the Project.)

GO!
Walk Thru
Project

PROJECT RESULTS

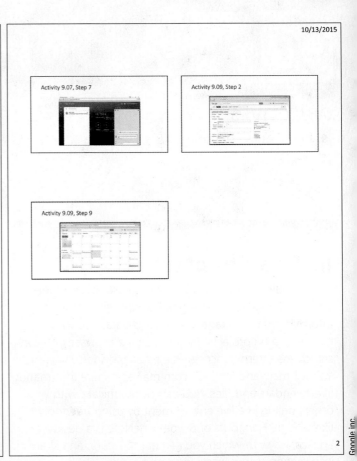

FIGURE 9.1 Project 9A Google Productivity

Event Planner

An Event Planner handles the details of planning an event that fits a client's budget and that meets the client's needs. A planner should be an effective communicator and well organized because he or she coordinates the setup, event activities, and follow-up after the event. Oro Jade Hotel Group employs Event Planners to efficiently plan personal and professional activities on the hotel grounds. Most hotels have indoor and outdoor venues in which they can house the special events with the help of the facilities and catering staff.

Objective 1 — Navigate the Web Using the Google Chrome Web Browser

A *web browser* is a software program that you use to display webpages and navigate the Internet. *Chrome* is the web browser software developed by Google and is available as a free download. It has become a very popular browser; some sources say that Chrome accounts for over 50 percent of all web browsing. Other popular web browsers include Internet Explorer, Firefox, and Microsoft's new browser named Edge.

Browsing is the term that describes the process of using your computer to view webpages. Browsing the web is one of the most common activities performed by individuals who use computers. *Surfing* refers to the process of navigating the Internet either for a particular item or for anything that is of interest, and quickly moving from one item to another. Chrome is the browser used on a *Chromebook*— a laptop that runs Google's Chrome operating system and Chrome web browser to provide a web-based environment for using applications; however, some apps may run offline as well. You can also take Chrome with you on your iOS or Android mobile device and browse the Internet at any time.

ALERT!   **You Must Have Google Chrome on Your Computer to Complete This Project**

You must have or download Google Chrome to complete this activity. To install, open your current browser, and navigate to **https://www.google.com/chrome/browser/desktop/** and download the new browser. Keep in mind that computer programs on the web receive continuous updates and improvements. Therefore, your screen may differ from the ones shown. You can often look at the screens and the information presented to determine how to complete the activities in this project.

3.01a (iii)
3.02a
3.02a (iv)

Activity 9.01 | Navigating the Web by Using the Google Chrome Web Browser

1 From your desktop, open **Google Chrome**, and if necessary, maximize the window. Compare your screen with Figure 9.2, and then take a moment to study the table in Figure 9.3 that describes the parts of the Google Chrome window.

If you have not set a *home page*, the default is Google's search engine. On your computer, the home page is whatever webpage you have selected—or is set by default—to display on your computer when you start Google Chrome. When visiting a website, the home page refers to the starting point for the remainder of the pages on that site.

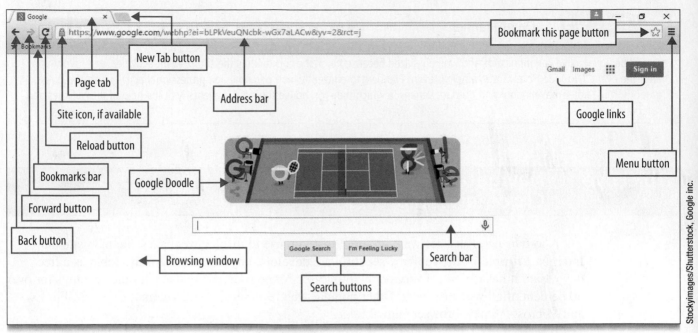

FIGURE 9.2

ALERT!	Websites Update Content Frequently

As you progress through the Projects in this chapter, the pictures of various websites may not match your screens exactly, because website administrators frequently update content. This will not affect your ability to complete the Projects successfully.

SCREEN ELEMENT	DESCRIPTION
Back button	Displays the previous page you visited; activates after you visit more than one webpage.
Forward button	Displays the next page if you have used the Back button.
Reload button	Reloads the current page.
Site icon	Displays the icon of the website currently displayed in the browsing window.
Address bar (also called the Omnibox)	Provides the area in which you type the URL for the site you want to visit, and which also works as a search box.
Page tab	Displays the name of the active webpage.
New Tab button	Opens a new tab.
Browsing window	Displays the webpage content for the site you are visiting.
Chrome Menu	Displays a list of features, including History, Print, Settings, and Help options.
Add Bookmark button	Identifies current page as a preferred site; marks it so it is easy to access the site again.
Bookmarks bar	Displays bookmarks on current page for easy access; can be turned off from the menu.
Google Links	Links to Gmail, Google Images, Google Apps, and a Sign-in screen used to access your Google account.
Google Doodle	An image that changes frequently, but always identifies the *Google* home page.
Search bar	Text box that enables you to enter search terms.
Search buttons	Buttons used to search for terms typed in the text box. I'm Feeling Lucky button automatically displays the first site in the results page.

FIGURE 9.3

2 Click the **Chrome Menu** ▤, and then click **Settings** to display the Chrome Settings. Notice settings related to *Sign in*, *Appearance*, *Search*, and *People*. Scroll to the bottom of the settings, and click **Show advanced settings** to display additional settings.

While you may not be able to change settings in a classroom lab, you can change them on your own computer to enhance your browsing experience and make it more secure.

3 Scroll down to display the information related to managing *Privacy* and *Passwords and forms* sections.

Under Privacy, click Clear browsing data to clear your browser history, a list of webpages that you have visited during browsing sessions that may include cookies and stored passwords. This may speed up browsing once it is complete.

Under Passwords and forms, be sure Enable Autofill to fill out web forms in a single click is selected if you want user data to automatically populate web forms. The offer to save your web passwords option allows you to save time when accessing password-protected sites. For safety reasons, use these options with caution.

4 On the **Settings tab**, click **Close** tab ⊠.

5 At the top of your screen, click in the **address bar** to select the current URL, type **www.nola.gov** and then press Enter to display the website for the city of New Orleans.

The area of the screen that displays the contents of the website is the ***browsing window***. At the top of the window is the ***address bar***—the area at the top of the browser window in which you can type a URL to visit a website. Google also refers to the address bar as the ***Omnibox***, because it serves as both an address bar and a search bar.

URL is the acronym for ***uniform resource locator***, which is an address that uniquely identifies a location on the Internet. By typing in the address bar and pressing Enter, the new URL opens. A URL contains the ***protocol prefix***—in this instance ***http***, which stands for ***HyperText Transfer Protocol***. HTTP represents the set of communication rules used by your computer to connect to servers on the web. Chrome defaults to the *http* prefix, so it is not necessary to type it, even though it is part of the URL for this site. The protocol prefix is followed by a colon and the separators //. A URL also contains the ***domain name***—in this instance *www.nola.gov*. A domain name is an organization's unique name on the Internet.

6 Click anywhere in the address bar to select the URL text, type **uoa.gov** and then press Enter.

When you type a new URL in the address bar, the new website opens to replace the existing website. You can also open a website on a new tab to keep multiple websites open.

7 In the **address bar**, on the left, click **Back** ⬅ one time. In the **address bar**, on the right, click **Forward** ➡ to move to the next page—the U.S. Government website.

The Back button takes you to the previous page that you visited—the city of New Orleans. The Back button is active after you visit more than one webpage. The Forward button takes you to the next page if you used the Back button.

8 Scroll to the bottom of the webpage to display the footer, and then compare your screen with Figure 9.4.

The bottom section of a webpage is referred to as the ***footer***. This area typically contains the name of the entity that publishes the website, copyright information, and basic navigation links, such as *About Us*, *Contact Information*, *Legal Information*, *Privacy Statements*, *Site Index*, and other similar titles.

FIGURE 9.4

9 Press [Ctrl] + [Home] to move to the top of the webpage, and notice the **navigation bar** across the top of the webpage.

A *navigation bar* is a set of buttons or images in a row or column that display on every webpage to link the user to sections on the website.

10 Point to one of the items in the **navigation bar**, and as you do so, notice that the item is selected and the 🖑 mouse pointer displays. Click **Health** to display that page below the **navigation bar**. On the **navigation bar**, point to **Travel and Immigration** and right-click.

11 On the shortcut menu, click **Open link in new tab** to open the Travel and Immigration page on its own tab.

When you use this method to open a new page, the existing page remains active in the browsing window, but the new tab does display.

🔄 **ANOTHER WAY**   Hold down [Ctrl] and click a location on the navigation bar to open the page on a new tab.

---

12 With the **Health | USA.gov** page displayed in the browsing window, above the **address bar**, on the **tab row**, click ✕ to close the tab and display only the **Travel and Immigration** page.

On the usa.gov website, a navigation bar and logo display at the top of every page and a footer displays at the bottom. On the navigation bar, clicking Home will display the home page again, and the other links will open other department pages.

13 Point to the *USA.gov* logo that displays above the **navigation bar** to display the 🖑 pointer, and then click one time to display this site's home page.

Some pages may not have a Home menu or button, so clicking the logo will usually take you to the home page. When you point to an item and the 🖑 displays, you know that it is an active link.

14 To the immediate right of the tab for the *U.S. Government*, point to the blank tab ▭ to display the ScreenTip *New tab*, and then click one time to open a new tab. Compare your screen with Figure 9.5.

A *ScreenTip* is a small text box that displays the name of an icon or button when a mouse pointer is hovered over it. Some ScreenTips provide details about the icon's or button's function. A new tab opens; the U.S. Government website remains open on the previous tab. Tiles for sites that you visit frequently or visited recently display so that you can go to them quickly when you open a new tab.

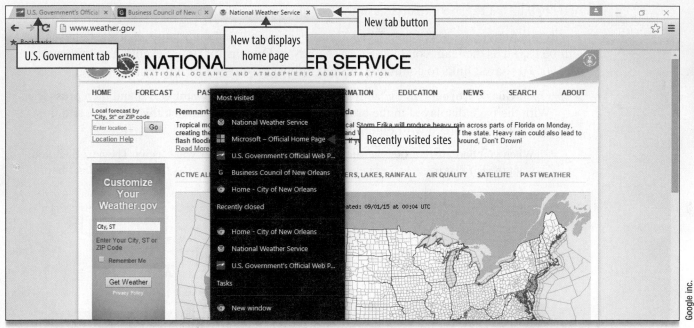

FIGURE 9.5

15 With the insertion point blinking in the **address bar**, type **bcno.org** and then press [Enter] to display the Business Council of New Orleans & the River Region.

16 Press [Ctrl] + [T] to open a new tab, type **weather.gov** and then press [Enter] to display the website for the National Weather Service.

As you type in the address bar, Chrome will use its autocomplete feature to assist you in reaching sites that you visited previously, sites that you have bookmarked, or sites that are popular URLs. The tiles for these sites may also display, and you can click or tap the tile to access the website.

Bookmarks are saved links to commonly visited webpages used to enable efficient browsing.

More Knowledge | **Cycling Through Open Tabs**

Hold down [Ctrl] and press [Tab] to cycle through and display all open tabs.

---

17 Start PowerPoint 2016. On the right, click **Blank Presentation**. Click the **Click to add title** box, and type **Project 9A** Click the **Click to add subtitle** box, and type your **Firstname Lastname** On the **Home tab**, in the **Slides** group, click the upper portion of the **New Slide** button to add a new slide in the presentation. Click the **Insert tab**. In the **Images** group, click **Screenshot**, and then click the image of the Google Chrome window to place the screenshot in the slide. Click the **Click to add title** box, and type **Activity 9.01, Step 17** Leave the PowerPoint presentation open.

18 Return to Google Chrome. On the **address bar**, in the **tab row**, point to the **National Weather Service tab**, right-click, then click **Close other tabs** to close all tabs *except* the National Weather Service. Point to the **National Weather Service tab** again, and then click its **Close** button [×].

3.02a
3.02a (iii)
3.01a (iii)

In this Activity, you will help Ellen Mouser organize a number of sites that she believes will be useful as the team conducts research on New Orleans for future events. You will create *bookmarks*—saved links to commonly visited webpages—to enable efficient browsing.

1 Open **Google Chrome**. In the **address bar**, type **neworleanschamber.org** and then press Enter. With the page displayed in the browsing window, click **Bookmark this page** ☆, and then compare your screen with Figure 9.6.

> When you bookmark a site, the site name is saved in the folder you specify. The next time you want to visit that page, you can click the name instead of typing the URL in the address bar.

FIGURE 9.6

Copyright 2015 New Orleans Chamber of Commerce. All Rights Reserved.

2 In the **Bookmark added!** dialog box, click the **Folder arrow**. Click **Bookmarks bar**, and then click **Done**. If the Bookmarks bar is not currently displayed below the address bar, click the **Chrome Menu** ☰, point to **Bookmarks**, and then click **Show bookmarks bar**.

> The Chrome Menu icon is commonly referred to as a *hamburger menu* or a *menu icon* or simply a *hamburger*. The name derives from the three lines that bring to mind a hamburger on a bun. This type of button is commonly used in mobile applications because it is compact to use on smaller screens. At the bottom of the Bookmark added! dialog box, you can click *Sign in to get your bookmarks everywhere* to sign in to your Google account if you want to be able to access your bookmarks from other computers.

3 Click in the **address bar** to select the URL text, type **lsu.edu** and then press Enter. In the upper right corner, click the **Chrome Menu** ☰. Point to **Bookmarks**, and then click **Bookmark this page**. In the **Bookmark added!** dialog box, click **Done**. On the right, notice that the star is gold when you are viewing a bookmarked site.

4 Click in the **address bar** to select the URL text, type **neworleansonline.com** and then press Enter. Press Ctrl + D to display the **Bookmark added!** dialog box, and then click **Done**.

> Three bookmarks display on the Bookmarks bar: New Orleans Chamber, Louisiana State University, and the New Orleans Official Tourism website.

5 Press Ctrl + T to open a new tab. Click the **Chrome Menu** ☰, and then point to **Bookmarks**. Compare your screen with Figure 9.7.

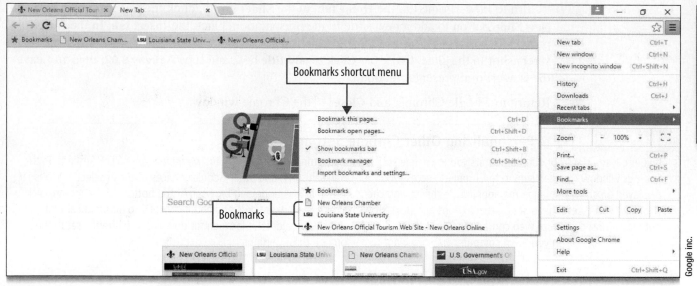

FIGURE 9.7

6 On the **Bookmarks menu**, click **Bookmark manager** to display the **Bookmark Manager**.

7 Under **Organize**, point to the area below the bookmarks and right-click. On the displayed shortcut menu, click **Add folder**. With *New folder* highlighted in blue, type **New Orleans Research** and then press Enter. Compare your screen with Figure 9.8.

The folder displays on the Bookmarks bar to organize your bookmarks for easy access. If your Bookmarks bar is not displayed, click the Chrome menu, point to Bookmarks, and then click Show bookmarks bar.

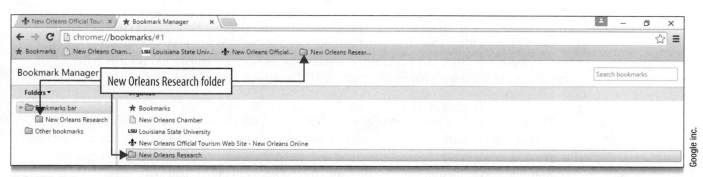

FIGURE 9.8

8 Under **Organize**, click to select the first website on the list, **New Orleans Chamber**. Hold down Shift, and then click the last website on the list, **New Orleans Official Tourism Website – New Orleans Online** to select all three bookmarks.

9 Point to the selected items until the ⬚ mouse pointer displays. Hold down the left mouse button, drag the items over the **New Orleans Research** folder until the ⬚ pointer displays, and then release the mouse button to drop the items into the folder. Double-click the **New Orleans Research** folder to display its contents.

Drag and drop is a mouse technique in which you select one or more objects and drag it to a different location. All three bookmarks are in the New Orleans Research folder.

10 ▶ Return to PowerPoint. On the **Home tab**, in the **Slides** group, click the upper portion of the **New Slide** button to add a new slide in the presentation. Click the **Insert tab**. In the **Images** group, click **Screenshot**, and then click the image of Google Chrome window to place the screenshot in the slide. Click the **Click to add title** box, and type **Activity 9.02, Step 10** Leave the PowerPoint presentation open.

11 ▶ Return to Google Chrome, and **Close** ☒ the Chrome window.

More Knowledge   **Personalizing Other Chrome Settings**

If your college classroom or lab permits you to change your personal settings, click the Chrome Menu, and then click Settings. In the Settings window, you can sign in to Chrome to access your bookmarks, history, and other Google services. You can select the tabs displayed on startup, change the appearance theme, and choose Chrome as your default browser. At the bottom of the screen, click Show advanced settings to set privacy options and clear browsing data, save passwords and enable Autofill to automatically fill out web forms, customize web content and language options, and choose the default location for downloads (currently set to the Downloads folder). On your own computer you may want to personalize these settings.

Objective 2 Search the Internet Using the Google Chrome Web Browser

The Internet can connect you to a vast amount of information, but first you have to find the information that you need. Larry Page and Sergey Brin, PhD students at Stanford University, recognized this in the mid-1990s, and Google began in March 1995 as their research project. Page and Brin built the search engine to help users navigate the web. It quickly became the most popular web search engine and also partners with other companies to provide search capabilities. In 2000, the search engine began selling advertising based on keywords used in a search.

3.01a (i)
3.02a

Activity 9.03 | **Searching the Internet Using the Google Chrome Web Browser**

A **search provider**—a website that provides search capabilities on the web—employs a **search engine** or computer program that searches for specific words and returns a list of webpages in which the search term was found. The default home page for Google Chrome is the Google search engine website.

1 ▶ Open the **Google Chrome** web browser; recall that the default home page is the Google search engine website. In the center of the window, click in the **Search** text box. Type **new orleans, la** and notice that your typing moves to the address bar. Press Enter. Notice the large number of results that are returned, and then compare your screen with Figure 9.9.

A search area displays at the top of the window. On the left, Google displays suggested related links to websites, and in the list of results, your search term, *new orleans, la*, displays in bold. On the right, Google displays a summary of information related to New Orleans, the city in Louisiana. It includes weather as well as links to upcoming events and points of interest.

You can click in the search text box to edit your search terms or click the Google logo—which may display as the current *Google doodle*—a modified Google search engine home page logo created to observe a special event, season, or holiday—to return to the Google home page.

Below the search text box, a navigation bar displays to assist you in customizing your search. For example, if you click News, you will see news stories about New Orleans. If you click Maps, you will go to Google Maps.

At the right edge of the navigation bar, the Settings button ⚙️▾ displays. Here you can select options to customize the search and set advanced search settings.

🔄 ANOTHER WAY   Click in the address bar, type the search terms, and then press Enter.

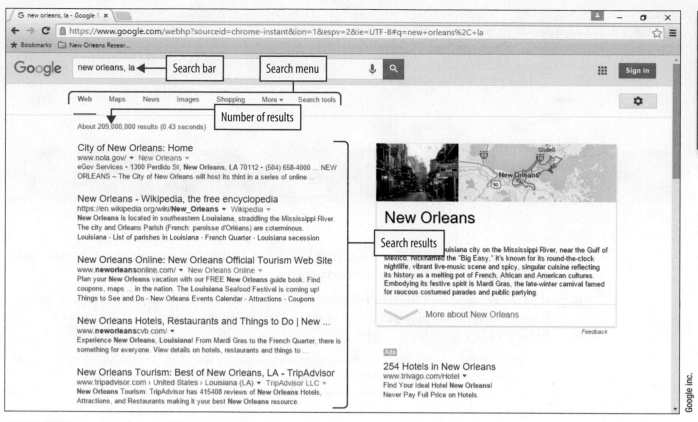

FIGURE 9.9

---

2 You can be more specific in your search to reduce the number of results. Click in the search text box, delete the text, type **travel new orleans** to display the search results, and then press ⏎ Enter. Notice that there are fewer results, although the number is still very large.

On the left, Google displays a map with links to places that might assist you. Below the map, there are other links to information you may find useful and to news related to your search terms. On the right, Google displays ***sponsored links***—paid advertisements shown as links, typically for products and services related to your search term. Sponsored links are the way that search sites like Google, Bing, and others earn revenue. When you hover your mouse pointer over or ***mouse over*** a blue title, a 🖑 pointer displays, and click to display the linked page.

3 On the navigation bar, click **Images** to display image search results related to *travel new orleans*. On the navigation bar, click **Search tools**, and compare your screen with Figure 9.10.

The links on the navigation bar narrow your search to specific *types* of information related to your search term, in this instance, images.

The search tools provide additional ways to narrow down your search, by size, color, image type, time (when image was added), usage rights related to permission, and more tools.

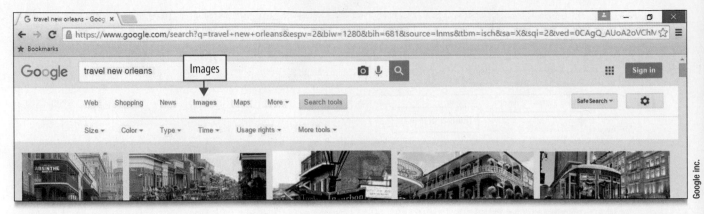

FIGURE 9.10

> 4 ▸ In the Search tools bar, click **Usage rights**, and then click **Labeled for reuse**. Click **Size**, click **Larger than…**, and then click **400x300** to narrow the image search results.

> 5 ▸ Point to or hover over the first image to display the size and location of the image. Click the first image to display details about the image, and then compare your screen with Figure 9.11.

> Details about the image include the website where it can be found and the resolution of the image. A set of related images is also displayed. All images are subject to copyright, so obtain any necessary permissions to use images appropriately.

FIGURE 9.11

> 6 ▸ Scroll to view the top of the page so your Search box displays. Return to PowerPoint. On the **Home tab**, in the **Slides** group, click the upper portion of the **New Slide** button to add a new slide in the presentation. Click the **Insert tab**. In the **Images** group, click **Screenshot**, and then click the image of Google Chrome window to place the screenshot in the slide. Click the **Click to add title** box, and type **Activity 9.03, Step 6** Leave the PowerPoint presentation open.

> 7 ▸ **Close** ✕ Google Chrome.

More Knowledge   **Hashtag Search**

In addition to searching for key words, you can search for a **hashtag**, a word or phrase preceded by the # symbol.

Email is a method of exchanging messages via the Internet in which the message resides in the recipient's mailbox until he or she signs in to read it. Free web-based email is available from many providers, including Microsoft's outlook.com and Yahoo!'s Yahoo! mail. *Gmail* is Google's free web-based email service. Gmail enables you send and receive email messages using your Google account. When using web-based email, there is no software to download or install on your computer.

ALERT! **You Must Work With a Partner to Exchange Email Messages, Chat Online, and Share Calendars**

In Objectives 3 through 5 of this Project, you will benefit from working with a classmate to exchange email messages and share documents. With the partner you have identified, agree on a convenient time and place to work on Activities 9.04 through 9.09 together.

3.02a (ii)
3.03b
3.03b (ii)
3.03b (i)
3.03b (iv)
3.02a (ii)
3.03e

Activity 9.04 | Sending and Receiving Email Messages in Gmail

Because email is such an important tool in business, study everything you can about creating effective email messages and about good email etiquette. One important habit to develop is to *add attachments first and type the names of the recipients last*. It may take time to craft your message, and you do not want to click the Send button before your message is completely thought out and proofread. By typing in the names of the recipients last, you lessen the risk of embarrassing errors in sending email. By adding attachments first—if there are attachments—you lessen the chance of forgetting to attach them, a common and embarrassing error. Additional good email practices include:

- Subject lines that indicate the content of the email—Help your email recipient know what the content of your email is by typing a clear and concise subject line.

- Revising the subject line if the topic changes—If you want to reply to a message but your reply is on a different topic, change the subject line accordingly.

- Single-topic content—Your email message should be about the topic in the subject line and nothing else. If you need to communicate about another topic, send another email with a clear subject line.

- A conversational tone that is informal, but not too informal—Write your message in a friendly tone, but avoid being as casual as you would be with your friends or family members. Within an organization, email messages are considered business communications.

- Concise writing—Write your message concisely. Get to the point without wordy phrases.

- Including only a few short paragraphs—If you cannot convey your message in a few short paragraphs of no more than two or three sentences each, you should probably call or meet with the person.

- Proofreading—Reread your message to make sure you have not made typing errors or omitted words that would change the context of your message entirely.

- Never using all capital letters—Writing in all capital letters is considered to be shouting. Additionally, it is very difficult to read messages in all capital letters.

- Never clicking the Send button without a final check—Before clicking the Send button, reread your message for clarity and appropriateness, take out any unnecessary text, attach any attachments, and be sure you have used the correct email addresses.

In this Activity, you will send, receive, and reply to an email message using your Gmail account.

<table>
<tr><td>ALERT!</td><td>**To Access Gmail, You Must Have a Google Account**</td></tr>
</table>

All Google services use the same account. If you do not currently have a Google account, click Create account. Complete the personal data form, type in the verification text, read the message and click to agree to the Google terms of service and privacy policy, and then click Next step. Then click Continue to Gmail.

1 Open **Google Chrome**. With the Google home page displayed, on the right, click **Gmail**, and then sign in using your Google account and password to display your Gmail window. Be sure that you and your partner are working at different computers and can access the Internet—the two of you can be in the same room or in separate locations, but you need to be working at the same time to complete the entire Activity. Write down the Gmail address for your partner.

2 In the upper left portion of the **Gmail** window, click **COMPOSE** to display the **New Message** box so that you can prepare an email to send to your classmate partner.

An *email header*—the first part of an email message generated by the email provider—displays at the top of the *New Message* window. In Gmail, it includes routing information and the subject line.

3 Be sure the insertion point is blinking in the **To** box, and then type the Gmail address for your classmate.

If you have corresponded with your classmate in the past, his or her email address may appear in the box after you have typed the first few characters, at which point you can click his or her name. To the right of your partner's email address, notice two additional recipient options—Cc and Bcc. Both Cc and Bcc are used to add one or more recipients in order to send a copy of a message to those who are interested in the message but will not be the primary recipient.

Cc is an abbreviation for *courtesy copy* or *carbon copy*, which is a reference to the days when paper copies were created using a typewriter and carbon paper. Use the Cc designation to send a copy of the email to one or more recipients who are interested in the message but not the primary recipient. All Cc'd recipients see the entire list of addressees when the message is received and read.

Bcc is an abbreviation for *blind carbon copy* (or blind courtesy copy) and is used to send a copy of the message to one or more recipients who would be interested in the message. When you add a message recipient in the Bcc box, the Bcc recipient receives a copy of the message, but the Bcc recipient's name is not visible to other recipients of the message. This can be useful for documenting that an email was sent.

4 Click in the **Subject** box, and then type **Writing an Email Message**

5 In the **Message window**, type your partner's name followed by a comma, and then press Enter two times. Type a short message to your partner identifying one good practice for writing professional email messages. Be sure to close your email with an appropriate closing and your name.

Always include a subject for email messages; it identifies to the recipient the reason for the email. Always begin with a greeting, and type the message using correct grammar, capitalization, and complete sentences. Proofread all messages before sending them.

6 At the bottom of the message window, notice the buttons to format the email and to add or insert items into the message. Mouse over each button to see what it is. Compare your screen with Figure 9.12.

ELEMENT	FUNCTIONS
Formatting options	Displays a toolbar with text formatting options that can be applied in the message.
Insert file	Allows the sender to attach a file from his or her computer to an email message. The recipient must download the file to open and read it.
Insert files using Drive	Allows the sender to share a file located on Google Drive by inserting a link to the file in the message or by attaching a copy of the file to the message.
Send and request money	Provides a link to Google Wallet to send money to or request money from the message recipient.
Insert photo	Allows the sender to share a photo he or she has uploaded or one from a URL that is shared. The image can be inserted inline or attached to the message.
Insert link	Inserts a hyperlink to a web address or an email address.
Insert emoticon	Displays a gallery of emoticons that can be inserted into the message window. An *emoticon* is an image that represents facial expressions. Emoticons should be used only in informal electronic communication to convey feelings.
Discard draft	Deletes the message without sending it.

FIGURE 9.12

Gaskin, Shelley. GO! All in One, 3E. Pearson Education, 2017.

7 Proofread your message, and make any necessary corrections. Click **Send**.

> **NOTE** Receiving an Error Message
>
> If an email message cannot be sent, an error message will display identifying a reason and instructions to continue. If you receive an email indicating the email was undeliverable, the message will state the reason, and then you can try again.

8 In the upper left portion of the Gmail window, to the right of **Inbox**, notice the number in parentheses, which notifies you how many new messages are in your Inbox. Compare your screen with Figure 9.13.

In your list of email messages, all unread email messages display in bold. If you read an email message without moving or deleting it, the message will remain in your Inbox, but the bold formatting will no longer display.

The tabs above the message list categorize your email messages; new messages are automatically categorized into one of the tabs based on the sender and/or content.

FIGURE 9.13

9 ▶ Point to the email sent by your partner, and then double-click to open it. Compare your screen with Figure 9.14, and then take a moment to study the commands you have available in email, which display along the top of the message area as described in the table in Figure 9.15.

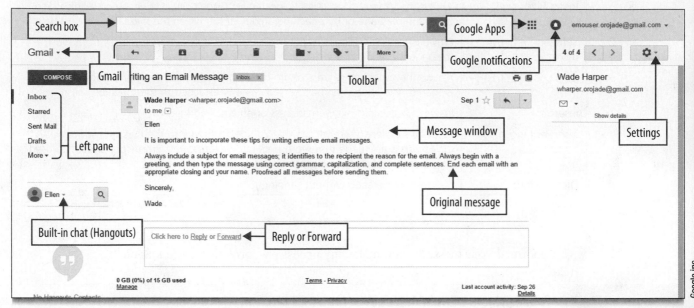

FIGURE 9.14

ELEMENT	FUNCTIONS
Search box	Searches your email to find search terms typed in the box.
Google Apps	Displays Google Apps that are available in your account.
Google Notifications	Displays notifications as identified in your account settings.
Toolbar	Displays features that enable you to • select messages • refresh the Inbox • mark messages as read or unread • archive messages • report spam • delete messages
Settings	Displays options to change the way the screen is displayed, to configure your Inbox, to set themes, and to set up your Gmail account; also displays Help.
Gmail Menu	Enables you to navigate to your Mail, Contacts, and Tasks list.
Left pane	Displays options that enable you compose, display, manage, and organize the messages in your Inbox.
Built-in Chat (Hangouts)	Provides a method to send instant messages by typing messages or creating voice recordings if you have a microphone attached; also includes phone calling options.
Message window	Displays the message text, the sender, the recipients, date of the message, star options, and reply options.
Reply or Forward box	Enables you to type a reply to the sender or to forward the message to another recipient.

FIGURE 9.15

Gaskin, Shelley. GO! All in One. 3E. Pearson Education. 2017.

10 In the Reply or Forward window, click **Reply**. Notice that the sender becomes the recipient. Click **Show trimmed content** [···] at the bottom of the window to display the original message. Scroll to display the entire original message, and then compare your screen with Figure 9.16.

> Forward is used to resend the message to someone else. If you were one of multiple recipients, *Reply to all* is an option. Reply all is used to send your reply to all messages. Be sure that all initial recipients need or should see your response before choosing Reply to all. On the left pane, notice the notification next to *Drafts*. A draft message is a message you have started but not yet sent.

> By default, Gmail hides—trims—the text of the message you just sent assuming that you only want to see the actual reply. *Trimmed content* contains the history of the Gmail message—sometimes this is referred to as the *email string* or the *email thread*.

> Sometimes an email message gets sent back and forth many times as you and your recipient exchange thoughts about a topic. That is why a Gmail message is referred to as *conversation*. After many exchanges, you may want to delete the email string when replying. This is frequently the case if you decide to forward the latest response to another recipient without the distraction of the entire email string. To do so, open the message, click Reply, press ⬇ to select the Show trimmed content button, and then press Delete.

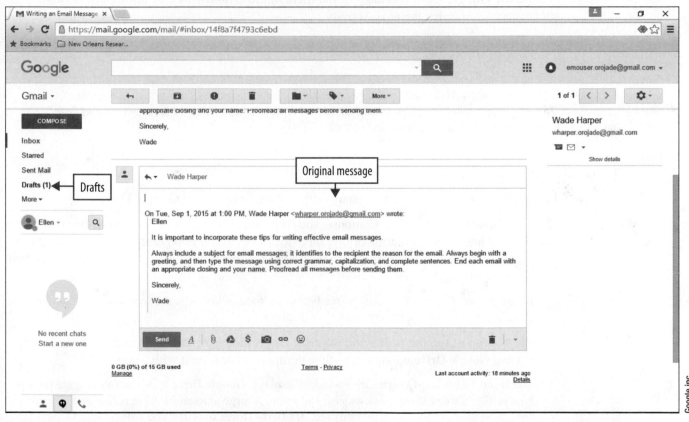

FIGURE 9.16

11 With the insertion point blinking inside the Message window, type a professional response about a potential problem you could encounter by *not* writing email messages in a professional manner. Be sure to include a greeting and closing.

> Because you clicked the *Show trimmed content* button, the original message displays below the reply. This enables the recipient to review the text of the original message, if necessary.

12 Return to PowerPoint. On the **Home tab**, in the **Slides** group, click the upper portion of the **New Slide** button to add a new slide in the presentation. Click the **Insert tab**. In the **Images** group, click **Screenshot**, and then click the image of Gmail window to place the screenshot in the slide. Click the **Click to add title** box, and type **Activity 9.04, Step 11** Leave the PowerPoint presentation open.

13 Return to **Gmail**. In the message window, click **Send** to send the reply email.

When you receive the email from your partner, notice you and your partner are listed as parties to that email conversation.

14 In the original message, point your mouse at your partner's name and hover or mouse over, and then, in the **Contact** box, click **Contact info**

Your partner's Contact information displays.

15 In the upper right, click **Edit contact** ✏ to display a list of fields that you can add to the contact information. Click **Add to contacts** 👤. Click the Back arrow to return to **Google Contacts**.

Google Contacts is a contact management application that integrates with all Google Apps, such as Gmail, Drive, and Calendar, for efficiency. Google Contacts is used to organize information about people you communicate with repeatedly. Each contact includes basic information like name, email addresses, and phone numbers, etc. You can then search for contacts, create groups that you communicate with regularly, and manage duplicate entries.

16 Close the **Google Contacts** tab ☒, and then, in the **Gmail** window, click **Back to Inbox** ↩. Remain signed in for the next Activity.

More Knowledge **Google Contacts**

Google Contacts is a contact management application that integrates with all Google Apps, such as Gmail, Drive, and Calendar, for efficiency. To access it, click Google Apps. At the bottom of the Apps, click More, and then click Contacts to display Google Contacts. Google Contacts is used to organize information about people you communicate with repeatedly. Each contact includes basic information like name, email addresses, phone numbers, and so forth.

1.05a (ii)
1.06c (i)
3.03d

Activity 9.05 | Inserting Files From Google Drive Into a Gmail Message

In this Activity, you will send an email with an attachment from Google Drive.

1 In your **Gmail** account, click **Compose**, and then compose a new email to your partner letting him or her know that you are working on a document about good email practices and that you are attaching the document to share and get feedback. Be sure to use the techniques that you practiced in the previous Activity.

Because you have emailed your partner before, as soon as you type the first few characters of your partner's email address, the entire address displays.

2 At the bottom of the message window, click **Insert files using Drive** 📁 to display the **Insert files using Google Drive** window, and then compare your screen with Figure 9.17.

The Insert files using Google Drive window displays. *Google Drive* provides free storage for any type of file: photos, documents, videos, and so on. A large amount of space is free and additional space can be purchased for a monthly fee. *My Drive* stores files that you create using Google applications. *Shared with Me* stores files that others have shared with you. *Upload* stores files that you have uploaded to Drive.

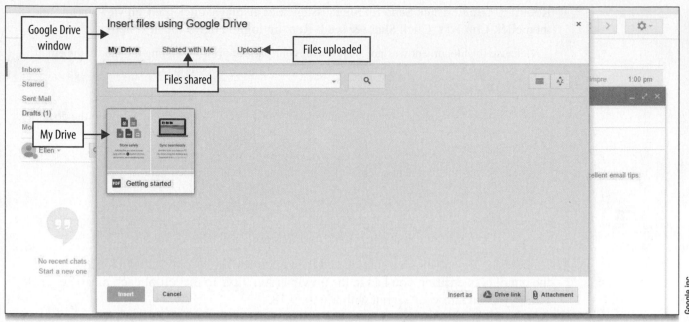

Google Drive window

Insert files using Google Drive

My Drive   Shared with Me   Upload ◄── Files uploaded

Files shared

My Drive ──►

Store safely

Sync seamlessly

PDF Getting started

Insert   Cancel   Insert as ☁ Drive link 📎 Attachment

FIGURE 9.17

3 At the top of the window, click **Upload**, and then in the center, click **Select files from your computer**.

4 Navigate to the location where you have stored the student data files for this chapter. In the **Open** dialog box, locate **w09A_Email_Info**, and double-click to add the file to the **Insert files using Google Drive** window.

5 In the lower right corner of the **Insert files using Google Drive** window, to the right of *Insert as*, click **Drive link** so that it is selected—instead of *Attachment* being selected—and then in the lower left corner, click the blue **Upload** button.

> This action uploads the document to your Google drive. The email message window displays, and the inserted file displays as a link to the file in your Google drive.

6 In the message window, click the link to the file, and notice that the file opens in your Google drive on a new tab in Chrome—in the address bar, the path to your Google drive displays.

> You can simply *attach* a file to an email message, but there are many benefits to inserting a link to your Google Drive. For example, the file size of an attachment is limited to 25 MB by many email providers, but you can *link* to a file that is up to 15 GB on Google Drive. Also, if you are collaborating on a document using attachments, you will likely end up with multiple versions of the document. When you link to Drive, all collaborators are working on the *same* document—and this is a very important distinction.

7 At the top of your screen, click **X** to close the tab and redisplay the **Gmail** window with the message open.

8 Return to PowerPoint. On the **Home tab**, in the **Slides** group, click the upper portion of the **New Slide** button to add a new slide in the presentation. Click the **Insert tab**. In the **Images** group, click **Screenshot**, and then click the image of Gmail window to place the screenshot in the slide. Click the **Click to add title** box, and type **Activity 9.05, Step 8** Leave the PowerPoint presentation open.

9 Return to Gmail. Click **Send**. In the message that displays, click the **Can view arrow**, and then click *Can edit*. Click **Share & send**. Remain logged in for the next activity.

Because this document was not shared with your partner prior to sending the link in the email message, you must set the sharing settings before the Send operation can complete.

There are three Share settings you can select:

- *Can view*—the recipient can view the document, but cannot comment on or edit the document
- *Can comment*—the recipient can view and comment on the document, but cannot edit the document
- *Can edit*—the recipient can view, comment on, and edit the document

3.03c (iv)

Activity 9.06 | Creating Labels and Starred Messages to Manage Email

In this Activity, you will manage email by starring messages and creating labels.

1 If necessary, open **Chrome**, sign in, and then open **Gmail**. Display your **Inbox** and locate the email conversation you had in the previous Activity. To the left of each message, click **Star** ☆. Compare your screen with Figure 9.18.

The star displays in gold to remind yourself that the message is important. *Labels* are used to organize messages into categories; labels function like folders in other email systems and in the Windows File Explorer program. However, labels have an added benefit that folders do not—you can assign more than one label to categorize a message; therefore, the message will be stored within each label. This makes it easier to find stored messages.

For example, perhaps you have labels for the name of each course you are taking and you also have a label for *Important Due Dates*. If you receive a message from your professor about the due date of a term paper, you could apply the label for the name of your course and also apply a label for your Important Due Dates. The message will display within both labels.

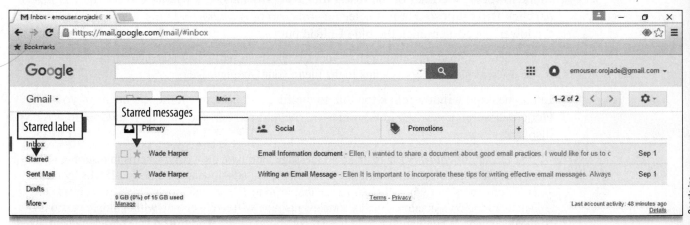

FIGURE 9.18

2 In the left pane, click **More** or **More labels**, and then click **Create new label**.

3 In the **New Label** dialog box, with the insertion point blinking in the **Please enter a new label name** box, type **All in One** to identify email messages related to this course. Notice that you can also nest one label under another. Click **Create**.

For additional levels of organization, you can nest labels—similar to storing a folder inside another folder.

4 To the left of each of the conversations created in this Project, click to select the check box. On the Gmail toolbar, click **Move to** 🗀▾, and then click **All in One** to add the label to the messages. Scroll to display the top of the left pane, if necessary. Notice that on the left, under **Drafts**, your labels—including *All in One*, which you just created—display.

5 > On the left, click **All in One** to display messages that have that label. At the top of your screen, under the address bar, notice the box that indicates *label:all-in-one*, which indicates where you are in the Gmail structure. Also notice that your starred message(s) display gold. Compare your screen with Figure 9.19.

> When you display messages with a specific label, that label does not display in the message list; rather, it displays at the top of the screen.

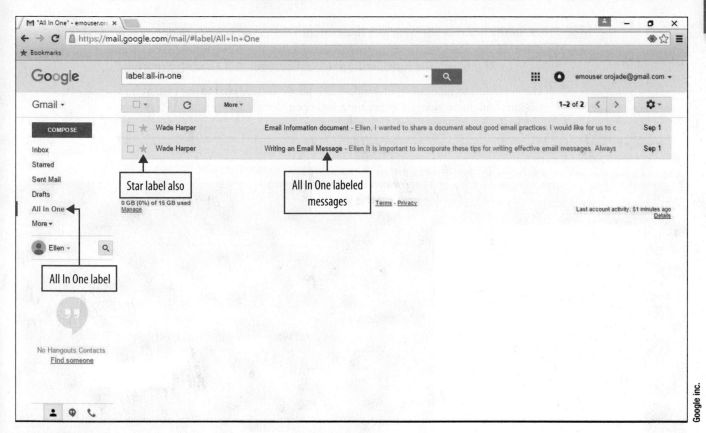

FIGURE 9.19

6 > Return to PowerPoint. On the **Home tab**, in the **Slides** group, click the upper portion of the **New Slide** button to add a new slide in the presentation. Click the **Insert tab**. In the **Images** group, click **Screenshot**, and then click the image of Gmail window to place the screenshot in the slide. Click the **Click to add title** box, and type **Activity 9.06, Step 6** Leave the PowerPoint presentation open.

7 > Return to Gmail. Display your **Inbox**, and remain signed in for the next activity.

More **Knowledge**   **Applying Labels**

When you add a label to a conversation, it applies only to the messages already in that conversation—not to messages sent after you applied the label.

Objective 4   Chat Online Using Google Hangouts

> *Hangouts* is a Google communication platform for video calls, phone calls, or messages using your Google account. Hangout conversations can occur between computers or other devices that have downloaded the Hangouts app on a mobile device.

Activity 9.07 | Participating in a Google Hangout

In this Activity, you will participate in a Google Hangout.

> **A L E R T !**   **Completing the Activity with Your Partner**
>
> Before starting the Activity, with your partner, determine which of you will initiate the first Google Hangout, and then follow the steps accordingly.

1 Click in the **address bar** to select the current URL, type **hangouts.google.com** and then press
Enter. If this is your first time visiting the site, click the **Next arrow** to the right of the message
box to scroll through the introduction. Compare your screen with Figure 9.20.

Use hangouts to participate in a video call, phone call, or chat using instant messaging. The
background photo changes every time you open Google Hangouts.

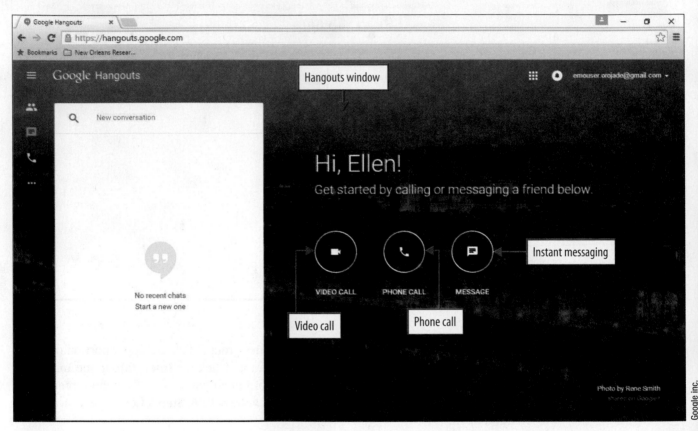

FIGURE 9.20

2 In the message pane, under *No recent chats*, click **Start a new one**. In the **Search for people**
text box, type your partner's name or email address.

Only one partner can start a chat.

3 In the list of people, click your partner, and then on the right, notice the invitation to start a
conversation. Click **Send Invite**.

Notifications of invitations sent will display, and the invitation will display for the recipient.

4 If you received the invitation in the lower left pane, click **Accept**.

Notifications are updated to display the last message received.

5 On the right, in the Hangout, in the **Send a message** box, click the **smiley face** to display emoticons, and then select an appropriate emoticon related to your feelings about using Hangouts. Click to the right of the emoticon, and then type a message to tell your partner how you feel about Hangouts. Compare your screen with Figure 9.21.

From the Hangout window, you can convert the conversation into a video call if you have a webcam and microphone installed. You can also add people to the hangout for a group Hangout.

FIGURE 9.21

6 Press Enter to send the message. Notice that all messages display in the Hangout window on the right, but only a portion of the most recent message received displays in the Conversation window.

7 Return to PowerPoint. On the **Home tab**, in the **Slides** group, click the upper portion of the **New Slide** button to add a new slide in the presentation. Click the **Insert tab**. In the **Images** group, click **Screenshot**, and then click the image of Hangout window to place the screenshot in the slide. Click the **Click to add title** box, and type **Activity 9.07, Step 7** Leave the PowerPoint presentation open.

8 Remain signed in for the next Activity.

More Knowledge | **Participating in More Than One Hangout at a Time**

Click New conversation to start additional hangouts. More than one Hangout window can be displayed at one time.

More Knowledge | **Hangouts On Air Using Google+**

With Hangouts On Air, you can host and broadcast live discussions and performances to the world through your Google+ page and YouTube channel. All Hangouts On Air are public by default, but you can make the event unlisted so that only people with the link can find and watch the video.

Google provides a web-based calendar that you can access from any Internet-connected device. Maintaining an electronic calendar keeps your life organized so that you can avoid scheduling overlapping activities. The Google calendar enables you to enter events on the calendar, manage multiple calendars, and share a calendar with others. Additionally, Google automatically captures events that it finds in your Gmail messages.

3.04a
3.04a (i)
3.04a (ii)

Activity 9.08 | Creating a Google Calendar

Ellen wants to use the Google calendar to track events for the next month. In this Activity, you will enter new events on the current month's calendar.

> 1 ▶ If necessary, sign in to your Google account. From any Google page, at the top of the window, click **Google Apps** ▦, and then click **Calendar** to display the calendar. If necessary, in the **What's new in Google Calendar** box, click **Got it**. Compare your screen to Figure 9.22.

By default, the calendar displays a week at a time; other view options are available above the calendar. Notice the orange line at the current date and time; on the left, the current date is outlined in the thumbnail of the current month. Google enables you to maintain more than one calendar at a time, and multiple calendars can be displayed simultaneously.

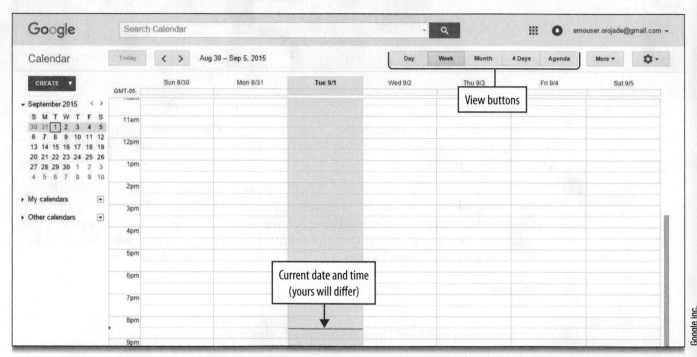

FIGURE 9.22

> 2 ▶ In the upper right corner, above the weekly calendar, click **Month**. In the upper left, to the left of the current month and year, click **Next period** ▶.

> 3 ▶ Click in the first Tuesday of next month to display the **Event** box. In the **What** box, type **11:30 am ABLE Awards Luncheon**

> 4 ▶ Click **Create event** to place the event in the calendar. At the top of your screen, notice the confirmation message that displays when an event is added. Compare your screen with Figure 9.23.

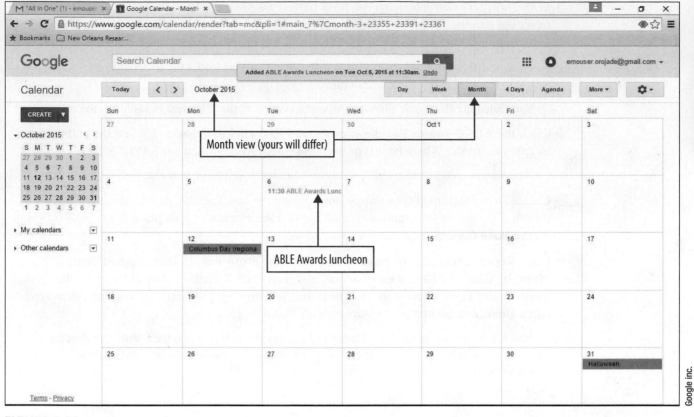

FIGURE 9.23

> **5** In the upper left, click **CREATE** to display the event window. Compare your screen with Figure 9.24.

This window enables you to enter the *details* of the event, for example, guests to include and in which calendar the event should be placed.

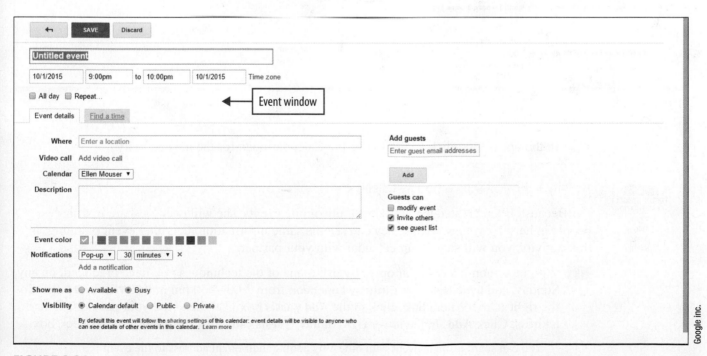

FIGURE 9.24

6 With *Untitled event* selected, type **Nalli-Gifford Wedding** Under the event name, use the boxes to set the date to any Saturday after the current date. Set the **From time** to **5:00 pm** and the **Until time** to **11:30 pm**. Click in the **Where** box, and type **Grand Ballroom A-C**

7 Click in the **Description** box, and type **Flower delivery at 3:00** At the top of the window, click **SAVE** to add the event to your calendar.

> Your calendar displays in Month view, and a portion of the What text is visible in the calendar.

8 Click the **ABLE Awards Luncheon** event, and then click **Edit event**. Update the ending time to **2:00 pm**. In the **Where** box, type **Metairie Room** At the top, click **SAVE**.

> To maintain an accurate calendar, you can edit events as information changes.

9 Create an event named **GBA Happy Hour** during the last Tuesday of this month or next month. Fill out the information to indicate that the event will take place from 5:30–7:00 pm on the **Rose Garden Patio**

10 Click **Repeat** to display the **Repeat** box. Click the arrow next to **Repeats**, and then click **Monthly**. Click the **Repeat every arrow**, and then click **3**. Next to **Repeat by**, click **day of the week**. Under **Ends**, click in the box next to *After*, highlight the existing text, and then type **3** Click **Done**, and compare your screen with Figure 9.25.

> This action schedules the GBA Happy Hour every three months, on the fourth Tuesday, for three times. When you schedule an event to repeat, all of the settings remain the same for each occurrence.

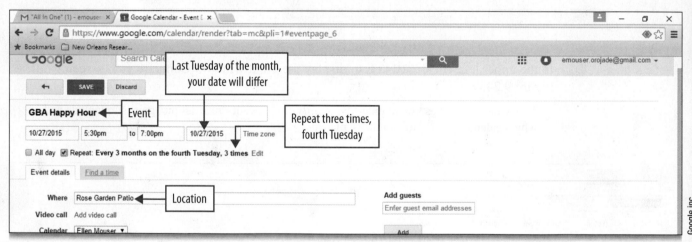

FIGURE 9.25

11 In the upper left, click **SAVE**. Leave the Calendar open for the next Activity.

Activity 9.09 | Sharing a Google Calendar

> Because Ellen created the calendar of upcoming events, she will need to share it with the people in her department so that they can see the same information regarding event planning. In this Activity, you will share your calendar with your partner.

1 With next month's calendar open, by using one of the techniques you have practiced, on any Sunday, add **Lyna Novack's Birthday Luncheon** from 2:00–4:30 pm in the **West End Salon** To the right of the Where box, click in the **Add guests** box, and then type your partner's Gmail address. Click **Add**. In the lower right, under **Guests can**, click the **modify event** check box.

> You can share a single event with others by adding their email address to the event.

2 Return to PowerPoint. On the **Home tab**, in the **Slides** group, click the upper portion of the **New Slide** button to add a new slide in the presentation. Click the **Insert tab**. In the **Images** group, click **Screenshot**, and then click the image of Google Calendar window to place the screenshot in the slide. Click the **Click to add title** box, and type **Activity 9.09, Step 2** Leave the PowerPoint presentation open.

3 Return to Calendar. In the upper left, **Save** the event. In the **Send invitations?** message box, click **Send**.

> An email invitation to the event will be sent to your partner, and you should receive an invitation from him or her.

4 In the left pane, to the right of **My calendars**, click the arrow.

> You can create a new calendar to maintain separate calendars. For example, you can create additional calendars to manage your work activities and your personal activities.

5 On the list, click **Settings**. In the calendar you are using for this activity, on the right under **SHARING**, click **Share this calendar** to display the Sharing settings.

> If you maintain multiple calendars in one Google account, verify that you are viewing the details of the correct calendar. By default, a calendar is private—not shared. You can choose to make a calendar public so that anyone can view it, or you can make your calendar visible in a way that others can view only your availability or free/busy schedule. It is probably not good practice to make your calendar public; keep it secure by choosing to share it only with specific people.

6 Under **Share with specific people**, click in the **Person** box, and type your partner's Gmail address. On the right, under **Permission Settings**, click the arrow to the right of *See all event details*, and compare your screen with Figure 9.26.

> The default option enables the person with whom you are sharing to see all event details. Other options include allowing the person to change the event and share it with others, only allowing the person to make changes to events, or restricting it further by only allowing the person to see the free/busy schedule.

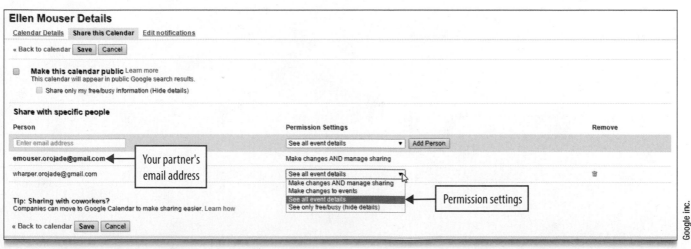

FIGURE 9.26

7 From the displayed list, select **Make changes to events** so that your partner can modify the events in the calendar, if necessary.

8 At the bottom of the window, click **Save**. Notice your events and your partner's events display on the same calendar; your partner's events are color coded to match the key under **Other calendars** in the left pane. To modify, add, or remove calendars from your view, click the calendar arrow, and select the appropriate option.

9 Return to PowerPoint. On the **Home tab**, in the **Slides** group, click the upper portion of the **New Slide** button to add a new slide in the presentation. Click the **Insert tab**. In the **Images** group, click **Screenshot**, and then click the image of Google Calendar window to place the screenshot in the slide. Click the **Click to add title** box, and type **Activity 9.09, Step 9**

10 Press Ctrl + Home to display **Slide 1**. On the **Quick Access** toolbar, click **Save** 🔲. Navigate to the location where you are saving your files for this chapter, and then create and open a new folder named **All in One Chapter 9** In the **File name** box, using your own name, replace the existing text with **Lastname_Firstname_9A_Google_Screens** and then click **Save**.

11 Click the **File tab** to display **Backstage** view, and then click **Print**. Under **Settings**, click **Full Page Slides**. Under **Handouts**, click **6 Slides Horizontal**. Notice that the **Print Preview** on the right displays the slide handout; your printout will require two pages. In the upper left portion of the screen, click **Print**. To create an electronic image of your document that looks like a printed document, on the left click **Export**. On the right, click **Create PDF/XPS** to display the **Publish as PDF or XPS** dialog box. Navigate to the location where you want to save your document, and then click **Publish**.

12 Return to Calendar. Click the arrow next to your email address, and click **Sign out**. Close **Chrome**.

13 As directed by your instructor, submit the PowerPoint file that includes all of screenshots from this project: 9A_Google_Screens

---

More Knowledge | **Adding Additional Calendars**

To add additional calendars, click the Other Calendars arrow, and then select the type of calendar you would like to add. Follow the prompts to display the contents on your calendar.

> **END | You have completed Project 9A**

Microsoft Cloud Computing and OneNote

PROJECT ACTIVITIES

Wanda Myers, a Special Events Coordinator for Oro Jade New Orleans, uses online tools to communicate with her team and share files. She also uses OneNote to organize information related to each project. In Activities 9.10 through 9.18, you will practice using OneDrive, Skype, and OneNote. Your completed documents and screen captures will look similar to Figure 9.27.

PROJECT FILES

For Project 9B, you will need the following files:

pdf09B_Renovation_Plan
e09B_Expense_Report
w09B_Project_Planner
jpg09B_Logo
w09B_Florist_List

You will save your files as:

**Lastname_Firstname_9B_Microsoft_
Screens (The PowerPoint file will include
3 screenshots that you will create while
completing the Project.)
Lastname_Firstname_9B_Special_Events**

PROJECT RESULTS

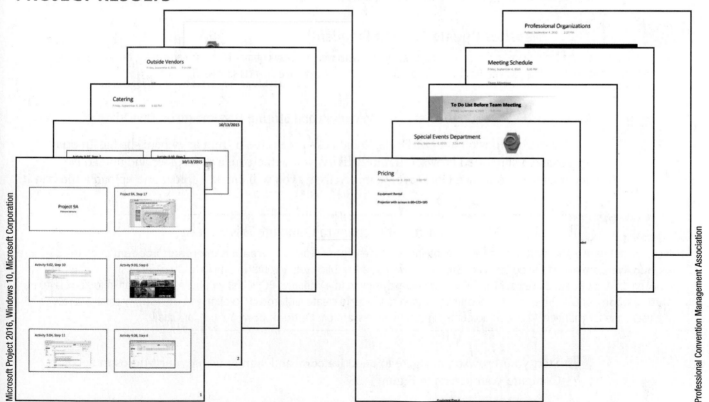

FIGURE 9.27 Project 9B Microsoft Cloud Computing and OneNote

Objective 6 — Use Your Microsoft Account's OneDrive for Storing and Sharing Files

When you create a free Microsoft account, it comes with **OneDrive**, a free file storage and file-sharing service with almost unlimited storage—a terabyte. In an organization, the compatible storage location for documents could be in **OneDrive** or in a **SharePoint** library—both of which provide high-level security features that businesses demand. SharePoint is a related group of technologies from Microsoft for collaboration, file sharing, and web publishing within organizations.

As an individual, your compatible storage location is OneDrive. Using web servers on the Internet—for example, OneDrive or a SharePoint library—to store files and run applications is referred to as **cloud computing**. By using OneDrive or a SharePoint library, your documents are easy to access from anywhere and easy to share with others using any Internet-connected device—and regardless of whether you have a version of Microsoft Office on your computer.

ALERT! | **Websites Update Content Frequently**

As you progress through the Projects in this chapter, the pictures of various websites may not match your screen exactly, because website administrators frequently update content. This will not affect your ability to complete the Projects successfully.

Activity 9.10 | **Creating Folders and Uploading and Storing Documents on OneDrive**

By storing files on her OneDrive, Wanda can access them from anywhere she has Internet access and a supported browser. In this activity, you will create a new folder and upload two documents to your own OneDrive. In this Activity, you will create a folder and upload a file into it.

NOTE | You Will Need a Microsoft Account to Complete This Project

If you do not have a Microsoft account, use an Internet search engine to search for **create a microsoft account** or go to **signup.live.com** and at the bottom click **Sign up now**. Use a free Microsoft account to sign in to Office 2016 so that you can work on different PCs and use your OneDrive. If you already sign in to a Windows PC, tablet, or phone, or you sign in to Xbox Live, **Outlook.com**, or OneDrive, use that account to sign in to Office. To create a Microsoft account, you can *use any* email address as the username for your new Microsoft account—including addresses from **Outlook.com**, Yahoo!, or Gmail.

1 ▶ Start your browser, navigate to **onedrive.com**, and sign in using your Microsoft account. Compare your screen to Figure 9.28.

Default folders display Files, Recent, Photos, Shared, and Recycle bin. In your OneDrive, you can create a new folder or create new documents using Microsoft's Office Online applications. You can use the Upload command to upload any type of file for storage in your OneDrive.

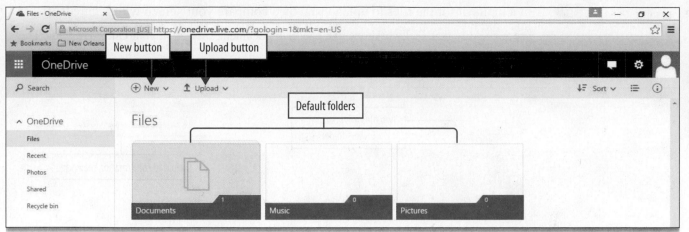

FIGURE 9.28

2 ▸ At the top of the window, click **New**, and then click **Folder**. In the box, type **Department Projects** and then press Enter or click **Create**.

This action creates a new folder on your OneDrive that is available only to you. If you already have folders, this folder will be positioned alphabetically.

3 ▸ Double-click the **Department Projects** folder to open it, and then compare your screen with Figure 9.29.

The new folder is open to enable you to add files. A path *Files > Department Projects* displays and you can navigate the path in the same manner that you navigate in File Explorer in Windows. Clicking the Change view button will toggle between icons and a file list.

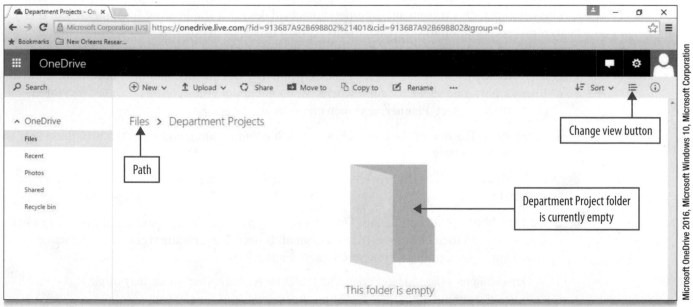

FIGURE 9.29

4 ▸ In the row of commands at the top of the window, click **Upload**, and then click **Files** to add files to this folder on your OneDrive.

5 ▸ In the **Open** dialog box, navigate to the location where your student data files for this chapter are stored, hold down Ctrl so that you can select multiple files, and then while holding down Ctrl, select the files **pdf09B_Renovation_Plan** and **e09B_Expense_Report**. Then, in the lower right corner of the dialog box, click **Open**.

6 Wait a moment for the files to upload, and then compare your screen with Figure 9.30.

The two files, one Excel workbook and one PDF document, display in your OneDrive folder and display tiles identifying the two document types.

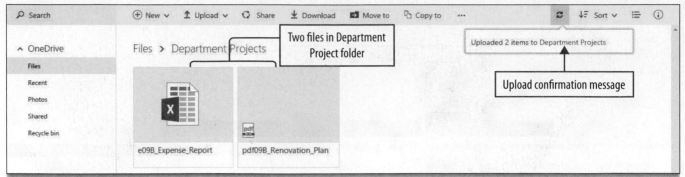

FIGURE 9.30

Microsoft OneDrive 2016, Microsoft Windows 10, Microsoft Corporation

7 In the file path, click **Files** to redisplay all the folders in your OneDrive. Remain signed in to OneDrive for the next Activity.

↻ BY TOUCH   Tap the location in the path.

Activity 9.11 | Saving a Document to OneDrive

When Wanda creates a document using Office 2016, she saves the document to her OneDrive so that she can access it from any Internet-connected device if she is away from the office. It is becoming less common to store documents on hard drives or in other locations that cannot be accessed from the Internet. In this Activity, you will save a Word document to OneDrive.

1 Start Microsoft Word. On the left, click **Open Other Documents**, and then under **Open**, click **Browse**. Navigate to the location where your student data files for this chapter are stored, click **w09B_Project_Planner**, and then click **Open**.

2 In the **PHASE 3** row of the table, click in the **Starting** column, and type **7/1/2019** Press ⟨Tab⟩ and type **10/22/2019**

3 In the **RIBBON CUTTING** row, click in the **Starting/Ending** merged column, and then type **11/5/2019**

4 On the ribbon, click the **File tab**. On the left, click **Save As**. Under **Save As**, if necessary click **OneDrive**, and then click **OneDrive – Personal**. If necessary, on the right, click the name of your OneDrive. Compare your screen with Figure 9.31.

Depending on what you have done with OneDrive recently, your screen may display different items.

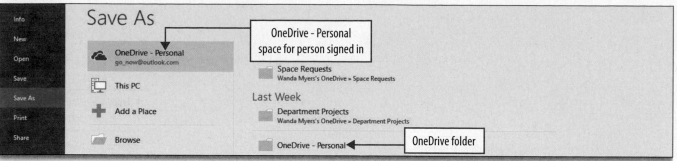

FIGURE 9.31

Microsoft OneDrive 2016, Microsoft Windows 10, Microsoft Corporation

---

ALERT! **Not Signed Into Your Microsoft Account in Word?**

If you are not signed into your Microsoft account in Word, under OneDrive, click Sign In. Type your Microsoft email address in the box, and click Next. In the Sign in box, type your password, and click Sign in. You must sign in before proceeding to the next step.

5 On the right, double-click the **Department Projects** folder. In the **Save As** dialog box, in the **File name** box, save the file as **Lastname_Firstname_9B_Planner_OneDrive** Click **Save**.

6 In the upper right corner, click **Close** [×] to close Word. Remain signed in to OneDrive for the next Activity.

Activity 9.12 | Sharing Files by Using Email

When Wanda wants to share a file stored on her OneDrive, she can use email to share that document. In this Activity, you will share a file with your partner.

1 Click the **Department Projects** folder to open it and display all of the documents stored there. Point to the upper right corner of the **9B_Planner_OneDrive** tile to display a small circle, and then click one time to select this file.

A blue circle with a check mark displays to indicate that the file is selected.

2 At the top of the window, click **Share** to display the **Share** dialog box. Compare your screen with Figure 9.32.

Here you can type the email address of the recipient in the To box and then add a quick note to explain why you are sharing the file. There is no Subject box, because when you click Share, the subject line is automatically created to let the recipient know who is sharing a file with them.

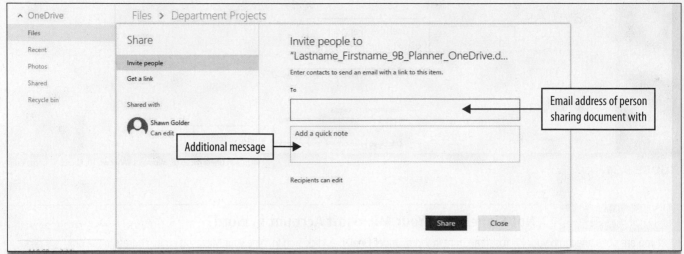

FIGURE 9.32

3 In the **To** box, type your partner's email address.

> If you have added your partner as a contact, you may notice his or her email address displays when you type the first few characters. Press Enter at any time to accept it.

4 Click in the **Add a quick note** box, type a greeting, and press Enter two times. Type **Here is the information you requested about the renovation project.**

> It is a good idea to include a message with shared files to provide information about the file or instructions.

5 Below the message box, click **Recipients can edit**.

> Two boxes display. The first enables the recipient to edit the document stored on your OneDrive. The second allows you to select whether or not the recipient must sign into his or her Microsoft account to be able to access the document.

6 With *Recipients can edit* and *Recipients don't need a Microsoft account* displayed, click the **Share** button.

> When you share a Word document, an Excel workbook, or a PowerPoint presentation using email, the recipient clicks the link in the message, and the document opens in his or her web browser.

More Knowledge	**Sharing a Folder**

To send a link to an entire folder, click the folder to select it, and then click Sharing to display the email window.

---

7 A window displays to confirm that your partner has editing rights in this document. Click **Close**.

> If your partner has shared the document with you, click the OneDrive arrow, and then click Mail to display your Inbox. Open the email message to see a link in the message.

8 Point to the **9B_Planner_OneDrive** file, right-click, and then click **Details** to display the **Information pane**. Compare your screen with Figure 9.33.

> The information about the document on your OneDrive displays on the right. Here you can see that the file is a Word document and that it has been shared with your partner.

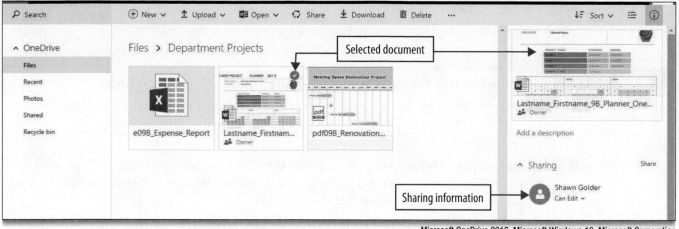

FIGURE 9.33

Microsoft OneDrive 2016, Microsoft Windows 10, Microsoft Corporation

9 ▶ Click the text *Add a description*, and then in the box type **Renovation Project Plan**

Recall that adding tags like this to documents enables you to search for them later by using the tag.

10 ▶ Start PowerPoint 2016. On the right, click **Blank Presentation**. Click the **Click to add title** box, and type **Project 9B** Click the **Click to add subtitle** box, and type your **Firstname Lastname** On the **Home tab**, in the **Slides** group, click the upper portion of the **New Slide** button to add a new slide in the presentation. Click the **Insert tab**. In the **Images** group, click **Screenshot**, and then click the image of Google Chrome window to place the screenshot in the slide. Click the **Click to add title** box, and type **Activity 9.12, Step 10** Leave the PowerPoint presentation open.

11 ▶ Return to OneDrive. Sign out of **OneDrive**, and **Close** ⊠ your browser.

Objective 7 | Communicate Using Skype

Skype is a software application you can use to make voice or video calls, share files, or send messages—including instant messages and text messages—over the Internet. *Instant messaging* is the real-time communication between two or more participants over the Internet. It is free to set up a basic Skype account, or you can pay for more sophisticated services, such as those you might need in a business. Free services include instant messaging, calls to other users within the Skype service, one-to-one video calls, and screen sharing. Other services, for example, calls to landline and mobile phones, can be made for a fee or with a subscription.

ALERT! | **Two Requirements to Complete the Following Skype Project**

There are two requirements to complete these Skype Activities:

1. You must have or download Skype and be able to sign in to your Microsoft account to complete this Activity. To install using Windows 10, go the Windows Store and download the Skype app. If you are using an earlier version of Windows, go to **www.skype.com** and download the free version for your type of device. Follow the directions to use your Microsoft account. Keep in mind that computer programs on the web receive continuous updates and improvements. Therefore, your screen may differ from the ones shown. You can often look at the screens and the information presented to determine how to complete the activity.

2. When completing Activities 9.13–9.15, identify a classmate or friend who has or can set up a Skype account. Then, partner with this individual to complete the Project. You will both need to be online at the same time, but you do not have to be in the same location.

Activity 9.13 | Adding Contacts in Skype

In this Activity, you will add a contact in Skype.

1 On the computer you are using, if necessary download and install Skype, and then start Skype and sign in with your Skype Name and password. Be sure that your partner has done the same. Compare your screen with Figure 9.34.

Your profile icon displays and identifies that you are currently online.

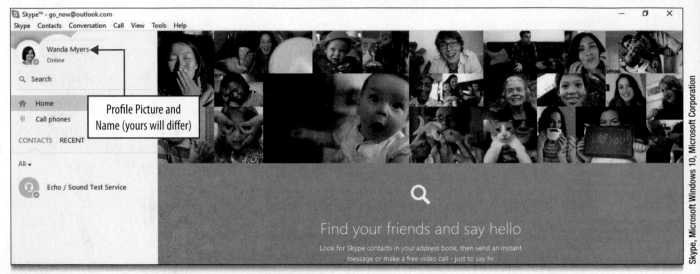

FIGURE 9.34

2 At the top of the Skype window, on the menu bar, click **Contacts**, point to **Add Contact**, and then click **Search Skype Directory**. With your insertion point blinking on the Search line, type your partner's email address or Skype name and then press Enter.

Before you can communicate with someone using Skype, you must add him or her as a contact. If your partner has a common name, it may be easier to search for his or her email address. Skype searches its users and displays information regarding anyone who has matching information.

3 When the correct match is found, click it, and then, on the right, click **add to contacts**—or right-click and click **Add to Contacts**. Compare your screen with Figure 9.35.

A contact request message will be sent to your partner via Skype. The request must be accepted before you can communicate using Skype.

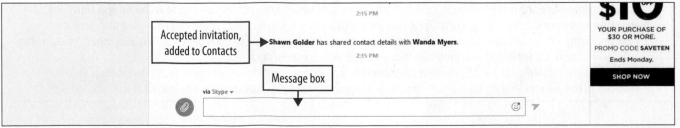

FIGURE 9.35

Skype, Microsoft Windows 10, Microsoft Corporation

4 ▶ Modify the message in the box, if you choose, and then click **send** to send the request to your partner.

 BY TOUCH   Tap inside the message window, and type new text to replace it. Tap send to send.

5 ▶ After you receive the request from your partner, on the left, click under **RECENT**, and click the request you receive from your partner. Click **accept**.

> When sending or accepting a contact request, the other person does not need to be online. However, both parties must be online to make and receive calls. If you are unsure about a request you receive, you can decline the request.

6 ▶ Remain signed in for the next Activity.

More Knowledge   **Uploading a Profile Picture**

Click the Skype menu, point to Profile, and then click Change Your Picture to either take a profile picture with your webcam or upload a picture from your device.

Activity 9.14 │ **Instant Messaging with Skype**

In this Activity, you will send and receive instant messages using Skype.

1 ▶ On the left, with **CONTACTS** selected, click your partner's name.

> Your contact's name and profile picture display. Verify you are sending your messages to the right person before you start typing. You may see earlier messages at the top of the window.

 BY TOUCH   Tap your partner's name.

2 ▶ In the message text box, click the icon on the right side, and select an emoticon that shows how you are feeling today.

> Recall that an emoticon is an image that represents facial expressions. Emoticons should be used only in informal electronic communication to convey feelings.

3 ▶ In the text box, type a short message to tell your partner about a benefit of instant messaging in the workplace. Press ⟨Enter⟩ to send the message to your partner.

> In the message window, you can see both the message you sent and the one you received identified by each person's display name and photo. You can continue the conversation by typing a new message in the message text box and pressing ⟨Enter⟩.

4 ▶ Return to PowerPoint. On the **Home tab**, in the **Slides** group, click the upper portion of the **New Slide** button to add a new slide in the presentation. Click the **Insert tab**. In the **Images** group, click **Screenshot**, and then click the image of instant messaging window to place the screenshot in the slide. Click the **Click to add title** box, and type **Activity 9.14, Step 4** Leave the PowerPoint presentation open.

5 ▶ Remain signed in to Skype for the next Activity.

Activity 9.15 │ **Participating in a Skype Call**

In this Activity, you will participate in a Skype call.

1 ▶ If necessary, under **Contacts**, click your partner's name. Next to his or her profile picture, click **Call** 📞 if you want to participate in an audio-only call; click **Video call** 📹

if you and the person you are calling have a webcam and want to include video in the Skype call.

2 ▶ Return to PowerPoint. On the **Home tab**, in the **Slides** group, click the upper portion of the **New Slide** button to add a new slide in the presentation. Click the **Insert tab**. In the **Images** group, click **Screenshot**, and then click the image of Skype window to place the screenshot in the slide. Click the **Click to add title** box, and type **Activity 9.15, Step 2** Leave PowerPoint open.

3 ▶ Press Ctrl + Home to display **Slide 1**. **Save** 🖫 the file in your **All in One Chapter 9** folder as **Lastname_Firstname_9B_Microsoft_Screens**

4 ▶ Return to Skype. When the call is complete, click **End Call** 🔽.

5 ▶ Click the **Skype** menu, and then click **Sign Out**.

For security of your account, be sure to sign out before leaving your computer.

6 ▶ If necessary, return to PowerPoint. Click the **File tab** to display **Backstage** view, and then click **Print**. Under **Settings**, click **Full Page Slides**. Under **Handouts**, click **4 Slides Horizontal**. Notice that the **Print Preview** on the right displays the slide handout. In the upper left portion of the screen, click **Print**. To create an electronic image of your document that looks like a printed document, on the left click **Export**. On the right, click **Create PDF/XPS** to display the **Publish as PDF or XPS** dialog box. Navigate to the location where you want to save your document, and then click **Publish**.

Objective 8 Use OneNote to Create a Notebook

OneNote is a Microsoft application with which you can create a digital notebook that provides a single location where you can gather and organize information in the form of *notes*. A note can include typed text, handwritten text if you have a tablet PC, pictures and graphics—including images and text that you capture from webpages—audio and video recordings, and documents from other applications such as Word or Excel. You can also share a OneNote notebook with others, or store your notebook on the web so that you can view and edit your notes from any computer with an Internet connection.

OneNote is an integrated part of Microsoft Office, so if you are familiar with the Microsoft Office programs, you will recognize the ribbon and tab layout as being similar to what you have used in Word, Excel, and PowerPoint.

The OneNote app is available for Windows mobile devices, Apple iOS devices, and Android devices, so you can access your notebooks from any Internet-connected device.

Activity 9.16 | Creating a Notebook

In this Activity, you will examine the elements of the OneNote window and create a notebook to store notes related to Wanda's Special Events department updates.

1 ▶ On the taskbar, in the Search box, type **onenote** In the **Apps** list, click **OneNote 2016 Desktop app**. Compare your screen with Figure 9.36, and then take a moment to study the OneNote window elements described in the table in Figure 9.37.

In OneNote, a *notebook* is a collection of files organized by major divisions and stored in a common folder. OneNote includes one pre-made notebook named *Personal* if you are not currently logged into your Microsoft account.

The *Personal* notebook contains one *section*—the *Quick Notes* section. A section is the primary division of a notebook, identifying a main topic and containing related *pages* of notes. A page is a subdivision of a section where notes are inserted. Think of a section just like the tabbed sections you would have in a three-ring notebook, and think of a page just like the paper pages you have in a notebook.

In the current notebook, the Quick Notes section contains two pages of notes, created by Microsoft, that explain features of OneNote.

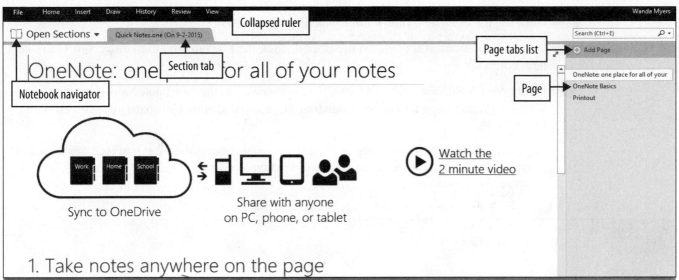

FIGURE 9.36

Microsoft OneNote 2016 Desktop App, Windows 10, Microsoft Corporation

WINDOW ELEMENT	DESCRIPTION
Ribbon	Groups, on tabs, the commands for performing related tasks, collapsed by default.
Notebook navigator	Displays the name of the active notebook. Click the arrow to open a new notebook or a quick note.
Section tab	Identifies a primary division of the active notebook.
Page tabs list	Displays the name of each page in the active section.
Page	Displays the content of the active page.

FIGURE 9.37

Gaskin, Shelley. GO! All in One, 3E. Pearson Education, 2017.

ALERT! **What If the Tutorial Notebook Does Not Display?**

When you open OneNote, the window displays as it was the last time OneNote was open at the computer at which you are working, so your screen may differ from Figure 9.36. The window elements, however, are the same. If another notebook displays, read the steps in this Activity, and then begin with Step 6.

---

2 On the ribbon, point to the **Insert tab** and right-click. On the displayed list, notice that a check mark displays to the left of **Collapse the Ribbon**.

The check mark indicates that the Collapse the Ribbon command is turned on. In OneNote, the ribbon is minimized by default to provide more space on the screen for inserting notes in the pages of your notebook.

ALERT! **Ribbon May Display Fully**

If someone else has already maximized the ribbon and it displays on your screen, you will not see a check mark to the left of Collapse the Ribbon. This feature is a toggle, so clicking it will collapse or restore the ribbon, depending on its current setting.

---

3 Click **Collapse the Ribbon** to remove the check mark and display the full ribbon.

4 On the right edge of the page, locate and then click the link **Watch the 2 minute video**. In the displayed window—your browser—maximize the window, click the **Play** button , and watch this short video.

Scroll down the page to see more information about OneNote and access additional 30-second videos.

5 **Close** ⊠ the browser window after watching the video.

6 With the notebook still open, on the ribbon, click the **File tab**, and then click **New** to create a new notebook.

7 Under *New Notebook*, click **This PC**. Under *This PC*, in the **Notebook Name** box, using your own name, type **Lastname_Firstname_9B_Special_Events** Compare your screen with Figure 9.38.

A notebook stored on your computer is only accessible from that device; however, a notebook created on the web can be accessed from other computers or mobile devices—from any Internet-connected device.

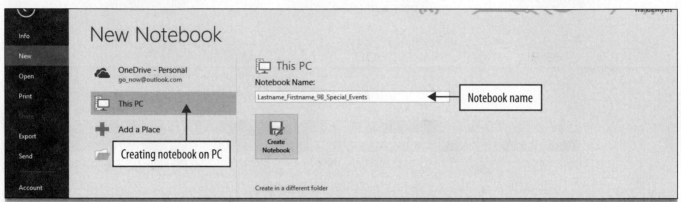

FIGURE 9.38

Microsoft OneNote 2016 Desktop App, Windows 10, Microsoft Corporation

8 Under the **Create Notebook** button, click **Create in a different folder**. Navigate to your **All in One Chapter 9** folder, and then click **Create**. Compare your screen with Figure 9.39.

Your new notebook becomes the active notebook, and its name displays at the top. The new notebook displays a section tab named *New Section 1* containing an *Untitled page* that includes the current date.

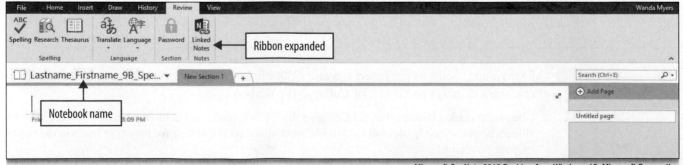

FIGURE 9.39

Microsoft OneNote 2016 Desktop App, Windows 10, Microsoft Corporation

Activity 9.17 | Creating Sections and Pages in a Notebook

By creating a section for different elements of the feasibility study, Wanda will be able to organize her notes. Then, she can add pages to each section to further organize her information.

1 Below the ribbon, point to the tab **New Section 1** and right-click. On the shortcut menu, click **Rename**.

2 With the text selected, type **Equipment** and then press Enter.

The new section name displays on the *section tab*—a tab that identifies a primary division of the active notebook.

3 To the right of the **Equipment tab**, click **Create a New Section** +. With *New Section 1* selected, type **Services** and then press Enter.

You can create as many sections as you need in a notebook. The Create a New Section tab will always display to the right of existing section tabs.

4 Using the technique you just practiced, create another new section tab named **Team**

5 Point to the **Services** section tab, hold down the left mouse button, and then drag the **Services** section tab to the left of the **Equipment** section tab. When a small black triangle displays at the top left of the **Equipment** section tab, compare your screen with Figure 9.40.

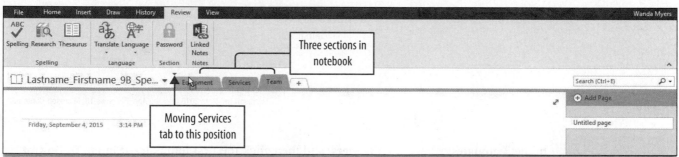

FIGURE 9.40

Microsoft OneNote 2016 Desktop App, Windows 10, Microsoft Corporation

6 Release the mouse button to move the **Services** section tab to the left of the **Equipment** section tab.

7 Click the **Services** section tab to make the section active. If necessary, click above the date and time to place the insertion point, and then type **Outside Vendors** and press Enter to title the page. On the right, notice that the title also displays on the *page tabs list*—a list on the right side of the OneNote notebook that displays the name of each page in the active section.

8 On the right, in the **page tabs list**, click **Add Page** to display a new untitled page. In the **Page Title** box above the date and time, type **Catering** and then compare your screen with Figure 9.41.

Your two new pages display in the page tabs list. The active Catering page tab is white; the other page tab displays in a lighter shade of the section color.

FIGURE 9.41

Microsoft OneNote 2016 Desktop App, Windows 10, Microsoft Corporation

9 In the **page tabs list**, point to **Outside Vendors**, hold down the left mouse button, and then drag down until a line displays below **Catering**. Release the mouse button to move the page.

↻ BY TOUCH   Tap and drag the tab to move it down.

10 Click the **Team** section tab. In the **Page Title** box, type **Special Events Department**

Each section that you create begins with a single untitled page.

11 With the **Team** section tab active, on the ribbon, click the **Insert tab**. In the **Pages group**, click the upper portion of the **Page Templates** button to display the **Templates** pane on the right. Compare your screen with Figure 9.42.

A *page template* is a file that serves as a pattern for creating a new page. Use a page template to ensure a uniform page layout and design. For example, a template might include background images, text formatting, and consistent use of color that you want for your notebook pages.

Page templates are arranged by categories. You can download additional templates from Microsoft or create your own.

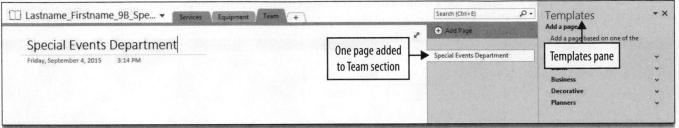

Microsoft OneNote 2016 Desktop App, Windows 10, Microsoft Corporation

FIGURE 9.42

12 In the **Templates** pane, click **Planners**, and then click the first template—**Simple To Do List**. **Close** ☒ the **Templates** pane, and then take a moment to study the page components.

13 In the **Page Title** box, click to the right of the text *To Do List* to place your insertion point, press Spacebar, and then type **Before Team Meeting** Press Enter.

14 With the **Team** section tab active, on the right, in the **page tabs list**, click **Add Page** to display a new untitled page. In the **Page Title** box above the date and time, and type **Meeting Schedule**

More Knowledge   **Changing Default Settings for Easy Viewing**

In OneNote, you can modify the Default font, Office background, and Office Theme. To do so, click the File tab, and then click Options. On the left, with General displayed, make any changes.

More Knowledge   **OneNote Saves Automatically and Continuously**

OneNote saves your work automatically and continuously while you take notes, when you switch to another page or section, and when you close a section or a notebook. You need not save any notes manually.

Activity 9.18 | **Inserting and Formatting Content**

In this Activity, you will add content to the pages of Wanda's notebook.

1 Click the **Team tab**, if necessary. Click the **Special Events Department** page to make it active. On the left side of the page, point approximately 1 inch below the date and time, and click one time to place the insertion point there. Type **Wanda Myers, Special Events Coordinator** and as you type, you will see a note container.

> When you click a page and then begin to type, a *note container*—a box that can contain text, pictures, video clips, and other types of notes—displays.

2 Select the text **Wanda Myers**. On the mini toolbar, click **Bold** [B] to apply bold to the selection.

3 Point approximately one inch to the right of the note container to display the [I] pointer, click one time, and then type **Ellen Mouser, Event Planner**

> Only one note container—the active container—displays at a time.

4 In the **page tabs list**, click the **Meeting Schedule** page tab. Click below the date and time to place the insertion point, and then type the following text, pressing [Enter] after each line:

> **Team Meetings**
> **January 3 Year in Review, Planning**
> **February 21 Renovation Update**
> **March 11 Summer Schedule Review**

5 Select the text **Team Meetings**, and then on the mini toolbar, click **Styles** [A]. On the displayed list, click **Heading 4**. Select the remaining three lines of text, and then on the mini toolbar, click **Bullets** [≡ ▾]. Press [Esc] to deselect the text. Compare your screen with Figure 9.43.

> *Styles* are combinations of formatting options that look attractive together. On the mini toolbar, the Styles are available without having to display any ribbon tabs.

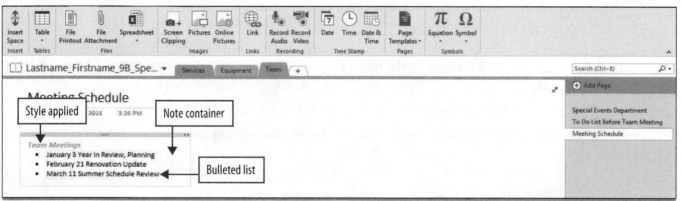

FIGURE 9.43

Microsoft OneNote 2016 Desktop App, Windows 10, Microsoft Corporation

6 Click the **Equipment section tab**, and then add a page named **Pricing**. Click approximately an inch below the date and time to open a new note container, and then type **Equipment Rental** Press [Enter] two times.

7 Type **Projector with screen is 60+125=** and then press [Spacebar]. Notice the result *185* displays to the right of the equal sign. Compare your screen with Figure 9.44.

> OneNote includes a calculator feature that supports simple arithmetic operations, mathematical functions such as square root, and trigonometric functions. Type the mathematical expression with no spaces, and then type an equal sign followed by a space to display the result.

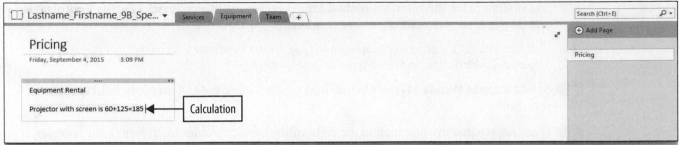

FIGURE 9.44

8 ▶ Click the **Team** section tab, and then click the **Special Events Department** page tab.

9 ▶ Click below the note container that contains Wanda's information. Type **Team Member** and then press Tab.

> Pressing Tab while typing text in a note container will begin a new table that you can expand as necessary. The Table Tools Layout commands display on the ribbon, from which you can select table-specific formatting and selection tools and control the display of the table borders.

10 ▶ With the insertion point blinking in the second column, type **Extension** and then press Enter. Type **Wade Harper** press Tab and then type **8390**

> After you start a new table, pressing Tab creates additional rows. To stop expanding the table, click outside it or press Enter two times.

11 ▶ In the table, click to position the insertion point to the left of **Team Member**, and then drag to the right to select all the text in the first row. On the **Home tab**, in the **Basic Text group**, click **Bold** B. Click in a blank area of the page to deselect the text.

12 ▶ With the **Special Events Department** page tab displayed, click to the right of the *Special Events Department* page title. On the ribbon, click the **Insert tab**, and then in the **Images group**, click **Pictures**. In the **Insert Picture** dialog box, navigate to the location where the student files for this chapter are stored. Click the file **jpg09B_Logo**.

> The Insert Picture command displays only files that are image file types.

13 ▶ In the **Insert Picture** dialog box, click **Insert**, and then compare your screen with Figure 9.45.

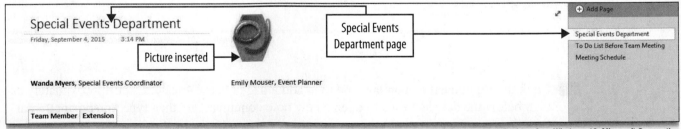

FIGURE 9.45

14 ▶ Click the **Services tab**, and then click the **Outside Vendors** page. If necessary, click below the date and time. On the ribbon, click **Insert tab**, and in the **Files group**, click **File Printout**.

> *File Printout* is a feature that inserts information from a file as a printed copy in the page. This feature is useful because text in the printout can be searched just like any other content in OneNote.

15 In the **Choose Document to Insert** dialog box, navigate to the location where your data files are stored. Select **w09B_Florist_List**, and then click **Insert**. Wait for the Inserting Documents indicator to complete. Scroll to display the top of the page, if necessary, and then compare your screen with Figure 9.46.

> The text from the selected file is inserted in the page as an image—it cannot be edited. A link to the actual file also displays.

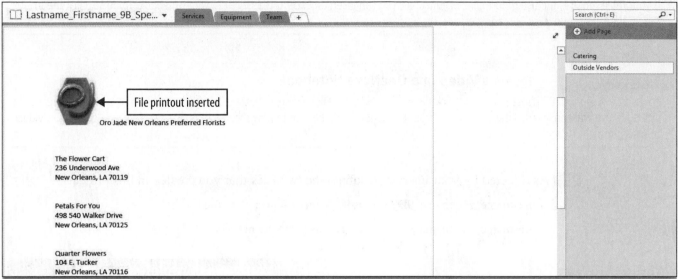

FIGURE 9.46

Microsoft OneNote 2016 Desktop App, Windows 10, Microsoft Corporation

16 Click the **Team tab**, and then add a page named **Professional Organizations** Click below the date and time.

17 On the taskbar, open your browser, and navigate to **pcma.org** Press ⊞ + Shift + S to insert a screen clipping.

> A *screen clipping* is what you are seeing on your screen, a webpage, or a document. The clipping is then sent to the active notebook page.

18 Select the logo area of the webpage. Notice the selected area displays on the **Professional Organizations** page. **Maximize** ☐ the **OneNote** window.

19 Click the **File tab**, and then click **Export**. Under *1. Export Current:*, click **Notebook**. Compare your screen with Figure 9.47.

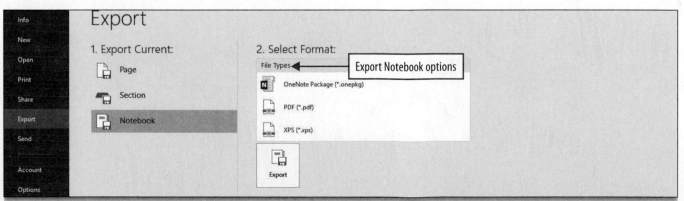

FIGURE 9.47

Microsoft OneNote 2016 Desktop App, Windows 10, Microsoft Corporation

20 Under *2. Select Format:* click **PDF**, and then click the **Export** button. Navigate to your **All in One Chapter 9** folder. Verify that the file name is **Lastname_Firstname_9B_Special_Events** and then click **Save**.

21 **Close** OneNote. **Close** your browser.

More **Knowledge**   **Insert a Spreadsheet in a OneNote Notebook**

If your table requires the use of formulas or functions, you can insert an Excel spreadsheet in your notebook. To do so, click the Insert tab. In the Files group, click Spreadsheet, and then select an existing or a new spreadsheet.

More **Knowledge**   **Insert a Video in a OneNote Notebook**

To insert a video in a OneNote notebook, click the Insert tab. In the Files group, click the File Attachment button, and then select the video file you want to insert. After the video is inserted, double-click the icon to play the video. With a webcam, you can record video to insert in the notebook.

---

22 As directed by your instructor, submit the two files that you created in this project:

Lastname_Firstname_9B_Microsoft_Screens PowerPoint file

Lastname_Firstname_9B_Special_Events OneNote notebook

END | You have completed Project 9B

Professional Social Networking Using LinkedIn and Twitter

PROJECT ACTIVITIES

In Activities 9.19 through 9.23, you will work with Paula Oliver, the Special Events Assistant at Oro Jade New Orleans, as she develops a LinkedIn profile for professional social networking and uses Twitter to follow the industry and inform others about events in the area. You will capture screens that will look similar to Figure 9.48.

PROJECT FILES

For Project 9C, you will not need any files

You will save your files as:

Lastname_Firstname_9C_Networking_Screens (The PowerPoint file will include 4 screenshots that you will create while completing the Project.)

PROJECT RESULTS

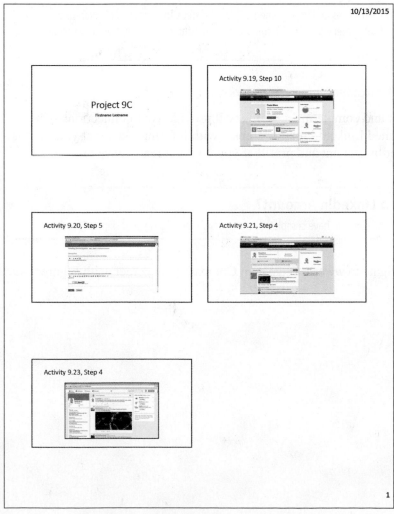

FIGURE 9.48 Project 9C Professional Social Networking

JOB FOCUS | Special Events Assistant

A Special Events Assistant handles the support functions for the event planners and special events coordinator. The assistant should have excellent communication skills and be well organized. The assistant is responsible for producing documents, communicating with vendors, and promoting the Oro Jade facilities through social media.

Objective 9 Create a LinkedIn Account

LinkedIn is a professional social networking site where you can find past and present colleagues and classmates, connect with appropriate people when seeking a new job or business opportunity, or get answers from industry experts. LinkedIn is widely accepted as the best place to become more active in your industry or search for a new career. LinkedIn summarizes what it does as *connecting people with opportunities.*

LinkedIn communication occurs within your list of *Connections*. Connections are the people with whom you have some level of online relationship using LinkedIn. To use LinkedIn, you develop a profile that includes information such as your recent work experience, education, photo, and specific skills that you have.

ALERT! | **Working with Web-Based Applications and Services**

Computer programs and services on the web receive continuous updates and improvements. Thus, the steps to complete this web-based Activity may differ from the ones shown. You can often look at the screens and the information presented to determine how to complete the Activity.

3.09c (ii)
3.05a (i)

Activity 9.19 | Creating a LinkedIn Account and Profile

Creating a LinkedIn account and completing a profile will provide your connections—the people with whom you have formed LinkedIn relationships—with information about you. In this Activity, you will create a LinkedIn account and profile if you do not already have one.

ALERT! | **Do You Already Have a LinkedIn Account?**

If you already have a LinkedIn account, review this Activity to be sure you have completed your profile. Then, sign in, and skip to Step 8.

1 ▷ Start your browser and navigate to **www.linkedin.com** Compare your screen with Figure 9.49.

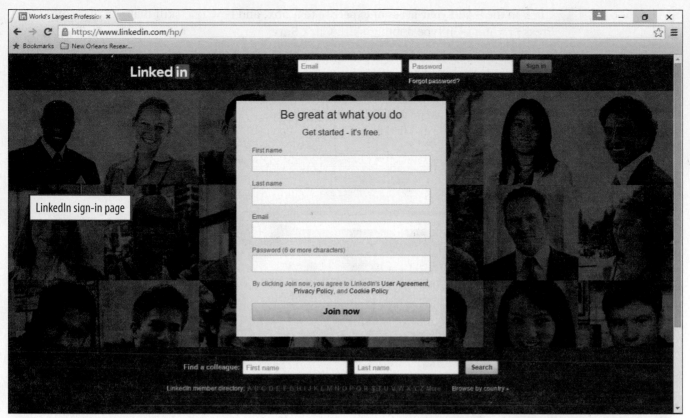

FIGURE 9.49

> **NOTE**
>
> For this activity, you can use any email address that you choose.

2 If you do not have a LinkedIn account, in the **Join now** box, type your first and last name, your email address, and a password of six or more characters, and then click the **Join now** button. If you have an account, sign in, review the steps below, and begin at Step 8

3 Fill out the required fields in each box, and then click **Create my profile**. If a box displays asking about your interests, click **Not sure yet. I'm open!**

4 In the **Email** connections box, click **Skip**, and then confirm by clicking **Skip** again.

> If you skip the email search at this point, you can perform the search later, after you finish creating your account. LinkedIn may require you to confirm your email address. If so, confirm it now so you can continue working with LinkedIn.

5 In the **Now, pick a few companies you'd like to follow** window, click the plus sign to add any you would like. Click the check mark of any company you do not really want to follow, and then click **Follow**. If you are not interested in following any of them, click **Skip**.

> When you follow a company, you may learn about developments, job openings, or even business development opportunities as soon as they are announced.

6 In the **Next, pick what you're interested in** window, click the plus sign to add any you would like. Click the check mark of any company you do not want to follow, and then click **Follow**. If you are not interested in following any of them, click **Skip**.

7 If you would like a link to the LinkedIn app, add your phone number, and then click **Get the app**. If you are not interested at this time, click **Skip**. Compare your screen with Figure 9.47.

> Your profile displays with options for updating it at the top.

8 ▸ Click in the **+Add your areas of expertise** text box, and type one skill that you currently have. Press Enter and then type another skill. Click **Save**.

9 ▸ Using the technique you just practiced, complete the information regarding your school, profile picture, and other profile questions. Skip any that do not apply. Compare your screen with Figure 9.50.

Keeping your profile up to date is a continual process. As you have new information to add, display your profile and find the section to be updated.

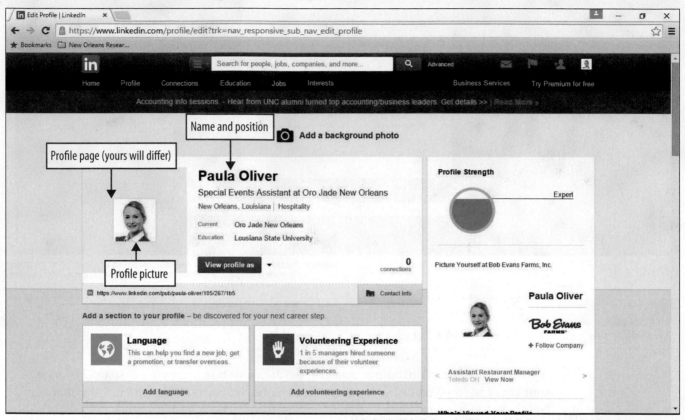

FIGURE 9.50

LinkedIn, the LinkedIn logo, the IN logo and InMail are registered trademarks or trademarks of LinkedIn Corporation and its affiliates in the United States and/or other countries.

10 ▸ Start PowerPoint 2016. On the right, click **Blank Presentation**. Click the **Click to add title** box, and type **Project 9C** Click the **Click to add subtitle** box, and type your **Firstname Lastname** On the **Home tab**, in the **Slides** group, click the upper portion of the **New Slide** button to add a new slide in the presentation. Click the **Insert tab**. In the **Images** group, click **Screenshot**, and then click the image of your LinkedIn window to place the screenshot in the slide. Click the **Click to add title** box, and type **Activity 9.19, Step 10** Leave the PowerPoint presentation open.

11 ▸ Return to LinkedIn, and remain signed in for the next Activity.

3.03b (iii)
3.09c (ii)

Activity 9.20 | Add a LinkedIn Profile Button to Your Email Signature

After you create a LinkedIn profile, you can provide a link to that profile from your email signature. In this Activity, add a LinkedInProfile button to your email signature.

1 ▸ At the bottom of the Name block, click the arrow to the right of **View profile as**, and then click **Manage public profile settings**. On the right, below *Your public profile badge*, click **Create a public profile badge**. Compare your screen with Figure 9.51.

Numerous button options display with the associated HTML code to the right.

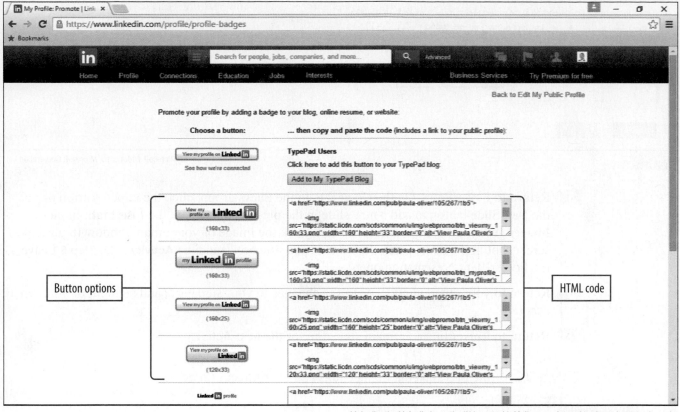

FIGURE 9.51

> **2** Review the button options. Locate the button you'd like to use, and click in the box with the HTML code to select it. Right-click and, from the shortcut menu, click **Copy**.
>
> To add the button to your email signature, you will paste the HTML code into the signature definition.
>
> **3** In your browser, open a new tab, and sign in to your email account. Using the features from your email provider, display your Signature options. If necessary, type your firstname lastname, and then press Enter. While options vary between different providers, your screen should look similar to Figure 9.52.

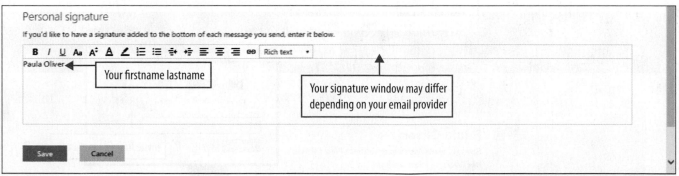

FIGURE 9.52

> **4** Choose the option to edit the signature in HTML. With the insertion point blinking below your name, right-click, and then click **Paste**. Return to the Rich text or default editing mode to display your signature with your LinkedIn profile button, and compare your screen to Figure 9.53.
>
> Here you can search your email accounts to find people who you know on LinkedIn or you can enter email addresses of people to invite them to be a connection.

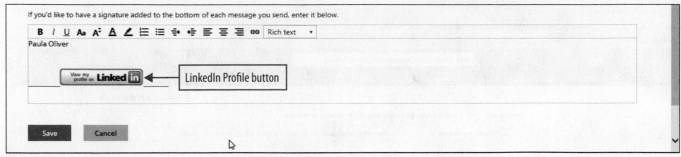

FIGURE 9.53

5 Return to PowerPoint. On the **Home tab**, in the **Slides** group, click the upper portion of the **New Slide** button to add a new slide in the presentation. Click the **Insert tab**. In the **Images** group, click **Screenshot**, and then click the image of your email window to place the screenshot in the slide. Click the **Click to add title** box, and type **Activity 9.20, Step 5** Leave the PowerPoint presentation open.

6 Return to your email window. **Save** the changes to your signature, and sign out of your email account.

7 Return to LinkedIn, and remain signed in for the next Activity.

Activity 9.21 | Inviting LinkedIn Connections and Sharing an Update

> **ALERT!** **Working with a Partner**
>
> When completing Activity 9.21, identify a classmate or friend with a LinkedIn account with whom you can partner to complete this Activity.

After you create a LinkedIn profile, you can build your connections by inviting contacts to connect with you using LinkedIn. In this Activity, you will begin building your connections.

1 If necessary, sign in to your LinkedIn account. At the top of the screen, click **Add Connections** 📇. Click **Invite your contacts**, and then click **Other**. Compare your screen with Figure 9.54.

Here you can search your email accounts to find people who you know on LinkedIn or you can enter email addresses of people to invite them to be a connection.

FIGURE 9.54

2 In the **Email** box, type the email address of your partner, and then click **Continue**.

After your invitation is accepted, you can click the Contacts menu and then click My Connections to see information about your contacts.

3 ▸ If necessary, on the navigation bar, click **Home** to display your LinkedIn home page. Scroll down to locate the **Share an update** box, if necessary. Click inside the box, and type a short message about learning to use LinkedIn.

> Use updates to share information with your connections. Because LinkedIn is a professional social networking site, be sure to write all your messages in a professional manner. Do not use the casual writing style that you might use on Facebook.

4 ▸ Return to PowerPoint. On the **Home tab**, in the **Slides** group, click the upper portion of the **New Slide** button to add a new slide in the presentation. Click the **Insert tab**. In the **Images** group, click **Screenshot**, and then click the image of your LinkedIn update window to place the screenshot in the slide. Click the **Click to add title** box, and type **Activity 9.21, Step 4** Leave the PowerPoint presentation open.

5 ▸ Return to LinkedIn. Below your update message, click **Share**. Scroll down to see any updates posted by your connections.

6 ▸ In the upper right corner of your screen, point to your profile picture, and then click **Sign Out**. **Close** ⊠ LinkedIn and **Close** ⊠ your browser.

More **Knowledge**	**Add Connections Based on Your Email Contacts**

To import your contacts, click the Connections menu, and then click Add Contacts. Follow the prompts to import your address book to select connections.

More **Knowledge**	**Additional and Valuable Features in LinkedIn**

As you build your career, try some other features of LinkedIn to connect with more people in your industry. For example, LinkedIn Groups enable you to follow influential people and join in groups in your area of interest. You can join a group or even start a group. Also try LinkedIn Answers to ask or answer questions. Finally, read and view the LinkedIn User Guides, especially the ones for New Users and for Students. There are many videos you can view to learn about getting started on your job search by using LinkedIn.

Objective 10 | Use Twitter

> ***Twitter*** is a microblogging platform for social networking that enables registered users to post and send messages to other registered users. The messages are called ***tweets***—short messages limited to 140 characters and spaces. Unregistered users can only read tweets—not post them. If you share another user's tweet giving them credit, it is called a ***retweet***. Twitter is useful for personal and professional networking.

Activity 9.22 | Creating a Twitter Profile That Includes Your Picture

1 ▸ Start your browser and navigate to **https://twitter.com** In the upper right, click **Sign up**, and then compare your screen with Figure 9.55.

> The information in this window establishes your account; you will choose a username after your account is established. If you already have a Twitter account, skip to Step 3.

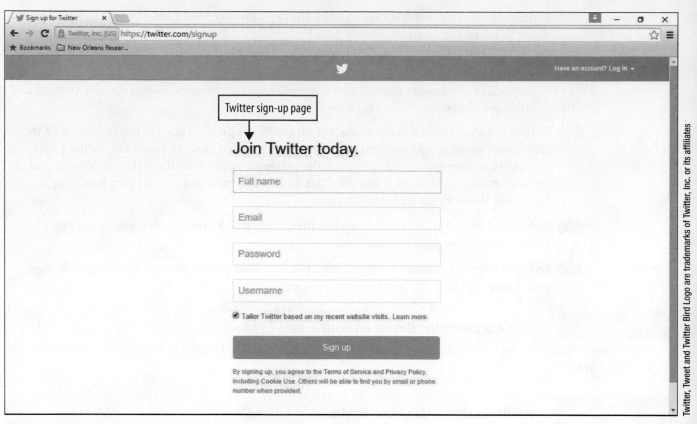

Twitter, Tweet and Twitter Bird Logo are trademarks of Twitter, Inc. or its affiliates

FIGURE 9.55

> **2** Complete the form, and then click **Sign up**. Enter your phone number or, below **Next**, click **Skip**. Click **Continue** to move through the steps to get started, choosing interests and suggestions as they apply to you (at least one in each step).

> **3** In Step 4 of the process, click **Upload your photo**. Notice the options, and then compare your screen with Figure 9.56.

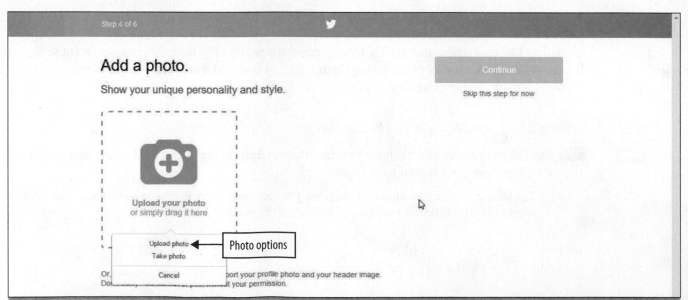

Twitter, Tweet and Twitter Bird Logo are trademarks of Twitter, Inc. or its affiliates

FIGURE 9.56

> **4** Click the option you want to use to add your profile picture, and follow the steps necessary to complete the process to display your image. Click **Continue**.

5 ▶ Skip finding people you know to display your timeline.

Below your name you will find statistics about how many times you have tweeted and how many people you are *following*—accounts to which you are subscribing or seeing tweets from in your *timeline*, the real-time stream of tweets that display in the center of the window.

Above the timeline is the What's happening? box; this is one place you can type your tweet. The *Who to follow* box displays on the left to suggest accounts you may want to follow. Trends tailored to your activity display on the left side of the screen.

6 ▶ Scroll down and review the tweets on your timeline. Notice the @ sign. It is used to identify usernames in a tweet, to send a message, or to link to a profile. @username is how you are identified on Twitter. Compare your screen with Figure 9.57.

You can also find a *hashtag*, a word or phrase preceded by the # symbol to group tweets based on a topic identified by the user. Because tweets are limited to 140 characters and spaces, web links are often shortened using online tools. You may also see messages that have been retweeted.

Twitter, Tweet and Twitter Bird Logo are trademarks of Twitter, Inc. or its affiliates, Twitter.com

FIGURE 9.57

| *More* Knowledge | **Twitter on a Mobile Device** |

While you can send and receive tweets via your computer, consider downloading an app to your phone or tablet. You can use Twitter or any number of third-party applications available for your platform.

---

7 ▶ Click in the **Search Twitter** text box. Type a search term related to something you are interested in, and then press Enter to display relevant Twitter accounts. Choose at least one account to follow.

Search results are categorized, with the Top results displayed by default. Click the other menu options to display additional results.

8 ▶ Using the same technique, search for another interest, and then select at least one account to follow.

9 ▶ Remain signed in for the next Activity.

Activity 9.23 │ Tweeting a Message

In this Activity, you will tweet a message.

1 ▶ Click in the What's happening text box, and type a tweet that you want to share. When you are finished click **Tweet**. In the message box, click **Close**.

Next to the Tweet button, you will see a countdown of available characters for this tweet. Remember that you need to keep the entire message to 140 characters or less. Click Add photos to include an image with your tweet.

As soon as you click Tweet, the Tweet is immediately posted to your timeline. Unless you specified that your tweets should remain private, all tweets are public and can be viewed by anyone.

> **2** In the upper right, click **Tweet**. In the **Compose new Tweet** dialog box, type a message that exceeds the 140 character limit, and then compare your screen with Figure 9.58.

When your message goes over 140 characters, the character count shows as a negative number to represent the number of characters that need to be removed. Any characters over 140 are also shaded in red.

FIGURE 9.58

Twitter, Tweet and Twitter Bird Logo are trademarks of Twitter, Inc. or its affiliates

> **3** Edit the message to meet the character restriction, and then click **Tweet** to post to your timeline.

> **4** Return to PowerPoint. On the **Home tab**, in the **Slides** group, click the upper portion of the **New Slide** button to add a new slide in the presentation. Click the **Insert tab**. In the **Images** group, click **Screenshot**, and then click the image of your Twitter window to place the screenshot in the slide. Click the **Click to add title** box, and type **Activity 9.23, Step 4**

> **5** Press Ctrl + Home to display **Slide 1**. Save 🖫 the file in your **All in One Chapter 9** folder as **Lastname_Firstname_9C_Networking_Screens**

> **6** Click the **File tab** to display **Backstage** view, and then click **Print**. Under **Settings**, click **Full Page Slides**. Under **Handouts**, click **6 Slides Horizontal**. Notice that the **Print Preview** on the right displays the slide handout. In the upper left portion of the screen, click **Print**. To create an electronic image of your document that looks like a printed document, on the left click **Export**. On the right, click **Create PDF/XPS** to display the **Publish as PDF or XPS** dialog box. Navigate to the location where you want to save your document, and then click **Publish**.

> **7** Return to Twitter. In the upper right corner, click your profile picture. The menu includes options to view your profile and modify your settings. Click **Log out**.

> **8** As directed by your instructor, submit the file that you created in this project:

Lastname_Firstname_9C_Networking_Screens

END | You have completed Project 9C

IC3 —MODULE 3: LIVING ONLINE

Project 9A

Section 3.01 Internet (Navigation)
  (a) Understand what the Internet is
    (ii) Be familiar with media literacy
    (iii) Understand browser functionality

Section 3.02 Common Functionality
  (a) Understand how to use common website navigation conventions
    (i) Click / delayed / double click
    (ii) Mouse over
    (iii) Drag and drop
    (iv) Basic web navigation principles

Section 3.03 Email Clients
  (b) Understand email etiquette
    (i) Reply vs. reply all, forward
    (ii) Cc vs. bcc
    (iv) Header
  (c) Understand email history and management
    (iv) Folders
  (d) Understand email attachments
    (i) Size limits
  (e) Understand contact management

Project 9B

Section 3.06 Communications
    (c) Know how to use chat platforms

Section 3.07 Online Conferencing
  (a) Understand and identify online conference offerings
    (iii) Phone conferencing

Project 9C

Section 3.03 Email Clients
  (b) Understand email etiquette
    (iii) Signature

Section 3.05 Social Media
  (a) Understand what a digital identity is (identity on social media)
    (i) Know what social networks are and how they are used (FB, LinkedIn, etc.)

Section 3.09 Digital Principles/Ethics/Skills/Citizenship
  (c) Understand an online identity management
    (ii) Managing profiles

GO! FOR JOB SUCCESS

Discussion: Job Satisfaction

Your instructor may assign this video to your class, and then ask you to think about, or discuss with your classmates, these questions:

Satisfied employees add value to businesses. They work harder and produce better results, and reduce costs related to hiring and training replacement workers. Especially in technology, companies provide benefits beyond great pay—like free food and fitness centers—to keep employees happy and engaged. But there is more to job satisfaction than pay and tangible items. Employee satisfaction surveys show that factors like opportunities for career growth and good relationships contribute to happy workers in all fields. Satisfaction surveys show that employees are motivated by good relationships with their coworkers, especially their supervisors. Work/life balance—the ability for employees to have a fulfilling personal life in addition to a satisfying job—is also a motivator for many employees.

FotoIEdhar / Fotolia

Do you think employers have a responsibility to provide work/life balance to their employees, and what responsibilities do employees have?

What can managers do to ensure that workers have opportunities to meet and interact with their coworkers?

What reasons beyond employee motivation would a supervisor want for regular open communications with their direct reports?

END OF CHAPTER

SUMMARY

Google offers users many options for productivity. Chrome is a web browser used to access the Internet. Creating a Google account allows you to communicate online using Gmail, a free email provider, and Hangouts, an instant messaging system. Google Drive also provides cloud storage with sharing options for your files.

OneDrive offers free online storage with your Microsoft account. Files can be uploaded from any location or saved from Microsoft Office. It is easy to share files for collaboration using OneDrive. Skype enables you to send and receive instant messages and phone calls using your computer.

OneNote is a Microsoft application with which you can create a digital notebook where you can gather notes. Notebooks can be stored locally or on the web, where they can be accessed via the Internet or on a mobile device.

LinkedIn and Twitter are professional social networking sites where you can share information with others. You can also use these platforms to follow others to gain new information.

GO! LEARN IT ONLINE

Review the concepts, key terms, and IC3 skills in this chapter by completing these online challenges, which you can find at **MyITLab**.

Matching and Multiple Choice: Answer matching and multiple-choice questions to test what you learned in this chapter.

Lessons on the GO!: Learn how to use all the new apps and features as they are introduced by Microsoft.

IC3 Prep Quiz: Answer questions to review the IC3 skills that you practiced in this chapter.

Your instructor may assign one or more of these projects to help you review the chapter and assess your mastery and understanding of the chapter.

	Project Guide for All in One Chapter 9		
Project	**Apply Skills from These Chapter Objectives**	**Project Type**	**Project Location**
9A **MyITLab**	Objectives 1–5 from Project 9A	**9A Instructional Project** Guided instruction to learn the skills in Project 9A.	In MyITLab and in text
9B **MyITLab**	Objectives 6–8 from Project 9B	**9B Instructional Project** Guided instruction to learn the skills in Project 9B.	In MyITLab and in text
9C **MyITLab**	Objectives 9–10 from Project 9C	**9C Instructional Project** Guided instruction to learn the skills in Project 9C.	In MyITLab and in text
9D **MyITLab**	Objectives 1–5 from Project 9A	**9D Mastering** **Mastery and Transfer of Learning** A demonstration of your mastery of the skills in Project 9A with extensive decision making.	In text
9E **MyITLab**	Objectives 6–8 from Project 9B	**9E Mastering** **Mastery and Transfer of Learning** A demonstration of your mastery of the skills in Project 9B with extensive decision making.	In text
9F **MyITLab**	Objectives 9-10 from Project 9C	**9F Mastering** **Mastery and Transfer of Learning** A demonstration of your mastery of the skills in Project 9C with extensive decision making.	In text
9G **MyITLab**	Objectives 1–10 from Projects 9A, 9B, and 9C	**9G Mastering** **Mastery and Transfer of Learning** A demonstration of your mastery of the skills in Projects 9A, 9B, and 9C with extensive decision making.	In text

GLOSSARY

GLOSSARY OF CHAPTER KEY TERMS

Address bar The area at the top of the browser window in which you can type a URL to visit a website.

Bcc An abbreviation for blind carbon copy (or blind courtesy copy), and is used to send a copy of the message to one or more recipients who would be interested in the message and whose name is not visible to other recipients of the message.

Bookmarks The term used to describe saved links to commonly visited webpages that allow for efficient web browsing.

Browsing The term used to describe the process of using your computer to view webpages.

Browsing window In Internet Explorer 10, the area of the screen in which the webpage displays.

Can comment A Gmail sharing setting applied when the recipient can view and comment on the document, but cannot edit the document.

Can edit A Gmail sharing setting applied when the recipient can view, comment on, and edit the document.

Can view A Gmail sharing setting applied when the recipient can view the document, but cannot comment on or edit the document.

Cc An abbreviation for *courtesy copy* or *carbon copy*, and is used to send a copy of the email to one or more recipients who are interested in the message but not the primary recipient.

Chrome A free web browser application developed by Google.

Chromebook A laptop that runs Google's Chrome operating system and Chrome web browser to provide a web-based environment for using applications; however, some apps may run offline as well.

Cloud computing The use of web servers on the Internet—for example, a OneDrive or SharePoint library—to store files and run applications.

Connections The people with whom you have some level of online relationship using LinkedIn.

Conversation A Gmail message that gets sent back and forth many times as you and your recipient exchange thoughts about a topic.

Domain name An organization's unique name on the Internet, which consists of a chosen name combined with a top-level domain such as *.com*,*.org*, or *.gov*.

Drag and drop A mouse gesture in which the user selects one or more objects and drags it to a different location.

Email A method of exchanging messages via the Internet in which the message resides in the recipient's mailbox until he or she signs in to read it.

Email header The first part of an email message generated by the email provider.

Email string (Email thread) The history of the email messages created through multiple responses and answers to an originating message in a thread.

Emoticon An image that represents facial expressions. An emoticon should be used only in informal electronic communication to convey feelings.

File Printout A OneNote feature that inserts information from a file as a printed copy in the page; this feature is useful because text in the printout can be searched just like any content in OneNote.

Following A term used to describe the accounts to which you are subscribing or seeing tweets from when using Twitter.

Footer The bottom section of a webpage that typically contains the name of the entity that publishes the website, copyright information, and basic navigation links.

Gmail Google's free web-based email service.

Google doodle A modified Google search engine home page logo created to observe a special event, season, or holiday.

Google Drive Free storage available for anyone with a Google account; it can be used to store any type of file.

Hamburger Another name for the hamburger menu.

Hamburger menu An icon made up of three lines that evoke a hamburger on a bun.

Hangouts A hangout is a private space where contacts can post status updates, chat, or initiate a video call using their Google accounts.

Hashtag A word or phrase preceded by the # symbol to group tweets based on a topic identified by the user.

Home page On your own computer, the webpage you have selected—or that is set by default—to display on your computer when you start Internet Explorer. When visiting a website, the starting point for the remainder of the pages on that site.

http The protocol prefix for HyperText Transfer Protocol.

HyperText Transfer Protocol The set of communication rules used by your computer to connect to servers on the web.

Instant messaging The real-time communication between two or more participants over the Internet.

Labels A storage system used to organize Gmail messages into categories; more than one label can be applied to a message.

LinkedIn A professional social networking site where you can find past and present colleagues and classmates, connect with appropriate people when seeking a new job or business opportunity, or get answers from industry experts.

Menu icon Another name for the hamburger menu.

Mouse over A term used to describe hovering your mouse pointer over text or an image on a webpage.

My Drive Google Drive location that stores files that you create using Google applications.

Navigation bar A set of buttons or images in a row or column that display on every webpage to link the user to sections on the website.

Note container A box in OneNote for text, pictures, video clips, and other types of notes.

Notebook In OneNote, a collection of files organized by major divisions and stored in a common folder.

Notes Typed text, handwritten text if you have a tablet PC, pictures and graphics—including images and text that you capture from webpages—audio and video recordings, and documents from other applications such as Word or Excel, that can be included in a OneNote notebook.

Omnibox Another name for the Address bar in Google Chrome, because it serves as both an address and a search bar.

OneDrive A free file storage and file sharing service provided to anyone with a Microsoft account.

OneNote A Microsoft application with which you can create a digital notebook that gives you a single location where you can gather and organize information in the form of notes.

Page A subdivision of a section where notes are inserted.

Page tabs list A list on the right side of the OneNote notebook that displays the name of each page in the active section.

Page template In OneNote, a file that serves as a pattern for creating a new page; ensures a uniform page layout and design.

Protocol prefix The letters that represent a set of communication rules used by a computer to connect to another computer.

Retweet The process of sharing another user's tweet, giving them credit for the original tweet.

Screen clipping A copy of what you are seeing on your screen, a webpage, or a document is then sent to the active notebook page.

ScreenTip A small text box that displays the name of an icon or button when a mouse pointer is hovered over it.

Search engine A computer program that searches for specific words and returns a list of documents in which the search term was found.

Search provider A website that provides search capabilities on the web.

Section The primary division of a notebook identifying a main topic and containing related pages of notes.

Section tab A tab that identifies a primary division of the active notebook.

Shared with Me Google Drive location that stores files that others have shared with you.

SharePoint A related group of technologies from Microsoft for collaboration, file sharing, and web publishing within organizations.

Skype A software application that users can download to create an account so they can make voice calls over the Internet as well as participate in web conferencing from any location in the world.

Sponsored links Paid advertisements shown as links, typically for products and services related to your search term. Sponsored links are the way that search sites like Bing, Google, and others earn revenue.

Styles Combinations of formatting options that look attractive together.

Surfing The process of navigating the Internet either for a particular item or for anything that is of interest, and quickly moving from one item to another.

Timeline The real-time stream of tweets that display in the center of the Twitter window.

Trimmed content The history of the Gmail conversation, sometimes referred to as the email string or the email thread.

Tweet A short message posted in Twitter, limited to 140 characters and spaces.

Twitter A microblogging platform used for social networking, which allows registered users to post and send messages to other registered users.

Uniform resource locator An address that uniquely identifies a location on the Internet.

Upload Google Drive location that stores files that you have uploaded to Drive.

URL The acronym for Uniform Resource Locator.

Web browser A software program with which you display webpages and navigate the Internet.

Apply 9A skills from these Objectives:

1 Navigate the Web Using the Google Chrome Web Browser

2 Search the Internet Using the Google Chrome Web Browser

3 Send and Receive Email Messages Using Gmail

4 Chat Online Using Google Hangouts

5 Manage a Google Calendar

Mastering | Project 9D Wedding Planning

In the following Mastering project, you will surf the Internet using Google Chrome and communicate online using Gmail and Google Hangouts. You will also manage an online calendar to assist Wade Harper, Senior Event Planner at Oro Jade Chicago. Your printed results will look similar to those in Figure 9.59.

PROJECT FILES

For Project 9D, you will need the following file:

w9D_Guide

You will save your file as:

Lastname_Firstname_9D_Event_Screens (The PowerPoint file will include 4 screenshots that you will create while completing the Project.)

PROJECT RESULTS

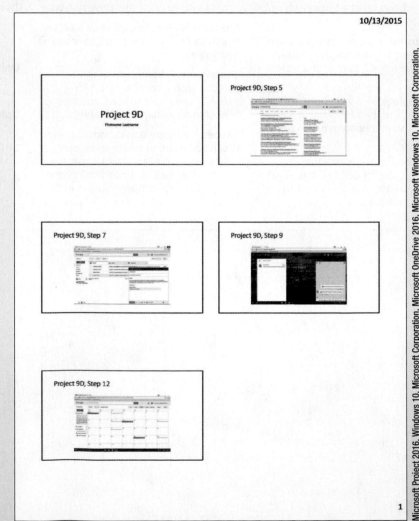

FIGURE 9.59

(Project 9D Wedding Planning continues on the next page)

Mastering | Project 9D Wedding Planning (continued)

ALERT! To complete this project, you will need to partner with a classmate in the same manner you did in the chapter project.

1 Start Google Chrome. Perform a search for resources related to wedding planning.

2 Visit two sites returned from the search, and Bookmark those sites so they display on the Bookmarks bar. Return to the Google search window.

3 On the Bookmarks bar, create a folder named **Wedding Planning**, and move the sites into that folder.

4 Right-click the **Wedding Planning** folder, and click **Open all bookmarks** to display tabs for each site.

5 Start PowerPoint 2016. On the right, click **Blank Presentation.** Click the **Click to add title** box, and type **Project 9D** Click the **Click to add subtitle** box, and type your **Firstname Lastname** On the **Home tab**, in the **Slides** group, click the upper portion of the **New Slide** button to add a new slide in the presentation. Click the **Insert tab**. In the **Images** group, click **Screenshot**, and then click the image of Bookmarks window to place the screenshot in the slide. Click the **Click to add title** box, and type **Project 9D, Step 5** Leave the PowerPoint presentation open.

6 Sign in to your **Gmail** account. Compose an email to your partner letting him or her know that you are reviewing the wedding planning guide and are sharing the document for feedback. Be sure to use the proper email techniques that you practiced in the project. Using **Drive**, insert the **w09D_Guide** file in the email as a **Drive link**.

7 Before sending the email, return to PowerPoint. On the **Home tab**, in the **Slides** group, click the upper portion of the **New Slide** button to add a new slide in the presentation. Click the **Insert tab**. In the **Images** group, click **Screenshot**, and then click the image of the Gmail window to place the screenshot in the slide. Click the **Click to add title** box, and type **Project 9D, Step 7** Leave the PowerPoint presentation open.

8 Send the email.

9 Navigate to **hangouts.google.com** Compose a message to your partner explaining one disadvantage to instant messaging. *Note*: If your partner is not currently online, you will see a message in the Hangout. Before sending the message, return to PowerPoint. On the

Home tab, in the **Slides** group, click the upper portion of the **New Slide** button to add a new slide in the presentation. Click the **Insert tab**. In the **Images** group, click **Screenshot**, and then click the image of Gmail window to place the screenshot in the slide. Click the **Click to add title** box, and type **Project 9D, Step 9** Leave the PowerPoint presentation open.

10 Send the message.

11 Display the Google Calendar that you used in Project 9A. With the month view displayed, click **Next period** two times, and add the following events to next month:

a. Spiro Golden Anniversary Party on the last Saturday, 7:00 pm–11:00 pm in the Mississippi River Ballroom

b. University Singers practice on the first Tuesday, will repeat every week for 3 weeks, 4:00 pm–7:00 pm in the Chamber Room with a stage set up

c. Ambrose-Green wedding on the second Saturday of the month, 2:00 pm–11:30 pm in the Lake Pontchartrain Room with dividers open

12 Return to PowerPoint. On the **Home tab**, in the **Slides** group, click the upper portion of the **New Slide** button to add a new slide in the presentation. Click the **Insert tab**. In the **Images** group, click **Screenshot**, and then click the image of Calendar window to place the screenshot in the slide. Click the **Click to add title** box, and type **Project 9D, Step 12**

13 In the presentation, display Slide 1. **Save** the presentation in your **All in One Chapter 9** folder as **Lastname_Firstname_9D_Event_Screens**

14 If you are instructed to submit this result, print **Handouts**, **6 Slides Horizontal** or create an electronic image. Close PowerPoint.

15 As directed by your instructor, submit the file that you created in this project: Lastname_Firstname_9D_Event_Screens

END | You have completed Project 9D

Apply **9B** skills from these Objectives:

6 Use Your Microsoft Account's OneDrive for Storing and Sharing Files

7 Communicate Using Skype

8 Use OneNote to Create a Notebook

Mastering | Project 9E Department Meeting

In the following mastering project, you will create folders and files on your OneDrive related to the upcoming department meeting and create a notebook for Gwen Hernandez to store information related to her presentation at the meeting. Your completed notebook will look similar to Figure 9.60.

PROJECT FILES

For Project 9E, you will need the following files:

w09E_Meeting_Agenda

w09E_Web_Sites

You will save your files as:

Lastname_Firstname_9E_OneDrive_Screen (The PowerPoint file will include 1 screenshot that you will create while completing the Project.)

Lastname_Firstname_9E_Notebook

PROJECT RESULTS

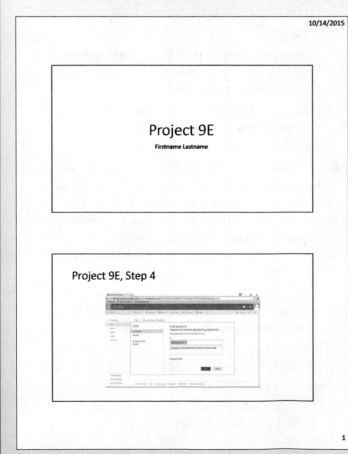
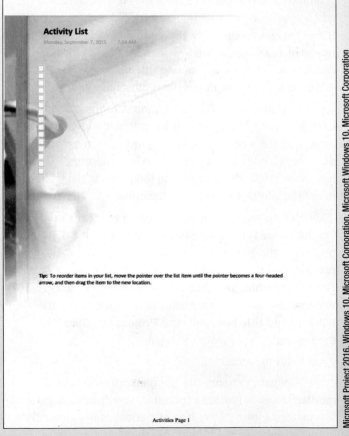

FIGURE 9.60

(Project 9E Department Meeting continues on the next page)

Mastering Project 9E Department Meeting (continued)

ALERT! To complete this project, you will need to partner with a classmate in the same manner you did in the chapter project.

1 Start your browser. Navigate to **OneDrive.com** and sign in using your Microsoft account.

2 Create a new folder named **Department Meeting** In that folder, from your student data files that accompany this chapter, upload **w09E_Meeting_Agenda**.

3 Rename the document as **Lastname_Firstname_9E_Meeting_Agenda**

4 With the **Department Meeting** folder, select the **Meeting Agenda** document, and then **Share** it with your partner. In the **message window**, type a short message about the benefits of OneDrive, and then start PowerPoint 2016. On the right, click **Blank Presentation**. Click the **Click to add title** box, and type **Project 9E** Click the **Click to add subtitle** box, and type your **Firstname Lastname** On the **Home tab**, in the **Slides** group, click the upper portion of the **New Slide** button to add a new slide in the presentation. Click the **Insert tab**. In the **Images** group, click **Screenshot**, and then click the image of the Bookmarks window to place the screenshot in the slide. Click the **Click to add title** box, and type **Project 9E, Step 4**

5 Save the presentation in your **All in One Chapter 9** folder as **Lastname_Firstname_9E_OneDrive_Screen**

6 If you are instructed to submit this result, print **Handouts, 2 Slides** or create an electronic image.

7 In the presentation, display Slide 1. **Save** the presentation in your **All in One Chapter 9** folder as **Lastname_Firstname_9E_OneDrive_Screen**

8 If you are instructed to submit this result, print **Handouts, 6 Slides Horizontal** or create an electronic image. **Close** PowerPoint. Sign out of **OneDrive**.

9 Open **Microsoft OneNote 2016**. Create a new notebook stored in your **All in One Chapter 9** folder. Using your name, save it as **Lastname_Firstname_9E_Notebook**

10 Create two sections: **Resources** and **Activities**

11 In the **Resources** section, rename the *Untitled page* as **Web Sites** Add a page named **Tips** Drag the **Tips** page up above **Web Sites**.

12 On the **Tips** page, insert a **note container** about an inch below the date and time. Add the following list and then format it as a bulleted list:

Be sure all team members are committed to the activity
Provide clear instructions before beginning
Debrief and discuss following each activity

13 On the **Web sites** page, insert a **File Printout** of **w09E_Web_Sites**.

14 In the **Activities** section, rename the *Untitled page* as **Planning** On that page, about an inch below the date and time, insert a note that displays **Group size is based on the number of attendees:** On the next line, insert a calculation to divide 24 by 4.

15 About an inch to the right of that note container, insert the following table:

Activity 1	15 minutes
Discussion	10 minutes
Activity 2	20 minutes
Discussion	10 minutes

16 In the **Activities** section, using a **Simple To Do List** page template, insert a new page. Replace the existing title with **Activity List**

17 **Print** your notebook or submit electronically as directed by your instructor. If submitting electronically, submit a PDF of your notebook.

18 As directed by your instructor, submit the two snip files that you created in this project:

Lastname_Firstname_9E_OneDrive_Screen   PowerPoint file
Lastname_Firstname_9E_Notebook   OneNote notebook

END | You have completed Project 9E

Apply 9C skills from these Objectives:

9 Create a LinkedIn Account

10 Use Twitter

Mastering Project 9F Networking Online

In the following Mastering project, you will update your LinkedIn Profile and post updates. You will also update your Twitter profile and tweet messages. Your completed notebook will look similar to Figure 9.61.

PROJECT FILES

For Project 9F, you will not need any files.

You will save your files as:

Lastname_Firstname_9F_Update_Screens (The PowerPoint file will include 2 screenshots that you will create while completing the Project.)

PROJECT RESULTS

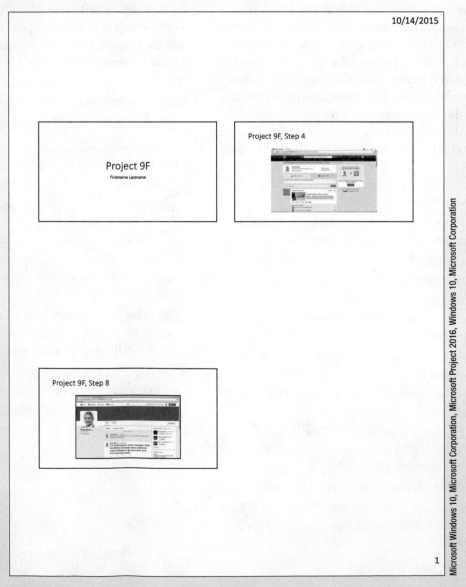

FIGURE 9.61

(Project 9F Networking Online continues on the next page)

Mastering   Project 9F Networking Online (continued)

1 Sign in to your LinkedIn account. In the menu bar at the top of the screen, click **Profile**, and then click **Edit Profile**.

2 Add a section to your profile, and then add the related information; for example, recommend someone who you know. **Save** the changes.

3 Post an update about how you plan to use LinkedIn professionally.

4 Start PowerPoint 2016. On the right, click **Blank Presentation**. Click the **Click to add title** box, and type **Project 9F** Click the **Click to add subtitle** box, and type your **Firstname Lastname** On the **Home tab**, in the **Slides** group, click the upper portion of the **New Slide** button to add a new slide in the presentation. Click the **Insert tab**. In the **Images** group, click **Screenshot**, and then click the image of the Bookmarks window to place the screenshot in the slide. Click the **Click to add title** box, and type **Project 9F, Step 4** Leave the PowerPoint presentation open.

5 Sign out of LinkedIn.

6 Sign in to your Twitter account. On the left, click your name to display your profile. Edit your profile to include a phrase that describes you as a **Bio**, and change the **Theme color** to a color of your choice. **Save** the changes.

7 Tweet a message about using Twitter from a mobile device.

8 Return to PowerPoint. On the **Home tab**, in the **Slides** group, click the upper portion of the **New Slide** button to add a new slide in the presentation. Click the **Insert tab**. In the **Images** group, click **Screenshot**, and then click the image of Calendar window to place the screenshot in the slide. Click the **Click to add title** box, and type **Project 9F, Step 8**

9 In the presentation, display Slide 1. **Save** the presentation in your **All in One Chapter 9** folder as **Lastname_Firstname_9F_Update_Screens**

10 If you are instructed to submit this result, print **Handouts**, **4 Slides Horizontal** or create an electronic image. Close PowerPoint.

11 Sign out of Twitter.

12 As directed by your instructor, submit the two files that you created in this project:

Lastname_Firstname_9F_Update_Screens Powerpoint file

END | You have completed Project 9F

Apply 9A, 9B, and 9C skills from these Objectives:

1 Navigate the Web Using the Google Chrome Browser

2 Search the Internet Using the Google Chrome Browser

3 Send and Receive Email Messages Using Gmail

4 Chat Online Using Google Hangouts

5 Manage a Google Calendar

6 Use Your Microsoft Account's OneDrive for Storing and Sharing Files

7 Communicate Using Skype

8 Use OneNote to Create a Notebook

9 Use LinkedIn for Networking

10 Use Twitter

Mastering   Project 9G Event Planning

In the following Mastering project, you will use cloud computing sites to store and share information. Your printed results will look similar to those in Figure 9.62.

PROJECT FILES

For Project 9G, you will need the following file:

w09G_Request

You will save your files as:

Lastname_Firstname_9G_Cloud_Screens (The PowerPoint file will include 3 screenshots that you will create while completing the Project.)

PROJECT RESULTS

FIGURE 9.62

(Project 9G Event Planning continues on the next page)

Mastering | Project 9G Event Planning (continued)

1 **Start** Google Chrome, and sign into your account. Display the **Google Calendar** that you used in Project 9A. With the calendar displayed in Month view, click **Next period** three times to display the calendar in three months. Add the following events to this month:

a. Smith-Lacy wedding on the first Saturday of the month, 3:00 pm–11:30 pm in the Grand Ballroom

b. Howard High Class Reunion on the third Saturday, 6:00 pm–10:00 pm in the Rose Garden Patio

c. ABD Annual Dinner Planning Group will meet on the first Thursday, will repeat every Tuesday and Thursday for 5 occurrences, 7:00 pm–9:00 pm in the Board Room

2 With the monthly calendar displayed, **start** PowerPoint 2016. On the right, click **Blank Presentation**. Click the **Click to add title** box, and type **Project 9G** Click the **Click to add subtitle** box, and type your **Firstname Lastname** On the **Home tab**, in the **Slides** group, click the upper portion of the **New Slide** button to add a new slide in the presentation. Click the **Insert tab**. In the **Images** group, click **Screenshot**, and then click the image of the Bookmarks window to place the screenshot in the slide. Click the **Click to add title** box, and type **Project 9G, Step 2** Leave the PowerPoint presentation open.

3 **Sign out** of your **Google** account.

4 With your browser displayed, navigate to **OneDrive.com** and sign in using your Microsoft account.

5 Create a new folder named **Space Requests** In that folder, from your student data files that accompany this chapter, upload **w09G_Request_Form**.

6 Rename the document as **Lastname_Firstname_9G_Request_Form**. Share the document with your partner. Display the information pane, and add a description **Request Form must be used for all events**

7 With the document displayed, including sharing information, return to PowerPoint. On the **Home tab**, in the **Slides** group, click the upper portion of the **New Slide** button to add a new slide in the presentation. Click the **Insert tab**. In the **Images** group, click **Screenshot**, and then click the image of the OneDrive window to place the screenshot in the slide. Click the **Click to add title** box, and type **Project 9G, Step 7**

8 **Sign out** of **OneDrive**.

9 **Sign in** to your Twitter account. Search for professional groups related to your career choice, and then follow at least three. Display your home page, and under your name, click **FOLLOWING** to display those accounts that you follow.

10 Return to PowerPoint. On the **Home tab**, in the **Slides** group, click the upper portion of the **New Slide** button to add a new slide in the presentation. Click the **Insert tab**. In the **Images** group, click **Screenshot**, and then click the image of Calendar window to place the screenshot in the slide. Click the **Click to add title** box, and type **Project 9G, Step 10**

11 In the presentation, display Slide 1. **Save** the presentation in your **All in One Chapter 9** folder as **Lastname_Firstname_9G_Cloud_Screens**

12 If you are instructed to submit this result, print **Handouts**, **4 Slides Horizontal** or create an electronic image. **Close** PowerPoint.

13 **Sign out** of **Twitter**.

14 As directed by your instructor, submit the file that you created in this project:

Lastname_Firstname_9G_Cloud_Screens

> **END | You have completed Project 9G**

Getting Started with Windows 10

PROJECT 10A

OUTCOMES
Sign in and out of Windows 10, identify the features of an operating system, create a folder and save a file, use Windows apps, and customize your Start menu.

OBJECTIVES

1. Explore the Windows 10 Environment
2. Use File Explorer and Desktop Apps to Create a New Folder and Save a File
3. Identify the Functions of the Windows 10 Operating System
4. Discover Windows 10 Features
5. Sign Out of Windows 10, Turn Off Your Computer, and Manage User Accounts
6. Manage Your Windows 10 System

PROJECT 10B

OUTCOMES
Start programs, search for and manage files and folders, copy and move files and folders, and use the Recycle Bin.

OBJECTIVES

7. Download and Extract Files and Folders
8. Use File Explorer to Display Locations, Folders, and Files
9. Start Programs and Open Data Files
10. Create, Rename, and Copy Files and Folders
11. Use OneDrive as Cloud Storage

Eugenio Marongiu/Shutterstock

In This Chapter 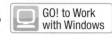 GO! to Work with Windows

In this chapter, you will use Microsoft Windows 10, which is software that manages your computer's hardware, software, communications, and data files. You will use the taskbar and Start menu features to get your work done with ease and use Windows apps to get your latest personal information and to find news and entertainment. You will sign in to your computer, explore the features of Windows 10, create folders and save files, use Windows apps, manage multiple windows, sign out of your computer, and examine user accounts.

The projects in this chapter relate to the **Bell Orchid Hotels**, headquartered in Boston, and which own and operate resorts and business-oriented hotels. Resort properties are located in popular destinations, including Honolulu, Orlando, San Diego, and Santa Barbara. The resorts offer deluxe accommodations and a wide array of dining options. Other Bell Orchid hotels are located in major business centers and offer the latest technology in their meeting facilities. Bell Orchid offers extensive educational opportunities for employees. The company plans to open new properties and update existing properties over the next decade.

PROJECT ACTIVITIES

In Activities 10.01 through 10.19, you will participate in training along with Steven Ramos and Barbara Hewitt, both of whom work for the Information Technology Department at the Boston headquarters office of the Bell Orchid Hotels. After completing this part of the training, you will be able to sign in and sign out of your computer, create folders and save files, use Windows apps, and manage your user account. You will capture two screens that will look similar to Figure 10.1.

 ## PROJECT FILES

For Project 10A, you will need the following files:

No Student Data Files are required to begin this project. When prompted to do so, you will create a new Snip file and a new Windows 10 screenshot using features in Windows 10.

You will save your files as:

Lastname_Firstname_10A_Get_Started_Snip
Lastname_Firstname_10A_Graph_Screenshot

PROJECT RESULTS

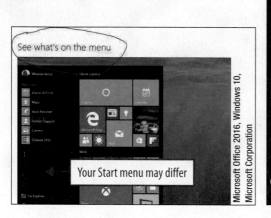

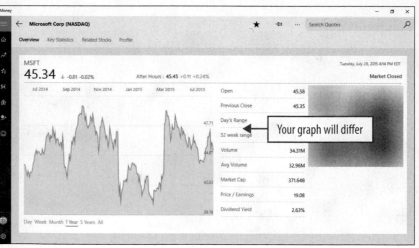

FIGURE 10.1 Project 10A Getting to Know Windows 10

A **program** is a set of instructions that a computer uses to accomplish a task. A computer program that helps you perform a task for a specific purpose is referred to as an **application**. For example, there are applications to create a document using word processing software, to play a game, to view the latest weather report, or to manage information.

An **operating system** is a specific type of computer program that manages the other programs on a computing device such as a desktop computer, a laptop computer, a smartphone, a tablet computer, or a game console. You need an operating system to:

- use application programs
- coordinate the use of your computer hardware such as a keyboard, mouse, touchpad, touchscreen, game controller, or printer
- organize data that you store on your computer and access data that you store on your own computer and in other locations

Windows 10 is an operating system developed by Microsoft Corporation that works with mobile computing devices and also with traditional desktop and laptop PCs.

Activity 10.01 | Identifying Apps and Platforms

The term **desktop app** commonly refers to a computer program that is installed on the hard drive of your personal computer—usually referred to as a PC—and requires a computer operating system like Microsoft Windows or Apple OSX (pronounced O-S-ten) to run. The programs in the full-featured versions of Microsoft Office such as Word and Excel are popular desktop apps. Adobe's Photoshop photo editing software and Adobe's Premiere video editing software are also popular desktop apps. Desktop apps typically have hundreds of features that take time to learn and use efficiently.

The shortened version of the term *application* is **app**, and this is typically a smaller application designed for a single purpose. Apps can run from the device operating system on a PC, a tablet computer, a game console, or a smartphone. You might already be familiar with apps that run on mobile devices like an Apple iPhone, an Apple iPad, an Android phone, an Android tablet, a Windows phone, or a Windows tablet. Examples include games like Monument Valley and Words with Friends; social networking and messaging apps like Instagram, Facebook, and WhatsApp; information apps like The Weather Channel and NFL Mobile; apps provided by your bank to enable you to conduct transactions; and services like Skype or Google Search.

Windows apps are apps that run not only on a Windows phone and a Windows tablet, but also on your Windows desktop PC. Most popular apps have versions for each major **mobile device platform**—the hardware and software environment for smaller-screen devices such as tablets and smartphones. For example, the NFL Mobile app is available for Apple mobile devices, Windows mobile devices, Android devices, and BlackBerry devices.

Increasingly, an operating system environment is referred to simply as a **platform**, which refers to an underlying computer system on which application programs can run. An **application developer**, which is anyone who writes a computer application, must write his or her application for one or more platforms, the most popular of which are the iOS platform, the Android platform, and the Windows platform.

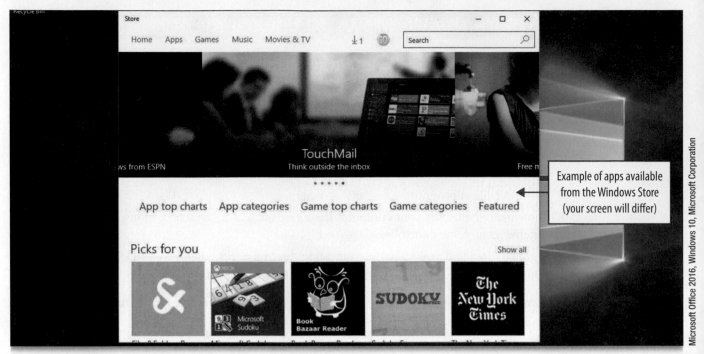

Example of apps available from the Windows Store (your screen will differ)

FIGURE 10.2

Some Windows apps are also referred to as *universal apps* because anyone that wants to develop an app for the Windows 10 platform can use a common code base to deliver the app to any Windows device—a desktop or laptop PC, a Windows phone, a Windows tablet, or an Xbox game console.

App developers can also use this code base to develop apps for Microsoft's new *HoloLens* see-through holographic computer and for devices on the *Internet of Things*, which refers to a growing network of physical objects that will have sensors connected to the Internet. Home automation devices like lights and appliances that you can control over the Internet are among the first objects connected to the *IoT*—the common acronym for the Internet of Things.

FIGURE 10.3

Self-Check | Answer These Questions to Check Your Understanding

1 A set of instructions that a computer uses to accomplish a task is a _____.

2 A specific type of computer program that manages the other programs on a computer is an _____ _____.

3 Computer programs installed on the hard drive of a computer, such as Microsoft Excel and Adobe Photoshop, and that typically have hundreds of features and take time to learn and use efficiently, are referred to as _____ apps.

4 The hardware and software environment for smaller-screen devices such as laptops, tablets, and smartphones is referred to as a mobile device _____.

5 The growing network of physical objects that have sensors connected to the Internet is called the _____ _____ _____.

Activity 10.02 | Recognizing User Accounts in Windows 10

On a single computer, Windows 10 can have multiple user accounts. This is useful because you can share a computer with other people in your family or organization and each person can have his or her own information and settings—none of which others can see. Each user on a single computer is referred to as a *user account*.

ALERT! **Variations in Screen Organization, Colors, and Functionality Are Common in Windows 10**

Individuals and organizations can determine how Windows 10 displays; therefore, the colors and the organization of various elements on the screen can vary. Your college or organization may customize Windows 10 to display a college picture or company logo, or restrict access to certain features. The basic functions and structure of Windows 10 are not changed by such variations. You can be confident that the skills you will practice in this instruction apply to Windows 10 regardless of available functionality or differences between the figures shown and your screen.

NOTE **Comparing Your Screen with the Figures in This Text**

Your screen will more closely match the figures shown in this text if you set your screen resolution to 1280 × 768. At other resolutions, your screen will closely resemble, but not match, the figures shown. To view your screen's resolution, on the desktop, right-click in a blank area, click *Display settings*, on the right click *Advanced display settings*, click the *Resolution arrow*, and then click the desired setting.

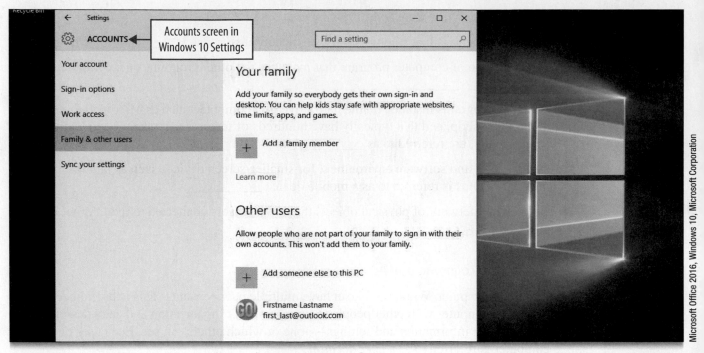

FIGURE 10.4

With Windows 10, you can create a *Microsoft account*, and then use that account to sign in to *any* Windows 10 computer on which you have, or create, a user account. By signing in with a Microsoft account you can:

- download apps from the Windows Store
- get your online content—email, social network updates, updated news—automatically displayed in an app when you sign in

Optionally, you can create a local account for use only on a specific PC. On your own Windows 10 computer, you must establish and then sign in with either a local account or a Microsoft account. Regardless of which one you select, you must provide an email address to associate with the user account name. If you create and then sign in with a local account, you can still connect to the Internet, but you will not have the advantage of having your personal arrangement of apps displayed on your Start menu every time you sign in to that PC. You can use any email address to create a local account—similar to other online services where an email address is your user ID. You can also use any email address to create a Microsoft account.

To enjoy and get the full benefit from Windows 10, Microsoft Office, Skype, and free unlimited OneDrive cloud storage, if you have not already done so, create a Microsoft account by going to www.microsoft.com/en-us/account and click *Create a free Microsoft account*. Here you can create an account using any email address and, if you want to do so, view a short video to learn about Microsoft accounts.

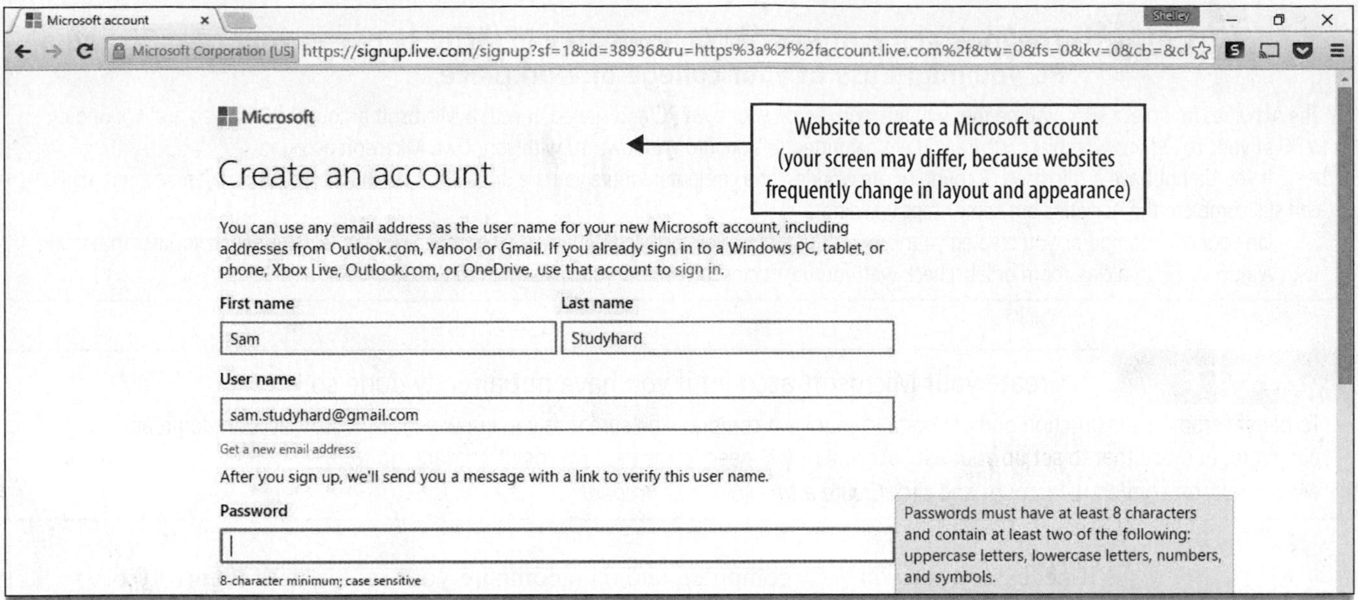

Website to create a Microsoft account (your screen may differ, because websites frequently change in layout and appearance)

FIGURE 10.5

Microsoft Office 2016, Windows 10, Microsoft Corporation

By signing in with a Microsoft account, your computer becomes your connected device where *you*—not your files—are the center of activity. At your college or place of employment, sign-in requirements will vary, because those computers are controlled by the organization's IT (Information Technology) professionals who are responsible for maintaining a secure computing environment for the entire organization.

Self-Check │ Answer These Questions to Check Your Understanding

1. On a single Windows 10 computer, multiple people can have a user account with their own information and _____.

2. On your own Windows 10 computer, it is recommended that you create a Microsoft account—if you do not have one—and then use that account to sign in because you will have your personal arrangement of _____ displayed on the Start menu every time you sign in to that PC.

3. To use your own Windows 10 computer, you must establish and then sign in with either a _____ account or a Microsoft account.

4. You can use any _____ address to set up a Microsoft account.

5. Sign-in requirements vary in organizations and colleges, because those computers are _____ by the organization's IT (Information Technology) professionals.

Activity 10.03 │ Turning On Your Computer, Signing In, and Exploring the Windows 10 Environment

Before you begin any computer activity, you must, if necessary, turn on your computer. This process is commonly referred to as ***booting the computer***. Because Windows 10 does not require you to completely shut down your computer except to install or repair a hardware device, in most instances moving the mouse or pressing a key will wake your computer in a few seconds. So most of the time you will skip the lengthier boot process.

In this Activity, you will turn on your computer and sign in to Windows 10. Within an organization, the sign-in process may differ from that of your own computer.

The look and features of Windows 10 will differ between your own PC and a PC you might use at your college or workplace.

The Activities in Project 10A assume that you are working on your own PC and signed in with a Microsoft account, or that you are working on a PC at your college or workplace where you are permitted to sign into Windows 10 with your own Microsoft account.

 If you do not have a Microsoft account, or are working at a computer where you are unable to sign in with your Microsoft account, you can still complete the Activities but some steps will differ.

 On your own computer, you created your user account when you installed Windows 10 or when you set up your new computer that came with Windows 10. In a classroom or lab, check with your instructor to see how you will sign in to Windows 10.

Create your Microsoft account if you have not already done so.

To benefit from this instruction and understand your own computer, be sure that you know your Microsoft account login and password, and use that to set up your user account. If you need to create a Microsoft account, go to www.microsoft.com/en-us/account and click *Create a free Microsoft account*.

---

1 ▶ If necessary, turn on your computer, and then compare your screen with Figure 10.6.

The Windows 10 *lock screen* displays a background—this might be a default picture from Microsoft or a picture that you selected if you have personalized your system already. You can also choose to have a slide show of your own photos display on the lock screen.

Your lock screen displays the time, day, and date. From the Personalization screen of Windows 10 Settings, you can choose *lock screen apps* to display, such as your calendar and mail. A lock screen app runs in the background and shows you quick status and notifications, even when your screen is locked. A lock screen app may also display a *badge*, which is an *icon*—small images that can represent commands, files, applications, or other windows—that shows status information such as your Internet connection or battery time remaining or summary information; for example, how many unread emails are in a mail app or the number of new posts in a social media app.

For example, one lock screen app that you can add is Skype so that you can answer a Skype call without having to sign in.

Your organization might have a custom sign-in screen with a logo or sign-in instructions, which will differ from the one shown. If you are using Windows 10 Pro, in the Accounts section of Settings, there is a feature named *Work access*, from which you may be able to connect to your work or school system based on established policies.

Windows 10 lock screen
(your image will vary)

FIGURE 10.6

Microsoft Office 2016, Windows 10, Microsoft Corporation

2 Determine whether you are working with a mouse and keyboard system or with a touchscreen system. If you are working with a touchscreen, determine whether you will use a stylus pen or the touch of your fingers.

Windows 10 is optimized for touchscreen computers and also works with a mouse and keyboard in the way you are probably most accustomed. If your device has a touchscreen, you can use the following gestures with your fingers in place of mouse and keyboard commands:

NOTE	If You Are Using a Touchscreen
	Tap an item to click it.
	Press and hold for a few seconds to right-click; release when the information or commands display.
	Touch the screen with two or more fingers and then pinch together to zoom in or stretch your fingers apart to zoom out.
	Slide your finger on the screen to scroll—slide left to scroll right and slide right to scroll left.
	Slide to rearrange—similar to dragging with a mouse.
	Swipe to select—slide an item a short distance with a quick movement—to select an item and bring up commands, if any.

3 ▷ Press Enter to display the Windows 10 sign-in screen.

🔄 **BY TOUCH**   On the lock screen, swipe upward to display the sign-in screen. Tap your user image if necessary to display the Password box.

4 ▷ If you are the displayed user, type your password (if you have established one) and press Enter. If you are not the displayed user, click your user image if it displays or click the Switch user arrow → and then click your user image. Type your password.

🔄 **BY TOUCH**   Tap the Password box to display the onscreen keyboard, type your password using the onscreen keyboard, and then at the right, tap the arrow.

The Windows 10 desktop displays with a default desktop background, a background you have selected, or perhaps a background set by your college or workplace.

5 ▷ In the lower left corner of your screen, move the mouse pointer over—*point to*—**Start** ⊞ and then *click*—press the left button on your mouse pointing device—to display the **Start menu**. Compare your screen with Figure 10.7, and then take a moment to study the table in Figure 10.8.

The *mouse pointer* is any symbol that displays on your screen in response to moving your mouse.

The Windows 10 *Start menu* displays a list of installed programs on the left and a customizable group of square and rectangular boxes—referred to as *tiles*—on the right. You can customize the arrangement of tiles from which you can access apps, websites, programs, folders, and tools for using your computer by simply clicking or tapping them.

Think of the right side of the Start menu as your connected *dashboard*—a one-screen view of links to information and programs that matter to *you*—through which you can connect with the people, activities, places, and apps that you care about.

Some tiles are referred to as *live tiles*, because they are constantly updated with fresh information relevant to you—the number of new email messages you have, new sports scores that you are interested in, or new updates to social networks such as Facebook or Twitter. Live tiles are at the center of your Windows 10 experience.

As you progress in your study of Windows 10, you will learn to customize the Start menu and add, delete, and organize tiles into meaningful groups. Your Start menu will not look like anyone else's; you will customize it to suit your own information needs.

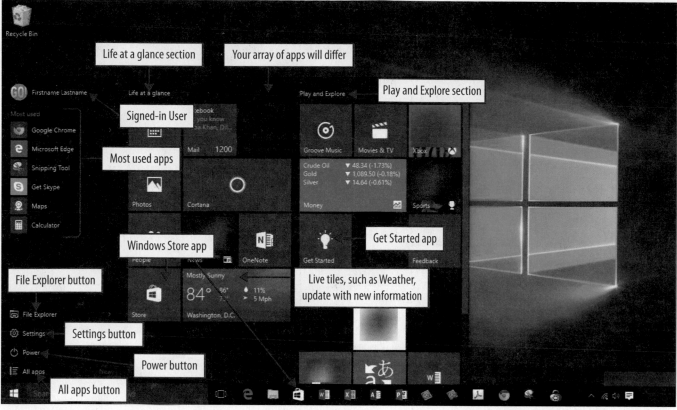

FIGURE 10.7

Microsoft Office 2016, Windows 10, Microsoft Corporation

PARTS OF THE WINDOWS 10 START MENU	
All apps button	Expands the list of apps to show all installed apps in alphabetic sections.
File Explorer button	Opens the File Explorer program.
Get Started app	Displays information to help you learn about Windows 10.
Life at a glance section	Apps pinned to the Start menu that related to your own information, for example, your Mail, your Calendar, and your contacts (People); you can change this heading or delete it.
Most used apps	Displays a list of the apps that you use the most; updates as you use Windows 10.
Play and Explore section	Apps pinned to the Start menu that relate to games or news apps that you have installed; you can change this heading or delete it.
Power button	Enables you to set your computer to Sleep, Shut down, or Restart.
Settings button	Displays the Settings window to change any Windows 10 setting.
Signed-in User	Displays the name of the signed-in user.
Windows Store app	Opens the Windows Store to locate and download more apps.

FIGURE 10.8

Gaskin, Shelley, Go! All in One, 3E. Pearson Education, 2017.

6 ▸ Click **Start** ⊞ again to close the Start menu. Compare your screen with Figure 10.9, and then take a moment to study the parts of the Windows desktop as shown in the table in Figure 10.10.

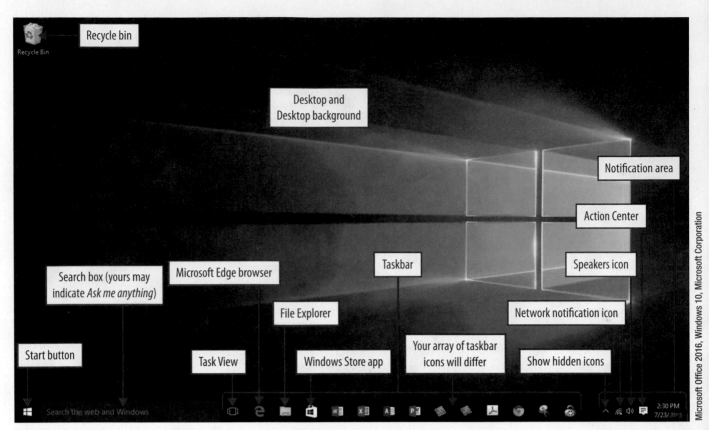

FIGURE 10.9

PARTS OF THE WINDOWS 10 DESKTOP	
Action Center	Displays the Action Center in a vertical pane on the right of your screen where you can see app notifications—such as new mail or new alerts from Microsoft or from social networks like Facebook—at the top and access commonly used settings at the bottom.
Desktop	Serves as a surface for your work, like the top of an actual desk. Here you can arrange icons—small pictures that represent a file, folder, program, or other object.
Desktop background	Displays the colors and graphics of your desktop; you can change the desktop background to look the way you want it, such as using a picture or a solid color. Also referred to as **wallpaper**.
File Explorer	Launches the File Explorer program, which displays the contents of folders and files on your computer and on connected locations, and also enables you to perform tasks related to your files and folders such as copying, moving, and renaming.
Microsoft Edge browser	Launches Microsoft Edge, the web browser program developed by Microsoft that is included with Windows 10.
Network notification icon	Displays the status of your network.
Notification area	Displays notification icons and the system clock and calendar; sometimes referred to as the **system tray**.
Recycle Bin	Contains files and folders that you delete. When you delete a file or folder from a location on your hard disk drive, it is not actually deleted; it stays in the Recycle Bin if you want it back, until you take an action to empty the Recycle Bin.
Search box	Before **Cortana**—Microsoft's intelligent personal assistant—is set up, this will indicate *Search the web and Windows*. After Cortana is set up, this will indicate *Ask me anything*. Regardless, you can type in the box to begin a search of your computer and the web.

FIGURE 10.10 *(continued)*

PARTS OF THE WINDOWS 10 DESKTOP (*continued*)	
Show hidden icons	Displays additional icons related to your notifications.
Speakers icon	Displays the status of your computer's speakers (if any).
Start button	Displays the Start menu.
Task View	Displays your desktop background with a small image of all open programs and apps. Click once to open, click again to close.
Taskbar	Contains buttons to launch programs and buttons for all open programs; by default, it is located at the bottom of the desktop, but you can move it. You can customize the number and arrangement of buttons.
Windows Store	Opens the Windows Store where you can select and download Windows apps.

Gaskin, Shelley. Go! All in One, 3E. Pearson Education, 2017.

FIGURE 10.10

> **NOTE** This Activity Is Optional
>
> Complete this Activity if you are able to do so. Some college labs may not enable these features. If you cannot practice in your college lab, practice this on another computer if possible.

Activity 10.04 | Changing Your Desktop Background and Lock Screen Image

As a way to personalize your computer, you can change the desktop background to a personal photo. You can also change your lock screen image to a personal photo.

1 Click **Start** ▦, just above the Start button click **Settings**, click **Personalization**, and then on the left click **Background**.

2 On the right, under **Choose your picture**, click **Browse**, and then select a personal photo from the **Pictures** folder on your PC—or navigate to some other location where you have stored a personal photo.

3 Click the picture, and then at the bottom of the Open dialog box, click **Choose picture**.

4 On the left, click **Lock screen**, on the right, click the **Background arrow**, and then click **Picture**.

5 Click **Browse**, and then select a personal photo from the **Pictures** folder on your PC—or navigate to some other location where you have stored a personal photo.

6 Click the picture, and then at the bottom of the Open dialog box, click **Choose picture**.

7 Close all open windows.

> **NOTE** This Activity Is Optional
>
> Complete this Activity if you are able to do so. Some college labs may not enable these features. If you cannot practice in your college lab, practice this on another computer if possible.

Activity 10.05 | Creating a PIN to Use in Place of Passwords

You can create a *PIN*—a personal identification number—to use in place of a password. Having a PIN makes it easier to sign in to Windows, apps, and services because it is short.

1 Click **Start** ▦, just above the Start button click **Settings**, click **Accounts**, and then on the left click **Sign-in options**.

2 On the right, under **PIN**, click **Add**. If necessary, enter the password for your Microsoft account and click **Sign in**.

3 In the **New PIN** box, type **1234**—or a PIN of your choice so long as you can remember it. In the **Confirm PIN** box, retype your PIN.

4 Click **OK**, and notice that you can use this PIN to sign in to Windows, apps, and services.

5 **Close** |×| the **Settings** window.

| Objective 2 | Use File Explorer and Desktop Apps to Create a New Folder and Save a File |

Activity 10.06 | Pinning a Program and Adding a Toolbar to the Taskbar

Snipping Tool is a program within Windows 10 that captures an image of all or part of your computer's screen. A *snip*, as the captured image is called, can be annotated, saved, copied, or shared via email.

1 In the lower left corner of your screen, click in the **Search box**.

Recall that your Search box may be set up for Cortana, in which case it will indicate *Ask me anything*; if Cortana is not set up, the Search box will indicate *Search the web and Windows*. If Cortana asks to be set up, you can indicate that you are not interested or go ahead and set it up.

Search relies on *Bing*, Microsoft's search engine, which enables you to conduct a search on your PC, your apps, and the web.

2 With your insertion point in the search box, type **snipping** Compare your screen with Figure 10.11.

BY TOUCH   On a touchscreen, tap in the Search box to display the onscreen keyboard, and then begin to type *snipping*.

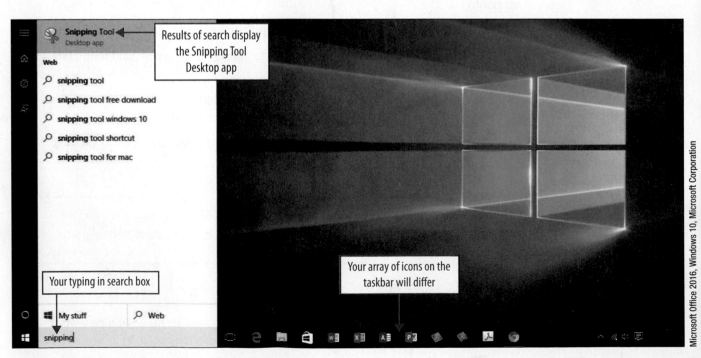

FIGURE 10.11

3 With **Snipping Tool** shaded and displayed at the top of the search results, press Enter one time.

The Snipping Tool *dialog box*—a small window that displays options for completing a task—displays on the desktop, and on the taskbar, the Snipping Tool program button displays underlined and framed in a lighter shade to indicate that the program is open.

BY TOUCH   In the search results, tap the Snipping Tool app.

4 On the taskbar, point to the **Snipping Tool** button 🖉 and then *right-click*—click the right mouse button one time. On the displayed **Jump List**, click **Pin this program to taskbar**.

A *Jump List* displays destinations and tasks from a program's taskbar icon when you right-click the icon.

BY TOUCH   On the taskbar, use the *Swipe to select* technique—swipe upward with a short quick movement—to display the Jump List. On the list, tap *Pin this program to taskbar*.

5 Point to the upper right corner of the **Snipping Tool** dialog box, and then click **Close** ×.

Because you will use Snipping Tool frequently while completing the projects in this instruction, it is recommended that you leave Snipping Tool pinned to your taskbar.

6 Point to an empty area of the taskbar, and then right-click to display a list that contains *Toolbars*—if your taskbar is crowded, you might have to try several times to find an empty area.

7 Point to **Toolbars**, click **Links**, and then on the taskbar, notice the text *Links*.

8 To the right of the text *Links*, click >> and then notice the links to websites you have visited.

It is good to know that these taskbar toolbars are available if you want to use them; however, it is now more common to add tiles to the Start menu for frequently used sites. There are some additional toolbars you might want to explore.

9 To remove the taskbar toolbar, right-click again in a blank area of the taskbar, point to **Toolbars**, and then click **Links** again to remove it from the taskbar.

Activity 10.07 │ Creating a New Folder to Store a File

A *file* is a collection of information stored on a computer under a single name. Examples of a file include a Word document, an Excel workbook, a picture, a song, or a program. A *folder* is a container in which you can store files. Windows 10 organizes and keeps track of your electronic files by letting you create and label electronic folders into which you can place your files.

In this Activity, you will create a new folder and save it in a location of your choice. You might decide to use a *removable storage device*, such as a USB flash drive, which is commonly used to transfer information from one computer to another. Such devices are also useful when you want to work with your files on different computers. For example, you probably have files that you work with at your college, at home, and possibly at your workplace.

A *drive* is an area of storage that is formatted with a file system compatible with your operating system and is identified by a drive letter. For example, your computer's *hard disk drive*—the primary storage device located inside your computer where some of your files and programs are typically stored—is usually designated as drive *C*. Removable storage devices that you insert into your computer will be designated with a drive letter—the letter designation varies from one computer to another.

As you progress in your study of Windows 10, you will also learn to use *cloud storage*—storage space on an Internet site that can also display as a drive on your computer. When you create a Microsoft account, free cloud storage called *OneDrive* is provided to you. If you are signed in with your Microsoft account, you can access OneDrive from File Explorer.

Increasingly, the use of removable storage devices for file storage is becoming less common, because having your files stored in the cloud where you can retrieve them from any device is more convenient and efficient.

ALERT!

The steps in this Activity use the example of storing on a USB flash drive. If you want to store your file in a different location, such as the Documents folder on your computer's hard drive or a folder on your OneDrive, you can still complete the steps, but your screens will not match exactly those shown.

---

1 Be sure your Windows desktop is still displayed. If you want to do so, insert your USB flash drive. If necessary, close any messages.

> Plugging in a device results in a chime sound—if sound is enabled. You might see a message in the taskbar or on the screen that the device software is being installed.

2 On the taskbar, click **File Explorer** 📁. If necessary, on the ribbon at the top of the window, on the View tab, in the Layout group, click Tiles. (You might have to expand your ribbon, as described in the table in Figure 10.13; also, you might have to scroll within the Layout group to view *Tiles*.) Compare your screen with Figure 10.12, and then take a moment to study the parts of the File Explorer window as shown in the table in Figure 10.13.

NOTE   Does your ribbon show only the tab names?

By default, the ribbon is minimized and appears as a menu bar, displaying only the ribbon tabs. If only the tabs of your ribbon are displayed, click the Expand the Ribbon arrow ⌄ on the right side to display the full ribbon.

The *File Explorer window* displays with the Quick access area selected by default. A File Explorer window displays the contents of the current location, and contains helpful parts so that you can *navigate*—explore within the file organizing structure of Windows. A *location* is any disk drive, folder, network, or cloud storage area in which you can store files and folders.

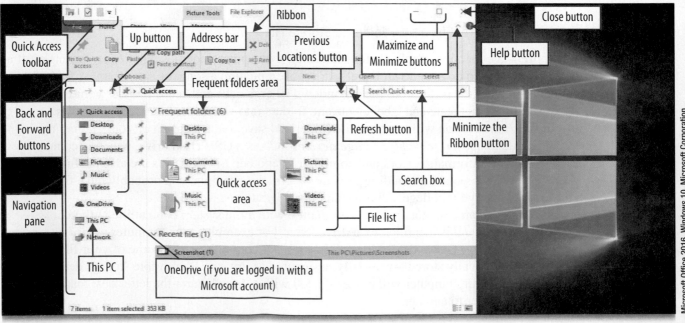

FIGURE 10.12

PARTS OF THE FILE EXPLORER WINDOW	
Address bar	Displays your current location in the folder structure as a series of links separated by arrows.
Back and Forward buttons	Provides the ability to navigate to other folders you have already opened without closing the current folder window. These buttons work with the address bar; that is, after you use the address bar to change folders, you can use the Back button to return to the previous folder.
Close button	Closes the window.
File list	Displays the contents of the current folder or location; if you type text into the Search box, only the folders and files that match your search will display here—including files in subfolders.
Frequent folders area	When Quick access is selected in the navigation pane, displays the folders you use frequently.
Help button	Opens a Bing search for Windows 10 help.
Maximize button	Increases the size of a window to fill the entire screen.
Minimize button	Removes the window from the screen without closing it; minimized windows can be reopened by clicking the associated button in the taskbar.
Minimize the Ribbon button	Collapses the ribbon so that only the tab names display.
Navigation pane	Displays—for the purpose of navigating to locations—the Quick access area, your OneDrive if you have one and are signed in, locations on the PC at which you are working, any connected storage devices, and network locations to which you might be connected.
OneDrive	Provides navigation to your free file storage and file sharing service provided by Microsoft that you get when you sign up for a Microsoft account; this is your personal cloud storage for files.
Previous Locations button	Displays the path to locations you have visited recently so that you can go back to a previously working directory quickly.
Quick access area	Displays commonly accessed locations—such as Documents and Desktop—that you want to access quickly.
Quick Access Toolbar	Displays commonly used commands; you can customize this toolbar by adding and deleting commands and by showing the toolbar below the ribbon instead of above the ribbon.
Refresh button	Refreshes the current path.
Ribbon	Groups common tasks on related tabs at the top of the window; for example, copying and moving, creating new folders, emailing and zipping items, and changing views.
Search box	Locates files stored within the current folder when you type a search term.
This PC	Provides navigation to your internal storage and attached storage devices including optical media such as a DVD drive.
Up button	Opens the location where the folder you are viewing is saved—also referred to as the *parent folder*.

FIGURE 10.13

Gaskin, Shelley, Go! All in One, 3E. Pearson Education, 2017.

3 If necessary, in the upper right corner of the **File Explorer** window, click **Expand the Ribbon** ⌄.

The *ribbon* is a user interface in Windows 10 that groups commands for performing related tasks on tabs across the upper portion of a window. Commands for common tasks include copying and moving, creating new folders, emailing and zipping items, and changing the view.

Use the *navigation pane*—the area on the left side of the File Explorer window—to get to locations—your OneDrive, folders on your PC, devices and drives connected to your PC, and other PCs on your network.

4 In the **navigation pane**, click **This PC**. On the right, under **Devices and drives**, locate **Windows (C:)**—or **OS (C:)**—point to the device name to display the ⇱ pointer, and then right-click to display a shortcut menu. Compare your screen with Figure 10.14.

A *shortcut menu* is a context-sensitive menu that displays commands and options relevant to the active object. The Windows logo on the C: drive indicates this is where the Windows 10 operating system is stored.

BY TOUCH   Press and hold briefly to display a shaded square and then release.

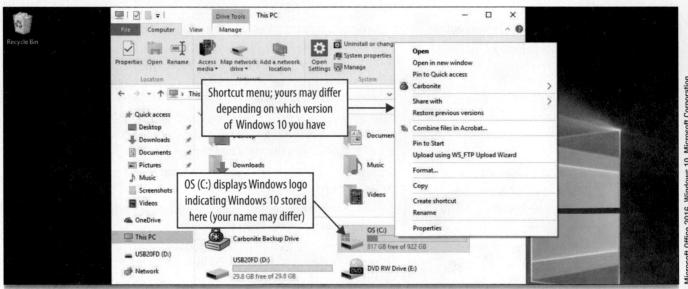

FIGURE 10.14

5 On the shortcut menu, click **Open** to display the *file list* for this drive.

A file list displays the contents of the current location. If you enter a search term in the search box, your results will also display here. Here, in the C: drive, Windows 10 stores various files related to your operating system.

ANOTHER WAY   Point to the device name and double-click to display the file list for the device.

6 On the ribbon, notice that the **Drive Tools tab** displays above the **Manage tab**.

This is a *contextual tab*, which is a tab added to the ribbon automatically when a specific object is selected and that contains commands relevant to the selected object.

7 To the left of the **address bar**, click **Up** [↑] to move up one level in the drive hierarchy and close the file list.

> The ***address bar*** displays your current location in the folder structure as a series of links separated by arrows. Use the address bar to enter or select a location. You can tap or click a part of the path to go to that level, or tap or click at the end of the path to select the path for copying.

8 Under **Devices and drives**, click your **USB flash drive** to select it—or click the folder or location where you want to store your files for this Project—and notice that the drive or folder is highlighted in blue, indicating it is selected. At the top of the window, on the ribbon, click the **Computer tab**, and then in the **Location group**, click **Open**. Compare your screen with Figure 10.15.

> The file list for the selected location displays. There may be no files or only a few files in the location you have selected. You can open a location by using the shortcut menu or by using this ribbon command.

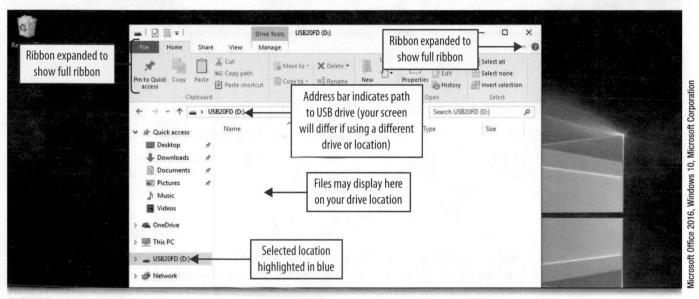

FIGURE 10.15

9 On the ribbon, in the **New group**, click **New folder**.

10 With the text *New folder* highlighted in blue, type **Windows 10 Chapter 10** and press [Enter] to confirm the folder name and select—highlight in blue—the new folder. With the folder selected, press [Enter] again to open the File Explorer window for your **Windows 10 Chapter 10** folder. Compare your screen with Figure 10.16.

> A new folder is created in the location you selected. The address bar indicates the ***path*** from This PC to your folder. A path is a sequence of folders that leads to a specific file or folder.

> To ***select*** means to specify, by highlighting, a block of data or text on the screen with the intent of performing some action on the selection.

⟳ BY TOUCH   You may have to tap the keyboard icon in the lower right corner of the taskbar to display the onscreen keyboard.

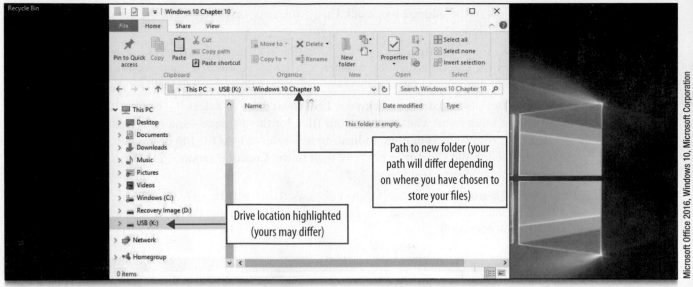

FIGURE 10.16

Activity 10.08 | Creating and Saving a File

1 In the upper right corner of your **Windows 10 Chapter 10** folder window, click **Close** ☒.

2 In the lower left corner, click **Start** ⊞, and then at the bottom of the menu, click **All apps**.

The **All apps** command displays the Start menu in an alphabetic arrangement showing every app—both desktop apps and Windows apps—that is installed on your computer. Many apps are installed by default and are part of the Windows 10 operating system.

3 Point to the right edge of the **menu list** to display a **scroll bar**, and then drag the **scroll box** down to view apps listed under **G**. Compare your screen with Figure 10.17.

To **drag** is to move something from one location on the screen to another while holding down the left mouse button; the action of dragging includes releasing the mouse button at the desired time or location.

FIGURE 10.17

More Knowledge   Jump to a Lettered Section of the All Apps List Quickly

To move quickly to an alphabetic section of the All apps list, click any alphabetic letter on the list to display an onscreen alphabet, and then click the letter of the alphabet to which you want to jump.

4 Click **Get Started**. If necessary, in the upper right, click **Maximize** ▫ so that the **Get Started** window fills your entire screen. On the list along the left side of the screen, click **Start**, and then click **See what's on the menu**. Then, move your mouse pointer to the right edge of the screen to display the **scroll bar**. Compare your screen with Figure 10.18.

A vertical *scroll bar* displays on the right side of this window. A scroll bar displays when the contents of a window are not completely visible. A scroll bar can be vertical as shown or horizontal and displayed at the bottom of a window.

Within the scroll bar, you can move the *scroll box* to bring the contents of the window into view. The position of the scroll box within the scroll bar indicates your relative position within the window's contents. You can click the *scroll arrow* at either end of the scroll bar to move within the window in small increments.

In any window, the *Maximize* button will maximize the size of the window to fill the entire screen.

It is worth your time to explore this *Get Started* feature in Windows 10 to learn about all the things that Windows 10 can do for you.

FIGURE 10.18

5 On the taskbar, click **Snipping Tool** 🖉 to display the small **Snipping Tool** dialog box over the screen.

6 On the **menu bar** of the **Snipping Tool** dialog box, click the **arrow** to the right of *New*— referred to as the **New arrow**—and then compare your screen with Figure 10.19.

An arrow attached to a button will display a menu when clicked. Such a button is referred to as a *split button*—clicking the main part of the button performs a command and clicking the arrow opens a menu with choices. A *menu* is a list of commands within a category, and a group of menus at the top of a program window is referred to as the *menu bar*.

FIGURE 10.19

7 On the menu, notice that there are four types of snips.

A *free-form snip* enables you to draw an irregular line such as a circle around an area of the screen. A *rectangular snip* enables you to draw a precise box by dragging the mouse pointer around an area of the screen to form a rectangle. A *window snip* captures the entire displayed window. A *full-screen snip* captures the entire screen.

8 On the menu, click **Rectangular Snip**, and move your mouse slightly. Notice that the screen dims and your pointer takes the shape of a plus sign ⊞.

9 Move the mouse pointer to the upper left corner of the white portion of the screen, hold down the left mouse button, and then drag down and to the right until you have captured the white portion of the screen with the Start menu picture as shown in Figure 10.20 and then release the mouse button. If you are not satisfied with your result, close the Snipping Tool window and begin again.

Your snip is copied to the Snipping Tool mark-up window. Here you can annotate—mark or make notes on—save, copy, or share the snip.

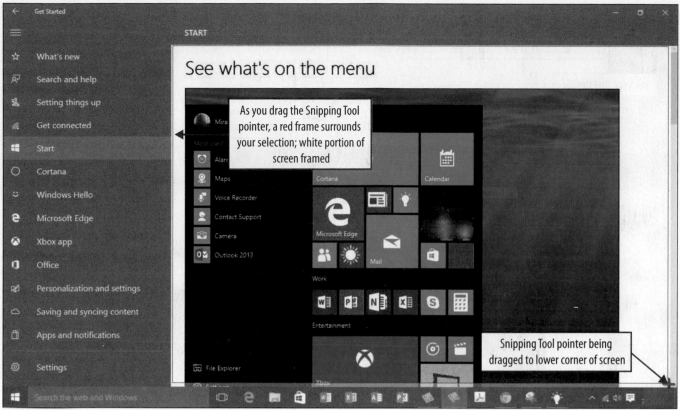

FIGURE 10.20

Microsoft Office 2016, Windows 10, Microsoft Corporation

10 ▶ On the toolbar of the displayed **Snipping Tool** mark-up window, click the **Pen button arrow** ⬜, and then click **Red Pen**. Notice that your mouse pointer displays as a red dot.

11 ▶ At the top of the snip—remember that you are now looking at a picture of the portion of the screen you captured—point to the words *See what's on the menu* and use the red mouse pointer to draw a circle around the text—the circle need not be precise. If you are not satisfied with your circle, on the toolbar, click the Eraser button ⬜, point anywhere on the red circle, click to erase, and then begin again. Compare your screen with Figure 10.21.

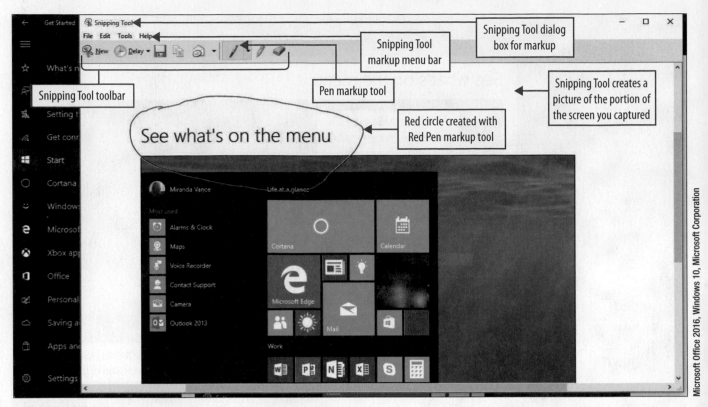

FIGURE 10.21

> **12** On the toolbar of the **Snipping Tool** mark-up window, click **Highlighter** 🖊. Notice that your mouse pointer displays as a small yellow rectangle.

> **13** Point to the text *See what's on the menu*, hold down the left mouse button, and then drag over the text to highlight it in yellow. If you are not satisfied with your yellow highlight, on the toolbar, click the Eraser button 🧽, point anywhere on the yellow highlight, click to erase, and then begin again. Compare your screen with Figure 10.22.

🔄 **BY TOUCH**   Use your finger to draw the circle and to highlight text.

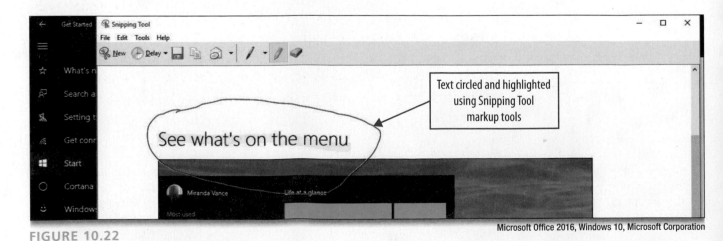

FIGURE 10.22

> **14** On the **Snipping Tool** mark-up window's toolbar, click **Save Snip** 💾 to display the **Save As** dialog box.

15 In the **Save As** dialog box, in the **navigation pane**, drag the scroll box down as necessary to find and then click the location where you created your **Windows 10 Chapter 10** folder.

16 In the **file list**, scroll as necessary, locate and *double-click*—press the left mouse button two times in rapid succession while holding the mouse still—your **Windows 10 Chapter 10** folder. Compare your screen with Figure 10.23.

 **ANOTHER WAY**   Right-click the folder name and click Open.

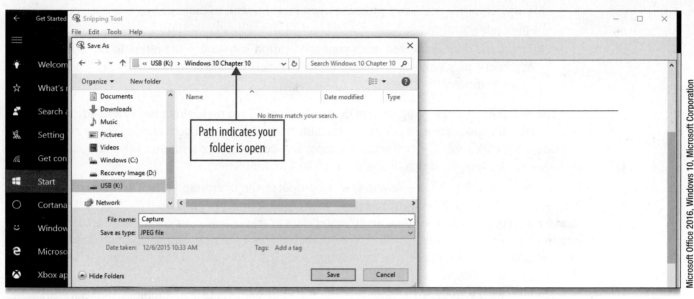

FIGURE 10.23

NOTE   Successful Double-Clicking Requires a Steady Hand

Double-clicking needs a steady hand. The speed of the two clicks is not as important as holding the mouse still between the two clicks. If you are not satisfied with your result, try again.

---

17 At the bottom of the **Save As** dialog box, locate **Save as type**, click anywhere in the box to display a list, and then on the displayed list click **JPEG file**.

JPEG, which is commonly pronounced *JAY-peg* and stands for Joint Photographic Experts Group, is a common file type used by digital cameras and computers to store digital pictures. JPEG is popular because it can store a high-quality picture in a relatively small file.

18 At the bottom of the **Save As** dialog box, click in the **File name** box to select the text *Capture*, and then using your own name, type **Lastname_Firstname_10A_Get_Started_Snip**

Within any Windows-based program, text highlighted in blue—selected—in this manner will be replaced by your typing.

NOTE   File Naming in This Text

Windows 10 recognizes file names with spaces. You can use spaces in file names, however, some programs, especially when transferring files over the Internet, may insert the extra characters *%20* in place of a space. In this instruction you will be instructed to save files using an underscore instead of a space. The underscore key is the shift of the ⎵ key—on most keyboards located two keys to the left of ⌫ Backspace.

---

19 In the lower right corner of the dialog box, click **Save**.

20 **Close** ☒ the **Snipping Tool** mark-up window, and then **Close** ☒ the **Get Started** window. Hold this file until you finish Project 10A, and then submit as directed by your instructor.

You have successfully created a folder and saved a file within that folder.

Traditionally, the three major tasks of an operating system are to:

- Manage your computer's hardware—the printers, scanners, disk drives, monitors, and other hardware attached to it.
- Manage the application software installed on your computer—programs like those in Microsoft Office and other programs you might install to manage your money, edit photos, or play games.
- Manage the *data* generated from your application software. Data refers to the documents, worksheets, pictures, songs, and so on that you create and store during the day-to-day use of your computer.

The Windows 10 operating system continues to perform these three tasks, and additionally is optimized for touchscreens; for example, tablets of all sizes and convertible laptop computers. Windows 10 works equally well with any input device, including a mouse, keyboard, touchscreen, and *pen*—a pen-shaped stylus that you tap on a computer screen.

In most instances, when you purchase a computer, the operating system software is already installed. The operating system consists of many smaller programs, stored as system files, which transfer data to and from the disk and transfer data in and out of your computer's memory. Other functions performed by the operating system include hardware-specific tasks such as checking to see if a key has been pressed on the keyboard and, if it has, displaying the appropriate letter or character on the screen.

When using a Windows 10 computer, you can write and create using traditional desktop apps, and you can also read and socialize and communicate by using the Windows Store apps. With Windows 10, as compared to earlier versions of Windows, your PC has some of the characteristics of a smartphone or tablet—it is connected, it is mobile, and it is centered on people and activities. If, as Microsoft predicts, the laptop and tablet will ultimately merge into one device—like the Microsoft Surface—then you will be well prepared by learning to use Windows 10 and the Windows apps.

Activity 10.09 | Identifying Operating System Functions and Windows App Functions

Windows 10, in the same manner as other operating systems and earlier versions of the Windows operating system, has a desktop that uses a *graphical user interface*—abbreviated as *GUI* and pronounced *GOO-ee*. A graphical user interface uses graphics such as an image of a file folder or wastebasket that you click to activate the item represented. A GUI commonly incorporates the following:

- A *pointer*—any symbol that displays on your screen in response to moving your mouse and with which you can select objects and commands.
- A *pointing device*, such as a mouse or touchpad, to control the pointer.
- *Icons*—small images that represent commands, files, applications, or other windows. You can select an object icon and drag it to move it or double-click a program icon to start a program.
- A *desktop*—a simulation of a real desk that represents your work area; here you can arrange icons such as shortcuts to programs, files, folders, and various types of documents in the same manner you would arrange physical objects on top of a desk.

In Windows 10, you also have a Start menu with tiles on the right. The array of tiles serves as a connected dashboard to all of your important programs, sites, and services. On the Start menu, your view is tailored to your information and activities.

The physical parts of your computer such as the central processing unit (CPU), memory, and any attached devices such as a printer, are collectively known as *resources*. The operating system keeps track of the status of each resource and decides when a resource needs attention and for how long.

There will be times when you want and need to interact with the functions of the operating system; for example, when you want to install a new hardware device like a color printer. Windows 10 provides tools with which you can inform the operating system of new hardware that you attach to your computer.

Software application programs are the programs that enable you to do work on, and be entertained by, your computer—programs such as Word and Excel found in the Microsoft Office suite of products, Adobe Photoshop, and computer games. No application program, whether a larger desktop app or smaller Windows app, can run on its own—it must run under the direction of an operating system.

For the everyday use of your computer, the most important and most often used function of the operating system is managing your files and folders—referred to as *data management*. In the same manner that you strive to keep your paper documents and file folders organized so that you can find information when you need it, your goal when organizing your computer files and folders is to group your files so that you can find information easily. Managing your data files so that you can find your information when you need it is one of the most important computing skills you can learn.

FIGURE 10.24

Managing the data on all of your devices is an important computing skill; storing your data in the cloud—for example, on OneDrive—enables you to access your data from any device

Hywards/Shutterstock

To check how well you can identify operating system functions, take a moment to answer the following questions:

Self-Check │ Answer These Questions to Check Your Understanding

1 Of the three major functions of the operating system, the first is to manage your computer's _____ such as disk drives, monitors, and printers.

2 The second major function of the operating system is to manage the application _____ such as Microsoft Office, Adobe PhotoShop, and video games.

3 The third major function of the operating system is to manage the _____ generated from your applications—the files such as Word documents, Excel workbooks, pictures, and songs that you create and store during the day-to-day use of your computer.

4 The Start menu's array of tiles is your connected _____ to all of your important programs, sites, and services.

5 One of the most important computing skills you can learn is how to manage your _____ _____ so that you can find your information quickly.

Objective 4 │ Discover Windows 10 Features

According to Microsoft, a billion people in the world use Windows and 93 percent of PCs in the world run some version of Windows. Increasingly people want to use Windows in a format that runs easily on mobile computing devices such as laptops, tablets, convertibles, and smartphones; research shows this is where people now spend more time.

With only desktop apps to choose from, Windows is centered around files—typing and creating things—and that will continue to be an important part of what you do on your computer, especially in the workplace.

Additionally, you are doing different kinds of things on your PC, and you probably expect your PC to be more like a smartphone—connected all the time, mobile, to have long battery life if it's a laptop, and be centered on the people and activities that are important to you. It is for those activities that the Windows apps will become important to you.

Think of Windows 10 as a way to do work on your desktop or laptop computer, and then to read and be entertained on your laptop, tablet, or Xbox game console. Windows 10 is both serious for work and fun for entertainment and social networking.

Activity 10.10 │ Using Windows Apps

On your own computer, an array of Windows apps displays on the Start menu immediately after you sign in to a Windows 10 computer. Keep in mind that a workplace computer may have a specific, locked-down arrangement of apps, or no apps at all.

On a new computer, the apps might be preselected by your computer manufacturer and by Microsoft. You can use these right away, and later you can add, delete, and rearrange the apps so that your Start menu tiles become your own personal dashboard. Recall that some apps are represented by live tiles that will update with information after you set them to do so. For example, the Mail app will show updates of incoming mail after you connect it to your email account.

Some of the built-in apps that will come with a new installation of Windows 10 on a consumer PC include:

- Mail, from which you can get email from all of your email accounts, all in one place!
- Weather, from which you can get hourly, daily, and 10-day forecasts.

- Sound Recorder, with which you can easily record a sound, and then trim, save, and replay it on your PC.
- Sports, where you can keep up with all the sports and teams you care about with Live Tile updates.
- News, which is a photo-rich app to keep up with what's happening in the world.

1 With your **desktop** displayed, to the right of Start ⊞, click in the Search box to display the insertion point, type **sports** and then compare your screen with Figure 10.25.

The *insertion point* is a blinking vertical line that indicates where text will be inserted when you type.

At the top of the results, the Windows Store app *Sports* is highlighted.

Windows 10 comes with some Windows apps already built-in—these include Sports, Weather, News, and Money. These are high-quality apps, and you might want to explore them and pin them to your Start menu. There are other apps in the Windows Store for these same categories, but the Microsoft apps are worth investigating.

> **NOTE** Don't Have the Sports App?
>
> You can use any app available on your system or from the Windows Store to complete this Activity. The Sports app and the Money app are used here as an example.

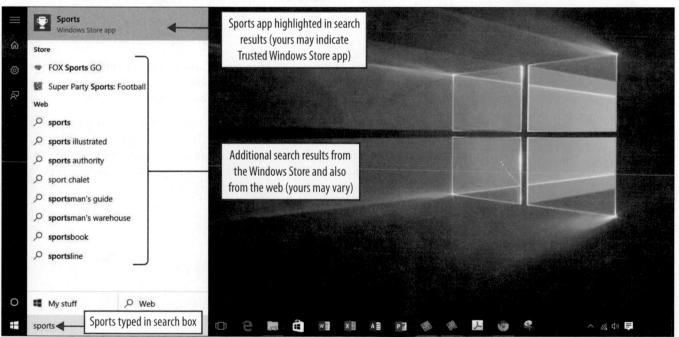

FIGURE 10.25

2 At the top of the list, point to the text *Sports Trusted Windows Store app*, right-click, and then click **Pin to Start**—or if *Unpin from Start* displays, click anywhere on your desktop to close the search results so that the app remains pinned to your Start menu.

3 Click **Start** ⊞ to display the **Start menu**, and then on the right, locate the **Sports** app, as shown in Figure 10.26.

Up-to-date information may already begin to display.

Your array of apps will differ

Sports app displaying updated information (yours will differ and may be in a different location)

Microsoft Office 2016, Windows 10, Microsoft Corporation

FIGURE 10.26

4 ▶ Click the **Sports** app tile; if necessary wait a moment if this is the first time you have used this app. In the upper right corner, if necessary, click **Maximize** ▢ to have the app fill the entire window.

> Here you can scroll down and click on many new sports stories. Across the top, you can click on *Scoreboard* to see up-to-date scores of games, or click *Slideshows* or *Videos* to see sports news stories portrayed in images or videos.

> The features in the Sports app are representative of the features in many Windows apps.

5 ▶ In the upper left corner, click the **Hamburger** icon ☰, and then compare your screen with Figure 10.27.

> This icon is commonly referred to as a ***hamburger menu*** or a ***menu icon*** or simply a ***hamburger***. The name derives from the three lines that bring to mind a hamburger on a bun. This type of button is often used in mobile applications because it is compact to use on smaller screens.

> When you click the hamburger icon, a menu displays that identifies the list of icons on the left so that you can navigate to more specific areas of the Microsoft Sports app. Sometimes this area is referred to as the ***app bar***. Regardless of the name, you can see that you can navigate directly to categories such as the NBA (National Basketball Association) or MLB (Major League Baseball). You can also create a list of favorite teams that you want to follow.

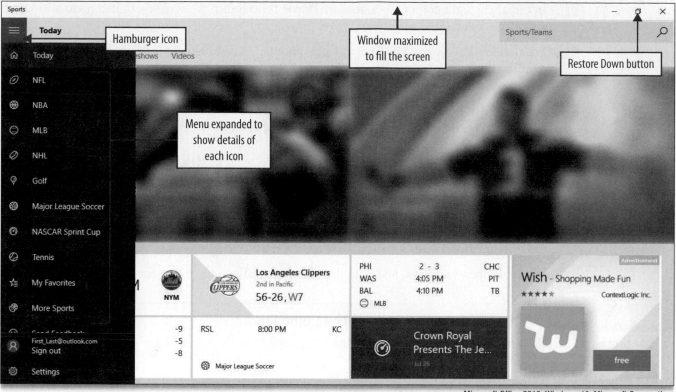

FIGURE 10.27

6 ▸ In the upper right corner, click *Restore Down* ⬚ to return the window to its previous size.

Use the Maximize command ⬚ to display a window in a full-screen view; use the *Restore Down command* ⬚ to resize a window to its previous size.

7 ▸ **Close** ✕ the Sports app.

8 ▸ With your **desktop** displayed, to the right of Start ⊞, click in the Search box to display the insertion point, type **money** and then at the top of the list of results, click the Window Store app **Money**.

9 ▸ **Maximize** ⬚ the window, and then on the navigation bar at the top of the window, click **Watchlist**. On the list of stocks, click **MSFT**. If *MSFT* does not display, at the upper right, click +, type MSFT, and then on the list that displays, click MSFT to add it to the list.

Information about Microsoft's stock and a graph displays.

10 ▸ Below the graph, click **1 Year** to see a graph representing one year.

11 ▸ With your Microsoft graph displayed, press and hold down ⊞ and then press ⌨PrintScrn⌨; release the two keys. Notice that your screen dims momentarily; you will view the screenshot at the end of this Activity.

Use this technique to create a *screenshot*. The screenshot file is automatically stored in the Pictures folder of your hard drive.

A screenshot captured in this manner from a Windows Store app is saved as a *.png* file, which is commonly pronounced PING, and stands for Portable Network Graphic. This is an image file type that can be transferred over the Internet.

A *keyboard shortcut* is a combination of two or more keyboard keys and is useful to perform a task that would otherwise require a mouse.

12 ▸ Point to the right edge of the screen to display a scroll bar, and then scroll down to see news stories about Microsoft.

13 In the upper right corner, click **Restore Down** ⬓ to return the window to its previous size, and then **Close** ✕ the Money app.

14 From the taskbar, open **File Explorer** ▣, and then navigate to **This PC**. In the file list, double-click **Pictures**, and then double-click **Screenshots**. On the ribbon, click the **View tab**, and then in the **Layout group**, if necessary, click **Large icons**.

15 In the **file list**, click one time to select the **Screenshot** file that you captured of the Microsoft graph; if more than one Screenshot file displays, click to select the file that has the highest number.

16 On the ribbon, on the **Home tab**, in the **Organize group**, click **Rename**, and then using your own name, type **Lastname_Firstname_10A_Graph_Screenshot** and then press ⏎.

17 With the renamed screenshot selected, on the **Home tab**, click **Copy**. In the **navigation pane**, navigate to the location of your **Windows 10 Chapter 10 folder**, open the folder, and then on the ribbon, click **Paste**.

18 Close all open windows, and hold this file until you complete Project 10A.

> **More Knowledge**   **Where Did the Hamburger Icon Come From?**
>
> For a brief history of the hamburger icon, visit http://blog.placeit.net/history-of-the-hamburger-icon

---

Activity 10.11 | Using Task View, Snap Assist, and Virtual Desktops

Use the **Task View** button on the taskbar to see and switch between open apps—including desktop apps. Use **Snap Assist** to display a 50/50 split screen view of two apps. Begin by dragging the **title bar**—the bar across the top of the window that displays the program or app name—to the right or left until it snaps into place. Or, hold down ⊞ and press → or ← to snap the window right or left. As soon as you snap the first window, Task View displays all your other open windows, and you need to click only one to have it snap to the other half of the screen. You can also snap four apps by dragging their title bars into the corners of your screen.

1 Be sure all windows are closed, and then on the taskbar, click **File Explorer** ▣. Navigate to the location for your **Windows 10 Chapter 10** folder, but do not open the folder. With your File Explorer window open, click **Start** ⊞ and then open one of the displayed apps; for example, Weather. From either the taskbar or the Start menu, open the Windows Store.

Three windows are open with the Windows Store app window on top.

2 On the taskbar, click **Task View** ▢, point to one of the windows, and then compare your screen with Figure 10.28.

Task View displays a **thumbnail**—a reduced image of a graphic—of each open window. This command is convenient when you want to see all of your open windows.

When you point to an open window, a Close button displays in the upper right corner so that you can close the window from Task View.

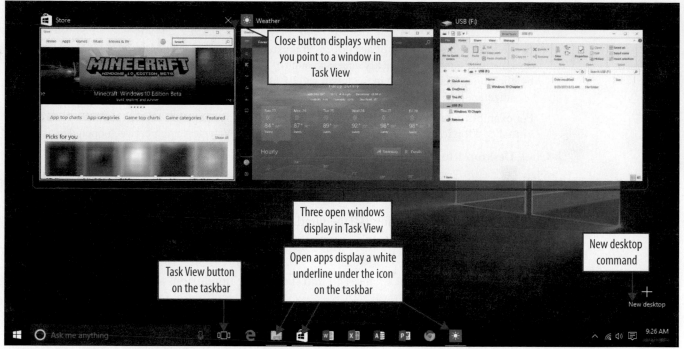

FIGURE 10.28

Microsoft Office 2016, Windows 10, Microsoft Corporation

3 Click the **File Explorer** window, hold down 🪟, and then press →.

The File Explorer window snaps to the right side of the screen, and Snap Assist displays the other two open windows on the left.

4 On the left, click the Weather app, and then compare your screen with Figure 10.29.

The Weather window snaps to the left side of the screen.

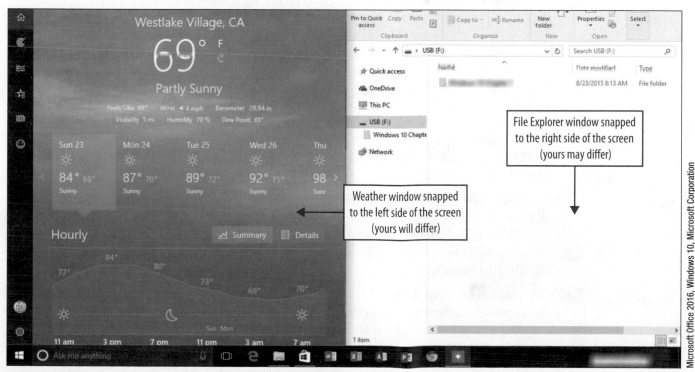

FIGURE 10.29

Microsoft Office 2016, Windows 10, Microsoft Corporation

5 On the taskbar, click **Task View** 🔲 again, in the lower right corner, click **New desktop**, and notice that two thumbnail images display—**Desktop 1** with your two apps snapped and **Desktop 2**.

If you have a large number of apps open, you can create another *virtual desktop*—an additional desktop to organize and quickly access groups of windows—to work with just the apps you want by clicking + New Desktop in the lower right corner of your screen. This can be a good way to organize and quickly access groups of windows.

For example, you could run your work email and Office apps on your desktop, and then open another virtual desktop for personal work. Then you can use Task View to switch between open desktops.

6 Click **Desktop 1** to bring that desktop back to full screen, and then on the taskbar, click **Task View** 🔲.

7 From your desktop, drag the Windows Store window down to **Desktop 2**.

8 Click **Desktop 2** and maximize 🔲 the window if necessary, and then click **Task View** 🔲. With **Desktop 2** active—its icon is framed above the taskbar—drag the app on the screen back down to **Desktop 1**.

9 Point to **Desktop 2** and click **Close** ✕, and then in the upper right corner of each open window, click **Close** ✕.

Create virtual desktops when you need to separate a group of windows while working on other things. Then you can close the virtual desktop when you no longer need it.

Activity 10.12 | Organizing Your Start Menu and Getting Apps from the Windows Store

On your own PC, you will want to organize your Start menu to become your personal dashboard. You will probably use your desktop apps like Microsoft Word and Microsoft Excel for work and school, but with the tiles on the Start menu, you can also use your PC like you use your smartphone—centered on the people and notifications that are important to you.

You can pin apps to the Start menu and then group your apps. You can also name your groups.

1 In the lower left corner, click in the **Search** box, type **store** and then at the top of the list, click **Store Trusted Windows Store app**. In the Store app, in the upper right corner, click in the **Search** box, type **travel** and then click the **Search** button 🔍. If necessary, click in a white area to close the suggested list, and then on the right, click **Show all**.

🔄 **ANOTHER WAY**   On the taskbar, click the Store icon 🛍; or, on the Start menu, click the Windows Store tile.

2 Click to select any free travel app (good ones include *Fodors*, *TripAdvisor*, and *tripwolf*), and then when the app displays, click **Free** (or click Install if your already own the app on another computer) to install the app; wait a few moments for the download and installation to complete ("Open" will display).

3 In the upper left corner of the app window, click the **Back** button ←. If necessary, click Show all again, and then find and install another travel app of your choice. When "Open" displays, meaning the app has finished downloading, in the upper left corner, click the Back button.

4 Using the techniques you just practiced, install a third travel app of your choice, and then **Close** ✕ the **Store** window.

5 Click **Start** ⊞ to display the Start menu. In the lower left corner, click **All apps**. In the Recently Added section at the top, right-click each travel app and pin it to the Start menu. Point anywhere in the list to display a scroll bar, and then compare your screen with Figure 10.30.

The *Recently added* section of the Start menu displays apps that you have recently downloaded and installed.

The *All apps* command displays all the apps installed on your computer in alphabetical order. You may see recently added apps display at the top.

FIGURE 10.30

Microsoft Office 2016, Windows 10, Microsoft Corporation

6 Scroll as necessary to locate one of the first travel apps that you installed, and notice that *New* displays under its name. Right-click the name of the app, and notice that from the All apps list, you can Unpin an app from the Start menu, pin it to the taskbar, or uninstall the app. Compare your screen with Figure 10.31.

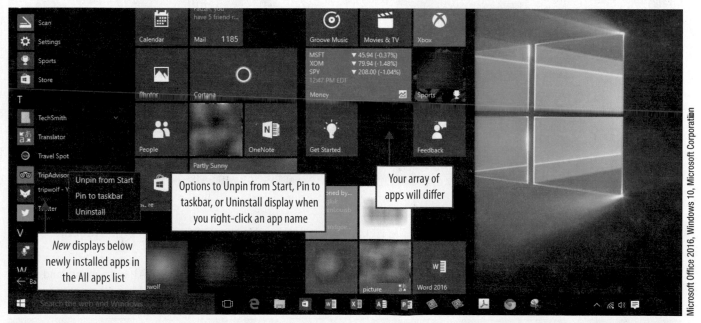

FIGURE 10.31

7 With your Start menu displayed, use the wheel on your mouse or the scroll bar at the right to scroll and locate one of your travel apps you pinned to the Start menu. Drag the app tile into a blank space, and notice that a shaded bar displays indicating that you can create a new section on your Start menu, as shown in Figure 10.32.

Your array of tiles and amount of space will differ from what is shown, because Windows 10 is *your* personal dashboard!

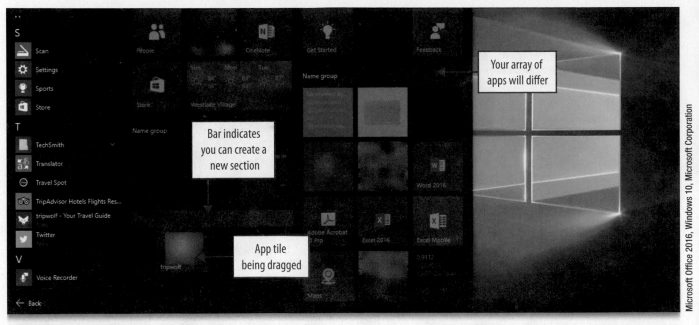

FIGURE 10.32

8 Drag the two remaining travel apps next to the first one, and then point to the area above the new group to display *Name group*, as shown in Figure 10.33.

FIGURE 10.33

9 Click the double lines at the right or click the text *New group*, and then type **Travel** to name the group. Press Enter, and then compare your screen with Figure 10.34.

You can use the techniques you just learned with the Windows Store, the All apps menu, and the tiles on the Start menu to customize Windows 10 to be your personal dashboard.

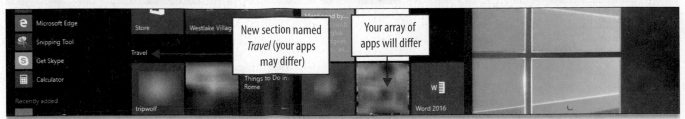

FIGURE 10.34

10 ▶ Point to one of the Travel app tiles, right-click, point to **Resize**, and then click **Small**. Point to another of the Travel app tiles, right-click, point to **Resize**, and then click **Wide**.

You might want to resize tiles on your Start menu to make them more or less visible—this is another way to personalize Windows 10 to make it work for you.

Activity 10.13 │ Using the Windows 10 Action Center

You probably want your PC to give you notifications—just like your smartphone does—and the Windows 10 Action Center does that. The **Action Center** is a vertical panel that displays on the right side of your screen when you click the icon in the notifications area of the taskbar. The upper portion displays notifications from apps you have installed and from which you have elected to receive notifications. The bottom portion displays Quick Actions—buttons that take you to frequently used system commands.

Both areas of the Action Center are customizable to suit your needs. When you have a new notification, the icon on the taskbar will light up white. There is even a Quiet Hours setting to turn off notifications when you don't want them.

1 ▶ At the right edge of your taskbar, to the left of the date and time, click **Action Center** ▣ to display the **Action Center** pane on the right side of your screen. Compare your screen with Figure 10.35.

Although your arrangement and list will differ from what is shown in the Figure, you can see that this is a convenient way to check mail and messages without leaving whatever you are working on.

You can add sites like Facebook and Twitter to your Action Center.

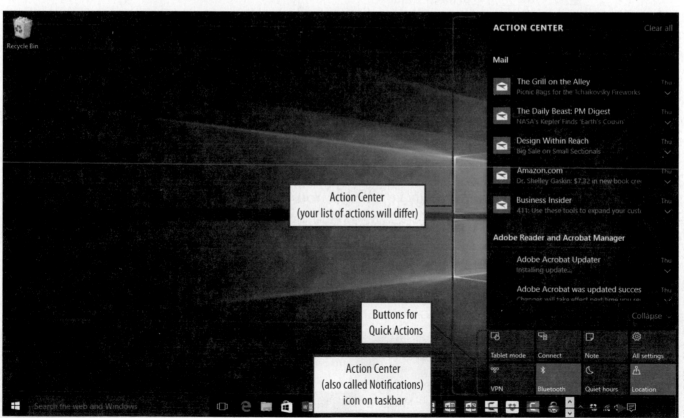

FIGURE 10.35

2 ▶ At the bottom of the **Action Center**, click **All settings**, and then in the **Settings** window, click **System**. On the left, click **Notifications & actions**, scroll down toward the bottom of the list on the right, and then compare your screen with Figure 10.36.

Here you can make decisions about what apps can send you notifications in the Action Center.

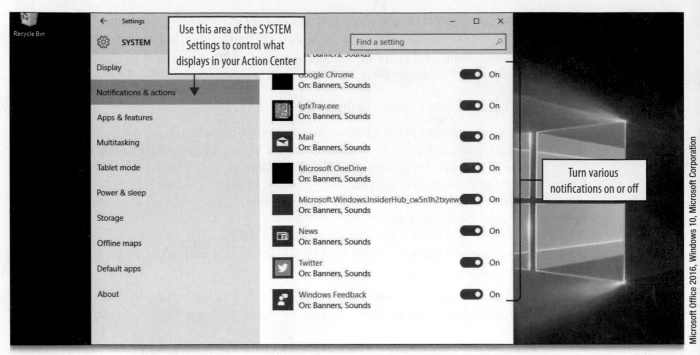

FIGURE 10.36

> **3** Close ✕ the **Settings** window.

Activity 10.14 | Using Cortana and Searching for Help

Cortana, the name for the intelligent female character in the *Halo* video game series, is also the name for the personal digital assistant in Windows 10. With use, Cortana becomes more useful to you, and you can add features—such as reminders—that Cortana delivers to you.

On your own PC, when you first use Windows 10 on a new installation or on a new system, Cortana might not be activated. You will benefit from activating and using this powerful feature that can search the web, find things on your PC, and keep track of your calendar.

ALERT!	Is Cortana Already Installed on Your System?

If Cortana is already active on your system—*Ask me anything* displays to the right of the Start button—skip to Step 5 of this Activity.

> **1** In the lower left corner of your desktop, determine whether Cortana is active, as shown in Figure 10.37.

> If this area indicates *Search the web and Windows*, then Cortana is not yet active on your system.

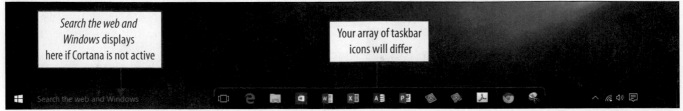

FIGURE 10.37

Microsoft Office 2016, Windows 10, Microsoft Corporation

> **2** If Cortana is not active, click **Start** ⊞, click **All apps**, scroll down to apps that begin with the letter **C**, and then point to **Cortana** as shown in Figure 10.38.

FIGURE 10.38

3 Click **Cortana**, and then in the upper left corner, click the **menu** icon ▤ to display the menu commands. At the bottom of the menu, click **Try Cortana**.

4 As necessary (note that the following sequence of steps may vary, but in general this is what you can expect), click **Next**, click **I agree**, and then type your first name or nickname. Click **Next**, as necessary, click **Got it**. Notice that your Search box now indicates *Ask me anything*, as shown in Figure 10.39.

> Usually you will also see a microphone icon so that you can speak your requests to Cortana instead of typing them.

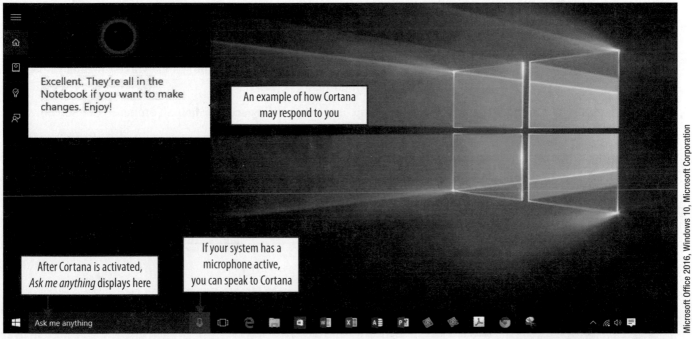

FIGURE 10.39

5 Click in the **Ask me anything** box, and then type **who is Cortana?** Then press `Enter`. If necessary, click *See more results on Bing.com*.

> Your *web browser*—software with which you display webpages and navigate the Internet—displays a Bing search with web links to information about Cortana.

6 **Close** ✕ the browser window.

7 Click again in the **Ask me anything** box, and then in the upper left corner, click the **menu** icon ▤. Compare your screen with Figure 10.40.

> On this menu, you can add Reminders to Cortana or add information to Cortana's notebook.

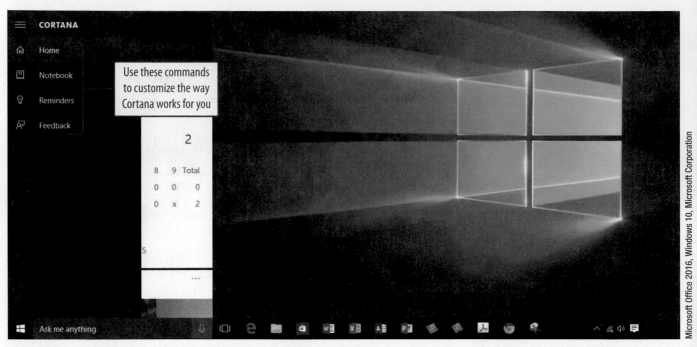

Use these commands to customize the way Cortana works for you

2

8 9 Total
0 0   0
0 x   2

5

Ask me anything

FIGURE 10.40

8 ▸ Click in an empty area of the desktop to dismiss Cortana, and then click **Start** ▉. Locate and click the tile **Get Started**. If you do not see this tile, ask Cortana to find it for you by typing *Get Started*.

9 ▸ **Maximize** ▢ the window, and then on the left, click **Cortana**. Click **Make Cortana yours**, and take a moment to read this information.

10 ▸ On the left, click **Search and help**, and then click **Search for help**. Compare your screen with Figure 10.41.

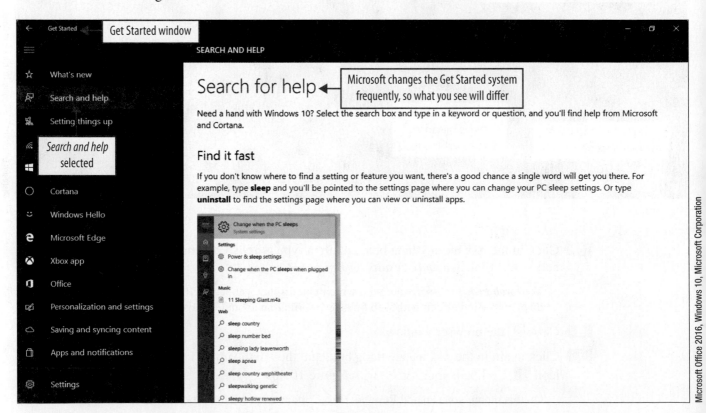

Get Started window

Search and help selected

SEARCH AND HELP

Search for help ◄ Microsoft changes the Get Started system frequently, so what you see will differ

Need a hand with Windows 10? Select the search box and type in a keyword or question, and you'll find help from Microsoft and Cortana.

Find it fast

If you don't know where to find a setting or feature you want, there's a good chance a single word will get you there. For example, type **sleep** and you'll be pointed to the settings page where you can change your PC sleep settings. Or type **uninstall** to find the settings page where you can view or uninstall apps.

FIGURE 10.41

Microsoft Office 2016, Windows 10, Microsoft Corporation

11 Scroll down and take a moment to read all of the important information.

Because Windows 10 will continue to grow and change and add new security features, rely on Cortana and the web information listed on this page to get help using Windows 10. You will always get the most current information.

12 **Close** ☒ the **Get Started** window and any other open windows.

Activity 10.15 │ Using the Microsoft Edge Browser

Microsoft Edge is the web browser program that comes with Windows 10. Among its many features are the ability to:

- Enter a search directly into the address bar
- Save sites and favorites and reading lists in the *Hub* feature
- Take notes and highlight directly on a webpage and then share that page with someone
- Pin a website to your Start menu

1 On the taskbar, click **Microsoft Edge** ⓔ. If the icon is not on your taskbar, search for the app in the search box. **Maximize** ☐ the window.

2 In the **Search or enter web address** box, or in the address bar, type the name of your college and then press Enter.

It is not necessary to type a web address; Edge will search for you and present the results.

3 In the search results, locate and click the link for your college's official website. On your college website, search for or navigate to information about the college library.

4 With the webpage for your college library displayed, in the upper right corner, click **Make a Web Note** ☒, and then compare your screen with Figure 10.42.

The Web Note toolbar displays tools for marking a webpage. Tools include a Pen, a Highlighter, an Eraser, a Note maker, and a Clip for cutting out a portion of a webpage as a file. On the right of the toolbar, there are tools for saving and sharing a webpage on which you have made markups or notes.

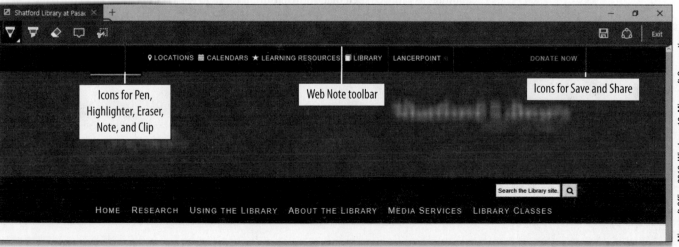

FIGURE 10.42

Microsoft Office 2016, Windows 10, Microsoft Corporation

5 On the toolbar, point to the **Pen** ▽, click the **small white triangle** in the lower right corner, and then on the displayed gallery, click the **yellow square**. Click the **white triangle** again, and then click the largest size.

6 With your mouse pointer, circle the name of—or some other information about—your college library. Compare your screen with Figure 10.43.

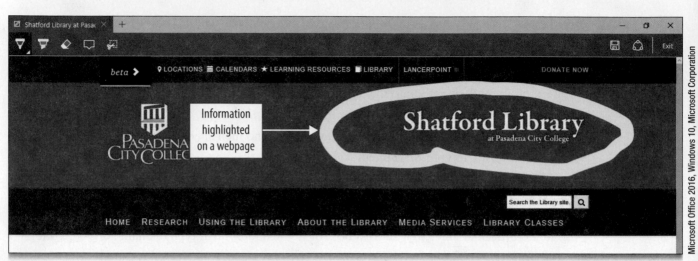

FIGURE 10.43

7 On the toolbar, click **Share** 🔗 to display the **Share** pane on the right, and notice the various ways you can share this marked-up webpage with others.

8 Click in a blank area of the webpage to close the Share pane. On the toolbar, click **Exit**.

9 In the upper right corner, click **More actions** ⋯ and then on the list, click **Pin to Start**. **Close** ✕ the browser window.

10 Click **Start** ⊞, and then scroll as necessary to locate the pinned website on your Start menu. Compare your screen with Figure 10.44.

Use this technique to pin websites that you visit often to your Start menu.

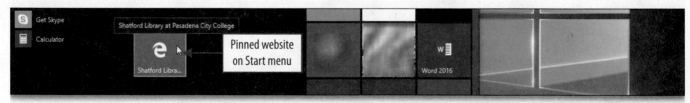

FIGURE 10.44

On your own computer, when you are done working, sign out from Windows 10, and then set your computer properly so that your data is saved, you save energy, and your computer remains secure.

When you turn off your computer by using the *Sleep* command, Windows 10 automatically saves your work, the screen goes dark, the computer's fan stops, and your computer goes to sleep. You need not close your programs or files because your work is saved. When you wake your computer by pressing a key, moving the mouse, or using whatever method is appropriate for your device, you need only to dismiss the lock screen and then enter your password; your screen will display exactly like it did when you initiated the Sleep command.

When you *shut down* your computer, all open programs and files close, network connections close, and the hard disk stops. No power is used. According to Microsoft, about half of all Windows users like to shut down so that they get a "fresh start" each time they turn on the computer. The other half use sleep.

Activity 10.16 | Locking, Signing Out of, and Shutting Down Your Computer

In an organization, there might be a specific process for signing out from Windows 10 and turning off the computer. The following steps will work on your own PC.

1 Click **Start** ⊞, and then in the upper left corner, click your user name. Compare your screen with Figure 10.45.

Here you can sign out of or lock your computer, in addition to changing your account settings. If you click Sign out, the lock screen will display, and then on the lock screen, if you press Enter, all the user accounts on the computer will display and you are able to sign in.

If you click Lock, the lock screen will display.

FIGURE 10.45

Microsoft Office 2016, Windows 10, Microsoft Corporation

2 Click **Lock**, and then with the lock screen displayed, press Enter. Sign in to your computer again if necessary.

3 If you want to shut down your computer, click **Start** ⊞, click Power, and then click Shut down.

Windows 10 supports multiple local account users on a single computer, and at least one user is the administrator—the initial administrator that was established when the system was purchased or when Windows 10 was installed.

As the administrator of your own computer, you can restrict access to your computer so that only people you authorize can use your computer or view its files. This access is managed through a local *user account*, which is a collection of information that tells Windows 10 what files and folders the account holder can access, what changes the account holder can make to the computer system, and what the account holder's personal preferences are.

Each person accesses his or her user account with a user name and password, and each user has his or her own desktop, files, and folders. Users with a local account should also establish a Microsoft account so that their Start menu arrangement—personal dashboard of tiles—displays when they sign in.

An *administrator account* allows complete access to the computer. Administrators can make changes that affect other users, change security settings, install software and hardware, access all files on the computer, and make changes to other user accounts.

1 Click **Start** ⊞. Above the Start button, click **Settings**, and then click **Accounts**. Compare your screen with Figure 10.46.

Here you can manage your Microsoft account, set various sign-in options, and change your account picture.

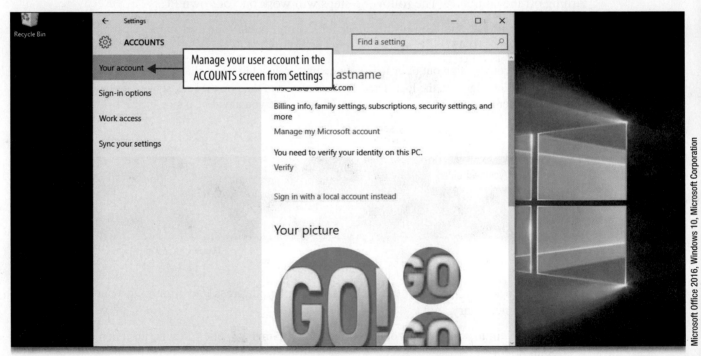

FIGURE 10.46

2 **Close** ⊠ the **Settings** window.

3 As directed by your instructor, submit the two files you created in this project:
Lastname_Firstname_10A_Get_Started_Snip and
Lastname_Firstname_10A_Graph_Screenshot

On your own computer, you can change the default settings of some basic functions that will help you manage your Windows 10 system.

NOTE	This Activity Is Optional

Complete this Activity if you are able to do so. Some college labs may not enable these features. If you cannot practice in your college lab, practice this on another computer if possible.

Activity 10.18 | Managing Windows Updates, Notifications, and Backup

Windows 10 is a modern operating system, and just like the operating system on your smartphone or tablet, Windows 10 will receive regular updates. These updates will include improvements, new features, and new security updates to address new security issues that emerge. Apps in the Windows Store will also be continuously updated.

Because updates will be automatically installed, you will not have to be concerned about keeping your Windows 10 system up to date; however, you can still view updates and see when they will be installed.

In Windows 10, notifications keep you informed about your apps and messages. You can manage what notifications you get and see in the notifications area of the taskbar from the Settings window.

The backup and recovery tools available in Windows 10 include: *File History*, which can automatically back up your most important files to a separate location; *PC Reset*, which lets you return your PC to the condition it was in the day you bought it; and *system image backup*, which creates a full system image backup from which you can restore your entire PC.

1 On the taskbar, click **Action Center** 🗨, and then at the bottom, in the **Quick Actions** area, click **All settings**. In the **Settings** window, *point to* **System**, and then notice that in this group of settings you can manage your display, your notifications, your apps, and the computer's power. Compare your screen with Figure 10.47.

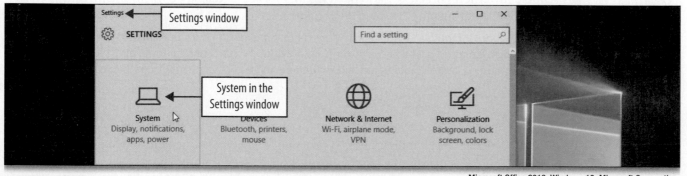

FIGURE 10.47   Microsoft Office 2016, Windows 10, Microsoft Corporation

2 Click **System**, and then on the left, click **Notifications & actions**. On the right, click **Select which icons appear on the taskbar**.

Here you can select the On and Off buttons to determine which icons display on your taskbar.

3 Without making any changes, click **Back** ← as many times as necessary to redisplay the **Settings** window. Click **Update & security**, and then on the left, click **Backup**. On the right, click **Add a drive**. (This may vary depending on what drives are attached to your system.)

> A list of drives connected to your computer displays, and you can select a drive onto which you could make a backup.

4 Close ☒ the **Settings** window without making a backup.

More Knowledge — **Consider a Commercial Backup Service Instead**

The backup system in Windows 10 is useful, but you might find it easier to use a commercial backup system like Carbonite or Mozy. For a small annual fee, these systems back up your files automatically on their servers—in the cloud—and if your computer suffers a misfortune, you can get your files back easily by simply downloading them to your new or repaired system.

NOTE — **This Activity Is Optional**

Complete this Activity if you are able to do so. Some college labs may not enable these features. If you cannot practice in your college lab, practice this on another computer if possible.

Activity 10.19 | Managing Windows Defender and Windows Firewall

Windows Defender is protection built into Windows 10 that helps prevent viruses, spyware, and malicious or unwanted software from being installed on your PC without your knowledge. You can rely on Windows Defender without assistance from other software products that might come preinstalled on a PC you purchase; you can confidently uninstall and not pay for these products.

Windows Firewall is protection built into Windows 10 that can prevent hackers or malicious software from gaining access to your computer through a network or the Internet.

1 In the lower left corner of your screen, click in the search box, type **windows defender** and then press Enter to display the **Windows Defender** dialog box.

> Here you can change settings related to real-time and cloud-based protection.

2 Close ☒ the **Windows Defender** window.

3 In the lower left corner, point to **Start** ▦, right-click to display a menu—sometimes referred to as the power menu—and then click **Control Panel**.

> The *Control Panel* is an area where you can manipulate some of the Windows 10 basic system settings. Control Panel is a carryover from previous versions of Windows, and over time, more and more of the Control Panel commands will move to and be accessible from the Settings window.

↻ **ANOTHER WAY**   Type *control panel* in the search box.

---

4 In the **Control Panel** window, click **System and Security**, and then click **Windows Firewall**. On the left, click **Change notification settings**—if necessary, enter your password; or, if you are unable to enter a password, just read the remaining steps in this Activity.

5 In the **Customize Settings** window, notice that you can receive notifications when Windows Firewall blocks a new app.

6 Close ☒ the window.

7 If you have not already done so, as directed by your instructor, submit the two files you created in this project: **Lastname_Firstname_10A_Get_Started_Snip** and **Lastname_Firstname_10A_Graph_Screenshot**.

END | You have completed Project 10A

Managing Files and Folders

In Activities 10.20 through 10.32, you will assist Barbara Hewitt and Steven Ramos, who work for the Information Technology Department at the Boston headquarters office of the Bell Orchid Hotels. Barbara and Steven have been asked to organize some of the files and folders that comprise the corporation's computer data. You will capture screens that will look similar to Figure 10.48.

PROJECT FILES

For Project 10B, you will need the following student data files:

Student Data Files may be provided by your instructor, or you can download them from www.pearsonhighered.com/go which you will learn to do in the next Activity. If you already have the Student Data Files stored in a location that you can access, then begin with Activity 10.21.

win10_10_Student_Data_Files

You will save your files as:

Lastname_Firstname_10B_WordPad_Snip

Lastname_Firstname_10B_Europe_Folders_Snip

Lastname_Firstname_10B_HR_Snip

Lastname_Firstname_10B_OneDrive_Snip (Optional)

PROJECT RESULTS

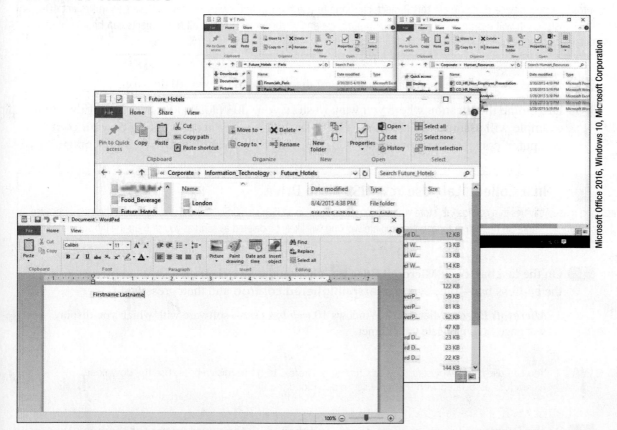

FIGURE 10.48 Project 10B Managing Files and Folders

Download refers to the action of transferring or copying a file from another location—such as a cloud storage location or from an Internet site—to your computer. Files that you download are frequently *compressed files*, which are files that have been reduced in size, take up less storage space, and can be transferred to other computers faster than uncompressed files.

A compressed folder might contain a group of files that were combined into one compressed folder, which makes it easier to share a group of files. To *extract* means to decompress, or pull out, files from a compressed form. The terms *zip* and *unzip* refer to the process of compressing (zipping) and extracting (unzipping). File Explorer includes *Compressed Folder Tools*, available on the ribbon, to assist you in extracting compressed files.

ALERT! **Already Have the Student Data Files?**

If your instructor has already provided you with the Student Data Files that accompany this chapter and you have stored them in a location that you can access, then skip to Activity 10.21. However, you can refer to these instructions when downloading files from other sites.

Activity 10.20 | Downloading Files from a Website

To complete this Project and the Projects at the end of this chapter, you will need the Student Data Files that accompany this chapter. Follow the steps in this Activity to download the Student Data Files from the publisher's website; or, your instructor might provide the Student Data Files to you, for example, in your learning management system.

NOTE **Using a Touchscreen**

If you are using a touchscreen device to complete this Project, continue to use the tap and swipe gestures presented in Project 10A. The remainder of this instruction will assume that you are using a mouse and keyboard setup, but all the Projects can be completed using a touchscreen without a mouse or keyboard.

---

1 If necessary, sign in to your computer and display the Windows 10 desktop.

2 Determine the location where you want to store your downloaded Student Data Files; this example will assume you are using a USB flash drive. If you are working on your own computer, consider the Documents folder on This PC or your OneDrive cloud storage.

ALERT! **In a College Lab, Use Your USB Flash Drive**

If you are completing these Activities in a college lab, store your Student Data Files on a USB flash drive and use it to complete the steps, because in a college lab, any work you store on the computer at which you are working will likely be deleted as soon as you sign off the lab computer.

---

3 On the taskbar, click **Microsoft Edge** , click in the **Search or enter web address** box or in the address bar—type **www.pearsonhighered.com/go** and then press Enter.

Microsoft Edge is Microsoft's Windows 10 *web browser*—software with which you display webpages and navigate the Internet.

ANOTHER WAY You can use other browsers, such as Chrome or Firefox, to go to this website. Use the download techniques associated with that browser to download the files.

---

4 At the Pearson site, on the right, locate and then click the cover image for the book you are using. In the window that opens, under **Student Resources**, click **Organized by chapter**.

5 Click the link for **win10_10_Student_Data_Files**. At the bottom of the screen, when the file has finished downloading, click **Open** to display the **File Explorer** window for the downloaded files, and then notice the path in the address bar.

> Typically, files that you download from an Internet site are stored in the *Downloads folder* on your PC.

6 In the **file list**, click the **win10_10_Student_Data_Files** folder one time to select it, and then on the right edge of the ribbon, with the **Compressed Folder Tools** active, click **Extract all**. In the displayed dialog box, click **Browse**.

7 In the **Select a destination** window, in the **navigation pane**, if necessary expand **This PC**, and then click your **USB flash drive** one time to select it—or click your desired storage location. In the lower right corner, click **Select Folder**. In the lower right corner of the displayed window, click **Extract**.

> After a few moments, the folder is extracted and placed in the location you selected.

8 **Close** ⊠ all open windows to redisplay your desktop.

Objective 8 Use File Explorer to Display Locations, Folders, and Files

A file is the fundamental unit of storage that enables Windows 10 to distinguish one set of information from another. A folder is the basic organizing tool for files. In a folder, you can store files that are related to one another. You can also place a folder inside another folder, which is then referred to as a *subfolder*.

Windows 10 arranges folders in a structure that resembles a *hierarchy*—an arrangement where items are ranked and where each level is lower in rank than the item above it. The hierarchy of folders is referred to as the *folder structure*. A sequence of folders in the folder structure that leads to a specific file or folder is a *path*.

Activity 10.21 │ Navigating with File Explorer

Recall that File Explorer is the program that displays the contents of locations, folders, and files on your computer and also in your OneDrive and other cloud storage locations. File Explorer also enables you to perform tasks related to your files and folders such as copying, moving, and renaming. When you open a folder or location, a window displays to show its contents. The design of the window helps you navigate—explore within the file structure for the purpose of finding files and folders—so that you can save and find your files and folders efficiently.

In this Activity, you will open a folder and examine the parts of its window.

1 Close any open windows. With your desktop displayed, on the taskbar, *point to* but do not click **File Explorer** 🗀, and notice the ScreenTip *File Explorer*.

> A *ScreenTip* displays useful information when you perform various mouse actions, such as pointing to screen elements.

2 Click **File Explorer** 🗀 to display the **File Explorer** window.

> File Explorer is at work anytime you are viewing the contents of a location or the contents of a folder stored in a specific location. By default, the File Explorer button on the taskbar opens with the *Quick access* location—a list of files you have been working on and folders you use often— selected in the navigation pane and in the address bar.

> The default list will likely display the Desktop, Downloads, Documents, Pictures, Music, Videos, and OneDrive folders, and then folders you worked on recently or work on frequently will be added automatically, although you can change this behavior.

The benefit of the Quick access list is that you can customize a list of folders that you go to often. To add a folder to the list quickly, you can right-click a folder in the file list and click Pin to Quick Access.

For example, if you are working on a project, you can pin it—or simply drag it—to the Quick access list. When you are done with the project and not using the folder so often, you can remove it from the list. Removing it from the list does not delete the folder, it simply removes it from the Quick access list.

3 On the left, in the **navigation pane**, scroll down if necessary, and then click **This PC** to display folders, devices, and drives in the **file list** on the right. Compare your screen with Figure 10.49.

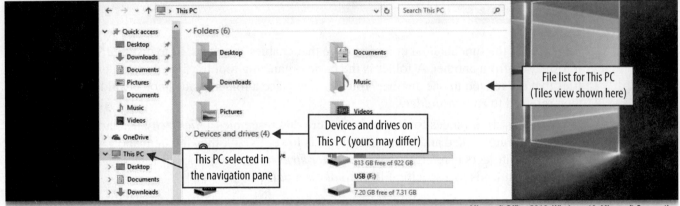

Microsoft Office 2016, Windows 10, Microsoft Corporation

FIGURE 10.49

4 If necessary, in the upper right corner, click Expand the Ribbon ⌄ . In the **File List,** under **Folders,** click **Documents** one time to select it, and then on the ribbon, on the **Computer tab,** in the **Location group,** click **Open**. On the ribbon, click the **View tab**, and then in the **Layout group,** if necessary, click **Details**.

The window for the Documents folder displays. You may or may not have files and folders already stored here.

⟳ ANOTHER WAY   Point to Documents, right-click to display a shortcut menu, and then click Open; or, point to Documents and double-click.

5 Compare your screen with Figure 10.50, and then take a moment to study the parts of the window as described in the table in Figure 10.51.

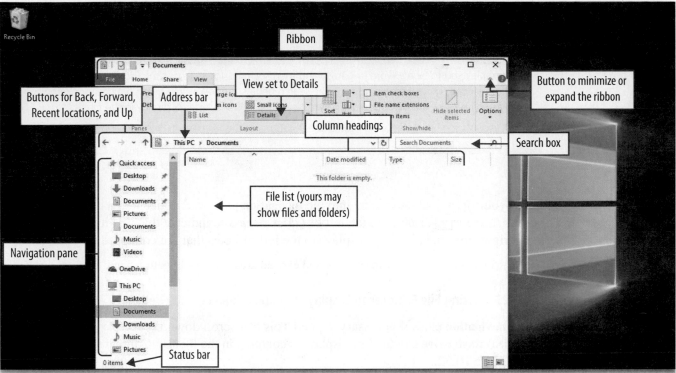

FIGURE 10.50

Microsoft Office 2016, Windows 10, Microsoft Corporation

PARTS OF THE FILE EXPLORER WINDOW	
WINDOW PART	**FUNCTION**
Address bar	Displays your current location in the file structure as a series of links separated by arrows. Tap or click a part of the path to go to that level or tap or click at the end to select the path for copying.
Back, Forward, Recent locations, and Up buttons	Enable you to navigate to other folders you have already opened without closing the current window. These buttons work with the address bar; that is, after you use the address bar to change folders, you can use the Back button to return to the previous folder. Use the Up button to open the location where the folder you are viewing is saved—also referred to as the *parent folder*.
Column headings	Identify the columns in Details view. By clicking the column heading name, you can change how the files in the file list are organized; by clicking the arrow on the right, you can select various sort arrangements in the file list. By right-clicking a column heading, you can select other columns to add to the file list.
File list	Displays the contents of the current folder or location. If you type text into the Search box, a search is conducted on the folder or location only, and only the folders and files that match your search will display here—including files in subfolders.
Minimize the Ribbon or Expand the Ribbon button	Changes the display of the ribbon. When minimized, the ribbon shows only the tab names and not the full ribbon.
Navigation pane	Displays locations to which you can navigate; for example, your OneDrive, folders on This PC, devices and drives connected to your PC, folders listed under Quick access, and possibly other PCs on your network. Use Quick access to open your most commonly used folders and searches. If you have a folder that you use frequently, you can drag it to the Quick access area so that it is always available.
Ribbon	Groups common tasks such as copying and moving, creating new folders, emailing and zipping items, and changing views of the items in the file list.

FIGURE 10.51 *(continued)*

PARTS OF THE FILE EXPLORER WINDOW (*continued*)	
WINDOW PART	**FUNCTION**
Search box	Enables you to type a word or phrase and then searches for a file or subfolder stored in the current folder that contains matching text. The search begins as soon as you begin typing; for example, if you type *G*, all the file and folder names that start with the letter *G* display in the file list.
Status bar	Displays the total number of items in a location, or the number of selected items and their total size.

FIGURE 10.51

Gaskin, Shelley. Go! All in One, 3E. Pearson Education, 2017.

6 Move your pointer anywhere into the **navigation pane**, and notice that a downward pointing arrow displays to the left of *Quick access* to indicate that this item is expanded, and a right-pointing arrow displays to the left of items that are collapsed.

You can click these arrows to collapse and expand areas in the navigation pane.

Activity 10.22 | Using File Explorer to Display Locations, Folders, and Files

1 In the **navigation pane**, if necessary expand **This PC**, scroll down if necessary, and then click your **USB flash drive** one time to display its contents in the **file list**. Compare your screen with Figure 10.52.

In the navigation pane, *This PC* displays all of the drive letter locations attached to your computer, including the internal hard drives, CD or DVD drives, and any connected devices such as a USB flash drive.

Your extracted student data files display if this is your storage location.

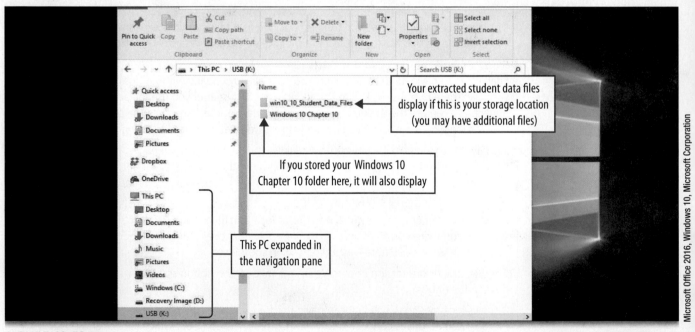

FIGURE 10.52

2 In the **file list**, double-click the uncompressed **win10_10_Student_Data_Files** folder to display the subfolders and files. Then double-click the folder for this Project— **win10_10B_Bell_Orchid**.

> Recall that the corporate office of the Bell Orchid Hotels is in Boston. The corporate office maintains subfolders labeled for each of its large hotels in Honolulu, Orlando, San Diego, and Santa Barbara.

🔄 **ANOTHER WAY**   Right-click the folder, and then click Open; or, select the folder and then on the ribbon, on the Home tab, in the Open group, click Open.

3 In the **file list**, double-click **Orlando** to display the subfolders, and then look at the **address bar** to view the path. Compare your screen with Figure 10.53.

> Within each city's subfolder, there is a structure of subfolders for the Accounting, Engineering, Food and Beverage, Human Resources, Operations, and Sales and Marketing departments.

> Because folders can be placed inside other folders, such an arrangement is common when organizing files on a computer.

> In the address bar, the path from the flash drive to the win10_10B_Bell_Orchid folder to the Orlando folder displays as a series of links.

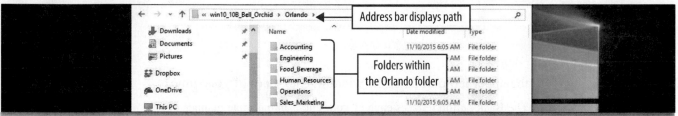

FIGURE 10.53

Microsoft Office 2016, Windows 10, Microsoft Corporation

4 In the **address bar**, to the right of **win10_10B_Bell_Orchid**, click the ⟩ arrow to display a list of the subfolders in the **win10_10B_Bell_Orchid** folder. On the list that displays, notice that **Orlando** displays in bold, indicating it is open in the file list. Then, on the list, click **Honolulu**.

> The subfolders within the Honolulu folder display.

5 In the **address bar**, to the right of **win10_10B_Bell_Orchid**, click the ⟩ arrow again to display the subfolders in that folder. Then, on the **address bar**—not on the list—point to **Honolulu** and notice that the list of subfolders in the **Honolulu** folder displays.

> After you display one set of subfolders in the address bar, all of the links are active and you need only point to them to display the list of subfolders.

> Clicking an arrow to the right of a folder name in the address bar displays a list of the subfolders in that folder. You can click a subfolder name to display its contents. In this manner, the address bar is not only a path, but it is also an active control with which you can step from the current folder directly to any other folder above it in the folder structure just by clicking a folder name.

6 On the list of subfolders for **Honolulu**, click **Sales_Marketing** to display its contents in the **file list**. On the **View tab**, in the **Layout group**, if necessary, click **Details**. Compare your screen with Figure 10.54.

🔄 ANOTHER WAY In the file list, double-click the Sales_Marketing folder.

The files in the Sales_Marketing folder for Honolulu display in the Details layout. To the left of each file name, an icon indicates the program that created each file. Here, there is one PowerPoint file, one Excel file, one Word file, and four JPEG images.

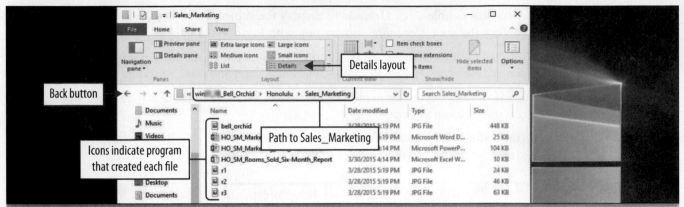

Microsoft Office 2016, Windows 10, Microsoft Corporation

FIGURE 10.54

7 In the upper left portion of the window, click **Back** ← one time.

The Back button retraces each of your clicks in the same manner as clicking the Back button when you are browsing the Internet.

8 In the **file list**, point to the **Human_Resources** folder, and then double-click to open the folder.

9 In the **file list**, click one time to select the PowerPoint file **HO_HR_New_Employee_Presentation**, and then on the ribbon, click the **View tab**. In the **Panes group**, click **Details pane**, and then compare your screen with Figure 10.55.

The *Details pane* displays the most common *file properties* associated with the selected file. File properties refer to information about a file, such as the author, the date the file was last changed, and any descriptive *tags*—properties that you create to help you find and organize your files.

Additionally, a thumbnail image of the first slide in the presentation displays, and the status bar displays the number of items in the folder.

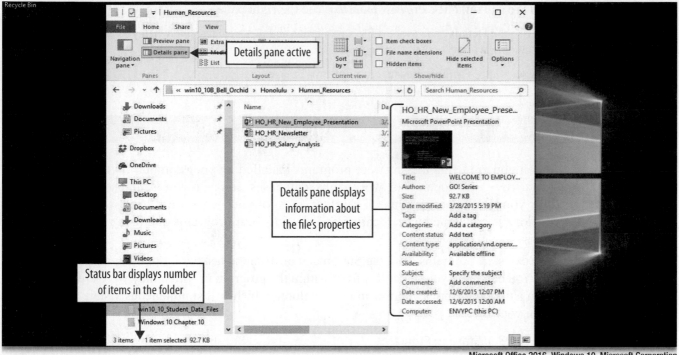

FIGURE 10.55

Microsoft Office 2016, Windows 10, Microsoft Corporation

> **10** On the right, in the **Details pane**, click **Add a tag**, type **New Employee meeting** and then at the bottom of the pane click **Save**.
>
> You can add tags to files to make them easier to find, because you can search for tags.

🔄 **ANOTHER WAY** With the file selected, on the Home tab, in the Open group, click Properties to display the Properties dialog box for the file.

> **11** On the ribbon, on the **View tab**, in the **Panes group**, click **Preview pane** to replace the **Details pane** with the **Preview pane**. Compare your screen with Figure 10.56.
>
> In the Preview pane that displays on the right, you can use the scroll bar to scroll through the slides in the presentation; or, you can click the up or down scroll arrow to view the slides as a miniature presentation.

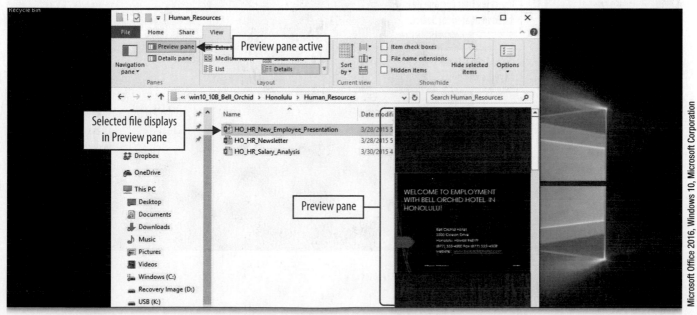

FIGURE 10.56

Microsoft Office 2016, Windows 10, Microsoft Corporation

12 On the ribbon, click **Preview pane** to close the right pane.

Use the Details pane to see a file's properties and the Preview pane when you want to look at a file quickly without actually opening it.

13 Close ☒ the **Human_Resources** window.

Objective 9 | Start Programs and Open Data Files

When you are using the software programs installed on your computer, you create and save data files—the documents, workbooks, databases, songs, pictures, and so on that you need for your job or personal use. Therefore, most of your work with Windows 10 desktop applications is concerned with locating and starting your programs and locating and opening your files.

You can start programs from the Start menu or from the taskbar by pinning a program to the taskbar. You can open your data files from within the program in which they were created, or you can open a data file from a window in File Explorer, which will simultaneously start the program and open your file.

Activity 10.23 | Starting Programs

1 Close any open windows. Click **Start** ⊞ to place the insertion point in the search box, and then type **paint** Compare your screen with Figure 10.57.

The Windows 10 search feature will immediately begin searching your PC and the web when you type in the search box. Here, Windows 10 searches your computer for applications and Documents containing the term *paint*, and searches Windows Store apps and the Web for the word *paint*.

Paint is a Windows desktop application that comes with Windows 10 with which you can create and edit drawings and display and edit stored photos.

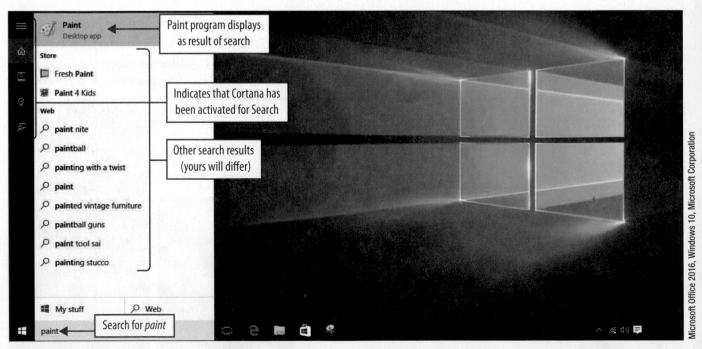

FIGURE 10.57

2 With the **Paint Desktop app** selected—also referred to as *in focus*—as the result of your search, press [Enter] to open this Windows desktop application.

3 On the ribbon of the Paint program, with the **Home tab** active, in the **Tools group**, click the **Pencil** icon. Move your mouse pointer into the white drawing area, hold down the left mouse button, and then with your mouse, try drawing the letters of your first name in the white area of the window.

⟳ BY TOUCH   Use your finger to draw on the screen.

4 In the upper left corner, to the left of the **Home tab**, click the **File tab** to display a menu of commands for things you can do with your picture.

5 At the bottom of the menu, click **Exit**. In the displayed message, click **Don't Save**.

Messages like this display in most programs to prevent you from forgetting to save your work. A file saved in the Paint program creates a graphic file in the JPEG format.

6 Click **Start** ⊞ to place the insertion point in the search box, type **wordpad** and then open the **WordPad Desktop app**. Notice that this program window has characteristics similar to the Paint program window; for example, it has a ribbon of commands.

7 With the insertion point blinking in the document window, type your first and last name.

8 From the taskbar, start **Snipping Tool**, and then create a **Window Snip**. Click anywhere in the WordPad window to display the **Snipping Tool** mark-up window. **Save** the snip as a **JPEG** in your **Windows 10 Chapter 10** folder as **Lastname_Firstname_10B_WordPad_Snip** Hold this file until you finish this project, and then submit this file as directed by your instructor.

9 **Close** ⊠ the **Snipping Tool** window. **Close** ⊠ **WordPad**, and then click **Don't Save**.

10 Search for the **windows journal** desktop app and open it—click **Cancel** if asked to install print information. Search for the **alarms & clock** Windows Store app and open it. Search for the **calculator** Windows Store app and open it. Search for **network and sharing center** and open it. Compare your screen with Figure 10.58.

Windows Journal is a desktop app that comes with Windows 10 with which you can type or handwrite—on a touch screen—notes and then store them or email them. The *Network and Sharing Center* is a Windows 10 feature in the Control Panel where you can view your basic network information.

You can open multiple programs and apps, and each one displays in its own window. Each open program displays an icon on the taskbar.

You can see that for both desktop apps that come with Windows 10 and Windows Store apps, the easiest way to find a program is to simply search for it, and then open it from the list of results.

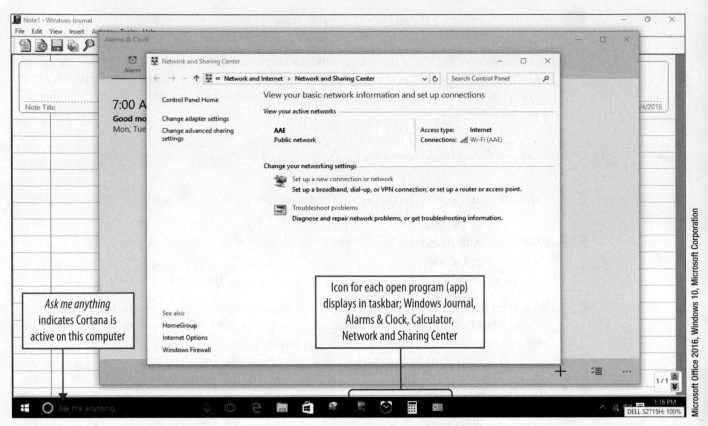

FIGURE 10.58

11 Click **Start** ⊞, and then directly above the Start button, click **All apps**. Click the letter **A** to display an onscreen alphabet, and then click **W** to quickly jump to the W section of the list. Click **Windows Accessories**. Compare your screen with Figure 10.59.

These are programs that come with Windows 10. You can open them from this list or search for them as you just practiced. Additionally, use the technique you just practiced to quickly jump to a section of the All apps list without scrolling.

W section of All apps menu

Programs (apps) included with Windows Accessories

FIGURE 10.59

Microsoft Office 2016, Windows 10, Microsoft Corporation

12 On the taskbar, click the **Windows Journal** icon , and then on the taskbar, click the **Alarms & Clocks** icon .

Use the taskbar to quickly move among open apps.

13 **Close** ✕ all open windows and redisplay the desktop.

Activity 10.24 | Opening Data Files

> **NOTE** You Need Microsoft Word 2016 or Word 2013
>
> For this Project you need Microsoft Word 2016 or Word 2013 on your computer; you can use a trial version if necessary.

1 Click **Start** , type **word 2016** (or type *word 2013* if that is the version of Word on your computer) and then open the **Word** desktop app. Maximize the window if necessary. Compare your screen with Figure 10.60.

The Word program window has features that are common to other programs you have opened; for example, commands are arranged on tabs. When you create and save data in Word, you create a Word document file.

FIGURE 10.60

Microsoft Office 2016, Windows 10, Microsoft Corporation

2 On the left, click **Open Other Documents**. Notice the list of places from which you can open a document, including your OneDrive if you are logged in. Click **Browse** to display the **Open** dialog box. Compare your screen with Figure 10.61, and then take a moment to study the table in Figure 10.62.

Recall that a dialog box is a window containing options for completing a task; its layout is similar to that of a File Explorer window. When you are working in a desktop application, use the Open dialog box to locate and open existing files that were created in the desktop application.

When you click Browse, typically the Documents folder on This PC displays. You can use the skills you have practiced to navigate to other locations on your computer, such as your removable USB flash drive.

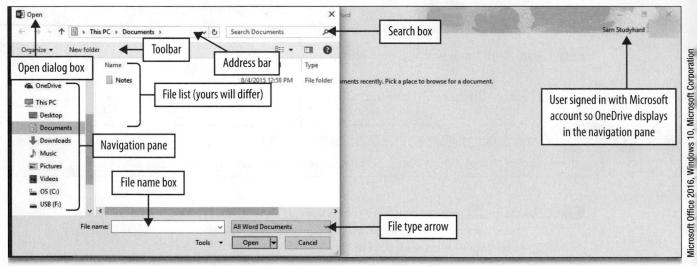

FIGURE 10.61

Microsoft Office 2016, Windows 10, Microsoft Corporation

DIALOG BOX ELEMENT	FUNCTION
Address bar	Displays the path in the folder structure.
File list	Displays the list of files and folders that are available in the folder indicated in the address bar.
File name box	Enables you to type the name of a specific file to locate it—if you know it.
File type arrow	Enables you to restrict the type of files displayed in the file list; for example, the default *All Word Documents* restricts (filters) the type of files displayed to only Word documents. You can click the arrow and adjust the restrictions (filters) to a narrower or wider group of files.
Navigation pane	Navigate to files and folders and get access to Quick access, OneDrive, and This PC.
Search box	Search for files in the current folder. Filters the file list based on text that you type; the search is based on text in the file name (and for files on the hard drive or OneDrive, in the file itself), and on other properties that you can specify. The search takes place in the current folder, as displayed in the address bar, and in any subfolders within that folder.
Toolbar	Displays relevant tasks; for example, creating a new folder.

FIGURE 10.62

Gaskin, Shelley. Go! All in One, 3E. Pearson Education, 2017.

3 In the **navigation pane**, scroll down as necessary, and then under **This PC**, click your **USB flash drive**. In the **file list**, double-click your **win10_10_Student_Data_Files** folder to open it and display its contents. Then double-click the **win10_10B_Bell_Orchid** folder to open it and display its contents.

4 In the upper right portion of the **Open** dialog box, click the **More options arrow** [▾], and then set the view to **Large icons**. Compare your screen with Figure 10.63.

The Live Preview feature indicates that each folder contains additional subfolders.

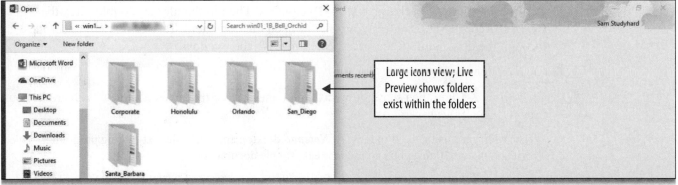

FIGURE 10.63

Microsoft Office 2016, Windows 10, Microsoft Corporation

5 In the **file list**, double-click the **Corporate** folder, and then double-click the **Accounting** folder.

The view returns to the Details view.

6 In the **file list**, notice that only one document—a Word document—displays. In the lower right corner, locate the **File type** button, and notice that *All Word Documents* displays as the file type. Click the **File type arrow**, and then on the displayed list, click **All Files**. Compare your screen with Figure 10.64.

> When you change the file type to *All Files*, you can see that the Word file is not the only file in this folder. By default, the Open dialog box displays only the files created in the *active program*; however, you can display variations of file types in this manner.

> Microsoft Office file types are identified by small icons, which is a convenient way to differentiate one type of file from another. Although you can view all the files in the folder, you can open only the files that were created in the active program, which in this instance is Microsoft Word.

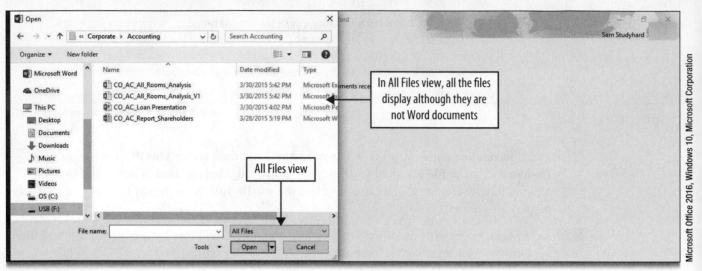

FIGURE 10.64

7 Change the file type back to **All Word Documents**. Then in the **file list**, double-click the **CO_AC_Report_Shareholders** Word file to open the document. Take a moment to scroll through the document. If necessary, Maximize ⬜ the window.

8 **Close** ⊠ the Word window.

9 Click **Start** ⊞, and then search for **.txt** Open one of the **Structure.txt** files, which are in your Student Data Files several times.

> The file opens using the Windows 10 *Notepad* desktop app—a basic text-editing program included with Windows 10 that you can use to create simple documents.

> In the search box, you can search for files on your computer, and you can search for a file by its *file name extension*—a set of characters at the end of a file name that helps Windows understand what kind of information is in a file and what program should open it. A *.txt file* is a simple file consisting of lines of text with no formatting and that almost any computer can open and display.

10 **Close** ⊠ all open windows.

Activity 10.25 | Searching, Pinning, Sorting, and Filtering in File Explorer

1 ▶ Click **File Explorer** 🗀. On the right, at the bottom, notice that under **Recent files**, you can see files that you have recently opened.

2 ▶ In the **navigation pane**, click your **USB flash drive**—or click the location where you have stored your student data files for this Project. In the upper right, click in the **Search** box, and then type **pool** Compare your screen with Figure 10.65.

> Files that contain the word *pool* in the title display. If you are searching a folder on your hard drive or OneDrive, files that contain the word *pool* within the document will also display. Additionally, Search Tools display on the ribbon.

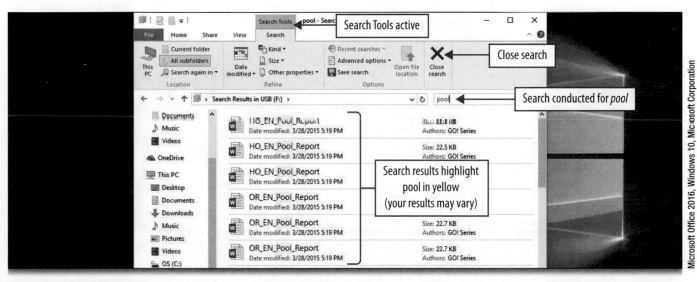

FIGURE 10.65

3 ▶ In the search box, clear the search by clicking ☒, and then in the search box type **dogs.jpg** Notice that you can also search by using a file extension as part of the search term.

4 ▶ **Clear** ☒ the search. In the **file list**, double-click your **win10_10_Student_Data_Files** folder to open it in the file list, and then click one time on your **win10_10B_Bell_Orchid** folder to select it.

5 On the **Home tab**, in the **Clipboard group**, click **Pin to Quick access**. Compare your screen with Figure 10.66.

> You can pin frequently used folders to the Quick access area, and then unpin them when you no longer need frequent access. Folders that you access frequently will also display in the Quick access area without the pin image. Delete them by right-clicking the name and clicking Unpin from Quick access.

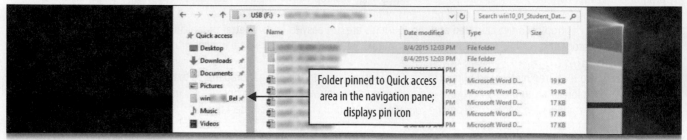

FIGURE 10.66

Microsoft Office 2016, Windows 10, Microsoft Corporation

🔄 **ANOTHER WAY**   In the file list, right-click a folder name, and then click Pin to Quick access; or, drag the folder to the Quick access area in the navigation pane and release the mouse button when the ScreenTip displays Pin to Quick access.

6 In the **file list**—or from the Quick access area—double-click your **win10_10B_Bell_Orchid** folder to display its contents in the file list. Double-click the **Corporate** folder and then double-click the **Engineering** folder.

7 Point to an empty area of the **file list**, right-click, point to **Sort by**, and then click **Type**. Compare your screen with Figure 10.67.

> Use this technique to sort files in the file list by type. Here, the JPG files display first, and then the Microsoft Excel files, and so on—in alphabetic order by file type.

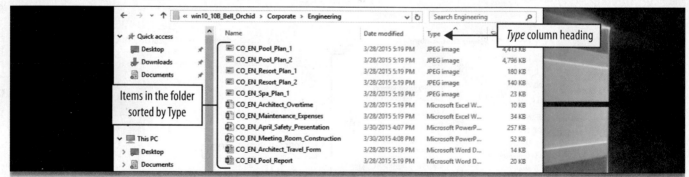

FIGURE 10.67

Microsoft Office 2016, Windows 10, Microsoft Corporation

8 Point to the column heading **Type**, and then click ∧.

9 Point to the column heading **Type** again, and on the right, click ⌄. On the displayed list, click **Microsoft PowerPoint Presentation**, and notice that the file list is filtered to show only PowerPoint files.

> A *filtered list* is a display of files that is limited based on specified criteria.

10 Click the check box to clear the Microsoft PowerPoint filter and redisplay all of the files.

11 **Close** ☒ all open windows.

Objective 10 Create, Rename, and Copy Files and Folders

File management includes organizing, copying, naming, renaming, moving, and deleting the files and folders you have stored in various locations—both locally and in the cloud.

Activity 10.26 | **Copying Files from a Removable Storage Device to the Documents Folder on the Hard Disk Drive**

Barbara and Steven have the assignment to transfer and then organize some of the corporation's files to a computer that will be connected to the corporate network. Data on such a computer can be accessed by employees at any of the hotel locations through the use of sharing technologies. For example, *SharePoint* is a Microsoft technology that enables employees in an organization to access information across organizational and geographic boundaries.

1 ▶ Close any open windows. If necessary, insert the USB flash drive that contains the Student Data Files that accompany this chapter that you downloaded from the Pearson website or obtained from your instructor.

2 ▶ Open **File Explorer** 📁. In the **navigation pane**, if necessary expand **This PC**, and then click your USB flash drive to display its contents in the file list.

> Recall that in the navigation pane, under This PC, you have access to all the storage areas inside your computer, such as your hard disk drives, and to any devices with removable storage, such as CDs, DVDs, or USB flash drives.

3 ▶ In the **file list**, double-click **win10_10_Student_Data_Files** (not the zipped folder if you still have it) to open it, and then click one time on the **win10_10B_Bell_Orchid** to select the folder. Compare your screen with Figure 10.68.

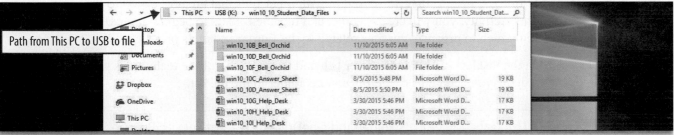

FIGURE 10.68

Microsoft Office 2016, Windows 10, Microsoft Corporation

4 With the **win10_10B_Bell_Orchid** folder on your USB drive selected, on the ribbon, on the **Home tab**, in the **Clipboard group**, click **Copy**.

The Copy command places a copy of your selected file or folder on the *Clipboard* where it will be stored until you use the Paste command to insert the copy somewhere else. The Clipboard is a temporary storage area for information that you have copied or moved from one place and plan to use somewhere else.

In Windows 10, the Clipboard can hold only one piece of information at a time. Whenever something is copied to the Clipboard, it replaces whatever was there before. In Windows 10, you cannot view the contents of the Clipboard nor place multiple items there in the manner that you can in Microsoft Word.

5 To the left of the address bar, click **Up** ↑ two times. In the **file list**, double-click your **Documents** folder to open it, and then on the **Home tab**, in the **Clipboard group**, click **Paste**.

A *progress bar* displays in a dialog box, and also displays on the File Explorer taskbar button with green shading. A progress bar indicates visually the progress of a task such as a copy process, a download, or a file transfer.

The Documents folder is one of several folders within your *personal folder* stored on the hard disk drive. For each user account—even if there is only one user on the computer—Windows 10 creates a personal folder labeled with the account holder's name.

6 Close ☒ the **Documents** window.

Activity 10.27 | Creating Folders, Renaming Folders, and Renaming Files

Barbara and Steven can see that various managers have been placing files related to the new European hotels in the *Future_Hotels* folder. They can also see that the files have not been organized into a logical structure. For example, files that are related to each other are not in separate folders; instead they are mixed in with other files that are not related to the topic.

In this Activity, you will create, name, and rename folders to begin a logical structure of folders in which to organize the files related to the European hotels project.

1 On the taskbar, click **File Explorer** ▭, and then use any of the techniques you have practiced to display the contents of the **Documents** folder in the **file list**.

NOTE   Using the Documents Folder and OneDrive Instead of Your USB Drive

In this modern computing era, you should limit your use of USB drives to those times when you want to quickly take some files to another computer without going online. Instead of using a USB drive, use your computer's hard drive, or better yet, your free OneDrive cloud storage that comes with your Microsoft account.

There are two good reasons to stop using USB flash drives. First, searching is limited on a USB drive—search does not look at the content inside a file. When you search files on your hard drive or OneDrive, the search extends to words and phrases actually *inside* the files. Second, if you delete a file or folder from a USB drive, it is gone and cannot be retrieved. Files you delete from your hard drive or OneDrive go to the Recycle Bin where you can retrieve them later.

---

2 In the **file list**, double-click the **win10_10B_Bell_Orchid** folder, double-click the **Corporate** folder, double-click the **Information_Technology** folder, and then double-click the **Future_Hotels** folder to display its contents in the file list; sometimes this navigation is written as *Documents* > *win10_10B_Bell_Orchid* > *Corporate* > *Information_Technology* > *Future_Hotels*.

Some computer users prefer to navigate a folder structure by double-clicking in this manner. Others prefer using the address bar as described in the following Another Way box. Use whatever method you prefer—double-clicking in the file list, clicking in the address bar, or expanding files in the navigation pane.

ANOTHER WAY   In the navigation pane, click Documents, and expand each folder in the navigation pane. Or, In the address bar, to the right of Documents, click >, and then on the list, click win10_10B_Bell_Orchid. To the right of win10_10B_Bell_Orchid, click > and then click Corporate. To the right of Corporate, click > and then click Information_Technology. To the right of Information_Technology, click >, and then click Future_Hotels.

3 In the **file list**, be sure the items are in alphabetical order by **Name**. If the items are not in alphabetical order, recall that by clicking the small arrow in the column heading name, you can change how the files in the file list are ordered.

4 On the ribbon, click the **View tab**, and then in the **Layout group**, be sure **Details** is selected.

The *Details view* displays a list of files or folders and their most common properties.

ANOTHER WAY   Right-click in a blank area of the file list, point to View, and then click Details.

5 On the ribbon, click the **Home tab**, and then in the **New group**, click **New folder**. With the text *New folder* selected, type **Paris** and press Enter. Click **New folder** again, and then type **Venice** and press Enter. Create a third **New folder** named **London**

In a Windows 10 file list, folders are listed first, in alphabetic order, followed by individual files in alphabetic order.

6 Click the **Venice** folder one time to select it, and then on the ribbon, in the **Organize group**, click **Rename**. Notice that the text *Venice* is selected. Type **Rome** and press Enter

ANOTHER WAY   Point to a folder or file name, right-click, and then on the shortcut menu, click Rename.

7 In the **file list**, click one time to select the Word file **Architects**. With the file name selected, click the file name again to select all the text. Click the file name again to place the insertion point within the file name, edit the file name to **Architects_Local** and press Enter. Compare your screen with Figure 10.69.

You can use any of the techniques you just practiced to change the name of a file or folder.

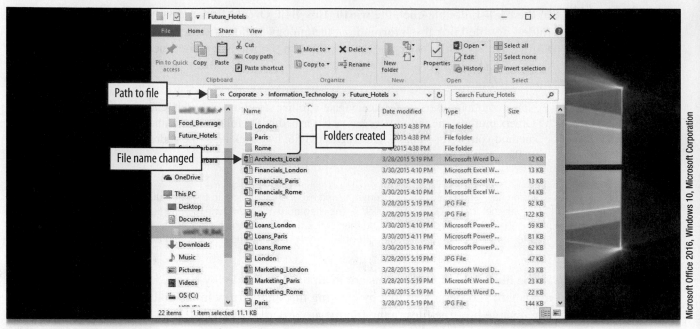

FIGURE 10.69

8 From the taskbar, start **Snipping Tool**; if necessary drag the *title bar*—the bar across the top of a window that displays the program name—of Snipping Tool into a blank area of the desktop. Click the **New arrow**, and then click **Window Snip**. Point anywhere in the **Future_Hotels** window and click one time. In the **Snipping Tool** mark-up window, click **Save Snip** 💾.

9 In the **Save As** dialog box, in the **navigation pane**, scroll down as necessary, and then click your USB flash drive so that it displays in the **address bar**.

10 In the **file list**, double-click your **Windows 10 Chapter 10** folder to open it. Click in the **File name** box, and then replace the selected text by typing **Lastname_Firstname_10B_Europe_Folders_Snip**

11 Be sure the file type is **JPEG**. Click **Save** or press Enter. **Close** ✕ the **Snipping Tool** window. Hold this file until you finish this Project.

12 **Close** ✕ all open windows.

Activity 10.28 | Copying Files

Copying, moving, renaming, and deleting files and folders comprise the most heavily used features within File Explorer. Probably half or more of the steps you complete in File Explorer relate to these tasks, so mastering these techniques will increase your efficiency.

When you *copy* a file or a folder, you make a duplicate of the original item and then store the duplicate in another location. In this Activity, you will assist Barbara and Steven in making copies of the Staffing_Plan file and then placing the copies in each of the three folders you created—London, Paris, and Rome.

1 From the taskbar, open **File Explorer** 📁, and then by double-clicking in the file list or following the links in the address bar, navigate to **This PC > Documents > win10_10B_Bell_Orchid > Corporate > Information_Technology > Future_Hotels**.

2 **Maximize** 🗖 the window. On the **View tab**, if necessary set the **Layout** to **Details**, and then in the **Current view group**, click **Size all columns to fit** ⊞.

3 In the **file list**, click the file **Staffing_Plan** one time to select it, and then on the **Home tab**, in the **Clipboard group**, click **Copy**.

4 At the top of the **file list**, double-click the **London folder** to open it, and then in the **Clipboard group**, click **Paste**. Notice that the copy of the **Staffing_Plan** file displays. Compare your screen with Figure 10.70.

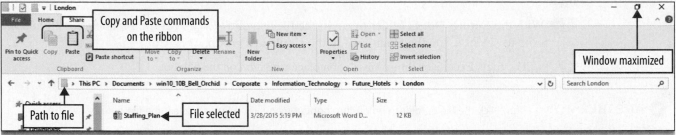

Microsoft Office 2016, Windows 10, Microsoft Corporation

FIGURE 10.70

ANOTHER WAY   Right-click the file you want to copy, and on the menu click Copy. Then right-click the folder into which you want to place the copy, and on the menu click Paste. Or, select the file you want to copy, press Ctrl + C to activate the Copy command, open the folder into which you want to paste the file, and then press Ctrl + V to activate the Paste command.

5 With the **London** window open, by using any of the techniques you have practiced, rename this copy of the **Staffing_Plan** file to **London_Staffing_Plan**

6 To the left of the **address bar**, click **Up** ↑ to move up one level in the folder structure and redisplay the file list for the **Future_Hotels** folder.

ANOTHER WAY   In the address bar, click Future_Hotels to redisplay this window and move up one level in the folder structure.

7 Click the **Staffing_Plan** file one time to select it, hold down Ctrl, and then drag the file upward over the **Paris** folder until the ScreenTip + *Copy to Paris* displays, and then release the mouse button and release Ctrl.

When dragging a file into a folder, holding down Ctrl engages the Copy command and places a *copy* of the file at the location where you release the mouse button. This is another way to copy a file or copy a folder.

8 Open the **Paris** folder, and then rename the **Staffing_Plan** file **Paris_Staffing_Plan** Then, move up one level in the folder structure to display the **Future_Hotels** window.

9 Double-click the **Rome** folder to open it. With your mouse pointer anywhere in the **file list**, right-click, and then from the shortcut menu click **Paste**.

A copy of the Staffing_Plan file is copied to the folder. Because a copy of the Staffing_Plan file is still on the Clipboard, you can continue to paste the item until you copy another item on the Clipboard to replace it.

10 Rename the file **Rome_Staffing_Plan**

11 On the **address bar**, click **Future_Hotels** to move up one level and open the **Future_Hotels** window—or click **Up** ↑ to move up one level. Leave this folder open for the next Activity.

Activity 10.29 | Moving Files

When you move a file or folder, you remove it from the original location and store it in a new location. In this Activity, you will move items from the Future_Hotels folder into their appropriate folders.

1 With the **Future_Hotels** folder open, in the **file list**, click the Excel file **Financials_London** one time to select it. On the **Home tab**, in the **Clipboard group**, click **Cut**.

The file's Excel icon dims. This action places the item on the Clipboard.

ANOTHER WAY   Right-click the file or folder, and on the shortcut menu, click Cut; or, select the file or folder, and then press Ctrl + X.

2 Double-click the **London** folder to open it, and then on the **Home tab**, in the **Clipboard group**, click **Paste**.

ANOTHER WAY   Right-click the folder, and on the shortcut menu, click Paste; or, select the folder, and then press Ctrl + V.

3 Click **Up** ↑ to move up one level and redisplay the **Future_Hotels** folder window. In the **file list**, point to **Financials_Paris**, hold down the left mouse button, and then drag the file upward over the **Paris** folder until the ScreenTip →*Move to Paris* displays, and then release the mouse button.

4 Open the **Paris** folder, and notice that the file was moved to this folder. Click **Up** ↑—or on the address bar, click Future_Hotels to return to that folder.

5 In the **file list**, click **Loans_London**, hold down Ctrl, and then click **London** and **Marketing_London** to select the three files. Release the Ctrl key. Compare your screen with Figure 10.71.

Use this technique to select a group of noncontiguous items in a list.

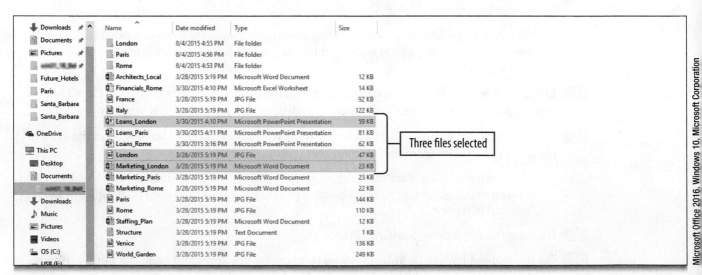

FIGURE 10.71

6 ▸ Point to any of the selected files, hold down the left mouse button, and then drag upward over the **London** folder until the ScreenTip ➔*Move to London* displays and *3* displays over the files being moved, and then release the mouse button.

> You can see that by keeping related files together—for example, all the files that relate to the London hotel—in folders that have an appropriately descriptive name, it will be easier to locate information later.

7 ▸ By dragging, move the **Architects_Local** file into the **London** folder.

8 ▸ In an empty area of the file list, right-click, and then click **Undo Move**. Leave the **Future_Hotels** window open for the next Activity.

> Any action that you make in a file list can be undone in this manner.

🔄 ANOTHER WAY   Press Ctrl + Z to undo an action in the file list.

More Knowledge   **Using Shift + Click to Select Files**

If files to be selected are contiguous (next to each other in the file list), click the first file to be selected and then press Shift and click the left mouse button on the last file to select all of the files between the top and bottom file selections.

Activity 10.30 │ **Copying and Moving Files by Snapping Two Windows**

Sometimes you will want to open, in a second window, another instance of a program that you are using; that is, two copies of the program will be running simultaneously. This capability is especially useful in the File Explorer program, because you are frequently moving or copying files from one location to another.

In this Activity, you will open two instances of File Explorer, and then use the *Snap* feature to display both instances on your screen.

To copy or move files or folders into a different level of a folder structure, or to a different drive location, the most efficient method is to display two windows side by side and then use drag and drop or copy (or cut) and paste commands.

In this Activity, you will assist Barbara and Steven in making copies of the Staffing_Plan files for the corporate office.

1 ▸ In the upper right corner, click **Restore Down** ▫ to restore the **Future_Hotels** window to its previous size and not maximized on the screen.

2 ▸ Hold down ⊞ and press ← to snap the window so that it occupies the left half of the screen.

3 ▸ On the taskbar, right-click **File Explorer** ▭, and then on the list, click **File Explorer** to open another instance of the program. With the new window active, hold down ⊞ and press → to snap the window so that it occupies the right half of the screen.

🔄 ANOTHER WAY   Drag the title bar of a window to the left or right side of the screen and when your mouse pointer reaches the edge, it will snap it into place.

4 ▸ In the window on the right, click in a blank area to make the window active. Then navigate to **Documents > win10_10B_Bell_Orchid > Corporate > Human_Resources**. Compare your screen with Figure 10.72.

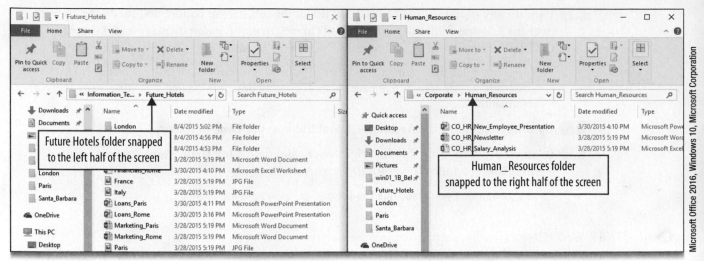

FIGURE 10.72

5 In the left window, double-click to open the **Rome** folder, and then click one time to select the file **Rome_Staffing_Plan**.

6 Hold down `Ctrl`, and then drag the file into the right window, into an empty area of the **Human_Resources file list**, until the ScreenTip + *Copy to Human_Resources* displays and then release the mouse button and `Ctrl`.

7 In the left window, on the **address bar**, click **Future_Hotels** to redisplay that folder. Open the **Paris** folder, point to **Paris_Staffing_Plan** and right-click, and then click **Copy**.

You can access the Copy command in various ways; for example, from the shortcut menu, on the ribbon, or by using the keyboard shortcut `Ctrl` + `C`.

8 In the right window, point anywhere in the **file list**, right-click, and then click **Paste**.

9 Start the **Snipping Tool** program, click the **New arrow**, and then click **Full-screen Snip**. In the **Snipping Tool** mark-up window, click **Save Snip** 🖫.

10 In the displayed **Save As** dialog box, notice the path in the **address bar**. If necessary, in the navigation pane, under **This PC**, click your USB flash drive, and then display the window for your **Windows 10 Chapter 10** folder.

11 Be sure the file type is **JPEG**. Using your own name, as the file name type **Lastname_Firstname_10B_HR_Snip** and press `Enter`. Hold this file until you have completed this Project.

12 **Close** ✕ all open windows.

Activity 10.31 | Deleting Files and Using the Recycle Bin

It is good practice to delete files and folders that you no longer need from your hard disk drive and removable storage devices. Doing so makes it easier to keep your data organized and also frees up storage space.

When you delete a file or folder from any area of your computer's hard disk drive or from OneDrive, the file or folder is not immediately deleted. Instead, the deleted item is stored in the *Recycle Bin* and remains there until the Recycle Bin is emptied. Thus, you can recover an item deleted from your computer's hard disk drive or OneDrive so long as the Recycle Bin has not been emptied. Items deleted from removable storage devices like a USB flash drive and from some network drives are immediately deleted and cannot be recovered from the Recycle Bin.

To permanently delete a file without first moving it to the Recycle Bin, click the item, hold down Shift, and then press Del. A message will display indicating *Are you sure you want to permanently delete this file?* Use caution when using Shift + Del to permanently delete a file because this action is not reversible.

You can restore items by dragging them from the file list of the Recycle Bin window to the file list of the folder window in which you want to restore them. Or, you can restore them to the location from which they were deleted by right-clicking the items in the file list of the Recycle Bin window and selecting Restore.

Self-Check | Answer These Questions to Check Your Understanding

1 When you delete a file or folder from any area of your computer's hard disk drive or from OneDrive, the file or folder is not deleted; it is automatically stored in the _____ _____.

2 Files deleted from the computer's hard drive or OneDrive can be recovered from the Recycle Bin until the Recycle Bin is _____.

3 Items deleted from removable storage devices such as a USB flash drive are immediately deleted and cannot be _____ from the Recycle Bin.

4 You can permanently delete a file from the hard drive or OneDrive without first moving it to the Recycle Bin, but a warning message will indicate *Are you sure you want to _____ delete this file?*

5 To restore items from the Recycle Bin to the location from which they were deleted, right-click the items and then click _____.

Objective 11 Use OneDrive as Cloud Storage

OneDrive is Microsoft's *cloud storage* product. Cloud storage means that your data is stored on a remote server that is maintained by a company so that you can access your files from anywhere and from any device. The idea of having all of your data on a single device—your desktop or laptop PC—has become old fashioned. Because cloud storage from large companies like Microsoft is secure, many computer users now store their information on cloud services like OneDrive. Anyone with a Microsoft account has a large amount of free storage on OneDrive, and if you have an Office 365 account—free to many college students if your college offers such a program—you have 1 terabyte or more of OneDrive storage that you can use across all Microsoft products. That amount of storage is probably all you will ever need—even if you store lots of photos on your OneDrive.

OneDrive is no longer just an app, as it was in Windows 8. Rather, OneDrive is integrated into the Windows 10 operating system. Similarly, Google's cloud storage called *Google Drive* is integrated into its Chrome operating system, and Apple's cloud storage called *iCloud* is integrated into both the Mac and iOS operating systems.

Activity 10.32 | Using OneDrive as Cloud Storage

When you install Windows 10 or use it for the first time, you will be prompted to set up your OneDrive. The setup process involves determining which folders—if not all—that you want to *sync* to OneDrive. Syncing—also called synchronizing—is the process of updating OneDrive data to match any updates you make on your device, and vice versa. This setup is optional, and you can always come back to it later. Your OneDrive storage, however, will be available from the navigation pane in File Explorer. Additionally, you will always have instant access to your OneDrive from any web browser.

1 **Close** ✕ any open windows. From the taskbar, start **File Explorer** 🗂 and then navigate to **Documents > win10_10B_Bell_Orchid > Santa_Barbara > Sales_Marketing > Media**.

2 Hold down Ctrl, click **Scenic1** and **Scenic2**, and then release Ctrl. With the two files selected, press Ctrl + C, which is the keyboard shortcut for the Copy command.

Although you see no screen action, the two files are copied to the Clipboard.

3 In the **navigation pane**, click **OneDrive**. If a dialog box regarding Customizing your OneDrive settings displays, in the lower right corner, click Cancel.

If you have decided on syncing options, you can do so in this dialog box; or, postpone these decisions by clicking Cancel.

Your OneDrive folders display in the file list.

4 On the ribbon, on the **Home tab**, in the **New group**, click **New folder**. Name the new folder **Marketing Photos** and then press Enter. Double-click the new folder to open it.

5 Press Ctrl + V, which is the keyboard shortcut for the Paste command, to paste the two photos into the folder. On the **View tab**, set the **Layout** to **Details**. Compare your screen with Figure 10.73.

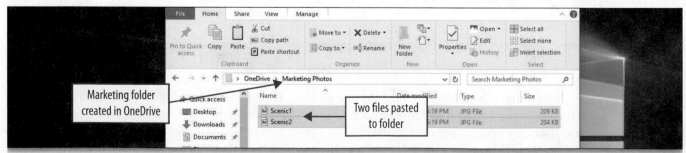

FIGURE 10.73

Microsoft Office 2016, Windows 10, Microsoft Corporation

6 Using the techniques you have practiced, create a window snip and save the snip in your chapter folder. Be sure the file type is **JPEG**. Using your own name, as the file name type **Lastname_Firstname_10B_OneDrive_Snip** and press Enter.

7 **Close** ✕ all open windows.

END | You have completed Project 10B

END OF CHAPTER

SUMMARY

Windows 10 is optimized for touchscreens and also works with a mouse and keyboard. You will probably use touch when you are reading or communicating on the web and a keyboard when creating files.

The Windows 10 Start menu is your connected dashboard—this is your one-screen view of information that updates continuously with new information and personal communications that are important to you.

The Windows Store apps you use from the Start menu display in separate Windows, similar to your other files, so you can move them on the desktop or display them side by side. These apps typically have a single purpose.

File Explorer is at work anytime you are viewing the contents of a location, a folder, or a file. Use File Explorer to navigate your Windows 10 structure that stores and organizes the files you create.

GO! LEARN IT ONLINE

Review the concepts and key terms in this chapter by completing these online challenges, which you can find in **MyITLab**.

Matching and Multiple Choice: Answer matching and multiple-choice questions to test what you learned in this chapter.

Lessons on the GO!: Learn how to use all the new apps and features as they are introduced by Microsoft.

GO! FOR JOB SUCCESS

Video: Email Etiquette

Your instructor may assign this video to your class, and then ask you to think about, or discuss with your classmates, these questions:

FotolEdhar/Fotolia

Why do you think it is important to follow specific etiquette when composing email?

Why is it important to include a greeting and sign every email you send?

What are the differences between sending a business email and a personal email, and what are three specific things you should never do in a business email?

PROJECT GUIDE FOR ALL IN ONE CHAPTER 10

Your instructor will assign Projects from this list to ensure your learning and assess your knowledge.

		Project Guide for All in One Chapter 10	
Project	Apply Skills from These Chapter Objectives	Project Type	Project Location
10A MyITLab	Objectives 1-6 from Project 10A	**10A Instructional Project (Grader Project)** Guided instruction to learn the skills in Project 10A.	In MYITLab and in text
10B MyITLab	Objectives 5-11 from Project 10B	**10B Instructional Project (Grader Project)** Guided instruction to learn the skills in Project 10B	In MYITLab and in text
10C	Objectives 1-6 from Project 10A	**10C Chapter Review** A guided review of the skills from Project 10A.	in text
10D	Objectives 7-11 from Project 10B	**10D Chapter Review** A guided review of the skills from Project 10B.	in text
10E MyITLab	Objectives 1-6 from Project 10A	**10E Mastery** **Mastery and Transfer of Learning** A demonstration of your mastery of the skills in Project 10A with decision-making.	in text
10F MyITLab	Objectives 7-11 from Project 10B	**10F Mastery** **Mastery and Transfer of Learning** A demonstration of your mastery of the skills in Project 10B with decision-making.	in text
10G	Combination of Objectives from Projects 10A and 10B	**10G GO! Think** **Critical Thinking** A demonstration of your understanding of the chapter concepts applied in a manner that you would outside of college. An analytic rubric helps you and your instructor grade the quality of your work by comparing it to the work an expert in the discipline would create.	in text
10H	Combination of Objectives from Projects 10A and 10B	**10H GO! Think** **Critical Thinking** A demonstration of your understanding of the chapter concepts applied in a manner that you would outside of college. An analytic rubric helps you and your instructor grade the quality of your work by comparing it to the work an expert in the discipline would create.	in text
10I	Combination of Objectives from Projects 10A and 10B	**10I GO! Think** **Critical Thinking** A demonstration of your understanding of the chapter concepts applied in a manner that you would outside of college. An analytic rubric helps you and your instructor grade the quality of your work by comparing it to the work an expert in the discipline would create.	in text

GLOSSARY

GLOSSARY OF CHAPTER KEY TERMS

.png An image file format, commonly pronounced *PING*, that stands for Portable Network Graphic; this is an image file type that can be transferred over the Internet.

.txt file A simple file consisting of lines of text with no formatting that almost any computer can open and display.

Action Center A vertical panel that displays on the right side of your screen when you click the icon in the notifications area of the taskbar; the upper portion displays notifications you have elected to receive such as mail and social network updates and the lower portion displays buttons for frequently used system commands.

Address bar (File Explorer) The area at the top of a File Explorer window that displays your current location in the folder structure as a series of links separated by arrows.

Administrator account A user account that lets you make changes that will affect other users of the computer; the most powerful of the three types of accounts, because it permits the most control over the computer.

All apps A command that displays all the apps installed on your computer in alphabetical order on the Start menu.

App The shortened version of the term *application*, and which typically refers to a smaller application designed for a single purpose.

App bar A term used to describe a horizontal or vertical array of command icons in a Windows app.

Application A set of instructions that a computer uses to accomplish a task; also called a program.

Application developer An individual who writes computer applications.

Badge An icon that displays on the Lock screen for lock screen apps that you have selected.

Bing Microsoft's search engine, which powers Cortana.

Booting the computer The process of turning on a computer when the computer has been completely shut down and during which the BIOS program will run.

Click The action of pressing the left mouse button.

Clipboard A temporary storage area for information that you have copied or moved from one place and plan to use somewhere else.

Cloud storage Storage space on an Internet site that may also display as a drive on your computer.

Compressed file A file that has been reduced in size and that takes up less storage space and can be transferred to other computers faster than uncompressed files.

Compressed Folder Tools File Explorer tools, available on the ribbon, to assist you in extracting compressed files.

Contextual tab A context-sensitive menu that displays commands and options relevant to the active object.

Control Panel An area of Windows 10 where you can manipulate some of the Windows 10 basic system settings—a carryover from previous versions of Windows.

Cortana Microsoft's intelligent personal assistant that is part of the Windows 10 operating system.

Dashboard A descriptive term for the Windows 10 Start menu because it provides a one-screen view of links to information and programs that matter most to the signed-in user.

Data All the files—documents, spreadsheets, pictures, songs, and so on—that you create and store during the day-to-day use of your computer.

Data management The process of managing your files and folders in an organized manner so that you can find information when you need it.

Desktop The main Windows 10 screen that serves as a starting point and surface for your work, like the top of an actual desk.

Desktop app A computer program that is installed on the hard drive of a personal computer and that requires a computer operating system like Microsoft Windows or Apple OSX to run.

Desktop background Displays the colors and graphics of your desktop; you can change the desktop background to look the way you want.

Desktop shortcuts Desktop icons that link to any item accessible on your computer or on a network, such as a program, file, folder, disk drive, printer, or another computer.

Details pane Displays the most common properties associated with the selected file.

Details view A view in File Explorer that displays a list of files or folders and their most common properties.

Dialog box A small window that displays options for completing a task.

Double-click The action of pressing the left mouse button twice in rapid succession while holding the mouse still.

Download The action of transferring or copying a file from another location—such as a cloud storage location or from an Internet site—to your computer.

Downloads folder A folder that holds items that you have downloaded from the Internet.

Drag The action of moving something from one location on the screen to another while holding down the left mouse button; the action of dragging includes releasing the mouse button at the desired time or location.

Drive An area of storage that is formatted with a file system compatible with your operating system and is identified by a drive letter.

Extract The action of decompressing—pulling out—files from a compressed form.

File A collection of information that is stored on a computer under a single name, for example, a text document, a picture, or a program.

File Explorer window A window that displays the contents of the current location and contains helpful parts so that you can navigate within the file organizing structure of Windows.

File History A backup and recovery tool that automatically backs up your files to a separate location.

File list Displays the contents of the current folder or location; if you type text into the Search box, only the folders and files that match your search will display here—including files in subfolders.

File name extension A set of characters at the end of a file name that helps Windows 10 understand what kind of information is in a file and what program should open it.

File properties Information about a file such as its author, the date the file was last changed, and any descriptive tags.

Filtered list A display of files that is limited based on specified criteria.

Folder A container in which you store files.

Folder structure The hierarchy of folders in Windows 10.

Free-form snip When using Snipping Tool, the type of snip that lets you draw an irregular line, such as a circle, around an area of the screen.

Full-screen snip When using Snipping Tool, the type of snip that captures the entire screen.

Get Started A feature in Windows 10 to learn about all the things that Windows 10 can do for you.

Google Drive Google's cloud storage.

Graphical user interface The system by which you interact with your computer and which uses graphics such as an image of a file folder or wastebasket that you click to activate the item represented.

GUI The acronym for a graphical user interface, pronounced *GOO-ee*.

Hamburger Another name for the hamburger menu.

Hamburger menu An icon made up of three lines that evoke a hamburger on a bun.

Hard disk drive The primary storage device located inside your computer and where most of your files and programs are typically stored; usually labeled as drive C.

Hierarchy An arrangement where items are ranked and where each level is lower in rank than the item above it.

HoloLens A see-through holographic computer developed by Microsoft.

Hub A feature in Microsoft Edge where you can save favorite websites and create reading lists.

iCloud Apple's cloud storage that is integrated into its Mac and iOS operating systems.

Icons Small images that represent commands, files, or other windows.

Insertion point A blinking vertical line that indicates where text or graphics will be inserted.

Internet of Things A growing network of physical objects that will have sensors connected to the Internet.

IoT The common acronym for the Internet of Things.

JPEG An acronym for Joint Photographic Experts Group, and which is a common file type used by digital cameras and computers to store digital pictures; JPEG is popular because it can store a high-quality picture in a relatively small file.

Jump list A list that displays when you right-click a button on the taskbar, and which displays locations (in the upper portion) and tasks (in the lower portion) from a program's taskbar button.

Keyboard shortcut A combination of two or more keyboard keys, used to perform a task that would otherwise require a mouse.

Live tiles Tiles on the Windows 10 Start menu that are constantly updated with fresh information relevant to the signed-in user; for example, the number of new email messages, new sports scores of interest, or new updates to social networks such as Facebook or Twitter.

Location Any disk drive, folder, or other place in which you can store files and folders.

Lock screen The first screen that displays after turning on a Windows 10 device and that displays the time, day, and date, and one or more icons representing the status of the device's Internet connection, battery status on a tablet or laptop, and any lock screen apps that are installed such as email notifications.

Lock screen apps Apps that display on a Windows 10 lock screen and that show quick status and notifications, even if the screen is locked.

Maximize The command to display a window in full-screen view.

Menu A list of commands within a category.

Menu bar A group of menus.

Menu icon Another name for the hamburger menu.

Microsoft account A single login account for Microsoft systems and services.

Microsoft Edge The web browser program included with Windows 10.

Mobile device platform The hardware and software environment for smaller-screen devices such as tablets and smartphones.

Mouse pointer Any symbol that displays on your screen in response to moving your mouse.

Navigate Explore within the file organizing structure of Windows 10.

Navigation pane The area on the left side of a folder window in File Explorer that displays the Quick Access area and an expandable list of drives and folders.

Network and Sharing Center A Windows 10 feature in the Control Panel where you can view your basic network information.

Notepad A basic text-editing program included with Windows 10 that you can use to create simple documents.

OneDrive A free file storage and file sharing service provided by Microsoft when you sign up for a free Microsoft account.

Operating system A specific type of computer program that manages the other programs on a computer—including computer devices such as desktop computers, laptop computers, smartphones, tablet computers, and game consoles.

Parent folder In the file organizing structure of File Explorer, the location where the folder you are viewing is saved—one level up in the hierarchy.

Path A sequence of folders (directories) that leads to a specific file or folder.

PC Reset A backup and recovery tool that returns your PC to the condition it was in the day you purchased it.

Pen A pen-shaped stylus that you tap on a computer screen.

Personal folder A folder created for each user account on a Windows 10 computer, labeled with the account holder's name, and which contains the subfolders *Documents, Pictures, Music.*

PIN Acronym for personal identification number; in Windows 10 Settings, you can create a PIN to use in place of a password.

Platform An underlying computer system on which application programs can run.

Point to The action of moving the mouse pointer over a specific area.

Pointer Any symbol that displays on your screen in response to moving your mouse and with which you can select objects and commands.

Pointing device A mouse, touchpad, or other device that controls the pointer position on the screen.

Program A set of instructions that a computer uses to accomplish a task; also called an application.

Progress bar In a dialog box or taskbar button, a bar that indicates visually the progress of a task such as a download or file transfer.

Quick access The navigation pane area in File Explorer where you can pin folders you use frequently and that also adds folders you are accessing frequently.

Quick Access Toolbar (File Explorer) The small row of buttons in the upper left corner of a File Explorer window from which you can perform frequently used commands.

Recently added On the Start menu, a section that displays apps that you have recently downloaded and installed.

Rectangular snip When using Snipping Tool, the type of snip that lets you draw a precise box by dragging the mouse pointer around an area of the screen to form a rectangle.

Recycle Bin A folder that stores anything that you delete from your computer, and from which anything stored there can be retrieved until the contents are permanently deleted by activating the Empty Recycle Bin command.

Removable storage device A portable device on which you can store files, such as a USB flash drive, a flash memory card, or an external hard drive, commonly used to transfer information from one computer to another.

Resources A term used to refer collectively to the parts of your computer such as the central processing unit (CPU), memory, and any attached devices such as a printer.

Restore Down A command to restore a window to its previous size before it was maximized.

Ribbon The area at the top of a folder window in File Explorer that groups common tasks such as copying and moving, creating new folders, emailing and zipping items, and changing views on related tabs.

Right-click The action of clicking the right mouse button.

Screenshot Another name for a screen capture.

ScreenTip Useful information that displays in a small box on the screen when you perform various mouse actions, such as pointing to screen elements.

Scroll arrow An arrow at the top, bottom, left, or right, of a scroll bar that when clicked, moves the window in small increments.

Scroll bar A bar that displays on the bottom or right side of a window when the contents of a window are not completely visible; used to move the window up, down, left, or right to bring the contents into view.

Scroll box The box in a vertical or horizontal scroll bar that you drag to reposition the document on the screen.

Select To specify, by highlighting, a block of data or text on the screen with the intent of performing some action on the selection.

SharePoint A Microsoft technology that enables employees in an organization to access information across organizational and geographic boundaries.

Shortcut menu A context-sensitive menu that displays commands and options relevant to the active object.

Shut down Turning off your computer in a manner that closes all open programs and files, closes your network connections, stops the hard disk, and discontinues the use of electrical power.

Sleep Turning off your computer in a manner that automatically saves your work, stops the fan, and uses a small amount of electrical power to maintain your work in memory.

Snap Assist The ability to drag windows to the edges or corners of your screen, and then having Task View display thumbnails of other open windows so that you can select what other windows you want to snap into place.

Snip The image captured using Snipping Tool.

Snipping Tool A program included with Windows 10 with which you can capture an image of all or part of a computer screen, and then annotate, save, copy, or share the image via email.

Split button A button that has two parts—a button and an arrow; clicking the main part of the button performs a command and clicking the arrow opens a menu with choices.

Start menu The menu that displays when you click the Start button, which consists of a list of installed programs on the left and a customizable group of app tiles on the right.

Subfolder A folder within another folder.

System image backup A backup and recovery tool that creates a full system image backup from which you can restore your entire PC.

System tray Another name for the notification area on the taskbar.

Tags A property that you create and add to a file to help you find and organize your files.

Taskbar The area of the desktop that contains program buttons, and buttons for all open programs; by default, it is located at the bottom of the desktop, but you can move it.

This PC An area on the navigation pane that provides navigation to your internal storage and attached storage devices including optical media such as a DVD drive.

Thumbnail A reduced image of a graphic.

Tiles Square and rectangular boxes on the Windows 10 Start menu from which you can access apps, websites, programs, and tools for using the computer by simply clicking or tapping them.

Title bar The bar across the top of the window that displays the program name.

Universal apps Windows apps that use a common code base to deliver the app to any Windows device.

Unzip Extracting files.

User account A collection of information that tells Windows 10 what files and folders the account holder can access, what changes the account holder can make to the computer system, and what the account holder's personal preferences are.

Virtual desktop An additional desktop display to organize and quickly access groups of windows.

Wallpaper Another term for the desktop background.

Web browser Software with which you display webpages and navigate the Internet.

Window snip When using Snipping Tool, the type of snip that captures the entire displayed window.

Windows 10 An operating system developed by Microsoft Corporation designed to work with mobile computing devices of all types and also with traditional PCs.

Windows apps Apps that run not only on a Windows phone and a Windows tablet, but also on your Windows desktop PC.

Windows Defender Protection built into Windows 10 that helps prevent viruses, spyware, and malicious or unwanted software from being installed on your PC without your knowledge.

Windows Firewall Protection built into Windows 10 that can prevent hackers or malicious software from gaining access to your computer through a network or the Internet.

Windows Journal A desktop app that comes with Windows 10 with which you can type or handwrite—on a touchscreen—notes and then store them or email them.

Windows Store The program where you can find and download Windows apps.

Work access A Windows 10 feature with which you can connect to your work or school system based on established policies.

Zip Compressing files.

Apply **10A** skills from
these Objectives:

1 Explore the Windows
10 Environment

2 Use File Explorer
and Desktop Apps to
Create a New Folder
and Save a File

3 Identify the Functions
of the Windows 10
Operating System

4 Discover Windows 10
Features

5 Sign Out of Windows
10, Turn Off Your
Computer, and
Manage User Accounts

6 Manage Your Windows
10 System

Skills Review | Project 10C Exploring Windows 10

PROJECT FILES

For Project 10C, you will need the following files:

Your USB flash drive—or other location—containing the student data files
win01_10C_Answer_Sheet (Word document)

You will save your file as:

Lastname_Firstname_10C_Answer_Sheet

1 Close all open windows. On the taskbar, click **File Explorer**, navigate to the location
where you are storing your student data files for this chapter, and then open the file
win10_10C_Answer_Sheet. If necessary, at the top click Enable editing; be sure the window is
maximized.

In the upper left corner, click **File**, click **Save As**, click **Browse**, and then navigate to your
Windows 10 Chapter 10 folder. Using your own name, save the document as
Lastname_Firstname_10C_Answer_Sheet

With the Word document displayed, on the taskbar, click the **Word** button to minimize
the window and leave your Word document accessible from the taskbar. **Close** the
File Explorer window. As you complete each step in this project, write the letter of your
answer on a piece of paper; you will fill in your Answer Sheet after you complete all the steps
in this project.

Click **Start**, and then with the insertion point blinking in the search box, type
lock screen Which of the following is true?

A. Search terms that include the text *lock screen* display in the search results.

B. The System settings dialog opens on the desktop.

C. From this screen, you can remove or change your lock screen picture from your
computer.

2 At the top of the search results, click **Lock screen settings**. What is your result?

A. Your lock screen picture fills the screen.

B. The PERSONALIZATION window displays with Background selected on the left.

C. The PERSONALIZATION window displays with Lock screen selected on the left.

3 **Close** the **Settings** window. Click **Start**, click **All apps**, scroll to the **G** section, click
Get Started, and then on the left, click **Windows Hello**. According to this information, which
of the following is true?

A. You cannot activate Windows Hello by using a fingerprint.

B. Windows Hello enables you to sign in to your computer without typing a password.

C. To set up Windows Hello, you must open a Windows Store app.

4 **Close** the **Get Started** window. On the taskbar, click **File Explorer**. What is your result?

A. The window for your USB flash drive displays.

B. The File Explorer window displays.

C. The Documents window displays.

(Project 10C Exploring Windows 10 continues on the next page)

5 ▸ On **This PC**, locate and open **Documents**. What is your result?

A. The first document in the folder opens in its application.

B. The contents of the Documents folder display in the file list.

C. The contents of the Documents folder display in the address bar.

6 ▸ In the **navigation pane**, click **This PC**. What is your result?

A. The storage devices attached to your computer display in the file list.

B. All of the files on the hard drive display in the file list.

C. Your computer restarts.

7 ▸ **Close** the **This PC** window. Click **Start**, and then in the search box, type **paint** Open the **Paint desktop app**, and then pin the program to the taskbar. **Close** the **Paint** window. Which of the following is true?

A. On the taskbar, the Paint program icon on the taskbar displays with shading and a white line under it.

B. The Paint program tile displays on the right side of the Start menu.

C. The Paint program icon displays on the taskbar with no shading.

8 ▸ On the taskbar, point to the **Paint** button, right-click, and then click **Unpin this program from taskbar**. Click **Start**, type **store** and then with the **Store app** at the top of the search results, press Enter. What is your result?

A. All the storage devices attached to your computer display on the Start menu.

B. The Store app displays.

C. A list of games that you can download displays.

9 ▸ **Close** the **Store** app. Click **Start**, type **maps** and press Enter; if necessary, enable your current location. Click **Start**, type **weather** and then press Enter. On the taskbar, click **Task View**. What is your result?

A. The Start menu displays.

B. The Weather app opens and fills the screen.

C. All the open apps display as smaller images.

10 ▸ Point to the **Weather** app, and then click its **Close** button. In the same manner, close the **Maps** app. What is your result?

A. Your Word document displays as a small image on the desktop.

B. The search results for *Weather* redisplay.

C. The Start menu displays.

To complete this project: On the taskbar, click the Word icon to redisplay your Word document. Type your answers into the correct boxes. Save and close your Word document, and submit as directed by your instructor. **Close** all open windows.

▸ END | You have completed Project 10C

Skills Review Project 10D Working with Windows, Programs, and Files

Apply 10B skills from these Objectives:

7 Download and Extract Files and Folders

8 Use File Explorer to Display Locations, Folders, and Files

9 Start Programs and Open Data Files

10 Create, Rename, and Copy Files and Folders

11 Use OneDrive as Cloud Storage

PROJECT FILES

For Project 10D, you will need the following files:

Your USB flash drive—or other location—containing the student data files
win01_10D_Answer_Sheet (Word document)

You will save your file as:

Lastname_Firstname_10D_Answer_Sheet

1 Close all open windows. On the taskbar, click **File Explorer**, navigate to the location where you are storing your student data files for this chapter, and then open the file **win10_10D_Answer_Sheet**. If necessary, at the top click Enable Editing; be sure the window is maximized.

In the upper left corner, click **File**, click **Save As**, click **Browse**, and then navigate to your **Windows 10 Chapter 10** folder. Using your own name, save the document as **Lastname_Firstname_10D_Answer_Sheet**

With the Word document displayed, on the taskbar, click the **Word** button to minimize the window and leave your Word document accessible from the taskbar. **Close** the **File Explorer** window. As you complete each step in this project, write the letter of your answer on a piece of paper; you will fill in your Answer Sheet after you complete all the steps in this project.

Open **File Explorer**, navigate to your student data files, and then open your **win10_10D_Bell_Orchid** folder. If necessary, on the **View tab**, set the **Layout** to **Details**.

In the **file list**, how many *folders* display?

A. Four

B. Five

C. Six

2 Navigate to **Corporate ▸ Food_Beverage**. If necessary, change the view to **Details**. How many *folders* are in the **Food_Beverage** folder?

A. Three

B. Two

C. One

3 Open the **Restaurants** folder, and then click one time to select the file **Breakfast_Continental**. On the ribbon, click the **Home tab**. In which group of commands can you change the name of this file?

A. New

B. Select

C. Organize

(Project 10D Working with Windows, Programs, and Files continues on the next page)

Project 10D Working with Windows, Programs, and Files (continued)

4 With the **Breakfast_Continental** file still selected, point to the file name and right-click. Which of the following is *not* true?

A. From this menu, you can rename the file.

B. From this menu, you can print the file.

C. From this menu, you can move the folder to another folder within Corporate.

5 Click on the desktop to close the shortcut menu, and then click the **Up** button to move up one level in the hierarchy and display the file list for the **Food_Beverage** folder. On the ribbon, click the **View tab**. In the **Layout group**, click **Large icons**. What is your result?

A. The window fills the entire screen.

B. Files that are pictures are visible as pictures.

C. Only picture files display in the file list.

6 On the **View tab**, return the **Layout** to **Details**. In the **file list**, click one time to select the file **CO_FB_Menu_Presentation**. In the **Panes group**, click the **Details pane** button. (*Hint*: You can point to a button to see its ScreenTip.) By looking at the displayed details about this file on the right, which of the following is an information item you can determine about this file?

A. The number of words on each slide

B. The number of slides in the presentation

C. The slide layout used in the title slide

7 In the **Panes group**, click **Preview pane**. In the **Preview pane**, *slowly* drag the scroll box to the bottom of the scroll bar. Which of the following is *not* true?

A. The slide title displays as you drag the scroll box.

B. The PowerPoint program opens as you drag the scroll box.

C. The slide number displays as you drag the scroll box.

8 On the ribbon, click **Preview pane** to turn off the display of the pane. Point to an empty area of the **file list**, right-click, point to **Sort by**, and then click **Type**. In the Type column, if necessary, click the arrow so that the column is sorted in ascending order. Which of the following is true?

A. The Restaurants folder displays at the bottom of the list.

B. The files are in alphabetic order by name.

C. The files are in alphabetic order by Type.

9 In the **Corporate ▸ Food_Beverage** folder, create a new folder named **Dining_Rooms** Select the three JPG files, and then move them into the new folder. Which of the following is true?

A. The status bar indicates that there are five items in the current folder.

B. The three JPG files display in the file list for Food_Beverage.

C. The Dining_Rooms folder is selected.

(Project 10D Working with Windows, Programs, and Files continues on the next page)

Skills Review Project 10D Working with Windows, Programs, and Files (continued)

10 Open the **Restaurants** folder, and then in the upper right portion of the window, in the **search** box, type **sales** and press Enter. How many files display with the word *Sales* in the document name?

A. Three

B. Four

C. Five

To complete this project: Close all open windows. On the taskbar, click the Word icon to redisplay your Word document. Type your answers into the correct boxes. Save and close your Word document, and submit as directed by your instructor. **Close** any open windows.

END | You have completed Project 10D

Project 10E Create a File and Use Windows Apps

Apply 10A skills from these Objectives:

1 Explore the Windows 10 Environment

2 Use File Explorer and Desktop Apps to Create a New Folder and Save a File

3 Identify the Functions of the Windows 10 Operating System

4 Discover Windows 10 Features

5 Sign Out of Windows 10, Turn Off Your Computer, and Manage User Accounts

6 Manage Your Windows 10 System

PROJECT ACTIVITIES

In the following Mastering Windows 10 project, you will capture and save a snip that will look similar to Figure 10.74.

PROJECT FILES

For Project 10E, you will need the following files:

Two new Snip files that you will create during the project

You will save your files as:

Lastname_Firstname_10E_Cortana_Snip
Lastname_Firstname_10E_Snap_Snip

PROJECT RESULTS

 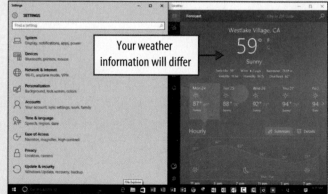

FIGURE 10.74

Microsoft Office 2016, Windows 10, Microsoft Corporation

Microsoft Office 2016, Windows 10, Microsoft Corporation

(Project 10E Create a File and Use Windows Apps continues on the next page)

Mastering Windows 10 | **Project 10E Create a File and Use Windows Apps** (continued)

1 Click **Start**, click **All apps**, click any letter to display an onscreen alphabet, click **G** to jump to the G section, and then click **Get Started**.

2 On the left, click **Cortana**, and then click **What is Cortana?** Scroll down to view the information about setting a reminder.

3 On the taskbar, click **Snipping Tool**, click the **New button arrow**, and then click **Window Snip**. Click anywhere in the window to capture the snip.

4 On the toolbar of the **Snipping Tool** mark-up window, click the **Highlighter**, and then highlight the text *Set a reminder*. Use the red **Pen** to circle the **hamburger menu** icon in the upper left corner. Click the **Save Snip** button.

5 In the displayed **Save As** dialog box, navigate to your **Windows 10 Chapter 10** folder. Using the jpeg file type and your own name, save the snip as
Lastname_Firstname_10E_Cortana_Snip

6 **Close** the **Snipping Tool** window, and then **Close** the **Get Started** window.

7 Click **Start**, click **All apps**, click any letter to display an onscreen alphabet, click **S** to jump to the S section, and then click **Settings**. Display the **All apps** list again, jump to the W section, and then click **Weather**.

8 Press ⊞ + → to snap the Weather app to the right side of the screen. Click the **Settings** window to snap it to the left side of the screen.

9 On the taskbar, click **Snipping Tool**, click the **New button arrow**, and then click **Full-screen Snip**.

10 Click the **Save Snip** button. In the displayed **Save As** dialog box, navigate to your **Windows 10 Chapter 10** folder. Using the jpeg file type and your own name, save the snip as
Lastname_Firstname_10E_Snap_Assist_Snip

11 Close all open windows, and then submit your two snip files to your instructor as directed.

> **END | You have completed Project 10E**

Project 10F Working with Windows, Programs, and Files

Apply 10B skills from these Objectives:

7 Download and Extract Files and Folders

8 Use File Explorer to Display Locations, Folders, and Files

9 Start Programs and Open Data Files

10 Create, Rename, and Copy Files and Folders

11 Use OneDrive as Cloud Storage

PROJECT ACTIVITIES

In the following Mastering Windows 10 project, you will capture and save a snip that will look similar to Figure 10.75.

PROJECT FILES

For Project 10F, you will need the following files:

Two new Snip files that you will create during the project

You will save your files as:

Lastname_Firstname_10F_San_Diego_Snip

Lastname_Firstname_10F_Filter_Snip

PROJECT RESULTS

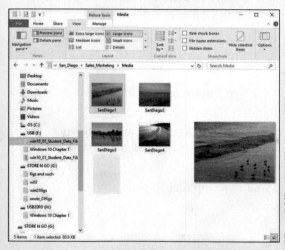

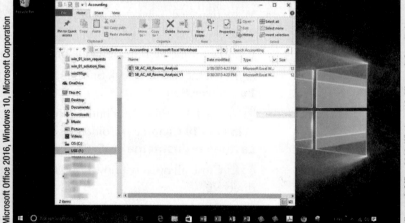

FIGURE 10.75

(Project 10F Working with Windows, Programs, and Files continues on the next page)

Mastering Windows 10 Project 10F Working with Windows, Programs, and Files (continued)

1 Close all open windows, and then on the taskbar, click **File Explorer**. Display the window for your **USB flash drive**—or the location of your student data files—and then navigate to **win10_10F_Bell_Orchid ▸ San_Diego ▸ Sales_Marketing ▸ Media**.

2 From the **View tab**, change the **Layout** to **Large icons**, and then in the **file list**, click one time to select the file **SanDiego1**.

3 Display the **Preview pane** for this file.

4 Start **Snipping Tool**, create a **Window Snip**, click anywhere in the **Media** window to capture it, and then click the **Save Snip** button.

5 In the displayed **Save As** dialog box, navigate to and open your **Windows 10 Chapter 10** folder so that its name displays in the **address bar**. Using the jpeg file type and your own name, save the snip as **Lastname_Firstname_10F_San_Diego_Snip**

6 **Close** the **Snipping Tool** window. Turn off the display of the **Preview pane**. **Close** the window.

7 Open **File Explorer**, and then from your student data files, navigate to **win10_10F_Bell_Orchid ▸ Santa_Barbara ▸ Accounting**.

8 From the **Type** column heading, filter the list to display only **Microsoft Excel Worksheet** files.

9 Create a **Full-screen snip**. Using the **jpeg** file type and your own name, save the snip as **Lastname_Firstname_10F_Filter_Snip**

10 **Close** the **Snipping Tool** window. **Close** the **File Explorer** window. Submit your two snip files as directed by your instructor.

END | You have completed Project 10F

OUTCOMES-BASED ASSESSMENTS

RUBRIC

The following outcomes-based assessments are *open-ended assessments*. That is, there is no specific correct result; your result will depend on your approach to the information provided. Make *Professional Quality* your goal. Use the following scoring rubric to guide you in *how* to approach the problem, and then to evaluate *how well* your approach solves the problem.

The *criteria*—Software Mastery, Content, Format and Layout, and Process—represent the knowledge and skills you have gained that you can apply to solving the problem. The *levels of performance*—Professional Quality, Approaching Professional Quality, or Needs Quality Improvements—help you and your instructor evaluate your result.

	Your completed project is of Professional Quality if you:	Your completed project is Approaching Professional Quality if you:	Your completed project Needs Quality Improvements if you:
1-Software Mastery	Choose and apply the most appropriate skills, tools, and features and identify efficient methods to solve the problem.	Choose and apply some appropriate skills, tools, and features, but not in the most efficient manner.	Choose inappropriate skills, tools, or features, or are inefficient in solving the problem.
2-Content	Construct a solution that is clear and well organized, contains content that is accurate, appropriate to the audience and purpose, and is complete. Provide a solution that contains no errors of spelling, grammar, or style.	Construct a solution in which some components are unclear, poorly organized, inconsistent, or incomplete. Misjudge the needs of the audience. Have some errors in spelling, grammar, or style, but the errors do not detract from comprehension.	Construct a solution that is unclear, incomplete, or poorly organized, contains some inaccurate or inappropriate content, and contains many errors of spelling, grammar, or style. Do not solve the problem.
3-Format and Layout	Format and arrange all elements to communicate information and ideas, clarify function, illustrate relationships, and indicate relative importance.	Apply appropriate format and layout features to some elements, but not others. Overuse features, causing minor distraction.	Apply format and layout that does not communicate information or ideas clearly. Do not use format and layout features to clarify function, illustrate relationships, or indicate relative importance. Use available features excessively, causing distraction.
4-Process	Use an organized approach that integrates planning, development, self-assessment, revision, and reflection.	Demonstrate an organized approach in some areas, but not others; or, use an insufficient process of organization throughout.	Do not use an organized approach to solve the problem.

GO! Think   Project 10G Help Desk

In this project, you will construct a solution by applying any combination of the skills you practiced from the Objectives in Projects 10A and 10B.

PROJECT FILES

For Project 10G, you will need the following file:

win01_10G_Help_Desk (Word file)

You will save your document as:

Lastname_Firstname_10G_Help_Desk

From the student files that accompany this chapter, open the Word document **win10_10G_Help_Desk**. Save the document in your chapter folder as **Lastname_Firstname_10G_Help_Desk**

The following email question arrived at the Help Desk from an employee at the Bell Orchid Hotel's corporate office. In the Word document, construct a response based on your knowledge of Windows 10. Although an email response is not as formal as a letter, you should still use good grammar, good sentence structure, professional language, and a polite tone. Save your document and submit the response as directed by your instructor.

To: Help Desk

We have a new employee in our department, and as her user picture, she wants to use a picture of her dog. I know that Corporate Policy says it is OK to use an acceptable personal picture on a user account. Can she change the picture herself within her standard user account, or does she need an administrator account to do that?

END | You have completed Project 10G

GO! Think   Project 10H Help Desk

In this project, you will construct a solution by applying any combination of the skills you practiced from the Objectives in Projects 10A and 10B.

PROJECT FILES

For Project 10H, you will need the following file:

win01_10H_Help_Desk (Word file)

You will save your document as:

Lastname_Firstname_10H_Help_Desk

From the student files that accompany this chapter, open the Word document **win10_10H_Help_Desk**. Save the document in your chapter folder as **Lastname_Firstname_10H_Help_Desk**

The following email question arrived at the Help Desk from an employee at the Bell Orchid Hotel's corporate office. In the Word document, construct a response based on your knowledge of Windows 10. Although an email response is not as formal as a letter, you should still use good grammar, good sentence structure, professional language, and a polite tone. Save your document and submit the response as directed by your instructor.

To: Help Desk

When I'm done using my computer at the end of the day, should I use the Sleep option or the Shut down option, and what's the difference between the two?

END | You have completed Project 10H

GO Think! | Project 10I Help Desk

In this project, you will construct a solution by applying any combination of the skills you practiced from the Objectives in Projects 10A and 10B.

PROJECT FILES

For Project 10I, you will need the following file:

win01_10I_Help_Desk (Word file)

You will save your document as:

Lastname_Firstname_10I_Help_Desk

From the student files that accompany this chapter, open the Word document **win10_10I_Help_Desk**. Save the document in your chapter folder as **Lastname_Firstname_10I_Help_Desk**

The following email question has arrived at the Help Desk from an employee at the Bell Orchid Hotel's corporate office. In the Word document, construct a response based on your knowledge of Windows 10. Although an email response is not as formal as a letter, you should still use good grammar, good sentence structure, professional language, and a polite tone. Save your document and submit the response as directed by your instructor.

To: Help Desk

I am not sure about the differences between copying and moving files and folders. When is it best to copy a file or a folder and when is it best to move a file or folder? Can you also describe some techniques that I can use for copying or moving files and folders? Which do you think is the easiest way to copy or move files and folders?

END | You have completed Project 10I

Introduction to Microsoft Office 2016 Features

PROJECT 11A

OUTCOMES
Create, save, and print a Microsoft Office 2016 document.

OBJECTIVES

1. Explore Microsoft Office 2016
2. Enter, Edit, and Check the Spelling of Text in an Office 2016 Program
3. Perform Commands from a Dialog Box
4. Create a Folder and Name and Save a File
5. Insert a Footer, Add Document Properties, Print a File, and Close a Desktop App

PROJECT 11B

OUTCOMES
Perform commands, apply formatting, and install apps for Office in Microsoft Office 2016.

OBJECTIVES

6. Open an Existing File and Save it with a New Name
7. Sign in to Office and Explore Options for a Microsoft Office Desktop App
8. Perform Commands from the Ribbon and Quick Access Toolbar
9. Apply Formatting in Office Programs and Inspect Documents
10. Compress Files and Get Help with Office
11. Install Apps for Office and Create a Microsoft Account

Imagewell10/Fotolia

In This Chapter GO! to Work with Office Features

In this chapter, you will practice using features in Microsoft Office 2016 that work similarly across Word, Excel, Access, and PowerPoint. These features include managing files, performing commands, adding document properties, signing in to Office, applying formatting to text, and searching for Office commands quickly. You will also practice installing apps from the Office Store and setting up a free Microsoft account so that you can use OneDrive.

The projects in this chapter relate to **Skyline Metro Grill**, which is a chain of 25 casual, full-service restaurants based in Boston. The Skyline Metro Grill owners are planning an aggressive expansion program. To expand by 15 additional restaurants in Chicago, San Francisco, and Los Angeles by 2020, the company must attract new investors, develop new menus, develop new marketing strategies, and recruit new employees, all while adhering to the company's quality guidelines and maintaining its reputation for excellent service. To succeed, the company plans to build on its past success and maintain its quality elements.

PROJECT
11A Note Form

MyITLab
Project 11A Training
Project 11A Grader

PROJECT ACTIVITIES

In Activities 11.01 through 11.08, you will create a note form using Microsoft Word 2016, save it in a folder that you create by using File Explorer, and then print the note form or submit it electronically as directed by your instructor. Your completed note form will look similar to Figure 11.1.

PROJECT FILES

MyITLab grader

If your instructor wants you to submit Project 11A in the MyITLab Grader system, log in to MyITLab, locate Grader Project11A, and then download the files for this Project.

For Project 11A, you will need the following file:
New blank Word document

You will save your file as:
Lastname_Firstname_11A_Note_Form

PROJECT RESULTS

Build From Scratch

GO! Walk Thru Project11A

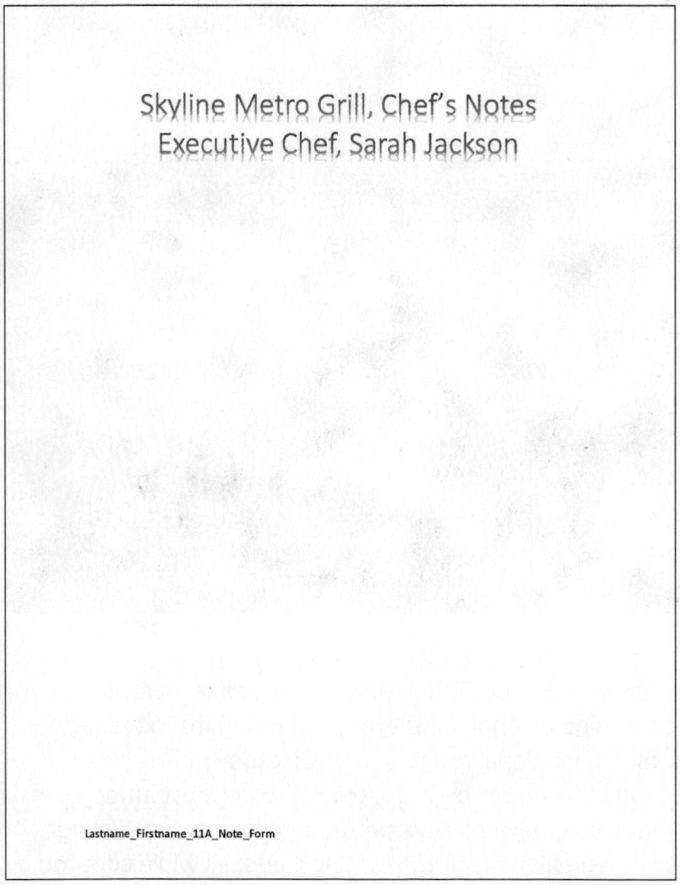
Skyline Metro Grill, Chef's Notes
Executive Chef, Sarah Jackson

Lastname_Firstname_11A_Note_Form

Word 2016, Windows 10, Microsoft Corporation

FIGURE 11.1 Project 11A Note Form

NOTE	If You Are Using a Touchscreen
	Tap an item to click it.
	Press and hold for a few seconds to right-click; release when the information or commands display.
	Touch the screen with two or more fingers and then pinch together to zoom out or stretch your fingers apart to zoom in.
	Slide your finger on the screen to scroll—slide left to scroll right and slide right to scroll left.
	Slide to rearrange—similar to dragging with a mouse.
	Swipe to select—slide an item a short distance with a quick movement—to select an item and bring up commands, if any.

Objective 1 Explore Microsoft Office 2016

NOTE	Creating a Microsoft Account

Use a free Microsoft account to sign in to Office 2016 so that you can work on different PCs and use your OneDrive. If you already sign in to a Windows PC, tablet, or phone, or you sign in to Xbox Live, Outlook.com, or OneDrive, use that account to sign in to Office. To create a Microsoft account, you can use *any* email address as the user name for your new Microsoft account—including addresses from Outlook.com, Yahoo! or Gmail.

GO! Learn How
Video OF11.1

The term *desktop application* or *desktop app* refers to a computer program that is installed on your PC and that requires a computer operating system such as Microsoft Windows. The programs in Microsoft Office 2016 are considered to be desktop apps. A desktop app typically has hundreds of features and takes time to learn.

An *app* refers to a self-contained program usually designed for a single purpose and that runs on smartphones and other mobile devices—for example, looking at sports scores or booking a flight on a particular airline. Microsoft's Windows 10 operating system supports both desktop apps that run only on PCs and *Windows apps* that run on all Windows device families—including PCs, Windows phones, Windows tablets, and the Xbox gaming system.

ALERT!	Is Your Screen More Colorful and a Different Size Than the Figures in This Text?

Your installation of Microsoft Office 2016 may use the default Colorful theme, where the ribbon in each application is a vibrant color and the ribbon tabs display with white text. In this text, figures shown use the White theme, but you can be assured that all the commands are the same. You can keep your Colorful theme, or if you prefer, you can change your theme to White to match the figures here. To do so, open any application and display a new document. On the ribbon, click the File tab, and then on the left, click Options. With General selected on the left, under Personalize your copy of Microsoft Office, click the Office Theme arrow, and then click White.

Additionally, the figures in this text were captured using a screen resolution of 1280 x 768. If that is not your screen resolution, your screen will closely resemble, but not match, the figures shown. To view or change your screen's resolution on a Windows 10 PC, on the desktop, right-click in a blank area, click Display settings, and then on the right, click Advanced display settings. On a Windows 7 PC, right-click the desktop, and then click Screen resolution.

ALERT!

To submit as an autograded project, log into MyITLab, download the files for this project, and then begin with those files instead of a new blank document.

1 On the computer you are using, start Microsoft Word 2016, and then compare your screen with Figure 11.2.

Depending on which operating system you are using and how your computer is set up, you might start Word from the taskbar in Windows 7, Windows 8, or Windows 10, or from the Start screen in Windows 8, or from the Start menu in Windows 10. On an Apple Mac computer, the program will display in the dock.

Documents that you have recently opened, if any, display on the left. On the right, you can select either a blank document or a *template*—a preformatted document that you can use as a starting point and then change to suit your needs.

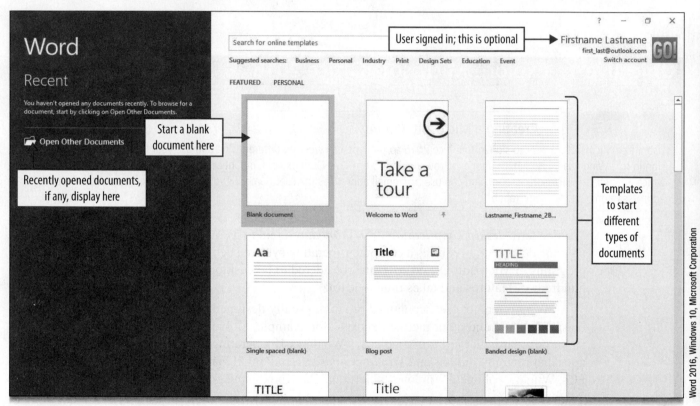

FIGURE 11.2

2 Click **Blank document**. Compare your screen with Figure 11.3, and then take a moment to study the description of these screen elements in the table in Figure 11.4.

NOTE | Displaying the Full Ribbon

If your full ribbon does not display, click any tab, and then at the right end of the ribbon, click ⊞ to pin the ribbon to keep it open while you work.

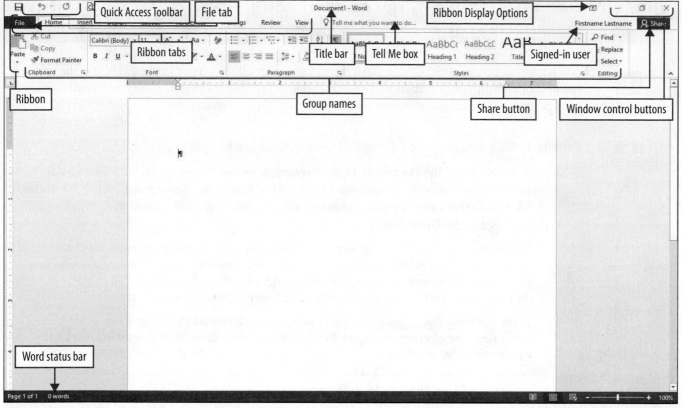

FIGURE 11.3

Word 2016, Windows 10, Microsoft Corporation

SCREEN ELEMENT	DESCRIPTION
File tab	Displays Microsoft Office Backstage view, which is a centralized space for all of your file management tasks such as opening, saving, printing, publishing, or sharing a file—all the things you can do *with* a file.
Group names	Indicate the name of the groups of related commands on the displayed tab.
Quick Access Toolbar	Displays buttons to perform frequently used commands and resources with a single click. The default commands include Save, Undo, and Redo. You can add and delete buttons to customize the Quick Access Toolbar for your convenience.
Ribbon	Displays a group of task-oriented tabs that contain the commands, styles, and resources you need to work in an Office 2016 desktop app. The look of your ribbon depends on your screen resolution. A high resolution will display more individual items and button names on the ribbon.
Ribbon Display Options	Displays three ways you can display the ribbon: Auto-hide Ribbon, Show Tabs, or Show Tabs and Commands.
Ribbon tabs	Display the names of the task-oriented tabs relevant to the open program.
Share button	Opens the Share pane from which you can save your file to the cloud—your OneDrive—and then share it with others so you can collaborate.
Signed-in user	Identifies the signed-in user.
Status bar	Displays file information on the left; on the right displays buttons for Read Mode, Print Layout, and Web Layout views; on the far right displays Zoom controls.
Tell Me box	Provides a search feature for Microsoft Office commands that you activate by typing what you are looking for in the Tell Me box; as you type, every keystroke refines the results so that you can click the command as soon as it displays.
Title bar	Displays the name of the file and the name of the program; the window control buttons are grouped on the right side of the title bar.
Window control buttons	Displays buttons for commands to change the Ribbon Display Options, Minimize, Restore Down, or Close the window.

FIGURE 11.4

GO! Learn How
Video OF11.2

DIGITAL LITERACY
CERTIFICATION
2.01f
2.02a
2.02e (v)

All of the programs in Office 2016 require some typed text. Your keyboard is still the primary method of entering information into your computer. Techniques to enter text and to *edit*—make changes to—text are similar across all of the Office 2016 programs.

Activity 11.02 | Entering and Editing Text in an Office 2016 Program

1 On the ribbon, on the **Home tab**, in the **Paragraph group**, if necessary, click **Show/Hide** ¶ so that it is active—shaded. If necessary, on the **View tab**, in the **Show group**, select the **Ruler** check box so that rulers display below the ribbon and on the left side of your window, and then redisplay the **Home tab**.

The *insertion point*—a blinking vertical line that indicates where text or graphics will be inserted—displays. In Office 2016 programs, the mouse *pointer*—any symbol that displays on your screen in response to moving your mouse device—displays in different shapes depending on the task you are performing and the area of the screen to which you are pointing.

When you press Enter, Spacebar, or Tab on your keyboard, characters display to represent these keystrokes. These screen characters do not print, and are referred to as *formatting marks* or *nonprinting characters*.

NOTE | Activating Show/Hide in Word Documents

When Show/Hide is active—the button is shaded—formatting marks display. Because formatting marks guide your eye in a document—like a map and road signs guide you along a highway—these marks will display throughout this instruction. Many expert Word users keep these marks displayed while creating documents.

---

2 Type **Skyline Grille Info** and notice how the insertion point moves to the right as you type. Point slightly to the right of the letter *e* in *Grille* and click one time to place the insertion point there. Compare your screen with Figure 11.5.

A *paragraph symbol* (¶) indicates the end of a paragraph and displays each time you press Enter. This is a type of formatting mark and does not print.

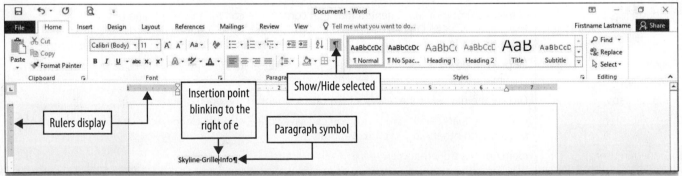

Word 2016, Windows 10, Microsoft Corporation

FIGURE 11.5

3 On your keyboard, locate and then press the Backspace key to delete the letter *e*.

Pressing Backspace removes a character to the left of the insertion point.

4 Press → one time to place the insertion point to the left of the *I* in *Info*. Type **Chef's** and then press Spacebar one time.

By *default*, when you type text in an Office program, existing text moves to the right to make space for new typing. Default refers to the current selection or setting that is automatically used by a program unless you specify otherwise.

5 Press **Del** four times to delete *Info* and then type **Notes**

Pressing **Del** removes a character to the right of the insertion point.

6 With your insertion point blinking after the word *Notes*, on your keyboard, hold down the **Ctrl** key. While holding down **Ctrl**, press **←** three times to move the insertion point to the beginning of the word *Grill*. Release **Ctrl**.

This is a ***keyboard shortcut***—a key or combination of keys that performs a task that would otherwise require a mouse. This keyboard shortcut moves the insertion point to the beginning of the previous word.

A keyboard shortcut is indicated as **Ctrl** + **←** (or some other combination of keys) to indicate that you hold down the first key while pressing the second key. A keyboard shortcut can also include three keys, in which case you hold down the first two and then press the third. For example, **Ctrl** + **Shift** + **←** selects one word to the left.

7 With the insertion point blinking at the beginning of the word *Grill*, type **Metro** and press **Spacebar**.

8 Press **Ctrl** + **End** to place the insertion point after the letter *s* in *Notes*, and then press **Enter** one time. With the insertion point blinking, type the following and include the spelling error:
Exective Chef, Madison Dunham

9 With your mouse, point slightly to the left of the *M* in *Madison*, hold down the left mouse button, and then ***drag***—hold down the left mouse button while moving your mouse—to the right to select the text *Madison Dunham* but not the paragraph mark following it, and then release the mouse button. Compare your screen with Figure 11.6.

The ***mini toolbar*** displays commands that are commonly used with the selected object, which places common commands close to your pointer. When you move the pointer away from the mini toolbar, it fades from view.

Selecting refers to highlighting—by dragging or clicking with your mouse—areas of text or data or graphics so that the selection can be edited, formatted, copied, or moved. The action of dragging includes releasing the left mouse button at the end of the area you want to select.

The Office programs recognize a selected area as one unit to which you can make changes. Selecting text may require some practice. If you are not satisfied with your result, click anywhere outside of the selection, and then begin again.

⟳ BY TOUCH Double-tap on *Madison* to display the gripper—a small circle that acts as a handle—directly below the word. This establishes the start gripper. If necessary, with your finger, drag the gripper to the beginning of the word. Then drag the gripper to the end of *Dunham* to select the text and display the end gripper.

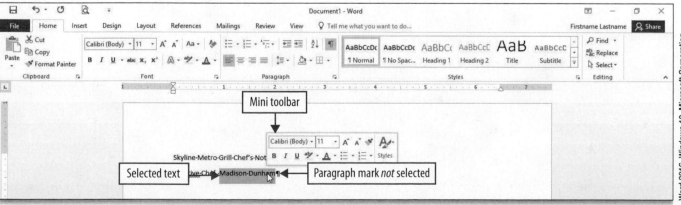

FIGURE 11.6

10 With the text *Madison Dunham* selected, type **Sarah Jackson**

In any Windows-based program, such as the Microsoft Office 2016 programs, selected text is deleted and then replaced when you begin to type new text. You will save time by developing good techniques for selecting and then editing or replacing selected text, which is easier than pressing the Del key numerous times to delete text.

Activity 11.03 | Checking Spelling

Office 2016 has a dictionary of words against which all entered text is checked. In Word and PowerPoint, words that are not in the dictionary display a wavy red line, indicating a possible misspelled word, a proper name, or an unusual word—none of which are in the Office 2016 dictionary.

In Excel and Access, you can initiate a check of the spelling, but red underlines do not display.

1 Notice that the misspelled word *Exective* displays with a wavy red underline.

2 Point to *Exective* and then ***right-click***—click your right mouse button one time.

A ***shortcut menu*** displays, which displays commands and options relevant to the selected text or object. These are ***context-sensitive commands*** because they relate to the item you right-clicked. These shortcut menus are also referred to as ***context menus***. Here, the shortcut menu displays commands related to the misspelled word.

 **BY TOUCH**   Tap and hold a moment—when a square displays around the misspelled word, release your finger to display the shortcut menu.

3 Press Esc to cancel the shortcut menu, and then in the lower left corner of your screen, on the status bar, click the ***Proofing*** icon ▣, which displays an *X* because some errors are detected. Compare your screen with Figure 11.7.

The Spelling pane displays on the right. Here you have many more options for checking spelling than you have on the shortcut menu. The suggested correct word, *Executive*, is highlighted.

You can click the speaker icon to hear the pronunciation of the selected word. If you have not already installed a dictionary, you can click *Get a Dictionary*—if you are signed in to Office with a Microsoft account—to find and install one from the online Office store; or if you have a dictionary app installed, it will display here and you can search it for more information.

In the Spelling pane, you can ignore the word one time or in all occurrences, change the word to the suggested word, select a different suggestion, or add a word to the dictionary against which Word checks.

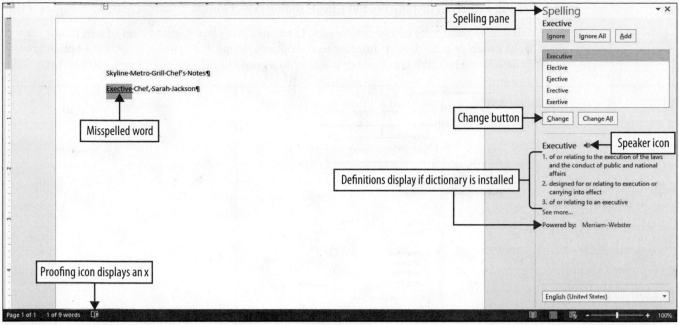

FIGURE 11.7

Word 2016, Windows 10, Microsoft Corporation

ANOTHER WAY Press F7 to display the Spelling pane; or, on the Review tab, in the Proofing group, click Spelling & Grammar.

4 In the *Spelling* pane, click **Change** to change the spelling to *Executive*. In the message box that displays, click **OK**.

Objective 3 Perform Commands from a Dialog Box

In a dialog box, you make decisions about an individual object or topic. In some dialog boxes, you can make multiple decisions in one place.

GO! Learn How
Video OF11.3

DIGITAL LITERACY
CERTIFICATION
2.02a

Activity 11.04 Performing Commands from a Dialog Box

1 On the ribbon, click the **Design tab**, and then in the **Page Background group**, click **Page Color**.

2 At the bottom of the menu, notice the command *Fill Effects* followed by an **ellipsis** (…). Compare your screen with Figure 11.8.

An *ellipsis* is a set of three dots indicating incompleteness. An ellipsis following a command name indicates that a dialog box will display when you click the command.

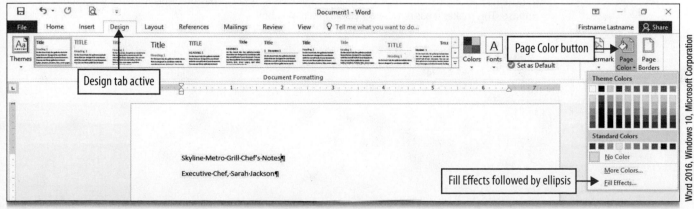

FIGURE 11.8

Word 2016, Windows 10, Microsoft Corporation

3 Click **Fill Effects** to display the **Fill Effects** dialog box. Compare your screen with Figure 11.9.

Fill is the inside color of a page or object. Here, the dialog box displays a set of tabs across the top from which you can display different sets of options. Some dialog boxes display the option group names on the left. The Gradient tab is active. In a *gradient fill*, one color fades into another.

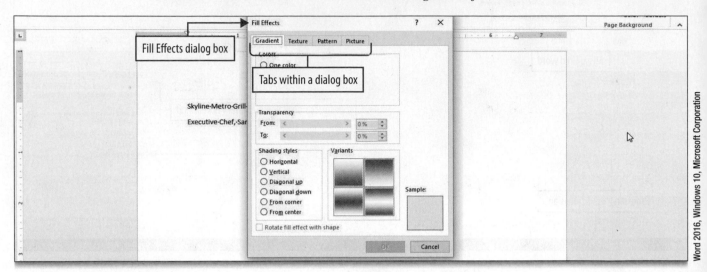

FIGURE 11.9

4 Under **Colors**, click the **One color** option button.

The dialog box displays settings related to the One color option. An *option button* is a round button that enables you to make one choice among two or more options.

5 Click the **Color 1 arrow**—the arrow under the text *Color 1*—and then in the third column, point to the second color to display the ScreenTip *Gray-25%, Background 2, Darker 10%*.

When you click an arrow in a dialog box, additional options display. A *ScreenTip* displays useful information about mouse actions, such as pointing to screen elements or dragging.

6 Click **Gray-25%, Background 2, Darker 10%**, and then notice that the fill color displays in the **Color 1** box. In the **Dark Light** bar, click the **Light arrow** as many times as necessary until the scroll box is all the way to the right. Under **Shading styles**, click the **Diagonal down** option button. Under **Variants**, click the **upper right variant**. Compare your screen with Figure 11.10.

This dialog box is a good example of the many different elements you may encounter in a dialog box. Here you have option buttons, an arrow that displays a menu, a slider bar, and graphic options that you can select.

↻ BY TOUCH

In a dialog box, you can tap option buttons and other commands just as you would click them with a mouse. When you tap an arrow to display a color palette, a larger palette displays than if you used your mouse. This makes it easier to select colors in a dialog box.

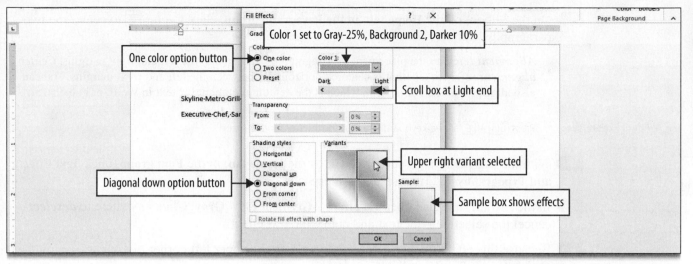

One color option button → Color 1 set to Gray-25%, Background 2, Darker 10%

Scroll box at Light end

Diagonal down option button →

Upper right variant selected

Sample box shows effects

FIGURE 11.10

7 At the bottom of the dialog box, click **OK**, and notice the subtle page color.

In Word, the gray shading page color will not print—even on a color printer—unless you set specific options to do so. However, a subtle background page color is effective if people will be reading the document on a screen. Microsoft's research indicates that two-thirds of people who open Word documents on a screen never print them; they only read them.

IC3
DIGITAL LITERACY
CERTIFICATION
2.01g
2.02a
2.02e (iv)

Activity 11.05 | Using Undo and Applying a Built-In Style to Text

1 Point to the *S* in *Skyline*, and then drag down and to the right to select both paragraphs of text and include the paragraph marks. On the mini toolbar, click **Styles**, and then *point to* but do not click **Title**. Compare your screen with Figure 11.11.

A *style* is a group of *formatting* commands, such as font, font size, font color, paragraph alignment, and line spacing that can be applied to a paragraph with one command. Formatting is the process of establishing the overall appearance of text, graphics, and pages in an Office file— for example, in a Word document.

Live Preview is a technology that shows the result of applying an editing or formatting change as you point to possible results—before you actually apply it.

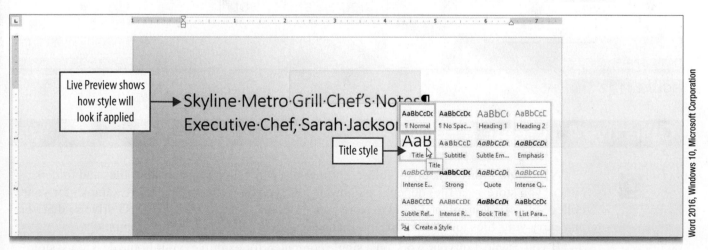

Live Preview shows how style will look if applied →

Title style

FIGURE 11.11

2 In the **Styles** gallery, click **Title**.

A *gallery* is an Office feature that displays a list of potential results.

3 On the ribbon, on the **Home tab**, in the **Paragraph group**, click **Center** 📃 to center the two paragraphs.

> *Alignment* refers to the placement of paragraph text relative to the left and right margins. *Center alignment* refers to text that is centered horizontally between the left and right margins. You can also align text at the left margin, which is the default alignment for text in Word, or at the right.

🔄 **ANOTHER WAY**   Press Ctrl + E as the keyboard shortcut for the Center command.

4 With the two paragraphs still selected, on the **Home tab**, in the **Font group**, click **Text Effects and Typography** 🄰▾ to display a gallery.

5 In the second row, click the first effect—**Gradient Fill – Gray**. Click anywhere to *deselect*—cancel the selection—the text and notice the text effect.

6 Because this effect might be difficult to read, in the upper left corner of your screen, on the ***Quick Access Toolbar***, click **Undo** ⟲.

> The *Undo* command reverses your last action.

🔄 **ANOTHER WAY**   Press Ctrl + Z as the keyboard shortcut for the Undo command.

7 With all of the text still selected, display the **Text Effects and Typography** 🄰▾ gallery again, and then in the second row, click the second effect—**Gradient Fill – Blue, Accent 1, Reflection**. Click anywhere to deselect the text and notice the text effect. Compare your screen with Figure 11.12.

> As you progress in your study of Microsoft Office, you will practice using many dialog boxes and commands to apply interesting effects such as this to your Word documents, Excel worksheets, Access database objects, and PowerPoint slides.

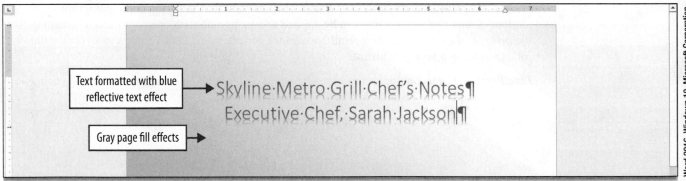

FIGURE 11.12

Objective 4   Create a Folder and Name and Save a File

GO! Learn How
Video OF11.5

A *location* is any disk drive, folder, or other place in which you can store files and folders. Where you store your files depends on how and where you use your data. For example, for your college classes, you might decide to store your work on a removable USB flash drive so that you can carry your files to different locations and access your files on different computers.

If you do most of your work on a single computer, for example, your home desktop system or your laptop computer that you take with you to school or work, then you can store your files in one of the folders—Documents, Music, Pictures, or Videos—on your hard drive provided by your Windows operating system.

The best place to store files if you want them to be available anytime, anywhere, from almost any device is on your **OneDrive**, which is Microsoft's free **cloud storage** for anyone with a free Microsoft account. Cloud storage refers to online storage of data so that you can access your data from different places and devices. **Cloud computing** refers to applications and services that are accessed over the Internet, rather than accessing applications installed on your local computer.

If you have an **Office 365** account—one of the versions of Microsoft Office to which you subscribe for an annual fee—your storage capacity on OneDrive is a terabyte or more, which is more than most individuals would ever require.

Because many people now have multiple computing devices—desktop, laptop, tablet, smartphone—it is common to store data *in the cloud* so that it is always available. **Synchronization**, also called *syncing*—pronounced SINK-ing—is the process of updating computer files that are in two or more locations according to specific rules. So if you create and save a Word document on your OneDrive using your laptop, you can open and edit that document on your tablet in OneDrive. When you close the document again, the file is properly updated to reflect your changes. Your OneDrive account will guide you in setting options for syncing files to your specifications.

You need not be connected to the Internet to access documents stored on OneDrive because an up-to-date version of your content is synched to your local system and available on OneDrive. You must, however, be connected to the Internet for the syncing to occur. Saving to OneDrive will keep the local copy on your computer and the copy in the cloud synchronized for as long as you need it. You can open and edit Office files by using Office apps available on a variety of device platforms, including iOS, Android, and Windows.

The Windows operating system helps you to create and maintain a logical folder structure, so always take the time to name your files and folders consistently.

Activity 11.06 | Creating a Folder and Naming and Saving a File

A Word document is an example of a file. In this Activity, you will create a folder in the storage location you have chosen to use for your files and then save your file. This example will use the Documents folder on the PC at which you are working. If you prefer to store on your OneDrive or on a USB flash drive, you can use similar steps.

1 Decide where you are going to store your files for this Project.

As the first step in saving a file, determine where you want to save the file, and if necessary, insert a storage device.

2 At the top of your screen, in the title bar, notice that *Document1 – Word* displays.

The Blank option on the opening screen of an Office 2016 program displays a new unsaved file with a default name— *Document1, Presentation1*, and so on. As you create your file, your work is temporarily stored in the computer's memory until you initiate a Save command, at which time you must choose a file name and a location in which to save your file.

3 In the upper left corner of your screen, click the **File tab** to display **Backstage** view. Compare your screen with Figure 11.13.

Backstage view is a centralized space that groups commands related to *file* management; that is why the tab is labeled *File*. File management commands include opening, saving, printing, publishing, or sharing a file. The *Backstage tabs*—Info, New, Open, Save, Save As, Print, Share, Export, and Close—display along the left side. The tabs group file-related tasks together.

Here, the *Info tab* displays information—*info*—about the current file, and file management commands display under Info. For example, if you click the Protect Document button, a list of options that you can set for this file that relate to who can open or edit the document displays.

On the right, you can also examine the *document properties*. Document properties, also known as *metadata*, are details about a file that describe or identify it, such as the title, author name, subject, and keywords that identify the document's topic or contents. To close Backstage view and return to the document, you can click ⬅ in the upper left corner or press [Esc].

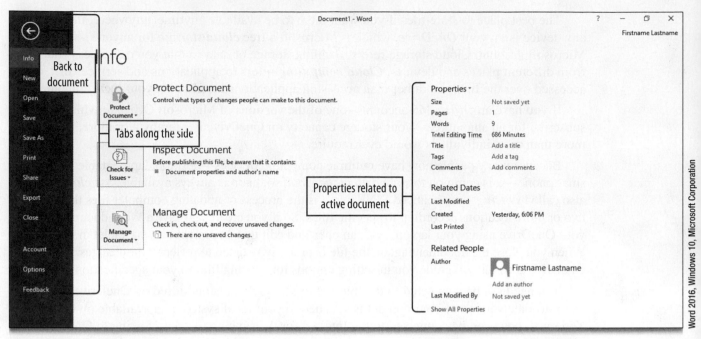

FIGURE 11.13

> **4** On the left, click **Save As**, and notice that the default location for storing Office files is your **OneDrive**—if you are signed in. Compare your screen with Figure 11.14.
>
> > When you are saving something for the first time, for example, a new Word document, the Save and Save As commands are identical. That is, the Save As commands will display if you click Save or if you click Save As.

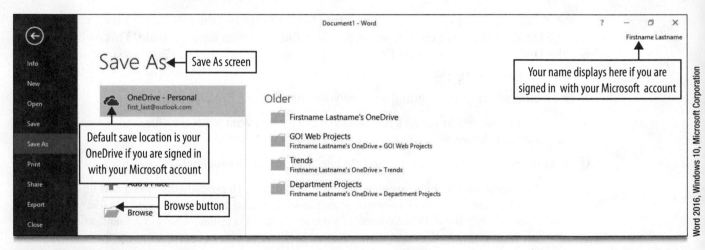

FIGURE 11.14

NOTE	Saving After Your File Is Named

After you name and save a file, the Save command on the Quick Access Toolbar saves any changes you make to the file without displaying Backstage view. The Save As command enables you to name and save a *new* file based on the current one—in a location that you choose. After you name and save the new document, the original document closes, and the new document—based on the original one—displays.

5 To store your Word file in the **Documents** folder on your PC, click **Browse** to display the **Save As** dialog box. On the left, in the **navigation pane**, scroll down; if necessary click > to expand This PC, and then click **Documents**, or navigate to your USB flash drive or other location. In a college lab, your work may be lost if you store in the Documents folder. Compare your screen with Figure 11.15.

In the Save As dialog box, you must indicate the name you want for the file and the location where you want to save the file. When working with your own data, it is good practice to pause at this point and determine the logical name and location for your file.

In the Save As dialog box, a *toolbar* displays, which is a row, column, or block of buttons or icons, that displays across the top of a window and that contains commands for tasks you perform with a single click.

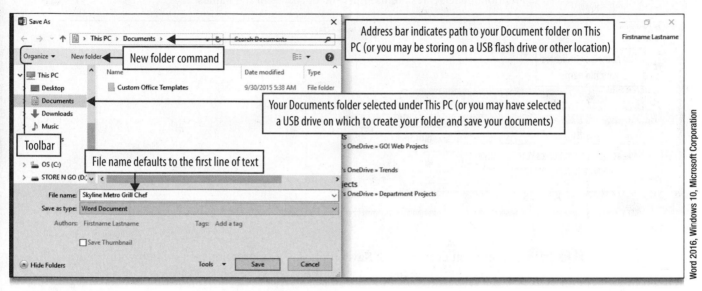

FIGURE 11.15

6 On the toolbar, click **New folder**.

In the file list, Windows creates a new folder, and the text *New folder* is selected.

7 Type **Office Features Chapter 11** and press Enter. Compare your screen with Figure 11.16.

In Windows-based programs, the Enter key confirms an action.

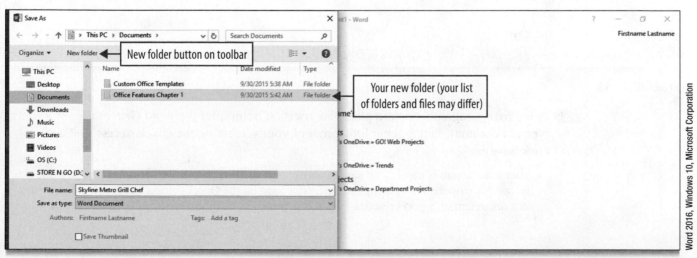

FIGURE 11.16

8 In the **file list**, double-click the name of your new folder to open it and display its name in the **address bar**.

9 In the lower portion of the dialog box, click in the **File name** box to select the existing text. Notice that as the suggested file name, Office inserts the text at the beginning of the document.

10 On your keyboard, locate the ⌐ key, to the right of zero on the number row. Notice that the Shift of this key produces the underscore character. With the text still selected and using your own name, type **Lastname_Firstname_11A_Note_Form** Compare your screen with Figure 11.17.

> You can use spaces in file names, however, some people prefer not to use spaces. Some programs, especially when transferring files over the Internet, may insert the extra characters *%20* in place of a space. In general, however, unless you encounter a problem, it is OK to use spaces. In this instruction, underscores are used instead of spaces in file names.

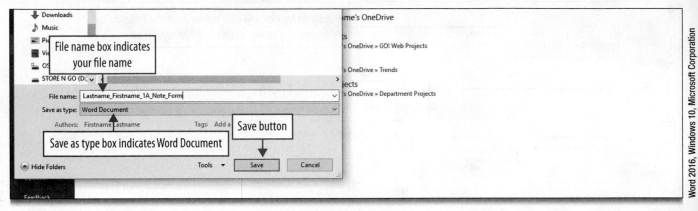

FIGURE 11.17

11 In the lower right corner, click **Save** or press Enter. Compare your screen with Figure 11.18.

> The Word window redisplays and your new file name displays in the title bar, indicating that the file has been saved to the location that you have specified.

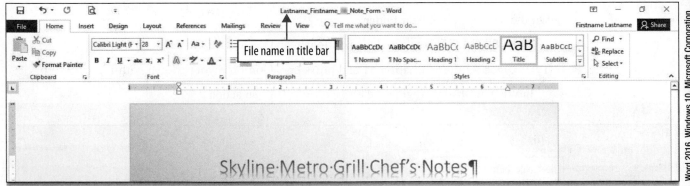

FIGURE 11.18

12 In the first paragraph, click to place the insertion point after the word *Grill* and type **,** (a comma). In the upper left corner of your screen, on the **Quick Access Toolbar**, click **Save** 🖫.

> After a document is named and saved in a location, you can save any changes you have made since the last Save operation by using the Save command on the Quick Access Toolbar. When working on a document, it is good practice to save your changes from time to time.

GO! Learn How
Video OF11.5

DIGITAL LITERACY
CERTIFICATION
2.02a

For most of your files, especially in a workplace setting, it is useful to add identifying information to help in finding files later. You might also want to print your file on paper or create an electronic printout. The process of printing a file is similar in all of the Office applications.

Activity 11.07 | Inserting a Footer, Inserting Document Info, and Adding Document Properties

1 On the ribbon, click the **Insert tab**, and then in the **Header & Footer group**, click **Footer**.

2 At the bottom of the list, click **Edit Footer**. On the ribbon, notice that the **Header & Footer Tools** display.

The *Header & Footer Tools Design* tab displays on the ribbon. The ribbon adapts to your work and will display additional tabs like this one—referred to as *contextual tabs*—when you need them.

A *footer* is a reserved area for text or graphics that displays at the bottom of each page in a document. Likewise, a *header* is a reserved area for text or graphics that displays at the top of each page in a document. When the footer (or header) area is active, the document area is dimmed, indicating it is unavailable.

3 On the ribbon, under **Header & Footer Tools**, on the **Design tab**, in the **Insert group**, click **Document Info**, and then click **File Name** to insert the name of your file in the footer, which is a common business practice. Compare your screen with Figure 11.19.

Ribbon commands that display ▼ will, when clicked, display a list of options for the command.

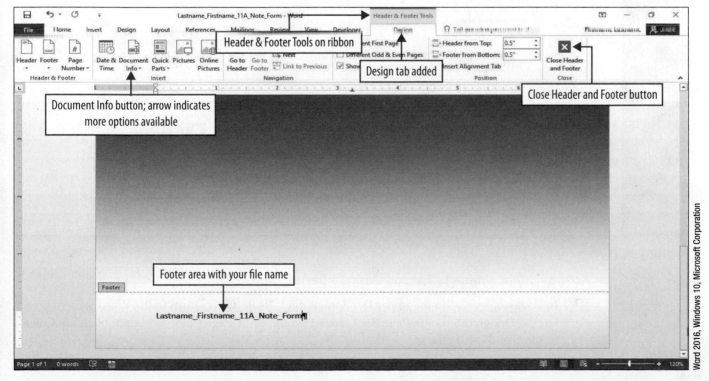

FIGURE 11.19

Word 2016, Windows 10, Microsoft Corporation

4 At the right end of the ribbon, click **Close Header and Footer**.

ANOTHER WAY   Double-click anywhere in the dimmed document to close the footer.

5 Click the **File tab** to display **Backstage** view. On the right, at the bottom of the **Properties** list, click **Show All Properties**.

ANOTHER WAY   Click the arrow to the right of Properties, and then click Advanced Properties to show and edit properties at the top of your document window.

6 On the list of **Properties**, click to the right of *Tags* to display an empty box, and then type **chef, notes, form**

> *Tags*, also referred to as ***keywords***, are custom file properties in the form of words that you associate with a document to give an indication of the document's content. Adding tags to your documents makes it easier to search for and locate files in File Explorer, on your OneDrive, and in systems such as Microsoft ***SharePoint*** document libraries. SharePoint is collaboration software with which people in an organization can set up team sites to share information, manage documents, and publish reports for others to see.

BY TOUCH   Tap to the right of Tags to display the Tags box and the onscreen keyboard.

7 Click to the right of *Subject* to display an empty box, and then type your course name and section #; for example, *CIS 10, #5543*.

8 Under **Related People**, be sure that your name displays as the author. If necessary, right-click the author name, click Edit Property, type your name, click outside of the Edit person dialog box, and then click OK. Compare your screen with Figure 11.20.

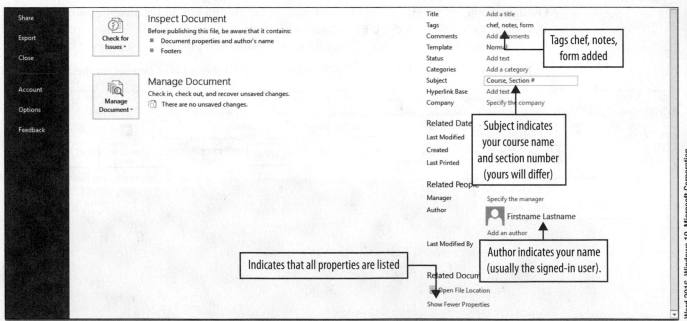

FIGURE 11.20

2.02f

Activity 11.08 | Printing a File and Closing a Desktop App

1 In **Backstage** view, in the upper left corner, click **Back** to return to the Word window. On the **Design tab**, in the **Page Background group**, click **Page Color**, and then click **No Color** to remove the fill effects.

> It's easy to remove formatting from your documents if you change your mind about how you want your document to look.

> **2** Click the **File tab** to return to **Backstage** view, on the left click **Print**, and then compare your screen with Figure 11.21.

Here you can select any printer connected to your system and adjust the settings related to how you want to print. On the right, the ***Print Preview*** displays, which is a view of a document as it will appear on paper when you print it.

At the bottom of the Print Preview area, in the center, the number of pages and page navigation arrows with which you can move among the pages in Print Preview display. On the right, the Zoom slider enables you to shrink or enlarge the Print Preview. ***Zoom*** is the action of increasing or decreasing the viewing area of the screen.

> **ANOTHER WAY**   From the document screen, press Ctrl + P or Ctrl + F2 to display Print in Backstage view.

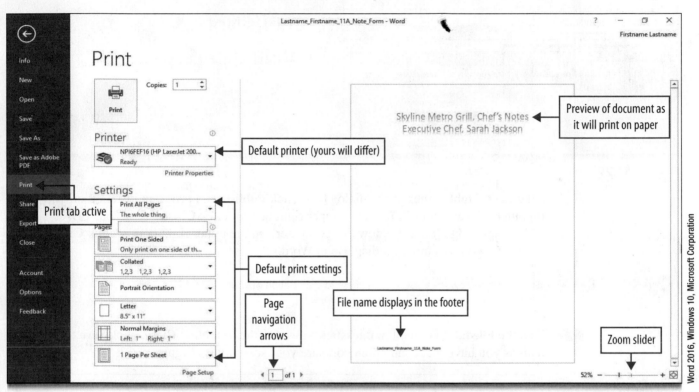

FIGURE 11.21

> **3** To create an electronic image of your document that looks like a printed document, skip this step and continue to Step 4. To print your document on paper using the default printer on your system, in the upper left portion of the screen, click **Print**.

The document will print on your default printer; if you do not have a color printer, the blue text will print in shades of gray. Backstage view closes and your file redisplays in the Word window.

> **4** To create an electronic image of your document that looks like a printed document, in **Backstage** view, on the left click **Export**. On the right, click the **Create PDF/XPS** button to display the **Publish as PDF or XPS** dialog box.

PDF stands for ***Portable Document Format***, which is a technology that creates an image that preserves the look of your file. This is a popular format for sending documents electronically, because the document will display on most computers.

XPS stands for ***XML Paper Specification***—a Microsoft file format that also creates an image of your document and that opens in the XPS viewer.

5 On the left in the **navigation pane**, if necessary expand > This PC, and then navigate to your **Office Features Chapter 11** folder in your **Documents** folder—or in whatever location you have created your Office Features Chapter 11 folder. Compare your screen with Figure 11.22.

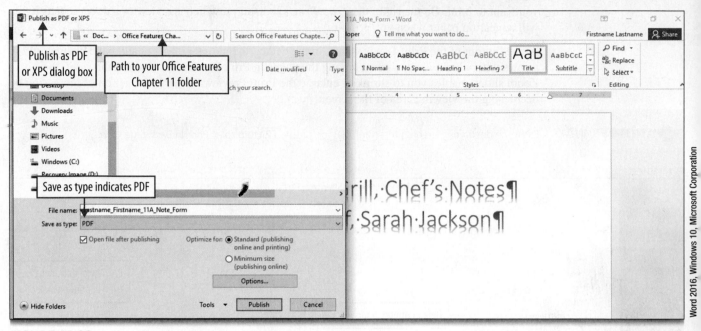

Word 2016, Windows 10, Microsoft Corporation

FIGURE 11.22

6 In the lower right corner of the dialog box, click **Publish**; if a program installed on your computer displays your PDF, in the upper right corner, click Close ⊠. If your PDF displays in Microsoft Edge (on a Windows 10 computer), in the upper right corner click Close ⊠. Notice that your document redisplays in Word.

ANOTHER WAY In Backstage view, click Save As, navigate to the location of your Chapter folder, click the Save as type arrow, on the list click PDF, and then click Save.

7 Click the **File tab** to redisplay **Backstage** view. On the left, click **Close**, click **Save** to save the changes you have made, and then compare your screen with Figure 11.23.

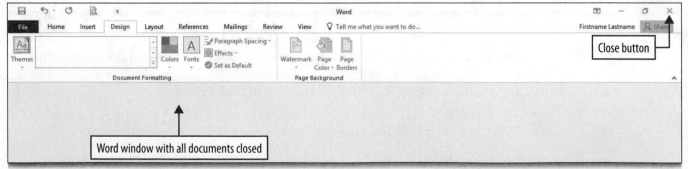

Word 2016, Windows 10, Microsoft Corporation

FIGURE 11.23

8 In the upper right corner of the Word window, click **Close** ⊠. If directed by your instructor to do so, submit your paper printout, your electronic image of your document that looks like a printed document, or your original Word file.

END | You have completed Project 11A

PROJECT ACTIVITIES

In Activities 11.09 through 11.24, you will open, edit, and then compress a Word file. You will also use the Tell Me help feature and install an app for Office. Your completed document will look similar to Figure 11.24.

PROJECT FILES

If your instructor wants you to submit Project 11B in the MyITLab Grader system, log in to MyITLab, locate Grader Project11B, and then download the files for this Project.

For Project 11B, you will need the following file:
of11B_Rehearsal_Dinner

You will save your file as:
Lastname_Firstname_11B_Rehearsal_Dinner

PROJECT RESULTS

Skyline Metro Grill

TO: Sarah Jackson, Executive Chef

FROM: Laura Mabry Hernandez, General Manager

DATE: February 17, 2019

SUBJECT: Wedding Rehearsal Dinners

In the spring and summer months, wedding rehearsal dinners provide a new marketing opportunity for Skyline Metro Grill at all of our locations. A rehearsal dinner is an informal meal following a wedding rehearsal at which the bride and groom typically thank those that have helped them make their wedding a special event.

Our smaller private dining rooms with sweeping city views are an ideal location for a rehearsal dinner. At each of our locations, I have directed the Sales and Marketing Coordinator to partner with local wedding planners to promote Skyline Metro Grill as a relaxed yet sophisticated venue for rehearsal dinners. The typical rehearsal dinner includes the wedding party, the immediate family of the bride and groom, and out-of-town guests.

Please develop six menus—in varying price ranges—to present to local wedding planners so that they can easily promote Skyline Metro Grill to couples who are planning a rehearsal dinner. In addition to a traditional menu, we should also include options for a buffet-style dinner and a family-style dinner.

This marketing effort will require extensive communication with our Sales and Marketing Coordinators and with local wedding planners. Let's meet to discuss the details and the marketing challenges, and to create a promotional piece that begins something like this:

Skyline Metro Grill for Your Rehearsal Dinner

Lastname_Firstname_11B_Rehearsal_Dinner

FIGURE 11.24 Project 11B Memo

In any Office program, you can display the **Open dialog box**, from which you can navigate to and then open an existing file that was created in that same program.

The Open dialog box, along with the Save and Save As dialog boxes, is a common dialog box. These dialog boxes, which are provided by the Windows programming interface, display in all Office programs in the same manner. So the Open, Save, and Save As dialog boxes will all look and perform the same regardless of the Office program in which you are working.

A L E R T !   **To Complete This Project, You Will Need the Student Data Files That Accompany This Chapter**

To complete this Project, you will need the Student Data Files that accompany this chapter. Possibly your instructor has provided these to you already; for example, in the learning management system used by your college. Alternatively, to download the files, go to **www.pearsonhighered.com/go** On the left, narrow your choice by selecting the appropriate topic, and then on the right, locate and click the image of this. In the window that displays, click Download Data Files, and then click the chapter name. Using the commands for your browser, store the zipped file in your storage location, and then use the Extract tools in File Explorer to extract the zipped folder. Instructions for extracting can be found in the Getting Started with Windows 10 chapter.

Activity 11.09 | Opening an Existing File and Saving It with a New Name

In this Activity, you will display the Open dialog box, open an existing Word document, and then save it in your storage location with a new name.

A L E R T !   **To submit as an autograded project, log into MyITLab, download the files for this project, and begin with those files instead of the student data file.**

---

1 Be sure you have saved the folder **of11_student_data_files** for this chapter in your storage location; you can download this folder from **www.pearsonhighered.com/go** or it may have been provided to you by your instructor.

2 Start Word, and then on Word's opening screen, on the left, click **Open Other Documents**. Under **Open**, click **Browse**.

3 In the **Open** dialog box, on the left in the **navigation pane**, navigate to the location where you stored the **of11_student_data_files** folder for this chapter, and then in the **file list**, double-click the folder name **of11_student_data_files** to open the folder.

4 In the **file list**, double-click the file **of11B_Rehearsal_Dinner** to open it in Word. If **PROTECTED VIEW** displays at the top of your screen, in the center click **Enable Editing**.

In Office 2016, a file will open in **Protected View** if the file appears to be from a potentially risky location, such as the Internet. Protected View is a security feature in Office 2016 that protects your computer from malicious files by opening them in a restricted environment until you enable them. **Trusted Documents** is another security feature that remembers which files you have already enabled.

You might encounter these security features if you open a file from an email or download files from the Internet; for example, from your college's learning management system or from the Pearson website. So long as you trust the source of the file, click Enable Editing or Enable Content—depending on the type of file you receive—and then go ahead and work with the file.

5 With the document displayed in the Word window, be sure that **Show/Hide** is active; if necessary, on the Home tab, in the Paragraph group, click Show/Hide to activate it; on the View tab, be sure that Rulers are active. Compare your screen with Figure 11.25.

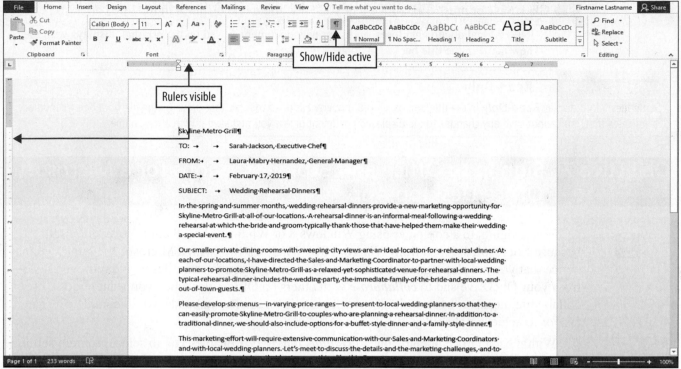

FIGURE 11.25

Word 2016, Windows 10, Microsoft Corporation

6 Click the **File tab** to display **Backstage** view, and then on the left, click **Save As**. Under **Save As**, click **Browse**.

7 In the **Save As** dialog box, use the **navigation pane** to navigate to and open the **Office Features Chapter 11** folder that you created to store your work from this chapter.

In Backstage view, on the right, you might also see your Office Features Chapter 11 folder listed, and if so, you can open it directly from there. The common dialog boxes Open, Save, and Save As remember your recently used locations and display them in Backstage view.

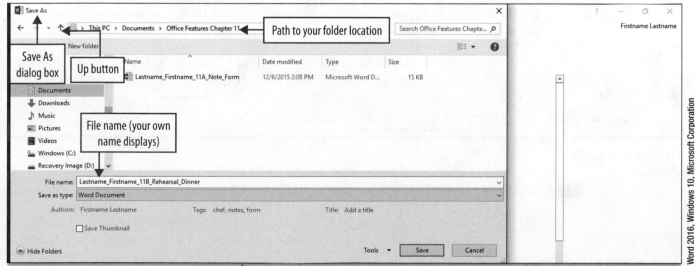

ANOTHER WAY   From the Word window, press F12 to display the Save As dialog box.

8 Click in the **File name** box to select the existing text, and then, using your own name, type **Lastname_Firstname_11B_Rehearsal_Dinner** Compare your screen with Figure 11.26.

FIGURE 11.26

Word 2016, Windows 10, Microsoft Corporation

9 Click **Save** or press [Enter]; notice that your new file name displays in the title bar.

The original document closes, and your new document, based on the original, displays with the new name in the title bar.

Objective 7   Sign In to Office and Explore Options for a Microsoft Office Desktop App

GO! Learn How
Video OF11.7

If you sign in to a computer using Windows 8 or Windows 10—there is no Windows 9, because Microsoft skipped from Windows 8 to Windows 10—with a Microsoft account, you may notice that you are also signed in to Office. This enables you to save files to and retrieve files from your OneDrive and to ***collaborate*** with others on Office files when you want to do so. To collaborate means to work with others as a team in an intellectual endeavor to complete a shared task or to achieve a shared goal.

Within each Office application, an ***Options dialog box*** enables you to select program settings and other options and preferences. For example, you can set preferences for viewing and editing files.

Activity 11.10 | Signing In to Office and Viewing Application Options

1 In the upper right corner of your screen, if you are signed in with a Microsoft account, click your name, and then compare your screen with Figure 11.27.

Here you can change your photo, go to About me to edit your profile, examine your Account settings, or switch accounts to sign in with a different Microsoft account.

ALERT!   **Not Signed In to Office or Have Not Yet Created a Microsoft Account?**

In the upper right corner, click Sign in, and then enter your Microsoft account. If you have not created a free Microsoft account, click Sign in, type any email address that you currently use, click Next, and then click Sign up now. If you are working in a college lab, this process may vary.

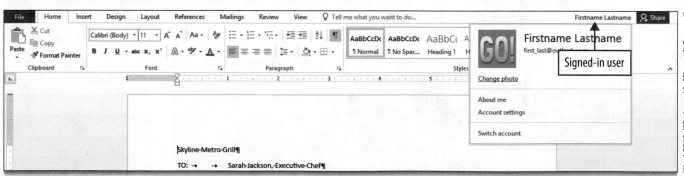

FIGURE 11.27

2 Click the **File tab** to display **Backstage** view. On the left, click **Options**.

3 In the **Word Options** dialog box, on the left, click **Display**, and then on the right, locate the information under **Always show these formatting marks on the screen**.

> The Word Options dialog box—or the similar Options dialog box in any of the Office applications—controls nearly every aspect of the application. Next to many of the items, you will see small *i* icons, which when you point to them display a ScreenTip.

> If you click each of the categories on the left side of the dialog box, you will see that the scope of each application is quite large and that you have a great deal of control over how the application behaves. For example, you can customize the tab names and group names in the ribbon.

> If you are not sure what a setting or option does, in the upper right corner of the title bar, click the Help button—the question mark icon.

4 Under **Always show these formatting marks on the screen**, be sure the last check box, **Show all formatting marks**, is selected—select it if necessary. Compare your screen with Figure 11.28.

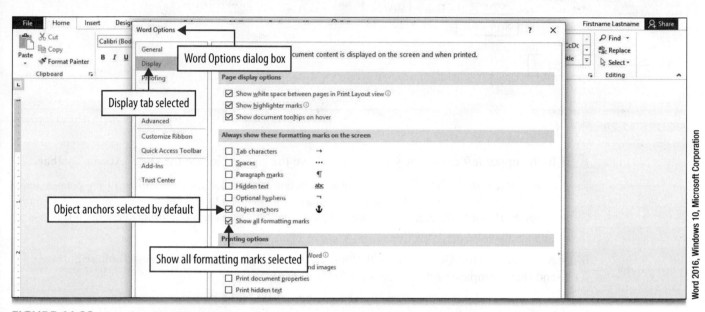

FIGURE 11.28

5 In the lower right corner of the dialog box, click **OK**.

Objective 8 Perform Commands from the Ribbon and Quick Access Toolbar

GO! Learn How
Video OF11.8

The ribbon that displays across the top of the program window groups commands in the way that you would most logically use them. The ribbon in each Office program is slightly different, but all contain the same three elements: *tabs*, *groups*, and *commands*.

Tabs display across the top of the ribbon, and each tab relates to a type of activity; for example, laying out a page. Groups are sets of related commands for specific tasks. Commands—instructions to computer programs—are arranged in groups and might display as a button, a menu, or a box in which you type information.

You can also minimize the ribbon so only the tab names display, which is useful when working on a smaller screen such as a tablet computer where you want to maximize your screen viewing area.

Activity 11.11 | Performing Commands from and Customizing the Quick Access Toolbar

1 Take a moment to examine the document on your screen. If necessary, on the ribbon, click the View tab, and then in the Show group, click to place a check mark in the Ruler check box. Compare your screen with Figure 11.29.

This document is a memo from the General Manager to the Executive Chef regarding a new restaurant promotion for wedding rehearsal dinners.

When working in Word, display the rulers so that you can see how margin settings affect your document and how text and objects align. Additionally, if you set a tab stop or an indent, its location is visible on the ruler.

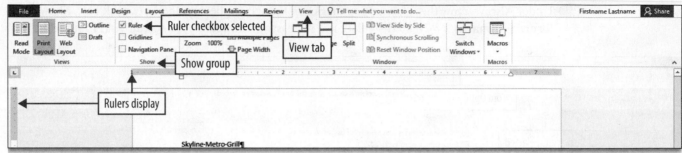

FIGURE 11.29

2 In the upper left corner of your screen, above the ribbon, locate the **Quick Access Toolbar**.

Recall that the Quick Access Toolbar contains commands that you use frequently. By default, only the commands Save, Undo, and Redo display, but you can add and delete commands to suit your needs. Possibly the computer at which you are working already has additional commands added to the Quick Access Toolbar.

3 At the end of the **Quick Access Toolbar**, click the **Customize Quick Access Toolbar** button 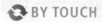, and then compare your screen with Figure 11.30.

A list of commands that Office users commonly add to their Quick Access Toolbar displays, including New, Open, Email, Quick Print, and Print Preview and Print. Commands already on the Quick Access Toolbar display a check mark. Commands that you add to the Quick Access Toolbar are always just one click away.

Here you can also display the More Commands dialog box, from which you can select any command from any tab to add to the Quick Access Toolbar.

BY TOUCH   Tap once on Quick Access Toolbar commands.

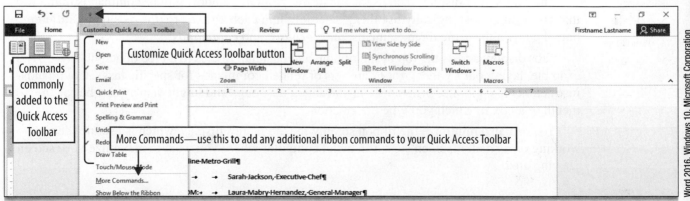

FIGURE 11.30

4 On the list, click **Print Preview and Print**, and then notice that the icon is added to the **Quick Access Toolbar**. Compare your screen with Figure 11.31.

The icon that represents the Print Preview command displays on the Quick Access Toolbar. Because this is a command that you will use frequently while building Office documents, you might decide to have this command remain on your Quick Access Toolbar.

ANOTHER WAY Right-click any command on the ribbon, and then on the shortcut menu, click Add to Quick Access Toolbar.

Icon for Print Preview and Print added to Quick Access Toolbar

FIGURE 11.31 Word 2016, Windows 10, Microsoft Corporation

Activity 11.12 | Performing Commands from the Ribbon

1 In the first line of the document, if necessary, click to the left of the *S* in *Skyline* to position the insertion point there, and then press Enter one time to insert a blank paragraph. Press ↑ one time to position the insertion point in the new blank paragraph. Compare your screen with Figure 11.32.

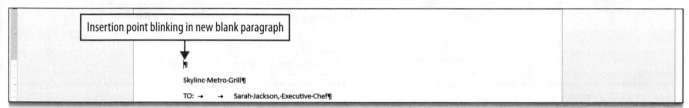

Insertion point blinking in new blank paragraph

Skyline·Metro·Grill¶

TO: →   →   Sarah·Jackson,·Executive·Chef¶

FIGURE 11.32 Word 2016, Windows 10, Microsoft Corporation

2 On the ribbon, click the **Insert tab**. In the **Illustrations group**, *point* to **Online Pictures** to display its ScreenTip.

Many buttons on the ribbon have this type of *enhanced ScreenTip*, which displays useful descriptive information about the command.

3 Click **Online Pictures**, and then compare your screen with Figure 11.33.

In the Insert Pictures dialog box, you can search for online pictures using Bing Image Search, and, if you are signed in with your Microsoft account, you can also find images on your OneDrive by clicking Browse. At the bottom, you can click a logo to download pictures from your Facebook and other types of accounts if you have them.

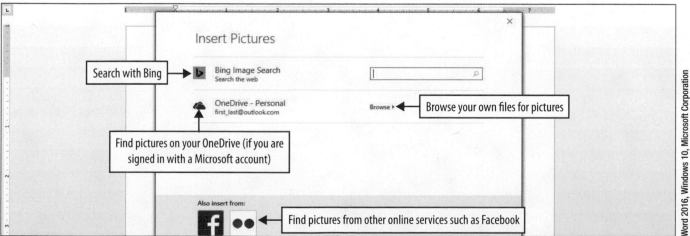

Insert Pictures

Search with Bing → Bing Image Search / Search the web

OneDrive - Personal / first_last@outlook.com — Browse ► ← Browse your own files for pictures

Find pictures on your OneDrive (if you are signed in with a Microsoft account)

Also insert from:

Find pictures from other online services such as Facebook

Word 2016, Windows 10, Microsoft Corporation

FIGURE 11.33

Project 11B: Memo | **GO! All in One**   **445**

4 With the insertion point positioned in the **Bing Image Search** box, type **salad** and press Enter. Point to any of the results, and notice that keywords display. Compare your screen with Figure 11.34.

> You can use various keywords to find images that are appropriate for your documents. The results shown indicate the images are licensed under *Creative Commons*, which, according to **www.creativecommons.org** is "a nonprofit organization that enables the sharing and use of creativity and knowledge through free legal tools."

> Creative Commons helps people share and use their photographs, but does not allow companies to sell them. For your college assignments, you can use these images so long as you are not profiting by selling the photographs.

> To find out more about Creative Commons, go to **https://creativecommons.org/about** and watch the video.

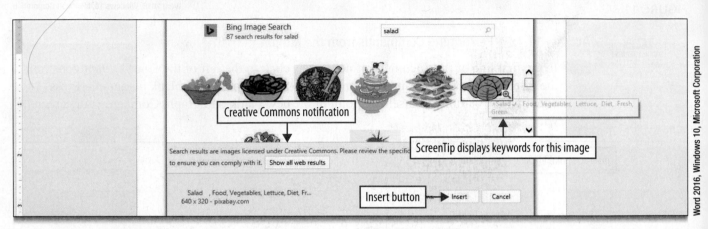

FIGURE 11.34

5 Locate an attractive picture of a salad on a plate or in a bowl that has a horizontal orientation—the picture is wider than it is tall—and then click that picture to select it. In the lower right corner, click **Insert**. In the upper right corner of the picture, point to the **Layout Options** button ▣ to display its ScreenTip, and then compare your screen with Figure 11.35.

> *Layout Options* enable you to choose how the *object*—in this instance an inserted picture—interacts with the surrounding text. An object is a picture or other graphic such as a chart or table that you can select and then move and resize.

> When a picture is selected, the Picture Tools become available on the ribbon. Additionally, *sizing handles*—small circles or squares that indicate an object is selected—surround the selected picture.

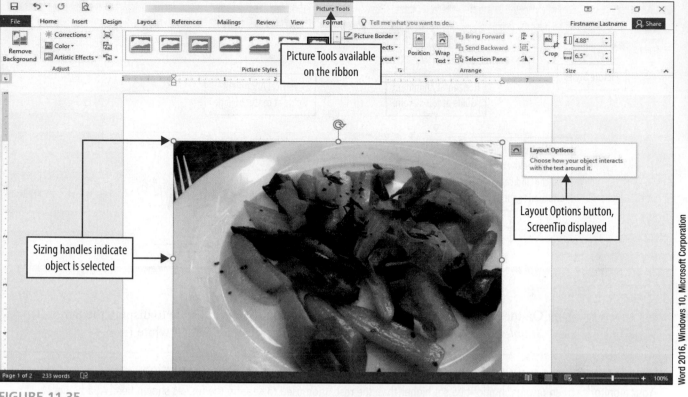

Sizing handles indicate object is selected

Picture Tools available on the ribbon

Layout Options button, ScreenTip displayed

Layout Options
Choose how your object interacts with the text around it.

Word 2016, Windows 10, Microsoft Corporation

FIGURE 11.35

6 With the image selected, click **Layout Options** 🖼, and then under **With Text Wrapping**, in the second row, click the first layout—**Top and Bottom**.

7 On the ribbon, with the **Picture Tools Format tab** active, at the right, in the **Size group**, click in the **Shape Height** box 🔲 to select the existing text. Type **2** and press Enter.

8 Point to the image to display the 🔀 pointer, hold down the left mouse button to display a green line at the left margin, and then drag the image to the right and slightly upward until a green line displays in the center of the image and at the top of the image, as shown in Figure 11.36, and then release the left mouse button. If you are not satisfied with your result, on the Quick Access Toolbar, click Undo 🔄 and begin again.

Alignment guides are green lines that display to help you align objects with margins or at the center of a page.

Inserted pictures anchor—attach to—the paragraph at the insertion point location—as indicated by an anchor symbol.

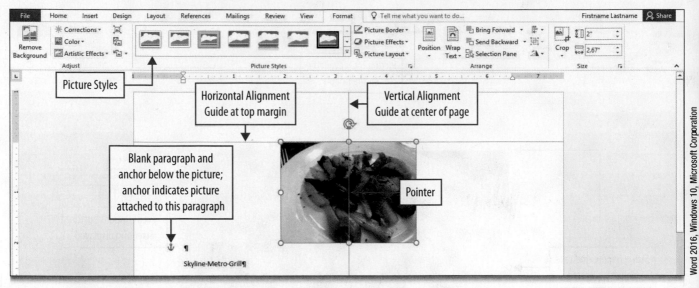

FIGURE 11.36

> **9** On the ribbon, in the **Picture Styles group**, point to the first style to display the ScreenTip *Simple Frame, White*, and notice that the image displays with a white frame.

<table>
<tr><td>**N O T E**</td><td>**The Size of Groups on the Ribbon Varies with Screen Resolution**</td></tr>
</table>

Your monitor's screen resolution might be set higher than the resolution used to capture the figures shown here. At a higher resolution, the ribbon expands some groups to show more commands than are available with a single click, such as those in the Picture Styles group. Or, the group expands to add descriptive text to some buttons, such as those in the Arrange group. Regardless of your screen resolution, all Office commands are available to you. In higher resolutions, you will have a more robust view of the ribbon commands.

> **10** Watch the image as you point to the second picture style, and then to the third, and then to the fourth.
>
> Recall that Live Preview shows the result of applying an editing or formatting change as you point to possible results—*before* you actually apply it.

> **11** In the **Picture Styles group**, click the second style—**Beveled Matte, White**—and then click anywhere outside of the image to deselect it. Notice that the Picture Tools no longer display on the ribbon. Compare your screen with Figure 11.37.
>
> Contextual tabs on the ribbon display only when you need them.

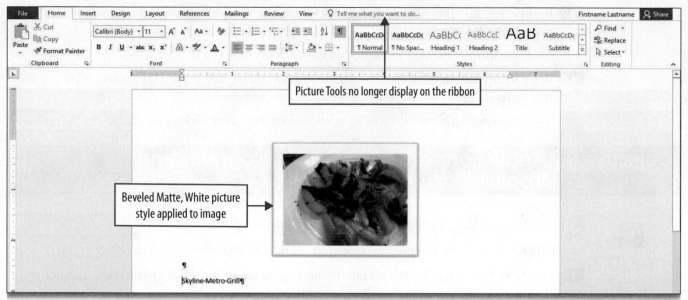

Picture Tools no longer display on the ribbon

Beveled Matte, White picture style applied to image

Skyline-Metro-Grill¶

Word 2016, Windows 10, Microsoft Corporation

FIGURE 11.37

12 On the **Quick Access Toolbar**, click **Save** 🔲 to save the changes you have made.

Activity 11.13 | Minimizing the Ribbon and Using the Keyboard to Control the Ribbon

Instead of a mouse, some individuals prefer to navigate the ribbon by using keys on the keyboard.

1 On your keyboard, press Alt, and then on the ribbon, notice that small labels display on the tabs. Press N to activate the commands on the **Insert tab**, and then compare your screen with Figure 11.38.

> Each label represents a *KeyTip*—an indication of the key that you can press to activate the command. For example, on the Insert tab, you can press F to open the Online Pictures dialog box.

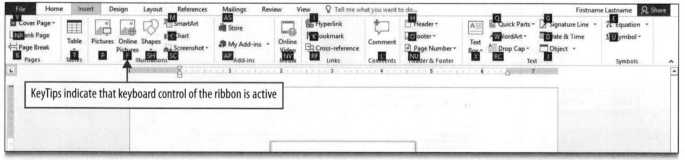

KeyTips indicate that keyboard control of the ribbon is active

Word 2016, Windows 10, Microsoft Corporation

FIGURE 11.38

2 Press Esc to redisplay the KeyTips for the tabs. Then, press Alt or Esc again to turn off keyboard control of the ribbon.

3 Point to any tab on the ribbon and right-click to display a shortcut menu.

> Here you can choose to display the Quick Access Toolbar below the ribbon or collapse the ribbon to maximize screen space. You can also customize the ribbon by adding, removing, renaming, or reordering tabs, groups, and commands, although this is not recommended until you become an expert Word user.

4 Click **Collapse the Ribbon**. Notice that only the ribbon tabs display. Click the **Home tab** to display the commands. Click anywhere in the document, and notice that the ribbon goes back to the collapsed display.

> **5** Right-click any ribbon tab, and then click **Collapse the Ribbon** again to remove the check mark from this command.

> Most expert Office users prefer the full ribbon display.

> **6** Point to any tab on the ribbon, and then on your mouse device, roll the mouse wheel. Notice that different tabs become active as you roll the mouse wheel.

> You can make a tab active by using this technique, instead of clicking the tab.

Objective 9 Apply Formatting in Office Programs and Inspect Documents

GO! Learn How
Video OF11.9

IC3
DIGITAL LITERACY
CERTIFICATION
2.01k
2.02b
2.02e (vi)

Activity 11.14 | Changing Page Orientation and Zoom Level

In this Activity, you will practice common formatting techniques used in Office applications.

> **1** On the ribbon, click the **Layout tab**. In the **Page Setup group**, click **Orientation**, and notice that two orientations display—*Portrait* and *Landscape*. Click **Landscape**.

> In *portrait orientation*, the paper is taller than it is wide. In *landscape orientation*, the paper is wider than it is tall.

> **2** In the lower right corner of the screen, locate the **Zoom slider**.

> Recall that to zoom means to increase or decrease the viewing area. You can zoom in to look closely at a section of a document, and then zoom out to see an entire page on the screen. You can also zoom to view multiple pages on the screen.

> **3** Drag the **Zoom slider** to the left until you have zoomed to approximately *60%*. Compare your screen with Figure 11.39.

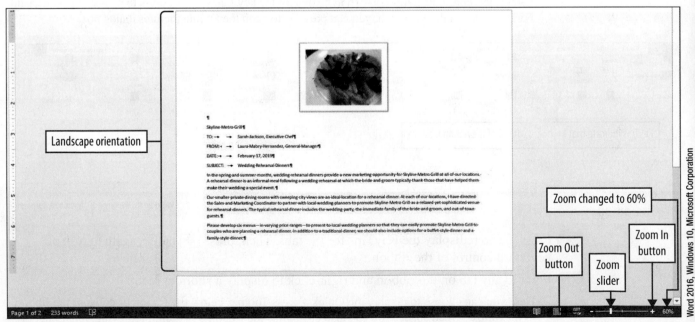

FIGURE 11.39

🔄 **BY TOUCH**   Drag the Zoom slider with your finger.

4 Use the technique you just practiced to change the **Orientation** back to **Portrait**.

The default orientation in Word is Portrait, which is commonly used for business documents such as letters and memos.

5 In the lower right corner, click the **Zoom In** button ➕ as many times as necessary to return to the **100%** zoom setting.

Use the zoom feature to adjust the view of your document for editing and for your viewing comfort.

⟳ ANOTHER WAY   You can also control Zoom from the ribbon. On the View tab, in the Zoom group, you can control the Zoom level and also zoom to view multiple pages.

6 On the **Quick Access Toolbar**, click **Save** 🖫.

More Knowledge   **Zooming to Page Width**

Some Office users prefer *Page Width*, which zooms the document so that the width of the page matches the width of the window. Find this command on the View tab, in the Zoom group.

Activity 11.15 | Formatting Text by Using Fonts, Alignment, Font Colors, and Font Styles

2.02a
2.02c

1 If necessary, on the right edge of your screen, drag the vertical scroll box to the top of the scroll bar. To the left of *Skyline Metro Grill*, point in the margin area to display the ⌐ pointer and click one time to select the entire paragraph. Compare your screen with Figure 11.40.

Use this technique to select complete paragraphs from the margin area—drag downward to select multiple-line paragraphs—which is faster and more efficient than dragging through text.

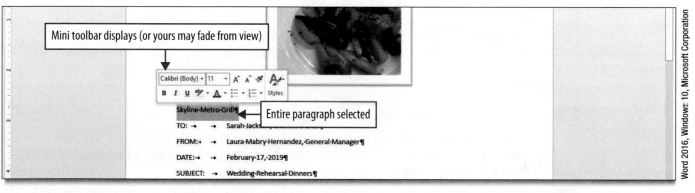

FIGURE 11.40

Word 2016, Windows 10, Microsoft Corporation

2 On the ribbon, click the **Home tab**, and then in the **Paragraph group**, click **Center** ≡ to center the paragraph.

3 On the **Home tab**, in the **Font group**, click the **Font button arrow** `Calibri (Body) ▾`. On the alphabetical list of font names, scroll down and then locate and *point to* **Cambria**.

A *font* is a set of characters with the same design and shape. The default font in a Word document is Calibri, which is a *sans serif font*—a font design with no lines or extensions on the ends of characters.

The Cambria font is a *serif font*—a font design that includes small line extensions on the ends of the letters to guide the eye in reading from left to right.

The list of fonts displays as a gallery showing potential results. For example, in the Font gallery, you can point to see the actual design and format of each font as it would look if applied to text.

4 Point to several other fonts and observe the effect on the selected text. Then, scroll back to the top of the **Font** gallery. Under **Theme Fonts**, click **Calibri Light**.

> A ***theme*** is a predesigned combination of colors, fonts, line, and fill effects that look good together and is applied to an entire document by a single selection. A theme combines two sets of fonts—one for text and one for headings. In the default Office theme, Calibri Light is the suggested font for headings.

5 With the paragraph *Skyline Metro Grill* still selected, on the **Home tab**, in the **Font group**, click the **Font Size button arrow** ⌷, point to **36**, and then notice how Live Preview displays the text in the font size to which you are pointing. Compare your screen with Figure 11.41.

FIGURE 11.41

6 On the list of font sizes, click **20**.

> Fonts are measured in ***points***, with one point equal to 1/72 of an inch. A higher point size indicates a larger font size. Headings and titles are often formatted by using a larger font size. The word *point* is abbreviated as ***pt***.

7 With *Skyline Metro Grill* still selected, on the **Home tab**, in the **Font group**, click the **Font Color button arrow** ⌷. Under **Theme Colors**, in the last column, click the last color—**Green, Accent 6, Darker 50%**. Click anywhere to deselect the text.

8 To the left of *TO:*, point in the left margin area to display the ⌷ pointer, hold down the left mouse button, drag down to select the four memo headings, and then release your mouse button. Compare your screen with Figure 11.42.

> Use this technique to select complete paragraphs from the margin area—drag downward to select multiple paragraphs—which is faster and more efficient than dragging through text.

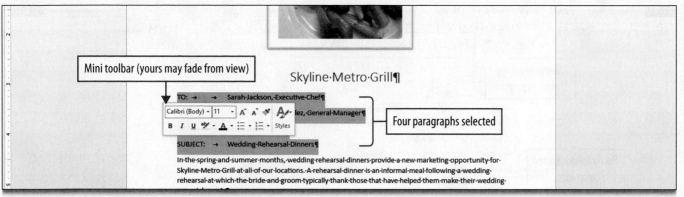

Mini toolbar (yours may fade from view)

Skyline·Metro·Grill¶

Four paragraphs selected

FIGURE 11.42

Word 2016, Windows 10, Microsoft Corporation

9 With the four paragraphs selected, on the mini toolbar, click the **Font Color** button ⬛▾, and notice that the text color of the four paragraphs changes.

The font color button retains its most recently used color—Green, Accent 6, Darker 50%. As you progress in your study of Microsoft Office, you will use other commands that behave in this manner; that is, they retain their most recently used format. This is commonly referred to as *MRU*—most recently used.

Recall that the mini toolbar places commands that are commonly used for the selected text or object close by so that you reduce the distance that you must move your mouse to access a command. If you are using a touch screen device, most commands that you need are close and easy to touch.

10 On the right edge of your screen, if necessary drag the vertical scroll box down slightly to position more of the text on the screen. Click anywhere in the paragraph that begins *In the spring*, and then *triple-click*—click the left mouse button three times—to select the entire paragraph. If the entire paragraph is not selected, click in the paragraph and begin again.

11 With the entire paragraph selected, on the mini toolbar, locate and then click the **Font Color button arrow** ⬛▾, and then under **Theme Colors**, in the sixth column, click the last color—**Orange, Accent 2, Darker 50%**.

12 In the memo headings, select the guide word **TO:** and then on the mini toolbar, click **Bold** [B] and **Italic** [I].

Font styles include bold, italic, and underline. Font styles emphasize text and are a visual cue to draw the reader's eye to important text.

13 On the mini toolbar, click **Italic** [I] again to turn off the Italic formatting.

A *toggle button* is a button that can be turned on by clicking it once, and then turned off by clicking it again.

IC3
DIGITAL LITERACY
CERTIFICATION
2.02a

Activity 11.16 | Using Format Painter

Use the Format Painter to copy the formatting of specific text or of a paragraph and then apply it in other locations in your document.

1 With TO: still selected, on the mini toolbar, click **Format Painter** 🖌. Then, move your mouse under the word *Sarah*, and notice the ▪I mouse pointer. Compare your screen with Figure 11.43.

The pointer takes the shape of a paintbrush, and contains the formatting information from the paragraph where the insertion point is positioned. Information about the Format Painter and how to turn it off displays in the status bar.

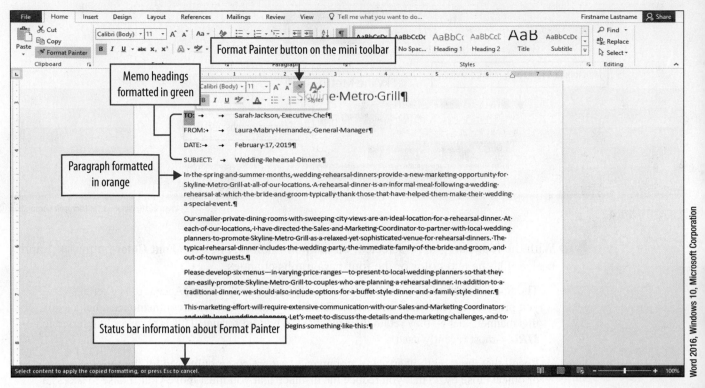

FIGURE 11.43

2 ▶ With the 📐 pointer, drag to select the guide word **FROM:** and notice that Bold formatting is applied. Then, point to the selected text *FROM:* and on the mini toolbar, *double-click* **Format Painter** 🖌️.

3 ▶ Select the guide word **DATE:** to copy the Bold formatting, and notice that the pointer retains the 📐 shape.

When you *double-click* the Format Painter button, the Format Painter feature remains active until you either click the Format Painter button again, or press Esc to cancel it—as indicated on the status bar.

4 ▶ With **Format Painter** still active, select the guide word **SUBJECT:**, and then on the ribbon, on the **Home tab**, in the **Clipboard group**, notice that **Format Painter** 🖌️ is selected, indicating that it is active. Compare your screen with Figure 11.44.

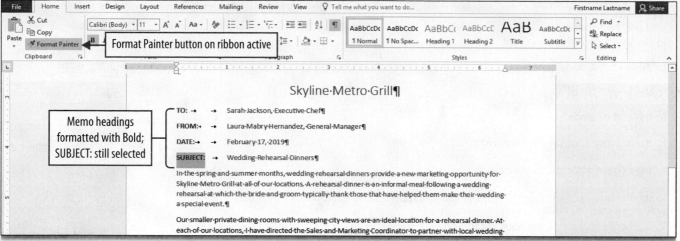

Word 2016, Windows 10, Microsoft Corporation

FIGURE 11.44

5 On the ribbon, click **Format Painter** to turn the command off.

🔄 **ANOTHER WAY**   Press Esc to turn off Format Painter.

6 In the paragraph that begins *In the spring*, triple-click again to select the entire paragraph. On the mini toolbar, click **Bold** B and **Italic** I. Click anywhere to deselect.

7 On the **Quick Access Toolbar**, click **Save** to save the changes you have made to your document.

2.01a

Activity 11.17 | Using Keyboard Shortcuts and Using the Clipboard to Copy, Cut, and Paste

The ***Clipboard*** is a temporary storage area that holds text or graphics that you select and then cut or copy. When you ***copy*** text or graphics, a copy is placed on the Clipboard and the original text or graphic remains in place. When you ***cut*** text or graphics, a copy is placed on the Clipboard, and the original text or graphic is removed—cut—from the document.

After copying or cutting, the contents of the Clipboard are available for you to ***paste***—insert—in a new location in the current document, or into another Office file.

1 On your keyboard, hold down Ctrl and press Home to move to the beginning of your document, and then take a moment to study the table in Figure 11.45, which describes similar keyboard shortcuts with which you can navigate quickly in a document.

TO MOVE	PRESS
To the beginning of a document	Ctrl + Home
To the end of a document	Ctrl + End
To the beginning of a line	Home
To the end of a line	End
To the beginning of the previous word	Ctrl + ←
To the beginning of the next word	Ctrl + →
To the beginning of the current word (if insertion point is in the middle of a word)	Ctrl + ←
To the beginning of the previous paragraph	Ctrl + ↑
To the beginning of the next paragraph	Ctrl + ↓
To the beginning of the current paragraph (if insertion point is in the middle of a paragraph)	Ctrl + ↑
Up one screen	PgUp
Down one screen	PgDn

FIGURE 11.45

2 To the left of *Skyline Metro Grill*, point in the left margin area to display the pointer, and then click one time to select the entire paragraph. On the **Home tab**, in the **Clipboard group**, click **Copy**.

Because anything that you select and then copy—or cut—is placed on the Clipboard, the Copy command and the Cut command display in the Clipboard group of commands on the ribbon. There is no visible indication that your copied selection has been placed on the Clipboard.

ANOTHER WAY   Right-click the selection, and then click Copy on the shortcut menu; or, use the keyboard shortcut Ctrl + C.

3 On the **Home tab**, in the **Clipboard group**, to the right of the group name *Clipboard*, click the **Dialog Box Launcher** button, and then compare your screen with Figure 11.46.

The Clipboard pane displays with your copied text. In any ribbon group, the *Dialog Box Launcher* displays either a dialog box or a pane related to the group of commands. It is not necessary to display the Clipboard in this manner, although sometimes it is useful to do so.

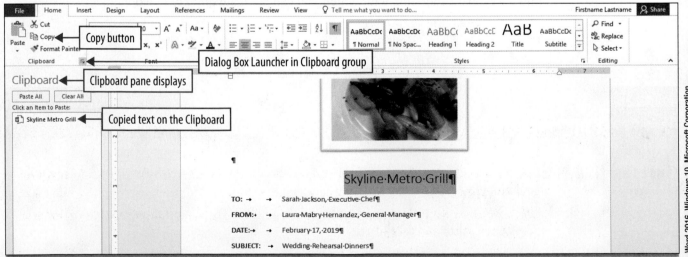

FIGURE 11.46

4 In the upper right corner of the **Clipboard** pane, click **Close** ☒.

5 Press `Ctrl` + `End` to move to the end of your document. Press `Enter` one time to create a new blank paragraph. On the **Home tab**, in the **Clipboard group**, point to **Paste**, and then click the *upper* portion of this split button.

> The Paste command pastes the most recently copied item on the Clipboard at the insertion point location. If you click the lower portion of the Paste button, a gallery of Paste Options displays. A *split button* is divided into two parts; clicking the main part of the button performs a command, and clicking the arrow displays a list or gallery with choices.

🔄 **ANOTHER WAY**   Right-click, on the shortcut menu under Paste Options, click the desired option button; or, press `Ctrl` + `V`.

6 Below the pasted text, click **Paste Options** 📋 as shown in Figure 11.47.

> Here you can view and apply various formatting options for pasting your copied or cut text. Typically you will click Paste on the ribbon and paste the item in its original format. If you want some other format for the pasted item, you can choose another format from the *Paste Options gallery*.

> The Paste Options gallery provides a Live Preview of the various options for changing the format of the pasted item with a single click. The Paste Options gallery is available in three places: on the ribbon by clicking the lower portion of the Paste button—the Paste button arrow; from the Paste Options button that displays below the pasted item following the paste operation; or on the shortcut menu if you right-click the pasted item.

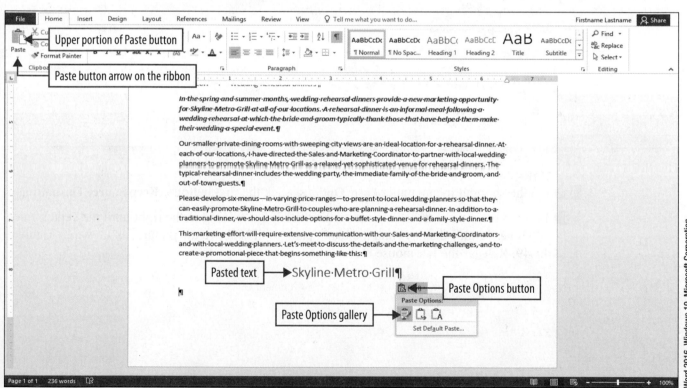

FIGURE 11.47

7 In the **Paste Options** gallery, *point* to each option to see the Live Preview of the format that would be applied if you clicked the button.

> The contents of the Paste Options gallery are contextual; that is, they change based on what you copied and where you are pasting.

8 Press [Esc] to close the gallery; the button will remain displayed until you take some other screen action.

9 On your keyboard, press [Ctrl] + [Home] to move to the top of the document, and then click the **salad image** one time to select it. While pointing to the selected image, right-click, and then on the shortcut menu, click **Cut**.

Recall that the Cut command cuts—removes—the selection from the document and places it on the Clipboard.

ANOTHER WAY   On the Home tab, in the Clipboard group, click the Cut button; or use the keyboard shortcut [Ctrl] + [X].

10 Press [Del] one time to remove the blank paragraph from the top of the document, and then press [Ctrl] + [End] to move to the end of the document.

11 With the insertion point blinking in the blank paragraph at the end of the document, right-click, and notice that the **Paste Options** gallery displays on the shortcut menu. Compare your screen with Figure 11.48.

FIGURE 11.48

12 On the shortcut menu, under **Paste Options**, click the first button—**Keep Source Formatting**.

13 Point to the picture to display the pointer, and then drag to the right until the center green **Alignment Guide** displays and the blank paragraph is above the picture, as shown in Figure 11.49. Release the left mouse button.

BY TOUCH   Drag the picture with your finger to display the Alignment Guide.

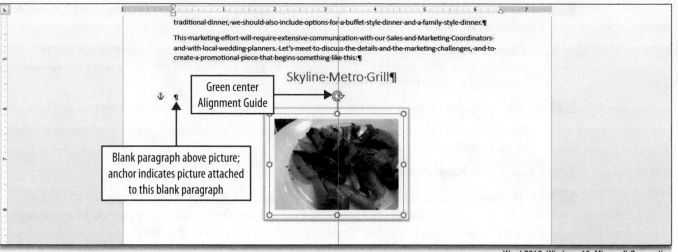

traditional·dinner,·we·should·also·include·options·for·a·buffet-style·dinner·and·a·family-style·dinner.¶

This·marketing·effort·will·require·extensive·communication·with·our·Sales·and·Marketing·Coordinators·and·with·local·wedding·planners.·Let's·meet·to·discuss·the·details·and·the·marketing·challenges,·and·to·create·a·promotional·piece·that·begins·something·like·this:¶

Skyline·Metro·Grill¶

Green center Alignment Guide

Blank paragraph above picture; anchor indicates picture attached to this blank paragraph

FIGURE 11.49

Activity 11.18 | Changing Text to WordArt and Adding Alternative Text for Accessibility

1 Above the picture, click to position the insertion point at the end of the word *Grill*, press Spacebar one time, and then type **for Your Rehearsal Dinner**

2 Select the text *Skyline Metro Grill for Your Rehearsal Dinner*, and then on the **Insert tab**, in the **Text group**, click **Insert WordArt** [4·].

> *WordArt* is an Office feature available in Word, Excel, and PowerPoint that enables you to change normal text into decorative stylized text.

3 In the displayed gallery, use the ScreenTips to locate and then click **Fill - Gold, Accent 4, Soft Bevel**.

4 With the WordArt surrounded with a solid line, on the **Home tab**, in the **Font group**, change the font size to **16**.

5 Point to the solid line surrounding the WordArt to display the [⊹] pointer, and then drag the WordArt slightly to the right until the green center alignment guides display, as shown in Figure 11.50, and then release the mouse button to center the WordArt above your picture. Click outside of the WordArt to deselect.

traditional·dinner,·we·should·also·include·options·for·a·buffet-style·dinner·and·a·family-style·dinner.¶

This·marketing·effort·will·require·extensive·communication·with·our·Sales·and·Marketing·Coordinators·and·with·local·wedding·planners.·Let's·meet·to·discuss·the·details·and·the·marketing·challenges,·and·to·create·a·promotional·piece·that·begins·something·like·this:¶

New heading → Skyline·Metro·Grill·for·Your·Rehearsal·Dinner¶

FIGURE 11.50

6 Point to the picture of the salad and right-click. On the shortcut menu, click **Format Picture**.

7 In the **Format Picture** pane that displays on the right, under **Format Picture**, click **Layout & Properties** ⊞, and then click **Alt Text**.

> *Alternative text* helps people using a *screen reader*, which is software that enables visually impaired users to read text on a computer screen to understand the content of pictures. *Alt text* is the term commonly used for this feature.

8 As the Title, type **Salad** and as the Description, type **Picture of salad on a plate**

> Anyone viewing the document with a screen reader will see the alternative text displayed instead of the picture.

9 Close ✕ the **Format Picture** pane.

10 On the **Insert tab**, in the **Header & Footer group**, click **Footer**. At the bottom of the list, click **Edit Footer**, and then with the **Header & Footer Tools Design tab** active, in the **Insert group**, click **Document Info**. Click **File Name** to add the file name to the footer.

11 On the right end of the ribbon, click **Close Header and Footer**.

12 On the **Quick Access Toolbar**, point to the **Print Preview and Print icon** 🔍 you placed there, right-click, and then click **Remove from Quick Access Toolbar**.

> If you are working on your own computer and you want to do so, you can leave the icon on the toolbar; in a college lab, you should return the software to its original settings.

13 Click **Save** 💾 and then click the **File tab** to display **Backstage** view. With the **Info tab** active, in the lower right corner, click **Show All Properties**. As **Tags**, type **weddings, rehearsal dinners, marketing**

14 As the **Subject**, type your course name and number—for example, *CIS 10, #5543*. Under **Related People**, be sure your name displays as the author (edit it if necessary), and then on the left, click **Print** to display the Print Preview. Compare your screen with Figure 11.51.

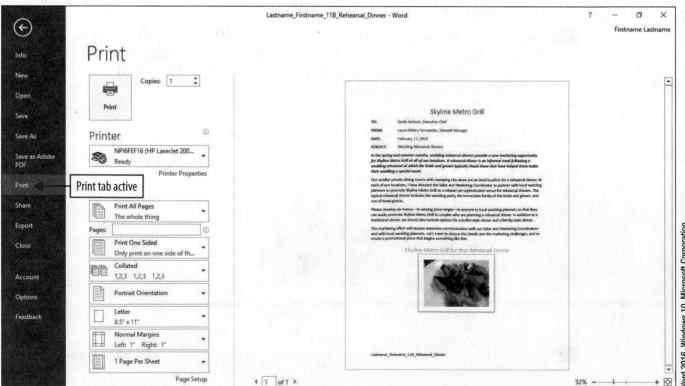

FIGURE 11.51

15 On the left side of **Backstage** view, click **Save**. In the upper right corner of the Word window, click **Close** ☒. If a message indicates *Do you want to keep the last item you copied?* click **No**.

> This message displays if you have copied some type of image to the Clipboard. If you click Yes, the items on the Clipboard will remain for you to use in another program or document.

16 As directed by your instructor, create and submit a paper printout or an electronic image of your document that looks like a printed document; or, submit your completed Word file. If necessary, refer to Activity 11.08 in Project 11A.

Activity 11.19 | Inspecting a Document

Word, Excel, and PowerPoint all have the same commands to inspect a file before sharing it.

1 If necessary, open your **Lastname_Firstname_11B_Rehearsal_Dinner** document.

2 Click the **File tab**, on the left, if necessary, click **Info**, and then on the right, click **Check for Issues**.

3 On the list, click **Inspect Document**.

> The *Inspect Document* command searches your document for hidden data or personal information that you might not want to share publicly. This information could reveal company details that should not be shared.

4 In the lower right corner of the **Document Inspector** dialog box, click **Inspect**.

> The Document Inspector runs and lists information that was found and that you could choose to remove.

5 Click **Close**, click **Check for Issues** again, and then click **Check Accessibility**.

> The *Check Accessibility* command checks the document for content that people with disabilities might find difficult to read. The Accessibility Checker pane displays on the right and lists two objects that might require attention: a text box (your WordArt) and your picture.

6 **Close** ☒ the **Accessibility Checker** pane, and then click the **File tab**.

7 Click **Check for Issues**, and then click **Check Compatibility**.

> The *Check Compatibility* command checks for features in your document that may not be supported by earlier versions of the Office program. This is only a concern if you are sharing documents with individuals with older software.

8 Click **OK**. Leave your Word document displayed for the next Activity.

Activity 11.20 | Inserting a Bookmark

A *bookmark* identifies a word, section, or place in your document so that you can find it quickly without scrolling. This is especially useful in a long document.

1 In the paragraph that begins *Please develop*, select the text *six menus*.

2 On the **Insert tab**, in the **Links group**, click **Bookmark**.

3 In the Bookmark name box, type **menus** and then click **Add**.

4 Press Ctrl + Home to move to the top of your document.

5 Press Ctrl + G, which is the keyboard shortcut for the Go To command.

6 Under **Go to what**, click **Bookmark**, and then with menus selected, click **Go To**. **Close** the **Find and Replace** dialog box, and notice that your bookmarked text is selected for you.

7 **Close** ☒ Word, and then click **Save**. Close any open windows.

GO! Learn How
Video OF11.10

A ***compressed file*** is a file that has been reduced in size. Compressed files take up less storage space and can be transferred to other computers faster than uncompressed files. You can also combine a group of files into one compressed folder, which makes it easier to share a group of files.

Within each Office program, you will see the ***Tell Me*** feature at the right end of the ribbon tabs, which is a search feature for Microsoft Office commands that you activate by typing what you are looking for in the Tell Me box.

Another method to get help with an Office command is to point to the command on the ribbon, and then at the bottom of the displayed ScreenTip, click Tell me more, which will display step-by-step assistance.

Activity 11.21 | Compressing Files

In this Activity, you will combine the two files you created in this chapter into one compressed file.

1 On the Windows taskbar, click **File Explorer** 📁. On the left, in the **navigation pane**, navigate to your storage location, and then open your **Office Features Chapter 11** folder. If you have been using this folder, it might appear under Quick access. Compare your screen with Figure 11.52.

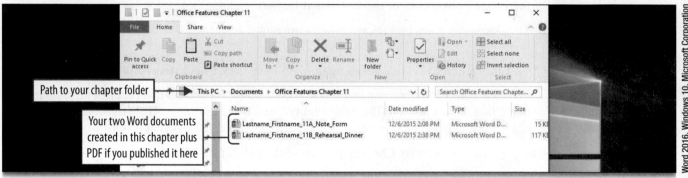

FIGURE 11.52

2 In the **file list**, click your **Lastname_Firstname_11A_Note_Form** Word file one time to select it. Then, hold down Ctrl, and click your **Lastname_Firstname_11B_Rehearsal_Dinner** file to select both files in the list.

In any Windows-based program, holding down Ctrl while selecting enables you to select multiple items.

3 On the **File Explorer** ribbon, click **Share**, and then in the **Send group**, click **Zip**. Compare your screen with Figure 11.53.

Windows creates a compressed folder containing a *copy* of each of the selected files. The folder name is selected—highlighted in blue—so that you can rename it. The default folder name is usually the name of the first file in the group that you select.

🔄 **BY TOUCH**   Tap the ribbon commands.

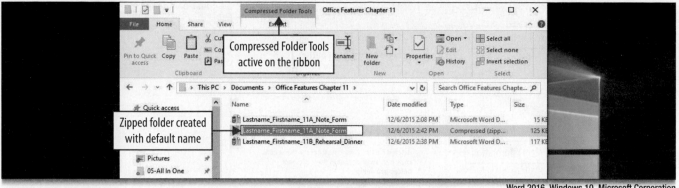

FIGURE 11.53

Word 2016, Windows 10, Microsoft Corporation

♻ ANOTHER WAY   Point to the selected files in the File List, right-click, point to Send to, and then click Compressed (zipped) folder.

4 ▶ With the folder name selected—highlighted in blue—using your own name, type **Lastname_Firstname_Office_Features_Chapter_11** and press Enter.

The compressed folder is ready to attach to an email or share in some other format.

5 ▶ In the upper right corner of the folder window, click **Close** ×.

Activity 11.22 | Using Microsoft Office Tell Me and Tell Me More to Get Help

In this Activity, you will use Tell Me to find information about formatting currency in Excel.

1 ▶ Start Excel and open a **Blank workbook**. With cell **A1** active, type **456789** and press Enter. Click cell **A1** again to make it the active cell.

2 ▶ At the top of the screen, click in the **Tell me what you want to do** box, and then type **format as currency** In the displayed list, point to **Accounting Number Formats**, and then click **$ English (United States)**.

As you type, every keystroke refines the results so that you can click the command as soon as it displays. This feature helps you apply the command immediately; it does not explain how to locate the command.

3 ▶ On the **Home tab**, in the **Alignment group**, *point to* **Merge & Center**, and then at the bottom of the displayed ScreenTip, click **Tell me more**. At the right edge of the displayed **Excel 2016 Help** window, use the scroll bar to scroll about halfway down the window, and then compare your screen with Figure 11.54.

The *Tell me more* feature opens the Office online Help system with explanations about how to perform the task.

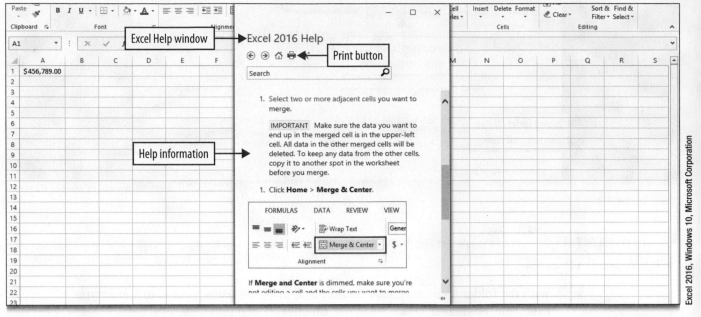

FIGURE 11.54

4 ▶ If you want to do so, at the top of the **Excel Help** window, click Print 🖶 to print a copy of this information for your reference.

5 ▶ In the upper right corner of the Help window, click **Close** ☒.

6 ▶ Leave Excel open for the next Activity.

Objective 11 | Install Apps for Office and Create a Microsoft Account

ALERT!	Working with Web-Based Applications and Services

Computer programs and services on the web receive continuous updates and improvements. Thus, the steps to complete the following web-based activities may differ from the ones shown. You can often look at the screens and the information presented to determine how to complete the Activity.

GO! Learn How
Video OF11.11

Apps for Office are a collection of downloadable apps that enable you to create and view information within your familiar Office programs. Apps for Office combine cloud services and web technologies within the user interface of Office. Some of these apps are developed by Microsoft, but many more are developed by specialists in different fields. As new apps are developed, they will be available from the online *Office Store*—a public marketplace that Microsoft hosts and regulates on Office.com.

A *task pane app* works side-by-side with an Office document by displaying a separate pane on the right side of the window. For example, a task pane app can look up and retrieve product information from a web service based on the product name or part number selected in the document.

A *content app* integrates web-based features as content within the body of a document. For example, in Excel, you can use an app to look up and gather search results for a new apartment by placing the information in an Excel worksheet, and then use maps to determine the distance of each apartment to work and to family members. *Mail apps* display next to an Outlook item. For example, a mail app could detect a purchase order number in an email message and then display information about the order or the customer.

Activity 11.23 | Installing Apps for Office

1 With cell **A1** active, on your keyboard, press [Delete] to clear the cell. On the Excel ribbon, click the **Insert tab**. In the **Add-ins group**, click **Store**.

2 In the **Office Add-ins** dialog box, in the upper right, click in the **Search the Office Store** box, type **bing maps** and then press [Enter].

3 Click the **Bing logo**, and then in the lower right corner, click **Trust It**.

4 If necessary, click Update. On the Welcome message, click **Insert Sample Data**.

Here, the Bing map displays information related to the sample data—this is a *content app*. Each city in the sample data displays a small pie chart that represents the two sets of data—revenue and expenses. Compare your screen with Figure 11.55.

This is just one example of many apps downloadable from the Office Store.

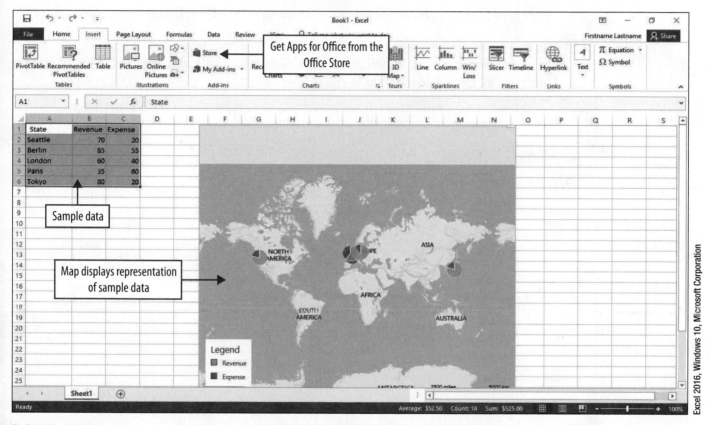

FIGURE 11.55

5 In the upper right corner of your screen, **Close** [×] Excel without saving.

Activity 11.24 | Creating a Microsoft Account

ALERT! This is an optional activity.

You will find both Windows and Office to be much more useful if you sign in with a Microsoft account. If you already have an email account from **msn.com**, **hotmail.com**, **live.com**, or **outlook.com**, then you already have a Microsoft account. If you do not, you can create a free Microsoft account by following the steps in this Activity.

In Windows 8 and Windows 10, you can use a Microsoft account to sign in to *any* Windows PC. Signing in with a Microsoft account is recommended because you can:

- Download Windows apps from the Windows Store.
- Get your online content—email, social network updates, updated news—automatically displayed in an app when you sign in.
- Synch settings online to make every Windows computer you use look and feel the same.
- Sign in to Office so that you can store documents on your OneDrive.

1 Use an Internet search engine to search for **create a microsoft account** or go to **signup.live.com** and at the bottom, click **Sign up now**. You will see a screen similar to Figure 11.56. Complete the form to create your account.

You can use any email address that you currently have for your Microsoft account. Or, on this screen, you can create a new outlook.com account.

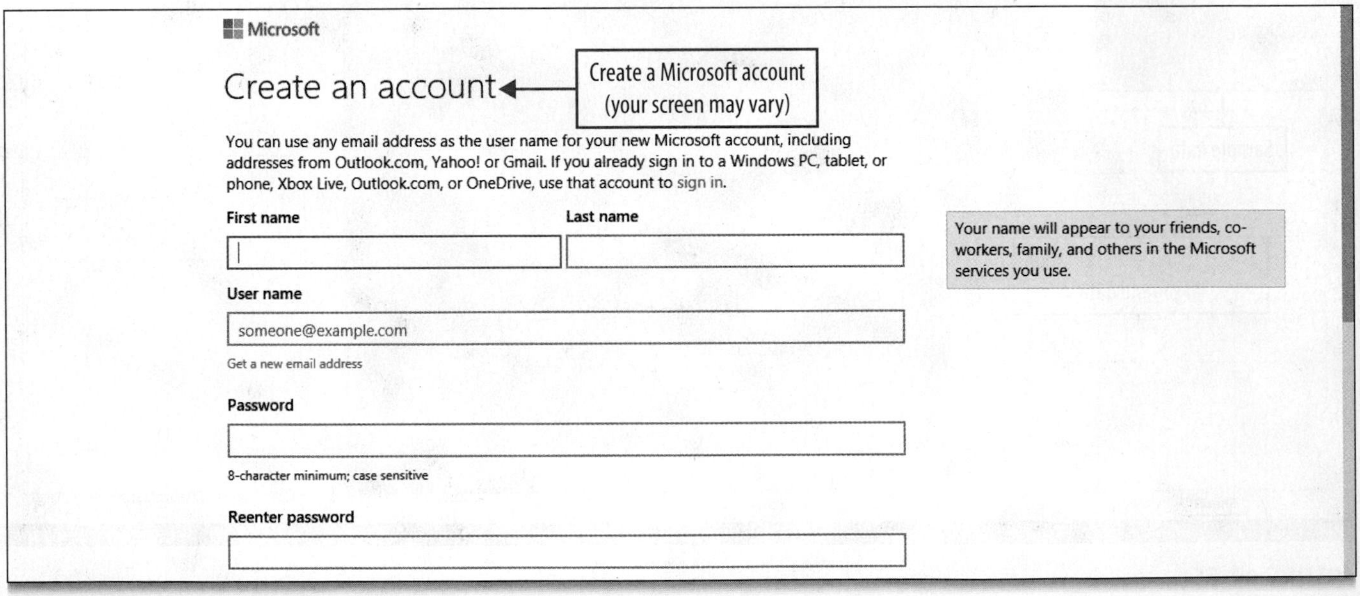

FIGURE 11.56

END | You have completed Project 11B

IC3 SKILLS IN THIS CHAPTER

IC3 — Key Applications

Project 11A

Section 2.01 Common Features
- (c) Know how to use spell check
- (f) Be able to select text or cells
- (g) Be able to redo and undo
- (j) Understand what protected mode means

Section 2.02 Word Processing
- (a) Perform basic formatting skills
- (d) Create and save files
- (e) Know page layout concepts
  - (iv) Alignment, text in paragraphs and tables
  - (v) Tabs and rulers
  - (vi) Orientation
- (f) Know how to print a word processing document

Project 11B

Section 2.01 Common Features
- (a) Know copy, cut, and paste keyboard equivalents
  - (i) Know the read-only view
- (k) Be able to use the zoom feature

Section 2.02 Word Processing
- (a) Perform basic formatting skills
- (b) Adjust margins, page sizes, and page orientation
- (c) Alter text and font styles

BUILD YOUR E-PORTFOLIO

An E-Portfolio is a collection of evidence, stored electronically, that showcases what you have accomplished while completing your education. Collecting and then sharing your work products with potential employers reflects your academic and career goals. Your completed documents from the following projects are good examples to show what you have learned: 11A and 11B.

END OF CHAPTER

SUMMARY

Many Office features and commands, such as accessing the Open and Save As dialog boxes, performing commands from the ribbon and from dialog boxes, and using the Clipboard, are the same in all Office desktop apps.

A desktop app is installed on your computer and requires a computer operating system such as Microsoft Windows or Apple's Mac OS-X to run. The programs in Microsoft Office 2016 are considered to be desktop apps.

An app refers to a self-contained program usually designed for a single purpose and that runs on smartphones and other mobile devices— for example, looking at sports scores or booking a flight on a particular airline.

Within an Office app, you can add Apps for Office from the Office Store, which combine cloud services and web technologies within the Office user interface. Apps can be task pane apps, content apps, or mail apps.

GO! LEARN IT ONLINE

Review the concepts, key terms, and IC3 skills in this chapter by completing these online challenges, which you can find at **MyITLab**.

Matching and Multiple Choice: Answer matching and multiple choice questions to test what you learned in this chapter.

Lessons on the GO!: Learn how to use all the new apps and features as they are introduced by Microsoft.

IC3 Prep Quiz: Answer questions to review the IC3 skills that you practiced in this chapter.

GLOSSARY

GLOSSARY OF CHAPTER KEY TERMS

Alignment The placement of text or objects relative to the left and right margins.

Alignment guides Green lines that display when you move an object to assist in alignment.

Alt text Another name for alternative text.

Alternative text Text added to a picture or object that helps people using a screen reader understand what the object is.

App A self-contained program usually designed for a single purpose and that runs on smartphones and other mobile devices.

Apps for Office A collection of downloadable apps that enable you to create and view information within Office programs, and that combine cloud services and web technologies within the user interface of Office.

Backstage tabs The area along the left side of Backstage view with tabs to display screens with related groups of commands.

Backstage view A centralized space for file management tasks; for example, opening, saving, printing, publishing, or sharing a file. A navigation pane displays along the left side with tabs that group file-related tasks together.

Bookmark A command that identifies a word, section, or place in a document so that you can find it quickly without scrolling.

Center alignment The alignment of text or objects that is centered horizontally between the left and right margin.

Check Accessibility A command that checks the document for content that people with disabilities might find difficult to read.

Check Compatibility A command that searches your document for features that may not be supported by older versions of Office.

Clipboard A temporary storage area that holds text or graphics that you select and then cut or copy.

Cloud computing Applications and services that are accessed over the Internet, rather than accessing applications that are installed on your local computer.

Cloud storage Online storage of data so that you can access your data from different places and devices.

Collaborate To work with others as a team in an intellectual endeavor to complete a shared task or to achieve a shared goal.

Commands Instructions to a computer program that cause an action to be carried out.

Compressed file A file that has been reduced in size and thus takes up less storage space and can be transferred to other computers quickly.

Content app An app for Office that integrates web-based features as content within the body of a document.

Context menus Menus that display commands and options relevant to the selected text or object; also called *shortcut menus*.

Context-sensitive commands Commands that display on a shortcut menu that relate to the object or text that you right-clicked.

Contextual tabs Tabs that are added to the ribbon automatically when a specific object, such as a picture, is selected, and that contain commands relevant to the selected object.

Copy A command that duplicates a selection and places it on the Clipboard.

Creative Commons A nonprofit organization that enables sharing and use of images and knowledge through free legal tools.

Cut A command that removes a selection and places it on the Clipboard.

Default The term that refers to the current selection or setting that is automatically used by a computer program unless you specify otherwise.

Deselect The action of canceling the selection of an object or block of text by clicking outside of the selection.

Desktop app A computer program that is installed on your PC and requires a computer operating system such as Microsoft Windows; also known as a *desktop application*.

Desktop application A computer program that is installed on your PC and requires a computer operating system such as Microsoft Windows; also known as a *desktop app*.

Dialog Box Launcher A small icon that displays to the right of some group names on the ribbon and that opens a related dialog box or pane providing additional options and commands related to that group.

Document properties Details about a file that describe or identify it, including the title, author name, subject, and keywords that identify the document's topic or contents; also known as *metadata*.

Drag The action of holding down the left mouse button while moving your mouse.

Edit The process of making changes to text or graphics in an Office file.

Ellipsis A set of three dots indicating incompleteness; an ellipsis following a command name indicates that a dialog box will display if you click the command.

Enhanced ScreenTip A ScreenTip that displays more descriptive text than a normal ScreenTip.

Fill The inside color of an object.

Font A set of characters with the same design and shape.

Font styles Formatting emphasis such as bold, italic, and underline.

Footer A reserved area for text or graphics that displays at the bottom of each page in a document.

Formatting The process of establishing the overall appearance of text, graphics, and pages in an Office file—for example, in a Word document.

Formatting marks Characters that display on the screen, but do not print, indicating where the Enter key, the Spacebar, and the Tab key were pressed; also called *nonprinting characters*.

Gallery An Office feature that displays a list of potential results instead of just the command name.

Gradient fill A fill effect in which one color fades into another.

Groups On the Office ribbon, the sets of related commands that you might need for a specific type of task.

Header A reserved area for text or graphics that displays at the top of each page in a document.

Info tab The tab in Backstage view that displays information about the current file.

Insertion point A blinking vertical line that indicates where text or graphics will be inserted.

Inspect Document A command that searches your document for hidden data or personal information that you might not want to share publicly.

Keyboard shortcut A combination of two or more keyboard keys, used to perform a task that would otherwise require a mouse.

KeyTip The letter that displays on a command in the ribbon and that indicates the key you can press to activate the command when keyboard control of the ribbon is activated.

Keywords Custom file properties in the form of words that you associate with a document to give an indication of the document's content; used to help find and organize files. Also called *tags*.

Landscape orientation A page orientation in which the paper is wider than it is tall.

Layout Options A button that displays when an object is selected and that has commands to choose how the object interacts with surrounding text.

Live Preview A technology that shows the result of applying an editing or formatting change as you point to possible results—*before* you actually apply it.

Location Any disk drive, folder, or other place in which you can store files and folders.

Mail app An app for Office that displays next to an Outlook item.

Metadata Details about a file that describe or identify it, including the title, author name, subject, and keywords that identify the document's topic or contents; also known as *document properties*.

Mini toolbar A small toolbar containing frequently used formatting commands that displays as a result of selecting text or objects.

MRU Acronym for *most recently used*, which refers to the state of some commands that retain the characteristic most recently applied; for example, the Font Color button retains the most recently used color until a new color is chosen.

Nonprinting characters Characters that display on the screen, but do not

print, indicating where the Enter key, the Spacebar, and the Tab key were pressed; also called *formatting marks*.

Object A text box, picture, table, or shape that you can select and then move and resize.

Office 365 A version of Microsoft Office to which you subscribe for an annual fee.

Office Store A public marketplace that Microsoft hosts and regulates on Office.com.

OneDrive Microsoft's free cloud storage for anyone with a free Microsoft account.

Open dialog box A dialog box from which you can navigate to, and then open on your screen, an existing file that was created in that same program.

Option button In a dialog box, a round button that enables you to make one choice among two or more options.

Options dialog box A dialog box within each Office application where you can select program settings and other options and preferences.

Page Width A view that zooms the document so that the width of the page matches the width of the window. Find this command on the View tab, in the Zoom group.

Paragraph symbol The symbol ¶ that represents the end of a paragraph.

Paste The action of placing text or objects that have been copied or cut from one location to another location.

Paste Options gallery A gallery of buttons that provides a Live Preview of all the Paste options available in the current context.

PDF The acronym for *Portable Document Format*, which is a file format that creates an image that preserves the look of your file, but that cannot be easily changed; a popular format for sending documents electronically, because the document will display on most computers.

Pointer Any symbol that displays on your screen in response to moving your mouse.

Points A measurement of the size of a font; there are 72 points in an inch.

Portable Document Format A file format that creates an image that preserves the look of your file, but that cannot be easily changed; a popular format for sending documents electronically, because the document

will display on most computers; also called a *PDF*.

Portrait orientation A page orientation in which the paper is taller than it is wide.

Print Preview A view of a document as it will appear when you print it.

Protected View A security feature in Office 2016 that protects your computer from malicious files by opening them in a restricted environment until you enable them; you might encounter this feature if you open a file from an email or download files from the Internet.

pt The abbreviation for *point*; for example, when referring to a font size.

Quick Access Toolbar In an Office program window, the small row of buttons in the upper left corner of the screen from which you can perform frequently used commands.

Read-only A property assigned to a file that prevents the file from being modified or deleted; it indicates that you cannot save any changes to the displayed document unless you first save it with a new name.

Right-click The action of clicking the right mouse button one time.

Sans serif font A font design with no lines or extensions on the ends of characters.

Screen reader Software that enables visually impaired users to read text on a computer screen to understand the content of pictures.

ScreenTip A small box that that displays useful information when you perform various mouse actions such as pointing to screen elements or dragging.

Selecting Highlighting, by dragging with your mouse, areas of text or data or graphics, so that the selection can be edited, formatted, copied, or moved.

Serif font A font design that includes small line extensions on the ends of the letters to guide the eye in reading from left to right.

Share button Opens the Share pane from which you can save your file to the cloud—your OneDrive—and then share it with others so you can collaborate.

SharePoint Collaboration software with which people in an organization can set up team sites to share information, manage documents, and publish reports for others to see.

Shortcut menu A menu that displays commands and options relevant to the selected text or object; also called a *context menu*.

Sizing handles Small squares or circles that indicate a picture or object is selected.

Split button A button divided into two parts and in which clicking the main part of the button performs a command and clicking the arrow opens a menu with choices.

Status bar The area along the lower edge of an Office program window that displays file information on the left and buttons to control how the window looks on the right.

Style A group of formatting commands, such as font, font size, font color, paragraph alignment, and line spacing that can be applied to a paragraph with one command.

Synchronization The process of updating computer files that are in two or more locations according to specific rules—also called *syncing*.

Syncing The process of updating computer files that are in two or more locations according to specific rules—also called *synchronization*.

Tabs (ribbon) On the Office ribbon, the name of each task-oriented activity area.

Tags Custom file properties in the form of words that you associate with a document to give an indication of the document's content; used to help find and organize files. Also called *keywords*.

Task pane app An app for Office that works side-by-side with an Office document by displaying a separate pane on the right side of the window.

Tell Me A search feature for Microsoft Office commands that you activate by typing what you are looking for in the Tell Me box.

Tell me more A prompt within a ScreenTip that opens the Office online Help system with explanations about how to perform the command referenced in the ScreenTip.

Template A preformatted document that you can use as a starting point and then change to suit your needs.

Theme A predesigned combination of colors, fonts, and effects that looks good together and is applied to an entire document by a single selection.

Title bar The bar at the top edge of the program window that indicates the name of the current file and the program name.

Toggle button A button that can be turned on by clicking it once, and then turned off by clicking it again.

Toolbar In a folder window, a row of buttons with which you can perform common tasks, such as changing the view of your files and folders.

Triple-click The action of clicking the left mouse button three times in rapid succession.

Trusted Documents A security feature in Office that remembers which files you have already enabled; you might encounter this feature if you open a file from an email or download files from the Internet.

Windows apps An app that runs on all Windows device families—including PCs, Windows phones, Windows tablets, and the Xbox gaming system.

WordArt An Office feature in Word, Excel, and PowerPoint that enables you to change normal text into decorative stylized text.

XML Paper Specification A Microsoft file format that creates an image of your document and that opens in the XPS viewer.

XPS The acronym for XML Paper Specification—a Microsoft file format that creates an image of your document and that opens in the XPS viewer.

Zoom The action of increasing or decreasing the size of the viewing area on the screen.

Introducing Microsoft Word 2016

devrim_pine_/fotolia

Word 2016: Introduction

Content! Defined by Merriam-Webster's online dictionary as "the topic or matter treated in a written work" and also as "the principal substance (as written matter, illustrations, or music) offered by a World Wide Web site," content is what you consume when you read on paper or online, when you watch video, or when you listen to any kind of music—live or recorded.

Content is what you *create* when your own words or performances are recorded in some form. For creating content in the form of words, Microsoft Office 2016 is a great choice. Rather than just a tool for word processing, Word is now a tool for you to communicate and collaborate with others. When you want to communicate with pictures or images in your Word document, Office 2016 has many features to help you do so. You can use Microsoft Word 2016 on a Windows desktop, laptop, or tablet. If your PC is touch-enabled, you will be able to use your fingers to work with Word. For example, the ribbon expands to make it easy to tap commands and you can resize images by moving your fingers on the screen.

Best of all, Microsoft Word 2016 is integrated into the cloud. If you save your documents to your cloud-based storage that comes with any free Microsoft account, you can retrieve them from any device and continue to work with and share your documents. Enjoy learning Word 2016!

Creating Documents with Microsoft Word 2016

PROJECT 12A

OUTCOMES
Create a flyer with a picture.

OBJECTIVES

1. Create a New Document and Insert Text
2. Insert and Format Graphics
3. Insert and Modify Text Boxes and Shapes
4. Preview and Print a Document

PROJECT 12B

OUTCOMES
Format text, paragraphs, and documents.

OBJECTIVES

5. Change Document and Paragraph Layout
6. Create and Modify Lists
7. Set and Modify Tab Stops
8. Insert a SmartArt Graphic and an Online Video

IvicaNS/Fotolia

In This Chapter 🖥️ GO! to Work with Word

In this chapter, you will begin your study of Microsoft Word, one of the most popular computer software applications and one that almost everyone has a reason to use. You will use many of the tools and features in Word 2016, such as applying attractive styles to your documents. You can use Microsoft Word to perform basic word processing tasks such as writing a memo, a report, or a letter. You can also use Word to complete complex tasks, such as creating sophisticated tables, embedding graphics, writing blogs, and creating publications. Word is a program that you can learn gradually, and then add more advanced skills one at a time.

The projects in this chapter relate to **Sturgeon Point Productions**, an independent film company based in Miami with offices in Detroit and Milwaukee. The film professionals produce effective broadcast and branded content for many industries, and provide a wide array of film and video production services. Sturgeon Point Productions has won awards for broadcast advertising, business media, music videos, and social media. The mission of the company is to help clients tell their stories—whether the story is about a social issue, a new product, a geographical location, a company, or a person.

PROJECT 12A Flyer

PROJECT ACTIVITIES

In Activities 12.01 through 12.16, you will create a flyer announcing two internships for a short documentary by Sturgeon Point Productions. Your completed document will look similar to Figure 12.1.

PROJECT FILES

MyITLab grader If your instructor wants you to submit Project 12A in the MyITLab Grader system, log in to MyITLab, locate Grader Project 12A, and then download the files for this project.

For Project 12A, you will need the following files:

New blank Word document
w012A_Text
w012A_Bird

You will save your document as:

Lastname_Firstname_12A_Flyer

PROJECT RESULTS

Build From Scratch

GO!
Walk Thru
Project 12A

FIGURE 12.1 Project 12A Internship Flyer

NOTE	If You Are Using a Touchscreen
	Tap an item to click it.
	Press and hold for a few seconds to right-click; release when the information or commands displays.
	Touch the screen with two or more fingers and then pinch together to zoom out or stretch your fingers apart to zoom in.
	Slide your finger on the screen to scroll—slide left to scroll right and slide right to scroll left.
	Slide to rearrange—similar to dragging with a mouse.
	Swipe to select—slide an item a short distance with a quick movement—to select an item and bring up commands, if any.

Objective 1　Create a New Document and Insert Text

GO! Learn How
Video W12-1

When you start Word, documents you have recently opened, if any, display on the left. On the right, you can select a *template*—a preformatted document that you can use as a starting point and then change to suit your needs. If you want to start a new, blank document, you can select the blank document template. When you create a new document, you can type all of the text, or you can type some of the text and then insert additional text from another source.

Activity 12.01　Starting a New Word Document

ALERT!	To submit as an autograded project, log into MyITLab and download the files for this project, and begin with those files instead of a new blank document.

1 Start Word and then click **Blank document**. On the **Home tab**, in the **Paragraph group**, if necessary click **Show/Hide** ¶ so that it is active and the formatting marks display. If the rulers do not display, click the View tab, and then in the Show group, select the Ruler check box.

2 Type **Internships Available** and then press Enter two times. Then type the following text: **This summer, Sturgeon Point Productions will be filming a short documentary in Costa Rica about its native birds and has positions available for two interns.**

As you type, the insertion point moves to the right, and when it approaches the right margin, Word determines whether the next word in the line will fit within the established right margin. If the word does not fit, Word moves the entire word down to the next line. This is *wordwrap* and means that you press Enter *only* when you reach the end of a paragraph—it is not necessary to press Enter at the end of each line of text.

NOTE	Spacing Between Sentences

Although you might have learned to add two spaces following end-of-sentence punctuation, the common practice now is to space only one time at the end of a sentence. Be sure to press Spacebar only one time following end-of-sentence punctuation.

3 Press Spacebar and then take a moment to study the table in Figure 12.2 to become familiar with the default document settings in Microsoft Word. Compare your screen with Figure 12.3.

When you press Enter, Spacebar, or Tab on your keyboard, characters display in your document to represent these keystrokes. These characters do not print and are referred to as *formatting marks* or *nonprinting characters*. These marks will display throughout this instruction.

DEFAULT DOCUMENT SETTINGS IN A NEW WORD DOCUMENT	
SETTING	**DEFAULT FORMAT**
Font and font size	The default font is Calibri, and the default font size is 11 points.
Margins	The default left, right, top, and bottom page margins are 1 inch.
Line spacing	The default line spacing is 1.08, which provides slightly more space between lines than single spacing does.
Paragraph spacing	The default spacing after a paragraph is 8 points, which is slightly less than the height of one blank line of text.
View	The default view is Print Layout view, which displays the page borders and displays the document as it will appear when printed.

FIGURE 12.2

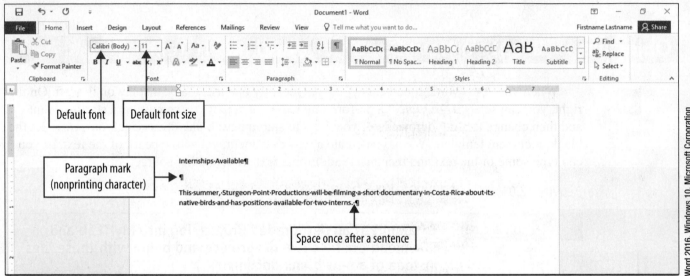

FIGURE 12.3

More Knowledge | **Word's Default Settings Are Easier to Read Online**

Until just a few years ago, word processing programs used single spacing, an extra blank paragraph to separate paragraphs, and 12 pt Times New Roman as the default formats. Now, studies show that individuals find the Word default formats described in Figure 12.2 to be easier to read online, where many documents are now viewed and read.

Activity 12.02 | Inserting Text from Another Document

1 On the ribbon, click the **Insert tab**. In the **Text group**, click the **Object button arrow**, and then click **Text from File**.

ALERT! | **Does the Object dialog box display?**

If the Object dialog box displays, you probably clicked the Object *button* instead of the Object *button arrow*. Close the Object dialog box, and then in the Text group, click the Object button arrow, as shown in Figure 12.4. Click *Text from File*, and then continue with Step 2.

---

2 In the **Insert File** dialog box, navigate to the student files that accompany this text, locate and select **w12A_Text**, and then click **Insert**. Compare your screen with Figure 12.4.

A *copy* of the text from the w12A_Text file displays at the insertion point location; the text is not removed from the original file.

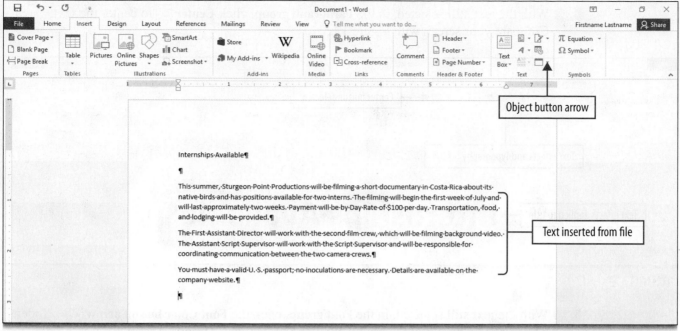

FIGURE 12.4

Word 2016, Windows 10, Microsoft Corporation

🔄 **ANOTHER WAY** Open the file, copy the required text, close the file, and then paste the text into the current document.

> **3** On the **Quick Access Toolbar**, click **Save** 🖫, and then under **Save As**, click **Browse**. Navigate to the location where you are saving your files for this chapter, and then create and open a new folder named **AIO Chapter 12** In the **File name** box, using your own name, replace the existing text with **Lastname_Firstname_12A_Flyer** and then click **Save**.

Objective 2 | Insert and Format Graphics

GO! Learn How
Video W12-2

To add visual interest to a document, insert *graphics*. Graphics include pictures, online pictures, charts, and *drawing objects*—shapes, diagrams, lines, and so on. For additional visual interest, you can apply an attractive graphic format to text; add, resize, move, and format pictures; and add a page border.

2.02a
2.02c

Activity 12.03 | Formatting Text by Using Text Effects

Text effects are decorative formats, such as shadowed or mirrored text, text glow, 3-D effects, and colors that make text stand out.

> **1** Including the paragraph mark, select the first paragraph of text—*Internships Available*. On the **Home tab**, in the **Font group**, click **Text Effects and Typography** 🅰·.

> **2** In the **Text Effects and Typography** gallery, in the third row, point to the first effect to display the ScreenTip *Fill – Black, Text 1, Outline – Background 1, Hard Shadow – Background 1*, and then click this effect.

> **3** With the text still selected, in the **Font group**, click in the **Font Size** box 11 · to select the existing font size. Type **52** and then press Enter.

> When you want to change the font size of selected text to a size that does not display in the Font Size list, type the number in the Font Size box and press Enter to confirm the new font size.

Project 12A: Flyer | **GO! All in One** 479

4 With the text still selected, in the **Paragraph group**, click **Center** ▤ to center the text. Compare your screen with Figure 12.5.

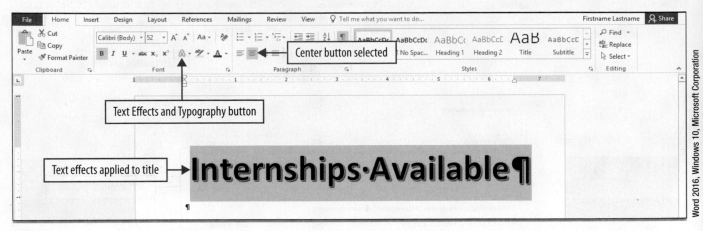

FIGURE 12.5

5 With the text still selected, in the **Font group**, click the **Font Color button arrow** ▲ ▾. Under **Theme Colors**, in the sixth column, click the first color—**Orange, Accent 2**.

6 With the text still selected, in the **Font group**, click **Text Effects and Typography** ▲ ▾. Point to **Shadow**, and then under **Outer**, in the second row, click the third style—**Offset Left**.

7 Click anywhere in the document to deselect the text, click **Save** 🖫, and then compare your screen with Figure 12.6.

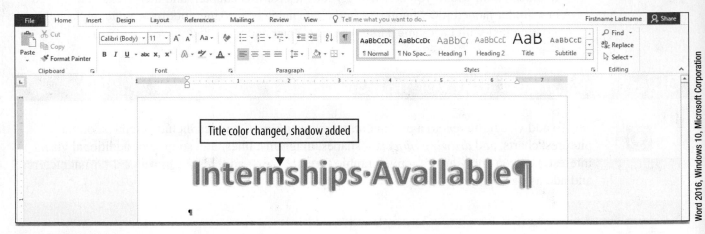

FIGURE 12.6

More Knowledge | **Clear Existing Formatting**

If you do not like your text effect, you can remove all formatting from any selected text. To do so, on the Home tab, in the Font group, click Clear All Formatting ▨.

Activity 12.04 | Inserting Pictures

1 In the paragraph that begins *This summer*, click to position the insertion point at the beginning of the paragraph.

2 On the **Insert tab**, in the **Illustrations group**, click **Pictures**. In the **Insert Picture** dialog box, navigate to your student data files, locate and click **w12A_Bird**, and then click **Insert**.

Word inserts the picture as an *inline object*; that is, the picture is positioned directly in the text at the insertion point, just like a character in a sentence. The Layout Options button displays to the right of the picture. You can change the *Layout Options* to control the manner in which text wraps around a picture or other object. Sizing handles surround the picture indicating it is selected.

3 Notice the round sizing handles around the selected picture, as shown in Figure 12.7.

The corner sizing handles resize the graphic proportionally. The center sizing handles resize a graphic vertically or horizontally only; however, sizing with these will distort the graphic. A *rotation handle*, with which you can rotate the graphic to any angle, displays above the top center sizing handle.

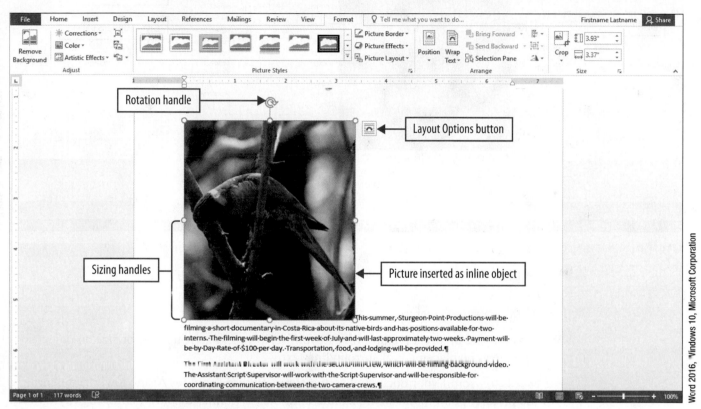

FIGURE 12.7

2.02a

Activity 12.05 | Wrapping Text Around a Picture Using Layout Options

Recall that Layout Options enable you to control *text wrapping*—the manner in which text displays around an object.

1 Be sure the picture is selected—you know it is selected if the sizing handles display.

2 To the right of the picture, click **Layout Options** 🖼 to display a gallery of text wrapping arrangements. Point to each icon layout option to view its ScreenTip.

Each icon visually depicts how text will wrap around an object.

ANOTHER WAY   On the Format tab, in the Arrange group, click Wrap Text.

3 From the gallery, under **With Text Wrapping**, click the first layout—**Square**. Compare your screen with Figure 12.8.

Select Square text wrapping when you want to wrap the text to the left or right of an image. To the left of the picture, an **object anchor** displays, indicating that the selected object is anchored to the text at this location in the document.

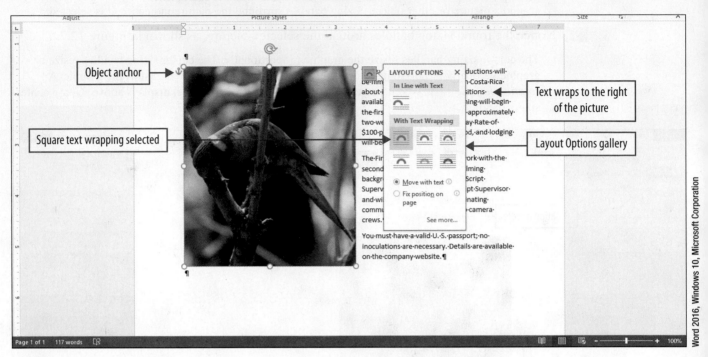

FIGURE 12.8

4 **Close** ✕ the **Layout Options**, and then **Save** 🖫 your document.

When you move or size a picture, **Live Layout** reflows text as you move or size an object so that you can view the placement of surrounding text.

1 If necessary, scroll your document so the entire picture displays. At the lower right corner of the picture, point to the sizing handle until the ⬚ pointer displays. Drag slightly upward and to the left. As you drag, a green alignment guide may display at the left margin. Compare your screen with Figure 12.9.

Alignment guides may display when you are moving or sizing a picture to help you with object placement, and Live Layout shows you how the document text will flow and display on the page.

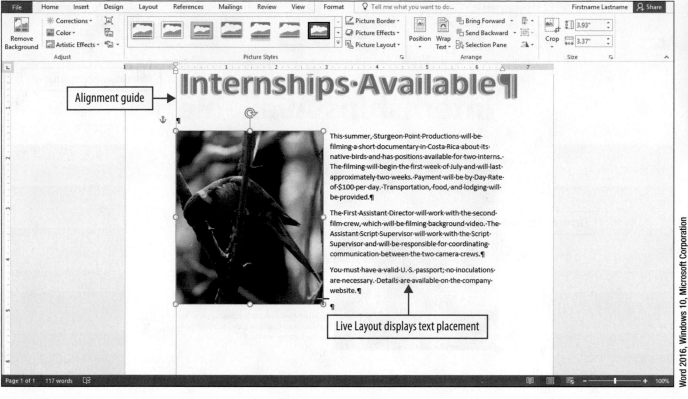

FIGURE 12.9

2 Continue to drag up and to the left until the bottom of the graphic is aligned at approximately **4 inches on the vertical ruler**. Notice that the graphic is proportionally resized.

3 On the **Quick Access Toolbar**, click **Undo** 🔄 to restore the picture to its original size.

ANOTHER WAY   On the Format tab, in the Adjust group, click Reset Picture.

4 On the ribbon, under **Picture Tools**, on the **Format tab**, in the **Size group**, click in the **Shape Height** box 🔲 0.29" ⬍. Type **3.8** and then press Enter. If necessary, scroll down to view the entire picture on your screen, and then compare your screen with Figure 12.10.

When you use the Shape Height and Shape Width boxes to change the size of a graphic, the graphic will always resize proportionally; that is, the width adjusts as you change the height and vice versa.

ANOTHER WAY   A *spin box* is a small box with an upward- and downward-pointing arrow that lets you move rapidly through a set of values by clicking. You can change the height or width of a picture object by clicking the Shape Height or Shape width spin box arrows.

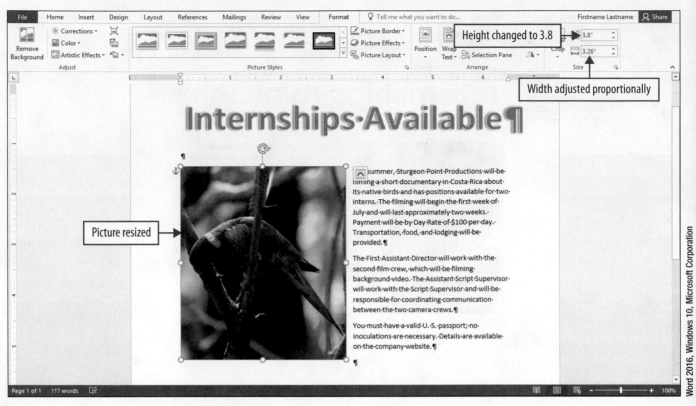

FIGURE 12.10

> **5** **Save** 🖫 your document.

Activity 12.07 | Positioning a Picture

There are two ways to move a picture in a document. You can point to the picture and then drag it to a new position. You can also change the picture settings in a dialog box, which gives you more precise control over the picture location.

> **1** Be sure the picture is selected. On the ribbon, click the **Format tab**. In the **Arrange group**, click **Position**, and then click **More Layout Options**.

> **2** In the **Layout** dialog box, be sure the **Position tab** is selected. Under **Horizontal**, click the **Alignment** option button. To the right of **Alignment**, click the **arrow**, and then click **Right**. To the right of **relative to**, click the **arrow**, and then click **Margin**.

> **3** Under **Vertical**, click the **Alignment** option button. Change the **Alignment** options to **Top relative to Line**. Compare your screen with Figure 12.11.

> > With these alignment settings, the picture will move to the right margin of the page and the top edge will align with the top of the first line of the paragraph to which it is anchored.

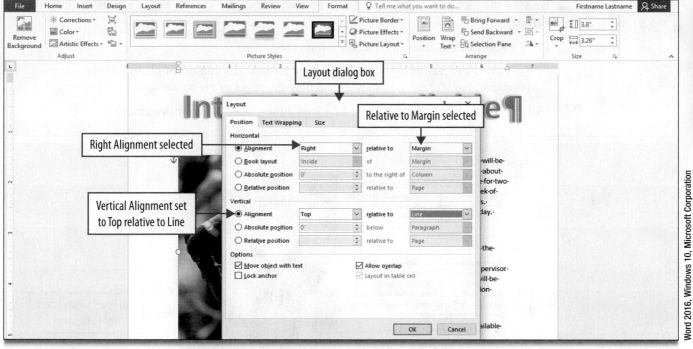

FIGURE 12.11

> **4** At the bottom of the **Layout** dialog box, click **OK**, and then on the **Quick Access Toolbar**, click **Save** 🔲. Notice that the picture moves to the right margin, and the text wraps on the left side of the picture. Compare your screen with Figure 12.12.

FIGURE 12.12

Activity 12.08 | Applying Picture Effects

Picture styles include shapes, shadows, frames, borders, and other special effects with which you can stylize an image. *Picture Effects* enhance a picture with effects such as a shadow, glow, reflection, or 3-D rotation.

1 Be sure the picture is selected. On the **Format tab**, in the **Picture Styles group**, click **Picture Effects**.

2 Point to **Soft Edges**, and then click **5 Point**.

The Soft Edges feature fades the edges of the picture. The number of points you choose determines how far the fade goes inward from the edges of the picture.

3 Compare your screen with Figure 12.13, and then **Save** 🖫 your document.

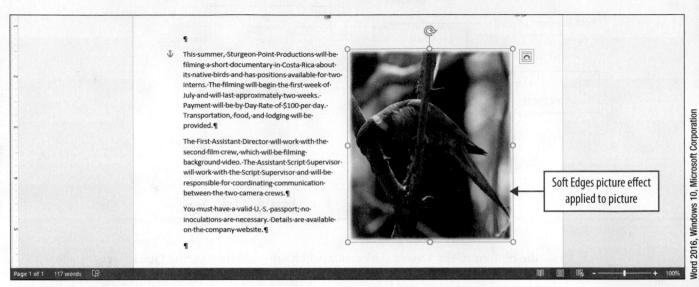

Soft Edges picture effect applied to picture

FIGURE 12.13

More Knowledge | **Applying Picture Styles**

To apply a picture style, select the picture. On the Picture Tools Format tab, in the Picture Styles group, click More, and then click the Picture Style that you want to apply.

Activity 12.09 | Applying Artistic Effects

Artistic effects are formats that make pictures look more like sketches or paintings.

1 Be sure the picture is selected. On the **Format tab**, in the **Adjust group**, click **Artistic Effects**.

2 In the first row of the gallery, point to, but do not click, the third effect—**Pencil Grayscale**.

Live Preview displays the picture with the *Pencil Grayscale* effect added.

3 In the second row of the gallery, click the third effect—**Paint Brush**. **Save** 🖫 your document, and then notice that the picture looks more like a painting than a photograph. Compare your screen with Figure 12.14.

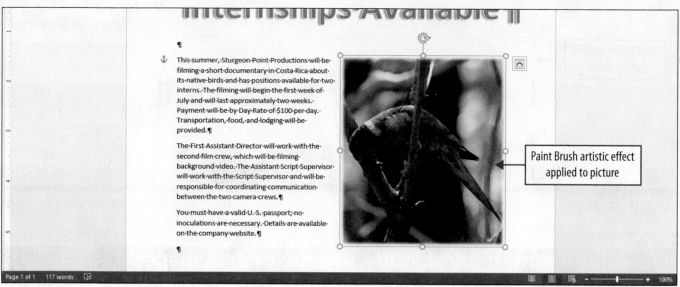

Paint Brush artistic effect applied to picture

FIGURE 12.14

2.02a

Activity 12.10 | Adding a Page Border

Page borders frame a page and help to focus the information on the page.

1 Click anywhere outside the picture to deselect it. On the **Design tab**, in the **Page Background group**, click **Page Borders**.

2 In the **Borders and Shading** dialog box, on the **Page Border tab**, under **Setting**, click **Box**. Under **Style**, scroll the list and click the seventh style—double lines.

3 Click the **Color arrow**, and then in the sixth column, click the first color—**Orange, Accent 2**.

4 Under **Apply to**, be sure *Whole document* is selected, and then compare your screen with Figure 12.15.

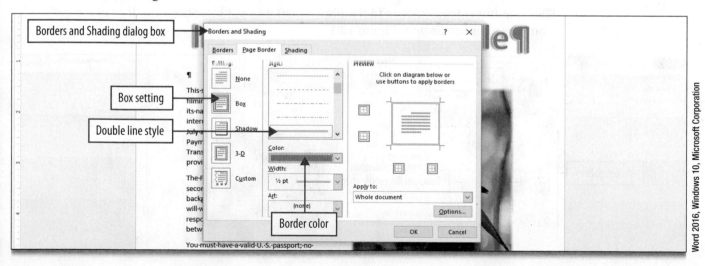

Borders and Shading dialog box

Box setting

Double line style

Border color

FIGURE 12.15

5 At the bottom of the **Borders and Shading** dialog box, click **OK**.

6 Press Ctrl + Home to move to the top of the document, click **Save** 💾, and then compare your screen with Figure 12.16.

Page border applied to document

FIGURE 12.16

Objective 3 | Insert and Modify Text Boxes and Shapes

GO! Learn How
Video W12-3

Word has predefined *shapes* and *text boxes* that you can add to your documents. A shape is an object such as a line, arrow, box, callout, or banner. A text box is a movable, resizable container for text or graphics. Use these objects to add visual interest to your document.

Activity 12.11 | Inserting, Sizing, and Positioning a Shape

1 Press ↓ one time to move to the blank paragraph below the title. Press Enter four times to create additional space for a text box, and notice that the picture anchored to the paragraph moves with the text.

2 Press Ctrl + End to move to the bottom of the document, and notice that your insertion point is positioned in the empty paragraph at the end of the document. Press Delete to remove the blank paragraph.

3 Click the **Insert tab**, and then in the **Illustrations group**, click **Shapes** to display the gallery. Compare your screen with Figure 12.17.

Shapes button

Shapes gallery

Rounded Rectangle shape

FIGURE 12.17

4 Under **Rectangles**, click the second shape—**Rounded Rectangle**, and then move your pointer. Notice that the ⊞ pointer displays.

5 Position the ⊞ pointer near the left margin at approximately **8 inches on the vertical ruler**. Click one time to insert a 1-inch by 1-inch rounded rectangle. The exact location is not important.

A blue rectangle with rounded edges displays.

6 To the right of the rectangle object, click **Layout Options** 🖾, and then at the bottom of the gallery, click **See more** to display the Layout dialog box.

🔁 **ANOTHER WAY**   On the Format tab, in the Arrange group, click Position, and then click More Layout Options.

7 In the **Layout** dialog box, under **Horizontal**, click **Alignment**. To the right of **Alignment**, click the **arrow**, and then click **Centered**. To the right of **relative to**, click the **arrow**, and then click **Page**. Under **Vertical**, select the existing number in the **Absolute position** box, and then type **1** To the right of **below**, be sure that **Paragraph** displays. Click **OK**.

> This action centers the rectangle on the page and positions the rectangle one inch below the last paragraph.

8 On the **Format tab**, click in the **Shape Height box** 🔲 0.29" ⬍ to select the existing text. Type **1.5** and then click in the **Shape Width box** 🔲 1.07" ⬍. Type **4.5** and then press ⏎.

9 Compare your screen with Figure 12.18, and then **Save** 🔲 your document.

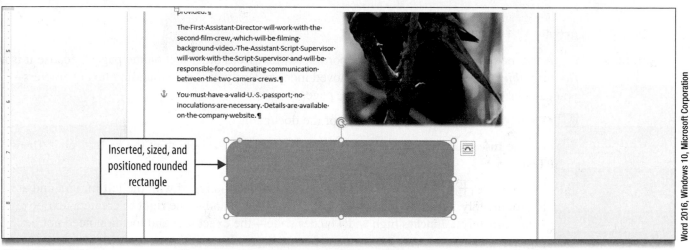

Inserted, sized, and positioned rounded rectangle

Word 2016, Windows 10, Microsoft Corporation

FIGURE 12.18

Activity 12.12 | Typing Text in a Shape and Formatting a Shape

1 If necessary, select the rectangle shape. Type **To set up an interview, apply online at:** and then press ⏎. Type **www.SturgeonPointProductions.com**

2 Press Ctrl + A to select the text you just typed. Right-click over the selected text to display the mini toolbar, and then click **Bold** B. With the text still selected, click **Increase Font Size** A˙ three times to increase the font size to **16 pt**.

> Use the keyboard shortcut Ctrl + A to select all of the text in a text box.

3 With the text still selected, on the mini toolbar, click the **Font Color button arrow**. Under **Theme Colors**, click **Black, Text 1**.

4 Click outside the shape to deselect the text. Click the border of the shape to select the shape but not the text. On the **Format tab**, in the **Shape Styles group**, click **Shape Fill**. In the sixth column, click the fourth color—**Orange, Accent 2, Lighter 40%**.

5 With the shape still selected, in the **Shape Styles group**, click **Shape Outline**. In the sixth column, click the first color—**Orange, Accent 2**. Compare your screen with Figure 12.19, and then **Save** 🔲 your document.

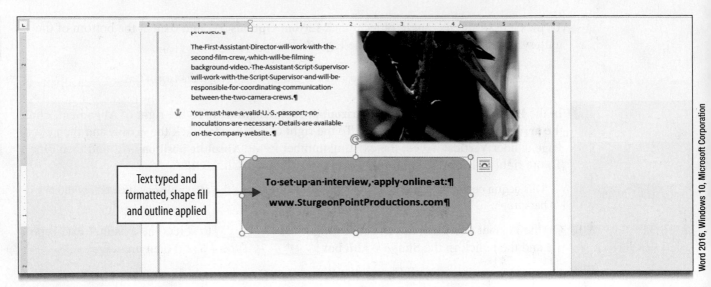

FIGURE 12.19

Activity 12.13 | Inserting a Text Box

A text box is useful to differentiate portions of text from other text on the page. Because it is a *floating object*—a graphic that can be moved independently of the surrounding text characters—you can place a text box anywhere on the page.

1 Press Ctrl + Home to move to the top of the document.

2 On the **Insert tab**, in the **Text group**, click **Text Box**. At the bottom of the gallery, click **Draw Text Box**.

3 Position the ⊞ pointer over the first blank paragraph—aligned with the left margin and at approximately 1 inch on the vertical ruler. Drag down and to the right to create a text box approximately **1.5 inches** high and **4 inches** wide—the exact size and location need not be precise.

4 With the insertion point blinking in the text box, type the following, pressing Enter after each of the first *two* lines to create a new paragraph:

> **Interviews will be held:**
> **Friday and Saturday, January 14 and 15**
> **In the Career Services Conference Room**

5 Compare your screen with Figure 12.20, and then **Save** 🖫 your document.

FIGURE 12.20

1 ▶ Point to the text box border to display the  pointer. In the space below the *Internships Available* title, by dragging, move the text box until a horizontal green alignment guide displays above the first blank paragraph mark and a vertical green alignment guide displays in the center of the page, as shown in Figure 12.21. If the alignment guides do not display, drag the text box to position it approximately as shown in the Figure.

FIGURE 12.21

Word 2016, Windows 10, Microsoft Corporation

2 ▶ To place the text box precisely, on the **Format tab**, in the **Arrange group**, click **Position**, and then click **More Layout Options**.

3 ▶ In the **Layout** dialog box, under **Horizontal**, click **Alignment**. To the right of **Alignment**, click the **arrow**, and then click **Centered**. To the right of **relative to**, click the **arrow**, and then click **Page**.

4 ▶ Under **Vertical**, click in the **Absolute position** box, select the existing number, and then type **1.25** To the right of **below**, click the **arrow**, and then click **Margin**.

5 ▶ In the **Layout** dialog box, click the **Size tab**. Under **Height**, select the number in the **Absolute** box. Type **1.25** and then under **Width**, select the number in the **Absolute** box. Type **4** and then click **OK**.

The text box is sized correctly, centered horizontally, and the top edge is positioned 1.25 inches below the top margin of the document.

6 ▶ On the ribbon, under **Drawing Tools**, click the **Format tab**. In the **Shape Styles group**, click **More** ⏷, and then in the first row, click the third style—**Colored Outline – Orange, Accent 2**.

7 ▶ On the **Format tab**, in the **Shape Styles group**, click **Shape Effects**. Point to **Shadow**, and then under **Outer**, in the first row, click the first effect—**Offset Diagonal Bottom Right**.

8 ▶ Click in the text box, and then press Ctrl + A to select all of the text. Right-click over the selected text to display the mini toolbar, change the **Font Size** to **16** and apply **Bold** B . Press Ctrl + E to center the text.

Ctrl + E is the keyboard shortcut to center text in a document or object.

9 ▶ Click anywhere in the document to deselect the text box. Compare your screen with Figure 12.22, and then **Save** 🖫 your document.

Text formatted and centered, text box sized and positioned, Shape Style and Shadow effect applied →

Internships·Available¶

Interviews·will·be·held:¶

Friday·and·Saturday,·January·14·and·15¶

In·the·Career·Services·Conference·Room¶

This·summer,·Sturgeon·Point·Productions·will·be·

FIGURE 12.22

Objective 4 Preview and Print a Document

GO! Learn How
Video W12-4

While you are creating your document, it is useful to preview your document periodically to be sure that you are getting the result you want. Then, before printing, make a final preview to be sure the document layout is what you intended.

Activity 12.15 Adding a File Name to the Footer by Inserting a Field

Information in headers and footers helps to identify a document when it is printed or displayed electronically. Recall that a header is information that prints at the top of every page; a footer is information that prints at the bottom of every page. In this text, you will insert the file name in the footer of every Word document.

> **1** Click the **Insert tab**, and then in the **Header & Footer group**, click **Footer**.

> **2** At the bottom of the gallery, click **Edit Footer**.

> The footer area displays with the insertion point blinking at the left edge, and on the ribbon, the Header & Footer Tools display.

⟳ ANOTHER WAY   At the bottom edge of the page, right-click; from the shortcut menu, click Edit Footer.

> **3** On the ribbon, under the **Header & Footer Tools**, on the **Design tab**, in the **Insert group**, click **Document Info**, and then click **File Name**. Compare your screen with Figure 12.23.

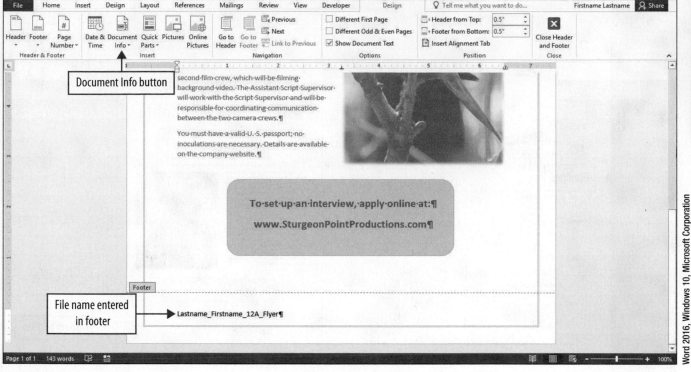

Document Info button

second·film·crew,·which·will·be·filming·
background·video.·The·Assistant·Script·Supervisor·
will·work·with·the·Script·Supervisor·and·will·be·
responsible·for·coordinating·communication·
between·the·two·camera·crews.¶

You·must·have·a·valid·U.·S.·passport;·no·
inoculations·are·necessary.·Details·are·available·
on·the·company·website.¶

To·set·up·an·interview,·apply·online·at:¶

www.SturgeonPointProductions.com¶

Footer

File name entered in footer → Lastname_Firstname_12A_Flyer¶

Page 1 of 1   143 words

Word 2016, Windows 10, Microsoft Corporation

FIGURE 12.23

> **4** On the **Design tab**, click **Close Header and Footer**, and then **Save** 🖫 your document.
>
> When the body of the document is active, the footer text is dimmed—it displays in gray. Conversely, when the footer area is active, the footer text is not dimmed; instead, the document text is dimmed.

🔁 **ANOTHER WAY**   Double-click in the document outside of the footer area to close the footer and return to the document.

IC3
DIGITAL LITERACY
CERTIFICATION
2.02f

Activity 12.16 | Adding Document Properties and Previewing and Printing a Document

> **1** Press Ctrl + Home to move the insertion point to the top of the document. In the upper left corner of your screen, click the **File tab** to display **Backstage** view. On the right, at the bottom of the **Properties** list, click **Show All Properties**.

> **2** On the list of **Properties**, click to the right of **Tags** to display an empty box, and then type **internship, documentary**

> **3** Click to the right of **Subject** to display an empty box, and then type your course name and section number. Under **Related People**, be sure that your name displays as the author. If necessary, right-click the author name, click Edit Property, type your name, and click OK.

> **4** On the left, click **Print** to display the **Print Preview**. Compare your screen with Figure 12.24.
>
> Here you can select any printer connected to your system and adjust the settings related to how you want to print. On the right, Print Preview displays your document exactly as it will print; the formatting marks do not display. At the bottom of the Print Preview area, in the center, the number of pages and arrows with which you can move among the pages in Print Preview displays. On the right, Zoom settings enable you to shrink or enlarge the Print Preview.

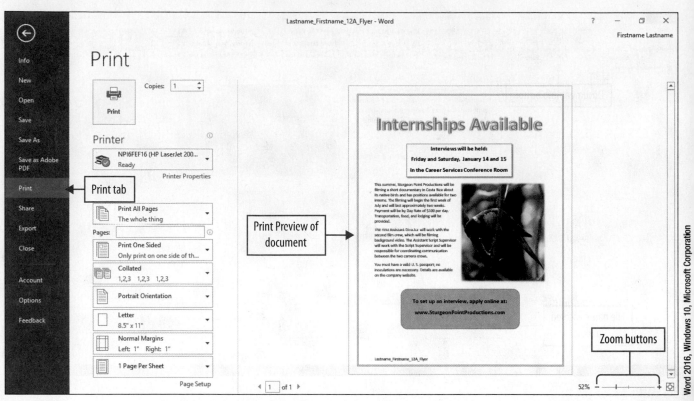

FIGURE 12.24

5 In the lower right corner of the window, click **Zoom In** several times to view the document at a larger size, and notice that a larger preview is easier to read. Click **Zoom to Page** 🔲 to view the entire page.

6 If you want to print your document on paper using the default printer on your system, in the upper left portion of the screen, click **Print**.

The document will print on your default printer; if you do not have a color printer, colors will print in shades of gray. Backstage view closes and your file redisplays in the Word window.

7 **Save** 🖫 your document. In the upper right corner of the Word window, click **Close** ⊠. If directed by your instructor to do so, submit your paper printout, your electronic image of your document that looks like a printed document, or your completed Word file.

END | You have completed Project 12A

Objective | Create a Flyer Using Google Docs

ALERT! | Working with Web-Based Applications and Services

Computer programs and services on the web receive continuous updates and improvements, so the steps to complete this web-based Activity may differ from the ones shown. You can often look at the screens and the information presented to determine how to complete the Activity.

If you do not already have a Google account, you will need to create one before you begin this Activity. Go to http://google.com and, in the upper right corner, click Sign In. On the Sign In screen, click Create Account. On the Create your Google Account page, complete the form, read and agree to the Terms of Service and Privacy Policy, and then click Next step. On the Welcome screen, click Get Started.

Activity | Creating a Flyer

In this Activity, you will use Google Docs to create a flyer.

1 From the desktop, open your browser, navigate to http://google.com, and then sign in to your Google account. In the upper right corner of your screen, click **Google Apps** ⊞ and then click **Drive** ☁.

2 To create a folder in which to store your web projects, click **NEW**, and then click **Folder**. In the **New folder** box, type **GO! Web Projects** and then click **Create** to create a folder on your Google drive. Double-click your **GO! Web Projects** folder to open it.

3 In the left pane, click **NEW**, and then click **Google Docs** to open a new tab in your browser and to start an Untitled document. At the top of the window, click **Untitled document** and then, using your own name as the file name, type **Lastname_Firstname_12A_Google_Doc** and then press [Enter] to change the file name.

4 To the right of the file name, point to the small file folder to display the ScreenTip **Move to folder** Click the file folder and notice that your file is saved in the GO! Web Projects folder. Compare your screen with Figure A.

5 Click in your document to close the Move to folder dialog box and to position the insertion point at the top of the document. Type **Internships Available** and then press [Enter] two times. Type **Interviews will be held Friday and Saturday, January 14 and 15 in the Career Services Conference Room.**

6 Press [Ctrl] + [A] to select all of the text. Click the **Font size arrow** ⏷, and then click **24**. With the text still selected, click **Center**.

7 Press [Ctrl] + [End] to move to the end of the document, and then press [Enter]. Click **Insert**, and then click **Image**. With **Upload** selected, click **Choose an image to upload**. Navigate to your student data files, click **w12A_Bird**, and then click **Open** to insert the picture.

8 Click the picture to select it, and then point to the square sizing handle at the upper left corner of the picture. Drag down and to the right until the sizing handle aligns with approximately **3 inches on the ruler**.

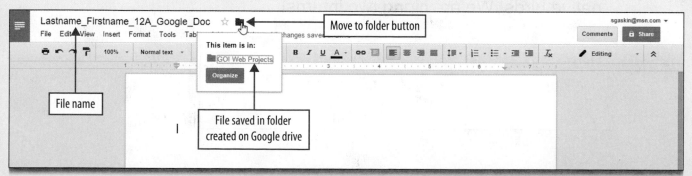

FIGURE A

(GO! With Google continues on the next page)

9 Click to the right of the picture and then press Enter twice. Type **Join our production crew in Costa Rica as we film a short documentary about its native birds. We are hiring two interns!**

10 Select the title **Internships Available** and then click **Text color** A. In the third column, click the sixth color—**dark orange 1**, and then apply **Bold** B. Your document will look similar to Figure B.

11 Your document will be saved automatically. Sign out of your Google account. Submit as instructed by your instructor.

Internships Available

Interviews will be held Friday and Saturday, January 14 and 15 in the Career Services Conference Room.

Join our production crew in Costa Rica as we film a short documentary about its native birds. We are hiring two interns!

FIGURE B

PROJECT ACTIVITIES

In Activities 12.17 through 12.29, you will format an information handout from Sturgeon Point Productions that describes internships available to students. Your completed document will look similar to Figure 12.25.

PROJECT FILES

MyITLab grader

If your instructor wants you to submit Project 12B in the MyITLab Grader system, log in to MyITLab, locate Grader Project 12B, and then download the files for this project.

For Project 12B, you will need the following file:
w012B_Programs

You will save your document as:
Lastname_Firstname_12B_Programs

PROJECT RESULTS

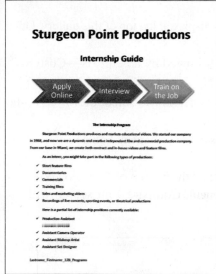

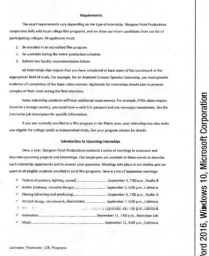

FIGURE 12.25 Project 12B Information Handout

GO! Learn How
Video W12-5

IC3
DIGITAL LITERACY
CERTIFICATION
2.02e (iii)

Document layout includes *margins*—the space between the text and the top, bottom, left, and right edges of the paper. Paragraph layout includes line spacing, indents, and tabs. In Word, the information about paragraph formats is stored in the paragraph mark at the end of a paragraph. When you press Enter, the new paragraph mark contains the formatting of the previous paragraph, unless you take steps to change it.

Activity 12.17 | Setting Margins

ALERT! To submit as an autograded project, log into MyITLab and download the files for this project, and begin with those files instead of w12B_Programs.

1 Start Word, and then click **Open Other Documents**. Navigate to the student files that accompany this text, and then open the document **w12B_Programs**. On the **Home tab**, in the **Paragraph group**, be sure **Show/Hide** ¶ is active so that you can view the formatting marks.

2 Click the **File tab**, and then click **Save As**. Navigate to your **AIO Chapter 12** folder, and then using your own name, **Save** the document as **Lastname_Firstname_12B_Programs**

3 Click the **Layout tab**. In the **Page Setup group**, click **Margins**, and then take a moment to study the settings in the Margins gallery.

> If you have recently used custom margins settings, they will display at the top of this gallery. Other commonly used settings also display.

4 At the bottom of the **Margins** gallery, click the command followed by an ellipsis—**Custom Margins** to display the **Page Setup** dialog box.

5 In the **Page Setup** dialog box, under **Margins**, press Tab as necessary to select the value in the **Left** box, and then, with *1.25"* selected, type **1**

> This action will change the left margin to 1 inch on all pages of the document. You do not need to type the inch (") mark.

6 Press Tab to select the margin in the **Right** box, and then type **1** At the bottom of the dialog box, notice that the new margins will apply to the **Whole document**. Compare your screen with Figure 12.26.

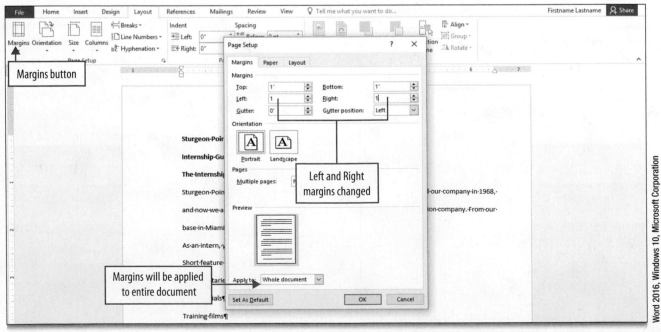

FIGURE 12.26

Word 2016, Windows 10, Microsoft Corporation

7 Click **OK** to apply the new margins and close the dialog box. If the ruler below the ribbon is not displayed, on the View tab, in the Show group, select the Ruler check box.

8 Scroll to position the bottom of **Page 1** and the top of **Page 2** on your screen. Notice that the page edges display, and the page number and total number of pages display on the left side of the status bar.

9 Near the bottom edge of **Page 1**, point anywhere in the bottom margin area, right-click, and then click **Edit Footer** to display the footer area.

10 On the ribbon, under the **Header & Footer Tools**, on the **Design tab**, in the **Insert group**, click **Document Info**, and then click **File Name**.

11 Double-click anywhere in the document to close the footer area, and then **Save** 🖫 your document.

Activity 12.18 | Aligning Paragraphs

Alignment refers to the placement of paragraph text relative to the left and right margins. Most paragraph text uses *left alignment*—aligned at the left margin, leaving the right margin uneven. Three other types of paragraph alignment are: *center alignment*—centered between the left and right margins; *right alignment*—aligned at the right margin with an uneven left margin; and *justified alignment*—text aligned evenly at both the left and right margins. The table in Figure 12.27 shows examples of these alignment types.

TYPES OF PARAGRAPH ALIGNMENT		
ALIGNMENT	**BUTTON**	**DESCRIPTION AND EXAMPLE**
Align Left	📄	Align Left is the default paragraph alignment in Word. Text in the paragraph aligns at the left margin, and the right margin is uneven.
Center	📄	Center alignment aligns text in the paragraph so that it is centered between the left and right margins.
Align Right	📄	Align Right aligns text at the right margin. Using Align Right, the left margin, which is normally even, is uneven.
Justify	📄	The Justify alignment option adds additional space between words so that both the left and right margins are even. Justify is often used when formatting newspaper-style columns.

FIGURE 12.27

Gaskin, Shelley. Go! All in One, 3E. Pearson Education, 2017.

1 Scroll to position the middle of **Page 2** on your screen, look at the left and right margins, and notice that the text is justified—both the right and left margins of multiple-line paragraphs are aligned evenly at the margins. On the **Home tab**, in the **Paragraph group**, notice that **Justify** 📄 is active.

> To achieve a justified right margin, Word adjusts the size of spaces between words, which can result in unattractive spacing in a document that spans the width of a page. Many individuals find such spacing difficult to read.

2 Press Ctrl + A to select all of the text in the document, and then on the **Home tab**, in the **Paragraph group**, click **Align Left** 📄.

ANOTHER WAY   On the Home tab, in the Editing group, click Select, and then click Select All.

3 Press Ctrl + Home to move to the beginning of the document. In the left margin area, point to the left of the first paragraph—*Sturgeon Point Productions*—until the 🡵 pointer displays, and then click one time to select the paragraph.

> Use this technique to select entire lines of text.

4 On the mini toolbar, in the **Font Size** box, select the existing number, type **40** and then press (Enter).

> Use this technique to change the font size to a size that is not available on the Font Size list.

5 Select the second paragraph—*Internship Guide*—and then on the mini toolbar, change the **Font Size** to **26 pt**. Point to the left of the first paragraph—*Sturgeon Point Productions*—to display the pointer again, and then drag down to select the first two paragraphs, which form the title and subtitle of the document.

6 On the **Home tab**, in the **Paragraph group**, click **Center** to center the title and subtitle between the left and right margins, and then compare your screen with Figure 12.28.

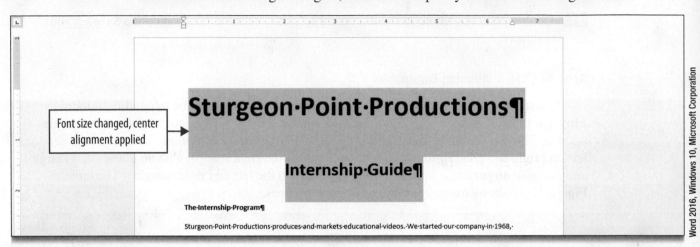

FIGURE 12.28

7 Near the top of **Page 1**, locate the first bold subheading—*The Internship Program*. Point to the left of the paragraph to display the pointer, and then click one time to select the text.

8 With *The Internship Program* selected, use your mouse wheel or the vertical scroll bar to bring the bottom portion of **Page 1** into view. Locate the subheading *Requirements*. Move the pointer to the left of the paragraph to display the pointer, hold down (Ctrl), and then click one time. Release (Ctrl), and then scroll to the middle of **Page 2**. Use the same technique to select the third subheading—*Introduction to Upcoming Internships*.

> Three subheadings are selected; in Windows-based programs, you can hold down (Ctrl) to select multiple items.

9 Click **Center** to center all three subheadings, and then click **Save**.

Activity 12.19 | Setting Line Spacing

Line spacing is the distance between lines of text in a paragraph. Three of the most commonly used line spacing options are shown in the table in Figure 12.29.

LINE SPACING OPTIONS	
ALIGNMENT	**DESCRIPTION, EXAMPLE, AND INFORMATION**
Single spacing	**This text in this example uses single spacing**. Single spacing was once the most commonly used spacing in business documents. Now, because so many documents are read on a computer screen rather than on paper, single spacing is becoming less popular.
Multiple 1.08 spacing	**This text in this example uses multiple 1.08 spacing**. The default line spacing in Microsoft Word 2016 is 1.08, which is slightly more than single spacing to make the text easier to read on a computer screen. Many individuals now prefer this spacing, even on paper, because the lines of text appear less crowded.
Double spacing	**This text in this example uses double spacing**. College research papers and draft documents that need space for notes are commonly double-spaced; there is space for a full line of text between each document line.

FIGURE 12.29

Gaskin, Shelley. Go! All in One, 3E. Pearson Education, 2017.

> **1** Press Ctrl + Home to move to the beginning of the document. Press Ctrl + A to select all of the text in the document.

> **2** With all of the text in the document selected, on the **Home tab**, in the **Paragraph group**, click **Line and Paragraph Spacing** ⬛, and notice that the text in the document is double-spaced—**2.0** is checked. Compare your screen with Figure 12.30.

↻ BY TOUCH   Tap the ribbon commands.

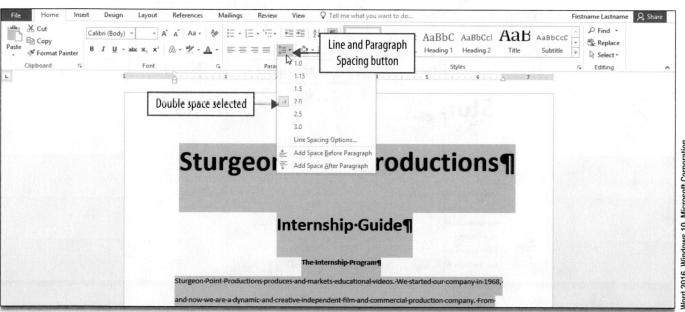

FIGURE 12.30

Word 2016, Windows 10, Microsoft Corporation

> **3** On the **Line Spacing** menu, click the *third* setting—**1.5**—and then click anywhere in the document to deselect the text. Compare your screen with Figure 12.31, and then **Save** 💾 your document.

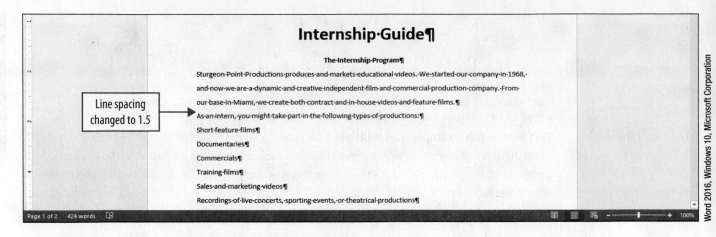

Line spacing changed to 1.5

FIGURE 12.31

Activity 12.20 | Indenting Text

Indenting the first line of each paragraph is a common technique to distinguish paragraphs.

1 Below the title and subtitle of the document, click anywhere in the paragraph that begins *Sturgeon Point Productions produces.*

2 On the **Home tab**, in the **Paragraph group**, click the **Dialog Box Launcher** ⬚.

3 In the **Paragraph** dialog box, on the **Indents and Spacing tab**, under **Indentation**, click the **Special arrow**, and then click **First line** to indent the first line by 0.5", which is the default indent setting. Compare your screen with Figure 12.32.

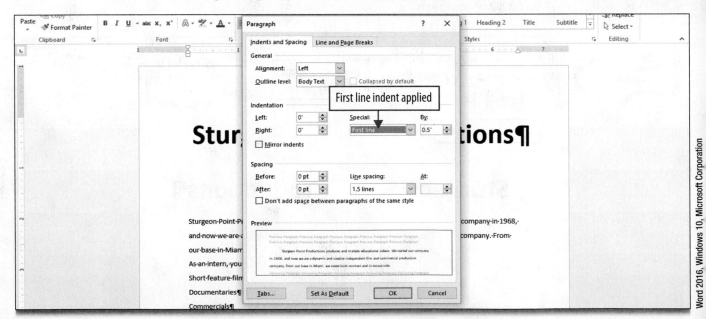

FIGURE 12.32

4 Click **OK**, and then click anywhere in the next paragraph, which begins *As an intern*. On the ruler under the ribbon, drag the **First Line Indent** marker ▽ to **0.5 inches on the horizontal ruler**, and then compare your screen with Figure 12.33.

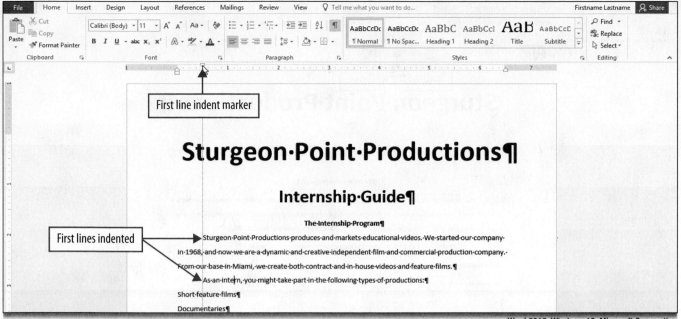

First line indent marker

First lines indented

FIGURE 12.33

5 By using either of the techniques you just practiced, or by using the Format Painter, apply a first line indent of **0.5"** to the paragraph that begins *Here is a partial* to match the indent of the remaining paragraphs in the document.

6 **Save** 💾 your document.

IC3
DIGITAL LITERACY
CERTIFICATION
2.02e (vii)

Activity 12.21 | Setting Space Before and After Paragraphs

Adding space after each paragraph is another technique to differentiate paragraphs.

1 Press Ctrl + A to select all of the text in the document. Click the **Layout tab**, and then in the **Paragraph group**, under **Spacing**, click the **After spin box up arrow** one time to change the value to **6 pt**.

To change the value in the box, you can also select the existing number, type a new number, and then press Enter. This document will use 6 pt spacing after paragraphs to add space.

🔄 ANOTHER WAY On either the Home tab or the Layout tab, display the Paragraph dialog box from the Paragraph group, and then under Spacing, click the spin box arrows as necessary.

2 Press Ctrl + Home, and then compare your screen with Figure 12.34.

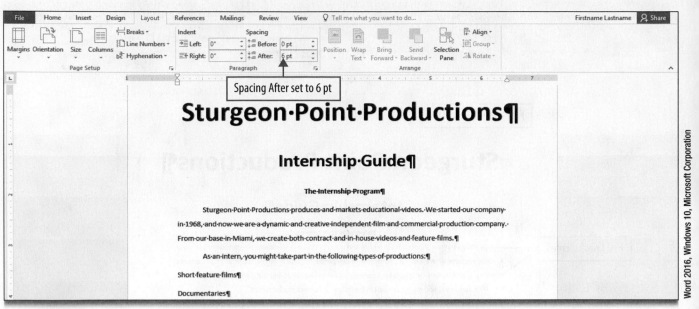

FIGURE 12.34

3 Near the top of **Page 1**, select the subheading **The Internship Program**, including the paragraph mark following it. Scroll down using the vertical scroll bar, hold down Ctrl, and then select the **Requirements** and **Introduction to Upcoming Internships** subheadings.

ALERT!   **Did your screen zoom when you were selecting?**

Holding down Ctrl and using the mouse wheel at the same time will zoom your screen.

4 With all three subheadings selected, in the **Paragraph group**, under **Spacing**, click the **Before up spin box arrow** two times to set the **Spacing Before** to **12 pt**. Compare your screen with Figure 12.35, and then **Save** 🖫 your document.

This action increases the amount of space above each of the subheadings, which will make them easy to distinguish in the document. The formatting is applied only to the selected paragraphs.

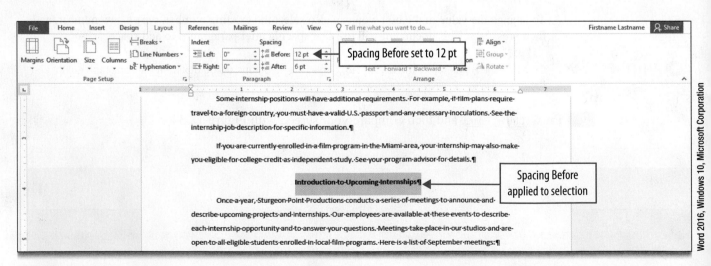

FIGURE 12.35

GO! Learn How
Video W12-6

To display a list of information, you can choose a **bulleted list**, which uses **bullets**—text symbols such as small circles or check marks—to introduce each item in a list. You can also choose a **numbered list**, which uses consecutive numbers or letters to introduce each item in a list.

Use a bulleted list if the items in the list can be introduced in any order; use a numbered list for items that have definite steps, a sequence of actions, or are in chronological order.

Activity 12.22 | Creating a Bulleted List

1 In the upper portion of **Page 1**, locate the paragraph *Short feature films*, and then point to this paragraph from the left margin area to display the ⟅ pointer. Drag down to select this paragraph and the next five paragraphs—ending with the paragraph *Recordings of live concerts*.

2 On the **Home tab**, in the **Paragraph group**, click **Bullets** ⊞ ▾ to change the selected text to a bulleted list.

The 6 pt spacing between each of the bulleted points is removed and each bulleted item is automatically indented.

3 On the ruler, point to **First Line Indent** ▽ and read the ScreenTip, and then point to **Hanging Indent** ⌂. Compare your screen with Figure 12.36.

By default, Word formats bulleted items with a first line indent of 0.25" and adds a Hanging Indent at 0.5". The hanging indent maintains the alignment of text when a bulleted item is more than one line.

You can modify the list indentation by using Decrease Indent ⇤ or Increase Indent ⇥. Decrease Indent moves your paragraph closer to the margin. Increase Indent moves your paragraph farther away from the margin.

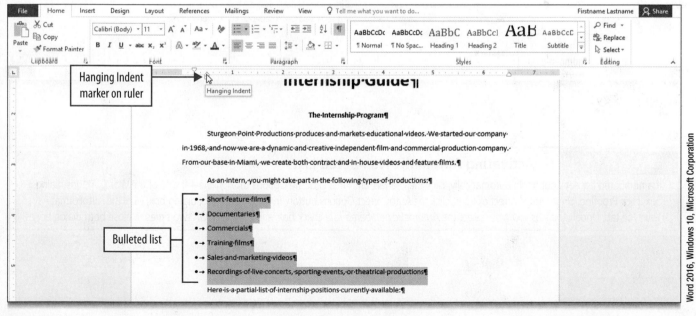

FIGURE 12.36

4 Scroll down slightly, and then by using the ⟅ pointer from the left margin area, select the five internship positions, beginning with *Production Assistant* and ending with *Assistant Set Designer*. In the **Paragraph group**, click **Bullets** ⊞ ▾.

5 Scroll down to view **Page 2**. Apply bullets to all of the paragraphs that indicate the September meetings and meeting dates, beginning with *Technical* and ending with *Music*.

6 **Save** 🖫 your document.

Activity 12.23 | Creating a Numbered List

1 Under the subheading *Requirements*, in the paragraph that begins *The exact requirements*, click to position the insertion point at the *end* of the paragraph, following the colon. Press Enter to create a blank paragraph. Notice that the paragraph is indented because the First Line Indent from the previous paragraph carried over to the new paragraph.

2 To change the indent formatting for this paragraph, on the ruler, drag the **First Line Indent** marker ▽ to the left so that it is positioned directly above the lower button.

3 Being sure to include the period, type **1.** and press Spacebar. Compare your screen with Figure 12.37.

Word determines that this paragraph is the first item in a numbered list and formats the new paragraph accordingly, indenting the list in the same manner as the bulleted list. The space after the number changes to a tab, and the AutoCorrect Options button displays to the left of the list item. The tab is indicated by a right arrow formatting mark.

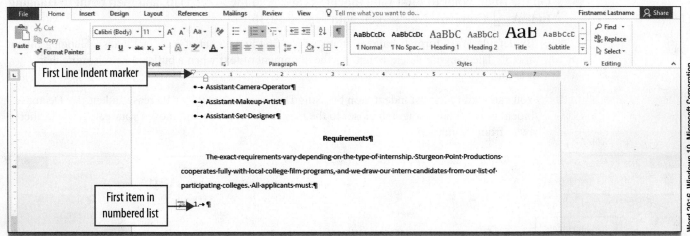

FIGURE 12.37

ALERT! **Activating Automatic Numbered Lists**

If a numbered list does not begin automatically, click the File tab, and then click the Options tab. On the left side of the Word Options dialog box, click Proofing. Under AutoCorrect options, click the AutoCorrect Options button. In the AutoCorrect dialog box, click the AutoFormat As You Type tab. Under *Apply as you type*, select the *Automatic numbered lists* check box, and then click OK two times to close both dialog boxes.

4 ▶ Click **AutoCorrect Options** [⚡], and then compare your screen with Figure 12.38.

From the displayed list, you can remove the automatic formatting here, or stop using the automatic numbered lists option in this document. You also have the option to open the AutoCorrect dialog box to *Control AutoFormat Options*.

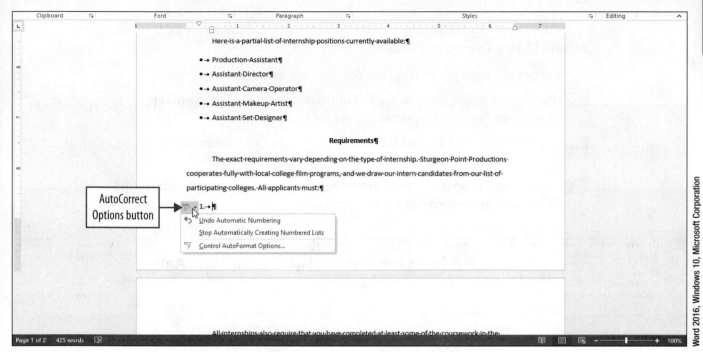

FIGURE 12.38

5 ▶ Click **AutoCorrect Options** [⚡] again to close the menu without selecting any of the commands. Type **Be enrolled in an accredited film program** and press [Enter]. Notice that the second number and a tab are added to the next line.

6 ▶ Type **Be available during the entire production schedule** and press [Enter]. Type **Submit two faculty recommendation letters** and then compare your screen with Figure 12.39. Save [💾] your document.

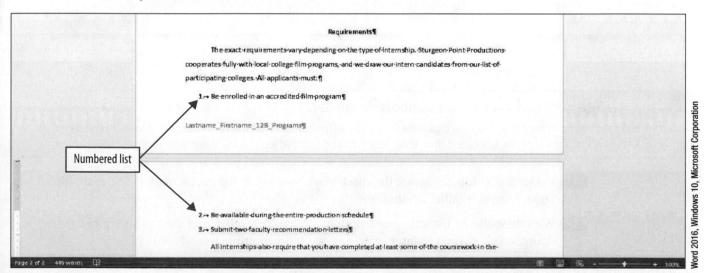

FIGURE 12.39

Activity 12.24 | Customizing Bullets

You can use any symbol from any font for your bullet characters.

1 Press Ctrl + End to move to the end of the document, and then scroll up as necessary to display the bulleted list containing the list of meetings.

2 Point to the left of the first list item to display the ◢ pointer, and then drag down to select all six meetings in the list—the bullet symbols are not selected.

3 On the mini toolbar, click the **Bullets button arrow** ≡ ▾ to display the Bullet Library, and then compare your screen with Figure 12.40.

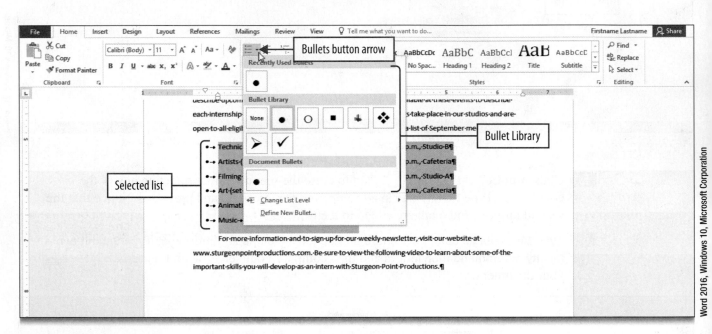

FIGURE 12.40

4 Under **Bullet Library**, click the **check mark** symbol. If the check mark is not available, choose another bullet symbol.

5 With the bulleted list still selected, right-click over the list, and then on the mini toolbar, double-click **Format Painter** to activate it for multiple use.

ANOTHER WAY   On the Home tab, in the Clipboard group, double-click Format Painter.

6 Use the vertical scroll bar or your mouse wheel to scroll to view **Page 1**. Move the pointer to the left of the first item in the first bulleted list to display the pointer, and then drag down to select all six items in the list and to apply the format of the third bulleted list—the check mark bullets—to this list. Repeat this procedure to change the bullets in the second list to check marks. Press Esc to turn off **Format Painter**, and then **Save** your document. Compare your screen with Figure 12.41.

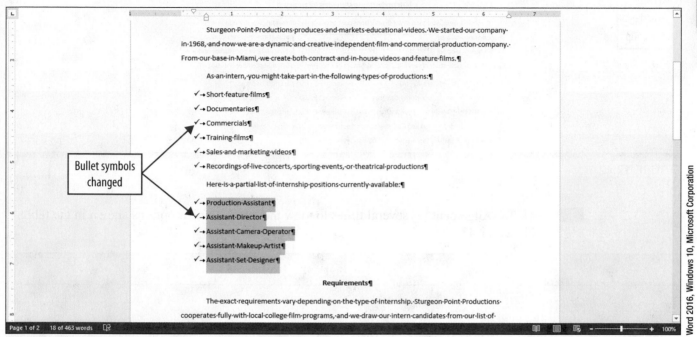

FIGURE 12.41

Objective 7 Set and Modify Tab Stops

GO! Learn How
Video W12-7

IC3
DIGITAL LITERACY
CERTIFICATION
2.02e (v)

Tab stops mark specific locations on a line of text. Use tab stops to indent and align text, and use the Tab key to move to tab stops.

Activity 12.25 | Setting Tab Stops

1 Scroll to view the lower portion of **Page 2**, and then by using the pointer at the left of the first item, select all of the items in the bulleted list. Notice that there is a tab mark between the name of the meeting and the date.

The arrow that indicates a tab is a nonprinting formatting mark.

2 To the left of the horizontal ruler, point to **Tab Alignment** to display the *Left Tab* ScreenTip, and then compare your screen with Figure 12.42.

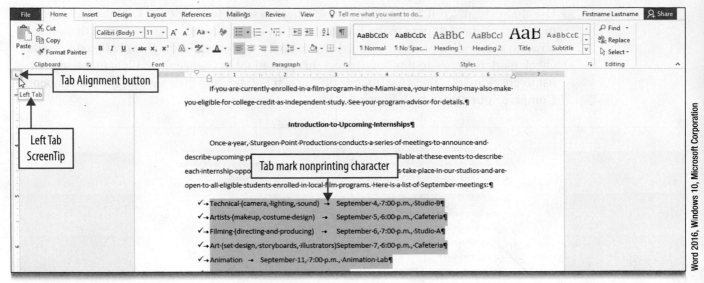

FIGURE 12.42

3 Click **Tab Alignment** ⌞ several times to view the tab alignment options shown in the table in Figure 12.43.

TAB ALIGNMENT OPTIONS		
TYPE	**TAB ALIGNMENT BUTTON DISPLAYS THIS MARKER**	**DESCRIPTION**
Left	⌞	Text is left aligned at the tab stop and extends to the right.
Center	⊥	Text is centered around the tab stop.
Right	⌟	Text is right aligned at the tab stop and extends to the left.
Decimal	⊥	The decimal point aligns at the tab stop.
Bar	∣	A vertical bar displays at the tab stop.
First Line Indent	▽	Text in the first line of a paragraph indents.
Hanging Indent	⌂	Text in all lines except the first line in the paragraph indents.

FIGURE 12.43

4 Display **Left Tab** ⌞. Along the lower edge of the horizontal ruler, point to and then click at **3.5 inches on the horizontal ruler**. Notice that all of the dates left align at the new tab stop location, and the right edge of the column is uneven.

5 Compare your screen with Figure 12.44, and then **Save** 🖫 your document.

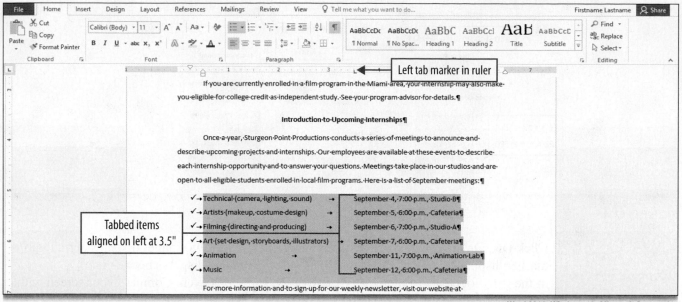

FIGURE 12.44

Word 2016, Windows 10, Microsoft Corporation

2.02e (v)

Activity 12.26 | Modifying Tab Stops

Tab stops are a form of paragraph formatting. Therefore, the information about tab stops is stored in the paragraph mark in the paragraphs to which they were applied.

1 With the bulleted list still selected, on the ruler, point to the new tab marker at *3.5 inches on the horizontal ruler*, and then when the *Left Tab* ScreenTip displays, drag the tab marker to **4 inches on the horizontal ruler**.

In all of the selected lines, the text at the tab stop left aligns at 4 inches.

2 On the ruler, point to the tab marker that you moved to display the *Left Tab* ScreenTip, and then double-click to display the **Tabs** dialog box.

 ANOTHER WAY On the Home tab, in the Paragraph group, click the Dialog Box Launcher. At the bottom of the Paragraph dialog box, click the Tabs button.

3 In the **Tabs** dialog box, under **Tab stop position**, if necessary select *4"* and then type **6**

4 Under **Alignment**, click the **Right** option button. Under **Leader**, click the **2** option button. Near the bottom of the **Tabs** dialog box, click **Set**.

Because the Right tab will be used to align the items in the list, the tab stop at 4" is no longer necessary.

5 In the **Tabs** dialog box, in the **Tab stop position** box, click **4"** to select this tab stop, and then in the lower portion of the **Tabs** dialog box, click the **Clear** button to delete this tab stop, which is no longer necessary. Compare your screen with Figure 12.45.

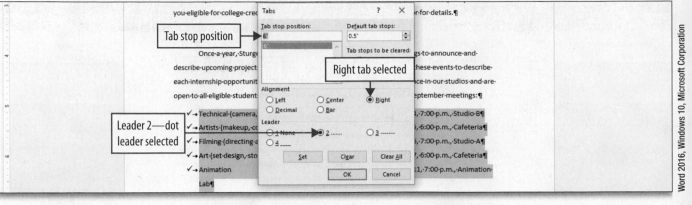

FIGURE 12.45

6 Click **OK**. On the ruler, notice that the left tab marker at *4"* no longer displays, a right tab marker displays at *6"*, and a series of dots—a ***dot leader***—displays between the columns of the list. Notice also that the right edge of the column is even. Compare your screen with Figure 12.46.

A ***leader character*** creates a solid, dotted, or dashed line that fills the space to the left of a tab character and draws the reader's eyes across the page from one item to the next. When the character used for the leader is a dot, it is commonly referred to as a dot leader.

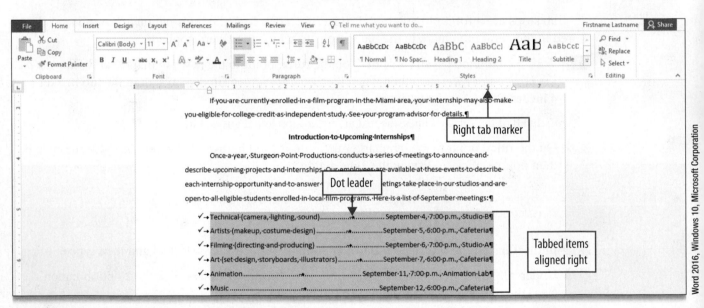

FIGURE 12.46

7 In the bulleted list that uses dot leaders, locate the *Art* meeting, and then click to position the insertion point at the end of that line, after the word *Cafeteria*. Press Enter to create a new blank bullet item.

8 Type **Video Editing** and press Tab. Notice that a dot leader fills the space to the tab marker location.

9 Type **September 10, 7:00 p.m., Cafeteria** and notice that the text moves to the left to maintain the right alignment of the tab stop.

10 **Save** 🖫 your document.

SmartArt graphics are designer-quality visual representations of information, and Word provides many different layouts from which you can choose. You can also insert a link to an online video from a variety of online sources, thus enabling the reader to view the video when connected to the Internet. SmartArt graphics and videos can communicate your messages or ideas more effectively than plain text, and these objects add visual interest to a document or web page.

Activity 12.27 | Inserting a SmartArt Graphic

1 Press Ctrl + Home to move to the top of the document, and then click to the right of the subtitle *Internship Guide*.

2 Click the **Insert tab**, and then in the **Illustrations group**, point to **SmartArt** to display its ScreenTip. Read the ScreenTip, and then click **SmartArt**.

3 In the center portion of the **Choose a SmartArt Graphic** dialog box, scroll down and examine the numerous types of SmartArt graphics available.

4 On the left, click **Process**, and then by using the ScreenTips, locate and click **Basic Chevron Process**. Compare your screen with Figure 12.47.

At the right of the dialog box, a preview and description of the SmartArt displays.

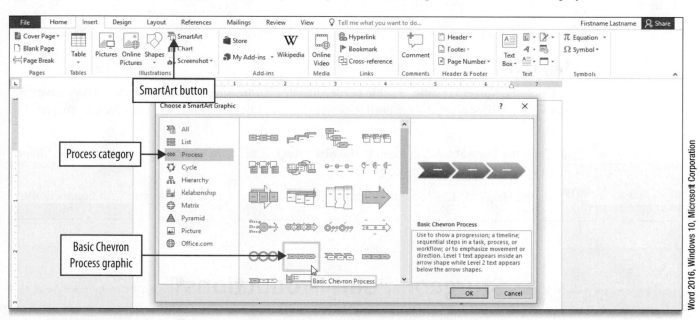

FIGURE 12.47

5 Click **OK** to insert the SmartArt graphic.

To the left of the inserted SmartArt graphic, the text pane may display. The text pane provides one method for entering text into your SmartArt graphic. If you choose not to use the text pane to enter text, you can close it.

6 On the ribbon, under **SmartArt Tools**, on the **Design tab**, in the **Create Graphic group**, notice the **Text Pane** button. If the text pane button is selected, click Text Pane to close the pane.

7 In the SmartArt graphic, in the first blue arrow, click **[Text]**, and notice that *[Text]* is replaced by a blinking insertion point.

The word *[Text]* is called *placeholder text*, which is nonprinting text that indicates where you can type.

8 Type **Apply Online**

9 Click the placeholder text in the middle arrow. Type **Interview** and then click the placeholder text in the third arrow. Type **Train on the Job** and then compare your screen with Figure 12.48.

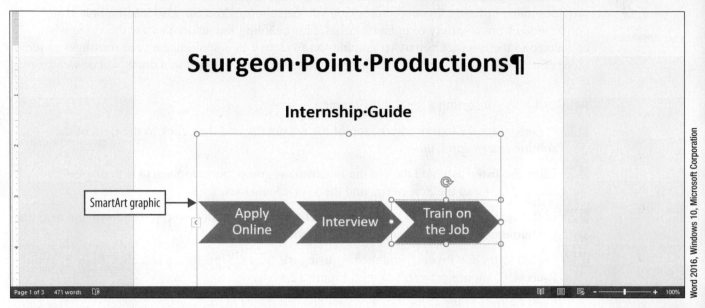

FIGURE 12.48

10 Save 🖫 your document.

Activity 12.28 | Sizing and Formatting a SmartArt Graphic

1 Click the **SmartArt solid graphic border** to select it. Be sure that none of the arrows have sizing handles around their border, which would indicate the arrow was selected, not the entire graphic.

2 Click the **Format tab**, and then in the **Size group**, if necessary click Size to display the Shape Height and Shape Width boxes.

3 Set the **Height** to **1.75"** and the **Width** to **6.5"**, and then compare your screen with Figure 12.49.

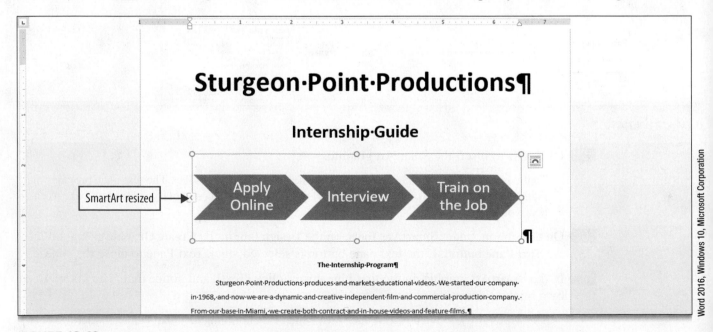

FIGURE 12.49

4 With the SmartArt graphic still selected, click the **SmartArt Tools Design tab**, and then in the **SmartArt Styles group**, click **Change Colors**. Under **Colorful**, click the fourth style—**Colorful Range - Accent Colors 4 to 5**.

5 On the **SmartArt Tools Design tab**, in the **SmartArt Styles group**, click **More** ⤓. Under **3-D**, click the second style—**Inset**. Click **Save** 🖫, and then compare your screen with Figure 12.50.

Word 2016, Windows 10, Microsoft Corporation

FIGURE 12.50

Activity 12.29 | Inserting an Online Video

Microsoft's research indicates that two-thirds of people who open Word documents never edit them; they only read them. So with more and more documents being read online—and not on paper—it makes sense that you may want to include videos in your Word documents.

1 Press Ctrl + End to move to the end of the document.

2 On the **Insert tab**, in the **Media group**, click **Online Video**.

Here you can search the web for an online video, search YouTube, or enter an *embed code* to insert a link to a video from a website. An embed code is a code that creates a link to a video, picture, or other type of *rich media* content. Rich media, also called *interactive media*, refers to computer interaction that responds to your actions; for example, by presenting text, graphics, animation, video, audio, or games.

3 In the **Bing Video Search** box, type **Go 1B Video** and then press Enter.

Several videos display based on the search term that you typed.

4 Point to several of the videos and notice that a ScreenTip displays a description of the video. Click one of the videos that includes the words *Go 1B Video* in the ScreenTip, and then click **Insert**. Compare your screen with Figure 12.51.

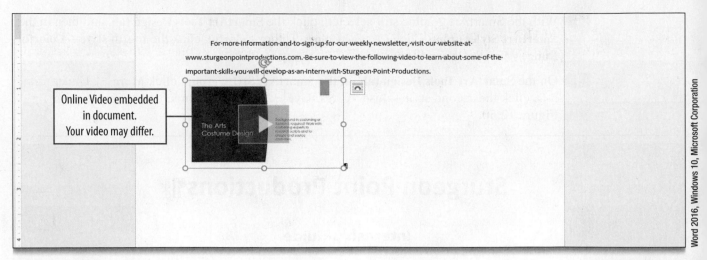

For·more·information·and·to·sign·up·for·our·weekly·newsletter,·visit·our·website·at·
www.sturgeonpointproductions.com.·Be·sure·to·view·the·following·video·to·learn·about·some·of·the·
important·skills·you·will·develop·as·an·intern·with·Sturgeon·Point·Productions.

Online Video embedded
in document.
Your video may differ.

The Arts
Costume Design

FIGURE 12.51

> **ALERT!**   **Are you unable to locate or play the video?**
>
> If you are unable to locate a video using the search words that you entered in Step 3, in the Bing Video Search box, type MyITLab and then insert the first video that displays. Depending upon your computer configuration, the video may not play.

5 ▶ On the **Picture Tools Format** tab, in the **Size** group, click in the **Height** box to select the value. Type **1.5** and then press Enter to change the size of the video.

6 ▶ Click **Save** 🖫, and then press Ctrl + Home to move to the top of your document.

7 ▶ Click the **File tab**, and then in the lower right portion of the screen, click **Show All Properties**. In the **Tags** box, type **internship** and in the **Subject** box, type your course name and section number. In the **Author** box, replace the existing text with your first and last name.

8 ▶ On the left, click **Print** to display **Print Preview**. At the bottom of the preview, click the **Next Page** ▶ and **Previous Page** ◀ buttons to move between pages. If necessary, return to the document and make any necessary changes.

9 ▶ **Save** 🖫 your document. In the upper right corner of the Word window, click **Close** ✕. If directed by your instructor to do so, submit your paper printout, your electronic image of your document that looks like a printed document, or your completed Word file.

END | You have completed Project 12B

Objective | Create an Information Handout

ALERT! **Working with Web-Based Applications and Services**

Computer programs and services on the web receive continuous updates and improvements, so the steps to complete this web-based Activity may differ from the ones shown. You can often look at the screens and the information presented to determine how to complete the Activity.

If you do not already have a Google account, you will need to create one before you begin this Activity. Go to http://google.com and, in the upper right corner, click Sign In. On the Sign In screen, click Create Account. On the Create your Google Account page, complete the form, read and agree to the Terms of Service and Privacy Policy, and then click Next step. On the Welcome screen, click Get Started.

Activity | Creating a Handout with Bulleted and Numbered Lists

In this Activity, you will use Google Docs to create an information handout.

1 From the desktop, open your browser, navigate to **http://google.com**, and then sign in to your Google account. In the upper right corner of your screen, click **Google Apps**, and then click **Drive**. Double-click your **GO! Web Projects** folder to open it. If you have not created this folder, refer to the instructions in the first Google Docs project in this chapter.

2 In the left pane, click **NEW**, and then click **Google Docs**. Click **File**, and then click **Open**. Click **Upload**, and then click **Select a file from your computer**. From your student data files, click **w12_12B_Web** and then click **Open** to open the file and upload it to your GO! Web Projects folder.

3 In the upper left corner of the Google Docs window, select **w12_12B_Web** and then type **Lastname_Firstname_12B_Google_Doc** and then press Enter to rename the file.

4 Press Ctrl + A to select all of the text. Click **Line spacing**, and then click **1.5**. Click **Left align**.

5 Select the six lines of text beginning with *Short feature films* and ending with *Recording of live concerts*, and then click **Bulleted list** to apply bullets to the selected text. Select the list of internship positions beginning with *Production Assistant* and ending with *Assistant Set Designer*, and then click **Bulleted list**. Compare your screen with Figure A.

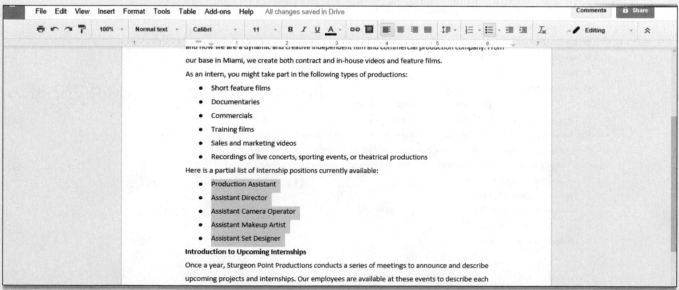

FIGURE A

(GO! With Google continues on the next page)

6 ▶ Select the last five lines of the document beginning with *Artists* and ending with *Music*. To create a numbered list from the selection, click **Numbered list** ▤.

7 ▶ Select the first three lines of text in the document, and then click **Center** ▤. Click in the *Introduction to Upcoming Internships* heading, and then click **Center** ▤.

8 ▶ Click at the beginning of the paragraph that begins *Sturgeon Point Production produces and markets*, and then press ⎄Tab. Look at the ruler and notice that the first line indent is applied.

9 ▶ With the insertion point in the same paragraph, double-click **Paint format** ▼. Then, click in the paragraphs that begin *As an intern*, *Here is a partial list*, and *Once a year* to apply the first line indent to each of the paragraphs. Click **Paint format** ▼ to turn it off. Compare your screen with Figure B.

10 ▶ Your document will be saved automatically. Sign out of your Google account, and then submit as instructed by your instructor.

Sturgeon Point Productions

Internship Guide

The Internship Program

Sturgeon Point Productions produces and markets educational videos. We started our company in 1968, and now we are a dynamic and creative independent film and commercial production company. From our base in Miami, we create both contract and in-house videos and feature films.

As an intern, you might take part in the following types of productions:

- Short feature films
- Documentaries
- Commercials
- Training films
- Sales and marketing videos
- Recordings of live concerts, sporting events, or theatrical productions

Here is a partial list of internship positions currently available:

- Production Assistant
- Assistant Director
- Assistant Camera Operator
- Assistant Makeup Artist
- Assistant Set Designer

Introduction to Upcoming Internships

Once a year, Sturgeon Point Productions conducts a series of meetings to announce and describe upcoming projects and internships. Our employees are available at these events to describe each internship opportunity and to answer your questions. Meetings take place in our studios and are open to all eligible students enrolled in local film programs. Here is a list of September meetings:

1. Artists—September 5, 6:00 p.m.
2. Filming—September 6, 7:00 p.m.
3. Art—September 7, 6:00 p.m.
4. Animation—September 11, 7:00 p.m.
5. Music—September 12, 6:00 p.m.

FIGURE B

IC3 SKILLS IN THIS CHAPTER

IC3 Key Applications

Project 12A
Section 2.02 Word Processing
    (a) Perform basic formatting skills
    (c) Alter text and font styles
Project 12B
Section 2.02 Word Processing
    (e) Know page layout concepts
        (iii) Margin
        (iv) Alignment, text in paragraphs and tables
        (v) Tabs and rulers
        (vii) Spacing
    (f) Know how to print a word processing document

BUILD YOUR E-PORTFOLIO

An E-Portfolio is a collection of evidence, stored electronically, that showcases what you have accomplished while completing your education. Collecting and then sharing your work products with potential employers reflects your academic and career goals. Your completed documents from the following projects are good examples to show what you have learned: 12G, 12K, and 12L.

GO! FOR JOB SUCCESS

Video: Personal Branding
Your instructor may assign this video to your class, and then ask you to think about, or discuss with your classmates, these questions:

FotolEdhar / Fotolia

How do you suggest job seekers communicate their unique value—their personal brand—to potential employers online?

What are the best ways to network online and offline?

What are some of the biggest pitfalls in using social media to communicate a personal brand?

END OF CHAPTER

SUMMARY

In this chapter, you started Word and practiced navigating the Word window, and you entered, edited, and formatted text. You also inserted text from another Word file.

Graphics include pictures, shapes, and text boxes. In this chapter, you formatted objects by applying styles, effects, and text-wrapping options, and you sized and positioned objects on the page.

SmartArt graphics visually represent your ideas, and there are many SmartArt graphics from which to choose. You can also use online videos in your documents to provide visual information to the reader.

Word documents can be formatted to display your information attractively. You can add a page border, add bulleted and numbered lists, change margins and tabs, and modify paragraph and line spacing.

GO! LEARN IT ONLINE

Review the concepts, key terms, and IC3 skills in this chapter by completing these online challenges, which you can find at **MyITLab**.

Matching and Multiple Choice: Answer matching and multiple-choice questions to test what you learned in this chapter.

Lessons on the GO!: Learn how to use all the new apps and features as they are introduced by Microsoft.

IC3 Prep Quiz: Answer questions to review the IC3 skills that you practiced in this chapter.

GO! COLLABORATIVE TEAM PROJECT (Available in **MyITLab** and Instructor Resource Center)

If your instructor assigns this project to your class, you can expect to work with one or more of your classmates—either in person or by using Internet tools—to create work products similar to those that you created in this chapter. A team is a group of workers who work together to solve a problem, make a decision, or create a work product. Collaboration is when you work together with others as a team in an intellectual endeavor to complete a shared task or achieve a shared goal.

Your instructor will assign Projects from this list to ensure your learning and assess your knowledge.

Project	Apply Skills from These Chapter Objectives	Project Type	Project Location
12A MyITLab	Objectives 1-4 from Project 12A	**12A Instructional Project (Grader Project)** Guided instruction to learn the skills in Project 12A.	In MyITLab and in text
12B MyITLab	Objectives 5-8 from Project 12B	**12B Instructional Project (Grader Project)** Guided instruction to learn the skills in Project 12B.	In MyITLab and in text
12C	Objectives 1-4 from Project 12A	**12C Skills Review (Scorecard Grading)** A guided review of the skills from Project 12A.	In text
12D	Objectives 5-8 from Project 12B	**12D Skills Review (Scorecard Grading)** A guided review of the skills from Project 12B.	In text
12E MyITLab	Objectives 1-4 from Project 12A	**12E Mastery (Grader Project)** **Mastery and Transfer of Learning** A demonstration of your mastery of the skills in Project 12A with extensive decision making.	In MyITLab and in text
12F MyITLab	Objectives 5-8 from Project 12B	**12F Mastery (Grader Project)** **Mastery and Transfer of Learning** A demonstration of your mastery of the skills in Project 12B with extensive decision making.	In MyITLab and in text
12G MyITLab	Objectives 1-8 from Project 12A and 12B	**12G Mastery (Grader Project)** **Mastery and Transfer of Learning** A demonstration of your mastery of the skills in Projects 12A and 12B with extensive decision making.	In MyITLab and in text
12H	Combination of Objectives from Projects 12A and 12B	**12H GO! Fix It (Scorecard Grading)** **Critical Thinking** A demonstration of your mastery of the skills in Projects 12A and 12B by creating a correct result from a document that contains errors you must find.	Instructor Resource Center (IRC) and MyITLab
12I	Combination of Objectives from Projects 12A and 12B	**12I GO! Make It (Scorecard Grading)** **Critical Thinking** A demonstration of your mastery of the skills in Projects 12A and 12B by creating a result from a supplied picture.	IRC and MyITLab
12J	Combination of Objectives from Projects 12A and 12B	**12J GO! Solve It (Rubric Grading)** **Critical Thinking** A demonstration of your mastery of the skills in Projects 12A and 12B, your decision-making skills, and your critical thinking skills. A task-specific rubric helps you self-assess your result.	IRC and MyITLab
12K	Combination of Objectives from Projects 12A and 12B	**12K GO! Solve It (Rubric Grading)** **Critical Thinking** A demonstration of your mastery of the skills in Projects 12A and 12B, your decision-making skills, and your critical thinking skills. A task-specific rubric helps you self-assess your result.	In text
12L	Combination of Objectives from Projects 12A and 12B	**12L GO! Think (Rubric Grading)** **Critical Thinking** A demonstration of your understanding of the chapter concepts applied in a manner that you would outside of college. An analytic rubric helps you and your instructor grade the quality of your work by comparing it to the work an expert in the discipline would create.	In text
12M	Combination of Objectives from Projects 12A and 12B	**12M GO! Think (Rubric Grading)** **Critical Thinking** A demonstration of your understanding of the chapter concepts applied in a manner that you would outside of college. An analytic rubric helps you and your instructor grade the quality of your work by comparing it to the work an expert in the discipline would create.	IRC and MyITLab
12N	Combination of Objectives from Projects 12A and 12B	**12N You and GO! (Rubric Grading)** **Critical Thinking** A demonstration of your understanding of the chapter concepts applied in a manner that you would in a personal situation. An analytic rubric helps you and your instructor grade the quality of your work.	IRC and MyITLab
12O	Combination of Objectives from Projects 12A and 12B	**12O Collaborative Team Project for AIO Chapter 12** **Critical Thinking** A demonstration of your understanding of concepts and your ability to work collaboratively in a group role-playing assessment, requiring both collaboration and self-management.	IRC and MyITLab

GLOSSARY

GLOSSARY OF CHAPTER KEY TERMS

Alignment The placement of paragraph text relative to the left and right margins.

Alignment guide A green vertical or horizontal line that displays when you are moving or sizing an object to assist you with object placement.

Artistic effects Formats applied to images that make pictures resemble sketches or paintings.

Bulleted list A list of items with each item introduced by a symbol such as a small circle or check mark, and which is useful when the items in the list can be displayed in any order.

Bullets Text symbols such as small circles or check marks that precede each item in a bulleted list.

Center alignment The alignment of text or objects that is centered horizontally between the left and right margin.

Dot leader A series of dots preceding a tab that guides the eye across the line.

Drawing objects Graphic objects, such as shapes, diagrams, lines, or circles.

Embed code A code that creates a link to a video, picture, or other type of rich media content.

Floating object A graphic that can be moved independently of the surrounding text characters.

Formatting marks Characters that display on the screen, but do not print, indicating where the Enter key, the Spacebar, and the Tab key were pressed; also called nonprinting characters.

Graphics Pictures, charts, or drawing objects.

Inline object An object or graphic inserted in a document that acts like a character in a sentence.

Interactive media Computer interaction that responds to your actions; for example, by presenting text, graphics, animation, video, audio, or games. Also referred to as rich media.

Justified alignment An arrangement of text in which the text aligns evenly on both the left and right margins.

Layout Options Picture formatting options that control the manner in which text wraps around a picture or other object.

Leader character Characters that form a solid, dotted, or dashed line that fills the space preceding a tab stop.

Left alignment An arrangement of text in which the text aligns at the left margin, leaving the right margin uneven.

Line spacing The distance between lines of text in a paragraph.

Live Layout A feature that reflows text as you move or size an object so that you can view the placement of surrounding text.

Margins The space between the text and the top, bottom, left, and right edges of the paper.

Nonprinting characters Characters that display on the screen, but do not print; also called formatting marks.

Numbered list A list that uses consecutive numbers or letters to introduce each item in a list.

Object anchor The symbol that indicates to which paragraph an object is attached.

Picture effects Effects that enhance a picture, such as a shadow, glow, reflection, or 3-D rotation.

Picture styles Frames, shapes, shadows, borders, and other special effects that can be added to an image to create an overall visual style for the image.

Placeholder text Nonprinting text that holds a place in a document where you can type.

Rich media Computer interaction that responds to your actions; for example, by presenting text, graphics, animation, video, audio, or games. Also referred to as interactive media.

Right alignment An arrangement of text in which the text aligns at the right margin, leaving the left margin uneven.

Rotation handle A symbol with which you can rotate a graphic to any angle; displays above the top center sizing handle.

Shapes Lines, arrows, stars, banners, ovals, rectangles, and other basic shapes with which you can illustrate an idea, a process, or a workflow.

SmartArt A designer-quality visual representation of your information that you can create by choosing from among many different layouts to effectively communicate your message or ideas.

Spin box A small box with an upward- and downward-pointing arrow that lets you move rapidly through a set of values by clicking.

Tab stop A specific location on a line of text, marked on the Word ruler, to which you can move the insertion point by pressing the Tab key, and which is used to align and indent text.

Template A preformatted document that you can use as a starting point and then change to suit your needs.

Text box A movable resizable container for text or graphics.

Text effects Decorative formats, such as shadowed or mirrored text, text glow, 3-D effects, and colors that make text stand out.

Text wrapping The manner in which text displays around an object.

Toggle button A button that can be turned on by clicking it once, and then turned off by clicking it again.

Wordwrap The feature that moves text from the right edge of a paragraph to the beginning of the next line as necessary to fit within the margins.

Apply 12A skills from these Objectives:

1 Create a New Document and Insert Text
2 Insert and Format Graphics
3 Insert and Modify Text Boxes and Shapes
4 Preview and Print a Document

In the following Skills Review, you will create a flyer advertising a photography internship with Sturgeon Point Productions. Your completed document will look similar to Figure 12.52.

PROJECT FILES

For Project 12C, you will need the following files:

New blank Word document
w012C_Building
w012C_Photographer

You will save your document as:

Lastname_Firstname_12C_Photography

PROJECT RESULTS

Build from Scratch

Internship Available for
Still Photographer

This position requires skill in the use of:

Professional full-frame DSLR cameras

Tilt-shift lenses for tall buildings

This fall, Sturgeon Point Productions will film a documentary on the historic architecture in and around Milwaukee, Wisconsin

The filming will take place during the last two weeks of September. If the weather is not conducive to outdoor shooting, it is possible that filming will continue into the first week of October.

The still photographer will accompany the director during the first two weeks of September to scout locations and take photographs for the purpose of planning the filming schedule. The photographer will also accompany the film crew throughout filming.

Photographs taken during pre-production and filming will be used for advertising and marketing and published in an upcoming book on the history of the city of Milwaukee.

Submit Your Application by June 30!

Lastname_Firstname_12C_Photography

Word 2016, Windows 10, Microsoft Corporation

FIGURE 12.52

(Project 12C Photography continues on the next page)

1 Start Word and then click **Blank document**. On the **Home tab**, in the **Paragraph group**, if necessary, click Show/Hide to display the formatting marks. If the rulers do not display, click the View tab, and then in the Show group, select the Ruler check box.

a. Type **Internship Available for Still Photographer** and then press Enter two times. Type the following text: **This fall, Sturgeon Point Productions will film a documentary on the historic architecture in and around Milwaukee, Wisconsin.** Press Enter.

b. On the ribbon, click the **Insert tab**. In the **Text group**, click the **Object button arrow**, and then click **Text from File**. In the **Insert File** dialog box, navigate to the student files that accompany this chapter, locate and select **w12C_Photographer**, and then click **Insert**. Delete the blank paragraph at the end of the document.

c. Including the paragraph mark, select the first paragraph of text—*Internship Available for Still Photographer*. On the **Home tab**, in the **Font group**, click **Text Effects and Typography**. In the **Text Effects and Typography** gallery, in the first row, click the fourth effect—**Fill – White, Outline – Accent 5, Shadow**.

d. With the text still selected, in the **Font group**, click in the **Font Size** box to select the existing font size. Type **44** and then press Enter. In the **Font group**, click the **Font Color button arrow**. Under **Theme Colors**, in the fourth column, click the first color—**Blue-Gray, Text 2**.

e. With the text still selected, in the **Font group**, click **Text Effects and Typography**. Point to **Shadow**, and then under **Outer**, in the second row, click the third style—**Offset Left**. In the **Paragraph group**, click **Center**.

f. On the **Quick Access Toolbar**, click **Save**. Under **Save As**, click **Browse**. Navigate to your **AIO Chapter 12** folder. In the **File name** box, replace the existing text with **Lastname_Firstname_12C_Photography** and then click **Save**.

2 In the paragraph that begins *The filming*, click to position the insertion point at the beginning of the paragraph. On the **Insert tab**, in the **Illustrations group**, click **Pictures**. In the **Insert Picture** dialog box, navigate to your student data files, locate and click **w12C_Building**, and then click **Insert**.

a. To the right of the selected picture, click the **Layout Options** button, and then under **With Text Wrapping**, click the first option—**Square**. **Close** the Layout Options.

b. On the **Format tab**, in the **Size group**, click in the **Shape Height** box to select the value, type **2.7** and then press Enter.

c. With the picture selected, on the **Format tab**, in the **Arrange group**, click **Position**, and then click **More Layout Options**. In the **Layout** dialog box, on the **Position tab**, in the middle of the dialog box under **Vertical**, click the **Alignment** option button. To the right of **Alignment**, click the arrow, and then click **Top**. To the right of **relative to**, click the arrow, and then click **Line**. Click **OK**.

d. On the **Format tab**, in the **Picture Styles group**, click **Picture Effects**. Point to **Soft Edges**, and then click **5 Point**. On the **Format tab**, in the **Adjust group**, click **Artistic Effects**. In the fourth row, click the third effect—**Crisscross Etching**.

e. Click anywhere outside the picture to deselect it. On the **Design tab**, in the **Page Background group**, click **Page Borders**. In the **Borders and Shading** dialog box, on the **Page Border tab**, under **Setting**, click **Box**. Under **Style**, scroll the list and then click the third style from the bottom—a black line that fades to gray.

f. Click the **Color arrow**, and then in the next to last column, click the first color—**Blue, Accent 5**. Under **Apply to**, be sure **Whole document** is selected, and then click **OK**. Click **Save**.

3 Click the **Insert tab**, and then in the **Illustrations group**, click **Shapes** to display the gallery. Under **Basic Shapes**, in the second row, click the fifth shape—**Frame**.

a. Position the ⊞ pointer anywhere in the blank area at the bottom of the document. Click one time to insert a 1" by 1" frame. The exact location need not be precise. To the right of the shape, click the **Layout Options** button, and at the bottom click **See more**.

b. In the **Layout** dialog box, under **Horizontal**, click the **Alignment** option button. To the right of **Alignment**, click the arrow, and then click **Centered**. To the right of **relative to**, click the arrow, and then click **Page**. Under **Vertical**, click the **Absolute**

(Project 12C Photography continues on the next page)

position option button. In the **Absolute position** box, select the existing number, and then type **1** To the right of **below**, click the arrow, and then click **Paragraph**. Click **OK**.

c. On the **Format tab**, click in the **Shape Height** box. Type **1.5** and then click in the **Shape Width** box. Type **5.5** and then press Enter.

d. If necessary, select the frame shape. On the **Format tab**, in the **Shape Styles group**, click **More** ▾. In the **Shape Styles** gallery, in the first row, click the sixth style—**Colored Outline - Blue, Accent 5**. Type **Submit Your Application by June 30!** Select the text you just typed, and then on the mini toolbar, change the **Font Size** to **22**.

4 ▸ Click outside of the frame to deselect it, and then press Ctrl + Home to move to the top of the document. Press ↓ two times to move to the blank paragraph below the title. Press Enter four times to make space for a text box.

a. On the **Insert tab**, in the **Text group**, click **Text Box**. At the bottom of the gallery, click **Draw Text Box**. Position the ✛ pointer over the first blank paragraph at the left margin. Drag down and to the right to create a text box approximately 1.5 inches high and 4 inches wide—the exact size and location need not be precise.

b. With the insertion point blinking in the text box, type the following, pressing Enter after the first two lines to create a new paragraph:

This position requires skill in the use of:

Professional full-frame DSLR cameras

Tilt-shift lenses for tall buildings

c. To precisely place the text box, on the **Format tab**, in the **Arrange group**, click **Position**, and then click **More Layout Options**. In the **Layout** dialog box, under **Horizontal**, click the **Alignment** button. To the right of **Alignment**, click the arrow, and then click **Centered**. To the right of **relative to**, click the arrow, and then click **Page**.

d. Under **Vertical**, click the **Absolute position** button. In the **Absolute position** box, select the existing number. Type **2** To the right of **below**, click the arrow, and then click **Margin**.

e. In the **Layout** dialog box, click the **Size tab**. Under **Height**, select the number in the **Absolute** box. Type **1** and then under **Width**, select the number in the **Absolute** box. Type **3.75** and then click **OK**.

f. In the text box, select all of the text. If necessary, right-click over the selected text to display the mini toolbar. Change the **Font Size** to **12**, apply **Bold**, and then press Ctrl + E to **Center** the text.

g. On the **Format tab**, in the **Shape Styles group**, click **Shape Effects**. Point to **Shadow**, and then under **Outer**, in the first row, click the first style—**Offset Diagonal Bottom Right**.

h. In the **Shape Styles group**, click **Shape Outline**. In the fifth column, click the first color—**Blue, Accent 1** to change the color of the text box border. Click **Shape Fill**, and then in the fifth column, click the second color—**Blue, Accent 1, Lighter 80%**. Click **Save**.

5 ▸ Click the **Insert tab**, and then in the **Header & Footer group**, click **Footer**. At the bottom of the menu, click **Edit Footer**. On the **Header & Footer Tools Design tab**, in the **Insert group**, click **Document Info**, and then click **File Name**. Double-click in the document outside of the footer area to close the footer and return to the document.

a. Press Ctrl + Home to move the insertion point to the top of the document. In the upper left corner of your screen, click the **File tab** to display **Backstage** view. On the right, at the bottom of the **Properties list**, click **Show All Properties**.

b. On the list of Properties, click to the right of **Tags** to display an empty box, and then type **internship, documentary** Click to the right of **Subject** to display an empty box, and then type your course name and section #. Under **Related People**, be sure that your name displays as the author. If necessary, right-click the author name, click Edit Property, type your name, and click OK.

c. **Save** your document. In the upper right corner of the Word window, click **Close**. If directed by your instructor to do so, submit your paper printout, your electronic image of your document that looks like a printed document, or your completed Word file.

END | You have completed Project 12C

Project 12D Internship

Apply 12B skills from these Objectives:

5 Change Document and Paragraph Layout

6 Create and Modify Lists

7 Set and Modify Tab Stops

8 Insert a SmartArt Graphic and an Online Video

In the following Skills Review, you will edit an information handout regarding production and development internships with Sturgeon Point Productions. Your completed document will look similar to Figure 12.53.

PROJECT FILES

For Project 12D, you will need the following file:

w012D_Internship

You will save your document as:

Lastname_Firstname_12D_Internship

PROJECT RESULTS

STURGEON POINT PRODUCTIONS

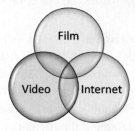

Sturgeon Point Productions is a full service film and video production facility located in Miami, Florida. Celebrating over 45 years of producing top quality commercial and independent film, our projects range from award winning documentaries and live action short features, to live concert and sporting events, to popular educational and training series of videos for schools, businesses, trade shows and multi-media presentations. We currently offer internships to film students in participating local colleges and universities, in both our development and production departments.

In-House Office Internships

Sturgeon Point Productions is looking for story analysts, research, post production and production assistants to work in our offices. We offer college credit as independent study at participating schools for one semester, which can be repeated for up to one year from the start date of the internship. To receive credit, interns must:

1. Be enrolled as a film major at a participating local college or university
2. Maintain a 3.0 GPA
3. Receive satisfactory monthly progress reports from their direct supervisor

Lastname_Firstname_12D_Internship

Following is a list of departments in our Miami office, currently seeking development and production interns:

✓ Development Department .... Researcher
✓ Development Department ....Asst. to Producer
✓ Development Department ....Writer's Assistant
✓ Post Production...Asst. Editor
✓ Post Production..Asst. Sound Editor
✓ Production...Asst. Office Manager

Additional Information

For more information and to sign up for our weekly newsletter, visit our website at www.sturgeonpointproductions.com. Be sure to view the following video to learn about some of the important skills you will develop as an intern with Sturgeon Point Productions.

Lastname_Firstname_12D_Internship

FIGURE 12.53

Word 2016, Windows 10, Microsoft Corporation

(Project 12D Internship continues on the next page)

1 Start Word, click **Open Other Documents**, and then click **Browse**. Navigate to your student files, and then open **w12D_Internship**. On the **Home tab**, in the **Paragraph group**, be sure **Show/Hide** is active. Click the **File tab**, and then click **Save As**. Navigate to your **AIO Chapter 12** folder, and then **Save** the document as **Lastname_Firstname_12D_Internship**

a. Click the **Layout tab**. In the **Page Setup group**, click **Margins**, and then click **Custom Margins**. In the **Page Setup** dialog box, press Tab as necessary to select the value in the **Left** box. Type **1** and then press Tab to select the value in the **Right** box. Type **1** and then click **OK**.

b. Scroll down to view the bottom of **Page 1**, point anywhere in the bottom margin area, right-click, and then click **Edit Footer** to display the footer area. On the **Header & Footer Tools Design tab**, in the **Insert group**, click **Document Info**, and then click **File Name**. Double-click anywhere in the document to close the footer area.

c. Press Ctrl + A to select all of the text in the document, and then on the **Home tab**, in the **Paragraph group**, click **Align Left**.

d. Press Ctrl + Home. Select the document title, and then on the **Home tab**, in the **Paragraph group**, click **Center**.

e. Locate the first bold subheading—*In-House Office Internships*. Point to the left of the paragraph to display the ⁂ pointer, and then click one time to select the text. With *In-House Office Internships* selected, locate the subheading *Additional Information*. Move the pointer to the left of the paragraph to display the ⁂ pointer, hold down Ctrl, and then click one time to select both paragraphs. In the **Paragraph group**, click **Center**.

f. Press Ctrl + A to select all of the text in the document. On the **Home tab**, in the **Paragraph group**, click **Line and Paragraph Spacing**, and then click **1.5**.

2 Below the title of the document, click anywhere in the paragraph that begins *Sturgeon Point Productions is a full service*. On the **Home tab**, in the **Paragraph group**, click the **Dialog Box Launcher**.

a. In the **Paragraph** dialog box, on the **Indents and Spacing tab**, under **Indentation**, click the **Special**

arrow, and then click **First line** to indent the first line by 0.5". Click **OK**, and then click anywhere in the paragraph that begins *Sturgeon Point Productions is looking for*. On the ruler under the ribbon, drag the **First Line Indent** marker to **0.5 inches on the horizontal ruler**.

b. Press Ctrl + A to select all of the text in the document. Click the **Layout tab**, and then in the **Paragraph group**, under **Spacing**, click the **After spin box up arrow** one time to change the value to **6 pt**.

c. Select the subheading **In-House Office Internships**, including the paragraph mark following it. Scroll down, hold down Ctrl, and then select the subheading **Additional Information**. With both subheadings selected, in the **Paragraph group**, under **Spacing**, click the **Before up spin box arrow** two times to set the **Spacing Before** to **12 pt**. **Save** your document.

3 Locate the first paragraph that begins *Development Department*, and then point to this paragraph from the left margin area to display the ⁂ pointer. Drag down to select this paragraph and the next five paragraphs so that six paragraphs are selected. On the **Home tab**, in the **Paragraph group**, click **Bullets** to change the selected text to a bulleted list.

a. Under the subheading *In-House Office Internships*, in the paragraph that begins *Sturgeon Point Productions is looking*, click to position the insertion point at the *end* of the paragraph, following the colon. Press Enter to create a blank paragraph. On the ruler, drag the **First Line Indent** marker to the left so that it is positioned directly above the lower button. Being sure to include the period, type **1.** and then press Spacebar to create the first item in a numbered list.

b. Type **Be enrolled as a film major at a participating local college or university** and then press Enter. Type **Maintain a 3.0 GPA** and then press Enter. Type **Receive satisfactory monthly progress reports from their direct supervisor**

c. Scroll down to view the bulleted list of departments, and then select all six bulleted items in the list. On the mini toolbar, click the **Bullets button arrow**, and then under **Bullet Library**, click the **check mark** symbol. If the check mark is not available, choose another bullet symbol.

(Project 12D Internship continues on the next page)

4 With the list selected, move the pointer to the horizontal ruler, and then point to and click at **3.5 inches on the horizontal ruler** to align the job titles at the tab mark.

a. With the bulleted list still selected, on the ruler, point to the new tab marker at **3.5 inches on the horizontal ruler**, and then when the *Left Tab* ScreenTip displays, drag the tab marker to **4 inches on the horizontal ruler**.

b. On the ruler, point to the tab marker that you moved to display the *Left Tab* ScreenTip, and then double-click to display the **Tabs** dialog box.

c. In the **Tabs** dialog box, under **Tab stop position**, if necessary select *4"*, and then type **6** Under **Alignment**, click the **Right** option button. Under **Leader**, click the **2** option button. Near the bottom of the **Tabs** dialog box, click **Set**.

d. Under **Tab stop position**, select **4"**, and then click **Clear** to delete the tab stop. Click **OK**. **Save** your document.

5 Press Ctrl + Home to move to the top of the document, and then in the title, click to the right of the *S* in *PRODUCTIONS*.

a. Click the **Insert tab**, and then in the **Illustrations group**, click **SmartArt**. On the left, click **Relationship**, and then scroll the list to the bottom. Locate and then click **Basic Venn**. Click **OK** to insert the SmartArt graphic. If necessary, close the Text Pane.

b. In the SmartArt graphic, click **[Text]** in the top circle shape. Type **Film** and then in the lower left shape, click the placeholder **[Text]**. Type **Video** and then in the third circle, type **Internet**

c. Click the SmartArt graphic border to select it. Click the **Format tab**, and then in the **Size group**, if

necessary click **Size** to display the **Shape Height** and **Shape Width** boxes. Set the **Height** to **3"** and the **Width** to **6.5"**.

d. With the SmartArt graphic still selected, on the ribbon, under **SmartArt Tools**, click the **Design tab**, and then in the **SmartArt Styles group**, click **Change Colors**. Under **Colorful**, click the third style—**Colorful Range - Accent Colors 3 to 4**. On the **Design tab**, in the **SmartArt Styles group**, click **More**. Under **3-D**, in the first row, click the third style—**Cartoon**.

6 Hold down Ctrl and then press End to move to the end of the document. On the **Insert tab**, in the **Media group**, click **Online Video**. Click in the **Bing Video Search** box. Including the quotation marks, type **"Go 2013 12B video"** and then press Enter. In the first row, click the first video, and then click **Insert**.

a. On the **Format tab**, in the **Size group**, change the **Height** to **2.0**

b. Click the **File tab**, and then on the right, click **Show All Properties**. In the **Tags** box, type **internship** and in the **Subject** box type your course name and section number. If necessary, in the **Author** box, replace the existing text with your first and last name. Click **Save**.

c. Click the **File tab**, and then click **Print** to display **Print Preview**. At the bottom of the preview, click the **Next Page** and **Previous Page** buttons to move between pages. If necessary, return to the document and make any necessary changes.

d. **Save** your document. In the upper right corner of the Word window, click **Close**. If directed by your instructor to do so, submit your paper printout, your electronic image of your document that looks like a printed document, or your completed Word file.

END | You have completed Project 12D

Mastering Word   Project 12E Documentary

In the following Mastery project, you will create a flyer announcing a special event being hosted by Sturgeon Point Productions. Your printed results will look similar to those in Figure 12.54.

Apply 12A skills from these Objectives:

1 Create a New Document and Insert Text

2 Insert and Format Graphics

3 Insert and Modify Text Boxes and Shapes

4 Preview and Print a Document

PROJECT FILES

For Project 12E, you will need the following files:

New blank Word document
w012E_Antarctica
w012E_Filmmaker

You will save your document as:

Lastname_Firstname_12E_Documentary

Build from Scratch

PROJECT RESULTS

Sturgeon Point Productions Presents Aria Pacheco

Sturgeon Point Productions will be hosting its *5th Annual Script to Screen* series, every Friday night this April in our Studio G screening room. All employees, interns, and film students with current school ID are welcome to share in this totally free, exciting evening, where our award-winning filmmakers from our Documentary and Short Feature Film Departments give a first-hand account of the filmmaking process and the challenges that went into their particular projects, from the script phase through production and finally, in distribution and marketing.

This year, we are proud to kick off the series with Aria Pacheco, who will discuss her multi-award winning documentary, **"Through the Cold."** This film documents the perils and triumphs of a team of scientists living in Antarctica. This compelling story, rich in visual complexity, follows the team as they prepare for the six months of darkness in the winter season. Celebrated film critic, Georges Harold, will be conducting an interview with Ms. Pacheco and select members of her crew following a screening of the film, which will take place on Friday, April 5th at 8 p.m. This event is guaranteed to fill up fast, so we suggest you get in line at least one hour prior to the screening.

"Through the Cold" has been heralded by critics across the country. Don't miss this chance to meet one of our greatest documentary filmmakers.

Date: April 5
Time: 8 p.m.
Place: Studio G Screening Room

Lastname_Firstname_12E_Documentary

Word 2016, Windows 10, Microsoft Corporation

FIGURE 12.54

(Project 12E Documentary continues on the next page)

1 Start Word and display a **Blank document** with the ruler and formatting marks displayed.

2 Type **Sturgeon Point Productions Presents Aria Pacheco** and then press Enter. From your student data files, insert the text file **w12E_Filmmaker**. Using your own name, **Save** the document in your **AIO Chapter 12** folder as **Lastname_Firstname_12E_Documentary**

3 To the document title, apply the **Fill – White, Outline – Accent 1, Glow – Accent 1** text effect, and then change the **Font Size** to 36.

4 Change the title **Font Color** to **Blue-Gray, Text 2**—in the fourth column, the first color. Apply an **Outer Shadow** using **Offset Left**—in the second row, the third style. **Center** the title.

5 Position the insertion point at the beginning of the paragraph that begins with *This year*, and then from your student data files, insert the picture **w012E_Antarctica**.

6 Change the **Layout Options** to **Square** and then change the **Height** of the picture to **2.25** Using the **Position** command, display the **Layout** dialog box, and then change the **Horizontal Alignment** to **Right relative to the Margin**.

7 Apply a **10 Point Soft Edges** picture effect to the image, and then display the **Artistic Effects** gallery. In the third row, apply the fourth effect—**Mosaic Bubbles**.

8 Deselect the picture. Apply a **Page Border** to the document using the **Shadow** setting. Select the first style,

and change the **Color** to **Blue-Gray, Text 2**. Change the **Width** to **3 pt**.

9 Below the last paragraph, draw a **Text Box** and then change the **Height** to **1.5** and the **Width** to **4.5**

10 To precisely place the text box, display the **Layout** dialog box. Change the **Horizontal Alignment** to **Centered**, **relative to** the **Page**, and then change the **Vertical Absolute position** to **0.5** below the **Paragraph**.

11 In the text box, type the following text:

> **Date: April 5**
>
> **Time: 8 p.m.**
>
> **Place: Studio G Screening Room**

12 In the text box, change the font size of all the text to **18**. Apply **Bold** and **Center**. Apply a **Shape Style** to the text box—under **Theme Styles**, in the last row, select the second style—**Intense Effect – Blue, Accent 1**. Change the **Shape Outline** to **Black, Text 1**.

13 Insert the **File Name** in the footer, and then display the document properties. As the **Tags** type **documentary, interview** and as the **Subject** type your course and section number. Be sure your name is indicated as the **Author**. **Save** your file.

14 Display the **Print Preview** and, if necessary, return to the document and make any necessary changes. **Save** your document and **Close** Word. If directed by your instructor to do so, submit your paper printout, your electronic image of your document that looks like a printed document, or your completed Word file.

END | You have completed Project 12E

Mastering Word **Project 12F Pitch Festival**

In the following Mastery project, you will edit a document with information regarding an event that Sturgeon Point Productions is holding for college students. Your printed results will look similar to those in Figure 12.55.

Apply 12B skills from these Objectives:

5 Change Document and Paragraph Layout

6 Create and Modify Lists

7 Set and Modify Tab Stops

8 Insert a SmartArt Graphic and an Online Video

PROJECT FILES

For Project 12F, you will need the following file:

w012F_Pitch_Festival

You will save your document as:

Lastname_Firstname_12F_Pitch_Festival

PROJECT RESULTS

Pitch Festival!

Do you have a story that must be told? Pitch us your project during the Sturgeon Point Productions annual Pitch Festival! We're setting up several days of conference video calls for college students that are currently enrolled in an accredited film production program anywhere in the United States. If your idea is selected, you will be flown to our studios in Miami, Florida to pitch your idea to our staff of producers and development executives. The following video provides additional information:

Sturgeon Point Productions is one of the leading independent film and video companies in the Miami area. We are currently looking for new, fresh, exciting ideas for short and full length feature films and documentaries. We like character driven stories that can be shot on an independent budget within one or two locations, preferably either in our studios or in the Miami area. We are currently looking for scripts, ideas, and concepts that are in one of the following categories:

1. Human interest or educational
2. Political or journalistic
3. Biographical or documentary

The Pitch Festival will take place at our secure website on the following dates and times. There are no entry fees to pitch; this unique opportunity to pitch to our staff of professional filmmakers is absolutely free for college film students. Sign up now at www.sturgeonpointproductions.com/pitchfest for one of the following pitch sessions:

- September 12, 11 a.m..Short and Feature Film Pitches
- September 13, 8 p.m. ....Biographical and Documentary Film Pitches
- September 14, 7 p.m. ....Educational Series Pitches

Lastname_Firstname_12F_Pitch_Festival

Word 2016, Windows 10, Microsoft Corporation

FIGURE 12.55

(Project 12F Pitch Festival continues on the next page)

1 Start Word, and then from your student files, open **w12F_Pitch_Festival**. Display formatting marks, and then **Save** the file in your **AIO Chapter 12** folder as **Lastname_Firstname_12F_Pitch_Festival**

2 Insert the **File Name** in the footer, and then change the **Line Spacing** for the entire document to **1.5**. **Center** the document title, and then change the title font size to **24**. Change the **Top** and **Bottom** margins to **0.5**

3 Select the three paragraphs below the title, and then apply a **First line** indent of **0.5"**.

4 Select the entire document, and then change the **Spacing Before** to **6 pt** and the **Spacing After** to **6 pt**.

5 Select the last three paragraphs containing the dates, and then apply filled square bullets. If the bullets are not available, choose another bullet style. With the bulleted list selected, set a **Right** tab with **dot leaders** at **6"**.

6 Locate the paragraph that begins *Sturgeon Point Productions*, and then click at the end of the paragraph, after the colon. Press [Enter] and remove the first line indent from the new paragraph.

7 In the blank line you inserted, create a numbered list with the following three numbered items:

Human interest or educational

Political or journalistic

Biographical or documentary

8 Position the insertion point at the end of the document after the word *Pitches*. Do *not* insert a blank line. Insert a **SmartArt** graphic from the **Process**

category. Toward the bottom of the gallery, select and insert the **Equation** SmartArt. Select the outside border of the SmartArt, and then change the **Height** of the SmartArt to **1** and the **Width** to **6.5**

9 With the SmartArt selected, change the layout to **Square**, and change the **Horizontal Alignment** to **Centered relative to** the **Page**. Change the **Vertical Alignment** to **Bottom relative to** the **Margin**.

10 In the first circle type **Your Ideas** and in the second circle type **Our Experts** In the third circle type **Pitch Festival!**

11 Change the SmartArt color to **Colorful Range – Accent Colors 4 to 5**. Apply the **3-D Polished** style.

12 Click at the end of the first paragraph below the title. Press [Enter], remove the first line indent, and then center the blank line. Insert an **Online Video**. In the **Bing Video Search** box, type **Go 1F Video** and then insert the video that displays a blue SmartArt. Change the height of the video to **1.5** and then **Save**.

13 Display the document properties. In the **Tags** box, type **pitch festival** and in the **Subject** box, type your course name and section number. In the **Author** box, replace the existing text with your first and last name. **Save** the file.

14 Display the **Print Preview** and if necessary, return to the document and make any necessary changes. **Save** your document and **Close** Word. If directed by your instructor to do so, submit your paper printout, your electronic image of your document that looks like a printed document, or your completed Word file.

END | You have completed Project 12F

In the following Mastery project, you will create a flyer that details a new educational website that Sturgeon Point Productions has developed for instructors. Your printed results will look similar to those in Figure 12.56.

Apply 12A and 12B skills from these Objectives:

1 Create a New Document and Insert Text

2 Insert and Format Graphics

3 Insert and Modify Text Boxes and Shapes

4 Preview and Print a Document

5 Change Document and Paragraph Layout

6 Create and Modify Lists

7 Set and Modify Tab Stops

8 Insert a SmartArt Graphic and an Online Video

Build from Scratch

PROJECT FILES

For Project 12G, you will need the following files:

New blank Word document
w012G_Education
w012G_Media

You will save your document as:

Lastname_Firstname_12G_Educational_Website

PROJECT RESULTS

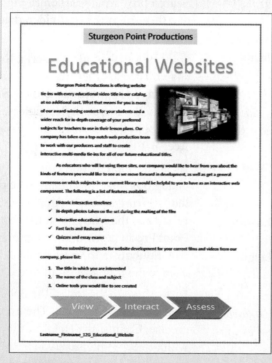

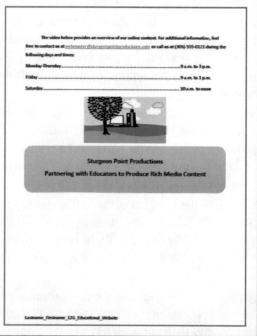

FIGURE 12.56

(Project 12G Educational Website continues on the next page)

1 Start Word and display a blank document. Display formatting marks and the ruler. **Save** the document in your **AIO Chapter 12** folder as **Lastname_Firstname_12G_Educational_Website**

2 Type **Educational Websites** and then press Enter. Type **Sturgeon Point Productions is offering website tie-ins with every educational video title in our catalog, at no additional cost.** Press Spacebar, and then with the insertion point positioned at the end of the sentence that you typed, insert the text from your student data file **w012G_Education**.

3 Change the **Line Spacing** for the entire document to **1.5** and the spacing **After** to **6 pt**. To each of the four paragraphs that begin *Sturgeon Point Productions*, *As educators*, *When submitting*, and *The video*, apply a **First Line** indent of **0.5"**.

4 Change the **font size** of the title to **50** and the **Line Spacing** to **1.0**. **Center** the title. With the title selected, display the **Text Effects and Typography** gallery. In the first row, apply the second effect—**Fill – Blue, Accent 1, Shadow**.

5 Click at the beginning of the paragraph below the title, and then from your student data files, insert the picture **w012G_Media**. Change the picture **Height** to **2** and the **Layout Options** to **Square**. Format the picture with **Soft Edges** in **10 Point**.

6 Use the **Position** command to display the **Layout** dialog box. Change the picture position so that the **Horizontal Alignment** is **Right relative to** the **Margin**. Change the **Vertical Alignment** to **Top relative to** the **Line**.

7 Select the five paragraphs beginning with *Historic interactive timelines* and ending with *Quizzes and essay exams*, and then apply check mark bullets.

8 In the paragraph below the bulleted list, click after the colon. Press Enter and remove the first line indent. Type a numbered list with the following three numbered items:

> **The title in which you are interested**
> **The name of the class and subject**
> **Online tools you would like to see created**

9 With the insertion point located at the end of the numbered list, insert a **SmartArt** graphic. In the **Process** category, locate and select the **Basic Chevron Process**. In the first shape type **View** In the second shape type **Interact** and in the third shape type **Assess**

10 Change the SmartArt color to **Colorful Range – Accent Colors 4 to 5**, and then apply the **3-D Flat Scene** style. Change the **Height** of the SmartArt to **1** and the **Width** to **6.5** Change the **Layout Options** to **Square**, the **Horizontal Alignment** to **Centered relative to** the **Page**, and the **Vertical Alignment** to **Bottom relative to** the **Margin**.

11 Select the days and times at the end of the document, and then set a **Right** tab with **dot leaders** at **6"**.

12 Click in the blank line below the tabbed list, and **Center** the line. Insert an **Online Video**. In the **Bing Video Search** box, type **Pearson Higher Education Learning** and then insert the first video that displays. Change the video **Height** to **1.5**

13 Below the video, insert a **Rounded Rectangle** shape. The exact location need not be precise. Change the **Shape Height** to **1.5** and the **Shape Width** to **6.5** Display the **Shape Styles** gallery, and then in the fourth row, apply the second style—**Subtle Effect - Blue, Accent 1**.

14 Use the **Position** command to display the **Layout** dialog box, and then change the position so that both the **Horizontal** and **Vertical Alignment** are **Centered relative to** the **Margin**. In the rectangle, type **Sturgeon Point Productions** and then press Enter. Type **Partnering with Educators to Produce Rich Media Content** and then change the font size of all of the text in the text box to **16**.

15 Move to the top of the document and insert a **Text Box** above the title. The exact location need not be precise. Change the **Height** of the text box to **0.5** and the width to **3.7** Type **Sturgeon Point Productions** and then change the font size to **22 Center** the text.

16 Use the **Position** command to display the **Layout** dialog box, and then position the text box so that the **Horizontal Alignment** is **Centered relative to** the **Page** and the **Vertical Absolute position** is **0.5 below** the **Page**.

17 With the text box selected, display the **Shape Fill** gallery, and then in the next to last column, select the second color—**Blue, Accent 5, Lighter 80%**. Change

(Project 12G Educational Website continues on the next page)

the **Shape Outline** to the same color—**Blue, Accent 5, Lighter 80%**.

18 Deselect the text box. Apply a **Page Border** to the document. Use the **Box** setting, and choose the first style. Change the **Color** to **Blue, Accent 5**.

19 Change the **Top** margin to **1.25** and insert the **File Name** in the footer.

20 Display the document properties. As the **Tags** type **website** and as the **Subject** type your course and section number. Be sure your name displays in the **Author** box. **Save** your document and **Close** Word. If directed by your instructor to do so, submit your paper printout, your electronic image of your document that looks like a printed document, or your completed Word file.

END | You have completed Project 12G

CONTENT-BASED ASSESSMENTS (CRITICAL THINKING)

| GO! Fix It | **Project 12H Casting Call** | MyITLab |

Build From Scratch

| GO! Make It | **Project 12I Development Team** | MyITLab |

| GO! Solve It | **Project 12J Softball** | MyITLab |

| GO! Solve It | **Project 12K Production** |

PROJECT FILES

For Project 12K, you will need the following files:

w012K_Production
w012K_Studio

You will save your document as:

Lastname_Firstname_12K_Production

From the student files that accompany this text, locate and open the file w12K_Production. Format the document using techniques you learned in this chapter to create an appropriate flyer aimed at filmmakers. From your student data files, insert the picture w12K_Studio, and then format the picture with an artistic effect. Insert a SmartArt graphic that illustrates two or three important points about the company. Use text effects and text wrapping so that the flyer is easy to read and understand and has an attractive design. Save the file in your AIO Chapter 12 folder as **Lastname_Firstname_12K_Production** and submit it as directed.

Performance Level

Performance Criteria		Exemplary: You consistently applied the relevant skills	Proficient: You sometimes, but not always, applied the relevant skills	Developing: You rarely or never applied the relevant skills
	Use text effects	Text effects applied to text in an attractive and appropriate manner.	Text effects are applied but do not appropriately display text.	Text effects not used.
	Insert and format a picture	The picture is inserted and text wrapping and an artistic effect are applied.	The picture is inserted but not formatted properly.	No picture is inserted in the document.
	Insert and format SmartArt	The SmartArt is inserted and appropriately formatted.	The SmartArt is inserted but no formatting is applied.	No SmartArt is inserted in the document.

END | You have completed Project 12K

OUTCOMES-BASED ASSESSMENTS (CRITICAL THINKING)

RUBRIC

The following outcomes-based assessments are *open-ended assessments*. That is, there is no specific correct result; your result will depend on your approach to the information provided. Make *Professional Quality* your goal. Use the following scoring rubric to guide you in *how* to approach the problem and then to evaluate *how well* your approach solves the problem.

The *criteria*—Software Mastery, Content, Format and Layout, and Process—represent the knowledge and skills you have gained that you can apply to solving the problem. The *levels of performance*—Professional Quality, Approaching Professional Quality, or Needs Quality Improvements—help you and your instructor evaluate your result.

	Your completed project is of Professional Quality if you:	Your completed project is Approaching Professional Quality if you:	Your completed project Needs Quality Improvements if you:
1-Software Mastery	Choose and apply the most appropriate skills, tools, and features and identify efficient methods to solve the problem.	Choose and apply some appropriate skills, tools, and features, but not in the most efficient manner.	Choose inappropriate skills, tools, or features, or are inefficient in solving the problem.
2-Content	Construct a solution that is clear and well organized, contains content that is accurate, appropriate to the audience and purpose, and is complete. Provide a solution that contains no errors of spelling, grammar, or style.	Construct a solution in which some components are unclear, poorly organized, inconsistent, or incomplete. Misjudge the needs of the audience. Have some errors in spelling, grammar, or style, but the errors do not detract from comprehension.	Construct a solution that is unclear, incomplete, or poorly organized, contains some inaccurate or inappropriate content, and contains many errors of spelling, grammar, or style. Do not solve the problem.
3-Format and Layout	Format and arrange all elements to communicate information and ideas, clarify function, illustrate relationships, and indicate relative importance.	Apply appropriate format and layout features to some elements, but not others. Overuse features, causing minor distraction.	Apply format and layout that does not communicate information or ideas clearly. Do not use format and layout features to clarify function, illustrate relationships, or indicate relative importance. Use available features excessively, causing distraction.
4-Process	Use an organized approach that integrates planning, development, self-assessment, revision, and reflection.	Demonstrate an organized approach in some areas, but not others; or, use an insufficient process of organization throughout.	Do not use an organized approach to solve the problem.

OUTCOMES-BASED ASSESSMENTS (CRITICAL THINKING)

Apply a combination of the 12A and 12B skills.

Build from Scratch

GO! Think | Project 12L Classes

PROJECT FILES

For Project 12L, you will need the following file:

New blank Word document

You will save your document as:

Lastname_Firstname_12L_Classes

The Human Resources director at Sturgeon Point Productions needs to create a flyer to inform full-time employees of educational opportunities beginning in September. The courses are taught each year by industry professionals and are designed to improve skills in motion picture and television development and production. Employees who have been with Sturgeon Point Productions for at least two years are eligible to take the courses free of cost. The classes provide employees with opportunities to advance their careers, gain valuable skills, and achieve technical certification. All courses take place in Studio G. Interested employees should contact Elana Springs in Human Resources to sign up. Information meetings are being held at 5:30 according to the following schedule: television development on June 15; motion picture production on June 17; and recording services on June 21.

Create a flyer with basic information about the courses and information meetings. Be sure the flyer is easy to read and understand and has an attractive design. Save the document as **Lastname_Firstname_12L_Classes** and submit it as directed.

> **END | You have completed Project 12L**

Build from Scratch

GO! Think | Project 12M Store   MyITLab

Build from Scratch

You and GO! | Project 12N Family Flyer   MyITLab

Build from Scratch

GO! Collaborative Team Project | Project 12O Bell Orchid Hotels   MyITLab

Creating Cover Letters and Using Tables to Create Resumes

PROJECT 13A	OUTCOMES Write a resume by using a Word table.

OBJECTIVES

1. Create a Table
2. Format a Table
3. Present a Word Document Online

PROJECT 13B	OUTCOMES Write a cover letter and print an envelope.

OBJECTIVES

4. Create a Custom Word Template
5. Correct and Reorganize Text
6. Use the Proofing Options and Print an Envelope

Kaspars Grinvalds/Fotolia

In This Chapter GO! to Work with Word

Tables are useful for organizing and presenting data. Because a table is so easy to use, many individuals prefer to arrange tabular information in a Word table rather than setting a series of tabs. For example, you can use a table when you want to present rows and columns of information or to create a format for a document such as a resume.

When using Word to write business or personal letters, use a commonly approved letter format, and always use a clear writing style. You will make a good impression on prospective employers if you use a standard business letter style when you are writing a cover letter for a resume.

The projects in this chapter relate to the **College Career Center at Florida Port Community College** in St. Petersburg, Florida, a coastal port city near the Florida High Tech Corridor. With 60 percent of Florida's high tech companies and a third of the state's manufacturing companies located in the St. Petersburg and Tampa Bay areas, the college partners with businesses to play a vital role in providing a skilled workforce. The College Career Center assists students in exploring careers, finding internships, and applying for jobs. The Center offers workshops for resume and cover letter writing and for practice interviews.

PROJECT ACTIVITIES

In Activities 13.01 through 13.11, you will create a table to use as the format for a resume. The director of the Career Center, Mary Walker-Huelsman, will use this model when assisting students with building their resumes. Your completed document will look similar to Figure 13.1.

PROJECT FILES

MyITLab grader

If your instructor wants you to submit Project 13A in the MyITLab Grader system, log in to MyITLab, locate Grader Project 13A, and then download the files for this project.

For Project 13A, you will need the following file:

New blank Word document
w013A_Experience

You will save your document as:

Lastname_Firstname_13A_Resume

PROJECT RESULTS

Build From
Scratch

GO!
Walk Thru
Project13A

Josh Hayes   (727) 555-0313
1541 Dearborn Lane, St. Petersburg, FL 33713   jhayes@alcona.net

OBJECTIVE   Technology writing and editing position in the robotics industry, using research
                   and advanced editing skills to communicate with customers.

SUMMARY OF   • Two years' experience in robotics lab for Aerospace Instruction Team
QUALIFICATIONS   • Excellent interpersonal and communication skills
                   • Proficiency using Microsoft Word
                   • Proficiency using page layout and design software
                   • Fluency in spoken and written Spanish

EXPERIENCE   **Instructional Lab Assistant**, Florida Port Community College, St. Petersburg, FL
                   July 2013 to June 2015
                   • Assist robotics professors with sophisticated experiments
                   • Set up robotics practice sessions for Aerospace Instruction Team

                   Assistant Executive Editor, Tech Today Newsletter, St. Petersburg, FL
                   September 2012 to June 2013
                   • Wrote and edited articles for popular college technology newsletter
                   • Responsible for photo editing, cropping, and resizing photos for newsletter
                   • Received Top College Technology Publication Award

                   Teacher's Assistant, Florida Port Community College, Aerospace Department,
                   St. Petersburg, FL July 2013 to June 2015
                   • Helped students with homework, explained assignments, organized
                     materials for professor
                   • Set up robotics lab assignments for students

EDUCATION   **University of South Florida, Tampa, FL**
                   Bachelor of Science, Mechanical Engineering, June 2015

                   Florida Port Community College, St. Petersburg, FL
                   Associate of Arts, Journalism, June 2013

HONORS AND   • Elected to Pi Tau Sigma, honor society for mechanical engineers
ACTIVITIES   • Qualified for Dean's List, six semesters
                   • Student Mentor, help other students in engineering programs

---

Lastname_Firstname_13A_Resume

FIGURE 13.1 Project 13A Resume

GO! Learn How
Video W13-1

IC3
DIGITAL LITERACY
CERTIFICATION
2.02i

A *table* is an arrangement of information organized into rows and columns. The intersection of a row and a column in a table creates a box called a *cell* into which you can type. Tables are useful to present information in a logical and orderly format.

Activity 13.01 | Creating a Table by Specifying Rows and Columns

> **ALERT!**
>
> **To submit as an autograded project, log into MyITLab, download the files for this project, and begin with those files instead of a new blank document.**

1 Start Word and then click **Blank document**. On the **Home tab**, in the **Paragraph group**, if necessary click Show/Hide to display the formatting marks. If the rulers do not display, click the View tab, and then in the Show group, select the Ruler check box.

2 Click the **File tab** to display **Backstage** view, click **Save As**, and then click **Browse**. In the **Save As** dialog box, navigate to the location where you are storing your projects for this chapter. Create a new folder named **AIO Chapter 13**

3 **Save** the file in the **AIO Chapter 13** folder as **Lastname_Firstname_13A_Resume**

4 On the **Insert tab**, in the **Header & Footer group**, click **Footer**, and then at the bottom of the list, click **Edit Footer**. On the ribbon, in the **Insert group**, click **Document Info**, click **File Name**, and then at the right end of the ribbon, click **Close Header and Footer**.

5 On the **Insert tab**, in the **Tables group**, click **Table**. In the **Insert Table** grid, in the fourth row, point to the second square, and notice that the cells are bordered in orange and *2x4 Table* displays at the top of the grid. Compare your screen with Figure 13.2.

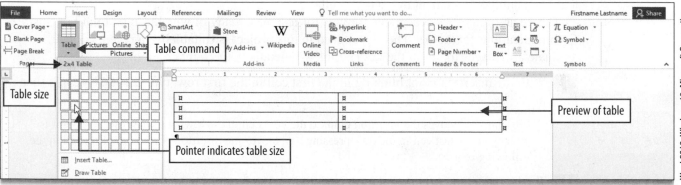

FIGURE 13.2

6 Click one time to create the table. Notice that formatting marks in each cell indicate the end of the contents of each cell; the mark to the right of each *row* indicates the row end. **Save** your document, and then compare your screen with Figure 13.3.

> A table with four rows and two columns displays at the insertion point location, and the insertion point displays in the upper left cell. The table fills the width of the page, from the left margin to the right margin. On the ribbon, Table Tools and two additional tabs—*Design* and *Layout*—display. Borders display around each cell in the table.

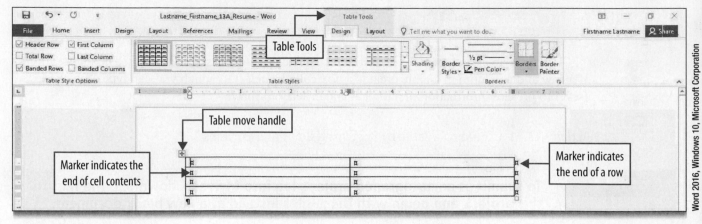

FIGURE 13.3

More Knowledge **Converting Text to a Table and Converting a Table to Text**

You can convert text you have already typed to a table. To do so, if necessary, first use commas or tabs within paragraphs to signal Word to create a column. Then, on the Insert tab, click Table, and click Convert Text to Table. In the Convert Text to Table dialog box, confirm the number of columns you want, indicate the delimiter character you used (e.g. Tab or Paragraph mark), and then click OK. You can convert a table to regular text and choose which text character to use to separate the columns. To do so, on the Table Tools Layout tab, in the Data group, click Convert to Text.

2.02c
2.02i

Activity 13.02 | **Typing Text in a Table**

In a Word table, each cell behaves similarly to a document. For example, as you type in a cell, when you reach the right border of the cell, wordwrap moves the text to the next line. When you press Enter, the insertion point moves down to a new paragraph in the same cell. You can also insert text from another document into a table cell.

There are numerous acceptable formats for resumes, many of which can be found in Business Communications textbooks. The layout used in this project is suitable for a recent college graduate and places topics in the left column and details in the right column.

1 With the insertion point blinking in the first cell in the first row, type **OBJECTIVE** and then press Tab.

Pressing Tab moves the insertion point to the next cell in the row, or, if the insertion point is already in the last cell in the row, pressing Tab moves the insertion point to the first cell in the following row.

2 Type **Technology writing and editing position in the robotics industry, using research and advanced editing skills to communicate with customers.** Notice that the text wraps in the cell and the height of the row adjusts to fit the text.

3 Press Tab to move to the first cell in the second row. Type **SUMMARY OF QUALIFICATIONS** and then press Tab. Type the following, pressing Enter at the end of each line *except* the last line:

Two years' experience in robotics lab for Aerospace Instruction Team
Excellent interpersonal and communication skills
Proficiency using Microsoft Word
Proficiency using page layout and design software
Fluency in spoken and written Spanish

The default font and font size in a table are the same as for a document—Calibri 11 pt. The default line spacing in a table is single spacing with no space before or after paragraphs, which differs from the defaults for a document.

4 **Save** 🖫 your document, and then compare your screen with Figure 13.4.

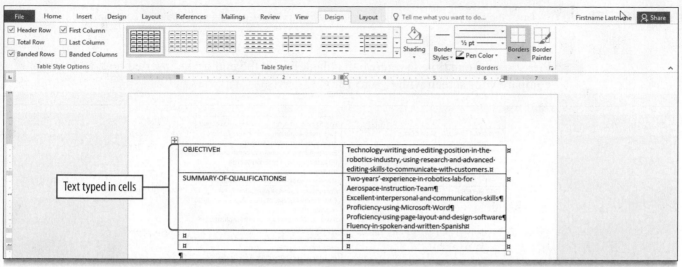

FIGURE 13.4

DIGITAL LITERACY CERTIFICATION
2.02c

Activity 13.03 | Inserting Text from a File and Removing Blank Paragraphs

1 Press [Tab] to move to the first cell in the third row. Type **EXPERIENCE** and then press [Tab].

2 Type the following, pressing [Enter] after each item, including the last item:

Instructional Lab Assistant, Florida Port Community College, St. Petersburg, FL July 2013 to June 2015
Assist robotics professors with sophisticated experiments
Set up robotics practice sessions for Aerospace Instruction Team

3 Be sure your insertion point is positioned in the second column to the left of the cell marker below *Instruction Team.* Compare your screen with Figure 13.5.

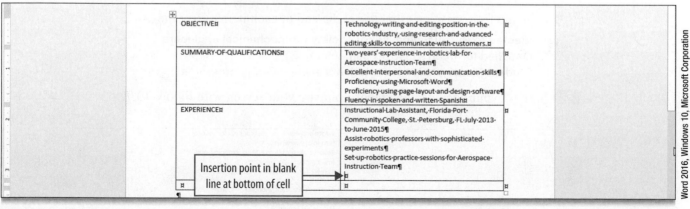

FIGURE 13.5

4 On the **Insert tab**, in the **Text group**, click the **Object button arrow**, and then click **Text from File**. Navigate to your student data files, select **w13A_Experience**, and then click **Insert**.

All of the text from the w13A_Experience document is added to the document at the insertion point.

↻ **ANOTHER WAY**   Open the second document and select the text you want. Copy the text, and then paste at the desired location.

5 Press Backspace one time to remove the blank line at the end of the inserted text, and then compare your screen with Figure 13.6.

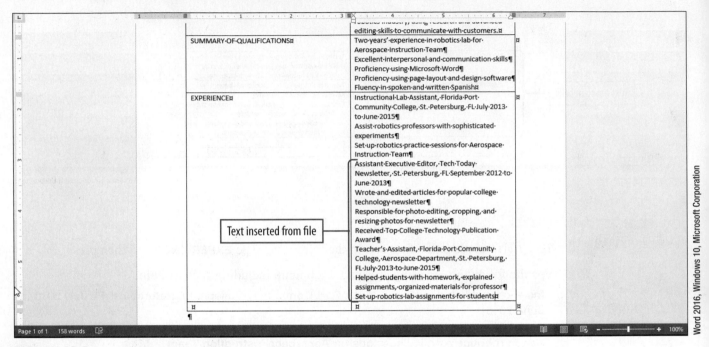

FIGURE 13.6

6 Press Tab to move to the first cell in the fourth row. Type **HONORS AND ACTIVITIES** and then press Tab.

7 Type the following, pressing Enter at the end of each item *except* the last one:

    Elected to Pi Tau Sigma, honor society for mechanical engineers
    Qualified for Dean's List, six semesters
    Student Mentor, help other students in engineering programs

8 **Save** 💾 your document, and then compare your screen with Figure 13.7.

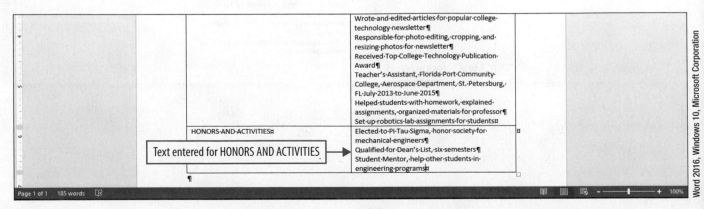

FIGURE 13.7

1 Press Ctrl + Home to move to the top of your document, and then in the cell to the right of *SUMMARY OF QUALIFICATIONS*, select all of the text.

2 On the **Home tab**, in the **Paragraph group**, click **Bullets** ☷▾.

> The selected text displays as a bulleted list to make each qualification more distinctive.

3 Click anywhere in the cell to deselect the bulleted text, and then drag to select all of the bulleted text again. In the **Paragraph group**, click **Decrease Indent** ☷ one time to align the bullets at the left edge of the cell.

4 Scroll as necessary so that you can view the entire *EXPERIENCE* and *HONORS AND ACTIVITIES* sections on your screen. With the bulleted text still selected, in the **Clipboard group**, double-click **Format Painter**.

5 In the cell to the right of *EXPERIENCE*, select the second and third paragraphs—beginning with *Assist* and *Set up*—to create the same style of bulleted list as you did in the previous step.

6 In the same cell, under *Assistant Executive Editor*, select the three paragraphs that begin *Wrote* and *Responsible* and *Received* to create another bulleted list aligned at the left edge of the cell.

7 In the same cell, select the paragraphs that begin *Helped* and *Set up* to create the same type of bulleted list.

8 In the cell below, select the paragraphs that begin *Elected*, *Qualified*, and *Student* to create a bulleted list.

9 Press Esc to turn off the **Format Painter**. Click anywhere in the table to deselect the text, **Save** 💾 your document, and then compare your screen with Figure 13.8.

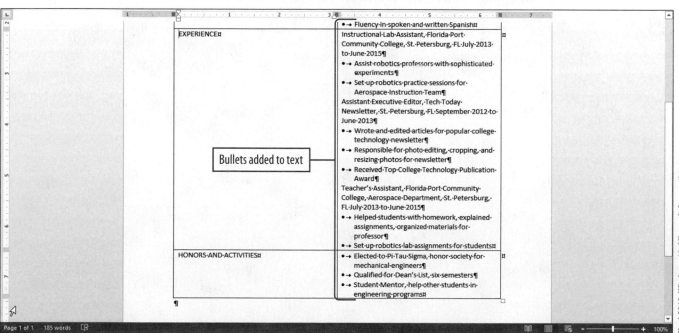

FIGURE 13.8

Use Word's formatting tools to make your tables attractive and easy to read. Types of formatting you can add to a table include changing the row height and the column width, removing or adding borders, increasing or decreasing the paragraph or line spacing, and enhancing the text.

Activity 13.05 | Changing the Width of Table Columns and Using AutoFit

When you create a table, all of the columns are of equal width. In this Activity, you will change the width of the columns.

1 Press `Ctrl` + `Home`. Click anywhere in the first column, and then on the ribbon, under **Table Tools**, click the **Layout tab**. In the **Cell Size group**, notice the **Width** box, which displays the width of the active column.

2 Look at the horizontal ruler and locate the **1.5-inch mark**. Then, in the table, in any row, point to the vertical border between the two columns to display the ⊣⊢ pointer.

3 Hold down the left mouse button and drag the column border to the left until the white arrow on the ruler is at approximately **1.5 inches on the horizontal ruler** and then release the left mouse button.

4 In the **Cell Size group**, click the **Width box down spin arrow** as necessary to set the column width to **1.4"** and notice that the right border of the table moves to the right.

Adjusting column width by dragging a column border adjusts only the width of the column; adjusting column width with the Width box simultaneously adjusts the right border of the table.

5 In the **Cell Size group**, click **AutoFit**, and then click **AutoFit Window** to stretch the table across the page within the margins so that the right border of the table is at the right margin. **Save** 🖫 and then compare your screen with Figure 13.9.

ANOTHER WAY You can adjust column widths by dragging the Move Table Column markers on the ruler. To maintain the right border of the table at the right margin, hold down `Shift` while dragging. To display measurements on the ruler, hold down `Alt` while dragging the marker.

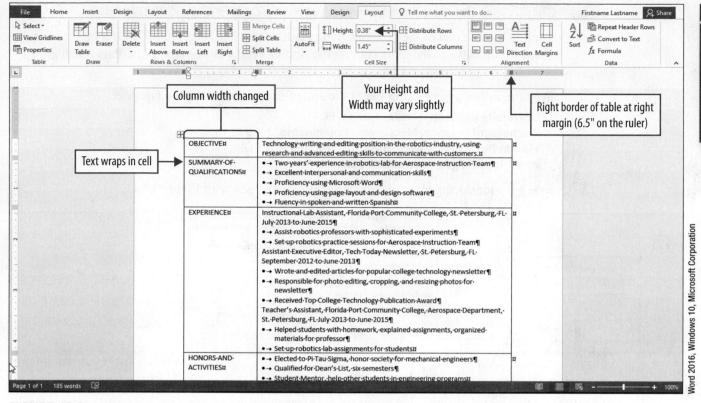

FIGURE 13.9

More Knowledge | **Changing Column Widths**

You will typically get the best results if you change the column widths starting at the left side of the table, especially in tables with three or more columns. Word can also calculate the best column widths for you. To do this, select the table. Then, on the Layout tab, in the Cell Size group, click the AutoFit button and click AutoFit Contents.

2.02i

Activity 13.06 | **Using One-Click Row/Column Insertion to Modify Table Dimensions**

One of the most common actions you will take in a table is adding another row or another column. By using *One-click Row/Column Insertion* you can do so in context by pointing to the left or top edge where you want the row or column to appear and then clicking the ⊕ button to add it.

1 ▶ Scroll to view the lower portion of the table. On the left border of the table, *point* to the upper left corner of the cell containing the text *HONORS AND ACTIVITIES* to display the **One-click Row/Column Insertion** button. Compare your screen with Figure 13.10.

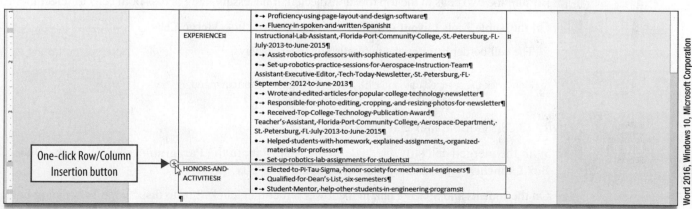

FIGURE 13.10

2 Click ⊕ one time to insert a new row above the *HONORS AND ACTIVITIES* row.

3 Click in the left cell of the new row, type **EDUCATION** and then press ⟨Tab⟩. If a bullet character displays in the table cell, on the ribbon, on the **Home tab**, in the **Paragraph group**, click **Bullets** to turn off Bullets.

4 Type the following, pressing ⟨Enter⟩ at the end of each item *except* the last one:

> **University of South Florida, Tampa, FL**
> **Bachelor of Science, Mechanical Engineering, June 2015**
> **Florida Port Community College, St. Petersburg, FL**
> **Associate of Arts, Journalism, June 2013**

5 **Save** 🖫 your document, and then compare your screen with Figure 13.11.

FIGURE 13.11

🔄 **ANOTHER WAY** When the insertion point is in the last cell in the bottom row of a table, you can add a row by pressing the Tab key; the insertion point will display in the first cell of the new row.

IC3
DIGITAL LITERACY
CERTIFICATION
2.02i
2.02e (iv)

Activity 13.07 | Merging Table Cells

The title of a table typically spans all of the columns. In this Activity, you will merge cells so that you can position the personal information across both columns.

1 Press ⟨Ctrl⟩ + ⟨Home⟩ to move to the top of your document, and then click anywhere in the top row of the table.

2 On the **Table Tools Layout tab**, in the **Rows & Columns group**, click **Insert Above**.

A new row displays above the row that contained the insertion point, and the new row is selected. This is another method to insert rows and columns in a table; use this method to insert a new row at the top of a table.

🔄 **ANOTHER WAY** Right-click in the top row, point to Insert, and then click Insert Rows Above.

3 Be sure the two cells in the top row are selected; if necessary, drag across both cells to select them.

4 On the **Table Tools Layout tab**, in the **Merge group**, click **Merge Cells**.

The cell border between the two cells no longer displays.

🔄 **ANOTHER WAY** Right-click the selected row and click Merge Cells on the shortcut menu.

IC3
DIGITAL LITERACY
CERTIFICATION
2.02e (iv)

Activity 13.08 | Setting Tabs in a Table

1 With the merged cell still selected, on the **Home tab**, in the **Paragraph group**, click the **Dialog Box Launcher** 🗗 to display the **Paragraph** dialog box.

2 On the **Indents and Spacing tab**, in the lower left corner, click **Tabs** to display the **Tabs** dialog box.

3 Under **Tab stop position**, type **6.5** and then under **Alignment**, click the **Right** option button. Click **Set**, and then click **OK** to close the dialog box.

4 Type **Josh Hayes** Hold down Ctrl and then press Tab. Notice that the insertion point moves to the right-aligned tab stop at 6.5".

In a Word table, you must use Ctrl + Tab to move to a tab stop, because pressing Tab is reserved for moving the insertion point from cell to cell.

5 Type **(727) 555-0313** and then press Enter.

6 Type **1541 Dearborn Lane, St. Petersburg, FL 33713** Hold down Ctrl and then press Tab.

7 Type **jhayes@alcona.net** Save 💾 your document, and then compare your screen with Figure 13.12.

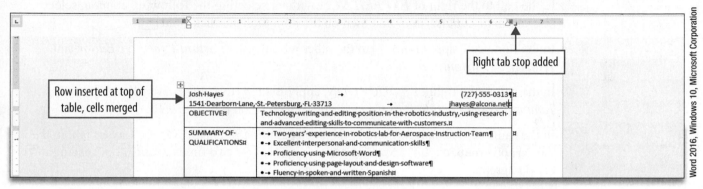

FIGURE 13.12

2.02c
2.02e (iv)

Activity 13.09 | Using Spacing After in a Table

1 In the first row of the table, select the name *Josh Hayes*, and then on the mini toolbar, apply **Bold** B and change the **Font Size** to **16**.

2 Under *Josh Hayes*, click anywhere in the second line of text, which contains the address and email address.

3 On the **Layout tab**, in the **Paragraph group**, click the **Spacing After up spin arrow** three times to add **18 pt** spacing between the first row of the table and the second row. Compare your screen with Figure 13.13.

This action separates the personal information from the body of the resume and adds focus to the name.

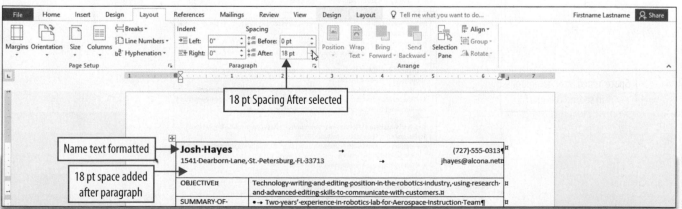

FIGURE 13.13

4 Using the technique you just practiced, in the second column, click in the last paragraph of *every cell* and add **18 pt Spacing After** including the last row; a border will be added to the bottom of the table, and spacing will be needed between the last row and the border.

5 In the second row, point to the word *OBJECTIVE*, hold down the left mouse button, and then drag downward in the first column only to select all the headings in uppercase letters. On the mini toolbar, click **Bold** B.

> **NOTE** Selecting Only One Column
>
> When you drag downward to select the first column, a fast mouse might also begin to select the second column when you reach the bottom. If this happens, drag upward slightly to deselect the second column and select only the first column.

6 In the cell to the right of *EXPERIENCE*, without selecting the following comma, select *Instructional Lab Assistant* and then on the mini toolbar, click **Bold** B.

7 In the same cell, apply **Bold** B to the other job titles—*Assistant Executive Editor* and *Teacher's Assistant.*

8 In the cell to the right of *EDUCATION*, apply **Bold** B to *University of South Florida, Tampa, FL* and *Florida Port Community College, St. Petersburg, FL.*

9 In the same cell, click anywhere in the line beginning *Bachelor*. On the **Layout tab**, in the **Paragraph group**, click the **Spacing After up spin arrow** two times to add **12 pt** spacing after the paragraph.

10 In the cell to the right of *EXPERIENCE*, under *Instructional Lab Assistant*, click anywhere in the second bulleted item, and then add **12 pt Spacing After** the item.

11 In the same cell, repeat this process for the last bulleted item under *Assistant Executive Editor.*

12 Scroll to view the top of your document, **Save** 💾 your document, and then compare your screen with Figure 13.14.

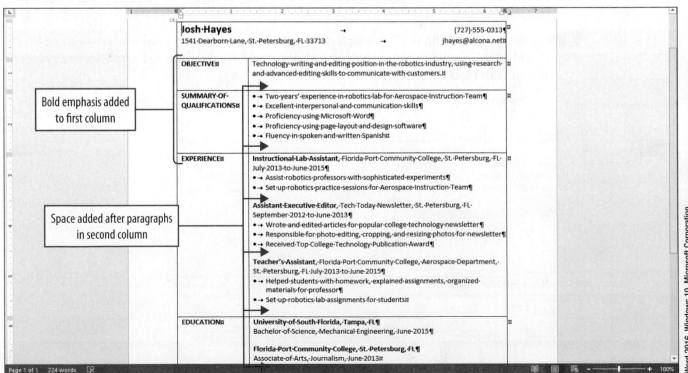

FIGURE 13.14

Activity 13.10 | Modifying Table Borders and Using Spacing Before

When you create a table, all of the cells have black 1/2-point, single-line, solid-line borders that print unless you remove them. Most resumes do not display any cell borders. A border at the top and bottom of the resume, however, is attractive and adds a professional look to the document.

1 Scroll as necessary to view the top margin area above the table, and then point slightly outside of the upper left corner of the table to display the **table move handle** ⊞.

2 Click the 🔝 pointer one time to select the entire table, and notice that the row markers at the end of each row are also selected.

Shaded row markers indicate that the entire row is selected. Use this technique to select the entire table.

3 On the ribbon, under **Table Tools**, click the **Design tab**. In the **Borders group**, click the **Borders button arrow**, and then click **No Border**.

The black borders no longer display.

4 Press Ctrl + P, which is the keyboard shortcut to view the Print Preview, and notice that no borders display in the preview. Then, press **Back** ⊙ to return to your document.

5 With the table still selected, on the **Design tab**, in the **Borders group**, click the **Borders button arrow**, and then at the bottom of the **Borders** gallery, click **Borders and Shading**.

6 In the **Borders and Shading** dialog box, on the **Borders tab**, under **Setting**, click **Custom**. Under **Style**, scroll down about one-third of the way, and then click the style with a **thick upper line and a thin lower line**.

7 In the **Preview** box at the right, point to the *top* border of the small preview and click one time.

🔄 **ANOTHER WAY**   Click the top border button, which is one of the buttons that surround the Preview.

8 Under **Style**, scroll down if necessary, click the opposite style—with the **thin upper line and the thick lower line**, and then in the **Preview** box, click the *bottom* border of the preview. Compare your screen with Figure 13.15.

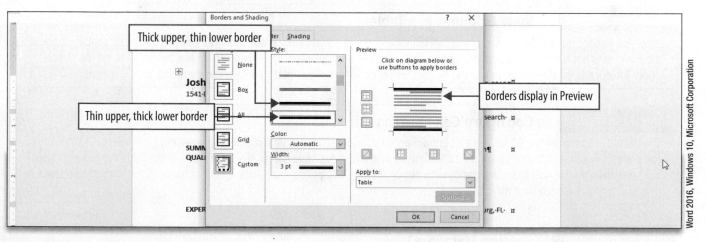

FIGURE 13.15

9 Click **OK**, click anywhere to cancel the selection, and then notice that there is only a small amount of space between the upper border and the first line of text.

10 ▸ Click anywhere in the text *Josh Hayes*, and then on the **Layout tab**, in the **Paragraph group**, click the **Spacing Before up spin arrow** as necessary to add **18 pt** spacing before the first paragraph.

11 ▸ Press Ctrl + P to display **Print Preview**. Compare your screen with Figure 13.16.

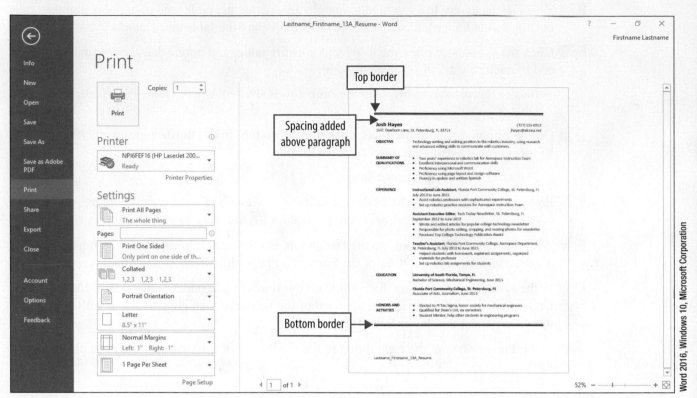

FIGURE 13.16

12 ▸ Press **Back** ⊙ to return to your document, and then on the Quick Access Toolbar, click **Save** 💾.

More Knowledge | **View Gridlines in a Table**

After you remove borders from a table, you can still view nonprinting gridlines, which show the cell boundaries of a table whenever the table does not have borders applied. Some people find this a useful visual aid. If you cannot see the gridlines, on the ribbon, under Table Tools, on the Design tab, in the Borders group, click the Borders button arrow, and then click View Gridlines.

More Knowledge | **Configure Cell Margins**

The default cell margins are 0" for Top and Bottom and 0.08" for Left and Right. To change the cell margins: Select the table (or you can select only some of the cells). On the Table Tools Layout tab, in the Table group, click Properties. In the Table Properties dialog box, click the Cell tab, and then click the Options button. In the Cell Options dialog box, clear the Same as the Whole Table check box, and then set your desired margins.

More Knowledge | **Sorting Data in a Table**

You can sort information in a table. To do so, click anywhere in the table, and then on the Table Tools Layout tab, click Sort. In the Sort dialog box, if the first row contains header information, select the Header Row option button in the lower left corner of the dialog box. In the Sort By list, select the column on which you want to sort, select the Type if necessary, select Ascending or Descending, and then click OK.

GO! Learn How
Video W13-3

Office Presentation Service enables you to present your Word document to others who can watch in a web browser. No preliminary setup is necessary; Word creates a link to your document that you can share with others via email or instant message. Anyone to whom you send the link can see your document while you are presenting online.

Individuals watching your presentation can navigate within the document independently of you or others in the presentation, so they can use a mouse, keyboard, or touch input to move around in the document while you are presenting it. If an individual is viewing a different portion of the document than the presenter, an alert displays on his or her screen. To return to the portion of the document that the presenter is showing, a Follow Presenter button displays.

While you are presenting, you can make minor edits to the document. If you want to share a copy of the document to the presentation attendees, you can select *Enable remote viewers to download the document* when you start the presentation. You can also share any meeting notes that you or others created in OneNote.

Activity 13.11 | Presenting a Word Document Online

If you are creating your own resume, it will be valuable to get feedback from your friends, instructors, or Career Center advisors before you submit your resume for a job application. In this Activity, you will present the resume document online for others to look at.

> **NOTE** **You may be asked to sign in with your Microsoft account.**
>
> You may be asked to sign in with your Microsoft account, even if you are already signed in, to present your document online.

1 With your resume document displayed, click **Save** 🖫.

2 Click the **File tab**, on the left click **Share**, and then under **Share**, click **Present Online**.

3 On the right, click **Present Online**. Wait a moment for the service to connect, and then compare your screen with Figure 13.17.

There are several methods to send your meeting invitation to others. You can click Copy Link to copy and paste the hyperlink; for example, you could copy the link into a *Skype* window. Skype is a Microsoft product with which you can make voice calls, make video calls, transfer files, or send messages—including instant messages and text messages—over the Internet.

You can also select Send in Email, which will open your Outlook email window if you use Outlook as your mail client.

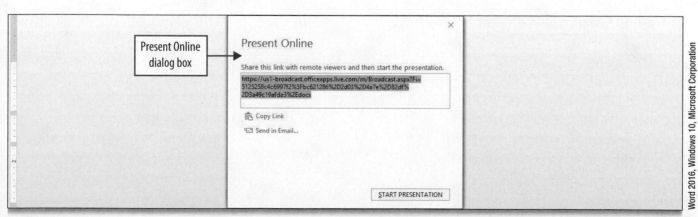

FIGURE 13.17

4 If you want to do so, identify a classmate or friend who is at a computer and available to view your presentation, select one of the methods to share, click **START PRESENTATION**, and when you are finished, on the ribbon, click **End Online Presentation**. If you are not ready to share your document right now, **Close** ⊠ the **Present Online** dialog box.

> If you present online, you will need to initiate voice communication using Skype or by simply phoning the other person.

5 Be sure you have closed the **Present Online** dialog box. On the ribbon, on the **Present Online tab**, click **End Online Presentation**, and then in the message, click **End Online Presentation**.

6 Press ⌈Ctrl⌉ + ⌈Home⌉ to move to the top of your document. In the lower right corner, click **Zoom In** ✚ as necessary to set the Zoom level to **100%**. If necessary, on the **Home tab**, redisplay the formatting marks by clicking **Show/Hide**.

7 Click the **File tab**, and then in the lower right portion of the screen, click **Show All Properties**. In the **Tags** box, type **resume, Word table** and in the **Subject** box, type your course name and section number. In the **Author** box, be sure your name is indicated and edit if necessary.

8 On the left, click **Print** to display **Print Preview**. If necessary, return to the document and make any necessary changes.

9 **Save** your document. In the upper right corner of the Word window, click **Close** ⊠. If directed by your instructor to do so, submit your paper printout, your electronic image of your document that looks like a printed document, or your original Word file.

END | You have completed Project 13A

Objective | Edit a Resume in Google Docs

ALERT! | **Working with Web-Based Applications and Services**

Computer programs and services on the web receive continuous updates and improvements, so the steps to complete this web-based Activity may differ from the ones shown. You can often look at the screens and the information presented to determine how to complete the Activity.

If you do not already have a Google account, you will need to create one before you begin this Activity. Go to http://google.com and, in the upper right corner, click Sign In. On the Sign In screen, click Create Account. On the Create your Google Account page, complete the form, read and agree to the Terms of Service and Privacy Policy, and then click Next step. On the Welcome screen, click Get Started.

Activity | Editing a Resume in Google Docs

In this Activity, you will use Google Docs to open and edit a Word table containing a resume similar to the resume you created in Project 13A.

1 From the desktop, open your browser, navigate to **http://google.com**, and then click the **Google Apps** menu ⊞. Click **Drive**, and then if necessary, sign in to your Google account.

2 Open your **GO! Web Projects** folder—or click New to create and then open this folder if necessary.

3 In the left pane, click **NEW**, and then click **File upload**. In the **Open** dialog box, navigate to your Student Data Files for this chapter, and then in the **File List**, double-click to open **w13_13A_Web**.

4 When the upload is complete, in the **Google Drive file list**, point to the file name, right-click, point to **Open with**, and then click **Google Docs** to open it in Google Docs.

5 Click anywhere in the word *OBJECTIVE*, right-click, and then click **Table properties**.

Under **Table border**, click the **Table border width arrow**, and then click **0.5 pt**. Click **OK** to display the table and cell borders in the default black color.

6 On the menu bar, click **Table**, and then click **Insert row above**. In the first cell of the new row, type **Daniela Frank** Select the text you just typed, and then on the toolbar, click the **Font size arrow**, and then click **18**.

7 Press Tab to move to the second cell of the new row, and then type **1343 Siena Lane, Deerfield, WI 53531** Hold down Shift and press Enter. Type **(608) 555-0588** Hold down Shift and press Enter. Type **dfrank@alcona.net** Select all the text in the second cell that you just typed, and then on the toolbar, click **Right align**. In Google Docs, the phone number and possibly the email address may remain as hyperlinks. Compare your screen with Figure A.

(GO! With Google continues on the next page)

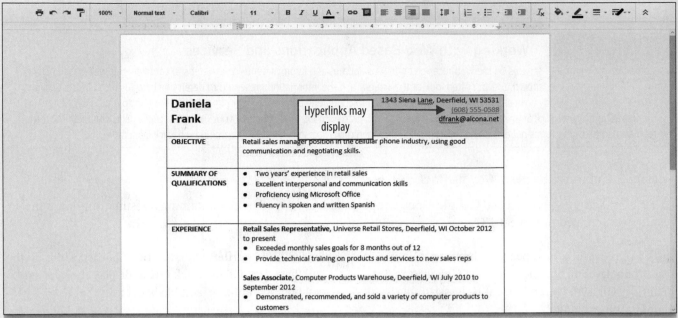

FIGURE A

8 ▶ Drag to select the two cells in the top row, right-click over the selection, and then click **Table properties**. Under **Cell background color**, click the arrow, and then in the top row, click the seventh color—**light gray 1**. Click **OK**.

9 ▶ Scroll down and click anywhere in the *EXPERIENCE* cell. Right-click, and then click **Insert row below**. In the first cell of the new row, type **EDUCATION**

10 ▶ Press Tab to move to the second cell in the new row, and then type **Madison Area Technical College, Madison, WI** Hold down Shift and press Enter.

11 ▶ On the toolbar, click **Bold** to turn off bold formatting, and then type **Associate of Arts in Information Systems, June 2014** and press Enter.

12 ▶ Right-click, click **Table properties**, and then change the **Table border width** to **0 pt** to remove the borders. Click **OK**.

13 ▶ Scroll as necessary to view the top of your document, and then compare your screen with Figure B.

(GO! With Google continues on the next page)

GO! With Google

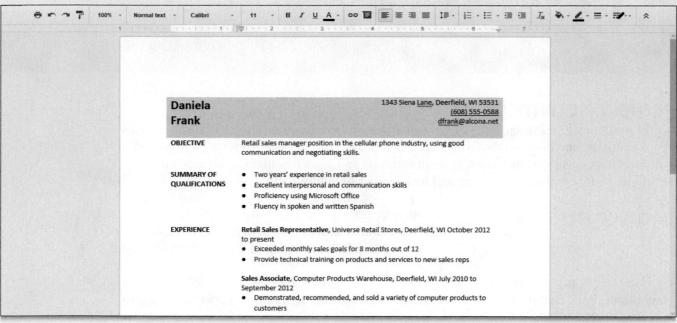

FIGURE B

14 Submit the file as directed by your instructor. In the upper right, click your user name, and then click **Sign out**. **Close** your browser window. Your file is automatically saved in your Google Drive.

PROJECT ACTIVITIES

In Activities 13.12 through 13.22, you will create a letterhead, save the letterhead as a custom Word template, and then use the letterhead to create a cover letter to accompany a resume. You will format an envelope, and if you have an envelope and printer available, you can print an envelope. Your completed document will look similar to Figure 13.18.

PROJECT FILES

If your instructor wants you to submit Project 13B in the MyITLab Grader system, log in to MyITLab, locate Grader Project 13B, and then download the files for this project.

For Project 13B, you will need the following files:

New blank Word document
w013B_Cover_Letter_Text

You will save your document as:

Lastname_Firstname_13B_Cover_Letter

PROJECT RESULTS

Build
From
Scratch

GO!
Walk Thru
Project13B

Jennifer Garcia

1776 Bay Cliff Drive, Tampa, FL 33602
(727) 555-0347 jgarcia@alcona.net

October 8, 2015

Ms. Mary Walker-Huelsman, Director
Florida Port Community College Career Center
2745 Oakland Avenue
St. Petersburg, FL 33713

Dear Ms. Walker-Huelsman:

I am seeking a position in which I can use my computer and communication skills. My education and experience, outlined on the enclosed resume, includes a Business Software Applications Specialist certificate from Florida Port Community College.

With a permanent position as my ultimate goal, I hope to use the Florida Port Community College Career Center to secure a temporary job. I can be available for a flexible number of hours or days and am willing to work in a variety of businesses or organizations.

As my resume illustrates, I have excellent computer skills. I am an honor student at Florida Port Community College and have outstanding references. In addition, I have part-time work experience as a software tester, where I perform the following computer activities:

Microsoft Access	Test database queries
Microsoft Excel	Enter software test data
Microsoft Word	Create and mail form letters

You can contact me by email at jgarcia@alcona.net or by telephone at (727) 555-0347. I am available for an interview at your convenience.

Sincerely,

Jennifer Garcia

Enclosure

Lastname_Firstname_13B_Cover_Letter

Word 2016, Windows 10, Microsoft Corporation

FIGURE 13.18 Project 13B Cover Letter and Envelope

GO! Learn How
Video W13-4

A *template* is a file you use as a starting point for a *new* document. A template has a predefined document structure and defined settings, such as font, margins, and available styles. On Word's opening screen, you can select from among many different templates—or you can create your own custom template.

When you open a template as the starting point for a new document, the template file opens a copy of itself, unnamed, and then you use the structure—and possibly some content, such as headings—as the starting point for a new document.

All documents are based on a template. When you create a new blank document, it is based on Word's *Normal template*, which serves as the starting point for all blank Word documents.

IC3
DIGITAL LITERACY
CERTIFICATION
2.02e (iv)

Activity 13.12 | Changing the Document Style Set for Paragraph Spacing and Applying a Bottom Border to a Paragraph

ALERT!	To submit as an autograded project, log into MyITLab, download the files for this project and then begin with those files instead of a new blank document.

A *letterhead* is the personal or company information that displays at the top of a letter, and which commonly includes a name, address, and contact information. The term also refers to a piece of paper imprinted with such information at the top. In this Activity, you will create a custom template for a personal letterhead.

1 Start Word and display a blank document; be sure that formatting marks and rulers display.

2 On the **Design tab**, in the **Document Formatting group**, click **Paragraph Spacing**.

The Paragraph Spacing command offers various options for setting the line and paragraph spacing of your entire document. A gallery of predefined values displays; or you can create your own custom paragraph spacing.

3 On the list *point* to **Default** and notice the settings in the ScreenTip.

Recall that the default spacing for a new Word document is 0 points of blank space before a paragraph, 8 points of blank space following a paragraph, and line spacing of 1.08.

4 Point to **No Paragraph Space** and notice the settings in the ScreenTip.

The *No Paragraph Space* style inserts *no* extra space before or after a paragraph and uses line spacing of 1. This is the same format used for the line spacing commonly referred to as *single spacing*. A *style set* is a collection of character and paragraph formatting that is stored and named.

5 Click **No Paragraph Space**.

By using the No Paragraph Space style, you will be able to follow the prescribed format of a letter, which Business Communications texts commonly describe in terms of single spacing.

 ANOTHER WAY

On Word's opening screen, select the Single-spaced (blank) document; or, in a blank document, select the entire document, and then on the Home tab, in the Styles group, click No Spacing. Also, so long as you leave an appropriate amount of space between the elements of the letter, you can use Word's default spacing. Finally, you could use one of Word's predesigned templates for a cover letter and observe all spacing requirements for a letter.

6 Type **Jennifer Garcia** and then press `Enter`.

7 Type **1776 Bay Cliff Drive, Tampa, FL 33602** and then press `Enter`.

8 Type **(727) 555-0347 jgarcia@alcona.net** and then press [Enter]. If the web address changes to blue text, right-click the web address, and then click **Remove Hyperlink**.

9 Select the first paragraph—*Jennifer Garcia*—and then on the mini toolbar, apply **Bold** [B] and change the **Font Size** to **16**.

10 Select the second and third paragraphs. On the mini toolbar, apply **Bold** [B] and change the **Font Size** to **12**.

11 With the two paragraphs still selected, on the **Home tab**, in the **Paragraph group**, click **Align Right** [≣].

ANOTHER WAY   Press [Ctrl] + [R] to align text to the right.

12 Click anywhere in the first paragraph—*Jennifer Garcia*. In the **Paragraph group**, click the **Borders button arrow** [⊞ ▾], and then at the bottom, click **Borders and Shading**.

13 In the **Borders and Shading** dialog box, on the **Borders tab**, under **Style**, be sure the first style—a single solid line—is selected.

14 Click the **Width arrow**, and then click **3 pt**. To the right, under **Preview**, click the bottom border of the diagram. Under **Apply to**, be sure *Paragraph* displays. Compare your screen with Figure 13.19.

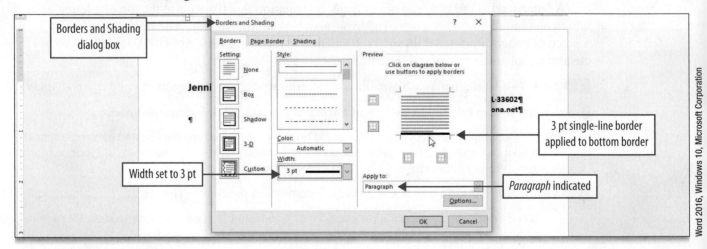

FIGURE 13.19

ANOTHER WAY   Alternatively, under Preview, click the bottom border button [⊞].

15 Click **OK** to display a 3 pt line below *Jennifer Garcia*, which extends from the left margin to the right margin.

The border is a paragraph command and uses the same margins of the paragraph to which it is applied.

Activity 13.13 | Saving a Document as a Custom Word Template

After you create a document format that you like and will use again, for example, a letterhead for personal letters during a job search, you can save it as a template and then use it as the starting point for any letter.

1 Display the **Save As** dialog box. In the lower portion of the dialog box, in the **Save as type** box, at the right edge, click the **arrow**, and then click **Word Template**.

2 At the top of the **Save As** dialog box, notice the path, and then compare your screen with Figure 13.20.

By default, Word stores template files on your hard drive in your user folder, in a folder named Custom Office Templates. By doing so, the template is available to you from the Word opening screen.

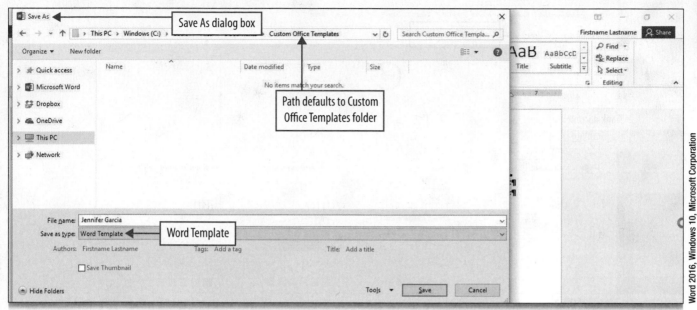

FIGURE 13.20

3 Click in the **File name** box, using your own name, type **Lastname_Firstname_13B_Letterhead_Template** and then click **Save**.

ALERT!	Are you unable to save in the Custom Word Templates folder?

Some college computer labs block you from saving on the hard drive. If you are unable to save your template in the Custom Word Templates folder, navigate to your AIO Chapter 13 folder in your storage location and save there. If you want to open a template that you stored in a location other than Word's default path, you must open the template directly from File Explorer—not from within Word—for it to open a new unnamed document based on the template.

---

4 Click the **File tab** to display **Backstage** view, and then click **Close** to close the file but leave Word open.

Activity 13.14 | Creating a Cover Letter from a Custom Word Template

A *cover letter* is a document that you send with your resume to provide additional information about your skills and experience. An effective cover letter includes specific information about why you are qualified for the job for which you are applying. Use the cover letter to explain your interest in the position and the organization.

ALERT!	Were you unable to save in the Custom Word Templates folder?

If you saved your template file at your storage location because you were blocked from saving in the default folder on the hard drive, open your saved document, press F12 to display the Save As dialog box, and then in your storage location, save the document—using your own name—as Lastname_Firstname_13B_Cover_Letter. Then move to Activity 13.15.

---

1 With Word open but no documents displayed, click the **File tab** to display **Backstage** view, and then click **New** to display the new document options. Compare your screen with Figure 13.21.

Here you can create a new document from a blank document or from one of Word's many built-in or online templates.

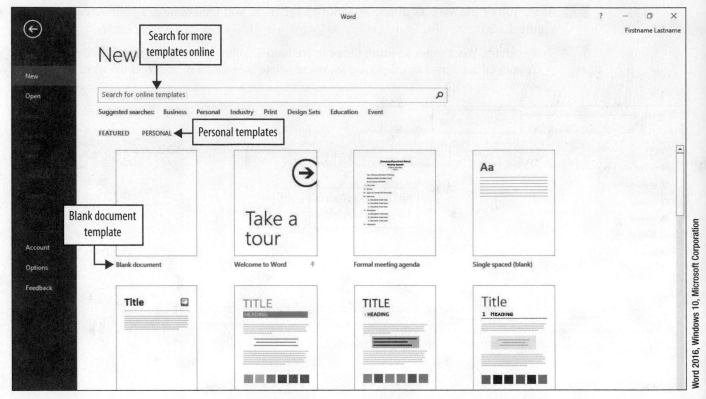

FIGURE 13.21

2 Under **Suggested searches**, click **Personal**, *point* to the name of your letterhead template, and then compare your screen with Figure 13.22.

Custom templates that you create and that are stored in the Custom Word Templates folder on your hard drive are accessible to you here whenever you want to create a new document from your stored template.

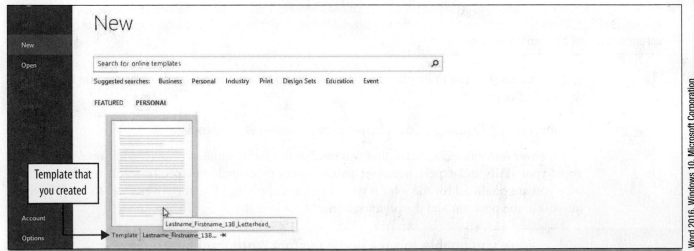

FIGURE 13.22

3 Click your letterhead template (or retrieve it from your storage location if you stored it elsewhere).

Word opens a copy of your 13B_Letterhead_Template in the form of a new Word document—the title bar indicates *Document* followed by a number. You are not opening the original template file, and changes that you make to this new document will not affect the contents of your stored 13B_Letterhead_Template file.

4 Display the **Save As** dialog box, and then navigate to your **AIO Chapter 13** folder. Using your own first and last name, **Save** the file as **Lastname_Firstname_13B_Cover_Letter**

5 On the **Insert tab**, in the **Header & Footer** group, click **Footer**, at the bottom click **Edit Footer**, and then in the **Insert group**, click **Document Info**. Click **File Name**, and then click **Close Header and Footer**.

6 **Save** 🖫 your document.

Objective 5   Correct and Reorganize Text

GO! Learn How
Video W13-5

Business letters follow a standard format and contain the following parts: the current date, referred to as the ***dateline***; the name and address of the person receiving the letter, referred to as the ***inside address***; a greeting, referred to as the ***salutation***; the text of the letter, usually referred to as the ***body*** of the letter; a closing line, referred to as the ***complimentary closing***; and the ***writer's identification***, which includes the name or job title (or both) of the writer and which is also referred to as the ***writer's signature block***.

Some letters also include the initials of the person who prepared the letter, an optional ***subject line*** that describes the purpose of the letter, or a list of ***enclosures***—documents included with the letter.

Activity 13.15 | Adding AutoCorrect Entries

Word's ***AutoCorrect*** feature corrects commonly misspelled words automatically; for example, *teh* instead of *the*. If you have words that you frequently misspell, you can add them to the list for automatic correction.

1 Click the **File tab** to display **Backstage** view. On the left, click **Options** to display the **Word Options** dialog box.

2 On the left side of the **Word Options** dialog box, click **Proofing**, and then under **AutoCorrect options**, click the **AutoCorrect Options** button.

3 In the **AutoCorrect** dialog box, click the **AutoCorrect tab**. Under **Replace**, type **resumee** and under **With**, type **resume**

   If another student has already added this AutoCorrect entry, a Replace button will display.

4 Click **Add**. If the entry already exists, click Replace instead, and then click Yes.

5 In the **AutoCorrect** dialog box, under **Replace**, type **computr** and under **With**, type **computer** Compare your screen with Figure 13.23.

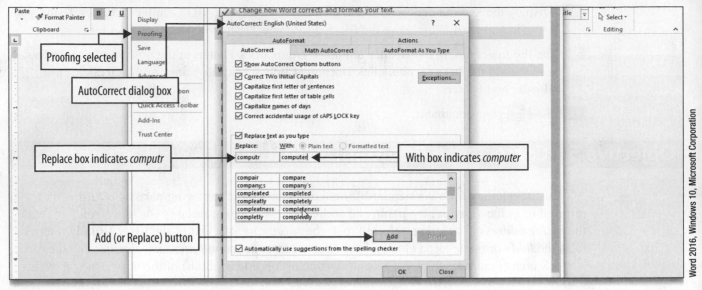

FIGURE 13.23

6 ▶ Click **Add** (or Replace) and then click **OK** two times to close the dialog boxes.

Activity 13.16 | Inserting the Current Date and Creating a Cover Letter

By using the ***Date & Time*** command, you can select from a variety of formats to insert the current date and time in a document.

For cover letters, there are a variety of accepted letter formats that you will see in reference manuals and Business Communications texts. The one used in this chapter is a block style cover letter following the style in Courtland Bovee and John Thill, *Business Communication Today*, Twelfth Edition, Pearson, 2014, p. 570.

1 ▶ Press Ctrl + End to move the insertion point to the blank line below the letterhead, and then press Enter three times.

2 ▶ On the **Insert tab**, in the **Text group**, click **Insert Date & Time** 📅, and then click the third date format. Click **OK** to create the dateline.

> Most Business Communication texts recommend that the dateline be positioned at least 0.5 inch (3 blank lines) below the letterhead; or, position the dateline approximately 2 inches from the top edge of the paper.

3 ▶ Press Enter four times, which leaves three blank lines. Type the following inside address on four lines, but do *not* press Enter following the last line:

Ms. Mary Walker-Huelsman, Director

Florida Port Community College Career Center

2745 Oakland Avenue

St. Petersburg, FL 33713

> The recommended space between the dateline and inside address varies slightly among experts in Business Communication texts and office reference manuals. However, all indicate that the space can be from one to 10 blank lines depending on the length of your letter.

4 ▶ Press Enter two times to leave one blank line, and then compare your screen with Figure 13.24.

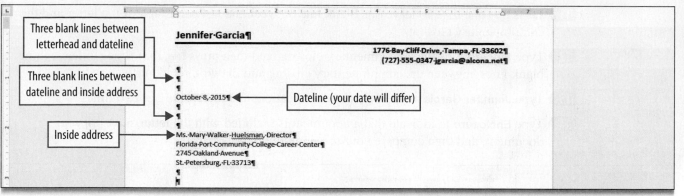

FIGURE 13.24

5 Type the salutation **Dear Ms. Walker-Huelsman:** and then press Enter two times.

Always leave one blank line above and below the salutation.

6 Type, exactly as shown, the following opening paragraph that includes an intentional word usage error: **I am seeking a position in witch I can use my** and press Spacebar. Type, exactly as shown, **computr** and then watch *computr* as you press Spacebar.

The AutoCorrect feature recognizes the misspelled word, and then changes *computr* to *computer* when you press Spacebar, Enter, or a punctuation mark.

7 Type the following, including the misspelled last word: **and communication skills. My education and experience, outlined on the enclosed resumee** and then type **,** (a comma). Notice that when you type the comma, AutoCorrect replaces *resumee* with *resume*.

8 Press Spacebar, and then complete the paragraph by typing **includes a Business Software Applications Specialist certificate from FPCC.** Compare your screen with Figure 13.25.

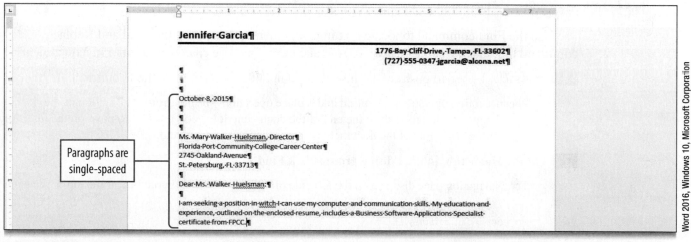

FIGURE 13.25

9 Press Enter two times. On the **Insert tab**, in the **Text group**, click the **Object button arrow**, and then click **Text from File**. From your student data files, locate and **Insert** the file **w13B_Cover_Letter_Text**.

Some of the words in the cover letter text display red or blue wavy underlines. These indicate potential spelling, grammar, or word usage errors, and will be addressed before the end of this project.

10 Scroll as necessary to display the lower half of the letter on your screen, and be sure your insertion point is positioned in the blank paragraph at the end of the document.

11 ▶ Press ⏎Enter one time to leave one blank line between the last paragraph of the letter and the complimentary closing.

12 ▶ Type **Sincerely,** as the complimentary closing, and then press ⏎Enter four times to leave three blank lines between the complimentary closing and the writer's identification.

13 ▶ Type **Jennifer Garcia** as the writer's identification, and then press ⏎Enter two times.

14 ▶ Type **Enclosure** to indicate that a document is included with the letter. **Save** 🖫 your document, and then compare your screen with Figure 13.26.

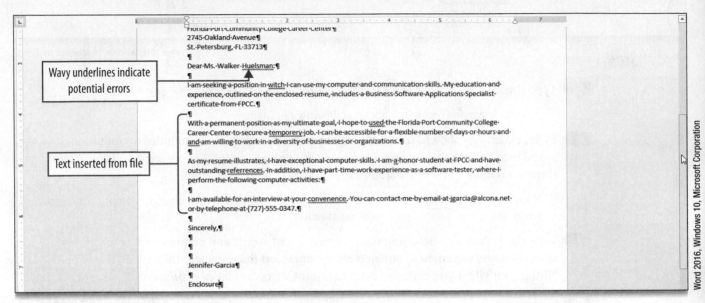

Florida Port Community College Career Center ¶
2745 Oakland Avenue ¶
St. Petersburg, FL 33713 ¶
¶
Dear Ms. Walker Huelsman: ¶

Wavy underlines indicate potential errors

I am seeking a position in witch I can use my computer and communication skills. My education and experience, outlined on the enclosed resume, includes a Business Software Applications Specialist certificate from FPCC. ¶

Text inserted from file

With a permanent position as my ultimate goal, I hope to used the Florida Port Community College Career Center to secure a temporary job. I can be accessible for a flexible number of days or hours and and am willing to work in a diversity of businesses or organizations. ¶
¶
As my resume illustrates, I have exceptional computer skills. I am a honor student at FPCC and have outstanding references. In addition, I have part-time work experience as a software tester, where I perform the following computer activities: ¶
¶
I am available for an interview at your convenence. You can contact me by email at jgarcia@alcona.net or by telephone at (727) 555-0347. ¶
¶
Sincerely, ¶
¶
¶
¶
Jennifer Garcia ¶
Enclosure ¶

FIGURE 13.26

Word 2016, Windows 10, Microsoft Corporation

IC3
DIGITAL LITERACY CERTIFICATION
2.01e

Activity 13.17 | Finding and Replacing Text

Use the Find command to locate text in a document quickly. Use the Find and Replace command to make the same change, or to make more than one change at a time, in a document.

1 ▶ Press Ctrl + Home to position the insertion point at the beginning of the document.

Because a find operation—or a find and replace operation—begins from the location of the insertion point and proceeds to the end of the document, it is good practice to position the insertion point at the beginning of the document before initiating the command.

2 ▶ On the **Home tab**, in the **Editing group**, click **Find**.

The Navigation pane displays on the left side of the screen with a search box at the top of the pane.

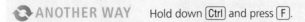

🔄 **ANOTHER WAY** Hold down Ctrl and press F.

3 ▶ In the search box, type **ac** If necessary, scroll down slightly in your document to view the entire body text of the letter, and then compare your screen with Figure 13.27.

In the document, the search letters *ac* are selected and highlighted in yellow for both words that begin with the letters *ac* and also for the word *contact*, which contains this letter combination. In the Navigation pane, the three instances are shown in context—*ac* displays in bold.

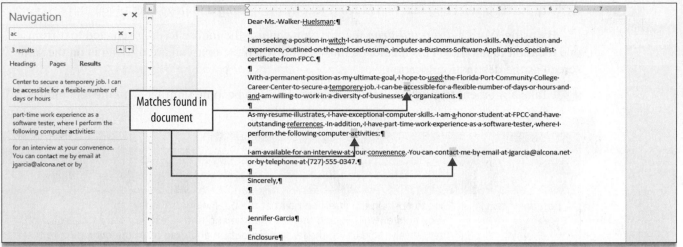

FIGURE 13.27

4 ▸ Click in the search box again, and type as necessary to display the word *accessible* in the search box.

> One match for the search term displays in context in the Navigation pane and is highlighted in the document.

5 ▸ In the document, double-click the yellow highlighted word *accessible*, and then type **available** to replace the word.

6 ▸ **Close** ☒ the **Navigation** pane, and then on the **Home tab**, in the **Editing group**, click **Replace**.

7 ▸ In the **Find and Replace** dialog box, in the **Find what** box, replace the existing text by typing **FPCC** In the **Replace with** box, type **Florida Port Community College** and then compare your screen with Figure 13.28.

FIGURE 13.28

8 ▸ In the lower left corner of the dialog box, click **More** to expand the dialog box, and then under **Search Options**, select the **Match case** check box.

> The acronym *FPCC* appears in the document two times. In a formal letter, the reader may not know what the acronym means, so you should include the full text instead of an acronym. In this instance, you must select the *Match case* check box so that the replaced text will match the case you typed in the Replace with box, and *not* display in all uppercase letters in the manner of *FPCC*.

9 ▸ In the **Find and Replace** dialog box, click **Replace All** to replace both instances of *FPCC*. Click **OK** to close the message box.

10 ▸ In the **Find and Replace** dialog box, clear the **Match case** check box, click **Less**, and then **Close** the dialog box.

> The Find and Replace dialog box opens with the settings used the last time it was open. Therefore, it is good practice to reset this dialog box to its default settings each time you use it.

11 ▸ **Save** 🖫 your document.

Activity 13.18 | Selecting Text and Moving Text by Using Drag and Drop

By using Word's *drag-and-drop* feature, you can use the mouse to drag selected text from one location to another. This method is most useful when the text you are moving is on the same screen as the destination location.

1 ▶ Take a moment to study the table in Figure 13.29 to become familiar with the techniques you can use to select text in a document quickly.

SELECTING TEXT IN A DOCUMENT	
TO SELECT THIS:	**DO THIS:**
A portion of text	Click to position the insertion point at the beginning of the text you want to select, hold down Shift, and then click at the end of the text you want to select. Alternatively, hold down the left mouse button and drag from the beginning to the end of the text you want to select.
A word	Double-click the word.
A sentence	Hold down Ctrl and click anywhere in the sentence.
A paragraph	Triple-click anywhere in the paragraph; or, move the pointer to the left of the paragraph, into the margin area. When the pointer displays, double-click.
A line	Move the pointer to the left of the line. When the pointer displays, click one time.
One character at a time	Position the insertion point to the left of the first character, hold down Shift, and press ← or → as many times as desired.
A string of words	Position the insertion point to the left of the first word, hold down Shift and Ctrl, and then press ← or → as many times as desired.
Consecutive lines	Position the insertion point to the left of the first word, hold down Shift and press ↑ or ↓.
Consecutive paragraphs	Position the insertion point to the left of the first word, hold down Shift and Ctrl and press ↑ or ↓.
The entire document	Hold down Ctrl and press A. Alternatively, move the pointer to the left of any line in the document. When the pointer displays, triple-click.

Gaskin, Shelley. Go! All in One, 3E. Pearson Education, 2017.

FIGURE 13.29

2 ▶ Be sure you can view the entire body of the letter on your screen. In the paragraph that begins *With a permanent position*, in the second line, locate and double-click *days*.

3 ▶ Point to the selected word to display the pointer.

4 ▶ Drag to the right until the dotted vertical line that floats next to the pointer is positioned to the right of the word *hours* in the same line, as shown in Figure 13.30.

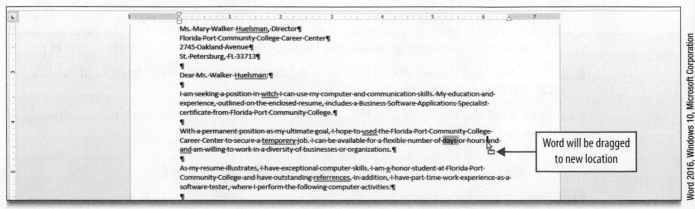

FIGURE 13.30

5 Release the mouse button to move the text. Select the word *hours* and drag it to the left of the word *or*—the previous location of the word *days*. Click anywhere in the document to deselect the text.

6 Examine the text that you moved, and add or remove spaces as necessary.

7 Hold down Ctrl, and then in the paragraph that begins *I am available*, click anywhere in the first sentence to select the entire sentence.

8 Release Ctrl. Drag the selected sentence to the end of the paragraph by positioning the small vertical line that floats with the pointer to the left of the paragraph mark. **Save** 🖫 your document, and then compare your screen with Figure 13.31.

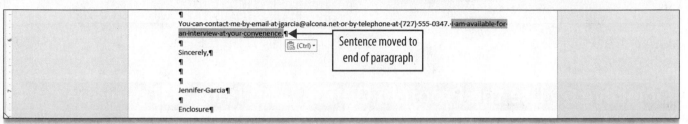

¶
You·can·contact·me·by·email·at·jgarcia@alcona.net·or·by·telephone·at·(727)·555-0347.·I·am·available·for·an·interview·at·your·convenence.·¶
¶
Sincerely,¶
¶
¶
Jennifer·Garcia¶
¶
Enclosure¶

📋 (Ctrl) ▾

Sentence moved to end of paragraph

FIGURE 13.31

Word 2016, Windows 10, Microsoft Corporation

IC3
DIGITAL LITERACY CERTIFICATION
2.02i

Activity 13.19 | Inserting a Table into a Document and Applying a Table Style

1 Locate the paragraph that begins *You can contact me*, and then click to position the insertion point in the blank paragraph above that paragraph. Press Enter one time.

2 On the **Insert tab**, in the **Tables group**, click **Table**. In the **Table** grid, in the third row, click the second square to insert a 2x3 table.

3 In the first cell of the table, type **Microsoft Access** and then press Tab. Type **Test database queries** and then press Tab. Complete the table using the following information:

Microsoft Excel	**Enter software test data**
Microsoft Word	**Create and mail form letters**

4 Point slightly outside of the upper left corner of the table to display the **table move handle** button ⊞. With the ⌖ pointer, click one time to select the entire table.

5 On the ribbon, under **Table Tools**, click the **Layout tab**. In the **Cell Size group**, click **AutoFit**, and then click **AutoFit Contents** to have Word choose the best column widths for the two columns based on the text you entered.

6 With the table still selected, under **Table Tools**, click the **Design tab**. In the **Table Styles group**, click **More** ▾. Under **Plain Tables**, click the second style—**Table Grid Light**.

Use Table Styles to change the visual style of a table.

7 With the table still selected, on the **Home tab**, in the **Paragraph group**, click **Center** ≡ to center the table between the left and right margins. Click anywhere to deselect the table.

8 Save and then compare your screen with Figure 13.32.

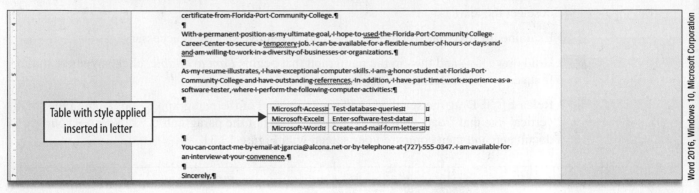

certificate-from-Florida-Port-Community-College.¶

¶

With-a-permanent-position-as-my-ultimate-goal,-I-hope-to-used-the-Florida-Port-Community-College-
Career-Center-to-secure-a-temporery-job.-I-can-be-available-for-a-flexible-number-of-hours-or-days-and-
and-am-willing-to-work-in-a-diversity-of-businesses-or-organizations.¶

¶

As-my-resume-illustrates,-I-have-exceptional-computer-skills.-I-am-a-honor-student-at-Florida-Port-
Community-College-and-have-outstanding-references.-In-addition,-I-have-part-time-work-experience-as-a-
software-tester,-where-I-perform-the-following-computer-activities:¶

¶

Microsoft·Access¤	Test·database·queries¤	¤
Microsoft·Excel¤	Enter·software·test·data¤	¤
Microsoft·Word¤	Create·and·mail·form·letters¤	¤

Table with style applied inserted in letter

¶

You-can-contact-me-by-email-at-jgarcia@alcona.net-or-by-telephone-at-(727)-555-0347.-I-am-available-for-
an-interview-at-your-convenence.¶

¶

Sincerely,¶

FIGURE 13.32

Word 2016, Windows 10, Microsoft Corporation

Objective 6 | Use the Proofing Options and Print an Envelope

GO! Learn How
Video W13-6

Word compares your typing to words in the Office dictionary and compares your phrases and punctuation to a list of grammar rules. This automatic proofing is set by default. Words that are not in the dictionary and words, phrases, and punctuation that differ from the grammar rules are marked with wavy underlines; for example, the misuse of *their*, *there*, and *they're*.

Word will not flag the word *sign* as misspelled even though you intended to type *sing a song* rather than *sign a song*, because both are words contained within Word's dictionary. Your own knowledge and proofreading skills are still required, even when using a sophisticated word processing program like Word.

IC3
DIGITAL LITERACY
CERTIFICATION
2.01c

Activity 13.20 | Checking for Spelling and Grammar Errors

There are two ways to respond to spelling and grammar errors flagged by Word. You can right-click a flagged word or phrase, and then from the shortcut menu choose a correction or action. Or, you can initiate the Spelling & Grammar command to display the Spelling and Grammar pane, which provides more options than the shortcut menus.

> **ALERT!** **Activating Spelling and Grammar Checking**
>
> If you do not see any wavy red or blue lines under words, the automatic spelling and/or grammar checking has been turned off on your system. To activate the spelling and grammar checking, display Backstage view, click Options, click Proofing, and then under *When correcting spelling in Microsoft Office programs*, select the first four check boxes. Under *When correcting spelling and grammar in Word*, select the first four check boxes, and then click the Writing Style arrow and click Grammar. Under *Exceptions for*, clear both check boxes. To display the flagged spelling and grammar errors, click the Recheck Document button, and then close the dialog box.

1 Position the body of the letter on your screen, and then examine the text to locate wavy underlines.

A list of grammar rules applied by a computer program like Word can never be exact, and a computer dictionary cannot contain all known words and proper names. Therefore, you will need to check any words flagged by Word with wavy underlines, and you will also need to proofread for content errors.

2 In the lower left corner of your screen, in the status bar, locate and point to but do not click the 🗏 icon to display the ScreenTip *Word found proofing errors. Click or tap to correct them.* Compare your screen with Figure 13.33.

If this button displays, you know there are potential errors identified in the document.

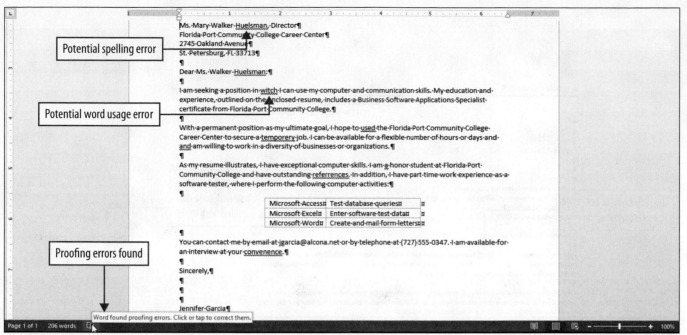

Potential spelling error

Potential word usage error

Proofing errors found

Ms.·Mary·Walker·Huelsman,·Director¶
Florida·Port·Community·College·Career·Center¶
2745·Oakland·Avenue¶
St.·Petersburg,·FL·33713¶
¶
Dear·Ms.·Walker·Huelsman:¶
¶
I·am·seeking·a·position·in·witch·I·can·use·my·computer·and·communication·skills.·My·education·and·
experience,·outlined·on·the·enclosed·resume,·includes·a·Business·Software·Applications·Specialist·
certificate·from·Florida·Port·Community·College.¶
¶
With·a·permanent·position·as·my·ultimate·goal,·I·hope·to·used·the·Florida·Port·Community·College·
Career·Center·to·secure·a·temporery·job.·I·can·be·available·for·a·flexible·number·of·hours·or·days·and·
and·am·willing·to·work·in·a·diversity·of·businesses·or·organizations.¶
¶
As·my·resume·illustrates,·I·have·exceptional·computer·skills.·I·am·a·honor·student·at·Florida·Port·
Community·College·and·have·outstanding·referrences.·In·addition,·I·have·part·time·work·experience·as·a·
software·tester,·where·I·perform·the·following·computer·activities:¶
¶

Microsoft·Access¤	Test·database·queries¤	¤
Microsoft·Excel¤	Enter·software·test·data¤	¤
Microsoft·Word¤	Create·and·mail·form·letters¤	¤

¶
You·can·contact·me·by·email·at·jgarcia@alcona.net·or·by·telephone·at·(727)·555-0347.·I·am·available·for·
an·interview·at·your·convenence.¶
¶
Sincerely,¶
¶
¶
¶
Jennifer·Garcia¶

Word found proofing errors. Click or tap to correct them.

Page 1 of 1   206 words   100%

FIGURE 13.33

3 In the paragraph that begins *With a permanent*, in the second line, locate the word *temporery* with the wavy red underline. Point to the word and right-click, and then click **temporary** to correct the spelling error.

4 In the next line, locate the word *and* that displays with a wavy red underline, point to the word and right-click, and then on the shortcut menu, click **Delete Repeated Word** to delete the duplicate word.

5 Press Ctrl + Home to move the insertion point to the beginning of the document. Click the **Review tab**, and then in the **Proofing group**, click **Spelling & Grammar** to check the spelling and grammar of the text in the document.

The Spelling pane displays on the right, and the proper name *Huelsman* is flagged. Word's dictionary contains only very common proper names—unusual names like this one will typically be flagged as a potential spelling error. If this is a name that you frequently type, consider adding it to the dictionary.

ANOTHER WAY Press F7 to start the Spelling & Grammar command.

6 In the **Spelling** pane, click **Ignore All**. Compare your screen with Figure 13.34.

The word *witch* is highlighted as a grammar error, and in the Grammar pane, *which* is suggested.

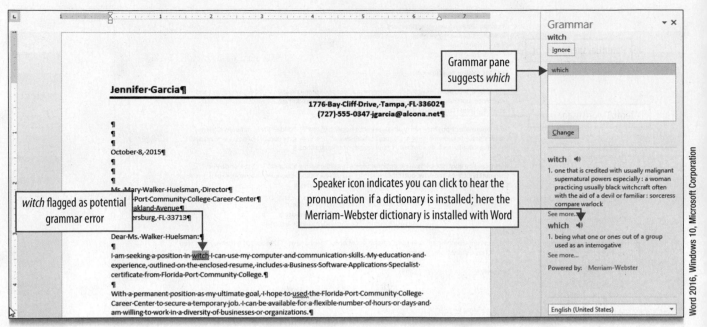

Grammar

witch

Ignore

which

Change

witch 🔊
1. one that is credited with usually malignant supernatural powers especially : a woman practicing usually black witchcraft often with the aid of a devil or familiar : sorceress compare warlock

See more...▼

which 🔊
1. being what one or ones out of a group used as an interrogative

See more...

Powered by: Merriam-Webster

English (United States)   ▼

Grammar pane suggests which

witch flagged as potential grammar error

Speaker icon indicates you can click to hear the pronunciation if a dictionary is installed; here the Merriam-Webster dictionary is installed with Word

Word 2016, Windows 10, Microsoft Corporation

FIGURE 13.34

7 In the **Grammar** pane, click **Change** to change to the correct usage *which*.

The next marked word—a possible grammar error—displays.

8 Click **Change** to change *used* to *use*. Notice that the next error is a potential Spelling error. In the **Spelling** pane, change *referrences* to the suggestion *references*. Notice that the next error is a possible grammar error.

9 Click **Change** to change *a* to *an*. Continue the spelling and grammar check and correct the spelling of *convenence*.

10 When Word displays the message *Spelling and grammar check is complete*, click **OK**.

11 Save 💾 your document.

Activity 13.21 | Using the Thesaurus

A *thesaurus* is a research tool that lists *synonyms*—words that have the same or similar meaning to the word you selected.

1 Scroll so that you can view the body of the letter. In the paragraph that begins *With a permanent*, double-click to select the word *diversity*, and then in the **Proofing** group, click **Thesaurus**.

The Thesaurus pane displays on the right with a list of synonyms; the list will vary in length depending on the selected word.

ANOTHER WAY   Right-click the word, on the shortcut menu, point to Synonyms, and then click Thesaurus.

2 In the **Thesaurus** pane, under **variety (n.)**, point to the word *variety*, and then click the arrow that displays. Click **Insert** to change *diversity* to *variety*.

3 In the paragraph that begins *As my resume*, double-click the word *exceptional*, and then on the ribbon, click **Thesaurus** again.

4 In the **Thesaurus** pane, under **excellent (adj.)**, point to *excellent*, click the **arrow**, and then click **Insert**. Compare your screen with Figure 13.35.

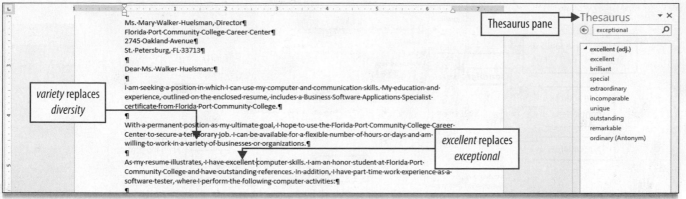

Thesaurus pane

Thesaurus
exceptional

▲ excellent (adj.)
excellent
brilliant
special
extraordinary
incomparable
unique
outstanding
remarkable
ordinary (Antonym)

Ms. Mary Walker-Huelsman, Director¶
Florida Port Community College Career Center¶
2745 Oakland Avenue¶
St. Petersburg, FL 33713¶
¶
Dear Ms. Walker-Huelsman:¶
¶
I am seeking a position in which I can use my computer and communication skills. My education and experience, outlined on the enclosed resume, includes a Business Software Applications Specialist certificate from Florida Port Community College.¶
¶
With a permanent position as my ultimate goal, I hope to use the Florida Port Community College Career Center to secure a temporary job. I can be available for a flexible number of hours or days and am willing to work in a variety of businesses or organizations.¶
¶
As my resume illustrates, I have excellent computer skills. I am an honor student at Florida Port Community College and have outstanding references. In addition, I have part-time work experience as a software tester, where I perform the following computer activities:¶

variety replaces *diversity*

excellent replaces *exceptional*

FIGURE 13.35

Word 2016, Windows 10, Microsoft Corporation

5 Close ☒ the **Thesaurus** pane.

6 Click the **File tab** to display **Backstage** view, and then on the **Info tab**, in the lower right portion of the screen, click **Show All Properties**. If you used your template, notice that it is indicated to the right of *Template*.

7 In the **Tags** box, type **cover letter** and in the **Subject** box, type your course name and section number. In the **Author** box, be sure your name is indicated and edit if necessary.

8 On the left, click **Print** to display **Print Preview**. If necessary, return to the document and make any necessary changes.

9 **Save** your document. If directed by your instructor to do so, submit your paper printout, your electronic image of your document that looks like a printed document, or your original Word file. In the upper right corner of the Word window, click **Close** ☒.

ALERT! **Because the next Activity is optional, if you are submitting your work in MyITLab, this is the file you will upload.**

Activity 13.22 | Addressing and Printing an Envelope

Use Word's Envelopes command on the Mailings label to format and print an envelope.

NOTE **This Is an Optional Activity**

This Activity is optional. If you do not have an envelope and printer, or do not want to complete the Activity at this time, then this project is complete.

---

1 Display your **13B_Cover_Letter**, and then select the four lines that comprise the inside address.

2 On the **Mailings tab**, in the **Create group**, click **Envelopes**. Notice that the **Delivery address** contains the selected inside address.

3 Click in the **Return address** box, and then type **Jennifer Garcia** and press [Enter]. Type **1776 Bay Cliff Drive** and then press [Enter]. Type **Tampa, FL 33602**

4 In the lower portion of the **Envelopes and Labels** dialog box, click **Options**, and then compare your screen with Figure 13.36.

The default envelope size is a standard business envelope referred to as a Size 10.

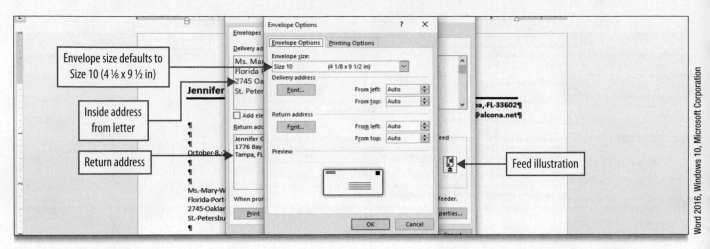

FIGURE 13.36

5 Click **OK** to close the **Envelope Options** dialog box. As shown under **Feed**, insert an envelope in your printer and then click **Print**.

Depending on the type and brand of printer you are using, your feed area may vary.

6 Close your **13B_Cover_Letter**, and then close Word.

END | You have completed Project 13B

GO! With Google

Objective   Create a Table in Google Docs

ALERT!   **Working with Web-Based Applications and Services**

Computer programs and services on the web receive continuous updates and improvements, so the steps to complete this web-based Activity may differ from the ones shown. You can often look at the screens and the information presented to determine how to complete the Activity.

If you do not already have a Google account, you will need to create one before you begin this Activity. Go to http://google.com and, in the upper right corner, click Sign In. On the Sign In screen, click Create Account. On the Create your Google Account page, complete the form, read and agree to the Terms of Service and Privacy Policy, and then click Next step. On the Welcome screen, click Get Started.

Activity | Creating a Table in Google Docs

In this Activity, you will use Google Docs to create a table within a document similar to Project 13B.

1 From the desktop, open your browser, navigate to **http://google.com**, and then click the **Google Apps** menu ⊞. Click **Drive**, and then if necessary, sign in to your Google account.

2 Open your **GO! Web Projects** folder—or click New to create and then open this folder if necessary.

3 In the left pane, click **NEW**, and then click **File upload**. In the **Open** dialog box, navigate to your Student Data Files for this chapter, and then in the **File List**, double-click to open **w13B_13B_Web**.

4 When the upload is complete, in the **Google Drive file list**, point to the document name, right-click, point

to **Open with**, and then click **Google Docs** to open it in Google Docs.

5 Click in the document and then press Ctrl + End to move to the end of the document, and then press Enter.

6 On the menu bar, click **Table**, point to **Insert table**, and then insert a **3x4 Table**.

7 Type **Position** and press Tab. Type **Type** and press Tab. Type **Location** and press Tab.

8 In the second row type **Paralegal** and press Tab. Type **Part-time** and press Tab. Type **Tampa** and press Tab. Compare your screen with Figure A.

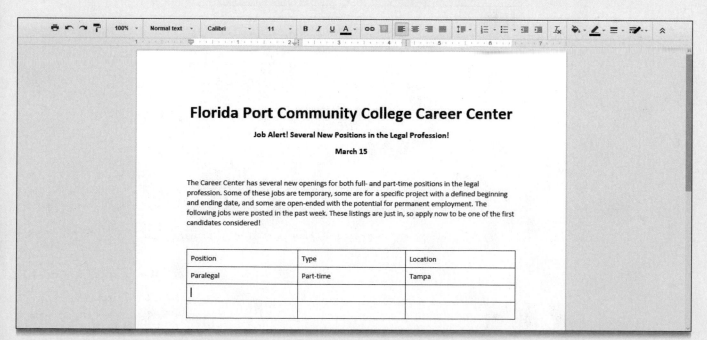

FIGURE A

(GO! With Google continues on the next page)

9 Type **Legal Records Clerk** and press [Tab]. Type **Full-time, 2 months** and press [Tab]. Type **North Tampa** and press [Tab].

10 Right-click in the last row of the table, and then click **Delete row**.

11 Drag to select all the cells in the first row, and then on the toolbar, click the **Normal text button arrow**, and then click **Heading 2**. With the three column titles still selected, on the toolbar, click **Center**.

12 Press [Ctrl] + [Home] to move to the top of the document, and then compare your screen with Figure B.

13 Submit the file as directed by your instructor. In the upper right, click your user name, and then click **Sign out**. **Close** your browser window. Your file is automatically saved in your Google Drive.

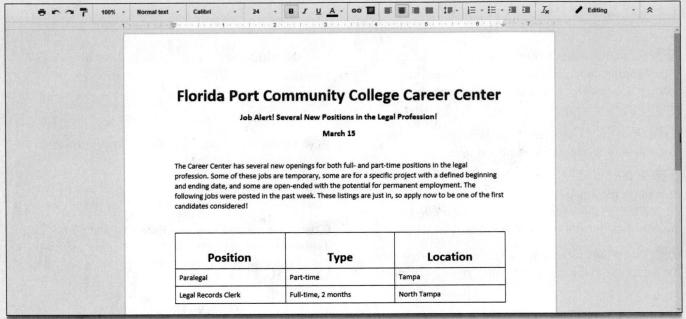

FIGURE B

IC3 SKILLS IN THIS CHAPTER

IC3 Key Applications

Project 13A

Section 2.02 Word Processing

    (c) Alter text and font styles

    (e) Know page layout concepts

        (iv) Alignment, text in paragraphs and tables

    (i) Be able to use tables

Project 13B

Section 2.01 Common Features

    (c) Know how to use spell check

    (e) Know the find/replace feature

    (h) Be able to drag and drop

Section 2.02 Word Processing

    (i) Be able to use tables

    (k) Use word processing template to increase productivity

BUILD YOUR E-PORTFOLIO

An E-Portfolio is a collection of evidence, stored electronically, that showcases what you have accomplished while completing your education. Collecting and then sharing your work products with potential employers reflects your academic and career goals. Your completed documents from the following projects are good examples to show what you have learned: 13G, 13K, and 13L.

GO! FOR JOB SUCCESS

Video: Cover Letter and Resume Tips

Your instructor may assign this video to your class, and then ask you to think about, or discuss with your classmates, these questions:

FotolEdhar / Fotolia

A cover letter should contain information that is different from but complementary to the information and facts on your resume and be tailored to the specific job you are applying for. Name two different things that you could mention in a cover letter.

What type of information belongs in the Career Objective portion of your resume?

When is it best to use a chronological resume layout, and when is it appropriate to use a functional resume layout?

END OF CHAPTER

SUMMARY

Word tables enable you to present information in a logical and orderly format. Each cell in a Word table behaves like a document; as you type in a cell, wordwrap moves text to the next line.

A good source of information for resume formats is a business communications textbook. A simple two-column table created in Word is suitable to create an appropriate resume for a recent college graduate.

Use Word's Office Presentation Service to present a Word document to others who can watch in a web browser. Word automatically creates a link to your document that you can share with others via email.

A template is useful because it has a predefined document structure and defined settings such as font and margins. Create your own custom template or, from Word's opening screen, select from thousands of templates.

GO! LEARN IT ONLINE

Review the concepts, key terms, and IC3 skills in this chapter by completing these online challenges, which you can find at **MyITLab**.

Matching and Multiple Choice: Answer matching and multiple choice questions to test what you learned in this chapter.

Lessons on the GO!: Learn how to use all the new apps and features as they are introduced by Microsoft.

IC3 Prep Quiz: Answer questions to review the IC3 skills that you practiced in this chapter.

GO! COLLABORATIVE TEAM PROJECT (Available in **MyITLab** and Instructor Resource Center)

If your instructor assigns this project to your class, you can expect to work with one or more of your classmates—either in person or by using Internet tools—to create work products similar to those that you created in this chapter. A team is a group of workers who work together to solve a problem, make a decision, or create a work product. Collaboration is when you work together with others as a team in an intellectual endeavor to complete a shared task or achieve a shared goal.

PROJECT GUIDE FOR ALL IN ONE CHAPTER 13

Your instructor will assign Projects from this list to ensure your learning and assess your knowledge.

	Project Guide for All in One Chapter 13		
Project	**Apply Skills from These Chapter Objectives**	**Project Type**	**Project Location**
13A MyITLab	Objectives 1–3 from Project 13A	**13A Instructional Project (Grader Project)** Guided instruction to learn the skills in Project 13A.	In MyITLab and in text
13B MyITLab	Objectives 4–6 from Project 13B	**13B Instructional Project (Grader Project)** Guided instruction to learn the skills in Project 13B.	In MyITLab and in text
13C	Objectives 1–3 from Project 13A	**13C Skills Review (Scorecard Grading)** A guided review of the skills from Project 13A.	In text
13D	Objectives 4–6 from Project 13B	**13D Skills Review (Scorecard Grading)** A guided review of the skills from Project 13B.	In text
13E MyITLab	Objectives 1–3 from Project 13A	**13E Mastery (Grader Project) Mastery and Transfer of Learning** A demonstration of your mastery of the skills in Project 13A with extensive decision making.	In MyITLab and in text
13F MyITLab	Objectives 4–6 from Project 13B	**13F Mastery (Grader Project) Mastery and Transfer of Learning** A demonstration of your mastery of the skills in Project 13B with extensive decision making.	In MyITLab and in text
13G MyITLab	Objectives 1–6 from Projects 13A and 13B	**13G Mastery (Grader Project) Mastery and Transfer of Learning** A demonstration of your mastery of the skills in Projects 13A and 13B with extensive decision making.	In MyITLab and in text
13H	Combination of Objectives from Projects 13A and13B	**13H GO! Fix It (Scorecard Grading) Critical Thinking** A demonstration of your mastery of the skills in Projects 13A and 13B by creating a correct result from a document that contains errors you must find.	Instructor Resource Center (IRC) and MyITLab
13I	Combination of Objectives from Projects 13A and 13B	**13I GO! Make It (Scorecard Grading) Critical Thinking** A demonstration of your mastery of the skills in Projects 13A and 13B by creating a result from a supplied picture.	IRC and MyITLab
13J	Combination of Objectives from Projects 13A and 13B	**13J GO! Solve It (Rubric Grading) Critical Thinking** A demonstration of your mastery of the skills in Projects 13A and 13B, your decision making skills, and your critical-thinking skills. A task-specific rubric helps you self-assess your result.	IRC and MyITLab
13K	Combination of Objectives from Projects 13A and 13B	**13K GO! Solve It (Rubric Grading) Critical Thinking** A demonstration of your mastery of the skills in Projects 13A and 13B, your decision-making skills, and your critical-thinking skills. A task-specific rubric helps you self-assess your result.	In text
13L	Combination of Objectives from Projects 13A and 13B	**13L GO! Think (Rubric Grading) Critical Thinking** A demonstration of your understanding of the chapter concepts applied in a manner that you would outside of college. An analytic rubric helps you and your instructor grade the quality of your work by comparing it to the work an expert in the discipline would create.	In text
13M	Combination of Objectives from Projects 13A and 13B	**13M GO! Think (Rubric Grading) Critical Thinking** A demonstration of your understanding of the chapter concepts applied in a manner that you would outside of college. An analytic rubric helps you and your instructor grade the quality of your work by comparing it to the work an expert in the discipline would create.	IRC and MyITLab
13N	Combination of Objectives from Projects 13A and 13B	**13N You and GO! (Rubric Grading) Critical Thinking** A demonstration of your understanding of the chapter concepts applied in a manner that you would in a personal situation. An analytic rubric helps you and your instructor grade the quality of your work.	IRC and MyITLab
13O	Combination of Objectives from Projects 13A and 13B	**13O Collaborative Team Project for AIO Chapter 13 Critical Thinking** A demonstration of your understanding of concepts and your ability to work collaboratively in a group role-playing assessment, requiring both collaboration and self-management.	IRC and MyITLab

GLOSSARY

GLOSSARY OF CHAPTER KEY TERMS

AutoCorrect A feature that corrects common typing and spelling errors as you type, for example, changing *teh* to *the*.

Body The text of a letter.

Cell The box at the intersection of a row and column in a Word table.

Complimentary closing A parting farewell in a business letter.

Cover letter A document that you send with your resume to provide additional information about your skills and experience.

Date & Time A command with which you can automatically insert the current date and time into a document in a variety of formats.

Dateline The first line in a business letter that contains the current date and which is positioned just below the letterhead if a letterhead is used.

Drag-and-drop A technique by which you can move, by dragging, selected text from one location in a document to another.

Enclosures Additional documents included with a business letter.

Inside address The name and address of the person receiving the letter and positioned below the date line.

Letterhead The personal or company information that displays at the top of a letter.

No Paragraph Space Style The built-in paragraph style—available from the Paragraph Spacing command—that inserts *no* extra space before or after a paragraph and uses line spacing of 1.

Normal template The template that serves as a basis for all Word documents.

Office Presentation Service A Word feature to present your Word document to others who can watch in a web browser.

One-click Row/Column Insertion A Word table feature with which you can insert a new row or column by pointing to the desired location and then clicking.

Salutation The greeting line of a business letter.

Single spacing The common name for line spacing in which there is *no* extra space before or after a paragraph and uses line spacing of 1.

Skype A Microsoft product with which you can make voice calls, make video calls, transfer files, or send messages—including instant messages and text messages—over the Internet.

Style set A collection of character and paragraph formatting that is stored and named.

Subject line The optional line following the inside address in a business letter that states the purpose of the letter.

Synonyms Words with the same or similar meaning.

Table An arrangement of information organized into rows and columns.

Template An existing document that you use as a starting point for a new document; it opens a copy of itself, unnamed, and then you use the structure—and possibly some content, such as headings—as the starting point for a new document.

Thesaurus A research tool that provides a list of synonyms.

Writer's identification The name and title of the author of a letter, placed near the bottom of the letter under the complimentary closing—also referred to as the *writer's signature block*.

Writer's signature block The name and title of the author of a letter, placed near the bottom of the letter, under the complimentary closing—also referred to as the *writer's identification*.

Apply 13A skills from these Objectives:

1 Create a Table
2 Format a Table
3 Present a Word Document Online

In the following Skills Review, you will use a table to create a resume for Ashley Kent. Your completed resume will look similar to the one shown in Figure 13.37.

PROJECT FILES

For Project 13C, you will need the following files:

New blank Word document
w013C_Skills
w013C_Experience

You will save your document as:

Lastname_Firstname_13C_Student_Resume

PROJECT RESULTS

Build
From
Scratch

Ashley Kent

2212 Bramble Road
St. Petersburg, FL 33713
(727) 555-0237
ashleykent@alcona.net

OBJECTIVE	A computer programmer position in a small startup company that requires excellent computer programming skills, systems analysis experience, and knowledge of database design.
SKILLS	**Computer Programming**
	• Advanced C/C++
	• Java
	• Ruby on Rails
	• SQL
	Leadership
	• Secretary, Florida Port Community College Computer Club
	• Vice President, Associated Students, Bay Hills High School
	Additional Skills
	• Microsoft Office
	• Adobe Creative Suite
	• Adobe Acrobat Pro
EXPERIENCE	**Database Designer** (part-time), Admissions and Records Florida Port Community College, St. Petersburg, FL September 2014 to present
	Software Tester (part-time), Macro Games Inc., Tampa, FL September 2011 to September 2014
EDUCATION	**Florida Port Community College**, Computer Science major September 2014 to present
	Graduate of Bay Hills High School June 2014

Lastname_Firstname_13C_Student_Resume

Word 2016, Windows 10, Microsoft Corporation

FIGURE 13.37

(Project 13C Student Resume continues on the next page)

1 Start Word and display a blank document. Be sure that formatting marks and rulers display. **Save** the document in your **AIO Chapter 13** folder as **Lastname_Firstname_13C_Student_Resume**

a. Add the file name to the footer, and then close the footer area. Click the **Insert tab**, and then in the **Tables group**, click **Table**. In the **Table** grid, in the fourth row, click the second square to insert a **2x4** table.

b. In the first cell of the table, type **Ashley Kent** and then press [Enter]. Type the following text, pressing [Enter] after each line *except* the last line:

2212 Bramble Road

St. Petersburg, FL 33713

(727) 555-0237

ashleykent@alcona.net

c. Press [↓] to move to the first cell in the second row. Type **SKILLS** and then press [↓] to move to the first cell in the third row.

d. Type **EXPERIENCE** and then press [↓]. Type **EDUCATION**

e. In the first cell, if the email address displays in blue, right-click the email address, and then on the shortcut menu, click **Remove Hyperlink**. **Save** your document.

2 Click in the cell to the right of *SKILLS*, and then type the following, pressing [Enter] after each line *including* the last line:

Computer Programming

Advanced C/C++

Java

Ruby on Rails

SQL

a. With the insertion point in the new line at the end of the cell, click the **Insert tab**. In the **Text group**, click the **Object button arrow**, and then click **Text from File**.

b. Navigate to your student data files, select **w13C_Skills**, and then click **Insert**. Press [Backspace] one time to remove the blank line.

c. Click in the cell to the right of *EXPERIENCE*, and then insert the file **w13C_Experience**. Press [Backspace] one time to remove the blank line.

d. Click in the cell to the right of *EDUCATION*, and then type the following, pressing [Enter] after all lines *except* the last line:

Florida Port Community College, Computer Science major

September 2014 to present

Graduate of Bay Hills High School

June 2014

3 Point to the upper left corner of the *SKILLS* cell, and then click the **Row Insertion** button. In the first cell of the new row, type **OBJECTIVE** and then press [Tab].

a. Type **A computer programmer position in a small startup company that requires excellent computer programming skills, systems analysis experience, and knowledge of database design.**

b. In any row, point to the vertical border between the two columns to display the [+] pointer. Drag the column border to the left to approximately **1.5 inches on the horizontal ruler**.

c. Under **Table Tools**, on the **Layout tab**, in the **Cell Size group**, click **AutoFit**, and then click **AutoFit Window** to be sure that your table stretches across the page within the margins.

d. In the first row of the table, drag across both cells to select them. On the **Layout tab**, in the **Merge group**, click **Merge Cells**. Right-click over the selected cell, and then on the mini toolbar, click **Center**.

e. In the top row, select the first paragraph of text— *Ashley Kent*. On the mini toolbar, increase the **Font Size** to **20** and apply **Bold**.

f. In the second row, point to the word *OBJECTIVE*, hold down the left mouse button, and then drag down to select the row headings in uppercase letters. On the mini toolbar, click **Bold**. **Save** your document.

4 Click in the cell to the right of *OBJECTIVE*. On the **Layout tab**, in the **Paragraph group**, click the **Spacing After up spin arrow** three times to change the spacing to **18 pt**.

a. In the cell to the right of *SKILLS*, apply **Bold** to the words *Computer Programming*, *Leadership*, and *Additional Skills*. Then, under each bold heading in the cell, select the lines of text, and create a bulleted list.

b. In the first two bulleted lists, click in the last bullet item, and then on the **Layout tab**, in the **Paragraph group**, set the **Spacing After** to **12 pt**.

(Project 13C Student Resume continues on the next page)

c. In the last bulleted list, click in the last bullet item, and then set the **Spacing After** to **18 pt**.

d. In the cell to the right of *EXPERIENCE*, apply **Bold** to *Database Designer* and *Software Tester*. Click in the line *September 2014 to present* and apply **Spacing After** of **12 pt**. Click in the line *September 2011 to September 2014* and apply **Spacing After** of **18 pt**.

e. In the cell to the right of *EDUCATION*, apply **Bold** to *Florida Port Community College* and *Graduate of Bay Hills High School*.

f. In the same cell, click in the line *September 2014 to present* and apply **Spacing After** of **12 pt**.

g. In the first row, click in the last line—*ashleykent@ alcona.net*—and then change the **Spacing After** to **18 pt**. Click in the first line—*Ashley Kent*—and set the **Spacing Before** to **30 pt** and the **Spacing After** to **6 pt**.

5 Point to the upper left corner of the table, and then click the **table move handle** ⊞ to select the entire table. Under **Table Tools**, on the **Design tab**, in the **Borders group**, click the **Borders button arrow**, and then click **No Border**.

a. In the **Borders group**, click the **Borders button arrow** again, and then at the bottom of the gallery, click **Borders and Shading**. In the **Borders and Shading** dialog box, under **Setting**, click **Custom**. Under **Style**, scroll down slightly, and then click the style with two equal lines.

b. Click the **Width arrow**, and then click **1 1/2 pt**. Under **Preview**, click the top border of the preview box, and then click **OK**.

c. Click the **File tab** to display **Backstage** view, and then in the lower right portion of the screen, click **Show All Properties**. In the **Tags** box, type **resume, table** and in the **Subject** box, type your course name and section number. In the **Author** box, be sure your name is indicated and edit if necessary.

d. On the left, click **Print** to display **Print Preview**. If necessary, return to the document and make any necessary changes.

e. Save 🖫 your document, and then if you want to do so, present your document online to a fellow classmate. If directed by your instructor to do so, submit your paper printout, your electronic image of your document that looks like a printed document, or your original Word file. Close Word.

END | You have completed Project 13C

Apply 13B skills from these Objectives:

4 Create a Custom Word Template

5 Correct and Reorganize Text

6 Use the Proofing Options and Print an Envelope

In the following Skills Review, you will create a letterhead, save the letterhead as a custom Word template, and then use the letterhead to create a cover letter to accompany a resume. If you have an envelope and printer available, you will format and print an envelope. Your completed document will look similar to Figure 13.38.

PROJECT FILES

For Project 13D, you will need the following files:

New blank Word document
w013D_Cover_Letter_Text

You will save your documents as:

Lastname_Firstname_13D_Cover_Letter

Build
From
Scratch

PROJECT RESULTS

Sarah Villmosky

7279 Rambling Brook Way, St. Petersburg, FL 33713
(727) 555-0117 svillmosky@alcona.net

October 7, 2015

Ms. Mary Walker-Huelsman, Director
Florida Port Community College Career Center
2745 Oakland Avenue
St. Petersburg, FL 33713

Dear Ms. Walker-Huelsman:

I am seeking the assistance of the Career Center in my job search.

Having recently graduated from Florida Port Community College with an Associate of Arts in Media Studies, I am interested in working for a newspaper, a magazine, or a publishing company.

I have previous work experience in the publishing industry as a writer and section editor for the local activities section of the St. Petersburg News and Times. I have the following skills that I developed while working at the St. Petersburg News and Times. I believe these skills would be a good fit with a local or national newspaper or publication:

Editorial experience:	Writing, editing, interviewing
Computer proficiency:	CS InDesign, QuarkXPress, Microsoft Publisher
Education focus:	Media Studies and Journalism

I am willing to consider temporary positions that might lead to a permanent position. Please contact me at sarahvillmosky@alcona.net or by phone at (727) 555-0117. I am available immediately for an interview or for further training at the Career Center that you think would be beneficial in my job search.

Sincerely,

Sarah Villmosky

Enclosure

Lastname_Firstname_13D_Cover_Letter

Word 2016, Windows 10, Microsoft Corporation

FIGURE 13.38

(Project 13D Cover Letter continues on the next page)

1 Start Word and display a blank document; be sure that formatting marks and rulers display. On the **Design tab**, in the **Document Formatting group**, click **Paragraph Spacing**, and then click **No Paragraph Space**.

a. Type **Sarah Villmosky** and then press Enter. Type **7279 Rambling Brook Way, St. Petersburg, FL 33713** and then press Enter.

b. Type **(727) 555-0117 svillmosky@alcona.net** and then press Enter. If the web address changes to blue text, right-click the web address, and then click **Remove Hyperlink**.

c. Select the first paragraph—*Sarah Villmosky*—and then on the mini toolbar, apply **Bold**, and change the **Font Size** to **16**.

d. Select the second and third paragraphs, and then on the mini toolbar, apply **Bold**, and change the **Font Size** to **12**.

e. Click anywhere in the first paragraph—*Sarah Villmosky*. On the **Home tab**, in the **Paragraph group**, click the **Borders button arrow**, and then click **Borders and Shading**. Under **Style**, click the first style—a single solid line. Click the **Width arrow**, and then click **3 pt**. In the **Preview** area, click the bottom border, and then click **OK**.

f. Click the **File tab**, click **Save As**, and then click **Browse** to display the **Save As** dialog box. In the lower portion of the dialog box, in the **Save as type** box, click the arrow, and then click **Word Template**. In the **File name** box, using your own name, type **Lastname_Firstname_13D_Letterhead_Template** and then click **Save** to save the custom Word template in the default path, which is the Templates folder on the hard drive of your computer.

g. Click the **File tab** to display **Backstage** view, and then click **Close** to close the file but leave Word open.

h. With Word open but no documents displayed, click the **File tab**, and then click **New**. Under **Suggested searches**, click **PERSONAL**, and then locate and click the letterhead template that you just created.

i. Click the **File tab**, click **Save As**, click **Browse** to display the **Save As** dialog box, navigate to your **AIO Chapter 13** folder, and then using your own name **Save** the file as **Lastname_Firstname_13D_Cover_Letter**

j. On the **Insert tab**, in the **Header & Footer group**, click **Footer**, click **Edit Footer**, and then in the

Insert group, click **Document Info**. Click **File Name**, and then click **Close Header and Footer**. Click **Save**.

2 Click the **File tab**. On the left, click **Options**. On the left side of the **Word Options** dialog box, click **Proofing**, and then under **AutoCorrect options**, click the **AutoCorrect Options** button.

a. In the **AutoCorrect** dialog box, click the **AutoCorrect tab**. Under **Replace**, type the misspelled word **assistence** and under **With**, type **assistance** Click **Add**. If the entry already exists, click Replace instead, and then click Yes. Click **OK** two times to close the dialog boxes.

b. Press Ctrl + End, and then press Enter three times. On the **Insert tab**, in the **Text group**, click **Date & Time**, and then click the third date format. Click **OK**.

c. Press Enter four times. Type the following inside address using four lines, but do *not* press Enter after the last line:

Ms. Mary Walker-Huelsman, Director

Florida Port Community College Career Center

2745 Oakland Avenue

St. Petersburg, FL 33713

d. Press Enter two times, type **Dear Ms. Walker-Huelsman:** and then press Enter two times. Type, exactly as shown with the intentional misspelling, and then watch *assistence* as you press Spacebar after typing it: **I am seeking the assistence**

e. Type **of the Career Center in my job search.** Press Enter two times.

f. On the **Insert tab**, in the **Text Group**, click the **Object button arrow**, and then click **Text from File**. From your student data files, locate and insert the file **w13D_Cover_Letter_Text**.

g. Scroll to view the lower portion of the page, and be sure your insertion point is in the empty paragraph mark at the end. Press Enter, type **Sincerely,** and then press Enter four times. Type **Sarah Villmosky** and press Enter two times. Type **Enclosure** and then **Save** your document.

h. Press Ctrl + Home. On the **Home tab**, in the **Editing group**, click **Find**. In the **Navigation** pane that opens on the left, click in the search box, and then type **journalism** In the letter, double-click the yellow highlighted word *Journalism* and type **Media Studies**

(Project 13D Cover Letter continues on the next page)

i. **Close** the **Navigation** pane, and then on the **Home tab**, in the **Editing group**, click **Replace**. In the **Find and Replace** dialog box, in the **Find what** box, replace the existing text by typing **SPNT** In the **Replace with** box, type **St. Petersburg News and Times** Click **More** to expand the dialog box, select the **Match case** check box, click **Replace All**, and then click **OK**. Two replacements are made. **Close** the **Find and Replace** dialog box.

j. In the paragraph that begins *I am available*, hold down Ctrl, and then click anywhere in the first sentence. Drag the selected sentence to the end of the paragraph by positioning the small vertical line that floats with the point to the left of the paragraph mark.

3 Below the paragraph that begins *I have previous*, click to position the insertion point in the blank paragraph, and then press Enter one time. On the **Insert tab**, in the **Tables group**, click **Table**. In the **Table grid**, in the third row, click the second square to insert a **2×3** table. Type the following information in the table:

Editorial experience:	Writing, editing, interviewing
Computer proficiency:	CS InDesign, QuarkXPress, Microsoft Publisher
Education focus:	Media Studies and Journalism

a. Point outside of the upper left corner of the table and click the **table move handle** button to select the entire table. On the **Layout tab**, in the **Cell Size group**, click **AutoFit**, and then click **AutoFit Contents**.

b. With the table selected, on the **Table Tools Design tab**, in the **Table Styles group**, click **More** ⊽. Under **Plain Tables**, click the second style—**Table Grid Light**.

c. With the table still selected, on the **Home tab**, in the **Paragraphs group**, click **Center**. **Save** your document.

4 Press Ctrl + Home. On the **Review tab**, in the **Proofing group**, click **Spelling & Grammar**. For the spelling of *Villmosky*, in the **Spelling** pane, click **Ignore All**. For the spelling of *Huelsman*, click **Ignore All**.

a. For the grammar error *a*, click **Change**. Click **Change** to correct the misspelling of *intrested*. Click **Delete** to delete the duplicated word *for*. Change *activitys* to *activities*. Change *benificial* to *beneficial*. Click **OK** when the Spelling & Grammar check is complete.

b. In the paragraph that begins *I am willing*, in the third line, double-click the word *preparation*. In the **Proofing group**, click **Thesaurus**.

c. In the **Thesaurus** pane, point to *training*, click the arrow, and then click **Insert**. **Close** the **Thesaurus** pane.

d. Click **File tab**, and then in the lower right portion of the screen, click **Show All Properties**. In the **Tags** box, type **cover letter** and in the **Subject** box, type your course name and section number.

e. In the **Author** box, be sure your name is indicated and edit if necessary. On the left, click **Print**. If necessary, return to the document and make any necessary changes. Save your document. If directed by your instructor to do so, submit your paper printout, your electronic image of your document that looks like a printed document, or your original Word file. **Close** Word.

END | You have completed Project 13D

Mastering Word | **Project 13E Table of Job Listings**

In the following Mastering Word project, you will create an announcement for new job postings at the Career Center. Your completed document will look similar to Figure 13.39.

MyITLab
grader

Apply 13A skills from these Objectives:

1 Create a Table

2 Format a Table

3 Present a Word Document Online

PROJECT FILES

For Project 13E, you will need the following files:

New blank Word document
w013E_New_Jobs

You will save your document as:

Lastname_Firstname_13E_Job_Listings

PROJECT RESULTS

Build
From
Scratch

Florida Port Community College Career Center

Job Alert! New Positions for Computer Science Majors!

April 11

Florida Port Community College Career Center has new jobs available for both part-time and full-time positions in Computer Science. Some of these jobs are temporary, some are for a specific project with a defined beginning and ending date, and some are open-ended with the potential for permanent employment. The following jobs were posted in the past week. These listings are just in, so apply now to be one of the first candidates considered!

For further information about any of these new jobs, or a complete listing of jobs that are available through the Career Center, please call Mary Walker-Huelsman at (727) 555-0030 or visit our website at www.fpcc.pro/careers.

New Computer Science Listings for the Week of April 11

POSITION	TYPE	LOCATION
Computer Engineer	Full-time, two months	Clearwater
Project Assistant	Full-time, three months	Coral Springs
Software Developer	Full-time, open-ended	Tampa
UI Designer	Part-time, two months	St. Petersburg

To help prepare yourself before applying for these jobs, we recommend that you review the following articles on our website at www.fpcc.pro/careers.

Topic	Article Title
Research	Working in Computer Science Fields
Interviewing	Interviewing in Startup Companies

Lastname_Firstname_13E_Job_Listings

Word 2016, Windows 10, Microsoft Corporation

FIGURE 13.39

(Project 13E Table of Job Listings continues on the next page)

1 Start Word and display a blank document; display formatting marks and rulers. **Save** the document in your **AIO Chapter 13** folder as **Lastname_Firstname_13E_Job_Listings** and then add the file name to the footer.

2 Type **Florida Port Community College Career Center** and press Enter. Type **Job Alert! New Positions for Computer Science Majors!** and press Enter. Type **April 11** and press Enter. **Insert** the file **w13E_New_Jobs**.

3 At the top of the document, select and **Center** the three title lines. Select the title *Florida Port Community College Career Center*, change the **Font Size** to **20 pt** and apply **Bold**. Apply **Bold** to the second and third title lines. Locate the paragraph that begins *For further*, and then below that paragraph, position the insertion point in the second blank paragraph. **Insert** a **3x4** table. Enter the following in the table:

POSITION	TYPE	LOCATION
Computer Engineer	Full-time, two months	Clearwater
Software Developer	Full-time, open-ended	Tampa
UI Designer	Part-time, two months	St. Petersburg

4 In the table, point to the upper left corner of the cell *Software Developer* to display the **Row Insertion** button, and then click to insert a new row. In the new row, type the following information so that the job titles remain in alphabetic order:

Project Assistant	Full-time, three months	Coral Springs

5 Select the entire table. On the **Table Tools Layout tab**, in the **Cell Size group**, click **AutoFit**, and then click **AutoFit Contents**. With the table still selected, on the **Home tab**, **Center** the table. With the table still selected, on the **Layout tab**, add **6 pt Spacing Before** and **6 pt Spacing After**.

6 With the table still selected, remove all table borders, and then add a **Custom 1 pt** solid line top border and bottom border. Select all three cells in the first row, apply **Bold**, and then **Center** the text. Click anywhere in the first row, and then on the **Table Tools Layout tab**, in the **Rows & Columns group**, insert a row above. Merge the three cells in the new top row, and then type **New Computer Science Listings for the Week of April 11** Notice that the new row keeps the formatting of the row from which it was created.

7 In the last blank paragraph at the bottom of the document, **Insert** a **2×3** table. Enter the following:

Topic	Article Title
Research	Working in Computer Science Fields
Interviewing	Interviewing in Startup Companies

8 Select the entire table. On the **Table Tools Layout tab**, in the **Cell Size group**, use the **AutoFit** button to **AutoFit Contents**. On the **Home tab**, **Center** the table. On the **Layout tab**, add **6 pt Spacing Before** and **6 pt Spacing After**. With the table still selected, remove all table borders, and then add a **Custom 1 pt** solid line top border and bottom border. Select the cells in the first row, apply **Bold**, and then **Center** the text.

9 Click the **File tab** to display **Backstage** view, and then in the lower right portion of the screen, click **Show All Properties**. In the **Tags** box type **new listings, computer science** and in the **Subject** box type your course name and section number. In the **Author** box, be sure your name is indicated and edit if necessary.

10 On the left, click **Print** to display **Print Preview**. If necessary, return to the document and make any necessary changes. **Save** your document, and then if you want to do so, present your document online to a fellow classmate. If directed by your instructor to do so, submit your paper printout, your electronic image of your document that looks like a printed document, or your original Word file. **Close** Word.

END | You have completed Project 13E

MyITLab grader

Mastering Word Project 13F Career Tips Memo

In the following Mastering Word project, you will create a memo that includes job tips for students and graduates using the services of the Florida Port Community College Career Center. Your completed document will look similar to Figure 13.40.

Apply 13B skills from these Objectives:

4 Create a Custom Word Template

5 Correct and Reorganize Text

6 Use the Proofing Options and Print an Envelope

PROJECT FILES

For Project 13F, you will need the following files:

w013F_Memo_Template

w013F_Memo_Text

You will save your documents as:

Lastname_Firstname_13F_Career_Tips

PROJECT RESULTS

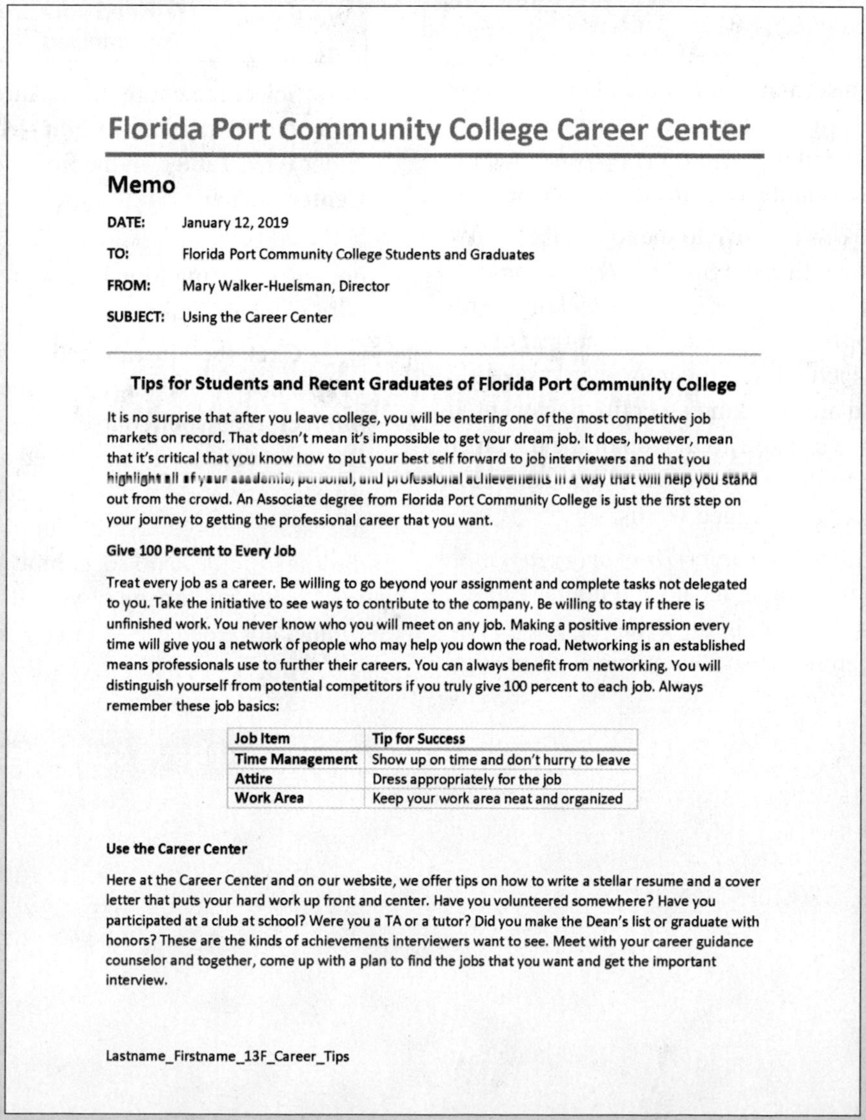

Florida Port Community College Career Center

Memo

DATE: January 12, 2019

TO: Florida Port Community College Students and Graduates

FROM: Mary Walker-Huelsman, Director

SUBJECT: Using the Career Center

Tips for Students and Recent Graduates of Florida Port Community College

It is no surprise that after you leave college, you will be entering one of the most competitive job markets on record. That doesn't mean it's impossible to get your dream job. It does, however, mean that it's critical that you know how to put your best self forward to job interviewers and that you highlight all of your academic, personal, and professional achievements in a way that will help you stand out from the crowd. An Associate degree from Florida Port Community College is just the first step on your journey to getting the professional career that you want.

Give 100 Percent to Every Job

Treat every job as a career. Be willing to go beyond your assignment and complete tasks not delegated to you. Take the initiative to see ways to contribute to the company. Be willing to stay if there is unfinished work. You never know who you will meet on any job. Making a positive impression every time will give you a network of people who may help you down the road. Networking is an established means professionals use to further their careers. You can always benefit from networking. You will distinguish yourself from potential competitors if you truly give 100 percent to each job. Always remember these job basics:

Job Item	Tip for Success
Time Management	Show up on time and don't hurry to leave
Attire	Dress appropriately for the job
Work Area	Keep your work area neat and organized

Use the Career Center

Here at the Career Center and on our website, we offer tips on how to write a stellar resume and a cover letter that puts your hard work up front and center. Have you volunteered somewhere? Have you participated at a club at school? Were you a TA or a tutor? Did you make the Dean's list or graduate with honors? These are the kinds of achievements interviewers want to see. Meet with your career guidance counselor and together, come up with a plan to find the jobs that you want and get the important interview.

Lastname_Firstname_13F_Career_Tips

Word 2016, Windows 10, Microsoft Corporation

FIGURE 13.40

(Project 13F Career Tips Memo continues on the next page)

1 Start Word. From your student data files, open the file **13F_Memo_Template**.

2 Display the **Save As** dialog box. Navigate to your **AIO Chapter 13** folder, and then in the **File name** box, using your own name, type **Lastname_Firstname_13F_Career_Tips**

3 Add the file name to the footer. At the top of your document, in the *DATE* paragraph, click to the right of the tab formatting mark, and then type **January 12, 2019** Use a similar technique to add the following information:

TO:	**Florida Port Community College Students and Graduates**
FROM:	**Mary Walker-Huelsman, Director**
SUBJECT:	**Using the CC**

4 Position the insertion point in the blank paragraph below the memo heading. **Insert** the file **w13F_Memo_Text**, and then press Backspace one time to remove the blank line at the end of the inserted text.

5 Press Ctrl + Home to move to the top of the document. By using either the **Spelling & Grammar** command on the Review tab or by right-clicking words that display blue or red wavy underlines, correct or ignore words flagged as spelling, grammar, or word usage errors. *Note*: If you are checking an entire document, it is usually preferable to move to the top of the document, and then use the Spelling & Grammar command so that you do not overlook any flagged words.

6 In the paragraph that begins *Treat every job*, in the second line of the paragraph, locate and double-click **donate**. On the **Review tab**, in the **Proofing group**, click **Thesaurus**, and then from the **Thesaurus** pane, change

the word to *contribute*. In the last line of the same paragraph, point to **fundamentals**, right-click, point to **Synonyms**, and then click **basics**.

7 In the paragraph that begins *An Associate degree*, move the first sentence to the end of the paragraph.

8 At the end of the paragraph that begins *Treat every job*, click in the blank paragraph, and then **Insert** a **2x4** table. Type the following information in the table:

Job Item	Tip for Success
Time Management	Show up on time and don't hurry to leave
Attire	Dress appropriately for the job
Work Area	Keep your work area neat and organized

9 Select the entire table. **AutoFit Contents**, and then apply the **Grid Table 1 Light – Accent 1** table style—under **Grid Tables**, in the first row, the second style. **Center** the table.

10 Press Ctrl + Home to move to the top of your document. Using Match Case, replace all instances of *CC* with *Career Center*.

11 Click the **File tab**, and then click **Show All Properties**. As the **Tags**, type **memo, job tips** As the **Subject**, type your course name and section number. Be sure your name is indicated as the **Author**, and edit if necessary. View the Print Preview, and make any necessary changes. Save your document. If directed by your instructor to do so, submit your paper printout, your electronic image of your document that looks like a printed document, or your original Word file. **Close** Word.

END | You have completed Project 13F

MyITLab grader

Mastering Word Project 13G Application Letter and Resume

Apply 13A and 13B skills from these Objectives:

1. Create a Table
2. Format a Table
3. Present a Word Document Online
4. Create a Custom Word Template
5. Correct and Reorganize Text
6. Use the Proofing Options and Print an Envelope

In the following Mastering Word project, you will create a letter and resume. Your completed document will look similar to Figure 13.41.

PROJECT FILES

For Project 13G, you will need the following files:

w013G_Letter_and_Resume
w013G_Letter_Text

You will save your documents as:

Lastname_Firstname_13G_Letter_and_Resume

PROJECT RESULTS

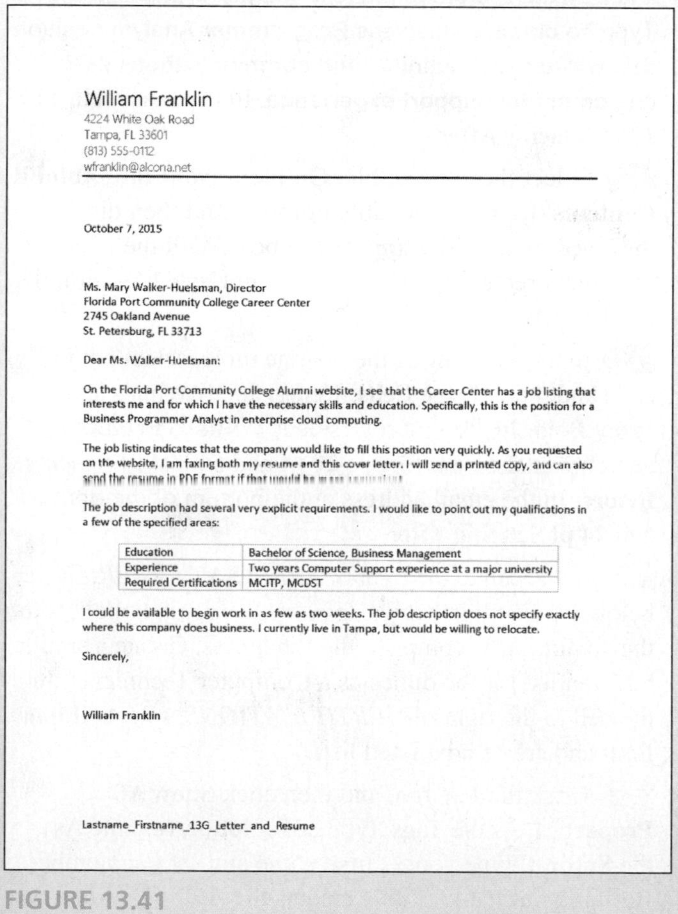

William Franklin
4224 White Oak Road
Tampa, FL 33601
(813) 555-0112
wfranklin@alcona.net

October 7, 2015

Ms. Mary Walker-Huelsman, Director
Florida Port Community College Career Center
2745 Oakland Avenue
St. Petersburg, FL 33713

Dear Ms. Walker-Huelsman:

On the Florida Port Community College Alumni website, I see that the Career Center has a job listing that interests me and for which I have the necessary skills and education. Specifically, this is the position for a Business Programmer Analyst in enterprise cloud computing.

The job listing indicates that the company would like to fill this position very quickly. As you requested on the website, I am faxing both my resume and this cover letter. I will send a printed copy, and can also send the resume in PDF format if that would be more convenient.

The job description had several very explicit requirements. I would like to point out my qualifications in a few of the specified areas:

Education	Bachelor of Science, Business Management
Experience	Two years Computer Support experience at a major university
Required Certifications	MCITP, MCDST

I could be available to begin work in as few as two weeks. The job description does not specify exactly where this company does business. I currently live in Tampa, but would be willing to relocate.

Sincerely,

William Franklin

Lastname_Firstname_13G_Letter_and_Resume

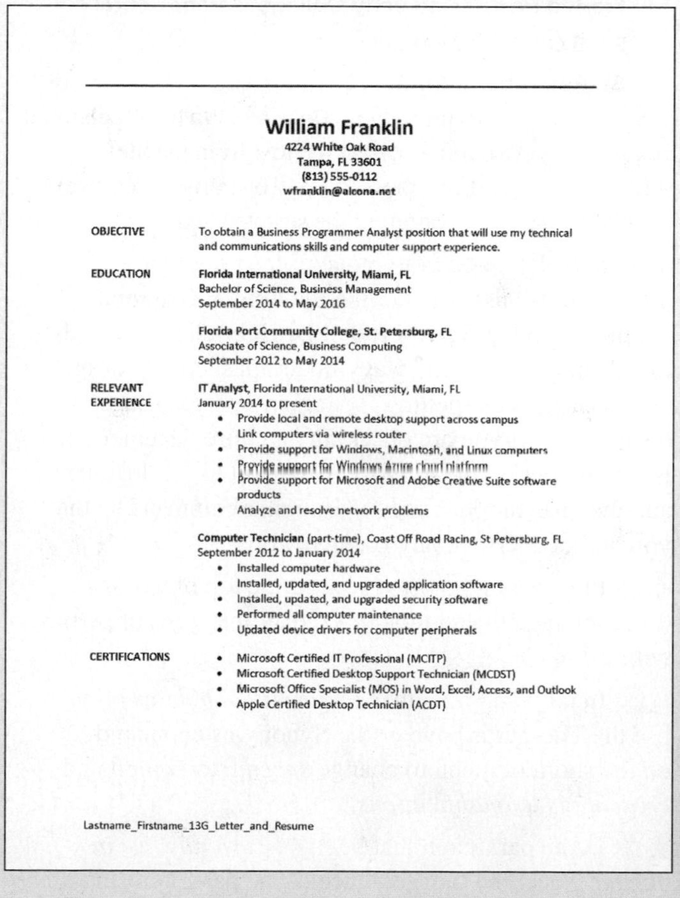

William Franklin
4224 White Oak Road
Tampa, FL 33601
(813) 555-0112
wfranklin@alcona.net

OBJECTIVE
To obtain a Business Programmer Analyst position that will use my technical and communications skills and computer support experience.

EDUCATION
Florida International University, Miami, FL
Bachelor of Science, Business Management
September 2014 to May 2016

Florida Port Community College, St. Petersburg, FL
Associate of Science, Business Computing
September 2012 to May 2014

RELEVANT EXPERIENCE
IT Analyst, Florida International University, Miami, FL
January 2014 to present
- Provide local and remote desktop support across campus
- Link computers via wireless router
- Provide support for Windows, Macintosh, and Linux computers
- Provide support for Windows Azure cloud platform
- Provide support for Microsoft and Adobe Creative Suite software products
- Analyze and resolve network problems

Computer Technician (part-time), Coast Off Road Racing, St Petersburg, FL
September 2012 to January 2014
- Installed computer hardware
- Installed, updated, and upgraded application software
- Installed, updated, and upgraded security software
- Performed all computer maintenance
- Updated device drivers for computer peripherals

CERTIFICATIONS
- Microsoft Certified IT Professional (MCITP)
- Microsoft Certified Desktop Support Technician (MCDST)
- Microsoft Office Specialist (MOS) in Word, Excel, Access, and Outlook
- Apple Certified Desktop Technician (ACDT)

Lastname_Firstname_13G_Letter_and_Resume

FIGURE 13.41

(Project 13G Application Letter and Resume continues on the next page)

MasteringWord | Project 13G Application Letter and Resume (continued)

1 Start Word. From your student data files, open the file **w13G_Letter_and_Resume**.

2 Display the **Save As** dialog box. Navigate to your **AIO Chapter 13** folder, and then in the **File name** box, using your own name, type **Lastname_Firstname_13G_Letter_and_Resume**

3 Add the file name to the footer. Be sure that rulers and formatting marks display. On **Page 1**, click in the blank paragraph below the letterhead, and then press Enter three times. Use the **Date & Time** command to insert the current date using the third format, and then press Enter four times. Type the following:

> **Ms. Mary Walker-Huelsman, Director**
>
> **Florida Port Community College Career Center**
>
> **2745 Oakland Avenue**
>
> **St. Petersburg, FL 33713**

4 Press Enter two times, type **Dear Ms. Walker-Huelsman:** and press Enter two times. **Insert** the text from the file **w13G_Letter_Text** and press Backspace one time to remove the blank line at the bottom of the selected text.

5 Press Ctrl + Home to move to the top of the document. By using either the **Spelling & Grammar** command on the **Review tab** or by right-clicking words that display blue or red wavy underlines, correct or ignore words flagged as spelling, grammar, or word usage errors. *Hint*: If you are checking an entire document, it is usually preferable to move to the top of the document, and then use the Spelling & Grammar command so that you do not overlook any flagged words.

6 Press Ctrl + Home to move to the top of the document again, and then replace all instances of **posting** with **listing**

7 In the paragraph that begins *The job description*, use the Thesaurus pane or the Synonyms command on the shortcut menu to change *specific* to *explicit* and *credentials* to *qualifications*.

8 In the paragraph that begins *I currently live in Tampa*, select the first sentence of the paragraph and drag it to the end of the same paragraph.

9 Click to position your insertion point in the *second* blank line below the paragraph that begins *The job description*. **Insert** a **2x3** table, and then type the text shown in Table 1.

TABLE 1

Education	Bachelor of Science, Business Management
Experience	Two years Computer Support experience at a major university
Required Certifications	MCITP, MCDST

10 Select the entire table. **AutoFit Contents**, and then apply the **Table Grid Light** table style—under **Plain Tables**, in the first row, the first style. **Center** the table.

11 In the resume on **Page 2**, insert a new second row in the table. In the first cell of the new row, type **OBJECTIVE** and then apply **Bold** to the text you just typed. Press Tab. Type **To obtain a Business Programmer Analyst position that will use my technical and communications skills and computer support experience.** In the same cell, add **12 pt Spacing After**.

12 Select the entire table. On the **Layout tab**, **AutoFit Contents**. Remove the table borders, and then display the **Borders and Shading** dialog box. With the table selected, create a **Custom** single solid line **1 1/2 pt** top border.

13 In the first row of the resume table, select both cells and then **Merge Cells**. **Center** the five lines and apply **Bold**. In the first row, select **William Franklin** and change the **Font Size** to **20 pt** and add **24 pt Spacing Before**. In the email address at the bottom of the first row, add **24 pt Spacing After**.

14 In the cell to the right of *RELEVANT EXPERIENCE*, below the line that begins *January 2014*, apply bullets to the six lines that comprise the job duties. Create a similar bulleted list for the duties as a Computer Technician. In the cell to the right of *CERTIFICATIONS*, select all four lines and create a bulleted list.

15 Click the **File tab**, and then click **Show All Properties**. As the **Tags**, type **cover letter, resume** As the **Subject**, type your course name and section number. Be sure your name is indicated as the **Author**, and edit if necessary. View the Print Preview, and make any necessary changes. If directed by your instructor to do so, submit your paper printout, your electronic image of your document that looks like a printed document, or your original Word file. **Close** Word.

END | You have completed Project 13G

Apply a combination of the 13A and 13B skills.

GO! Fix It	Project 13H New Jobs	**MyITLab**
GO! Make It	Project 13I Training	**MyITLab**
GO! Solve It	Project 13J Job Postings	**MyITLab**
GO! Solve It	Project 13K Agenda	

Build
From
Scratch

PROJECT FILES

For Project 13K, you will need the following file:

Agenda template from Word's Online templates

You will save your document as:

Lastname_Firstname_13K_Agenda

On Word's opening screen, search for an online template using the search term **formal meeting agenda** Create the agenda and then save it in your AIO Chapter 13 folder as **Lastname_Firstname_13K_Agenda** Use the following information to prepare an agenda for an FPCC Career Center meeting.

The meeting will be chaired by Mary Walker-Huelsman. It will be the monthly meeting of the Career Center's staff—Kevin Rau, Marilyn Kelly, André Randolph, Susan Nguyen, and Charles James. The meeting will be held on March 15, 2016, at 3:00 p.m. The old business agenda items (open issues) include 1) seeking more job listings related to the printing and food service industries; 2) expanding the alumni website, and 3) the addition of a part-time trainer. The new business agenda items will include 1) writing a grant so the center can serve more students and alumni; 2) expanding the training area with 20 additional workstations; 3) purchase of new computers for the training room; and 4) renewal of printing service contract.

Add the file name to the footer, add your name, your course name, the section number, and then add the keywords **agenda, monthly staff meeting** to the Properties area. Submit as directed.

Performance Level

Performance Criteria	Exemplary: You consistently applied the relevant skills.	Proficient: You sometimes, but not always, applied the relevant skills.	Developing: You rarely or never applied the relevant skills.
Select an agenda template	Agenda template is appropriate for the information provided for the meeting.	Agenda template is used, but does not fit the information provided.	No template is used for the agenda.
Add appropriate information to the template	All information is inserted in the appropriate places.	All information is included, but not in the appropriate places.	Information is missing.
Format template information	All text in the template is properly aligned and formatted.	All text is included, but alignment or formatting is inconsistent.	No additional formatting has been added.

END | You have completed Project 13K

OUTCOMES-BASED ASSESSMENTS

RUBRIC

The following outcomes-based assessments are *open-ended assessments*. That is, there is no specific correct result; your result will depend on your approach to the information provided. Make *Professional Quality* your goal. Use the following scoring rubric to guide you in *how* to approach the problem and then to evaluate *how well* your approach solves the problem.

The *criteria*—Software Mastery, Content, Format and Layout, and Process—represent the knowledge and skills you have gained that you can apply to solving the problem. The *levels of performance*—Professional Quality, Approaching Professional Quality, or Needs Quality Improvements—help you and your instructor evaluate your result.

	Your completed project is of Professional Quality if you:	Your completed project is Approaching Professional Quality if you:	Your completed project Needs Quality Improvements if you:
1-Software Mastery	Choose and apply the most appropriate skills, tools, and features and identify efficient methods to solve the problem.	Choose and apply some appropriate skills, tools, and features, but not in the most efficient manner.	Choose inappropriate skills, tools, or features, or are inefficient in solving the problem.
2-Content	Construct a solution that is clear and well organized, contains content that is accurate, appropriate to the audience and purpose, and is complete. Provide a solution that contains no errors of spelling, grammar, or style.	Construct a solution in which some components are unclear, poorly organized, inconsistent, or incomplete. Misjudge the needs of the audience. Have some errors in spelling, grammar, or style, but the errors do not detract from comprehension.	Construct a solution that is unclear, incomplete, or poorly organized, contains some inaccurate or inappropriate content, and contains many errors of spelling, grammar, or style. Do not solve the problem.
3-Format and Layout	Format and arrange all elements to communicate information and ideas, clarify function, illustrate relationships, and indicate relative importance.	Apply appropriate format and layout features to some elements, but not others. Overuse features, causing minor distraction.	Apply format and layout that does not communicate information or ideas clearly. Do not use format and layout features to clarify function, illustrate relationships, or indicate relative importance. Use available features excessively, causing distraction.
4-Process	Use an organized approach that integrates planning, development, self-assessment, revision, and reflection.	Demonstrate an organized approach in some areas, but not others; or, use an insufficient process of organization throughout.	Do not use an organized approach to solve the problem.

Apply a combination of the 13A and 13B skills.

Build From Scratch

GO! Think   Project 13L Workshops

PROJECT FILES

For Project 13L, you will need the following files:

New blank Word document
w013L_Workshop_Information

You will save your document as:

Lastname_Firstname_13L_Workshops

The Florida Port Community College Career Center offers a series of workshops for both students and alumni. Any eligible student or graduate can attend the workshops, and there is no fee. Currently, the Career Center offers a three-session workshop covering Excel and Word, a two-session workshop covering Business Communication, and a one-session workshop covering Creating a Resume.

Print the w13L_Workshop_Information file and use the information to complete this project. Create an announcement with a title, an introductory paragraph, and a table listing the workshops and the topics covered in each workshop. Use the file w13L_Workshop_Information for help with the topics covered in each workshop. Format the table cells appropriately. Add an appropriate footer and document properties. Save the document as **Lastname_Firstname_13L_Workshops** and submit it as directed.

> **END | You have completed Project 13L**

Build from Scratch

GO! Think!   Project 13M Planner   MyITLab

Build from Scratch

You and GO!   Project 13N Personal Resume   MyITLab

Build from Scratch

GO! Collaborative Team Project   Project 13O Bell Orchid Hotels   MyITLab

Build from Scratch

Creating Research Papers, Newsletters, and Merged Mailing Labels

14

PROJECT 14A

OUTCOMES
Create a research paper that includes citations and a bibliography.

OBJECTIVES

1. Create a Research Paper
2. Insert Footnotes in a Research Paper
3. Create Citations and a Bibliography in a Research Paper
4. Use Read Mode and PDF Reflow

PROJECT 14B

OUTCOMES
Create a multiple-column newsletter and merged mailing labels.

OBJECTIVES

5. Format a Multiple-Column Newsletter
6. Use Special Character and Paragraph Formatting
7. Create Mailing Labels Using Mail Merge

Guschenkova/Shutterstock

In This Chapter

Microsoft Word provides many tools for creating complex documents. For example, Word has tools that enable you to create a research paper that includes citations, footnotes, and a bibliography. You can also create multiple-column newsletters, format the nameplate at the top of the newsletter, use special character formatting to create distinctive title text, and add borders and shading to paragraphs to highlight important information.

In this chapter, you will edit and format a research paper, create a two-column newsletter, and optionally create a set of mailing labels to mail the newsletter to multiple recipients.

The projects in this chapter relate to **University Medical Center**, which is a patient-care and research institution serving the metropolitan area of Memphis, Tennessee. Because of its outstanding reputation in the medical community and around the world, University Medical Center is able to attract top physicians, scientists, and researchers in all fields of medicine and achieve a level of funding that allows it to build and operate state-of-the-art facilities. A program in biomedical research was recently added. Individuals throughout the eastern United States travel to University Medical Center for diagnosis and care.

PROJECT
14A
Research Paper

MyITLab
Project 14A Training
Project 14A Grader

PROJECT ACTIVITIES

In Activities 14.01 through 14.14, you will edit and format a research paper that contains an overview of a new area of study. This paper was created by Gerard Foster, a medical intern at University Medical Center, for distribution to his classmates studying various physiologic monitoring devices. Your completed document will look similar to Figure 14.1.

PROJECT FILES

MyITLab
grader

If your instructor wants you to submit Project 14A in the MyITLab Grader system, log in to MyITLab, locate Grader Project 14A, and then download the files for this project.

For Project 14A, you will need the following file:
w14A_Quantitative_Technology

You will save your document as:
Lastname_Firstname_14A_Quantitative_Technology

PROJECT RESULTS

GO!
Walk Thru
Project14A

Word 2016, Windows 10, Microsoft Corporation

FIGURE 14.1 Project 14A Quantitative Technology

GO! Learn How
Video W14-1

When you write a research paper or a report for college or business, follow a format prescribed by one of the standard *style guides*—a manual that contains standards for the design and writing of documents. The two most commonly used styles for research papers are those created by the ***Modern Language Association (MLA)*** and the ***American Psychological Association (APA)***; there are several others.

IC3
DIGITAL LITERACY
CERTIFICATION
2.02e (vii)

Activity 14.01 │ Formatting the Spacing and First-Page Information for a Research Paper

> **ALERT!** **To submit as an autograded project, log into MyITLab, download the files for this project, and then use those files instead of w14A_Quantitative_Technology.**

When formatting the text for your research paper, refer to the standards for the style guide that you have chosen. In this Activity, you will create a research paper using the MLA style. The MLA style uses 1-inch margins, a 0.5" first line indent, and double spacing throughout the body of the document with no extra space above or below paragraphs.

1 Start Word. On the left, click **Open Other Documents**, click **Browse**, and then navigate to the student data files that accompany this chapter. Locate and open the document **w14A_Quantitative_Technology**. If necessary, display the formatting marks and rulers. In the location where you are storing your projects for this chapter, create a new folder named **AIO Chapter 14** and then **Save** the file in the folder as **Lastname_Firstname_14A_Quantitative_Technology**

2 Press Ctrl + A to select the entire document. On the **Home tab**, in the **Paragraph group**, click **Line and Paragraph Spacing** , and then change the line spacing to **2.0**. On the **Layout tab**, in the **Paragraph group**, change the **Spacing After** to **0 pt**.

3 Press Ctrl + Home to deselect and move to the top of the document. Press Enter one time to create a blank paragraph at the top of the document, and then click to position the insertion point in the blank paragraph. Type **Gerard Foster** and press Enter.

4 Type **Dr. Hillary Kim** and press Enter. Type **Biomedical Research 617** and press Enter. Type **February 15, 2016** and press Enter.

5 Type **Quantified Self Movement Gains Momentum** and then press Ctrl + E, which is the keyboard shortcut to center a paragraph of text. Click **Save** , and then compare your screen with Figure 14.2.

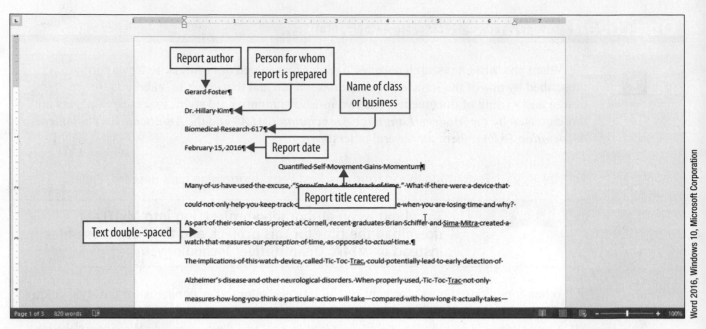

FIGURE 14.2

Word 2016, Windows 10, Microsoft Corporation

| *More* **Knowledge** | **Creating a Document Heading for a Research Paper** |

On the first page of an MLA-style research paper, on the first line, type the report author. On the second line, type the person for whom the report is prepared—for example, your professor or supervisor. On the third line, type the name of the class or business. On the fourth line, type the date. On the fifth line, type the report title and center it.

IC3
DIGITAL LITERACY
CERTIFICATION
2.02e (i)
2.02e (iv)

Activity 14.02 | Formatting the Page Numbering and Paragraph Indents for a Research Paper

1 On the **Insert tab**, in the **Header & Footer group**, click **Header**, and then at the bottom of the list, click **Edit Header**.

2 Type **Foster** and then press ⎵Spacebar.

Recall that the text you insert into a header or footer displays on every page of a document. Within a header or footer, you can insert many different types of information; for example, automatic page numbers, the date, the time, the file name, or pictures.

3 Under **Header and Footer Tools**, on the **Design tab**, in the **Header & Footer group**, click **Page Number**, and then point to **Current Position**. In the gallery, under **Simple**, click **Plain Number**. Compare your screen with Figure 14.3.

Word will automatically number the pages using this number format.

FIGURE 14.3

Word 2016, Windows 10, Microsoft Corporation

4 On the **Home tab**, in the **Paragraph group**, click **Align Right** 🗏. Double-click anywhere in the document to close the Header area.

5 Near the top of **Page 1**, locate the paragraph beginning *Many of us*, and then click to position the insertion point at the beginning of the paragraph. By moving the vertical scroll bar, scroll to view the end of the document, hold down Shift, and then click to the right of the last paragraph mark to select all of the text from the insertion point to the end of the document. Release Shift.

6 With the text selected, in the **Paragraph group**, click the **Dialog Box Launcher** button 🗗 to display the **Paragraph** dialog box.

7 On the **Indents and Spacing tab**, under **Indentation**, click the **Special arrow**, and then click **First line**. In the **By** box, be sure **0.5"** displays. Click **OK**. Compare your screen with Figure 14.4.

The MLA style uses 0.5-inch indents at the beginning of the first line of every paragraph. *Indenting*—moving the beginning of the first line of a paragraph to the right or left of the rest of the paragraph—provides visual cues to the reader to help divide the document text and make it easier to read.

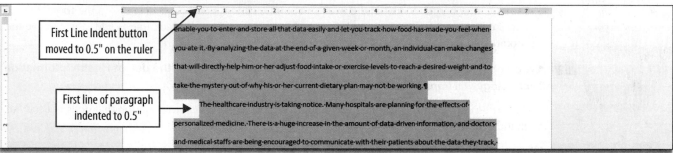

> First Line Indent button moved to 0.5" on the ruler

> First line of paragraph indented to 0.5"

FIGURE 14.4

🔄 **ANOTHER WAY**   On the ruler, point to the First Line Indent button ▽, and then drag the button to 0.5" on the horizontal ruler.

8 Press Ctrl + Home to deselect and move to the top of the document. On the **Insert tab**, in the **Header & Footer group**, click **Footer**, and then at the bottom of the list click **Edit Footer**.

9 In the **Insert group**, click **Document Info**, and then click **File Name**. On the ribbon, click **Close Header and Footer**.

The file name in the footer is *not* part of the research report format, but it is included in projects in this chapter so that you and your instructor can identify your work.

10 Save 🖫 your document.

More Knowledge | **Suppressing the Page Number on the First Page of a Document**

Some style guidelines require that the page number and other header and footer information on the first page be hidden from view—***suppressed***. To hide the information contained in the header and footer areas on Page 1 of a document, double-click in the header or footer area. Then, under Header and Footer Tools, on the Design tab, in the Options group, select the Different First Page check box.

GO! Learn How
Video W14-2

Within report text, numbers mark the location of *notes*—information that expands on the topic being discussed but that does not fit well in the document text. The numbers refer to *footnotes*—notes placed at the bottom of the page containing the note, or to *endnotes*—notes placed at the end of a document or chapter.

Activity 14.03 | Inserting Footnotes

You can add footnotes as you type your document or after your document is complete. Word renumbers the footnotes automatically, so footnotes do not need to be entered in order, and if one footnote is removed, the remaining footnotes automatically renumber.

1 Scroll to view the upper portion of **Page 2**, and then locate the paragraph that begins *Accurate records*. In the third line of the paragraph, click to position the insertion point to the right of the period after *infancy*.

2 On the **References tab**, in the **Footnotes group**, click **Insert Footnote**.

Word creates space for a footnote in the footnote area at the bottom of the page and adds a footnote number to the text at the insertion point location. Footnote *1* displays in the footnote area, and the insertion point moves to the right of the number. A short black line is added just above the footnote area. You do not need to type the footnote number.

3 Type **The Department of Health & Human Services indicates that the use of Health Information Technology will improve the quality of health care.**

This is an explanatory footnote; the footnote provides additional information that does not fit well in the body of the report.

4 Click the **Home tab**, and then in the **Font group** and **Paragraph group**, examine the font size and line spacing settings. Notice that the new footnote displays in 10 pt font size and is single-spaced, even though the font size of the document text is 11 pt and the text is double-spaced, as shown in Figure 14.5.

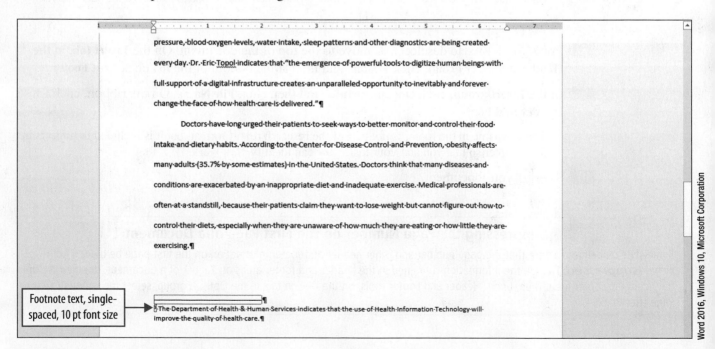

Footnote text, single-spaced, 10 pt font size

Word 2016, Windows 10, Microsoft Corporation

FIGURE 14.5

5 Scroll to view the top of **Page 1**, and then locate the paragraph that begins *Many of us*. At the end of the paragraph, click to position the insertion point to the right of the period following *time*.

6 On the **References tab**, in the **Footnotes group**, click **Insert Footnote**. Type **Organizations such as airlines and the military could benefit because many employees are involved in time-sensitive operations.** Notice that the footnote you just added becomes the new footnote *1*. Click **Save** 🖫, and then compare your screen with Figure 14.6.

> The first footnote that you typed, which is on Page 2 and begins *The Department of Health*, is renumbered as footnote *2*.

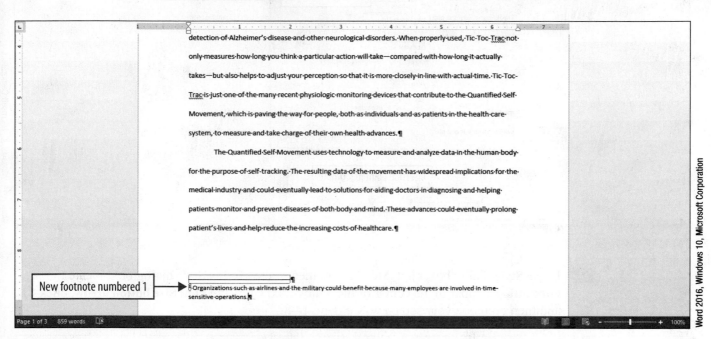

detection·of·Alzheimer's·disease·and·other·neurological·disorders.·When·properly·used,·Tic-Toc·Trac·not·only·measures·how·long·you·think·a·particular·action·will·take—compared·with·how·long·it·actually·takes—but·also·helps·to·adjust·your·perception·so·that·it·is·more·closely·in·line·with·actual·time.·Tic-Toc-Trac·is·just·one·of·the·many·recent·physiologic·monitoring·devices·that·contribute·to·the·Quantified·Self·Movement,·which·is·paving·the·way·for·people,·both·as·individuals·and·as·patients·in·the·health·care·system,·to·measure·and·take·charge·of·their·own·health·advances.¶

The·Quantified·Self·Movement·uses·technology·to·measure·and·analyze·data·in·the·human·body·for·the·purpose·of·self-tracking.·The·resulting·data·of·the·movement·has·widespread·implications·for·the·medical·industry·and·could·eventually·lead·to·solutions·for·aiding·doctors·in·diagnosing·and·helping·patients·monitor·and·prevent·diseases·of·both·body·and·mind.·These·advances·could·eventually·prolong·patient's·lives·and·help·reduce·the·increasing·costs·of·healthcare.¶

New footnote numbered 1 → ⁵·Organizations·such·as·airlines·and·the·military·could·benefit·because·many·employees·are·involved·in·time-sensitive·operations.¶

Page 1 of 3   859 words

Word 2016, Windows 10, Microsoft Corporation

FIGURE 14.6

More Knowledge   **Using Symbols Rather Than Numbers for Notes**

Instead of using numbers to designate footnotes, you can use standard footnote symbols. The seven traditional symbols, available from the Footnote and Endnote dialog box, in order, are * (asterisk), † (dagger), ‡ (double dagger), § (section mark), || (parallels), ¶ (paragraph mark), and # (number or pound sign). This sequence can be continuous (this is the default setting), or it can begin anew with each page.

IC3
DIGITAL LITERACY
CERTIFICATION
2.02c

Activity 14.04 | Modifying a Footnote Style

Microsoft Word contains built-in paragraph formats called ***styles***—groups of formatting commands, such as font, font size, font color, paragraph alignment, and line spacing—that can be applied to a paragraph with one command.

The default style for footnote text is a single-spaced paragraph that uses a 10-point Calibri font and no paragraph indents. MLA style specifies double-spaced text in all areas of a research paper—including footnotes. According to the MLA style, first lines of footnotes must also be indented 0.5 inch and use the same font size as the report text.

1 At the bottom of **Page 1**, point anywhere in the footnote text you just typed, right-click, and then on the shortcut menu, click **Style**. Compare your screen with Figure 14.7.

The Style dialog box displays, listing the styles currently in use in the document, in addition to some of the word processing elements that come with special built-in styles. Because you right-clicked in the footnote text, the selected style is the Footnote Text style.

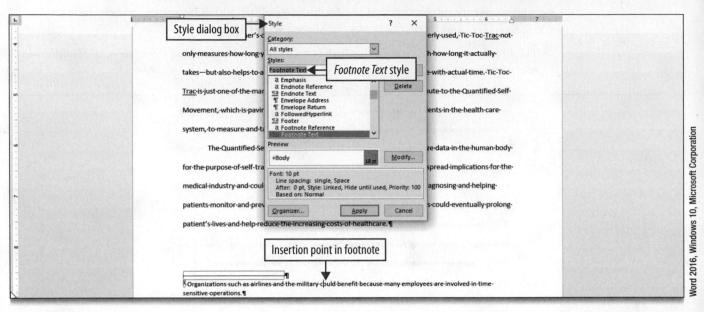

FIGURE 14.7

2 In the **Style** dialog box, click **Modify**, and then in the **Modify Style** dialog box, locate the **Formatting** toolbar in the center of the dialog box. Click the **Font Size button arrow**, click **11**, and then compare your screen with Figure 14.8.

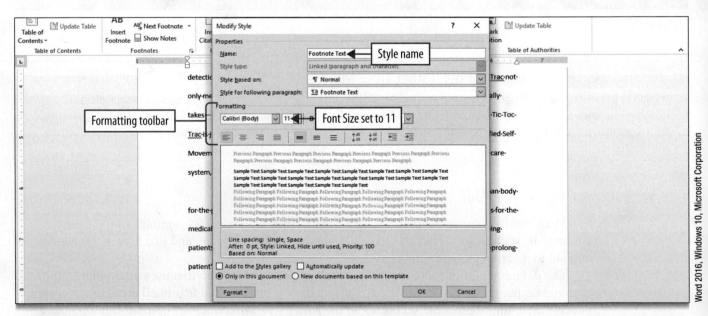

FIGURE 14.8

3 In the lower left corner of the dialog box, click **Format**, and then click **Paragraph**. In the **Paragraph** dialog box, on the **Indents and Spacing tab**, under **Indentation**, click the **Special arrow**, and then click **First line**.

4 Under **Spacing**, click the **Line spacing arrow**, and then click **Double**. Compare your dialog box with Figure 14.9.

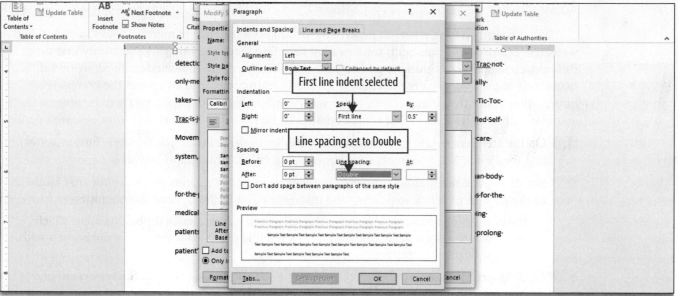

FIGURE 14.9

Word 2016, Windows 10, Microsoft Corporation

5 Click **OK** to close the **Paragraph** dialog box, click **OK** to close the **Modify Style** dialog box, and then click **Apply** to apply the new style and close the dialog box. Compare your screen with Figure 14.10.

> Your inserted footnotes are formatted with the modified Footnote Text paragraph style; any new footnotes that you insert will also use this format.

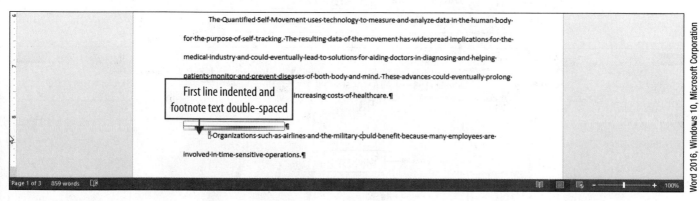

FIGURE 14.10

Word 2016, Windows 10, Microsoft Corporation

6 Scroll to view the bottom of **Page 2** to confirm that the new format was also applied to the second footnote, and then **Save** 🖫 your document.

Objective 3 Create Citations and a Bibliography in a Research Paper

GO! Learn How
Video W14-3

Reports and research papers typically include information that you find in other sources, and these sources of information must be credited. When you use quotations from or detailed summaries of other people's work, you must specify the source of the information. A *citation* is a note inserted into the text of a report or research paper that refers the reader to a source in the bibliography. Create a *bibliography* at the end of a research paper to list the sources you have referenced. Such a list is typically titled *Works Cited* (in MLA style), *Bibliography*, *Sources*, or *References*.

When writing a long research paper, you will likely reference numerous books, articles, and websites. Some of your research sources may be referenced many times, others only one time. References to sources within the text of your research paper are indicated in an *abbreviated* manner. However, as you enter a citation for the first time, you can also enter the *complete* information about the source. Then, when you have finished your paper, you will be able to automatically generate the list of sources that must be included at the end of your research paper.

1 On the **References tab**, in the **Citations & Bibliography group**, click the **Style button arrow**, and then click **MLA** to insert a reference using MLA bibliography style.

2 Scroll to view the middle of **Page 2**. In the paragraph that begins *Accurate records*, at the end of the paragraph, click to position the insertion point to the right of the quotation mark.

The citation in the document points to the full source information in the bibliography, which typically includes the name of the author, the full title of the work, the year of publication, and other publication information.

3 Click **Insert Citation**, and then click **Add New Source**. Click the **Type of Source arrow**, and then if necessary, click **Book**. Add the following information, and then compare your screen with Figure 14.11:

Author	Sopol, Eric J.
Title	The Creative Destruction of Medicine
Year	2012
City	New York
Publisher	Basic Books
Medium	Print

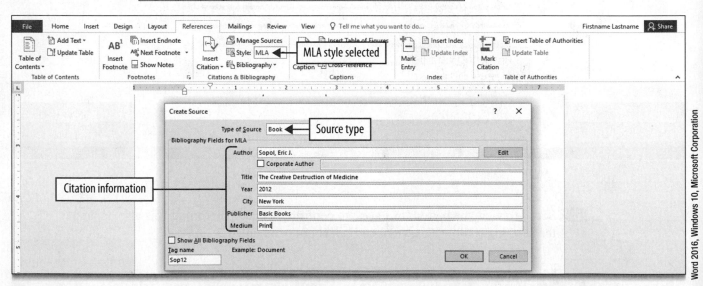

FIGURE 14.11

4 Click **OK** to insert the citation. Point to *(Sopol)* and click one time to select the citation.

In the MLA style, citations that refer to items on the *Works Cited* page are placed in parentheses and are referred to as **parenthetical references**—references that include the last name of the author or authors and the page number in the referenced source, which you add to the reference. No year is indicated, and there is no comma between the name and the page number.

Both MLA and APA styles use parenthetical references for source citations rather than using footnotes.

5 **Save** the document.

Citing Corporate Authors and Indicating the Medium

If the author of a document is only identified as the name of an organization, select the Corporate Author check box and type the name of the organization in the Corporate Author box.

In the 7th edition of the *MLA Handbook for Writers of Research Papers*, the category Medium was added and must be included for any item on the Works Cited page. Entries for this category can include Print, Web, Performance, and Photograph, among many others.

Activity 14.06 | Editing Citations

1 In the lower right corner of the box that surrounds the selected reference, point to the small arrow to display the ScreenTip *Citation Options*. Click the **Citation Options arrow**, and then on the list of options, click **Edit Citation**.

2 In the **Edit Citation** dialog box, under **Add**, in the **Pages** box, type **5** to indicate that you are citing from page 5 of this source. Compare your screen with Figure 14.12.

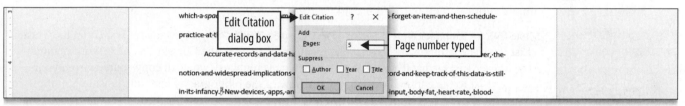

FIGURE 14.12

Word 2016, Windows 10, Microsoft Corporation

3 Click **OK** to display the page number of the citation. Click outside of the citation box to deselect it.

4 Type a period to the right of the citation, and delete the period to the left of the quotation mark.

In the MLA style, if the reference occurs at the end of a sentence, the parenthetical reference always displays to the left of the punctuation mark that ends the sentence.

5 Press Ctrl + End to move to the end of the document, and then click to position the insertion point after the letter *e* in *disease* and to the left of the period.

6 In the **Citations & Bibliography group**, click **Insert Citation**, and then click **Add New Source**. Click the **Type of Source arrow**, if necessary scroll to the top of the list, click **Book**, and then add the following information:

Author	Glaser, John P., and Claudia Salzberg
Title	The Strategic Application of Information Technology in Health Care Organizations
Year	2011
City	San Francisco
Publisher	Jossey-Bass
Medium	Print

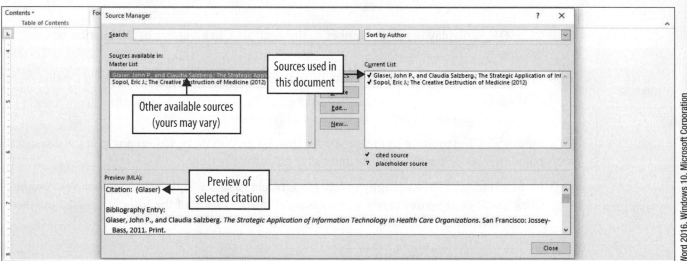

ANOTHER WAY In the Create Source dialog box, if you prefer, you can enter each author name separately by using the Edit command to the right of the Author box. Initiate the command for each author of the work, and then Word will automatically format all the names properly and in the correct order in the Works Cited list.

> **NOTE** MLA Style for Two or More Authors
>
> According to MLA Style, to cite a book by two or more authors, reverse only the name of the first author, add a comma, and give the other name or names in normal form. Place a period after the last name.

7 ▸ Click **OK**. Click the inserted citation to select it, click the **Citation Options arrow**, and then click **Edit Citation**.

8 ▸ In the **Edit Citation** dialog box, under **Add**, in the **Pages** box, type **28** to indicate that you are citing from page 28 of this source. Click **OK**.

9 ▸ On the **References tab**, in the **Citations & Bibliography group**, click **Manage Sources**, and then compare your screen with Figure 14.13.

The Source Manager dialog box displays. Other citations on your computer display in the Master List box. The citations for the current document display in the Current List box. Word maintains the Master List so that if you use the same sources regularly, you can copy sources from your Master List to the current document. A preview of the bibliography entry also displays at the bottom of the dialog box.

FIGURE 14.13

10 ▸ At the bottom of the **Source Manager** dialog box, click **Close**. Click anywhere in the document to deselect the parenthetical reference, and then **Save** your document.

Activity 14.07 | Adding Citations for a Website

1 ▸ In the lower portion of **Page 2**, in the paragraph that begins *Doctors have long urged*, in the third line, click to position the insertion point after the s in *States* and to the left of the period.

2 In the **Citations & Bibliography group**, click **Insert Citation**, and then click **Add New Source**. Click the **Type of Source arrow**, scroll down as necessary, and then click **Web site**. Type the following information:

Author	Ogden, C. L.
Name of Web Page	NCHS Data Brief Number 82
Year	2012
Month	January
Day	01
Year Accessed	2016
Month Accessed	January
Day Accessed	17
Medium	Web

3 Click **OK**. Save 🖫, and then compare your screen with Figure 14.14.

A parenthetical reference is added. Because the cited Web page has no page numbers, only the author name is used in the parenthetical reference.

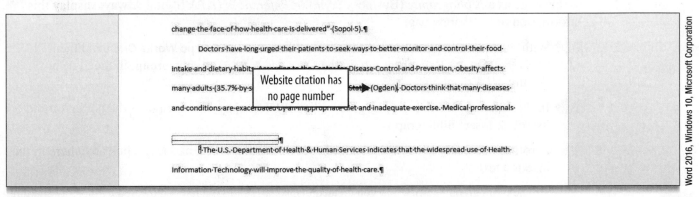

change·the·face·of·how·health·care·is·delivered"·(Sopol·5).¶

Doctors·have·long·urged·their·patients·to·seek·ways·to·better·monitor·and·control·their·food·

intake·and·dietary·habits.·According·to·the·Center·for·Disease·Control·and·Prevention,·obesity·affects·

many·adults·(35.7%·by·s   Stat   (Ogden).·Doctors·think·that·many·diseases·

and·conditions·are·exacerbated·by·an·inappropriate·diet·and·inadequate·exercise.·Medical·professionals·

Website citation has no page number

¶·The·U.S.·Department·of·Health·&·Human·Services·indicates·that·the·widespread·use·of·Health·

Information·Technology·will·improve·the·quality·of·health·care.¶

Word 2016, Windows 10, Microsoft Corporation

FIGURE 14.14

More Knowledge **Including URLs of Web Sources**

With the 7th edition of the *MLA Handbook for Writers of Research Papers*, including the URL of Web sources is recommended only when the reader would have difficulty finding the source without it or if your instructor requires it. Otherwise, readers will likely find the resource by using search tools. If you include the URL, enclose it in angle brackets and end with a period.

IC3
DIGITAL LITERACY
CERTIFICATION
2.02e

Activity 14.08 | Inserting Page Breaks

Your bibliography must begin on a new page, so at the bottom of the last page of your report, you must insert a manual page break.

1 Press Ctrl + End to move the insertion point to the end of the document.

If there is a footnote on the last page, the insertion point will display at the end of the final paragraph, but above the footnote—a footnote is always associated with the page that contains the footnote information.

2 Press ⌈Ctrl⌉ + ⌈Enter⌉ to insert a manual page break.

A *manual page break* forces a page to end at the insertion point location, and then places any subsequent text at the top of the next page. Recall that the new paragraph retains the formatting of the previous paragraph, so in this instance the first line is indented.

A *page break indicator*, which shows where a manual page break was inserted, displays at the bottom of Page 3.

3 On the **Home tab**, in the **Paragraph group**, click the **Dialog Box Launcher** button ⌐ to display the **Paragraph** dialog box.

4 On the **Indents and Spacing tab**, under **Indentation**, click the **Special arrow**, and then click **(none)**. Click **OK**, and then **Save** 🔲 your document.

↻ ANOTHER WAY On the ruler, point to the First Line Indent button ▽ , and then drag the button to 0" on the horizontal ruler.

Activity 14.09 | Creating a Reference Page

At the end of a report or research paper, include a list of each source referenced. *Works Cited* is the reference page heading used in the MLA style guidelines. Other styles may refer to this page as a *Bibliography* (Business Style) or *References* (APA Style). Always display this information on a separate page.

1 With the insertion point blinking in the first line of **Page 4**, type **Works Cited** and then press ⌈Enter⌉. On the **References tab**, in the **Citations & Bibliography group**, in the **Style** box, be sure *MLA* displays.

2 In the **Citations & Bibliography group**, click **Bibliography**, and then near the bottom of the list, click **Insert Bibliography**.

3 Scroll as necessary to view the entire list of three references, and then click anywhere in the inserted text.

The bibliography entries that you created display as a field, which is indicated by the gray shading. This field links to the Source Manager for the citations. The references display alphabetically by the author's last name.

4 In the bibliography, point to the left of the first entry—beginning *Glaser, John P.*—to display the ⍗ pointer. Drag down to select all three references in the field but not the blank paragraph.

5 On the **Home tab**, in the **Paragraph group**, change the **Line spacing** to **2.0**, and then on the **Layout tab**, in the **Paragraph group**, change the **Spacing After** to **0 pt**.

The entries display according to MLA guidelines; the text is double-spaced, the extra space between paragraphs is removed, and each entry uses a *hanging indent*—the first line of each entry extends 0.5 inch to the left of the remaining lines of the entry.

↻ ANOTHER WAY Display the Paragraph dialog box. Under Spacing, click the Line spacing arrow, and then click Double. Under Spacing, in the After box, type 0.

---

6 At the top of **Page 4**, click anywhere in the title text *Works Cited*, and then press ⌈Ctrl⌉ + ⌈E⌉ to center the title. Compare your screen with Figure 14.15, and then **Save** 🔲 your document.

In MLA style, the *Works Cited* title is centered.

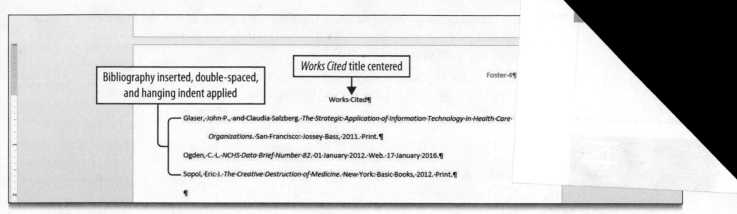

Foster-4¶

Works·Cited¶

Glaser,·John·P.,·and·Claudia·Salzberg.·*The·Strategic·Application·of·Information·Technology·in·Health·Care·*

Organizations.·San·Francisco:·Jossey-Bass,·2011.·Print.¶

Ogden,·C.·L.·*NCHS·Data·Brief·Number·82.*·01·January·2012.·Web.·17·January·2016.¶

Sopol,·Eric·J.·*The·Creative·Destruction·of·Medicine.*·New·York:·Basic·Books,·2012.·Print.¶

¶

FIGURE 14.15

Word 2016, Windows 10, Microsoft Corporation

Activity 14.10 | Managing and Modifying Sources for a Document

Use the Source Manager to organize the sources cited in your document. For example, in the Source Manager dialog box, you can copy sources from the master list to the current list, delete a source, edit a source, or search for a source. You can also display a preview of how your citations will appear in your document.

1 On the **References tab**, in the **Citations & Bibliography group**, click **Manage Sources**.

2 On the left, in the **Master List**, click the entry for *Sopol, Eric J.* and then between the **Master List** and the **Current List**, click **Edit**.

The name of this source should be *Topol* instead of *Sopol*.

3 In the **Edit Source** dialog box, in the **Author** box, delete *S* and type **T**

4 Click **OK**. When the message box indicates *This source exists in your master list and current document. Do you want to update both lists with these changes?* click **Yes**. Compare your screen with Figure 14.16.

In the lower portion of the Source Manager dialog box, a preview of the corrected entry displays.

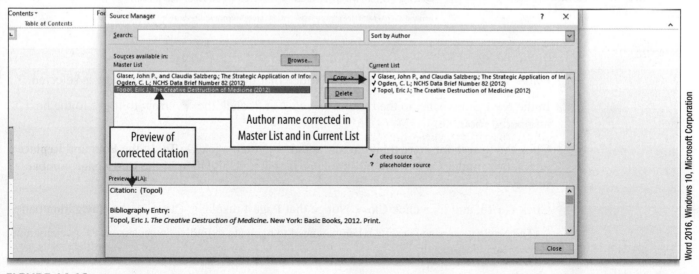

FIGURE 14.16

Word 2016, Windows 10, Microsoft Corporation

5 In the lower right corner, click **Close**. On your **Works Cited page**, notice that the author name is *not* corrected. Scroll to view the lower portion of **Page 2**, and notice that the author name *is* corrected and the citation is selected.

6 On the selected citation *(Topol 5)*, click the **Citation Options arrow**, and then click **Update Citations and Bibliography**. Press Ctrl + End, and notice that this action updates the Works Cited page with the corrected name.

> Editing a source in Source Manager updates only the sources in the document; to update the Works Cited page, use the Update Citations and Bibliography command on the citation.

7 Click **Save** ◻.

Activity 14.11 | Using the Navigation Pane to Go to a Specific Page

In a multipage document, use the Navigation pane to move to a specific page or to find specific objects in the document.

1 Press Ctrl + Home to move to the top of the document. Click the **View tab**, and then in the **Show group**, select the **Navigation Pane** check box.

2 In the **Navigation** pane, on the right end of the **Search document** box, click the **Search for more things arrow**, and then compare your screen with Figure 14.17.

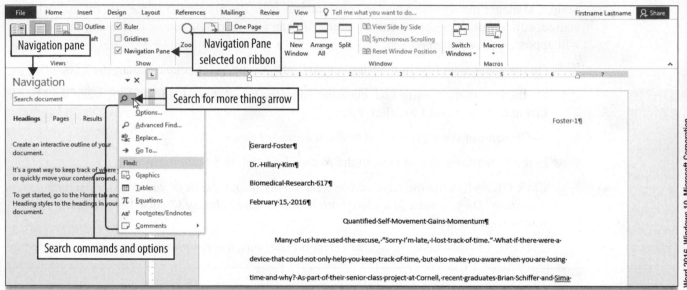

FIGURE 14.17

3 Under **Find**, click **Footnotes/Endnotes**. Notice that the first numbered footnote is selected.

4 In the **Navigation** pane, to the right of *Result 1 of 2*, click the ▼ arrow to move to the next numbered footnote.

5 Click the **Search for more things arrow** again, and then click **Go To**. In the **Find and Replace** dialog box, under **Go to what**, be sure **Page** is selected, and then in the **Enter page number** box, type **4**

6 Click **Go To**, and then click **Close**. Notice that **Page 4** displays. **Close** ✕ the **Navigation** pane.

> The Navigation pane is useful when you need to navigate to find various elements, especially in a very long document.

ANOTHER WAY You can also initiate the Go To command from the ribbon or by using a keyboard shortcut. To do so, on the Home tab, in the Editing group, click the Find arrow, and then click Go To; or, hold down Ctrl and press G to display the Go To tab of the Find and Replace dialog box.

For a research paper, you may want to add additional document properties.

1 Press `Ctrl` + `Home` to return to the top of your document. Click the **File tab** to display **Backstage** view, and then in the lower right corner of the screen, click **Show All Properties**.

2 As the document **Title**, type **Quantified Self Movement Gains Momentum** and then as the **Tags**, type **quantified self, research paper**

3 Click in the **Comments** box and type **draft copy of report for class** and then in the **Categories** box, type **biomedical research**

4 In the **Subject** box, type your course name and section number. In the **Company** box, select and delete any existing text, and then type **University Medical Center**

5 Click in the **Manager** box and type **Dr. Hillary Kim** Be sure your name displays as the **Author** and edit if necessary.

6 At the top of the **Properties** list, click the text *Properties*, and then click **Advanced Properties**. In the dialog box, if necessary click the **Summary tab**, and then compare your screen with Figure 14.18.

In the Advanced Properties dialog box, you can view and modify additional document properties.

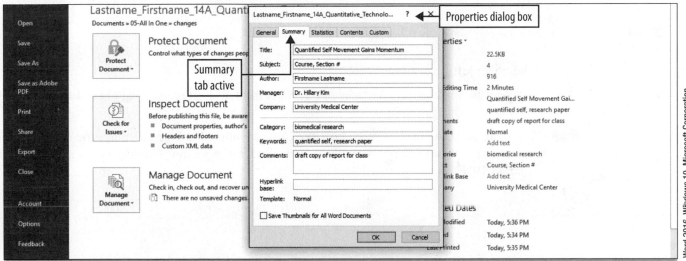

FIGURE 14.18

7 Click the **Statistics tab**.

The document statistics show the number of revisions made to the document, the last time the document was edited, and the number of paragraphs, lines, words, and characters in the document. Additional information categories are available by clicking the Custom tab.

8 **Close** ☒ the dialog box, and then on the left, click **Save** to save and return to your document.

> **More Knowledge** | **Inserting a Watermark**
>
> A **watermark** is a text or graphic element that displays behind document text. Until you know your research paper is final—for example, you have others reviewing it—you might want to display the word DRAFT on each page. To do so, on the Design tab, in the Page Background group, click Watermark, and then at the bottom, click Custom Watermark. In the Printed Watermark dialog box, click the Text watermark option button, click the Text arrow, and then click DRAFT. Click OK. To remove the watermark—after you are sure your research paper is final—click the Watermark command again, and then click Remove Watermark.

GO! Learn How
Video W14-4

Read Mode optimizes the view of the Word screen for the times when you are *reading* Word documents on the screen and not creating or editing them. Microsoft's research indicates that two-thirds of user sessions in Word contain no editing—meaning that people are simply reading the Word document on the screen. The Column Layout feature of Read Mode reflows the document to fit the size of the device you are reading so that the text is as easy to read on a tablet device as on a 24-inch screen. The Object Zoom feature of Read Mode resizes graphics to fit the screen you are using, but you can click or tap to zoom in on the graphic.

PDF Reflow provides the ability to import PDF files into Word so that you can transform a PDF back into a fully editable Word document. This is useful if you have lost the original Word file or if someone sends you a PDF that you would like to modify. PDF Reflow is not intended to act as a viewer for PDF files—for that you will still want to use a PDF reader such as Adobe Reader. In Windows 10, the Microsoft Edge browser also serves as a PDF reader.

Activity 14.13 | Using Read Mode

1 If necessary, press Ctrl + Home to move to the top of your document. On the **View tab**, in the **Views group**, click **Read Mode**, and notice that Read Mode keeps footnotes displayed on the page associated with the footnote.

ANOTHER WAY   On the right side of the status bar, click the Read Mode button 📖.

2 In the upper left corner, click **Tools**.

You can use these tools to find something within the document or use Bing to conduct an Internet search.

3 Click **Find**, and then in the **Search** box, type **Topol** Notice that Word displays the first page where the search term displays and highlights the term in yellow. Compare your screen with Figure 14.19.

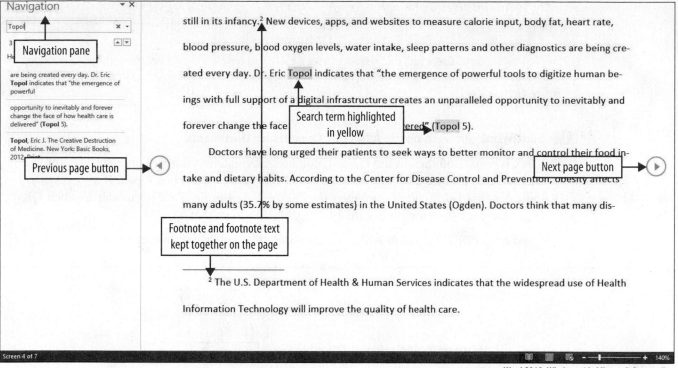

FIGURE 14.19

Word 2016, Windows 10, Microsoft Corporation

> 4 ▸ In the upper left corner, click **View**, and then take a moment to study the table in Figure 14.20.

VIEW COMMANDS IN READ MODE	
VIEW COMMAND	**ACTION**
Edit Document	Return to Print Layout view to continue editing the document.
Navigation Pane	Search for specific text or click a heading or page to move to that location.
Show Comments	See comments, if any, within the document.
Column Width	Change the display of the document to fit more or less text on each line.
Page Color	Change the colors used to show the document to make it easier to read. Some readers prefer a sepia (brownish-gray) shading as the background or a black background with white text.
Layout	Read in different layouts. Select Column Layout, which is the default, or Paper Layout, which mimics the 8.5 x 11 format but without the ribbon.

Gaskin, Shelley. Go! All in Cne, 3E. Pearson Education, 2017.

FIGURE 14.20

> 5 ▸ On the **View** menu, click **Edit Document** to return to **Print Layout** view. **Close** ☒ the **Navigation** pane.

> 6 ▸ In the upper right corner of the Word window, click **Close** ☒. If directed by your instructor to do so, submit your paper printout, your electronic image of your document that looks like a printed document, or your original Word file. If you are submitting this Project as a MyITLab grader, submit this file.

More Knowledge | **Highlighting Text in a Word Document**

You can highlight text in a Word document. Select the text you want to highlight, and then on the Home tab, in the Font group, click the Text Highlight Color arrow 🖌▾. Click the color you want to use for your highlight to apply it to the selected text. Or, click the Text Highlight Color button arrow 🖌▾, click a color, and then use the 🖌 pointer to select text that you want to highlight.

> ### ALERT!   This Activity Is Optional
>
> This Activity is optional. Check with your instructor to see if you should complete this Activity. This Activity is not included in the MyITLab Grader system for this project; however, you may want to practice this on your own to see how PDF Reflow works.

1 Start Word, and then on the left, click **Open Other Documents**.

2 Click **Browse**, and then in the **Open** dialog box, navigate to your student data files for this chapter. Click **w14A_PDF_optional**. In the lower right corner, click **Open**. If a message indicates that *Word will now convert the PDF to an editable Word document ...*, click OK. Compare your screen with Figure 14.21.

> With the PDF displayed in Word, you can make edits, and then re-save as a PDF.

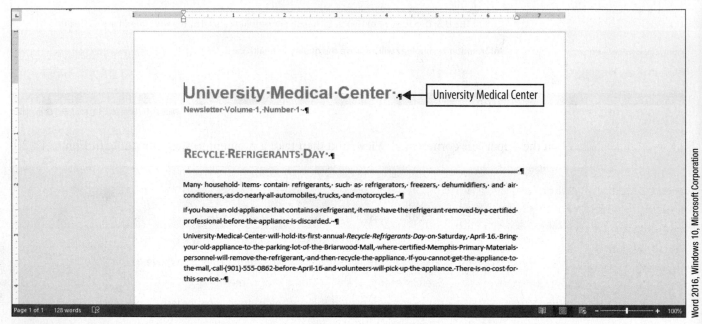

FIGURE 14.21

Word 2016, Windows 10, Microsoft Corporation

3 **Close** ✕ Word.

> ### More Knowledge   Saving Documents in Alternative File Formats
>
> You can save a Word document in a variety of other document formats, including a PDF. To do so, with your Word document open, display the Save As dialog box. Click the Save as type arrow, and then click the desired file type. Commonly used file types are PDF and Rich Text Format.

END | You have completed Project 14A

GO! With Google

Objective | Use the Research Bar in Google Docs

ALERT! **Working with Web-Based Applications and Services**

Computer programs and services on the web receive continuous updates and improvements, so the steps to complete this web-based Activity may differ from the ones shown. You can often look at the screens and the information presented to determine how to complete the Activity.

If you do not already have a Google account, you will need to create one before you begin this Activity. Go to http://google.com and, in the upper right corner, click Sign In. On the Sign In screen, click Create Account. On the Create your Google Account page, complete the form, read and agree to the Terms of Service and Privacy Policy, and then click Next step. On the Welcome screen, click Get Started.

Activity | Using the Research Bar in Google Docs

Google Docs provides a research tool that you can use to find studies and academic papers on many topics. You can narrow your search results by selecting "Scholar" from the menu in the search bar. After you find the study, you can insert it as a citation or a footnote. You can also choose to use the MLA, APA, or Chicago citation formatting.

1 From the desktop, open your browser, navigate to **http://google.com**, and then click the **Google Apps** menu ⊞. Click **Drive**, and then if necessary, sign in to your Google account.

2 Open your **GO! Web Projects** folder—or click NEW to create and then open this folder if necessary.

3 In the left pane, click **NEW**, and then click **File upload**. In the **Open** dialog box, navigate to your student data files for this chapter, and then in the **File List**, double-click to open **w14_14A_Web**.

4 Point to the uploaded file **w14_14A_Web**, and then right-click. On the shortcut menu, scroll as necessary, and then click **Rename**. Using your own last name and first name, type **Lastname_Firstname_WD_14A_Web** and use the default .docx extension. Click **OK** to rename the file.

5 Point to the file you just renamed, right-click, point to **Open with**, and then click **Google Docs**.

6 Press Ctrl + End to move to the end of the document, and then press Enter one time. Type **There are many studies related to the quantified self movement conducted by Melanie Swan, who is interested in crowdsourced health research.**

7 On the menu bar, click **Tools**, and then click **Research** to open the **Research pane** on the right. At the top of the **Research pane**, click the arrow to the right of *G*, click the arrow a second time to filter the results, and then on the list click **Scholar**.

8 In the search box at the top, delete any existing text, type **Melanie Swan** and then press Enter. *Point to the first item in the list, and then compare your screen with Figure A.*

(GO! With Google continues on the next page)

GO! With Google

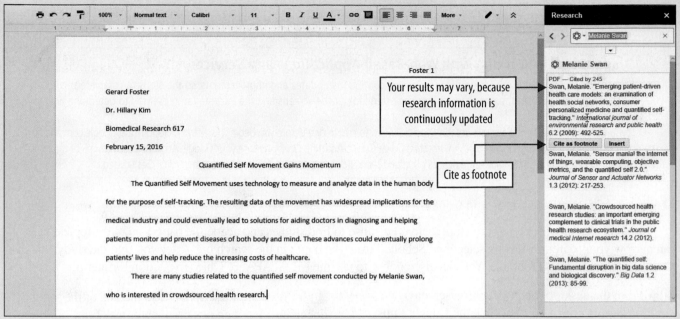

FIGURE A

9 Click **Cite as footnote**. Notice that a footnote number is inserted at the end of the sentence. Scroll down to view the bottom of the page, and then compare your screen with Figure B.

10 Submit the file as directed by your instructor. In the upper right, click your user name, and then click **Sign out**. **Close** your browser window. Your file is automatically saved in your Google Drive.

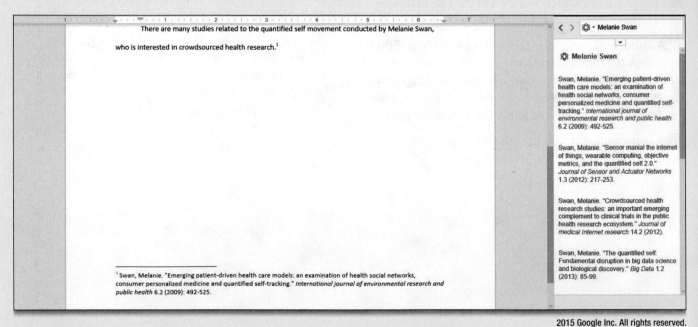

FIGURE B

Newsletter with Optional Mailing Labels

PROJECT ACTIVITIES

In Activities 14.15 through 14.29, you will edit a newsletter that University Medical Center is sending to the board of directors; optionally, you can create the necessary mailing labels. Your completed documents will look similar to Figure 14.22.

PROJECT FILES

MyITLab grader If your instructor wants you to submit Project 14B in the MyITLab Grader system, log in to MyITLab, locate Grader Project 14B, and then download the files for this project.

For Project 14B, you will need the following files:

w14B_Environment_Newsletter
w14B_Addresses (Optional if assigned)

You will save your documents as:

Lastname_Firstname_14B_Environment_Newsletter
Lastname_Firstname_14B_Mailing_Labels (Optional if assigned)

PROJECT RESULTS

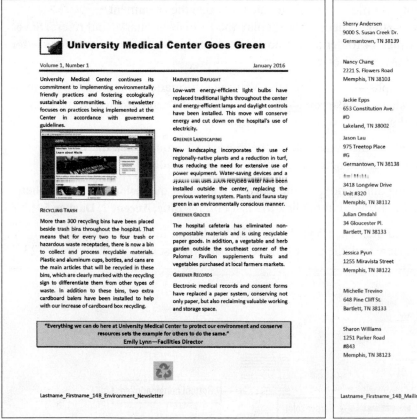

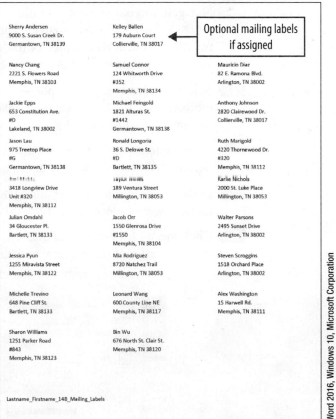

FIGURE 14.22 Project 14B Environment Newsletter

Objective 5   Format a Multiple-Column Newsletter

GO! Learn How
Video W14-5

A *newsletter* is a periodical that communicates news and information to a specific group. Newsletters, as well as all newspapers and most magazines, use multiple columns for articles because text in narrower columns is easier to read than text that stretches across a page.

You can create a newsletter in Word by changing a single column of text into two or more columns. If a column does not end where you want it to, you can end the column at a location of your choice by inserting a *manual column break*—an artificial end to a column to balance columns or to provide space for the insertion of other objects.

Activity 14.15 | Changing One Column of Text to Two Columns

ALERT!   **To submit as an autograded project, log into MyITLab, download the files for this project, and then begin with those files instead of with w14B_Environment_Newsletter.**

IC3
DIGITAL LITERACY
CERTIFICATION
2.02e (ii)

Newsletters are usually two or three columns wide. When using 8.5 × 11-inch paper in portrait orientation, avoid creating four or more columns because they are so narrow that word spacing looks awkward, often resulting in one long word on a line by itself.

1 Start Word. On Word's opening screen, in the lower left, click **Open Other Documents**. Navigate to your student data files, and then locate and open the document **w14B_Environment_Newsletter**. If necessary, display the formatting marks and rulers. **Save** the file in your **AIO Chapter 14** folder as **Lastname_Firstname_14B_Environment_Newsletter** and then add the file name to the footer.

2 Select the first two paragraphs—the title and the Volume information and date. On the mini toolbar, click the **Font Color button arrow** [A▾], and then under **Theme Colors**, in the fifth column, click the last color—**Blue, Accent 1, Darker 50%**.

3 With the text still selected, on the **Home tab**, in the **Paragraph group**, click the **Borders button arrow** [▦▾], and then at the bottom, click **Borders and Shading**.

4 In the **Borders and Shading** dialog box, on the **Borders tab**, click the **Color arrow**, and then under **Theme Colors**, in the fifth column, click the last color—**Blue, Accent 1, Darker 50%**.

5 Click the **Width arrow**, and then click **3 pt**. In the **Preview** box at the right, point to the *bottom* border of the preview and click one time. Compare your screen with Figure 14.23.

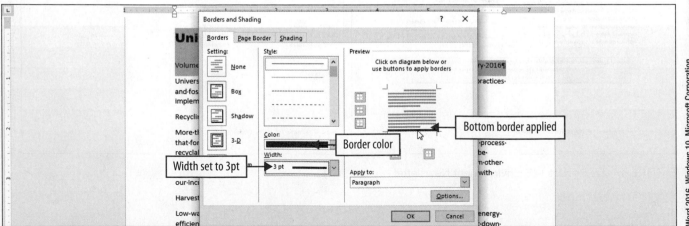

FIGURE 14.23

6 In the **Borders and Shading** dialog box, click **OK**.

The line visually defines the newsletter's *nameplate*—the banner on the front page of a newsletter that identifies the publication.

7 Below the Volume information, click at the beginning of the paragraph that begins *University Medical Center continues*. By using the vertical scroll box, scroll to view the lower portion of the document, hold down Shift, and then click after the paragraph mark at the end of the paragraph that begins *Electronic medical records* to select all of the text between the insertion point and the sentence ending with the word *space*. Be sure that the paragraph mark is included in the selection. Compare your screen with Figure 14.24.

Use Shift to define a selection that may be difficult to select by dragging.

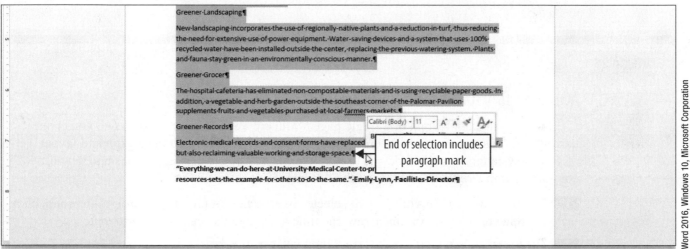

Greener·Landscaping¶

New·landscaping·incorporates·the·use·of·regionally·native·plants·and·a·reduction·in·turf,·thus·reducing· the·need·for·extensive·use·of·power·equipment.·Water-saving·devices·and·a·system·that·uses·100%· recycled·water·have·been·installed·outside·the·center,·replacing·the·previous·watering·system.·Plants· and·fauna·stay·green·in·an·environmentally-conscious·manner.¶

Greener·Grocer¶

The·hospital·cafeteria·has·eliminated·non-compostable·materials·and·is·using·recyclable·paper·goods.·In· addition,·a·vegetable·and·herb·garden·outside·the·southeast·corner·of·the·Palomar·Pavilion· supplements·fruits·and·vegetables·purchased·at·local·farmers·markets.¶

Greener·Records¶

Electronic·medical·records·and·consent·forms·have·replaced
but·also·reclaiming·valuable·working·and·storage·space.¶

End of selection includes paragraph mark

"Everything·we·can·do·here·at·University·Medical·Center·to·p
resources·sets·the·example·for·others·to·do·the·same."·Emily·Lynn,·Facilities·Director¶

Calibri (Body) ▾ 11 ▾ A˄ A˅ ✦ A⧸

Word 2016, Windows 10, Microsoft Corporation

FIGURE 14.24

8 On the **Layout tab**, in the **Page Setup group**, click **Columns**, and then click **Two**. Compare your screen with Figure 14.25, and then **Save** 🖫 your newsletter.

Word divides the selected text into two columns and inserts a *section break* at the end of the selection, dividing the one-column section of the document from the two-column section of the document. A *section* is a portion of a document that can be formatted differently from the rest of the document. A section break marks the end of one section and the beginning of another section.

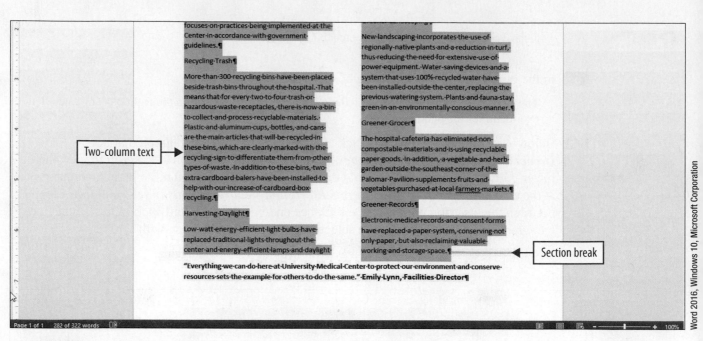

Two-column text

focuses·on·practices·being·implemented·at·the·Center·in·accordance·with·government·guidelines.¶

Recycling·Trash¶

More·than·300·recycling·bins·have·been·placed·beside·trash·bins·throughout·the·hospital.·That·means·that·for·every·two·to·four·trash·or·hazardous·waste·receptacles,·there·is·now·a·bin·to·collect·and·process·recyclable·materials.·Plastic·and·aluminum·cups,·bottles,·and·cans·are·the·main·articles·that·will·be·recycled·in·these·bins,·which·are·clearly·marked·with·the·recycling·sign·to·differentiate·them·from·other·types·of·waste.·In·addition·to·these·bins,·two·extra·cardboard·balers·have·been·installed·to·help·with·our·increase·of·cardboard·box·recycling.¶

Harvesting·Daylight¶

Low-watt·energy-efficient·light·bulbs·have·replaced·traditional·lights·throughout·the·center·and·energy-efficient·lamps·and·daylight·

New·landscaping·incorporates·the·use·of·regionally·native·plants·and·a·reduction·in·turf,·thus·reducing·the·need·for·extensive·use·of·power·equipment.·Water-saving·devices·and·a·system·that·uses·100%·recycled·water·have·been·installed·outside·the·center,·replacing·the·previous·watering·system.·Plants·and·fauna·stay·green·in·an·environmentally·conscious·manner.¶

Greener·Grocer¶

The·hospital·cafeteria·has·eliminated·non-compostable·materials·and·is·using·recyclable·paper·goods.·In·addition,·a·vegetable·and·herb·garden·outside·the·southeast·corner·of·the·Palomar·Pavilion·supplements·fruits·and·vegetables·purchased·at·local·farmers·markets.¶

Greener·Records¶

Electronic·medical·records·and·consent·forms·have·replaced·a·paper·system,·conserving·not·only·paper,·but·also·reclaiming·valuable·working·and·storage·space.¶ **← Section break**

"Everything·we·can·do·here·at·University·Medical·Center·to·protect·our·environment·and·conserve·resources·sets·the·example·for·others·to·do·the·same."·**Emily·Lynn,·Facilities·Director**¶

Page·1·of·1   282·of·322·words   100%

Word 2016, Windows 10, Microsoft Corporation

FIGURE 14.25

IC3 DIGITAL LITERACY CERTIFICATION
2.02e (ii)

Activity 14.16 | Formatting Multiple Columns

The uneven right margin of a single page-width column is easy to read. When you create narrow columns, justified text is sometimes preferable. Depending on the design and layout of your newsletter, you might decide to reduce extra space between paragraphs and between columns to improve the readability of the document.

1 With the two columns of text still selected, on the **Layout tab**, in the **Paragraph group**, click the **Spacing After down spin arrow** one time to change the spacing after to **6 pt**.

2 On the **Home tab**, in the **Paragraph group**, click **Justify** ▤.

3 Click anywhere in the document to deselect the text, compare your screen with Figure 14.26, and then **Save** 🖫.

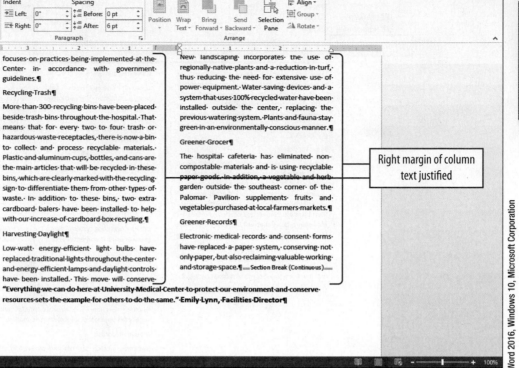

New· landscaping· incorporates· the· use· of·
regionally·native·plants·and·a·reduction·in·turf,·
thus· reducing· the· need· for· extensive· use· of·
power·equipment.·Water-saving·devices·and·a·
system·that·uses·100%·recycled·water·have·been·
installed· outside· the· center,· replacing· the·
previous·watering·system.·Plants·and·fauna·stay·
green·in·an·environmentally-conscious·manner.¶

Right margin of column text justified

focuses·on·practices·being·implemented·at·the·
Center· in· accordance· with· government·
guidelines.¶

Recycling·Trash¶

More·than·300·recycling·bins·have·been·placed·
beside·trash·bins·throughout·the·hospital.·That·
means· that· for· every· two· to· four· trash· or·
hazardous·waste·receptacles,·there·is·now·a·bin·
to· collect· and· process· recyclable· materials.·
Plastic·and·aluminum·cups,·bottles,·and·cans·are·
the·main·articles·that·will·be·recycled·in·these·
bins,·which·are·clearly·marked·with·the·recycling·
sign·to·differentiate·them·from·other·types·of·
waste.· In· addition· to· these· bins,· two· extra·
cardboard· balers· have· been· installed· to· help·
with·our·increase·of·cardboard·box·recycling.¶

Greener·Grocer¶

The· hospital· cafeteria· has· eliminated· non-
compostable· materials· and· is· using· recyclable·
paper·goods.·In·addition,·a·vegetable·and·herb·
garden· outside· the· southeast· corner· of· the·
Palomar· Pavilion· supplements· fruits· and·
vegetables·purchased·at·local·farmers·markets.¶

Greener·Records¶

Harvesting·Daylight¶

Low-watt· energy-efficient· light· bulbs· have·
replaced·traditional·lights·throughout·the·center·
and·energy-efficient·lamps·and·daylight·controls·
have· been· installed.· This· move· will· conserve·

Electronic· medical· records· and· consent· forms·
have· replaced· a· paper· system,· conserving· not·
only·paper,·but·also·reclaiming·valuable·working·
and·storage·space.¶ ══ Section Break (Continuous) ══

"Everything·we·can·do·here·at·University·Medical·Center·to·protect·our·environment·and·conserve·
resources·sets·the·example·for·others·to·do·the·same."·Emily·Lynn,·Facilities·Director¶

Page 1 of 1   322 words

FIGURE 14.26

| **More Knowledge** | **Justifying Column Text** |

Although many magazines and newspapers still justify text in columns, there are a variety of opinions about whether to justify the columns, or to use left alignment and leave the right edge uneven. Justified text tends to look more formal and cleaner, but in a word processing document, it also results in uneven spacing between words. It is the opinion of some authorities that justified text is more difficult to read, especially in a page-width document. Let the overall look and feel of your newsletter be your guide.

IC3
DIGITAL LITERACY
CERTIFICATION
2.02e (ii)

Activity 14.17 | Inserting a Column Break

1 Near the bottom of the first column, click to position the insertion point at the beginning of the line *Harvesting Daylight*.

2 On the **Layout tab**, in the **Page Setup group**, click **Breaks**. Under **Page Breaks**, click **Column**, and then if necessary, scroll to view the bottom of the first column.

A column break displays at the bottom of the first column; text to the right of the column break moves to the top of the next column.

3 Compare your screen with Figure 14.27, and then **Save** 🖫.

A *column break indicator*—a dotted line containing the words *Column Break*—displays at the bottom of the column.

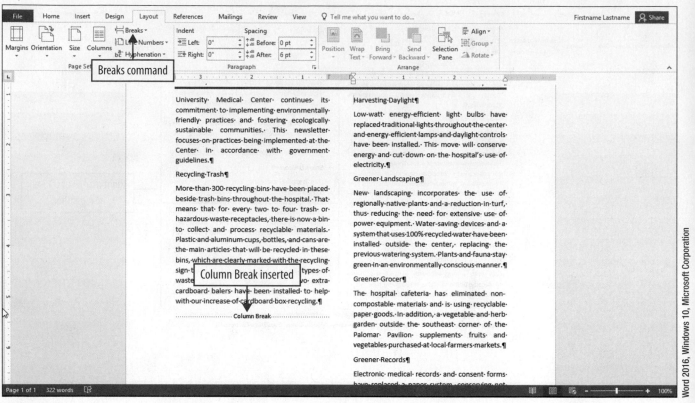

FIGURE 14.27

Activity 14.18 | Inserting an Online Picture

You can search for and insert online pictures in your document without saving the images to your computer. Pictures can make your document visually appealing and more interesting.

1 ▶ Press Ctrl + End to move to the end of the document. Compare your screen with Figure 14.28.

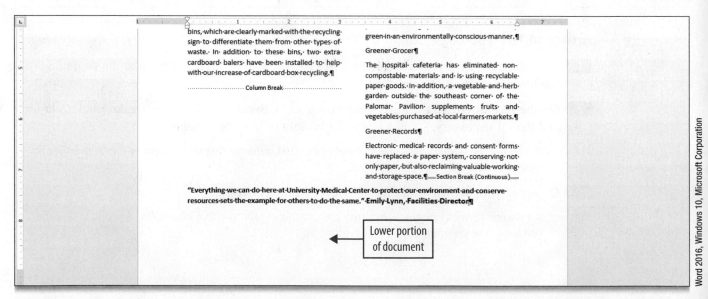

FIGURE 14.28

2 ▶ On the **Insert tab**, in the **Illustrations group**, click **Online Pictures**. With your insertion point blinking in the **Bing Image Search** box, type **green recycling symbol** and then press Enter. Compare your screen with Figure 14.29.

You can use various keywords to find images that are appropriate for your documents. The results shown indicate the images are licensed under *Creative Commons*, which, according to **www.creativecommons.org** is "a nonprofit organization that enables the sharing and use of creativity and knowledge through free legal tools."

Creative Commons helps people share and use their photographs, but does not allow users to sell them. For your college assignments, you can use these images so long as you are not profiting by selling the images.

To find out more about Creative Commons, go to **https://creativecommons.org/about** and watch their video.

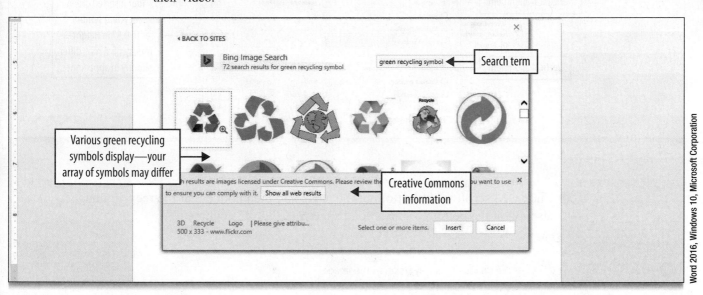

FIGURE 14.29

3 Click one of the green recycling symbols in the first row, and then in the lower right corner click **Insert**; your picture may display in a large size and create a new page.

4 With the picture selected, on the **Picture Tools Format tab**, in the **Size group**, click in the **Height** box. Type **0.5** and then press Enter. To the right of the picture, click **Layout Options** 🖼, and then click **Square** 🖼, which is the first button under **With Text Wrapping**. At the bottom of the **Layout Options gallery**, click **See more** to display the **Layout** dialog box. Compare your screen with Figure 14.30.

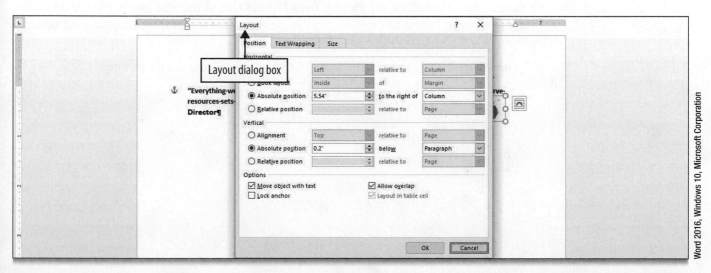

FIGURE 14.30

5 In the **Layout** dialog box, on the **Position tab**, under **Horizontal**, click the **Alignment** option button. Click the **Alignment arrow**, and then click **Centered**. Click the **relative to arrow** and then click **Page**. Under **Vertical**, click the **Alignment** option button. Click the **Alignment arrow**, and then click **Bottom**. Click the **relative to arrow**, and then click **Margin**. Compare your screen with Figure 14.31.

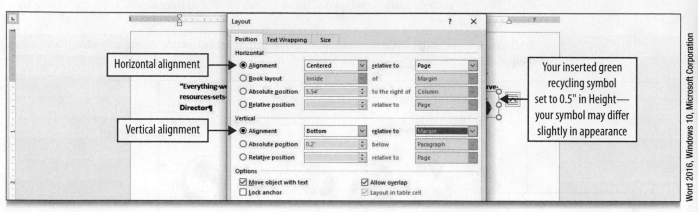

FIGURE 14.31

6 Click **OK**, scroll to the bottom of the page, and then notice that the recycle image displays at the bottom of the second page. **Save** 🖫 the document.

🔄 ANOTHER WAY   Drag the image to visually position the image.

Activity 14.19 | Cropping a Picture and Resizing a Picture by Scaling

In this Activity, you will insert a picture and edit the picture by cropping and scaling. When you *crop* a picture, you remove unwanted or unnecessary areas of the picture. When you *scale* a picture, you resize it to a percentage of its size.

1 Press Ctrl + Home to move to the top of the document. On the **Insert tab**, in the **Illustrations group**, click **Pictures**. In the **Insert Picture** dialog box, navigate to the location of your student data files, and then double-click **w14B_Recycling** to insert it.

2 With the picture selected, on the **Picture Tools Format tab**, in the **Size group**, click the upper portion of the **Crop** button to display crop handles around the picture. Compare your screen with Figure 14.32.

Crop handles are used like sizing handles to define unwanted areas of the picture.

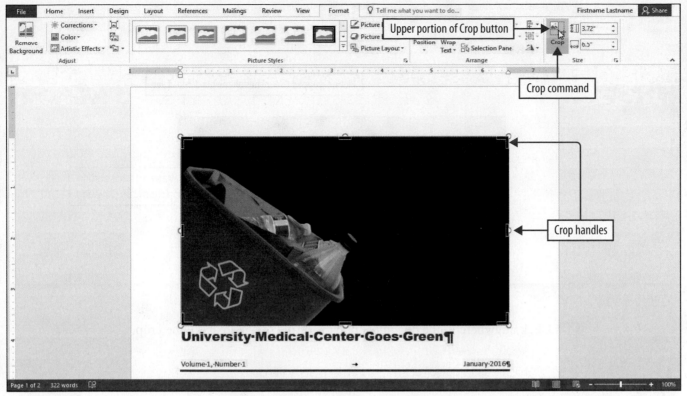

Upper portion of Crop button

Crop command

Crop handles

University·Medical·Center·Goes·Green¶

Volume·1,·Number·1 → January·2016¶

Page 1 of 2   322 words   100%

FIGURE 14.32

Word 2016, Windows 10, Microsoft Corporation

3 ▶ Point to the center right crop handle to display the ⊢ pointer. Compare your screen with Figure 14.33.

Use the ***crop pointer*** to crop areas of a picture.

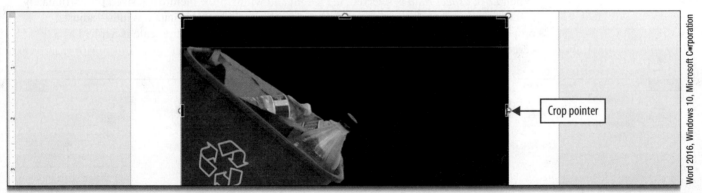

Crop pointer

Word 2016, Windows 10, Microsoft Corporation

FIGURE 14.33

4 ▶ With the crop pointer displayed, hold down the left mouse button and drag to the left to approximately **5 inches on the horizontal ruler**, and then release the mouse button. Compare your screen with Figure 14.34.

The portion of the image to be removed displays in gray.

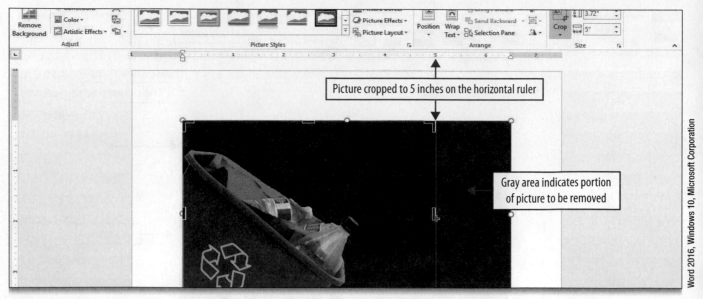

Picture cropped to 5 inches on the horizontal ruler

Gray area indicates portion of picture to be removed

Word 2016, Windows 10, Microsoft Corporation

FIGURE 14.34

5 ▶ Click anywhere in the document outside of the image to apply the crop.

🔄 **ANOTHER WAY**   Click the upper portion of the Crop button to apply the crop.

6 ▶ Click to select the picture again. On the **Picture Tools Format tab**, in the **Size group**, click the **Dialog Box Launcher** button 🗔.

7 ▶ In the **Layout** dialog box, on the **Size tab**, under **Scale**, be sure that the **Lock aspect ratio** and **Relative to original picture size** check boxes are selected. Under **Scale**, select the percentage in the **Height box**, type **10** and then press Tab. Compare your screen with Figure 14.35.

When *Lock aspect ratio* is selected, the height and width of the picture are sized proportionately and only one scale value is necessary. The second value—in this instance Width—adjusts proportionately. When *Relative to original picture size* is selected, the scale is applied as a percentage of the original picture size.

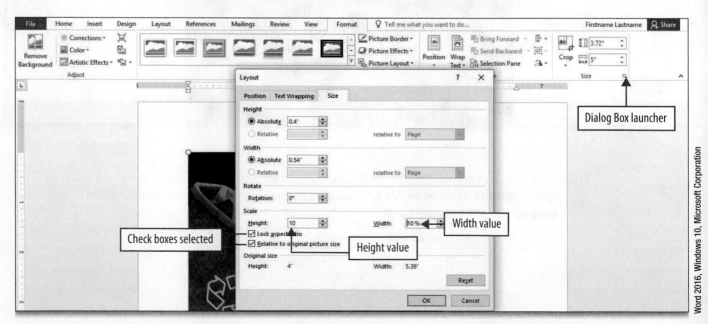

Dialog Box launcher

Check boxes selected

Width value

Height value

Word 2016, Windows 10, Microsoft Corporation

FIGURE 14.35

8 In the **Layout** dialog box, click the **Text Wrapping tab**. Under **Wrapping style**, click **Square**.

9 Click the **Position tab**, and then under **Horizontal**, click the **Alignment** option button. Be sure that the **Alignment** indicates **Left** and **relative to Column**. Under **Vertical**, click the **Alignment** option button, and then change the alignment to **Top relative to Margin**. Click **OK**, and then compare your screen with Figure 14.36.

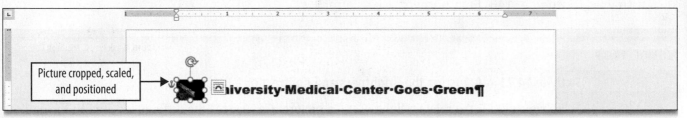

Picture cropped, scaled, and positioned → **iversity·Medical·Center·Goes·Green¶**

FIGURE 14.36

Activity 14.20 | Setting Transparent Color and Recoloring a Picture

You can make one color in a picture transparent using the Set Transparent Color command. When you *recolor* a picture, you change all the colors in the picture to shades of a single color.

1 On the **View tab**, in the **Zoom group**, click **Zoom**, and then click **200%**. Click **OK**. Drag the scroll bars as necessary so that you can view the recycle bin picture at the top of the document.

2 If necessary, select the recycle bin picture. Click the **Picture Tools Format tab**. In the **Adjust group**, click **Color**, and then below the gallery, click **Set Transparent Color**. Move the pointer into the document to display the 🖉 pointer.

3 Point anywhere in the black background of the recycle bin picture, and then click to apply the transparent color to the background. Compare your screen with Figure 14.37.

Transparent color applied to black background

University·Medical·Center·Goes·G

Volume·1,·Number·1

FIGURE 14.37

4 Press Ctrl + End to move to the end of your document, and then select the picture of the recycle symbol. On the **Format tab**, in the **Adjust group**, click **Color** to display a gallery of recoloring options. Under **Recolor**, in the last row, click the fourth option—**Olive Green, Accent color 3 Light**. Compare your screen with Figure 14.38, and then **Save** 🖫 the document.

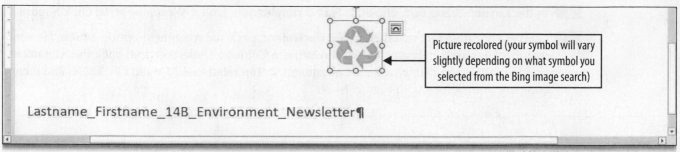

Picture recolored (your symbol will vary slightly depending on what symbol you selected from the Bing image search)

Lastname_Firstname_14B_Environment_Newsletter¶

FIGURE 14.38

Activity 14.21 | Adjusting the Brightness and Contrast of a Picture

Brightness is the relative lightness of a picture. *Contrast* is the difference between the darkest and lightest area of a picture.

1 If necessary, select the recycle symbol. On the **Format tab**, in the **Adjust group**, click **Corrections**. Under **Brightness/Contrast**, point to several of the options to view the effect that the settings have on the picture.

2 Under **Brightness/Contrast**, in the last row, click the first setting—**Brightness: –40% Contrast: +40%**. Compare your screen with Figure 14.39.

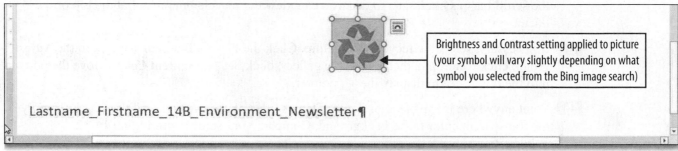

Brightness and Contrast setting applied to picture (your symbol will vary slightly depending on what symbol you selected from the Bing image search)

Lastname_Firstname_14B_Environment_Newsletter¶

FIGURE 14.39

3 On the **View tab**, in the **Zoom group**, click **100%**, if necessary click **OK**, and then **Save** 🖫 the document.

Activity 14.22 | Applying a Border to a Picture and Flipping a Picture

The *flip* commands create a reverse image of a picture or object.

1 Press Ctrl + Home to move to the top of the document, and then select the picture of the recycle bin. On the **Format tab**, in the **Picture Styles group**, click **Picture Border**. Under **Theme Colors**, in the fourth column, click the first color—**Dark Blue, Text 2**.

2 Click **Picture Border** again, and then point to **Weight**. Click **1 ½ pt** to change the thickness of the border.

3 On the **Format tab**, in the **Arrange group**, click **Rotate Objects** 🔄, and then click **Flip Horizontal**. Click anywhere in the document to deselect the picture. **Save** 🖫, and then compare your screen with Figure 14.40.

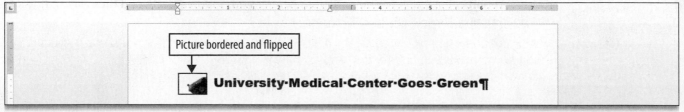

Picture bordered and flipped

University·Medical·Center·Goes·Green¶

FIGURE 14.40

Activity 14.23 | Inserting and Formatting a Screenshot

A *screenshot* is an image of an active window on your computer that you can paste into a document. Screenshots are especially useful when you want to insert an image of a website into your Word document. You can insert a screenshot of any open window on your computer.

1 In the paragraph that begins *University Medical Center continues*, click after the period at the end of the paragraph. Start your web browser, and then navigate to **www.epa.gov** and press [Enter].

2 From the taskbar, redisplay your **14B_Environment_Newsletter** document.

3 With the insertion point positioned at the end of the paragraph, on the **Insert tab**, in the **Illustrations group**, click **Screenshot**.

All of your open windows display in the Available Windows gallery and are available to paste into the document.

4 In the **Screenshot** gallery, click the browser window that contains the EPA site to insert the screenshot at the insertion point. If a message box displays asking if you want to hyperlink the screenshot, click No, and then notice that the image is inserted and is sized to fit between the margins of the first column. Compare your screen with Figure 14.41.

By selecting No in the message box, you are inserting a screenshot without links to the actual website. Choose Yes if you want to link the image to the website.

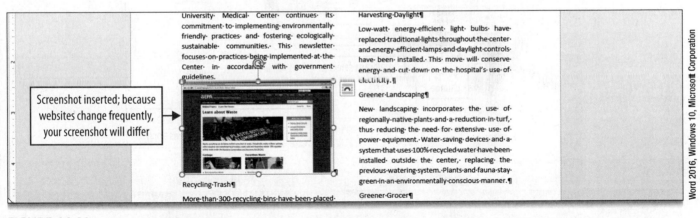

FIGURE 14.41

5 With the inserted screenshot selected, on the **Format tab**, in the **Picture Styles group**, click **Picture Border**, and then under **Theme Colors**, in the second column, click the first color—**Black, Text 1**.

6 Save the document.

GO! Learn How
Video W14-6

By using special text and paragraph formatting, you can emphasize text and make your newsletter look more professional. For example, you can place a border around one or more paragraphs or add shading to a paragraph. When adding shading, use light colors; dark shading can make the text difficult to read.

2.02c

Activity 14.24 | Applying the Small Caps Font Effect

For headlines and titles, *small caps* is an attractive font effect. The effect changes lowercase letters to uppercase letters, but with the height of lowercase letters.

1 Under the screenshot, select the paragraph *Recycling Trash* including the paragraph mark.

2 Right-click the selected text, and then on the shortcut menu, click **Font** to display the **Font** dialog box. Click the **Font color arrow**, and then change the color to **Blue, Accent 1, Darker 50%**—in the fifth column, the last color.

3 Under **Font style**, click **Bold**. Under **Effects**, select the **Small caps** check box. Compare your screen with Figure 14.42.

The Font dialog box provides more options than are available on the ribbon and enables you to make several changes at the same time. In the Preview box, the text displays with the selected formatting options applied.

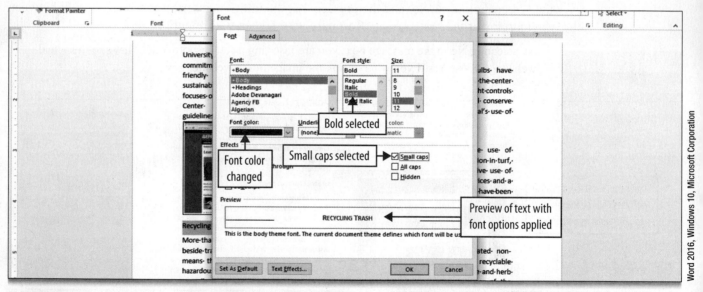

FIGURE 14.42

4 Click **OK**. With the text still selected, right-click, and then on the mini toolbar, double-click **Format Painter** so that you can apply the format multiple times. Then, in the second column, with the pointer, select each of the heading paragraphs—*Harvesting Daylight*, *Greener Landscaping*, *Greener Grocer*, and *Greener Records*—to apply the same formats. Press Esc to turn off Format Painter.

5 In the first column, below the screenshot, notice that the space between the *Recycling Trash* subheading and the screenshot is fairly small. Click anywhere in the *Recycling Trash* subheading, and then on the **Layout tab**, in the **Paragraph group**, click the **Before up spin arrow** two times to set the spacing to **12 pt**.

6 Compare your screen with Figure 14.43, and then **Save** your document.

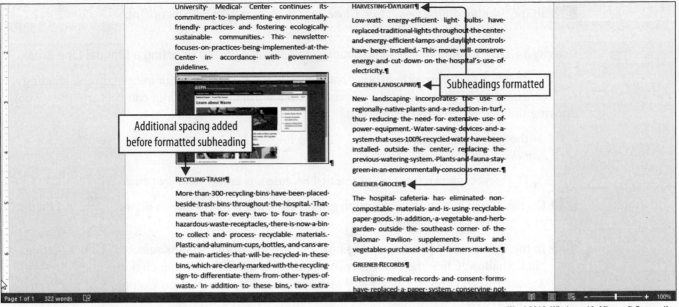

FIGURE 14.43

Word 2016, Windows 10, Microsoft Corporation

Activity 14.25 | Inserting Symbols and Special Characters

You can insert symbols and special characters in a Word document, including copyright symbols, trademark symbols, and em dashes. An *em dash* is a punctuation symbol used to indicate an explanation or emphasis.

1 Press Ctrl + End to move to the end of the document, and then after the name *Emily Lynn* delete the comma and the space that separates her name from her job title—*Facilities Director*.

2 With the insertion point positioned before the *F* in *Facilities*, on the **Insert tab**, in the **Symbols group**, click **Symbol**. Below the gallery, click **More Symbols** to display the **Symbol** dialog box.

Here you can choose the symbol that you want to insert in your document.

3 In the **Symbol** dialog box, click the **Special Characters tab**. Scroll the list to view the types of special characters that you can insert; notice that some of the characters can be inserted using a Shortcut key.

4 Click **Em Dash**, and then in the lower right portion of the dialog box, click **Insert**. If necessary, drag the title bar of the Symbol window up or to the side, and then compare your screen with Figure 14.44.

An em dash displays between the name *Lynn* and the word *Facilities*.

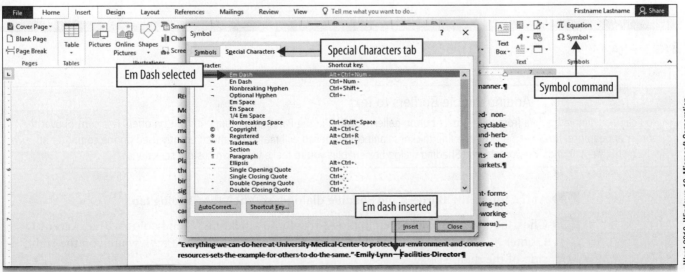

FIGURE 14.44

Word 2016, Windows 10, Microsoft Corporation

5 ▶ In the **Symbol** dialog box, click **Close**, and then **Save** 🖫 your document.

Activity 14.26 | Adding Borders and Shading to a Paragraph and Inserting a Manual Line Break

Paragraph borders provide strong visual cues to the reader. You can use paragraph shading with or without borders; however, combined with a border, light shading can be very effective in drawing the reader's eye to specific text.

1 ▶ At the end of the document, select the two lines of bold text that begin *"Everything we can do*.

The recycle picture may also be selected because it is anchored to the paragraph.

2 ▶ On the **Home tab**, in the **Paragraph group**, click the **Borders button arrow** 🔲 ▾, and then click **Borders and Shading**.

3 ▶ In the **Borders and Shading** dialog box, be sure the **Borders tab** is selected. Under **Setting**, click **Shadow**. Click the **Color arrow**, and then in the fifth column, click the last color—**Blue, Accent 1, Darker 50%**. Click the **Width arrow**, and then click **1 pt**. Compare your screen with Figure 14.45.

In the lower right portion of the Borders and Shading dialog box, the *Apply to* box indicates *Paragraph*. The *Apply to* box directs where the border will be applied—in this instance, the border will be applied only to the selected paragraph.

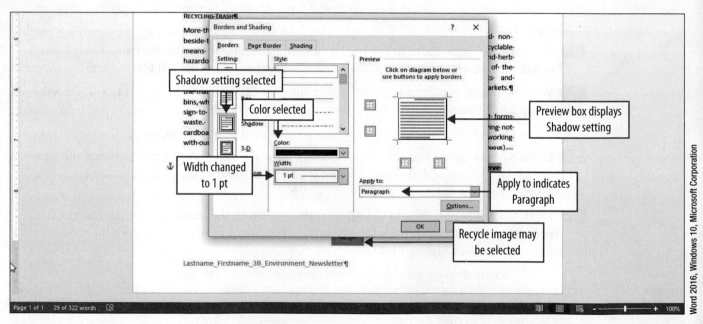

FIGURE 14.45

NOTE	Adding Simple Borders to Text

You can add simple borders from the Borders button gallery, located in the Paragraph group. This button offers less control over the border appearance, however, because the line thickness and color applied will match the most recently used on the computer at which you are working. The Borders and Shading dialog box enables you to make your own custom selections.

---

4 ▶ At the top of the **Borders and Shading** dialog box, click the **Shading tab**.

5 ▶ Click the **Fill arrow**, and then in the fifth column, click the second color—**Blue, Accent 1, Lighter 80%**. Notice that the shading change is reflected in the Preview area on the right side of the dialog box.

6 ▸ Click **OK**. On the **Home tab**, in the **Paragraph group**, click **Center** 🔳.

7 ▸ Click anywhere in the document to deselect, and then compare your screen with Figure 14.46.

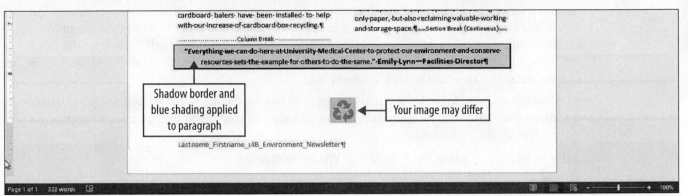

cardboard· balers· have· been· installed· to· help·
with·our·increase·of·cardboard·box·recycling.¶

·········· Column Break ··········

"Everything·we·can·do·here·at·University·Medical·Center·to·protect·our·environment·and·conserve·
resources·sets·the·example·for·others·to·do·the·same."·Emily·Lynn—Facilities·Director¶

only·paper, ·but·also·reclaiming·valuable·working·
and·storage·space.¶——Section Break (Continuous)——

Shadow border and
blue shading applied
to paragraph

Your image may differ

Lastname_Firstname_14B_Environment_Newsletter¶

Page 1 of 1   322 words

100%

Word 2016, Windows 10, Microsoft Corporation

FIGURE 14.46

8 ▸ In the shaded paragraph, in the second line, click in front of the *E* in the name *Emily*. Hold down Shift and then press Enter.

Holding down Shift while pressing Enter inserts a **manual line break**, which moves the text to the right of the insertion point to a new line while keeping the text in the same paragraph. A **line break indicator**, in the shape of a bent arrow, indicates a manual line break.

9 ▸ Press Ctrl + Home to move the insertion point to the top of the document. Click the **File tab** to display **Backstage** view. On the right, at the bottom of the **Properties** list, click **Show All Properties**.

10 ▸ On the list of **Properties**, click to the right of **Tags**, and then type **newsletter, January**

11 ▸ Click to the right of **Subject**, and then type your course name and section number. Under **Related People**, be sure that your name displays as the author. If necessary, right-click the author name, click Edit Property, type your name, and click OK.

12 ▸ On the left, click **Print** to display the **Print Preview**, and then on the left click Save to save your document and return to the document window. In the upper right corner of the Word window, click **Close** ✕. If directed by your instructor to do so, submit your paper printout, your electronic image of your document that looks like a printed document, or your completed Word file. If you are submitting this Project as a MyITLab grader, submit this file.

ALERT!   **The Remaining Activities in This Chapter Are Optional**

Activities 14.27, 14.28, and 14.29, in which you create a set of mailing labels for the newsletter, are optional. Check with your instructor to see if you should complete these three Activities. These Activities *are* included in the MyITLab Grader system as a separate Grader exercise.

GO! Learn How
Video W14-7

Word's *mail merge* feature joins a *main document* and a *data source* to create customized letters or labels. The main document contains the text or formatting that remains constant. For labels, the main document contains the formatting for a specific label size. The data source contains information including the names and addresses of the individuals for whom the labels are being created. Names and addresses in a data source might come from an Excel worksheet, an Access database, or your Outlook contacts list.

The easiest way to perform a mail merge is to use the Mail Merge Wizard, which asks you questions and, based on your answers, walks you step by step through the mail merge process.

Activity 14.27 | Starting the Mail Merge Wizard Template

In this Activity, you will open the data source for the mail merge, which is an Excel worksheet containing names and addresses.

1 Start Word and display a new blank document. Display formatting marks and rulers. **Save** the document in your **AIO Chapter 14** folder as **Lastname_Firstname_14B_Mailing_Labels**

2 With your new document open on the screen, from the taskbar, open **File Explorer** 📁. Navigate to the student data files that accompany this chapter, and then double-click the Excel file **w14B_Addresses** to open it in Excel. Compare your screen with Figure 14.47.

This Excel worksheet contains the addresses. Each row of information that contains data for one person is referred to as a *record*. The column headings, for example *First Name* and *Last Name*, are referred to as *fields*.

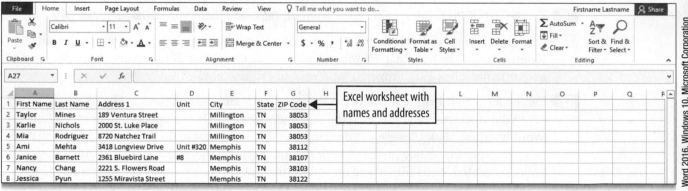

FIGURE 14.47

3 **Close** Excel and if necessary, close the File Explorer window. Be sure that your blank **Lastname_Firstname_14B_Mailing_Labels** document displays.

4 Click the **Mailings tab**. In the **Start Mail Merge group**, click **Start Mail Merge**, and then click **Step-by-Step Mail Merge Wizard** to display the **Mail Merge** pane on the right.

5 In the **Mail Merge** pane, under **Select document type**, click **Labels**. At the bottom of the **Mail Merge** pane, click **Next: Starting document** to display Step 2 of 6.

6 Under **Select starting document**, be sure **Change document layout** is selected, and then under **Change document layout**, click **Label options**.

7 In the **Label Options** dialog box, under **Printer information**, click the **Tray arrow**, and then if necessary, click **Default tray (Automatically Select)**—the exact wording may vary depending on your printer, but select the *Default* or *Automatic* option so that you can print the labels on regular paper rather than manually inserting labels in the printer.

8 Under **Label information**, click the **Label vendors arrow**, and then click **Avery US Letter**. Under **Product number**, scroll about halfway down the list, and then click **5160 Easy Peel Address Labels**. Compare your screen with Figure 14.48.

> The Avery 5160 address label is a commonly used label. The precut sheets contain three columns of 10 labels each—for a total of 30 labels per sheet.

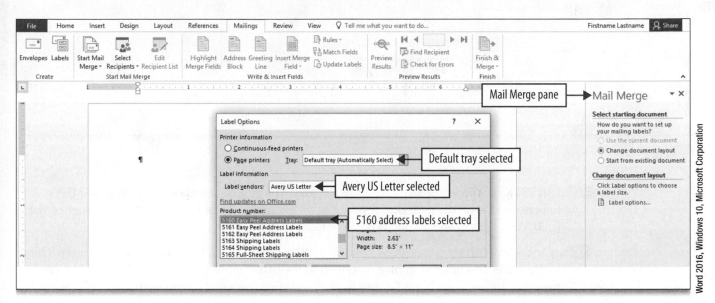

FIGURE 14.48

9 At the bottom of the **Label Options** dialog box, click **OK**. If a message box displays, click OK to set up the labels. If the gridlines do not display, on the Table Tools Layout tab, in the Table group, click View Gridlines. At the bottom of the **Mail Merge** pane, click **Next: Select recipients**.

> The label page is set up with three columns and ten rows. Here, in Step 3 of the Mail Merge Wizard, you must identify the recipients—the data source. For your recipient data source, you can choose to use an existing list—for example, a list of names and addresses that you have in an Access database, an Excel worksheet, or your Outlook contacts list. If you do not have an existing data source, you can type a new list at this point in the wizard.

10 In the **Mail Merge** pane, under **Select recipients**, be sure the **Use an existing list** option button is selected. Under **Use an existing list**, click **Browse**.

11 In the **Select Data Source** dialog box, navigate to the student data files that accompany this chapter, click the Excel file **w14B_Addresses** one time to select it, and then click **Open** to display the **Select Table** dialog box. Compare your screen with Figure 14.49.

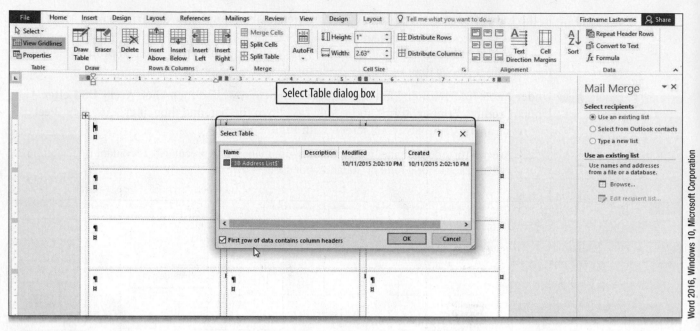

FIGURE 14.49

12 Click **OK**. In the lower left portion of the **Mail Merge Recipients** dialog box, in the **Data Source** box, click the path that contains your file name. Then in the lower left corner of the **Mail Merge Recipients** dialog box, click **Edit**.

13 In the lower left corner of the displayed **Edit Data Source** dialog box, click **New Entry**. Click in the blank box shaded in blue, and then in the blank record, type the following new record, pressing Tab to move from field to field. Then compare your screen with Figure 14.50.

FIRST_NAME	LAST_NAME	ADDRESS_1	UNIT	CITY	STATE	ZIP CODE
Sharon	Williams	1251 Parker Road	#843	Memphis	TN	38123

FIGURE 14.50

14 In the lower right corner of the **Edit Data Source** dialog box, click **OK**, and then in the displayed message, click **Yes**. Scroll to the end of the recipient list to confirm that the record for *Sharon Williams* that you just added is in the list. At the bottom of the **Mail Merge Recipients** dialog box, click **OK**.

Activity 14.28 | Completing the Mail Merge

Not only can you add and edit names and addresses while completing the Mail Merge, but you can also match your column names with preset names used in Mail Merge.

1 At the bottom of the **Mail Merge** pane, click **Next: Arrange your labels**.

2 Under **Arrange your labels**, click **Address block**. In the **Insert Address Block** dialog box, under **Specify address elements**, examine the various formats for names. If necessary, under *Insert recipient's name in this format*, select the *Joshua Randall Jr.* format. Compare your dialog box with Figure 14.51.

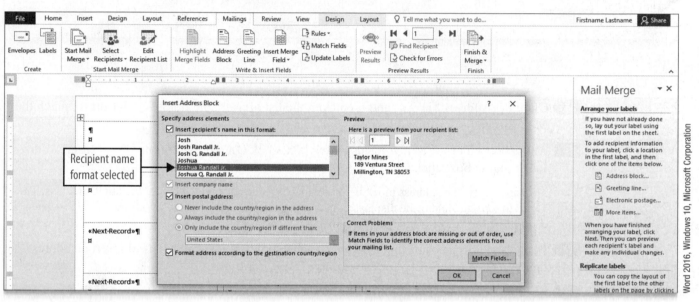

FIGURE 14.51

3 In the lower right corner of the **Insert Address Block** dialog box, click **Match Fields**, and then compare your screen with Figure 14.52.

If your field names are descriptive, the Mail Merge program will identify them correctly, as is the case with most of the information in the *Required for Address Block* section. However, the Address 2 field is unmatched—in the source file, this column is named *Unit*.

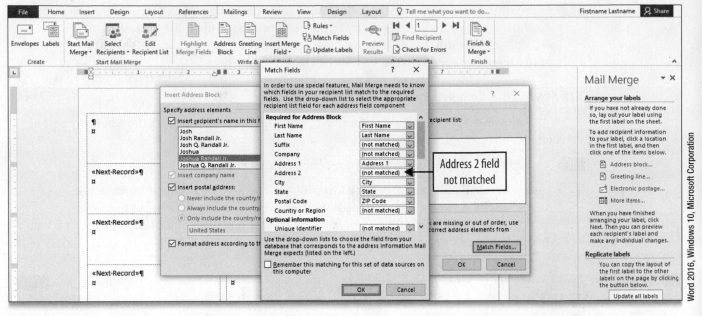

FIGURE 14.52

4 Click the **Address 2 arrow**, and then from the list of available fields, click **Unit** to match the Mail Merge field with the field in your data source.

5 At the bottom of the **Match Fields** dialog box, click **OK**. At the bottom of the **Insert Address Block** dialog box, click **OK**.

Word inserts the Address block in the first label space surrounded by double angle brackets. The *AddressBlock* field name displays, which represents the address block you saw in the Preview area of the Insert Address Block dialog box.

6 In the **Mail Merge** pane, under **Replicate labels**, click **Update all labels** to insert an address block in each label space for each subsequent record.

7 At the bottom of the **Mail Merge** pane, click **Next: Preview your labels**. Notice that for addresses with four lines, the last line of the address is cut off.

8 Press Ctrl + A to select all of the label text, click the **Layout tab**, and then in the **Paragraph group**, click in the **Spacing Before** box. Type **3** and press Enter.

9 Click in any label to deselect, and notice that 4-line addresses are no longer cut off. Compare your screen with Figure 14.53.

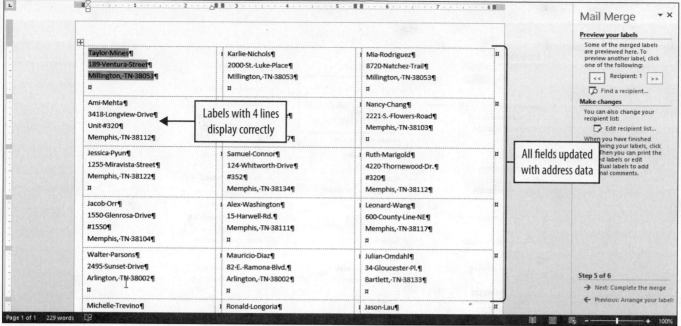

FIGURE 14.53

10 At the bottom of the **Mail Merge** pane, click **Next: Complete the merge**.

Step 6 of the Mail Merge displays. At this point you can print or edit your labels, although this is done more easily in the document window.

11 Save 🖫 your labels, and then on the right, **Close** ⊠ the **Mail Merge** pane.

Activity 14.29 | Previewing and Printing Mail Merge Results

If you discover that you need to make further changes to your labels, you can still make them even though the Mail Merge task pane is closed.

1 Add the file name to the footer, close the footer area, and then move to the top of **Page 2**. Click anywhere in the empty table row, and then click the **Table Tools Layout tab**. In the **Rows & Columns group**, click **Delete**, and then click **Delete Rows**.

Adding footer text to a label sheet replaces the last row of labels on a page with the footer text, and moves the last row of labels to the top of the next page. In this instance, a blank second page is created, which you can delete by deleting the blank row.

2 Notice that the labels do not display in alphabetical order. Click the **Mailings tab**, and then in the **Start Mail Merge group**, click **Edit Recipient List** to display the list of names and addresses.

3 In the **Mail Merge Recipients** dialog box, click the **Last Name** field heading, and notice that the names are sorted alphabetically by the recipient's last name.

Mailing labels are often sorted by either last name or by ZIP Code.

4 Click the **Last Name** field heading again, and notice that the last names are sorted in descending order. Click the **Last Name** field one more time to return to ascending order, and then click **OK**. Press Ctrl + Home, and then compare your screen with Figure 14.54.

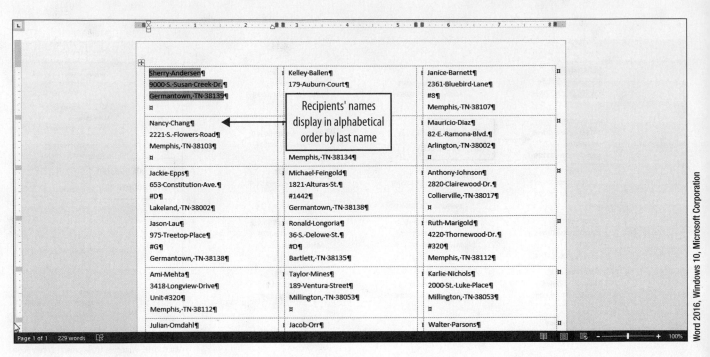

FIGURE 14.54

5 ▶ Click the **File tab**. On the right, at the bottom of the **Properties** list, click **Show All Properties**. On the list of **Properties**, click to the right of **Tags**, and then type **labels**

6 ▶ Click to the right of **Subject**, and then type your course name and section number. Be sure that your name displays as the author. If necessary, right-click the author name, click Edit Property, type your name, and click OK.

7 ▶ On the left, click **Save**. In the upper right corner of the Word window, click **Close** [✕]. If directed by your instructor to do so, submit your Lastname_Firstname_14B_Mailing_Labels file as a paper printout, an electronic image of your document that looks like a printed document, or your completed Word file.

> If you print, the labels will print on whatever paper is in the printer; unless you have preformatted labels available, the labels will print on a sheet of paper. Printing the labels on plain paper enables you to proofread the labels before you print them on more expensive label sheets.

END | You have completed Project 14B

GO! With Google

> **ALERT!** **Working with Web-Based Applications and Services**
>
> Computer programs and services on the web receive continuous updates and improvements, so the steps to complete this web-based Activity may differ from the ones shown. You can often look at the screens and the information presented to determine how to complete the Activity.
>
> If you do not already have a Google account, you will need to create one before you begin this Activity. Go to http://google.com and, in the upper right corner, click Sign In. On the Sign In screen, click Create Account. On the Create your Google Account page, complete the form, read and agree to the Terms of Service and Privacy Policy, and then click Next step. On the Welcome screen, click Get Started.

Activity | Formatting a Single-Column Newsletter in Google Docs

In this Activity, you will use Google Docs to edit a single-column newsletter similar to the one you edited in Project 14B. You can create columns in a Google Doc by inserting a table with two columns, and then typing in the two columns.

1 From the desktop, open your browser, navigate to **http://google.com**, and then click the **Google Apps** menu. Click **Drive**, and then if necessary, sign in to your Google account.

2 Open your **GO! Web Projects** folder—or click New to create and then open this folder if necessary.

3 In the left pane, click **NEW**, and then click **File upload**. In the **Open** dialog box, navigate to your student data files for this chapter, and then in the **File List**, double-click to open **w14_14B_Web**.

4 Point to the uploaded file **w14_14B_Web**, and then right-click. On the shortcut menu, scroll as necessary, and then click **Rename**. Using your own last name and first

name, type **Lastname_Firstname_WD_14B_Web** (leave the file extension .docx) and then click **OK** to rename the file.

5 Right-click the file you just renamed, point to **Open with**, and then click **Google Docs.**

6 Drag to select the newsletter title—*University Medical Center Goes Green*. On the toolbar, click the **Font size arrow**, and then click **18**. With the newsletter title still selected, on the toolbar, click the **Text color arrow**, and then in the second row, click the third from last color—**blue**.

7 Apply the same **Font Color** to the five subheadings—*Recycling Trash, Harvesting Daylight, Greener Landscaping, Greener Grocer,* and *Greener Records*. Compare your screen with Figure A.

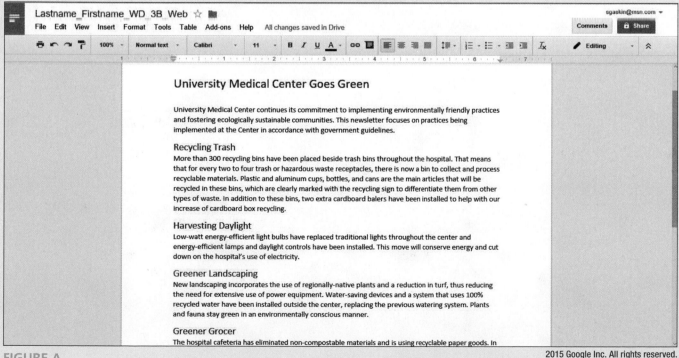

FIGURE A

(GO! With Google continues on the next page)

8 ▶ Press `Ctrl` + `End` to move to the end of the document, and then press `Enter`. On the menu bar, click **Insert**, and then click **Image**. In the **Insert image** dialog box, in the upper right, click **Search**, and then click in the Google search box. Type **green recycle symbol** and then press `Enter`.

9 ▶ Click an image of a green recycle symbol similar to the one you used in Project 14B, and then at the bottom click **Select**.

10 ▶ Click the inserted image to select it, point to a corner of the image to display the sizing arrow, and then drag to resize the image until it displays at the bottom of the first page. On the toolbar, click the **Center** icon to center the image. Click anywhere in the text to deselect the image.

11 ▶ Submit the file as directed by your instructor. In the upper right, click your user name, and then click **Sign out**. **Close** your browser window. Your file is automatically saved in your Google Drive.

IC3 SKILLS IN THIS CHAPTER

IC3 Key Applications

Project 14A
Section 2.02 Word Processing
- (c) Alter text and font styles
- (e) Know page layout concepts
    - (i) Page numbering
    - (iv) Alignment, text in paragraphs and tables
    - (vii) Spacing

Project 14B
Section 2.02 Word Processing
- (c) Alter text and font styles
- (e) Know page layout concepts
    - (ii) Columns
    - (iv) Alignment, text in paragraphs and tables

BUILD YOUR E-PORTFOLIO

An E-Portfolio is a collection of evidence, stored electronically, that showcases what you have accomplished while completing your education. Collecting and then sharing your work products with potential employers reflects your academic and career goals. Your completed documents from the following projects are good examples to show what you have learned: 14G, 14K, 14L.

GO! FOR JOB SUCCESS

Video: Email Etiquette
Your instructor may assign this video to your class, and then ask you to think about, or discuss with your classmates, these questions:

FotolEdhar / Fotolia

> Why do you think it is important to follow specific etiquette when composing email?

> Why is it important to include a greeting and sign every email that you send?

> What are the differences between sending a business email and a personal email, and what are three specific things you should never do in a business email?

GO! COLLABORATIVE TEAM PROJECT (Available in MyITLab and Instructor Resource Center)

If your instructor assigns this project to your class, you can expect to work with one or more of your classmates—either in person or by using Internet tools—to create work products similar to those that you created in this chapter. A team is a group of workers who work together to solve a problem, make a decision, or create a work product. Collaboration is when you work together with others as a team in an intellectual endeavor to complete a shared task or achieve a shared goal.

END OF CHAPTER

SUMMARY

Word assists you in formatting a research paper for college or business by providing built-in styles and formats for the most commonly used footnote and citation styles for research papers—MLA and APA.

Word helps you create the bibliography for your research paper by recording all of your citations in the Source Manager, and then generating the bibliography—in MLA, called Works Cited—for you.

Newsletters are often used by organizations to communicate information to a specific group. A newsletter can be formatted in two columns with a nameplate at the top that identifies the publication.

The Mail Merge Wizard enables you to easily merge a main document and a data source to create customized letters or labels. The data source can be an Excel spreadsheet, an Access database, or Outlook contacts.

GO! LEARN IT ONLINE

Review the concepts, key terms, and IC3 skills in this chapter by completing these online challenges, which you can find at **MyITLab**.

Matching and Multiple Choice: Answer matching and multiple choice questions to test what you learned in this chapter.

Lessons on the GO!: Learn how to use all the new apps and features as they are introduced by Microsoft.

IC3 Prep Quiz: Answer questions to review the IC3 skills you practiced in this chapter.

Your instructor will assign Projects from this list to ensure your learning and assess your knowledge.

Project	Apply Skills from These Chapter Objectives	Project Type	Project Location
Project Guide for All in One Chapter 14			
14A **MyITLab**	Objectives 1–4 from Project 14A	**14A Instructional Project (Grader Project)** Guided instruction to learn the skills in Project 14A	In MyITLab and in text
14B **MyITLab**	Objectives 5–7 from Project 14B	**14B Instructional Project (Grader Project)** Guided instruction to learn the skills in Project 14B	In MyITLab and in text
14C	Objectives 1–4 from Project 14A	**14C Skills Review** A guided review of the skills from Project 14A.	In text
14D	Objectives 5–7 from Project 14B	**14D Skills Review** A guided review of the skills from Project 14B.	In text
14E **MyITLab**	Objectives 1–4 from Project 14A	**14E Mastery (Grader Project)** **Mastery and Transfer of Learning** A demonstration of your mastery of the skills in Project 14A with extensive decision making.	In MyITLab and in text
14F **MyITLab**	Objectives 5–7 from Project 14B	**14F Mastery (Grader Project)** **Mastery and Transfer of Learning** A demonstration of your mastery of the skills in Project 14B with extensive decision making.	In MyITLab and in text
14G **MyITLab**	Objectives 1–7 from Projects 14A and 14B	**14G Mastery (Grader Project)** **Mastery and Transfer of Learning** A demonstration of your mastery of the skills in Projects 14A and 14B with extensive decision making.	In MyITLab and in text
14H	Combination of Objectives from Projects 14A and 14B	**14H GO! Fix It** **Critical Thinking** A demonstration of your mastery of the skills in Projects 14A and 14B by creating a correct result from a document that contains errors you must find.	Instructor Resource Center (IRC) and MyITLab
14I	Combination of Objectives from Projects 14A and 14B	**14I GO! Make It** **Critical Thinking** A demonstration of your mastery of the skills in Projects 14A and 14B by creating a result from a supplied picture.	IRC and MyITLab
14J	Combination of Objectives from Projects 14A and 14B	**14J GO! Solve It** **Critical Thinking** A demonstration of your mastery of the skills in Projects 14A and 14B, your decision-making skills, and your critical-thinking skills. A task-specific rubric helps you self-assess your result.	IRC and MyITLab
14K	Combination of Objectives from Projects 14A and 14B	**14K GO! Solve It** **Critical Thinking** A demonstration of your mastery of the skills in Projects 14A and 14B, your decision-making skills, and your critical-thinking skills. A task-specific rubric helps you self-assess your result.	In text
14L	Combination of Objectives from Projects 14A and 14B	**14L GO! Think** **Critical Thinking** A demonstration of your understanding of the chapter concepts applied in a manner that you would outside of college. An analytic rubric helps you and your instructor grade the quality of your work by comparing it to the work an expert in the discipline would create.	In text
14M	Combination of Objectives from Projects 14A and 14B	**14M GO! Think** **Critical Thinking** A demonstration of your understanding of the chapter concepts applied in a manner that you would outside of college. An analytic rubric helps you and your instructor grade the quality of your work by comparing it to the work an expert in the discipline would create.	IRC and MyITLab
14N	Combination of Objectives from Projects 14A and 14B	**14N You and GO!** **Critical Thinking** A demonstration of your understanding of the chapter concepts applied in a manner that you would in a personal situation. An analytic rubric helps you and your instructor grade the quality of your work.	IRC and MyITLab
14O	Combination of Objectives from Projects 14A and 14B	**14O Collaborative Team Project for AIO Chapter 14** **Critical Thinking** A demonstration of your understanding of concepts and your ability to work collaboratively in a group role-playing assessment, requiring both collaboration and self-management.	IRC and MyITLab

GLOSSARY

GLOSSARY OF CHAPTER KEY TERMS

American Psychological Association (APA) One of two commonly used style guides for formatting research papers.

Bibliography A list of cited works in a report or research paper; also referred to as Works Cited, Sources, or References, depending upon the report style.

Brightness The relative lightness of a picture.

Citation A note inserted into the text of a research paper that refers the reader to a source in the bibliography.

Column break indicator A dotted line containing the words *Column Break* that displays at the bottom of the column.

Contrast The difference between the darkest and lightest area of a picture.

Crop A command that removes unwanted or unnecessary areas of a picture.

Crop handles Handles used to define unwanted areas of a picture.

Crop pointer The pointer used to crop areas of a picture.

Data source A document that contains a list of variable information, such as names and addresses, that is merged with a main document to create customized form letters or labels.

Em dash A punctuation symbol used to indicate an explanation or emphasis.

Endnote In a research paper, a note placed at the end of a document or chapter.

Fields In a mail merge, the column headings in the data source.

Flip A command that creates a reverse image of a picture or object.

Footnote In a research paper, a note placed at the bottom of the page.

Hanging indent An indent style in which the first line of a paragraph extends to the left of the remaining lines and that is commonly used for bibliographic entries.

Line break indicator A nonprinting character in the shape of a bent arrow that indicates a manual line break.

Mail merge A feature that joins a main document and a data source to create customized letters or labels.

Main document In a mail merge, the document that contains the text or formatting that remains constant.

Manual column break An artificial end to a column to balance columns or to provide space for the insertion of other objects.

Manual line break A break that moves text to the right of the insertion point to a new line while keeping the text in the same paragraph.

Manual page break The action of forcing a page to end and placing subsequent text at the top of the next page.

Modern Language Association (MLA) One of two commonly used style guides for formatting research papers.

Nameplate The banner on the front page of a newsletter that identifies the publication.

Newsletter A periodical that communicates news and information to a specific group.

Note In a research paper, information that expands on the topic, but that does not fit well in the document text.

Page break indicator A dotted line with the text *Page Break* that indicates where a manual page break was inserted.

Parenthetical references References that include the last name of the author or authors, and the page number in the referenced source.

PDF Reflow The ability to import PDF files into Word so that you can transform a PDF back into a fully editable Word document.

Read Mode A view in Word that optimizes the Word screen for the times when you are reading Word documents on the screen and not creating or editing them.

Recolor A feature that enables you to change all colors in the picture to shades of a single color.

Record Each row of information that contains data for one person.

Scale A command that resizes a picture to a percentage of its size.

Screenshot An image of an active window on your computer that you can paste into a document.

Section A portion of a document that can be formatted differently from the rest of the document.

Section break A double dotted line that indicates the end of one section and the beginning of another section.

Small caps A font effect that changes lowercase letters to uppercase letters, but with the height of lowercase letters.

Style A group of formatting commands, such as font, font size, font color, paragraph alignment, and line spacing, that can be applied to a paragraph with one command.

Style guide A manual that contains standards for the design and writing of documents.

Suppress A Word feature that hides header and footer information, including the page number, on the first page of a document.

Watermark A text or graphic element that displays behind document text.

Works Cited In the MLA style, a list of cited works placed at the end of a research paper or report.

Skills Review Project 14C Diet and Exercise Report

In the following Skills Review, you will edit and format a research paper that contains information about the effects of diet and exercise. This paper was created by Rachel Holder, a medical intern at University Medical Center, for distribution to her classmates studying physiology. Your completed document will look similar to the one shown in Figure 14.55.

PROJECT FILES

For Project 14C, you will need the following file:

w14C_Diet_Exercise

You will save your document as:

Lastname_Firstname_14C_Diet_Exercise

PROJECT RESULTS

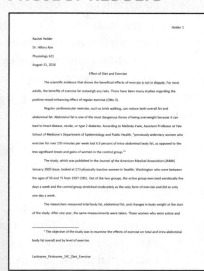

Word 2016, Windows 10, Microsoft Corporation

FIGURE 14.55

(Project 14C Diet and Exercise Report continues on the next page)

1 Start Word. On Word's opening screen, in the lower left, click **Open Other Documents**. Navigate to your student data files, and then locate and open the document **w14C_Diet_Exercise**. Display the formatting marks and rulers. Save the file in your **AIO Chapter 14** folder as **Lastname_Firstname_14C_Diet_Exercise**

a. Press Ctrl + A to select all the text. On the **Home tab**, in the **Paragraph group**, click **Line and Paragraph Spacing**, and then change the line spacing to **2.0**. On the **Layout tab**, in the **Paragraph group**, change the **Spacing After** to **0 pt**.

b. Press Ctrl + Home, press Enter to create a blank line at the top of the document, and then click to position the insertion point in the new blank line. Type **Rachel Holder** and press Enter. Type **Dr. Hillary Kim** and press Enter. Type **Physiology 621** and press Enter. Type **August 31, 2016** and press Enter.

c. Type **Effects of Diet and Exercise** and then press Ctrl + E to center the title you just typed.

2 On the **Insert tab**, in the **Header & Footer group**, click **Header**, and then at the bottom of the list, click **Edit Header**. Type **Holder** and then press Spacebar.

a. Under **Header and Footer Tools**, on the **Design tab**, in the **Header & Footer group**, click **Page Number**, and then point to **Current Position**. Under **Simple**, click **Plain Number**.

b. On the **Home tab**, in the **Paragraph group**, click **Align Right**. Double-click anywhere in the document to close the Header area.

c. Near the top of **Page 1**, locate the paragraph beginning *The scientific evidence*, and then click to position the insertion point at the beginning of that paragraph. Scroll to the end of the document, hold down Shift, and then click to the right of the last paragraph mark to select all of the text from the insertion point to the end of the document.

d. On the **Home tab**, in the **Paragraph group**, click the **Dialog Box Launcher** button. In the **Paragraph** dialog box, on the **Indents and Spacing tab**, under **Indentation**, click the **Special arrow**, and then click **First line**. Click **OK**.

e. On the **Insert tab**, in the **Header & Footer group**, click **Footer**, and then click **Edit Footer**. In the **Insert group**, click **Document Info**, and then click **File Name**. Click **Close Header and Footer**.

3 Scroll to view the top of **Page 2**, locate the paragraph that begins *Exercise also has*, and then at the end of that paragraph, click to position the insertion point to the right of the period following *Irwin*. On the **References tab**, in the **Footnotes group**, click **Insert Footnote**.

a. As the footnote text, type **Physical activity may provide a low-risk method of preventing weight gain. Unlike diet-induced weight loss, exercise-induced weight loss increases cardiorespiratory fitness levels.**

b. In the upper portion of **Page 1**, locate the paragraph that begins *Regular cardiovascular exercise*. Click to position the insertion point at the end of the paragraph and insert a footnote.

c. As the footnote text, type **The objective of the study was to examine the effects of exercise on total and intra-abdominal body fat overall and by level of exercise. Save** your document.

4 At the bottom of **Page 1**, right-click in the footnote you just typed. On the shortcut menu, click **Style**. In the **Style** dialog box, click **Modify**. In the **Modify Style** dialog box, locate the Formatting toolbar in the center of the dialog box, click the **Font Size button arrow**, and then click **11**.

a. In the lower left corner of the dialog box, click **Format**, and then click **Paragraph**. In the **Paragraph** dialog box, under **Indentation**, click the **Special arrow**, and then click **First line**. Under **Spacing**, click the **Line spacing button arrow**, and then click **Double**.

b. Click **OK** to close the **Paragraph** dialog box, click **OK** to close the **Modify Style** dialog box, and then click **Apply** to apply the new style. **Save** your document.

5 Scroll to view the top of **Page 1**, and then in the paragraph that begins *The scientific evidence*, click to position the insertion point to the left of the period at the end of the paragraph.

a. On the **References tab**, in the **Citations & Bibliography group**, click the **Style button arrow**, and then click **MLA** to insert a reference using MLA style. Click **Insert Citation**, and then click **Add New Source**. Click the **Type of Source arrow**, scroll as

(Project 14C Diet and Exercise Report continues on the next page)

necessary to locate and click **Book**, and then add the following information:

Author	Otto, Michael, and Jasper A. J. Smits
Title	Exercise for Mood and Anxiety: Proven Strategies for Overcoming Depression and Enhancing Well-Being
Year	2011
City	New York
Publisher	Oxford University Press, USA
Medium	Print

b. Click **OK** to insert the citation. In the paragraph, click to select the citation, click the **Citation Options arrow**, and then click **Edit Citation**. In the **Edit Citation** dialog box, under **Add**, in the **Pages** box, type **3** and then click **OK**.

c. On the upper portion of **Page 2**, in the paragraph that begins *Other positive effects*, in the second line, click to position the insertion point to the left of the period following *substantially*. In the **Citations & Bibliography group**, click **Insert Citation**, and then click **Add New Source**. Click the **Type of Source arrow**, click **Book**, and then add the following information:

Author	Lohrman, David, and Lois Heller
Title	Cardiovascular Physiology, Seventh Edition
Year	2010
City	New York
Publisher	McGraw-Hill Professional
Medium	Print

d. Click **OK**. Click to select the citation in the paragraph, click the **Citation Options arrow**, and then click **Edit Citation**. In the **Edit Citation** dialog box, under **Add**, in the **Pages** box, type **195** and then click **OK**.

6 Press Ctrl + End to move to the end of the last paragraph in the document. Click to the left of the period following *loss*. In the **Citations & Bibliography group**, click **Insert Citation**, and then click **Add New Source**. Click the **Type of Source arrow**,

click **Web site**, and then select the **Corporate Author** check box. Add the following information:

Corporate Author	U.S. Department of Health and Human Services
Name of Web Page	NIH News
Year	2012
Month	October
Day	15
Year Accessed	2016
Month Accessed	July
Day Accessed	21
Medium	Web

a. Click **OK**. Press Ctrl + End to move the insertion point to the end of the document. Press Ctrl + Enter to insert a manual page break. On the **Home tab**, in the **Paragraph group**, click the **Dialog Box Launcher** button. In the **Paragraph** dialog box, on the **Indents and Spacing tab**, under **Indentation**, click the **Special arrow**, and then click **(none)**. Click **OK**.

b. Type **Works Cited** and then press Enter. On the **References tab**, in the **Citations & Bibliography group**, be sure **MLA** displays in the **Style** box. In the **Citations & Bibliography group**, click **Bibliography**, and then at the bottom, click **Insert Bibliography**.

c. In the bibliography, move the pointer to the left of the first entry—beginning *Lohrman*—to display the pointer. Drag down to select all three references in the field. On the **Home tab**, in the **Paragraph group**, set the **Line spacing** to **2.0**. On the **Layout tab**, set the **Spacing After** to **0 pt**.

d. Click anywhere in the *Works Cited* title, and then press Ctrl + E to center the title. **Save** your document.

7 On the **References tab**, in the **Citations & Bibliography group**, click **Manage Sources**. On the left, on the **Master List**, click the entry for *Lohrman, David*, and then click **Edit**. In the **Edit Source** dialog box, in the **Author** box, change the *L* in *Lohrman* to **M** Click **OK**, click **Yes**, and then click **Close**.

a. On **Page 2**, in the paragraph that begins *Other positive effects*, in the second line, on the selected citation, click the **Citation Options arrow**, and then click **Update Citations and Bibliography**.

(Project 14C Diet and Exercise Report continues on the next page)

b. Click the **File tab**, and then in the lower right corner, click **Show All Properties**. Add the following information:

Title	Diet and Exercise
Tags	weight loss, exercise, diet
Comments	Draft copy of report for class
Categories	biomedical research
Company	University Medical Center
Manager	Dr. Hillary Kim

c. In the **Subject** box, type your course name and section number. Be sure that your name displays as the Author and edit if necessary. On the left, click **Save** to redisplay your document. On the **View tab**, in the **Views group**, click **Read Mode**. In the upper left, click **Tools**, click **Find**, and then in the search box, type **Yale** and notice that the text you searched for is highlighted in the document.

d. In the upper left, click **View**, and then click **Edit Document** to return to Print Layout view. **Close** the **Navigation** pane. **Save** your document, and view the Print Preview. If directed by your instructor to do so, submit your paper printout, your electronic image of your document that looks like a printed document, or your original Word file. **Close** Word.

END | You have completed Project 14C

Skills Review Project 14D Career Newsletter

In the following Skills Review, you will format a newsletter regarding professional development opportunities offered by University Medical Center, and you will create mailing labels for staff interested in these opportunities. Your completed document will look similar to Figure 14.56.

PROJECT FILES

For Project 14D, you will need the following files:

w14D_Career_Newsletter

w14D_Career_Sign (optional)

w14D_Medical_Symbol

w14D_Addresses (Optional: Use only if you are completing the Mailing Labels portion of this project)

You will save your documents as:

Lastname_Firstname_14D_Career_Newsletter

Lastname_Firstname_14D_Mailing_Labels (Optional: Create only if you are completing the Mailing Labels portion of this project)

PROJECT RESULTS

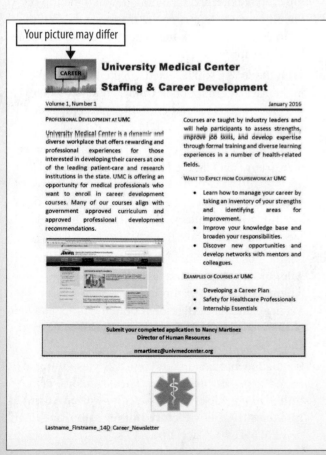

FIGURE 14.56

(Project 14D Career Newsletter continues on the next page)

Skills Review **Project 14D Career Newsletter** (continued)

1 Start Word. On Word's opening screen, in the lower left, click **Open Other Documents**. Navigate to your student files, and then locate and open **w14D_Career_Newsletter**. Save the file in your **AIO Chapter 14** folder as **Lastname_Firstname_14D_Career_Newsletter** and then add the file name to the footer.

a. Select the first two lines of the document. On the mini toolbar, change the **Font** to **Arial Black** and the **Font Size** to **18**. Select the first three lines of the document. Click the **Font Color button arrow**, and then under **Theme Colors**, in the fifth column, click the last color—**Blue, Accent 1, Darker 50%**.

b. With the text still selected, on the **Home tab**, in the **Paragraph group**, click the **Borders button arrow**, and then at the bottom, click **Borders and Shading**. In the **Borders and Shading** dialog box, on the **Borders tab**, click the **Color arrow**, and then under **Theme Colors**, in the fifth column, click the last color—**Blue, Accent 1, Darker 50%**.

c. Click the **Width arrow**, and then click **3 pt**. In the **Preview** box, click the bottom border. Click **OK**.

d. Click at the beginning of the paragraph that begins *Professional Development*. Scroll the document, hold down Shift, and then click after the paragraph mark at the end of the *Internship Essentials* line. On the **Layout tab**, in the **Page Setup group**, click **Columns**, and then click **Two**. With the two columns of text selected, on the **Home tab**, in the **Paragraph group**, click **Justify**.

e. In the first column, click at the beginning of the paragraph that begins *Courses are taught*. On the **Layout tab**, in the **Page Setup group**, click **Breaks**. Under **Page Breaks**, click **Column**.

2 Press Ctrl + Home. On the **Insert tab**, in the **Illustrations group**, click **Online Pictures**. In the **Bing Image Search** box, type **career sign** and then press Enter. Find the image of a green sign with the text *Your Career* with an arrow pointing to the right, and then click **Insert**. If you cannot find this image, from your student data files, insert w14D_Career_Sign.

a. With the image selected, on the **Format tab**, in the **Size group**, click the **Dialog Box Launcher** button. In the **Layout** dialog box, on the **Size tab**, under **Scale**, be sure the **Lock aspect ratio** and **Relative to original picture size** check boxes are selected. Under

Scale, select the percentage in the **Height box**, type **90** and then press Tab.

b. In the **Layout** dialog box, click the **Text Wrapping tab**. Under **Wrapping style**, click **Square**.

c. Click the **Position tab**, and then under **Horizontal**, click the **Alignment** option button. Be sure that the **Alignment** indicates **Left** and **relative to Column**. Under **Vertical**, click the **Alignment** option button, and then change the alignment to **Top relative to Margin**. Click **OK**. Compare the picture size and placement with Figure 14.56 and adjust the size of the image if necessary. **Save** your newsletter.

3 Press Ctrl + End to move to the end of the document. On the **Insert tab**, in the **Illustrations group**, click **Pictures**, and then from your student data files, insert the picture **w14D_Medical_Symbol**.

a. On the **Format tab**, in the **Size group**, click the upper portion of the **Crop** button. Point to the center top crop handle, and then drag down to the top of the blue rectangle. Repeat on the lower edge of the picture, and then click the upper portion of the **Crop** button to apply the crop.

b. With the image still selected, on the **Format tab**, in the **Adjust group**, click **Color**, and then under **Recolor**, in the last row, click **Blue, Accent color 1 Light**.

c. With the picture selected, on the **Format tab**, in the **Size group**, click in the **Height** box. Type **1** and then press Enter. To the right of the picture, click **Layout Options**, and then click **Square**. At the bottom of the **Layout Options gallery**, click **See more** to display the **Layout** dialog box.

d. On the **Position tab**, under **Horizontal**, click the **Alignment** option button, and then change the **Alignment** to **Centered relative to Page**. Under **Vertical**, click the **Alignment** option button, and then change **Alignment** to **Bottom relative to Margin**. Click **OK**.

e. On the **Format tab**, in the **Picture Styles group**, click **Picture Border**. Under **Theme Colors**, in the fifth column, click the second color—**Blue Accent 1, Lighter 80%**. Click **Picture Border** again, and then point to **Weight**. Click **1 pt**.

(Project 14D Career Newsletter continues on the next page)

4 In the paragraph that begins *University Medical Center is a dynamic*, click after the period at the end of the paragraph, and then press Enter one time. With the insertion point in the new blank paragraph, open your web browser, and then navigate to **www.ahrq.gov/clinic/**

a. From the taskbar, redisplay your **14D_Career_Newsletter** document. With the insertion point positioned at the end of the first paragraph in the body of the newsletter, on the **Insert tab**, in the **Illustrations group**, click **Screenshot**. In the **Screenshot** gallery, click the browser window that contains the website you just opened.

b. Select the subheading **Professional Development at UMC** including the paragraph mark. Right-click the selected text, and then on the shortcut menu, click **Font**. In the **Font** dialog box, click the **Font color arrow**, and then in the fifth column, click the last color—**Blue, Accent 1, Darker 50%**. Under **Font style**, click **Bold**, and then under **Effects**, select **Small caps**. Click **OK**.

c. With the text still selected, right-click, and then on the mini toolbar, double-click **Format Painter**. In the second column, with the ⒶI pointer, select each of the subheadings—**What to Expect from Coursework at UMC** and **Examples of Courses at UMC**. Press Esc to turn off Format Painter.

5 Press Ctrl + End to move to the end of the document, and then select the two lines of bold text—the graphic will also be selected. On the **Home tab**, in the **Paragraph group**, click the **Borders button arrow**, and then click **Borders and Shading**.

a. In the **Borders and Shading** dialog box, on the **Borders tab**, under **Setting**, click **Shadow**. Click the **Color arrow**, and then in the fifth column, click the last color—**Blue, Accent 1, Darker 50%**. Click the **Width arrow**, and then click **1 pt**.

b. In the **Borders and Shading** dialog box, click the **Shading tab**. Click the **Fill arrow**, and then in the fifth column, click the second color—**Blue, Accent 1, Lighter 80%**. Click **OK**. On the **Home tab**, in the **Paragraph group**, click **Center**. In the shaded paragraph, click in front of the *D* in the word *Director*. Hold down Shift and then press Enter.

c. Press Ctrl + Home, and then click the **File tab**. At the bottom of the **Properties** list, click **Show All Properties**. Click to the right of **Tags**, and then type **newsletter, careers** Click to the right of **Subject**, and then type your course name and section number. Under **Related People**, if necessary, type your name in the Author box. Display the **Print Preview** and make any necessary corrections. **Save** the document; close Word and close your browser window.

6 (NOTE: The remainder of this project, which is the creation of mailing labels, is optional. Complete if assigned by your instructor.) Start Word and display a new blank document. **Save** the document in your **AIO Chapter 14** folder as **Lastname_Firstname_14D_Mailing_Labels**

a. Click the **Mailings tab**. In the **Start Mail Merge group**, click **Start Mail Merge**, and then click **Step-by-Step Mail Merge Wizard**. In the **Mail Merge** pane, under **Select document type**, click **Labels**. At the bottom of the **Mail Merge** pane, click **Next: Starting document**.

b. Under **Select starting document**, under **Change document layout**, click **Label options**. In the **Label Options** dialog box, under **Printer information**, be sure that the **Default tray** is selected.

c. Under **Label information**, click the **Label vendors arrow**, and then click **Avery US Letter**. Under **Product number**, scroll about halfway down the list, and then click **5160 Easy Peel Address Labels**. At the bottom of the **Label Options** dialog box, click **OK**. At the bottom of the **Mail Merge** pane, click **Next: Select recipients**.

d. In the **Mail Merge** pane, under **Select recipients**, under **Use an existing list**, click **Browse**. In the **Select Data Source** dialog box, navigate to the student data files that accompany this chapter, click the Excel file **w14D_Addresses** one time to select it, and then click **Open** to display the **Select Table** dialog box. Click **OK**.

7 In the lower left portion of the **Mail Merge Recipients** dialog box, in the **Data Source** box, click the path that contains your file name. Then, at the bottom of the **Mail Merge Recipients** dialog box, click **Edit**. In the lower left corner of the displayed **Edit Data Source** dialog box, click **New Entry**. In the blank record, which

(Project 14D Career Newsletter continues on the next page)

is shaded, type the following, pressing Tab to move from field to field:

First Name	Mia
Last Name	Orr
Address 1	1378 Lima Ave.
Unit	#82
City	Memphis
State	TN
ZIP Code	38123

a. In the lower right corner of the **Edit Data Source** dialog box, click **OK**, and then in the displayed message, click **Yes**. At the bottom of the **Mail Merge Recipients** dialog box, click **OK**.

b. At the bottom of the **Mail Merge** pane, click **Next: Arrange your labels**. Under **Arrange your labels**, click **Address block**. In the lower right corner of the **Insert Address Block** dialog box, click **Match Fields**.

c. Click the **Address 2 arrow**, and then from the list of available fields, click **Unit**. Click **OK** two times.

d. In the **Mail Merge** pane, under **Replicate labels**, click **Update all labels**. At the bottom of the **Mail**

Merge pane, click **Next: Preview your labels**. Press Ctrl + A to select all of the label text, click the **Layout tab**, and then in the **Paragraph group**, click in the **Spacing Before** box. Type **3** and press Enter. At the bottom of the **Mail Merge** pane, click **Next: Complete the merge**.

e. Click the **Mailings tab**, and then in the **Start Mail Merge group**, click **Edit Recipient List** to display the list of names and addresses. In the **Mail Merge Recipients** dialog box, click the **Last Name** field heading to sort the names. Click **OK**. **Close** the **Mail Merge** pane.

f. Scroll the document and then click anywhere in the empty table row at the bottom. Click the **Table Tools Layout tab**. In the **Rows & Columns group**, click **Delete**, and then click **Delete Rows**. Add the file name to the footer, close the footer area, and then click the **File tab**. Click **Show All Properties**. As the **Tags**, type **labels** and as the **Subject**, type your course name and section number. Be sure your name displays as the **Author**, and then **Save** your file.

g. If directed by your instructor to do so, submit your paper printout, your electronic image of your document, or your original Word file. **Close** Word.

END | You have completed Project 14D

Mastering Word | Project 14E Skin Protection Report

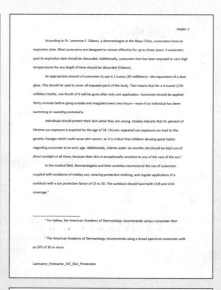

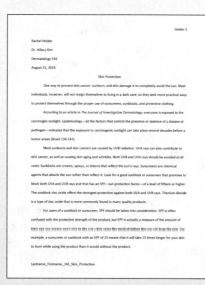

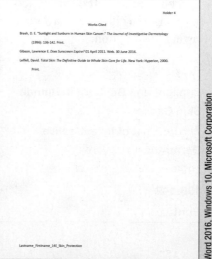

Apply 14A skills from these Objectives:

1 Create a Research Paper
2 Insert Footnotes in a Research Paper
3 Create Citations and a Bibliography in a Research Paper
4 Use Read Mode and PDF Reflow

In the following Mastering Word project, you will edit and format a research paper that contains information about skin protection and the use of sunblocks and sunscreens. This paper was created by Rachel Holder, a medical intern at University Medical Center, for distribution to her classmates studying dermatology. Your completed document will look similar to the one shown in Figure 14.57.

PROJECT FILES

For Project 14E, you will need the following file:

w14E_Skin_Protection

You will save your document as:

Lastname_Firstname_14E_Skin_Protection

PROJECT RESULTS

FIGURE 14.57

Word 2016, Windows 10, Microsoft Corporation

(Project 14E Skin Protection Report continues on the next page)

Mastering Word | Project 14E Skin Protection Report (continued)

1 Start Word, and on the left click **Open Other Documents**. From your student data files, locate and open the document **w14E_Skin_Protection**. Display formatting marks and rulers. Save the file in your **AIO Chapter 14** folder as **Lastname_Firstname_14E_Skin_Protection**

2 Select all the text, change the **Line Spacing** to **2.0**, and then change the **Spacing After** to **0 pt**.

3 At the top of the document, insert a new blank paragraph, and then in the new paragraph, type **Rachel Holder** Press Enter. Type **Dr. Hillary Kim** and press Enter. Type **Dermatology 544** and press Enter. Type **August 31, 2016** and press Enter. Type **Skin Protection** and then press Ctrl + E to center the title you just typed.

4 Insert a header, type **Holder** and then press Spacebar. Display the **Page Number gallery**, and then in the **Current Position**, add the **Plain Number** style. Apply **Align Right** formatting to the header. Insert a footer with the file name.

5 To the paragraph that begins *One way to prevent*, apply a **First line** indent of **0.5"**.

6 On **Page 2**, at the end of the paragraph that begins *In the medical field*, insert a footnote with the following text: **The American Academy of Dermatology recommends using a broad spectrum sunscreen with an SPF of 30 or more.**

7 Modify the **Footnote Text** style so that the **Font Size** is **11**, there is a **First line indent** of **0.5"**, and the spacing is **Double**, and then apply the style.

8 On **Page 1**, at the end of the paragraph that begins *According to an article*, click to the left of the period, and then using **MLA** format, insert a citation for a **Journal Article** with the following information:

Author	Brash, D. E.
Title	Sunlight and Sunburn in Human Skin Cancer
Journal Name	The Journal of Investigative Dermatology
Year	1996
Pages	136-142
Medium	Print

9 In the report, select the citation you just created, display the **Citation Options**, and then edit the citation to include **Pages 136-142**

10 At the top of **Page 2**, at the end of the paragraph that begins *According to Dr.*, click to the left of the period, and then insert a citation for a **Web site** with the following information:

Author	Gibson, Lawrence E.
Name of Web Page	Does Sunscreen Expire?
Year	2011
Month	April
Day	01
Year Accessed	2016
Month Accessed	June
Day Accessed	30
Medium	Web

11 On **Page 3**, at the end of the last paragraph of the report that begins *Because the effect*, click to the left of the period, and then insert a citation for a **Book** with the following information:

Author	Leffell, David.
Title	Total Skin: The Definitive Guide to Whole Skin Care for Life
Year	2000
City	New York
Publisher	Hyperion
Medium	Print

12 In the report, select the citation you just created, display the **Citation Options**, and then edit the citation to include **Page 96**

13 Move to the end of the document, and then insert a manual page break to create a new page. Display the **Paragraph** dialog box, and then change the **Indentation** under **Special** to **(none)**. Add a **Works Cited** title, press Enter, and then **Insert Bibliography**. Select the references, apply **Double** line spacing, and then set the **Spacing After** paragraphs to **0 pt**. **Center** the *Works Cited* title.

(Project 14E Skin Protection Report continues on the next page)

Mastering Word Project 14E Skin Protection Report (continued)

14 Update the **Document Properties** with the following information:

Title	**Skin Protection**
Tags	**sunscreen, sun exposure**
Comments	**Draft copy of report for class**
Categories	**Dermatology**
Company	**University Medical Center**
Manager	**Dr. Hillary Kim**

15 In the **Subject** box, type your course name and section number. Be sure that your name displays as the **Author** and edit if necessary. On the left, click **Print** to view the **Print Preview**. Click **Save** to redisplay your document. If directed by your instructor to do so, submit your paper printout, your electronic image of your document that looks like a printed document, or your original Word file. **Close** Word.

END | You have completed Project 14E

Mastering Word Project 14F Dogs Newsletter and Mailing Labels

Apply 14B skills from these Objectives:

5 Format a Multiple-Column Newsletter

6 Use Special Character and Paragraph Formatting

7 Create Mailing Labels Using Mail Merge

In the following Mastering Word project, you will format a newsletter with information about the therapy dogs handled by volunteers at the University Medical Center. Optionally, you will create mailing labels so that the newsletter can be sent to the volunteer staff. Your completed documents will look similar to Figure 14.58.

PROJECT FILES

For Project 14F, you will need the following files:

w14F_Dogs_Newsletter

w14F_Dog

w14F_Addresses (Optional: Use only if you are completing the Mailing Labels portion of this project)

You will save your documents as:

Lastname_Firstname_14F_Dogs_Newsletter

Lastname_Firstname_14F_Mailing_Labels (Optional: Create only if you are completing the Mailing Labels portion of this project)

PROJECT RESULTS

FIGURE 14.58

(Project 14F Dogs Newsletter and Mailing Labels continues on the next page)

Mastering Word Project 14F Dogs Newsletter and Mailing Labels (continued)

1 Start Word. From your student files, open **w14F_Dogs_Newsletter**. **Save** the file in your **AIO Chapter 14** folder as **Lastname_Firstname_14F_Dogs_Newsletter** and then add the file name to the footer. Select the first three lines of the document, and then change the **Font Color** to **Olive Green, Accent 3, Darker 25%**—in the seventh column, the fifth color. With the text selected, display the **Borders and Shading** dialog box. Apply a **3 pt** bottom border using the color **Black, Text 1**.

2 Click at the beginning of the newsletter title *University Medical Center*. Insert an online picture from **Bing Image Search** by searching for **physician symbol** and then insert one of the symbols that is not bordered or framed.

3 Set the image **Height** to **1"**. Change the **Brightness/Contrast** to **Brightness: 0% (Normal) Contrast: +40%**.

4 Change the **Text Wrapping** to **Square**. Change the **Horizontal Alignment** to **Left relative** to **Margin** and the **Vertical Alignment** to **Top relative** to **Margin**. If necessary, drag a corner of the inserted physician symbol to decrease its size so that the newsletter title displays on two lines.

5 Starting with the paragraph that begins *Dogs for Healing*, select all of the text from that point to the end of the document. Change the **Spacing After** to **10 pt**, format the text in two columns, and apply **Justify** alignment. Insert a **Column** break before the subheading *Cuddles*.

6 Click at the beginning of the sentence that begins with *Brandy is a 6-year-old Beagle*. From your student data files, insert the picture **w14F_Dog**. Rotate the picture using **Flip Horizontal**.

7 Change the picture **Width** to **1** and then apply the **Square** layout option. Change the **Horizontal Alignment**

to **Right relative** to **Margin** and the **Vertical Alignment** to **Top relative** to **Line**. Apply a **Black, Text 1 Picture Border** and change the **Weight** to **2 ¼ pt**.

8 Start your web browser and if necessary, maximize the window. Navigate to **www.ada.gov/qasrvc.htm** From the taskbar, redisplay your **Lastname_Firstname_14F_Dogs_Newsletter** file, click at the end of the paragraph below the *Dogs for Healing* subheading. Insert a **Screenshot** of the website. Apply a **Black, Text 1 Picture Border** and change the **Weight** to **1 pt**.

9 Select the subheading **Dogs for Healing** including the paragraph mark. By using the **Font** dialog box, change the **Size** to **16**, apply **Bold**, apply the **Small caps** effect, and change the **Font color** to **Olive Green, Accent 3, Darker 50%**—in the seventh column, the last color. Apply the same formatting to the subheadings **Benefits to Patients**, **Cuddles**, and **Brandy**.

10 Select the last paragraph in the newsletter including the paragraph mark, and then apply a **1 pt Shadow** border, in **Black, Text 1**. Shade the paragraph with a **Fill** color of **Olive Green, Accent 3, Lighter 80%**—in the seventh column, the second color.

11 Click the **File tab**, and then click **Show All Properties**. As the **Tags**, type **dogs, newsletter** As the **Subject**, type your course name and section number. Under **Related People**, if necessary, type your name in the Author box. **Print Preview** the document and make any necessary corrections.

12 On the left, click **Print** to view the **Print Preview**. Click **Save** to redisplay your document. If directed by your instructor to do so, submit your paper printout, your electronic image of your document that looks like a printed document, or your original Word file. **Close** Word.

END | You have completed Project 14F

ALERT! **Optional Project to Produce Mailing Labels**

Your instructor may ask you to complete the optional project on the following page to produce mailing labels. Check with your instructor to see if you should complete the mailing labels. This project is not included in the MyITLab Grader system.

1 Start Word and display a new blank document. **Save** the document in your **AIO Chapter 14** folder as **Lastname_Firstname_14F_Mailing_Labels** From your student files, **Open** the file **w14F_Addresses**. **Save** the address file in your **AIO Chapter 14** folder as **Lastname_Firstname_14F_Addresses**

2 Start the **Step-by-Step Mail Merge Wizard** to create **Labels**. Display the **Label Options** dialog box, and be sure that the **Default tray** is selected and that the label vendor is **Avery US Letter**. The **Product number** is **5160 Easy Peel Address Labels**. Select the **Use an existing list** option, click **Browse**, and then in the **Select Data Source** dialog box, navigate to your student data files and open **w14F_Addresses**. In the **Select Table** dialog box, click **OK**. Add the following record to your file:

First Name	Miranda
Last Name	Yanos
Address 1	1256 Loma Ave.
Unit	#34
City	Memphis
State	TN
ZIP Code	38123

3 Insert an **Address block** and match the fields. Match the **Address 2** field to the **Unit** field, and then update the labels. Preview the labels, and then select the entire document. Change the **Spacing Before** to **3** and then **Complete the merge**. Delete the last row from the bottom of the table, and then add the file name to the footer.

4 Display the document properties. As the **Tags** type **labels** and as the **Subject** type your course name and section number. Be sure your name displays in the **Author box**, and then **Save** your file. As directed by your instructor, print or submit electronically. **Close** Word and close your browser window.

END | You have completed the optional portion of this project

MyITLab grader

Mastering Word | Project 14G Research Paper, Newsletter, and Mailing Labels

Apply **14A** and **14B** skills from these Objectives:

1 Create a Research Paper

2 Insert Footnotes in a Research Paper

3 Create Citations and a Bibliography in a Research Paper

4 Use Read Mode and PDF Reflow

5 Format a Multiple-Column Newsletter

6 Use Special Character and Paragraph Formatting

7 Create Mailing Labels Using Mail Merge

In the following Mastering Word project, you will edit and format a research paper and a newsletter. Optionally, you will create mailing labels. Your completed documents will look similar to Figure 14.59.

PROJECT FILES

For Project 14G, you will need the following files:

w14G_Newsletter_and_Research_Paper

w14G_Addresses (Optional: For use if you are completing the Mailing Labels portion of this project)

You will save your documents as:

Lastname_Firstname_14G_Newsletter_and_Research_Paper

Lastname_Firstname_14G_Mailing_Labels (Optional: Create only if you are completing the Mailing Labels portion of this project)

PROJECT RESULTS

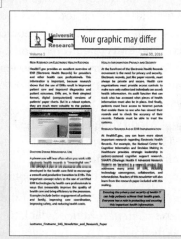

FIGURE 14.59

(Project 14G Research Paper, Newsletter, and Mailing Labels continues on the next page)

Mastering Word | Project 14G Research Paper, Newsletter, and Mailing Labels (continued)

1 From your student files, open **w14G_Newsletter_and_Research_Paper**. **Save** the file in your **AIO Chapter 14** folder as **Lastname_Firstname_14G_Newsletter_and_Research_Paper** and then add the file name to the footer. Click anywhere on Page 2, and because this is a separate section, add the File Name to the footer again so that it appears in both sections of the document. Redisplay **Page 1**, select the first three lines of the newsletter heading, and then apply a **3 pt** bottom border in **Black, Text 1**.

2 Click at the beginning of the newsletter title *University Medical Center*. Insert an online picture from **Bing Image Search** by searching for **microscope** and then insert an image of a black—or a black and white—microscope. Set the **Height** of the image to **.7"** and then **Recolor** the picture by applying **Blue, Accent color 1 Light**. Apply a **Black, Text 1 Picture Border** and change the **Weight** to **2 ¼ pt**.

3 Change the **Text Wrapping** of the inserted image to **Square**. Change the **Horizontal Alignment** to **Left relative** to **Margin** and the **Vertical Alignment** to **Top relative** to **Margin**.

4 Starting with the subheading paragraph *New Research on Electronic Health Records*, select all of the text from that point to the end of the page—include the paragraph mark but do not include the Section Break in your selection. Format the text in two columns, and apply **Justify** alignment. Insert a **Column** break before the subheading *Health Information Privacy and Security*.

5 Start your web browser, and then navigate to **www.healthit.gov** If necessary, close the message about subscribing. Redisplay your document, click at the end of the paragraph below the *New Research on Electronic Health Records* subheading. Insert a **Screenshot** of the website. Apply a **Black, Text 1 Picture Border** and change the **Weight** to **1 pt**.

6 Select the subheading *New Research on Electronic Health Records* including the paragraph mark. From the **Font** dialog box, apply **Bold** and **Small Caps** and change the **Font color** to **Dark Blue, Text 2**—in the fourth column, the first color. Apply the same formatting to the subheadings *Doctors Define Meaningful Use*, *Health Information and Privacy and Security* and *Research*

Sources Aid in EHR Implementation. Select the *Doctors Define Meaningful Use* subheading and then change the **Spacing Before** to **18 pt**.

7 Select the last paragraph in the newsletter—the text in bold italic that begins *Ensuring the privacy* including the paragraph mark but not the Section Break lines—and then apply a **1 pt Shadow** border using **Black, Text 1**. Shade the paragraph with the **Fill** color **Dark Blue, Text 2, Lighter 80%**—in the fourth column, the second color. **Center** the text. **Save** your document.

8 On **Page 2**, beginning with **Janet Eisler**, select all of the text on the page. With the text on Page 2 selected, change the **Line Spacing** to **2.0**, and then change the **Spacing After** to **0 pt**. To the paragraph that begins *There is often a discrepancy*, apply a **First line** indent of **0.5"** inches.

9 At the bottom of **Page 2**, in the next to last line of text, after the period at the end of the sentence that ends *if they had it*, insert a footnote with the following text: **The EMR (electronic medical record) is the patient record created in hospitals and ambulatory environments; it serves as a data source for other systems.**

10 Modify the **Footnote Text** style to set the **Font Size** to **11** and the format of the Footnote Text paragraph to include a **First line** indent of **0.5"** and **Double** spacing. Apply the new style to the footnote text.

11 On **Page 2**, at the end of the paragraph that begins *Those clinical practices*, click to the left of the period, and then using **MLA** format, insert a citation for a **Web site** with the following information:

Author	Gabriel, Barbara A.
Name of Web Page	Do EMRS Make You a Better Doctor?
Year	2008
Month	July
Day	15
Year Accessed	2016
Month Accessed	June
Day Accessed	30
Medium	Web

(Project 14G Research Paper, Newsletter, and Mailing Labels continues on the next page)

Mastering Word | Project 14G Research Paper, Newsletter, and Mailing Labels (continued)

12 On **Page 3**, at the end of the paragraph that begins *Further research*, click to the left of the period, and then using **MLA** format, insert a citation for a **Book** with the following information:

Author	DeVore, Amy.
Title	The Electronic Health Record for the Physician's Office, 1e
Year	2010
City	Maryland Heights
Publisher	Saunders
Medium	Print

13 In the report, select the citation you just created, display the **Citation Options**, and then edit the citation to include **Pages 253**

14 On **Page 4**, click in the blank paragraph. On the **References tab**, click **Bibliography**, and then click **Insert Bibliography**.

15 Update the **Document Properties** with the following information:

Title	Electronic Health Records
Tags	EMR, health records
Subject	(insert your course name and section number)
Company	University Medical Center
Manager	Dr. Hillary Kim

16 On the left, click **Print** to display the **Print Preview**, and then click **Save** to redisplay your document. If directed by your instructor to do so, submit your paper printout, your electronic image of your document that looks like a printed document, or your original Word file. **Close** Word.

END | You have completed Project 14G

ALERT! **Optional Project to Produce Mailing Labels**

Your instructor may ask you to complete the optional project on the next page to produce mailing labels. Check with your instructor to see if you should complete the mailing labels. This project is not included in the MyITLab Grader system.

1 Start Word and display a new blank document. **Save** the document in your **AIO Chapter 14** folder as **Lastname_Firstname_14G_Mailing_Labels**

2 Start the **Step-by-Step Mail Merge Wizard** to create **Labels**. Display the **Label Options** dialog box, and be sure that the **Default tray** is selected and that the label vendor is **Avery US Letter**. The **Product number** is **5160 Easy Peel Address Labels**. Select the **Use an existing list option**, click **Browse**, and then in the **Select Data Source** dialog box, navigate to your student data files and open **w14G_Addresses**. In the **Select Table** dialog box, click **OK**. Add the following record to your file:

First Name	Mason
Last Name	Zepeda
Address 1	134 Atlantic Ave.
Unit	#21
City	Memphis
State	TN
ZIP Code	38123

3 Insert an **Address block** and match the fields. Match the **Address 2** field to the **Unit** field, and then update the labels. Preview the labels, and then select the entire document. Change the **Spacing Before** to **3** and then **Complete the merge**. Delete the last row from the bottom of the table, and then add the file name to the footer.

4 Display the document properties. As the **Tags** type **labels** and as the **Subject** type your course name and section number. Be sure your name displays in the **Author box**, and then **Save** your file. As directed by your instructor, print or submit your work electronically. Close all open windows.

END | You have completed the optional portion of this project

CONTENT-BASED ASSESSMENTS (CRITICAL THINKING)

GO! Fix It	Project 14H Hospital Materials	MyITLab

GO! Make It	Project 14I Health Newsletter	MyITLab

GO! Solve It	Project 14J Colds and Flu	MyITLab

GO! Solve It	Project 14K Cycling Newsletter	

PROJECT FILES

For Project 14K, you will need the following file:

w14K_Cycling_Newsletter

You will save your document as:

Lastname_Firstname_14K_Cycling_Newsletter

The University Medical Center Emergency Department publishes a monthly newsletter focusing on safety and injury prevention. The topic for the current newsletter is bicycle safety. From your student data files, open **w14K_Cycling_Newsletter**, add the file name to the footer, and then save the file in your **AIO Chapter 14** folder as **Lastname_Firstname_14K_Cycling_Newsletter**

Using the techniques that you practiced in this chapter, format the document in two-column newsletter format. Format the nameplate so that it is clearly separate from the body of the newsletter and is easily identified as the nameplate. Insert column breaks as necessary and apply appropriate formatting to subheadings. Insert and format at least one online picture that is appropriate to the topic, and insert a screenshot of a relevant website. Apply a border and shading to the last paragraph so that it is formatted attractively.

Add your name, your course name and section number, and the keywords **agenda, monthly staff meeting** to the Properties area. Submit as directed.

(Project 14K Cycling Newsletter continues on the next page)

Performance Level

Performance Criteria	Exemplary: You consistently applied the relevant skills	Proficient: You sometimes, but not always, applied the relevant skills	Developing: You rarely or never applied the relevant skills
Format nameplate	The nameplate is formatted attractively and in a manner that clearly indicates that it is the nameplate.	The nameplate includes some formatting but is not clearly separated from the body of the newsletter.	The newsletter does not include a nameplate.
Insert and format at least one online picture	An appropriate online picture image is included. The image is sized and positioned appropriately.	A clip art image is inserted but is either inappropriate, or is formatted or positioned poorly.	No clip art image is included.
Border and shading added to a paragraph	The last paragraph displays an attractive border with shading that enables the reader to read the text.	A border or shading is displayed but not both; or the shading is too dark to enable the reader to easily read the text.	No border or shading is added to a paragraph.
Insert a screenshot	A screenshot is inserted in one of the columns; the screenshot is related to the content of the article.	A screenshot is inserted in the document but does not relate to the content of the article.	No screenshot is inserted.

END | You have completed Project 14K

OUTCOMES-BASED ASSESSMENTS

RUBRIC

The following outcomes-based assessments are *open-ended assessments*. That is, there is no specific correct result; your result will depend on your approach to the information provided. Make *Professional Quality* your goal. Use the following scoring rubric to guide you in *how* to approach the problem and then to evaluate *how well* your approach solves the problem.

The *criteria*—Software Mastery, Content, Format and Layout, and Process—represent the knowledge and skills you have gained that you can apply to solving the problem. The *levels of performance*—Professional Quality, Approaching Professional Quality, or Needs Quality Improvements—help you and your instructor evaluate your result.

	Your completed project is of Professional Quality if you:	Your completed project is Approaching Professional Quality if you:	Your completed project Needs Quality Improvements if you:
1-Software Mastery	Choose and apply the most appropriate skills, tools, and features and identify efficient methods to solve the problem.	Choose and apply some appropriate skills, tools, and features, but not in the most efficient manner.	Choose inappropriate skills, tools, or features, or are inefficient in solving the problem.
2-Content	Construct a solution that is clear and well organized, contains content that is accurate, appropriate to the audience and purpose, and is complete. Provide a solution that contains no errors in spelling, grammar, or style.	Construct a solution in which some components are unclear, poorly organized, inconsistent, or incomplete. Misjudge the needs of the audience. Have some errors in spelling, grammar, or style, but the errors do not detract from comprehension.	Construct a solution that is unclear, incomplete, or poorly organized; contains some inaccurate or inappropriate content; and contains many errors in spelling, grammar, or style. Do not solve the problem.
3-Format & Layout	Format and arrange all elements to communicate information and ideas, clarify function, illustrate relationships, and indicate relative importance.	Apply appropriate format and layout features to some elements, but not others. Overuse features, causing minor distraction.	Apply format and layout that does not communicate information or ideas clearly. Do not use format and layout features to clarify function, illustrate relationships, or indicate relative importance. Use available features excessively, causing distraction.
4-Process	Use an organized approach that integrates planning, development, self-assessment, revision, and reflection.	Demonstrate an organized approach in some areas, but not others; or, use an insufficient process of organization throughout.	Do not use an organized approach to solve the problem.

OUTCOMES-BASED ASSESSMENTS

Apply a combination of the 14A and 14B skills.

Build from Scratch

GO! Think   Project 14L Influenza Report

PROJECT FILES

For Project 14L, you will need the following file:

New blank Word document

You will save your document as:

Lastname_Firstname_14L_Influenza

As part of the ongoing research conducted by University Medical Center in the area of community health and contagious diseases, Dr. Hillary Kim has asked Sarah Stanger to create a report on influenza—how it spreads, and how it can be prevented in the community.

Create a new Word document and save it as **Lastname_Firstname_14L_Influenza** Conduct your research and then create the report in MLA format. The report should include at least two footnotes, at least two citations, and should include a *Works Cited* page.

The report should contain an introduction, and then information about what influenza is, how it spreads, and how it can be prevented. A good place to start is at **http://health.nih.gov/topic/influenza**.

Add the file name to the footer. Add appropriate information to the Document Properties and submit as directed.

END | You have completed Project 14L

Build From Scratch

GO! Think   Project 14M Volunteer Newsletter   **MyITLab**

You and GO!   Project 14N College Newsletter   **MyITLab**

Build from Scratch

GO! Collaborative Team Project   Project 14O Bell Orchid Hotels   **MyITLab**

Introducing Microsoft Excel 2016

Georgejmclittle/Fotolia

Excel 2016: Introduction

Quantitative information! Defined as a type of information that can be counted or that communicates the quantity of something, quantitative information can be either easy or hard to understand—depending on how it is presented. According to Stephen Few, in his book *Show Me the Numbers*: "Quantitative information forms the core of what businesses must know to operate effectively."

Excel 2016 is a tool to communicate quantitative business information effectively. Sometimes you need to communicate quantitative relationships. For example, the number of units sold per geographic region shows a relationship of sales to geography. Sometimes you need

to summarize numbers. A list of every student enrolled at your college with his or her major indicated is not as informative as a summary of the total number of students in each major. In business, the most common quantitative information is some measure of money—costs, sales, payroll, expenses—and so on.

Rather than just a tool for making calculations, Excel is now a tool for you to communicate and collaborate with others. When you want to communicate visually with tables and graphs, Excel 2016 has many features to help you do so. If you engage in Business Intelligence activities, you will find rich tools for forecasting and analysis. Excel is the world's most widely used and familiar data analysis tool.

Creating a Worksheet and Charting Data

15

PROJECT 15A

OUTCOMES
Create a sales report with an embedded column chart and sparklines.

OBJECTIVES

1. Create, Save, and Navigate an Excel Workbook
2. Enter Data in a Worksheet
3. Construct and Copy Formulas and Use the SUM Function
4. Format Cells with Merge & Center, Cell Styles, and Themes
5. Chart Data to Create a Column Chart and Insert Sparklines
6. Print a Worksheet, Display Formulas, and Close Excel

PROJECT 15B

OUTCOMES
Calculate the value of an inventory.

OBJECTIVES

7. Check Spelling in a Worksheet
8. Enter Data by Range
9. Construct Formulas for Mathematical Operations
10. Edit Values in a Worksheet
11. Format a Worksheet

In This Chapter

In this chapter, you will use Microsoft Excel 2016 to create and analyze data organized into columns and rows. After entering data in a worksheet, you can perform complex calculations, analyze the data to make logical decisions, and create attractive charts that help readers visualize your data in a way they can understand and that is meaningful. In this chapter, you will create and modify Excel workbooks. You will practice the basics of worksheet design, create a footer, enter and edit data in a worksheet, and chart data. You will save, preview, and print workbooks, and you will construct formulas for mathematical operations.

The projects in this chapter relate to **Pro Fit Marietta**, a distributor of fitness equipment and apparel to private gyms, personal trainers, health clubs, corporate wellness centers, hotels, college athletic facilities, physical therapy practices, and multi-unit residential properties. The company's mission is to find, test, and distribute the highest-quality fitness products in the world to its customers for the benefit of consumers. Their popular blog provides useful tips on how to use the latest workout and fitness equipment. The company is located in Marietta, Georgia, which is metropolitan Atlanta's largest suburb.

PROJECT 15A Sales Report with Embedded Column Chart and Sparklines

PROJECT ACTIVITIES

In Activities 15.01 through 15.17, you will create an Excel worksheet for Michelle Barry, the President of Pro Fit Marietta. The worksheet displays the second quarter sales of cardio equipment for the current year and includes a chart to visually represent the data. Your completed worksheet will look similar to Figure 15.1.

PROJECT FILES

MyITLab grader If your instructor wants you to submit Project 15A in the MyITLab Grader system, log in to MyITLab, locate Grader Project 15A, and then download the files for this project.

For Project 15A, you will need the following file:
New blank Excel workbook

You will save your workbook as:
Lastname_Firstname_15A_Quarterly_Sales
Lastname_Firstname_15A_Quarterly_Sales_formulas (if your instructor requires)

PROJECT RESULTS

 Build From Scratch

 GO! Walk Thru Project 15A

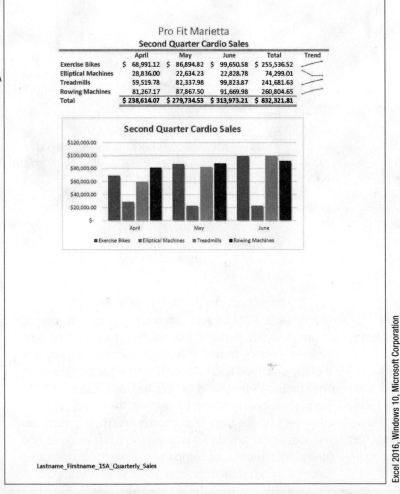

FIGURE 15.1 Project 15A Quarterly Sales

NOTE	If You Are Using a Touchscreen
	Tap an item to click it.
	Press and hold for a few seconds to right-click; release when the information or commands display.
	Touch the screen with two or more fingers and then pinch together to zoom out or stretch your fingers apart to zoom in.
	Slide your finger on the screen to scroll—slide left to scroll right and slide right to scroll left.
	Slide to rearrange—similar to dragging with a mouse.
	Swipe to select—slide an item a short distance with a quick movement—to select an item and bring up commands, if any.

Objective 1 Create, Save, and Navigate an Excel Workbook

GO! Learn How
Video E15-1

On startup, Excel displays a new blank **workbook**—the Excel document that stores your data—which contains one or more pages called a **worksheet**. A worksheet—or **spreadsheet**—is stored in a workbook, and is formatted as a pattern of uniformly spaced horizontal rows and vertical columns. The intersection of a column and a row forms a box referred to as a **cell**.

IC3
DIGITAL LITERACY
CERTIFICATION

2.03a (i)
2.03a (ii)
2.03a (iii)
2.03a (v)
2.03a (vi)
2.03a (vii)

Activity 15.01 | Starting Excel, Navigating Excel, and Naming and Saving a Workbook

> **ALERT!**   **To submit as an autograded project, log into MyITLab, download the files for this project, and begin with those files instead of a new blank workbook.**

1 Start Excel, and on the opening screen, click **Blank workbook**. In the lower right corner of the window, on the status bar, if necessary, click the Normal button ⊞, and then to the right, locate the zoom—magnification—level.

> Your zoom level should be 100%, although some figures in this text may be shown at a higher zoom level. The **Normal view** maximizes the number of cells visible on your screen and keeps the column letters and row numbers closer to the cells.

BY TOUCH On Excel's opening screen, tap Blank workbook.

2 On the ribbon, click the **File tab**, on the left click **Save As**, under **Save As**, click **Browse** to display the **Save As** dialog box, and then navigate to the location where you will store your workbooks for this chapter.

3 In your storage location, create a new folder named **AIO Chapter 15** and then open the new folder to display its folder window. In the **File name** box, notice that *Book1* displays as the default file name.

4 In the **File name** box, click **Book1** to select it, and then using your own name, type **Lastname_Firstname_15A_Quarterly_Sales** being sure to include the underscore (_) instead of spaces between words.

5 Click **Save**. Compare your screen with Figure 15.2, and then take a moment to study the parts of the Excel window described in the table in Figure 15.3.

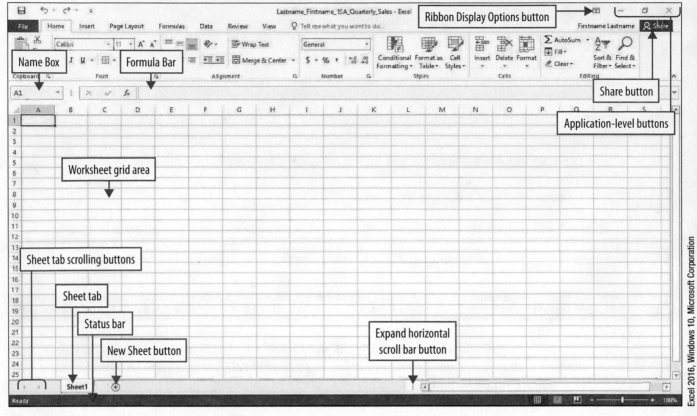

FIGURE 15.2

PARTS OF THE EXCEL WINDOW	
SCREEN PART	**DESCRIPTION**
Horizontal scroll bar button	Increases or decreases the width of the horizontal scroll bar by sliding left or right.
Formula Bar	Displays the value or formula contained in the active cell; also permits entry or editing.
Sheet tab	Identifies the worksheet in the workbook.
New sheet button	Inserts an additional worksheet.
Name Box	Displays the name of the selected cell, table, chart, or object.
Share button	Opens the Share pane from which you can save your file to the cloud—your OneDrive—and then share it with others so you can collaborate.
Sheet tab scrolling buttons	Display sheet tabs that are not in view when there are numerous sheet tabs.
Status bar	Displays the current cell mode, page number, worksheet information, view and zoom buttons, and for numerical data, common calculations such as Sum and Average.
Application-level buttons	Minimize, close, or restore the previous size of the displayed workbook window.
Ribbon Display Options button	Displays various ways you can display the ribbon—the default is Show Tabs and Commands.
Worksheet grid area	Displays the columns and rows that intersect to form the worksheet's cells.

FIGURE 15.3

6 ▶ Take a moment to study Figure 15.4 and the table in Figure 15.5 to become familiar with the Excel worksheet window.

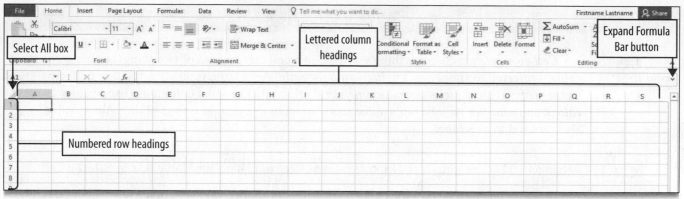

FIGURE 15.4

PARTS OF THE EXCEL WORKSHEET WINDOW	
WORKBOOK WINDOW ELEMENT	**DESCRIPTION**
Excel pointer	Displays the location of the pointer.
Expand Formula Bar button	Increases the height of the Formula Bar to display lengthy cell content.
Lettered column headings	Indicate the column letter.
Numbered row headings	Indicate the row number.
Select All box	Selects all the cells in a worksheet.

FIGURE 15.5

7 In the lower right corner of the screen, in the horizontal scroll bar, click the **right scroll arrow** one time to shift **column A** out of view.

A *column* is a vertical group of cells in a worksheet. Beginning with the first letter of the alphabet, *A*, a unique letter identifies each column—this is called the *column heading*. Clicking one of the horizontal scroll bar arrows shifts the window either left or right one column at a time.

8 Point to the **right scroll arrow**, and then hold down the left mouse button until the columns begin to scroll rapidly to the right; release the mouse button when you begin to see pairs of letters as the column headings.

BY TOUCH Anywhere on the worksheet, slide your finger to the left to view columns to the right.

9 Slowly drag the horizontal scroll box to the left, and notice that just above the scroll box, ScreenTips with the column letters display as you drag. Drag the horizontal scroll box left or right—or click the left or right scroll arrow—as necessary to position **column Z** near the center of your screen.

Column headings after column Z use two letters starting with AA, AB, and so on through ZZ. After that, columns begin with three letters beginning with AAA. This pattern provides 16,384 columns. The last column is XFD.

10 In the vertical scroll bar, click the **down scroll arrow** one time to move **Row 1** out of view.

A *row* is a horizontal group of cells. Beginning with number 1, a unique number identifies each row—this is the *row heading*, located at the left side of the worksheet. A single worksheet can have 1,048,576 rows of data.

11 Use the skills you just practiced to scroll horizontally to display **column A**, and if necessary, **row 1**.

12 Click **Save** 💾.

GO! Learn How
Video E15-2

Cell content, which is anything you type in a cell, can be one of two things: either a *constant value*—referred to simply as a *value*—or a *formula*. A formula is an equation that performs mathematical calculations on values in your worksheet. The most commonly used values are *text values* and *number values*, but a value can also include a date or a time of day. A text value is also referred to as a *label*.

IC3
DIGITAL LITERACY
CERTIFICATION
2.03f

Activity 15.02 | Entering Text, Using AutoComplete, and Using the Name Box to Select a Cell

A text value usually provides information about number values in other worksheet cells. For example, a title such as Second Quarter Cardio Sales gives the reader an indication that the data in the worksheet relates to information about sales of cardio equipment during the three-month period April through June.

1 Point to and then click the cell at the intersection of **column A** and **row 1** to make it the *active cell*—the cell is outlined and ready to accept data.

The intersecting column letter and row number form the *cell reference*—also called the *cell address*. When a cell is active, its column letter and row number are highlighted. The cell reference of the selected cell, *A1*, displays in the Name Box.

2 With cell **A1** as the active cell, type the worksheet title **Pro Fit Marietta** and then press `Enter`. Compare your screen with Figure 15.6.

Text or numbers in a cell are referred to as *data*. You must confirm the data you type in a cell by pressing `Enter` or by some other keyboard movement, such as pressing `Tab` or an arrow key. Pressing `Enter` moves the active cell to the cell below.

FIGURE 15.6

Excel 2016, Windows 10, Microsoft Corporation

3 In cell **A1**, notice that the text does not fit; the text extends into cell **B1** to the right.

If text is too long for a cell and cells to the right are empty, the text will display. If the cells to the right contain other data, only the text that will fit in the cell displays.

4 In cell **A2**, type the worksheet subtitle **Second Quarter Cardio Sales** and then press `Enter`. Compare your screen with Figure 15.7.

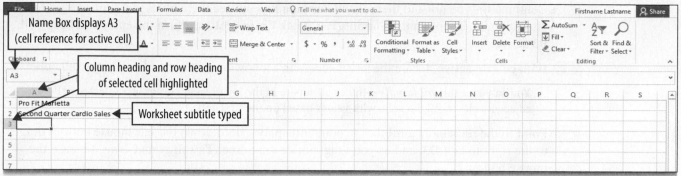

FIGURE 15.7

Excel 2016, Windows 10, Microsoft Corporation

5 Above **column A**, click in the **Name Box** to select the cell reference *A3*. Type **a4** and then press Enter to make cell **A4** the active cell. In cell **A4**, type **Exercise Bikes** to form the first row title, and then press Enter.

The text characters that you typed align at the left edge of the cell—referred to as *left alignment*—and cell A5 becomes the active cell. Left alignment is the default for text values. You can type a cell address in the Name Box and press Enter to move to a specific cell quickly.

6 In cell **A5**, type **E** and notice the text from the previous cell displays.

If the first characters you type in a cell match an existing entry in the column, Excel fills in the remaining characters for you. This feature, called *AutoComplete*, assists only with alphabetic values.

7 Continue typing the remainder of the row title **lliptical Machines** and press Enter.

The AutoComplete suggestion is removed when the entry you are typing differs from the previous value.

8 In cell **A6**, type **Treadmills** and press Enter. In cell **A7**, type **Rowing Machines** and press Enter. In cell **A8**, type **Total** and press Enter. On the Quick Access Toolbar, click **Save** 🖫.

🔄 **ANOTHER WAY**   Use the keyboard shortcut Ctrl + S to save changes to your workbook.

Activity 15.03 | Using Auto Fill and Keyboard Shortcuts

1 Click cell **B3**. Type **A** and notice that when you begin to type in a cell, on the **Formula Bar**, the **Cancel** and **Enter** buttons become active, as shown in Figure 15.8.

FIGURE 15.8

Excel 2016, Windows 10, Microsoft Corporation

2 Continue to type **pril** and then on the **Formula Bar**, notice that values you type in a cell also display there. Then, on the **Formula Bar**, click **Enter** ☑ to confirm the entry and keep cell **B3** active.

3 With cell **B3** active, locate the small square in the lower right corner of the selected cell.

You can drag this **fill handle**—the small square in the lower right corner of a selected cell—to adjacent cells to fill the cells with values based on the first cell.

4 Point to the **fill handle** until the ⊞ pointer displays, hold down the left mouse button, drag to the right to cell **D3**, and as you drag, notice the ScreenTips *May* and *June*. Release the mouse button.

5 Under the text that you just filled, click the **Auto Fill Options** button ⊞ that displays, and then compare your screen with Figure 15.9.

Auto Fill generates and extends a *series* of values into adjacent cells based on the value of other cells. A series is a group of things that come one after another in succession; for example, *April*, *May*, *June*.

The Auto Fill Options button displays options to fill the data; options vary depending on the content and program from which you are filling, and the format of the data you are filling.

Fill Series is selected, indicating the action that was taken. Because the options are related to the current task, the button is referred to as being *context sensitive*.

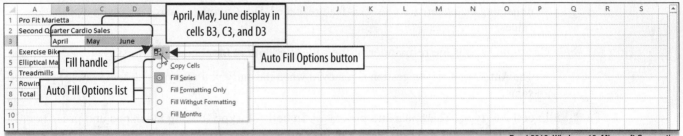

FIGURE 15.9

Excel 2016, Windows 10, Microsoft Corporation

6 Click in any cell to cancel the display of the list.

The list no longer displays; the button will display until you perform some other screen action.

7 Press Ctrl + Home, which is the keyboard shortcut to make cell **A1** active.

8 On the Quick Access Toolbar, click **Save** 🖫 to save the changes you have made to your workbook.

9 Take a moment to study the table in Figure 15.10 to become familiar with keyboard shortcuts with which you can navigate the Excel worksheet.

KEYBOARD SHORTCUTS TO NAVIGATE THE EXCEL WORKSHEET	
TO MOVE THE LOCATION OF THE ACTIVE CELL:	**PRESS:**
Up, down, right, or left one cell	↑, ↓, →, ←
Down one cell	Enter
Up one cell	Shift + Enter
Up one full screen	PageUp
Down one full screen	PageDown
To column A of the current row	Home
To the last cell in the last column of the active area (the rectangle formed by all the rows and columns in a worksheet that contain entries)	Ctrl + End
To cell A1	Ctrl + Home
Right one cell	Tab
Left one cell	Shift + Tab
To the cell one worksheet window to the right	Alt + PageDown
To the cell one worksheet window to the left	Alt + PageUp
To the cell containing specific content that you enter in the Find and Replace dialog box	Shift + F5
To the cell that corresponds with the cell reference you enter in the Go To dialog box	F5

FIGURE 15.10

Gaskin, Shelley. Go! All in One, 3E. Pearson Education, 2017.

2.03j (i)

Activity 15.04 | Aligning Text and Adjusting the Size of Columns

1 In the **column heading area**, point to the vertical line between **column A** and **column B** to display the ⊞ pointer, press and hold down the left mouse button, and then compare your screen with Figure 15.11.

A ScreenTip displays information about the width of the column. The default width of a column is 64 *pixels*. A pixel, short for *picture element*, is a point of light measured in dots per square inch. Sixty-four pixels equal 8.43 characters, which is the average number of characters that will fit in a cell using the default font. The default font in Excel is Calibri and the default font size is 11.

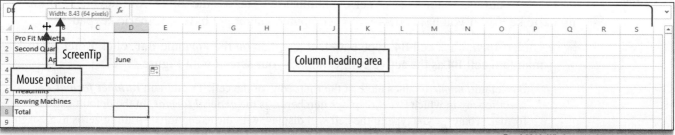

FIGURE 15.11

Excel 2016, Windows 10, Microsoft Corporation

2 Drag to the right, and when the number of pixels indicated in the ScreenTip reaches **120 pixels**, release the mouse button. If you are not satisfied with your result, click Undo ↻ on the Quick Access Toolbar and begin again.

This width accommodates the longest row title in cells A4 through A8—*Elliptical Machines*. The worksheet subtitle in cell A2 spans more than one column and still does not fit in column A.

3 > Point to cell **B3** and then drag across to select cells **B3**, **C3**, and **D3**. Compare your screen with Figure 15.12; if you are not satisfied with your result, click anywhere and begin again.

The three cells, B3 through D3, are selected and form a *range*—two or more cells on a worksheet that are adjacent (next to each other) or nonadjacent (not next to each other). This range of cells is referred to as *B3:D3*. When you see a colon (:) between two cell references, the range includes all the cells between the two cell references.

A range of cells you select this way is indicated by a dark border, and Excel treats the range as a single unit so you can make the same changes to more than one cell at a time. The selected cells in the range are highlighted except for the first cell in the range, which displays in the Name Box.

When you select a range of data, the *Quick Analysis tool* displays in the lower right corner of the selected range, with which you can analyze your data by using Excel tools such as charts, color-coding, and formulas.

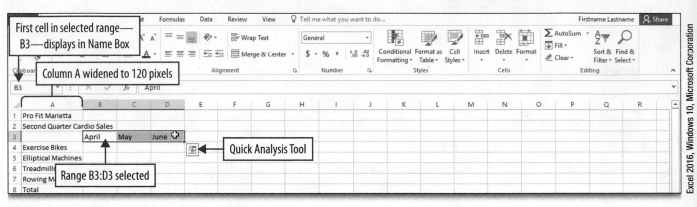

FIGURE 15.12

BY TOUCH — To select a range, tap a cell to display a circular gripper in the upper left and lower right corners of the cell, and then drag one of the grippers as necessary to select the desired range.

4 > With the range **B3:D3** selected, point anywhere over the selected range, right-click, and then on the mini toolbar, click **Center** 🔲. On the Quick Access Toolbar, click **Save** 🔲.

The column titles *April*, *May*, *June* align in the center of each cell.

Activity 15.05 | Entering Numbers

To type number values, use either the number keys across the top of your keyboard or the numeric keypad if you have one—laptop computers might not have a numeric keypad.

1 > Under *April*, click cell **B4**, type **68991.12** and then on the **Formula Bar**, click **Enter** ✓ to maintain cell **B4** as the active cell. Compare your screen with Figure 15.13.

By default, *number* values align at the right edge of the cell. The default *number format*—a specific way in which Excel displays numbers—is the *general format*. In the default general format, whatever you type in the cell will display, with the exception of trailing zeros to the right of a decimal point. For example, in the number 237.50 the *0* following the *5* is a trailing zero and would not display.

Data that displays in a cell is the *displayed value*. Data that displays in the Formula Bar is the *underlying value*. The number of digits or characters that display in a cell—the displayed value—depends on the width of the column. Calculations on numbers will always be based on the underlying value, not the displayed value.

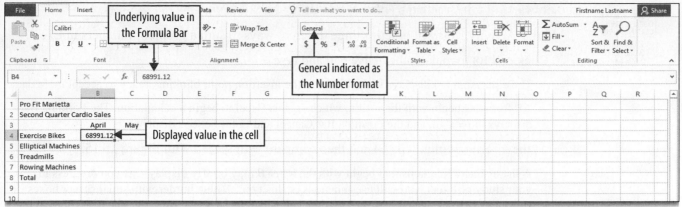

FIGURE 15.13

Excel 2016, Windows 10, Microsoft Corporation

2 ▸ Press Tab to make cell **C4** active. Type **86894.82** and then press Tab to move to cell **D4**. Type **99650.58** and then press Enter to move to cell **B5** in the next row. Then, by using the same technique, enter the remaining sales numbers as shown:

	APRIL	MAY	JUNE
Elliptical Machines	28836	22634.23	22828.78
Treadmills	59519.78	82337.98	99823.87
Rowing Machines	81267.17	87867.50	91669.98

3 ▸ Compare the numbers you entered with Figure 15.14, and then **Save** 🖫 your workbook.

In the default General format, trailing zeros to the right of a decimal point will not display. For example, when you type *87867.50*, the cell displays 87867.5 instead.

FIGURE 15.14

Excel 2016, Windows 10, Microsoft Corporation

Objective 3 Construct and Copy Formulas and Use the SUM Function

GO! Learn How
Video E15-3

A cell contains either a constant value (text or numbers) or a formula. A formula is an equation that performs mathematical calculations on values in other cells, and then places the result in the cell containing the formula. You can create formulas or use a *function*—a prewritten formula that looks at one or more values, performs an operation, and then returns a value.

Activity 15.06 | Constructing a Formula and Using the SUM Function

2.03e (i)
2.03e (ii)
2.03e (iii)

In this Activity, you will practice three different ways to sum a group of numbers in Excel.

1 Click cell **B8** to make it the active cell and type **=**

The equal sign (=) displays in the cell with the insertion point blinking, ready to accept more data.

All formulas begin with the = sign, which signals Excel to begin a calculation. The Formula Bar displays the = sign, and the Formula Bar Cancel and Enter buttons display.

2 At the insertion point, type **b4** and then compare your screen with Figure 15.15.

A list of Excel functions that begin with the letter *B* may briefly display—as you progress in your study of Excel, you will use functions of this type. A blue border with small corner boxes surrounds cell B4, which indicates that the cell is part of an active formula. The color used in the box matches the color of the cell reference in the formula.

Excel 2016, Windows 10, Microsoft Corporation

FIGURE 15.15

3 At the insertion point, type **+** and then type **b5**

A border of another color surrounds cell B5, and the color matches the color of the cell reference in the active formula. When typing cell references, it is not necessary to use uppercase letters.

4 At the insertion point, type **+b6+b7** and then press Enter.

The result of the formula calculation—*238614.1*—displays in the cell. Recall that in the default General format, trailing zeros do not display.

5 Click cell **B8** again, look at the **Formula Bar**, and then compare your screen with Figure 15.16.

The formula adds the values in cells B4 through B7, and the result displays in cell B8. In this manner, you can construct a formula by typing. Although cell B8 displays the *result* of the formula, the formula itself displays in the Formula Bar. This is referred to as the ***underlying formula***.

Always view the Formula Bar to be sure of the exact content of a cell—*a displayed number may actually be a formula.*

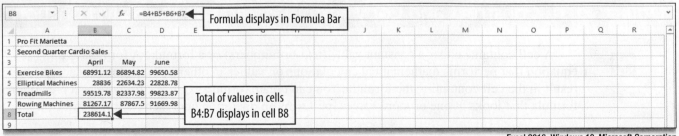

Excel 2016, Windows 10, Microsoft Corporation

FIGURE 15.16

6 Click cell **C8** and type **=** to signal the beginning of a formula. Then, point to cell **C4** and click one time.

> The reference to the cell C4 is added to the active formula. A moving border surrounds the referenced cell, and the border color and the color of the cell reference in the formula are color coded to match.

7 At the insertion point, type **+** and then click cell **C5**. Repeat this process to complete the formula to add cells **C6** and **C7**, and then press Enter.

> The result of the formula calculation—*279734.5*—displays in the cell. This method of constructing a formula is the ***point and click method***.

8 Click cell **D8**. On the **Home tab**, in the **Editing group**, click **AutoSum**, and then compare your screen with Figure 15.17.

> SUM is an Excel function—a prewritten formula. A moving border surrounds the range D4:D7 and =*SUM(D4:D7)* displays in cell D8.

> The = sign signals the beginning of a formula, *SUM* indicates the type of calculation that will take place (addition), and *(D4:D7)* indicates the range of cells on which the sum calculation will be performed. A ScreenTip provides additional information about the action.

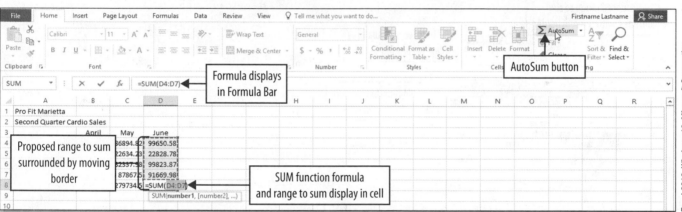

FIGURE 15.17

🔄 **ANOTHER WAY**   Use the keyboard shortcut Alt + =; or, on the Formulas tab, in the Function Library group, click the AutoSum button.

---

9 Look at the **Formula Bar**, and notice that the formula also displays there. Then, look again at the cells surrounded by the moving border.

> When you activate the ***Sum function***, Excel first looks *above* the active cell for a range of cells to sum. If no range is above the active cell, Excel will look to the *left* for a range of cells to sum. If the proposed range is not what you want to calculate, you can select a different group of cells.

10 Press Enter to construct a formula by using the prewritten SUM function.

> Your total is *313973.2*. Because the Sum function is frequently used, it has its own button in the Editing group on the Home tab of the ribbon. A larger version of the button also displays on the Formulas tab in the Function Library group. This button is also referred to as ***AutoSum***.

11 Notice that the totals in the range **B8:D8** display only one decimal place. Click **Save** 🖫.

> Number values that are too long to fit in the cell do *not* spill over into the unoccupied cell to the right in the same manner as text values. Rather, Excel rounds the number to fit the space.

> ***Rounding*** is a procedure that determines which digit at the right of the number will be the last digit displayed and then increases it by one if the next digit to its right is 5, 6, 7, 8, or 9.

Activity 15.07 | Copying a Formula by Using the Fill Handle

You have practiced three ways to create a formula—by typing, by using the point-and-click technique, and by using a Function button from the ribbon. You can also copy formulas. When you copy a formula from one cell to another, Excel adjusts the cell references to fit the new location of the formula.

1 Click cell **E3**, type **Total** and then press Enter.

The text in cell E3 is centered because the centered format continues from the adjacent cell.

2 With cell **E4** as the active cell, hold down Alt, and then press =. Compare your screen with Figure 15.18.

Alt + = is the keyboard shortcut for the SUM function. Recall that Excel first looks above the selected cell for a proposed range of cells to sum, and if no data is detected, Excel looks to the left and proposes a range of cells to sum.

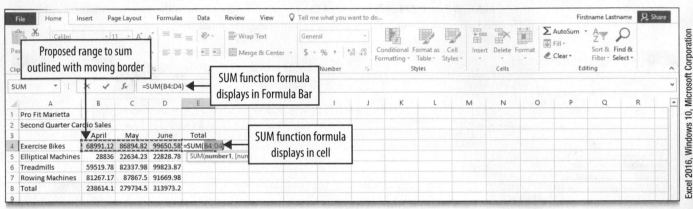

FIGURE 15.18

3 On the **Formula Bar**, click **Enter** ✓ to display the result and keep cell **E4** active.

The total dollar amount of *Exercise Bikes* sold in the quarter is *255536.5*. In cells E5:E8, you can see that you need a formula similar to the one in E4, but formulas that refer to the cells in row 5, row 6, and so on.

4 With cell **E4** active, point to the fill handle in the lower right corner of the cell until the + pointer displays. Then, drag down through cell **E8**; if you are not satisfied with your result, on the Quick Access Toolbar, click Undo ↺ and begin again. Compare your screen with Figure 15.19.

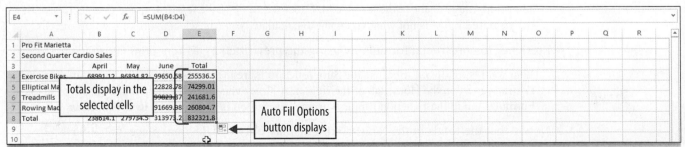

FIGURE 15.19

5 Click cell **E5**, look at the **Formula Bar**, and notice the formula =*SUM(B5:D5)*. Click cell **E6**, look at the **Formula Bar**, and then notice the formula =*SUM(B6:D6)*.

In each row, Excel copied the formula but adjusted the cell references *relative to* the row number. This is called a ***relative cell reference***—a cell reference based on the relative position of the cell that contains the formula and the cells referred to in the formula.

The calculation is the same, but it is performed on the cells in that particular row. Use this method to insert numerous formulas into spreadsheets quickly.

6 Click cell **F3**, type **Trend** and then press [Enter]. **Save** 💾 your workbook.

Objective 4 | Format Cells with Merge & Center, Cell Styles, and Themes

GO! Learn How
Video E15-4

IC3
DIGITAL LITERACY
CERTIFICATION
2.03i
2.03i (i)

Format—change the appearance of—cells to make your worksheet attractive and easy to read.

Activity 15.08 | Using Merge & Center and Applying Cell Styles

1 Select the range **A1:F1**, and then in the **Alignment group**, click **Merge & Center**. Then, select the range **A2:F2** and click **Merge & Center**.

The *Merge & Center* command joins selected cells into one larger cell and centers the contents in the merged cell; individual cells in the range B1:F1 and B2:F2 can no longer be selected—they are merged into cell A1 and A2, respectively.

🔄 **ANOTHER WAY**   Select the range, right-click over the selection, and then on the mini toolbar, click the Merge & Center command.

2 Click cell **A1**. In the **Styles group**, click **Cell Styles**, and then compare your screen with Figure 15.20.

A *cell style* is a defined set of formatting characteristics, such as font, font size, font color, cell borders, and cell shading.

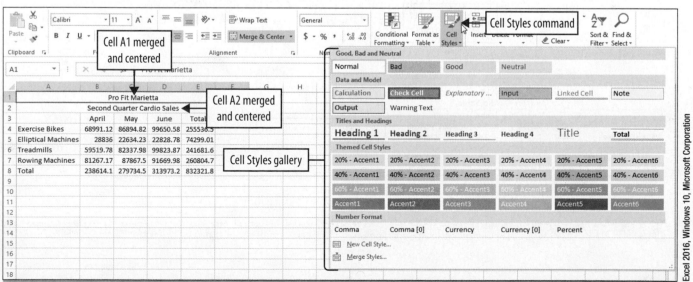

FIGURE 15.20

3 In the displayed gallery, under **Titles and Headings**, click **Title** and notice that the row height adjusts to accommodate the larger font size.

4 Click cell **A2**, display the **Cell Styles** gallery, and then under **Titles and Headings**, click **Heading 1**.

Use cell styles to maintain a consistent look in a worksheet and across worksheets in a workbook.

5 Select the horizontal range **B3:F3**, hold down Ctrl, and then select the vertical range **A4:A8** to select the column titles and the row titles. Release Ctrl.

Use this technique to select two or more ranges that are nonadjacent—not next to each other.

6 With the two ranges selected, display the **Cell Styles** gallery, click **Heading 4** to apply this cell style to the column titles and row titles, and then **Save** 🖫 your workbook.

Activity 15.09 | Formatting Financial Numbers

1 Select the range **B4:E4**, hold down Ctrl, and then select the range **B8:E8**. Release Ctrl.

This range is referred to as *b4:e4,b8:e8* with a comma separating the references to the two nonadjacent ranges.

🔄 ANOTHER WAY   In the Name Box type b4:e4,b8:e8 and then press Enter.

2 With the two ranges selected, on the **Home tab**, in the **Number group**, click **Accounting Number Format** $ ·. Compare your screen with Figure 15.21.

The *Accounting Number Format* applies a thousand comma separator where appropriate, inserts a fixed U.S. dollar sign aligned at the left edge of the cell, applies two decimal places, and leaves a small amount of space at the right edge of the cell to accommodate a parenthesis when negative numbers are present. Excel widens the columns to accommodate the formatted numbers.

At the bottom of your screen, in the status bar, Excel displays the results for some common calculations that might be made on the range; for example, the Average of the numbers selected and the Count—the number of items selected.

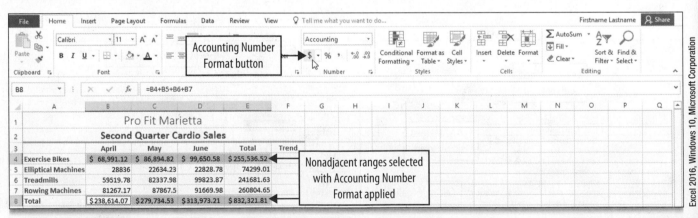

FIGURE 15.21

🔄 ANOTHER WAY   Display the Cell Styles gallery, and under Number Format, click Currency.

3 Select the range **B5:E7**, and then in the **Number group**, click **Comma Style** ⟨,⟩.

The **Comma Style** inserts a thousand comma separator where appropriate and applies two decimal places. Comma Style also leaves space at the right to accommodate a parenthesis when negative numbers are present.

When preparing worksheets with financial information, the first row of dollar amounts and the total row of dollar amounts are formatted in the **Accounting Number Format**; that is, with thousand comma separators, dollar signs, two decimal places, and space at the right to accommodate a parenthesis for negative numbers, if any. Rows that are *not* the first row or the total row should be formatted with the Comma Style.

4 Select the range **B8:E8**. In the **Styles group**, display the **Cell Styles** gallery, and then under **Titles and Headings**, click **Total**. Click any blank cell to cancel the selection, and then compare your screen with Figure 15.22.

This is a common way to apply borders to financial information. The single border indicates that calculations were performed on the numbers above, and the double border indicates that the information is complete. Sometimes financial documents do not display values with cents; rather, the values are rounded up. You can do this by selecting the cells, and then clicking the Decrease Decimal button two times.

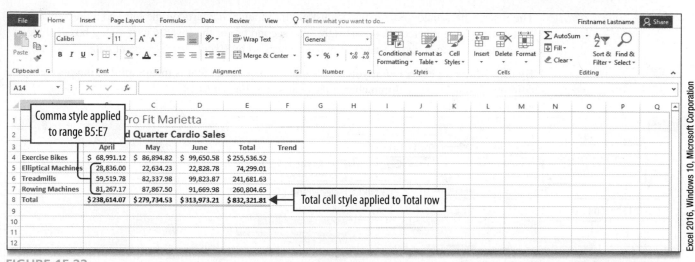

FIGURE 15.22

Activity 15.10 | Changing the Workbook Theme

A **theme** is a predefined set of colors, fonts, lines, and fill effects that coordinate for an attractive look.

1 Click the **Page Layout tab**, and then in the **Themes group**, click **Themes**.

2 Click the **Retrospect** theme, and notice that the cell styles change to match the new theme. Click **Save** 🖫.

More Knowledge | **Formatting a Cell's Font, Style, Size, or Color with Individual Commands**

Instead of using Cell Styles, you could use a combination of individual commands to format a cell. For example, on the Home tab, in the Font group, you can change a cell's font by clicking the Font arrow and selecting a different font. You can change the font size by clicking the Font Size arrow and selecting a size. From the same group, you can apply various styles to the cell—such as Bold or Italic or Underline. To change a cell's font color, in the Font Group, click the Font Color arrow and select a different color.

GO! Learn How
Video E15-5

DIGITAL LITERACY
CERTIFICATION

2.03g
2.03g (i)
2.03g (ii)

A *chart* is a graphic representation of data in a worksheet. Data in a chart is easier to understand than a table of numbers. *Sparklines* are tiny charts embedded in a cell that give a visual trend summary alongside your data. A sparkline makes a pattern more obvious to the eye.

Activity 15.11 | Charting Data and Using Recommended Charts to Select and Insert a Column Chart

Recommended Charts is an Excel feature that displays a customized set of charts that, according to Excel's calculations, will best fit your data based on the range of data that you select. In this Activity, you will create a *column chart* showing the monthly sales of cardio equipment by category during the second quarter. A column chart is useful for illustrating comparisons among related numbers. The chart will enable the company president, Michelle Barry, to see a pattern of overall monthly sales.

1 Select the range **A3:D7**.

When charting data, typically you should *not* include totals—include only the data you want to compare.

2 With the data that you want to compare selected, click the **Insert tab**, and then in the **Charts group**, click **Recommended Charts**. Compare your screen with Figure 15.23.

The Insert Chart dialog box displays a list of recommended charts on the left and a preview of the first chart, which is selected, on the right. The second tab of the Insert Chart dialog box includes all chart types—even those that are not recommended by Excel for this type of data.

By using different *chart types*, you can display data in a way that is meaningful to the reader—common examples are column charts, pie charts, and line charts.

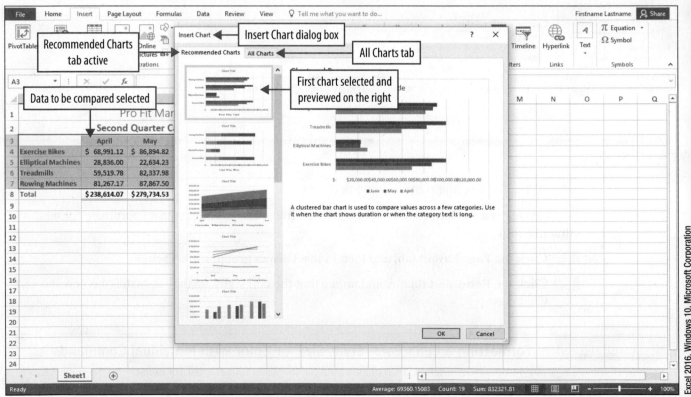

FIGURE 15.23

3 In the **Insert Chart** dialog box, use the scroll bar to scroll down about one-third of the way, and then click the second Clustered Column chart. Compare your screen with Figure 15.24.

Here, *each type of cardio equipment* displays its *sales for each month*. A clustered column chart is useful to compare values across a few categories, especially if the order of categories is not important.

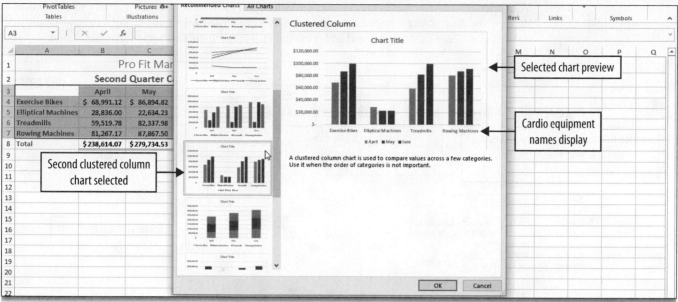

FIGURE 15.24

4 In the **Insert Chart** dialog box, click the chart directly above the selected chart—the first clustered column chart. Compare your screen with Figure 15.25.

In this clustered column chart, *each month* displays its *sales for each type of cardio equipment*. When constructing a chart, you can switch the row and column data in this manner to display the data in a way that is most useful to the reader. Here, the president of Pro Fit Marietta wants to compare sales of each type of equipment by month to detect patterns.

The comparison of data—either by month or by type of equipment—depends on the type of analysis you want to perform. You can select either chart, or, after your chart is complete, you can use the *Switch/Row Column* command on the ribbon to swap the data over the axis; that is, data being charted on the vertical axis will move to the horizontal axis and vice versa.

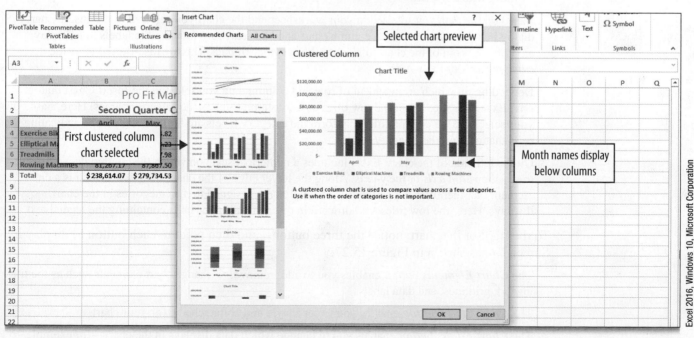

FIGURE 15.25

5 In the lower right corner of the **Insert Chart** dialog box, click **OK** to insert the selected chart into the worksheet. Compare your screen with Figure 15.26.

Your selected column chart displays in the worksheet, and the charted data is bordered by colored lines. Because the chart object is selected—surrounded by a border and displaying sizing handles—contextual tools named *Chart Tools* display and add contextual tabs next to the standard tabs on the ribbon.

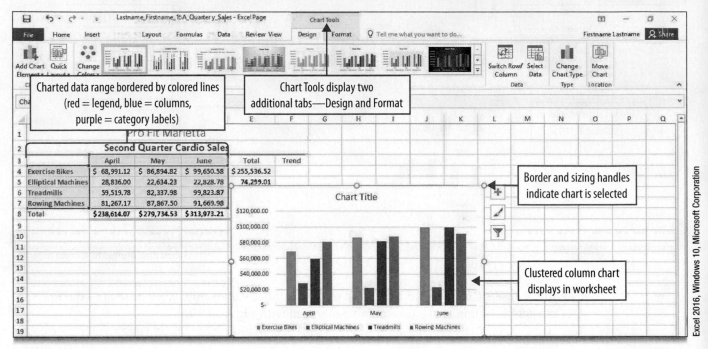

FIGURE 15.26

DIGITAL LITERACY
CERTIFICATION
2.03g (iii)

Activity 15.12 | Using the Chart Tools to Apply Chart Styles

1 On the ribbon, locate the contextual tabs under **Chart Tools—Design** and **Format**.

When a chart is selected, Chart Tools become available and these two tabs provide commands for working with the chart.

Based on the data you selected in your worksheet and the chart you selected in the Insert Chart dialog box, Excel constructs a column chart and adds *category labels*—the labels that display along the bottom of the chart to identify the category of data. This area is referred to as the *category axis* or the *x-axis*.

Depending on which arrangement of row and column data you select in the Insert Chart dialog box, Excel arranges either the row titles or the column titles as the category names. Here, based on your selection, the column titles that form the category labels are bordered in purple, indicating the cells that contain the category names.

On the left side of the chart, Excel includes a numerical scale on which the charted data is based; this is the *value axis* or the *y-axis*. Along the lower edge of the chart, a *legend*, which is a chart element that identifies the patterns or colors that are assigned to the categories in the chart, displays. Here, the row titles are bordered in red, indicating the cells containing the legend text.

2 To the right of the chart, notice the three buttons, and then point to each button to display its ScreenTip, as shown in Figure 15.27.

The *Chart Elements button* enables you to add, remove, or change chart elements such as the title, legend, gridlines, and data labels.

The *Chart Styles button* enables you to set a style and color scheme for your chart.

The *Chart Filters button* enables you to change which data displays in the chart—for example, to see only the data for *May* and *June* or only the data for *Treadmills* and *Rowing Machines*.

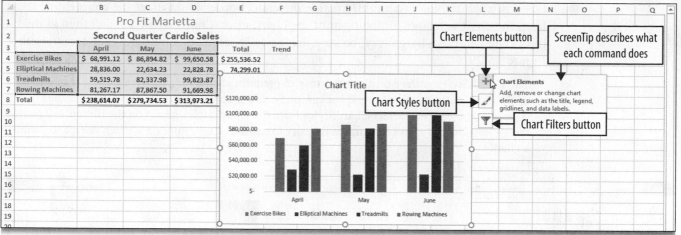

FIGURE 15.27

Excel 2016, Windows 10, Microsoft Corporation

3 ▸ In the worksheet data, locate the group of cells bordered in blue.

Each of the twelve cells bordered in blue is referred to as a ***data point***—a value that originates in a worksheet cell. Each data point is represented in the chart by a ***data marker***—a column, bar, area, dot, pie slice, or other symbol in a chart that represents a single data point.

Related data points form a ***data series***; for example, there is a data series for *April*, for *May*, and for *June*. Each data series has a unique color or pattern represented in the chart legend.

4 ▸ On the **Design tab**, in the **Chart Layouts group**, click **Quick Layout**, and then compare your screen with Figure 15.28.

In the Quick Layout gallery, you can change the overall layout of the chart by selecting a predesigned ***chart layout***—a combination of chart elements, which can include a title, legend, labels for the columns, and the table of charted cells.

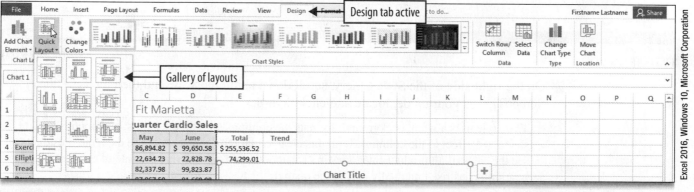

FIGURE 15.28

Excel 2016, Windows 10, Microsoft Corporation

5 ▸ *Point* to several different layouts to see how Live Preview displays the effect on your chart, and then click the **Quick Layout** button again without changing the layout.

6 ▸ In the chart, click anywhere in the text *Chart Title* to select the title box, watch the **Formula Bar** as you begin to type **Second** and notice that AutoComplete fills in the subtitle for you. Press Enter at any point to insert the worksheet subtitle as the chart title.

7 Click in a white area just slightly *inside* the chart border to deselect the chart title but keep the chart selected. To the right of the chart, click **Chart Styles** [✎], and then at the top of the **Chart Styles** gallery, be sure that **Style** is selected. Compare your screen with Figure 15.29.

The *Chart Styles gallery* displays an array of predefined *chart styles*—the overall visual look of the chart in terms of its colors, backgrounds, and graphic effects such as flat or shaded columns. You can also select Chart Styles from the Chart Styles group on the ribbon, but having the gallery closer to the chart makes it easier to use a touch gesture on a touch device to format a chart.

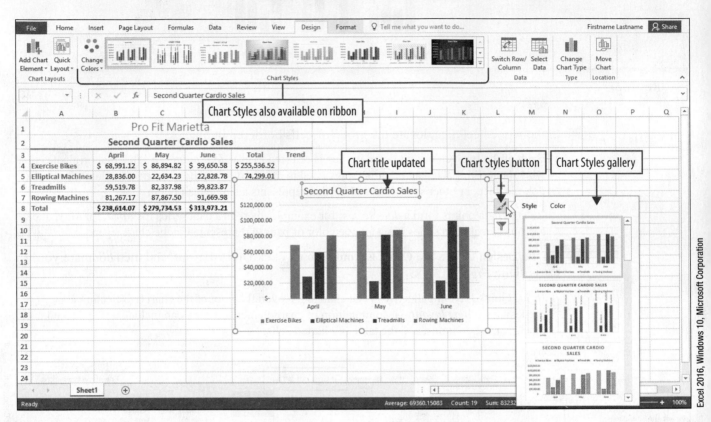

FIGURE 15.29

8 On the right side of the **Style** gallery, scroll down about halfway, and then by using the ScreenTips as your guide, locate and click **Style 6**.

This style uses a white background, formats the columns with theme colors, and applies a slight shadowed effect to the columns. With this clear visual representation of the data, the president can see the sales of all product categories in each month, and can see that the sale of exercise bikes and treadmills has risen markedly during the quarter.

9 At the top of the gallery, click **Color**. Under **Colorful**, point to the third row of colors to display the ScreenTip *Color 3*, and then click to apply the **Color 3** variation of the theme colors.

10 Point to the top border of the chart to display the [↖️] pointer, and then drag the upper left corner of the chart just inside the upper left corner of cell **A10**, approximately as shown in Figure 15.30.

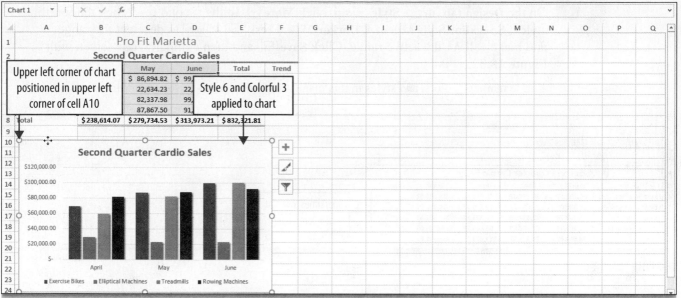

FIGURE 15.30

Excel 2016, Windows 10, Microsoft Corporation

11 Click any cell to deselect the chart, and notice that the chart buttons no longer display to the right of the chart and the Chart Tools no longer display on the ribbon. Click **Save** 🔲.

> Contextual tabs display when an object is selected and then are removed from view when the object is deselected.

Activity 15.13 | Creating and Formatting Sparklines

By creating sparklines, you provide a context for your numbers. Your readers will be able to see the relationship between a sparkline and its underlying data quickly.

1 Select the range **B4:D7**, which represents the monthly sales figures for each product and for each month. Click the **Insert tab**, and then in the **Sparklines group**, click **Line**. In the displayed **Create Sparklines** dialog box, notice that the selected range *B4:D7* displays.

2 With the insertion point blinking in the **Location Range** box, type **f4:f7** which is the range of cells where you want the sparklines to display. Compare your screen with Figure 15.31.

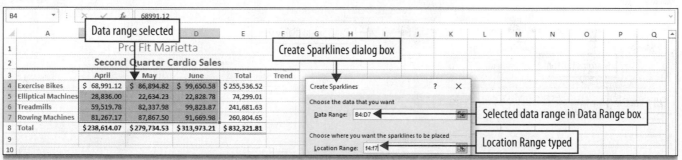

FIGURE 15.31

Excel 2016, Windows 10, Microsoft Corporation

🔄 **ANOTHER WAY**   In the worksheet, select the range F4:F7 to insert it into the Location Range box.

3 Click **OK** to insert the sparklines in the range **F4:F7**, and then on the **Design tab**, in the **Show group**, click the **Markers** check box to select it.

> Alongside each row of data, the sparkline provides a quick visual trend summary for sales of each cardio item over the three-month period. For example, you can see instantly that of the four items, only Elliptical Machines had declining sales for the period.

4 ▸ On the **Design tab**, in the **Style group**, click **More** ⊡. In the second row, click the fourth style—**Sparkline Style Accent 4, Darker 25%**. Press Ctrl + Home to deselect the range and make cell **A1** the active range. Click **Save** 🖫, and then compare your screen with Figure 15.32.

Use markers, colors, and styles in this manner to further enhance your sparklines.

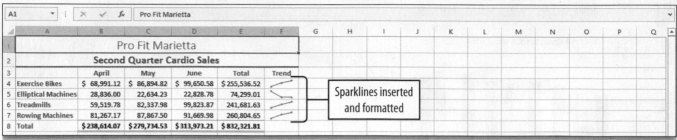

FIGURE 15.32

Objective 6 | Print a Worksheet, Display Formulas, and Close Excel

GO! Learn How
Video E15-6

Use the **Show Formulas** command to display the formula in each cell instead of the resulting value. Use the commands on the Page Layout tab to prepare for printing.

2.03j
2.03j (i)

Activity 15.14 | Creating a Footer and Centering a Worksheet

For each Excel project in this text, you will create a footer containing the file name, which includes your name and the project name. You will also center the data horizontally on the page to create an attractive result if your worksheet is printed.

1 ▸ If necessary, click cell **A1** to deselect the chart. Click the **Page Layout tab**, and then in the **Page Setup group**, click **Margins**. At the bottom of the **Margins** gallery, click **Custom Margins**, to display the **Page Setup** dialog box. Compare your screen with Figure 15.33.

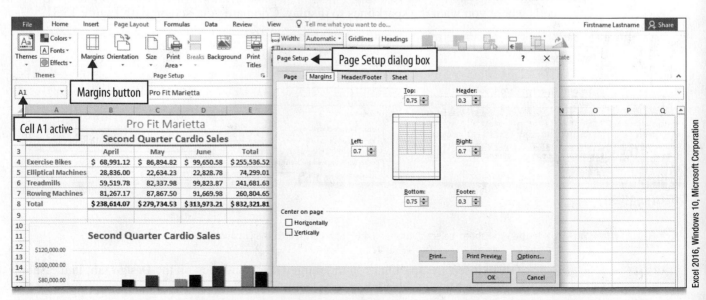

FIGURE 15.33

2 On the **Margins tab**, under **Center on page**, select the **Horizontally** check box.

This action will center the data and chart horizontally on the page, as shown in the Preview area.

3 In the **Page Setup** dialog box, click the **Header/Footer tab**, and then in the center of the dialog box, click **Custom Footer**. In the **Footer** dialog box, with your insertion point blinking in the **Left section**, on the row of buttons, click **Insert File Name** 🗋. Compare your screen with Figure 15.34.

&[File] displays in the Left section. Here you can type or insert information from the row of buttons into the left, middle, or right section of the footer. The Custom Header button displays a similar screen to enter information in the header of the worksheet.

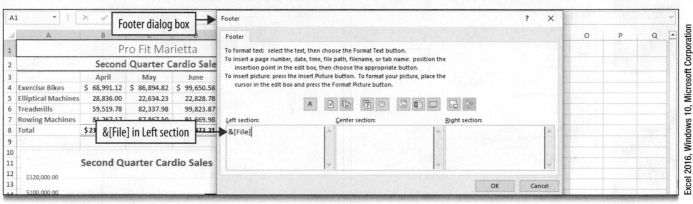

FIGURE 15.34

4 Click **OK** two times.

The vertical dotted line between columns indicates that as currently arranged, only the columns to the left of the dotted line will print on the first page. The exact position of the vertical line may depend on your default printer setting.

ANOTHER WAY Deselect the chart. On the Insert tab, in the Text group, click Header & Footer to display Page Layout view. Click in the left section of the displayed footer, and then in the Header & Footer Elements group, click File Name. Click any cell in the workbook to deselect the footer area, and then on the status bar, click the Normal button to return to Normal view.

Activity 15.15 | Adding Document Properties and Printing a Workbook

1 In the upper left corner of your screen, click the **File tab** to display **Backstage** view. In the lower right corner, click **Show All Properties**.

2 As the **Tags**, type **cardio sales** In the **Subject** box, type your course name and section number. Be sure your name displays in the **Author** box and edit if necessary.

3 On the left, click **Print** to view the **Print Preview**. Compare your screen with Figure 15.35.

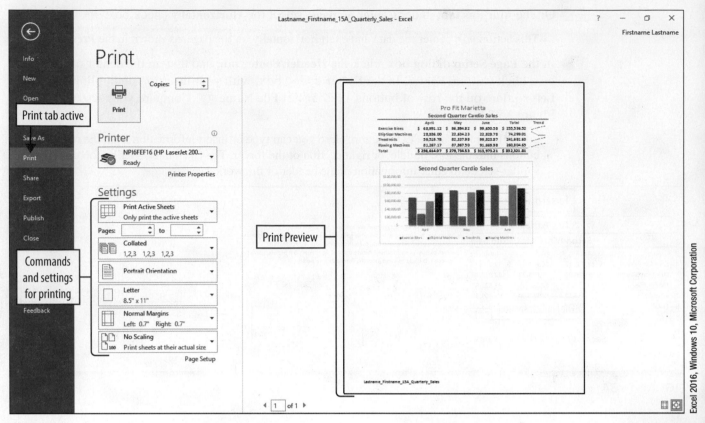

FIGURE 15.35

> **4** ▷ Note any adjustments that need to be made, and then on the left, click **Save** to save and return to the workbook.

NOTE **What Does Your Instructor Require for Submission? A Paper Printout, an Image That Looks Like a Printed Document, or Your Excel File?**

You can produce a paper printout of your worksheet or an electronic image of your worksheet that looks like a printed document. Or, your instructor may want only your completed Excel file.

> **5** ▷ If you are directed to print on paper, be sure that a printer is available to your system. Press `Ctrl` + `F2`, which is the keyboard shortcut to display the **Print Preview**, and then under **Print**, click the **Print** button.

> **6** ▷ If you are directed to create an electronic image of your worksheet that looks like a printed document, click the **File tab**, on the left click **Export**, and then on the right, click **Create PDF/XPS**. In the **Publish as PDF or XPS** dialog box, navigate to your storage location, in the **Save as type** box, be sure **PDF** is indicated, and then click **Publish** to create the PDF file.

Activity 15.16 | Printing a Section of the Worksheet

From Backstage view, you can print only the portion of the worksheet that you select, and there are times you might want to do this.

> **1** ▷ Select the range **A2:F5** to select only the subtitle and the data for *Exercise Bikes* and *Elliptical Machines* and the column titles.

2 Press [Ctrl] + [F2], which is the keyboard shortcut to display **Print Preview**, and then under **Settings**, click the first arrow, which currently displays *Print Active Sheets*. On the list that displays, click **Print Selection**, and then compare your screen with Figure 15.36.

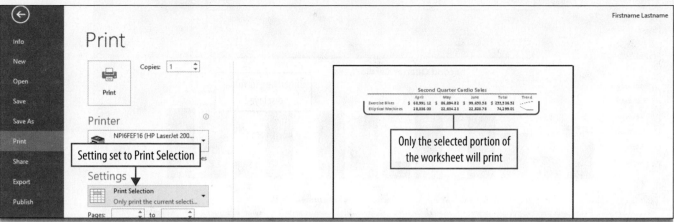

FIGURE 15.36

Excel 2016, Windows 10, Microsoft Corporation

3 If directed by your instructor, print the selection on paper; otherwise, in the upper left corner, click **Back** ⊙ to return to your workbook.

4 Press [Ctrl] + [Home], and then click **Save** 🔲.

Activity 15.17 | Changing Page Orientation and Displaying, Printing, and Hiding Formulas

When you type a formula in a cell, the cell displays the *results* of the formula calculation. Recall that this value is called the displayed value. You can view and print the underlying formulas in the cells. When you do so, a formula often takes more horizontal space to display than the result of the calculation.

1 If necessary, redisplay your worksheet. Because you will make some temporary changes to your workbook, on the Quick Access Toolbar, click **Save** 🔲 to be sure your work is saved up to this point.

2 On the **Formulas tab**, in the **Formula Auditing group**, click **Show Formulas**.

🔄 **ANOTHER WAY** Hold down [Ctrl], and then press [~] (usually located below [Esc]).

3 In the **column heading area**, point to the **column A** heading to display the ⬇ pointer, hold down the left mouse button, and then drag to the right to select columns **A:F**. Compare your screen with Figure 15.37.

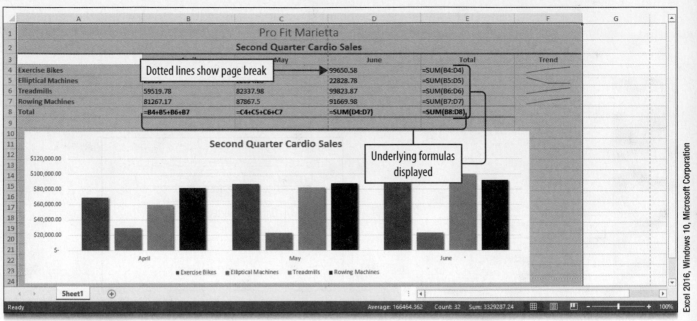

FIGURE 15.37

> **NOTE** Turning the Display of Formulas On and Off
>
> The Show Formulas button is a toggle button. Clicking it once turns the display of formulas on—the button will be shaded. Clicking the button again turns the display of formulas off.

4 ▸ Point to the column heading boundary between any two of the selected columns to display the ⊞ pointer, and then double-click to AutoFit the selected columns.

AutoFit adjusts the width of a column to fit the cell content of the *widest* cell in the column.

> ↻ **ANOTHER WAY** With the columns selected, on the Home tab, in the Cells group, click Format, and then click AutoFit Column Width.

5 ▸ On the **Page Layout tab**, in the **Page Setup group**, click **Orientation**, and then click **Landscape**. In the **Scale to Fit** group, click the **Width arrow**, and then click **1 page** to scale the data to fit onto one page.

Scaling shrinks the width or height of the printed worksheet to fit a maximum number of pages and is convenient for printing formulas. Although it is not always the case, formulas frequently take up more space than the actual data.

> ↻ **ANOTHER WAY** In the Scale to Fit group, click the Dialog Box Launcher button to display the Page tab of the Page Setup dialog box. Then, under Scaling, click the Fit to option button.

6 ▸ In the **Page Setup group**, click **Margins**, click **Custom Margins**, and then on the **Margins tab**, under **Center on page**, be sure the **Horizontally** check box is selected—select it if necessary.

7 ▸ Click **OK** to close the dialog box. Check to be sure your chart is centered below the data and the left and right edges are slightly inside column A and column F—use the ⛶ pointer to drag a chart edge and then deselect the chart if necessary.

8 ▶ Click any cell so that the chart is not selected, and then press ⌈Ctrl⌉ + ⌈F2⌉ to display the **Print Preview**. Under **Settings**, if necessary switch back to the option to **Print Active Sheets**. If directed to do so by your instructor, print on paper; or, to save the workbook in this format, click Save As and name the worksheet **Lastname_Firstname_15A_Quarterly_Sales_formulas**

   If you save the workbook with this new name, your original workbook is automatically saved and closed.

9 ▶ If you did not save your formulas worksheet, on the left, click **Close**, and when prompted, click **Don't Save** so that you do *not* save the changes you made—displaying formulas, changing column widths and orientation, and scaling—to print your formulas.

10 ▶ In the upper right corner of your screen, click **Close** ⌈✕⌉ to close Excel.

> **END | You have completed Project 15A**

GO! With Google

Objective | Create a Sales Report with an Embedded Column Chart Using Google Sheets

> **ALERT!** **Working with Web-Based Applications and Services**
>
> Computer programs and services on the web receive continuous updates and improvements, so the steps to complete this web-based Activity may differ from the ones shown. You can often look at the screens and the information presented to determine how to complete the Activity.
>
> If you do not already have a Google account, you will need to create one before you begin this Activity. Go to http://google.com and in the upper right corner, click Sign In. On the Sign In screen, click Create Account. On the Create your Google Account page, complete the form, read and agree to the Terms of Service and Privacy Policy, and then click Next step. On the Welcome screen, click Get Started.

Activity | Creating a Sales Report with an Embedded Column Chart Using Google Sheets

In this Activity, you will use Google Sheets to create a sales report and chart similar to the one you created in Project 15A.

1 From the desktop, open your browser, (use a browser other than Edge), navigate to **http://google.com** and then click the **Google Apps** menu ⊞. Click **Drive**, and then if necessary, sign in to your Google account.

2 Open your **GO! Web Projects** folder—or click NEW to create and then open this folder if necessary.

3 In the left pane, click **NEW**, and then click **Google Sheets**. From your Windows taskbar, open **File Explorer**, navigate to your Student Data Files for this chapter, and then in the **File List**, double-click to open **e15_15A_Web**.

4 In the displayed Excel worksheet, select the range **A1:E8**, right-click over the selection, click **Copy**, and then **Close** Excel. **Close** the **File Explorer** window.

5 In your blank Google Sheet, with cell **A1** active, point to cell **A1**, right-click, and then click **Paste**; by copying and pasting the data, you can create this project more quickly without having to do extra typing. In the column heading area, point to the border between **column A** and **column B** to display the ↔ pointer, and then widen **column A** slightly so that all of the data in rows 4–8 displays.

6 Select the range **A1:E1**. On the toolbar, click **Merge cells** ⊞. On the toolbar, click the **Align arrow** ▾, and then click **Center** ≣. Repeat for the range **A2:E2**, and then apply **Bold** **B** to cells **A1** and **A2**.

7 Select the range with the month names, center them, and apply **Bold** **B**. Apply **Bold** **B** to the totals in the range **B8:E8**.

8 Select the range **A3:D7** (the data without the totals and without the titles). On the menu bar, click **Insert**, and

then click **Chart**. In the **Chart Editor** dialog box, notice the three tabs.

9 In the **Chart Editor** window, with the first chart type selected, click the **Chart types tab**, and then select the **Switch rows/columns** check box.

10 Click the **Customization tab**. In the **Title** box, replace the existing text with **Second Quarter Cardio Sales**

11 Click the **Legend arrow**, and then click **None**. Click the **Background arrow**, and then in the fourth column, click the third color—**light yellow 3**.

12 In the lower left corner, click **Insert**. Point anywhere inside the selected chart, hold down the left mouse button to display the 🖑 pointer, and then drag the chart slightly below the data. Then using the corner sizing handles resize and reposition the chart attractively below the data.

13 At the top of the worksheet, click the text *Untitled spreadsheet*, and then using your own name, type **Lastname_Firstname_EX_15A_Web** and press ENTER.

14 If you are instructed to submit your file to your instructor, you can either share the file through Google Drive, or create a PDF or Excel file. Click the File menu, point to Download as, and click the format you want. The file will download to your default download folder as determined by your browser settings. Ask your instructor in what format he or she would like to receive your file.

15 **Close** the browser tab—a new Google Sheet always opens in a new window in your browser; your work is automatically saved. Notice that your new Google Sheet displays in the file list on your Google Drive. Sign out of your Google account.

PROJECT
15B

Inventory Valuation

MyITLab
Project 15B Training
Project 15B Grader

PROJECT ACTIVITIES

In Activities 15.18 through 15.27 you will create a workbook for Josh Feingold, Operations Manager, which calculates the retail value of an inventory of plyometric training products. Your completed worksheet will look similar to Figure 15.38.

PROJECT FILES

MyITLab
grader

If your instructor wants you to submit Project 15B in the MyITLab Grader system, log in to MyITLab, locate Grader Project 15B, and then download the files for this project.

For Project 15B, you will need the following file:
New blank Excel workbook

You will save your workbook as:
Lastname_Firstname_15B_Plyo_Products

PROJECT RESULTS

Pro Fit Marietta
Plyometric Products Inventory Valuation
As of September 30

	Warehouse Location	Quantity in Stock	Retail Price	Total Retail Value	Percent of Total Retail Value
Power Hurdle	Atlanta	125	$ 32.95	$ 4,118.75	1.41%
Speed Hurdle	Atlanta	995	59.95	59,650.25	20.37%
Stackable Steps	Marietta	450	251.59	113,215.50	38.65%
Pro Jump Rope	Marietta	1,105	49.95	55,194.75	18.84%
Plyometric Box Set	Marietta	255	158.05	40,302.75	13.76%
Plyometric Mat	Atlanta	215	94.99	20,422.85	6.97%
Total Retail Value for All Products				$ 292,904.85	

Lastname_Firstname_15B_Plyo_Products

FIGURE 15.38 Project 15B Plyo Products

Excel 2016, Windows 10, Microsoft Corporation

GO! Learn How
Video E15-7

In Excel, the spelling checker performs similarly to the other Microsoft Office programs.

Activity 15.18 | Checking Spelling in a Worksheet

> **ALERT!** To submit as an autograded project, log into MyITLab, download the files for this project, and begin with those files instead of a new blank workbook.

1 Start Excel and display a new blank workbook. In cell **A1**, type **Pro Fit Marietta** and press Enter. In cell **A2**, type **Plyometric Products Inventory** and press Enter.

2 Click the **File tab**, on the left click **Save As**, under **Save As**, click **Browse** to display the **Save As** dialog box, and then navigate to your **AIO Chapter 15** folder. As the **File name**, using your own name, type **Lastname_Firstname_15B_Plyo_Products** and then click **Save**.

3 Press Tab to move to cell **B3**, type **Quantity** and press Tab. In cell **C3**, type **Average Cost** and press Tab. In cell **D3**, type **Retail Price** and press Tab.

4 Click cell **C3**, and then look at the **Formula Bar**. Notice that in the cell, the displayed value is cut off; however, in the **Formula Bar**, the entire text value—the underlying value—displays. Compare your screen with Figure 15.39.

> Text that is too long to fit in a cell extends into cells on the right only if they are empty. If the cell to the right contains data, the text in the cell to the left is truncated—cut off. The entire value continues to exist, but it is not completely visible.

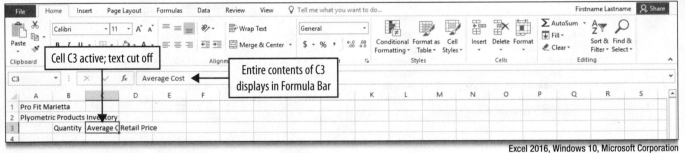

Excel 2016, Windows 10, Microsoft Corporation

FIGURE 15.39

5 Click cell **E3**, type **Total Retail Value** and press Tab. In cell **F3**, type **Percent of Total Retail Value** and press Enter.

6 Click cell **A4**. *Without* correcting the spelling error, type **Powr Hurdle** Press Enter. In the range **A5:A10**, type the remaining row titles shown below. Then compare your screen with Figure 15.40.

Speed Hurdle
Stackable Steps
Pro Jump Rope
Plyometric Box Set
Plyometric Mat
Total Retail Value for All Products

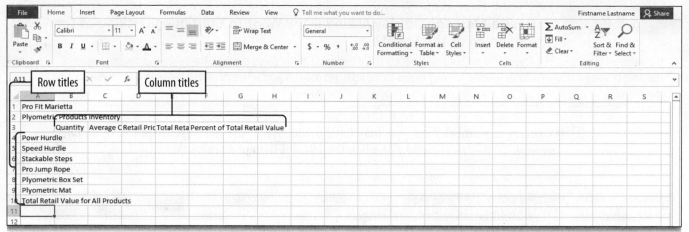

FIGURE 15.40

Excel 2016, Windows 10, Microsoft Corporation

7 In the **column heading area**, point to the right boundary of **column A** to display the ⊞ pointer, and then drag to the right to widen **column A** to **215** pixels.

8 Select the range **A1:F1**, **Merge & Center** the text, and then from the **Cell Styles** gallery, apply the **Title** style.

9 Select the range **A2:F2**, **Merge & Center** the text, and then from the **Cell Styles** gallery, apply the **Heading 1** style. Press Ctrl + Home to move to the top of your worksheet.

10 With cell **A1** as the active cell, click the **Review tab**, and then in the **Proofing group**, click **Spelling**. Compare your screen with Figure 15.41.

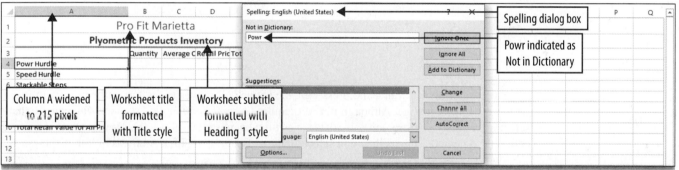

FIGURE 15.41

Excel 2016, Windows 10, Microsoft Corporation

ANOTHER WAY Press F7, which is the keyboard shortcut for the Spelling command.

11 In the **Spelling** dialog box, under **Not in Dictionary**, notice the word *Powr*.

The spelling tool does not have this word in its dictionary. Under *Suggestions*, Excel provides a list of suggested spellings.

12 Under **Suggestions**, click **Power**, and then click **Change**.

Powr, a typing error, is changed to *Power*. A message box displays *The spelling check is complete for the entire sheet*—unless you have additional unrecognized words. Because the spelling check begins its checking process starting with the currently selected cell, it is good practice to return to cell A1 before starting the Spelling command.

13 Correct any other errors you may have made. When the message displays, *Spell check complete. You're good to go!*, click **OK**. **Save** 🖫 your workbook.

Objective 8 Enter Data by Range

GO! Learn How
Video E15-8

IC3
DIGITAL LITERACY
CERTIFICATION
2.03f

You can enter data by first selecting a range of cells. This is a time-saving technique, especially if you use the numeric keypad to enter the numbers.

Activity 15.19 | Entering Data by Range

1 Select the range **B4:D9**, type **125** and then press Enter.

The value displays in cell B4, and cell B5 becomes the active cell.

2 With cell **B5** active in the range, and pressing Enter after each entry, type the following, and then compare your screen with Figure 15.42:

1125
450
1105
255
215

After you enter the last value and press Enter, the active cell moves to the top of the next column within the selected range. Although it is not required to enter data in this manner, you can see that selecting the range before you enter data saves time because it confines the movement of the active cell to the selected range. When you select a range of data, the Quick Analysis button displays.

FIGURE 15.42

Excel 2016, Windows 10, Microsoft Corporation

3 With the selected range still active, from the following table, beginning in cell **C4** and pressing Enter after each entry, enter the data for the **Average Cost** column and then the **Retail Price** column. If you prefer, deselect the range to enter the values— typing in a selected range is optional.

AVERAGE COST	RETAIL PRICE
15.50	32.95
29.55	59.95
125.95	251.59
18.75	49.95
85.25	159.05
49.95	94.99

Recall that the default number format for cells is the *General* number format, in which numbers display exactly as you type them and trailing zeros do not display, even if you type them.

4 Click any blank cell, and then compare your screen with Figure 15.43. Correct any errors you may have made while entering data, and then click **Save** 🖫.

	A	B	C	D	E	F	G
1	Pro Fit Marietta						
2	Plyometric Products Inventory						
3		Quantity	Average C	Retail Pric	Total Reta	Percent of Total Retail Value	
4	Power Hurdle	125	15.5	32.95			
5	Speed Hurdle	1125	29.55	59.95			
6	Stackable Steps	450	125.95	251.59			
7	Pro Jump Rope	1105	18.75	49.95			
8	Plyometric Box Set	255	85.25	159.05			
9	Plyometric Mat	215	49.95	94.99			
10	Total Retail Value for All Products						
11							

Data entered

Excel 2016, Windows 10, Microsoft Corporation

FIGURE 15.43

Objective 9 Construct Formulas for Mathematical Operations

GO! Learn How
Video E15-9

DIGITAL LITERACY
CERTIFICATION

2.03e
2.03e (i)
2.03e (iii)

Operators are symbols with which you can specify the type of calculation you want to perform in a formula.

Activity 15.20 | Using Arithmetic Operators

1 Click cell **E4**, type **=b4*d4** and notice that the two cells are outlined as part of an active formula. Then press Enter.

The *Total Retail Value* of all *Power Hurdle* items in inventory—*4118.75*—equals the *Quantity* (125) times the *Retail Price* (selling price) of 32.95. In Excel, the asterisk (*) indicates multiplication.

2 Take a moment to study the symbols you will use to perform basic mathematical operations in Excel as shown in the table in Figure 15.44, which are referred to as *arithmetic operators*.

SYMBOLS USED IN EXCEL FOR ARITHMETIC OPERATORS	
OPERATOR SYMBOL	OPERATION
+	Addition
–	Subtraction (also negation)
*	Multiplication
/	Division
%	Percent
^	Exponentiation

FIGURE 15.44

Gaskin, Shelley. Go! All in One, 3E. Pearson Education, 2017.

3 Click cell **E4**.

> You can see that in cells E5:E9 you need a formula similar to the one in E4, but one that refers to the cells in row 5, row 6, and so forth. Recall that you can copy formulas and the cell references will change *relative to* the row number.

4 With cell **E4** selected, position your pointer over the fill handle in the lower right corner of the cell until the + pointer displays. Then, drag down through cell **E9** to copy the formula.

5 Select the range **B4:B9**, and then on the **Home tab**, in the **Number group**, click **Comma Style** ⟨ , ⟩. In the **Number group**, click **Decrease Decimal** two times to remove the decimal places from these values.

> Comma Style formats a number with two decimal places; because these are whole numbers referring to quantities, no decimal places are necessary.

ANOTHER WAY   Select the range, display the Cell Styles gallery, and then under Number Format, click Comma [0].

6 Select the range **E4:E9**, and then at the bottom of your screen, in the status bar, notice the displayed values for **Average**, **Count**, and **Sum**—*50158.89167, 6* and *300953.35*.

> When you select a range of numerical data, Excel's *AutoCalculate* feature displays three calculations in the status bar by default—Average, Count, and Sum. Here, Excel indicates that if you averaged the selected values, the result would be *50158.89167*, there are *6* cells in the selection that contain values, and that if you added the values the result would be *300953.35*.

> You can display three additional calculations to this area by right-clicking the status bar and selecting them—Numerical Count, Minimum, and Maximum.

Activity 15.21 | Using the Quick Analysis Tool

Recall that the Quick Analysis button displays when you select a range of data. Quick Analysis is convenient because it keeps common commands close to your mouse pointer and also displays commands in a format that is easy to touch with your finger if you are using a touchscreen device.

1 Be sure the range **E4:E9** is still selected. In the lower right corner of the selected range, click **Quick Analysis**, and then in the displayed gallery, click **Totals**. *Point to*, but do not click, the first **Sum** button, which shows blue cells at the bottom. Compare your screen with Figure 15.45.

> Here, the shaded cells on the button indicate what will be summed and where the result will display, and a preview of the result displays in the cell bordered with a gray shadow.

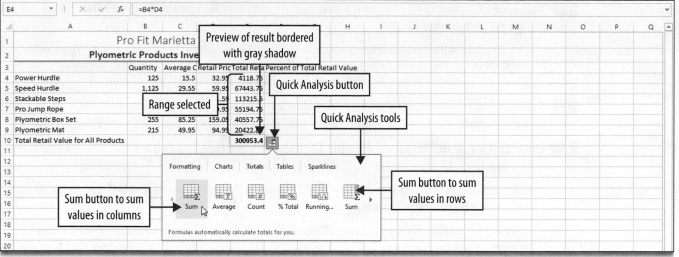

FIGURE 15.45

Excel 2016, Windows 10, Microsoft Corporation

2 Click the first **Sum** button to display the column total *300953.4* formatted in Bold.

Sums calculated using the Quick Analysis tool are formatted in Bold.

3 Select the range **C5:E9** and apply the **Comma Style** [,]; notice that Excel widens the columns to accommodate the data.

4 Select the range **C4:E4**, hold down Ctrl, and then click cell **E10**. Release Ctrl, and then apply the **Accounting Number Format** [$ ▾]. Notice that Excel widens the columns as necessary.

5 Click cell **E10**, and then from the **Cell Styles** gallery, apply the **Total** style. Click any blank cell, **Save** [🖫] your workbook, and then compare your screen with Figure 15.46.

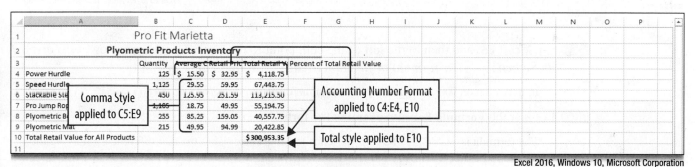

FIGURE 15.46

Excel 2016, Windows 10, Microsoft Corporation

2.03e (i)

Activity 15.22 | Copying Formulas Containing Absolute Cell References

In a formula, a *relative cell reference* refers to a cell by its position *relative to* the cell that contains the formula. An ***absolute cell reference***, on the other hand, refers to a cell by its *fixed* position in the worksheet, for example, the total in cell E10.

A relative cell reference automatically adjusts when a formula is copied. In some calculations, you do *not* want the cell reference to adjust; rather, you want the cell reference to remain the same when the formula is copied.

1 Click cell **F4**, type **=** and then click cell **E4**. Type **/** and then click cell **E10**.

The formula *=E4/E10* indicates that the value in cell E4 will be *divided* by the value in cell E10. Why? Because Mr. Feingold wants to know the percentage by which each product's Total Retail Value makes up the Total Retail Value for All Products.

Arithmetically, the percentage is computed by dividing the *Total Retail Value* for each product by the *Total Retail Value for All Products*. The result will be a percentage expressed as a decimal.

2 Press `Enter`. Click cell **F4** and notice that the formula displays in the **Formula Bar**. Then, point to cell **F4** and double-click.

> The formula, with the two referenced cells displayed in color and bordered with the same color, displays in the cell. This feature, called the *range finder*, is useful for verifying formulas because it visually indicates which workbook cells are included in a formula calculation.

3 Press `Enter` to redisplay the result of the calculation in the cell, and notice that .013686, which is approximately 1% of the total retail value of the inventory, is made up of Power Hurdles.

4 Click cell **F4** again, and then drag the fill handle down through cell **F9**. Compare your screen with Figure 15.47.

> Each cell displays an error message—*#DIV/0!* and a green triangle in the upper left corner of each cell indicates that Excel detects an error.

> Like a grammar checker, Excel uses rules to check for formula errors and flags errors in this manner. Additionally, the Auto Fill Options button displays, from which you can select formatting options for the copied cells.

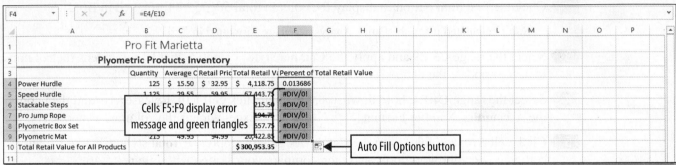

FIGURE 15.47

Excel 2016, Windows 10, Microsoft Corporation

5 Click cell **F5**, and then to the left of the cell, point to the **Error Checking** button ⬦ to display its ScreenTip—*The formula or function used is dividing by zero or empty cells*.

> In this manner, Excel suggests the cause of an error.

6 Look at the **Formula Bar** and examine the formula.

> The formula is =E5/E11. The cell reference to E5 is correct, but the cell reference following the division operator (/) is *E11*, and E11 is an *empty* cell.

7 Click cell **F6**, point to the **Error Checking** button ⬦, and in the **Formula Bar** examine the formula.

> Because the cell references are relative, Excel builds the formulas by increasing the row number for each equation. But in this calculation, the divisor must always be the value in cell E10—the *Total Retail Value for All Products*.

8 Point to cell **F4**, and then double-click to place the insertion point within the cell.

9 Within the cell, use the arrow keys as necessary to position the insertion point to the left of *E10*, and then press `F4`. Compare your screen with Figure 15.48.

> Dollar signs ($) display, which changes the reference to cell E10 to an absolute cell reference. The use of the dollar sign to denote an absolute reference is not related in any way to whether or not the values you are working with are currency values. It is simply the symbol that Excel uses to denote an absolute cell reference.

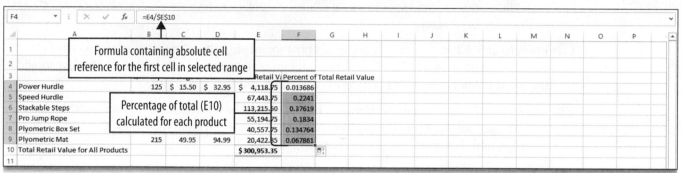

Edited formula with dollar signs indicating an absolute cell reference

FIGURE 15.48

Excel 2016, Windows 10, Microsoft Corporation

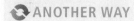 **ANOTHER WAY**   Edit the formula so that it indicates =E4/$E$10.

10 On the **Formula Bar**, click **Enter** ✓ so that **F4** remains the active cell. Then, drag the fill handle to copy the new formula down through cell **F9**. Compare your screen with Figure 15.49.

Formula containing absolute cell reference for the first cell in selected range

Percentage of total (E10) calculated for each product

FIGURE 15.49

Excel 2016, Windows 10, Microsoft Corporation

11 Click cell **F5**, examine the formula in the **Formula Bar**, and then examine the formulas for cells **F6**, **F7**, **F8**, and **F9**.

For each formula, the cell reference for the *Total Retail Value* of each product changed relative to its row; however, the value used as the divisor—*Total Retail Value for All Products* in cell E10—remained absolute. You can see that by using either relative or absolute cell references, it is easy to duplicate formulas without typing them.

12 Save 🖫 your workbook.

| *More* Knowledge | **Calculate a Percentage if You Know the Total and the Amount** |

Using the equation *amount/total = percentage*, you can calculate the percentage by which a part makes up a total—with the percentage formatted as a decimal. For example, if on a test you score 42 points correctly out of 50, your percentage of correct answers is 42/50 = 0.84 or 84%.

Objective 10 | Edit Values in a Worksheet

GO! Learn How
Video E15-10

Excel performs calculations on numbers; that is why you use Excel. If you make changes to the numbers, Excel automatically *re*-calculates the results. This is one of the most powerful and valuable features of Excel.

2.03f

Activity 15.23 | Editing Values in a Worksheet

You can edit text and number values directly within a cell or in the Formula Bar.

1 In cell **E10**, notice the column total *$300,953.35*. Click cell **B5**. To change its value, type **995** and watch cell E5 as you press Enter.

Excel formulas *recalculate* if you change the value in a cell that is referenced in a formula. It is not necessary to delete the old value in a cell; selecting the cell and typing a new value replaces the old value with your new typing.

The *Total Retail Value* of all *Speed Hurdle* items recalculates to *59,650.25* and the total in cell E10 recalculates to *$293,159.85*. Additionally, all of the percentages in column F recalculate.

2 Point to cell **D8**, and then double-click to place the insertion point within the cell. Use the arrow keys to move the insertion point to the left or right of *9*, and use either Del or Backspace to delete *9* and then type **8** so that the new Retail Price is *158.05*.

3 Watch cell **E8** and **E10** as you press Enter, and then notice the recalculation of the formulas in those two cells.

Excel recalculates the value in cell E8 to *40,302.75* and the value in cell E10 to *$292,904.85*. Additionally, all of the percentages in column F recalculate because the *Total Retail Value for All Products* recalculated.

4 Point to cell **A2** so that the ⊕ pointer is positioned slightly to the right of the word *Inventory*, and then double-click to place the insertion point in the cell. Edit the text to add the word **Valuation** pressing Spacebar as necessary, and then press Enter.

5 Click cell **B3**, and then in the **Formula Bar**, click to place the insertion point after the letter *y*. Press Spacebar one time, type **in Stock** and then on the **Formula Bar**, click **Enter** ✓. Click **Save** 🖫, and then compare your screen with Figure 15.50.

Recall that if text is too long to fit in the cell and the cell to the right contains data, the text is truncated—cut off—but the entire value still exists as the underlying value.

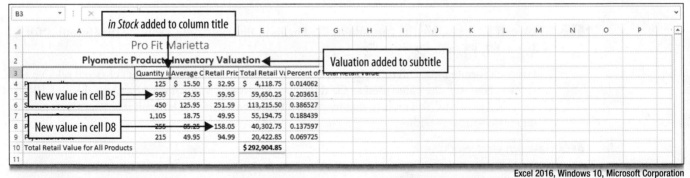

Excel 2016, Windows 10, Microsoft Corporation

FIGURE 15.50

2.03j
2.03j (i)

Activity 15.24 | Formatting Cells with the Percent Style

A percentage is part of a whole expressed in hundredths. For example, 75 cents is the same as 75 percent of one dollar. The Percent Style button formats the selected cell as a percentage rounded to the nearest hundredth.

1 Click cell **F4**, and then in the **Number group**, click **Percent Style** %.

Your result is 1%, which is *0.014062* rounded to the nearest hundredth and expressed as a percentage. Percent Style displays the value of a cell as a percentage.

2 Select the range **F4:F9**, right-click over the selection, and then on the mini toolbar, click **Percent Style** %, click **Increase Decimal** .00 two times, and then click **Center** ≡.

Percent Style may not offer a percentage precise enough to analyze important financial information—adding additional decimal places to a percentage makes data more precise.

3 Click any cell to cancel the selection, **Save** your workbook, and then compare your screen with Figure 15.51.

	A	B	C	D	E	F	G
1	Pro Fit Marietta						
2	Plyometric Products Inventory Valuation						
3		Quantity i	Average C	Retail Pric	Total Retail V	Percent of Total Retail Value	
4	Power Hurdle	125	$ 15.50	$ 32.95	$ 4,118.75	1.41%	
5	Speed Hurdle	995	29.55	59.95	59,650.25	20.37%	
6	Stackable Steps	450	Percentages formatted		.50	38.65%	
7	Pro Jump Rope	1,105			.75	18.84%	
8	Plyometric Box Set	255	85.25	158.05	40,302.75	13.76%	
9	Plyometric Mat	215	49.95	94.99	20,422.85	6.97%	
10	Total Retail Value for All Products				$ 292,904.85		
11							

FIGURE 15.51

Excel 2016, Windows 10, Microsoft Corporation

Objective 11 Format a Worksheet

GO! Learn How
Video E15-11

Formatting refers to the process of specifying the appearance of cells and the overall layout of your worksheet. Formatting is accomplished through various commands on the ribbon, for example, applying Cell Styles, and also from commands on shortcut menus, using keyboard shortcuts, and in the Format Cells dialog box.

IC3
DIGITAL LITERACY
CERTIFICATION
2.03b

Activity 15.25 | Inserting and Deleting Rows and Columns

1 In the **row heading area** on the left side of your screen, point to the row heading for **row 3** to display the [→] pointer, and then right-click to simultaneously select the row and display a shortcut menu.

2 On the shortcut menu, click **Insert** to insert a new **row 3** above the selected row.

The rows below the new row 3 move down one row, and the Insert Options button displays. By default, the new row uses the formatting of the row *above*.

 **ANOTHER WAY** Select the row, on the Home tab, in the Cells group, click the Insert button arrow, and then click Insert Sheet Rows. Or, select the row and click the Insert button—the default setting of the button inserts a new sheet row above the selected row.

3 Click cell **E11**. On the **Formula Bar**, notice that the range changed to sum the new range **E5:E10**. Compare your screen with Figure 15.52.

If you move formulas by inserting additional rows or columns in your worksheet, Excel automatically adjusts the formulas. Excel adjusted all of the formulas in the worksheet that were affected by inserting this new row.

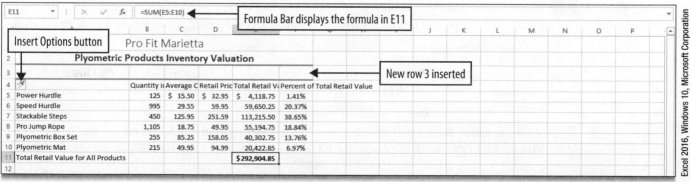

E11			fx	=SUM(E5:E10)		Formula Bar displays the formula in E11								
	Insert Options button		B	C	D			J	K	L	M	N	O	P
1			Pro Fit Marietta											
2			Plyometric Products Inventory Valuation											
3							New row 3 inserted							
4			Quantity i	Average C	Retail Pric	Total Retail V	Percent of Total Retail Value							
5	Power Hurdle		125	$ 15.50	$ 32.95	$ 4,118.75	1.41%							
6	Speed Hurdle		995	29.55	59.95	59,650.25	20.37%							
7	Stackable Steps		450	125.95	251.59	113,215.50	38.65%							
8	Pro Jump Rope		1,105	18.75	49.95	55,194.75	18.84%							
9	Plyometric Box Set		255	85.25	158.05	40,302.75	13.76%							
10	Plyometric Mat		215	49.95	94.99	20,422.85	6.97%							
11	Total Retail Value for All Products					$ 292,904.85								
12														

FIGURE 15.52

Excel 2016, Windows 10, Microsoft Corporation

4 ▶ Click cell **A3**, type **As of September 30** and then on the **Formula Bar**, click **Enter** ✓ to maintain **A3** as the active cell. **Merge & Center** the text across the range **A3:F3**, and then apply the **Heading 2** cell style.

5 ▶ In the **column heading area**, point to **column B** to display the ⬇ pointer, right-click, and then click **Insert**.

A column is inserted to the left of column B. By default, the new column uses the formatting of the column to the *left*.

🔄 **ANOTHER WAY** Select the column, on the Home tab, in the Cells group, click the Insert button arrow, and then click Insert Sheet Columns. Or, select the column and click the Insert button—the default setting of the button inserts a new sheet column to the right of the selected column.

---

6 ▶ Click cell **B4**, type **Warehouse Location** and then press [Enter].

7 ▶ In cell **B5**, type **Atlanta** and then type **Atlanta** again in cells **B6** and **B10**. Use AutoComplete to speed your typing by pressing [Enter] as soon as the AutoComplete suggestion displays. In cells **B7**, **B8**, and **B9**, type **Marietta**

8 ▶ In the **column heading area**, point to **column D**, right-click, and then click **Delete**.

The remaining columns shift to the left, and Excel adjusts all the formulas in the worksheet accordingly. You can use a similar technique to delete a row in a worksheet.

9 ▶ Compare your screen with Figure 15.53, and then **Save** 💾 your workbook.

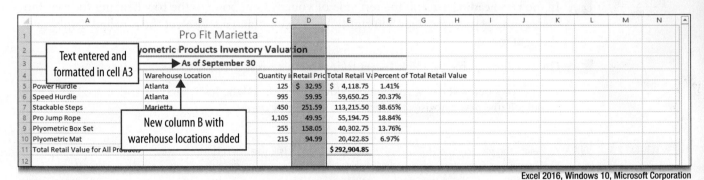

Excel 2016, Windows 10, Microsoft Corporation

FIGURE 15.53

IC3
DIGITAL LITERACY
CERTIFICATION
2.03j (i)

Activity 15.26 │ Adjusting Column Widths and Wrapping Text

Use the Wrap Text command to display the contents of a cell on multiple lines.

1 ▶ In the **column heading area**, point to the **column B** heading to display the ⬇ pointer, and then drag to the right to select **columns B:F**.

2 ▶ With the columns selected, in the **column heading area**, point to the right boundary of any of the selected columns to display the ➕ pointer, and then drag to set the width to **95 pixels**.

Use this technique to format multiple columns or rows simultaneously.

3 ▶ Select the range **B4:F4** that comprises the column headings, and then on the **Home tab**, in the **Alignment group**, click **Wrap Text** 📑. Notice that the row height adjusts to display the titles on multiple lines.

4 ▶ With the range **B4:F4** still selected, in the **Alignment group**, click **Center** ≡ and **Middle Align** ▤. With the range **B4:F4** still selected, apply the **Heading 4** cell style.

The Middle Align command aligns text so that it is centered between the top and bottom of the cell.

5 Select the range **B5:B10**, right-click, and then on the mini toolbar, click **Center** ☰. Click cell **A11**, and then from the **Cell Styles** gallery, under **Themed Cell Styles**, click **40% - Accent1**. **Save** 🖫 your workbook.

2.03j (i)

Activity 15.27 | Changing Theme Colors

You can change only the theme *colors* of a workbook—without changing the theme fonts or effects.

1 On the **Page Layout tab**, in the **Themes group**, click **Colors**, and then click **Green** to change the Theme Color. Click any blank cell, and then compare your screen with Figure 15.54.

		C	D	E	F	G	H	I	J	K	L	M	N
1	Theme colors changed to Green Pro Fit Marietta												
2	Plyometric Products Inventory Valuation												
3	As of September 30												
4		Warehouse Location	Quantity in Stock	Retail Price	Total Retail Value	Percent of Total Retail Value							
5	Power Hurdle	Atlanta	125	$ 32.95	$ 4,118.75	1.41%							
6	Speed Hurdle	Atlanta	995	59.95	59,650.25	20.37%							
7	Stackable Steps	Marietta	450	251.59	113,215.50	38.65%							
8	Pro Jump Rope	Marietta	1,105	49.95	55,194.75	18.84%							
9	Plyometric Box Set	Marietta	255	158.05	40,302.75	13.76%							
10	Plyometric Mat	Atlanta	215	94.99	20,422.85	6.97%							
11	Total Retail Value for All Products				$ 292,904.85								
12													

Excel 2016, Windows 10, Microsoft Corporation

FIGURE 15.54

2 On the **Page Layout tab**, in the **Page Setup group**, click **Margins**, and then click **Custom Margins**.

3 In the **Page Setup** dialog box, on the **Margins tab**, under **Center on page**, select the **Horizontally** check box.

This action will center the data horizontally on the page, as shown in the Preview area.

4 Click the **Header/Footer tab**, and then in the center of the dialog box, click **Custom Footer**. In the **Footer** dialog box, with your insertion point blinking in the **Left section**, on the row of buttons, click **Insert File Name** 🗎.

&[File] displays in the Left section. Here you can type or insert information from the row of buttons into the left, middle, or right section of the footer. The Custom Header button displays a similar screen to enter information in the header of the worksheet.

5 Click **OK** two times.

6 Click the **File tab** to display Backstage view, and then in the lower right corner, click **Show All Properties**.

7 As the **Tags**, type **plyo products, inventory** and as the **Subject**, type your course name and section number. Be sure your name displays in the **Author** box, or edit it if necessary.

8 On the left, click **Print** to view the **Print Preview**. At the bottom of the **Print Preview**, click **Next Page** ▶, and notice that as currently formatted, the worksheet occupies two pages.

9 Under **Settings**, click **Portrait Orientation**, and then click **Landscape Orientation**. Compare your screen with Figure 15.55.

You can change the orientation on the Page Layout tab, or here, in Print Preview. Because it is in the Print Preview that you will often see adjustments that need to be made, commonly used settings display on the Print tab in Backstage view.

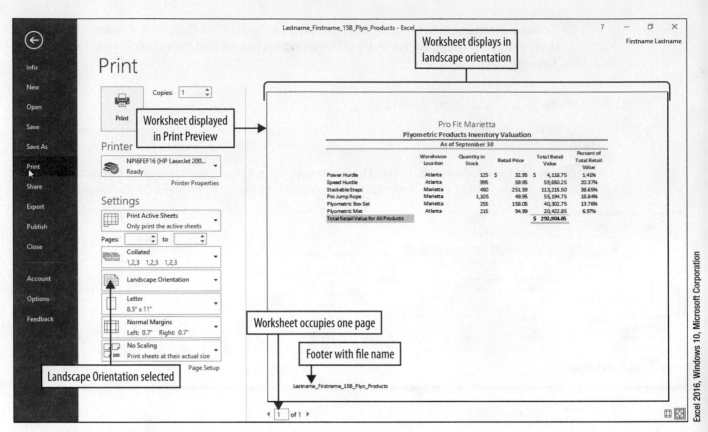

FIGURE 15.55

10 On the left, click **Save**. By using the techniques you practiced in Project 15A and as directed by your instructor, print, create a PDF image that looks like a printed document, or submit your completed Excel file. If required by your instructor, print or create an electronic version of your worksheet with formulas displayed.

11 In **Backstage** view, click **Close** to close your workbook, and then **Close** ☒ Excel.

END | You have completed Project 15B

GO! With Google

Objective | Creating an Inventory Valuation Report

> **ALERT!** **Working with Web-Based Applications and Services**
>
> Computer programs and services on the web receive continuous updates and improvements, so the steps to complete this web-based Activity may differ from the ones shown. You can often look at the screens and the information presented to determine how to complete the Activity.
>
> If you do not already have a Google account, you will need to create one before you begin this Activity. Go to http://google.com and in the upper right corner, click Sign In. On the Sign In screen, click Create Account. On the Create your Google Account page, complete the form, read and agree to the Terms of Service and Privacy Policy, and then click Next step. On the Welcome screen, click Get Started.

Activity | Creating an Inventory Valuation Report Using Google Sheets

In this Activity, you will use Google Sheets to create an inventory valuation report similar to the one you created in Project 15B.

1 From the desktop, open your browser (a browser other than Edge), navigate to **http://google.com** and then click the **Google Apps** menu ▦. Click **Drive**, and then if necessary, sign in to your Google account.

2 Open your **GO! Web Projects** folder—or click New to create and then open this folder if necessary.

3 In the left pane, click **NEW**, and then click **Google Sheets**. From your Windows taskbar, open **File Explorer**, navigate to your Student Data Files for this chapter, and then in the **File List**, double-click the Word document **e15_15B_Web**; to complete this project quickly and eliminate extra typing, you will copy the data from a Word document.

4 In the displayed Word document, click anywhere in the text, and then in the upper left corner, click to select the **Table Select** ⊞ to select the entire Word table. Right-click anywhere over the selection, and then click **Copy**. **Close** Word. **Close** the **File Explorer** window.

5 In your blank Google Sheet, with cell **A1** active, point to cell **A1**, right-click, and then click **Paste**. In the column heading area, point to the border between **column A** and **column B** to display the ↔ pointer, and then widen **column A** slightly so that all of the data in rows 4–10 displays.

6 Select the range **A1:E1**. On the toolbar, click **Merge cells** ⊞. On the toolbar, click the **Align arrow** ▾, and then click **Center** ☰. Repeat for the range **A2:E2**, and then apply **Bold** **B** to cells **A1** and **A2**.

7 Select the range **B3:E3**, on the menu bar click **Format**, point to **Text wrapping**, and then click **Wrap**. Center these column titles and apply **Bold** **B**.

8 Select the range **C4:C9**, on the menu bar click **Format**, point to **Number**, on the fly-out menu click **Number**, and then if necessary, on the toolbar, click **Decrease decimal places** two times.

9 Click cell **E4**, type **=** and then click cell **C4**. Type * and then click cell **D4**. Press Enter. Click cell **E4**, point to the fill handle in the lower right corner of the cell, and then drag down to cell **E9**.

10 Select the range **E4:E9**. On the toolbar, click **Functions** Σ ▾, click **SUM**, and then press Enter.

11 Select the range **D4:E4**, hold down Ctrl, and then select cell **E10**. On the menu bar, click **Format**, point to **Number**, and then in the fly-out menu click **Currency**.

12 Select cell **A10**, hold down Ctrl, and then click cell **E10**. Apply **Bold** **B**.

13 Click cell **A1**, hold down Ctrl, and then click cell **A2**, cell **A10**, and cell **E10**. With the four cells selected, on the toolbar, click **Fill color** ▾, and then in the fourth column, click the third color—**light yellow 3**.

14 At the top of the worksheet, click the text *Untitled spreadsheet*, and then using your own name, type **Lastname_Firstname_EX_15B_Web** and press ENTER.

(GO! With Google continues on the next page)

GO! With Google

15 If you are instructed to submit your file to your instructor, you can either share the file through Google Drive, or create a PDF or Excel file as described in the Note box below. Ask your instructor in what format he or she would like to receive your file.

16 **Close** the browser tab—a new Google Sheet always opens in a new window in your browser; your work is automatically saved. Notice that your new Google Sheet displays in the file list on your Google Drive. Sign out of your Google account.

NOTE   Downloading Google Files

You can download your file in several formats, including PDF or PowerPoint. Click the File menu, point to Download as, and click the format directed by your instructor. The file will download to your default download folder as determined by your browser settings.

	A	B	C	D	E
1	Pro Fit Marietta				
2	Plyometric Products Inventory Valuation				
3		Warehouse Location	Quantity In Stock	Retail Price	Total Retail Value
4	Power Hurdle	Atlanta	125	$32.95	$4,118.75
5	Speed Hurdle	Atlanta	995	59.95	59650.25
6	Stackable Steps	Marietta	450	251.59	113215.5
7	Pro Jump Rope	Marietta	1,105	49.95	55194.75
8	Plyometric Box Set	Marietta	255	158.05	40302.75
9	Plyometric Mat	Atlanta	215	94.99	20422.85
10	Total Retail Value for All Products				$292,904.85
11					

FIGURE A

GO! To Work

IC3 SKILLS IN THIS CHAPTER

IC3 Key Applications

Project 15A
Section 2.03 Spreadsheets

(a) Understand common spreadsheet terms
  (i) Cell
  (ii) Column
  (iii) Row
  (iv) Range
  (v) Worksheet
  (vi) Workbook
  (vii) Navigation
(e) Understand functions, formulas, and operators
  (i) Understand their purpose and how they are used
  (ii) Recognize syntax
(f) Be able to enter data in a spreadsheet
(g) Use and create spreadsheet charts
  (i) Recognize charts
  (ii) Read and interpret charts
  (iii) Create simple charts
(i) Manipulate data within a spreadsheet
  (i) Merge and unmerge cells
(j) Format data within spreadsheets
  (i) Modify borders, fill color, text color, alignment, data type

Project 15B
Section 2.03 Spreadsheets

(b) Be able to insert/delete rows and columns
(e) Understand functions, formulas, and operators
  (i) Understand their purpose and how they are used
  (iii) Be able to create simple formulas
(f) Be able to enter data in a spreadsheet
(j) Format data within spreadsheets
  (i) Modify borders, fill color, text color, alignment, data type

BUILD YOUR E-PORTFOLIO

An E-Portfolio is a collection of evidence, stored electronically, that showcases what you have accomplished while completing your education. Collecting and then sharing your work products with potential employers reflects your academic and career goals. Your completed documents from the following projects are good examples to show what you have learned: 15G, 15K, and 15L.

GO! FOR JOB SUCCESS

Video: Customer Service

Your instructor may assign this video to your class, and then ask you to think about, or discuss with your classmates, these questions:

FotolEdhar / Fotolia

If you were interviewing people for your company, what would you look for in terms of their dress and personal presentation?

What might you want to change about your personal dress for work or for an interview?

Do you feel that it's right to "judge a book by its cover"? Why or why not?

END OF CHAPTER

SUMMARY

In Excel, you work with worksheets that are contained in a workbook. A worksheet is formatted as a pattern of uniformly spaced horizontal rows and vertical columns, the intersection of which forms a cell.

A cell can contain a constant value—referred to as a value—or a formula, which is an equation that performs mathematical calculations on the values in your worksheet. Common values are text and numbers.

You can insert sparklines in an Excel worksheet, which are tiny charts embedded in a cell that give a visual trend summary alongside your data. A sparkline makes a pattern more obvious to the eye.

Charts provide a graphic representation of data in a worksheet. Use the Recommended Charts feature to display customized charts that, according to Excel's calculations, will best represent your data.

GO! LEARN IT ONLINE

Review the concepts, key terms, and IC3 skills in this chapter by completing these online challenges, which you can find at MyITLab.

Matching and Multiple Choice: Answer matching and multiple choice questions to test what you learned in this chapter.

Lessons on the GO!: Learn how to use all the new apps and features as they are introduced by Microsoft.

IC3 Prep Quiz: Answer questions to review the IC3 skills that you practiced in this chapter.

GO! COLLABORATIVE TEAM PROJECT (Available in MyITLab and Instructor Resource Center)

If your instructor assigns this project to your class, you can expect to work with one or more of your classmates—either in person or by using Internet tools—to create work products similar to those that you created in this chapter. A team is a group of workers who work together to solve a problem, make a decision, or create a work product. Collaboration is when you work together with others as a team in an intellectual endeavor to complete a shared task or achieve a shared goal.

PROJECT GUIDE FOR ALL IN ONE CHAPTER 15

Your instructor will assign Projects from this list to ensure your learning and assess your knowledge.

		Project Guide for All in One Chapter 15	
Project	**Apply Skills from These Chapter Objectives**	**Project Type**	**Project Location**
15A MyITLab	Objectives 1–6 from Project 15A	**15A Instructional Project (Grader Project)** Guided instruction to learn the skills in Project 15A.	In MyITLab and in text
15B MyITLab	Objectives 7–11 from Project 15B	**15B Instructional Project (Grader Project)** Guided instruction to learn the skills in Project 15B.	In MyITLab and in text
15C	Objectives 1–6 from Project 15A	**15C Skills Review (Scorecard Grading)** A guided review of the skills from Project 15A.	In text
15D	Objectives 7–11 from Project 15B	**15D Skills Review (Scorecard Grading)** A guided review of the skills from Project 15B.	In text
15E MyITLab	Objectives 1–6 from Project 15A	**15E Mastery (Grader Project)** **Mastery and Transfer of Learning** A demonstration of your mastery of the skills in Project 15A with extensive decision making.	In MyITLab and in text
15F MyITLab	Objectives 7–11 from Project 15B	**15F Mastery (Grader Project)** **Mastery and Transfer of Learning** A demonstration of your mastery of the skills in Project 15B with extensive decision making.	In MyITLab and in text
15G MyITLab	Objectives 1–11 from Projects 15A and 15B	**15G Mastery (Grader Project)** **Mastery and Transfer of Learning** A demonstration of your mastery of the skills in Projects 15A and 15B with extensive decision making.	In MyITLab and in text
15H	Combination of Objectives from Projects 15A and 15B	**15H GO! Fix It (Scorecard Grading)** **Critical Thinking** A demonstration of your mastery of the skills in Projects 15A and 15B by creating a correct result from a document that contains errors you must find.	Instructor Resource Center (IRC) and MyITLab
15I	Combination of Objectives from Projects 15A and 15B	**15I GO! Make It (Scorecard Grading)** **Critical Thinking** A demonstration of your mastery of the skills in Projects 15A and 15B by creating a result from a supplied picture.	IRC and MyITLab
15J	Combination of Objectives from Projects 15A and 15B	**15J GO! Solve It (Rubric Grading)** **Critical Thinking** A demonstration of your mastery of the skills in Projects 15A and 15B, your decision-making skills, and your critical-thinking skills. A task-specific rubric helps you self-assess your result.	IRC and MyITLab
15K	Combination of Objectives from Projects 15A and 15B	**15K GO! Solve It (Rubric Grading)** **Critical Thinking** A demonstration of your mastery of the skills in Projects 15A and 15B, your decision-making skills, and your critical-thinking skills. A task-specific rubric helps you self-assess your result.	In text
15L	Combination of Objectives from Projects 15A and 15B	**15L GO! Think (Rubric Grading)** **Critical Thinking** A demonstration of your understanding of the chapter concepts applied in a manner that you would outside of college. An analytic rubric helps you and your instructor grade the quality of your work by comparing it to the work an expert in the discipline would create.	In text
15M	Combination of Objectives from Projects 15A and 15B	**15M GO! Think (Rubric Grading)** **Critical Thinking** A demonstration of your understanding of the chapter concepts applied in a manner that you would outside of college. An analytic rubric helps you and your instructor grade the quality of your work by comparing it to the work an expert in the discipline would create.	IRC and MyITLab
15N	Combination of Objectives from Projects 15A and 15B	**15N You and GO! (Rubric Grading)** **Critical Thinking** A demonstration of your understanding of the chapter concepts applied in a manner that you would in a personal situation. An analytic rubric helps you and your instructor grade the quality of your work.	IRC and MyITLab
15O	Combination of Objectives from Projects 15A and 15B	**15O Cumulative Group Project for AIO Chapter 15** A demonstration of your understanding of concepts and your ability to work collaboratively in a group role-playing assessment, requiring both collaboration and self-management.	IRC and MyITLab

GLOSSARY

GLOSSARY OF CHAPTER KEY TERMS

Absolute cell reference A cell reference that refers to cells by their fixed position in a worksheet; an absolute cell reference remains the same when the formula is copied.

Accounting Number Format The Excel number format that applies a thousand comma separator where appropriate, inserts a fixed U.S. dollar sign aligned at the left edge of the cell, applies two decimal places, and leaves a small amount of space at the right edge of the cell to accommodate a parenthesis for negative numbers.

Active cell The cell, surrounded by a border, ready to receive data or be affected by the next Excel command.

Arithmetic operators The symbols +, −, *, /, %, and ^ used to denote addition, subtraction (or negation), multiplication, division, percentage, and exponentiation in an Excel formula.

Auto Fill An Excel feature that generates and extends values into adjacent cells based on the values of selected cells.

AutoCalculate A feature that displays three calculations in the status bar by default—Average, Count, and Sum—when you select a range of numerical data.

AutoComplete A feature that speeds your typing and lessens the likelihood of errors; if the first few characters you type in a cell match an existing entry in the column, Excel fills in the remaining characters for you.

AutoFit An Excel feature that adjusts the width of a column to fit the cell content of the widest cell in the column.

AutoSum A button that provides quick access to the SUM function.

Category axis The area along the bottom of a chart that identifies the categories of data; also referred to as the x-axis.

Category labels The labels that display along the bottom of a chart to identify the categories of data; Excel uses the row titles as the category names.

Cell The intersection of a column and a row.

Cell address Another name for a cell reference.

Cell content Anything typed into a cell.

Cell reference The identification of a specific cell by its intersecting column letter and row number.

Cell style A defined set of formatting characteristics, such as font, font size, font color, cell borders, and cell shading.

Chart The graphic representation of data in a worksheet; data presented as a chart is usually easier to understand than a table of numbers.

Chart Elements button A button that enables you to add, remove, or change chart elements such as the title, legend, gridlines, and data labels.

Chart Filters button A button that enables you to change which data displays in the chart.

Chart layout The combination of chart elements that can be displayed in a chart such as a title, legend, labels for the columns, and the table of charted cells.

Chart style The overall visual look of a chart in terms of its graphic effects, colors, and backgrounds; for example, you can have flat or beveled columns, colors that are solid or transparent, and backgrounds that are dark or light.

Chart Styles button A button that enables you to set a style and color scheme for your chart.

Chart Styles gallery A group of predesigned chart styles that you can apply to an Excel chart.

Chart types Various chart formats used in a way that is meaningful to the reader; common examples are column charts, pie charts, and line charts.

Column A vertical group of cells in a worksheet.

Column chart A chart in which the data is arranged in columns and that is useful for showing data changes over a period of time or for illustrating comparisons among items.

Column heading The letter that displays at the top of a vertical group of cells in a worksheet; beginning with the first letter of the alphabet, a unique letter or combination of letters identifies each column.

Comma Style The Excel number format that inserts thousand comma separators where appropriate and applies two decimal places; Comma Style also leaves space at the right to accommodate a parenthesis when negative numbers are present.

Constant value Numbers, text, dates, or times of day that you type into a cell.

Context sensitive A command associated with the currently selected or active object; often activated by right-clicking a screen item.

Data Text or numbers in a cell.

Data marker A column, bar, area, dot, pie slice, or other symbol in a chart that represents a single data point; related data points form a data series.

Data point A value that originates in a worksheet cell and that is represented in a chart by a data marker.

Data series Related data points represented by data markers; each data series has a unique color or pattern represented in the chart legend.

Displayed value The data that displays in a cell.

Excel pointer An Excel window element with which you can display the location of the pointer.

Expand Formula Bar button An Excel window element with which you can increase the height of the Formula Bar to display lengthy cell content.

Expand horizontal scroll bar button An Excel window element with which you can increase the width of the horizontal scroll bar.

Fill handle The small square in the lower right corner of a selected cell.

Format Changing the appearance of cells and worksheet elements to make a worksheet attractive and easy to read.

Formula An equation that performs mathematical calculations on values in a worksheet.

Formula Bar An element in the Excel window that displays the value or formula contained in the active cell; here you can also enter or edit values or formulas.

Function A predefined formula—a formula that Excel has already built for you—that performs calculations by using specific values in a particular order.

General format The default format that Excel applies to numbers; this format has no specific characteristics—whatever you type in the cell will display, with the exception that trailing zeros to the right of a decimal point will not display.

Label Another name for a text value, and which usually provides information about number values.

Left alignment The cell format in which characters align at the left edge of the cell; this is the default for text entries and is an example of formatting information stored in a cell.

Legend A chart element that identifies the patterns or colors that are assigned to the categories in the chart.

Lettered column headings The area along the top edge of a worksheet that identifies each column with a unique letter or combination of letters.

Merge & Center A command that joins selected cells in an Excel worksheet into one larger cell and centers the contents in the merged cell.

Name Box An element of the Excel window that displays the name of the selected cell, table, chart, or object.

Normal view A screen view that maximizes the number of cells visible on your screen and keeps the column letters and row numbers close to the columns and rows.

Number format A specific way in which Excel displays numbers in a cell.

Number values Constant values consisting of only numbers.

Numbered row headings The area along the left edge of a worksheet that identifies each row with a unique number.

Operators The symbols with which you can specify the type of calculation you want to perform in an Excel formula.

Picture element A point of light measured in dots per square inch on a screen; 64 pixels equals 8.43 characters, which is the average number of characters that will fit in a cell in an Excel worksheet using the default font.

Pixel The abbreviated name for a picture element.

Point and click method The technique of constructing a formula by pointing to and then clicking cells; this method

is convenient when the referenced cells are not adjacent to one another.

Quick Analysis Tool A tool that displays in the lower right corner of a selected range, with which you can analyze your data by using Excel tools such as charts, color-coding, and formulas.

Range Two or more selected cells on a worksheet that are adjacent or nonadjacent; because the range is treated as a single unit, you can make the same changes or combination of changes to more than one cell at a time.

Range finder An Excel feature that outlines cells in color to indicate which cells are used in a formula; useful for verifying which cells are referenced in a formula.

Recommended Charts An Excel feature that displays a customized set of charts that, according to Excel's calculations, will best fit your data based on the range of data that you select.

Relative cell reference In a formula, the address of a cell based on the relative positions of the cell that contains the formula and the cell referred to in the formula.

Rounding A procedure in which you determine which digit at the right of the number will be the last digit displayed and then increase it by one if the next digit to its right is 5, 6, 7, 8, or 9.

Row A horizontal group of cells in a worksheet.

Row heading The numbers along the left side of an Excel worksheet that designate the row numbers.

Scaling The process of shrinking the width and/or height of printed output to fit a maximum number of pages.

Select All box A box in the upper left corner of the worksheet grid that, when clicked, selects all the cells in a worksheet.

Series A group of things that come one after another in succession; for example, January, February, March, and so on.

Sheet tab scrolling buttons Buttons to the left of the sheet tabs used to display Excel sheet tabs that are not in view; used when there are more sheet tabs than will display in the space provided.

Sheet tabs The labels along the lower border of the Excel window that identify each worksheet.

Show Formulas A command that displays the formula in each cell instead of the resulting value.

Sparkline A tiny chart in the background of a cell that gives a visual trend summary alongside your data; makes a pattern more obvious.

Spreadsheet Another name for a worksheet.

Status bar The area along the lower edge of the Excel window that displays, on the left side, the current cell mode, page number, and worksheet information; on the right side, when numerical data is selected, common calculations such as Sum and Average display.

SUM function A predefined formula that adds all the numbers in a selected range of cells.

Switch Row/Column A charting command to swap the data over the axis—data being charted on the vertical axis will move to the horizontal axis and vice versa.

Text values Constant values consisting of only text, and which usually provide information about number values; also referred to as labels.

Theme A predefined set of colors, fonts, lines, and fill effects that coordinate with each other.

Underlying formula The formula entered in a cell and visible only on the Formula Bar.

Underlying value The data that displays in the Formula Bar.

Value Another name for a constant value.

Value axis A numerical scale on the left side of a chart that shows the range of numbers for the data points; also referred to as the Y-axis.

Workbook An Excel file that contains one or more worksheets.

Worksheet The primary document that you use in Excel to work with and store data, and which is formatted as a pattern of uniformly spaced horizontal and vertical lines.

Worksheet grid area A part of the Excel window that displays the columns and rows that intersect to form the worksheet's cells.

X-axis Another name for the horizontal (category) axis.

Y-axis Another name for the vertical (value) axis.

Apply 15A **skills from these Objectives:**

1 Create, Save, and Navigate an Excel Workbook

2 Enter Data in a Worksheet

3 Construct and Copy Formulas and Use the SUM Function

4 Format Cells with Merge & Center, Cell Styles, and Themes

5 Chart Data to Create a Column Chart and Insert Sparklines

6 Print a Worksheet, Display Formulas, and Close Excel

Skills Review   Project 15C Step Sales

In the following Skills Review, you will create a new Excel worksheet with a chart that summarizes the first quarter sales of fitness equipment for step training. Your completed worksheet will look similar to Figure 15.56.

PROJECT FILES

For Project 15C, you will need the following file:

New blank Excel workbook

You will save your workbook as:

Lastname_Firstname_15C_Step_Sales

PROJECT RESULTS

Build From
Scratch

	January	February	March	Total	Trend
Basic Step Box	$ 75,826.99	$ 81,657.32	$ 72,431.22	$ 229,915.53	
Step Storage Box	85,245.90	92,618.95	88,337.68	266,202.53	
Stackable Steps	68,751.64	71,997.48	78,951.23	219,700.35	
Step Mats	63,255.10	58,742.67	67,995.20	189,992.97	
Total	$ 293,079.63	$ 305,016.42	$ 307,715.33	$ 905,811.38	

Pro Fit Marietta
First Quarter Step Sales

First Quarter Step Sales

Lastname_Firstname_15C_Step_Sales

FIGURE 15.56

(Project 15C Step Sales continues on the next page)

Excel 2016, Windows 10, Microsoft Corporation

Skills Review Project 15C Step Sales (continued)

1 ▶ Start Excel and open a new blank workbook. Click the **File tab** to display **Backstage** view, click **Save As**, and then navigate to your **AIO Chapter 15** folder. In the **File name** box, using your own name, type **Lastname_Firstname_15C_Step_Sales** and then press Enter.

a. With cell **A1** as the active cell, type the worksheet title **Pro Fit Marietta** and then press Enter. In cell **A2**, type the worksheet subtitle **First Quarter Step Sales** and then press Enter.

b. Click in cell **A4**, type **Basic Step Box** and then press Enter. In cell **A5**, type **Step Storage Box** and then press Enter. In cell **A6**, type **Stackable Steps** and then press Enter. In cell **A7**, type **Step Mats** and then press Enter. In cell **A8**, type **Total** and then press Enter.

c. Click cell **B3**. Type **January** and then in the **Formula Bar**, click **Enter** to keep cell **B3** the active cell. With **B3** as the active cell, point to the fill handle in the lower right corner of the selected cell, drag to the right to cell **D3**, and then release the mouse button to enter the text *February* and *March*.

d. Press Ctrl + Home to make cell **A1** the active cell. In the **column heading area**, point to the vertical line between **column A** and **column B** to display the ✛ pointer, hold down the left mouse button, and drag to the right to increase the column width to **130 pixels**.

e. Point to cell **B3**, and then drag across to select cells **B3** and **C3** and **D3**. With the range **B3:D3** selected, point anywhere over the selected range, right-click, and then on the mini toolbar, click **Center**.

f. Click cell **B4**, type **75826.99** and press Tab to make cell **C4** active. Enter the remaining values, as shown in **Table 1**, pressing Tab to move across the rows and Enter to move down the columns.

TABLE 1

	January	February	March
Basic Step Box	75826.99	81657.32	72431.22
Step Storage Box	85245.90	92618.95	88337.68
Stackable Steps	68751.64	71997.48	78951.23
Step Mats	63255.10	58742.67	67995.20

2 ▶ Click cell **B8** to make it the active cell and type =

a. At the insertion point, type **b4** and then type + Type **b5** and then type **+b6+b7** Press Enter. Your result is *293079.6*.

b. Click in cell **C8**. Type = and then click cell **C4**. Type + and then click cell **C5**. Repeat this process to complete the formula to add cells **C6** and **C7** to the formula, and then press Enter. Your result is *305016.4*.

c. Click cell **D8**. On the **Home tab**, in the **Editing group**, click **AutoSum**, and then press Enter to construct a formula by using the SUM function. Your result is *307715.3*.

d. In cell **E3** type **Total** and press Enter. With cell **E4** as the active cell, hold down Alt, and then press =. On the **Formula Bar**, click **Enter** to display the result and keep cell **E4** active.

e. With cell **E4** active, point to the fill handle in the lower right corner of the cell. Drag down through cell **E8**, and then release the mouse button to copy the formula with relative cell references down to sum each row.

3 ▶ Click cell **F3**. Type **Trend** and then press Enter.

a. Select the range **A1:F1**, and then on the **Home tab**, in the **Alignment group**, click **Merge & Center**. Select the range **A2:F2** and **Merge & Center** the selection.

b. Click cell **A1**. In the **Styles group**, click **Cell Styles**. Under **Titles and Headings**, click **Title**. Click cell **A2**, display the **Cell Styles** gallery, and then click **Heading 1**.

c. Select the range **B3:F3**, hold down Ctrl, and then select the range **A4:A8**. From the **Cell Styles** gallery, click **Heading 4** to apply this cell style to the column and row titles.

d. Select the range **B4:E4**, hold down Ctrl, and then select the range **B8:E8**. On the **Home tab**, in the **Number group**, click **Accounting Number Format**. Select the range **B5:E7**, and then in the **Number group**, click **Comma Style**. Select the range **B8:E8**. From the **Styles group**, display the **Cell Styles** gallery, and then under **Titles and Headings**, click **Total**.

e. On the ribbon, click the **Page Layout tab**, and then in the **Themes group**, click **Themes** to display the **Themes** gallery. Click the **Basis** theme. (This theme widens the columns slightly). On the Quick Access Toolbar, click **Save**.

(Project 15C Step Sales continues on the next page)

4 Select the range **A3:D7**, which includes the row titles, the column titles, and the data without the totals. Click the **Insert tab**, and then in the **Charts group**, click **Recommended Charts**. In the **Insert Chart** dialog box, scroll down and click the fifth recommended chart—a **Clustered Column** chart in which *each month* displays its *sales for each type of step training equipment*. Click **OK**.

a. In the chart, click anywhere in the text *Chart Title* to select the text box. Watch the **Formula Bar** as you type **First** and then let AutoComplete complete the title by pressing Enter.

b. Click in a white area just slightly *inside* the chart border to deselect the chart title but keep the chart selected. To the right of the chart, click the second button—the **Chart Styles** button .

Be sure the **Style** tab is selected. Use the scroll bar to scroll down, and then by using the ScreenTips, locate and click **Style 6**.

c. At the top of the gallery, click **COLOR**. Under **Colorful**, point to the fourth row of colors to display the ScreenTip *Color 4*, and then click to apply the **Color 4** variation of the theme colors.

d. Point to the top border of the chart to display the pointer, and then drag the upper left corner of the chart just to the center of cell **A10** to visually center it below the data.

5 Select the range **B4:D7**. Click the **Insert tab**, and then in the **Sparklines group**, click **Line**. In the **Create Sparklines** dialog box, in the **Location Range** box, type **f4:f7** and then click **OK** to insert the sparklines.

a. On the **Design tab**, in the **Show group**, select the **Markers** check box to display markers in the sparklines.

b. On the **Design tab**, in the **Style group**, click **More** and then in the second row, click the fourth style—**Sparkline Style Accent 4, Darker 25%**.

6 Click cell **A1** to deselect the chart. Click the **Page Layout tab**, and then in the **Page Setup group**, click **Margins**. Click **Custom Margins**. In the **Page Setup** dialog box, on the **Margins tab**, under **Center on page**, select the **Horizontally** check box.

a. Click the **Header/Footer tab**, and then click **Custom Footer**. With your insertion point in the **Left section**, click **Insert File Name**. Click **OK** two times.

b. Click the **File tab** to display **Backstage** view. In the lower right corner, click **Show All Properties**. As the **Tags**, type **step sales, 1st quarter** In the **Subject** box, type your course name and section number. Be sure your name displays as the author—edit if necessary.

c. On the left, click **Save**.

d. By using the techniques you practiced in Project 15A and as directed by your instructor, print, create a PDF image that looks like a printed document, or submit your completed Excel file. If required by your instructor, print or create an electronic version of your worksheet with formulas displayed. In the upper right corner of your Excel window, click Close.

END | You have completed Project 15C

Apply 15B skills from these Objectives:

7 Check Spelling in a Worksheet
8 Enter Data by Range
9 Construct Formulas for Mathematical Operations
10 Edit Values in a Worksheet
11 Format a Worksheet

Skills Review Project 15D Band and Tubing Inventory

In the following Skills Review, you will create a worksheet that summarizes the inventory of band and tubing exercise equipment. Your completed worksheet will look similar to Figure 15.57.

PROJECT FILES

For Project 15D, you will need the following file:

New blank Excel workbook

You will save your workbook as:

Lastname_Firstname_15D_Band_Inventory

Build From Scratch

PROJECT RESULTS

Pro Fit Marietta

Band and Tubing Inventory

As of June 30

	Material	Quantity in Stock	Retail Price	Total Retail Value	Percent of Total Retail Value
Super Strength Bands	Latex	225	$ 48.98	$ 11,020.50	25.16%
Medium Tubing	Rubber	198	27.95	5,534.10	12.64%
Resistance Band, Average	Latex	165	42.95	7,086.75	16.18%
Mini Bands, Medium	Latex	245	25.95	6,357.75	14.52%
Mini Bands, Heavy	Rubber	175	32.95	5,766.25	13.17%
Heavy Tubing	Latex	187	42.95	8,031.65	18.34%
Total Retail Value for All Products				**$ 43,797.00**	

Lastname_Firstname_15D_Band_Inventory

FIGURE 15.57

(Project 15D Band and Tubing Inventory continues on the next page)

1 Start Excel and display a new blank workbook. **Save** the workbook in your **AIO Chapter 15** folder as **Lastname_Firstname_15D_Band_Inventory** In cell **A1** type **Pro Fit Marietta** and in cell **A2** type **Band and Tubing Inventory**

a. Click cell **B3**, type **Quantity in Stock** and press Tab. In cell **C3** type **Average Cost** and press Tab. In cell **D3**, type **Retail Price** and press Tab. In cell **E3**, type **Total Retail Value** and press Tab. In cell **F3** type **Percent of Total Retail Value** and press Enter.

b. Click cell **A4**, type **Super Strength Bands** and press Enter. In the range **A5:A10**, type the remaining row titles as shown below, including any misspelled words.

Medium Tubing

Resistnce Band, Average

Mini Bands, Medium

Mini Bands, Heavy

Heavy Tubing

Total Retail Value for All Products

c. Press Ctrl + Home to move to the top of your worksheet. On the **Review tab**, in the **Proofing group**, click **Spelling**. Correct *Resistnce* to **Resistance** and any other spelling errors you may have made, and then when the message displays, *Spell check complete. You're good to go!* click **OK**.

d. In the **column heading area**, point to the right boundary of **column A** to display the ➕ pointer, and then drag to the right to widen **column A** to **225** pixels.

e. In the **column heading area**, point to the **column B** heading to display the ⬇ pointer, and then drag to the right to select **columns B:F**. With the columns selected, in the **column heading area**, point to the right boundary of any of the selected columns, and then drag to the right to set the width to **100 pixels**.

f. Select the range **A1:F1**. On the **Home tab**, in the **Alignment group**, click **Merge & Center**, and then in the **Cell Styles** gallery, apply the **Title** style. Select the range **A2:F2**. **Merge & Center** the text across the selection, and then in the **Cell Styles** gallery, apply the **Heading 1** style.

2 On the **Page Layout tab**, in the **Themes group**, change the **Colors** to **Blue Green**. Select the empty range

B4:D9. With cell **B4** active in the range, type **225** and then press Enter.

a. With cell **B5** active in the range, and pressing Enter after each entry, type the following data in the *Quantity in Stock* column:

198
265
245
175
187

b. With the selected range still active, from the following table, beginning in cell **C4** and pressing Enter after each entry, enter the following data for the **Average Cost** column and then the **Retail Price** column. If you prefer, type without selecting the range first; recall that this is optional.

Average Cost	Retail Price
22.75	48.98
15.95	27.95
26.90	42.95
12.95	25.95
18.75	32.95
26.90	42.95

3 In cell **E4**, type **=b4*d4** and then press Enter to construct a formula that calculates the *Total Retail Value* of the *Super Strength Bands* (Quantity in Stock X Retail Price).

a. Click cell **E4**, position your pointer over the fill handle, and then drag down through cell **E9** to copy the formula with relative cell references.

b. Select the range **B4:B9**, and then on the **Home tab**, in the **Number group**, click **Comma Style**. Then, in the **Number group**, click **Decrease Decimal** two times to remove the decimal places from these non-currency values.

c. To calculate the *Total Retail Value for All Products*, select the range **E4:E9**, and then in the lower right corner of the selected range, click the **Quick Analysis** button 📊.

(Project 15D Band and Tubing Inventory continues on the next page)

d. In the gallery, click **Totals**, and then click the *first* **Sum** button, which visually indicates that the column will be summed with a result at the bottom of the column.

e. Select the range **C5:E9** and apply the **Comma Style**. Select the range **C4:E4**, hold down Ctrl, and then click cell **E10**. With the nonadjacent cells selected, apply the **Accounting Number Format**. Click cell **E10**, and then from the **Cell Styles** gallery, apply the **Total** style.

f. Click cell **F4**, type = and then click cell **E4**. Type / and then click cell **E10**. Press F4 to make the reference to cell *E10* absolute, and then on the **Formula Bar**, click **Enter** so that cell **F4** remains the active cell. Drag the fill handle to copy the formula down through cell **F9**.

g. Point to cell **B6**, and then double-click to place the insertion point within the cell. Use the arrow keys to move the insertion point to the left or right of *2*, and use either Delete or Backspace to delete *2*, and then type **1** and press Enter so that the new *Quantity in Stock* is *165*. Notice the recalculations in the worksheet.

4 Select the range **F4:F9**, right-click over the selection, and then on the mini toolbar, click **Percent Style**. Click **Increase Decimal** two times, and then **Center** the selection.

a. In the **row heading area** on the left side of your screen, point to **row 3** to display the ➡ pointer, and then right-click to simultaneously select the row and display a shortcut menu. On the shortcut menu, click **Insert** to insert a new **row 3**.

b. Click cell **A3**, type **As of June 30** and then on the **Formula Bar**, click **Enter** to keep cell **A3** as the active cell. **Merge & Center** the text across the range **A3:F3**, and then apply the **Heading 2** cell style.

5 In the **column heading area**, point to **column B**. When the ⬇ pointer displays, right-click, and then click **Insert** to insert a new column.

a. Click cell **B4**, type **Material** and then press Enter. In cell **B5**, type **Latex** and then press Enter. In cell **B6,** type **Rubber** and then press Enter.

b. Using AutoComplete to speed your typing by pressing Enter as soon as the AutoComplete suggestion displays, in cells **B7**, **B8**, and **B10** type **Latex** and in cell **B9** type **Rubber**

c. In the **column heading area**, point to the right boundary of **column B**, and then drag to the left and set the width to **90 pixels**. In the **column heading area**, point to **column D**, right-click, and then click **Delete**.

d. Select the column titles in the range **B4:F4**, and then on the **Home tab**, in the **Alignment group**, click **Wrap Text**, **Center**, and **Middle Align**. With the range still selected, apply the **Heading 4** cell style.

e. Click cell **A11**, and then in the **Cell Styles** gallery, under **Themed Cell Styles**, click **40% - Accent1**.

6 Click the **Page Layout tab**, and then in the **Page Setup group**, click **Margins**. Click **Custom Margins**. In the **Page Setup** dialog box, on the **Margins tab**, under **Center on page**, select the **Horizontally** check box.

a. Click the **Header/Footer tab**, and then click **Custom Footer**. With your insertion point in the **Left section**, click **Insert File Name**. Click **OK** two times.

b. In the **Page Setup group**, click **Orientation**, and then click **Landscape**.

c. Click the **File tab** to display **Backstage** view. In the lower right corner, click **Show All Properties**. As the Tags, type **bands, tubing, inventory** In the **Subject** box, type your course name and section number. Be sure your name displays as the author—edit if necessary.

d. On the left, click **Save**.

e. By using the techniques you practiced in Project 15A and as directed by your instructor, print, create a PDF image that looks like a printed document, or submit your completed Excel file. If required by your instructor, print or create an electronic version of your worksheet with formulas displayed. In the upper right corner of your Excel window, click Close.

End | You have completed Project 15D

Mastering Excel Project 15E Gym Sales

In the following Mastering Excel project, you will create a worksheet comparing the sales of different types of home gym equipment sold in the second quarter. Your completed worksheet will look similar to Figure 15.58.

Apply 15A skills from these Objectives:

1 Create, Save, and Navigate an Excel Workbook

2 Enter Data in a Worksheet

3 Construct and Copy Formulas and Use the SUM Function

4 Format Cells with Merge & Center, Cell Styles, and Themes

5 Chart Data to Create a Column Chart and Insert Sparklines

6 Print a Worksheet, Display Formulas, and Close Excel

PROJECT FILES

For Project 15E, you will need the following file:

e15E_Gym_Sales

You will save your workbook as:

Lastname_Firstname_15E_Gym_Sales

PROJECT RESULTS

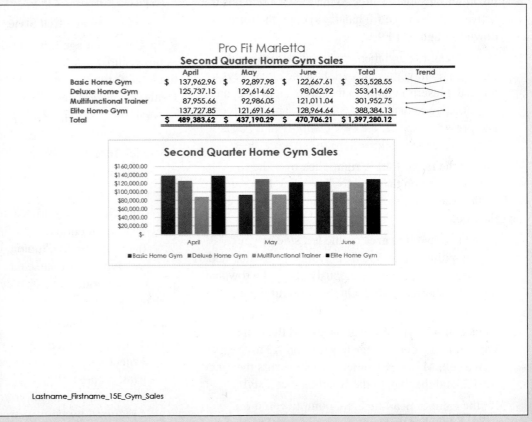

FIGURE 15.58

(Project 15E Gym Sales continues on the next page)

Mastering Excel | Project 15E Gym Sales (continued)

1 Start Excel, and then on the opening screen, in the lower left, click **Open Other Workbooks**. Click **Browse**, and then navigate to your student data files for this chapter. Open the file **e15E_Gym_Sales**. Click the **File tab**, on the left click **Save As**, and then click **Browse**. In the **Save As** dialog box, navigate to your **AIO Chapter 15** folder, and then using your own name, save the file as **Lastname_Firstname_15E_Gym_Sales**

2 Change the theme to **Wisp**.

3 In cell **B3**, use the fill handle to fill the months *May* and *June* in the range **C3:D3**.

4 **Merge & Center** the title across the range **A1:F1**, and then apply the **Title** cell style. **Merge & Center** the subtitle across the range **A2:F2**, and then apply the **Heading 1** cell style. **Center** the column titles in the range **B3:F3**.

5 Widen **column A** to **180 pixels**, and then widen columns **B:F** to **115 pixels**. In the range **B7:D7**, enter the monthly sales figures for the Elite Home Gym as shown in the table below:

	April	May	June
Elite Home Gym	137727.85	121691.64	128964.64

6 In cell **B8**, on the **Home tab**, use the **AutoSum** command to sum the April sales. Copy the resulting formula across to cells **C8:D8** to sum the May monthly sales and the June monthly sales. In cell **E4**, use the **AutoSum** button to sum the *Basic Home Gym* sales. Copy the formula down to cells **E4:E8**.

7 Apply the **Heading 4** cell style to the row titles and the column titles. Apply the **Total** cell style to the totals in the range **B8:E8**.

8 Apply the **Accounting Number Format** to the first row of sales figures and to the total row. Apply the **Comma Style** to the remaining sales figures.

9 To compare the monthly sales of each product visually, select the range that represents the sales figures for the three months, including the month names and the product names—do not include any totals in the range. With this data selected, use the **Recommended Charts** command to insert a **Clustered Column** chart with the month names displayed on the category axis and the product names displayed in the legend.

10 Move the chart so that its upper left corner is positioned in the center of cell **A10**. Then drag the center right sizing handle to the right until the right edge of the chart aligns with the right edge of **column E**; this will display the legend on one row and, after you add the sparklines, center the chart below the data.

11 Apply **Chart Style 6** and **Color 2** under **Colorful**. Change the **Chart Title** to **Second Quarter Home Gym Sales**

12 In the range **F4:F7**, insert **Line** sparklines that compare the monthly data. Do not include the totals. Show the sparkline **Markers** and apply **Sparkline Style Accent 2, Darker 50%** in the first row, the second style.

13 Center the worksheet **Horizontally** on the page, and then insert a **Footer** with the **File Name** in the **left section**.

14 Change the **Orientation** to **Landscape**. Display the document properties, and then as the **Tags** type **home gym, sales** As the **Subject**, type your course name and section number. Be sure your name displays as the **Author**. Check your worksheet by previewing it in **Print Preview**, and then make any necessary corrections.

15 **Save** your workbook. By using the techniques you practiced in Project 15A and as directed by your instructor, print, create a PDF image that looks like a printed document, or submit your completed Excel file. If required by your instructor, print or create an electronic version of your worksheet with formulas displayed. In the upper right corner of your Excel window, click **Close**.

END | You have completed Project 15E

Mastering Excel Project 15F Balance Sales

In the following Mastering Excel project, you will create a worksheet that summarizes the sales of balance and stabilization equipment that Pro Fit Marietta is marketing. Your completed worksheet will look similar to Figure 15.59.

PROJECT FILES

For Project 15F, you will need the following file:

e15F_Balance_Sales

You will save your workbook as:

Lastname_Firstname_15F_Balance_Sales

PROJECT RESULTS

Pro Fit Marietta
Balance and Stabilization Sales

	Month Ending March 31			
	Quantity Sold	Retail Price	Total Sales	Percent of Total Sales
Balance Pillow	275	$ 22.95	$ 6,311.25	5.43%
Slide Board	382	75.50	28,841.00	24.82%
Foam Roller	251	39.50	9,914.50	8.53%
Rebounder	162	139.95	22,671.90	19.51%
Stability Ball	380	51.50	19,570.00	16.84%
Balance Board	206	84.95	17,499.70	15.06%
Balance Pad	150	75.99	11,398.50	9.81%
Total Sales for All Products			$ 116,206.85	

Lastname_Firstname_15F_Balance_Sales

Excel 2016, Windows 10, Microsoft Corporation

FIGURE 15.59

(Project 15F Balance Sales continues on the next page)

1 Start Excel, and then on the opening screen, in the lower left, click **Open Other Workbooks**. Click **Browse**, and then navigate to your student data files for this chapter. Open the file **e15F_Balance_Sales**. Click the **File tab**, on the left click **Save As**, and then click **Browse**. In the **Save As** dialog box, navigate to your **AIO Chapter 15** folder, and then using your own name, save the file as **Lastname_Firstname_15F_Balance_Sales**

2 **Merge & Center** the title and the subtitle across **columns A:F**. Apply the **Title** and **Heading 1** cell styles respectively.

3 Make cell **A1** the active cell, and then check spelling in your worksheet. Correct *Silde* to **Slide**. Widen **column A** to **180 pixels** and **columns B:F** to **95 pixels**.

4 In cell **E4**, construct a formula to calculate the *Total Sales* of the *Balance Pillow* by multiplying the *Quantity Sold* times the *Retail Price*. Copy the formula down for the remaining products.

5 Select the range **E4:E10**, and then use the **Quick Analysis** tool to **Sum** the *Total Sales for All Products*, which will be formatted in Bold. To the total in cell **E11**, apply the **Total** cell style.

6 Using absolute cell references as necessary so that you can copy the formula, in cell **F4**, construct a formula to calculate the *Percent of Total Sales* for the first product. Copy the formula down for the remaining products.

7 To the computed percentages, apply **Percent Style** with two decimal places, and then **Center** the percentages.

8 Apply the **Comma Style** with no decimal places to the *Quantity Sold* figures. To cells **D4**, **E4**, and **E11** apply the **Accounting Number Format**.

9 To the range **D5:E10**, apply the **Comma Style**.

10 Change the *Retail Price* of the *Slide Board* to **75.50** and the *Quantity Sold* of the *Balance Pad* to **150**

11 Delete **column B**.

12 Insert a new **row 3**. In cell **A3**, type **Month Ending March 31** and then **Merge & Center** the text across the range **A3:E3**. Apply the **Heading 2** cell style.

13 To cell **A12**, apply the **20%-Accent1** cell style.

14 Select the four column titles, apply **Wrap Text**, **Middle Align**, and **Center** formatting, and then apply the **Heading 3** cell style.

15 Center the worksheet **Horizontally** on the page, and then insert a **Footer** with the **File Name** in the **left section**.

16 Display the document properties, and then as the **Tags**, type **balance, stability, sales** In the **Subject** box, add your course name and section number. Be sure your name displays as the Author.

17 **Save** your workbook. By using the techniques you practiced in Project 15A and as directed by your instructor, print, create a PDF image that looks like a printed document, or submit your completed Excel file. If required by your instructor, print or create an electronic version of your worksheet with formulas displayed. In the upper right corner of your Excel Window, click **Close**.

END | You have completed Project 15F

MyITLab® grader

Mastering Excel Project 15G Regional Sales

Apply a combination of 15A and 15B skills:

1. Create, Save, and Navigate an Excel Workbook
2. Enter Data in a Worksheet
3. Construct and Copy Formulas and Use the SUM Function
4. Format Cells with Merge & Center, Cell Styles, and Themes
5. Chart Data to Create a Column Chart and Insert Sparklines
6. Print a Worksheet, Display Formulas, and Close Excel
7. Check Spelling in a Worksheet
8. Enter Data by Range
9. Construct Formulas for Mathematical Operations
10. Edit Values in a Worksheet
11. Format a Worksheet

In the following Mastering Excel project, you will create a new worksheet that compares annual sales by region. Your completed worksheet will look similar to Figure 15.60.

PROJECT FILES

For Project 15G, you will need the following file:

e15G_Regional_Sales

You will save your workbook as

Lastname_Firstname_15G_Regional_Sales

PROJECT RESULTS

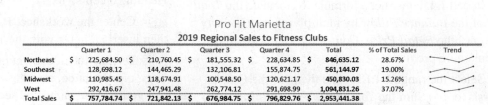

Pro Fit Marietta

2019 Regional Sales to Fitness Clubs

	Quarter 1	Quarter 2	Quarter 3	Quarter 4	Total	% of Total Sales	Trend
Northeast	$ 225,684.50	$ 210,760.45	$ 181,555.32	$ 228,634.85	$ 846,635.12	28.67%	
Southeast	128,698.12	144,465.29	132,106.81	155,874.75	561,144.97	19.00%	
Midwest	110,985.45	118,674.91	100,548.50	120,621.17	450,830.03	15.26%	
West	292,416.67	247,941.48	262,774.12	291,698.99	1,094,831.26	37.07%	
Total Sales	$ 757,784.74	$ 721,842.13	$ 676,984.75	$ 796,829.76	$ 2,953,441.38		

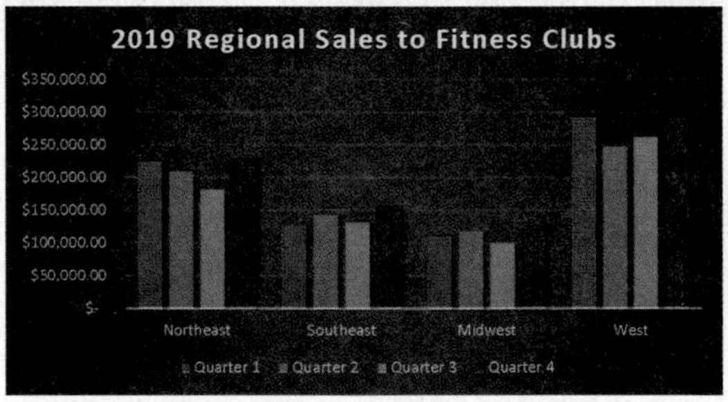

Lastname_Firstname_15G_Regional_Sales

FIGURE 15.60

Excel 2016, Windows 10, Microsoft Corporation

(Project 15G Regional Sales continues on the next page)

Mastering Excel Project 15G Regional Sales Project 15G (continued)

1 Start Excel, and then on the opening screen, in the lower left, click **Open Other Workbooks**. Click **Browse**, and then navigate to your student data files for this chapter. Open the file **e15G_Regional_Sales**. Click the **File tab**, on the left click **Save As**, and then click **Browse**. In the **Save As** dialog box, navigate to your **AIO Chapter 15** folder, and then using your own name, save the file as **Lastname_Firstname_15G_Regional_Sales**

2 Change the **Theme** to **Retrospect**. Set the width of **column A** to **80 pixels** and the width of columns **B:H** to **110 pixels**.

3 **Merge & Center** the title across the range **A1:H1**, and then apply the **Title** cell style. **Merge & Center** the subtitle across the range **A2:H2**, and then apply the **Heading 1** cell style.

4 Select the seven column titles, apply **Center** formatting, and then apply the **Heading 4** cell style.

5 By using the **Quick Analysis** tool, **Sum** the *Quarter 1* sales, and then copy the formula across for the remaining Quarters; the Quick Analysis tool formats totals in Bold.

6 Select the *Northeast* sales for the four quarters, and then display the **Quick Analysis** gallery for **Totals**. Click the second **Sum** option—the sixth item in the gallery—which displays the column selection in yellow. Copy the formula down through cell **F7**; recall that the Quick Analysis tool formats sums in Bold.

7 Apply the **Accounting Number Format** to the first row of sales figures and to the total row. Apply the **Comma Style** to the remaining sales figures. Format the totals in **row 7** with the **Total** cell style.

8 Insert a new **row 6** with the row title **Midwest** and the following sales figures for each quarter: **110985.45** and **118674.91** and **100548.50** and **120621.17** Copy the formula in cell **F5** down to cell **F6** to sum the new row.

9 Using absolute cell references as necessary so that you can copy the formula, in cell **G4** construct a formula to calculate the *Percent of Total Sales* for the first region. Copy the formula down for the remaining regions.

10 To the computed percentages, apply **Percent Style** with two decimal places, and then **Center** the percentages.

11 Insert **Line** sparklines in the range **H4:H7** that compare the quarterly data. Do not include the totals. Show the sparkline **Markers** and apply the second style in the second row—**Sparkline Style Accent 2, Darker 25%**.

12 **Save** your workbook. To compare the quarterly sales of each region visually, select the range that represents the sales figures for the four quarters, including the quarter names and each region—do not include any totals in the range. With this data selected, by using the **Recommended Charts** command, insert a **Clustered Column** with the regions as the category axis and the Quarters as the legend.

13 Apply **Chart Style 8** and **Color 3** under **Colorful**. Position the chart so that its upper right corner aligns with the upper right corner of cell **F10**.

14 Change the **Chart Title** to **2019 Regional Sales to Fitness Clubs**

15 Deselect the chart. Change the page **Orientation** to **Landscape**, center the worksheet **Horizontally** on the page, and then insert a footer with the file name in the left section.

16 Show the document properties. As the **Tags**, type **fitness clubs, sales** In the **Subject** box, type your course name and section number. Be sure your name displays as the Author.

17 **Save** your workbook. By using the techniques you practiced in Project 15A and as directed by your instructor, print, create a PDF image that looks like a printed document, or submit your completed Excel file. If required by your instructor, print or create an electronic version of your worksheet with formulas displayed. In the upper right corner of your Excel Window, click **Close**.

> **END | You have completed Project 15G**

GO! Fix It	Project 15H Team Sales	**MyITLab**
GO! Make It	Project 15I Agility Sales	**MyITLab**
GO! Solve It	Project 15J Kettlebell Sales	**MyITLab**
GO! Solve It	Project 15K Commission	

Apply a combination of the 15A and 15B skills.

Build From Scratch

PROJECT FILES

For Project 15K, you will need the following file:

e15K_Commission

You will save your workbook as:

Lastname_Firstname_15K_Commission

Open the file e15K_Commission and save it as **Lastname_Firstname_15K_Commission** Complete the worksheet by using Auto Fill to complete the month headings, and then calculating the Total Commission for each month and for each region. Insert and format appropriate sparklines in the Trend column. Format the worksheet attractively with a title and subtitle, check spelling, adjust column width, and apply appropriate financial formatting. Insert a chart that compares the total sales commission for each region with the months displaying as the categories, and format the chart attractively. Include the file name in the footer, add appropriate properties, and submit as directed.

Performance Level

		Exemplary: You consistently applied the relevant skills	Proficient: You sometimes, but not always, applied the relevant skills	Developing: You rarely or never applied the relevant skills
Performance Criteria	**Create formulas**	All formulas are correct and are efficiently constructed.	Formulas are correct but not always constructed in the most efficient manner.	One or more formulas are missing or incorrect; or only numbers were entered.
	Create a chart	Chart created properly.	Chart was created but incorrect data was selected.	No chart was created.
	Insert and format sparklines	Sparklines inserted and formatted properly.	Sparklines were inserted but incorrect data was selected or sparklines were not formatted.	No sparklines were inserted.
	Format attractively and appropriately	Formatting is attractive and appropriate.	Adequately formatted but difficult to read or unattractive.	Inadequate or no formatting.

END | You have completed Project 15K

RUBRIC

The following outcomes-based assessments are *open-ended assessments*. That is, there is no specific correct result; your result will depend on your approach to the information provided. Make *Professional Quality* your goal. Use the following scoring rubric to guide you in *how* to approach the problem and then to evaluate *how well* your approach solves the problem.

The *criteria*—Software Mastery, Content, Format and Layout, and Process—represent the knowledge and skills you have gained that you can apply to solving the problem. The *levels of performance*—Professional Quality, Approaching Professional Quality, or Needs Quality Improvements—help you and your instructor evaluate your result.

	Your completed project is of Professional Quality if you:	Your completed project is Approaching Professional Quality if you:	Your completed project Needs Quality Improvements if you:
1-Software Mastery	Choose and apply the most appropriate skills, tools, and features and identify efficient methods to solve the problem.	Choose and apply some appropriate skills, tools, and features, but not in the most efficient manner.	Choose inappropriate skills, tools, or features, or are inefficient in solving the problem.
2-Content	Construct a solution that is clear and well organized, contains content that is accurate, appropriate to the audience and purpose, and is complete. Provide a solution that contains no errors of spelling, grammar, or style.	Construct a solution in which some components are unclear, poorly organized, inconsistent, or incomplete. Misjudge the needs of the audience. Have some errors in spelling, grammar, or style, but the errors do not detract from comprehension.	Construct a solution that is unclear, incomplete, or poorly organized, contains some inaccurate or inappropriate content, and contains many errors of spelling, grammar, or style. Do not solve the problem.
3-Format and Layout	Format and arrange all elements to communicate information and ideas, clarify function, illustrate relationships, and indicate relative importance.	Apply appropriate format and layout features to some elements, but not others. Overuse features, causing minor distraction.	Apply format and layout that does not communicate information or ideas clearly. Do not use format and layout features to clarify function, illustrate relationships, or indicate relative importance. Use available features excessively, causing distraction.
4-Process	Use an organized approach that integrates planning, development, self-assessment, revision, and reflection.	Demonstrate an organized approach in some areas, but not others; or, use an insufficient process of organization throughout.	Do not use an organized approach to solve the problem.

Apply a combination of the 15A and 15B skills.

GO! Think | Project 15L Video Sales

PROJECT FILES

Build From Scratch For Project 15L, you will need the following file:

New blank Excel workbook

You will save your workbook as:

Lastname_Firstname_15L_Video_Sales

Michelle Barry, President of Pro Fit Marietta, needs a worksheet that summarizes the following data regarding the first quarter sales of training videos. Michelle would like the worksheet to include a calculation of the total sales for each type of video and a total of the sales of all of the videos. She would also like to know each type of video's percentage of total sales.

	Number Sold	Price
Pilates	156	29.99
Step	392	14.99
Weight Training	147	54.99
Kickboxing	282	29.99
Yoga	165	34.99

Create a worksheet that provides Michelle with the information needed. Include appropriate worksheet, column, and row titles. Using the formatting skills that you practiced in this chapter, format the worksheet in a manner that is professional and easy to read and understand. Insert a footer with the file name and add appropriate document properties. Save the file as **Lastname_Firstname_15L_Video_Sales** and print or submit as directed by your instructor.

END | You have completed Project 15L

GO! Think | Project 15M Expenses **MyITLab**

Build From Scratch

You and GO! | Project 15N Personal Expenses **MyITLab**

Build From Scratch

GO! Collaborative Team Project | Project 15O Bell Orchid Hotels **MyITLab**

Build From Scratch

Functions, Tables, Large Workbooks, and Pie Charts

PROJECT 16A

OUTCOMES
Analyze inventory by applying statistical and logical calculations to data and by sorting and filtering data.

OBJECTIVES

1. Use Flash Fill and the SUM, AVERAGE, MEDIAN, MIN, and MAX Functions
2. Move Data, Resolve Error Messages, and Rotate Text
3. Use COUNTIF and IF Functions and Apply Conditional Formatting
4. Use Date & Time Functions and Freeze Panes
5. Create, Sort, and Filter an Excel Table
6. View, Format, and Print a Large Worksheet

PROJECT 16B

OUTCOMES
Summarize the data on multiple worksheets.

OBJECTIVES

7. Navigate a Workbook and Rename Worksheets
8. Enter Dates, Clear Contents, and Clear Formats
9. Copy and Paste by Using the Paste Options Gallery
10. Edit and Format Multiple Worksheets at the Same Time
11. Create a Summary Sheet with Column Sparklines
12. Format and Print Multiple Worksheets in a Workbook

PROJECT 16C

OUTCOMES
Present fund data in a pie chart.

OBJECTIVES

13. Chart Data with a Pie Chart
14. Format a Pie Chart
15. Edit a Workbook and Update a Chart
16. Use Goal Seek to Perform What-If Analysis

Jbd30/Shutterstock

In This Chapter
GO! to Work with Excel

In this chapter, you will use several types of Excel functions, including Statistical, Date & Time, and Logical functions. You will also use Excel's Flash Fill feature to automatically fill in values, and you will apply different types of conditional formatting to make data easy to visualize. You will create a pie chart in a separate chart sheet to show how the parts of a fund contribute to a total fund, and you will create a table to organize, sort, and filter related information. You will also create formulas to summarize a workbook that contains multiple worksheets.

The projects in this chapter relate to **Rosedale Landscape and Garden** and the **City of Pacifica Bay**. Rosedale Landscape and Garden grows and sells trees and plants suitable for all areas of North America. The company has nurseries and stores in the major metropolitan areas in the United States and Canada. The City of Pacifica Bay is a coastal city south of San Francisco. The city's access to major transportation provides both residents and businesses an opportunity to compete in the global marketplace. The city's mission is to create a more beautiful and more economically viable community for its residents.

Inventory Status Report

PROJECT ACTIVITIES

In Activities 16.01 through 16.20, you will edit a worksheet for Holman Hill, President of Rosedale Landscape and Garden, detailing the current inventory of trees at the Pasadena nursery. Your completed worksheet will look similar to Figure 16.1.

PROJECT FILES

MyITLab grader — If your instructor wants you to submit Project 16A in the MyITLab Grader system, log in to MyITLab, locate Grader Project 16A, and then download the files for this project.

For Project 16A, you will need the following file:
e16A_Tree_Inventory

You will save your workbook as:
Lastname_Firstname_16A_Tree_Inventory

PROJECT RESULTS

GO!
Walk Thru
Project 16A

Quantity in Stock	Item #	Tree Name	Retail Price	Light	Landscape Use	Category	Stock Level
93	38700	Pacific Fire	103.75	Full Shade	Erosion Control	Oak	OK
45	38744	Cheals Weeping	104.99	Partial Shade	Erosion Control	Cherry	Order
58	39704	Embers	105.99	Partial Sun	Erosion Control	Oak	Order
90	42599	Beurre	109.98	Partial Sun	Border	Pear	OK
350	43153	Bradford	104.99	Full Shade	Border	Pear	OK

12/6/2015 15:09

Pasadena Tree Nursery
As of December 31

Tree Statistics

Total Items in Stock		3,022
Average Price	$	107.89
Median Price	$	107.99
Lowest Price	$	102.99
Highest Price	$	117.98

Oak Trees   13
Maple Trees   6 (571 total items in stock)

Quantity in Stock	Item #	Tree Name	Retail Price	Light	Landscape Use	Category	Stock Level
78	13129	Golden Oak	108.99	Partial Sun	Erosion Control	Oak	OK
35	13358	Columnar English	106.95	Full Shade	Border	Oak	Order
60	15688	Coral Bark	106.25	Partial Shade	Erosion Control	Oak	Order
20	16555	Crimson King	105.50	Full Shade	Border	Oak	Order
75	21683	Japanese Blooming	103.99	Partial Shade	Erosion Control	Cherry	OK
60	22189	Crimson Queen	109.95	Filtered Sun	Erosion Control	Oak	Order
68	23677	Black Japanese	107.99	Partial Sun	Border	Maple	Order
71	23688	Artist Flowering	109.95	Partial Sun	Erosion Control	Pear	Order
159	24896	Bing Small Sweet	105.99	Partial Shade	Border	Cherry	OK
60	25678	Bartlett	109.75	Partial Sun	Erosion Control	Pear	Order
179	25844	Bloodgood	110.99	Partial Shade	Border	Maple	OK
90	26787	Sentry	108.50	Partial Sun	Border	Oak	OK
81	32544	Burgundy Bell	110.95	Partial Sun	Border	Maple	OK
81	34266	Lace Maple	109.99	Partial Sun	Border	Maple	OK
113	34793	Emerald Elf	103.98	Full Shade	Erosion Control	Oak	OK
191	34878	Ginger Pear	107.78	Partial Sun	Border	Pear	OK
102	34982	Fernleaf	105.99	Partial Shade	Border	Oak	OK
170	35677	Flamingo	109.99	Partial Sun	Border	Oak	OK
170	35690	Bing Sweet	107.99	Partial Sun	Erosion Control	Cherry	OK
70	35988	Butterfly Japanese	111.75	Partial Sun	Border	Maple	Order
92	36820	Ever Red	110.95	Partial Sun	Border	Maple	OK
173	37803	Osakazuki	103.88	Full Shade	Erosion Control	Oak	OK
113	37845	Anna	117.98	Partial Sun	Woodland Garden	Magnolia	OK
75	38675	Palo Alto	102.99	Partial Shade	Erosion Control	Oak	OK

Lastname_Firstname_16A_Tree_Inventory

FIGURE 16.1 Project 16A Tree Inventory

Objective 1 | Use Flash Fill and the SUM, AVERAGE, MEDIAN, MIN, and MAX Functions

GO! Learn How
Video E16-1

Flash Fill recognizes a pattern in your data, and then automatically fills in values when you enter examples of the output that you want. Use Flash Fill to split data into two or more cells or to combine data from two cells.

A *function* is the name given to a predefined formula—a formula that Excel has already built for you—that performs calculations by using specific values that you insert in a particular order or structure. *Statistical functions*, which include the AVERAGE, MEDIAN, MIN, and MAX functions, are useful to analyze a group of measurements.

Activity 16.01 | Using Flash Fill

> **ALERT!**
>
> **To submit as an autograded project, log into MyITLab and download the files for this project, and begin with those files instead of e16A_Tree_Inventory.**

1. Start Excel, and then in the lower left corner of Excel's opening screen, click **Open Other Workbooks**.

2. Click **Browse**. Navigate to the student files that accompany this chapter, and then locate and open **e16A_Tree_Inventory**. Display the **Save As** dialog box, and then navigate to the location where you are storing your projects for this chapter.

3. Create a new folder named **AIO Chapter 16** and then open the new folder. In the **File name** box, type **Lastname_Firstname_16A_Tree_Inventory** and then click **Save** or press Enter.

4. Scroll down. Notice that the worksheet contains data related to types of trees in inventory, including information about the *Quantity in Stock*, *Item #/Category*, *Tree Name*, *Retail Price*, *Light*, and *Landscape Use*.

5. In the **column heading area**, point to **column C** to display the ↓ pointer, and then drag to the right to select **columns C:D**. On the **Home tab**, in the **Cells group**, click the **Insert button arrow**, and then click **Insert Sheet Columns**.

   New columns for C and D display and the remaining columns move to the right.

> **ANOTHER WAY** Select the columns, right-click anywhere over the selected columns, and then on the shortcut menu, click Insert.

6. Click cell **C11**, type **13129** and then on the **Formula Bar**, click **Enter** ✓ to confirm the entry and keep **C11** as the active cell.

7. On the **Home tab**, in the **Editing group**, click **Fill**, and then click **Flash Fill**. Compare your screen with Figure 16.2.

   Use this technique to split a column of data based on what you type. Flash Fill looks to the left and sees the pattern you have established, and then fills the remaining cells in the column with only the Item #. The Flash Fill Options button displays.

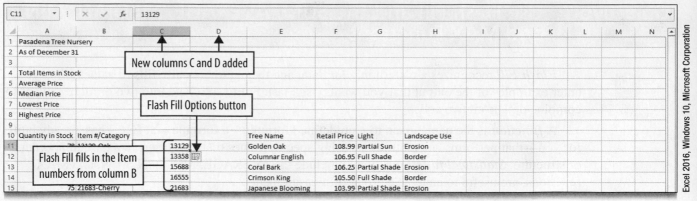

FIGURE 16.2

8 Near the lower right corner of cell **C11**, click the **Flash Fill Options** button, and notice that here you can *Undo Flash Fill*, *Accept suggestions*, or *Select all 28 changed cells*, for example, to apply specific formatting. Click the button again to close it.

> If Excel is not sure what pattern to use, it suggests a pattern by filling with pale gray characters, and then you can use the Accept suggestions command to accept or start again.

9 Click cell **D11**, type **Oak** and then on the **Formula Bar**, click ☑ to confirm the entry and keep **D11** as the active cell. Press Ctrl + E, which is the keyboard shortcut for Flash Fill.

> Flash Fill extracts the text from the *Item#/Category* column and also inserts *Category* as the column name. Now that *Item #* and *Category* are in two separate columns, the data can be sorted and filtered by both Item # and Category.

10 Select **column B**, and then in the **Cells group**, click the **Delete button arrow**. Click **Delete Sheet Columns**. On the Quick Access Toolbar, click **Save** 🖫.

↻ ANOTHER WAY   Select the column, right-click anywhere over the selected column, and then on the shortcut menu, click Delete.

Activity 16.02 │ Moving a Column

1 In cell **B10**, type **Item #** and then press Enter. Select **column C**, and then on the **Home tab**, in the **Clipboard group**, click **Cut** ✂. Click cell **H1**, and then in the **Clipboard group**, click the upper portion of the **Paste** button.

↻ ANOTHER WAY   Press Ctrl + X to cut and Ctrl + V to paste.

2 Select and then delete **column C**. Select **columns A:G**. In the **Cells group**, click **Format**, and then click **AutoFit Column Width**.

↻ ANOTHER WAY   Select the columns, in the column heading area point to any of the selected column borders to display the ⊹ pointer, and then double-click to AutoFit the columns.

3 **Merge & Center** cell A1 across the range **A1:H1**, and then apply the **Title** cell style. **Merge & Center** cell A2 across the range **A2:H2**, and then apply the **Heading 1** cell style. Compare your screen with Figure 16.3. **Save** 🖫 your workbook.

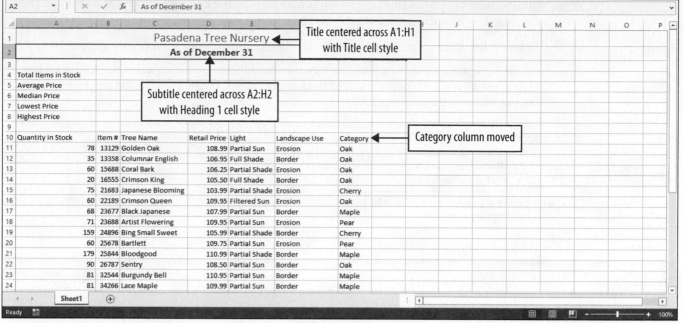

FIGURE 16.3

Excel 2016, Windows 10, Microsoft Corporation

IC3
DIGITAL LITERACY
CERTIFICATION

2.03e (i)
2.03e (ii)
2.03e (iii)

Activity 16.03 | Using the SUM and AVERAGE Functions

In this Activity, you will use the SUM and AVERAGE functions to gather information about the product inventory.

1 Click cell **B4**. Click the **Formulas tab**, and then in the **Function Library group**, click the upper portion of the **AutoSum** button. Compare your screen with Figure 16.4.

The *SUM function* is a predefined formula that adds all the numbers in a selected range of cells. Because it is frequently used, there are several ways to insert the function. For example, you can insert the function from the Home tab's Editing group, or by using the keyboard shortcut Alt + =, or from the Function Library group on the Formulas tab, or from the Math & Trig button in that group.

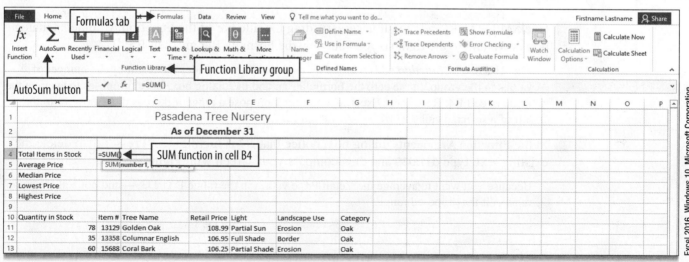

FIGURE 16.4

Excel 2016, Windows 10, Microsoft Corporation

> **2** With the insertion point blinking in the function, type the cell range **a11:a39** to sum all the values in the *Quantity in Stock* column, and then press Enter; your result is *3022*.

> **3** Click cell **B4**, look at the **Formula Bar**, and then compare your screen with Figure 16.5.

> *SUM* is the name of the function. The values in parentheses are the ***arguments***—the values that an Excel function uses to perform calculations or operations. In this instance, the argument consists of the values in the range A11:A39.

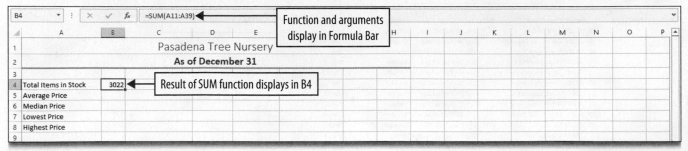

FIGURE 16.5

> **4** Click cell **B5**. In the **Function Library group**, click **More Functions**, point to **Statistical**, point to **AVERAGE**, and notice the ScreenTip. Compare your screen with Figure 16.6.

> The ScreenTip describes how the AVERAGE function will compute the calculation.

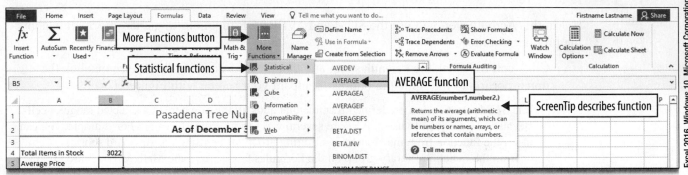

FIGURE 16.6

> **5** Click **AVERAGE**, and then if necessary, drag the title bar of the Function Arguments dialog box down and to the right so you can view the Formula Bar and cell B5.

> The ***AVERAGE function*** adds a group of values, and then divides the result by the number of values in the group. In the cell, the Formula Bar, and the dialog box, Excel proposes to average the value in cell B4. Recall that Excel functions will propose a range if there is data above or to the left of a selected cell.

> **6** In the **Function Arguments** dialog box, notice that *B4* is highlighted. Press Del to delete the existing text, type **d11:d39** and then compare your screen with Figure 16.7.

> Because you want to average the Retail Price values in the range D11:D39—and not cell B4—you must edit the proposed range.

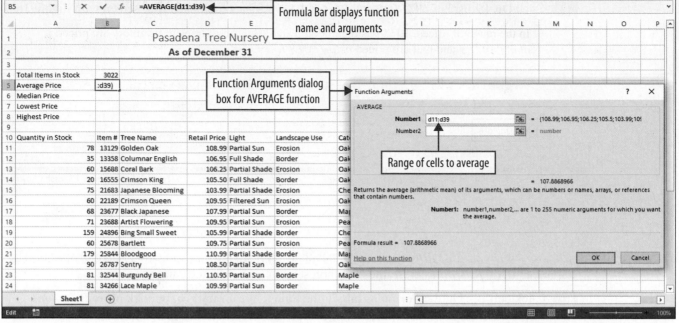

FIGURE 16.7

Excel 2016, Windows 10, Microsoft Corporation

7 In the **Function Arguments** dialog box, click **OK**, and then click **Save** 💾.

The result indicates that the average Retail Price of all products is *107.89*.

Activity 16.04 | Using the MEDIAN Function

The **MEDIAN function** is a statistical function that describes a group of data—it is commonly used to describe the price of houses in a particular geographical area. The MEDIAN function finds the middle value that has as many values above it in the group as are below it. It differs from AVERAGE in that the result is not affected as much by a single value that is greatly different from the others.

1 Click cell **B6**. In the **Function Library group**, click **More Functions**, display the list of **Statistical** functions, scroll down as necessary, and then click **MEDIAN**.

2 Press Del to delete the text in the **Number1** box. Type **d11:d39** and then compare your screen with Figure 16.8.

When indicating which cells you want to use in the function's calculation—known as *defining the arguments*—you can either select the values with your mouse or type the range of values, whichever you prefer.

10	Quantity in Stock		Item #	Tree Name	Retail Price			egory	Function Arguments	?	×
11		78	13129	Golden Oak	108.99						
12		35	13358	Columnar English	106.95				MEDIAN		
13		60	15688	Coral Bark	106.25						
14		20	16555	Crimson King	105.50	Full Shade	Border	Oak	Number1 d11:d39	= {108.99;106.95;106.25;105.5;103.99;10	
15		75	21683	Japanese Blooming	103.99	Partial Shade	Erosion	Cherry	Number2	= number	
16		60	22189	Crimson Queen	109.95	Filtered Sun	Erosion	Oak			
17		68	23677	Black Japanese	107.99	Partial Sun	Border	Maple			
18		71	23688	Artist Flowering	109.95	Partial Sun	Erosion	Pear		= 107.99	
19		159	24896	Bing Small Sweet	105.99	Partial Shade	Border	Cherry	Returns the median, or the number in the middle of the set of given numbers.		
20		60	25678	Bartlett	109.75	Partial Sun	Erosion	Pear			
21		179	25844	Bloodgood	110.99	Partial Shade	Border	Maple	Number1: number1,number2,... are 1 to 255 numbers or names, arrays, or references that contain numbers for which you want the median.		
22		90	26787	Sentry	108.50	Partial Sun	Border	Oak			
23		81	32544	Burgundy Bell	110.95	Partial Sun	Border	Maple			
24		81	34266	Lace Maple	109.99	Partial Sun	Border	Maple	Formula result = 107.99		
25		113	34793	Emerald Elf	103.98	Full Shade	Erosion	Oak	Help on this function	OK	Cancel
26		191	34878	Ginger Pear	107.78	Partial Sun	Border	Pear			

FIGURE 16.8

Excel 2016, Windows 10, Microsoft Corporation

3 Click **OK** to display *107.99* in cell **B6**. Click **Save** 🖫 and compare your screen with Figure 16.9.

In the range of prices, 107.99 is the middle value. Half of all trees in inventory are priced *above* 107.99 and half are priced *below* 107.99.

FIGURE 16.9

Activity 16.05 | Using the MIN and MAX Functions

The statistical ***MIN function*** determines the smallest value in a selected range of values. The statistical ***MAX function*** determines the largest value in a selected range of values.

1 Click cell **B7**. On the **Formulas tab**, in the **Function Library group**, click **More Functions**, display the list of **Statistical** functions, scroll as necessary, and then click **MIN**.

2 Press ⌑Del⌑, and then in the **Number1** box, type **d11:d39** Click **OK**.

The lowest Retail Price is *102.99*.

3 Click cell **B8**, and then by using a similar technique, insert the **MAX** function to determine the highest **Retail Price**, and then check to see that your result is *117.98*.

4 Press ⌑Ctrl⌑ + ⌑Home⌑. Point to cell **B4**, right-click, and then on the mini toolbar, click **Comma Style** ⌑ one time and **Decrease Decimal** ⌑ two times.

5 Select the range **B5:B8**, apply the **Accounting Number Format** ⌑$ ·⌑, click **Save** 🖫, and then compare your screen with Figure 16.10.

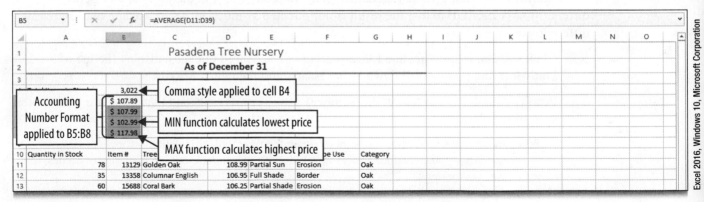

FIGURE 16.10

When you move a formula, the cell references within the formula do not change, no matter what type of cell reference you use.

If you move cells into a column that is not wide enough to display number values, Excel will display a message so that you can adjust as necessary.

You can reposition data within a cell at an angle by rotating the text.

Activity 16.06 | Moving Data and Resolving a # # # # # Error Message

1 Select **column E** and set the width to **50 pixels**. Select the range **A4:B8**. Point to the right edge of the selected range to display the ⬚ pointer, and then compare your screen with Figure 16.11.

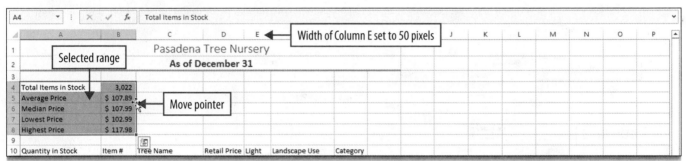

FIGURE 16.11

Excel 2016, Windows 10, Microsoft Corporation

2 Drag the selected range to the right until the ScreenTip displays *D4:E8*, release the mouse button, and then notice that a series of # symbols displays in **column E**. Point to any of the cells that display # symbols, and then compare your screen with Figure 16.12.

Using this technique, cell contents can be moved from one location to another; this is referred to as **drag and drop**.

If a cell width is too narrow to display the entire number, Excel displays the ##### message, because displaying only a portion of a number would be misleading. The underlying values remain unchanged and are displayed in the Formula Bar for the selected cell. An underlying value also displays in the ScreenTip if you point to a cell containing # symbols.

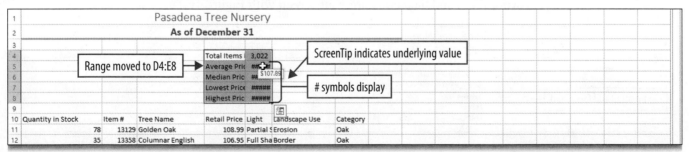

FIGURE 16.12

Excel 2016, Windows 10, Microsoft Corporation

3 Select **columns D:E**, and then in the **column heading area**, point to the right boundary of **column E** to display the ⊞ pointer. Double-click to AutoFit the column to accommodate the widest entry.

4 Select the range **D4:E8**. On the **Home tab**, in the **Styles group**, display the **Cell Styles** gallery. Under **Themed Cell Styles**, click **20%-Accent1**. Click **Save** 🖫.

1 In cell **C6**, type **Tree Statistics** and then press Enter.

2 Select cell **C6**. On the **Home tab**, in the **Font group**, change the **Font Size** `11 ▾` to **14**, and then apply **Bold** `B` and **Italic** `I`. Click the **Font Color arrow** `A ▾`, and then in the fifth column, click the first color—**Blue, Accent 1**.

3 In the **Alignment group**, apply **Align Right** `☰`.

4 Select the range **C4:C8**, right-click over the selection, and then on the shortcut menu, click **Format Cells**. In the **Format Cells** dialog box, click the **Alignment tab**. Under **Text control**, select the **Merge cells** check box.

5 Under **Orientation**, click in the **Degrees** box to select the value, type **30** and then compare your screen with Figure 16.13.

🔄 **ANOTHER WAY**   In the upper right portion of the dialog box, under Orientation, point to the red diamond, and then drag the diamond upward until the Degrees box indicates 30.

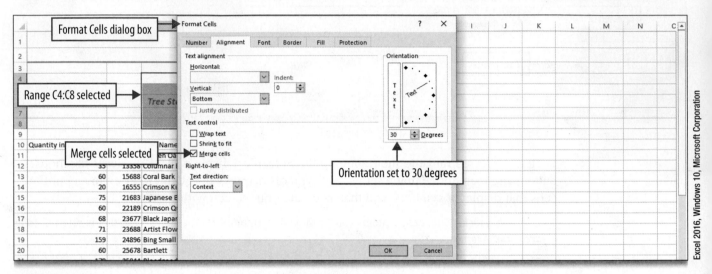

FIGURE 16.13

6 In the lower right corner of the **Format Cells** dialog box, click **OK**. Press Ctrl + Home, **Save** `💾` your workbook, and then compare your screen with Figure 16.14.

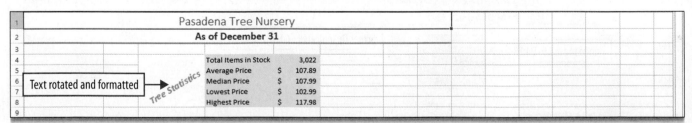

FIGURE 16.14

Excel 2016, Windows 10, Microsoft Corporation

7 In the **row heading area**, point to **row 9** and right-click to select the row and display the shortcut menu. Click **Insert**, and then press F4 two times to repeat the last action and insert two additional blank rows.

F4 is useful to repeat commands in Microsoft Office programs. Most commands can be repeated in this manner.

8 From the **row heading area**, select **rows 9:11**. On the **Home tab**, in the **Editing group**, click **Clear** ✐ and then click **Clear Formats** to remove the blue accent color in columns D and E from the new rows. Click **Save** 🖫.

> When you insert rows or columns, formatting from adjacent rows or columns repeats in the new cells.

9 Click cell **E4**, look at the **Formula Bar**, and then notice that the arguments of the **SUM** function adjusted and refer to the appropriate cells in rows 14:42.

> The referenced range updates to *A14:A42* after you insert the three new rows. In this manner, Excel adjusts the cell references in a formula relative to their new locations.

Objective 3 | Use COUNTIF and IF Functions and Apply Conditional Formatting

GO! Learn How
Video E16-3

Recall that statistical functions analyze a group of measurements. Another group of Excel functions, referred to as *logical functions*, test for specific conditions. Logical functions typically use conditional tests to determine whether specified conditions—called *criteria*—are true or false.

Activity 16.08 | Using the COUNTIF Function

The *COUNT function* counts the number of cells in a range that contain numbers. The *COUNTIF function* is a statistical function that counts the number of cells within a range that meet the given condition—the criteria that you provide. The COUNTIF function has two arguments—the range of cells to check and the criteria.

The trees of Rosedale Landscape and Garden will be featured on an upcoming segment of a TV gardening show. In this Activity, you will use the COUNTIF function to determine the number of *Oak* trees currently available in inventory that can be featured in the TV show.

1 In cell **A10**, type **Oak Trees** and then press Tab.

2 With cell **B10** as the active cell, on the **Formulas tab**, in the **Function Library group**, click **More Functions**, and then display the list of **Statistical** functions. Click **COUNTIF**.

> Recall that the COUNTIF function counts the number of cells within a range that meet the given condition.

3 In the **Range** box, type **g14:g42** Click in the **Criteria** box, type **Oak** and then compare your screen with Figure 16.15.

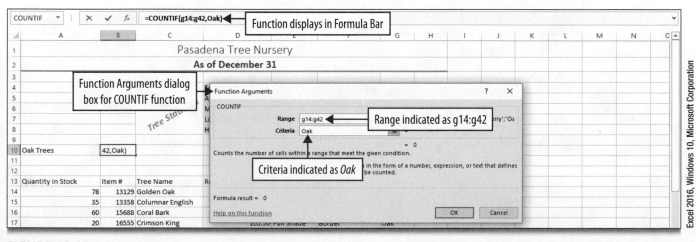

FIGURE 16.15

4 In the lower right corner of the **Function Arguments** dialog box, click **OK**.

There are *13* different *Oak* trees available to feature on the TV show.

5 On the **Home tab**, in the **Alignment group**, click **Align Left** to place the result closer to the row title. **Save** your workbook.

Activity 16.09 | Using the IF Function

A *logical test* is any value or expression that you can evaluate as being true or false. The *IF function* uses a logical test to check whether a condition is met, and then returns one value if true, and another value if false.

For example, *C14=228* is an expression that can be evaluated as true or false. If the value in cell C14 is equal to 228, the expression is true. If the value in cell C14 is not 228, the expression is false.

In this Activity, you will use the IF function to evaluate the inventory levels and determine if more products should be ordered.

1 Click cell **H13**, type **Stock Level** and then press Enter.

2 In cell **H14**, on the **Formulas tab**, in the **Function Library group**, click **Logical**, and then in the list, click **IF**. Drag the title bar of the **Function Arguments** dialog box up or down to view **row 14** on your screen.

3 With the insertion point in the **Logical_test** box, type **a14<75**

This logical test will look at the value in cell A14, which is *78*, and then determine if the number is less than 75. The expression *<75* includes the *comparison operator*, which means *less than*. Comparison operators compare values.

4 Examine the table in Figure 16.16 for a list of comparison operator symbols and their definitions.

COMPARISON OPERATORS	
COMPARISON OPERATORS	**SYMBOL DEFINITION**
=	Equal to
>	Greater than
<	Less than
>=	Greater than or equal to
<=	Less than or equal to
<>	Not equal to

FIGURE 16.16

Gaskin, Shelley. Go! All in One, 3E. Pearson Education, 2017.

5 Press Tab to move the insertion point to the **Value_if_true** box, and then type **Order**

If the result of the logical test is true—the Quantity in Stock is less than 75—cell H14 will display the text *Order* indicating that additional trees must be ordered.

6 Press Tab to move to the **Value_if_false** box, type **OK** and then compare your screen with Figure 16.17.

If the result of the logical test is false—the Quantity in Stock is *not* less than 75—then Excel will display *OK* in the cell.

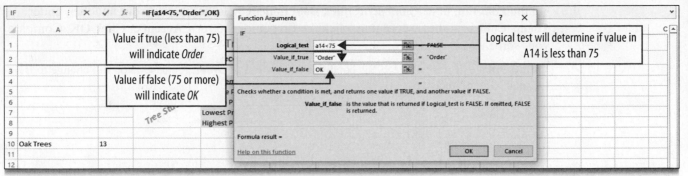

FIGURE 16.17

Excel 2016, Windows 10, Microsoft Corporation

7 ▸ Click **OK** to display the result *OK* in cell **H14**.

8 ▸ Using the fill handle, copy the function in cell **H14** down through cell **H42**. Then scroll as necessary to view cell **A18**, which contains the value *75*. Look at cell **H18** and notice that the **Stock Level** is indicated as *OK*. **Save** 🖫 your workbook. Compare your screen with Figure 16.18.

The comparison operator indicated <75 (less than 75) and therefore a value of *exactly* 75 is indicated as OK.

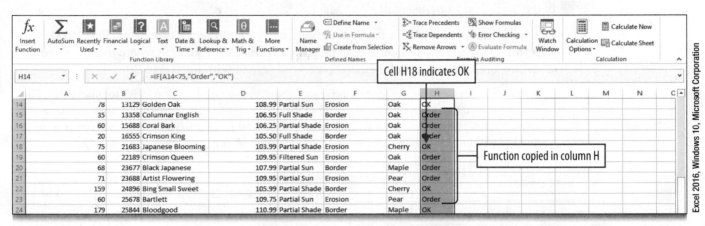

FIGURE 16.18

Activity 16.10 | Applying Conditional Formatting by Using Highlight Cells Rules and Data Bars

A **conditional format** changes the appearance of a cell based on a condition—a criteria. If the condition is true, the cell is formatted based on that condition; if the condition is false, the cell is *not* formatted. In this Activity, you will use conditional formatting as another way to draw attention to the Stock Level of trees.

1 ▸ Be sure the range **H14:H42** is selected. On the **Home tab**, in the **Styles group**, click **Conditional Formatting**. In the list, point to **Highlight Cells Rules**, and then click **Text That Contains**.

2 ▸ In the **Text That Contains** dialog box, with the insertion point blinking in the first box, type **Order** and notice that in the selected range, the text *Order* displays with the default format— Light Red Fill with Dark Red Text.

3 ▸ In the second box, click the **arrow**, and then in the list, click **Custom Format**.

Here, in the Format Cells dialog box, you can select any combination of formats to apply to the cell if the condition is true. The custom format you specify will be applied to any cell in the selected range if it contains the text *Order*.

4 On the **Font tab**, under **Font style**, click **Bold Italic**. Click the **Color arrow**, and then under **Theme Colors**, in the last column, click the first color—**Green, Accent 6**. Click **OK**. Compare your screen with Figure 16.19.

In the range, if the cell meets the condition of containing *Order*, the font color will change to Bold Italic, Green, Accent 6.

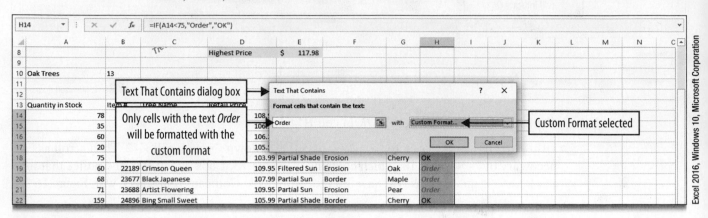

FIGURE 16.19

5 In the **Text That Contains** dialog box, click **OK**.

6 Select the range **A14:A42**. In the **Styles group**, click **Conditional Formatting**. Point to **Data Bars**, and then under **Gradient Fill**, click **Orange Data Bar**. Click anywhere to cancel the selection, click **Save** 💾, and then compare your screen with Figure 16.20.

A ***data bar*** provides a visual cue to the reader about the value of a cell relative to other cells. The length of the data bar represents the value in the cell. A longer bar represents a higher value and a shorter bar represents a lower value. Data bars are useful for identifying higher and lower numbers quickly within a large group of data, such as very high or very low levels of inventory.

FIGURE 16.20

Excel 2016, Windows 10, Microsoft Corporation

2.03a (vii)

Activity 16.11 | Using Find and Replace

The ***Find and Replace*** feature searches the cells in a worksheet—or in a selected range—for matches, and then replaces each match with a replacement value of your choice.

Comments from customers on the company's blog indicate that using the term *Erosion Control* would be clearer than *Erosion* when describing the best landscape use for specific trees. Therefore, all products of this type will be relabeled accordingly. In this Activity, you will replace all occurrences of *Erosion* with *Erosion Control*.

1 Select the range **F14:F42**. On the **Home tab**, in the **Editing group**, click **Find & Select**, and then click **Replace**.

Restrict the find and replace operation to a specific range in this manner, especially if there is a possibility that the name occurs elsewhere.

2 Type **Erosion** to fill in the **Find what** box. In the **Replace with** box, type **Erosion Control** and then compare your screen with Figure 16.21.

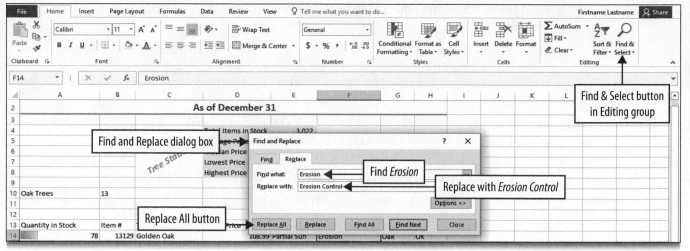

FIGURE 16.21

Excel 2016, Windows 10, Microsoft Corporation

3 ▷ Click **Replace All**. In the message box, notice that 13 replacements were made, and then click **OK**. In the lower right corner of the **Find and Replace** dialog box, click **Close**. Click **Save** 🔲.

Objective 4 | Use Date & Time Functions and Freeze Panes

GO! Learn How
Video E16-4

Excel can obtain the date and time from your computer's calendar and clock and display this information on your worksheet.

By freezing or splitting panes, you can view two areas of a worksheet and lock rows and columns in one area. When you freeze panes, you select the specific rows or columns that you want to remain visible when scrolling in your worksheet.

Activity 16.12 | Using the NOW Function to Display a System Date

The *NOW function* retrieves the date and time from your computer's calendar and clock and inserts the information into the selected cell. The result is formatted as a date and time.

1 ▷ To the left of the **Formula Bar**, click in the **Name Box**, type **a44** and then press Enter. Notice that cell A44 is the active cell.

2 ▷ With cell **A44** as the active cell, on the **Formulas tab**, in the **Function Library group**, click **Date & Time**. In the list of functions, click **NOW**. Compare your screen with Figure 16.22.

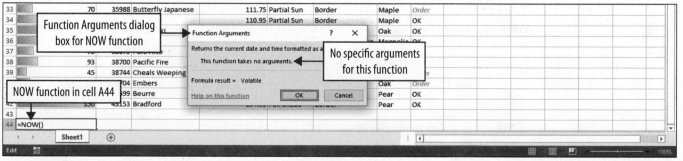

FIGURE 16.22

Excel 2016, Windows 10, Microsoft Corporation

3 Read the description in the **Function Arguments** dialog box, and notice that this result is *Volatile*.

> The Function Arguments dialog box displays a message indicating that this function does not require an argument. It also states that this function is *volatile*, meaning the date and time will not remain as entered, but rather the date and time will automatically update each time you open this workbook.

4 In the **Function Arguments** dialog box, click **OK** to close the dialog box to display the current date and time in cell **A44**. **Save** 🖫 your workbook.

More Knowledge | **NOW Function Recalculates Each Time a Workbook Opens**

The NOW function updates each time the workbook is opened. With the workbook open, you can force the NOW function to update by pressing ⌗ F9 , for example, to update the time.

Activity 16.13 │ Freezing and Unfreezing Panes

In a large worksheet, if you scroll down more than 25 rows or scroll beyond column O (the exact row number and column letter varies, depending on your screen size and screen resolution), you will no longer see the top rows or first column of your worksheet where identifying information about the data is usually placed. You will find it easier to work with your data if you can always view the identifying row or column titles.

The *Freeze Panes* command enables you to select one or more rows or columns and then freeze (lock) them into place. The locked rows and columns become separate panes. A *pane* is a portion of a worksheet window bounded by and separated from other portions by vertical or horizontal bars.

1 Press ⌗ Ctrl + ⌗ Home to make cell **A1** the active cell. Scroll down until **row 21** displays at the top of your Excel window, and notice that all of the identifying information in the column titles is out of view.

2 Press ⌗ Ctrl + ⌗ Home again, and then from the **row heading area**, select **row 14**. Click the **View tab**, and then in the **Window group**, click **Freeze Panes**. In the list, click **Freeze Panes**. Click any cell to deselect the row, and then notice that a line displays along the upper border of **row 14**.

> By selecting row 14, the rows above—rows 1–13—are frozen in place and will not move as you scroll down.

3 Watch the row numbers below **row 13**, and then begin to scroll down to bring **row 21** into view again. Notice that rows 1:13 are frozen in place. Compare your screen with Figure 16.23.

> The remaining rows of data continue to scroll. Use this feature when you have long or wide worksheets.

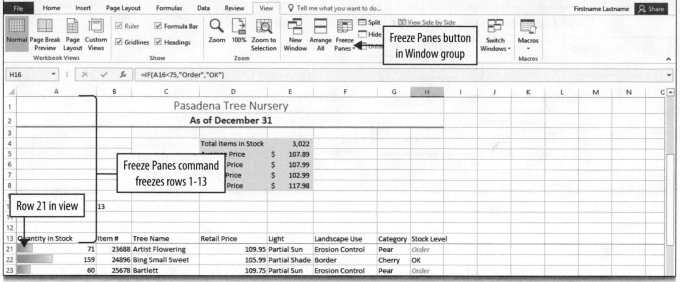

	A	B	C	D	E	F	G	H	I	J	K	L	M	N
1			Pasadena Tree Nursery											
2			As of December 31											
3														
4				Total Items in Stock	3,022									
5				Average Price	$ 107.89									
6				Price	$ 107.99									
7				Price	$ 102.99									
8				Price	$ 117.98									
			13											
12														
13	Quantity in Stock	Item #	Tree Name	Retail Price	Light	Landscape Use	Category	Stock Level						
21	71	23688	Artist Flowering	109.95	Partial Sun	Erosion Control	Pear	Order						
22	159	24896	Bing Small Sweet	105.99	Partial Shade	Border	Cherry	OK						
23	60	25678	Bartlett	109.75	Partial Sun	Erosion Control	Pear	Order						

Freeze Panes button in Window group

Freeze Panes command freezes rows 1-13

Row 21 in view

FIGURE 16.23

Excel 2016, Windows 10, Microsoft Corporation

4 In the **Window group**, click **Freeze Panes**, and then click **Unfreeze Panes** to unlock all rows and columns. **Save** 🖫 your workbook.

More **Knowledge** | **Freeze Columns or Freeze Both Rows and Columns**

You can freeze columns that you want to remain in view on the left. Select the column to the right of the column(s) that you want to remain in view while scrolling to the right, and then click the Freeze Panes command. You can also use the command to freeze both rows and columns; click a *cell* to freeze the rows *above* the cell and the columns to the *left* of the cell.

Objective 5 | Create, Sort, and Filter an Excel Table

GO! Learn How
Video E16-5

To analyze a group of related data, you can convert a range of cells to an ***Excel table***. An Excel table is a series of rows and columns that contains related data that is managed independently from the data in other rows and columns in the worksheet.

DIGITAL LITERACY
CERTIFICATION

2.03h (i)
2.03h (ii)
2.03h (iii)
2.03m

Activity 16.14 | Creating an Excel Table and Applying a Table Style

1 Be sure that you have applied the Unfreeze Panes command—no rows on your worksheet are locked. Click any cell in the data below row 13. Click the **Insert tab**. In the **Tables group**, click **Table**. In the **Create Table** dialog box, if necessary, click to select the My table has headers check box, and then compare your screen with Figure 16.24.

The column titles in row 13 will form the table headers. By clicking in a range of contiguous data, Excel will suggest the range as the data for the table. You can adjust the range if necessary.

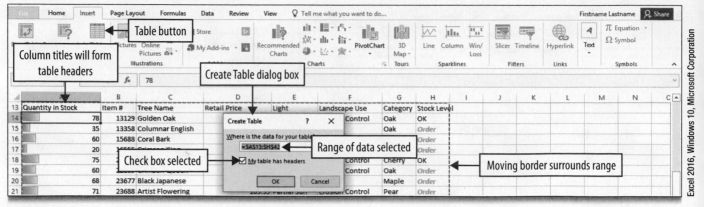

FIGURE 16.24

🔄 **ANOTHER WAY**   Select the range of cells that make up the table, including the header row, and then click the Table button.

> **2** Click **OK**. With the range still selected, on the ribbon notice that the **Table Tools** are active.

> **3** On the **Design tab**, in the **Table Styles group**, click **More** ⬇, and then under **Light**, locate and click **Table Style Light 16**.

> **4** Press Ctrl + Home. Click **Save** 💾, and then compare your screen with Figure 16.25.

Sorting and filtering arrows display in the table's header row.

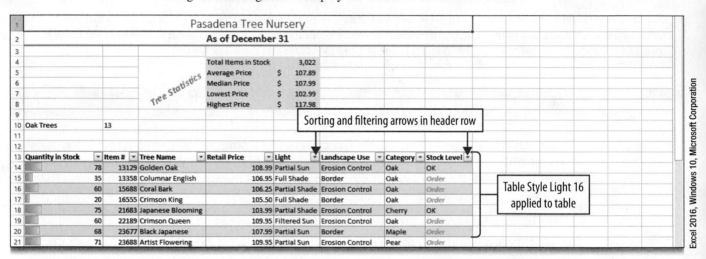

FIGURE 16.25

Activity 16.15 | Sorting an Excel Table

You can *sort* tables—arrange all the data in a specific order—in ascending or descending order.

> **1** In the header row of the table, click the **Retail Price arrow**, and then on the menu, click **Sort Smallest to Largest**. Next to the arrow, notice the small **up arrow** indicating an ascending (smallest to largest) sort.

> This action sorts the rows in the table from the lowest retail price to highest retail price.

> **2** In the table's header row, click the **Category arrow**, and then click **Sort Z to A**.

> This action sorts the rows in the table in reverse alphabetic order by Category name, and the small arrow points downward, indicating a descending (Z to A) sort. The Retail Price continues to be sorted from smallest to largest within each category.

3 Click the **Category arrow**, and then sort from **A to Z**. Next to the arrow, notice the small **up arrow** indicating an ascending (A to Z) sort.

> This action sorts the rows in the table alphabetically by Category, and within a Category sorts the rows from smallest to largest by Retail Price.

4 In the table header row, click the **Item # arrow**, and then click **Sort Smallest to Largest**, which will apply an ascending sort to the data using the *Item #* column.

Activity 16.16 | Filtering an Excel Table and Displaying a Total Row

You can *filter* tables—display only a portion of the data based on matching a specific value—to show only the data that meets the criteria that you specify.

1 Click the **Category arrow**. On the menu, click the **(Select All)** check box to clear all the check boxes. Click to select only the **Maple** check box, and then click **OK**. Compare your screen with Figure 16.26.

> Only the rows containing *Maple* in the Category column display—the remaining rows are hidden from view. A small funnel—the filter icon—indicates that a filter is applied to the data in the table. Additionally, the row numbers display in blue to indicate that some rows are hidden from view. A filter hides entire rows in the worksheet.

			Name	Retail Price	Light	Landscape Use	Category	Stock Level
9								
10	Oak Trees	13						
11								
12								
18	Qu		Name	Retail Price	Light	Landscape Use	Category	Stock Level
20		68	23077 Black Japanese	107.99	Partial Sun	Border	Maple	Order
24	179	25844 Bloodgood	1				Maple	OK
26	81	32544 Burgundy Bell	1				Maple	OK
27	81	34266 Lace Maple	1				Maple	OK
33	70	35988 Butterfly Japanese	1				Maple	Order
34	92	36820 Ever Red	110.95	Partial Sun	Border	Maple	OK
43								

Blue row numbers indicate some rows hidden

Only products in Maple category display

Funnel indicates filter applied

FIGURE 16.26

Excel 2016, Windows 10, Microsoft Corporation

2 Point to the right of *Category*, and notice that *Equals "Maple"* displays to indicate the filter criteria.

3 Click any cell in the table so that the table is selected. Click the **Design tab**, and then in the **Table Style Options group**, select the **Total Row** check box.

> *Total* displays in cell A43. In cell H43, the number *6* indicates that six rows currently display.

4 Click cell **A43**, click the **arrow** that displays to the right of cell **A43**, and then in the list, click **Sum**.

> Excel sums only the visible rows in Column A, and indicates that 571 products in the Maple category are in stock. In this manner, you can use an Excel table to quickly find information about a group of data.

5 Click cell **A11**, type **Maple Trees** and press Tab. In cell **B11**, type **6 (571 total items in stock)** and then press Enter.

6 In the table header row, click the **Category arrow**, and then on the menu, click **Clear Filter From "Category"**.

> All the rows in the table redisplay.

7 Click the **Landscape Use arrow**, click the **(Select All)** check box to clear all the check boxes, and then click to select the **Erosion Control** check box. Click **OK**.

Click the **Category arrow**, click the **(Select All)** check box to clear all the check boxes, and then click the **Oak** check box. Click **OK**, **Save** 🖫 your workbook, and then compare your screen with Figure 16.27.

By applying multiple filters, you can determine quickly that eight tree names identified with a *Landscape Use* of *Erosion Control* are in the *Oak* tree category with a total of 710 such trees in stock.

	Quantity in Stock	Item #	Tree Name	Retail Price	Light	Landscape Use	Category	Stock Level
11	Maple Trees	6 (571 total items in stock)						
12								
14	78	13129	Golden Oak	108.99	Partial Sun	Erosion Control	Oak	OK
16	60	15688	Coral Bark	106.25	Partial Shade	Erosion Control	Oak	Order
19	60	22189	Crimson Queen	109.95	Filtered Sun	Erosion Control	Oak	Order
28	113	34793	Emerald Elf	103.98	Full Shade	Erosion Control	Oak	OK
35	173	37803	Osakazuki	103.88	Full Shade	Erosion Control	Oak	OK
37	75	38675	Palo Alto	102.99	Partial Shade	Erosion Control	Oak	OK
38	93	38700	Pacific Fire	103.75	Full Shade	Erosion Control	Oak	OK
40	58	39704	Embers	105.99	Partial Sun	Erosion Control	Oak	Order
43	710							8
44	10/1/2015 15:38							

8 tree types in Oak category can be used for Erosion Control

FIGURE 16.27

Excel 2016, Windows 10, Microsoft Corporation

More Knowledge **Band Rows and Columns in a Table**

You can band rows to format even rows differently from odd rows, making them easier to read. To band rows or columns, on the Design tab, in the Table Style Options group, select the Banded Rows or Banded Columns check box.

Activity 16.17 | **Clearing Filters**

When you are finished answering questions about the data in a table, you can clear the filters and remove the total row.

1 Click the **Category arrow**, and then click **Clear Filter From "Category"**. Use the same technique to remove the filter from the **Landscape Use** column.

2 Click anywhere in the table to activate the table and display the **Table Tools** on the ribbon. Click the **Design tab**, and then in the **Table Style Options group**, click the **Total Row** check box to clear the check mark and remove the Total row from the table.

3 Click **Save** 🖫, and then compare your screen with Figure 16.28.

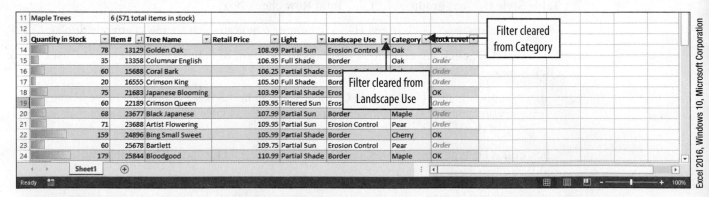

FIGURE 16.28

Excel 2016, Windows 10, Microsoft Corporation

More Knowledge **Converting a Table to a Range**

When you are finished answering questions about the data in a table by sorting, filtering, and totalling, you can convert the table into a normal range. Doing so is useful if you want to use the Table feature only to apply an attractive Table Style to a range of cells. For example, you can insert a table, apply a Table Style, and then convert the table to a normal range of data but keep the formatting. To convert a table to a range, on the Design tab, in the Tools group, click Convert to Range. In the message box, click Yes. Or, with any table cell selected, right-click, point to Table, and then click Convert to Range.

GO! Learn How
Video E16-6

You can magnify or shrink the view of a worksheet on your screen to either zoom in to view specific data or zoom out to see the entire worksheet. You can also split a worksheet window into panes to view different parts of a worksheet at the same time.

A worksheet might be too wide, too long—or both—to print on a single page. Use Excel's *Print Titles* and *Scale to Fit* commands to create pages that are attractive and easy to read.

The Print Titles command enables you to specify rows and columns to repeat on each printed page. Scale to Fit commands enable you to stretch or shrink the width, height, or both, of printed output to fit a maximum number of pages.

Activity 16.18 | Modifying and Shrinking the Worksheet View

1 Press Ctrl + Home to display the top of your worksheet. On the **View tab**, in the **Zoom group**, click **Zoom**.

2 In the **Zoom** dialog box, click the **75%** option button, and then click **OK.** Notice that by zooming out in this manner, you can see additional rows of your worksheet on the screen.

3 In the lower right corner of your worksheet, in the status bar, click **Zoom In** + until the worksheet redisplays at 100%.

Activity 16.19 | Splitting a Worksheet Window into Panes

The *Split* command splits the window into multiple resizable panes that contain views of your worksheet. This is useful to view multiple distant parts of your worksheet at one time.

1 Click cell **F9**. On the **View tab**, in the **Window group**, click **Split**.

Horizontal and vertical split bars display. You can drag the split bars to view any four portions of the worksheet. On the right, separate vertical scroll bars display for the upper and lower panes and at the bottom, separate horizontal scroll bars display for the left and right panes.

2 Drag the lower vertical scroll box down to the bottom of the scroll bar to view **row 43**. Compare your screen with Figure 16.29.

Here it could be useful to isolate the Tree Statistics at the top and then scroll to the bottom to browse the inventory items.

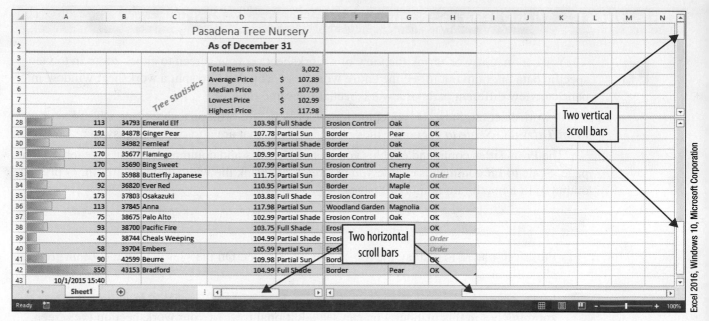

FIGURE 16.29

3 ▸ Click **Split** again to remove the split bars.

4 ▸ Press ⎈ Ctrl + ⎄ Home to display the top of your worksheet. On the **Page Layout tab**, in the **Themes group**, click **Themes**, and then click **Slice**.

5 ▸ Select the range **A13:H13**. On the **Home tab**, from the **Styles group**, apply the **Heading 4** cell style, and then apply **Center** ☰. Click cell **A1**.

Activity 16.20 │ Printing Titles and Scaling to Fit

1 ▸ Click the **Page Layout tab**, and then in the **Page Setup group**, click **Margins**. At the bottom of the gallery, click **Custom Margins** to display the **Page Setup** dialog box. Under **Center on page**, select the **Horizontally** check box.

2 ▸ Click the **Header/Footer tab**, and then in the center of the dialog box, click **Custom Footer**. In the **Footer** dialog box, with your insertion point blinking in the **Left section**, on the row of buttons, click **Insert File Name** 🗐. Click **OK** two times.

3 ▸ In the **Page Setup group**, click **Orientation**, and then click **Landscape**.

The dotted line indicates that as currently formatted, column H will not fit on the page.

4 ▸ Press ⎈ Ctrl + ⎄ F2 to display the **Print Preview**. At the bottom of the **Print Preview**, click **Next Page** ▸.

As currently formatted, the worksheet will print on four pages, and the columns will span multiple pages. Additionally, after Page 1, no column titles are visible to identify the data in the columns.

5 ▸ Click **Next Page** ▸ two times to display **Page 4**, and notice that one column moves to an additional page.

6 ▸ In the upper left corner of **Backstage** view, click **Back** ⊙ to return to the worksheet. In the **Page Setup group**, click **Print Titles**. Under **Print titles**, click in the **Rows to repeat at top** box, and then at the right, click **Collapse Dialog** 🖳.

7 From the **row heading area**, select **row 13**, and then in the **Page Setup – rows to repeat at top:** dialog box, click **Expand Dialog** 🖳. Click **OK** to print the column titles in row 13 at the top of every page.

You can collapse and then expand dialog boxes on your screen to enable a better view of your data.

8 Press Ctrl + F2 to display the **Print Preview** again. At the bottom of the **Settings group**, click the **No Scaling arrow**, and then on the displayed list, point to **Fit All Columns on One Page**. Compare your screen with Figure 16.30.

This action will shrink the width of the printed output to fit all the columns on one page. You can make adjustments like this on the Page Layout tab, or here, in the Print Preview.

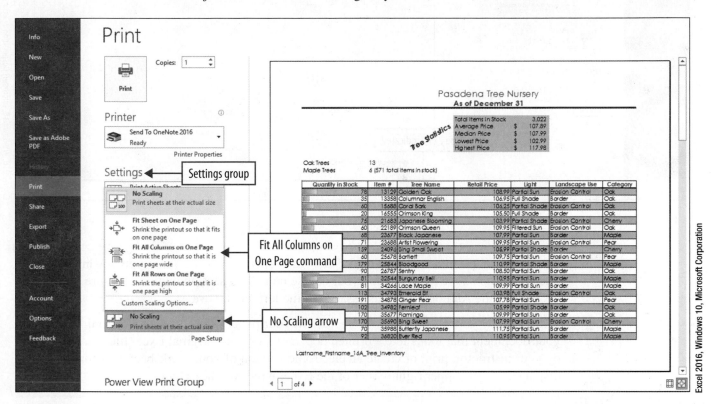

FIGURE 16.30

9 Click **Fit All Columns on One Page**. Notice in the **Print Preview** that all the columns display on one page.

♻ **ANOTHER WAY**   With the worksheet displayed, on the Page Layout tab, in the Scale to Fit group, click the Width button arrow, and then click 1 page.

10 At the bottom of the **Print Preview**, click **Next Page** ▶ one time. Notice that the output will now print on two pages and that the column titles display at the top of **Page 2**. Compare your screen with Figure 16.31.

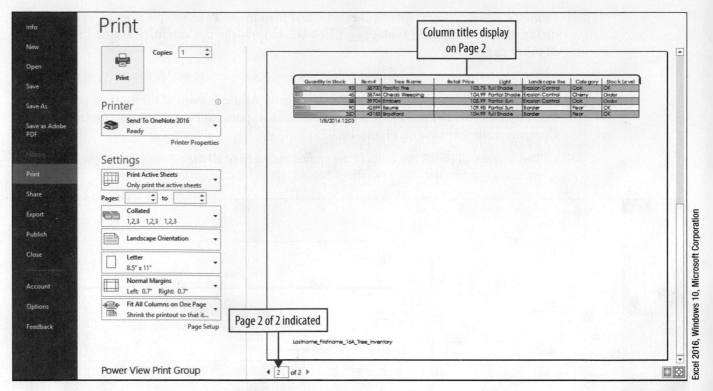

FIGURE 16.31

11 On the left, click **Info**, and then click **Show All Properties**. As the **Tags**, type **tree inventory, Pasadena** and as the **Subject**, type your course name and section number. Be sure your name displays as the Author; edit if necessary. On the left, click **Save**.

12 If directed by your instructor to do so, submit your paper printout, your electronic image of your document that looks like a printed document, or your original Excel file. If required by your instructor, print or create an electronic version of your worksheet with formulas displayed. In the upper right corner of the Excel window, click **Close** ☒.

More **Knowledge** **Scaling for Data That Is Slightly Larger Than the Printed Page**

If your data is just a little too large to fit on a printed page, you can scale the worksheet to make it fit. Scaling reduces both the width and height of the printed data to a percentage of its original size or by the number of pages that you specify. On the Page Layout tab, in the Scale to Fit group, click the Scale arrows to select a percentage.

END | You have completed Project 16A

GO! With Google

Objective | Summarize an Inventory List

ALERT! | **Working with Web-Based Applications and Services**

Computer programs and services on the web receive continuous updates and improvements, so the steps to complete this web-based Activity may differ from the ones shown. You can often look at the screens and the information presented to determine how to complete the Activity.

If you do not already have a Google account, you will need to create one before you begin this Activity. Go to http://google.com and, in the upper right corner, click Sign In. On the Sign In screen, click Create Account. On the Create your Google Account page, complete the form, read and agree to the Terms of Service and Privacy Policy, and then click Next step. On the Welcome screen, click Get Started.

Activity | Create SUM, AVERAGE, COUNTIF, and IF functions

1 From the desktop, open your browser, navigate to **http://google.com**, and then click the **Google Apps** menu ⊞. Click **Drive** ⚪, and then if necessary, sign in to your Google account.

2 Open your **GO! Web Projects** folder—or click New to create and then open this folder if necessary. In the left pane, click **NEW**, and then click **File upload**. Navigate to your student data files, click **e16_16A_Web**, and then click **Open**.

3 Right-click the file you uploaded, point to **Open with**, and then click **Google Sheets**.

4 Select the range **A1:H1**. Click **Merge cells** ⊞. Click **Format**, point to **Align**, and then click **Center**. With **A1** selected, click **Paint format** 🖌, and then click cell **A2**.

5 Select **A1:A2**, and then click the **Font size arrow** ▾. Click **18**.

6 Click cell **B4**. On the ribbon, click **Functions** Σ ▾, and then click **SUM**. Within the formula's parentheses, type **a11:a33** and press Enter for a result of *2311*. Click **B4**, and then on the ribbon, click **More formats** 123 ▾. Click **Number**, and then click **Decrease decimal places** .0. two times.

7 Click cell **B5**, click **Functions** Σ ▾, and then click **AVERAGE**. Within the parentheses, type **d11:d33** and press Enter. Click **B5**, and then on the ribbon, click **Format as currency** $.

8 Click cell **B7**. Type **=countif(g11:g33,"Oak")** and then press Enter to create a function that counts the number of Oak trees in the category column.

9 Click cell **H11**. Type **=if(a11<75,"Order","OK")** and then press Enter. Click cell **H11**, and then drag the fill handle down through cell **H33**.

10 With the range **H11:H33** selected, click **Format**, and then click **Conditional formatting**. On the right side of the window, in the **Apply to range** box, make sure that **H11:H33** displays. Under **Format cells if…**, click the displayed box, and then click **Text contains**. Click in the **Value or formula** box, and then type **Order** Under **Formatting style,** click **Bold**. Click **Done** to apply the default green background conditional format and bold to all cells containing the word *Order*. Click cell **A1** and compare your screen with Figure A.

11 Submit your file as directed by your instructor. Sign out of your Google account and close your browser.

1			Austin Tree Nursery					
2			As of March 30					
3								
4	Total Items in Stock	2,311						
5	Average Price	$108.52						
6								
7	Oak Trees:	10						
8								
9								
10	Quantity in Stock	Item #	Tree Name	Retail Price	Light	Landscape Use	Category	Stock Level
11	78	13129	Golden Oak	108.99	Partial Sun	Erosion	Oak	OK
12	35	13358	Columnar English	106.95	Full Shade	Border	Oak	Order
13	60	15688	Coral Bark	106.25	Partial Shade	Erosion	Oak	Order
14	20	16555	Crimson King	105.5	Full Shade	Border	Oak	Order
15	75	21683	Japanese Blooming	103.99	Partial Shade	Erosion	Cherry	OK
16	60	22189	Crimson Queen	109.95	Filtered Sun	Erosion	Oak	Order

FIGURE A

Weekly Sales Summary

PROJECT ACTIVITIES

In Activities 16.21 through 16.35, you will edit an existing workbook for the Sales Director, Mariam Daly. The workbook summarizes the online and in-store sales of products during a one-week period in April. The worksheets of your completed workbook will look similar to Figure 16.32.

PROJECT FILES

If your instructor wants you to submit Project 16B in the MyITLab Grader system, log in to MyITLab, locate Grader Project 16B, and then download the files for this project.

For Project 16B, you will need the following file:
e16B_Weekly_Sales

You will save your workbook as:
Lastname_Firstname_16B_Weekly_Sales

PROJECT RESULTS

GO!
Walk Thru
Project 16B

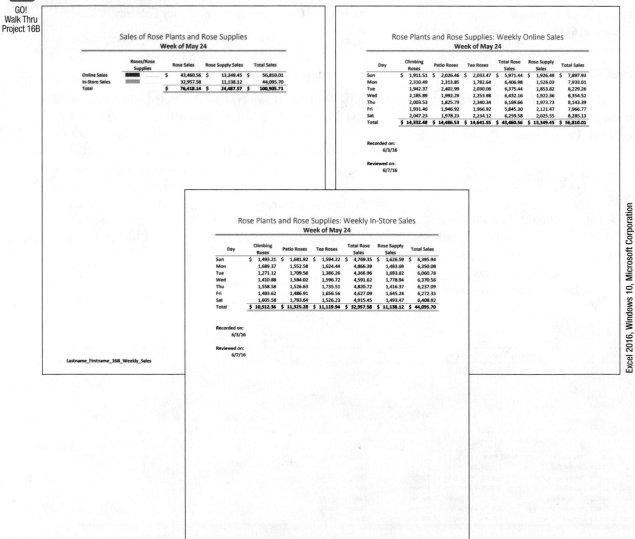

FIGURE 16.32 Project 16B Weekly Sales

GO! Learn How
Video E16-7

Use multiple worksheets in a workbook to organize data in a logical arrangement. When you have more than one worksheet in a workbook, you can *navigate* (move) among worksheets by clicking the *sheet tabs*. Sheet tabs identify each worksheet in a workbook and display along the lower left edge of the workbook window. When you have more worksheets in the workbook than can display in the sheet tab area, use the sheet tab scrolling buttons to move sheet tabs into and out of view.

IC3
DIGITAL LITERACY
CERTIFICATION
2.03a (vii)

Activity 16.21 | Navigating Among Worksheets, Renaming Worksheets, and Changing the Tab Color of Worksheets

> **A L E R T !**   **To submit as an autograded project, log into MyITLab and download the files for this project, and begin with those files instead of e16B_Weekly_Sales.**

Excel names the first worksheet in a workbook *Sheet1* and each additional worksheet that you add in order—*Sheet2*, *Sheet3*, and so on. Most Excel users rename their worksheets with meaningful names. In this Activity, you will navigate among worksheets, rename worksheets, and change the tab color of sheet tabs.

1 Start Excel. In the lower left corner of Excel's opening screen, click **Open Other Workbooks**, and then click **Browse**.

🔄 **ANOTHER WAY**   Press Ctrl + F12 to display the Open dialog box.

2 Navigate to the student files that accompany this chapter, and then open **e16B_Weekly_Sales**. Display the **Save As** dialog box, and then navigate to your **AIO Chapter 16** folder. In the **File name** box, using your own name, type **Lastname_Firstname_16B_Weekly_Sales** and then click **Save** or press Enter.

In this workbook, two worksheets display, into which some data has already been entered. For example, on the first worksheet, the days of the week and sales data for the one-week period display.

3 Along the bottom of the Excel window, point to and then click the **Sheet2 tab**.

The second worksheet in the workbook displays and becomes the active worksheet. *Sheet2* displays in bold.

4 In cell **A1**, notice the text *In-Store*—this worksheet will contain data for in-store sales.

5 Click the **Sheet1 tab**. Then, point to the **Sheet1 tab**, and double-click to select the sheet tab name. Type **Online Sales** and press Enter.

The first worksheet becomes the active worksheet, and the sheet tab displays *Online Sales*.

6 Point to the **Online Sales sheet tab** and right-click. Point to **Tab Color**, and then in the next to last column, point to the first color—**Blue, Accent 5**. Compare your screen with Figure 16.33.

🔄 **ANOTHER WAY**   On the Home tab, in the Cells group, click the Format button, and then on the displayed list, point to Tab Color.

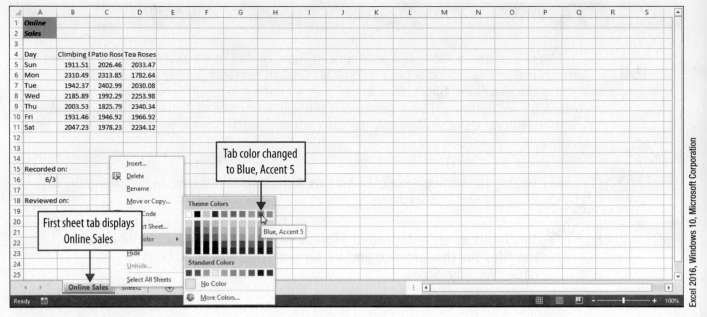

FIGURE 16.33

7 ▶ Click **Blue, Accent 5** to change the tab color.

8 ▶ Point to the **Sheet2 tab**, right-click, and then from the shortcut menu, click **Rename**. Type **In-Store Sales** and press Enter.

> You can either double-click the sheet name or use the shortcut menu to rename a sheet tab.

9 ▶ Point to the **In-Store Sales sheet tab** and right-click. Point to **Tab Color**, and then in the last column, click the first color—**Green, Accent 6**. Save your workbook.

More **Knowledge** | **Copying a Worksheet**

To copy a worksheet to the same workbook, right-click the sheet tab, on the shortcut menu click Move or Copy, click the sheet before which you want to insert the copied sheet, select the Create a copy check box, and then click OK. To copy to a different, opened workbook, in the Move or Copy dialog box, click the To book arrow, and then select the workbook into which you want to insert the copy.

Objective 8 | Enter Dates, Clear Contents, and Clear Formats

GO! Learn How
Video E16-8

Dates represent a type of value that you can enter in a cell. When you enter a date, Excel assigns a serial value—a number—to the date. This makes it possible to treat dates like other numbers. For example, if two cells contain dates, you can find the number of days between the two dates by subtracting the older date from the more recent date.

Activity 16.22 | Entering and Formatting Dates

In this Activity, you will examine the various ways that Excel can format dates in a cell. Date values entered in any of the following formats will be recognized by Excel as a date:

VALUE TYPED	EXAMPLE
m/d/yy	7/4/2016
d-mmm	4-Jul
d-mmm-yy	4-Jul-16
mmm-yy	Jul-16

Pearson Education, Inc.

On your keyboard, ⌐ (the hyphen key) and ⌐ (the forward slash key) function identically in any of these formats and can be used interchangeably. You can abbreviate the month name to three characters or spell it out. You can enter the year as two digits, four digits, or even leave it off. When left off, the current year is assumed but does not display in the cell.

A two-digit year value of 30 through 99 is interpreted by the Windows operating system as the four-digit years of 1930 through 1999. All other two-digit year values are assumed to be in the 21st century. If you always type year values as four digits, even though only two digits may display in the cell, you can be sure that Excel interprets the year value as you intended. Examples are shown in Figure 16.34.

HOW EXCEL INTERPRETS DATES	
DATE TYPED AS:	COMPLETED BY EXCEL AS:
7/4/15	7/4/2015
7/4/98	7/4/1998
7/4	4-Jul (current year assumed)
7-4	4-Jul (current year assumed)
July 4	4-Jul (current year assumed)
Jul 4	4-Jul (current year assumed)
Jul/4	4-Jul (current year assumed)
Jul-4	4-Jul (current year assumed)
July 4, 1998	4-Jul-98
July 2012	Jul-12 (first day of month assumed)
July 1998	Jul-98 (first day of month assumed)

Gaskin, Shelley. Go! All in One, 3E. Pearson Education, 2017.

FIGURE 16.34

1 Click the **Online Sales sheet tab** to make it active. Click cell **A16** and notice that the cell displays *6/3*. In the **Formula Bar**, notice that the full date of June 3, 2016, displays in the format *6/3/2016*.

2 With cell **A16** selected, on the **Home tab**, in the **Number group**, click the **Number Format arrow**. At the bottom, click **More Number Formats** to display the **Number tab** of the **Format Cells** dialog box.

> Under Category, *Date* is selected, and under Type, *3/14* is selected. Cell A16 uses this format type; that is, only the month and day display in the cell.

3 In the displayed dialog box, under **Type**, click several other date types and watch the **Sample** area to see how applying the selected date format will format your cell. When you are finished, click the **3/14/12** type, and then compare your screen with Figure 16.35.

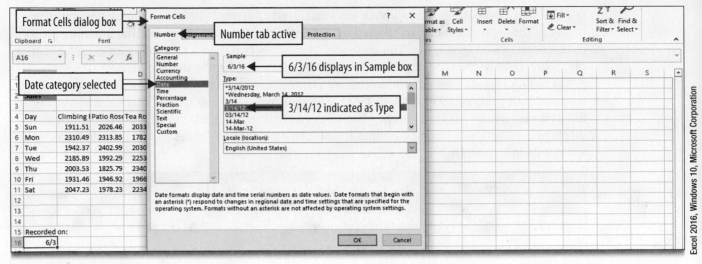

FIGURE 16.35

4 At the bottom of the dialog box, click **OK**. Click cell **A19**, type **6-7-16** and then press Enter.

Cell A19 has no special date formatting applied, and displays in the default date format *6/7/2016*.

5 Click cell **A19** again. Hold down Ctrl and press ; (semicolon). Press Enter to confirm the entry.

Excel enters the current date, obtained from your computer's internal calendar, in the selected cell using the default date format. Ctrl + ; is a quick method to enter the current date.

6 Click cell **A19** again, type **6/7/16** and then press Enter.

Because the year *16* is less than 30, Excel assumes a 21st century date and changes *16* to *2016* to complete the four-digit year. Typing *98* would result in *1998*. For two-digit years that you type that are between 30 and 99, Excel assumes a 20th century date.

7 Click cell **A16**, and then on the **Home tab**, in the **Clipboard group**, click **Format Painter**. Click cell **A19**, and notice that the date format from cell **A16** is copied to cell **A19**. **Save** your workbook.

Activity 16.23 | Clearing Cell Contents and Formats

A cell has *contents*—a value or a formula—and a cell may also have one or more *formats* applied, for example, bold and italic font styles, fill color, font color, and so on. You can choose to clear—delete—the *contents* of a cell, the *formatting* of a cell, or both.

Clearing the contents of a cell deletes the value or formula typed there, but it does *not* clear formatting applied to a cell. In this Activity, you will clear the contents of a cell and then clear the formatting of a cell that contains a date to see its underlying content.

1 In the **Online Sales** worksheet, click cell **A1**. In the **Editing group**, click **Clear**, and then click **Clear Contents**. Notice that the text is cleared, but the green formatting remains.

2 Click cell **A2**, and then press Delete.

You can use either of these two methods to delete the *contents* of a cell. Deleting the contents does not, however, delete the formatting of the cell; you can see that the green fill color format applied to the two cells still displays.

3 In cell **A1**, type **Online Sales** and then on the **Formula Bar**, click **Enter** ☑ so that cell **A1** remains the active cell.

In addition to the green fill color, the bold italic text formatting remains with the cell.

4 In the **Editing group**, click **Clear** 🧹, and then click **Clear Formats**.

Clearing the formats deletes formatting from the cell—the green fill color and the bold and italic font styles—but does not delete the cell's contents.

5 Use the same technique to clear the green fill color from cell **A2**. Click cell **A16**, click **Clear** 🧹, and then click **Clear Formats**. In the **Number group**, notice that *General* displays as the number format of the cell.

The box in the Number group indicates the current Number format of the selected cell. Clearing the date formatting from the cell displays the date's serial number. The date, June 3, 2016, is stored as a serial number that indicates the number of days since January 1, 1900. This date is the 42,524th day since the reference date of January 1, 1900.

6 On the Quick Access Toolbar, click **Undo** ↩ to restore the date format. **Save** 💾 your workbook, and then compare your screen with Figure 16.36.

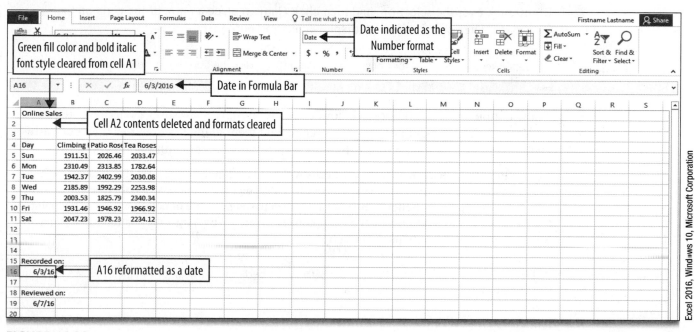

FIGURE 16.36

More Knowledge   **Clearing an Entire Worksheet**

To clear an entire worksheet, in the upper left corner of the worksheet, click the Select All button, and then on the Home tab, in the Editing group, click Clear, and then click Clear All.

Objective 9 | Copy and Paste by Using the Paste Options Gallery

GO! Learn How
Video E16-9

DIGITAL LITERACY
CERTIFICATION
2.03i (ii)

Data in cells can be copied to other cells in the same worksheet, to other sheets in the same workbook, or to sheets in another workbook. The action of placing cell contents that have been copied or moved to the Clipboard into another location is called ***paste***.

Activity 16.24 | Copying and Pasting by Using the Paste Options Gallery

Recall that the Clipboard is a temporary storage area maintained by your Windows operating system. When you select one or more cells, and then perform the Copy command or the Cut command, the selected data is placed on the Clipboard. From the Clipboard storage area, the data is available for pasting into other cells, other worksheets, other workbooks, and even into other Office programs. When you paste, the ***Paste Options gallery*** displays, which includes Live Preview to preview the Paste formatting that you want.

1 With the **Online Sales** worksheet active, select the range **A4:A19**.

A range of cells identical to this one is required for the *In-Store Sales* worksheet.

2 Right-click over the selection, and then click **Copy** to place a copy of the cells on the Clipboard. The copied cells may display a moving border.

>  **ANOTHER WAY**   Use the keyboard shortcut for Copy, which is Ctrl + C; or click the Copy button in the Clipboard group on the Home tab.

3 At the bottom of the workbook window, click the **In-Store Sales sheet tab** to make it the active worksheet. Point to cell **A4**, right-click, and then on the shortcut menu, under **Paste Options**, *point* to the first button—**Paste**. Compare your screen with Figure 16.37.

Live Preview displays how the copied cells will be placed in the worksheet if you click the Paste button. In this manner, you can experiment with different paste options, and then be sure you are selecting the paste operation that you want. When pasting a range of cells, you need only point to or select the cell in the upper left corner of the ***paste area***—the target destination for data that has been cut or copied using the Clipboard.

> **ANOTHER WAY**   Use the keyboard shortcut for Paste, which is Ctrl + V; or click the Paste button in the Clipboard group on the Home tab.

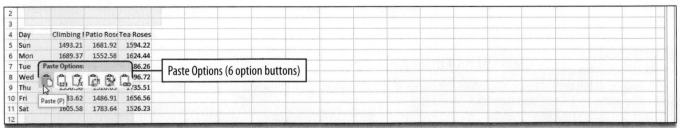

Excel 2016, Windows 10, Microsoft Corporation

FIGURE 16.37

4 Click the first button, **Paste**. In the status bar, notice the message that displays, indicating that your selected range remains available on the Office Clipboard.

5 Display the **Online Sales** worksheet. Press Esc to cancel the moving border. **Save** your workbook.

The status bar no longer displays the message.

Objective 10 Edit and Format Multiple Worksheets at the Same Time

GO! Learn How
Video E16-10

You can enter or edit data on several worksheets at the same time by selecting and grouping multiple worksheets. Data that you enter or edit on the active sheet is reflected in all selected sheets. If the sheet tab displays with a solid background color, you know the sheet is not selected.

Activity 16.25 | Grouping Worksheets for Editing

In this Activity, you will group the two worksheets, and then format both worksheets at the same time.

1 With the **Online Sales** sheet active, press Ctrl + Home to make cell **A1** the active cell. Point to the **Online Sales sheet tab**, right-click, and then click **Select All Sheets**.

2 At the top of your screen, notice that *[Group]* displays in the title bar. Compare your screen with Figure 16.38.

Both worksheets are selected, as indicated by *[Group]* in the title bar and the sheet tab names underlined. Data that you enter or edit on the active sheet will also be entered or edited in the same manner on all the selected sheets in the same cells.

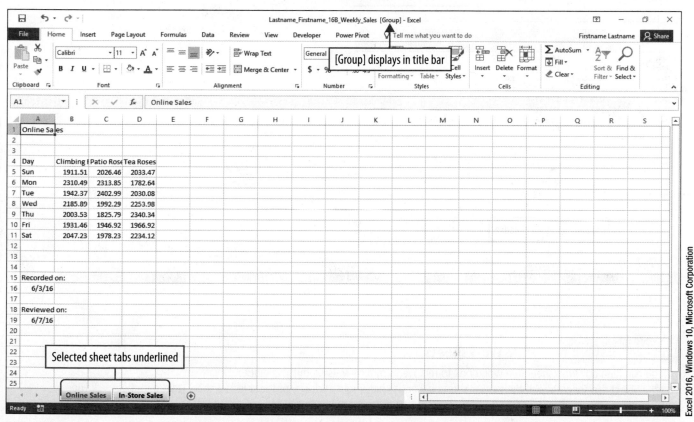

FIGURE 16.38

3 Select **columns A:G**, and then set their width to **85 pixels**.

4 Click cell **A2**, type **Week of May 24** and then on the **Formula Bar**, click **Enter** ✓ to keep cell **A2** as the active cell. **Merge & Center** the text across the range **A2:G2**, and then apply the **Heading 1** cell style.

5 Click cell **E4**, type **Total Rose Sales** and then press Tab. In cell **F4**, type **Rose Supply Sales** and then press Tab. In cell **G4**, type **Total Sales** and then press Enter.

6 Select the range **A4:G4**, and then apply the **Heading 3** cell style. In the **Alignment group**, click **Center** 🔲, **Middle Align** 🔲, and **Wrap Text**. **Save** 🔲 your workbook.

7 Display the **In-Store Sales** worksheet to cancel the grouping, and then compare your screen with Figure 16.39.

> As soon as you select a single sheet, the grouping of the sheets is cancelled and *[Group]* no longer displays in the title bar. Because the sheets were grouped, the same new text and formatting were applied to both sheets. In this manner, you can make the same changes to all the sheets in a workbook at one time.

↻ **ANOTHER WAY**   Right-click any sheet tab, and then click Ungroup Sheets.

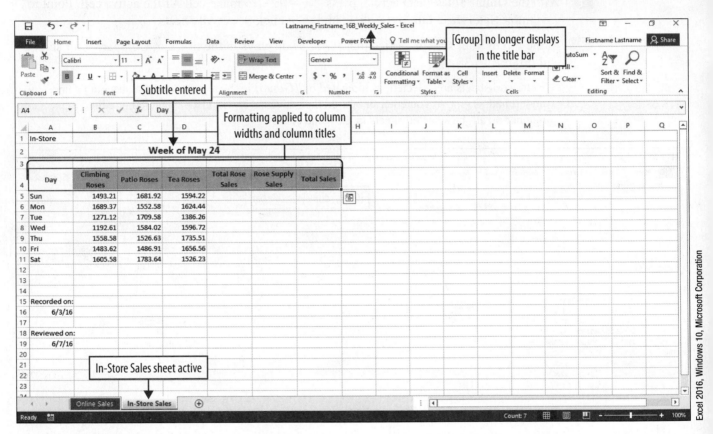

FIGURE 16.39

More **Knowledge**   **Hide Worksheets**

You can hide any worksheet in a workbook to remove it from view using this technique:
  Select the sheet tabs of the worksheets you want to hide, right-click any of the selected sheet tabs, and then click Hide.

Activity 16.26 | Formatting and Constructing Formulas on Grouped Worksheets

Recall that formulas are equations that perform calculations on values in your worksheet and that a formula starts with an equal sign (=). Operators are the symbols with which you specify the type of calculation that you want to perform on the elements of a formula. In this Activity, you will enter sales figures for Rose Supply items from both Online and In-Store sales, and then calculate the total sales.

1 Display the **Online Sales** worksheet. Verify that the sheets are not grouped—*[Group]* does *not* display in the title bar.

2 Click cell **A1**, replace *Online Sales* by typing **Rose Plants and Rose Supplies: Weekly Online Sales** and then on the **Formula Bar**, click **Enter** ✓ to keep cell **A1** as the active cell. **Merge & Center** the text across the range **A1:G1**, and then apply the **Title** cell style.

3 In the column titled *Rose Supply Sales*, click cell **F5**. In the range **F5:F11**, type the following data for Rose Supply Sales, and then compare your screen with Figure 16.40.

	ROSE SUPPLY SALES
Sun	**1926.49**
Mon	**1526.03**
Tue	**1853.82**
Wed	**1922.36**
Thu	**1973.73**
Fri	**2121.47**
Sat	**2025.55**

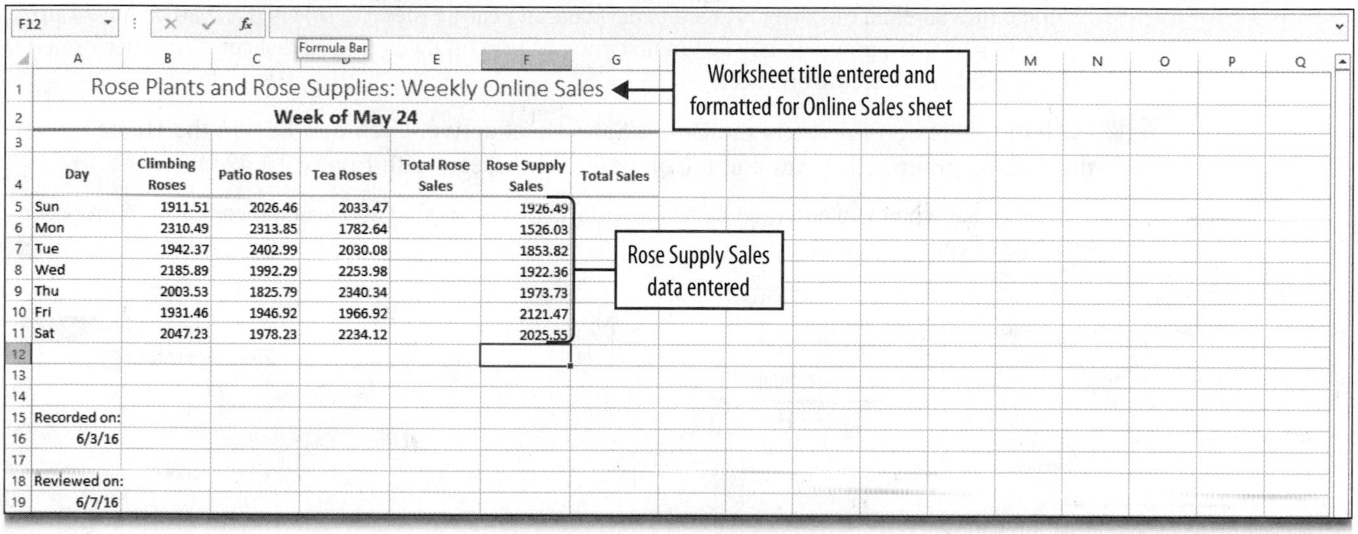

Excel 2016, Windows 10, Microsoft Corporation

FIGURE 16.40

4 Display the **In-Store Sales** sheet. In cell **A1**, replace *In-Store* by typing **Rose Plants and Rose Supplies: Weekly In-Store Sales** and then on the **Formula Bar**, click **Enter** ✓ to keep cell **A1** as the active cell. **Merge & Center** the text across the range **A1:G1**, and then apply the **Title** cell style.

5 In the column titled *Rose Supply Sales*, click cell **F5**. In the range **F5:F11**, type the following data for Rose Supply Sales, and then compare your screen with Figure 16.41.

	ROSE SUPPLY SALES
Sun	**1626.59**
Mon	**1483.69**
Tue	**1693.82**
Wed	**1778.94**
Thu	**1416.37**
Fri	**1645.24**
Sat	**1493.47**

The worksheet data shown in Figure 16.41:

Rose Plants and Rose Supplies: Weekly In-Store Sales

Week of May 24

Day	Climbing Roses	Patio Roses	Tea Roses	Total Rose Sales	Rose Supply Sales	Total Sales
Sun	1493.21	1681.92	1594.22		1626.59	
Mon	1689.37	1552.58	1624.44		1483.69	
Tue	1271.12	1709.58	1386.26		1693.82	
Wed	1192.61	1584.02	1596.72		1778.94	
Thu	1558.58	1526.63	1735.51		1416.37	
Fri	1483.62	1486.91	1656.56		1645.24	
Sat	1605.58	1783.64	1526.23		1493.47	

Recorded on:
6/3/16

Worksheet title entered and formatted for In-Store Sales sheet

Rose Supply Sales data entered

FIGURE 16.41

6 Save 🖫 your workbook. Right-click the **Online Sales sheet tab**, and then click **Select All Sheets**.

The first worksheet becomes the active sheet, and the worksheets are grouped. *[Group]* displays in the title bar, and the sheet tabs are underlined, indicating they are selected as part of the group. Recall that when grouped, any action that you perform on the active worksheet is *also* performed on any other selected worksheets.

7 With the sheets *grouped* and the **Online Sales** sheet active, click cell **E5**. On the **Home tab**, in the **Editing group**, click **AutoSum**. Compare your screen with Figure 16.42.

Recall that when you enter the SUM function, Excel looks first above and then left for a proposed range of cells to sum.

The worksheet data shown in Figure 16.42:

...upplies: Weekly Online Sales

...k of May 24

Day	Climbing Roses	Patio Roses	Tea Roses	Total Rose Sales	Rose Supply Sales	Total Sales
Sun	1911.51	2026.46	2033.47	=SUM(B5:D5)	1926.49	
Mon	2310.49	2313.85	1782.64		1853.82	
Tue	1942.37	2402.99	2030.08			
Wed	2185.89	1992.29	2253.98		1922.36	
Thu	2003.53	1825.79	2340.34		1973.73	
Fri	1931.46	1946.92	1966.92		2121.47	
Sat	2047.23	1978.23	2234.12		2025.55	

[Group] indicates the worksheets are grouped

Proposed range of cells to sum surrounded by moving border

SUM function in cell

FIGURE 16.42

8 Press Enter to display Total Rose Sales for Sunday, which is *5971.44*.

9 Click cell **E5**, and then drag the fill handle down to copy the formula through cell **E11**.

10 Click cell **G5**, type = click cell **E5**, type + click cell **F5**, and then compare your screen with Figure 16.43.

Using the point-and-click technique to construct this formula is only one of several techniques you can use. Alternatively, you could use any other method to enter the SUM function to add the values in these two cells.

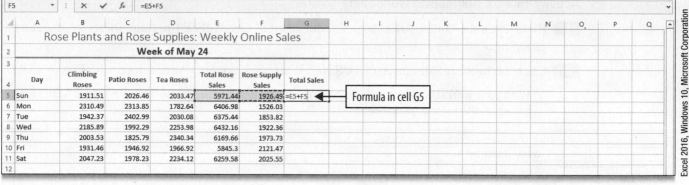

Excel 2016, Windows 10, Microsoft Corporation

FIGURE 16.43

11 Press Enter to display the result *7897.93*, and then copy the formula down through cell **G11**. **Save** 🖫 your workbook.

Activity 16.27 | Determining Multiple Totals at the Same Time

You can select a contiguous range of cells adjacent to rows or columns of numbers and then click the AutoSum button—or use Alt + =—to enter the SUM function for each row or column.

1 With the two worksheets still grouped, in cell **A12**, type **Total** and then select the range **B5:G12**, which is all of the sales data and the empty cells at the bottom of each column of sales data.

2 With the range **B5:G12** selected, hold down Alt and press = to enter the **SUM** function in each empty cell. Click **Save** 🖫.

Selecting a range in this manner and then clicking the AutoSum button, or entering the SUM function with the keyboard shortcut Alt + =, places the SUM function in the empty cells at the bottom of each column.

Activity 16.28 | Formatting Grouped Worksheets

1 With the two worksheets still grouped, select the range **A5:A12**, and then apply the **Heading 4** cell style.

2 To apply financial formatting to the worksheets, select the range **B5:G5**, hold down Ctrl, and then select the range **B12:G12**. With the nonadjacent ranges selected, apply the **Accounting Number Format** $ -.

3 Select the range **B6:G11** and apply **Comma Style** 𝟵. Select the range **B12:G12** and apply the **Total** cell style. Press Ctrl + Home to move to the top of the worksheet; compare your screen with Figure 16.44.

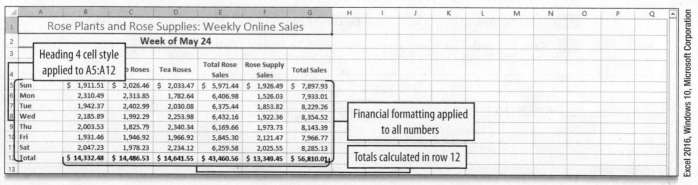

Excel 2016, Windows 10, Microsoft Corporation

FIGURE 16.44

Activity 16.29 | Ungrouping Worksheets

1 Right-click the **Online Sales sheet**. On the shortcut menu, click **Ungroup Sheets** to cancel the grouping.

2 Click the **In-Store Sales sheet**. Click **Save**, and then compare your screen with Figure 16.45.

With your worksheets grouped, the calculations and formatting on the first worksheet were also added on the second worksheet.

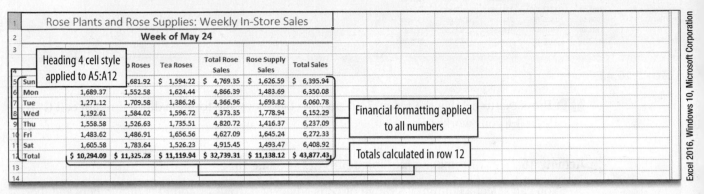

FIGURE 16.45

Objective 11 Create a Summary Sheet with Column Sparklines

GO! Learn How
Video E16-11

A *summary sheet* is a worksheet where totals from other worksheets are displayed and summarized. Recall that sparklines are tiny charts within a single cell that show a data trend.

Activity 16.30 | Inserting a Worksheet

1 To the right of the **In-Store Sales** sheet tab, click **New sheet**.

2 Rename the new worksheet tab **Summary** and change its **Tab Color** to **Gold, Accent 4**—in the eighth column, the first color.

3 Widen **columns A:E** to **110** pixels. In cell **A1**, type **Sales of Rose Plants and Rose Supplies** and then **Merge & Center** the title across the range **A1:E1**. Apply the **Title** cell style.

4 In cell **A2**, type **Week of May 24** and then **Merge & Center** across **A2:E2**; apply the **Heading 1** cell style.

5 Leave **row 3** blank. To form column titles, in cell **B4**, type **Roses/Rose Supplies** and press Tab. In cell **C4**, type **Rose Sales** and press Tab. In cell **D4**, type **Rose Supply Sales** and press Tab. In cell **E4**, type **Total Sales** and press Enter.

6 Select the range **B4:E4**. Apply the **Heading 3** cell style. In the **Alignment group**, click **Center**, **Middle Align**, and **Wrap Text**.

7 To form row titles, in cell **A5**, type **Online Sales** In cell **A6**, type **In-Store Sales**

8 **Save**, and then compare your screen with Figure 16.46.

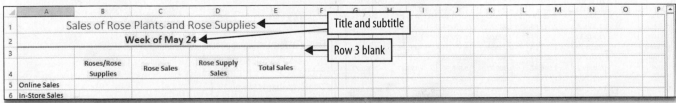

FIGURE 16.46

Excel 2016, Windows 10, Microsoft Corporation

Activity 16.31 | Constructing Formulas that Refer to Cells in Another Worksheet

In this Activity, you will construct formulas in the Summary worksheet to display the total sales for both online sales and in-store sales that will update the Summary worksheet whenever changes are made to the other worksheet totals.

1 Click cell **C5**. Type **=** and then click the **Online Sales sheet tab**. On the **Online Sales** worksheet, click cell **E12**, and then press Enter to redisplay the **Summary** worksheet and insert the total **Rose Sales** amount of *$43,460.56*.

2 Click cell **C5** to select it again. Look at the **Formula Bar**, and notice that instead of a value, the cell contains a formula that is equal to the value in another cell in another worksheet. Compare your screen with Figure 16.47.

The value in this cell is equal to the value in cell E12 of the *Online Sales* worksheet. The Accounting Number Format applied to the referenced cell is carried over. By using a formula of this type, changes in cell E12 on the *Online Sales* worksheet will be automatically updated in this *Summary* worksheet.

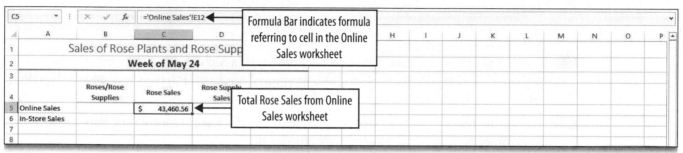

FIGURE 16.47

Excel 2016, Windows 10, Microsoft Corporation

3 Click cell **D5**. Type **=** and then click the **Online Sales sheet tab**. Click cell **F12**, and then press Enter to redisplay the **Summary** worksheet and insert the total **Rose Supply Sales** amount of *$13,349.45*.

4 By using the techniques you just practiced, in cells **C6** and **D6** insert the total **Rose Sales** and **Rose Supply Sales** data from the **In-Store Sales** worksheet. Click **Save** ⊞, and then compare your screen with Figure 16.48.

FIGURE 16.48

Excel 2016, Windows 10, Microsoft Corporation

Activity 16.32 | Changing Values in a Detail Worksheet to Update a Summary Worksheet

The formulas in cells C5:D6 display the totals from the other two worksheets. Changes made to any of the other two worksheets—sometimes referred to as ***detail sheets*** because the details of the information are contained there—that affect their totals will display on this Summary worksheet. In this manner, the Summary worksheet accurately displays the current totals from the other worksheets.

1 In cell **A7**, type **Total** Select the range **C5:E6**, and then on the **Home tab**, in the **Editing group**, click **AutoSum** to total the two rows.

This technique is similar to selecting the empty cells at the bottom of columns and then inserting the SUM function for each column. Alternatively, you could use any other method to sum the rows. Recall that cell formatting carries over to adjacent cells unless two cells are left blank.

2 Select the range **C5:E7**, and then click **AutoSum** to total the three columns. Compare your screen with Figure 16.49.

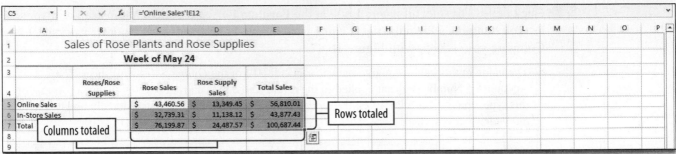

FIGURE 16.49

3 Notice that in cell C6, Rose Sales for In-Store Sales is $32,739.31, and in cell C7, the total is $76,199.87. Display the **In-Store Sales** worksheet, click cell **B8**, type **1410.88** and then press Enter. Notice that the formulas in the worksheet recalculate.

4 Display the **Summary** worksheet, and notice that in the **Rose Sales** column, both the total for the *In-Store Sales* and the *Total* were recalculated.

In this manner, a Summary sheet recalculates any changes made in the other worksheets.

5 On the **Summary** worksheet, select the range **C6:E6** and change the format to **Comma Style**. Select the range **C7:E7**, and then apply the **Total** cell style. Select the range **A5:A7** and apply the **Heading 4** cell style. **Save** 💾 your workbook. Click cell **A1**, and then compare your screen with Figure 16.50.

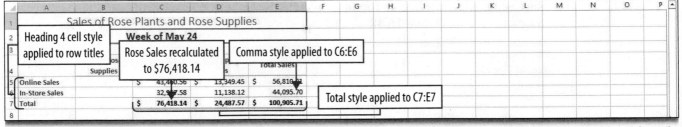

FIGURE 16.50

Activity 16.33 | Inserting Column Sparklines

In this Activity, you will insert column sparklines to visualize the ratio of Rose sales to Rose Supply sales for both Online and In-Store.

1 On the **Summary** worksheet, click cell **B5**. On the **Insert tab**, in the **Sparklines group**, click **Column**. In the **Create Sparklines** dialog box, with the insertion point blinking in the **Data Range** box, type **c5:d5** and then compare your screen with Figure 16.51.

FIGURE 16.51

2 Click **OK**. Click cell **B6**, and then **Insert** a **Column Sparkline** for the range **c6:d6**

3 With cell **B6** selected, on the **Design tab**, in the **Style group**, click **More** ⌄, and then click **Sparkline Style Accent 4, (no dark or light)**—in the third row, the fourth style. Press Ctrl + Home, click **Save** ⊟, and then compare your screen with Figure 16.52.

> You can see, at a glance, that for both Online and In-Store sales, Rose sales are greater than Rose Supply sales.

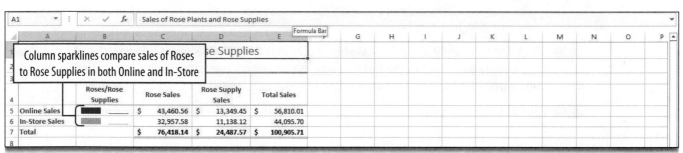

FIGURE 16.52

Objective 12 Format and Print Multiple Worksheets in a Workbook

GO! Learn How
Video E16-12

Each worksheet within a workbook can have different formatting, for example, different headers or footers. If all the worksheets in the workbook will have the same header or footer, you can select all the worksheets and apply formatting common to all of the worksheets; for example, you can set the same footer in all of the worksheets.

Activity 16.34 | Moving a Worksheet, Repeating Footers, and Formatting Multiple Worksheets in a Workbook

In this Activity, you will move the Summary sheet to become the first worksheet in the workbook. Then you will format and prepare your workbook for printing. The three worksheets containing data can be formatted simultaneously.

1 Point to the **Summary sheet tab**, hold down the left mouse button to display a small black triangle—a caret—and then notice that a small paper icon attaches to the mouse pointer.

2 Drag to the left until the caret and mouse pointer are to the left of the **Online Sales sheet tab**, as shown in Figure 16.53, and then release the left mouse button.

> Use this technique to rearrange the order of worksheets within a workbook.

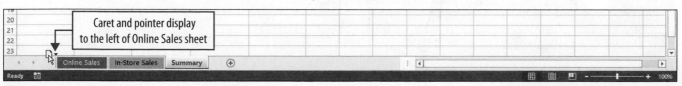

FIGURE 16.53

3 Be sure the **Summary** worksheet is the active sheet, point to its sheet tab, right-click, and then click **Select All Sheets** to display *[Group]* in the title bar.

4 Click the **Page Layout tab**. In the **Page Setup group**, click **Margins**, and then at the bottom of the gallery, click **Custom Margins** to display the **Page Setup** dialog box.

5 In the **Page Setup** dialog box, on the **Margins tab**, under **Center on page**, select the **Horizontally** check box.

6 Click the **Header/Footer tab**, and then in the center of the dialog box, click **Custom Footer**. In the **Footer** dialog box, with your insertion point blinking in the **Left section**, on the row of buttons, click **Insert File Name** 📄.

7 Click **OK** two times.

The dotted line indicates the page break as currently formatted.

8 Press [Ctrl] + [Home]; verify that *[Group]* still displays in the title bar.

By selecting all sheets, you can apply the same formatting to all the worksheets at the same time, for example, to repeat headers or footers.

9 Click the **File tab** to display **Backstage** view, and then click **Show All Properties**. As the **Tags**, type **weekly sales** and in the **Subject** box, type your course name and section number. Be sure your name displays as the **Author**; edit if necessary.

10 On the left, click **Print** to display the **Print Preview**, and then compare your screen with Figure 16.54.

By grouping, you can view all sheets in Print Preview. If you do not see *1 of 3* at the bottom of the Preview, redisplay the workbook, select all the sheets again, and then redisplay Print Preview.

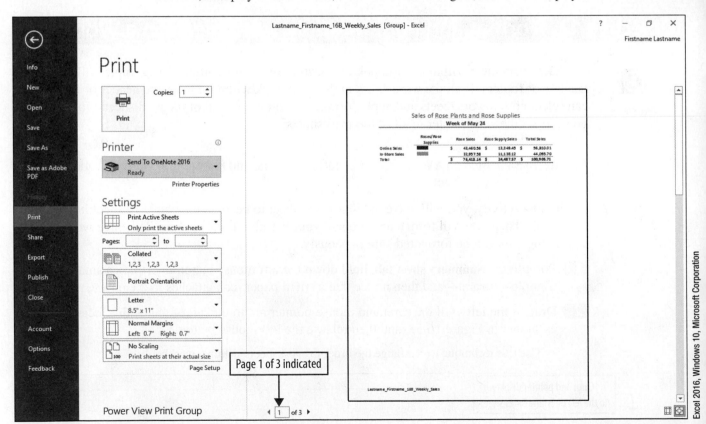

FIGURE 16.54

11 At the bottom of the **Print Preview**, click **Next Page** ▶ as necessary and take a moment to view each page of your workbook.

Activity 16.35 | Printing All or Individual Worksheets in a Workbook

1 In **Backstage** view, click **Save** to save your workbook before printing. In the displayed workbook, right-click the **Summary sheet tab**, and then click **Ungroup Sheets**.

2 Press Ctrl + F2 to display **Print Preview**, and then at the bottom of the window, notice that *1 of 1* is indicated.

Because the worksheets are no longer grouped, only the active sheet is available for printing.

3 On the left, under **Settings**, click **Print Active Sheets**, and then click **Print Entire Workbook**.

At the bottom of the window, *1 of 3* is indicated. You can use this command to print an entire workbook.

4 If directed by your instructor to do so, submit your paper printout, your electronic image of your document that looks like a printed document, or your original Excel file. If required by your instructor, print or create an electronic version of your worksheet with formulas displayed. In the upper right corner of the Excel window, click **Close** ⊠.

END | You have completed Project 16B

GO! With Google

Objective | Calculate Weekly Sales

> **ALERT!** Working with Web-Based Applications and Services
>
> Computer programs and services on the web receive continuous updates and improvements, so the steps to complete this web-based Activity may differ from the ones shown. You can often look at the screens and the information presented to determine how to complete the Activity.
>
> If you do not already have a Google account, you will need to create one before you begin this Activity. Go to http://google.com and, in the upper right corner, click Sign In. On the Sign In screen, click Create Account. On the Create your Google Account page, complete the form, read and agree to the Terms of Service and Privacy Policy, and then click Next step. On the Welcome screen, click Get Started.

Activity | Calculating Weekly Sales with Google Sheets

1 From the desktop, open your browser, navigate to **http://google.com**, and then click the **Google Apps** menu ⊞. Click **Drive**, and then if necessary, sign in to your Google account.

2 Open your **GO! Web Projects** folder—or click New to create and then open this folder if necessary. In the left pane, click **NEW**, and then click **File upload**. Navigate to your student data files, click **e16_16B_Web**, and then click **Open**.

3 Right-click the file you uploaded, point to **Open with**, and then click **Google Sheets**.

4 Click cell **E5**. On the ribbon, click **Functions** Σ ⌄, and then click **SUM**. Select **B5:D5** and then press Enter to total the rose sales for Sunday. Click cell **E5**, and then drag the fill handle down through cell **E11**. Select **E6:E11**, and then on the ribbon, click **More Formats** 123 ⌄. Click **Number**.

5 Click cell **G5** and then enter a formula to add cells **E5** and **F5**. Fill the formula down through cell **G11**, and then format the range **G6:G11** with **Number** format.

6 Select the range **B5:B11**. Click **Functions** Σ ⌄, click **SUM**, and then press Enter to sum the selected range and place the result in cell **B12**. With **B12** selected, fill the formula across to cell **G12**.

7 Click cell **H5**. To calculate the percent that the Sunday sales are of the total sales, type **=g5/g12** and then press F4 to make the cell reference to G12 absolute. Press Enter and then fill the formula down through cell **H11**. With the range **H5:H11** selected, click **Format as percent** % .

8 Click cell **A1** and then compare your screen with Figure A.

9 Submit your file as directed by your instructor. Sign out of your Google account and close your browser.

	A	B	C	D	E	F	G	H	I	J	K	L	M	N	O	P	Q
1		Rose Plants and Rose Supplies: Austin Sales															
2		Week of May 24															
3																	
4	Day	Climbing Roses	Patio Roses	Tea Roses	Total Rose Sales	Rose Supply Sales	Total Sales	Percent of Sales									
5	Sun	$911.51	$26.46	$33.47	$971.44	$1,926.49	$2,897.93	12.17%									
6	Mon	310.49	313.85	782.64	1,406.98	1,526.03	2,933.01	12.32%									
7	Tue	942.37	402.99	30.08	1,375.44	1,853.82	3,229.26	13.56%									
8	Wed	185.89	992.29	253.98	1,432.16	1,922.36	3,354.52	14.09%									
9	Thu	3.53	825.79	340.34	1,169.66	1,973.73	3,143.39	13.20%									
10	Fri	931.46	946.92	966.92	2,845.30	2,121.47	4,966.77	20.86%									
11	Sat	47.23	978.23	234.12	1,259.58	2,025.55	3,285.13	13.80%									
12	Total Sales	$3,332.48	$4,486.53	$2,641.55	$10,460.56	$13,349.45	$23,810.01										
13																	
14																	
15																	

FIGURE A

Enterprise Fund Pie Chart

PROJECT ACTIVITIES

In Activities 16.36 through 16.47, you will edit a worksheet for Michael Larsen, City Manager, that reports the adjusted figures for Enterprise Fund Expenditures for the next fiscal year, and then present the data in a pie chart. Your completed worksheets will look similar to Figure 16.55.

PROJECT FILES

If your instructor wants you to submit Project 16C in the MyITLab Grader system, log in to MyITLab, locate Grader Project 16C, and then download the files for this project.

For Project 16C, you will need the following file:
e16C_Enterprise_Fund

You will save your workbook as:
Lastname_Firstname_16C_Enterprise_Fund

PROJECT RESULTS

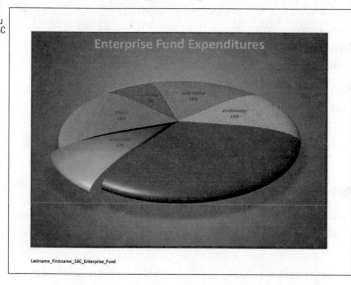

	Pacifica Bay		
	Enterprise Fund Expenditures		
	Recommended Adjustments		
	Originally Proposed	Adjusted	% of Total Fund Expenditures
Airport	$ 17,610,810	$ 18,121,067	18.12%
Parking	6,824,865	7,897,526	7.90%
Solid Waste	18,695,222	17,845,287	17.85%
Wastewater	12,657,765	13,985,695	13.99%
Water Usage	30,457,903	32,356,236	32.36%
Waterfront	10,976,843	9,794,189	9.79%
Total	$ 97,223,408	$ 100,000,000	

Lastname_Firstname_16C_Enterprise_Fund

FIGURE 16.55 Project 16C Enterprise Fund Pie Chart

GO! Learn How
Video E16-13

A *pie chart* shows the relationship of each part to a whole. The size of each pie slice is equal to its value compared to the total value of all the slices. A pie chart displays data that is arranged in a single column or single row, and shows the size of items in a single data series proportional to the sum of the items. Whereas a column or bar chart can have two or more data series in the chart, a pie chart can have only one data series.

Consider using a pie chart when you have only one data series to plot, you do not have more than seven categories, and the categories represent parts of a total value.

Activity 16.36 | Calculating Values for a Pie Chart

> **ALERT!** **To submit as an autograded project, log into MyITLab and download the files for this project, and begin with those files instead of e16C_Enterprise_Fund.**

A *fund* is a sum of money set aside for a specific purpose. In a municipal government like the City of Pacifica Bay, the *general fund* is money set aside for the normal operating activities of the city, such as police, fire, and administering the everyday functions of the city.

Municipal governments also commonly establish an *enterprise fund* to report income and expenditures related to municipal services for which a fee is charged in exchange for goods or services. For example, Pacifica Bay receives income from airport landing fees, parking fees, water usage fees, and rental fees along public beaches, but there are costs—expenditures—related to building and maintaining these facilities and services from which income is received.

1 Start Excel. From the student files that accompany this chapter, open **e16C_Enterprise_Fund**. Display the **Save As** dialog box, and then navigate to your **AIO Chapter 16** folder. In the **File name** box, type **Lastname_Firstname_16C_Enterprise_Fund** and then click **Save** or press Enter.

The worksheet indicates the originally proposed and adjusted expenditures from the Enterprise Fund for the next fiscal year.

2 Click cell **D5**, and then type **=** to begin a formula.

3 Click cell **C5**, which is the first value that is part of the total adjusted Fund Expenditures, to insert it into the formula. Type **/** to indicate division, and then click cell **C11**, which is the total adjusted expenditures.

Recall that to determine the percentage by which a value makes up a total, you must divide the value by the total. The result will be a percentage expressed as a decimal.

4 Press F4 to make the reference to the value in cell **C11** absolute, which will enable you to copy the formula. Compare your screen with Figure 16.56.

Recall that an *absolute cell reference* refers to a cell by its fixed position in the worksheet—the cell reference will not change when you copy the formula. The reference to cell C5 is a *relative cell reference*, because when you copy the formula, you want the reference to change *relative* to its row. In the formula, the dollar signs display to indicate that a cell reference is absolute.

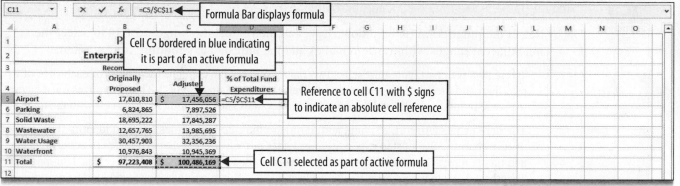

FIGURE 16.56

Excel 2016, Windows 10, Microsoft Corporation

5 ▶ On the **Formula Bar**, click **Enter** ☑ to confirm the entry and to keep cell **D5** the active cell.

6 ▶ Copy the formula down through cell **D10**, and then compare your screen with Figure 16.57.

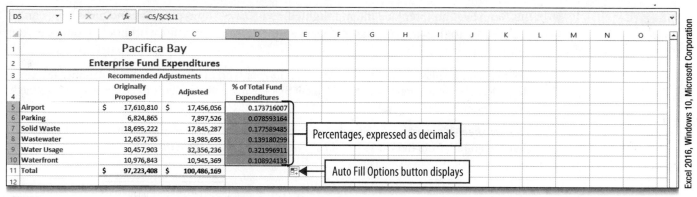

FIGURE 16.57

Excel 2016, Windows 10, Microsoft Corporation

7 ▶ With the range **D5:D10** still selected, right-click over the selection, and then on the mini toolbar, click **Percent Style** ⅔ and **Center** ☰. Click cell **A1** to cancel the selection, and then **Save** 🖫 your workbook. Compare your screen with Figure 16.58.

	A	B	C	D	E	F	G	H	I	J	K	L	M	N	O
1		Pacifica Bay													
2		Enterprise Fund Expenditures													
3			Recommended Adjustments												
4		Originally Proposed	Adjusted	% of Total Fund Expenditures											
5	Airport	$ 17,610,810	$ 17,456,056	17%											
6	Parking	6,824,865	7,897,526	8%											
7	Solid Waste	18,695,222	17,845,287	18%											
8	Wastewater	12,657,765	13,985,695	14%											
9	Water Usage	30,457,903	32,356,236	32%											
10	Waterfront	10,976,843	10,945,369	11%											
11	Total	$ 97,223,408	$ 100,486,169												
12															

Percent of Total for each item calculated, expressed as percentages

FIGURE 16.58

Excel 2016, Windows 10, Microsoft Corporation

IC3
DIGITAL LITERACY
CERTIFICATION
2.03g (i)
2.03g (ii)
2.03g (iii)

Activity 16.37 | Creating a Pie Chart and Moving a Chart to a Chart Sheet

1 Select the range **A5:A10**, hold down Ctrl, and then select the range **C5:C10** to select the nonadjacent ranges with the item names and the adjusted expenditure for each item.

To create a pie chart, you must select two ranges. One range contains the labels for each slice of the pie chart, and the other range contains the values that add up to a total. The two ranges must have the same number of cells and the range with the values should *not* include the cell with the total.

The item names (Airport, Parking, and so on) are the category names and will identify the slices of the pie chart. Each adjusted expenditure is a *data point*—a value that originates in a worksheet cell and that is represented in a chart by a *data marker*. In a pie chart, each pie slice is a data marker. Together, the data points form the *data series*—related data points represented by data markers—and determine the size of each pie slice.

2 With the nonadjacent ranges selected, click the **Insert tab**, and then in the **Charts group**, click **Insert Pie or Doughnut Chart**. Under **3-D Pie**, click the chart **3-D Pie** to create the chart on your worksheet and to display the Chart Tools contextual tabs on the ribbon.

3 On the **Design tab**, at the right end of the ribbon in the **Location group**, click **Move Chart**. In the **Move Chart** dialog box, click the **New sheet** option button.

4 In the **New sheet** box, replace the highlighted text *Chart1* by typing **Expenditures Chart** and then click **OK** to display the chart on a separate worksheet in your workbook. Compare your screen with Figure 16.59.

The pie chart displays on a separate new sheet in your workbook, and a *legend* identifies the pie slices. Recall that a legend is a chart element that identifies the patterns or colors assigned to the categories in the chart.

A *chart sheet* is a workbook sheet that contains only a chart; it is useful when you want to view a chart separately from the worksheet data. The sheet tab indicates *Expenditures Chart*.

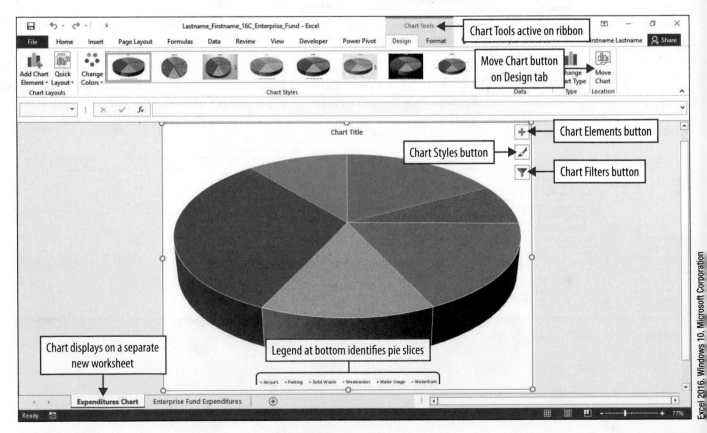

FIGURE 16.59

GO! Learn How
Video E16-14

Activity 16.38 | Formatting a Chart Title by Applying a WordArt Style and Changing Font Size

1 Click the text **Chart Title** to surround it with selection handles, and then watch the **Formula Bar** as you type **Enterprise Fund Expenditures** Press [Enter] to create the new chart title in the box.

2 Click the **Format tab**, and then in the **WordArt Styles group**, click **More** ⊡. In the first row, click the last style—**Fill – Gold, Accent 4, Soft Bevel**.

3 With the ⊡ pointer, drag to select the chart title text, and then on the mini toolbar, change the **Font Size** to **32**. Click the edge of the chart to deselect the title, and then compare your screen with Figure 16.60.

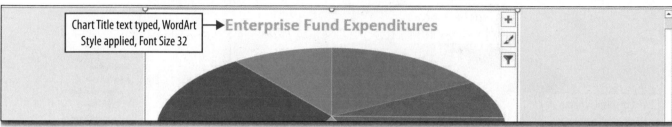

> Chart Title text typed, WordArt Style applied, Font Size 32 → **Enterprise Fund Expenditures**

Excel 2016, Windows 10, Microsoft Corporation

FIGURE 16.60

4 **Save** 🖫 your workbook.

Activity 16.39 | Formatting Chart Elements by Removing a Legend and Adding and Formatting Data Labels

In your worksheet, for each budget item, you calculated the percent of the total in column D. These percentages can also be calculated by the Chart feature and added to the pie slices as labels.

1 If necessary, click the edge of the chart to display the three chart buttons on the right, and then click **Chart Elements** ⊞. Compare your screen with Figure 16.61.

Use the Chart Elements button to add, remove, or change chart elements such as the chart title, the legend, and the data labels.

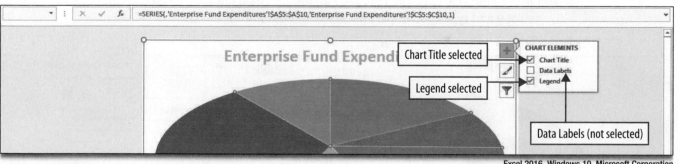

=SERIES(,'Enterprise Fund Expenditures'!$A$5:$A$10,'Enterprise Fund Expenditures'!$C$5:$C$10,1)

Enterprise Fund Expendi...

Chart Title selected → CHART ELEMENTS
☑ Chart Title
☐ Data Labels
☑ Legend

Legend selected →

Data Labels (not selected)

Excel 2016, Windows 10, Microsoft Corporation

FIGURE 16.61

2 Click the **Legend** check box to deselect it and remove the legend from the bottom of the chart.

3 *Point* to **Data Labels**, and then click the ▶ **arrow** to display a menu. At the bottom of the menu, click **More Options** to display the **Format Data Labels** pane on the right.

The Format Data Labels pane displays and data labels representing the values display on each pie slice.

4 In the **Format Data Labels** pane, under **Label Options**, click as necessary to select the **Category Name** and **Percentage** check boxes. Click to *clear* any other check boxes in this group. Under **Label Position**, click the **Center** option button. Compare your screen with Figure 16.62.

All of the data labels are selected and display both the category name and the percentage. In the worksheet, you calculated the percent of the total in column D. Here, the percentage will be calculated by the Chart feature and added to the chart as a label.

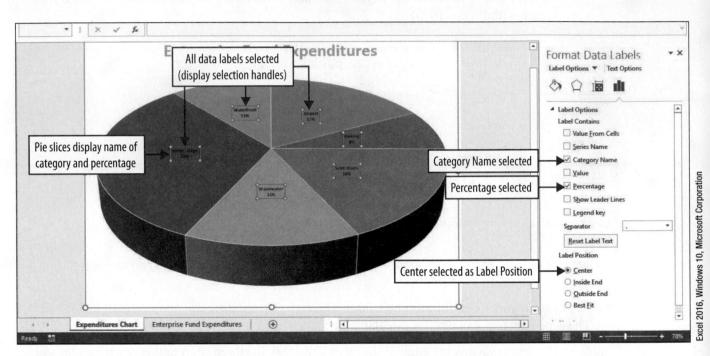

FIGURE 16.62

5 Point to any of the selected data labels, right-click to display a shortcut menu, and then click **Font** to display the **Font** dialog box.

6 On the **Font tab**, click the **Font style arrow**, and then click **Bold Italic**. In the **Size** box, drag to select **9** and type **11** Compare your screen with Figure 16.63.

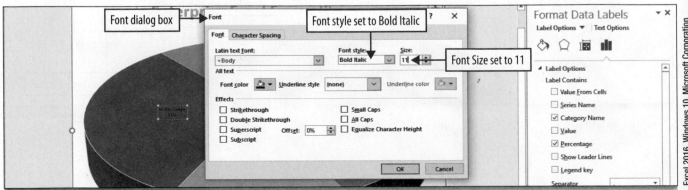

FIGURE 16.63

7 Click **OK** to close the dialog box and apply the formatting to the data labels. In the upper right corner of the **Format Data Labels** pane, click **Close** [X]. **Save** [💾] your workbook.

Activity 16.40 | Formatting a Data Series with 3-D Effects

3-D, which is short for *three-dimensional*, refers to an image that appears to have all three spatial dimensions—length, width, and depth.

1 In any pie slice, point anywhere outside of the selected label, and then double-click to display the **Format Data Series** pane on the right.

> **ANOTHER WAY** Right-click outside the label of any pie slice, and then click Format Data Series to display the Format Data Series pane. Or, on the Format tab, in the Current Selection group, click the Chart Elements arrow, click Series 1, and then click Format Selection.

2 In the **Format Data Series** pane, under **Series Options**, click **Effects** [⬠], and then click **3-D Format**. Compare your screen with Figure 16.64.

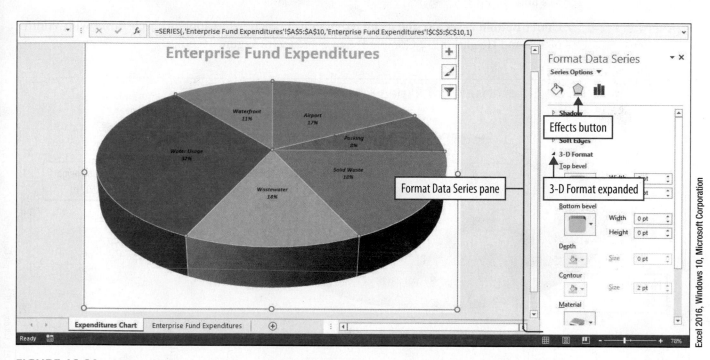

FIGURE 16.64

3 Click the **Top bevel arrow**, and then in the gallery, under **Bevel**, click the first bevel—**Circle**—as shown in Figure 16.65.

> *Bevel* is a shape effect that uses shading and shadows to make the edges of a shape appear to be curved or angled.

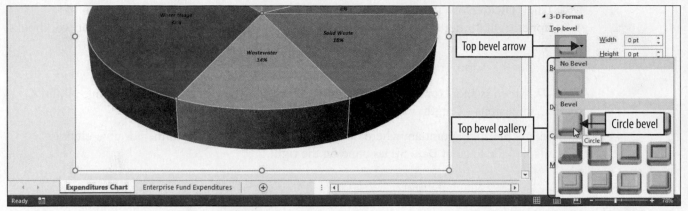

FIGURE 16.65

4 Under **Top bevel**, in the **Width** box, select the existing text and type **512** Change the **Height** to **512** and then press Enter.

5 Under **Bottom bevel**, use the technique you just practiced to apply a **Circle** bevel with **Width** of **512** and **Height** of **512** Compare your screen with Figure 16.66.

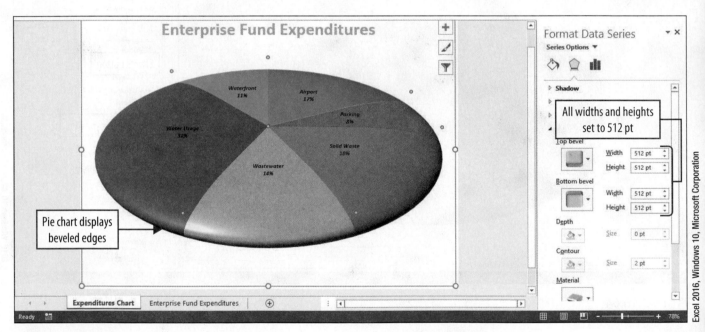

FIGURE 16.66

6 In the **Format Data Series** pane, scroll down as necessary, and then click the **Material arrow**. Under **Standard**, click the third material—**Plastic**.

7 **Save** your workbook.

Activity 16.41 | Formatting a Data Series with a Shadow Effect

1 In the **Format Data Series** pane, scroll back to the top of the pane, and then click **Shadow** to expand the options for this effect.

2 Under **Shadow**, click the **Presets arrow**, use the scroll bar to move to the bottom of the gallery, and then under **Perspective**, in the first row, point to the third effect to display the ScreenTip *Below*. Compare your screen with Figure 16.67.

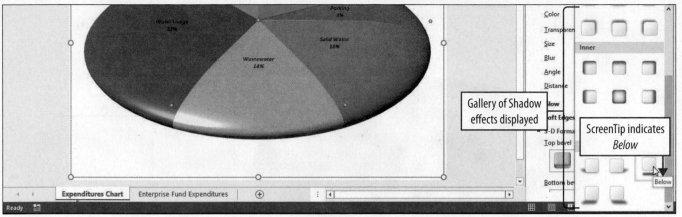

FIGURE 16.67

3 ▶ Click **Below** to apply the shadow to the chart. **Save** 🔲 your workbook.

Activity 16.42 | Rotating a Pie Chart by Changing the Angle of the First Slice

The order in which the data series in pie charts are plotted in Excel is determined by the order of the data on the worksheet. To gain a different view of the chart, you can rotate the chart within the 360 degrees of the circle of the pie shape to present a different visual perspective of the chart.

1 ▶ Notice the position of the **Water Usage** and **Waterfront** slices in the chart. Then, with the pie chart still selected—sizing handles surround the pie—in the **Format Data Series** pane, under **Series Options**, click **Series Options** 📊.

2 ▶ Under **Angle of first slice**, in the box to the right, drag to select **0°**, type **250** and then press [Enter] to rotate the chart 250 degrees to the right.

🔁 **ANOTHER WAY**   Drag the slider to 250°, or click the spin box up arrow as many times as necessary.

3 ▶ Click **Save** 🔲, and then compare your screen with Figure 16.68.

Rotating the chart can provide a better perspective to the chart. Here, rotating the chart in this manner emphasizes that Water Usage is the largest enterprise fund expenditure.

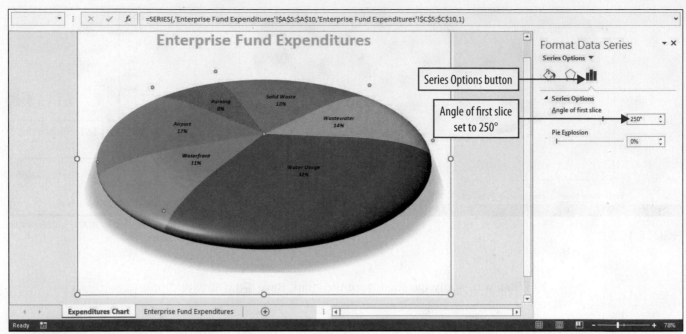

Formula bar: `=SERIES(,'Enterprise Fund Expenditures'!$A$5:$A$10,'Enterprise Fund Expenditures'!$C$5:$C$10,1)`

Enterprise Fund Expenditures

Parking 8%
Solid Waste 18%
Wastewater 14%
Airport 17%
Waterfront 11%
Water Usage 12%

Format Data Series
Series Options ▼

Series Options button

Series Options
Angle of first slice

Angle of first slice set to 250° → 250°

Pie Explosion 0%

Expenditures Chart | Enterprise Fund Expenditures

Ready   78%

Excel 2016, Windows 10, Microsoft Corporation

FIGURE 16.68

Activity 16.43 | Exploding and Coloring a Pie Slice

You can pull out—*explode*—one or more slices of a pie chart to emphasize a specific slice or slices.

1 In the **Format Data Series** pane, under **Series Options**, notice the slider and box for *Pie Explosion*.

When all the pie slices are selected, as they currently are, you can use this command to explode *all* of the pie pieces away from the center by varying degrees to emphasize all the individual slices of the pie chart. An exploded pie chart visualizes the contribution of each value to the total, while at the same time emphasizing individual values.

2 On the pie chart, click the **Waterfront** slice to select only that slice, and then on the right, notice that the **Format Data Point** pane displays.

Excel adjusts the pane, depending on what you have selected, so that the commands you need are available.

3 In the **Format Data Point** pane, in the **Point Explosion** box, select the existing text, type **10%** and then press Enter.

4 With the **Waterfront** slice still selected, in the **Format Data Point** pane, under **Series Options**, click **Fill & Line** ◇, and then click **Fill** to expand its options.

5 Click the **Gradient fill** option button, click the **Preset gradients arrow**, and then in the fourth row, click the last gradient—**Bottom Spotlight – Accent 6**. Click **Save** 🖫, and then compare your screen with Figure 16.69.

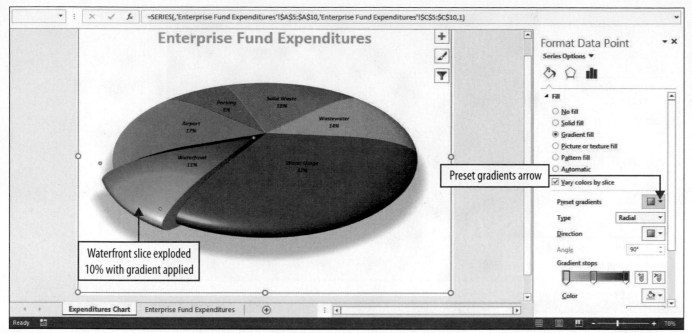

Enterprise Fund Expenditures

=SERIES(,'Enterprise Fund Expenditures'!$A$5:$A$10,'Enterprise Fund Expenditures'!$C$5:$C$10,1)

Preset gradients arrow

Waterfront slice exploded
10% with gradient applied

Format Data Point

Series Options ▼

◢ Fill
○ No fill
○ Solid fill
◉ Gradient fill
○ Picture or texture fill
○ Pattern fill
○ Automatic
☑ Vary colors by slice

Preset gradients
Type   Radial
Direction
Angle   90°
Gradient stops

Color

Expenditures Chart   Enterprise Fund Expenditures

Ready

FIGURE 16.69

Activity 16.44 | Formatting the Chart Area

The entire chart and all of its elements comprise the ***chart area***.

1 Point to the white area just inside the border of the chart to display the ScreenTip *Chart Area*. Click one time, and notice that on the right, the **Format Chart Area** pane displays.

2 Under **Chart Options**, click **Fill & Line** 🖊, and be sure the **Fill** options are still displayed.

3 Click the **Gradient fill** option button, click the **Preset gradients arrow**, and then in the fourth row, click the first gradient—**Bottom Spotlight – Accent 1**.

4 In the **Format Chart Area** pane, click **Fill** to collapse the options, and then click **Border** to expand its options.

5 Under **Border**, click **Solid line**, click the **Color arrow** to display the Outline colors, and then in the fourth column, click the first color—**Blue – Gray, Text 2**. In the **Width** box, drag to select the existing width, and then type **5**

6 **Close** ☒ the **Format Chart Area** pane, and then click outside of the Chart Area to deselect the chart. Click **Save** 💾, and then compare your screen with Figure 16.70.

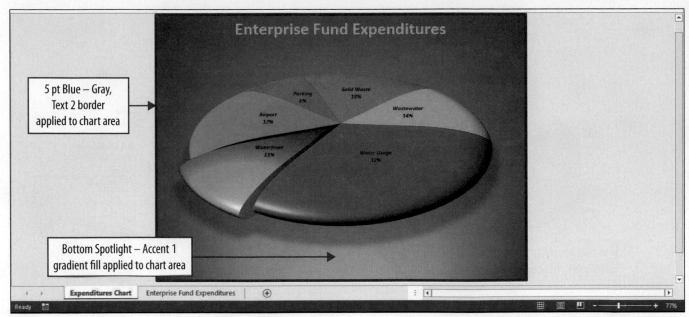

5 pt Blue – Gray, Text 2 border applied to chart area

Bottom Spotlight – Accent 1 gradient fill applied to chart area

FIGURE 16.70

Objective 15 Edit a Workbook and Update a Chart

GO! Learn How
Video E16-15

Activity 16.45 | Editing a Workbook and Updating a Chart

If you edit the data in your worksheet, the chart data markers—in this instance, the pie slices—will adjust automatically to accurately represent the new values.

1 On the pie chart, notice that *Airport* represents 17% of the total projected expenses.

2 In the sheet tab area at the bottom of the workbook, click the **Enterprise Fund Expenditures tab** to redisplay the worksheet.

3 Click cell **C5**, type **18,121,067** and then press Enter. Notice that the Accounting Number Format is retained in the cell.

ANOTHER WAY Double-click the cell to position the insertion point in the cell and edit.

4 Notice that the total in cell **C11** recalculated to *$101,151,180* and the percentages in **column D** also recalculated.

5 Display the **Expenditures Chart** sheet. Notice that the pie slices adjust to show the recalculation—*Airport* is now *18%* of the adjusted expenditures. Click **Save** ⊟, and then compare your screen with Figure 16.71.

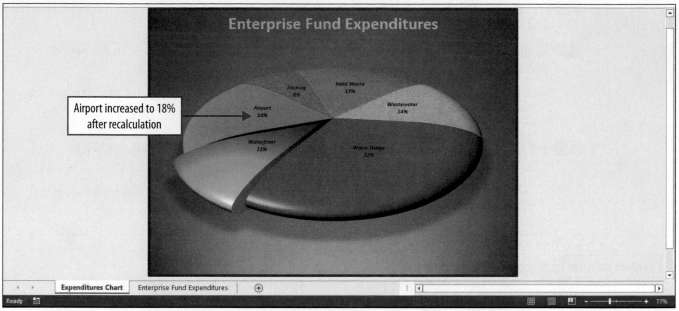

Airport increased to 18%
after recalculation

Excel 2016, Windows 10, Microsoft Corporation

FIGURE 16.71

Objective 16 Use Goal Seek to Perform What-If Analysis

GO! Learn How
Video E16-16

Activity 16.46 | Using Goal Seek to Perform What-If Analysis

The process of changing the values in cells to see how those changes affect the outcome of formulas in your worksheet is referred to as *what-if analysis*. One what-if analysis tool in Excel is *Goal Seek*, which finds the input needed in one cell to arrive at the desired result in another cell.

1 Click the **Enterprise Fund Expenditures sheet tab** to redisplay the worksheet.

2 Select the range **D5:D10**, and then increase the number of decimal places to two. Compare your screen with Figure 16.72.

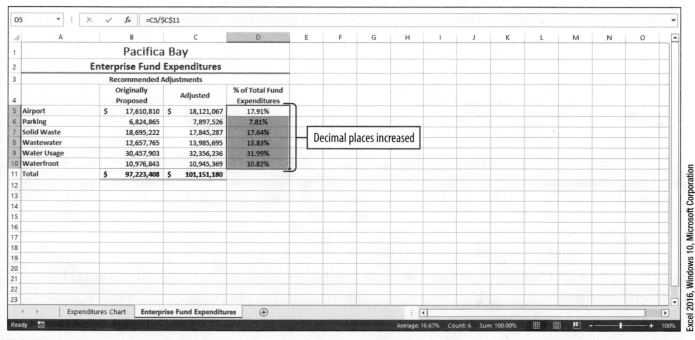

Decimal places increased

FIGURE 16.72

3 Click cell **C11**. On the **Data tab**, in the **Forecast group**, click **What-If Analysis**, and then click **Goal Seek**.

4 In the **Goal Seek** dialog box, notice that the active cell, **C11**, is indicated in the **Set cell** box. Press Tab to move to the **To value** box, and then type **100,000,000**

C11 is the cell in which you want to set a specific value; $100,000,000 is the total expenditures budgeted for the Enterprise Fund. The Set cell box contains the formula that calculates the information you seek.

5 Press Tab to move the insertion point to the **By changing cell** box, and then click cell **C10**. Compare your screen with Figure 16.73.

Cell C10 contains the value that Excel changes to reach the goal. In the Goal Seek dialog box, Excel formats this cell as an absolute cell reference.

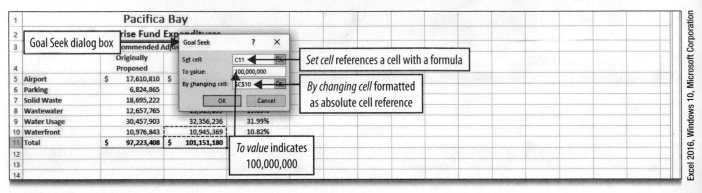

FIGURE 16.73

6 Click **OK**. In the displayed **Goal Seek Status** dialog box, click **OK**.

7 Press Ctrl + Home, click **Save** 🖫, and then compare your screen with Figure 16.74.

Excel calculates that the city must budget for *$9,794,189* in Waterfront expenditures in order to maintain a total Enterprise Fund Expenditure budget of $100,000,000.

	A	B	C	D
1		**Pacifica Bay**		
2		**Enterprise Fund Expenditures**		
3		Recommended Adjustments		
4		Originally Proposed	Adjusted	% of Total Fund Expenditures
5	Airport	$ 17,610,810	$ 18,121,067	18.12%
6	Parking	6,824,865	7,897,526	7.90%
7	Solid Waste	18,695,222	17,845,287	17.85%
8	Wastewater	12,657,765	13,985,695	13.99%
9	Water Usage	30,457,903	32,356,236	32.36%
10	Waterfront	10,976,843	9,794,189	9.79%
11	Total	$ 97,223,408	$ 100,000,000	

Goal of $100,000,000   Waterfront changed to 9,794,189

FIGURE 16.74

Activity 16.47 | Preparing and Printing a Workbook with a Chart Sheet

1 Click the **Page Layout tab**. In the **Page Setup group**, click the Dialog Box Launcher 🖻.

2 In the **Page Setup** dialog box, on the **Margins tab**, under **Center on page**, select the **Horizontally** check box.

3 Click the **Header/Footer tab**, and then in the center of the dialog box, click **Custom Footer**. In the **Footer** dialog box, with the insertion point blinking in the **Left section**, on the row of buttons, click **Insert File Name** 🗋. Click **OK** two times.

The dotted line indicates the page break as currently formatted.

4 Display the **Expenditures Chart**, which must have its footer formatted separately. In the **Page Setup group**, click the **Dialog Box Launcher** ⬚.

Chart sheets are automatically centered on the page.

5 Click the **Header/Footer tab**, and then in the center of the dialog box, click **Custom Footer**. In the **Footer** dialog box, with the insertion point blinking in the **Left section**, on the row of buttons, click **Insert File Name** 🗋. Click **OK** two times.

6 Right-click the **Expenditures Chart sheet tab**, and then click **Select All Sheets**. Verify that *[Group]* displays in the title bar.

Recall that by selecting all sheets, you can view all of the workbook pages in Print Preview.

7 Press ⌃Ctrl + F2 to display the **Print Preview**. Examine the first page, and then at the bottom of the **Print Preview**, click **Next Page** ▶ to view the second page of your workbook.

NOTE | Printing a Chart Sheet Uses More Toner

Printing a chart that displays on a chart sheet will use more toner or ink than a small chart that is part of a worksheet. If you are printing your work, check with your instructor to verify whether or not you should print the chart sheet.

---

8 Click **Info**, and then click **Show All Properties**. As the **Tags**, type **enterprise fund, expenditures** As the **Subject**, type your course name and section number. Be sure your name displays as the **Author**. **Save** 🖫 the workbook.

9 If directed by your instructor to do so, submit your paper printout, your electronic image of your document that looks like a printed document, or your original Excel file. If required by your instructor, print or create an electronic version of your worksheet with formulas displayed. In the upper right corner of the Excel window, click **Close** ☒.

END | You have completed Project 16C

Go! With Google

> **ALERT!** **Working with Web-Based Applications and Services**
>
> Computer programs and services on the web receive continuous updates and improvements, so the steps to complete this web-based Activity may differ from the ones shown. You can often look at the screens and the information presented to determine how to complete the Activity.
>
> If you do not already have a Google account, you will need to create one before you begin this Activity. Go to http://google.com and, in the upper right corner, click Sign In. On the Sign In screen, click Create Account. On the Create your Google Account page, complete the form, read and agree to the Terms of Service and Privacy Policy, and then click Next step. On the Welcome screen, click Get Started.

Activity | Create a Pie Chart

1 From the desktop, open your browser, navigate to **http://google.com**, and then click the **Google Apps** menu ⦙⦙⦙. Click **Drive**, and then if necessary, sign in to your Google account.

2 Open your **GO! Web Projects** folder—or click New to create and then open this folder if necessary. In the left pane, click **NEW**, and then click **File upload**. Navigate to your student data files, click **e16_16C_Web**, and then click **Open**.

3 Right-click the file you uploaded, point to **Open with**, and then click **Google Sheets**.

4 Click cell **D5**. Type **=** and then click cell **C5**. Type **/** and then click **C11** and press F4 to make the cell reference absolute. Press Enter to create a formula to calculate % of Total Fund Expenditures.

5 Click cell **D5**, and then apply percent formatting. Fill the formula down through cell **D10**. Click **Format**, point to **Align**, and then click **Center**.

6 Select the range **A5:A10**, hold down Ctrl, and then select **C5:C10**. Click **Insert**, and then click **Chart**. To the right of the chart gallery, point to the vertical scroll bar

and drag down to display the Pie charts. Click the third chart—**3D pie chart**, and then click **Insert**.

7 Point to the chart and then drag down and to the left to position the pie chart under the worksheet data so that its left edge aligns with the left edge of cell **A13**. Click the **Chart title** to display a box in which you can type the chart title. Type **Enterprise Fund Expenditures** and then press Enter. In the chart title ribbon, click the **Font Size arrow**, and then click **20**. Click anywhere in the chart outside of the title so that the title is not selected.

8 In the upper right corner of the chart area, click the **down-pointing triangle**, and then click **Advanced edit**. Under **Legend**, click **Right**, and then in the list, click **Labeled**. To the right of **Background**, click the **Background color arrow**, and then in the seventh column, click the third color—**light cornflower blue 3**. Click **Update** to apply the formatting changes and close the **Chart Editor**.

9 Click cell **A1** and then scroll down to view the entire chart. Compare your screen with Figure A.

10 Submit your file as directed by your instructor. Sign out of your Google account and close your browser.

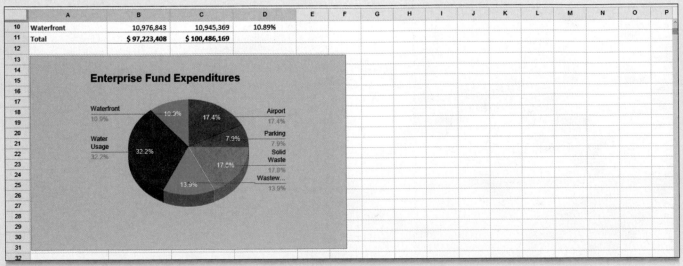

FIGURE A

16
EXCEL 2016

IC3 SKILLS IN THIS CHAPTER

IC3 Key Applications

Project 16A
Section 2.03 Spreadsheets

(a) Understand common spreadsheet terms
   (vii) Navigation
(d) Be able to filter and sort data
(e) Understand functions, formulas, and operators
   (i) Understand their purpose and how they are used
   (ii) Recognize syntax
   (iii) Be able to create simple formulas
(h) Create spreadsheet tables
   (i) Recognize tables
   (ii) Use and manipulate tables
   (iii) Create simple tables
(m) Understand how a spreadsheet can be used as a simple database

Project 16B
Section 2.03 Spreadsheets

(i) Manipulate data within a spreadsheet
   (i) Cut, copy, and paste data

Project 16C
Section 2.03 Spreadsheets

(g) Use and create spreadsheet charts
   (i) Recognize charts
   (ii) Read and interpret charts
   (iii) Create simple charts

BUILD YOUR E-PORTFOLIO

An E-Portfolio is a collection of evidence, stored electronically, that showcases what you have accomplished while completing your education. Collecting and then sharing your work products with potential employers reflects your academic and career goals. Your completed documents from the following projects are good examples to show what you have learned: 16G, 16K, and 16L.

GO! FOR JOB SUCCESS

Video: Customer Service
Your instructor may assign this video to your class, and then ask you to think about, or discuss with your classmates, these questions:

FotolEdhar / Fotolia

How could Lee have been more helpful to the customer?

What did the supervisor, Christine, do to calm the customer?

What might SunTel do on a company-wide basis to create a better customer service experience?

END OF CHAPTER

SUMMARY

Use Flash Fill to recognize a pattern in data and automatically fill in values when you enter examples of desired output. Flash Fill can split data from two or more cells or combine data from two cells.

Functions are formulas that Excel provides and that perform calculations by using specific values in a particular order or structure. Statistical functions are useful to analyze a group of measurements.

You can navigate among worksheets in a workbook by clicking the sheet tabs, which identify each worksheet in a workbook. Use multiple worksheets in a workbook to organize data in a logical arrangement.

To create a pie chart, you must select two ranges. One range contains the labels for each pie slice; the other contains the values that add up to a total. Both ranges must have the same number of cells.

GO! LEARN IT ONLINE

Review the concepts, key terms, and IC3 skills in this chapter by completing these online challenges, which you can find at **MyITLab**.

Matching and Multiple Choice: Answer matching and multiple-choice questions to test what you learned in this chapter.

Lessons on the GO!: Learn how to use all the new apps and features as they are introduced by Microsoft.

IC3 Prep Quiz: Answer questions to review the IC3 skills that you practiced in this chapter.

GO! COLLABORATIVE TEAM PROJECT (Available in MyITLab and Instructor Resource Center)

If your instructor assigns this project to your class, you can expect to work with one or more of your classmates—either in person or by using Internet tools—to create work products similar to those that you created in this chapter. A team is a group of workers who work together to solve a problem, make a decision, or create a work product. Collaboration is when you work together with others as a team in an intellectual endeavor to complete a shared task or achieve a shared goal.

PROJECT GUIDE FOR ALL IN ONE CHAPTER 16

Your instructor will assign Projects from this list to ensure your learning and assess your knowledge.

Project	Apply Skills from These Chapter Objectives	Project Type	Project Location
16A MyITLab	Objectives 1–6 from Project 16A	**16A Instructional Project (Grader Project)** Guided instruction to learn the skills in Project 16A.	In MyITLab and in text
16B MyITLab	Objectives 7–12 from Project 16B	**16B Instructional Project (Grader Project)** Guided instruction to learn the skills in Project 16B.	In MyITLab and in text
16C MyITLab	Objectives 13–16 from Project 16C	**16C Instructional Project (Grader Project)** Guided instruction to learn the skills in Project 16C.	In MyITLab and in text
16D	Objectives 1–6 from Project 16A	**16D Skills Review (Scorecard Grading)** A guided review of the skills from Project 16A.	Instructor Resource Center (IRC) and MyITLab
16E	Objectives 7–12 from Project 16B	**16E Skills Review (Scorecard Grading)** A guided review of the skills from Project 16B.	IRC and MyITLab
16F	Objectives 13–16 from Project 16C	**16F Skills Review (Scorecard Grading)** A guided review of the skills from Project 16C.	IRC and MyITLab
16G MyITLab	Objectives 1–6 from Project 16A	**16G Mastery (Grader Project)** **Mastery and Transfer of Learning** A demonstration of your mastery of the skills in Project 16A with extensive decision making.	In MyITLab and in text
16H MyITLab	Objectives 7–12 from Project 16B	**16H Mastery (Grader Project)** **Mastery and Transfer of Learning** A demonstration of your mastery of the skills in Project 16B with extensive decision making.	In MyITLab and in text
16I MyITLab	Objectives 13–16 from Project 16C	**16I Mastery (Grader Project)** **Mastery and Transfer of Learning** A demonstration of your mastery of the skills in Project 16C with extensive decision making.	In MyITLab and in text
16J MyITLab	Objectives 1–16 from Projects 16A, 16B, and 16C	**16J Mastery (Grader Project)** **Mastery and Transfer of Learning** A demonstration of your mastery of the skills in Projects 16A, 16B, and 16C with extensive decision making.	In MyITLab and in text
16K	Combination of Objectives from Projects 16A, 16B, and 16C	**16K GO! Fix It (Scorecard Grading)** **Critical Thinking** A demonstration of your mastery of the skills in Projects 16A, 16B, and 16C by creating a correct result from a document that contains errors you must find.	IRC and MyITLab
16L	Combination of Objectives from Projects 16A, 16B, and 16C	**16L GO! Make It (Scorecard Grading)** **Critical Thinking** A demonstration of your mastery of the skills in Projects 16A, 16B, and 16C by creating a result from a supplied picture.	IRC and MyITLab
16M	Combination of Objectives from Projects 16A, 16B, and 16C	**16M GO! Solve It (Rubric Grading)** **Critical Thinking** A demonstration of your mastery of the skills in Projects 16A, 16B, and 16C your decision-making skills, and your critical-thinking skills. A task-specific rubric helps you self-assess your result.	IRC and MyITLab
16N	Combination of Objectives from Projects 16A, 16B, and 16C	**16N GO! Solve It (Rubric Grading)** **Critical Thinking** A demonstration of your mastery of the skills in Projects 16A, 16B, and 16C your decision-making skills, and your critical-thinking skills. A task-specific rubric helps you self-assess your result.	In text
16O	Combination of Objectives from Projects 16A, 16B, and 16C	**16O GO! Think (Rubric Grading)** **Critical Thinking** A demonstration of your understanding of the chapter concepts applied in a manner that you would outside of college. An analytic rubric helps you and your instructor grade the quality of your work by comparing it to the work an expert in the discipline would create.	In text
16P	Combination of Objectives from Projects 16A, 16B, and 16C	**16M GO! Think (Rubric Grading)** **Critical Thinking** A demonstration of your understanding of the chapter concepts applied in a manner that you would outside of college. An analytic rubric helps you and your instructor grade the quality of your work by comparing it to the work an expert in the discipline would create.	IRC and MyITLab
16Q	Combination of Objectives from Projects 16A, 16B, and 16C	**16N You and GO! (Rubric Grading)** **Critical Thinking** A demonstration of your understanding of the chapter concepts applied in a manner that you would in a personal situation. An analytic rubric helps you and your instructor grade the quality of your work.	IRC and MyITLab
16R	Combination of Objectives from Projects 16A, 16B, and 16C	**16O Collaborative Team Project for AIO Chapter 16** **Critical Thinking** A demonstration of your understanding of concepts and your ability to work collaboratively in a group role-playing assessment, requiring both collaboration and self-management.	IRC and MyITLab

GLOSSARY

GLOSSARY OF CHAPTER KEY TERMS

3-D The shortened term for three-dimensional, which refers to an image that appears to have all three spatial dimensions—length, width, and depth.

Absolute cell reference A cell reference that refers to cells by their fixed position in a worksheet; an absolute cell reference remains the same when the formula is copied.

Arguments The values that an Excel function uses to perform calculations or operations.

AVERAGE function An Excel function that adds a group of values, and then divides the result by the number of values in the group.

Bevel A shape effect that uses shading and shadows to make the edges of a shape appear to be curved or angled.

Chart area The entire chart and all of its elements.

Chart sheet A workbook sheet that contains only a chart.

Comparison operators Symbols that evaluate each value to determine if it is the same (=), greater than (>), less than (<), or in between a range of values as specified by the criteria.

Conditional format A format that changes the appearance of a cell—for example, by adding cell shading or font color—based on a condition; if the condition is true, the cell is formatted based on that condition, and if the condition is false, the cell is not formatted.

COUNT function A statistical function that counts the number of cells in a range that contains numbers.

COUNTIF function A statistical function that counts the number of cells within a range that meet the given condition and that has two arguments—the range of cells to check and the criteria.

Criteria Conditions that you specify in a logical function.

Data bar A cell format consisting of a shaded bar that provides a visual cue to the reader about the value of a cell relative to other cells; the length of the bar represents the value in the cell—a longer bar represents a higher value and a shorter bar represents s lower value.

Data marker A column, bar, area, dot, pie slice, or other symbol in a chart that represents a single data point; related data points form a data series.

Data point A value that originates in a worksheet cell and that is represented in a chart by a data marker.

Data series Related data points represented by data markers; each data series has a unique color or pattern represented in the chart legend.

Detail sheets The worksheets that contain the details of the information summarized on a summary sheet.

Drag and drop The action of moving a selection by dragging it to a new location.

Enterprise fund A municipal government fund that reports income and expenditures related to municipal services for which a fee is charged in exchange for goods or services.

Excel table A series of rows and columns that contains related data that is managed independently from the data in other rows and columns in the worksheet.

Explode The action of pulling out one or more pie slices from a pie chart for emphasis.

Filter The process of displaying only a portion of the data based on matching a specific value to show only the data that meets the criteria that you specify.

Find and Replace A command that searches the cells in a worksheet—or in a selected range—for matches and then replaces each match with a replacement value of your choice.

Flash Fill Recognizes a pattern in your data, and then automatically fills in values when you enter examples of the output that you want. Use it to split data from two or more cells or to combine data from two cells.

Freeze Panes A command that enables you to select one or more rows or columns and freeze (lock) them into place; the locked rows and columns become separate panes.

Function A predefined formula—a formula that Excel has already built for you—that performs calculations by using specific values in a particular order or structure.

General fund The term used to describe money set aside for the normal operating activities of a government entity such as a city.

Goal Seek A feature that finds the input needed in one cell to arrive at the desired result in another cell.

IF function A function that uses a logical test to check whether a condition is met, and then returns one value if true, and another value if false.

Legend A chart element that identifies the patterns or colors that are assigned to the categories in the chart.

Logical functions A group of functions that test for specific conditions and that typically use conditional tests to determine whether specified conditions are true or false.

Logical test Any value or expression that can be evaluated as being true or false.

MAX function An Excel function that determines the largest value in a selected range of values.

MEDIAN function An Excel function that finds the middle value that has as many values above it in the group as are below it; it differs from AVERAGE in that the result is

not affected as much by a single value that is greatly different from the others.

MIN function An Excel function that determines the smallest value in a selected range of values.

Navigate The process of moving within a worksheet or workbook.

NOW function An Excel function that retrieves the date and time from your computer's calendar and clock and inserts the information into the selected cell.

Pane A portion of a worksheet window bounded by and separated from other portions by vertical and horizontal bars.

Paste The action of placing cell contents that have been copied or moved to the Clipboard into another location.

Paste area The target destination for data that has been cut or copied using the Office Clipboard.

Paste Options gallery A gallery of buttons that provides a Live Preview of all the Paste options available in the current context.

Pie chart A chart that shows the relationship of each part to a whole.

Print Titles An Excel command that enables you to specify rows and columns to repeat on each printed page.

Relative cell reference In a formula, the address of a cell based on the relative position of the cell that contains the formula and the cell referred to.

Scale to Fit Excel commands that enable you to stretch or shrink the width, height, or both, of printed output to fit a maximum number of pages.

Sheet tabs The labels along the lower border of the workbook window that identify each worksheet.

Sort The process of arranging data in a specific order based on the value in each field.

Split Splits the window into multiple resizable panes that contain views of your worksheet. This is useful to view multiple distant parts of your worksheet at one time.

Statistical functions Excel functions, including the AVERAGE, MEDIAN, MIN, and MAX functions, which are useful to analyze a group of measurements.

SUM function A predefined formula that adds all the numbers in a selected range of cells.

Summary sheet A worksheet where totals from other worksheets are displayed and summarized.

Volatile A term used to describe an Excel function that is subject to change each time the workbook is reopened; for example, the NOW function updates itself to the current date and time each time the workbook is opened.

What-if analysis The process of changing the values in cells to see how those changes affect the outcome of formulas in a worksheet.

Mastering Excel Project 16G Plants

Apply 16A skills from these Objectives:

1 Use Flash Fill and the SUM, AVERAGE, MEDIAN, MIN, and MAX Functions

2 Move Data, Resolve Error Messages, and Rotate Text

3 Use COUNTIF and IF Functions and Apply Conditional Formatting

4 Use Date & Time Functions and Freeze Panes

5 Create, Sort, and Filter an Excel Table

6 View, Format, and Print a Large Worksheet

In the following project, you will edit a worksheet detailing the current inventory of plants at the Pasadena facility. Your completed worksheet will look similar to Figure 16.75.

PROJECT FILES

For Project 16G, you will need the following file:

e16G_Plants

You will save your workbook as:

Lastname_Firstname_16G_Plants

PROJECT RESULTS

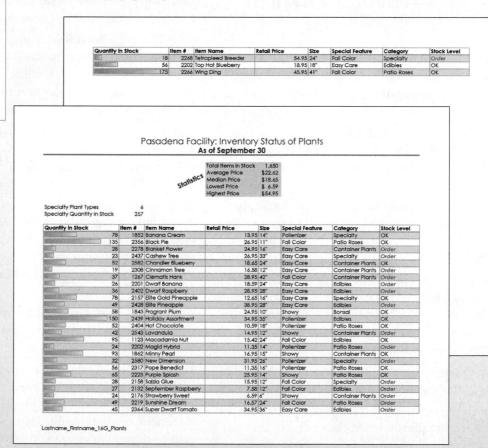

Excel 2016, Windows 10, Microsoft Corporation

FIGURE 16.75

(Project 16G Plants continues on the next page)

1 Start Excel. From your student files, locate and open **e16G_Plants**, and then **Save** the file in your **AIO Chapter 16** folder as **Lastname_Firstname_16G_Plants**

2 To the right of **column B**, insert two new columns to create **new blank columns C and D**. By using **Flash Fill** in the two new columns, split the data in **column B** into a column for *Item #* in **column C** and *Category* in **column D**. As necessary, type **Item #** as the column title in **column C** and **Category** as the column title in **column D**. Delete **column B**.

3 By using the **Cut** and **Paste** commands, cut **column C**—*Category*—and paste it to **column H**, and then delete the empty **column C**. Apply **AutoFit** to **columns A:G**.

4 In cell **B4**, insert a function to calculate the **Total Items in Stock** by summing the **Quantity in Stock** data, and then apply **Comma Style** with zero decimal places to the result.

5 In each cell in the range **B5:B8**, insert functions to calculate the Average, Median, Lowest, and Highest retail prices, and then apply the **Accounting Number Format** to each result.

6 Move the range **A4:B8** to the range **D4:E8**, apply the **40% - Accent4** cell style to the range, and then select **columns D:E** and **AutoFit**.

7 In cell **C6**, type **Statistics** and then select the range **C4:C8**. In the **Format Cells** dialog box, merge the selected cells, and change the text **Orientation** to **25 Degrees**. Format the cell with **Bold**, a **Font Size** of **14 pt**, and then change the **Font Color** to **Blue-Gray, Text 2**. Apply **Middle Align** and **Align Right**.

8 In the **Category** column, **Replace All** occurrences of **Vine Roses** with **Patio Roses**

9 In cell **B10**, use the **COUNTIF** function to count the number of **Specialty** plant types in the **Category** column.

10 In cell **H13**, type **Stock Level** In cell **H14**, enter an **IF** function to determine the items that must be ordered.

If the **Quantity in Stock** is less than **50** the **Value_if_true** is **Order** Otherwise the **Value_if_false** is **OK** Fill the formula down through cell **H42**.

11 Apply **Conditional Formatting** to the **Stock Level** column so that cells that contain the text *Order* are formatted with **Bold Italic** and with a **Color of Green, Accent 6**. Apply conditional formatting to the **Quantity in Stock** column by applying a **Gradient Fill Green Data Bar**.

12 Format the range **A13:H42** as a **Table** with headers, and apply the style **Table Style Light 20**. Sort the table from **A to Z** by **Item Name**, and then filter on the **Category** column to display the **Specialty** types.

13 Display a **Total Row** in the table, and then in cell **A43**, **Sum** the **Quantity in Stock** for the **Specialty** items. Type the result in cell **B11**. Click in the table, and then on the **Design tab**, remove the total row from the table. Clear the **Category** filter.

14 **Merge & Center** the title and subtitle across **columns A:H**, and apply **Title** and **Heading 1** styles, respectively. Change the theme to **Mesh**, and then select and **AutoFit** all the columns.

15 Set the orientation to **Landscape**. In the **Page Setup** dialog box, center the worksheet **Horizontally**, insert a custom footer in the **left section** with the file name, and set **row 13** to repeat at the top of each page. Display the **Print Preview**. Apply the **Fit All Columns on One Page** setting.

16 As the **Tags**, type **plants inventory, Pasadena** As the **Subject**, type your course name and section number. Be sure your name displays as the **Author**.

17 **Save** your workbook. If directed by your instructor to do so, submit your paper printout, your electronic image of your document that looks like a printed document, or your original Excel file. If required by your instructor, print or create an electronic version of your worksheet with formulas displayed. In the upper right corner of the Excel window, click **Close**.

END | You have completed Project 16G

Mastering Excel **Project 16H Bonus**

Apply 16B skills from these Objectives:

7 Navigate a Workbook and Rename Worksheets

8 Enter Dates, Clear Contents, and Clear Formats

9 Copy and Paste by Using the Paste Options Gallery

10 Edit and Format Multiple Worksheets at the Same Time

11 Create a Summary Sheet with Column Sparklines

12 Format and Print Multiple Worksheets in a Workbook

In the following project, you will edit a workbook that summarizes the compensation for the commercial salespersons who qualified for bonuses in the Western and Eastern Canadian regions. Your completed worksheets will look similar to Figure 16.76.

PROJECT FILES

For Project 16H, you will need the following file:

e16H_Bonus

You will save your workbook as:

Lastname_Firstname_16H_Bonus

PROJECT RESULTS

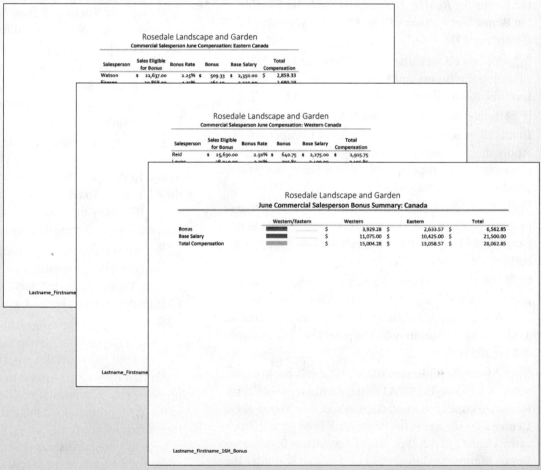

Excel 2016, Windows 10, Microsoft Corporation

FIGURE 16.76

(Project 16H Bonus continues on the next page)

Mastering Excel   Project 16H Bonus (continued)

1 Start Excel. From your student files, open **e16H_Bonus**, and then save the file in your **AIO Chapter 16** folder as **Lastname_Firstname_16H Bonus**

2 Rename **Sheet1** as **Western** and change the **Tab Color** to **Brown, Accent 2**. Rename **Sheet2** as **Eastern** and change the **Tab Color** to **Orange, Accent 1**.

3 Click the **Western sheet tab** to make it the active sheet, and then group the worksheets. In cell **A1**, type **Rosedale Landscape and Garden** and then **Merge & Center** the text across the range **A1:F1**. Apply the **Title** cell style. **Merge & Center** the text in cell **A2** across the range **A2:F2**, and then apply the **Heading 3** cell style.

4 With the sheets still grouped, in cell **D5** calculate the **Bonus** for *Reid* by multiplying the **Sales Eligible for Bonus** by the **Bonus Rate**. **Copy** the formula down through cell **D8**.

5 In cell **F5**, calculate **Total Compensation** by summing the **Bonus** and **Base Salary** for *Reid*. Copy the formula down through the cell **F8**.

6 In **row 9**, sum the columns for **Sales Eligible for Bonus**, **Bonus**, **Base Salary**, and **Total Compensation**. Apply the **Accounting Number Format** with two decimal places to the appropriate cells in **row 5** and **row 9** (do not include the percentages).

7 Apply the **Comma Style** with two decimal places to the appropriate cells in **rows 6:8** (do not include the percentages). Apply the **Total** cell style to the appropriate cells in the Total row.

8 Click the Eastern sheet tab to ungroup the sheets, and then insert a new worksheet. Change the sheet name to **Summary** and then change the **Tab Color** to **Brown, Text 2**. Widen **column A** to **210** pixels, widen **columns B:E** to **155** pixels.

9 Move the **Summary** sheet so that it is the first sheet in the workbook. In cell **A1** of the **Summary** sheet, type **Rosedale Landscape and Garden** and then **Merge & Center** the title across the range **A1:E1**. Apply the **Title** cell style. In cell **A2**, type **June Commercial Salesperson Bonus Summary: Canada** and then **Merge & Center** the text across the range **A2:E2**. Apply the **Heading 1** cell style.

10 In the range **A5:A7**, type the following row titles and then apply the **Heading 4** cell style:

> **Bonus**
>
> **Base Salary**
>
> **Total Compensation**

11 In the range **B4:E4**, type the following column titles, and then **Center** and apply the **Heading 3** cell style.

> **Western/Eastern**
>
> **Western**
>
> **Eastern**
>
> **Total**

12 In cell **C5**, enter a formula that references cell **D9** in the **Western** worksheet so that the total bonus amount for the Western region displays in cell **C5**. Create similar formulas to enter the total **Base Salary** for the Western region in cell **C6**. Using the same technique, enter formulas in the range **D5:D6** so that the **Eastern** totals display.

13 Sum the **Bonus** and **Base Salary** rows, and then calculate **Total Compensation** for the **Western**, **Eastern**, and **Total** columns.

14 In cell **B5**, insert a **Column Sparkline** for the range **C5:D5**. In cells **B6** and **B7**, insert **Column** sparklines for the appropriate ranges to compare Western totals with Eastern totals.

15 To the sparkline in cell **B5**, apply the second style in the third row—**Sparkline Style Accent 2, (no dark or light)**. To the sparkline in cell **B6**, apply the first style in the fifth row—**Sparkline Style Dark #1**. To the sparkline in cell **B7**, apply the first style in the fourth row— **Sparkline Style Accent 1, Lighter 40%**.

16 **Group** the three worksheets, and then center the worksheets **Horizontally** on the page, and insert a **Custom Footer** in the **left section** with the file name. Change the **Orientation** to **Landscape**.

17 As the **Tags**, type **June, bonus, compensation** As the **Subject**, type your course name and section number. Be sure your name displays as the **Author** and then **Save**. If directed by your instructor to do so, submit your paper printout, your electronic image of your document that looks like a printed document, or your original Excel file. If required by your instructor, print or create an electronic version of your worksheet with formulas displayed. In the upper right corner of the Excel window, click **Close**.

END | You have completed Project 16H

Mastering Excel | Project 16I Revenue

In the following project, you will edit a worksheet that summarizes the revenue budget for the City of Pacifica Bay. Your completed worksheets will look similar to Figure 16.77.

Apply 16C skills from these Objectives:

13 Chart Data with a Pie Chart

14 Format a Pie Chart

15 Edit a Workbook and Update a Chart

16 Use Goal Seek to Perform What-If Analysis

PROJECT FILES

For Project 16I, you will need the following file:

e16I_Revenue

You will save your workbook as:

Lastname_Firstname_16I_Revenue

PROJECT RESULTS

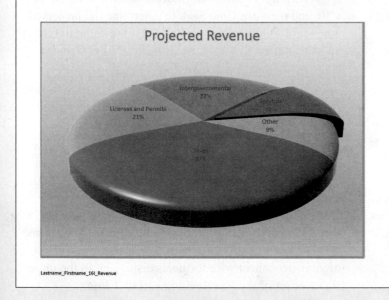

FIGURE 16.77

Excel 2016, Windows 10, Microsoft Corporation

(Project 16I Revenue continues on the next page)

1 Start Excel. From your student data files, locate and open **e16I_Revenue**. **Save** the file in your **AIO Chapter 16** folder as **Lastname_Firstname_16I_Revenue**

2 In cell **D5**, construct a formula to calculate the **% of Total Projected Revenue** from **Taxes** by dividing the **Projected Revenue for Next Fiscal Year** for **Taxes** by the **Total Projected Revenue for Next Fiscal Year**. Use absolute cell references as necessary, format the result in **Percent Style**, and **Center** the percentage. Fill the formula down through cell **D9**.

3 Select the nonadjacent ranges **A5:A9** and **C5:C9** as the data for a pie chart, and then insert a **3-D Pie** chart. Move the chart to a **New sheet** named **Projected Revenue Chart**

4 As the text for the **Chart Title** element, type **Projected Revenue** Format the **Chart Title** using the **WordArt Style Fill – Aqua, Accent 1, Shadow**—in the first row, the second style and a **Font Size** of **32**.

5 Remove the **Legend** chart element, and then add the **Data Labels** chart element formatted so that only the **Category Name** and **Percentage** display positioned in the **Center**. Format the data labels with a **Font style** of **Bold** and a **Font Size** of **14**.

6 Format the **Data Series** using a **3-D Format** effect. Change the **Top bevel** and **Bottom bevel** to **Art Deco**. Set the **Top bevel Width** and **Height** to **350 pt** and then set the **Bottom bevel Width** and **Height** to **0 pt** Change the **Material** to the second **Special Effect—Soft Edge**.

7 Display the **Series Options**, and then set the **Angle of first slice** to **115** so that the **Taxes** slice is in the front of the pie.

8 Select the **Services** slice, and then explode the slice **10%**. Change the **Fill Color** of the **Services** slice to a **Solid fill** using **Gray-50%, Accent 4**—in the eighth column, the first color.

9 Format the **Chart Area** by applying a **Gradient fill** using the **Preset gradients Light Gradient – Accent 4**. Format the **Border** of the **Chart Area** by applying a **Solid line** border using **Gray-50%, Accent 4** and a **5 pt Width**. Close any panes that are open on the right.

10 Display the **Page Setup** dialog box, and then for this chart sheet, insert a **Custom Footer** in the **left section** with the file name.

11 Display the **Revenue Sources sheet**. Click cell **C10**, and then use **Goal Seek** to determine the projected amount of Other revenue in cell **C9** if the value in **C10** is **150,125,000**

12 Display the **Page Setup** dialog box, center the worksheet **Horizontally**, and then insert a custom footer in the **left section** with the file name.

13 Show all the properties, and then as the **Tags**, type **revenue sources** As the **Subject**, type your course name and section number. Be sure your name displays as the **Author**. **Save** your workbook. If directed by your instructor to do so, submit your paper printout, your electronic image of your document that looks like a printed document, or your original Excel file. If required by your instructor, print or create an electronic version of your worksheet with formulas displayed. In the upper right corner of the Excel window, click **Close**.

END | You have completed Project 16I

Mastering Excel | Project 16J Inventory

In the following project, you will edit a worksheet that summarizes the inventory of bulbs and trees at the Pasadena facility. Your completed workbook will look similar to Figure 16.78.

Apply a combination of 16A, 16B, and 16C skills:

1 Use Flash Fill and the SUM, AVERAGE, MEDIAN, MIN, and MAX Functions

2 Move Data, Resolve Error Messages, and Rotate Text

3 Use COUNTIF and IF Functions and Apply Conditional Formatting

4 Use Date & Time Functions and Freeze Panes

5 Create, Sort, and Filter an Excel Table

6 View, Format and Print a Large Worksheet

7 Navigate a Workbook and Rename Worksheets

8 Enter Dates, Clear Contents, and Clear Formats

9 Copy and Paste by Using the Paste Options Gallery

10 Edit and Format Multiple Worksheets at the Same Time

11 Create a Summary Sheet with Column Sparklines

12 Format and Print Multiple Worksheets in a Workbook

13 Chart Data with a Pie Chart

14 Format a Pie Chart

15 Edit a Workbook and Update a Chart

16 Use Goal Seek to Perform What-If Analysis

PROJECT FILES

For Project 16J, you will need the following file:

e16J_Inventory

You will save your workbook as:

Lastname_Firstname_16J_Inventory

PROJECT RESULTS

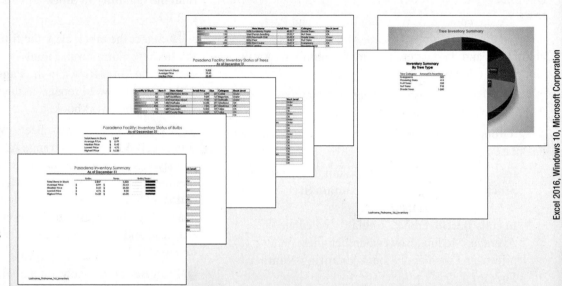

FIGURE 16.78

(Project 16J Inventory continues on the next page)

1 Start Excel. From your student files, open **e16J_Inventory**. Save the file in your **AIO Chapter 16** folder as **Lastname_Firstname_16J_Inventory**

2 Change the **Theme** to **Slice**. Rename **Sheet1** as **Bulbs** and **Sheet2** as **Trees** and then make the **Bulbs sheet** the active sheet.

3 To the right of **column B**, insert two new columns to create **new blank columns C and D**. By using **Flash Fill** in the two new columns, split the data in **column B** into a column for *Item #* in **column C** and *Category* in **column D**. Type **Item #** as the column title in **column C** and **Category** as the column title in **column D**.

4 Delete **column B**. By using the **Cut** and **Paste** commands, cut **column C**—*Category*—and paste it to **column G**, and then delete the empty **column C**. Apply **AutoFit** to **columns A:F**.

5 Display the **Trees** worksheet, and then repeat Steps 3 and 4 on this worksheet.

6 Group the worksheets and then make the following calculations:

- In cell **B4**, enter a function to sum the **Quantity in Stock** data, and then apply **Comma Style** with zero decimal places to the result.
- In cells **B5:B8**, enter formulas to calculate the Average, Median, Lowest, and Highest retail prices, and then apply the **Accounting Number Format**.

7 Ungroup the worksheets. In each of the two worksheets, make the following calculations *without* grouping the sheets:

- In cell **B10**, enter a COUNTIF function to determine how many different types of **Tulips** are in stock on the **Bulbs** sheet and how many different types of **Evergreens** are in stock on the **Trees** worksheet.
- In cell **G14**, type **Stock Level** In cell **G15**, enter an **IF** function to determine the items that must be ordered. If the **Quantity in Stock** is less than **75** the **Value_if_true** is **Order** Otherwise the **Value_if_false** is **OK** Fill the formula down through all the rows.
- Apply **Conditional Formatting** to the **Stock Level** column so that cells that contain the text *Order* are formatted with **Bold Italic** with a **Font Color** of **Dark Blue, Text 2**. Apply **Gradient Fill Blue Data Bars** to the **Quantity in Stock** column.

8 In the **Bulbs** sheet, format the range **A14:G42** as a table with headers and apply **Table Style Light 20**. Insert a **Total Row**, filter by **Category** for **Tulips**, and then **Sum** the **Quantity in Stock** column. Record the result in cell **B11**.

9 Select the table, clear the filter, **Sort** the table on the **Item #** column from **Smallest to Largest**, and then remove the **Total Row**. On the **Page Layout tab**, set **Print Titles** so that **row 14** repeats at the top of each page.

10 In the **Trees** sheet, format the range **A14:G42** as a table with headers and apply **Table Style Light 19**. Insert a **Total Row**, filter by **Category** for **Evergreens**, and then **Sum** the **Quantity in Stock** column. Record the result in cell **B11**.

11 Select the table, clear the filter, **Sort** the table on the **Item #** column from **Smallest to Largest**, and then remove the **Total Row**. On the **Page Layout tab**, set **Print Titles** so that **row 14** repeats at the top of each page, and then **Save** your workbook.

12 **Group** the two worksheets. **Merge & Center** the title in cell **A1** across the range **A1:G1** and apply the **Title** cell style. **Merge & Center** the subtitle in cell **A2** across the range **A2:G2** and apply the **Heading 1** cell style. **AutoFit** Column A. **Center** the worksheets **Horizontally**, change the **Orientation** to **Landscape**, display the **Print Preview**, and then change the **Settings** to **Fit All Columns on One Page**.

13 In **Backstage** view, on the left click **Save**, and then ungroup the sheets. Make the **Trees** sheet the active sheet, and then insert a new worksheet. Change the sheet name to **Summary** and then widen **columns A:D** to **170** pixels. Move the **Summary** sheet so that it is the first sheet in the workbook.

14 In cell **A1**, type **Pasadena Inventory Summary** and then **Merge & Center** the title across the range **A1:D1**. Apply the **Title** cell style. In cell **A2**, type **As of December 31** and then **Merge & Center** the text across the range **A2:D2**. Apply the **Heading 1** cell style.

15 On the **Bulbs** sheet, **Copy** the range **A4:A8**. Display the **Summary** sheet and **Paste** the selection to cell **A5**. Apply the **Heading 4** cell style to the selection.

16 In the **Summary** sheet, in cell **B4**, type **Bulbs** In cell **C4** type **Trees** In cell **D4** type **Bulbs/Trees** and then **Center** the column titles. Apply the **Heading 3** cell style.

(Project 16J Inventory continues on the next page)

Mastering Excel Project 16J Inventory (continued)

17 In cell **B5**, enter a formula that references cell **B4** in the **Bulbs sheet** so that the **Bulbs Total Items in Stock** displays in **B5**. Create similar formulas to enter the **Average Price**, **Median Price**, **Lowest Price**, and **Highest Price** from the **Bulbs sheet** into the **Summary** sheet in the range **B6:B9**.

18 Enter formulas in the range **C5:C9** that reference the appropriate cells in the **Trees** worksheet.

19 In cells **D5**, **D6**, **D7**, **D8**, and **D9**, insert **Column** sparklines using the values in the *Bulbs* and *Trees* columns. Format each sparkline using the first five Sparkline styles in the first row.

20 To the range **B5:C5**, apply **Comma Style** with zero decimal places, and to the range **B6:C9**, apply **Accounting Number Format**. Center the **Summary** worksheet **Horizontally** and change the **Orientation** to **Landscape**. **Group** the worksheets and insert a footer in the left section with the **File Name**.

21 Add a new worksheet after the Trees sheet and **Rename** the sheet **Tree Summary**

22 In **A1** type **Inventory Summary** and then **Merge & Center** across **A1:B1**. In **A2** type **By Tree Type** and then **Merge & Center** across **A2:B2**. Change the **Font Size** for **A1:A2** to 16 and apply **Bold**. In the range **A4:B9**, type the following data:

Tree Category	Amount in Inventory
Evergreens	583
Flowering Trees	414
Fruit Trees	328
Nut Trees	918
Shade Trees	1260

23 **AutoFit** columns **A:B** and apply **Comma Style** with zero decimal places to the numbers in **Column B**. Apply the Heading 3 style to A4:B4.

24 Create a **3-D Pie** chart from the data in the range **A5:B9** and move the chart to a **New Sheet** named **Tree Summary Chart**

25 Apply **Chart Style 3**. Remove the **Legend**, and display the **Data Labels** with the **Category Name** and **Percentage** displayed in the **Center**. Change the font size of the data labels to **12**. Change the **Chart Title** to **Tree Inventory Summary** and then insert the **File Name** in the left section of the footer. If necessary, move the **Tree Summary Chart** sheet so that it is the last sheet in the workbook.

26 Select the **Tree Summary** sheet and then center the worksheet **Horizontally** on the page. **Group** the worksheets and insert a footer in the left section with the **File Name**.

27 As the **Tags**, type **Pasadena inventory** As the **Subject**, type your course name and section number. Be sure your name displays as the **Author**.

28 In **Backstage** view, on the left click **Save**. If directed by your instructor to do so, submit your paper printout, your electronic image of your document that looks like a printed document, or your original Excel file. If required by your instructor, print or create an electronic version of your worksheet with formulas displayed. In the upper right corner of the Excel window, click **Close**.

END | You have completed Project 16J

Apply a combination of the 16A and 16B skills.

GO! Fix It	**Project 16K Planters**	**MyITLab**
GO! Make It	**Project 16L Salary**	**MyITLab**
GO! Solve It	**Project 16M Sod**	**MyITLab**
GO! Solve It	**Project 16N Products**	

PROJECT FILES

For Project 16N, you will need the following file:

e16N_Products

You will save your workbook as:

Lastname_Firstname_16N_Products

From your student data files, open the file e16N_Products and save it as **Lastname_Firstname_16N_Products** This workbook contains two worksheets: one for U.S. sales data by product and one for Canadian sales data by product. Complete the two worksheets by calculating totals by product and by month. Then calculate the Percent of Total for each product, using absolute cell references as necessary. Format the worksheet, percentages, and values appropriately. Insert a new worksheet that summarizes the monthly totals for the United States and Canada. Enter the months as the column titles and the countries as the row titles. Include a Product Total column and a column for sparklines comparing the months. Format the Summary worksheet appropriately, including a title and subtitle. Include the file name in the footer, add appropriate document properties, and submit as directed.

Performance Level

Performance Criteria		Exemplary: You consistently applied the relevant skills	Proficient: You sometimes, but not always, applied the relevant skills	Developing: You rarely or never applied the relevant skills
	Create formulas	All formulas are correct and are efficiently constructed.	Formulas are correct but not always constructed in the most efficient manner.	One or more formulas are missing or incorrect; or only numbers were entered.
	Create Summary worksheet	Summary worksheet created properly.	Summary worksheet was created but some elements were incorrect.	No Summary worksheet was created.
	Format appropriately	Formatting is appropriate.	Not all worksheets were appropriately formatted.	No formatting was applied.

END | You have completed Project 16N

OUTCOMES-BASED ASSESSMENTS

RUBRIC

The following outcomes-based assessments are open-ended assessments. That is, there is no specific correct result; your result will depend on your approach to the information provided. Make Professional Quality your goal. Use the following scoring rubric to guide you in how to approach the problem and then to evaluate how well your approach solves the problem.

The *criteria*—Software Mastery, Content, Format and Layout, and Process—represent the knowledge and skills you have gained that you can apply to solving the problem. The *levels of performance*—Professional Quality, Approaching Professional Quality, or Needs Quality Improvements—help you and your instructor evaluate your result.

	Your completed project is of Professional Quality if you:	Your completed project is Approaching Professional Quality if you:	Your completed project Needs Quality Improvements if you:
1-Software Mastery	Choose and apply the most appropriate skills, tools, and features and identify efficient methods to solve the problem.	Choose and apply some appropriate skills, tools, and features, but not in the most efficient manner.	Choose inappropriate skills, tools, or features, or are inefficient in solving the problem.
2-Content	Construct a solution that is clear and well organized, contains content that is accurate, appropriate to the audience and purpose, and is complete. Provide a solution that contains no errors in spelling, grammar, or style.	Construct a solution in which some components are unclear, poorly organized, inconsistent, or incomplete. Misjudge the needs of the audience. Have some errors in spelling, grammar, or style, but the errors do not detract from comprehension.	Construct a solution that is unclear, incomplete, or poorly organized; contains some inaccurate or inappropriate content; and contains many errors in spelling, grammar, or style. Do not solve the problem.
3-Format & Layout	Format and arrange all elements to communicate information and ideas, clarify function, illustrate relationships, and indicate relative importance.	Apply appropriate format and layout features to some elements, but not others. Overuse features, causing minor distraction.	Apply format and layout that does not communicate information or ideas clearly. Do not use format and layout features to clarify function, illustrate relationships, or indicate relative importance. Use available features excessively, causing distraction.
4-Process	Use an organized approach that integrates planning, development, self-assessment, revision, and reflection.	Demonstrate an organized approach in some areas, but not others; or, use an insufficient process of organization throughout.	Do not use an organized approach to solve the problem.

Apply a combination of the 16A and 16B skills.	**GO! Think** Project 16O Palms

PROJECT FILES

For Project 16O, you will need the following file:

e16O_Palms

You will save your workbook as:

Lastname_Firstname_16O_Palms

Melanie Castillo, Product Manager for Rosedale Landscape and Garden, has requested a worksheet that summarizes the current palm tree inventory data. Melanie would like the worksheet to include the total Quantity in Stock and Number of Items for each of the four categories of palm trees, and she would like the items to be sorted from lowest to highest retail price. She would also like a separate column for Item # and for Category.

Edit the file e16O_Palms to provide Melanie with the information requested, and use the Table feature to find the data requested. Format the worksheet titles and data and include an appropriately formatted table so that the worksheet is professional and easy to read and understand. Insert a footer with the file name and add appropriate document properties. Save the file as **Lastname_Firstname_16O_Palms** and print or submit as directed by your instructor.

END | You have completed Project 16O

GO! Think Project 16P Contracts	**MyITLab**

You and GO! Project 16Q Annual Expenses	**MyITLab**

Build from Scratch

GO! Collaborative Team Project	Project 16R Bell Orchid Hotels **MyITLab**

Build from Scratch

Introduction to Microsoft Access 2016

Christy Thompson/Shutterstock

Introduction to Access 2016

Microsoft Access 2016 provides a convenient way to organize data that makes it easy for you to utilize and present information. Access uses tables to store the data; like Excel spreadsheets, data is stored in rows and columns in a table. So why use a database rather than an Excel spreadsheet? By using a database, you can manipulate and work with data in a more robust manner. For example, if you have thousands of records about patients in a hospital, you can easily find all of the records that pertain to the patients who received a specific type of medicine on a particular day. Information from one table can be used to retrieve information from another

table. For example, by knowing a patient's ID number, you can view immunization records, insurance information, or hospitalization records. Having information stored in an Access database enables you to make bulk changes to data at one time even when it is stored in different tables.

It's easy to get started with Access by using one of the many prebuilt database templates. For example, a nonprofit organization can track events, donors, members, and donations. A small business can use a prebuilt database to track inventory, create invoices, monitor projects, manage pricing, track competitors, and manage quotes.

Using Microsoft Access 2016

17

PROJECT 17A

OUTCOMES
Create a new database.

OBJECTIVES

1. Identify Good Database Design
2. Create a Table and Define Fields in a Blank Desktop Database
3. Change the Structure of Tables and Add a Second Table
4. Create a Query, Form, and Report
5. Close a Database and Close Access

PROJECT 17B

OUTCOMES
Sort and query a database.

OBJECTIVES

6. Open and Save an Existing Database
7. Create Table Relationships
8. Sort Records in a Table
9. Create a Query in Design View
10. Create a New Query From an Existing Query
11. Sort Query Results
12. Specify Criteria in a Query

PROJECT 17C

OUTCOMES
Create complex queries.

OBJECTIVES

13. Specify Numeric Criteria in a Query
14. Use Compound Criteria in a Query
15. Create a Query Based on More Than One Table
16. Use Wildcards in a Query
17. Create Calculated Fields in a Query
18. Calculate Statistics and Group Data in a Query
19. Create a Crosstab Query
20. Create a Parameter Query

Rawpixel.com/Shutterstock

In This Chapter
GO! to Work with Access

In this chapter, you will use Microsoft Access 2016 to organize related information. You will learn to apply good database design principles to your Access database and to define the structure of a database. You will create new databases, create tables, enter data into the tables, sort data, define relationships, and create queries.

The projects in this chapter relate to **Texas Lakes Community College**. Its four campuses serve over 30,000 students and offer more than 140 certificate programs and degrees. Popular fields of study include nursing and health care, solar technology, computer technology, and graphic design.

Student Advising Database with Two Tables

PROJECT ACTIVITIES

In Activities 17.01 through 17.17, you will assist Dr. Daniel Martinez, Vice President of Student Services at Texas Lakes Community College, in creating a new database for tracking students and their faculty advisors. Your completed database objects will look similar to Figure 17.1.

PROJECT FILES

If your instructor wants you to submit Project 17A in the MyITLab Grader system, log in to MyITLab, locate Grader Project 17A, and then download the files for this project.

For Project 17A, you will need the following files:

Blank desktop database
a17A_Students (Excel workbook)
a17A_Faculty_Advisors (Excel workbook)

You will save your database as:

Lastname_Firstname_17A_Advising

PROJECT RESULTS

FIGURE 17.1 Project 17A Advising

N O T E	**If You Are Using a Touchscreen**
	Tap an item to click it.
	Press and hold for a few seconds to right-click; release when the information or commands displays.
	Touch the screen with two or more fingers and then pinch together to zoom out or stretch your fingers apart to zoom in
	Slide your finger on the screen to scroll—slide left to scroll right and slide right to scroll left.
	Slide to rearrange—similar to dragging with a mouse.
	Swipe to select—slide an item a short distance with a quick movement—to select an item and bring up commands, if any.

PROJECT RESULTS

In this project, using your own name, you will create the following database and objects. Your instructor may ask for printouts or PDF electronic images:

Lastname_Firstname_17A_Advising	Database file
Lastname Firstname 17A Students	Table
Lastname Firstname 17A Faculty Advisors	Table
Lastname Firstname 17A All Students Query	Query
Lastname Firstname 17A Student Form	Form
Lastname Firstname 17A Faculty Advisors Report	Report

Objective 1 | Identify Good Database Design

GO! Learn How
video A17-1

IC3
DIGITAL LITERACY
CERTIFICATION
1.04d
2.04a (i)
2.04c (ii)

A **database** is an organized collection of **data**—facts about people, events, things, or ideas—related to a specific topic or purpose. **Information** is data that is accurate, timely, and organized in a useful manner. **Metadata** is data that describes the properties or characteristics of other data; it refers to information like size or formatting of data. Your contact list is a type of database, because it is a collection of data about one topic—the people with whom you communicate. A simple database of this type is called a **flat database** because it is not related or linked to any other collection of data. Another example of a simple database is your music collection. You do not keep information about your music collection in your contact list because the data is not related to the people in your contact list.

A more sophisticated type of database is a **relational database**, because multiple collections of data in the database are related to one another—for example, data about the students, the courses, and the faculty members at a college. Microsoft Access 2016 is a relational **database management system**—also referred to as a **DBMS**—which is software that controls how related collections of data are stored, organized, retrieved, and secured.

IC3
DIGITAL LITERACY
CERTIFICATION
1.04d
2.04c (i)
2.04c (ii)

Activity 17.01 | Using Good Design Techniques to Plan a Database

Before creating a new database, the first step is to determine the information you want to keep track of by asking yourself, *What questions should this database be able to answer?* The purpose of a database is to store the data in a manner that makes it easy to find the information you need by asking questions. For example, in a student database for Texas Lakes Community College, the questions to be answered might include:

- How many students are enrolled at the college?
- How many students have not yet been assigned a faculty advisor?

- Which students live in Austin, Texas?
- Which students owe money for tuition?
- Which students are majoring in Information Systems Technology?

Tables are the foundation of an Access database because all of the data is stored in one or more tables. A table is similar in structure to an Excel worksheet because data is organized into rows and columns. Each table row is a *record*—all of the categories of data pertaining to one person, place, event, thing, or idea. Each table column is a *field*—a single piece of information for every record. For example, in a table storing student contact information, each row forms a record for only one student. Each column forms a field for every record—for example, the student ID number or the student last name.

When organizing the fields of information in your table, break each piece of information into its smallest, most useful part. For example, create three fields for the name of a student—one field for the last name, one field for the first name, and one field for the middle name or initial.

The *first principle of good database design* is to organize data in the tables so that *redundant*—duplicate—data does not occur. For example, record the student contact information in only *one* table, so that if a student's address changes, you can change the information in just one place. This conserves space, reduces the likelihood of errors when inputting new data, and does not require remembering all of the places where a student's address is stored.

The *second principle of good database design* is to use techniques that ensure the accuracy and consistency of data as it is entered into the table. Proofreading data is critical to maintaining accuracy in a database. Typically, many different people enter data into a database—think of all the people who enter data about students at your college. When entering a state in a student contacts table, one person might enter the state as *Texas*, while another might enter the state as *TX*. Use design techniques to help those who enter data into a database to enter the data more accurately and consistently.

Normalization is the process of applying design rules and principles to ensure that your database performs as expected. Taking the time to plan and create a database that is well designed will ensure that you can retrieve meaningful information from the database. A database may be stored for local use or on the web to collect and share data. Some Access features are not accessible in a web database, like relationships and some query types.

The tables of information in a relational database are linked or joined to one another by a *common field*—a field in two or more tables that stores the same data. For example, a Students table includes the Student ID, name, and full address of every student. The Student Activities table includes the club name and the Student ID of members, but not the name or address, of each student in the club. Because the two tables share a common field—Student ID—you can use the data together to create a list of names and addresses of all of the students in a particular club. The names and addresses are stored in the Students table, and the Student IDs of the club members are stored in the Student Activities table.

Objective 2 Create a Table and Define Fields in a Blank Desktop Database

GO! Learn How
video A17-2

Three methods are used to create a new Access database. One method is to create a new database using a *database template*—a preformatted database designed for a specific purpose. A second method is to create a new database from a *blank desktop database*. A blank desktop database is stored on your computer or other storage device. Initially, it has no data and has no database tools; you create the data and the tools as you need them. A third method is to create a *custom web app* database from scratch or by using a template that you can publish and share with others over the Internet.

Regardless of the method you use, you must name and save the database before you can create any *objects* in it. Objects are the basic parts of a database; you create objects to store your data, to work with your data, and to display your data. The most common database objects are tables, queries, forms, and reports. Think of an Access database as a container for the objects that you create.

Activity 17.02 | Starting with a Blank Desktop Database

> **ALERT!**
>
> To submit as an autograded project, log into MyITLab and download the files for this project and begin with those files instead of a new blank database. For Project 17A using Grader, read Activities 17.01 and 17.02 carefully. Begin working with the database in Activity 17.03. For Grader to award points accurately, when saving an object, do not include your Lastname Firstname at the beginning of the object name.

1 Start Microsoft Access 2016. Take a moment to compare your screen with Figure 17.2 and study the parts of the Microsoft Access opening screen described in the table in Figure 17.3.

From this Access opening screen, you can open an existing database, create a custom web app, create a blank desktop database, or create a new database from a template.

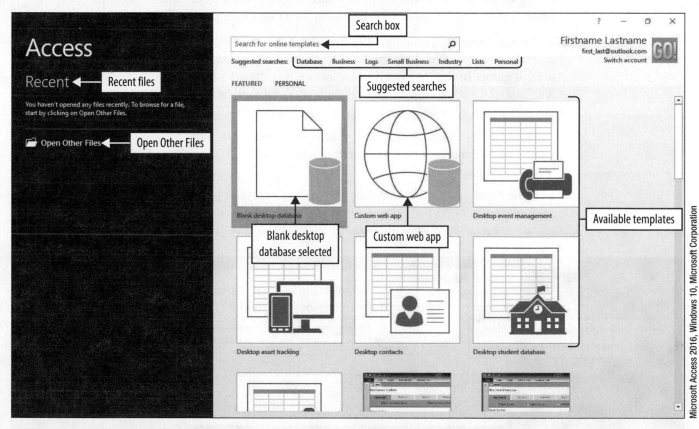

FIGURE 17.2

MICROSOFT ACCESS OPENING SCREEN ELEMENTS	
SCREEN ELEMENT	**DESCRIPTION**
Available templates	Starts a database for a specific purpose that includes built-in objects and tools ready for use.
Blank desktop database	Starts a blank database that is stored on your computer or on a portable storage device.
Custom web app	Starts a web app database that can be published and shared on the Internet.
Open Other Files	Enables you to open a database file from your computer, a shared location, or other location that you have designated.
Recent files	Displays a list of database files that have been recently opened.
Search box	Enables you to search the Microsoft Office website for templates.
Suggested searches	Enables you to click on a category to start an online search for a template.

FIGURE 17.3

2 > In the Access opening screen, click **Blank desktop database**. In the **Blank desktop database** dialog box, to the right of the **File Name** box, click **Browse** . In the **File New Database** dialog box, navigate to the location where you are saving your databases for this chapter, create a **New folder** named **All In One Chapter 17** and then press Enter.

3 > In the **File name** box, notice that *Database1* displays as the default file name—the number at the end of your file name might differ if you have saved a database previously with the default name. In the **Save as type** box, notice that the default database type is *Microsoft Access 2007 – 2016 Databases*, which means that you can open a database created in Access 2016 by using Access 2007, Access 2010, or Access 2013.

4 > Click in the **File name** box. Using your own name, replace the existing text with **Lastname_Firstname_17A_Advising** and then click **OK** or press Enter. Compare your screen with Figure 17.4.

> In the Blank desktop database dialog box, in the File Name box, the name of your database displays. Under the File Name box, the drive and folder where the database will be stored displays. An Access database has a file extension of *.accdb*.

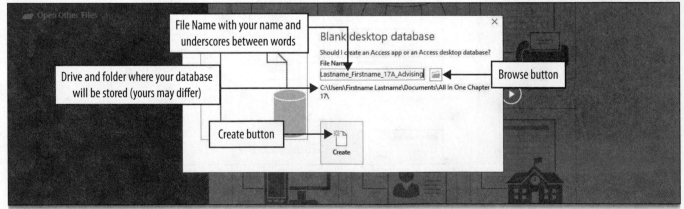

FIGURE 17.4

Microsoft Access 2016, Windows 10, Microsoft Corporation

5 > In the **Blank desktop database** dialog box, click **Create**. Compare your screen with Figure 17.5, and then take a moment to study the screen elements described in the table in Figure 17.6.

> Access creates the new database and opens *Table1*. Recall that a table is an Access object that stores data in columns and rows, similar to the format of an Excel worksheet. Table objects are the foundation of a database because tables store data that is used by other database objects.

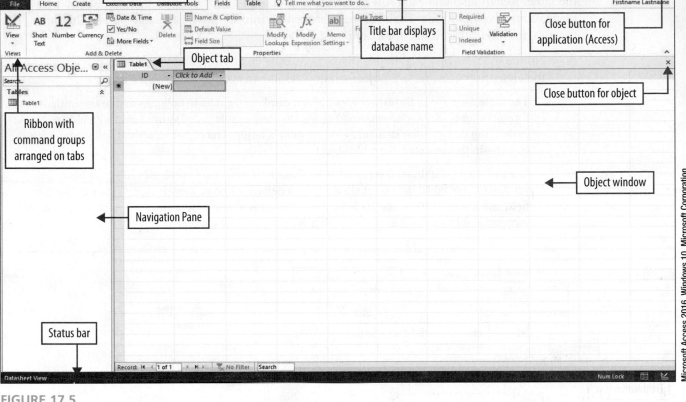

FIGURE 17.5

MICROSOFT ACCESS DATABASE WINDOW ELEMENTS	
ACCESS WINDOW ELEMENT	**DESCRIPTION**
Navigation Pane	Displays the database objects that can be opened in the object window.
Object tab	Identifies the open object.
Object window	Displays the active or open object(s), including tables, queries, or other objects.
Close button for object	Closes the active object.
Ribbon	Displays commands grouped by related tasks and stored on different tabs.
Status bar	Indicates the active view and the status of action occurring within the database on the left; provides buttons on the right to switch between Datasheet view and Design view.
Table Tools	Provides tools on two tabs for working with the active table object, these are contextual tabs—only available when a table object is active.
Close button for application (Access)	Closes the active database and Access.

FIGURE 17.6

Activity 17.03 | Assigning the Data Type and Name to Fields

After you have named and saved your database, the next step is to consult your database design plan and then create the tables for your data. Limit the data in each table to *one* subject. For example, in this project, your database will have two tables—one for student information and one for faculty advisor information.

Recall that each column in a table is a field; field names display at the top of each column of the table. Recall also that each row in a table is a record—all of the data pertains to one person, place, thing, event, or idea. Each record is broken up into its smallest usable parts—the fields. Use meaningful names for fields; for example, *Last Name*.

1 Notice the new blank table that displays in Datasheet view, and then take a moment to study the elements of the table's object window. Compare your screen with Figure 17.7.

The table displays in *Datasheet view*, which displays the data in columns and rows similar to the format of an Excel worksheet. Another way to view a table is in *Design view*, which displays the underlying design—the *structure*—of the table's fields. The *object window* displays the open object—in this instance, the table object.

In a new blank database, there is only one object—a new blank table. Because you have not yet named this table, the object tab displays a default name of *Table1*. Access creates the first field and names it *ID*. In the ID field, Access assigns a unique sequential number—each number incremented by one—to each record as it is entered into the table.

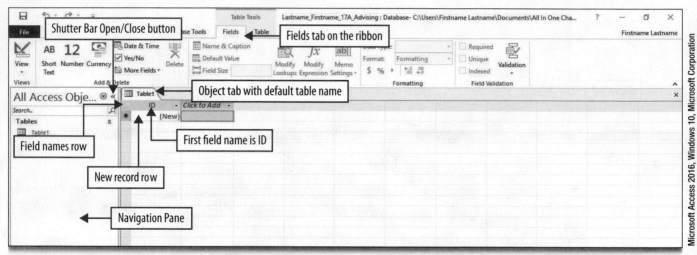

FIGURE 17.7

2 In the **Navigation Pane**, click **Shutter Bar Open/Close** $\boxed{«}$ to collapse the **Navigation Pane** to a narrow bar on the left.

The *Navigation Pane* displays and organizes the names of the objects in a database. From the Navigation Pane, you can open objects. Collapse or close the Navigation Pane to display more of the object—in this case, the table.

ANOTHER WAY Press F11 to close or open the Navigation Pane.

3 In the field names row, click anywhere in the text *Click to Add* to display a list of data types. Compare your screen with Figure 17.8.

A *data type* classifies the kind of data that you can store in a field, such as numbers, text, or dates. A field in a table can have only one data type. The data type of each field should be included in your database design. After selecting the data type, you can name the field.

ANOTHER WAY To the right of *Click to Add*, click the arrow.

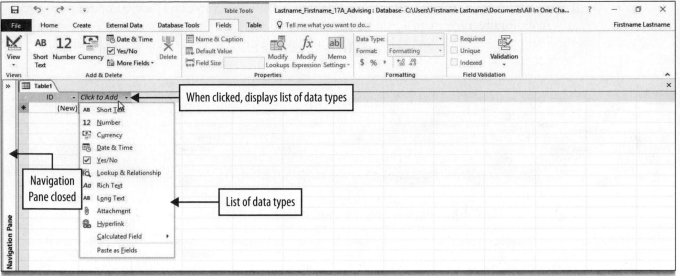

FIGURE 17.8

Microsoft Access 2016, Windows 10, Microsoft Corporation

4 In the list of data types, click **Short Text**, and notice that in the second column, *Click to Add* changes to *Field1*, which is selected. Type **Last Name** and then press Enter.

The second column displays *Last Name* as the field name, and, in the third column, the data types list displays. The **Short Text data type** describes text, a combination of text and numbers, or numbers that do not represent a quantity or are not used in calculations, such as the Postal Code. This data type enables you to enter up to 255 characters in the field. The **Number data type** describes numeric data used in mathematical calculations with varying field sizes.

ANOTHER WAY With the list of data types displayed, type the character that is underscored to select the data type. For example, type *t* to select Short Text or type *u* to select Currency.

5 In the third field name box, type **t** to select *Short Text*, type **First Name** and then press Enter.

6 In the fourth field name box, click **Short Text**, type **Middle Initial** and then press Enter.

7 Create the remaining fields from the table below by first selecting the data type, typing the field name, and then pressing Enter. The field names in the table will display on one line--do not be concerned if the field names do not completely display in the column; you will adjust the column widths later.

Data Type		Short Text	Short Text	Short Text	Short Text	Short Text	Short Text	Short Text	Short Text	Short Text	Short Text	Currency
Field Name	ID	Last Name	First Name	Middle Initial	**Address**	**City**	**State**	**Postal Code**	**Phone**	**Email**	**Faculty Advisor ID**	**Amount Owed**

The Postal Code and Phone fields are assigned a data type of Short Text because the numbers are never used in calculations. The Amount Owed field is assigned the **Currency data type**, which describes monetary values and numeric data that can be used in calculations and that have one to four decimal places. A U.S. dollar sign ($) and two decimal places are automatically included for all of the numbers in a field with the Currency data type.

8 If necessary, scroll to bring the first column—ID—into view, and then compare your screen with Figure 17.9.

Access automatically created the ID field, and you created 11 additional fields in the table.

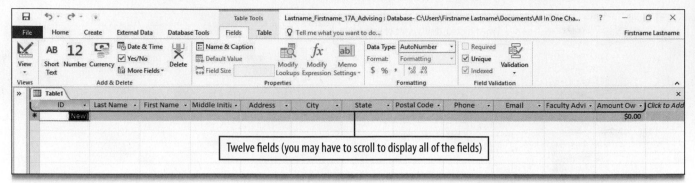

FIGURE 17.9

Microsoft Access 2016, Windows 10, Microsoft Corporation

More Knowledge **Create Fields by Entering Data**

You can create a new field in Datasheet view by typing the data in a new column. Access automatically assigns a data type based on the data you enter. For example, if you enter a date, Access assigns the Date & Time data type. If you enter a monetary amount, Access assigns the Currency data type. If Access cannot determine the data type based on the data entered, the Short Text data type is assigned. You can always change the data type if an incorrect data type is assigned. If you use this method to create fields, you must check the assigned data types to be sure they are correct. You must also rename the fields because Access assigns the names as *Field1*, *Field2*, and so on.

Activity 17.04 | **Renaming Fields and Changing Data Types in a Table**

1 In the first column, click anywhere in the text *ID*. On the ribbon, under **Table Tools**, on the **Fields tab**, in the **Properties group**, click **Name & Caption**. In the **Enter Field Properties** dialog box, in the **Name** box, change *ID* to **Student ID**

The field name *Student ID* is a more precise description of the data contained in this field. In the Enter Field Properties dialog box, you have the option to use the *Caption* property to display a name for a field different from the one that displays in the Name box. Many database designers do not use spaces in field names; instead, they might name a field *LastName* or *LName* and then create a caption for the field so it displays as *Last Name* in tables, forms, or reports. In the Enter Field Properties dialog box, you can also provide a description for the field.

ANOTHER WAY   Right-click the field name to display the shortcut menu, and then click Rename Field; or, double-click the field name to select the existing text, and then type the new field name.

2 Click **OK** to close the **Enter Field Properties** dialog box. On the ribbon, in the **Formatting group**, notice that the **Data Type** for the **Student ID** field is *AutoNumber*. Click the **Data Type arrow**, click **Short Text**, and then compare your screen with Figure 17.10.

In the new record row, the Student ID field is selected. By default, Access creates an ID field for all new tables and sets the data type for the field to AutoNumber. The *AutoNumber data type* describes a unique sequential or random number assigned by Access as each record is entered. Changing the data type of this field to Short Text enables you to enter a custom student ID number.

When records in a database have *no* unique value, such as a book ISBN or a license plate number, the AutoNumber data type is a useful way to automatically create a unique number. In this manner, you are sure that every record is different from the others.

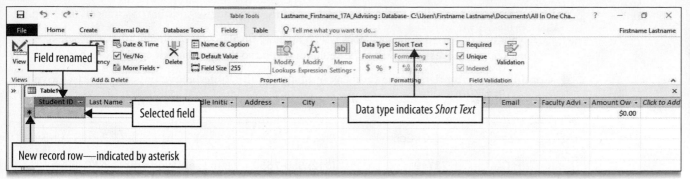

FIGURE 17.10

Activity 17.05 | Adding a Record to a Table

A new contact list is not useful until you fill it with names and phone numbers. Likewise, a new database is not useful until you **populate** it by filling one or more tables with data. You can populate a table with records by typing data directly into the table.

1 In the new record row, click in the **Student ID** field to display the insertion point, type **1023045** and then press Enter. Compare your screen with Figure 17.11.

The pencil icon ✎ in the **record selector box** indicates that a record is being entered or edited. The record selector box is the small box at the left of a record in Datasheet view. When clicked, the entire record is selected.

ANOTHER WAY Press Tab to move the insertion point to the next field.

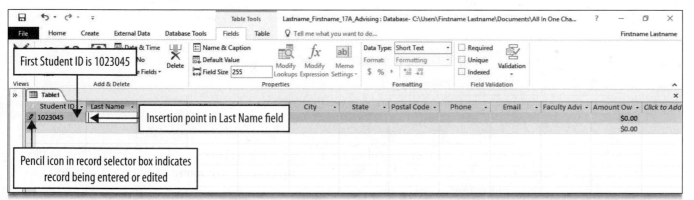

FIGURE 17.11

2 With the insertion point positioned in the **Last Name** field, type **Fresch** and then press Enter.

> **NOTE** **Correcting Typing Errors**
>
> Correct any typing errors you make by using the techniques you have practiced in other Office applications. For example, use Backspace to remove characters to the left of the insertion point. Use Del to remove characters to the right of the insertion point. Or select the text you want to replace and type the correct information. Press Esc to exit out of a record that has not been completely entered.

3 In the **First Name** field, type **Jenna** and then press Enter.

4 In the **Middle Initial** field, type **A** and then press Enter.

5 In the **Address** field, type **7550 Douglas Ln** and then press Enter.

> Do not be concerned if the data does not completely display in the column. As you progress in your study of Access, you will adjust column widths so that you can view all of the data.

6 Continue entering data in the fields as indicated in the table below, pressing Enter to move to the next field.

City	State	Postal Code	Phone	Email	Faculty Advisor ID
Austin	**TX**	**78749**	**(512) 555-7550**	**jfresch@tlcc.edu**	**FAC-2289**

NOTE   Format for Typing Telephone Numbers in Access

Access does not require a specific format for typing telephone numbers in a record. The examples in this textbook use the format of Microsoft Outlook. Using such a format facilitates easy transfer of Outlook information to and from Access.

---

7 In the **Amount Owed** field, type **250** and then press Enter. Compare your screen with Figure 17.12.

> Pressing Enter or Tab in the last field moves the insertion point to the next row to begin a new record. Access automatically saves the record as soon as you move to the next row; you do not have to take any specific action to save a record.

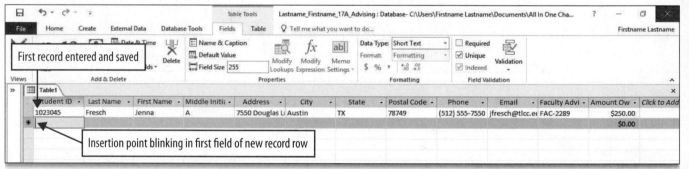

FIGURE 17.12   Microsoft Access 2016, Windows 10, Microsoft Corporation

8 To give your table a meaningful name, on the Quick Access Toolbar, click **Save** 🔲. In the **Save As** dialog box, in the **Table Name** box, using your own name, replace the selected text by typing **Lastname Firstname 17A Students**

> Save each database object with a name that identifies the data that it contains. When you save objects within a database, it is not necessary to use underscores in place of the spaces between words. Your name is included as part of the object name so that you and your instructor can identify your printouts or electronic files easily.

9 In the **Save As** dialog box, click **OK**. Notice that the object tab—located directly above the *Student ID* field name—displays the new table name that you just entered.

More Knowledge   **Renaming or Deleting a Table**

To change the name of a table, close the table, display the Navigation Pane, right-click the table name, and then click Rename. Type the new name or edit as you would any selected text. To delete a table, close the table, display the Navigation Pane, right-click the table name, and then click Delete.

Activity 17.06 | Adding Additional Records to a Table

1 In the new record row, click in the **Student ID** field, and then enter the data for two additional students as shown in the table below. Press Enter or Tab to move from field to field. The data in each field will display on one line in the table.

Student ID	Last Name	First Name	Middle Initial	Address	City	State	Postal Code	Phone	Email	Faculty Advisor ID	Amount Owed
2345677	Ingram	Joseph	S	621 Hill-top Dr	Leander	TX	78646	(512) 555-0717	jingram@tlcc.edu	FAC-2377	378.5
3456889	Snyder	Amanda	J	4786 Bluff St	Buda	TX	78610	(512) 555-9120	asnyder@tlcc.edu	FAC-9005	0

2 Press Enter, and compare your screen with Figure 17.13

FIGURE 17.13

Microsoft Access 2016, Windows 10, Microsoft Corporation

Activity 17.07 | Importing Data from an Excel Workbook into an Existing Access Table

You can type records directly into a table. You can also *import* data from a variety of sources. Importing is the process of copying data from one source or application to another application. For example, you can import data from a Word table or an Excel spreadsheet into an Access database because the data is arranged in columns and rows, similar to a table in Datasheet view.

In this Activity, you will *append*—add on—data from an Excel spreadsheet to your *17A Students* table. To append data, the table must already be created, and it must be closed.

1 In the upper right corner of the table, below the ribbon, click **Object Close** ✕ to close your **17A Students** table. Notice that no objects are open.

2 On the ribbon, click the **External Data tab**. In the **Import & Link group**, click **Excel**. In the **Get External Data – Excel Spreadsheet** dialog box, click **Browse**.

3 In the **File Open** dialog box, navigate to your student files, double-click the Excel file **a17A_ Students**, and then compare your screen with Figure 17.14.

The path to the *source file*—the file being imported—displays in the File name box. There are three options for importing data from an Excel spreadsheet: import the data into a *new* table in the current database, append a copy of the records to an existing table, or link the data from the spreadsheet to a linked table in the database. A *link* is a connection to data in another file. When linking, Access creates a table that maintains a link to the source data, so that changes to the data in one file are automatically made in the other—linked—file.

 **ANOTHER WAY** Click the file name, and then in the File Open dialog box, click Open.

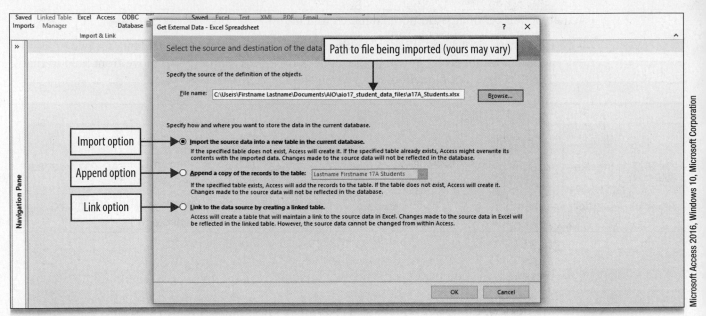

FIGURE 17.14

4 ▶ Click the **Append a copy of the records to the table** option button, and then, in the box to the right, click the **arrow**.

Currently, your database has only one table, so no other tables display on the list. However, when a database has multiple tables, click the arrow to select the table to which you want to append records. The table into which you import or append data is referred to as the *destination table*.

5 ▶ Press Esc to cancel the list, and in the dialog box, click **OK**. Compare your screen with Figure 17.15.

The first screen of the Import Spreadsheet Wizard displays. A *wizard* is a feature in a Microsoft Office program that walks you step by step through a process. The presence of scroll bars in the window indicates that records and fields are out of view. To append records from an Excel workbook to an existing database table, the column headings in the Excel worksheet or spreadsheet must be identical to the field names in the table. The wizard identified the first row of the spreadsheet as column headings, which are equivalent to field names.

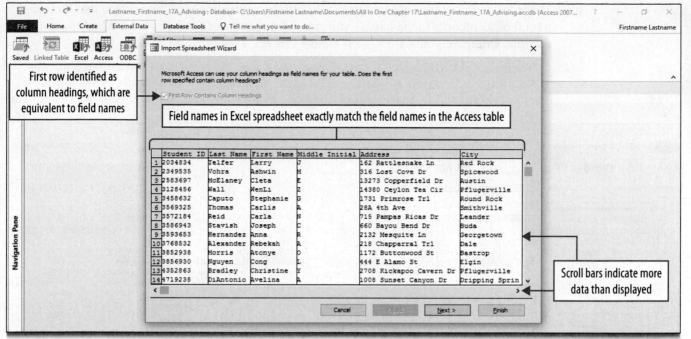

FIGURE 17.15

6 ▶ In the lower right corner of the wizard, click **Next**. Notice that the name of your table displays under **Import to Table**. In the lower right corner of the wizard, click **Finish**.

7 ▶ In the **Get External Data – Excel Spreadsheet** dialog box, click **Close**. Open ⏩ the **Navigation Pane**.

8 ▶ Point to the right edge of the **Navigation Pane** to display the ⟷ pointer. Drag to the right to increase the width of the **Navigation Pane** so that the entire table name displays, and then compare your screen with Figure 17.16.

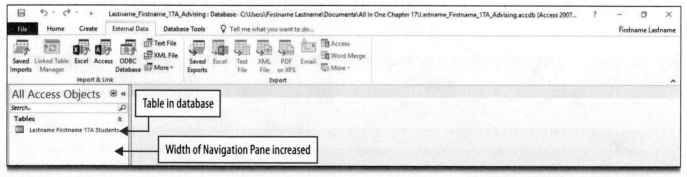

FIGURE 17.16

9 ▶ In the **Navigation Pane**, double-click your **17A Students** table to open the table in Datasheet view, and then **Close** ⏪ the **Navigation Pane**.

🔄 **ANOTHER WAY**   To open an object from the Navigation Pane, right-click the object name, and then click Open.

10 In the lower left corner of your screen, locate the navigation area, and notice that there are a total of **25** records in the table—you entered three records and imported 22 additional records. Compare your screen with Figure 17.17.

The records that you entered and the records you imported from the Excel spreadsheet display in your table; the first record in the table is selected. The *navigation area* indicates the number of records in the table and has controls in the form of arrows that you click to move through the records.

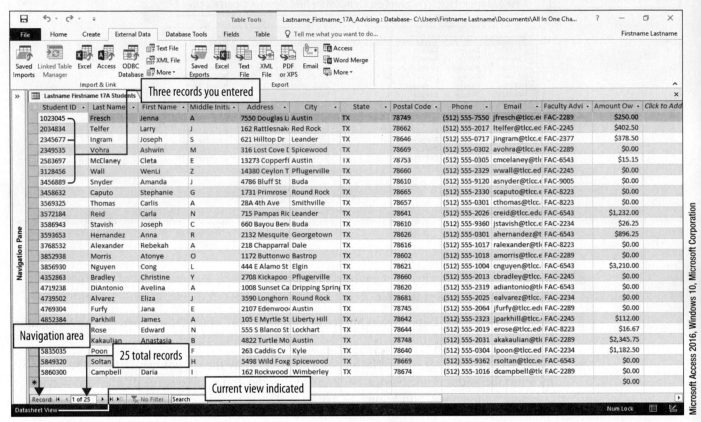

FIGURE 17.17

Objective 3 | Change the Structure of Tables and Add a Second Table

GO! Learn How
video A17-3

Recall that the structure of a table is the underlying design of the table and includes field names and data types. You can create or modify a table in Datasheet view. To define and modify fields, many database experts prefer to work in Design view, where you have more options for defining fields in a table.

Activity 17.08 | Deleting a Table Field in Design View

In this Activity, you will delete the *Middle Initial* field from the table.

1 Click the **Home tab**, and then in the **Views group**, click the **View arrow** to display a list of views.

There are two views for tables: Datasheet view and Design view. Other objects have different views. On the list, Design view is represented by a picture of a pencil, a ruler, and an angle. Datasheet view is represented by a picture of a table arranged in columns and rows. In the Views group, if the top of the View button displays the pencil, ruler, and angle, clicking View will switch your view to Design view. Likewise, clicking the top of the View button that displays as a datasheet will switch your view to Datasheet view.

2 ▸ On the list, click **Design View**, and then compare your screen with Figure 17.18.

Design view displays the underlying design—the structure—of the table and its fields. In Design view, the records in the table do not display. You can only view the information about each field's attributes. Each field name is listed, along with its data type. You can add explanatory information about a field in the Description column, but it is not required.

You can decide how each field should look and behave in the Field Properties area. For example, you can set a specific field size in the Field Properties area. In the lower right corner, information displays about the active selection—in this case, the Field Name.

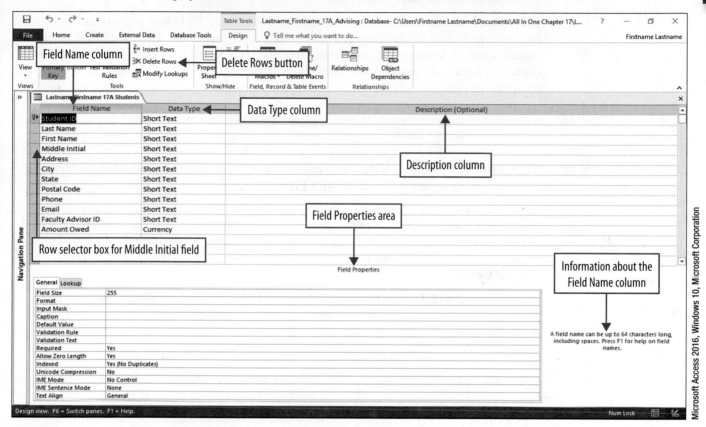

FIGURE 17.18

3 ▸ In the **Field Name** column, to the left of **Middle Initial**, point to the row selector box to display the ➡ pointer, and then click one time to select the entire row.

4 ▸ On the **Design tab**, in the **Tools group**, click **Delete Rows**. Read the warning in the message box, and then click **Yes**.

Deleting a field deletes both the field and its data. After you save the changes, you cannot undo this action, so Access prompts you to be sure you want to proceed. If you change your mind after deleting a field and saving the changes, you must add the field back into the table and then reenter the data for that field for every record.

ANOTHER WAY In Design view, right-click the selected row, and then click Delete Rows; or, in Datasheet view, select the field—column—and on the Home tab, in the Records group, click Delete.

Activity 17.09 | Changing a Field Size and Adding a Description

Typically, many different individuals have the ability to enter data into a table. For example, at your college, many Registration Assistants enter and modify student and course information daily. Two ways to help reduce errors are to restrict what can be typed in a field and to add descriptive information to help the individuals when entering the data.

> **1** With your table still displayed in **Design** view, in the **Field Name** column, click anywhere in the **Student ID** field name.

> **2** In the lower area of the screen, under **Field Properties**, click **Field Size** to select the text *255*, and then type **7**

This action limits the size of the Student ID field to no more than seven characters. *Field properties* control how the field displays and how data can be entered into the field. You can define properties for each field in the Field Properties area by first clicking on the field name to display the properties for that specific data type.

The default field size for a Short Text field is 255. Limiting the Field Size property to 7 ensures that no more than seven characters can be entered for each Student ID. However, this does not prevent someone from entering seven characters that are incorrect or entering fewer than seven characters. Setting the proper data type for the field and limiting the field size are two ways to help reduce errors during data entry.

⟳ ANOTHER WAY   In Datasheet view, click in the field. Under Table Tools, on the Fields tab, in the Properties group, click in the Field Size box, and then type the number that represents the maximum number of characters for that field.

> **3** In the **Student ID** row, click in the **Description** box, type **Seven-digit Student ID number** and then press Enter. Compare your screen with Figure 17.19.

Descriptions for fields in a table are optional. Include a description if the field name does not provide an obvious explanation of the type of data to be entered. If a description is provided for a field, when data is being entered in that field in Datasheet view, the text in the Description displays on the left side of the status bar to provide additional information for the individuals who are entering the data.

When you enter a description for a field, a Property Update Options button displays below the text you typed, which enables you to copy the description for the field to all other database objects that use this table as an underlying source.

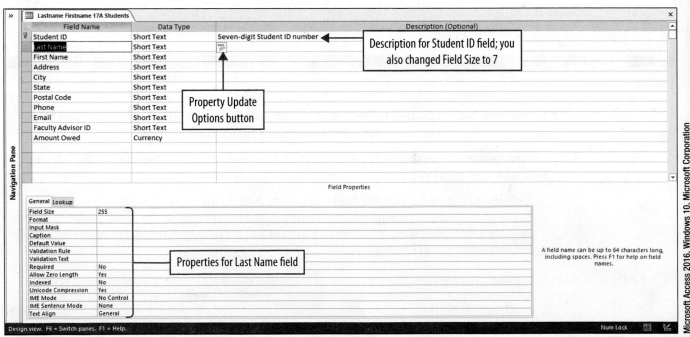

FIGURE 17.19

4 Click in the **State** field name box. In the **Field Properties** area, change the **Field Size** to **2** and in the **Description** box for this field, type **Two-character state abbreviation** and then press Enter.

5 Click in the **Faculty Advisor ID** field name box. In the **Field Properties** area, change the **Field Size** to **8** and in the **Description** box for this field, type **Eight-character ID of the instructor assigned as advisor** and then press Enter.

6 On the Quick Access Toolbar, click **Save** 🖫 to save the design changes to your table, and then notice the message.

The message indicates that the field size property of one or more fields has changed to a shorter size. If more characters are currently present in the Student ID, State, or Faculty Advisor ID fields than you have allowed, the data will be *truncated*—cut off or shortened—because the fields were not previously restricted to these specific numbers of characters.

7 In the message box, click **Yes**.

More **Knowledge** | **Add a Table Description**

You can create a description to provide more information to users regarding the entire table. With the table displayed in Design view, click the Design tab. In the Show/Hide group, click Property Sheet. Click in the Description box, type the table description, and then press Enter. Close the Property Sheet.

Activity 17.10 | Viewing the Primary Key in Design View

Primary key refers to the required field in the table that uniquely identifies a record. For example, in a college registration database, your Student ID number identifies you as a unique individual—every student has a student number and no other student at the college has your exact student number. In the 17A Students table, the Student ID uniquely identifies each student.

When you create a table using the blank desktop database template, Access designates the first field as the primary key field and names the field ID. It is good database design practice to establish a primary key for every table, because doing so ensures that you do not enter the same record more than once. You can imagine the confusion if another student at your college had the same Student ID number as you do.

1 With your table still displayed in **Design** view, in the **Field Name** column, click in the **Student ID** box. To the left of the box, notice the small icon of a key, as shown in Figure 17.20.

Access automatically designates the first field as the primary key field, but you can set any field as the primary key by clicking the field name, and then in the Tools group, clicking Primary Key.

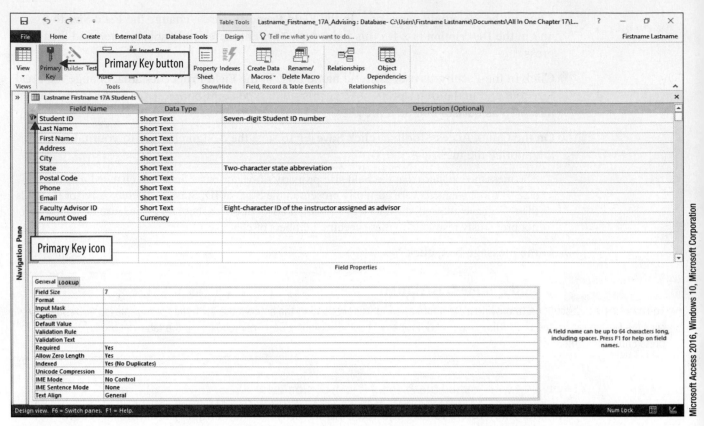

FIGURE 17.20

2 On the **Design tab**, in the **Views group**, notice that the View button displays a picture of a datasheet, indicating that clicking View will switch the view to Datasheet view. Click the top of the **View** button.

> If you make design changes to a table and switch views without first saving the table, Access will prompt you to save the table before changing views.

Activity 17.11 | Adding a Second Table to a Database by Importing an Excel Spreadsheet

Many Microsoft Office users track data in an Excel spreadsheet. The sorting and filtering capabilities of Excel are useful for a simple database where all of the information resides in one large Excel spreadsheet. However, Excel is limited as a database management tool because it cannot *relate* the information in multiple spreadsheets in a way that you can ask a question and get a meaningful result. Because data in an Excel spreadsheet is arranged in columns and rows, the spreadsheet can easily convert to an Access table by importing the spreadsheet.

1 On the ribbon, click the **External Data tab**, and then in the **Import & Link group**, click **Excel**. In the **Get External Data – Excel Spreadsheet** dialog box, to the right of the **File name** box, click **Browse**.

2 In the **File Open** dialog box, navigate to the location where your student data files are stored, and then double-click **a17A_Faculty_Advisors**. Compare your screen with Figure 17.21.

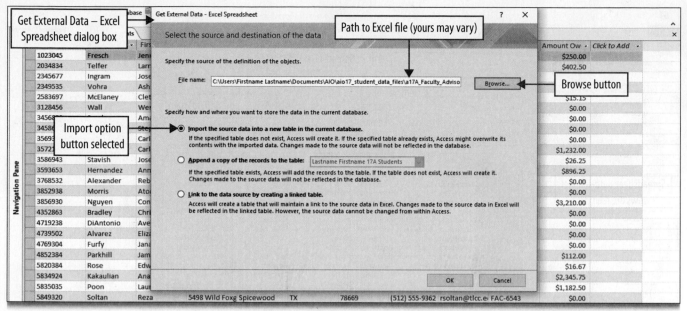

FIGURE 17.21

Microsoft Access 2016, Windows 10, Microsoft Corporation

3 Be sure that the **Import the source data into a new table in the current database** option button is selected, and click **OK**.

The Import Spreadsheet Wizard displays the spreadsheet data.

4 In the upper left corner of the wizard, select the **First Row Contains Column Headings** check box.

The Excel data is framed, indicating that the first row of Excel column titles will become the Access table field names, and the remaining rows will become the individual records in the new Access table.

5 Click **Next**. Notice that the first column—*Faculty ID*—is selected, and in the upper area of the wizard, the **Field Name** and the **Data Type** display. Compare your screen with Figure 17.22.

In this step, under Field Options, you can review and change the name or the data type of each selected field. You can also identify fields in the spreadsheet that you do not want to import into the Access table by selecting the Do not import field (Skip) check box.

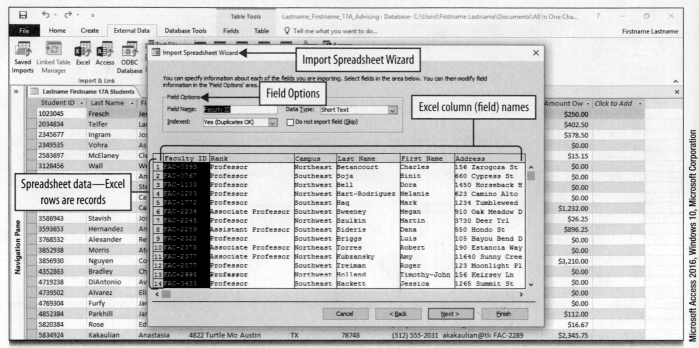

FIGURE 17.22

6 ▸ Click **Next**. In the upper area of the wizard, click the **Choose my own primary key** option button, and then be sure that **Faculty ID** displays.

> In the new table, Faculty ID will be the primary key. Every faculty member has a Faculty ID and no two faculty members have the same Faculty ID. By default, Access selects the first field as the primary key, but you can click the arrow and select a different field.

7 ▸ Click **Next**. In the **Import to Table** box, using your own name, type **Lastname Firstname 17A Faculty Advisors** and then click **Finish**.

8 ▸ In the **Get External Data – Excel Spreadsheet** dialog box, click **Close**. Open ⟩⟩ the **Navigation Pane**.

9 ▸ In the **Navigation Pane**, double-click your **17A Faculty Advisors** table to open it in Datasheet view, and then **Close** ⟨⟨ the **Navigation Pane**.

> Two tables that are identified by their object tabs are open in the object window. Your 17A Faculty Advisors table is the active table and displays the 29 records that you imported from the Excel spreadsheet.

10 ▸ In your **17A Faculty Advisors** table, click in the **Postal Code** field in the first record. On the ribbon, under **Table Tools**, click the **Fields tab**. In the **Formatting group**, click the **Data Type arrow**, and then click **Short Text**. Compare your screen with Figure 17.23.

> When you import data from an Excel spreadsheet, check the data types of all fields to ensure they are correct. Recall that if a field, such as the Postal Code, contains numbers that do not represent a quantity or are not used in calculations, the data type should be set to Short Text. To change the data type of a field, click in the field in any record.

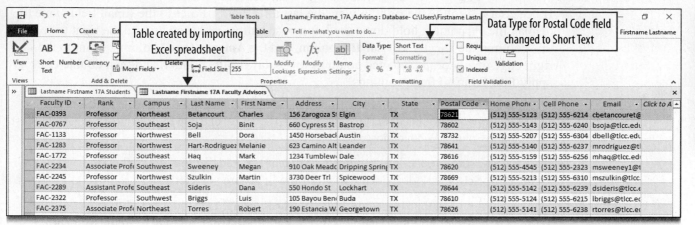

FIGURE 17.23

Microsoft Access 2016, Windows 10, Microsoft Corporation

Activity 17.12 | Adjusting Column Widths

You can adjust the column widths in a table displayed in Datasheet view by using techniques similar to those you use for Excel spreadsheets.

1 In the object window, click the **object tab** for your **17A Students** table to make it the active object and to display it in the object window.

Clicking an object tab along the top of object window enables you to display the open object and make it active so that you can work with it. All of the columns in the datasheet are the same width, regardless of the length of the data in the field, the length of the field name, or the field size that was set. If you print the table as currently displayed, some of the data or field names will not print completely, so you will want to adjust the column widths.

2 In the column headings row, point to the right edge of the **Address** field to display the ⊞ pointer, and then compare your screen with Figure 17.24.

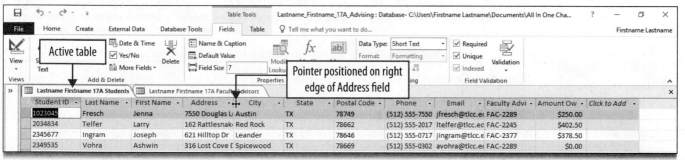

FIGURE 17.24

Microsoft Access 2016, Windows 10, Microsoft Corporation

3 With the ⊞ pointer positioned as shown in Figure 17.24, double-click the right edge of the **Address** field.

The column width of the Address field widens to display the longest entry in the field fully. In this manner, the width of a column can be increased or decreased to fit its contents in the same manner as a column in an Excel spreadsheet. In Access, adjusting the column width to fit the contents is referred to as *Best Fit*.

4 Point to the **City** field name to display the ⬇ pointer, and right-click to select the entire column and display the shortcut menu. Click **Field Width**, and then in the **Column Width** dialog box, click **Best Fit**.

This is a second way to adjust column widths.

5 If necessary, scroll to the right to view the last three fields. Point to the **Email** field name to display the ⬇ pointer, hold down the left mouse button, and then drag to the right to select this column, the **Faculty Advisor ID** column, and the **Amount Owed** column. Point to the right edge of any of the selected columns to display the ⊞ pointer, and then double-click to apply **Best Fit** to all three columns.

> You can select multiple columns and adjust the widths of all of them at one time by using this technique or by right-clicking any of the selected columns, clicking Field Width, and clicking Best Fit in the Column Width dialog box.

6 If necessary, scroll to the left to view the **Student ID** field. To the left of the **Student ID** field name, click **Select All** ▨. Notice that all of the fields are selected.

7 On the ribbon, click the **Home tab**. In the **Records group**, click **More**, and then click **Field Width**. In the **Column Width** dialog box, click **Best Fit**. Click anywhere in the **Student ID** field, and then compare your screen with Figure 17.25.

> Using the More command is a third way to adjust column widths. By using Select All, you can adjust the widths of all of the columns at one time. Adjusting the width of columns does not change the data in the table's records; it only changes the *display* of the data.

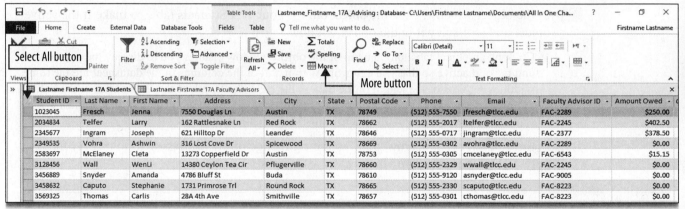

FIGURE 17.25

Microsoft Access 2016, Windows 10, Microsoft Corporation

NOTE **Adjusting Column Widths**

After adjusting column widths, scroll horizontally and vertically to be sure that all of the data displays in all of the fields. Access adjusts column widths to fit the screen size based on the displayed data. If data is not displayed on the screen when you adjust column widths—even if you use Select All—the column width may not be adjusted adequately to display all of the data in the field. After adjusting column widths, click in any field to remove the selection of the column or columns, and then save the table before performing other tasks.

---

8 On the Quick Access Toolbar, click **Save** 🖫 to save the table design changes—changing the column widths.

> If you do not save the table after making design changes, Access prompts you to save it when you close the table.

Activity 17.13 | Printing a Table

There are times when you will want to print a table, even though a report may look more professional. For example, you may need a quick reference, or you may want to proofread the data that has been entered.

1 > On the ribbon, click the **File tab**, click **Print**, and then click **Print Preview**. Compare your screen with Figure 17.26.

> The table displays in Print Preview with the default zoom setting of One Page, a view that enables you to see how your table will print on the page. It is a good idea to view any object in Print Preview before printing so that you can make changes to the object if needed before actually printing it. In the navigation area, the Next Page button is darker (available), an indication that more than one page will print.

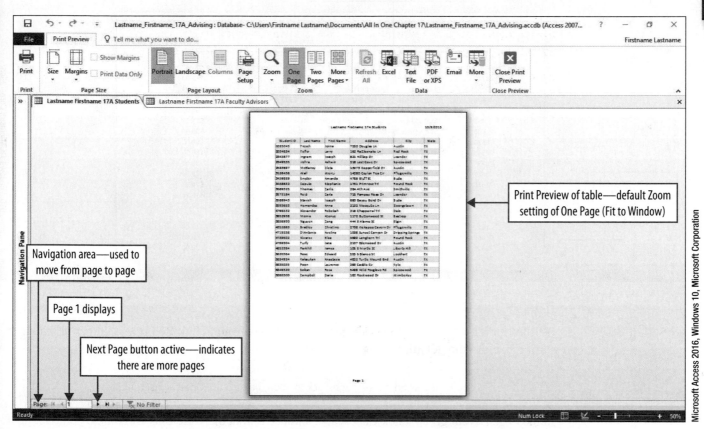

Print Preview of table—default Zoom setting of One Page (Fit to Window)

Navigation area—used to move from page to page

Page 1 displays

Next Page button active—indicates there are more pages

FIGURE 17.26

2 > In the navigation area, click **Next Page** ▶ to display Page 2. Point to the top of the page to display the 🔍 pointer, click one time to zoom in, and then compare your screen with Figure 17.27.

> The Print Preview display enlarges, and the Zoom Out pointer displays. The second page of the table displays the last five fields. The Next Page button is dimmed, indicating that the button is unavailable because there are no more pages after Page 2. The Previous Page button is available, indicating that a page exists before this page.

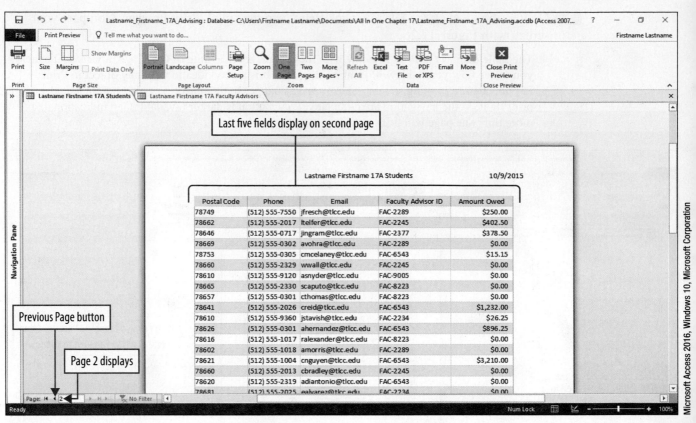

FIGURE 17.27

3 On the ribbon, on the **Print Preview tab**, in the **Zoom group**, click **Zoom** to change the zoom setting back to the default setting of One Page.

🔄 **ANOTHER WAY**   With the 🔍 pointer displayed on the page, click to zoom back to the One Page setting.

---

4 In the **Page Layout group**, click **Landscape**, and notice that there are only three fields on Page 2. In the navigation area, click **Previous Page** ◄ to display Page 1, and then compare your screen with Figure 17.28.

> The orientation of the page to be printed changes. The header on the page includes the table name and current date, and the footer displays the page number. The change in orientation from portrait to landscape is not saved with the table. Each time you print, you must check the page orientation, the margins, and any other print parameters so that the object prints as you intend.

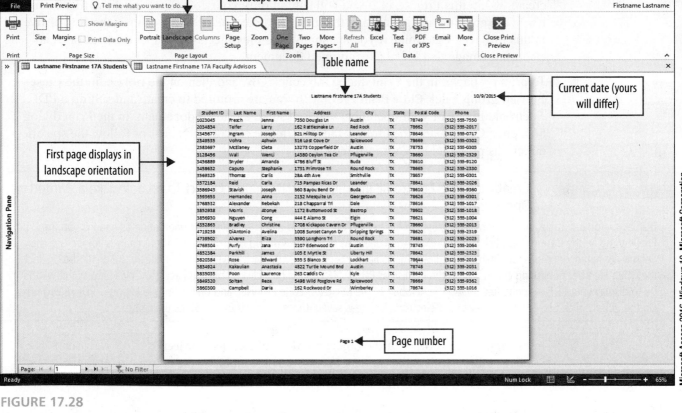

FIGURE 17.28

NOTE	**Headers and Footers in Access Objects**

The headers and footers in Access tables and queries are controlled by default settings; you cannot enter additional information or edit the information. The object name displays in the center of the header area, and the current date displays on the right. Adding your name to the object name is helpful in identifying your paper printouts or electronic results. The page number displays in the center of the footer area. The headers and footers in Access forms and reports are more flexible; you can add to and edit the information.

---

5 On the **Print Preview tab**, in the **Print group**, click **Print**. In the **Print** dialog box, under **Print Range**, verify that **All** is selected. Under **Copies**, verify that the **Number of Copies** is **1**. Compare your screen with Figure 17.29.

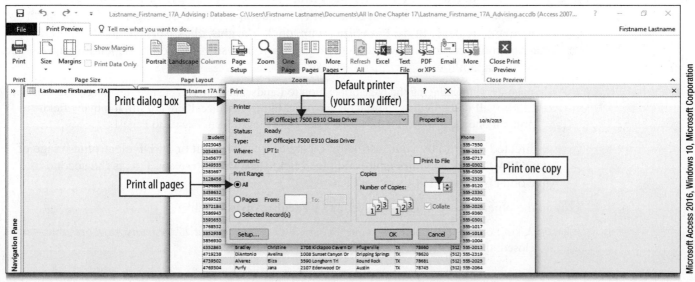

FIGURE 17.29

6 Determine if your instructor wants you to submit the individual database objects that you create within this Project, or if you will submit only your completed database file. Then, if you are creating and submitting the individual database objects—this is the first of five in this Project—determine if you are submitting the objects as a paper printout or as an electronic image that looks like a printed document.

7 To print on paper, in the **Print** dialog box, click **OK**, and then on the ribbon, in the **Close Preview group**, click **Close Print Preview**. If you are required to create and submit a PDF electronic image of your document that looks like a printed document, in the Print dialog box, click Cancel, and then follow the steps in the following Note—or follow the specific directions provided by your instructor.

NOTE   Creating a PDF Electronic Image of Your Database Object That Looks Like a Printed Document

Display the object (table, query, form, report, and so on) in Print Preview and adjust margins and orientation as needed. On the Print Preview tab, in the Data group, click PDF or XPS. In the Publish as PDF or XPS dialog box, navigate to your chapter folder. Use the default file name, or follow your instructor's directions to name the object. If you wish to view the PDF file, in the dialog box, select the Open file after publishing check box. In the Publish as PDF or XPS dialog box, click Publish. If necessary, close any windows that try to display your PDF—Adobe Reader, Adobe Acrobat, or the Microsoft Edge browser, and then close the Export – PDF dialog box. On the ribbon, click Close Print Preview; your electronic image is saved. Close the Save Export Steps dialog box.

---

8 In the upper right corner of the object window, click **Close Object** ☒ to close your **17A Students** table. Notice that the **17A Faculty Advisors** table is the active object in the object window.

↻ ANOTHER WAY   In the object window, right-click the 17A Students object tab, and then click Close.

9 In your **17A Faculty Advisors** table, to the left of the **Faculty ID** field name, click **Select All** ☐ to select all of the columns. On the **Home tab**, in the **Records group**, click **More**, and then click **Field Width**. In the **Column Width** dialog box, click **Best Fit** to adjust the widths of all of the columns so that all of the data displays. Click in any field in the table to cancel the selection. Scroll horizontally and vertically to be sure that all of the data displays in each field; if necessary, use the techniques you practiced to apply Best Fit to individual columns. **Save** ☐ the changes you made to the table's column widths, and then click in any record to cancel the selection, if necessary.

10 On the ribbon, click the **File tab**, click **Print**, and then click **Print Preview**. On the **Print Preview tab**, in the **Page Layout group**, click **Landscape**. Notice that the table will print on more than one page. In the **Page Size group**, click **Margins**, click **Normal**, and then notice that one more column moved to the first page—your results may differ depending upon your printer's capabilities.

In addition to changing the page orientation to Landscape, you can change the margins to Normal to see if all of the fields will print on one page. In this instance, there are still too many fields to print on one page, although the Postal Code field moved from Page 2 to Page 1.

11 If directed to do so by your instructor, create a paper printout or a PDF electronic image of your **17A Faculty Advisors** table, and then click **Close Print Preview**. This is the second of five objects printed in this project.

12 In the object window, **Close** ☒ your **17A Faculty Advisors** table.

All of your database objects—your *17A Students* table and your *17A Faculty Advisors* table—are closed; the object window is empty.

Recall that tables are the foundation of an Access database because all of the data is stored in one or more tables. You can use the data stored in tables in other database objects such as queries, forms, and reports.

2.04c (iv)

Activity 17.14 │ Creating a Query by Using the Simple Query Wizard

A *query* is a database object that retrieves specific data from one or more database objects—either tables or other queries—and then, in a single datasheet, displays only the data that you specify when you design the query. Because the word *query* means *to ask a question*, think of a query as a question formed in a manner that Access can answer.

A *select query* is one type of Access query. A select query, also called a *simple select query*, retrieves (selects) data from one or more tables or queries and then displays the selected data in a datasheet. A select query creates a subset of the data to answer specific questions; for example, *Which students live in Austin, TX?*

The objects from which a query selects the data are referred to as the query's *data source*. In this Activity, you will create a simple query using a wizard that walks you step by step through the process. The process involves selecting the data source and indicating the fields that you want to include in the query results. The query—the question you want to ask—is *What is the name, email address, phone number, and Student ID of every student?*

1 On the ribbon, click the **Create tab**, and then in the **Queries group**, click **Query Wizard**. In the **New Query** dialog box, be sure **Simple Query Wizard** is selected, and then click **OK**. Compare your screen with Figure 17.30.

In the wizard, the displayed table or query name is the object that was last selected on the Navigation Pane. The last object you worked with was your 17A Faculty Advisors table, so that object name displayed in the wizard.

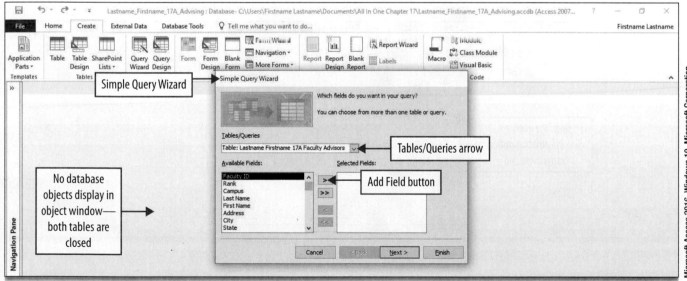

FIGURE 17.30

Microsoft Access 2016, Windows 10, Microsoft Corporation

2 In the wizard, click the **Tables/Queries arrow**, and then click your **Table: Lastname Firstname 17A Students**.

To create a query, first select the data source—the object from which the query is to select the data. The information you need to answer the question is stored in your 17A Students table, so this table is your data source.

3 Under **Available Fields**, click **Last Name**, and then click **Add Field** `>` to move the field to the **Selected Fields** list on the right. Double-click the **First Name** field to add the field to the **Selected Fields** list.

> Use either method to add fields to the Selected Fields list—you can add fields in any order.

4 By using **Add Field** `>` or by double-clicking the field name, add the following fields to the **Selected Fields** list in the order specified: **Email**, **Phone**, and **Student ID**. Compare your screen with Figure 17.31.

> Selecting these five fields will answer the question, *What is the name, email address, phone number, and Student ID of every student?*

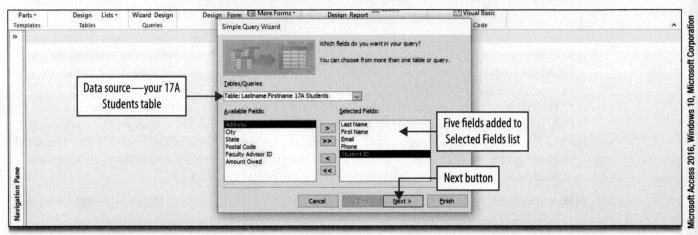

FIGURE 17.31

5 In the wizard, click **Next**. Click in the **What title do you want for your query?** box. Using your own name, edit as necessary so that the query name is **Lastname Firstname 17A All Students Query** and then compare your screen with Figure 17.32.

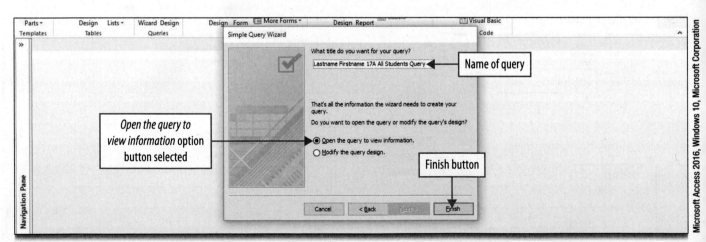

FIGURE 17.32

6 ▶ In the wizard, click **Finish**. Select all of the columns, apply **Best Fit**, and then **Save** ⊟ the query. In the first record, click in the **Last Name** field to cancel the selection. Compare your screen with Figure 17.33

> Access *runs* the query—performs the actions indicated in your query design—by searching the records in the specified data source, and then finds the records that match specified criteria. The records that match the criteria display in a datasheet. A select query *selects*—pulls out and displays—*only* the information from the data source that you request, including the specified fields.
>
> In the object window, Access displays every student from your 17A Students table—the data source—but displays *only* the five fields that you moved to the Selected Fields list in the Simple Query Wizard.

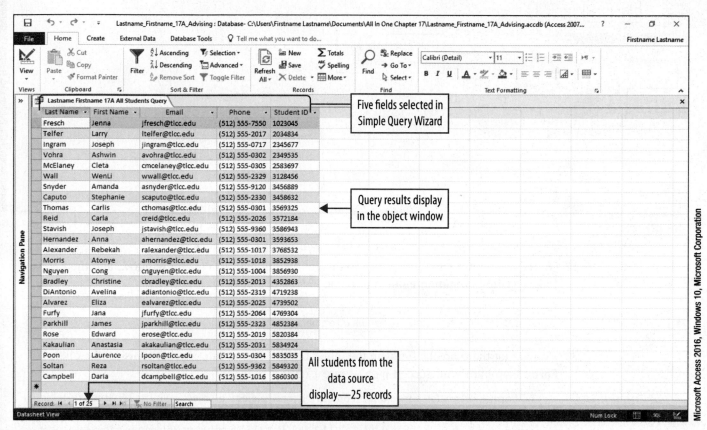

FIGURE 17.33

7 ▶ On the ribbon, click the **File tab**, click **Print**, and then click **Print Preview**. Notice that the query results will print on one page. As directed by your instructor, create a paper printout or PDF electronic image. Click **Close Print Preview**. This is the third of five objects printed in this project.

8 ▶ In the object window, **Close** ⊠ the query.

IC3
DIGITAL LITERACY
CERTIFICATION
2.04c (v)

Activity 17.15 | Creating and Printing a Form

A *form* is an Access object with which you can enter data, edit data, or display data from a table or query. In a form, the fields are laid out in an attractive format on the screen, which makes working with the database easier for those who must enter and look up data.

One type of form displays only one record at a time. Such a form is useful not only to the individual who performs the data entry—typing in the records—but also to anyone who has the job of viewing information in the database. For example, when you visit the Records office at your college to obtain a transcript, someone displays your record on the screen. For the viewer, it is much easier to look at one record at a time using a form than to look at all of the student records in the database table.

1 Open ⏵»⏴ the **Navigation Pane**. Drag the right edge of the **Navigation Pane** to the right to increase the width of the pane so that all object names display fully. Notice that a table name displays with a datasheet icon, and a query name displays an icon of two overlapping datasheets. Right-click your **17A Students** table, and then compare your screen with Figure 17.34.

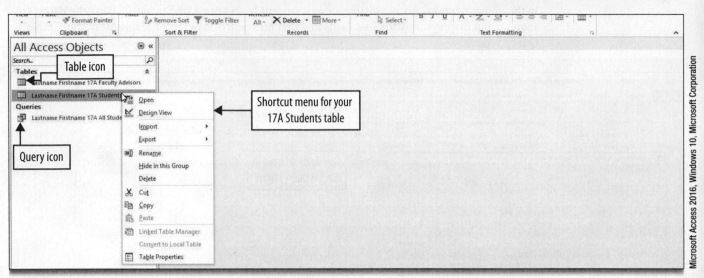

FIGURE 17.34

2 On the shortcut menu, click **Open** to display the table in the object window, and then **Close** ⏴«⏵ the **Navigation Pane** to maximize your object window space.

ANOTHER WAY   In the Navigation Pane, double-click the object name to open it.

3 Notice that there are 11 fields in the table. On the **Create tab**, in the **Forms group**, click **Form**. Compare your screen with Figure 17.35.

The Form tool creates a form based on the currently selected object—your 17A Students table. The form displays all of the fields from the underlying data source—one record at a time—in a simple top-to-bottom format with all 11 fields in a single column. You can use this form as it displays, or you can modify it. Records that you create or edit in a form are automatically added to or updated in the underlying table or data source.

The new form displays in *Layout view*—the Access view in which you can make changes to elements of an object while it is open and displaying the data from the data source. Each field in the form displayed in Figure 17.35 displays the data for the first student record—*Jenna Fresch*—in your 17A Students table.

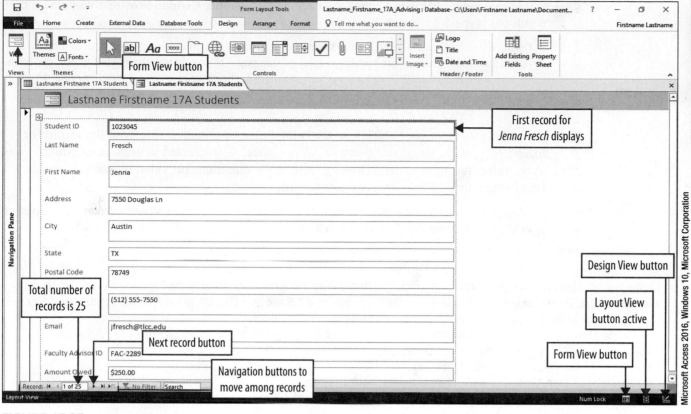

FIGURE 17.35

4 At the right side of the status bar, notice the three buttons. Point to each button to display its ScreenTip, and notice that **Layout View** ▣ is active, indicating that the form is displayed in Layout view.

5 In the status bar, click **Form View** ▣.

In *Form view*, you can view the records, create a new record, edit a record, and delete a record. You cannot change the layout or design of the form. Form view is useful for individuals who *access records* in your database. Layout view is useful for individuals who *design* the form.

ANOTHER WAY On the Design tab, or on the Home tab, in the Views group, click View when the button displays an icon of a form.

6 In the navigation area, click **Next record** ▶ two times to display the third record—the record for *Joseph Ingram*.

Use the navigation buttons to scroll among the records and to display any single record.

7 Using your own name, **Save** ▣ the form as **Lastname Firstname 17A Student Form**

8 On the ribbon, click the **File tab**, click **Print**, and then on the right, click **Print**—do *not* click Print Preview because you are going to print a *single* record—not all of the records.

9 In the **Print** dialog box, under **Print Range**, click the **Selected Record(s)** option button, and then click **Setup**.

10 In the **Page Setup** dialog box, click the **Columns tab**. Under **Column Size**, double-click in the **Width** box, type **7.5** and then click **OK**.

> Forms are usually not printed, so the default width for a form created with the Form command is larger than most printers can handle to print on one page. If you do not change the width, the form will print on two pages because the column flows over the margins allowed by the printer. If, after changing the Width to 7.5, your form still prints on two pages, try entering a different value for Width; for example, 7 or 6.5.

11 If instructed to print your objects, in the **Print** dialog box, click **OK** to print the record for *Joseph Ingram* on one page; otherwise, click Cancel. If instructed to print an electronic copy, follow the steps in the following Note or the directions provided by your instructor. This is the fourth of five objects printed in this project.

> After printing, along the left edge of the record, the narrow bar—the ***record selector bar***—displays in black, indicating that the record is selected.

NOTE | **Printing a Single Form in PDF**

On the File tab, click Print, and then on the right, click Print. In the Print dialog box, click Setup. In the Page Setup dialog box, click the Columns tab. Under Column Size, double-click in the Width box, type **7.5** and then click OK. In the Print dialog box, click Cancel. On the left edge of the form, click the record selector bar so that it is black—selected.

On the ribbon, click the External Data tab. In the Export group, click PDF or XPS. In the Publish as PDF or XPS dialog box, navigate to your chapter folder, and at the lower right corner of the dialog box, click Options. In the Options dialog box, under Range, click the Selected records option button, and then click OK. In the Publish as PDF or XPS dialog box, click Publish. If necessary, close Adobe Reader, Adobe Acrobat, or the Microsoft Edge browser.

---

12 **Close** ⊠ the form object; leave your **17A Students** table open.

Activity 17.16 | Creating, Modifying, and Printing a Report

A ***report*** is a database object that displays the fields and records from a table or query in an easy-to-read format suitable for printing. Create professional-looking reports to summarize database information.

1 **Open** ⊮ the **Navigation Pane**, and then open your **17A Faculty Advisors** table by double-clicking the table name or by right-clicking the table name and clicking Open. **Close** ⧏ the **Navigation Pane**.

2 On the **Create tab**, in the **Reports group**, click **Report**.

> The Report tool creates a report in Layout view and includes all of the fields and all of the records in the data source—your 17A Faculty Advisors table. Dotted lines indicate how the report would break across pages if you print it now. In Layout view, you can make quick changes to the report layout while viewing the data from the table.

3 Click the **Faculty ID** field name, and then on the ribbon, under **Report Layout Tools**, click the **Arrange tab**. In the **Rows & Columns group**, click **Select Column**, and then press Del. Using the same technique, delete the **Rank** field.

> The Faculty ID and Rank fields, along with the data, are deleted from the report. The fields readjust by moving to the left. Deleting the fields from the report does *not* delete the fields and data from the data source—your 17A Faculty Advisors table.

ANOTHER WAY | Right-click the field name, click Select Entire Column, and then press Del.

4 Click the **Address** field name, and then by using the scroll bar at the bottom of the screen, scroll to the right to display the **Cell Phone** field; be careful not to click in the report.

5 Hold down ⇧Shift, and then click the **Cell Phone** field name to select all of the fields from *Address* through *Cell Phone*. With the field names selected—surrounded by a colored border—in the **Rows & Columns group**, click **Select Column**, and then press ⌦Del.

> Use this method to select and delete multiple columns in Layout view.

6 Scroll to the left, and notice that the four remaining fields display within the dotted lines—they are within the margins of the report. Click the **Campus** field name. Hold down ⇧Shift, and then click the **First Name** field name to select the first three fields. In the **Rows & Columns group**, click **Select Column** to select all three fields.

7 On the ribbon, under **Report Layout Tools**, click the **Design tab**, and then in the **Tools group**, click **Property Sheet**.

> The *Property Sheet* for the selected columns displays on the right side of the screen. Every object and every item in an object has an associated Property Sheet where you can make precise changes to the properties—characteristics—of selected items.

8 In the **Property Sheet**, if necessary, click the **Format tab**. Click **Width**, type **1.5** and then press ⏎Enter. Compare your screen with Figure 17.36.

> The width of the three selected fields changes to 1.5″, and the fields readjust by moving to the left. You can change the Width property if you need to move columns within the margins of a report. In this report, the fields already displayed within the margins, but some reports may need this minor adjustment to print on one page.

🔄 ANOTHER WAY   Select the column, and then drag the right edge of the column to the left to decrease the width of the field, or drag to the right to increase the width of the field.

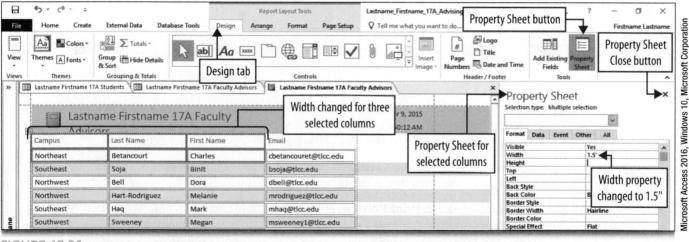

FIGURE 17.36

9 Close ⊠ the **Property Sheet**. Click the **Last Name** field name. On the ribbon, click the **Home tab**, and then in the **Sort & Filter group**, click **Ascending**.

> Access sorts the report in ascending alphabetical order by the Last Name field. By default, tables are sorted in ascending order by the primary key field—in this instance, the Faculty ID field. Changing the sort order in the report does *not* change the sort order in the underlying table.

10 At the top of the report, to the right of the green report icon, click anywhere in the title of the report to select the title. On the **Home tab**, in the **Text Formatting group**, click the **Font Size arrow**, and then click **14**. Save 🖫 the report. In the **Save As** dialog box, in the **Report Name** box, add **Report** to the end of *Lastname Firstname 17A Faculty Advisors*, and then click **OK**.

> **11** On the **File tab**, click **Print**, and then click **Print Preview**. On the **Print Preview tab**, in the **Zoom group**, click **Two Pages**, and then compare your screen with Figure 17.37.

As currently formatted, the report will print on two pages, because the page number at the bottom of the report is positioned beyond the right margin of the report.

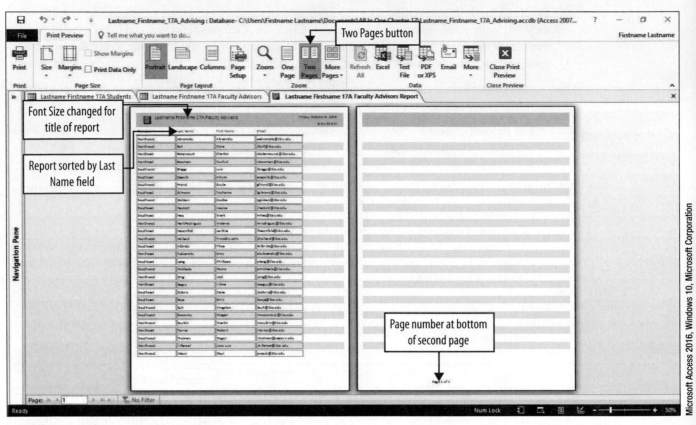

FIGURE 17.37

> **12** In the **Close Preview group**, click **Close Print Preview**. Scroll down to display the bottom of the report, and then, if necessary, scroll right to display the page number. Click the page number—**Page 1 of 1**—and then press ⌈Del⌉.

Because all of the data will print on one page, the page number is not necessary for this report. If you want the page number to display, you can drag it within the margins of the report.

> **13** Display the report in **Print Preview**, and notice that the report will now print on one page. In the **Zoom group**, click **One Page**. Click **Save** to save the changes to the design of the report, and then create a paper printout or PDF electronic image as directed. Click **Close Print Preview**. This is the fifth or last object printed in this project.

When you create a report by using the Report tool, the default margins are 0.25 inch. Some printers require a greater margin, so your printed report may result in two pages. As you progress in your study of Access, you will practice making these adjustments. Also, if a printer is not installed on your system, the electronic PDF printout might result in a two-page report.

> **14** In the object window, right-click any **object tab**, and then click **Close All** to close all of the open objects. Notice that the object window is empty.

GO! Learn How
video A17-5

When you close a table, any changes made to the records are saved automatically. If you made changes to the structure or adjusted column widths, you will be prompted to save the table when you close the table or when you switch views. Likewise, you will be prompted to save queries, forms, and reports if you make changes to the layout or design. If the Navigation Pane is open when you close Access, it will display when you reopen the database. When you are finished using your database, close the database, and then close Access.

Activity 17.17 | Closing a Database and Closing Access

1 **Open** ⏵ the **Navigation Pane**. If necessary, increase the width of the Navigation Pane so that all object names display fully. Notice that your report object displays with a green report icon. Compare your screen with Figure 17.38.

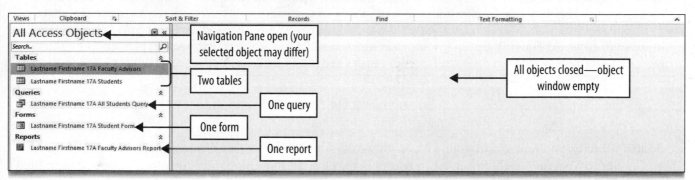

FIGURE 17.38

Microsoft Access 2016, Windows 10, Microsoft Corporation

2 On the **File tab**, click **Close** to close the database but leave Access open. This action enables you to continue working in Access with another database if you want to do so. In the Access application window, in the upper right corner, click **Close** ☒ to close Access. As directed by your instructor, submit your database and the paper printouts or PDF electronic images of the five objects—two tables, one query, one form, and one report—that are the results of this project.

> **END | You have completed Project 17A**

GO! With Google

Objective	Export an Access Table to an Excel Spreadsheet, Open as a Google Sheet, Edit a Record, and Save to Your Computer

Access web apps are designed to work with Microsoft's **SharePoint**, a service for setting up websites to share and manage documents. Your college may not have SharePoint installed, so you will use other tools to share objects from your database so that you can work collaboratively with others. Recall that Google Drive is Google's free, web-based word processor, spreadsheet, slide show, form, and data storage and sharing service. For Access, you can **export** a database object to an Excel worksheet, a PDF file, or a text file, and then save the file to Google Drive.

ALERT!   **Working with Web-Based Applications and Services**

Computer programs and services on the web receive continuous updates and improvements, so the steps to complete this web-based activity may differ from the ones shown. You can often look at the screens and the information presented to determine how to complete the activity.

    If you do not already have a Google account, you will need to create one before you doing this activity. Go to http://google.com and in the upper right corner, click Sign In. On the Sign In screen, click Create Account. On the Create your Google Account page, complete the form, read and agree to the Terms of Service and Privacy Policy, and then click Next step. On the Welcome screen, click Get Started.

Activity | Exporting an Access Table to an Excel Spreadsheet, Saving the Spreadsheet to Google Drive, Editing a Record in Google Drive, and Saving to Your Computer

In this Activity, you will export your 17A Faculty Advisors table to an Excel spreadsheet, upload your Excel file to Google Drive as a Google Sheet, edit a record in the Google Sheet, and then download a copy of the edited spreadsheet to your computer.

1 Start Access, navigate to your **All In One Chapter 17** folder, and then **Open** your **17A_Advising** database file. If necessary, on the Message Bar, click **Enable Content**. In the **Navigation Pane**, click your **17A Faculty Advisors** table to select it—do not open it.

2 On the ribbon, click the **External Data tab**, and then in the **Export group**, click **Excel**. In the **Export – Excel Spreadsheet** dialog box, click **Browse**, and then navigate to your **All In One Chapter 17** folder. In the **File Save** dialog box, click in the **File name** box, type **Lastname_Firstname_a17A_Web** and then click **Save**.

3 In the **Export – Excel Spreadsheet** dialog box, under **Specify export options**, select the first two check boxes—**Export data with formatting and layout** and **Open the destination file after the export operation is complete**—and then click **OK**. Take a moment to examine the data in the file, and then **Close** Excel. In the **Export – Excel Spreadsheet** dialog box, click **Close**, and then **Close** Access.

4 Open your browser software, navigate to **http://drive.google.com**, and sign in to your Google account. On the right side of the screen, click **Settings** ⚙▾ , and then click **Settings**. In the **Settings** dialog box, to the

right of *Convert uploads*, if necessary, select the **Convert uploaded files to Google Docs editor format** check box. In the upper right, click **Done**.

It is necessary to select this setting; otherwise, your document will upload as a pdf file and cannot be edited without further action.

5 Open your **GO! Web Projects** folder—or create and then open this folder by clicking **NEW** and then **Folder**. On the left, click **NEW**, and then click **File upload**. In the **Open** dialog box, navigate to your **All In One Chapter 17** folder, and then double-click your **a17A_Web** Excel file to upload it to Google Drive. When the message *Uploads completed* displays, **Close** the message box.

6 Double-click your **Lastname_Firstname_a17A_Web** file to display the file, and then compare your screen with Figure A.

The worksheet displays column letters, row numbers, and data.

7 Click in cell **C2**, and replace the current Campus with **Southwest** Click in cell **D2** and replace *Betancourt* with your last name. Press ⨂Tab⨂ and then replace Charles with your first name.

(GO! With Google continues on the next page)

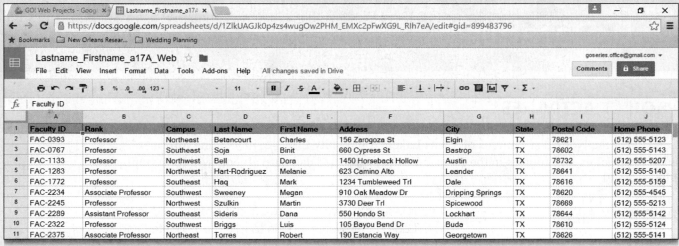

FIGURE A

Google inc.

8 Above row **1** and to the left of column **A**, click **Select All** [ ]. On the menu bar, click **Format**, and then click **Clear formatting** so that the font is the same for all data; the cell borders are removed, and the formatting of the field names are removed.

9 In the column headings row, click **I** to select the entire column. On the menu bar, click **Format**, point to **Number**, and then click **Plain Text** to format every number in the column as text. Click in cell **A1** to deselect the column.

Recall that in Access, numbers that are not used in calculations should be formatted as Short Text.

Because the formatting is cleared, you can enter new records into the spreadsheet in the same format as the existing records.

10 Click **File** to display the menu, point to **Download as**, and then click **Microsoft Excel (.xlsx)**. In the message box—usually displayed at the bottom of your screen—click the **Save arrow**, and then click **Save As**. In the **Save As** dialog box, navigate to your **All In One Chapter 17** folder, click in the **File name** box, and type **Lastname_Firstname_a17A_Web_Download** and then click **Save**. **Close** the message box.

> **NOTE** Saving The Downloaded File to the All In One Chapter 17 Folder
>
> Depending on the browser you are using, you may need to open the file in Excel and then save the a17A_Web_Download worksheet to your All In One Chapter 17 folder.

11 In Google Drive, at the top right corner of your screen, click your user name, and then click **Sign out**. **Close** your browser window.

12 Start Excel. In the Excel opening screen, click **Open Other Workbooks**, and then click **Browse**. Navigate to your **All In One Chapter 17** folder, and then double-click your **a17A_Web** Excel file. Notice that this file is the original file—the new record is not entered. If you are required

to print your documents, use one of the methods in the following Note. **Close** your Excel file; if prompted, save the changes to your worksheet. Then **Open** and print your **a17A_Web_Download** Excel file using one of the methods in the following Note. **Close** Excel; if prompted, save the changes to your worksheet. As directed by your instructor, submit your two workbooks and the two paper printouts or PDF electronic images that are the results of this project.

> **NOTE** Adding the File Name to the Footer and Printing or Creating a PDF Electronic Image of an Excel Spreadsheet on One Page
>
> Click the FILE tab, click Print, and then click Page Setup. In the Page Setup dialog box, on the Page tab, under Orientation, click Landscape. Under Scaling, click the Fit to option button. In the Page Setup dialog box, click the Header/Footer tab, and then click Custom Footer. With the insertion point blinking in the Left section box, click the Insert File Name button, and then click OK. In the Page Setup dialog box, click OK.
>
> To print on paper, click Print. To create a PDF electronic image of your printout, on the left side of your screen, click Export. Under Export, be sure Create PDF/XPS Document is selected, and then click Create PDF/XPS. Navigate to your All In One Chapter 17 folder, and then click Publish to save the file with the default name and an extension of pdf.

PROJECT
17B

Instructors and Courses Database

MyITLab
Project 17B Training
Project 17B Grader

PROJECT ACTIVITIES

In Activities 17.18 through 17.34, you will assist Dr. Carolyn Judkins, Dean of the Business Division at the Northeast Campus of Texas Lakes Community College, in locating information about instructors and courses in the Division. Your completed database objects will look similar to Figure 17.39.

PROJECT FILES

 If your instructor wants you to submit Project 17B in the MyITLab grader system, log in to MyITLab, locate Grader Project 17B, and then download the files for this project.

For Project 17B, you will need the following file:

a17B_Instructors_Courses

You will save your database as:

Lastname_Firstname_17B_Instructors_Courses

PROJECT RESULTS

GO!
Walk Thru
Project 17B

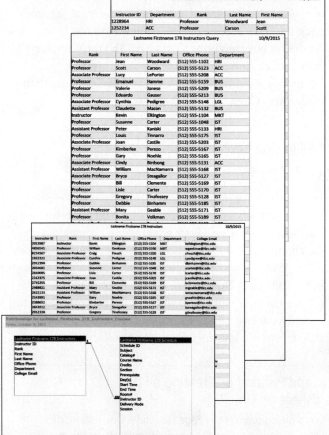

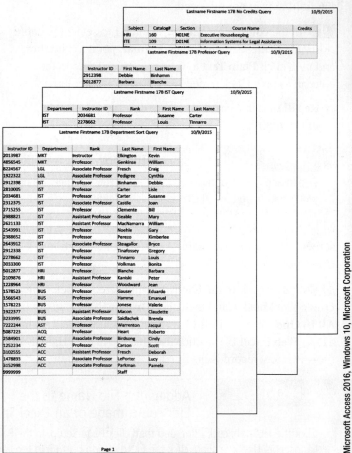

FIGURE 17.39 Project 17B Instructors and Courses

Microsoft Access 2016, Windows 10, Microsoft Corporation

PROJECT RESULTS

In this project, using your own name, you will create the following database and objects. Your instructor may ask you to submit printouts or PDF electronic images:

Lastname_Firstname_17B_Instructors_Courses	Database file
Relationships for Lastname_Firstname_17B_Instructors_Courses	Relationships Report
Lastname Firstname 17B Instructors table sorted (not saved)	Table sorted (Page 1)
Lastname Firstname 17B Instructors Query	Query
Lastname Firstname 17B Instructor IDs Query	Query
Lastname Firstname 17B Department Sort Query	Query
Lastname Firstname 17B IST Query	Query
Lastname Firstname 17B Professor Query	Query
Lastname Firstname 17B No Credits Query	Query

Objective 6 | Open and Save an Existing Database

GO! Learn How
video A17-6

There will be instances where you need to work with a database and still keep the original, unaltered version of the database. Like the other Microsoft Office 2016 applications, you can open a database file and save it with another name.

Activity 17.18 | Opening and Saving an Existing Database

ALERT!

To submit as an autograded project, log into MyITLab and download the files for this project and begin with those files instead of the a17B_Instructors_Courses file. For Project 17B using the Grader, read Activity 17.18 carefully. Begin working with the database in Activity 17.19. For Grader to award points accurately, when saving an object, do not include your Lastname Firstname at the beginning of the object name.

1 Start Access. In the Access opening screen, click **Open Other Files**. Under **Open**, click **Browse**. In the **Open** dialog box, navigate to the location where your student data files for this chapter are stored, and then double-click **a17B_Instructors_Courses** to open the database.

2 On the ribbon, click the **File tab**, and then click **Save As**. Under **File Types**, be sure **Save Database As** is selected. On the right, under **Database File Types**, be sure **Access Database** is selected, and then at the bottom of the screen, click **Save As**.

The Access Database file type saves your database in a format that enables the database to be opened with Access 2007, Access 2010, Access 2013, or Access 2016. If you are sharing your database with individuals who have an earlier version of Access, you can save the database in a version that will be compatible with that application, although some functionality might be lost since earlier versions of Access do not have the same features as later versions of Access. None of the features added to Access since that earlier version will be available in a database saved with backward compatibility.

3 In the **Save As** dialog box, navigate to your **All In One Chapter 17** folder, type **Lastname_Firstname_17B_Instructors_Courses** and then click **Save** or press [Enter].

> Use this technique when you need to keep a copy of the original database file.

4 On the **Message Bar**, notice the **SECURITY WARNING**. In the **Navigation Pane**, notice that this database contains two table objects. Compare your screen with Figure 17.40.

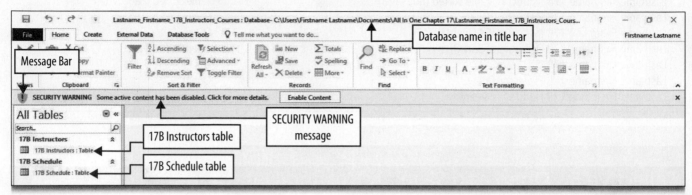

FIGURE 17.40

Microsoft Access 2016, Windows 10, Microsoft Corporation

Activity 17.19 | Resolving Security Alerts and Renaming Tables

The *Message Bar* is the area directly below the ribbon that displays information such as security alerts when there is potentially unsafe, active content in an Office document that you open. Settings that determine the alerts that display on your Message Bar are set in the Access *Trust Center*, an area in Access where you can view the security and privacy settings for your Access installation.

You may not be able to change the settings in the Trust Center, depending upon decisions made by your organization. To display the Trust Center, click the File tab, click Options, and then click Trust Center.

1 On the **Message Bar**, click **Enable Content**.

> When working with the student data files that accompany this chapter, repeat this action each time you see the security warning. Databases for this textbook are safe to use on your computer.

2 In the **Navigation Pane**, right-click the **17B Instructors** table, and then click **Rename**. With the table name selected and using your own name, type **Lastname Firstname 17B Instructors** and then press [Enter] to rename the table. Use the same technique to **Rename** the **17B Schedule** table to **Lastname Firstname 17B Schedule**

> Including your name in the table enables you and your instructor to easily identify your work, because Access includes the table name in the header of your paper or PDF electronic image.

3 Point to the right edge of the **Navigation Pane** to display the [↔] pointer. Drag to the right to increase the width of the pane until both table names display fully.

Objective 7 | Create Table Relationships

GO! Learn How
video A17-7

Access databases are relational databases because the tables in the database can relate—actually connect—to other tables through common fields. Recall that common fields are fields in one or more tables that store the same data; for example, a Student ID number may be stored in two tables in the same database.

After you have a table for each subject in your database, you must provide a way to connect the data in the tables when you need to obtain meaningful information from the stored data. To do this, create common fields in the related tables, and then define table *relationships*. A relationship is an association that you establish between two tables based on common fields. After the relationship is established, you can create a query, form, or report that displays information from more than one related table.

Activity 17.20 | Selecting the Tables and Common Field to Establish the Table Relationship

In this Activity, you will select the two tables in the database that will be used to establish the table relationship and identify the common field that is used to connect the tables.

1 In the **Navigation Pane**, double-click your **17B Instructors** table to open it in the object window. Examine the fields in the table. Double-click your **17B Schedule** table to open it, and examine the fields in the table.

In the 17B Instructors table, *Instructor ID* is the primary key field, which ensures that each instructor has only one record in the table. No two instructors have the same Instructor ID, and the table is sorted by Instructor ID.

In the 17B Schedule table, *Schedule ID* is the primary key field. Every scheduled course section during an academic term has a unique Schedule ID. The courses are sorted by Schedule ID.

2 In the **17B Schedule** table, scroll to display the **Instructor ID** field, and then compare your screen with Figure 17.41.

Both the 17B Instructors table and the 17B Schedule table include the *Instructor ID* field, which is the common field of the two tables. Because *one* instructor can teach *many* different courses, *one* Instructor ID can be present *many* times in the 17B Schedule table. When the relationship is established, it will be a *one-to-many relationship*, which is the most common type of relationship in Access.

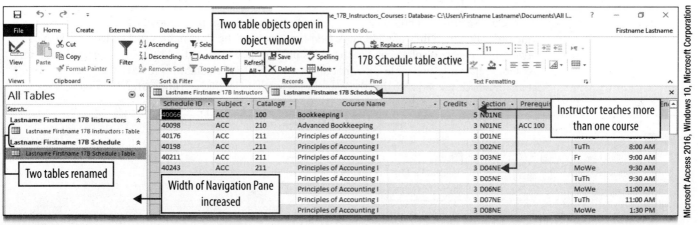

FIGURE 17.41

3 In the object window, right-click either **object tab**, and then click **Close All** to close both tables. Click the **Database Tools tab**, and then in the **Relationships group**, click **Relationships**. Compare your screen with Figure 17.42.

The Show Table dialog box displays in the Relationships window. In the Show Table dialog box, the Tables tab displays the two tables that are in this database.

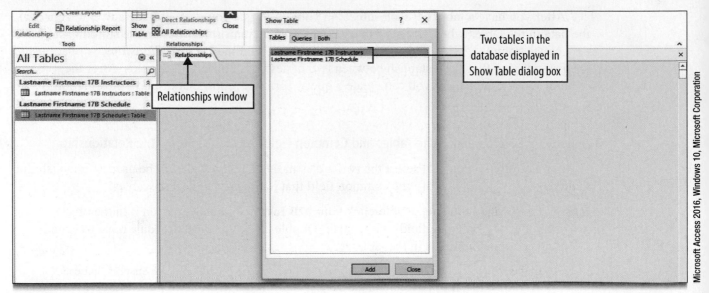

FIGURE 17.42

Microsoft Access 2016, Windows 10, Microsoft Corporation

4 ▶ Point to the title bar of the **Show Table** dialog box, and then, holding down the left mouse button, drag downward and slightly to the right to move the dialog box away from the top of the **Relationships** window. Release the mouse button.

Moving the Show Table dialog box enables you to see the tables as they are added to the Relationships window.

5 ▶ In the **Show Table** dialog box, if necessary, click your **17B Instructors** table, and then click **Add**. In the **Show Table** dialog box, double-click your **17B Schedule** table to add it to the **Relationships** window. In the **Show Table** dialog box, click **Close**, and then compare your screen with Figure 17.43.

You can use either technique to add a table to the Relationships window; tables are displayed in the order in which they are added. A *field list*—a list of the field names in a table—for each of the two table objects displays, and each table's primary key is identified by a key icon. Although this database has only two tables, it is not uncommon for larger databases to have many tables. Scroll bars in a field list indicate that there are fields in the table that are not currently in view.

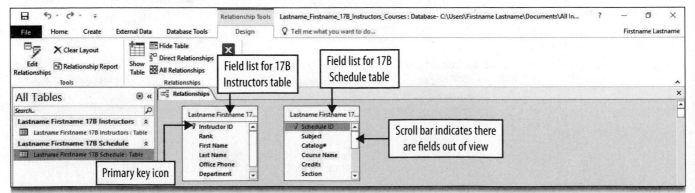

FIGURE 17.43

Microsoft Access 2016, Windows 10, Microsoft Corporation

ALERT! **Are there more than two field lists in the Relationships window?**

In the Show Table dialog box, if you double-click a table name more than one time, a duplicate field list displays in the Relationships window. To remove a field list from the Relationships window, right-click the title bar of the field list, and then click Hide Table. Alternatively, click anywhere in the field list, and then on the Design tab, in the Relationships group, click Hide Table.

---

6 In the **17B Schedule** field list—the field list on the right—point to the title bar to display the ⇖ pointer. Drag the field list to the right until there are about two inches of space between the field lists.

7 In the **17B Instructors** field list—the field list on the left—point to the lower right corner of the field list to display the ⬿ pointer, and then, holding down the left mouse button, drag downward and to the right to increase the height and width of the field list until the entire name of the table in the title bar displays and all of the field names display. Release the mouse button.

This action enables you to see all of the available fields and removes the vertical scroll bar.

8 Use the same technique to resize the **17B Schedule** field list so that the table name and all of the field names display as shown in Figure 17.44.

Recall that *one* instructor can teach *many* scheduled courses. The arrangement of field lists in the Relationships window displays the *one table* on the left side and the *many table* on the right side. Recall also that the primary key in each table is the required field that contains the data that uniquely identifies each record in the table. In the 17B Instructors table, each instructor is uniquely identified by the Instructor ID. In the 17B Schedule table, each scheduled course section is uniquely identified by the Schedule ID.

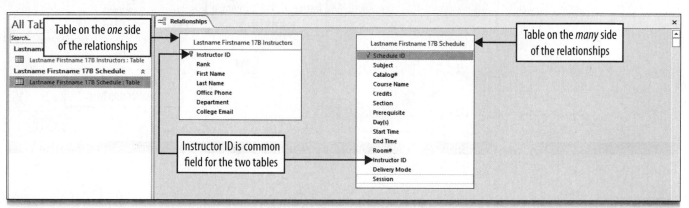

FIGURE 17.44

Microsoft Access 2016, Windows 10, Microsoft Corporation

> **NOTE** The Field That is Highlighted Does Not Matter
>
> After you rearrange the field lists in the Relationships window, the highlighted field name indicates the active field list, which is the list that you moved last. This is of no consequence for this activity.

9 In the **17B Instructors** field list, point to **Instructor ID**, and then, holding down the left mouse button, drag the field name downward and to the right into the **17B Schedule** field list until the ⬚ pointer's arrow is on top of **Instructor ID**. Release the mouse button to display the **Edit Relationships** dialog box.

As you drag, a small graphic displays to indicate that you are dragging a field name from one field list to another. A table relationship works by matching data in two fields—the common field. In these two tables, the common field has the same name—*Instructor ID*. Common fields are not required to have the same name; however, they must have the same data type and field size.

🔄 **ANOTHER WAY**   On the Design tab, in the Tools group, click Edit Relationships. In the Edit Relationships dialog box, click Create New. In the Create New dialog box, designate the tables and fields that will create the relationship.

10 Point to the title bar of the **Edit Relationships** dialog box, and then, holding down the left mouse button, drag the dialog box downward and to the right below the two field lists as shown in Figure 17.45. Release the mouse button.

By dragging the common field, you create the *one-to-many* relationship. In the 17B Instructors table, Instructor ID is the primary key. In the 17B Schedule table, Instructor ID is the *foreign key* field. The foreign key is the field in the related table used to connect to the primary key in another table. The field on the *one* side of the relationship is typically the primary key.

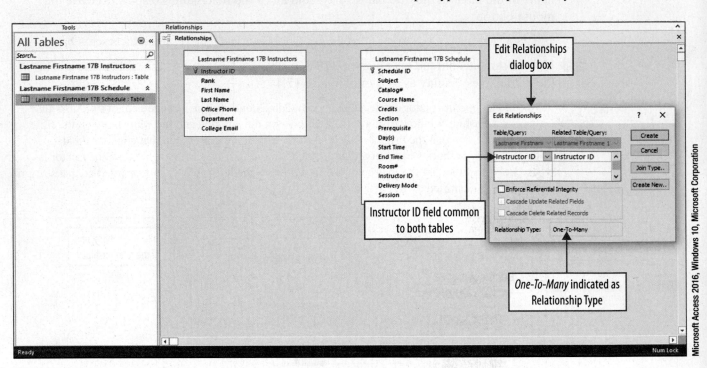

FIGURE 17.45

Activity 17.21 | Setting Relationship Options

In this Activity, you will set relationship options that will enable you to work with records in the related tables.

1 In the **Edit Relationships** dialog box, click to select the **Enforce Referential Integrity** check box. Notice that the two options under **Enforce Referential Integrity** are now available.

Referential integrity is a set of rules that Access uses to ensure that the data between related tables is valid. Enforcing referential integrity ensures that an Instructor ID cannot be added to a course in the 17B Schedule table if the Instructor ID is *not* included in the 17B Instructors table first. Similarly, enforcing referential integrity ensures that you cannot delete an instructor from the 17B Instructors table if there is a course that has been assigned to that instructor in the 17B Schedule table.

After selecting Enforce Referential Integrity, *cascade options*—relationship options that enable you to update records in related tables when referential integrity is enforced—become available for use.

2 In the **Edit Relationships** dialog box, click to select the **Cascade Update Related Fields** check box.

The *Cascade Update Related Fields* option enables you to change the data in the primary key field for the table on the *one* side of the relationship, and updates automatically change any fields in the related table that store the same data. For example, in the 17B Instructors table, if you change the data in the Instructor ID field for one instructor, Access automatically finds every scheduled course assigned to that instructor in the 17B Schedule table and changes the data in the common field, in this case, the Instructor ID field. Without this option, if you try to change the ID number for an instructor, an error message displays if there is a related record in the related table on the *many* side of the relationship.

3 In the **Edit Relationships** dialog box, click to select the **Cascade Delete Related Records** check box, and then compare your screen with Figure 17.46

The *Cascade Delete Related Records* option enables you to delete a record in the table on the *one* side of the relationship and also delete all of the related records in related tables. For example, if an instructor retires or leaves the college and the courses that the instructor teaches must be canceled because no other instructor can be found, you can delete the instructor's record from the 17B Instructors table, and then all of the courses that are assigned to that instructor in the 17B Schedule table are also deleted. Without this option, an error message displays if you try to delete the instructor's record from the 17B Instructors table. Use caution when applying this option; in many instances another instructor would be found so you would not want the course to be deleted. In this instance, you would need to change the Instructor ID in the related records before deleting the original instructor from the 17B Instructors table.

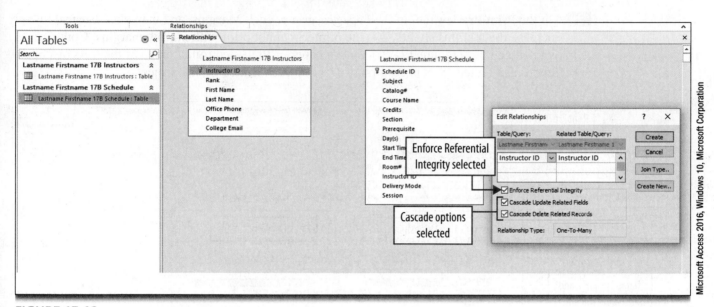

FIGURE 17.46

4 In the **Edit Relationships** dialog box, click **Create**, and then compare your screen with Figure 17.47.

A *join line*—the line connecting or joining the two tables—displays between the two tables. The join line connects the primary key field—Instructor ID—in the 17B Instructors field list to the common field—Instructor ID—in the 17B Schedule field list. On the join line, *1* indicates the *one* side of the relationship, and the infinity symbol (∞) indicates the *many* side of the relationship. These symbols display when referential integrity is enforced.

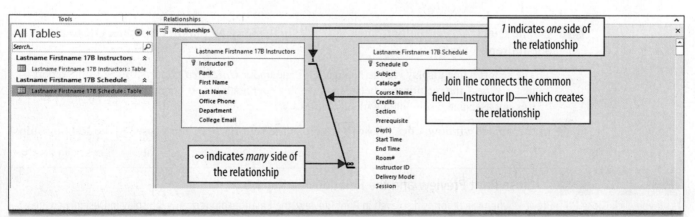

FIGURE 17.47

Microsoft Access 2016, Windows 10, Microsoft Corporation

Activity 17.22 | Printing and Saving a Relationship Report

The Relationships window provides a map of how your database tables are related, and you can print and save this information as a report.

1 On the **Design tab**, in the **Tools group**, click **Relationship Report**.

The report is created and displays in the object window in Print Preview.

2 On the **Print Preview tab**, in the **Page Size group**, click **Margins**, and then click **Normal** to increase the margins slightly—some printers cannot print with narrow margins. Compare your screen with Figure 17.48. Create a paper or PDF electronic image of the relationship report as directed. This is the first of eight objects printed in this project.

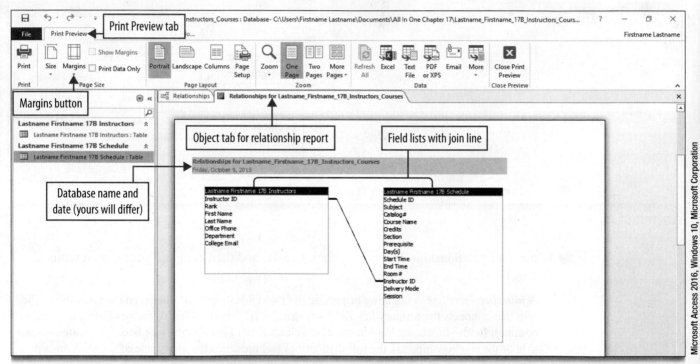

FIGURE 17.48

3 On the **Quick Access Toolbar**, click **Save** 🖫. In the **Save As** dialog box, click **OK** to accept the default report name.

The report name displays in the Navigation Pane under *Unrelated Objects*. Because the report is just a map of the relationship between the tables, and not a report containing records from a table, it is not associated or related with any tables.

4 In the object window, click **Close** ✕ to close the report, and then **Close** ✕ the **Relationships** window.

Activity 17.23 | Displaying Subdatasheet Records

When you open the table on the *one* side of the relationship, the related records from the table on the *many* side are available for you to view and to modify.

1 In the **Navigation Pane**, double-click your **17B Instructors** table to open it in the object window, and then **Close** the **Navigation Pane**.

2 On the left side of the first record—*Instructor ID* of *1224567*—click **+**, and then compare your screen with Figure 17.49.

A plus sign (+) to the left of a record in a table indicates that *related* records may exist in another table. Click the plus sign to display the related records in a ***subdatasheet***. In the first record for *Craig Fresch*, you can see that related records exist in the 17B Schedule table—he is scheduled to teach five LGL (Legal) courses. The plus signs display because you created a relationship between the two tables using the Instructor ID field—the common field.

When you click + to display the subdatasheet, the symbol changes to a minus sign (–), an indication that the subdatasheet is expanded. Click - to collapse the subdatasheet.

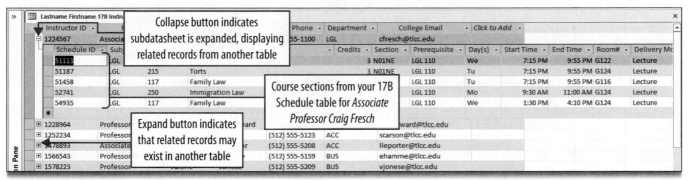

FIGURE 17.49

Microsoft Access 2016, Windows 10, Microsoft Corporation

More Knowledge | Other Types of Relationships: One-to-One and Many-to-Many

The type of relationship is determined by the placement of the primary key field. A one-to-one relationship exists between two tables when a record in one table is related to only one record in a second table. In this case, both tables use the same field as the primary key. This is most often used when data is placed in a separate table because access to that information is restricted; for example, using an Employee ID field as the primary key field, there is one table for contact information, and a second table with payroll information.

A many-to-many relationship between tables exists where many records in one table can be related to many records in another table. For example, many students can enroll in many courses. To create a many-to-many relationship, you must create a third table that contains the primary key fields from both tables. In the Relationships window, you create a join line from this table to the other two tables. In effect, you create multiple one-to-many relationships.

Activity 17.24 | Testing Cascade Options

Recall that cascade options enable you to make changes to records on the *one* side table of the relationship and update or delete records in the table on the *many* side of the relationship. In this Activity, you will change the data in the Instructor ID field—the primary key field—for one instructor, and then delete all of the records associated with another instructor from both tables.

1 In the subdatasheet for the first record—*Instructor ID* of *1224567*—notice that the first course that the instructor is scheduled to teach has a *Schedule ID* of *51113—LGL 216*. In the **17B Instructors** table, to the left of the first record, click **–** (minus sign) to collapse the subdatasheet.

2 If necessary, in the first record, in the **Instructor ID** field, select the data—**1224567**. Type **8224567** and then press ⬇ to save the record.

> If you had not enabled Cascade Update Related Fields in the Edit Relationships dialog box, an error message would have displayed.

3 Open » the **Navigation Pane**. In the **Navigation Pane**, double-click your **17B Schedule** table to open it, and then **Close** « the **Navigation Pane**.

🔄 ANOTHER WAY   Press F11 to open or close the Navigation Pane.

4 Scroll to locate the record with a **Schedule ID** of **51113**—*LGL 216*. If necessary, scroll to the right to display the **Instructor ID** field, and notice that for this record, the **Instructor ID** is **8224567**. Compare your screen with Figure 17.50.

> The Cascade Update Related Fields option enables you to change the data in the primary key field in your 17B Instructors table, and the five related records for *Craig Fresch* in the 17B Schedule table were updated to store his Instructor ID of *8224567*.

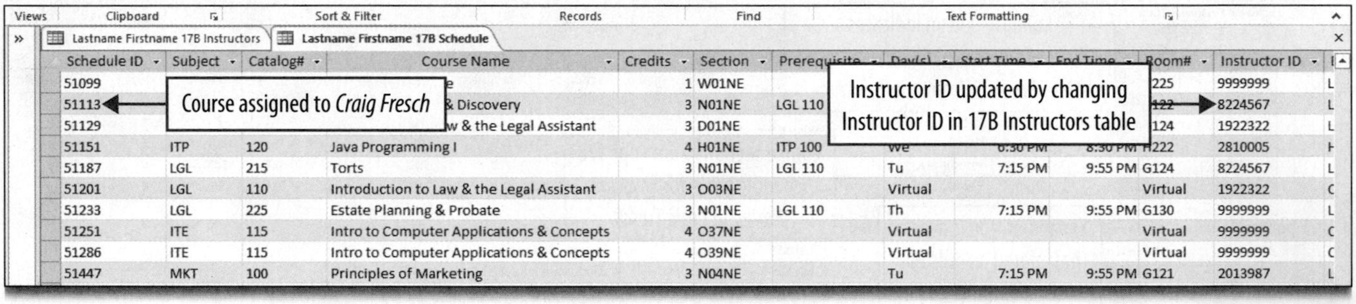

Schedule ID	Subject	Catalog#	Course Name	Credits	Section	Prerequisite	Day(s)	Start Time	End Time	Room#	Instructor ID	
51099			e	1	W01NE					225	9999999	L
51113		Course assigned to *Craig Fresch*	& Discovery	3	N01NE	LGL 110	Instructor ID updated by changing Instructor ID in 17B Instructors table		122	8224567	L
51129			w & the Legal Assistant	3	D01NE				124	1922322	L
51151	ITP	120	Java Programming I	4	H01NE	ITP 100	We	6:30 PM	8:30 PM	H222	2810005	F
51187	LGL	215	Torts	3	N01NE	LGL 110	Tu	7:15 PM	9:55 PM	G124	8224567	L
51201	LGL	110	Introduction to Law & the Legal Assistant	3	O03NE		Virtual		Virtual	1922322	C
51233	LGL	225	Estate Planning & Probate	3	N01NE	LGL 110	Th	7:15 PM	9:55 PM	G130	9999999	L
51251	ITE	115	Intro to Computer Applications & Concepts	4	O37NE		Virtual		Virtual	9999999	C
51286	ITE	115	Intro to Computer Applications & Concepts	4	O39NE		Virtual		Virtual	9999999	C
51447	MKT	100	Principles of Marketing	3	N04NE		Tu	7:15 PM	9:55 PM	G121	2013987	L

FIGURE 17.50   Microsoft Access 2016, Windows 10, Microsoft Corporation

5 **Close** ✕ your **17B Schedule** table. In your **17B Instructors** table, scroll to display the last few records. On the left side of the record for **Instructor ID** of **6145288**—*Professor Ivey Clarke*—click **+** to display the subdatasheet. Notice that this instructor is scheduled to teach two courses—*Schedule ID* of *42837* and *42930*.

6 Click **–** to collapse the subdatasheet. For the same record—*Instructor ID* of *6145288*—point to the record selector box to display the ➡ pointer, and then click to select the record. On the **Home tab**, in the **Records group**, click **Delete**.

> A message displays warning you that this record and related records in related tables will be deleted. The record you selected does not display in the table, and the next record is selected. If you had not enabled Cascade Delete Related Records, an error message would have displayed, and you would not be able to delete the record for Professor Ivey Clarke without assigning her courses to another instructor first.

🔄 ANOTHER WAY   With the record selected, press Del ; or with the record selected, right-click, and then click Delete Record.

7 In the message box, click **Yes**.

> The record for *Instructor ID* of *6145288* is deleted. On the Quick Access Toolbar, the Undo button is unavailable—if you mistakenly delete the wrong record and the related records, you must enter them again in both tables. Access cannot use Undo to undo a Delete.

8 Open » the **Navigation Pane**, open your **17B Schedule** table, and then **Close** « the **Navigation Pane**. Scroll through the records and notice that the records for a **Schedule ID** of **42837** and **42930** have been deleted from the table.

The Cascade Delete Related Records option in the Edit Relationships dialog box enables you to delete a record in the table on the *one* side of the relationship—17B Instructors—and simultaneously delete the records in the table on the *many* side of the relationship—17B Schedule—that are related to the deleted record.

9 In the object window, right-click either **object tab**, and then click **Close All** to close both tables.

> **NOTE**   Cascade Options—Record Must Be Edited or Deleted in Correct Table
>
> Changes in the data in the common field must be made in the primary key field in the table on the *one* side of the relationship— you cannot change the data in the common field in the table on the *many* side of the relationship. To delete a record and all of its associated records in another table, you must delete the record in the table on the *one* side of the relationship. You can, however, delete a related record from the table on the *many* side of the relationship—the related record in the table on the *one* side of the relationship is not deleted.

Objective 8   Sort Records in a Table

GO! Learn How
video A17-8

Sorting is the process of arranging data in a specific order based on the value in a field. For example, you can sort the names in your contact list alphabetically by each person's last name, or you can sort your music collection by the artist. As records are entered into an Access table, they display in the order in which they are added to the table. After you close the table and reopen it, the records display in order by the primary key field.

Activity 17.25 | Sorting Records in a Table in Ascending or Descending Order

In this Activity, you will determine the departments of the faculty in the Business Division by sorting the data. Data can be sorted in either ***ascending order*** or ***descending order***. Ascending order sorts text alphabetically (A to Z) and sorts numbers from the lowest number to the highest number. Descending order sorts text in reverse alphabetical order (Z to A) and sorts numbers from the highest number to the lowest number.

1 Open ⟩⟩ the **Navigation Pane**, open your **17B Instructors** table, and then **Close** ⟨⟨ the **Navigation Pane**. Notice that the records in the table are sorted in ascending order by the **Instructor ID** field, which is the primary key field.

2 In the field names row, click the **Department arrow**, click **Sort A to Z**, and then compare your screen with Figure 17.51.

To sort records in a table, click the arrow to the right of the field name in the column on which you want to sort, and then click the sort order. After a field is sorted, a small arrow in the field name box indicates the sort order. For the Department field, the small arrow points up, indicating an ascending sort, and on the ribbon, Ascending is selected.

The records display in alphabetical order by the Department field. Because the department names are now grouped together, you can quickly scroll through the table to see the instructors for each department. The first record in the table has no data in the Department field because the *Instructor ID* of *9999999* is reserved for *Staff*, a designation that is used until a scheduled course has been assigned to a specific instructor.

ANOTHER WAY   Click in the field in any record, and then on the Home tab, in the Sort & Filter group, click Ascending; or right-click in the field in any record, and then click Sort A to Z.

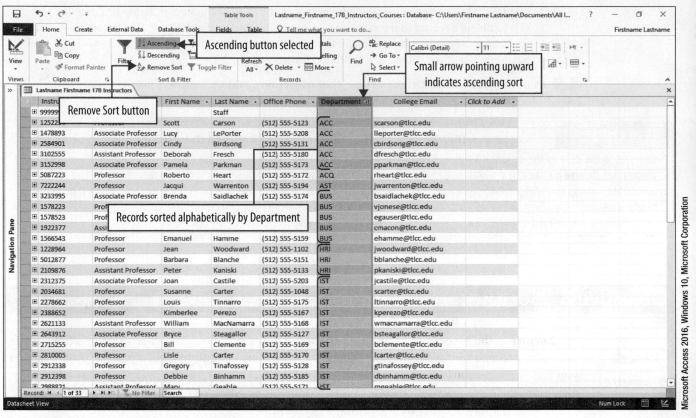

FIGURE 17.51

3 On the **Home tab**, in the **Sort & Filter group**, click **Remove Sort** to clear the sort and return the records to the default sort order, which is by the primary key field—*Instructor ID*.

4 Click the **Last Name arrow**, and then click **Sort Z to A**.

The records in the table are sorted by the Last Name field in reverse alphabetical order. The small arrow in the field name box points down, indicating a descending sort. On the ribbon, Descending is selected.

5 In the **Sort & Filter group**, click **Remove Sort** to clear the sort.

Activity 17.26 | Sorting Records in a Table on Multiple Fields

To sort a table on two or more fields, first identify the fields that will act as the ***outermost sort field*** and the ***innermost sort field***. The outermost sort field is the first level of sorting, and the innermost sort field is the second or final level of sorting. To alphabetize a table by Last Name and then First Name (also called First Name within Last Name), the Last Name field is identified as the outermost sort field. If there are duplicate last names, the records should be further sorted by the First Name field—the innermost sort field. For tables, you sort the innermost field first and then sort the outermost field.

In this Activity, you will sort the records by Last Name (innermost sort field) within the Department (outermost sort field).

1 In the **Last Name** field, click in any record. On the **Home tab**, in the **Sort & Filter group**, click **Ascending**.

The records are sorted in ascending order by Last Name—the innermost sort field.

2 ▶ Point anywhere in the **Department** field, right-click, and then click **Sort Z to A**. Compare your screen with Figure 17.52.

> The records are sorted in descending order first by Department—the outermost sort field. Within each Department grouping, the records are sorted in ascending order by Last Name— the innermost sort field. Records can be sorted on multiple fields using both ascending and descending order.

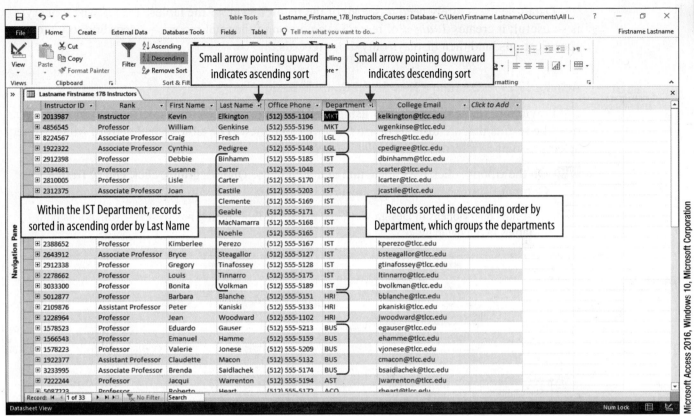

FIGURE 17.52

3 ▶ On the ribbon, click the **File tab**, click **Print**, and then click **Print Preview**. In the **Page Layout** group, click **Landscape**. In the **Zoom group**, click **Two Pages**, and notice that the table will print on two pages.

4 ▶ In the **Print group**, click **Print**. In the **Print** dialog box, under **Print Range**, click in the **From** box, type **1** and then click in the **To** box and type **1** to print only the first page. This is the second of eight objects printed in this project. If directed to submit a paper printout, click **OK**. If directed to create a PDF electronic image, in the **Publish as PDF or XPS** dialog box, click **Options**, then under **Range**, click the **Page(s)** option button, and then click **OK**.

5 ▶ In the **Close Preview group**, click **Close Print Preview**. In the object window, **Close** ☒ the table. In the message box, click **Yes** to save the changes to the sort order.

6 ▶ Open ⟫ the **Navigation Pane**, double-click your **17B Instructors** table to open it, and then **Close** ⟪ the **Navigation Pane**. Notice that the table displays the sort order you specified.

7 ▶ On the **Home tab**, in the **Sort & Filter group**, click **Remove Sort**. **Close** ☒ the table, and in the message box, click **Yes** to save the table with the sort removed.

> Generally, tables are not stored with the data sorted. Instead queries are created that sort the data, and then reports are created to display the sorted data.

Objective 9 | Create a Query in Design View

GO! Learn How
video A17-9

Recall that a select query is a database object that retrieves (selects) specific data from one or more tables and then displays the specified data in a table in Datasheet view. A query answers a question such as *Which instructors teach courses in the IST department?* Unless a query has already been designed to ask this question, you must create a new query.

Database users rarely need to see all of the records in all of the tables. That is why a query is so useful; it creates a *subset* of records—a portion of the total records—according to your specifications, and then displays only those records.

IC3
DIGITAL LITERACY
CERTIFICATION
2.04c (iv)

Activity 17.27 | Creating a New Select Query in Design View

Previously, you created a query using the Query Wizard. To create queries with more control over the results that are displayed, use Query Design view. The table or tables from which a query selects its data is referred to as the *data source*.

1 On the ribbon, click the **Create tab**, and then in the **Queries group**, click **Query Design**. Compare your screen with Figure 17.53.

A new query opens in Design view, and the Show Table dialog box displays, which lists both tables in the database.

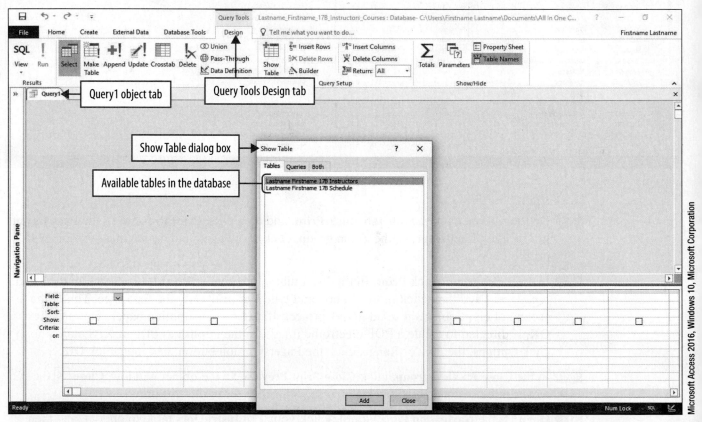

FIGURE 17.53

2 In the **Show Table** dialog box, double-click **17B Instructors**, and then, in the dialog box, click **Close**.

A field list for your 17B Instructors table displays in the upper area of the Query window. Instructor ID is the primary key field in this table. The Query window has two parts: the *table area* (upper area), which displays the field lists for tables that are used in the query, and the *design grid* (lower area), which displays the design of the query.

3 ▶ Point to the lower right corner of the field list to display the ⬉ pointer, and then, holding down the left mouse button, drag downward and to the right to resize the field list, displaying all of the field names and the entire table name. Release the mouse button. In the **17B Instructors** field list, double-click **Rank**, and then look at the design grid.

The Rank field name displays in the design grid in the Field row. You limit the fields that display in the query results by placing only the desired field names in the design grid.

4 ▶ In the **17B Instructors** field list, point to **First Name**, holding down the left mouse button, drag the field name down into the design grid until the ⬇ pointer displays in the **Field** row in the second column, and then release the mouse button. Compare your screen with Figure 17.54.

This is a second way to add field names to the design grid. When you release the mouse button, the field name displays in the Field row.

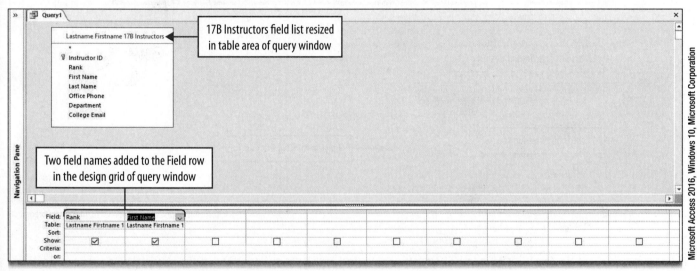

FIGURE 17.54

5 ▶ In the design grid, in the **Field** row, click in the third column, and then click the **arrow** that displays. From the list, click **Last Name** to add the field to the design grid.

This is a third way to add field names to the design grid.

6 ▶ Using one of the three techniques you just practiced, add the **Office Phone** field to the fourth column and the **Department** field to the fifth column in the design grid.

Microsoft Access 2016, Windows 10, Microsoft Corporation

IC3
DIGITAL LITERACY
CERTIFICATION
2.04c (iv)

Activity 17.28 | Running, Saving, Printing, and Closing a Query

Once a query is designed, you **run** it to display the results. When you run a query, Access looks at the records in the table (or tables) you have included in the query, finds the records that match the specified conditions (if any), and displays only those records in a datasheet. Only the fields that you have added to the design grid display in the query results. The query always runs using the current table or tables, presenting the most up-to-date information.

1 On the **Design tab**, in the **Results group**, click **Run**, and then compare your screen with Figure 17.55.

This query answers the question, *What is the rank, first name, last name, office phone number, and department of all of the instructors in the 17B Instructors table?* A query is a subgroup of the records in the table, arranged in Datasheet view, using the fields and conditions that you specify in the design grid. The five fields you specified in the design grid display in columns, and the records from the 17B Instructors table display in rows.

ANOTHER WAY On the Design tab, in the Results group, click the upper portion of the View button, which runs the query by switching to Datasheet view.

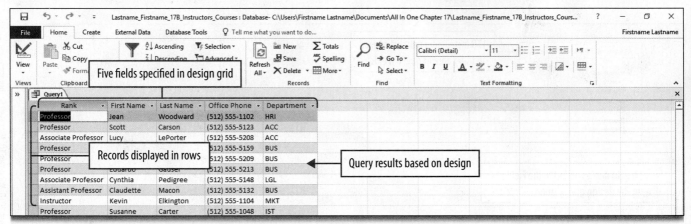

FIGURE 17.55

Microsoft Access 2016, Windows 10, Microsoft Corporation

2 On the **Quick Access Toolbar**, click **Save** 🖫. In the **Save As** dialog box, type **Lastname Firstname 17B Instructors Query** and then click **OK**.

The query name displays on the object tab in the object window. Save your queries if you are likely to ask the same question again; doing so will save you the effort of creating the query again to answer the same question—just run the query again.

ALERT! **Does a message display after entering a query name?**

Query names are limited to 64 characters. For all projects, if you have a long last name or first name that results in your query name exceeding the 64-character limit, ask your instructor how you should abbreviate your name.

---

3 Click the **File tab**, click **Print**, and then click **Print Preview**. Create a paper or PDF electronic image as directed, and then click **Close Print Preview**. This is the third of eight objects printed in this project.

Queries answer questions and gather information from the data in tables. Typically, queries are created as a basis for a report, but query results can be printed like any table of data.

4 ▶ Close ⊠ the query. **Open** ⊗ the **Navigation Pane**, and then notice that your **17B Instructors Query** object displays under your **17B Instructors** table object.

The new query name displays in the Navigation Pane under the table with which it is related—the 17B Instructors table, which is the data source. Only the design of the query is saved; the records reside in the table object. Each time you open a query, Access runs it and displays the results based on the data stored in the data source. Thus, the results of the query always reflect the most up-to-date information.

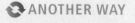

Objective 10 ⟩ Create a New Query From an Existing Query

GO! Learn How
video A17-10

You can create a new query from scratch or you can open an existing query, save it with a new name, and modify the design to answer another question. Using an existing query saves you time if your new query uses all or some of the same fields and conditions in an existing query.

Activity 17.29 │ Copying an Existing Query

1 ▶ In the **Navigation Pane**, right-click your **17B Instructors Query**, and then click **Copy**.

2 ▶ In the **Navigation Pane**, point to a blank area, right-click, and then click **Paste**.

The Paste As dialog box displays, which enables you to name the copied query.

🔁 ANOTHER WAY To create a copy of the query, in the Navigation Pane, click the query name to select it. On the Home tab, in the Clipboard group, click Copy. On the Home tab, in the Clipboard group, click the upper portion of the Paste button.

3 ▶ In the **Paste As** dialog box, type **Lastname Firstname 17B Instructor IDs Query** and then click **OK**.

A new query, based on a copy of your 17B Instructors Query, is created and displays in the object window and in the Navigation Pane under its data source—your 17B Instructors table.

More Knowledge │ **Rename a Query**

If the query name is not correct, you can rename it as long as the query is closed. In the Navigation Pane, right-click the query name, and then click Rename. Edit the current name or type a new name, and then press [Enter] to accept the change.

4 ▶ In the **Navigation Pane**, double-click your **17B Instructor IDs Query** to run the query and display the query results in **Datasheet** view. **Close** ⊗ the **Navigation Pane**.

🔁 ANOTHER WAY To create a copy of a query using a new name, click the File tab, and then click Save As. Under Save As, double-click Save Object As. In the Save As dialog box, click in the Name box and type the name of the new query.

IC3
DIGITAL LITERACY
CERTIFICATION
2.04c (iv)

Activity 17.30 │ Modifying the Design of a Query

1 ▶ On the **Home tab**, in the **Views group**, click **View** to switch to **Design** view.

🔁 ANOTHER WAY On the Home tab, in the Views group, click the View arrow, and then click Design View; or on the right side of the status bar, click the Design View button.

2 In the design grid, point to the thin gray selection bar above the **Office Phone** field name to display the ⬇ pointer, and then compare your screen with Figure 17.56.

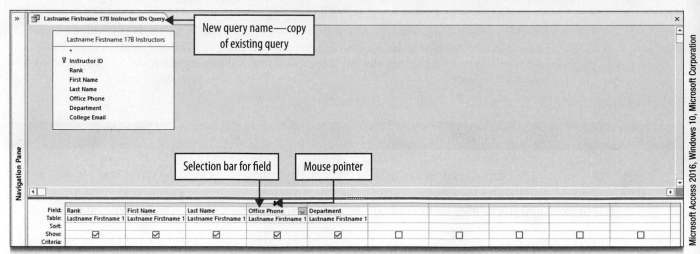

Lastname Firstname 17B Instructor IDs Query

New query name—copy of existing query

Lastname Firstname 17B Instructors

Instructor ID
Rank
First Name
Last Name
Office Phone
Department
College Email

Selection bar for field

Mouse pointer

Field:	Rank	First Name	Last Name	Office Phone	Department					
Table:	Lastname Firstname 1	Lastname Firstname 1	Lastname Firstname 1	Lastname Firstname 1	Lastname Firstname 1					
Sort:										
Show:	☑	☑	☑	☑	☑	☐	☐	☐	☐	☐
Criteria:										

FIGURE 17.56

3 With the ⬇ pointer displayed in the selection bar above the **Office Phone** field name, click to select the column, and then press (Del).

This action deletes the field from the query design only—it has no effect on the field in the data source—17B Instructors table. The Department field moves to the left. Similarly, by using the selection bar, you can drag to select multiple fields and delete them at one time.

🔄 **ANOTHER WAY**   In the design grid, click in the field name. On the Design tab, in the Query Setup group, click Delete Columns; or right-click the field name, and then click Cut; or click in the field name, and on the Home tab, in the Records group, click Delete.

4 Point to the selection bar above the **First Name** column, and then click to select the column. In the selected column, point to the selection bar to display the ▨ pointer, and then drag to the right until a dark vertical line displays on the right side of the **Last Name** column. Release the mouse button to position the **First Name** field in the third column.

To rearrange fields in a query, first select the field to move, and then drag it to a new position in the design grid.

5 Using the technique you just practiced, move the **Department** field to the left of the **Rank** field.

6 From the field list, drag the **Instructor ID** field down to the first column in the design grid until the ▨ pointer displays, and then release the mouse button. Compare your screen with Figure 17.57.

The Instructor ID field displays in the first column, and the remaining four fields move to the right. Use this method to insert a field to the left of a field already displayed in the design grid.

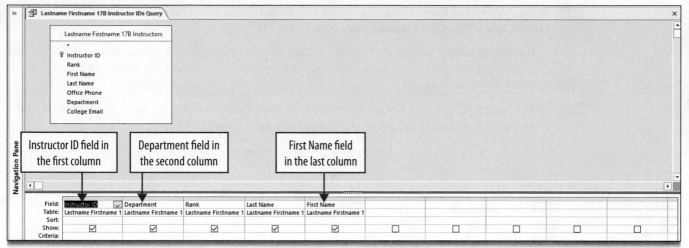

Figure 17.57 shows the Access query design grid with the following callouts:

- **Instructor ID field in the first column**
- **Department field in the second column**
- **First Name field in the last column**

The query window title is "Lastname Firstname 17B Instructor IDs Query" with a table "Lastname Firstname 17B Instructors" containing fields: Instructor ID, Rank, First Name, Last Name, Office Phone, Department, College Email.

Design grid:

Field:	Instructor ID	Department	Rank	Last Name	First Name				
Table:	Lastname Firstname 1	Lastname Firstname 1	Lastname Firstname 1	Lastname Firstname 1	Lastname Firstname 1				
Sort:									
Show:	☑	☑	☑	☑	☑	☐	☐	☐	☐
Criteria:									

FIGURE 17.57

7 On the **Design tab**, in the **Results group**, click **Run**.

This query answers the question, *What is the instructor ID, department, rank, last name, and first name of every instructor in the 17B Instructors table?* The results of the query are a subgroup of the records stored in the 17B Instructors table. The records are sorted by the table's primary key field—Instructor ID.

8 On the **File tab**, click **Print**, and then click **Print Preview**. Create a paper or PDF electronic image as directed, and then click **Close Print Preview**. This is the fourth of eight objects printed in this project.

9 Close ⊠ the query. In the message box, click **Yes** to save the changes to the query design—deleting a field, moving two fields, and adding a field. **Open** ⟩⟩ the **Navigation Pane**.

The query is saved and closed, and the query name displays in the Navigation Pane under the related table. Recall that only the *design* of the query is saved; the records reside in the related table or tables.

Objective 11 Sort Query Results

GO! Learn How
video A17-11

You can sort the results of a query in ascending or descending order in either Datasheet view or Design view. Use Design view if your query results should always display in a specified sort order, or if you intend to use the sorted results in a report.

Activity 17.31 │ Sorting Query Results

In this Activity, you will save an existing query with a new name, and then sort the query results by using the Sort row in Design view.

1 In the **Navigation Pane**, right-click your **17B Instructor IDs Query**, and then click **Copy**. In the **Navigation Pane**, point to a blank area, right-click, and then click **Paste**.

2 In the **Paste As** dialog box, type **Lastname Firstname 17B Department Sort Query** and then click **OK**. Increase the width of the **Navigation Pane** so that the names of all of the objects display fully.

A new query is created based on a copy of your 17B Instructor IDs Query; that is, the new query includes the same fields in the same order as the query on which it is based. The query does not need to be open to save it with another name; you can select the object name in the Navigation Pane.

3 In the **Navigation Pane**, right-click your **17B Department Sort Query**, and then click **Design View**. **Close** ‹‹ the **Navigation Pane**.

Use this technique to display the query in Design view if you are redesigning the query. Recall that if you double-click a query name in the Navigation Pane, Access runs the query and displays the query results in Datasheet view.

4 In the design grid, in the **Sort** row, under **Last Name**, click to display the insertion point and an arrow. Click the **arrow**, click **Ascending**, and then compare your screen with Figure 17.58.

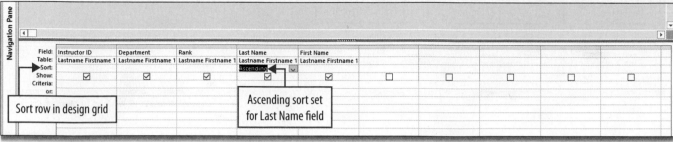

FIGURE 17.58   Microsoft Access 2016, Windows 10, Microsoft Corporation

5 On the **Design tab**, in the **Results group**, click **Run**.

In the query results, the records are sorted in ascending order by the Last Name field, and two instructors have the same last name of *Carter*—*Susanne* and *Lisle*.

6 On the **Home tab**, in the **Views group**, click the upper portion of the **View** button to switch to **Design** view.

7 In the design grid, click in the **Sort** row under **First Name**, click the **arrow**, and then click **Ascending**. **Run** the query.

In the query results, the records are sorted first by the Last Name field. If two instructors have the same last name, then those records are sorted by the First Name field. The two instructors with the same last name of *Carter* are sorted by their first names, and the two records with the same last name of *Fresch* are sorted by their first names.

8 Switch to **Design** view. In the design grid, click in the **Sort** row under **Department**, click the **arrow**, and then click **Descending**. **Run** the query, and then compare your screen with Figure 17.59.

In Design view, fields with a Sort setting are sorted from left to right. That is, the sorted field on the left becomes the outermost sort field, and the sorted field on the right becomes the innermost sort field. Thus, the records in this query are sorted first in descending order by the Department field—the leftmost sort field. Then, within each department, the records are sorted in ascending order by the Last Name field. And, finally, within each duplicate last name, the records are sorted in ascending order by the First Name field.

If you run a query and the sorted results are not what you intended, be sure the fields are displayed from left to right according to the groupings that you desire.

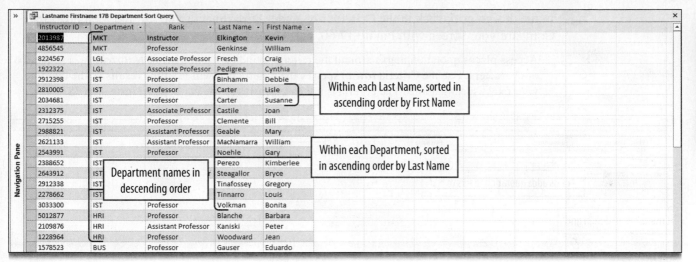

Within each Last Name, sorted in ascending order by First Name

Within each Department, sorted in ascending order by Last Name

Department names in descending order

FIGURE 17.59

Microsoft Access 2016, Windows 10, Microsoft Corporation

9 Display the query results in **Print Preview**. Create a paper or PDF electronic image as directed, and then click **Close Print Preview**. This is the fifth of eight objects printed in this project. **Close** ☒ the query. In the message box, click **Yes** to save the changes to the query design.

More **Knowledge**   **Sorting in Design View or Datasheet View**

If you add a sort order to the *design* of a query, it remains as a permanent part of the query design. If you use the sort buttons in Datasheet view, the sort order will override the sort order of the query design and can be saved as part of the query. A sort order designated in Datasheet view does not display in the Sort row of the query design grid. As with sorting tables, in Datasheet view, a small arrow displays to the right of the field name to indicate the sort order of the field.

Objective 12   Specify Criteria in a Query

GO! Learn How
video A17-12

Queries locate information in a table based on *criteria* that you specify as part of the query design. Criteria are conditions that identify the specific records for which you are looking. Criteria enable you to ask a more specific question; therefore, you will get a more specific result. For example, to find out how many instructors are in the IST department, limit the results to display only that specific department by entering criteria in the design grid.

DIGITAL LITERACY
CERTIFICATION
2.04c (iv)

Activity 17.32 │ **Specifying Text Criteria in a Query**

In this Activity, you will assist Dean Judkins by creating a query to answer the question, *Which instructors are in the IST Department?*.

1 On the ribbon, click the **Create tab**, and then in the **Queries group**, click **Query Design**.

2 In the **Show Table** dialog box, double-click your **17B Instructors** table to add it to the table area, and then **Close** the **Show Table** dialog box.

3 By dragging the lower right corner, resize the field list to display all of the field names and the table name. Add the following fields to the design grid in the order given: **Department**, **Instructor ID**, **Rank**, **First Name**, and **Last Name**.

4 In the design grid, click in the **Criteria** row under **Department**, type **IST** and then press Enter. Compare your screen with Figure 17.60.

Access places quotation marks around the criteria to indicate that this is a *text string*—a sequence of characters. Use the Criteria row to specify the criteria that will limit the results of the query to your exact specifications. The criteria is not case sensitive; you can type *ist* instead of *IST*.

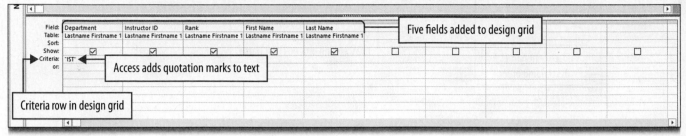

FIGURE 17.60

5 **Run** the query, and then compare your screen with Figure 17.61.

Thirteen records display. There are 13 instructors in the IST Department; or, more specifically, there are 13 records that have *IST* in the Department field.

Department	Instructor ID	Rank	First Name	Last Name
IST	2034681	Professor	Susanne	Carter
IST	2278662	Professor	Louis	Tinnarro
IST	2312375	Associate Professor	Joan	Castile
IST	2388652	Professor	Kimberlee	Perezo
IST	2543991	Professor	Gary	Noehle
IST	2621133	Assistant Professor	William	MacNamarra
IST	2643912	Associate Professor	Bryce	Steagallor
IST	2715255	Professor	Bill	Clemente
IST	2810005	Professor	Lisle	Carter
IST	2912338	Professor	Gregory	Tinafossey
IST	2912398	Professor	Debbie	Binhamm
IST	2988821	Assistant Professor	Mary	Geable
IST	3033300	Professor	Bonita	Volkman

Records sorted in ascending order by the Last Name field

Within Last Name field, records sorted in ascending order by the First Name field

Thirteen records match criteria—*IST* in the Department field

FIGURE 17.61

6 **Save** the query as **Lastname Firstname 17B IST Query** and then display the query results in **Print Preview**. Create a paper or PDF electronic image as directed, and then click **Close Print Preview**. This is the sixth of eight objects printed in this project.

7 **Close** the query, **Open** the **Navigation Pane**, and then notice that your **17B IST Query** object name displays under your **17B Instructors** table—its data source.

Recall that in the Navigation Pane, queries display an icon of two overlapping datasheets.

Activity 17.33 | Specifying Criteria and Hiding the Field in the Query Results

So far, all of the fields that you included in the query design have also been included in the query results. There are times when you need to use the field in the query design, but you do not need to display that field in the results—usually, when the data in the field is the same for all of the records. In this Activity, you will create a query to answer the question, *Which instructors have a rank of Professor?*

1 ▶ **Close** ⟨«⟩ the **Navigation Pane.** On the **Create tab**, in the **Queries group**, click **Query Design**.

2 ▶ In the **Show Table** dialog box, double-click your **17B Instructors** table to add it to the table area, and then **Close** the **Show Table** dialog box.

3 ▶ Resize the field list, and then add the following fields to the design grid in the order given: **Instructor ID**, **First Name**, **Last Name**, and **Rank**.

4 ▶ Click in the **Sort** row under **Last Name**, click the **arrow**, and then click **Ascending**.

5 ▶ Click in the **Criteria** row under **Rank**, type **professor** and then press Enter. Compare your screen with Figure 17.62.

> Recall that criteria are not case sensitive. As you start typing *professor*, a list of functions displays, from which you can select if a function is included in your criteria. After pressing Enter, the insertion point moves to the next criteria box, and quotation marks are added around the text string that you entered.

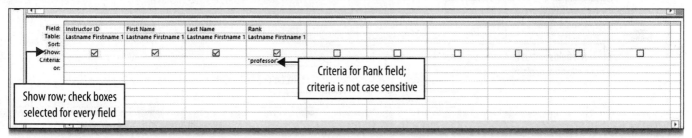

FIGURE 17.62   Microsoft Excel 2016, Windows 10, Microsoft Corporation

6 ▶ In the design grid, in the **Show** row, notice that a check box is selected for every field. **Run** the query.

> Eighteen records meet the criteria—*professor* in the *Rank* field. In the Rank column, every record displays *Professor*, and the records are sorted in ascending order by the Last Name field.

7 ▶ Switch to **Design** view. In the design grid, in the **Show** row under **Rank**, click to clear the check box.

> Because it is repetitive and not particularly useful to display *Professor* for every record in the query results, clear the Show check box so that the field is hidden or does not display. You should, however, always run the query first before clearing the Show check box to be sure that the correct records display.

8 ▶ **Run** the query, and then notice that the *Rank* field does not display even though it was used to specify criteria in the query.

> The same 18 records display, but the *Rank* field is hidden from the query results. Although the Rank field is included in the query design so that you could specify the criteria of *professor*, it is not necessary to display the field in the results. When appropriate, clear the Show check box to avoid cluttering the query results with data that is not useful.

9 ▶ **Save** 🖫 the query as **Lastname Firstname 17B Professor Query** and then display the query results in **Print Preview**. Create a paper or PDF electronic image as directed, and then click **Close Print Preview**. This is the seventh of eight objects printed in this project. **Close** ⟨X⟩ the query.

Activity 17.34 | Using *Is Null* Criteria to Find Empty Fields

Sometimes you must locate records where data is missing. You can locate such records by using *Is Null* as the criteria in a field. *Is Null* is used to find empty fields. Additionally, you can display only the records where data has been entered in the field by using the criteria of *Is Not Null*, which excludes records where the specified field is empty. In this Activity, you will design a query to answer the question, *Which scheduled courses have no credits listed?*

1 On the **Create tab**, in the **Queries group**, click **Query Design**. In the **Show Table** dialog box, double-click your **17B Schedule** table to add it to the table area, and then **Close** the **Show Table** dialog box.

2 Resize the field list, and then add the following fields to the design grid in the order given: **Subject, Catalog#, Section, Course Name**, and **Credits**.

3 Click in the **Criteria** row under **Credits**, type **is null** and then press Enter.

Access capitalizes *is null*. The criteria *Is Null* examines the Credits field and locates records that do *not* have any data entered in the field.

4 Click in the **Sort** row under **Subject**, click the **arrow**, and then click **Ascending**. **Sort** the **Catalog#** field in **Ascending** order, and then **Sort** the **Section** field in **Ascending** order. Compare your screen with Figure 17.63.

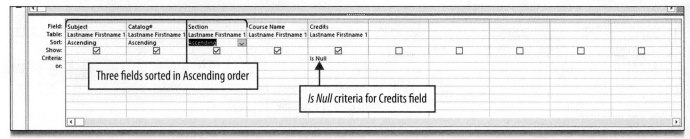

FIGURE 17.63   Microsoft Access 2016, Windows 10, Microsoft Corporation

5 **Run** the query, and then compare your screen with Figure 17.64.

Four scheduled courses do not have credits listed—the Credits field is empty. The records are sorted in ascending order first by the Subject field, then by the Catalog# field, and then by the Section field. Using the information displayed in the query results, a course scheduler can more easily locate the records in the table and enter the credits for these courses.

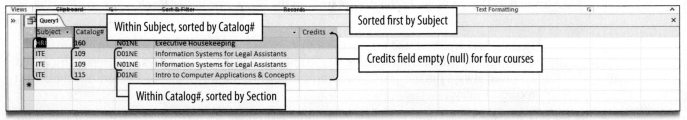

FIGURE 17.64   Microsoft Access 2016, Windows 10, Microsoft Corporation

6 Save 🖫 the query as **Lastname Firstname 17B No Credits Query**, and then display the query results in **Print Preview**. Create a paper or PDF electronic image as instructed, and then click **Close Print Preview**. This is the eighth of eight objects printed in this project.

7 Close ☒ the query. **Open** ⟫ the **Navigation Pane**, and resize it so all object names are fully visible. Notice that your **17B No Credits Query** object displays under your **17B Schedule** table object, its data source.

8 On the right side of the title bar, click **Close** ☒ to close the database and **Close** Access. As directed by your instructor, submit your database and the paper or PDF electronic images of the eight objects—relationship report, sorted table, and six queries—that are the results of this project.

END | You have completed Project 17B

GO! With Google

Objective	Export a Relationship Report to a PDF File, Save the PDF File to Google Drive, and then Share the File

Access web apps are designed to work with Microsoft's SharePoint, a service for setting up websites to share and manage documents. Your college may not have SharePoint installed, so you will use other tools to share objects from your database so that you can work collaboratively with others. Recall that Google Drive is Google's free, web-based word processor, spreadsheet, slide show, form, and data storage and sharing service. For Access, you can export a database object to an Excel worksheet, a PDF file, or a text file, and then save the file to Google Drive.

ALERT!	Working with Web-Based Applications and Services

Computer programs and services on the web receive continuous updates and improvements, so the steps to complete this web-based activity may differ from the ones shown. You can often look at the screens and the information presented to determine how to complete the activity.

If you do not already have a Google account, you will need to create one before doing this activity. Go to http://google.com and in the upper right corner, click Sign In. On the Sign In screen, click Create Account. On the Create your Google Account page, complete the form, read and agree to the Terms of Service and Privacy Policy, and then click Next step. On the Welcome screen, click Get Started.

Activity | Exporting a Relationship Report to a PDF File, Saving the PDF File to Google Drive, and Sharing the File

In this Activity, you will export your Relationships Report object to a PDF file, upload your PDF file to Google Drive, and then share the file.

1 Start Access, navigate to your **All In One Chapter 17** folder, and then open your **17B_Instructors_Courses** database file. On the **Message Bar**, click **Enable Content**. In the **Navigation Pane**, click your **Relationships for 17B Instructors Courses** object to select it.

2 On the ribbon, click the **External Data tab**, and then in the **Export group**, click **PDF or XPS**. In the **Publish as PDF or XPS** dialog box, navigate to your **All In One Chapter 17** folder. In the **File Save** dialog box, click in the **File name** box, and then using your own name, type **Lastname_Firstname_AC_17B_Web** and be sure that the **Open file after publishing** check box is selected and the **Minimum size (publishing online)** option button is selected. Click **Publish.** If necessary, choose the application with which you want to display the file.

The PDF file is created and opens in Microsoft Edge, Adobe Reader, or Adobe Acrobat, depending on the software that is installed on your computer.

3 If necessary, close the view of the PDF file. In the **Export – PDF** dialog box, click **Close**, and then **Close** ☒ Access.

4 From the desktop, open your browser, navigate to **http://google.com**, and then sign in to your Google account. Click the **Google Apps** menu ⦙⦙⦙, and then click **Drive** ☁. Open your **GO! Web Projects** folder—or click New to create and then open this folder if necessary.

5 On the left, click **NEW**, click **File upload**. In the **Open** dialog box, navigate to your **All In One Chapter 17** folder, and then double-click your **Lastname_Firstname_AC_17B_Web** file to upload it to Google Drive. When the title bar of the message box indicates *Uploads completed*, **Close** the message box. A second message box may display temporarily.

6 In the file list, click your **Lastname_Firstname_AC_17B_Web** PDF file one time to select it.

7 At the top of the window, click **Share** 👤.

8 In the **Share with others** dialog box, with your insertion point blinking in the **Enter names or email addresses** box, type the email address that you use at your college. Click **Can edit**, and click **Can comment**. Click in the **Add a note** box, and then type **This relationship report identifies tables that can be used together to create other objects in the database.** Compare your screen with Figure A.

(GO! With Google continues on the next page)

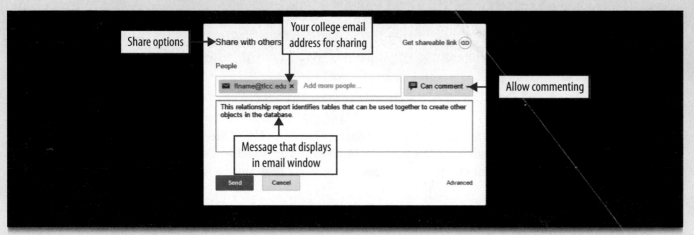

FIGURE A

Google inc.

If you upload a table that you exported as an Excel spreadsheet or Word document and that you want to enable others to add records, be sure that you change the Sharing permission to *Can edit*.

9 In the **Share with others** dialog box, click **Send**.

If your college is not using Google accounts, you may have to confirm sending the message with a link.

10 At the top of the window, click **Share** 👤. In the **Share with others** dialog box, notice that the file has been shared with your college email account. Start the **Snipping Tool**. In the **Snipping Tool** dialog box, click the **New arrow**, and then click **Full-screen Snip**.

11 On the **Snipping Tool** toolbar, click the **Save Snip** button 💾. In the **Save As** dialog box, navigate to your **All**

In One Chapter 17 folder. Click in the **File name** box, type **Lastname_Firstname_a17B_Web_Snip** and then be sure that the **Save as type** box displays **JPEG file**, and then click **Save**. **Close** ✕ the **Snipping Tool** window.

12 In the **Share with Others** dialog box, click **Done** in Google Drive, click your Google Drive name, and then click **Sign out**. **Close** your browser window.

13 If directed to submit a paper printout of your PDF and snip file, follow the directions given in the Note below. As directed by your instructor, submit your pdf file and your snip file that are the results of this project. Your instructor may also request that you submit a copy of the email that was sent to you notifying you of the shared file.

> **NOTE** Printing your PDF and Snip .JPG File
>
> Using File Explorer, navigate to your All In One Chapter 17 folder. Locate and double-click your a17B_Google file. On the toolbar, click the Print file button. Then Close your default PDF reader. In your All In One Chapter 17 folder, locate and double-click your a17B_Web_Snip file. If this is the first time you have tried to open a .jpg file, you will be asked to identify a program. If you are not sure which program to use, select Paint or Windows Photo Viewer. From the ribbon, menu bar, or toolbar, click the Print command, and then Close the program window.

Athletic Scholarships Database

PROJECT ACTIVITIES

In Activities 17.35 through 17.50, you will assist Roberto Garza, Athletic Director for Texas Lakes Community College, in creating queries to locate information about athletic scholarships that have been awarded to students. Your completed database objects will look similar to Figure 17.65.

PROJECT FILES

 If your instructor wants you to submit Project 17C in the MyITLab grader system, log in to MyITLab, locate Grader Project 17C, and then download the files for this project.

For Project 17C, you will need the following files:

a17C_Athletes_Scholarships
a17C_Athletes (Excel workbook)

You will save your document as:

Lastname_Firstname_17C_Athletes_Scholarships

PROJECT RESULTS

GO!
Walk Thru
Project 17C

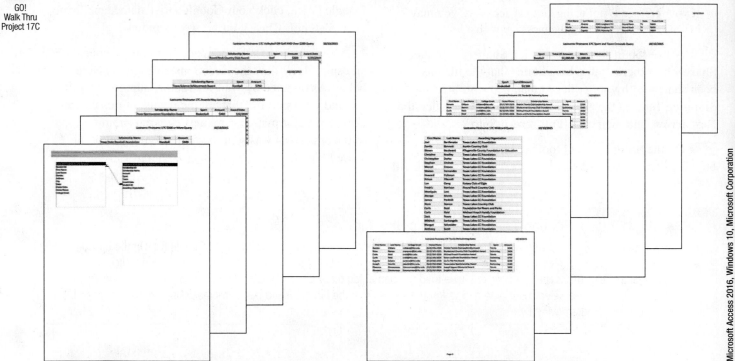

FIGURE 17.65 Project 17C Athletic Scholarships

Microsoft Access 2016, Windows 10, Microsoft Corporation

In this project, using your own name, you will create the following database and objects. Your instructor may ask you to submit printouts or PDF electronic images:

Lastname_Firstname_17C_Athletes_Scholarships	Database file
Lastname Firstname 17C Relationships	Relationships Report
Lastname Firstname 17C $300 or More Query	Query
Lastname Firstname 17C Awards May-June Query	Query
Lastname Firstname 17C Football AND Over $500	Query
Lastname Firstname 17C Volleyball OR Golf AND Over $200 Query	Query
Lastname Firstname 17C Tennis OR Swimming Query	Query
Lastname Firstname 17C Wildcard Query	Query
Lastname Firstname 17C Alumni Donations Query	Query
Lastname Firstname 17C Total by Sport Query	Query
Lastname Firstname 17C Sport and Team Crosstab Query	Query
Lastname Firstname 17C City Parameter Query	Query (Round Rock)

Objective 13 Specify Numeric Criteria in a Query

GO! Learn How
video A17-13

Criteria can be set for fields containing numeric data. When you design your table, set the appropriate data type for fields that will contain numbers, currency, or dates so that mathematical calculations can be performed.

Activity 17.35 | Opening, Renaming, and Saving an Existing Database and Importing a Spreadsheet as a New Table

> **ALERT!** **To submit as an autograded project, log into MyITLab and download the files for this project and begin with those files instead of the a17C_ Athletes_Scholarships file. For Project 17C using the Grader, begin working with the database in Step 3. For Grader to award points accurately, when saving an object, do not include your Lastname Firstname at the beginning of the object name.**

In this Activity, you will open, rename, and save an existing database, and then import an Excel spreadsheet as a new table in the database.

1 Start Access. In the Access opening screen, click **Open Other Files**. Under **Open**, click **Browse** and then navigate to the location where your student data files are stored. Double-click **a17C_Athletes_Scholarships** to open the database.

2 On the **File tab**, click **Save As**. Under **File Types**, be sure **Save Database As** is selected, and on the right, under **Database File Types**, be sure **Access Database** is selected, and then click **Save As**. In the **Save As** dialog box, navigate to your **All In One Chapter 17** folder, click in the **File name** box, type **Lastname_Firstname_17C_Athletes_Scholarships** and then press Enter.

3 On the **Message Bar**, click **Enable Content**. In the **Navigation Pane**, right-click **17C Scholarships Awarded**, and then click **Rename**. Type **Lastname Firstname 17C Scholarships Awarded** and then double-click the table name to open it in **Datasheet** view. **Close** [«] the **Navigation Pane**, and then examine the data in the table. Compare your screen with Figure 17.66.

In this table, Mr. Garza tracks the names and amounts of scholarships awarded to student athletes. Students are identified only by their Student ID numbers, and the primary key is the Scholarship ID field.

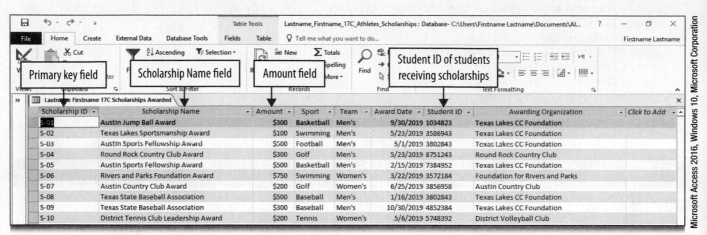

FIGURE 17.66

4 **Close** [×] the table. On the ribbon, click the **External Data tab**, and then in the **Import & Link group**, click **Excel**. In the **Get External Data – Excel Spreadsheet** dialog box, to the right of the **File name** box, click **Browse**.

5 In the **File Open** dialog box, navigate to your student data files, and then double-click **a17C_ Athletes**. Be sure that the **Import the source data into a new table in the current database** option button is selected, and then click **OK**.

The Import Spreadsheet Wizard opens and displays the spreadsheet data.

6 In the upper left area of the wizard, select the **First Row Contains Column Headings** check box. In the wizard, click **Next**, and then click **Next** again.

7 In the wizard, click the **Choose my own primary key** option button, and then be sure that **Student ID** displays in the box.

In the new table, Student ID will be designated as the primary key. No two students have the same Student ID.

8 Click **Next**. With the text selected in the **Import to Table** box, type **Lastname Firstname 17C Athletes** and then click **Finish**. In the **Get External Data – Excel Spreadsheet** dialog box, click **Close**.

9 **Open** [»] the **Navigation Pane**, and increase the width of the pane so that the two table names display fully. In the **Navigation Pane**, right-click your **17C Athletes** table, and then click **Design View**. **Close** [«] the **Navigation Pane**.

10 To the right of **Student ID**, click in the **Data Type** box, click the **arrow**, and then click **Short Text**. For the **Postal Code** field, change the **Data Type** to **Short Text**, and in the **Field Properties** area, click **Field Size**, type **5** and then press [Enter]. In the **Field Name** column, click **State**, set the **Field Size** to **2** and then press [Enter]. Compare your screen with Figure 17.67.

Recall that numeric data that does not represent a quantity and is not used in a calculation, such as the Student ID and Postal Code, should be assigned a data type of Short Text.

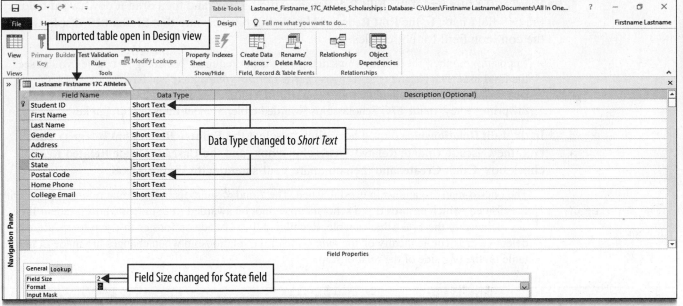

FIGURE 17.67

Microsoft Access 2016, Windows 10, Microsoft Corporation

11 On the **Design tab**, in the **Views group**, click the top half of the **View button** to switch to **Datasheet** view. In the message box, click **Yes** to save the table. In the second message box, click **Yes**—no data will be lost. Take a moment to examine the data in the imported table.

12 In the datasheet, to the left of the **Student ID** field name, click the **Select All** button. On the **Home tab**, in the **Records group**, click **More**, and then click **Field Width**. In the **Column Width** dialog box, click **Best Fit**. Click in any record to cancel the selection, **Save** the table, and then **Close** the table.

Activity 17.36 | Creating a One-to-Many Table Relationship

In this Activity, you will create a one-to-many relationship between your 17C Athletes table and your 17C Scholarships Awarded table by using the common field—*Student ID*.

1 Click the **Database Tools tab**, and then in the **Relationships group**, click **Relationships**.

2 In the **Show Table** dialog box, double-click your **17C Athletes** table, and then double-click your **17C Scholarships Awarded** table to add both tables to the **Relationships** window. **Close** the **Show Table** dialog box.

3 Point to the title bar of the field list on the right, and drag the field list to the right until there are approximately three inches of space between the field lists. By dragging the lower right corner of the field list, resize each field list to display all of the field names and the entire table name.

> Repositioning and resizing the field lists are not required, but doing so makes it easier for you to view the field names and the join line when creating relationships.

4 In the **17C Athletes** field list, point to **Student ID**, and then, holding down the left mouse button, drag the field name into the **17C Scholarships Awarded** field list on top of **Student ID**. Release the mouse button to display the **Edit Relationships** dialog box.

5 Point to the title bar of the **Edit Relationships** dialog box, and then drag it downward below the two field lists. In the **Edit Relationships** dialog box, be sure that **Student ID** displays as the common field for both tables.

> Repositioning the Edit Relationships dialog box is not required, but doing so enables you to see the field lists. The Relationship Type is *One-To-Many*—one athlete can have *many* scholarships. The common field in both tables is the *Student ID* field. In the 17C Athletes table, Student ID is the primary key. In the 17C Scholarships Awarded table, Student ID is the foreign key.

6 In the **Edit Relationships** dialog box, click to select the **Enforce Referential Integrity** check box, the **Cascade Update Related Fields** check box, and the **Cascade Delete Related Records** check box. Click **Create**, and then compare your screen with Figure 17.68.

> The one-to-many relationship is established. The *1* and ∞ symbols indicate that referential integrity is enforced, which ensures that a scholarship cannot be awarded to a student whose Student ID is not included in the 17C Athletes table. Recall that the Cascade options enable you to update and delete records automatically on the *many* side of the relationship when changes are made in the table on the *one* side of the relationship.

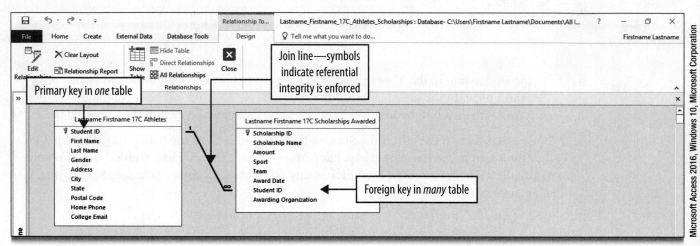

FIGURE 17.68

7 On the **Design tab**, in the **Tools group**, click **Relationship Report**. On the **Print Preview tab**, in the **Page Size group**, click **Margins**, and then click **Normal**. Save 🖫 the report as **Lastname Firstname 17C Relationships** and then create a paper or PDF electronic image as directed. This is the first of eleven objects printed in this project.

8 In the object window, right-click either **object tab**, and then click **Close All** to close the Relationships Report and the Relationships window.

9 **Open** 〉〉 the **Navigation Pane**, double-click your **17C Athletes** table to open it, and then **Close** 〈〈 the **Navigation Pane**. On the left side of the first record, click + (plus sign) to display the subdatasheet for the record.

> In the first record, for *Joel Barthmaier*, one related record exists in the 17C Scholarships Awarded table. Joel has been awarded the *Austin Jump Ball Award* in the amount of *$300*. The subdatasheet displays because you created a relationship between the two tables using Student ID as the common field.

10 **Close** ✕ the **17C Athletes** table.

> When you close the table, the subdatasheet will collapse—you do not need to click – (minus sign) before closing a table.

IC3
DIGITAL LITERACY
CERTIFICATION
2.04c (iv)

Activity 17.37 | Specifying Numeric Criteria in a Query

In this Activity, you will create a query to answer the question, *Which scholarships are in the amount of $300, and for which sports?*

1 Click the **Create tab**. In the **Queries group**, click **Query Design**.

2 In the **Show Table** dialog box, double-click your **17C Scholarships Awarded** table to add it to the table area, and then **Close** the **Show Table** dialog box. Resize the field list to display all of the fields and the entire table name.

3 Add the following fields to the design grid in the order given: **Scholarship Name**, **Sport**, and **Amount**.

4 Click in the **Sort** row under **Sport**, click the **arrow**, and then click **Ascending**.

5 Click in the **Criteria** row under **Amount**, type **300** and then press Enter. Compare your screen with Figure 17.69.

> When you enter currency values as criteria, do not type the dollar sign. Include a decimal point only if you are looking for a specific amount that includes cents; for example, 300.49. Access does not insert quotation marks around the criteria because the data type of the field is Currency, which is a numeric format.

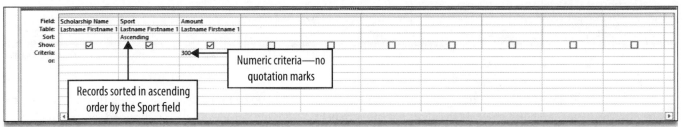

FIGURE 17.69

Microsoft Access 2016, Windows 10, Microsoft Corporation

6 On the **Design tab**, in the **Results group**, click **Run** to display the query results.

> Five scholarships in the exact amount of $300 were awarded to student athletes. In the navigation area, *1 of 5* displays—1 represents the first record that is selected, and 5 represents the total number of records that meet the criteria.

7 On the **Home tab**, in the **Views group**, click **View** to switch to **Design** view.

Activity 17.38 | Using Comparison Operators in Criteria

Comparison operators are symbols that are used to evaluate data in the field to determine if it is the same (=), greater than (>), less than (<), or in between a range of values as specified by the criteria. If no comparison operator is specified, equal (=) is assumed. For example, in the previous Activity, you created a query to display only those records where the *Amount* is *300*. The comparison operator of = was assumed, and the query results displayed only those records that had values in the Amount field equal to 300.

1 In the design grid, in the **Criteria** row under **Amount**, select the existing criteria—*300*—and then type **>300** and press Enter. **Run** the query.

> Fourteen records display, and each has a value *greater than* $300 in the Amount field; there are no records for which the Amount is *equal to* $300.

2 Switch to **Design** view. In the **Criteria** row under **Amount**, select the existing criteria—*>300*. Type **<300** and then press Enter. **Run** the query.

> Eleven records display, and each has a value *less than* $300 in the Amount field; there are no records for which the Amount is *equal to* $300.

3 Switch to **Design** view. In the **Criteria** row under **Amount**, select the existing criteria—*<300*. Type **>=300** and then press Enter. **Run** the query, and then compare your screen with Figure 17.70.

Nineteen records display, including the records for scholarships in the exact amount of $300. The records include scholarships *greater than* or *equal to* $300. In this manner, comparison operators can be combined. This query answers the question, *Which scholarships have been awarded in the amount of $300 or more, and for which sports, arranged alphabetically by sport?*

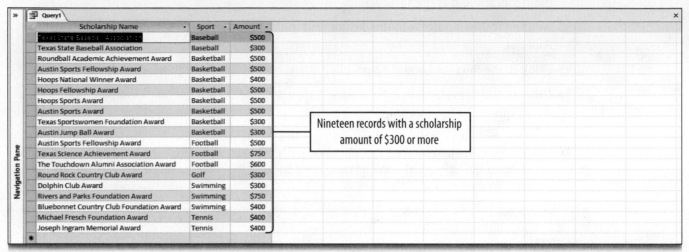

Scholarship Name	Sport	Amount
Texas State Baseball Association	Baseball	$500
Texas State Baseball Association	Baseball	$300
Roundball Academic Achievement Award	Basketball	$500
Austin Sports Fellowship Award	Basketball	$500
Hoops National Winner Award	Basketball	$400
Hoops Fellowship Award	Basketball	$500
Hoops Sports Award	Basketball	$500
Austin Sports Award	Basketball	$500
Texas Sportswomen Foundation Award	Basketball	$300
Austin Jump Ball Award	Basketball	$300
Austin Sports Fellowship Award	Football	$500
Texas Science Achievement Award	Football	$750
The Touchdown Alumni Association Award	Football	$600
Round Rock Country Club Award	Golf	$300
Dolphin Club Award	Swimming	$300
Rivers and Parks Foundation Award	Swimming	$750
Bluebonnet Country Club Foundation Award	Swimming	$400
Michael Fresch Foundation Award	Tennis	$400
Joseph Ingram Memorial Award	Tennis	$400

Nineteen records with a scholarship amount of $300 or more

FIGURE 17.70   Microsoft Access 2016, Windows 10, Microsoft Corporation

4 Save the query as **Lastname Firstname 17C $300 or More Query** and then display the query results in **Print Preview**. Create a paper or PDF electronic image as directed, and then click **Close Print Preview**. This is the second of eleven objects printed in this project.

5 Close the query. Open the **Navigation Pane**, and notice that this new query displays under *17C Scholarships Awarded*, its data source.

Activity 17.39 | Using the Between … And Comparison Operator

The **Between … And operator** is a comparison operator that looks for values within a range. It is useful when you need to locate records that are within a range of dates; for example, scholarships awarded between May 1 and June 30.

In this Activity, you will create a new query from an existing query, and then add criteria to look for values within a range of dates. The query will answer the question, *Which scholarships were awarded between May 1 and June 30?*

1 In the **Navigation Pane**, click your **17C $300 or More Query** object to select it. On the **Home tab**, in the **Clipboard** group, click **Copy**. In the **Navigation Pane**, point to a blank area, right-click, and then click **Paste**.

2 In the **Paste As** dialog box, type **Lastname Firstname 17C Awards May-June Query** and then click **OK**.

A new query, based on a copy of your 17C $300 or More Query, is created and displays in the Navigation Pane under its data source—your 17C Scholarships Awarded table.

3 In the **Navigation Pane**, right-click your **17C Awards May-June Query**, click **Design View**, and then **Close** the **Navigation Pane**.

4 In the **17C Scholarships Awarded** field list, double-click **Award Date** to add it to the fourth column in the design grid.

5 In the **Criteria** row under **Amount**, select the existing criteria—>=*300*—and then press ⌦ so that the query is not restricted by a monetary value.

6 Click in the **Criteria** row under **Award Date**, type **between 5/1/19 and 6/30/19** and then press Enter.

7 In the selection bar of the design grid, point to the right edge of the **Award Date** column to display the ➕ pointer, and then double-click to apply Best Fit to this column. Compare your screen with Figure 17.71.

The width of the Award Date column is increased to fit the longest entry in the column, which enables you to see all of the criteria. Access places pound signs (#) around the dates and capitalizes *between* and *and*. This criteria instructs Access to look for values in the Award Date field that begin with 5/1/19 and end with 6/30/19. Both the beginning and ending dates will be included in the query results.

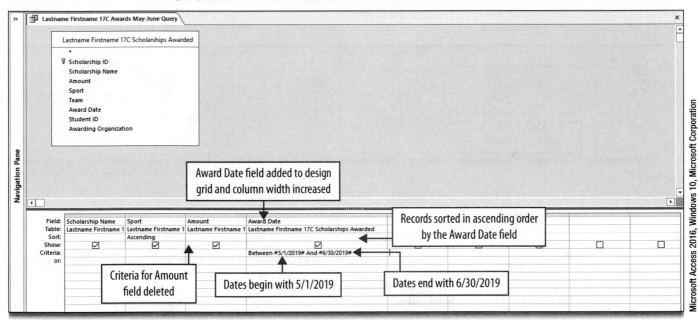

FIGURE 17.71

8 **Run** the query, and notice that eight scholarships were awarded between 5/1/2019 and 6/30/2019.

9 Display the query results in **Print Preview**, create a paper or PDF electronic image as directed, and then click **Close Print Preview**. This is the third of eleven objects printed in this project. **Close** ✕ the query, and in the message box, click **Yes** to save the changes to the query design.

Objective 14 | Use Compound Criteria in a Query

GO! Learn How
video A17-14

You can specify more than one condition—criteria—in a query; this is called **compound criteria**. Compound criteria use AND and OR **logical operators**. Logical operators enable you to enter multiple criteria for the same field or for different fields.

2.04c (iv)

Activity 17.40 | Using AND Criteria in a Query

The **AND condition** is an example of a compound criteria used to display records that match all parts of the specified criteria. In this Activity, you will help Mr. Garza answer the question, *Which scholarships over $500 were awarded for football?*

1 Click the **Create tab**, and in the **Queries group**, click **Query Design**. In the **Show Table** dialog box, double-click your **17C Scholarships Awarded** table to add it to the table area, and then **Close** the **Show Table** dialog box. Resize the field list to display all of the fields and the table name.

2 Add the following fields to the design grid in the order given: **Scholarship Name**, **Sport**, and **Amount**.

3 Click in the **Criteria** row under **Sport**, type **football** and then press Enter.

4 In the **Criteria** row under **Amount**, type **>500** and then press Enter. Compare your screen with Figure 17.72.

> You create the AND condition by placing the criteria for both fields on the same line in the Criteria row. The criteria indicates that records should be located that contain *Football* in the Sport field AND a value greater than *500* in the Amount field. Both conditions must exist or be true for the records to display in the query results.

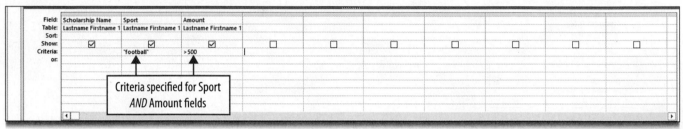

FIGURE 17.72

Microsoft Access 2016, Windows 10, Microsoft Corporation

5 **Run** the query, and notice that two records display that match both conditions—*Football* in the Sport field AND a value greater than *$500* in the Amount field.

6 **Save** the query as **Lastname Firstname 17C Football AND Over $500 Query** and then **Close** the query.

7 **Open** the **Navigation Pane**, and then click to select your **17C Football AND Over $500 Query** object. Click the **File tab**, click **Print**, and then click **Print Preview**.

> You can view an object in Print Preview or print any selected object in the Navigation Pane—the object does not need to be open in the object window to print it.

8 Create a paper or PDF electronic image as directed, and then click **Close Print Preview**. This is the fourth of eleven objects printed in this project. **Close** the **Navigation Pane**.

Activity 17.41 | Using OR Criteria in a Query

The **OR condition** is an example of a compound criteria used to display records that meet one or more parts of the specified criteria. The OR condition can specify criteria in a single field or in different fields. In this Activity, you will help Mr. Garza answer the question, *Which scholarships over $200 were awarded for volleyball or golf, and what is the award date of each?*

1 On the **Create tab**, in the **Queries group**, click **Query Design**.

2 In the **Show Table** dialog box, double-click your **17C Scholarships Awarded** table to add it to the table area, and then **Close** the **Show Table** dialog box. Resize the field list, and then add the following fields to the design grid in the order given: **Scholarship Name**, **Sport**, **Amount**, and **Award Date**.

3 In the design grid, click in the **Criteria** row under **Sport**, type **volleyball** and then press ↓.

> The insertion point is blinking in the *or* row under Sport.

4 In the **or** row under **Sport**, type **golf** and then press Enter. **Run** the query.

Six records were located in the 17C Scholarships Awarded table that have either *volleyball* OR *golf* stored in the Sport field. This is an example of using the OR condition to locate records that meet one or more parts of the specified criteria in a single field–*Sport*.

5 Switch to **Design** view. In the **or** row under **Sport**, select *golf* and then press Del. In the **Criteria** row under **Sport**, select and delete *volleyball*. Type **volleyball or golf** and then press Enter.

6 In the **Criteria** row under **Amount**, type **>200** and then press Enter. Compare your screen with Figure 17.73.

This is an alternative way to enter the OR condition in the Sport field and is a good method to use when you add an AND condition to the criteria. Access will locate records where the Sport field contains *volleyball* OR *golf* AND where the Amount field contains a value greater than *200*.

If you enter *volleyball* in the Criteria row and *golf* in the OR row for the Sport field, then you must enter *>200* in both the Criteria row and the OR row for the Amount field so that the correct records are located when the query is run.

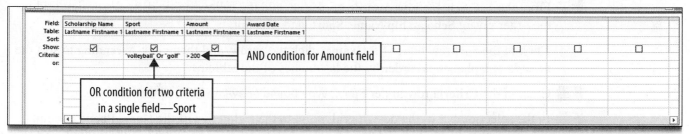

FIGURE 17.73

Microsoft Access 2016, Windows 10, Microsoft Corporation

7 **Run** the query.

Two records were located in the 17C Scholarships Awarded table that have either *Volleyball* OR *Golf* stored in the Sport field AND a value greater than $200 in the Amount field. This is an example of using the OR condition in combination with an AND condition.

8 Save 💾 the query as **Lastname Firstname 17C Volleyball OR Golf AND Over $200 Query** and then display the query results in **Print Preview**. Create a paper or PDF electronic image as directed, click **Close Print Preview**, and then **Close** ☒ the query. This is the fifth of eleven objects printed in this project.

Objective 15 | Create a Query Based on More Than One Table

GO! Learn How
video A17-15

In a relational database, you can retrieve information from more than one table. Recall that a table in a relational database contains all of the records about a single topic. Tables are joined to one another by relating the primary key in one table to the foreign key in another table. This common field is used to create the relationship and is used to find records from multiple tables when the query is created and run.

For example, the Athletes table stores all of the data about the student athletes—name, address, and so on. The Scholarships Awarded table stores data about the scholarship name, the amount, and so on. When an athlete receives a scholarship, only the Student ID of the athlete is used to identify the athlete in the Scholarships Awarded table. It is not necessary to include any other data about the athlete in the Scholarships Awarded table; doing so would result in redundant data.

2.04c (iv)

Activity 17.42 | Creating a Query Based on More Than One Table

In this Activity, you will create a query that selects records from two tables. This is possible because you created a relationship between the two tables in the database. The query will answer the questions, *What is the name, email address, and phone number of athletes who have received a scholarship for tennis or swimming, and what is the name and amount of the scholarship?*

1 On the **Create tab**, in the **Queries group**, click **Query Design**. In the **Show Table** dialog box, double-click your **17C Athletes** table, and then double-click your **17C Scholarships Awarded** table to add both tables to the table area. In the **Show Table** dialog box, click **Close**. Drag the **17C Scholarships Awarded** field list to the right so that there are approximately three inches of space between the two field lists, and then resize each field list to display all of the field names and the entire table name.

> The join line displays because you created a one-to-many relationship between the two tables using the common field of Student ID; *one* athlete can have *many* scholarships.

2 From the **17C Athletes** field list, add the following fields to the design grid in the order given: **First Name**, **Last Name**, **College Email**, and **Home Phone**.

3 From the **17C Scholarships Awarded** field list, add the following fields to the design grid in the order given: **Scholarship Name**, **Sport**, and **Amount**.

4 Click in the **Sort** row under **Last Name**, click the **arrow**, and then click **Ascending** to sort the records in alphabetical order by the last names of the athletes.

5 Click in the **Criteria** row under **Sport**, type **tennis or swimming** and then press Enter.

6 In the selection bar of the design grid, point to the right edge of the **Home Phone** column to display the ⊞ pointer, and then double-click to increase the width of the column and to display the entire table name on the **Table** row. Using the same technique, increase the width of the **Scholarship Name** column. If necessary, scroll to the right to display both of these columns in the design grid, and then compare your screen with Figure 17.74.

> When locating data from multiple tables, the information in the Table row is helpful, especially when different tables include the same field name, such as Address. Although the field name is the same, the data may be different—for example, an athlete's address or a coach's address from two different related tables.

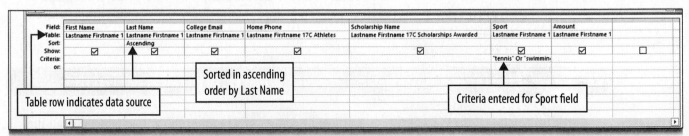

FIGURE 17.74

Microsoft Access 2016, Windows 10, Microsoft Corporation

7 **Run** the query, and then compare your screen with Figure 17.75.

> Eight records display for athletes who received either a Swimming *or* Tennis scholarship, and the records are sorted in ascending order by the Last Name field. Because the common field of Student ID is included in both tables, Access can locate the specified fields in both tables by using one query. Two students—*Carla Reid* and *Florence Zimmerman*—received two scholarships, one for swimming and one for tennis. Recall that *one* student athlete can receive *many* scholarships.

FIGURE 17.75

8. Save the query as **Lastname Firstname 17C Tennis OR Swimming Query** and then display the query results in **Print Preview**. Change the orientation to **Landscape**, and the **Margins** to **Normal**. Create a paper or PDF electronic image as directed, and then click **Close Print Preview**. This is the sixth of eleven objects printed in this project.

9. Close ⊠ the query, Open ≫ the **Navigation Pane**, increase the width of the **Navigation Pane** to display all object names fully, and then compare your screen with Figure 17.76.

Your *17C Tennis OR Swimming Query* object name displays under both tables from which it selected records.

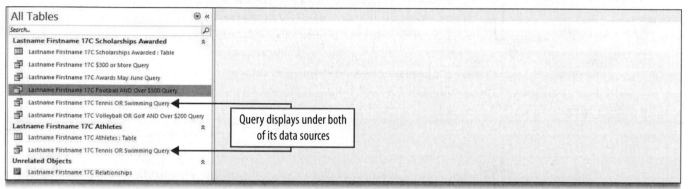

FIGURE 17.76

10. Close ≪ the **Navigation Pane**.

Objective 16 | Use Wildcards in a Query

GO! Learn How
video A17-16

A **wildcard character** is used to represent one or more unknown characters in a string. When you are unsure of the specific character or set of characters to include in the criteria for a query, use a wildcard character in place of the character.

IC3
DIGITAL LITERACY
CERTIFICATION
2.04c (iv)

Activity 17.43 | Using a Wildcard in a Query

Use the asterisk (*) wildcard character to represent one or more unknown characters. For example, entering Fo* as the criteria in a last name field will result in displaying records containing last names of Foster, Forrester, Fossil, or any other last name that begins with *Fo*. In this Activity, you will use the asterisk (*) wildcard character in criteria to answer the question, *Which athletes received scholarships from local rotary clubs, country clubs, or foundations?*

1 On the **Create tab**, in the **Queries group**, click **Query Design**. In the **Show Table** dialog box, double-click your **17C Athletes** table, and then double-click your **17C Scholarships Awarded** table to add both tables to the table area. In the **Show Table** dialog box, click **Close**. Drag the **17C Scholarships Awarded** field list to the right so that there are approximately three inches of space between the two field lists, and then resize each field list to display all of the field names and the entire table name.

2 From the **17C Athletes** field list, add the following fields to the design grid in the order given: **First Name** and **Last Name**. From the **17C Scholarships Awarded** field list, add the **Awarding Organization** field to the design grid.

3 Click in the **Sort** row under **Last Name**, click the **arrow**, and then click **Ascending** to sort the records in alphabetical order by the last names of the athletes.

4 Click in the **Criteria** row under **Awarding Organization**, type **rotary*** and then press Enter.

The * wildcard character is a placeholder used to match one or more unknown characters. After pressing Enter, Access adds *Like* to the beginning of the criteria.

5 **Run** the query, and then compare your screen with Figure 17.77.

Three athletes received scholarships from a rotary club from different cities. The results are sorted alphabetically by the Last Name field.

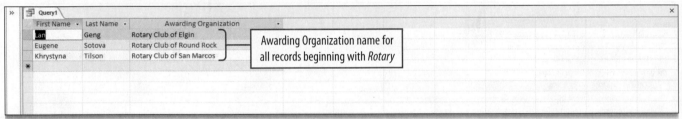

FIGURE 17.77

Microsoft Access 2016, Windows 10, Microsoft Corporation

6 Switch to **Design** view. Click in the **or** row under **Awarding Organization**, type ***country club** and then press Enter.

The * wildcard character can be used at the beginning, middle, or end of the criteria. The position of the * determines the location of the unknown characters. By entering *country club*, you will locate records where the Awarding Organization name ends in *Country Club*.

7 **Run** the query.

Six records display for students receiving scholarships; three from organizations with a name that begins with *Rotary*, and three from organizations with a name that ends with *Country Club*.

8 Switch to **Design** view. In the design grid under **Awarding Organization** and under **Like "*country club"**, type ***foundation*** and then press Enter. Compare your screen with Figure 17.78.

This query will also display records where the Awarding Organization has *Foundation* anywhere in the organization name—at the beginning, middle, or end. Three *OR* criteria have been entered for the Awarding Organization field. When run, this query will locate records where the Awarding Organization has a name that begins with *Rotary*, OR ends with *Country Club*, OR that has *Foundation* anywhere in its name.

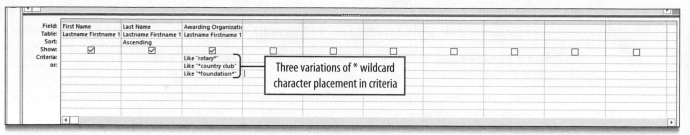

FIGURE 17.78

Microsoft Access 2016, Windows 10, Microsoft Corporation

Three variations of * wildcard character placement in criteria

9 **Run** the query.

Twenty-eight scholarships were awarded from organizations where the name of the organization begins with Rotary, ends with Country Club, or has Foundation anywhere in its name. The records are sorted alphabetically by the Last Name field.

10 Save 🖫 the query as **Lastname Firstname 17C Wildcard Query** and then display the query results in **Print Preview**. Create a paper or PDF electronic image as directed, and then click **Close Print Preview**. This is the seventh of eleven objects printed in this project.

11 Close ☒ the query, and then **Open** ⟩⟩ the **Navigation Pane**. Notice that your **17C Wildcard Query** displays under both tables because the query selected data from both tables—the data sources.

More Knowledge | **Using the ? Wildcard Character to Search for a Single Unknown Character**

The question mark (?) wildcard character is used to search for a single unknown character. For each question mark included in the criteria, any character can be located. For example, entering *b?d* as the criteria will result in the display of words such as *bed*, *bid*, or *bud*, or any three-character word that begins with *b* and ends with *d*. Entering *b??d* as the criteria will results in the display of words such as *bard*, *bend*, or *bind*, or any four-character word that begins with *b* and ends with *d*.

Objective 17 | Create Calculated Fields in a Query

GO! Learn How
video A17-17

Queries can create calculated values that are stored in a *calculated field*. A calculated field stores the value of a mathematical operation. For example, you can multiply the value stored in a field named Total Hours Worked by the value stored in a field named Hourly Pay to display the Gross Pay value for each work study student.

There are two steps to create a calculated field in a query. First, name the field that will store the results of the calculation. Second, enter the *expression*—the formula—that will perform the calculation. When entering the information for the calculated field in the query, the new field name must be followed by a colon (:), and each field name from the table used in the expression must be enclosed within its own pair of brackets.

Activity 17.44 | Creating a Calculated Field in a Query

For each scholarship received by student athletes, the Texas Lakes Community College Alumni Association will donate an amount equal to 50 percent of each scholarship. In this Activity, you will create a calculated field to determine the amount that the alumni association will donate for each scholarship. The query will answer the question, *How much money will the alumni association donate for each student athlete who is awarded a scholarship?*

1 Close ⟨⟨ the **Navigation Pane**. On the **Create tab**, in the **Queries group**, click **Query Design**. In the **Show Table** dialog box, double-click your **17C Scholarships Awarded** table to add the table to the table area, **Close** the **Show Table** dialog box, and then resize the field list.

2 Add the following fields to the design grid in the order given: **Student ID**, **Scholarship Name**, and **Amount**. Click in the **Sort** row under **Student ID**, click the **arrow**, and then click **Ascending**.

3 In the **Field** row, right-click in the first empty column to display a shortcut menu, and then click **Zoom**.

Although the calculation can be typed directly in the empty Field box, the Zoom dialog box gives you more working space and enables you to see the entire calculation as you enter it.

4 In the **Zoom** dialog box, type **Alumni Donation:[Amount]*0.5** and then compare your screen with Figure 17.79.

The first element, *Alumni Donation*, is the new field name that will identify the result of the calculation when the query is run; the field is not added back to the table. The new field name is followed by a colon (:), which separates the new field name from the expression. *Amount* is enclosed in brackets because it is an existing field name in your 17C Scholarships Awarded table; it contains the numeric data on which the calculation is performed. Following the right square bracket is the asterisk (*), the mathematical operator for multiplication. Finally, the percentage expressed as a decimal—*0.5*—displays.

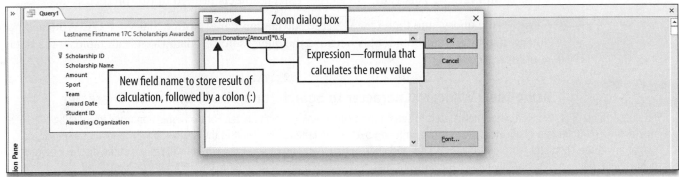

FIGURE 17.79

5 In the **Zoom** dialog box, click **OK**. **Run** the query, and then compare your screen with Figure 17.80.

The query results display three fields from your 17C Scholarships Awarded table and a fourth field—*Alumni Donation*—that displays a calculated value. Each calculated value equals the value in the Amount field multiplied by 0.5 or 50%.

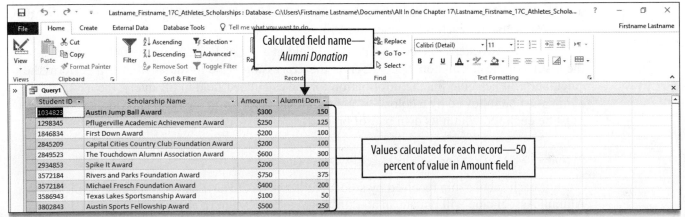

FIGURE 17.80

ALERT! **Do your query results differ from Figure 17.80?**

If your new field name does not display or if the results of the calculation do not display as shown in Figure 17.80, switch to Design view and carefully examine the expression you entered. Spelling or syntax errors prevent calculated fields from working properly.

---

6 Notice the formatting of the values in the **Alumni Donation** field—there are no dollar signs to match the formatting in the **Amount** field; you will adjust the formatting of this field later.

> When using a number, such as 0.5, in an expression, the values that display in the calculated field may not be formatted the same as the existing field that was part of the calculation.

Activity 17.45 | Creating a Second Calculated Field in a Query

In this Activity, you will create a calculated field to determine the total value of each scholarship after the alumni association donates an additional 50% based on the amount awarded by various organizations. The query will answer the question, *What is the total value of each scholarship after the alumni association donates an additional 50%?*

1 Switch to **Design** view. In the **Field** row, right-click in the first empty column to display a shortcut menu, and then click **Zoom**.

2 In the **Zoom** dialog box, type **Total Scholarship:[Amount]+[Alumni Donation]** and then compare your screen with Figure 17.81.

> Each existing field name—*Amount* and *Alumni Donation*—must be enclosed in separate pairs of brackets.

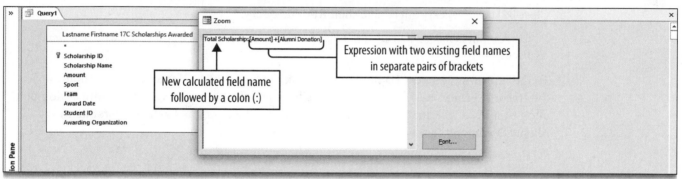

FIGURE 17.81   Microsoft Access 2016, Windows 10, Microsoft Corporation

3 In the **Zoom** dialog box, click **OK**, and then **Run** the query.

> The value in the *Total Scholarship* field is calculated by adding together the values in the Amount field and the Matching Donation field. The values in the Total Scholarship field are formatted with dollar signs, commas, and decimal points, which is carried over from the Currency format in the Amount field.

Activity 17.46 | Formatting Calculated Fields

In this Activity, you will format the calculated fields so that the values display in a consistent manner.

1 Switch to **Design** view. In the **Field** row, click in the **Alumni Donation** field name box.

2 On the **Design tab**, in the **Show/Hide group**, click **Property Sheet**.

> The Property Sheet displays on the right side of your screen. Recall that a Property Sheet enables you to make precise changes to the properties—characteristics—of selected items, in this case, a field.

↻ **ANOTHER WAY**   In the design grid, on the Field row, right-click in the Alumni Donation field name box, and then click Properties.

3 In the **Property Sheet**, with the **General tab** active, click **Format**. In the property setting box, click the **arrow**, and then compare your screen with Figure 17.82.

> A list of available formats for the Alumni Donation field displays.

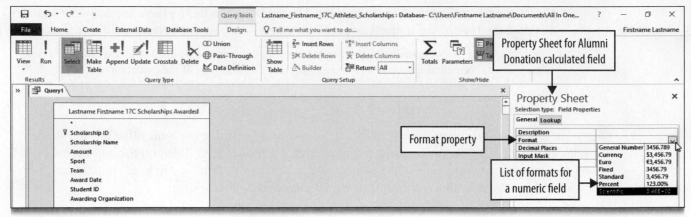

FIGURE 17.82

4 In the list, click **Currency**. In the **Property Sheet**, click **Decimal Places**. In the property setting box, click the **arrow**, and then click **0**.

5 In the design grid, in the **Field** row, click in the **Total Scholarship** field name. In the **Property Sheet**, set the **Format** property setting to **Currency** and the **Decimal Places** property setting to **0**.

6 Close ⊠ the **Property Sheet**, and then **Run** the query.

The Alumni Donation and Total Scholarship fields are formatted as Currency with 0 decimal places.

7 To the left of the **Student ID** field name, click the **Select All** ▢ button. On the **Home tab**, in the **Records group**, click **More**, and then click **Field Width**. In the **Column Width** dialog box, click **Best Fit**. Click in any field, and then **Save** 🖫 the query as **Lastname Firstname 17C Alumni Donations Query**

The field widths are adjusted to display fully the calculated field names.

8 Display the query results in **Print Preview**. Change the **Margins** to **Normal**. Create a paper or PDF electronic image as directed, and then click **Close Print Preview**. This is the eighth of eleven objects printed in this project. **Close** ⊠ the query.

Objective 18 Calculate Statistics and Group Data in a Query

GO! Learn How
video A17-18

Queries can be used to perform statistical calculations known as ***aggregate functions*** on a group of records. For example, you can find the total or average amount for a group of records, or you can find the lowest or highest number in a group of records.

DIGITAL LITERACY
CERTIFICATION
2.04c (iv)

Activity 17.47 | Using the Min, Max, Avg, and Sum Functions in a Query

In this Activity, you will use aggregate functions to find the lowest and highest scholarship amounts and the average and total scholarship amounts. The last query in this Activity will answer the question, *What is the total dollar amount of all scholarships awarded?*

1 On the **Create tab**, in the **Queries group**, click **Query Design**. In the **Show Table** dialog box, double-click your **17C Scholarships Awarded** table to add the table to the table area, **Close** the **Show Table** dialog box, and then resize the field list.

2 Add the **Amount** field to the design grid.

Include only the field to summarize in the design grid, so that the aggregate function is applied only to that field.

3 On the **Design tab**, in the **Show/Hide group**, click **Totals** to add a **Total** row as the third row in the design grid. Notice that in the design grid, on the **Total** row under **Amount**, *Group By* displays.

Use the Total row to select an aggregate function for the selected field.

4 In the **Total** row under **Amount**, click in the box that displays *Group By*, and then click the **arrow** to display a list of aggregate functions. Compare your screen with Figure 17.83, and then take a moment to review the available aggregate functions and the purpose of each function as shown in Table 17.84.

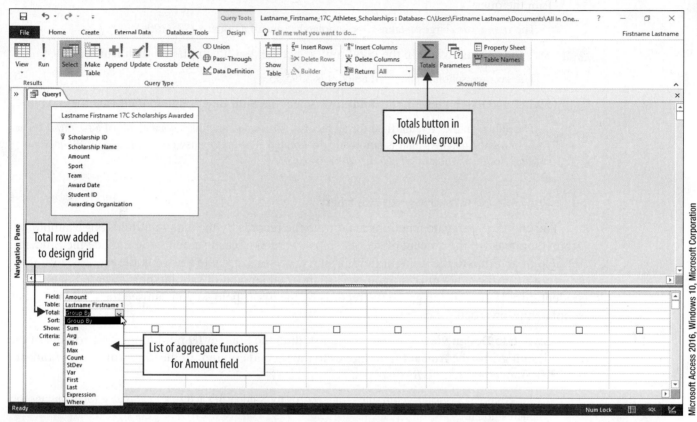

FIGURE 17.83

AGGREGATE FUNCTIONS	
FUNCTION NAME	**PURPOSE**
Group By	Combines data based on matching data in the selected field.
Sum	Totals the values in a field.
Avg	Averages the values in a field.
Min	Locates the smallest value in a field.
Max	Locates the largest value in a field.
Count	Displays the number of records based on a field.
StDev	Calculates the standard deviation for the values in a field.
Var	Calculates the variance for the values in a field.
First	Displays the first value in a field for the first record.
Last	Displays the last value in a field for the last record.
Expression	Creates a calculated field that includes an aggregate function.
Where	Limits the records to those that match a condition specified in the Criteria row of a field.

FIGURE 17.84

5 In the list of functions, click **Min**, and then **Run** the query. Point to the right edge of the first column to display the ⊞ pointer, and then double-click to apply Best Fit to the field.

Access locates the minimum (smallest) value–*$100*—in the Amount field for all of the records in the 17C Scholarships Awarded table. The field name *MinOfAmount* is automatically created. This query answers the question, *What is the minimum (smallest) scholarship amount awarded to athletes?*

6 Switch to **Design** view. In the **Total** row under **Amount**, click the **arrow**, and then click **Max**. **Run** the query.

The maximum (largest) value for a scholarship award amount is *$750.00*.

7 Switch to **Design** view. In the **Total** row, select the **Avg** function, and then **Run** the query.

The average scholarship award amount is *$395.33*.

8 Switch to **Design** view. In the **Total** row, select the **Sum** function, and then **Run** the query.

The values in the Amount field for all records is summed and displays a result of *$10,750.00*. The field name *SumOfAmount* is automatically created. The query answers the question, *What is the total dollar amount of all scholarships awarded?*

Activity 17.48 | Grouping Records in a Query

You can use aggregate functions and group the records by the data in a field. For example, to group (summarize) the amount of scholarships awarded to each student, you include the Student ID field in addition to the Amount field. Using the Sum aggregate function, the records will be grouped by the Student ID so you can see the total amount of scholarships awarded to each student. Similarly, you can group the records by the Sport field so you can see the total amount of scholarships awarded for each sport.

1 Switch to **Design** view. From the field list, drag the **Student ID** field to the first column of the design grid—the **Amount** field moves to the second column. In the **Total** row under **Student ID**, notice that *Group By* displays.

This query will group—combine—the records by Student ID and will calculate a total amount for each student.

2 **Run** the query, and then compare your screen with Figure 17.85.

The query calculates the total amount of all scholarships for each student.

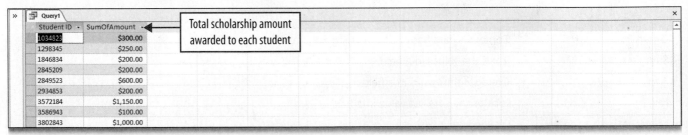

FIGURE 17.85

Microsoft Access 2016, Windows 10, Microsoft Corporation

3 Switch to **Design** view. In the design grid, above **Student ID**, point to the selection bar to display the ↓ pointer. Click to select the column, and then press Del to remove the **Student ID** field from the design grid.

4 From the field list, drag the **Sport** field to the first column in the design grid—the **Amount** field moves to the second column. Click in the **Sort** row under **Amount**, click the **arrow**, and then click **Descending**.

5 On the **Design tab**, in the **Show/Hide group**, click **Property Sheet**. In the **Property Sheet**, set the **Format** property to **Currency**, and then set the **Decimal Places** property to **0**. **Close** ☒ the **Property Sheet**.

6 **Run** the query, and then compare your screen with Figure 17.86.

Access groups—summarizes—the records by each sport and displays the groupings in descending order by the total amount of scholarships awarded for each sport. Basketball scholarships were awarded the largest total amount–*$3,500*—and Volleyball scholarships were awarded the smallest total amount–*$650*.

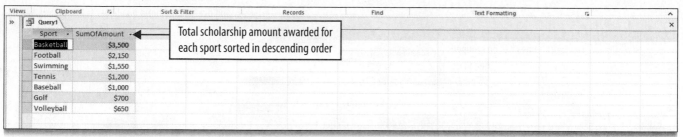

Sport	SumOfAmount
Basketball	$3,500
Football	$2,150
Swimming	$1,550
Tennis	$1,200
Baseball	$1,000
Golf	$700
Volleyball	$650

Total scholarship amount awarded for each sport sorted in descending order

FIGURE 17.86

7 **Save** 🖫 the query as **Lastname Firstname 17C Total by Sport Query** and then display the query results in **Print Preview**. Create a paper or PDF electronic image as directed, click **Close Print Preview**, and then **Close** ☒ the query. This is the ninth of eleven objects printed in this project.

Objective 19 Create a Crosstab Query

GO! Learn How
video A17-19

A **crosstab query** uses an aggregate function for data that can be grouped by two types of information, and displays the data in a compact, spreadsheet-like format with column headings and row headings. A crosstab query always has at least one row heading, one column heading, and one summary field. Use a crosstab query to summarize a large amount of data in a compact space that is easy to read.

Activity 17.49 │ Creating a Crosstab Query Using the Query Wizard

In this Activity, you will create a crosstab query that displays the total amount of scholarships awarded for each sport and for each type of team—men's or women's.

1 On the **Create tab**, in the **Queries group**, click **Query Wizard**.

2 In the **New Query** dialog box, click **Crosstab Query Wizard**, and then click **OK**.

3 In the **Crosstab Query Wizard**, click your **Table: 17C Scholarships Awarded**, and then click **Next**.

4 In the wizard under **Available Fields**, double-click **Sport** to group the scholarship amounts by the sports—the sports will display as row headings. Click **Next**, and then compare your screen with Figure 17.87.

The sport names will be grouped and displayed as row headings, and you are prompted to select column headings.

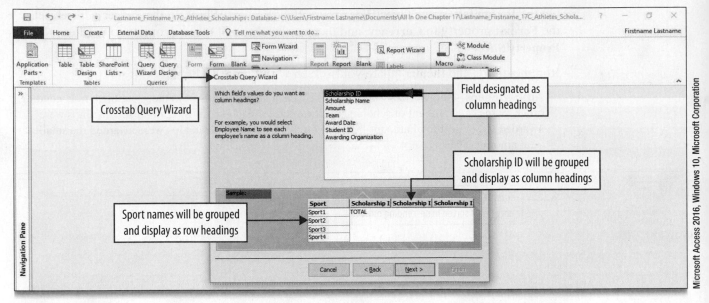

FIGURE 17.87

5 In the wizard, in the field list, click **Team** to select the column headings. Click **Next**, and then compare your screen with Figure 17.88.

The Team types—*Men's* and *Women's*—will display as column headings, and you are prompted to select a field to summarize.

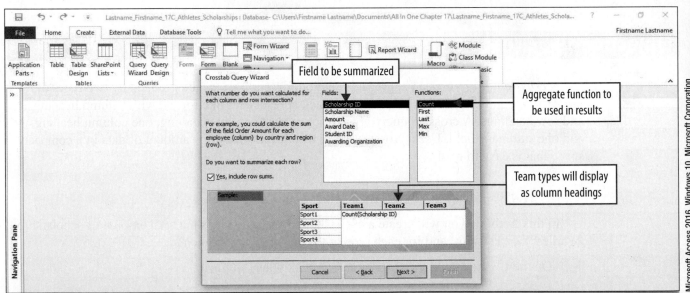

FIGURE 17.88

6 In the wizard under **Fields**, click **Amount**. Under **Functions**, click **Sum**.

The crosstab query will calculate the total scholarship amount for each sport and for each type of team.

7 Click **Next**. In the **What do you want to name your query?** box, select the existing text, type **Lastname Firstname 17C Sport and Team Crosstab Query** and then click **Finish**. Apply **Best Fit** to the datasheet, click in any field to cancel the selection, **Save** 🖫 the query, and then compare your screen with Figure 17.89.

The field widths are adjusted to display fully the calculated field names.

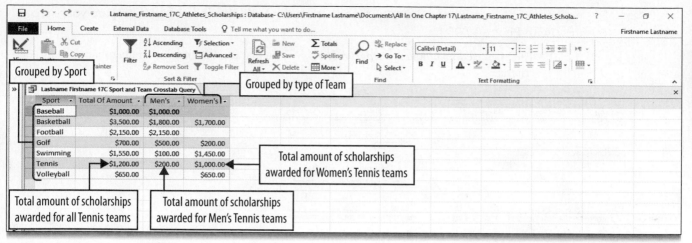

Baseball $1,000.00 $1,000.00

Basketball $3,500.00 $1,800.00 $1,700.00

Football $2,150.00 $2,150.00

Golf $700.00 $500.00 $200.00

Swimming $1,550.00 $100.00 $1,450.00

Tennis $1,200.00 $200.00 $1,000.00

Volleyball $650.00 $650.00

Grouped by Sport

Grouped by type of Team

Total amount of scholarships awarded for Women's Tennis teams

Total amount of scholarships awarded for all Tennis teams

Total amount of scholarships awarded for Men's Tennis teams

FIGURE 17.89

Microsoft Access 2016, Windows 10, Microsoft Corporation

8 Display the query results in **Print Preview**. Create a paper or PDF electronic image as directed, click **Close Print Preview**, and then **Close** ☒ the query. This is the tenth of eleven objects printed in this project.

More Knowledge	Creating a Crosstab Query Using Data From Two Related Tables

To create a crosstab query using fields from more than one table, you must first create a select query with the fields from both tables, and then use the query as the data source for the crosstab query.

Objective 20 Create a Parameter Query

GO! Learn How
video A17-20

A ***parameter query*** prompts you for criteria before running the query. For example, you need to display the records for students who live in different cities serviced by Texas Lakes Community College. You can create a select query and enter the criteria for a city such as Austin, but when you open the query, only the records for those students who live in Austin will display. To find the students who live in Round Rock, you must open the query in Design view, change the criteria, and then run the query again.

A parameter query eliminates the need to change the design of a select query. You create a single query that prompts you to enter the city; the results are based upon the criteria you enter when prompted.

IC3
DIGITAL LITERACY
CERTIFICATION
2.04c (iv)

Activity 17.50 │ Creating a Parameter Query With One Criteria

In this Activity, you will create a parameter query that displays student athletes from a specific city in the areas serviced by Texas Lakes Community College.

1 On the **Create tab**, in the **Queries group**, click **Query Design**.

2 In the **Show Table** dialog box, double-click your **17C Athletes** table to add it to the table area, **Close** the **Show Table** dialog box, and then resize the field list.

3 Add the following fields to the design grid in the order given: **First Name**, **Last Name Address**, **City**, **State**, and **Postal Code**.

4 In the **Sort** row under **Last Name**, click the **arrow**, and then click **Ascending**.

5 In the **Criteria** row under **City**, type **[Enter a City]** and then press ⏎. Compare your screen with Figure 17.90.

The bracketed text indicates a *parameter*—a value that can be changed—rather than specific criteria.

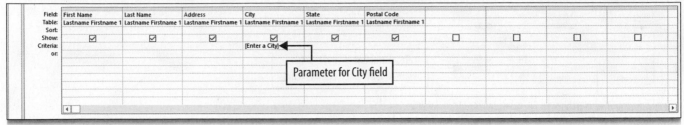

FIGURE 17.90

Microsoft Access 2016, Windows 10, Microsoft Corporation

6 **Run** the query. In the **Enter Parameter Value** dialog box, type **austin** and then compare your screen with Figure 17.91.

The Enter Parameter Value dialog box prompts you to *Enter a City*, which is the text enclosed in brackets that you entered in the criteria row under City. The city you enter will be set as the criteria for the query. Because you are prompted for the criteria, you can reuse this query without having to edit the criteria row in Design view. The value you enter is not case sensitive—you can enter *austin*, *Austin*, or *AUSTIN*.

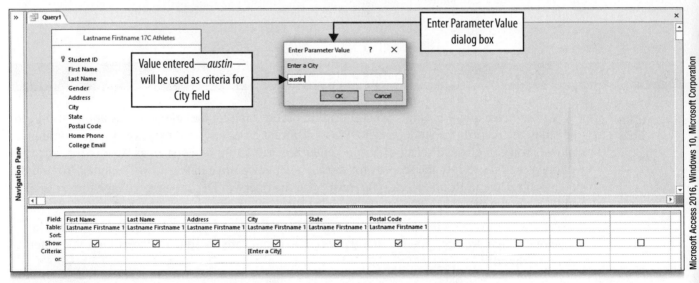

Microsoft Access 2016, Windows 10, Microsoft Corporation

FIGURE 17.91

ALERT! **Did the Enter Parameter Value dialog box not display?**

If the Enter Parameter Value dialog box does not display, you may have typed the parameter incorrectly in the design grid. Common errors include using parentheses or curly braces instead of brackets around the parameter text, which Access interprets as specific criteria, resulting in no records matching the criteria. If you typed curly braces instead of brackets, the query will not run. To correct, display the query in Design view and change the parameter entered in the Criteria row.

7 In the **Enter Parameter Value** dialog box, click **OK**.

Twenty-three students live in the city of Austin, and the records are sorted in alphabetical order by the Last Name field.

8 **Save** 💾 the query as **Lastname Firstname 17C City Parameter Query**, and then **Close** ✕ the query.

9 ▸ **Open** » the **Navigation Pane**. In the **Navigation Pane**, under your **17C Athletes** table, double-click your **17C City Parameter Query**. In the **Enter Parameter Value** dialog box, type **round rock** and then click **OK**. **Close** « the **Navigation Pane**. Compare your screen with Figure 17.92.

Nine students live in the city of Round Rock. Every time you open a parameter query, you are prompted to enter criteria. You may have to apply Best Fit to the columns if all of the data in the fields does not display and you wish to print the query results—the length of the data in the fields changes as new records display depending upon the criteria entered. Recall that only the query design is saved; each time you open a query, it is run using the most up-to-date information in the data source.

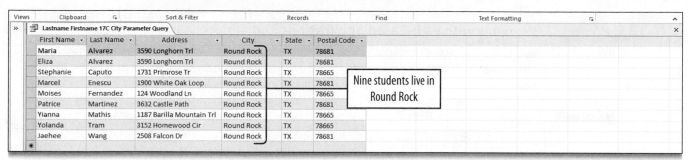

First Name	Last Name	Address	City	State	Postal Code
Maria	Alvarez	3590 Longhorn Trl	Round Rock	TX	78681
Eliza	Alvarez	3590 Longhorn Trl	Round Rock	TX	78681
Stephanie	Caputo	1731 Primrose Tr	Round Rock	TX	78665
Marcel	Enescu	1900 White Oak Loop	Round Rock	TX	78681
Moises	Fernandez	124 Woodland Ln	Round Rock	TX	78665
Patrice	Martinez	3632 Castle Path	Round Rock	TX	78681
Yianna	Mathis	1187 Barilla Mountain Trl	Round Rock	TX	78665
Yolanda	Tram	3152 Homewood Cir	Round Rock	TX	78665
Jaehee	Wang	2508 Falcon Dr	Round Rock	TX	78681

Nine students live in Round Rock

FIGURE 17.92

Microsoft Access 2016, Windows 10, Microsoft Corporation

10 ▸ Display the query results in **Print Preview**, and change the orientation to **Landscape**. Create a paper or PDF electronic image as directed, click **Close Print Preview**, and then **Close** ✕ the query. This is the eleventh of eleven objects printed in this project.

More Knowledge — **Parameter Query Prompts**

Be sure that the parameter you enter in the Criteria row as a prompt is not the same as the field name. For example, do not use *[City]* as the parameter. Access interprets this as the field name of *City*. Recall that you entered a field name in brackets when creating a calculated field in a query. If you use a field name as the parameter, the Enter Parameter Value dialog box will not display, and all of the records will display.

The parameter should inform the individual running the query of the data required to display the correct results. If you want to use the field name by itself as the prompt, type a question mark at the end of the text; for example, *[City?]*. You cannot use a period, exclamation mark (!), curly braces ({ }), another set of brackets ([ ]), or the ampersand (&) as part of the parameter.

---

11 ▸ **Open** » the **Navigation Pane**, and, if necessary increase the width of the pane so that all object names display fully. On the right side of the title bar, click **Close** ✕ to close the database and **Close** Access. As directed by your instructor, submit your database and the paper or PDF electronic images of the 11 objects—relationship report and 10 queries—that are the results of this project.

END | You have completed Project 17C

GO! With Google

Access web apps are designed to work with Microsoft's SharePoint, a service for setting up websites to share and manage documents. Your college may not have SharePoint installed, so you will use other tools to share objects from your database so that you can work collaboratively with others. Recall that Google Drive is Google's free, web-based word processor, spreadsheet, slide show, form, and data storage and sharing service. For Access, you can export a database object to an Excel worksheet, a PDF file, or a text file, and then save the file to Google Drive.

ALERT!	**Working with Web-Based Applications and Services**

Computer programs and services on the web receive continuous updates and improvements, so the steps to complete this web-based activity may differ from the ones shown. You can often look at the screens and the information presented to determine how to complete the activity.

    If you do not already have a Google account, you will need to create one before you doing this activity. Go to http://google.com and in the upper right corner, click Sign In. On the Sign In screen, click Create Account. On the Create your Google Account page, complete the form, read and agree to the Terms of Service and Privacy Policy, and then click Next step. On the Welcome screen, click Get Started.

Activity | Exporting an Access Query to an Excel Spreadsheet, Saving the Spreadsheet to Google Drive, Editing a Record in Google Drive, and Saving to Your Computer

In this Activity, you will export your 17C Sport and Team Crosstab Query table to an Excel spreadsheet, upload the Excel file to your Google Drive as a Google Sheet, edit a record in Google Drive, and then download a copy of the edited spreadsheet to your computer.

1 Start Access, navigate to your **All In One Chapter 17** folder, and then open your **17C_Athletes_Scholarships** database file. If necessary, on the Message Bar, click **Enable Content**. In the **Navigation Pane**, click your **17C Sport and Team Crosstab Query** one time to select it—do not open it.

2 Click the **External Data tab**, and then in the **Export group**, click **Excel**. In the **Export – Excel Spreadsheet** dialog box, click **Browse**, and then navigate to your **All In One Chapter 17** folder. In the **File Save** dialog box, click in the **File name** box, type **Lastname_Firstname_AC_17C_Web** and then click **Save**.

3 In the **Export – Excel Spreadsheet** dialog box, under **Specify export options**, select the first two check boxes—**Export data with formatting and layout** and **Open the destination file after the export operation is complete**—and then click **OK**. Take a moment to examine the data in the file, and then **Close** Excel. In the **Export – Excel Spreadsheet** dialog box, click **Close**, and then **Close Access**.

4 From the desktop, open your browser, navigate to **http://google.com**, and then sign in to your Google account. Click the **Google Apps** menu ⊞, and then click

Drive ☁. Open your **GO! Web Projects** folder—or click New to create and then open this folder if necessary.

5 In the upper right corner, click **Settings** [icon requested], and then on the menu click **Settings**. In the **Settings** dialog box, next to *Convert uploads*, be sure that **Convert uploaded files to Google Docs editor format** is selected. In the upper right, click **Done**.

    If this setting is not selected, your document will upload as a pdf file and cannot be edited without further action.

6 On the left, click **NEW**, and then click **File upload**. In the **Open** dialog box, navigate to your **All In One Chapter 17** folder, and then double-click your **Lastname_Firstname_a17C_Web** Excel file to upload it to Google Drive. In the lower right corner, when the title bar of the message box indicates *Uploads completed*, **Close** [icon requested] the message box. A second message box may display temporarily.

7 In the file list, double-click your **Lastname_Firstname_AC_17C_Web** file to open it in Google Sheets. Compare your screen with Figure A.

    The worksheet displays column letters, row numbers, and data.

(GO! With Google continues on the next page)

GO! With Google

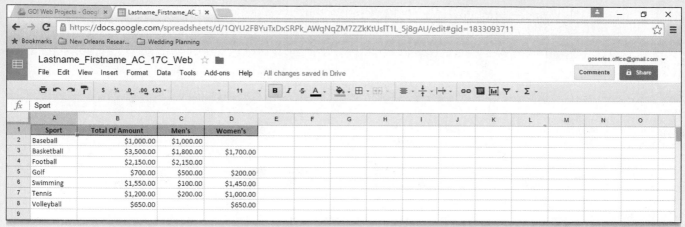

FIGURE A

Google inc.

8 Select the range **A1:B8**. On the menu bar, click **Insert**, and then click **Chart**. At the bottom of the **Chart Editor** dialog box, click **Insert** to insert the column chart in the spreadsheet.

The chart is placed in the spreadsheet, covering some of the data.

9 Click the **Chart title**, type **Lastname Firstname Total Scholarships by Sport** Above the title, click the **font size arrow**, click **12** and then press Enter to apply the title. On the right side of the chart, point to the legend, right-click, and click **Clear legend**.

10 Click to select the chart, if necessary. Point to the top of the chart window until the 🖑 pointer displays. Hold down the left mouse button, and then drag the chart below the data in the spreadsheet.

11 On the menu, click **File**, point to **Download as**, and then click **Microsoft Excel (.xlsx)**. Use your browser commands to save the file in your **All In One Chapter 17** folder as **Lastname_Firstname_AC_17C_Web_Download**

> **NOTE** Saving The Downloaded File to the All In One Chapter 17 Folder
>
> Depending on the browser you are using, you may need to open the file in Excel and then save the AC_17C_Web_Download worksheet to your All In One Chapter 17 folder.

12 In Google Drive, in the upper right corner, click your name, and then click **Sign out. Close** your browser window.

13 Start Excel. In the Excel opening screen, in the lower left corner, click **Open Other Workbooks**. Navigate to your **Lastname_Firstname_AC_17C_Web_Download** file and then open the file.

14 If directed to submit a paper printout of your AC_17C_Web_Download file, follow the directions given in the Note below. As directed by your instructor, submit your Excel file created of this project. Your instructor may also request that you submit a copy of the email that was sent to you notifying you of the shared file.

> **NOTE** Printing or Creating an PDF electronic image of an Excel Spreadsheet
>
> To print on paper, click Print. To create a PDF electronic image of your printout, on the left side of your screen, click Export. Under Export, be sure Create PDF/XPS Document is selected, and then click Create PDF/XPS. Navigate to your All In One Chapter 17 folder, and then click Publish to save the file with the default name and an extension of pdf.

Andrew Rodriguez/Fotolia; FotolEdhar/Fotolia; apops/Fotolia; Yuri Arcurs/Fotolia

IC3 SKILLS IN THIS CHAPTER

Project 17A

Section 2.04 Databases
    (a) Understand what data is
    (b) Understand how websites utilize databases
    (c) Know basic concepts of a relational
        database
        (i)   Field
        (ii)   Table
        (iii)   Data
        (iv)   Query
        (v)   Form
    (d) Know what metadata is

Project 17B

Section 2.04 Databases
    (c) Know basic concepts of a relational
        database
        (iv)   Query

Project 17C

Section 2.04 Databases
    (c) Know basic concepts of a relational
        database
        (iv)   Query

BUILD YOUR E-PORTFOLIO

An E-Portfolio is a collection of evidence, stored electronically, that showcases what you have accomplished while completing your education. Collecting and then sharing your work products with potential employees reflects your academic and career goals. Your completed documents from the following projects are good examples to show what you have learned: 17G.

GO! FOR JOB SUCCESS

Video: Making Ethical Choices

Your instructor may assign this video to your class, and then ask you to think about, or discuss with your classmates, these questions:

FotolEdhar / Fotolia

Which behaviors in this video do you think were unethical?

Is it unethical to "borrow" things from your employer? Why? What would you do if you saw this behavior going on?

What do you think an employer could do to prevent unethical behavior?

END OF CHAPTER

SUMMARY

Principles of good database design, also known as normalization, help ensure that the data in your database is accurate and organized in a way that you can retrieve information that is useful.

Tables are the foundation of a database; forms are used to enter data into a table or view the data. Queries retrieve information from tables, and reports display information in a professional-looking format.

Table relationships are created by joining the common fields in tables providing a means for you to modify data simultaneously and use data from multiple tables to create queries, forms, and reports.

Queries can ask a single question or ask complex queries where you use compound criteria, wildcard characters, logical operators, calculated fields, crosstab design, and including parameters.

GO! LEARN IT ONLINE

Review the concepts, key terms, and IC3 skills in this chapter by completing these online challenges, which you can find at **MyITLab**.

Matching and Multiple Choice: Answer matching and multiple choice questions to test what you learned in this chapter.

Lessons on the GO!: Learn how to use all the new apps and features as they are introduced by Microsoft.

IC3 Prep Quiz: Answer questions to review the IC3 skills that you have practiced in this chapter.

PROJECT GUIDE FOR ALL IN ONE CHAPTER 17

Your instructor will assign Projects from this list to ensure your learning and assess your knowledge.

Project Guide for All In One Chapter 17

Project	Apply Skills from These Chapter Objectives	Project Type	Project Location
17A MyITLab	Objectives 1–5 from Project 17A	**17A Instructional Project (Grader Project)** Guided instruction to learn the skills in Project 17A.	In text and in MyITLab
17B MyITLab	Objectives 6–12 from Project 17B	**17B Instructional Project (Grader Project)** Guided instruction to learn the skills in Project 17B.	In text and in MyITLab
17C MyITLab	Objectives 13–20 from Project 17C	**17C Instructional Project (Grader Project)** Guided instruction to learn the skills in Project 17C.	In text and in MyITLab
17D	Objectives 1–5 from Project 17A	**17D Skills Review (Scorecard Grading)** A guided review of the skills from Project 17A.	Instructor Resource Center (IRC) and in MyITLab
17E	Objectives 6–12 from Project 17B	**17E Skills Review (Scorecard Grading)** A guided review of the skills from Project 17B.	IRC and in MyITLab
17F	Objectives 13–20 from Project 17C	**17F Skills Review (Scorecard Grading)** A guided review of the skills from Project 17C.	IRC and in MyITLab
17G MyITLab	Objectives 1–5 from Project 17A	**17G Mastery (Grader Project)** **Mastery and Transfer of Learning** A demonstration of your mastery of the skills in Project 17A with extensive decision-making.	In text and in MyITLab
17H MyITLab	Objectives 6–12 from Project 17B	**17H Mastery (Grader Project)** **Mastery and Transfer of Learning** A demonstration of your mastery of the skills in Project 17B with extensive decision-making.	In text and in MyITLab
17I MyITLab	Objectives 13–20 from Project 17C	**17I Mastery (Grader Project)** **Mastery and Transfer of Learning** A demonstration of your mastery of the skills in Project 17C with extensive decision-making.	In text and in MyITLab
17J MyITLab	Combination of Objectives from Projects 17A, 17B, and 17C	**17J Mastery (Grader Project)** **Mastery and Transfer of Learning** A demonstration of your mastery of the skills in Projects 17A, 17B, and 17C with extensive decision-making.	In text and in MyITLab
17K	Combination of Objectives from Projects 17A, 17B, and 17C	**17K GO! Fix It (Scorecard Grading)** **Critical Thinking** A demonstration of your mastery of the skills in Projects 17A, 17B, and 17C by creating a correct result from a document that contains errors you must find.	IRC and in MyITLab
17L	Combination of Objectives from Projects 17A, 17B, and 17C	**17L GO! Make It (Scorecard Grading)** **Critical Thinking** A demonstration of your mastery of the skills in Projects 17A, 17B, and 17C by creating a result from a supplied picture.	IRC and in MyITLab
17M	Combination of Objectives from Projects 17A, 17B, and 17C	**17M GO! Solve It (Rubric Grading)** **Critical Thinking** A demonstration of your mastery of the skills in Projects 17A, 17B, and 17C, your decision-making skills, and your critical thinking skills. A task-specific rubric helps you self-assess your result.	IRC and in MyITLab
17N	Combination of Objectives from Projects 17A, 17B, and 17C	**17N GO! Solve It (Rubric Grading)** **Critical Thinking** A demonstration of your mastery of the skills in Projects 17A, 17B, and 17C, your decision-making skills, and your critical thinking skills. A task-specific rubric helps you self-assess your result.	IRC and in MyITLab
17O	Combination of Objectives from Projects 17A, 17B, and 17C	**17O GO! Think (Rubric Grading)** **Critical Thinking** A demonstration of your understanding of the Chapter concepts applied in a manner that you would outside of college. An analytic rubric helps you and your instructor grade the quality of your work by comparing it to the work an expert in the discipline would create.	IRC and in MyITLab

(PROJECT Guide for All In One Chapter 17 continues on the next page)

Project	Apply Skills from These Chapter Objectives	Project Type	Project Location
17P	Combination of Objectives from Projects 17A, 17B, and 17C	**17P GO! Think (Rubric Grading)** **Critical Thinking** A demonstration of your understanding of the Chapter concepts applied in a manner that you would outside of college. An analytic rubric helps you and your instructor grade the quality of your work by comparing it to the work an expert in the discipline would create.	IRC and in MyITLab
17Q	Combination of Objectives from Projects 17A, 17B, and 17C	**17Q You and GO! (Rubric Grading)** **Critical Thinking** A demonstration of your understanding of the Chapter concepts applied in a manner that you would in a personal situation. An analytic rubric helps you and your instructor grade the quality of your work.	IRC and in MyITLab
17R	Combination of Objectives from Projects 17A, 17B, and 17C	**17R Collaborative Team Project for AIO Chapter 17** **Critical Thinking** A demonstration of your understanding of concepts and your ability to work collaboratively in a group role-playing assessment, requiring both collaboration and self-management.	IRC and in MyITLab

GLOSSARY

GLOSSARY OF CHAPTER KEY TERMS

Aggregate functions Calculations such as Min, Max, Avg, and Sum that are performed on a group of records.

AND condition A compound criteria used to display records that match all parts of the specified criteria.

Append To add on to the end of an object; for example, to add records to the end of an existing table.

Ascending order A sorting order that arranges text alphabetically (A to Z) and numbers from the lowest number to the highest number.

AutoNumber data type A data type that describes a unique sequential or random number assigned by Access as each record is entered and that is useful for data that has no distinct field that can be considered unique.

Best Fit An Access command that adjusts the width of a column to accommodate the column's longest entry.

Between … And operator A comparison operator that looks for values within a range.

Blank desktop database A database that has no data and has no database tools—you must create the data and tools as you need them; the database is stored on your computer or other storage device.

Calculated field A field that stores the value of a mathematical operation.

Caption A property setting that displays a name for a field in a table, query, form, or report different from the one listed as the field name.

Cascade Delete Related Records A cascade option that enables you to delete a record in a table and also delete all of the related records in related tables.

Cascade options Relationship options that enable you to update records in related tables when referential integrity is enforced.

Cascade Update Related Fields A cascade option that enables you to change the data in the primary key field in the table on the *one* side of the relationship and update that change to any fields storing that same data in related tables.

Common field A field included in two or more tables that stores the same data.

Comparison operators Symbols that are used to evaluate data in the field to determine if it is the same (=), greater than (>), less than (<), or in between a range of values as specified by the criteria.

Compound criteria Multiple conditions in a query or filter.

Criteria Conditions in a query that identify the specific records you are looking for.

Crosstab query A query that uses an aggregate function for data that can be grouped by two types of information and displays the data in a compact, spreadsheet-like format with column headings and row headings.

Currency data type An Access data type that describes monetary values and numeric data that can be used in mathematical calculations involving values with one to four decimal places.

Custom web app A database that you can publish and share with others over the Internet.

Data Facts about people, events, things, or ideas.

Data source The table or tables from which a form, query, or report retrieves its data.

Data type Classification identifying the kind of data that can be stored in a field, such as numbers, text, or dates.

Database An organized collection of facts about people, events, things, or ideas related to a specific topic or purpose.

Database management system (DBMS) Database software that controls how related collections of data are stored, organized, retrieved, and secured; also known as a DBMS.

Database template A preformatted database that contains prebuilt tables, queries, forms, and reports that perform a specific task, such as tracking events.

Datasheet view The Access view that displays data organized in columns and rows similar to an Excel worksheet.

DBMS An acronym for database management system.

Descending order A sorting order that arranges text in reverse alphabetical order (Z to A) and numbers from the highest number to the lowest number.

Design grid The lower area of the query window that displays the design of the query.

Design view An Access view that displays the detailed structure of a table, query, form, or report. For forms and reports, may be the view in which some tasks must be performed, and only the controls, and not the data, display in this view.

Destination table The table to which you import or append data.

Export The process of copying data from one file into another file, such as an Access table into an Excel spreadsheet.

Expression A formula that will perform the calculation.

Field A single piece of information that is stored in every record; represented by a column in a database table.

Field list A list of field names in a table.

Field properties Characteristics of a field that control how the field displays and how data can be entered in the field; vary for different data types.

First principle of good database design A principle of good database design stating that data is organized in tables so that there is no redundant data.

Flat database A simple database file that is not related or linked to any other collection of data.

Foreign key The field that is included in the related table so the field can be joined with the primary key in another table for the purpose of creating a relationship.

Form An Access object you can use to enter new records into a table, edit or delete existing records in a table, or display existing records.

Form view The Access view in which you can view records, but you cannot change the layout or design of the form.

Import The process of copying data from another file, such as a Word table or an Excel workbook, into a separate file, such as an Access database.

Information Data that is accurate, timely, and organized in a useful manner.

Innermost sort field When sorting on multiple fields in Datasheet view, the field that will be used for the second level of sorting.

Is Not Null A criteria that searches for fields that are not empty.

Is Null A criteria that searches for fields that are empty.

Join line In the Relationships window, the line connecting two tables that visually indicates the common fields and the type of relationship.

Layout view The Access view in which you can make changes to a form or report while the data from the underlying data source displays.

Link A connection to data in another file.

Logical operators Operators that combine criteria using AND and OR. With two criteria, AND requires that both conditions be met and OR requires that either condition be met for the record to display in the query results.

Message Bar The area directly below the ribbon that displays information such as security alerts when there is potentially unsafe, active content in an Office document that you open.

Metadata Data that describes the properties or characteristics of other data; it refers to information like size or formatting of data.

Navigation area An area at the bottom of the Access window that indicates the number of records in the table and contains controls in the form of arrows that you click to move among the records.

Navigation Pane An area of the Access window that displays and organizes the names of the objects in a database; from here, you open objects for use.

Normalization The process of applying design rules and principles to ensure that your database performs as expected.

Number data type An Access data type that represents a quantity, how much or how many, and may be used in calculations.

Object tab In the object window, a tab that identifies the object and which enables you to make an open object active.

Object window An area of the Access window that displays open objects, such as tables, queries, forms, or reports; by default, each object displays on its own tab.

Objects The basic parts of a database that you create to store your data and to work with your data; for example, tables, queries, forms, and reports.

One-to-many relationship A relationship between two tables where one record in the first table corresponds to many records in the

second table—the most common type of relationship in Access.

OR condition A compound criteria used to display records that match at least one of the specified criteria.

Outermost sort field When sorting on multiple fields in Datasheet view, the field that will be used for the first level of sorting.

Parameter A value that can be changed.

Parameter query A query that prompts you for criteria before running the query.

Populate The action of filling a database table with records.

Primary key A required field that uniquely identifies a record in a table; for example, a Student ID number at a college.

Property Sheet A list of characteristics—properties—for fields or controls on a form or report in which you can make precise changes to each property associated with the field or control.

Query A database object that retrieves specific data from one or more database objects—either tables or other queries—and then, in a single datasheet, displays only the data you specify.

Record All of the categories of data pertaining to one person, place, event, thing, or idea; represented by a row in a database table.

Record selector bar The bar at the left edge of a record when it is displayed in a form, and which is used to select an entire record.

Record selector box The small box at the left of a record in Datasheet view that, when clicked, selects the entire record.

Redundant In a database, information that is duplicated in a manner that indicates poor database design.

Referential integrity A set of rules that Access uses to ensure that the data between related tables is valid.

Relational database A sophisticated type of database that has multiple collections of data within the file that are related to one another.

Relationship An association that you establish between two tables based on common fields.

Report A database object that summarizes the fields and records from a table or query in an easy-to-read format suitable for printing.

Run The process in which Access looks at the records in the table(s) included in the query design, finds the records that match the specified criteria, and then displays the records in a

datasheet; only the fields included in the query design display.

Second principle of good database design A principle stating that appropriate database techniques are used to ensure the accuracy and consistency of data as it is entered into the table.

Select query A type of Access query that retrieves (selects) data from one or more tables or queries, displaying the selected data in a datasheet; also known as a simple select query.

SharePoint A Microsoft application used for setting up websites to share and manage documents.

Short Text data type An Access data type that describes text, a combination of text and numbers, or numbers that are not used in calculations, such as the Postal Code.

Simple select query Another name for a select query.

Sorting The process of arranging data in a specific order based on the value in a field.

Source file When importing a file, refers to the file being imported.

Structure In Access, the underlying design of a table, including field names, data types, descriptions, and field properties.

Subdatasheet A format for displaying related records when you click the plus sign (+) next to a record in a table on the *one* side of the relationship.

Subset A portion of the total records available.

Table A format for information that organizes and presents text and data in columns and rows; the foundation of a database.

Table area The upper area of the query window that displays field lists for the tables that are used in a query.

Text string A sequence of characters.

Truncated Data that is cut off or shortened because the field or column is not wide enough to display all of the data or the field size is too small to contain all of the data.

Trust Center An area of Access where you can view the security and privacy settings for your Access installation.

Wildcard character In a query, a character that represents one or more unknown characters in criteria; an asterisk (*) represents one or more unknown characters, and a question mark (?) represents a single unknown character.

Wizard A feature in Microsoft Office that walks you step by step through a process.

17

ACCESS 2016

Mastering Access Project 17G Kiosk Inventory

In the following Mastering Access project, you will create a database to track information about the inventory of items for sale in the kiosk located in the Snack Bar at the Southeast Campus of Texas Lakes Community College. Your completed database objects will look similar to Figure 17.93.

Apply 17A skills from these Objectives:

1 Identify Good Database Design
2 Create a Table and Define Fields in a Blank Desktop Database
3 Change the Structure of Tables and Add a Second Table
4 Create a Query, Form, and Report
5 Close a Database and Close Access

PROJECT FILES

For Project 17G, you will need the following files:

Blank desktop database
a17G_Inventory (Excel workbook)
a17G_Inventory_Storage (Excel workbook)

You will save your database as:

Lastname_Firstname_17G_Kiosk_Inventory

Build From Scratch

PROJECT RESULTS

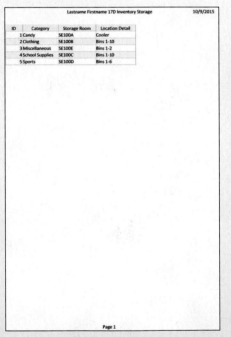

FIGURE 17.93

(Project 17G Kiosk Inventory continues on the next page)

Mastering Access Project 17G Kiosk Inventory (continued)

1 **Start** Access. Create a **Blank desktop database** in your **All In One Chapter 17** folder. Name the database **Lastname_Firstname_17G_Kiosk_Inventory** and then **Close** the **Navigation Pane**. Create the fields shown in Table 1.

2 For the **ID** field, change the **Data Type** to **Short Text**, rename the field to **Item ID** and then enter the records shown in **Table 2**.

3 **Save** the table as **Lastname Firstname 17G Inventory** and then **Close** the table. From your student data files, import and then **Append** the data in the Excel file **a17G_Inventory** to your **17G Inventory** table. After importing, open your **17G Inventory** table—17 records display.

4 In **Design** view, delete the **Campus** field, which is redundant data. For the **Category** field, change the **Field Size** to **25** and enter a **Description** of **Enter the category of the item** For the **Item ID** field, change the **Field Size** to **10** and then **Save** the changes to your table. Switch to **Datasheet** view, apply **Best Fit** to all of the fields in the table, and then **Save** your changes. Display the table in **Print Preview**, change the orientation to **Landscape**, and then create a paper printout or PDF electronic image as directed by your instructor. **Close Print Preview**, and then **Close** the table.

5 From your student data files, import the **Excel** file **a17G_Inventory_Storage** into the database as a new table; designate the first row as column headings and the **Category** field as the primary key. In the wizard, name

the table **Lastname Firstname 17G Inventory Storage** and then open your **17G Inventory Storage** table—five records display. In **Design** view, for the **Location Detail** field, change the **Field Size** to **35** and enter a **Description** of **Room and bin number or alternate location of inventory item** Save the design changes, switch to **Datasheet** view, apply **Best Fit** to all of the fields, and then **Save** your changes. Display the table in **Print Preview**, create a paper printout or PDF electronic image as directed, **Close Print Preview**, and then **Close** the table.

6 **Create** a **Simple Query**, by using the **Query Wizard**, based on your **17G Inventory** table. Include only the three fields that will answer the question, *For all items, what is the storage location and quantity in stock?* In the wizard, accept the default name for the query. Display the query in **Print Preview**, create a paper printout or PDF electronic image as directed, **Close Print Preview**, and then **Close** the query.

7 Open your **17G Inventory** table, and then **Create** a **Form** for this table. **Save** the form as **Lastname Firstname 17G Inventory Form** and then display and select the fifth record. By using the instructions in Activity 17.15, create a paper printout or PDF electronic image of only this record on one page as directed by your instructor. **Close** the form object, saving changes if prompted.

8 With your **17G Inventory** table open, **Create** a **Report**. Delete the **Category** and **Price** fields, and then

TABLE 1

Data Type		Short Text	Short Text	Short Text	Short Text	Currency	Number
Field Name	ID	**Item**	**Category**	**Campus**	**Storage Location**	**Price**	**Quantity in Stock**

(Return to Step 1)

TABLE 2

Item ID	Item	Category	Campus	Storage Location	Price	Quantity in Stock
C-1	**Chocolate Bar**	**Candy**	**Southeast**	**SE100A**	**.89**	**250**
C-2	**Lollipop**	**Candy**	**Southeast**	**SE100A**	**.5**	**500**
T-1	**T-shirt**	**Clothing**	**Southeast**	**SE100B**	**17.5**	**100**

(Return to Step 2)

(Project 17G Kiosk Inventory continues on the next page)

sort the **Item ID** field in **Ascending** order. Using the **Property Sheet**, for the **Item ID** field, change the **Width** to **0.75** and then for the **Storage Location** field, change the **Width** to **1.5** Scroll to display the bottom of the report, if necessary, and then delete the page number— **Page 1 of 1**. **Save** the report as **Lastname Firstname 17G Inventory Report** and then display the report in **Print Preview**. Create a paper printout or PDF electronic image as directed. Click **Close Print Preview.**

9 **Close All** open objects. **Open** the **Navigation Pane** and be sure that all object names display fully. **Close** the database, and then **Close** Access. As directed by your instructor, submit your database and the paper printouts or PDF electronic images of the five objects—two tables, one query, one form, and one report—that are the results of this project. Specifically, in this project, using your own name, you created the following database and printouts or PDF electronic images:

1	Lastname_Firstname_17G_Kiosk_Inventory	Database file
2	Lastname Firstname 17G Inventory	Table
3	Lastname Firstname 17G Inventory Storage	Table
4	Lastname Firstname 17G Inventory Query	Query
5	Lastname Firstname 17G Inventory Form	Form
6	Lastname Firstname 17G Inventory Report	Report

END You have completed Project 17G

MyITLab
grader

Mastering Access Project 17H Biology Supplies

In the following Mastering Access project, you will assist Greg Franklin, Chair of the Biology Department at the Southwest Campus, in using his database to answer questions about biology laboratory supplies. Your completed database objects will look similar to Figure 17.94.

PROJECT FILES

For Project 17H, you will need the following file:

a17H_Biology_Supplies

You will save your database as:

Lastname_Firstname_17H_Biology_Supplies

PROJECT RESULTS

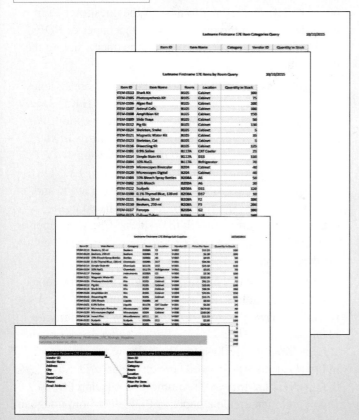

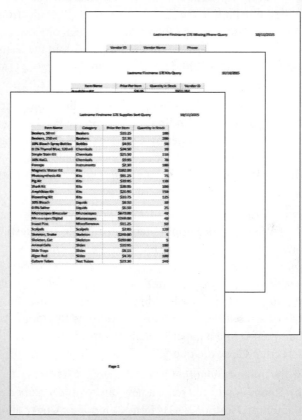

FIGURE 17.94

Microsoft Access 2016, Windows 10, Microsoft Corporation

(Project 17H Biology Supplies continues on the next page)

1 **Start** Access. From your student data files, open **a17H_Biology_Supplies**. Save the database in your **All In One Chapter 17** folder as **Lastname_Firstname_17H_Biology_Supplies** and then enable the content. In the **Navigation Pane**, **Rename** each table by adding **Lastname Firstname** to the beginning of the table name. Increase the width of the **Navigation Pane** so that all object names display fully.

2 Open both tables to examine the fields and data, and then **Close** both tables. Create a *one-to-many* relationship between your **17H Vendors** table and your **17H Biology Lab Supplies** table using the common field **Vendor ID**. **Enforce Referential Integrity**, and enable both cascade options. *One* vendor can supply *many* supplies. Create a **Relationship Report** with **Normal Margins**, saving it with the default name. Create a paper or PDF electronic image as directed, and then **Close All** open objects. Open your **17H Vendors** table. In the last record, in the **Vendor ID** field, select **V-100**, type **V-001** and then press ⬇ to save the record. **Close** the table.

3 Open your **17H Biology Lab Supplies** table. Sort the records first in **Descending** order by **Price Per Item** and then in **Ascending** order by **Category**. Using **Landscape** orientation, create a paper or PDF electronic image as directed. **Close** the table, and do *not* save changes to the table.

4 **Create** a query in **Query Design** view using your **17H Biology Lab Supplies** table to answer the question, *What is the item ID, item name, room, location, and quantity in stock for all of the items, sorted in ascending order by the Room field and the Location field?* Display the fields in the order listed in the question. **Save** the query as **Lastname Firstname 17H Items by Room Query** and then create a paper or PDF electronic image as directed. **Close** the query.

5 In the **Navigation Pane**, use your **17H Items by Room Query** to create a new query object named **Lastname Firstname 17H Item Categories Query** and then redesign the query to answer the question, *What*

is the item ID, item name, category, vendor ID, and quantity in stock for all items, sorted in ascending order by the Category field and the Vendor ID field? Display only the fields necessary to answer the question and in the order listed in the question. Create a paper or PDF electronic image as directed. **Close** the query, saving the design changes.

6 In the **Navigation Pane**, use your **17H Items by Room Query** to create a new query object named **Lastname Firstname 17H Supplies Sort Query** and then open the new query in **Design** view. Redesign the query to answer the question, *What is the item name, category, price per item, and quantity in stock for all supplies, sorted in ascending order by the Category field and then in descending order by the Price Per Item field?* Display only the fields necessary to answer the question and in the order listed in the question. Create a paper or PDF electronic image as directed. **Close** the query, saving the design changes.

7 Using your **17H Supplies Sort Query**, create a new query object named **Lastname Firstname 17H Kits Query** and then redesign the query to answer the question, *What is item name, category, price per item, quantity in stock, and vendor ID for all items that have a category of kits, sorted in ascending order by the Item Name field?* Do not display the **Category** field in the query results, and display the rest of the fields in the order listed in the question. Six records match the criteria. Create a paper or PDF electronic image as directed. **Close** the query, saving the design changes.

8 **Create** a query in **Query Design** view using your **17H Vendors** table to answer the question, *What is the vendor ID, vendor name, and phone number where the phone number is blank, sorted in ascending order by the Vendor Name field?* Display the fields in the order listed in the question. Two records match the criteria. **Save** the query as **Lastname Firstname 17H Missing Phone Query** and then create a paper or PDF electronic image as directed. **Close** the query.

(Project 17H Biology Supplies continues on the next page)

Mastering Access | Project 17H Biology Supplies (continued)

9 ▸ Be sure all objects are closed. **Open** the **Navigation Pane**, be sure that all object names display fully, and then **Close Access**. As directed by your instructor, submit your database and the paper or PDF electronic images of the seven objects—relationship report, sorted table, and five queries—that are the results of this project.

1	Lastname_Firstname_17H_Biology_Supplies	Database file
2	Relationships for Lastname_Firstname_17H_Biology_Supplies Relationships	Report
3	Lastname Firstname 17H Biology Lab Supplies table sorted (not saved)	Table sorted
4	Lastname Firstname 17H Items by Room Query	Query
5	Lastname Firstname 17H Item Categories Query	Query
6	Lastname Firstname 17H Supplies Sort Query	Query
7	Lastname Firstname 17H Kits Query	Query
8	Lastname Firstname 17H Missing Phone Query	Query

END | You have completed Project 17H

Apply 17C skills from these Objectives:

13 Specify Numeric Criteria in a Query

14 Use Compound Criteria in a Query

15 Create a Query Based on More Than One Table

16 Use Wildcards in a Query

17 Create Calculated Fields in a Query

18 Calculate Statistics and Group Data in a Query

19 Create a Crosstab Query

20 Create a Parameter Query

In the following Mastering Access project, you will assist Siabhon Reiss, the English Writing Lab Coordinator, in using her database to answer questions about student publications. Your completed database objects will look similar to Figure 17.95.

PROJECT FILES

For Project 17I, you will need the following files:

a17I_Student_Publications

a17I_Student_Papers (Excel workbook)

You will save your database as:

Lastname_Firstname_17I_Student_Publications

PROJECT RESULTS

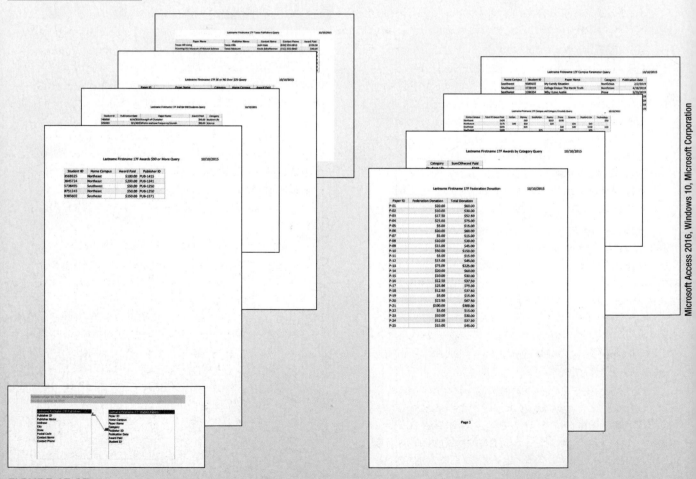

FIGURE 17.95

Microsoft Access 2016, Windows 10, Microsoft Corporation

(Project 17I Student Publications continues on the next page)

Mastering Access Project 17I Student Publications (continued)

1 **Start** Access. From your student data files, open **a17I_Student_Publications**. Save the database in your **All In One Chapter 17** folder as **Lastname_Firstname_17I_Student_Publications** and then enable the content. In the **Navigation Pane**, **Rename** the table by adding **Lastname Firstname** to the beginning of the table name. From your student data files, import **a17I_Student_Papers** as a new table in the database. Designate the first row of the spreadsheet as column headings, and designate **Paper ID** as the primary key. Name the new table **Lastname Firstname 17I Student Papers** and then increase the width of the **Navigation Pane** so that all object names display fully.

Open your **17I Student Papers** table in **Design** view. For the **Student ID** field, change the **Data Type** to **Short Text**. Switch to **Datasheet** view, apply **Best Fit** to all of the columns, and then **Save** the table. Examine the fields and data in this table. Open your **17I Publishers** table, examine the fields and data, and then **Close All** open objects.

Create a *one-to-many* relationship between your **17I Publishers** table and your **17I Student Papers** table using the common field **Publisher ID**. **Enforce Referential Integrity**, and enable both cascade options. *One* publisher can publish *many* student papers. Create a **Relationship Report** with **Normal Margins**, saving it as **Lastname Firstname 17I Relationships** and then create a paper or PDF electronic image as directed. **Close All** open objects.

2 **Create** a query in **Query Design** view using your **17I Student Papers** table to answer the question, *What is the student ID, home campus, award paid, and publisher ID for awards greater than or equal to $50, sorted in ascending order by the Student ID field?* Display the fields in the order listed in the question. Five records match the criteria. **Save** the query as **Lastname Firstname 17I Awards $50 or More Query** and then create a paper or PDF electronic image as directed.

3 Using your **17I Awards $50 or More Query**, create a new query object named **Lastname Firstname 17I 2nd Qtr NW Students Query** and then redesign the query to answer the questions, *Which students (Student ID) from the Northwest campus had papers published between 4/1/19 and 6/30/19, and what was the paper name, the award paid, and the category, sorted in ascending order*

by the Publication Date field? Do not restrict the results by **Award Paid**. Do not display the **Home Campus** field in the query results, and display the rest of the fields in the order listed in the question. Three records match the criteria. Using **Landscape** orientation, create a paper or PDF electronic image as directed. **Close** the query, saving the design changes.

4 **Create** a query in **Query Design** view using your **17I Student Papers** table to answer the question, *Which paper IDs, paper names, and category for students from the Southeast and Northeast campuses were published that had an award paid greater than $25, sorted in descending order by the Award Paid field?* Display the fields in the order listed in the question. Six records match the criteria. **Save** the query as **Lastname Firstname 17I SE or NE Over $25 Query** and then using **Normal Margins**, create a paper or PDF electronic image as directed. **Close** the query.

5 **Create** a query in **Query Design** view using both tables to answer the questions, *Which paper names were published with a publisher name that has Texas as part of its name, what is the contact name and contact phone number, and what was the award paid, sorted in descending order by the Award Paid field? Hint:* Use a wildcard character in the criteria row. Display the fields in the order listed in the question. Eight records match the criteria. **Save** the query as **Lastname Firstname 17I Texas Publishers Query** and then using **Landscape** orientation, create a paper or PDF electronic image as directed. **Close** the query.

6 The college's Federation of English Faculty will donate money to the English Writing Lab based on 50 percent of the awards paid to the students. **Create** a query in **Query Design** view using your **17I Student Papers** table to answer the question, *In ascending order by the Paper ID field, what will be the total of each donation to the Writing Lab if the Federation donates an additional 50 percent of each award paid to students? Hint:* First calculate the amount of the donation, naming the new field **Federation Donation**, and then run the query to be sure the correct results display. Then calculate the total donation, naming the new field **Total Donation**. Change the property settings of the **Federation Donation** field to display with a **Format** of **Currency** and with **Decimal Places** set to **2**. For the **Publisher ID** of **P-20**, the

(Project 17I Student Publications continues on the next page)

Federation Donation is *$22.50*, and the *Total Donation* is *$67.50*. Apply **Best Fit** to all of the columns, **Save** the query as **Lastname Firstname 17I Federation Donation Query** and then create a paper or PDF electronic image as directed. **Close** the query.

7 Create a query in **Query Design** view using your **17I Student Papers** table and the **Sum** aggregate function to answer the question, *What are the total awards paid for each category, sorted in descending order by the Award Paid field?* Display the fields in the order listed in the question. Change the property settings of the **Award Paid** field to display with a **Format** of **Currency** and with **Decimal Places** set to **0**. For the **Category** of **Student Life**, total awards paid are *$265*. Apply **Best Fit** to the **SumOfAward Paid** column. **Save** the query as **Lastname Firstname 17I Awards by Category Query** and then create a paper or PDF electronic image as directed. **Close** the query.

8 By using the **Query Wizard**, create a crosstab query based on your **17I Student Papers** table. Select **Home Campus** as the row headings and **Category** as the column headings. **Sum** the **Award Paid** field. Name the query **Lastname Firstname 17I Campus and Category Crosstab Query** In **Design** view, change the property settings of the last two fields to display with a **Format** of

Currency and with **Decimal Places** set to **0**. This query answers the question, *What are the total awards paid for student publications by each home campus and by each category?* Apply **Best Fit** to all of the columns, and then **Save** the query. Using **Landscape** orientation and **Normal Margins**, create a paper or PDF electronic image as directed. **Close** the query.

9 Create a query in **Query Design** view using your **17I Student Papers** table that prompts you to enter the **Home Campus**, and then answers the question, *What is the home campus, student ID, paper name, category, and publication date for student publications, sorted in ascending order by the Publication Date field?* Display the fields in the order listed in the question. **Run** the query, entering **southwest** when prompted for criteria. Seven records match the criteria. **Save** the query as **Lastname Firstname 17I Campus Parameter Query** and then using **Normal Margins**, create a paper or PDF electronic image as directed. **Close** the query.

10 Open the **Navigation Pane**, and be sure that all object names display fully. **Close Access**. As directed by your instructor, submit your database and the paper or PDF electronic images of the nine objects—relationship report and eight queries—that are the results of this project.

1	Lastname_Firstname_17I_Student_Publications	Database file
2	Lastname Firstname 17I Relationships Relationships	Report
3	Lastname Firstname 17I Awards $50 or More Query	Query
4	Lastname Firstname 17I 2nd Qtr NW Students Query	Query
5	Lastname Firstname 17I SE OR NE Over $25 Query	Query
6	Lastname Firstname 17I Texas Publishers Query	Query
7	Lastname Firstname 17I Federation Donation Query	Query
8	Lastname Firstname 17I Awards by Category Query	Query
9	Lastname Firstname 17I Campus and Category Crosstab Query	Query
10	Lastname Firstname 17I Campus Parameter Query	Query

END| You have completed Project 17I

Mastering Access | **Project 17J Student Scholarships**

In the following Mastering Access project, you will assist Kim Ngo, Director of Academic Scholarships, in using her database to answer questions about scholarships awarded to students. Your completed database objects will look similar to Figure 17.96.

PROJECT FILES

For Project 17J, you will need the following file:

a17J_Student_Scholarships

You will save your database as:

Lastname_Firstname_17J_Student_Scholarships

PROJECT RESULTS

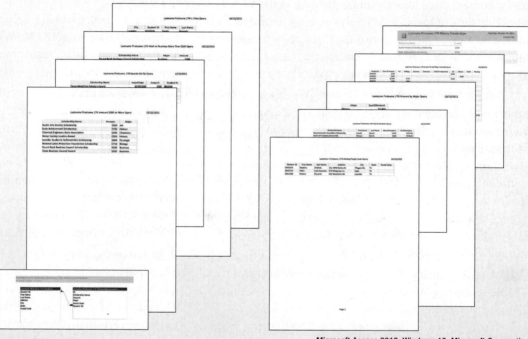

FIGURE 17.96

Microsoft Access 2016, Windows 10, Microsoft Corporation

(Project 17J Student Scholarships continues on the next page)

1 **Start** Access. From your student data files, open **a17J_Student_Scholarships**. Save the database in your **All In One Chapter 17** folder as **Lastname_Firstname_17J_Student_Scholarships** and then enable the content. In the **Navigation Pane**, **Rename** each table by adding **Lastname Firstname** to the beginning of the table name. Increase the width of the **Navigation Pane** so that all object names display fully.

2 Open your **17J Students** table in **Design view**. Change the data type for the **Student ID** field to **Short Text**. Change the data type for the **Postal Code** field to **Short Text**. Change the field size for the **State** field to 2. Switch to **Datasheet view**, saving changes. In the message box, click **Yes**. Examine the data in the **17J Students** table. Open the **17J Scholarships Awarded** table to examine the fields and data, and then **Close** both tables.

3 Create a *one-to-many* relationship between your **17J Students** table and your **17J Scholarships Awarded** table using the common field **Student ID**. **Enforce Referential Integrity**, and enable both cascade options. *One* student can have *many* scholarships. Create a **Relationship Report** with **Normal Margins**, saving it with the default name. Create a paper or PDF electronic image as directed, and then **Close All** open objects. Open your **17J Students** table. In the last record, in the **Student ID** field, select **9999999**, type **2839403** and then press ↓ to save the record. **Close** the table.

4 **Create** a query in **Query Design** view using your **17J Scholarships Awarded** table to answer the question, *What is the scholarship name, amount, and major for scholarships greater than or equal to $500, sorted in ascending order by the Scholarship Name field?* Display the fields in the order listed in the question. Eight records match the criteria. **Save** the query as **Lastname Firstname 17J Amount $500 or More Query** and then create a paper or PDF electronic image as directed. Click **Close Print Preview**, and leave the query open.

5 Use your **17J Amount $500 or More Query** to create a new query object named **Lastname Firstname 17J Awards 4th Qtr Query** and then redesign the query to answer the question, *Which scholarships (Scholarship Name) were awarded between 10/1/19 and 12/31/19, for what amount, and for which student (Student ID), sorted in ascending order by the Award Date field?* Display

only the fields necessary to answer the question and in the order listed in the question. Do not restrict the results by amount, and sort only by the field designated in the question. Five records match the criteria. Create a paper or PDF electronic image as directed. **Close** the query, saving the design changes.

6 **Create** a query in **Query Design** view using your **17J Scholarships Awarded** table to answer the question, *Which scholarships (Scholarship Name) were awarded for either Math or Business majors for amounts of more than $200, sorted in descending order by the Amount field?* Display the fields in the order listed in the question. Four records match the criteria. (Hint: If six records display, switch to Design view and combine the majors on one criteria line using OR.) **Save** the query as **Lastname Firstname 17J Math or Business More Than $200 Query** and then create a paper or PDF electronic image as directed. **Close** the query.

7 **Create** a query in **Query Design** view using your **17J Students** table to answer the question, *What is the city, student ID, first name, and last name of students from cities that begin with the letter L, sorted in ascending order by the City field and by the Last Name field?* Display the fields in the order listed in the question. Five records match the criteria. **Save** the query as **Lastname Firstname 17J L Cities Query** and then create a paper or PDF electronic image as directed. **Close** the query.

8 **Create** a query in **Query Design** view using your **17J Students** table and all of the fields to answer the question, *For which students is the Postal Code missing?* Three records match the criteria. **Save** the query as **Lastname Firstname 17J Missing Postal Code Query** and then using **Normal Margins**, create a paper or PDF electronic image as directed. **Close** the query.

9 The Board of Trustees for the college will donate an amount equal to 50 percent of each scholarship amount. **Create** a query in **Query Design** view using both tables to answer the question, *In ascending order by the Scholarship Name field, and including the first name and last name of the scholarship recipient, what will be the total value of each scholarship if the Board of Trustees donates an additional 50 percent of each award paid to students?* Hint: First calculate the amount of the donation, naming the new field **Board Donation**, and then run the query to be sure the correct results display.

(Project 17J Student Scholarships continues on the next page)

Then calculate the total donation, naming the new field **Total Donation**. Change the property settings of the appropriate fields to display with a **Format** of **Currency** and with **Decimal Places** set to **0**. For the **Scholarship Name** of **Amanda Snyder Foundation Scholarship**, the *Board Donation* is *$125*, and the *Total Donation* is *$375*. Apply **Best Fit** to all of the columns, **Save** the query as **Lastname Firstname 17J Board Donation Query** and then using **Landscape** orientation, create a paper or PDF electronic image as directed. **Close** the query.

10 **Create** a query in **Query Design** view using your **17J Scholarships Awarded** table and the **Sum** aggregate function to answer the question, *For each major, what is the total scholarship amount, sorted in descending order by the Amount field?* Display the fields in the order listed in the question. Change the property settings of the **Amount** field to display with a **Format** of **Currency** and with **Decimal Places** set to **0**. For the **Major** of **History**, the total scholarship amount is *$1,850*. Apply **Best Fit** to all of the columns. **Save** the query as **Lastname Firstname 17J Amount by Major Query** and then create a paper or PDF electronic image as directed. **Close** the query.

11 By using the **Query Wizard**, create a crosstab query based on your **17J Scholarships Awarded** table. Select **Student ID** as the row headings and **Major** as the column headings. **Sum** the **Amount** field. Name the query **Lastname Firstname 17J Student ID and Major Crosstab Query** In Design view, change the property settings of the last two fields to display with a **Format** of **Currency** and with **Decimal Places** set to **0**. This query answers the question, *What are the total scholarship amounts paid*

by each student ID and by each major? Apply **Best Fit** to all of the columns, and then **Save** the query. Using **Landscape** orientation, create a paper or PDF electronic image as directed—two pages result. **Close** the query.

12 **Create** a query in **Query Design** view using your **17J Scholarships Awarded** table that prompts you to enter the **Major** of the student, and then answers the question, *What is the scholarship name and amount for a major, sorted in ascending order by the Scholarship Name field?* Display the fields in the order listed in the question. **Run** the query, entering **history** when prompted for criteria. Four records match the criteria. Hide the **Major** field from the results, and then **Run** the query again, entering **history** when prompted for criteria. **Save** the query as **Lastname Firstname 17J Major Parameter Query** With the query results displayed, create a report.

13 Select the title, and replace it with **Lastname Firstname 17J History Scholarships** Change the font size to **14**. Delete the **Page Number** control. Sort the report in **Ascending** order by **Scholarship Name**. Resize the width of the **Scholarship Name** column to **3.25** Save the report as **Lastname Firstname 17J History Scholarships Report** Create a paper or PDF electronic image as directed. **Close** all open objects.

14 Open the **Navigation Pane**, and be sure that all object names display fully. **Close Access**. As directed by your instructor, submit your database and the paper or PDF electronic images of the ten objects—relationship report and nine queries, one of which prints on two pages—that are the results of this project.

1	Lastname_Firstname_17J_Student_Scholarships	Database file
2	Relationships for Lastname_Firstname_17J_Student_Scholarships Relationships	Report
3	Lastname Firstname 17J Amount $500 or More Query	Query
4	Lastname Firstname 17J Awards 4th Qtr Query	Query
5	Lastname Firstname 17J Math OR Business Over $200 Query	Query
6	Lastname Firstname 17J L Cities Query	Query
7	Lastname Firstname 17J Missing Postal Code Query	Query
8	Lastname Firstname 17J Board Donation Query	Query
9	Lastname Firstname 17J Amount by Major Query	Query
10	Lastname Firstname 17J Student ID and Major Crosstab Query	Query (2 pages)
11	Lastname Firstname 17J History Majors Report	Report

END | You have completed Project 17J

OUTCOMES-BASED ASSESSMENTS (CRITICAL THINKING)

| GO! Fix It | Project 17K Social Sciences | MyITLab |

| GO! Make It | Project 17L Faculty Awards | MyITLab |

| GO! Solve It | Project 17M Student Refunds | MyITLab |

| GO! Solve It | Project 17N Leave | MyITLab |

| GO! Think | Project 17O Coaches | MyITLab |

| GO! Think | Project 17P Club Donations | MyITLab |

| You and GO! | Project 17Q Personal Inventory | MyITLab |

| GO! Collaborative Team Project | Project 17R Bell Orchid Hotels | MyITLab |

Introducing Microsoft PowerPoint 2016

Surpasspro/Fotolia

PowerPoint 2016: Introduction

Communication skills are critical to your success in a business career, and when it comes to communicating *your* ideas, presentation is everything! Whether you are planning to deliver your presentation in person or online—to a large audience or to a small group—Microsoft PowerPoint 2016 is a versatile business tool that will help you create presentations that make a lasting impression. Additionally, collaborating with others to develop a presentation is easy because you can share the slides you create by using your free Microsoft OneDrive cloud storage.

Microsoft PowerPoint 2016 includes a variety of themes that you can apply to a new presentation. Each theme includes several theme variants that coordinate colors, fonts, and effects. The benefit of this approach is that the variations evoke different moods and responses, yet the basic design remains the same. As a result, you can use a similar design within your company to brand your presentations, while still changing the colors to make the presentation appropriate to the audience and topic. You do not have to determine which colors work well together in the theme you choose, because professional designers have already done that for you. So you can concentrate on how best to communicate your message. Focus on creating dynamic, interesting presentations that keep your audience engaged!

Getting Started with Microsoft PowerPoint

PROJECT 18A

OUTCOMES
Create a company overview presentation.

OBJECTIVES

1. Create a New Presentation
2. Edit a Presentation in Normal View
3. Add Pictures to a Presentation
4. Print and View a Presentation

PROJECT 18B

OUTCOMES
Create a new product announcement presentation.

OBJECTIVES

5. Edit an Existing Presentation
6. Format a Presentation
7. Use Slide Sorter View
8. Apply Slide Transitions

PROJECT 18C

OUTCOMES
Format a presentation to add visual interest and clarity.

OBJECTIVES

9. Format Numbered and Bulleted Lists
10. Insert Online Pictures
11. Insert Text Boxes and Shapes
12. Format Objects

Jeff McGraw/Fotolia

In This Chapter

GO! to Work with PowerPoint

In this chapter, you will study presentation skills, which are among the most important skills you will learn. Good presentation skills enhance your communications—written, electronic, and interpersonal. In this technology-enhanced world, communicating ideas clearly and concisely is a critical personal skill. Microsoft PowerPoint 2016 is presentation software with which you create electronic slide presentations. Use PowerPoint to present information to your audience effectively. You can start with a new, blank presentation and add content, pictures, and themes, or you can collaborate with colleagues by inserting slides that have been saved in other presentations.

Projects 18A and 18B relate to **Kodiak West Travel**, which is a travel agency with offices in Juneau, Anchorage, and Victoria. Kodiak West Travel works closely with local vendors to provide clients with specialized adventure travel itineraries. The company was established in 2001 in Juneau and built a loyal client base that led to the expansion into Anchorage and Victoria. Project 18C relates to **Sensation Park Entertainment Group**, an entertainment company that operates 15 regional theme parks across the United States, Mexico, and Canada. Park types include traditional theme parks, water parks, and animal parks.

PROJECT

18A

Company Overview

MyITLab

Project 18A Training
Project 18A Grader

PROJECT ACTIVITIES

In Activities 18.01 through 18.16, you will create the first five slides of a new presentation that Kodiak West Travel tour manager Ken Dakona is developing to introduce the tour services that the company offers. Your completed presentation will look similar to Figure 18.1.

PROJECT FILES

MyITLab
grader

If your instructor wants you to submit Project 18A in the MyITLab Grader system, log in to MyITLab, locate Grader Project 18A, and then download the files for this project.

Build From
Scratch

For Project 18A, you will need the following files:

New blank PowerPoint presentation
p18A_Glacier
p18A_Bay

You will save your presentation as:

Lastname_Firstname_18A_KWT_Overview

PROJECT RESULTS

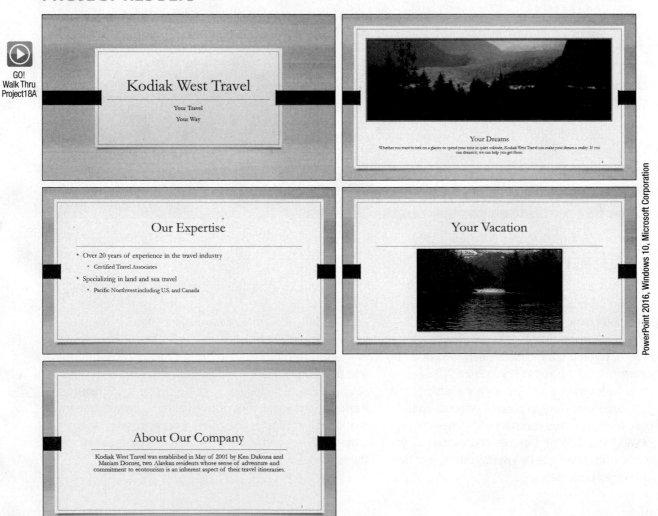

FIGURE 18.1 Project 18A KWT Overview

NOTE	If You Are Using a Touchscreen
	Tap an item to click it.
	Press and hold for a few seconds to right-click; release when the information or command displays.
	Touch the screen with two or more fingers and then pinch together to zoom out or stretch your fingers apart to zoom in.
	Slide your finger on the screen to scroll—slide left to scroll right and slide right to scroll left.
	Slide to rearrange—similar to dragging with a mouse.
	Swipe to select—slide an item a short distance with a quick movement—to select an item and bring up commands, if any.

Objective 1 | Create a New Presentation

GO! Learn How
Video P18-1

Microsoft PowerPoint 2016 is software you can use to present information to your audience effectively. You can edit and format a blank presentation by adding text, a presentation theme, and pictures. When you start PowerPoint, presentations you have recently opened, if any, display on the left. On the right you can select either a blank presentation or a *theme*—a set of unified design elements that provides a look for your presentation by applying colors, fonts, and effects. A presentation consists of one or more slides. Similar to a page in a document—a presentation *slide* can contain text, pictures, tables, charts, and other multimedia or graphic objects.

Activity 18.01 | Identifying Parts of the PowerPoint Window

ALERT!	To submit as an autograded project, log into MyITLab, download the files for this project, and begin with those files instead of a new blank presentation.

IC3
DIGITAL LITERACY
CERTIFICATION

2.05f
2.05g (i)

In this Activity, you will start PowerPoint and identify the parts of the PowerPoint window.

1. Start PowerPoint. On the right, click **Facet** to view a preview of the Facet theme and the color variations associated with this theme. Below the theme preview, click either the left- or right-pointing **More Images** ◀ and ▶ arrows to view how various types of slides in this theme display. To the right of the preview, click each of the color variations. After you have viewed each color, click the original green color.

2. On either the left or right side of the preview window, notice the arrow, and then compare your screen with Figure 18.2.

> You can use the arrows to the left and right of the preview window to scroll through the available themes.

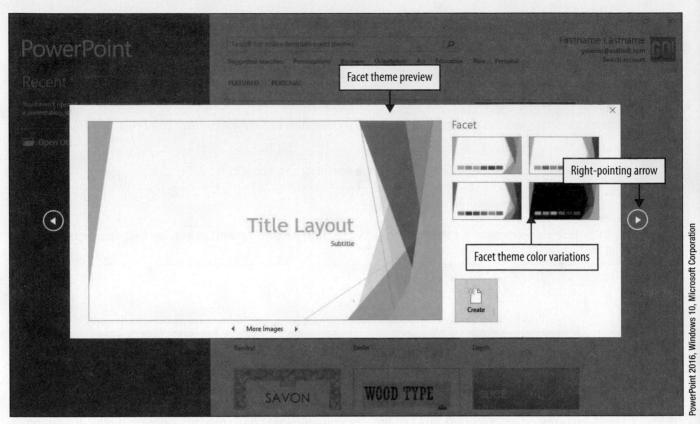

FIGURE 18.2

3 ▸ Click the right- or left-pointing arrow several times to view other available themes, and then return to the **Facet** theme. In the lower right area of the preview window, click **Create** to begin a new presentation using the **Facet** theme.

4 ▸ Compare your screen with Figure 18.3, and then take a moment to study the parts of the PowerPoint window described in the table in Figure 18.4.

The presentation displays in ***Normal view***, which is the primary editing view in PowerPoint where you write and design your presentations. On the left, a pane displays miniature images—***thumbnails***—of the slides in your presentation. On the right, the ***Slide pane*** displays a larger image of the active slide.

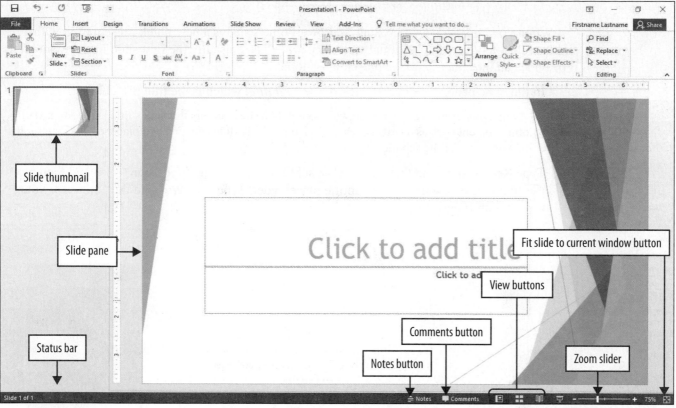

FIGURE 18.3

PowerPoint 2016, Windows 10, Microsoft Corporation

MICROSOFT POWERPOINT SCREEN ELEMENTS	
SCREEN ELEMENT	**DESCRIPTION**
Slide pane	Displays a large image of the active slide.
Slide thumbnails	Miniature images of each slide in the presentation. Clicking a slide thumbnail displays the slide in the Slide pane.
Status bar	Displays, in a horizontal bar at the bottom of the presentation window, the current slide number, number of slides in a presentation, Notes button, Comments button, View buttons, Zoom slider, and Fit slide to current window button; you can customize this area to include additional information.
Notes button	When clicked, displays an area below the Slide pane in which presentation notes can be typed.
Comments button	When clicked, displays a Comments pane to the right of the Slide pane, in which reviewers can type comments.
View buttons	Controls the look of the presentation window with a set of commands.
Zoom slider	Zooms the slide displayed in the Slide pane, in and out.
Fit slide to current window button	Fits the active slide to the maximum view in the Slide pane.

FIGURE 18.4

Gaskin, Shelley. Go! All in One, 3E. Pearson Education, 2017.

When you create a new presentation, PowerPoint displays a new blank presentation with a single slide—a title slide in Normal view. The **title slide** is usually the first slide in a presentation; it provides an introduction to the presentation topic.

1 In the **Slide** pane, click in the text *Click to add title*, which is the title placeholder.

A **placeholder** is a box on a slide with dotted or dashed borders that holds title and body text or other content such as charts, tables, and pictures. This slide contains two placeholders, one for the title and one for the subtitle.

2 Type **Kodiak West** and then click in the subtitle placeholder. Type **Your Travel** and then press Enter to create a new line in the subtitle placeholder. Type **Your Way** and then compare your screen with Figure 18.5.

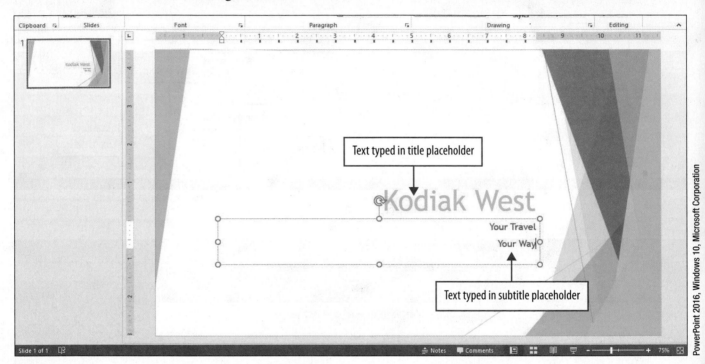

FIGURE 18.5

3 On the **Quick Access Toolbar**, click **Save** 🖫. Under **Save As**, click **Browse**. Navigate to the location where you are saving your files for this chapter, and then create and open a new folder named **AIO Chapter 18** In the **File name** box, using your own name, replace the existing text with **Lastname_Firstname_18A_KWT_Overview** and then click **Save**.

Activity 18.03 | Applying a Presentation Theme

A theme is a set of unified design elements that provides a look for your presentation by applying colors, fonts, and effects. After you create a presentation, you can change the look of your presentation by applying a different theme. Kodiak West Travel wants a theme that evokes a feeling of nature.

1 On the ribbon, click the **Design tab**. In the **Themes group**, click **More** ⊡ to display the **Themes** gallery. Compare your screen with Figure 18.6.

The themes displayed on your system may differ from Figure 18.6.

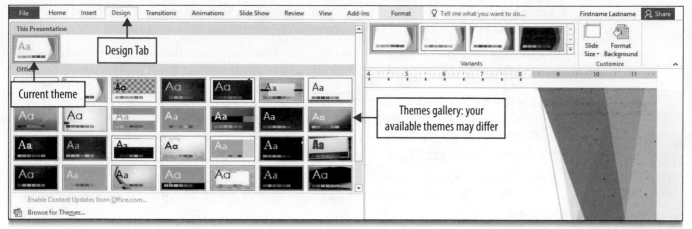

FIGURE 18.6

PowerPoint 2016, Windows 10, Microsoft Corporation

> **2** Under **Office**, point to several of the themes and notice that a ScreenTip displays the name of each theme, and the Live Preview feature displays how each theme would look if applied to your presentation.
>
> The first theme that displays is the Office Theme.
>
> **3** Use the ScreenTips to locate the **Organic** theme shown in Figure 18.7.

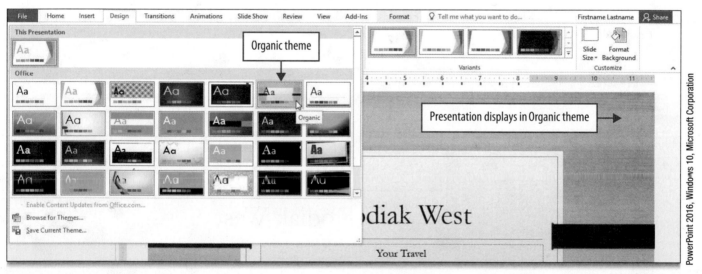

FIGURE 18.7

PowerPoint 2016, Windows 10, Microsoft Corporation

> **4** Click **Organic** to change the presentation theme and then **Save** 🔲 your presentation.

Objective 2 | Edit a Presentation in Normal View

GO! Learn How
Video P18-2

IC3
DIGITAL LITERACY
CERTIFICATION

2.05e (i)
2.05g (ii)
2.05g (v)

Editing is the process of modifying a presentation by adding and deleting slides or by changing the contents of individual slides.

Activity 18.04 | Inserting a New Slide

Your presentation consists of a single slide. You can insert additional slides in any order. If you have more than one slide, to insert a new slide in a presentation, display the slide that will come before the slide that you want to insert.

1 On the **Home tab**, in the **Slides group**, point to the **New Slide arrow**—the lower part of the New Slide button. Compare your screen with Figure 18.8.

The New Slide button is a ***split button***—a type of button in which clicking the main part of the button performs a command and clicking the arrow opens a menu, list, or gallery. The upper, main part of the New Slide button, when clicked, inserts a slide without displaying any options. The lower part—the New Slide arrow—when clicked, displays a gallery of slide ***layouts***—the arrangement of elements, such as title and subtitle text, lists, pictures, tables, charts, shapes, and movies, on a slide.

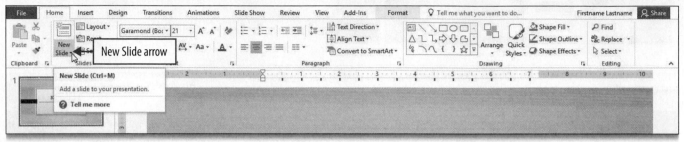

FIGURE 18.8

PowerPoint 2016, Windows 10, Microsoft Corporation

2 In the **Slides group**, click the lower portion of the **New Slide** button—the **New Slide arrow**—to display the gallery, and then compare your screen with Figure 18.9.

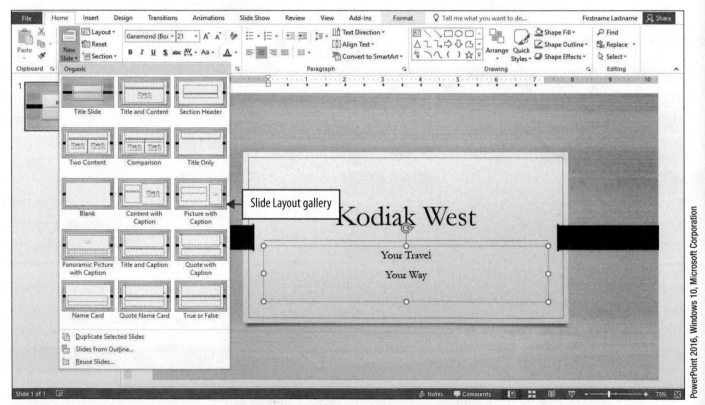

FIGURE 18.9

3 In the gallery, click the **Panoramic Picture with Caption** layout to insert a new slide. Notice that the new blank slide displays in the Slide pane, and a slide thumbnail displays at the left. Compare your screen with Figure 18.10.

🔄 **BY TOUCH**   In the gallery, tap the desired layout to insert a new slide.

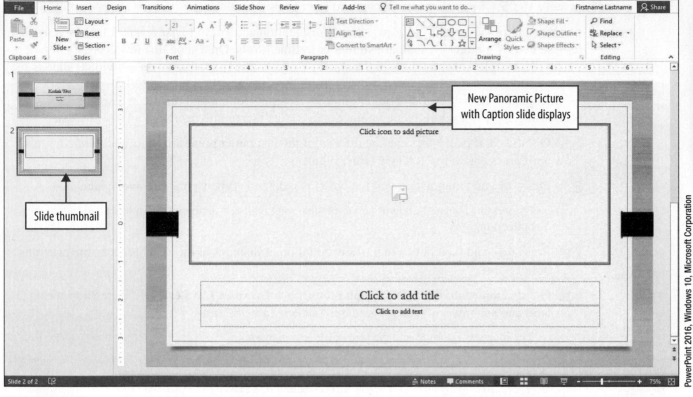

FIGURE 18.10

4 ▸ On the new slide, below the picture placeholder, click the text *Click to add title*, and then type **Your Dreams**

5 ▸ Below the title placeholder, click in the text placeholder. Type **Whether you want to trek on a glacier or spend your time in quiet solitude, Kodiak West Travel can make your dream a reality.** Compare your screen with Figure 18.11.

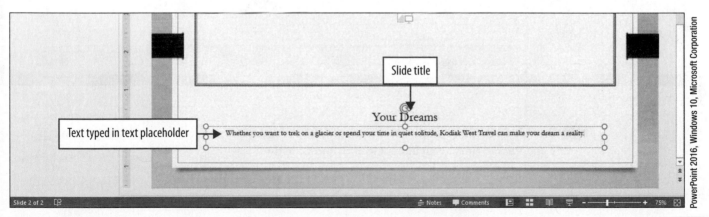

FIGURE 18.11

6 ▸ On the **Home tab**, in the **Slides group**, click the **New Slide arrow** to display the gallery, and then click **Title and Content**. In the title placeholder, type **Our Expertise** and then below the title placeholder, click in the content placeholder. Type **Over 20 years of experience in the travel industry**

7 ▸ **Save** 🖫 your presentation.

You can organize text in a PowerPoint presentation according to *list levels*. List levels, each represented by a bullet symbol, are similar to outline levels. On a slide, list levels are identified by the bullet style, indentation, and the size of the text. The first level on an individual slide is the title.

Increasing the list level of a bullet point increases its indent and results in a smaller text size. Decreasing the list level of a bullet point decreases its indent and results in a larger text size.

1 On **Slide 3**, if necessary, click at the end of the last bullet point after the word *industry*, and then press Enter to insert a new bullet point.

2 Press Tab, and then notice that the bullet is indented. Type **Certified Travel Associates**

By pressing Tab at the beginning of a bullet point, you can increase the list level and indent the bullet point.

3 Press Enter, and then notice that a new bullet point displays at the same level as the previous bullet point.

4 On the **Home tab**, in the **Paragraph group**, click **Decrease List Level**. Type **Specializing in land and sea travel** and then compare your screen with Figure 18.12.

The indent is removed and the size of the text increases.

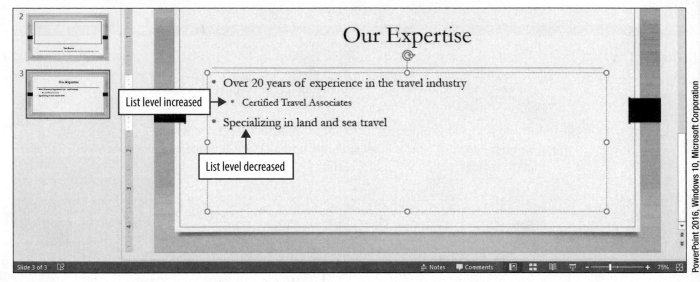

FIGURE 18.12

5 Press Enter, and then on the **Home tab**, in the **Paragraph group**, click **Increase List Level**. Type **Pacific Northwest including U.S. and Canada**

You can use the Increase List Level button to indent the bullet point.

6 Compare your screen with Figure 18.13, and then **Save** your presentation.

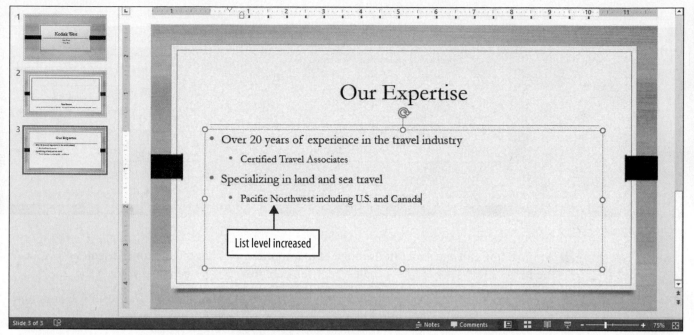

FIGURE 18.13

PowerPoint 2016, Windows 10, Microsoft Corporation

Activity 18.06 | Adding Speaker Notes to a Presentation

The **Notes pane** is an area of the Normal view window that displays below the Slide pane with space to type notes regarding the active slide. You can refer to these notes while making a presentation, reminding you of the important points that you want to discuss.

1 With **Slide 3** displayed, in the **Status bar**, click **Notes** ≜, and then notice that below the Slide pane, the Notes pane displays. Click in the **Notes** pane, and then type **Kodiak West Travel has locations in Juneau, Anchorage, and Victoria.**

2 Compare your screen with Figure 18.14, and then **Save** 🖫 your presentation.

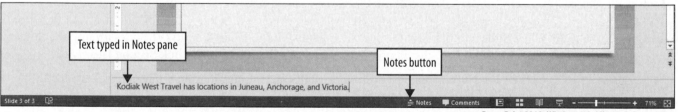

FIGURE 18.14

PowerPoint 2016, Windows 10, Microsoft Corporation

Activity 18.07 | Displaying and Editing Slides in the Slide Pane

1 At the left side of the PowerPoint window, look at the slide thumbnails, and then notice that the presentation contains three slides. At the right side of the PowerPoint window, in the vertical scroll bar, point to the scroll box, and then hold down the left mouse button to display a ScreenTip indicating the slide number and title.

2 Drag the scroll box up until the ScreenTip displays *Slide: 2 of 3 Your Dreams*. Compare your screen with Figure 18.15, and then release the mouse button to display **Slide 2**.

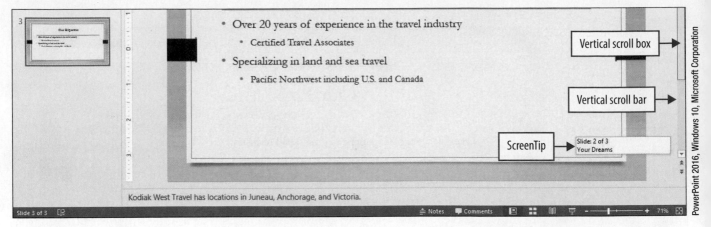

Kodiak West Travel has locations in Juneau, Anchorage, and Victoria.

Slide 3 of 3

≙ Notes 💬 Comments 71%

FIGURE 18.15

3 At the bottom of the slide, in the content placeholder, click at the end of the sentence, after the period. Press Spacebar, and then type **If you can dream it, we can help you get there.**

4 On the left side of the PowerPoint window, in the slide thumbnails, point to **Slide 3**, and then notice that a ScreenTip displays the slide title. Compare your screen with Figure 18.16.

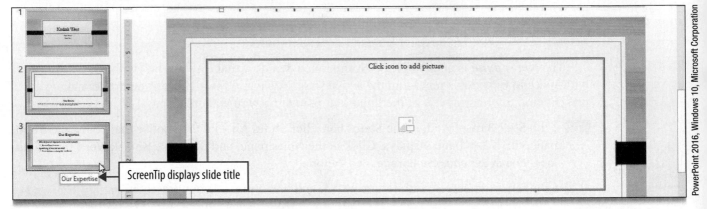

FIGURE 18.16

5 Click **Slide 3** to display it in the Slide pane. On the **Home tab**, in the **Slides group**, click the **New Slide arrow** to display the **Slide Layout** gallery, and then click **Section Header**.

A *section header* is a type of slide layout that changes the look and flow of a presentation by providing text placeholders that do not contain bullet points.

6 Click in the title placeholder, and then type **About Our Company**

7 Click in the content placeholder below the title, and then type **Kodiak West Travel was established in May of 2001 by Ken Dakona and Mariam Dorner, two Alaskan residents whose sense of adventure and commitment to ecotourism is an inherent aspect of their travel itineraries.** Compare your screen with Figure 18.17.

The placeholder text is resized to fit within the placeholder. The AutoFit Options button displays.

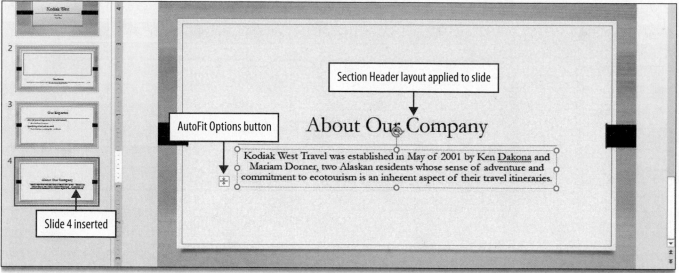

FIGURE 18.17

PowerPoint 2016, Windows 10, Microsoft Corporation

8 ▶ Click **AutoFit Options** 🔆, review the AutoFit options, and then click outside the menu to close it.

The *AutoFit Text to Placeholder* option keeps the text contained within the placeholder by reducing the size of the text. The *Stop Fitting Text to This Placeholder* option turns off the AutoFit option so that the text can flow beyond the placeholder border; the text size remains unchanged. You can also choose to split the text between two slides, continue on a new slide, or divide the text into two columns.

9 ▶ In the slide thumbnails, click **Slide 1** to display it in the Slide pane, and then in the slide title, click at the end of the word *West*. Press [Spacebar], and then type **Travel**

Clicking a slide thumbnail is the most common method used to display a slide in the Slide pane.

10 ▶ **Save** 🔲 your presentation.

Objective 3 Add Pictures to a Presentation

GO! Learn How
Video P18-3

IC3
DIGITAL LITERACY
CERTIFICATION
2.05e (ii)

Photographic images add impact to a presentation and help the audience visualize your message.

Activity 18.08 │ Inserting a Picture from a File

Many slide layouts in PowerPoint accommodate digital picture files so that you can easily add pictures you have stored. The agency has a collection of photographs to be inserted in the presentation that highlight the beauty of the region.

1 ▶ Display **Slide 2**, and then compare your screen with Figure 18.18.

In the center of the picture placeholder, the *Pictures* button displays.

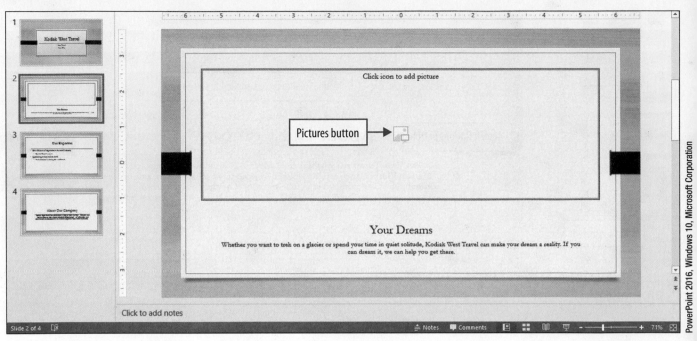

FIGURE 18.18

> **2** In the picture placeholder, click **Pictures** to open the **Insert Picture** dialog box. Navigate to the location where your student data files are stored, click **p18A_Glacier**, and then click **Insert** to insert the picture in the placeholder. Compare your screen with Figure 18.19.
>
>> Small circles—*sizing handles*—surround the inserted picture and indicate that the picture is selected and can be modified or formatted. The *rotation handle*—a circular arrow above the picture—provides a way to rotate a selected image. The Picture Tools are added to the ribbon, providing picture formatting commands.

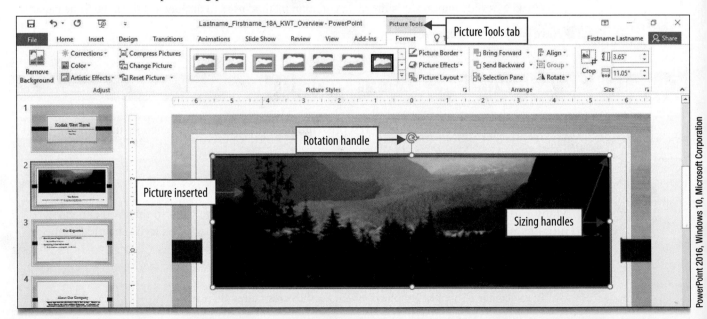

FIGURE 18.19

> **3** Display **Slide 3**. On the **Home tab**, in the **Slides group**, click the **New Slide arrow**, and then click **Title and Content**. In the title placeholder, type **Your Vacation**
>
> **4** In the content placeholder, click **Pictures** . Navigate to your student data files, and then click **p18A_Bay**. Click **Insert**, and then compare your screen with Figure 18.20. **Save** the presentation.

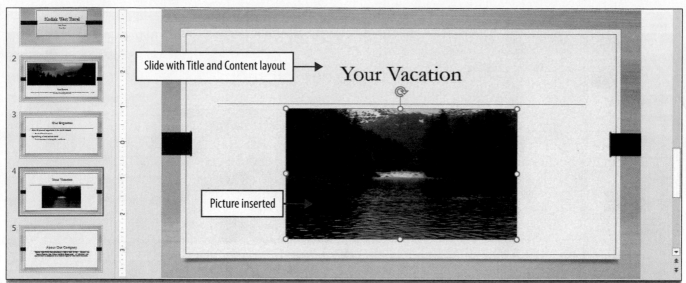

FIGURE 18.20

Activity 18.09 | Applying a Style to a Picture

When you select a picture, the Picture Tools display, adding the Format tab to the ribbon. The Format tab provides numerous styles that you can apply to your pictures. A *style* is a collection of formatting options that you can apply to a picture, text, or an object.

1 With **Slide 4** displayed, if necessary, click the picture to select it. On the ribbon, notice that the Picture Tools are active and the Format tab displays.

2 On the **Format tab**, in the **Picture Styles group**, click **More** ⏷ to display the **Picture Styles** gallery, and then compare your screen with Figure 18.21.

FIGURE 18.21

3 In the gallery, point to several of the picture styles to display the ScreenTips and to view the effect on your picture. In the second row, click the second style—**Simple Frame, Black**. Click in a blank area of the slide, compare your screen with Figure 18.22, and then **Save** 🖫 the presentation.

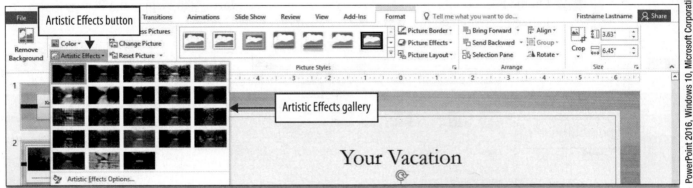

FIGURE 18.22

PowerPoint 2016, Windows 10, Microsoft Corporation

Activity 18.10 | Applying and Removing Picture Artistic Effects

Artistic effects are formats applied to images that make pictures resemble sketches or paintings.

> **1** On **Slide 4**, click the picture to select it. On the **Format tab**, in the **Adjust group**, click **Artistic Effects** to display the **Artistic Effects** gallery. Compare your screen with Figure 18.23.

FIGURE 18.23

PowerPoint 2016, Windows 10, Microsoft Corporation

> **2** In the gallery, point to several of the artistic effects to display the ScreenTips and to have Live Preview display the effect on your picture. Then, in the second row, click the **Glow Diffused** effect.

> **3** With the picture still selected, on the **Format tab**, in the **Adjust group**, click **Artistic Effects** again to display the gallery. In the first row, click the first effect—**None**—to remove the effect from the picture and restore the previous formatting.

> **4** **Save** 🖫 the presentation.

GO! Learn How
Video P18-4

There are several print options in PowerPoint. For example, you can print full page images of your slides, presentation handouts to provide your audience with copies of your slides, or Notes pages displaying speaker notes below an image of the slide.

IC3
DIGITAL LITERACY
CERTIFICATION
2.05c

Activity 18.11 | Viewing a Slide Show

When you view a presentation as an electronic slide show, the entire slide fills the computer screen, and an audience can view your presentation if your computer is connected to a projection system.

1 On the **Slide Show tab**, in the **Start Slide Show group**, click **From Beginning**. Compare your slide with Figure 18.24.

The first slide fills the screen, displaying the presentation as the audience would see it if your computer was connected to a projection system.

ANOTHER WAY Press [F5] to start the slide show from the beginning. Or, display the first slide you want to show and click the Slide Show button on the lower right side of the status bar.

FIGURE 18.24

2 Click the left mouse button or press [Spacebar] to advance to the second slide.

3 Continue to click or press [Spacebar] until the last slide displays, and then click or press [Spacebar] one more time to display a *black slide*—a slide that displays after the last slide in a presentation, indicating that the presentation is over.

4 With the black slide displayed, click the left mouse button to exit the slide show and return to the presentation.

↻ **ANOTHER WAY**　　Press `Esc` to exit the slide show.

2.05b
2.05c

Activity 18.12 │ Using Presenter View

Presenter View shows the full-screen slide show on one monitor or projection screen for the audience to see, while enabling the presenter to view a preview of the next slide, notes, and a timer on another monitor.

1 On the **Slide Show tab**, in the **Monitors** group, if necessary, select the Use Presenter View check box. Hold down `Alt` and press `F5`. Take a moment to study the parts of the PowerPoint Presenter View window described in the table in Figure 18.25.

If you do not have two monitors, you can practice using Presenter View by pressing `Alt` + `F5`. You will only see the presenter's view—not the audience view—in this mode.

MICROSOFT POWERPOINT PRESENTER VIEW ELEMENTS	
SCREEN ELEMENT	**DESCRIPTION**
`0:00:00 ‖ ↻`	**Timer:** running time, pause timer, and reset timer options
✎	**Pen and laser pointer tools:** point to or annotate slides during a presentation
▦	**See all slides:** display all slides on the screen to easily navigate between them
🔍	**Zoom into the slide:** focus on a part of a slide while presenting
▨	**Black or unblack slide show:** hide or unhide the presentation
⊙	**More slide show options:** including hide presenter view, help, pause, and end show
◀ **and** ▶	**Navigation buttons:** move back and forth through the presentation
SHOW TASKBAR　DISPLAY SETTINGS ▼　END SLIDE SHOW	**Presenter View ribbon:** control slide presentation display options
A˅ **or** A˄	**Notes pane text size adjustment:** make notes text larger or smaller

FIGURE 18.25

2 Below the current slide, click the **Advance to the next slide arrow** ⊙ to display **Slide 2**.

↻ **BY TOUCH**　　Advance to the next slide by swiping the current slide to the left.

3 In the upper right corner of the **Presenter View** window, point to the next slide—*Our Expertise*—and then click. Notice that the notes that you typed on **Slide 3** display. Compare your screen with Figure 18.26.

Clicking the image of the next slide advances the presentation.

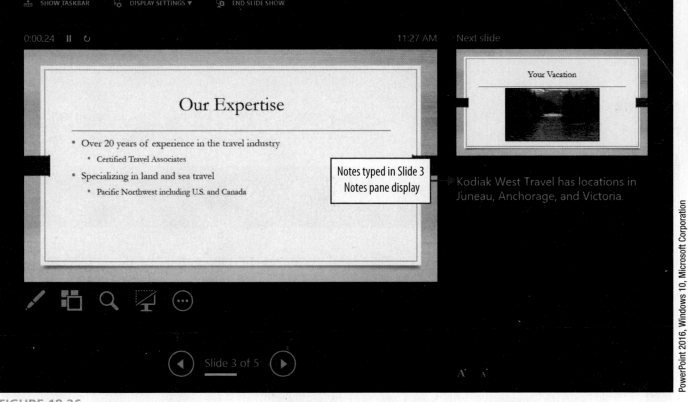

FIGURE 18.26

4 Below the notes, click **Make the text larger** to increase the font size of the notes in Presenter view to make the notes easier to read.

5 Below the current slide, click the second button—**See all slides** . Compare your screen with Figure 18.27.

A thumbnail view of all of the slides in your presentation displays. Here you can quickly move to another slide, if, for example, you want to review a concept or answer a question related to a slide other than the current slide.

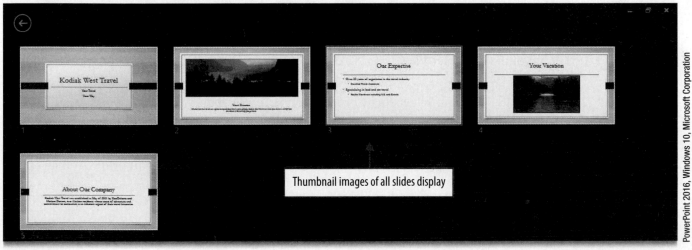

FIGURE 18.27

> **6** Click **Slide 4** to make Slide 4 the current slide in Presenter View. Below the current slide, click the third button—**Zoom into the slide** 🔍. Move the 🔍 pointer to the middle of the picture on the current slide, and then click to zoom in on the picture. Notice that the 🖐 pointer displays. Compare your slide with Figure 18.28.
>
> With the 🖐 pointer displayed, you can move the zoomed image to draw close-up attention to a particular part of your slide.

♻ BY TOUCH Touch the current slide with two fingers and then pinch together to zoom out or stretch your fingers apart to zoom in.

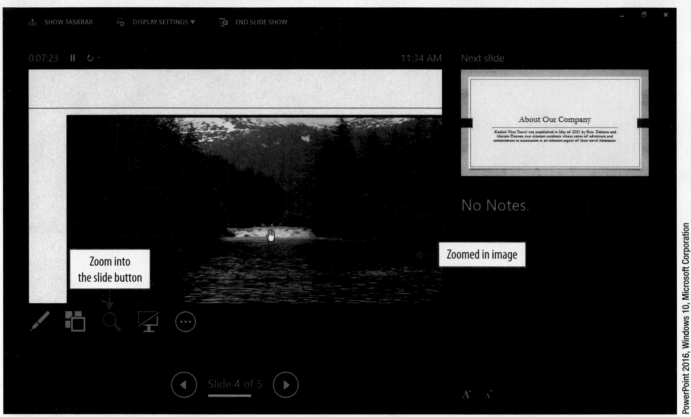

FIGURE 18.28

> **7** Below the current slide, click the **Advance to the next slide arrow** 🔘 to display **Slide 5.** At the top of the Presenter View window, click **END SLIDE SHOW** to return to your presentation.

Activity 18.13 | Inserting Headers and Footers on Slide Handouts

A **header** is text that prints at the top of each sheet of **slide handouts** or **notes pages**. Slide handouts are printed images of slides on a sheet of paper. Notes pages are printouts that contain the slide image on the top half of the page and notes that you have created in the Notes pane in the lower half of the page.

In addition to headers, you can insert **footers**—text that displays at the bottom of every slide or that prints at the bottom of a sheet of slide handouts or notes pages.

> **1** On the **Insert tab**, in the **Text group**, click **Header & Footer** to display the **Header and Footer** dialog box.

2 In the **Header and Footer** dialog box, click the **Notes and Handouts tab**. Under **Include on page**, select the **Date and time** check box, and as you do so, watch the Preview box in the upper right corner of the Header and Footer dialog box.

> The two narrow rectangular boxes at the top of the Preview box are placeholders for the header text and date. When you select the Date and time check box, the placeholder in the upper right corner is outlined, indicating the location in which the date will display.

3 Be sure that the **Update automatically** option button is selected so that the current date prints on the notes and handouts each time the presentation is printed. If it is not selected, click the Update automatically option button.

4 Verify that the **Page number** check box is selected and select it if it is not. If necessary, clear the Header check box to omit this element. Notice that in the **Preview** box, the corresponding placeholder is not selected.

5 Select the **Footer** check box, and then click in the **Footer** box. Using your own name, type **Lastname_Firstname_18A_KWT_Overview** so that the file name displays as a footer, and then compare your dialog box with Figure 18.29.

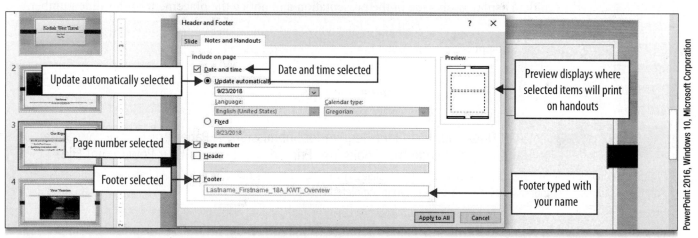

FIGURE 18.29

6 In the lower right corner of the dialog box, click **Apply to All**. Save ⊟ your presentation.

Activity 18.14 | Inserting Slide Numbers on Slides

In this Activity, you will insert the slide numbers on the presentation slides.

1 Display **Slide 1**. On the **Insert tab**, in the **Text group**, click **Header & Footer** to display the **Header and Footer** dialog box.

2 In the **Header and Footer** dialog box, if necessary, click the Slide tab. Under **Include on slide**, select the **Slide number** check box, and then select the **Don't show on title slide** check box. Verify that all other check boxes are cleared, and then compare your screen with Figure 18.30.

> Selecting the *Don't show on title slide* check box omits the slide number from the first slide in a presentation.

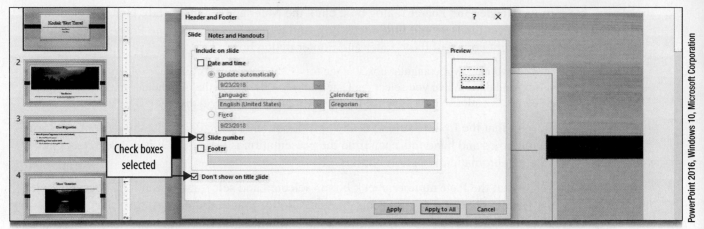

PowerPoint 2016, Windows 10, Microsoft Corporation

Check boxes selected

FIGURE 18.30

3 ▸ Click **Apply to All**, and then notice that on the first slide, the slide number does not display.

4 ▸ Display **Slide 2**, and then notice that the slide number displays in the lower right area of the slide. Display each slide in the presentation and notice the placement of the slide number.

> The position of the slide number and other header and footer information is determined by the theme applied to the presentation.

2.05a (i)
2.05a (ii)

Activity 18.15 │ **Printing Presentation Handouts**

NOTE	**What Does Your Instructor Require for Submission? A Paper Printout of Your Slide Handouts, an Image That Looks Like Printed Handouts, or Your PowerPoint File?**

In this Activity, you can produce a paper printout of your Slides, Handouts, or an electronic image of your handouts that looks like a printed document. Or, your instructor may want only your completed PowerPoint file.

Use Backstage view to preview the arrangement of slides and to print your presentation.

1 ▸ Display **Slide 1**. Click the **File tab** to display **Backstage** view, and then click **Print**.

> The Print tab in Backstage view displays the tools you need to select your settings and also to view a preview of your presentation. On the right, Print Preview displays your presentation exactly as it will print. If your system is not connected to a color printer, your slide may display in black and white.

2 ▸ Under **Settings**, click **Full Page Slides**, and then compare your screen with Figure 18.31.

> The gallery displays either the default print setting—Full Page Slides—or the most recently selected print setting. This button might indicate the presentation Notes Pages, Outline, or one of several arrangements of slide handouts—depending on the most recently used setting.

PowerPoint 2016, Windows 10, Microsoft Corporation

Print Layout

Full Page Slides   Notes Pages   Outline

Handouts

1 Slide   2 Slides   3 Slides

...es Horizontal   6 Slides Horizontal   9 Slides Horizontal

4 Slides Vertical   6 Slides Vertical   9 Slides Vertical

Frame Slides
✓ Scale to Fit Paper
High Quality
Print Comments and Ink Markup

Full Page Slides
Print 1 slide per page

Collated
1,2,3   1,2,3   1,2,3

Color

Edit Header & Footer

Info
New
Open
Save
Save As
Print
Share
Export
Close

Account
Options
Feedback

Print layout options

Print tab

Full Page Slides

Slide 1 displays in preview window

Kodiak West Travel

Your Travel
Your Way

Current page number

Number of pages to be printed

| 1 | of 5

71% − ——|—— +

FIGURE 18.31

---

3 In the gallery, under **Handouts**, click **6 Slides Horizontal**. Notice that the **Print Preview** on the right displays the slide handout, and that the current date, file name, and page number display in the header and footer. Compare your screen with Figure 18.32.

In the Settings group, the Portrait Orientation option displays; here you can change the print orientation from Portrait to Landscape. The Portrait Orientation option does not display when Full Page Slides is chosen.

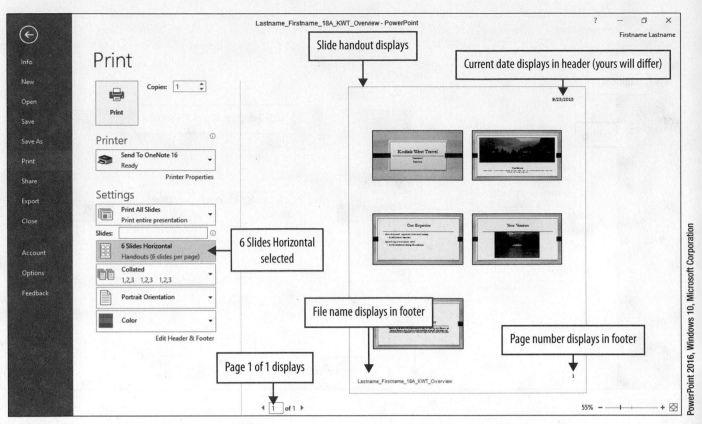

FIGURE 18.32

4 To create an electronic image of your handouts that looks like printed handouts, skip this step and continue to Step 5. To print your handout document on paper using the default printer on your system, in the upper left portion of the screen, click **Print**.

> The handout will print on your default printer—on a black and white printer, the colors will print in shades of gray. To save the cost of color ink, you can print in grayscale by clicking the Color button. Backstage view closes and your file redisplays in the PowerPoint window.

5 To create an electronic image of your document that looks like a printed document, on the left click **Export**. On the right, click the **Create PDF/XPS** button to display the **Publish as PDF or XPS** dialog box.

6 In the **Publish as PDF or XPS** dialog box, click **Options**. Under **Publish what**, click the **Slides arrow**, and then click **Handouts**. Be sure **Slides per page** is set to **6**, and **Order** is set to **Horizontal**. Click **OK**.

> **ANOTHER WAY** Under Printer, click the printer arrow, click Print as a PDF, and then click Print to print your presentation to a PDF file. Microsoft Print to PDF is an automatically installed printer option in Windows 10, which enables you to create an image that looks like a printed document.

7 Navigate to your **AIO Chapter 18** folder, and then click **Publish**. If your Adobe Acrobat or Reader program displays your PDF, close the PDF file. If your PDF displays in Microsoft Edge (on a Windows 10 computer), in the upper right corner, click Close ⊠. Notice that your presentation redisplays in PowerPoint.

IC3
DIGITAL LITERACY
CERTIFICATION
2.05a (i)

Activity 18.16 │ **Printing Speaker Notes**

1 On the **File tab**, click **Print**. Under **Settings**, click **6 Slides Horizontal**, and then under **Print Layout**, click **Notes Pages** to view the presentation notes for **Slide 1**; recall that you created notes for **Slide 3**.

> Indicated below the Notes page are the current slide number and the number of pages that will print when Notes Pages is selected. You can use the Next Page and Previous Page arrows to display each Notes page in the presentation.

2 At the bottom of the **Print Preview**, click **Next Page** ▶ two times so that **Page 3** displays. Notice that the notes that you typed for Slide 3 display below the image of the slide. Compare your screen with Figure 18.33.

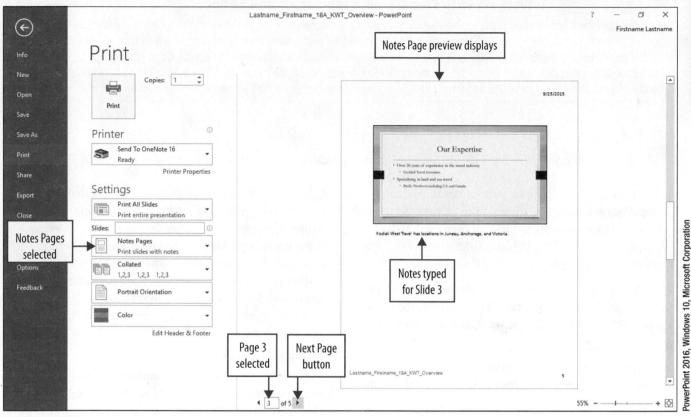

FIGURE 18.33

3 Under **Settings**, click in the **Slides box**. Type **3** and then click **Notes Pages**. In the lower section, click **Frame Slides**. Under **Printer**, click the printer arrow, click **Print as a PDF**, and then click **Print** to print your presentation to a PDF file.

> Microsoft Print to PDF is an automatically installed printer option in Windows 10, which enables you to create an image that looks like a printed document.

ALERT!   **No Print as a PDF Printer Option Available**

If you are using Windows 7 or 8, select the Microsoft XPS Document Writer printer instead to print your presentation to the XPS format, a Microsoft file format that also creates an image of your document and that opens in the XPS viewer.

---

4 Navigate to the location where you store your files for this chapter, name the file **Lastname_ Firstname_18A_KWT_Overview_Notes**, and then click **Save**.

5 Redisplay **Backstage** view. On the right, at the bottom of the **Properties** list, click **Show All Properties**. On the list of **Properties**, click to the right of **Tags**, and then type **company overview**

6 Click to the right of **Subject**, and then type your course name and section number. Under **Related People**, be sure that your name displays as the author, and edit if necessary.

7 Click **Save**. On the right end of the title bar, click **Close** ☒ to close the presentation and close PowerPoint.

END | You have completed Project 18A

GO! With Google

Build From
Scratch

ALERT! **Working with Web-Based Applications and Services**

Computer programs and services on the web receive continuous updates and improvements, so the steps to complete this web-based activity may differ from the ones shown. You can often look at the screens and the information presented to determine how to complete the activity.

If you do not already have a Google account, you will need to create one before you begin this activity. Go to http://google.com and in the upper right corner, click Sign In. On the Sign In screen, click Create Account. On the Create your Google Account page, complete the form, read and agree to the Terms of Service and Privacy Policy, and then click Next step. On the Welcome screen, click Get Started.

Activity | Creating a Company Overview Presentation in Google Slides

In this Activity, you will use Google Slides to create a presentation similar to the one you created in Project 18A.

1 From the desktop, open your browser, navigate to **http://google.com**, and then sign in to your Google account. Click **Google Apps** , and then click **Drive** . Open your **GO! Web Projects** folder—or click New to create and then open this folder if necessary.

2 In the left pane, click **NEW**, and then click **Google Slides**. In the **Themes** pane, click **Tropic**. If this theme is not available, select another theme. **Close** the **Themes** pane.

3 At the top of the window, click **Untitled presentation** and then, using your own name, type **Lastname_Firstname_18A_Web** as the file name and then press Enter.

4 In the title placeholder, type **Kodiak West Travel** and then in the subtitle placeholder type **Your Travel - Your Way**

5 On the **toolbar**, click the **New slide arrow** + , and then click **Caption**.

6 On the **toolbar**, click **Image** . In the **Insert image** dialog box, click **Choose an image to upload**. Navigate to your student data files, and then click **p18_1A_Web_Glacier**. Click **Open**.

7 Type **Your Dreams** in the text placeholder.

8 On the **toolbar**, click the **New slide arrow** + , and then click **Title and body**. Type **Our Expertise** in the title placeholder.

9 Click in the content placeholder. On the toolbar, if necessary, click More More , click **Bulleted list** . In the placeholder, type **Over 20 years of experience in the travel industry** and then press Enter. Press Tab. Type **Certified Travel Associates** and then press Enter. On toolbar, if necessary, click More, and then click **Decrease indent** . Type **Specializing in land and sea travel** and then press Enter. Press Tab and then type **Pacific Northwest including U.S. and Canada**

10 Below the slide, click in the Notes pane. Type **Kodiak West Travel has locations in Juneau, Anchorage, and Victoria.** Compare your screen to Figure A.

11 In the upper right, click the **Present arrow**, click **Present from beginning**. Click the left mouse button to progress through the presentation. When the last slide displays, press Esc or click **Exit**.

12 Your presentation will be saved automatically. If you are instructed to submit your file, click the **File** menu, point to **Download as**, and then click Microsoft PowerPoint, PDF Document, or another format as directed by your instructor. The file will download to your default download folder as determined by your browser settings. Sign out of your Google account and close your browser.

(GO! With Google continues on the next page)

GO! With Google

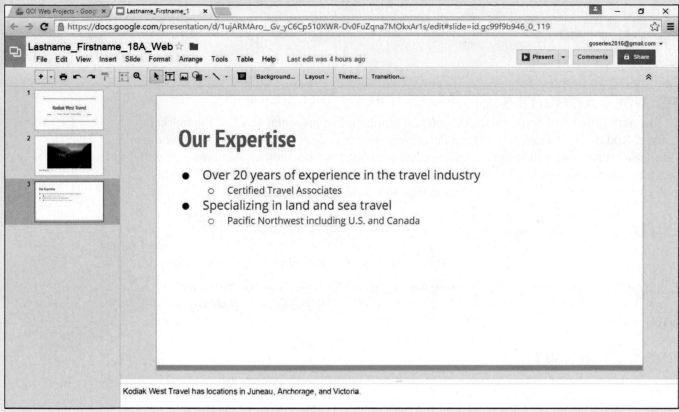

PROJECT ACTIVITIES

In Activities 18.17 through 18.33, you will combine two presentations that the marketing team at Kodiak West Travel developed describing itinerary ideas when visiting Seattle before or after a cruise. You will insert slides from one presentation into another, and then you will rearrange and delete slides. You will also apply font formatting and slide transitions to the presentation. Your completed presentation will look similar to Figure 18.34.

PROJECT FILES

MyITLab grader If your instructor wants you to submit Project 18B in the MyITLab Grader system, log in to MyITLab, locate Grader Project 18B, and then download the files for this project.

For Project 18B, you will need the following files:

p18B_Seattle
p18B_Slides

You will save your presentation as:

Lastname_Firstname_18B_Seattle

PROJECT RESULTS

GO!
Walk Thru
Project18B

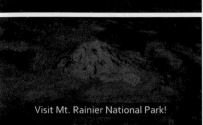

PowerPoint 2016, Windows 10, Microsoft Corporation

FIGURE 18.34 Project 18B Seattle

GO! Learn How
Video P18-5

Recall that editing refers to the process of adding, deleting, and modifying presentation content. You can edit presentation content in either the Slide pane or in the presentation outline.

Activity 18.17 | Changing Slide Size

ALERT! **To submit as an autograded project, log into MyITLab, download the files for this project, and begin with those files instead of the student data files.**

Presentations created with one of the new themes in PowerPoint 2016 default to a widescreen format using a 16:9 *aspect ratio*—the ratio of the width of a display to the height of the display. This slide size is similar to most television and computer monitor screens. PowerPoint 2010 and earlier versions of PowerPoint used a squarer format with a 4:3 aspect ratio. The widescreen format utilizes screen space more effectively.

1 Start PowerPoint. On the left, under the list of recent presentations, click **Open Other Presentations**. Under **Open**, click **Browse**. In the **Open** dialog box, navigate to your student data files, and then click **p18B_Seattle**. Click **Open**. On the **File tab**, click **Save As**, navigate to your **AIO Chapter 18** folder, and then using your own name, save the file as **Lastname_Firstname_18B_Seattle**

2 Notice that **Slide 1** displays in a square format.

3 On the **Design tab**, in the **Customize group**, click **Slide Size**, and then click **Widescreen (16:9)**. Compare your screen with Figure 18.35, and notice that the slide fills the slide pane. **Save** 🖫 the presentation.

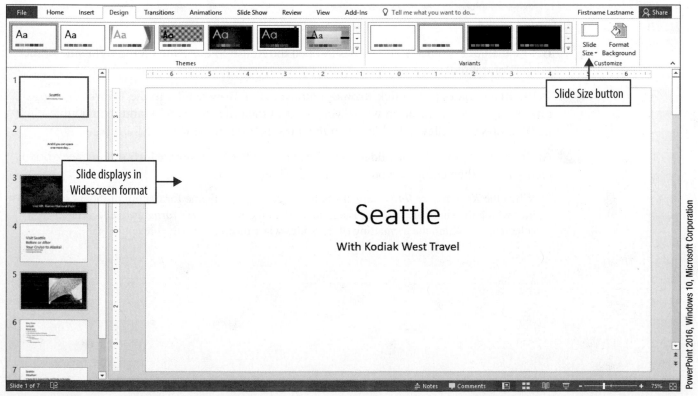

FIGURE 18.35

PowerPoint 2016, Windows 10, Microsoft Corporation

IC3
DIGITAL LITERACY
CERTIFICATION
2.05g (i)

Activity 18.18 | Inserting Slides from an Existing Presentation

Presentation content is commonly shared among group members in an organization. Rather than re-creating slides, you can insert slides from an existing presentation into the current presentation. In this Activity, you will insert slides from an existing presentation into your 1B_Seattle presentation.

1 With **Slide 1** displayed, on the **Home tab**, in the **Slides group**, click the **New Slide arrow** to display the **Slide Layout** gallery and additional commands for inserting slides. Compare your screen with Figure 18.36.

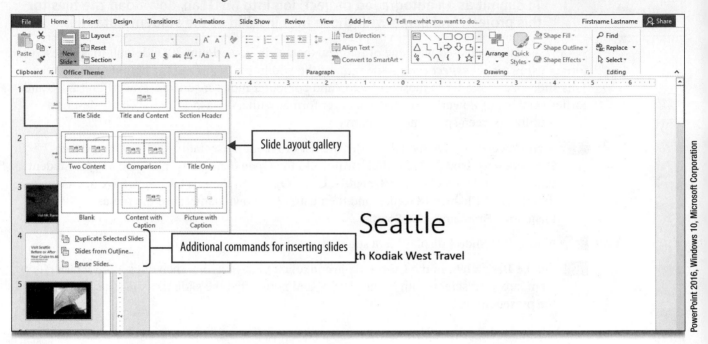

FIGURE 18.36

2 Below the gallery, click **Reuse Slides** to open the Reuse Slides pane on the right side of the PowerPoint window.

3 In the **Reuse Slides** pane, click **Browse**, and then click **Browse File**. In the **Browse** dialog box, navigate to the location where your student data files are stored, and then double-click **p18B_Slides** to display the slides from this presentation in the Reuse Slides pane.

4 At the bottom of the **Reuse Slides** pane, be sure that the **Keep source formatting** check box is *cleared*, and then compare your screen with Figure 18.37.

When the *Keep source formatting* check box is cleared, the theme formatting of the presentation into which the slides are inserted is applied. When the *Keep source formatting* check box is selected, you retain the formatting of the slides when inserted into the presentation.

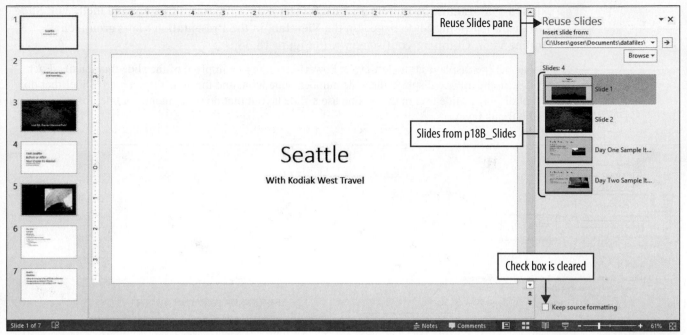

FIGURE 18.37

PowerPoint 2016, Windows 10, Microsoft Corporation

5 In the **Reuse Slides** pane, point to each slide to view a ScreenTip displaying the file name and the slide title.

6 In the **Reuse Slides** pane, click the first slide to insert the slide after **Slide 1** in your Seattle presentation. Notice that the inserted slide adopts the color of your Seattle presentation theme.

> **NOTE**   Inserting Slides
>
> You can insert slides into your presentation in any order; remember to display the slide that will come before the slide that you want to insert.

7 In your **18B_Seattle** presentation, in the slide thumbnails, click **Slide 7** to display it in the Slide pane.

8 In the **Reuse Slides** pane, click the fourth slide to insert it after **Slide 7**.

Your presentation contains nine slides. When a presentation contains a large number of slides, a scroll box displays to the right of the slide thumbnails so that you can scroll and then select the thumbnails.

9 **Close** ✕ the **Reuse Slides** pane, and then **Save** 🖫 the presentation.

> **More Knowledge**   Inserting All Slides
>
> You can insert all of the slides from an existing presentation into the current presentation at one time. In the Reuse Slides pane, right-click one of the slides that you want to insert, and then click Insert All Slides.

Activity 18.19 | Displaying and Editing the Presentation Outline

Outline View displays the presentation outline to the left of the Slide pane. You can use the outline to edit the presentation text. Changes that you make in the outline are immediately displayed in the Slide pane.

1 To the right of the slide thumbnails, if necessary, drag the scroll box up, and then click **Slide 1** to display it in the Slide pane. On the **View tab**, in the **Presentation Views group**, click **Outline View**. Compare your screen with Figure 18.38.

The outline displays at the left of the PowerPoint window in place of the slide thumbnails. Each slide in the outline displays the slide number, slide icon, and the slide title in bold. Slides that do not display a slide title in the outline use a slide layout that does not include a title, for example, the Blank layout.

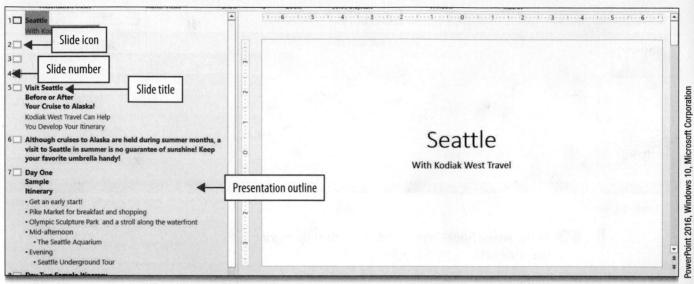

FIGURE 18.38

2 In the **Outline**, in **Slide 7**, drag to select the text of the second and third bullet points—*Pike Market for breakfast and shopping*, and *Olympic Sculpture Park and a stroll along the waterfront*. Compare your screen with Figure 18.39.

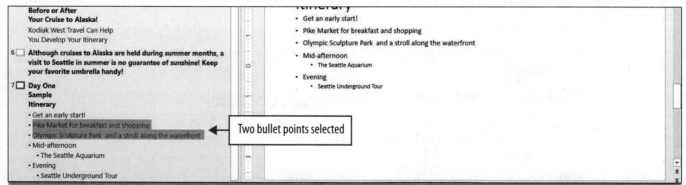

FIGURE 18.39

PowerPoint 2016, Windows 10, Microsoft Corporation

3 On the **Home tab**, in the **Paragraph group**, click **Increase List Level** one time to increase the list level of the selected bullet points.

When you type in the outline or change the list level, the changes also display in the Slide pane.

4 In the **Outline**, in **Slide 7**, click at the end of the last bullet point after the word *Tour*. Press Enter to create a new bullet point at the same list level as the previous bullet point. Type **Pike Place Market for dinner** and then compare your screen with Figure 18.40.

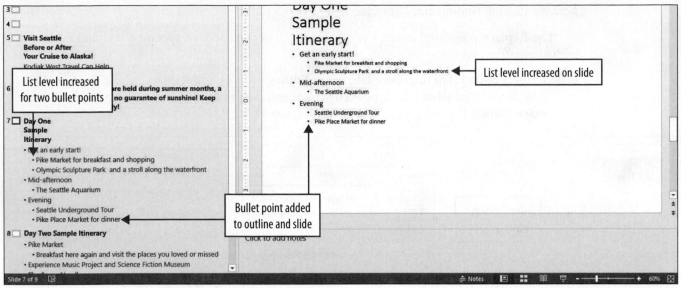

List level increased
for two bullet points

Bullet point added
to outline and slide

List level increased on slide

Slide 7 of 9

FIGURE 18.40

5 In the **Status bar**, click **Normal** ▣ to close Outline View and redisplay the slide thumbnails. **Save** ▣ the presentation.

You can type text in the Slide pane or in the Outline. Displaying the Outline enables you to view the entire flow of the presentation text.

IC3
DIGITAL LITERACY
CERTIFICATION
2.05g (i)
2.05g (iii)
2.05g (iv)

Activity 18.20 | Deleting and Moving a Slide

1 To the right of the slide thumbnails, locate the vertical scroll bar and scroll box. If necessary, drag the scroll box down so that Slide 9 displays in the slide thumbnails. Click **Slide 9** to display it in the Slide pane. Press Delete to delete the slide from the presentation.

Your presentation contains eight slides.

2 If necessary, scroll the slide thumbnails so that **Slide 4** displays. Point to **Slide 4**, hold down the left mouse button, and then drag down to position the **Slide 4** thumbnail below the **Slide 8** thumbnail. Release the mouse button, and then compare your screen with Figure 18.41. **Save** ▣ the presentation.

You can easily rearrange your slides by dragging a slide thumbnail to a new location in the presentation.

🔄 **BY TOUCH**   Use your finger to drag the slide you want to move to a new location in the presentation.

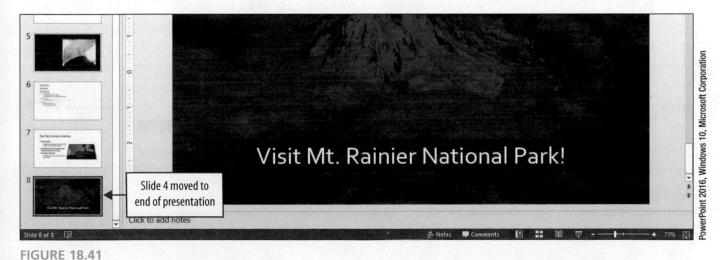

Slide 4 moved to
end of presentation

Visit Mt. Rainier National Park!

Slide 8 of 8

FIGURE 18.41

Activity 18.21 | Finding and Replacing Text

The Replace command enables you to locate all occurrences of specified text and replace it with alternative text.

1 Display **Slide 1**. On the **Home tab**, in the **Editing group**, click **Replace**. In the **Replace** dialog box, in the **Find what** box, type **Pike Market** and then in the **Replace with** box, type **Pike Place Market** Compare your screen with Figure 18.42.

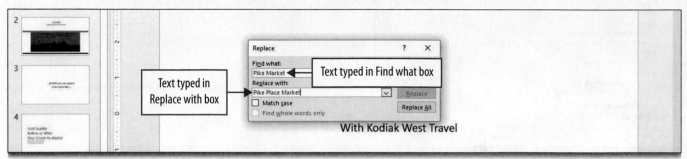

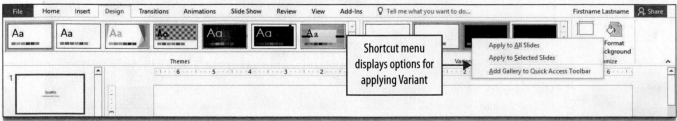

FIGURE 18.42

2 In the **Replace** dialog box, click **Replace All** to display a message box indicating that two replacements were made.

3 In the message box, click **OK**. **Close** the **Replace** dialog box, and then click **Save** 🖫.

Objective 6 | Format a Presentation

GO! Learn How
Video P18-6

2.05f (i)

Formatting refers to changing the appearance of the text, layout, and design of a slide.

Activity 18.22 | Applying a Theme Variant

Recall that a theme is a set of unified design elements that provides a look for your presentation by applying colors, fonts, and effects. Each PowerPoint theme includes several ***variants***—variations on the theme style and color. The themes and variants that are available on your system may vary.

1 On the **Design tab**, in the **Variants group**, notice that four variants of the current theme display and the second variant is applied.

2 Point to each of the variants to view the change to **Slide 1**.

If you do not see the same variants, refer to the figures for this activity.

3 With **Slide 1** displayed, in the **Variants group**, point to the **third variant**, and then right-click. Compare your screen with Figure 18.43.

The shortcut menu displays options for applying the variant.

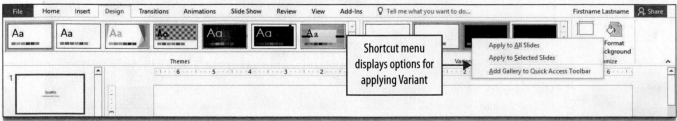

FIGURE 18.43

4. Click **Apply to Selected Slides** to apply the variant to **Slide 1** only.

5. In the **Variants group**, right-click the **second variant**. On the shortcut menu, click **Apply to All Slides** so that the original variant color is applied to all of the slides in the presentation. Compare your screen with Figure 18.44. **Save** 🖫 your presentation.

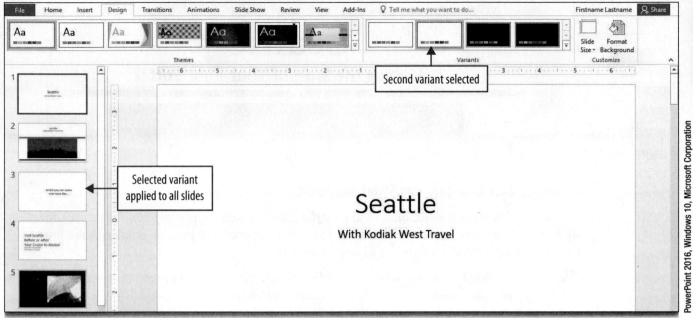

FIGURE 18.44

🔄 **ANOTHER WAY**   Click Undo to remove the variant you applied in step 4.

Activity 18.23 | Changing Fonts and Font Sizes

A font is a set of characters with the same design and shape, and fonts are measured in points.

1. Display **Slide 2**. Select all of the text in the title placeholder, point to the mini toolbar, and then click the **Font arrow** to display the available fonts. Scroll the font list, and then click **Georgia**.

2. Select the first line of the title—*Seattle*. On the mini toolbar, click the **Font Size arrow** and then click **80**.

3. Select the second line of the title—*Making the Most of Your First Port*. On the **Home tab**, in the **Font group**, click the **Font Size arrow**, and then click **36**. Click in a blank area of the slide to cancel your selection, and then compare your screen with Figure 18.45. **Save** 🖫 your presentation.

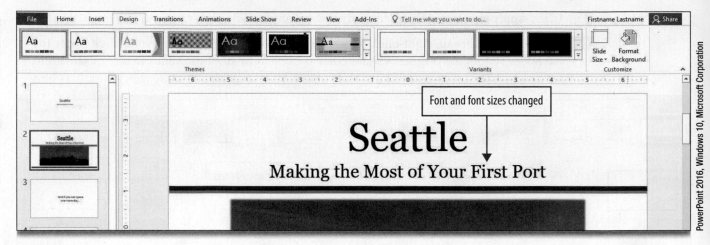

FIGURE 18.45

Activity 18.24 | Changing Font Styles and Font Colors

Font styles include bold, italic, and underline, and you can apply any combination of these styles to presentation text. Font styles and font color are useful to provide emphasis and are a visual cue to draw the reader's eye to important text.

1 Display **Slide 3**, and then select both lines of text. On the **Home tab**, in the **Font group**, click the **Font Color arrow** **A** ▾ and then compare your screen with Figure 18.46.

The colors in the top row of the color gallery are the colors associated with the presentation theme. The colors in the rows below the first row are light and dark variations of the theme colors.

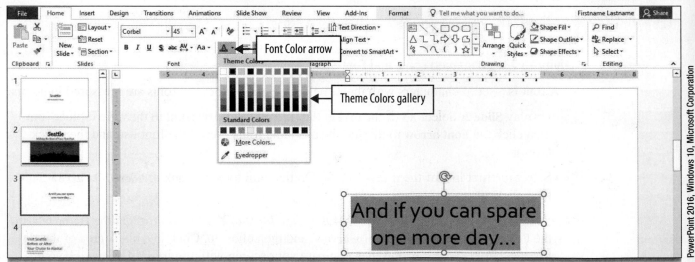

FIGURE 18.46

2 Point to several of the colors and notice that a ScreenTip displays the color name and Live Preview displays the selected text in the color to which you are pointing.

3 In the fifth column of colors, click the last color—**Dark Green, Accent 1, Darker 50%**—to change the font color. Notice that on the **Home tab**, the lower part of the **Font Color** button displays the most recently applied font color— *Dark Green, Accent 1, Darker 50%*.

> When you click the Font Color button instead of the Font Color button arrow, the color displayed in the lower part of the Font Color button is applied to selected text without displaying the color gallery.

4 With the two lines of text still selected, right-click within the selected text to redisplay the mini toolbar, and then from the mini toolbar, apply **Bold** and **Italic**.

5 Display **Slide 4**, and then select the title—*Visit Seattle Before or After Your Cruise to Alaska!* On the mini toolbar, click **Font Color** to apply the font color **Dark Green, Accent 1, Darker 50%** to the selection. Select the subtitle—*Kodiak West Travel Can Help You Develop Your Itinerary*—and then change the **Font Color** to **Dark Green, Accent 1, Darker 50%**. Click anywhere on the slide to cancel the selection, and then compare your screen with Figure 18.47. **Save** your presentation.

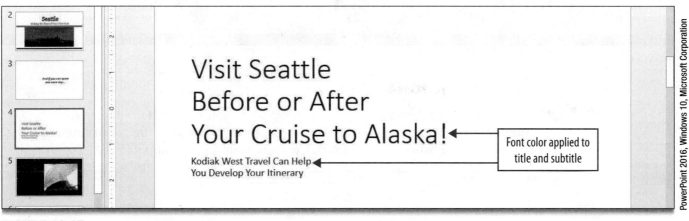

FIGURE 18.47

PowerPoint 2016, Windows 10, Microsoft Corporation

Activity 18.25 | Aligning Text

In PowerPoint, *text alignment* refers to the horizontal placement of text within a placeholder. You can align text left, centered, right, or justified.

1 Display **Slide 5**, and then click anywhere in the paragraph. On the **Home tab**, in the **Paragraph group**, click **Center** to center the text within the placeholder.

2 Display **Slide 4**, and then click anywhere in the slide title. Press Ctrl + E to use the keyboard shortcut to center the text.

3 On **Slide 4**, using one of the methods that you practiced, **Center** the subtitle. Click in a blank area of the slide. Compare your screen with Figure 18.48, and then **Save** the presentation.

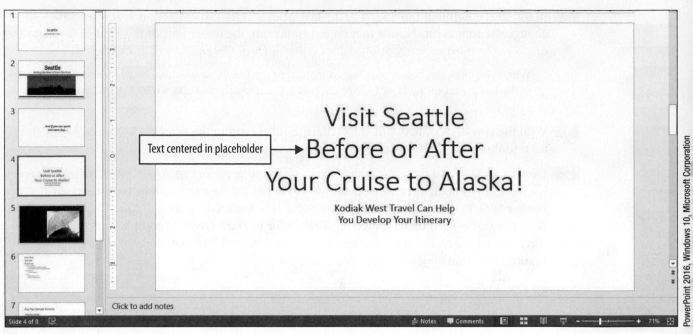

FIGURE 18.48

Activity 18.26 | Changing Line Spacing

1 Display **Slide 5**, and then click anywhere in the paragraph. On the **Home tab**, in the **Paragraph group**, click **Line Spacing** . In the list, click **2.0** to change from single spacing to double spacing between lines of text. Compare your screen with Figure 18.49.

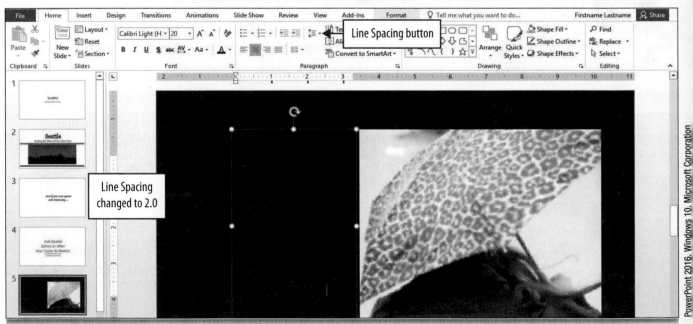

FIGURE 18.49

2 **Save** your presentation.

Activity 18.27 | Changing the Slide Layout

The slide layout defines the placement of the content placeholders on a slide. PowerPoint includes predefined layouts that you can apply to your slide for the purpose of arranging slide elements. For example, a Title Slide contains two placeholder elements—the title and the subtitle. When you design your slides, consider the content that you want to include, and then choose a layout with the elements that will display the message you want to convey in the best way.

1 Display **Slide 1**. On the **Home tab**, in the **Slides group**, click **Layout** to display the **Slide Layout** gallery. Notice that *Title Slide* is selected, indicating the layout of the current slide.

2 Click **Section Header** to change the slide layout. Compare your screen with Figure 18.50, and then **Save** 🖫 your presentation.

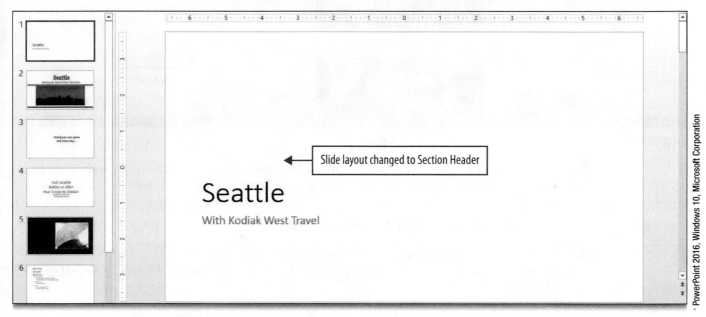

Slide layout changed to Section Header

FIGURE 18.50

Objective 7 | Use Slide Sorter View

Slide Sorter view displays thumbnails of all of the slides in a presentation. Use Slide Sorter view to rearrange and delete slides and to apply formatting to multiple slides.

Activity 18.28 | Deleting Slides in Slide Sorter View

1 In the lower right corner of the PowerPoint window, click **Slide Sorter** ⊞ to display all of the slide thumbnails. Compare your screen with Figure 18.51.

Your slides may display larger or smaller than those shown in Figure 18.51.

🔄 **ANOTHER WAY**   On the View tab, in the Presentation Views group, click Slide Sorter.

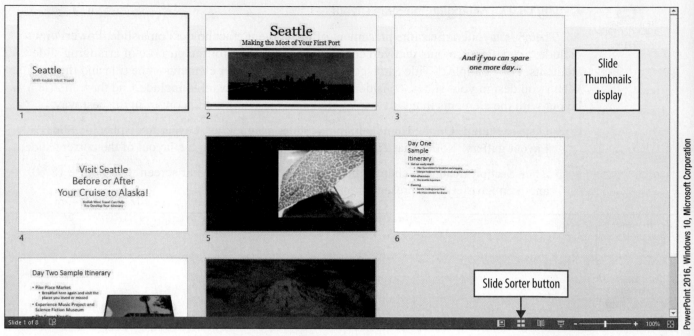

FIGURE 18.51

2.05g (iv)

2 If necessary, click **Slide 1**, and notice that a thick outline surrounds the slide, indicating that it is selected. On your keyboard, press Delete to delete the slide. Click **Save** 🖫 .

Activity 18.29 | Moving a Single Slide in Slide Sorter View

1 With the presentation displayed in **Slide Sorter** view, point to **Slide 2**. Hold down the left mouse button, and then drag to position the slide to the right of **Slide 6**, as shown in Figure 18.52.

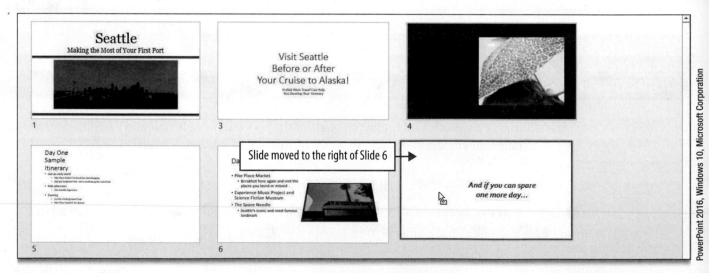

FIGURE 18.52

2 Release the mouse button to move the slide to the **Slide 6** position in the presentation. **Save** 🖫 your presentation.

Activity 18.30 | Selecting Contiguous and Noncontiguous Slides and Moving Multiple Slides

Contiguous slides are slides that are adjacent to each other in a presentation. *Noncontiguous slides* are slides that are not adjacent to each other in a presentation.

1 ▶ Click **Slide 2**, hold down Ctrl, click **Slide 4**, and then release Ctrl. Notice that both slides are selected.

The noncontiguous slides—Slides 2 and 4—are outlined, indicating that both are selected. By holding down Ctrl, you can select noncontiguous slides.

2 ▶ Click **Slide 3**, so that only Slide 3 is selected. Hold down Shift, click **Slide 5**, and then release Shift. Compare your screen with Figure 18.53.

The contiguous slides—Slides 3, 4, and 5—are outlined, indicating that all three slides are selected. By holding down Shift, you can create a group of contiguous selected slides.

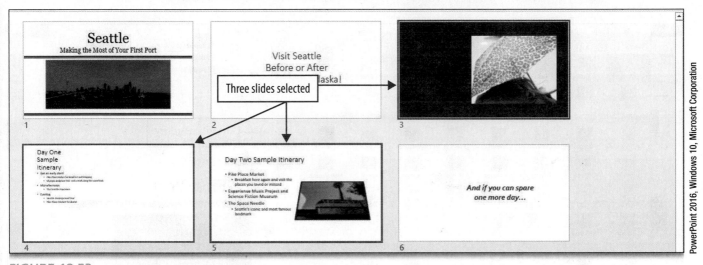

FIGURE 18.53

3 ▶ With **Slides 3, 4,** and **5** selected, hold down Ctrl, and then click **Slide 3**. Notice that only **Slides 4** and **5** are selected.

With a group of selected slides, you can press Ctrl and then click a selected slide to *deselect* it.

4 ▶ Point to either of the selected slides, hold down the left mouse button, and then drag to position the two slides to the right of **Slide 2**. Compare your screen with Figure 18.54.

The selected slides are dragged as a group, and the number 2 in the upper left area of the selected slides indicates the number of slides that you are moving.

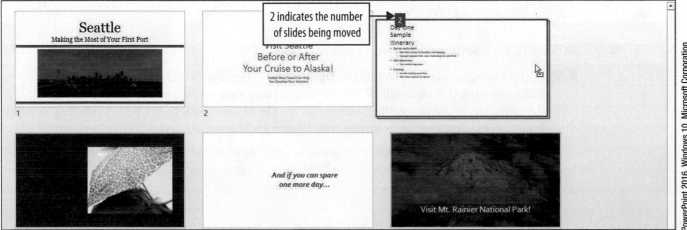

FIGURE 18.54

5 In the status bar, click **Normal** to return to Normal view. **Save** 🔲 your presentation.

Objective 8 Apply Slide Transitions

GO! Learn How
Video P18-8

Slide transitions are the motion effects that occur in Slide Show view when you move from one slide to the next during a presentation. You can choose from a variety of transitions, and you can control the speed and method with which the slides advance.

IC3
DIGITAL LITERACY
CERTIFICATION
2.05d

Activity 18.31 | Applying Slide Transitions to a Presentation

1 Display **Slide 1**. On the **Transitions tab**, in the **Transition to This Slide group**, click **More** ⏷ to display the **Transitions** gallery. Compare your screen with Figure 18.55.

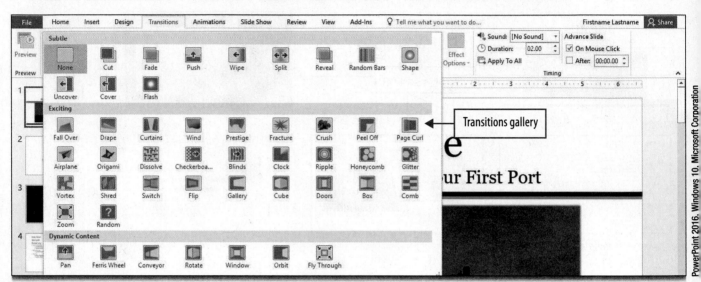

FIGURE 18.55

2 Under **Subtle**, click **Fade** to apply and view the transition. In the **Transition to This Slide group**, click **Effect Options** to display the way the slide enters the screen. Click **Smoothly**. In the **Timing group**, click **Apply To All** to apply the *Fade, Smoothly* transition to all of the slides in the presentation. **Save** 🔲 your presentation.

The Effect Options vary depending on the selected transition and include the direction from which the slide enters the screen or the shape in which the slide displays during the transition. In the slide thumbnails, a star displays below the slide number, providing a visual cue that a transition has been applied to the slide.

IC3
DIGITAL LITERACY
CERTIFICATION
2.05d

Activity 18.32 | Setting Slide Transition Timing Options

1 In the **Timing group**, notice that the **Duration** box displays *00.70*, indicating that the transition lasts 0.70 seconds. Click the **Duration up spin arrow** several times until *01.75* displays. Under **Advance Slide**, verify that the **On Mouse Click** check box is selected; select it if necessary. Compare your screen with Figure 18.56.

With On Mouse Click selected, the presenter controls when the current slide advances to the next slide by clicking the mouse button or by pressing Spacebar.

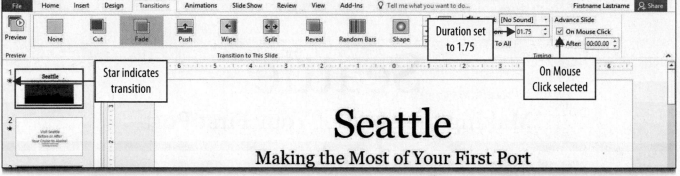

FIGURE 18.56

PowerPoint 2016, Windows 10, Microsoft Corporation

2 In the **Timing group**, click **Apply To All** so that the Duration of *1.75* seconds transition is applied to all of the slides in the presentation.

3 Click the **Slide Show tab**. In the **Start Slide Show group**, click **From Beginning**, and then view your presentation, clicking the mouse button to advance through the slides. When the black slide displays, click the mouse button one more time to display the presentation in Normal view. **Save** ⊟ your presentation.

More Knowledge	**Applying Multiple Slide Transitions**

You can apply more than one type of transition in your presentation by displaying the slides one at a time, and then clicking the transition that you want to apply instead of clicking Apply To All.

2.05c

Activity 18.33 | Displaying a Presentation in Reading View

Organizations frequently conduct online meetings when participants are unable to meet in one location. The **Reading view** in PowerPoint displays a presentation in a manner similar to a slide show, but the taskbar, title bar, and status bar remain available in the presentation window. Thus, a presenter can easily facilitate an online conference by switching to another window without closing the slide show.

1 In the lower right corner of the PowerPoint window, click **Reading View** 📖. Compare your screen with Figure 18.57.

In Reading view, the status bar contains the Next and Previous buttons, which are used to navigate in the presentation, and the Menu button, which is used to print, copy, and edit slides.

⟳ ANOTHER WAY   On the View tab, in the Presentation Views group, click Reading View.

FIGURE 18.57

2 Press Spacebar to display **Slide 2**. Click the left mouse button to display **Slide 3**. In the status bar, click **Previous** ◀ to display **Slide 2**.

3 In the status bar, click **Menu** 🔳 to display the Reading view menu, and then click **End Show** to return to Normal view.

🔄 **ANOTHER WAY**   Press Esc to exit Reading view and return to Normal view.

4 On the **Insert tab**, in the **Text group**, click **Header & Footer**, and then click the **Notes and Handouts tab**. Under **Include on page**, select the **Date and time** check box, and if necessary, select Update automatically. If necessary, select the Page number check box and clear the Header check box. Select the **Footer** check box, in the **Footer** box, using your own name, type **Lastname_Firstname_18B_Seattle** and then click **Apply to All**.

5 Display **Backstage** view, and then on the right, at the bottom of the **Properties** list, click **Show All Properties**. On the list of properties, click to the right of **Tags**, and then type **Seattle** To the right of **Subject**, type your course name and section number. Under **Related People**, be sure that your name displays as the author; edit if necessary.

6 On the left, scroll up as necessary, and then click **Save**. As directed by your instructor, create and submit a paper printout or an electronic image of your presentation that looks like a printed document; or, submit your completed PowerPoint file.

7 **Close** ☒ PowerPoint.

END | You have completed Project 18B

GO! With Google

Objective   Create an Itinerary Presentation in Google Slides

ALERT!   **Working with Web-Based Applications and Services**

Computer programs and services on the web receive continuous updates and improvements, so the steps to complete this web-based activity may differ from the ones shown. You can often look at the screens and the information presented to determine how to complete the activity. If you do not already have a Google account, you will need to create one before you begin this activity.

Activity | Creating an Itinerary Presentation in Google Slides

In this Activity, you will use Google Slides to create a presentation similar to the one you created in Project 18B.

1 From the desktop, open your browser, navigate to **http://google.com**, and then sign in to your Google account. Click **Google Apps** [⠿] and then click **Drive**. Open your **GO! Web Projects** folder—or create and then open this folder if necessary.

2 In the left pane, click **NEW**, and then click **File upload** [🖹]. Navigate to your student data files, click **p18_18B_Web**, and then click **Open**.

3 Wait a moment for the upload to complete, point to the uploaded file **p18_18B_Web.pptx**, and then right-click. On the shortcut menu, click **Rename**. Delete the existing text, and then using your own last name and first name, type **Lastname_Firstname_18B_Web** Click **OK** to rename the file.

4 Right-click the file that you just renamed, point to **Open with**, and then click **Google Slides**.

5 On **Slide 1**, in the Title placeholder, drag to select the two lines of text. On the **toolbar**, click the **Font arrow** [▾] and then click **Georgia**.

6 Select the text *Making the Most of Your First Port*. On the **toolbar**, click the **Font Size arrow**, and then click **24**.

7 Click **Slide 2**. Click the **Edit menu**, and then click **Delete** to remove the slide from the presentation.

8 With **Slide 2**—*Seattle Weather*—displayed, press Delete to remove the slide from your presentation. Notice that the presentation contains seven slides.

9 Display **Slide 3**, and then click in the paragraph on the left side of the slide. Drag to select the text, and then on the **toolbar**, click the **Text color arrow** [A]. Under **Theme**, click the second color—**Theme Color white**. With the paragraph still selected, on the toolbar, click **Bold** [B] and **Italic** [I]. Click the **Align** button [≡ ▾] and click **Center** [≡]. Click anywhere in a blank area of the slide to cancel the selection and view your changes.

10 In the slide thumbnails, point to **Slide 4**, hold down the left mouse button, and then drag up slightly. Notice that a black bar displays above **Slide 4**. Continue to drag up until the black bar displays above **Slide 3**. Release the mouse button to move the slide.

11 Using the technique that you just practiced, move **Slide 5** to position it above **Slide 4**.

12 Display **Slide 6**. Select all three lines of text. Click the **Align** button [≡ ▾], and then click **Center** [≡]. Click anywhere on the slide to cancel the selection. Click **Slide 1** and compare your screen with Figure A.

(GO! With Google continues on the next page)

GO! With Google

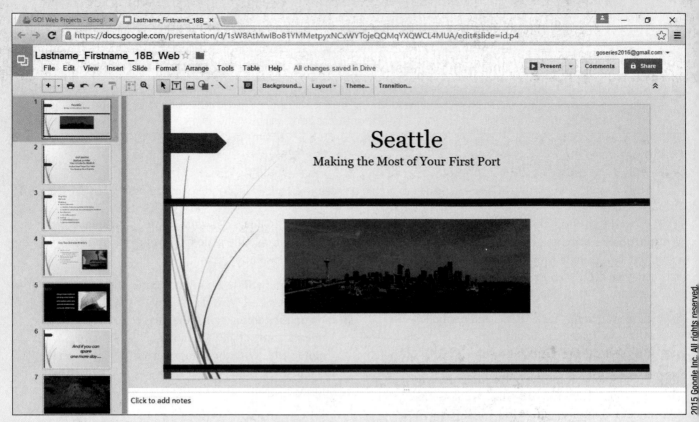

FIGURE A

13 At the right end of the toolbar, click **Transition** to open the **Animations** pane. On the right, in the Animations pane, click the **No transition button**, click **Slide from right**, and then click **Apply to all slides**.

14 To the right of the **menu bar**, click the **Present button arrow**, and then click **Present from beginning**. If necessary, click Allow. Click the left mouse button to progress through the presentation. When the last slide displays, press [Esc], or in the lower left corner, click **Exit**.

15 Your presentation will be saved automatically. Download as Microsoft PowerPoint, PDF Document, or another format and submit as directed by your instructor. Sign out of your Google account and close your browser.

PROJECT
18C Employee Training
Presentation

MyITLab
Project 18C Training
Project 18C Grader

PROJECT ACTIVITIES

In Activities 18.34 through 18.54 , you will format a presentation for Marc Johnson, Director of Operations for Sensation Park Entertainment Group, which describes important safety guidelines for employees. Your completed presentation will look similar to Figure 18.58.

PROJECT FILES

MyITLab
grader
If your instructor wants you to submit Project 18C in the MyITLab Grader system, log in to MyITLab, locate Grader Project 18C, and then download the files for this project.

For Project 18C, you will need the following file:
p18C_Safety

You will save your presentation as:
Lastname_Firstname_18C_Safety

PROJECT RESULTS

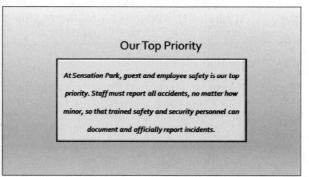

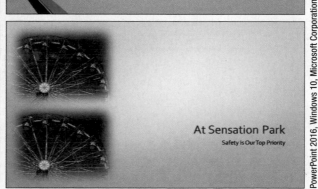

PowerPoint 2016, Windows 10, Microsoft Corporation

FIGURE 18.58 Project 18C Safety

GO! Learn How
Video P18-9

The font, color, and style of a numbered or bulleted list are determined by the presentation theme; however, you can format these elements by changing the bulleted and numbered list styles and colors. A **bulleted list**, sometimes called an unordered list, is a list of items preceded by small dots or other shapes, which do not indicate order or rank. In a **numbered list**, or ordered list, items are preceded by numbers, which indicate sequence or rank of the items.

Activity 18.34 | Selecting Placeholder Text

> **ALERT!** **To submit as an autograded project, log into MyITLab, download the files for this project, and begin with those files instead of the student data files.**

A placeholder is a box on a slide with dotted or dashed borders that holds title and body text or other content such as charts, tables, and pictures. You can format placeholder contents by selecting text or by selecting the entire placeholder.

1 Start PowerPoint. From the student data files for this chapter, locate and open **p18C_Safety**. Display the **Save As** dialog box, and then using your own name, save the file in your **AIO Chapter 18** folder as **Lastname_Firstname_18C_Safety**

2 Display **Slide 2**, and then click anywhere in the content placeholder with the single bullet point.

3 Point to the dashed border surrounding the placeholder to display the [pointer icon] pointer, and then click one time to display the border as a solid line. Compare your screen with Figure 18.59.

When a placeholder's border displays as a solid line, all of the text in the placeholder is selected, and any formatting changes that you make will be applied to *all* of the text in the placeholder.

Placeholder border displays as solid line

PowerPoint 2016, Windows 10, Microsoft Corporation

FIGURE 18.59

4 With the border of the placeholder displaying as a solid line, change the **Font Size** `60` to **24**. Notice that the font size of *all* of the placeholder text increases.

5 **Save** 🖫 your presentation.

Activity 18.35 | Changing a Bulleted List to a Numbered List

You can easily change a bulleted list to a numbered list. In this safety presentation, the list of steps to follow should be a numbered list.

1 Display **Slide 3**, and then click anywhere in the bulleted list. Point to the placeholder dashed border to display the 🖟 pointer, and then click one time to display the border as a solid line indicating that all of the text is selected.

2 On the **Home tab**, in the **Paragraph group**, click **Numbering** ☰▾, and then compare your slide with Figure 18.60. **Save** 🖫 your presentation.

All of the bullet symbols are converted to numbers. The color of the numbers is determined by the presentation theme.

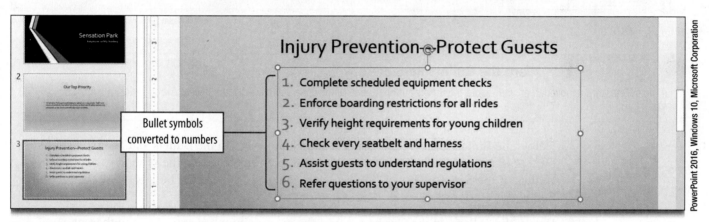

FIGURE 18.60

> **ALERT!** **Did You Display the Numbering Gallery?**
>
> If you clicked the Numbering arrow instead of the Numbering button, the Numbering gallery displays. Click the Numbering arrow again to close the gallery, and then click the Numbering button to convert the bullets to numbers.

Activity 18.36 | Changing the Shape and Color of a Bulleted List Symbol

The presentation theme includes default styles for the bullet points in content placeholders. You can customize a bullet by changing its style, color, and size.

1 Display **Slide 4**, and then select the three second-level bullet points—*Ride entrances*, *Visitor center*, and *Rest areas*.

2 On the **Home tab**, in the **Paragraph group**, click the **Bullets button arrow** ☰▾ to display the **Bullets** gallery, and then compare your screen with Figure 18.61.

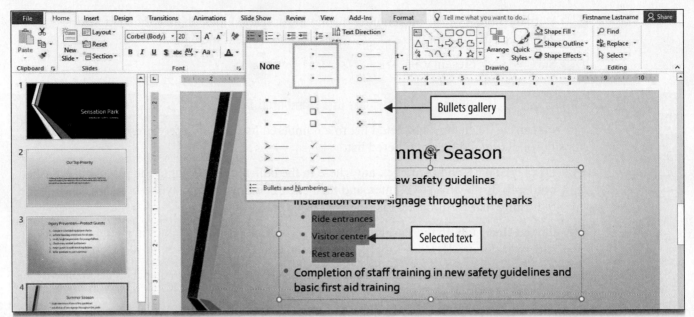

FIGURE 18.61

PowerPoint 2016, Windows 10, Microsoft Corporation

ALERT! **Were the Bullets Removed?**

If the bullets were removed, then you clicked the Bullets button instead of the Bullets arrow. Click the Bullets arrow, and then continue with Step 3.

> **3** Below the **Bullets** gallery, click **Bullets and Numbering**. In the **Bullets and Numbering** dialog box, point to each bullet style to display its ScreenTip. Then, in the second row, click **Star Bullets**. If the Star Bullets are not available, in the second row of bullets, click the second bullet style, and then click the Reset button.

> **4** Below the gallery, in the **Size** box, select the existing number, type **100** and then click **Color** 🖊. Under **Theme Colors**, in the eighth column, click the last color—**Red, Accent 4, Darker 50%**, and then compare your dialog box with Figure 18.62.

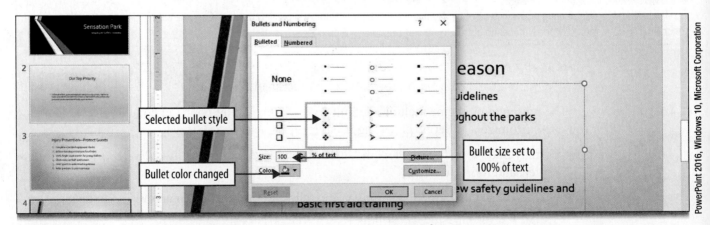

FIGURE 18.62

PowerPoint 2016, Windows 10, Microsoft Corporation

> **5** Click **OK** to apply the bullet style, and then **Save** 🖫 your presentation.

More Knowledge | **Using Other Symbols as Bullet Characters**

Many bullets styles are available to insert in your presentation. In the Bullets and Numbering dialog box, click Customize to view additional bullet styles.

Activity 18.37 | Removing a Bullet Symbol from a Bullet Point

The Bullets button is a toggle, enabling you to turn the bullet symbol on and off. A slide that contains a single bullet point can be formatted as a single paragraph *without* a bullet symbol.

> **1** Display **Slide 2**, and then click in the paragraph. On the **Home tab**, in the **Paragraph group**, click **Bullets** ☷ ▾. Compare your screen with Figure 18.63.

> The bullet symbol no longer displays, and the Bullets button is no longer selected. Additionally, the indentation associated with the list level is removed.

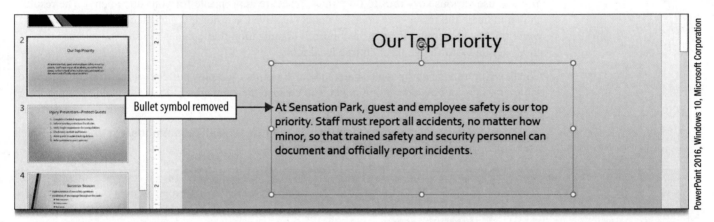

FIGURE 18.63

> **2** Click the dashed border to display the solid border and to select all of the text in the paragraph, and then apply **Bold** **B** and **Italic** *I*. **Center** ≡ the paragraph. On the **Home tab**, in the **Paragraph group**, click **Line Spacing** ☷ ▾, and then click **2.0**. **Save** 🖫 your presentation.

Objective 10 Insert Online Pictures

GO! Learn How
Video P18-10

There are many sources from which you can insert images and other media into a presentation. One type of image that you can insert is a *clip*—a single media file such as art, sound, animation, or a movie.

IC3
DIGITAL LITERACY
CERTIFICATION
2.05e (ii)
2.07a

Activity 18.38 | Inserting Online Pictures in a Content Placeholder

> **1** Display **Slide 5**. In the placeholder on the right side of the slide, click **Online Pictures** 🖼 to display the **Insert Pictures** dialog box, and then compare your screen with Figure 18.64.

FIGURE 18.64

2 With the insertion point in the **Bing Image Search** box, type **pouring water** and then press Enter to search for images that contain the keywords *pouring water*. Point to any of the results, and notice that keywords display. Select a vertical image of water being poured, similar to Figure 18.65.

> You can use various keywords to find images that are appropriate for your documents. The results shown indicate the images are licensed under Creative Commons, which, according to **www.creativecommons.org**, is "a nonprofit organization that enables the sharing and use of creativity and knowledge through free legal tools."
>
> Creative Commons helps people share and use their photographs, but does not allow companies to sell them. For your college assignments, you can use these images so long as you are not profiting by selling the images.
>
> To find out more about Creative Commons, go to **https://creativecommons.org/about** and watch their video.

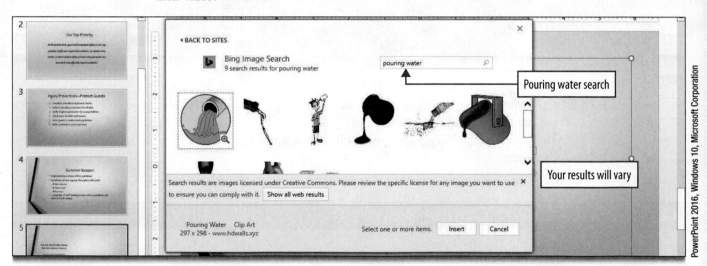

FIGURE 18.65

3 With the water picture selected, click **Insert**. Compare your screen with Figure 18.66, and then **Save** 🖫 your presentation.

On the ribbon, the Picture Tools display, and the pouring water image is surrounded by sizing handles, indicating that it is selected.

🔄 **BY TOUCH**   Tap the picture that you want to insert, and then tap Insert.

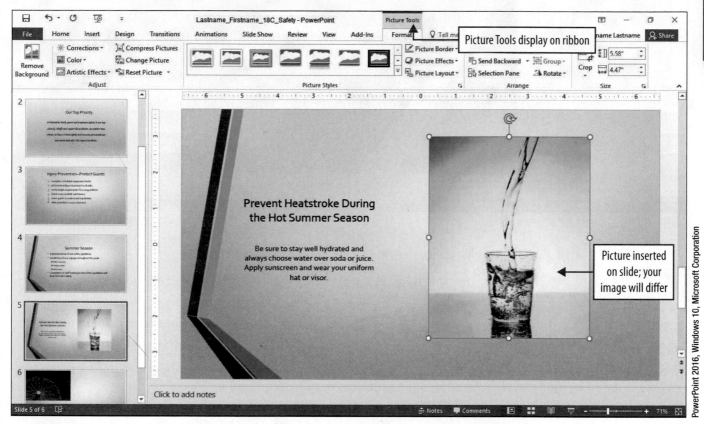

FIGURE 18.66

IC3
DIGITAL LITERACY
CERTIFICATION
2.05e (ii)
2.07a

Activity 18.39 │ Inserting Online Pictures in Any Location on a Slide

1 Display **Slide 1**. On the **Insert tab**, in the **Images group**, click **Online Pictures**.

2 In the **Insert Pictures** dialog box, in the **Bing Image Search** box, type **red lights** and then press Enter. Click a picture of a single red light, and then click **Insert**. Compare your screen with Figure 18.67. **Save** 🖫 your presentation.

When you use the Online Pictures button on the ribbon instead of the Online Pictures button in a content placeholder, PowerPoint inserts the image in the center of the slide.

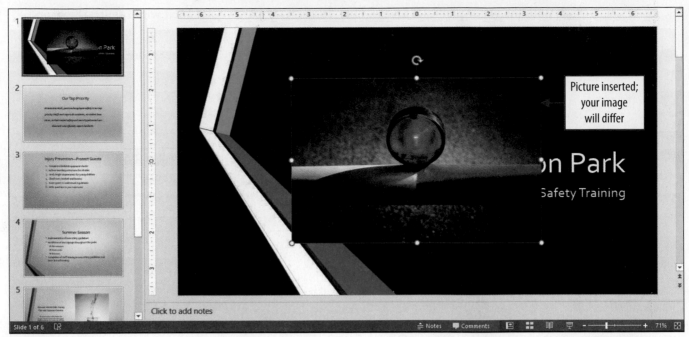

FIGURE 18.67

Activity 18.40 | Sizing a Picture

A selected image displays sizing handles that you can drag to resize the image. You can also resize an image using the Shape Height and Shape Width boxes on the Format tab.

1 If necessary, select the picture of the red light. On the **Picture Tools Format tab**, in the **Size group**, click in the **Shape Height** box, and then replace the selected number with **3.5**

2 Press Enter to resize the image. Notice that the picture is resized proportionately, and the **Width** box of this image displays *5.26*—or another measurement; your width will vary depending upon the image you select. Compare your screen with Figure 18.68, and then **Save** your presentation.

When a picture is resized in this manner, the width adjusts in proportion to the picture height.

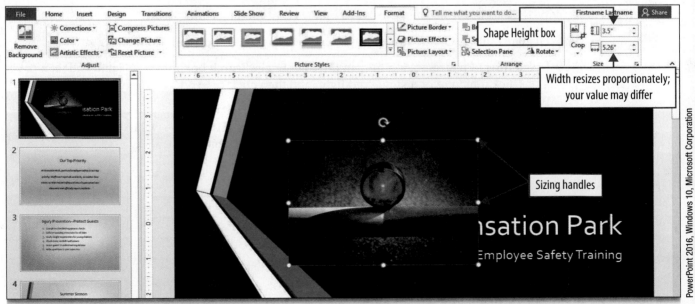

FIGURE 18.68

⟳ BY TOUCH Drag the corner sizing handle with your finger or mouse to resize the picture proportionately.

Activity 18.41 | Using Smart Guides and the Ruler to Position a Picture

Smart Guides are dashed lines that display on your slide when you are moving an object to assist you with alignment.

1 On **Slide 1**, on the **View tab**, in the **Show group**, verify that the **Ruler** check box is selected and if necessary, select the check box. On the horizontal and vertical rulers, notice that *0* displays in the center. Point to the picture, and then drag up so that the top edge of the picture aligns with the top edge of the slide.

Horizontally, the PowerPoint ruler indicates measurements from the center of the slide *out* to the left and to the right. Vertically, the PowerPoint ruler indicates measurements from the center up and down.

2 Point to the picture to display the 🔆 pointer. Hold down Shift, and then slowly drag the picture to the right and notice that dashed red Smart Guides periodically display along the edges of the picture. When the dashed red Smart Guide displays on the right edge of the picture at approximately **6 inches to the right of zero on the horizontal ruler**, compare your screen with Figure 18.69.

Smart Guides display when you move an object and it is aligned with another object on the slide. Here, the Smart Guide displays because the right edge of the picture is aligned with the right edge of the title placeholder. Pressing Shift while dragging an object constrains object movement in a straight line either vertically or horizontally. Here, pressing Shift maintains the vertical placement of the picture at the top edge of the slide.

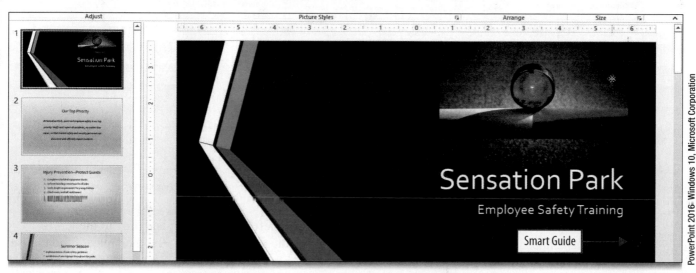

FIGURE 18.69

3 Release the mouse button and Shift key, and then **Save** 🖫 the presentation.

More Knowledge | **Moving an Object by Using the Arrow Keys**

You can use the directional arrow keys on your keyboard to move a picture, shape, or other object in small increments. Select the object so that its outside border displays as a solid line. Then, on your keyboard, press the directional arrow keys to move the selected object in small, precise increments.

Activity 18.42 | Cropping a Picture

When you **crop** a picture you remove unwanted or unnecessary areas of the picture.

1 Display **Slide 6**, and then select the Ferris wheel picture. On the **Picture Tools Format tab**, in the **Size group**, click the upper portion of the **Crop** button to display the crop handles on the edges of the picture. Compare your screen with Figure 18.70.

Use the **crop handles** like sizing handles to remove unwanted areas of the picture.

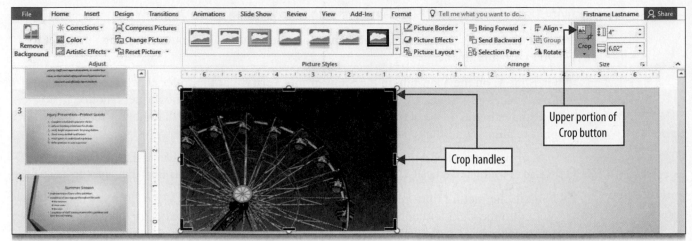

2 ▸ Point to the center right crop handle to display the crop pointer ⊢. Compare your screen with Figure 18.71.

The *crop pointer* is the mouse pointer that displays when cropping areas of a picture.

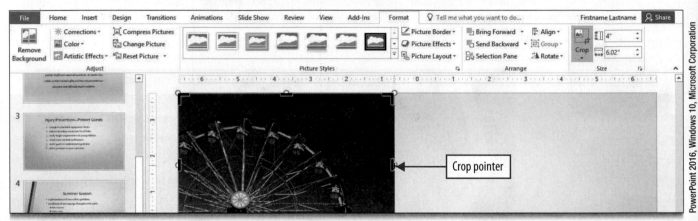

3 ▸ With the crop pointer displayed, hold down the left mouse button and drag to the left to approximately **1.5 inches to the left of zero on the horizontal ruler**, and then release the mouse button. Compare your screen with Figure 18.72.

The portion of the picture to be removed by the crop displays in gray.

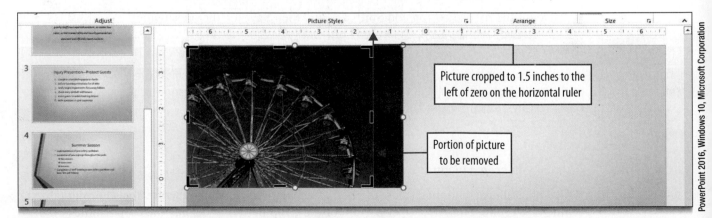

> **4** On the **Picture Tools Format tab**, in the **Size group**, click the upper portion of the **Crop** button to apply the crop, and then **Save** 🔲 your presentation.

🔄 **ANOTHER WAY**   Press [Enter] or click outside the picture to apply the crop.

IC3
DIGITAL LITERACY
CERTIFICATION
2.07b

Activity 18.43 | Using the Crop to Shape Command to Change the Shape of a Picture

An inserted picture is typically rectangular in shape; however, you can modify a picture by changing its shape.

> **1** Display **Slide 1**, and then select the picture. On the **Picture Tools Format tab**, in the **Size group**, click the lower portion of the **Crop** button—the **Crop arrow**—and then compare your screen with Figure 18.73.

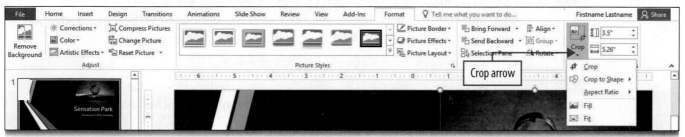

PowerPoint 2016, Windows 10, Microsoft Corporation

FIGURE 18.73

> **2** Point to **Crop to Shape** to display a gallery of shapes. Under **Basic Shapes**, in the first row, click the first shape—**Oval**—to change the picture's shape to an oval. Compare your screen with Figure 18.74.

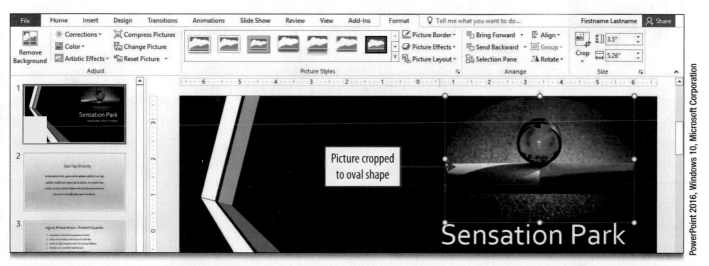

PowerPoint 2016, Windows 10, Microsoft Corporation

FIGURE 18.74

> **3** **Save** 🔲 your presentation.

GO! Learn How
Video P18-11

You can use objects, including text boxes and shapes, to draw attention to important information or to serve as containers for slide text. Many shapes, including lines, arrows, ovals, and rectangles, are available to insert and position anywhere on your slides.

Activity 18.44 | Inserting a Text Box

A *text box* is an object with which you can position text anywhere on a slide.

1 Display **Slide 3** and verify that the rulers display. On the **Insert tab**, in the **Text group**, click **Text Box**.

2 Move the ⬇ pointer to several different places on the slide, and as you do so, in the horizontal and vertical rulers, notice that *ruler guides*—dotted red vertical and horizontal lines that display in the rulers indicating the pointer's position—move also.

Use the ruler guides to help you position objects on a slide.

3 Position the pointer so that the ruler guides are positioned on the **left half of the horizontal ruler at 4.5 inches** and on the **lower half of the vertical ruler at 2 inches**, and then compare your screen with Figure 18.75.

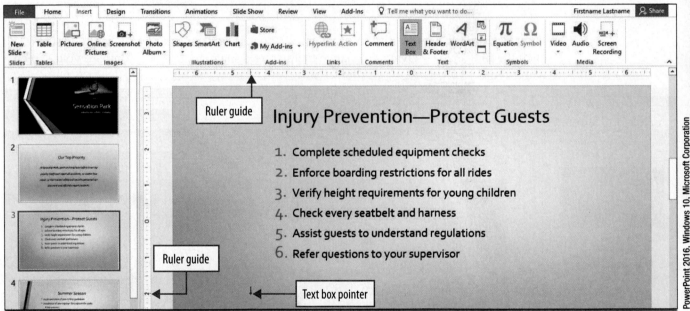

FIGURE 18.75

4 Click one time to create a narrow rectangular text box surrounded by sizing handles. With the insertion point blinking inside the text box, type **If Safety is Questionable** Notice that as you type, the width of the text box expands to accommodate the text. Compare your screen with Figure 18.76.

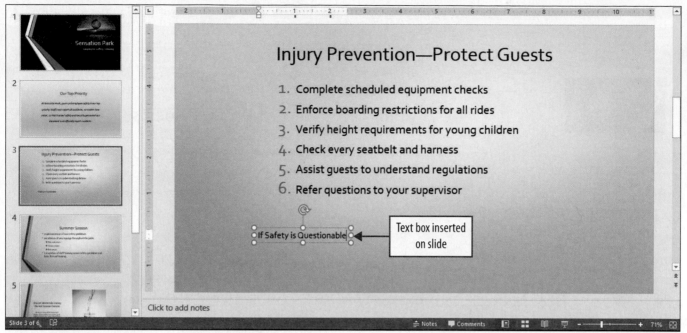

FIGURE 18.76

PowerPoint 2016, Windows 10, Microsoft Corporation

ALERT! **Does the Text in the Text Box Display Vertically, One Character at a Time?**

If you move the pointer when you click to create the text box, PowerPoint sets the width of the text box and does not widen to accommodate the text. If this happens, your text may display vertically instead of horizontally or it may display on two lines. Click Undo, and then repeat the steps again, being sure that you do not move the mouse when you click to insert the text box.

5 Select the text that you typed, change the **Font Size** to **24**, and then **Save** 🖫 your presentation.

You can format the text in a text box by using the same techniques that you use to format text in any other placeholder. For example, you can change the font, font style, font size, and font color.

Activity 18.45 │ Inserting and Sizing a Shape

Shapes are slide objects such as lines, arrows, boxes, callouts, and banners. You can size and move a shape using the same techniques that you use to size and move pictures.

1 With **Slide 3** displayed, on the **Insert tab**, in the **Illustrations group**, click **Shapes** to display the **Shapes** gallery. Under **Block Arrows**, click the first shape—**Right Arrow**. Move the pointer into the slide until the ⊞ pointer—called the *crosshair pointer*—displays, indicating that you can draw a shape.

2 Move the ⊞ pointer to position the ruler guides at approximately **0 on the horizontal ruler** and on the **lower half of the vertical ruler at 2 inches**. Compare your screen with Figure 18.77.

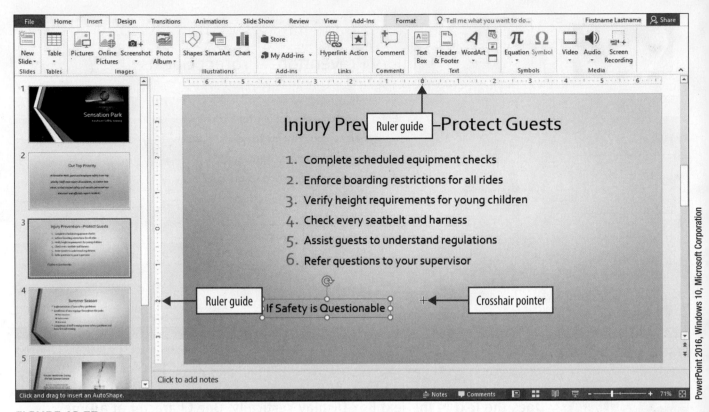

FIGURE 18.77

3 Click to insert the arrow. On the **Drawing Tools Format tab**, in the **Size group**, click in the **Shape Height** box ⬆️ to select the number. Type **0.5** and then press Enter. Click in the **Shape Width** box ↔️. Type **2** and then press Enter to resize the arrow. Compare your screen with Figure 18.78.

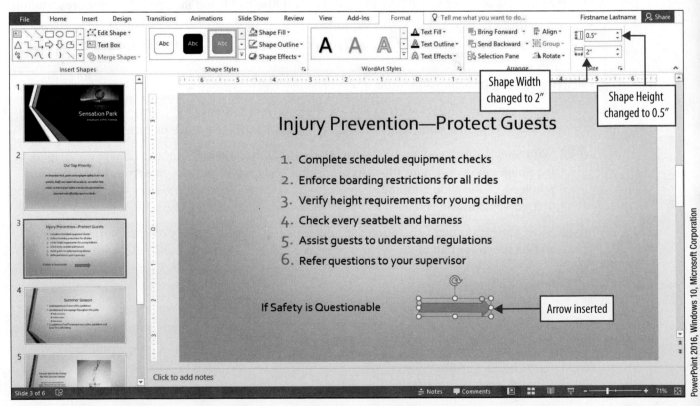

FIGURE 18.78

> **4** On the **Drawing Tools Format tab**, in the **Insert Shapes group**, click **More** ⊡. In the gallery, under **Basic Shapes**, in the first row, click the second to last shape—**Octagon**.

> **5** Move the ⊞ pointer to position the ruler guides on the **right half of the horizontal ruler at 3.5 inches** and on the **lower half of the vertical ruler at 1 inch**, and then click one time to insert an octagon.

> **6** On the **Drawing Tools Format tab**, in the **Size group**, click in the **Shape Height** box ⬚ to select the number. Type **2** and then press Enter. Click in the **Shape Width** box ⬚. Type **2** and then press Enter to resize the octagon. Compare your slide with Figure 18.79.

> Do not be concerned if your shapes are not positioned exactly as shown in the figure.

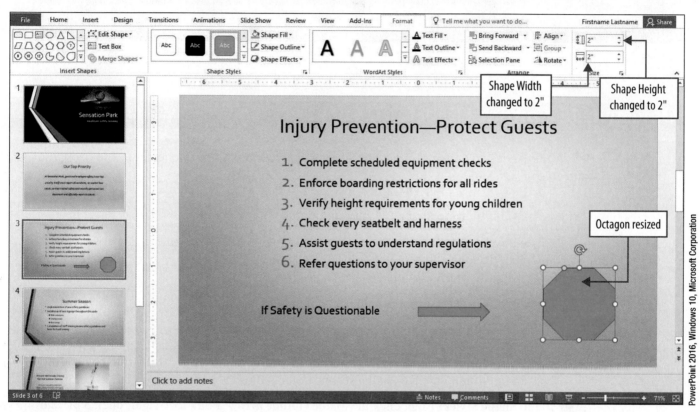

FIGURE 18.79

> **7** **Save** ⊟ your presentation.

Activity 18.46 │ Adding Text to Shapes

Shapes can serve as a container for text. After you add text to a shape, you can change the font and font size, apply font styles, and change text alignment.

> **1** On **Slide 3**, if necessary, click the octagon so that it is selected. Type **STOP** and notice that the text is centered within the octagon.

> **2** Select the text **STOP**, and then change the **Font Size** to **32**.

> **3** Click in a blank area of the slide to cancel the selection, and then compare your screen with Figure 18.80. **Save** ⊟ your presentation.

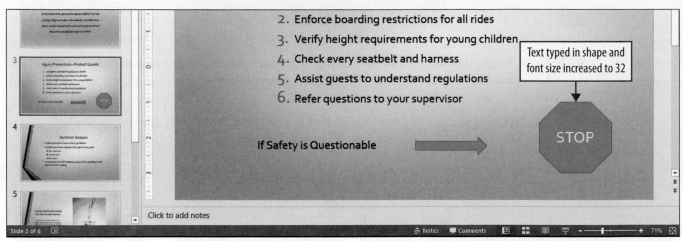

FIGURE 18.80

PowerPoint 2016, Windows 10, Microsoft Corporation

Objective 12 Format Objects

GO! Learn How
Video P18-12

Apply styles and effects to pictures, shapes, and text boxes to complement slide backgrounds and colors.

Activity 18.47 | Applying Shape Fills and Outlines

A distinctive way to format a shape is by changing the *fill color*—the inside color of text or of an object—and the outside line color. Use the Shape Styles gallery to apply predefined combinations of these fill and line colors and also to apply other effects.

1 Display **Slide 2**, and then click anywhere in the paragraph of text to select the content placeholder.

2 On the **Drawing Tools Format tab**, in the **Shape Styles group**, click the **Shape Fill arrow**. Point to several of the theme colors and watch as Live Preview changes the inside color of the text box. In the fifth column, click the second color—**Blue, Accent 1, Lighter 80%**.

3 In the **Shape Styles group**, click the **Shape Outline arrow**. Point to **Weight**, click **3 pt**, and notice that a thick outline surrounds the text placeholder. Click in a blank area of the slide so that nothing is selected, and then compare your slide with Figure 18.81. **Save** 🖫 your presentation.

You can use combinations of shape fill, outline colors, and weights to format an object.

FIGURE 18.81

Activity 18.48 | Using the Eyedropper to Change Color

The *eyedropper* is a tool that captures the exact color from an object on your screen and then applies it to any shape, picture, or text. You can use the eyedropper to give your presentation a cohesive look by matching a font color, fill color, border color, or other slide element to any color on any slide.

1 Display **Slide 6**, and then select the title text—**At Sensation Park**.

2 On the **Home tab**, in the **Font group**, click the **Font Color arrow**. Below the gallery, click **Eyedropper**, and then move the ✏ pointer into the upper right corner of the Ferris wheel picture. Compare your screen with Figure 18.82.

A small square displays next to the pointer indicating the exact color to which you are pointing. When you hover over a color, its *RGB* color coordinates display in a ScreenTip, replacing the block of color. RGB is a color model in which the colors red, green, and blue are added together to form another color.

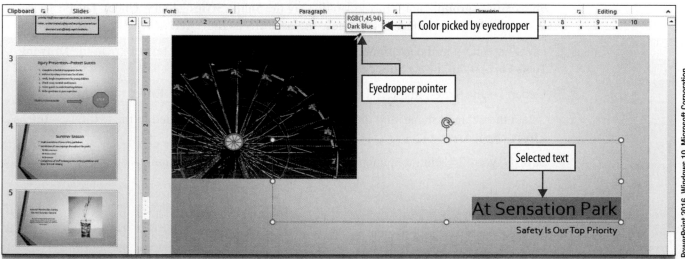

FIGURE 18.82

3 With the ✏ pointer in the upper right corner of the picture, click one time. Notice that the color is applied to the selected text. Click a blank area of the slide to deselect the text and compare your screen with Figure 18.83.

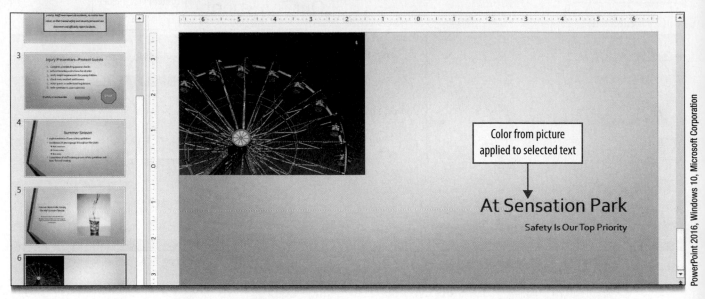

Color from picture applied to selected text

At Sensation Park

Safety Is Our Top Priority

PowerPoint 2016, Windows 10, Microsoft Corporation

FIGURE 18.83

4 Display **Slide 5**, and then select the title. On the mini toolbar, click the **Font Color arrow**. Under **Recent Colors**, notice that the color you selected with the eyedropper displays. Point to the color to display the ScreenTip—*Dark Blue*. Click **Dark Blue** to apply the color to the selection.

> After a color has been selected with the eyedropper, it remains available in the presentation each time the color gallery is displayed. When you use the eyedropper in this manner, you can consistently apply the same color throughout your presentation.

5 Save 🖫 your presentation.

Activity 18.49 | Applying Shape Styles

1 Display **Slide 3**, and then select the **arrow shape**. On the **Drawing Tools Format tab**, in the **Shape Styles group**, click **More** ⟱ to display the **Shape Styles** gallery. Under **Theme Styles**, in the last row, click the second style—**Intense Effect - Blue, Accent 1**.

2 Click anywhere in the text *If Safety is Questionable* to select the text box. On the **Drawing Tools Format tab**, in the **Shape Styles group**, click **More** ⟱.

3 Under **Theme Styles**, in the last row, click the fifth style—**Intense Effect - Red, Accent 4**.

4 Select the **octagon shape**, and then apply the same style you applied to the text box—**Intense Effect - Red, Accent 4**.

5 Save 🖫 your presentation, and then compare your screen with Figure 18.84.

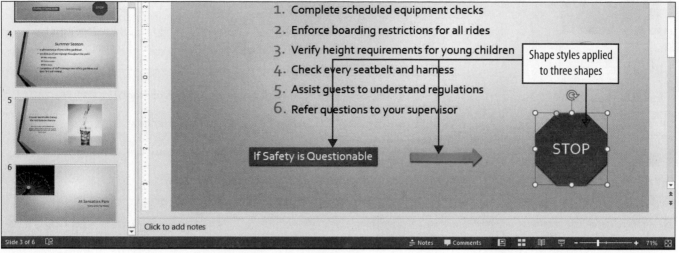

FIGURE 18.84

PowerPoint 2016, Windows 10, Microsoft Corporation

Activity 18.50 | Applying Shape and Picture Effects

1 Display **Slide 1**, and then select the picture. On the **Picture Tools Format tab**, in the **Picture Styles group**, click **Picture Effects**.

> A list of effects that you can apply to pictures displays. These effects can also be applied to shapes and text boxes.

2 Point to **Soft Edges**, and then in the **Soft Edges** gallery, point to each style to view its effect on the picture. Click the last **Soft Edges** effect—**50 Point**, and then compare your screen with Figure 18.85.

> The soft edges effect softens and blurs the outer edge of the picture so that it blends into the slide background.

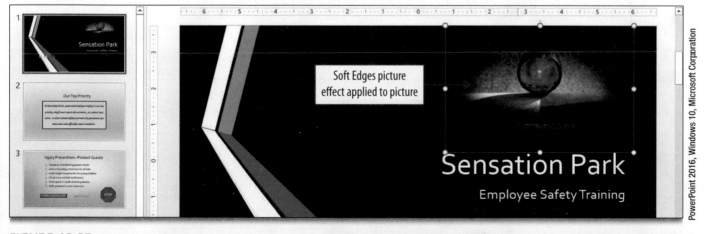

FIGURE 18.85

PowerPoint 2016, Windows 10, Microsoft Corporation

3 Display **Slide 2**, and then select the light blue content placeholder. On the **Drawing Tools Format tab**, in the **Shape Styles group**, click **Shape Effects**. Point to **Bevel** to display the **Bevel** gallery. Point to each bevel to view its ScreenTip and to use Live Preview to examine the effect of each bevel on the content placeholder. Then, in the last row, click the last bevel—**Art Deco**.

4 Click in a blank area of the slide and then compare your screen with Figure 18.86.

FIGURE 18.86

PowerPoint 2016, Windows 10, Microsoft Corporation

5 Display **Slide 5**, and then select the picture. On the **Picture Tools Format tab**, in the **Picture Styles group**, click **Picture Effects**, and then point to **Glow**.

6 Point to several of the effects to view the effect on the picture, and then under **Glow Variations**, in the second row, click the first glow effect—**Blue, 8 pt glow, Accent color 1**.

The glow effect applies a colored, softly blurred outline to the selected object.

7 **Save** 🖫 your presentation.

Activity 18.51 | Duplicating Objects

1 Display **Slide 6**, and then select the picture.

2 Press and hold down ⌃Ctrl, and then press D one time. Release ⌃Ctrl.

⌃Ctrl + D is the keyboard shortcut to duplicate an object. A duplicate of the picture overlaps the original picture and the duplicated image is selected.

3 **Save** 🖫 your presentation, click a blank area of the slide, and then compare your screen with Figure 18.87.

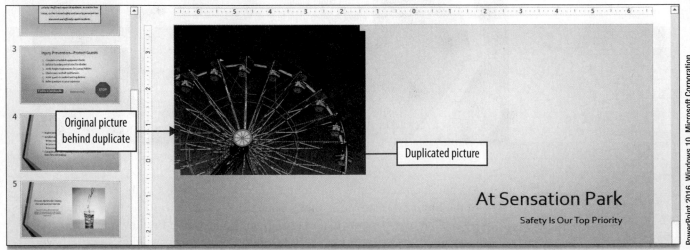

FIGURE 18.87

PowerPoint 2016, Windows 10, Microsoft Corporation

You can select multiple slide objects, and then use ribbon commands to align and distribute the objects precisely.

1 With **Slide 6** displayed, click the image in the upper left corner of the slide to select it. Hold down Shift and then click the second image so that both images are selected. Release the Shift key, and then compare your screen with Figure 18.88.

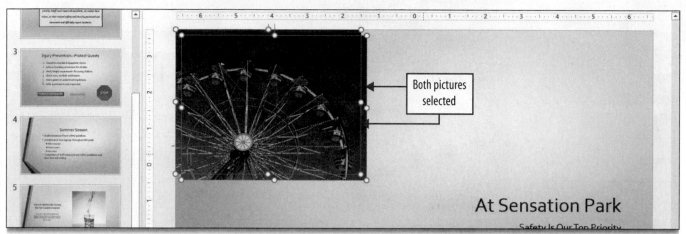

Both pictures selected

FIGURE 18.88

ANOTHER WAY Position the pointer in the gray area of the Slide pane just outside the upper left corner of the slide to display the pointer. Drag down and to the right to draw a transparent, gray selection rectangle that encloses both pictures.

2 On the **Picture Tools Format tab**, in the **Arrange group**, click **Align**. At the bottom of the menu, click **Align to Slide** to activate this setting. In the **Arrange group**, click **Align** again, click **Align Left**, and then compare your screen with Figure 18.89.

The Align to Slide setting tells PowerPoint to align each selected object with the slide, rather than with each other. In combination with the Align Left option, this aligns the left edge of each picture with the left edge of the slide.

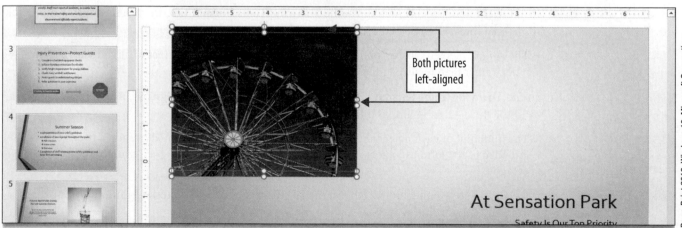

Both pictures left-aligned

FIGURE 18.89

3 With both pictures still selected, on the **Picture Tools Format tab**, in the **Arrange group**, click **Align** again, and then click **Distribute Vertically**.

The pictures are distributed evenly down the left edge of the slide between the top and bottom edges of the slide.

> **4** With both pictures selected, on the **Picture Tools Format tab**, in the **Picture Styles group**, click **Picture Effects**. Point to **Soft Edges**, and then click **50 Point** to apply the picture effect to both images. Click in a blank area of the slide and compare your screen with Figure 18.90.

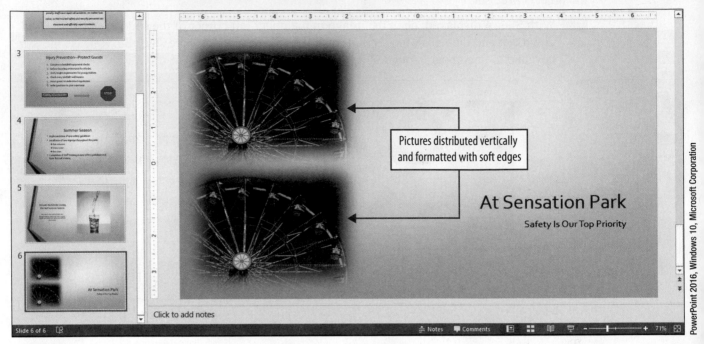

FIGURE 18.90

> **5** **Save** 🖫 the presentation.

Activity 18.53 | Aligning and Distributing Objects Relative to Each Other

> **1** Display **Slide 3**, hold down Shift, and then at the bottom of the slide, click the **text box**, the **arrow**, and the **octagon** to select all three objects. Release Shift.

🔁 BY TOUCH   Tap the text box, hold down Shift, and then tap the arrow and the octagon.

> **2** With the three objects selected, on the **Drawing Tools Format tab**, in the **Arrange group**, click **Align** 🖫. Click **Align Selected Objects**.
>
> The Align Selected Objects option will cause the objects that you select to align relative to each other, rather than relative to the edges of the slide.

> **3** On the **Drawing Tools Format tab**, in the **Arrange group**, click **Align** 🖫, and then click **Align Middle**. Click **Align** again, and then click **Distribute Horizontally**.
>
> The midpoint of each object aligns and the three objects are distributed evenly between the left edge of the leftmost object—the text box—and the right edge of the rightmost object—the octagon.

> **4** Click anywhere on the slide so that none of the objects are selected. Compare your screen with Figure 18.91, and then **Save** 🖫 the presentation.

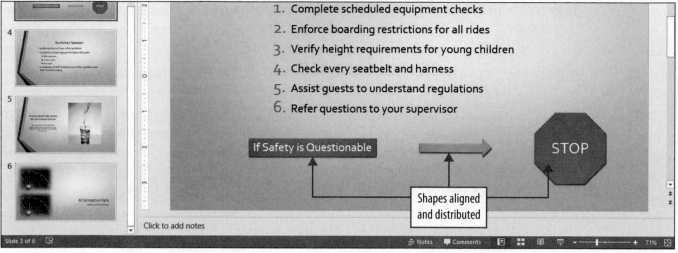

FIGURE 18.91

Activity 18.54 │ Grouping Objects

You can select multiple objects and group them so that they can be formatted and edited as one object.

1 With **Slide 3** displayed, click the **text box**, hold down Shift, and then click the **arrow** and the **octagon** so that all three objects are selected.

Sizing handles surround each individual object.

2 On the **Drawing Tools Format tab**, in the **Arrange group**, click **Group** 🖼, and then click **Group**. Compare your screen with Figure 18.92.

The sizing handles surround all three shapes as one, indicating that the three shapes are grouped into one object. The individual objects are not selected. The grouped object can be formatted, aligned, and moved as one object.

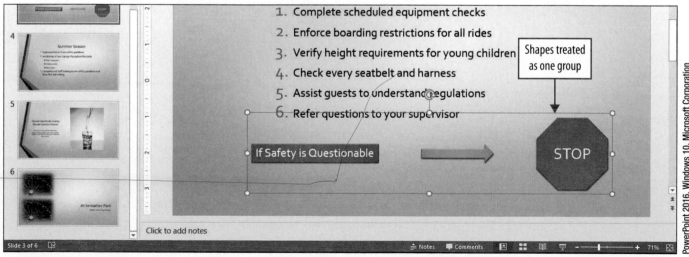

FIGURE 18.92

3 On the **Drawing Tools Format tab**, in the **Arrange group**, click **Align** 🖼, and then click **Align Center**.

The group is centered horizontally on the slide.

4 On the **Slide Show tab**, in the **Start Slide Show group**, click **From Beginning**, and then view the slide show. When the black slide displays, press (Esc).

5 On the **Insert tab**, in the **Text group**, click **Header & Footer** to display the **Header and Footer** dialog box. Click the **Notes and Handouts tab**. Under **Include on page**, select the **Date and time** check box, and then select **Update automatically**. If necessary, clear the Header check box. Select the **Page number** and **Footer** check boxes. In the **Footer** box, using your own name, type **Lastname_Firstname_18C_Safety** and then click **Apply to All**.

6 Display the document properties. As the **Tags** type **safety presentation** and as the **Subject**, type your course and section number. Be sure your name displays as author, and then **Save** your file. As directed by your instructor, create and submit a paper printout or an electronic image of your presentation that looks like a printed document—either as the Notes and Handouts or as the presentation slides—or, submit your completed PowerPoint file.

7 **Close** PowerPoint.

END | You have completed Project 18C

Objective   Create an Informational Presentation in Google Slides

Activity | **Creating an Informational Presentation in Google Slides**

In this Activity, you will use Google Slides to create a presentation similar to the one you created in Project 18C.

1 From the desktop, open your browser, navigate to **http://google.com**, and then sign in to your Google account. Click **Google Apps** [⠿], and then click **Drive** [△]. Open your **GO! Web Projects** folder—or if necessary, click New to create and then open this folder.

2 In the left pane, click **NEW**, click **File upload** [↥], and then in the **Open** dialog box, navigate to your student data files. Select **p18_C_Web**. Click **Open**. When the upload is complete and the file name displays in the file list, right-click **p18_C_Web**, and then click **Rename**. In the **Rename** dialog box, select and delete the text. Using your own name, as the file name type **Lastname_Firstname_18C_Web** and then press Enter. Right-click your file, click **Open with**, and then click **Google Slides**.

3 Display **Slide 5**. On the **toolbar**, click **Image** [▣]. In the **Insert image** dialog box, click **Search**. In the **Search** box, type **pouring water** and then press Enter. Select a picture similar to the one that you inserted in Project 18A, and then in the lower left, click **Select**. Drag the image to the right and use the sizing handles to position and resize the image so that there is an even amount of space above, below, and to the right of the image.

4 Display **Slide 2**, and then click anywhere in the paragraph. At the right end of the toolbar, if necessary, click More [More ▾], and then click **Bulleted list** [☰] to remove the bullet symbol from the paragraph. Click **More** [More ▾] to close the menu.

5 Click **Align** [☰], click **Center**, and then select the entire paragraph. Change the **Font size** to **24** and apply **Bold**.

6 With **Slide 2** displayed and the paragraph selected, on the **toolbar**, click **Fill color** [▨ ▾], and then in the eighth column, select the fifth color— **light blue 1**.

7 Click **Line color** [✎], and then, in the eighth column, select the second color—**blue**. Click **Line weight** [☰], and then click **4px**. Click a blank area of the slide to deselect the text box, and then compare your screen with Figure A.

FIGURE A

(GO! With Google continues on the next page)

8 ▶ Display **Slide 3**, and then click in the bulleted list. Click **More** More ▾ , and then click **Numbered list** ⊞ to apply numbers to all of the bullet points. It is not necessary to select the text; bullets and numbering are applied to all of the bullet points in a content placeholder. Click **More** to close the menu.

9 ▶ With **Slide 3** displayed, on the **toolbar**, click **Text box** to insert a text box in your slide. Click below the content placeholder and drag to create the textbox near the bottom of the slide—the exact size and placement need not be precise.

10 ▶ With the insertion point blinking in the text box, type **If Safety is Questionable** and then on the **toolbar**, click **Fill color** 🖎 ▾ . In the first column, click the fourth color—**light red berry 2**. If necessary, drag the sizing handles of the text box to shorten the text box to fit the text. Click outside the text box to deselect it.

11 ▶ On the **toolbar**, click **Shape** 🖾 , point to **Arrows**, and then click **Right Arrow**. Position the mouse pointer to the right of the text box and click to insert an arrow in the middle of your slide. Drag the arrow so that it is aligned horizontally with the text box—a red guide will

display to assist you—and its left edge aligns with the *y* in *your*, and then on the **toolbar**, click **Fill color** 🖎 ▾ . In the eight column, click the second color—**blue**.

12 ▶ On the **toolbar**, click **Shape** 🖾 , point to **Shapes**, and then click **Octagon**. Position the mouse pointer to the right of the arrow, and then click to insert an octagon on your slide. Drag the octagon so that its center sizing handle aligns with the arrow point and its left edge aligns with the *s* in *regulations*, and then on the **toolbar**, click **Fill color** 🖎 ▾ . In the first column, click the fourth color—**light red berry 2**.

13 ▶ Click in the octagon. Type **STOP** select the text, change the **Font size** to 18, **Align Center**, and then click in a blank area of the slide. Compare your screen with Figure B and make adjustments to the position of the shapes as necessary.

14 ▶ Your presentation will be saved automatically. If you are instructed to submit your file, click the File menu, point to Download, and then click PDF or PowerPoint as directed by your instructor. The file will download to your default download folder as determined by your browser settings. Sign out of your Google account.

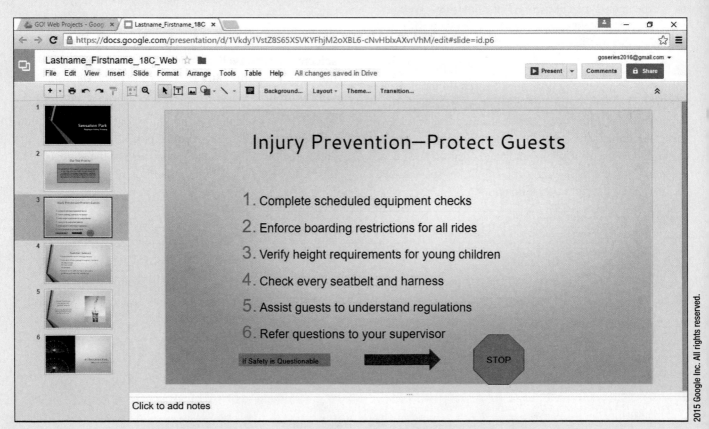

FIGURE B

GO! To Work

Andrew Rodriguez/Fotolia; FotolEdhar/Fotolia; apops/Fotolia; Yuri Arcurs/Fotolia

IC3 SKILLS IN THIS CHAPTER

IC3 – Module 2: Key Applications

Project 18A
Section 2.05   Presentations
(a) Understand file types compatible with presentation software
  (i) Sharing (presentation, handout, outlines, video)
  (ii) Publishing (pptx, pdf, jpg, show, png)
(b) Understand how to connect to external/extended monitors to display presentation
(c) Be able to use presentation views and modes
(e) Know how to create and organize slides
  (i) Slide management
  (ii) Inserting and managing media files
(f) Know how to design slides
  (i) Be able to use templates
(g) Identify presentation software options
  (i) Presentations
  (ii) Add slides
  (v) Layout

Project 18B
Section 2.05   Presentations
(a) Understand file types compatible with presentation software
  (i) Sharing (presentation, handout, outlines, video)
(c) Be able to use presentation views and modes
(d) Know how to add animations, effects, and slide transitions
(f) Know how to design slides
  (i) Be able to use templates
(g) Identify presentation software options
  (i) Presentations
  (ii) Add slides
  (iii) Delete slides
  (iv) Revise slide order
  (v) Layout

Project 18C
Section 2.05   Presentations
(e) Know how to create and organize slides
  (ii) Inserting and managing media files
Section 2.07 Graphic Modification
(a) Be able to import and insert images into documents
(b) Understand how to crop images

BUILD YOUR E-PORTFOLIO

An E-Portfolio is a collection of evidence, stored electronically, that showcases what you have accomplished while completing your education. Collecting and then sharing your work products with potential employers reflects your academic and career goals. Your completed documents from the following projects are good examples to show what you have learned: 18J, 18O, and 18N.

GO! FOR JOB SUCCESS

Video: Managing Priorities and Workspace

Your instructor may assign this video to your class, and then ask you to think about, or discuss with your classmates, these questions:

FotolEdhar / Fotolia

What kind of scheduling tool do you use? Is it on your computer, your cell phone, or other electronic device, or do you write in a notebook or physical calendar? Which kind of scheduling tool will be most effective for you and why?

Name one lifestyle change that you can make today that will help you create more time for your work projects.

What is the one touch rule and how do you think it will help you be more efficient?

END OF CHAPTER

SUMMARY

In this chapter, you started a new presentation in PowerPoint. You inserted slides with various layouts and you entered, edited, and formatted text. You also inserted text from another PowerPoint file.

Use a presentation theme to establish a unified presentation design. You can change the color of the presentation theme by applying one of the predefined variants that are supplied with each theme.

Presentations are often organized in a manner similar to outlines. List levels represent outline levels and are identified by the bullet style, indentation, and text size.

Use pictures to illustrate an idea. The Online Pictures feature enables you to search the web for images that emphasize important points. Using good keywords is critical to a successful search to find a great picture!.

GO! LEARN IT ONLINE

Review the concepts, key terms, and IC3 skills in this chapter by completing these online challenges, which you can find at **MyITLab**.

Matching and Multiple Choice: Answer matching and multiple choice questions to test what you learned in this chapter.

Lessons on the GO!: Learn how to use all the new apps and features as they are introduced by Microsoft.

IC3 Prep Quiz: Answer questions to review the IC3 skills that you practiced in this chapter.

GO! COLLABORATIVE TEAM PROJECT (Available in MyITLab and Instructor Resource Center)

If your instructor assigns this project to your class, you can expect to work with one or more of your classmates—either in person or by using Internet tools—to create work products similar to those that you created in this chapter. A team is a group of workers who work together to solve a problem, make a decision, or create a work product. Collaboration is when you work together with others as a team in an intellectual endeavor to complete a shared task or achieve a shared goal.

PROJECT GUIDE FOR ALL IN ONE CHAPTER 18

Your instructor will assign Projects from this list to ensure your learning and assess your knowledge.

	Project Guide for All in One Chapter 18		
Project	**Apply Skills from These Chapter Objectives**	**Project Type**	**Project Location**
18A MyITLab	Objectives 1–4 from Project 18A	**18A Instructional Project (Grader Project)** Guided instruction to learn the skills in Project 18A.	In MyITLab and in text
18B MyITLab	Objectives 5–8 from Project 18B	**18B Instructional Project (Grader Project)** Guided instruction to learn the skills in Project 18B.	In MyITLab and in text
18C MyITLab	Objectives 9–12 from Project 18C	**18C Instructional Project (Grader Project)** Guided instruction to learn the skills in Project 18C.	In MyITLab and in text
18D	Objectives 1–4 from Project 18A	**18D Skills Review (Scorecard Grading)** A guided review of the skills from Project 18A.	Instructor Resource Center (IRC) and MyITLab
18E	Objectives 5–8 from Project 18B	**18E Skills Review (Scorecard Grading)** A guided review of the skills from Project 18B.	In MyITLab
18F	Objectives 9–12 from Project 18C	**18F Skills Review (Scorecard Grading)** A guided review of the skills from Project 18C.	In MyITLab
18G MyITLab	Objectives 1–4 from Project 18A	**18G Mastery (Grader Project)** **Mastery and Transfer of Learning** A demonstration of your mastery of the skills in Project 18A with extensive decision making.	In MyITLab and in text
18H MyITLab	Objectives 5–8 from Project 18B	**18H Mastery (Grader Project)** **Mastery and Transfer of Learning** A demonstration of your mastery of the skills in Project 18B with extensive decision making.	In MyITLab and in text
18I MyITLab	Objectives 9-12 from Project 18C	**18I Mastery (Grader Project)** **Mastery and Transfer of Learning** A demonstration of your mastery of the skills in Project 18C with extensive decision making.	In MyITLab and in text
18J MyITLab	Objectives 1–12 from Projects 18A, 18B, and 18C	**18J Mastery (Grader Project)** **Mastery and Transfer of Learning** A demonstration of your mastery of the skills in Projects 18A, 18B, and 18C with extensive decision making.	In MyITLab and in text
18K	Combination of Objectives from Projects 18A, 18B, and 18C	**18K GO! Fix It (Scorecard Grading)** **Critical Thinking** A demonstration of your mastery of the skills in Projects 18A, 18B, and 18C by creating a correct result from a document that contains errors you must find.	IRC and in MyITLab
18L	Combination of Objectives from Projects 18A, 18B, and 18C	**18L GO! Make It (Scorecard Grading)** **Critical Thinking** A demonstration of your mastery of the skills in Projects 18A, 18B, and 18C by creating a result from a supplied picture.	IRC and in MyITLab
18M	Combination of Objectives from Projects 18A, 18B, and 18C	**18M GO! Solve It (Rubric Grading)** **Critical Thinking** A demonstration of your mastery of the skills in Projects 18A, 18B, and 18C, your decision-making skills, and your critical thinking skills. A task-specific rubric helps you self-assess your result.	IRC and in MyITLab
18N	Combination of Objectives from Projects 18A, 18B, and 18C	**18N GO! Solve It (Rubric Grading)** **Critical Thinking** A demonstration of your mastery of the skills in Projects 18A, 18B, and 18C, your decision-making skills, and your critical thinking skills. A task-specific rubric helps you self-assess your result.	IRC and in MyITLab
18O	Combination of Objectives from Projects 18A, 18B, and 18C	**18O GO! Think (Rubric Grading)** **Critical Thinking** A demonstration of your understanding of the chapter concepts applied in a manner that you would outside of college. An analytic rubric helps you and your instructor grade the quality of your work by comparing it to the work an expert in the discipline would create.	IRC and in MyITLab
18P	Combination of Objectives from Projects 18A, 18B, and 18C	**18P GO! Think (Rubric Grading)** **Critical Thinking** A demonstration of your understanding of the chapter concepts applied in a manner that you would outside of college. An analytic rubric helps you and your instructor grade the quality of your work by comparing it to the work an expert in the discipline would create.	IRC and in MyITLab
18Q	Combination of Objectives from Projects 18A, 18B, and 18C	**18Q You and GO! (Rubric Grading)** **Critical Thinking** A demonstration of your understanding of the chapter concepts applied in a manner that you would in a personal situation. An analytic rubric helps you and your instructor grade the quality of your work.	IRC and in MyITLab
18R	Combination of Objectives from Projects 18A, 18B, and 18C	**18R Collaborative Team Project for PowerPoint Chapter 18** **Critical Thinking** A demonstration of your understanding of concepts and your ability to work collaboratively in a group role-playing assessment, requiring both collaboration and self-management.	IRC and in MyITLab

GLOSSARY

GLOSSARY OF CHAPTER KEY TERMS

Artistic effects Formats applied to images that make pictures resemble sketches or paintings.

Aspect ratio The ratio of the width of a display to the height of the display.

Black slide A slide that displays after the last slide in a presentation, indicating that the presentation is over.

Bulleted list A list of items preceded by small dots or other shapes, which do not indicate order or rank. Sometimes called unordered lists.

Clip A single media file such as art, sound, animation, or a movie.

Contiguous slides Slides that are adjacent to each other in a presentation.

Crop A command that removes unwanted or unnecessary areas of a picture.

Crop handles Handles used to remove unwanted areas of a picture.

Crop pointer The pointer used to crop areas of a picture.

Crosshair pointer The pointer used to draw a shape.

Editing The process of modifying a presentation by adding and deleting slides or by changing the contents of individual slides.

Eyedropper A tool that captures the exact color from an object on your screen and then applies it to any shape, picture, or text.

Fill color The inside color of text or of an object.

Footer Text that displays at the bottom of every slide or that prints at the bottom of a sheet of slide handouts or notes pages.

Formatting The process of changing the appearance of the text, layout, and design of a slide.

Header Text that prints at the top of each sheet of slide handouts or notes pages.

Layout The arrangement of elements, such as title and subtitle text, lists, pictures, tables, charts, shapes, and movies, on a slide.

List level An outline level in a presentation represented by a bullet symbol and identified in a slide by the indentation and the size of the text.

Noncontiguous slides Slides that are not adjacent to each other in a presentation.

Normal view The primary editing view in PowerPoint where you write and design your presentations.

Notes page A printout that contains the slide image on the top half of the page and notes that you have created on the Notes pane in the lower half of the page.

Notes pane An area of the Normal view window that displays below the Slide pane with space to type notes regarding the active slide.

Numbered list A list of items preceded by numbers, which indicate sequence or rank of the items. Sometimes called ordered lists.

Outline view A PowerPoint view that displays the presentation outline to the left of the Slide pane.

Placeholder A box on a slide with dotted or dashed borders that holds title and body text or other content such as charts, tables, and pictures.

Presenter view A view that shows the full-screen slide show on one monitor or projection screen while enabling the presenter to view a preview of the next slide, notes, and a timer on another monitor.

Reading view A view in PowerPoint that displays a presentation in a manner similar to a slide show but in which the taskbar, title bar, and status bar remain available in the presentation window.

RGB A color model in which the colors red, green, and blue are added together to form another color.

Rotation handle A circular arrow that provides a way to rotate a selected image.

Ruler guides Dotted red vertical and horizontal lines that display in the rulers indicating the pointer's position.

Section header A type of slide layout that changes the look and flow of a presentation by providing text

placeholders that do not contain bullet points.

Shape A slide object such as a line, arrow, box, callout, or banner.

Sizing handles Small circles surrounding a picture that indicate that the picture is selected.

Slide A presentation page that can contain text, pictures, tables, charts, and other multimedia or graphic objects.

Slide handout Printed images of slides on a sheet of paper.

Slide pane A PowerPoint screen element that displays a large image of the active slide.

Slide Sorter view A presentation view that displays thumbnails of all of the slides in a presentation.

Slide transitions Motion effects that occur in Slide Show view when you move from one slide to the next during a presentation.

Smart guides Dashed lines that display on your slide when you are moving an object to assist you with alignment.

Split button A type of button in which clicking the main part of the button performs a command and clicking the arrow opens a menu, list, or gallery.

Style A collection of formatting options that you can apply to a picture, text, or an object.

Text alignment The horizontal placement of text within a placeholder.

Text box An object with which you can position text anywhere on a slide.

Theme A set of unified design elements that provides a look for your presentation by applying colors, fonts, and effects.

Thumbnails Miniature images of presentation slides.

Title slide A slide layout—most commonly the first slide in a presentation—that provides an introduction to the presentation topic.

Variant A variation on the presentation theme style and color.

Mastering PowerPoint Project 18G Juneau

In the following Mastering PowerPoint project, you will create a new presentation that Kodiak West Travel will use in their promotional materials to describe activities in the city of Juneau. Your completed presentation will look similar to Figure 18.93.

PROJECT FILES

For Project 18G, you will need the following files:

New blank PowerPoint presentation

p18G_Aerial_View

p18G_Whale

p18G_Falls

Build From Scratch

You will save your presentation as:

Lastname_Firstname_18G_Juneau

PROJECT RESULTS

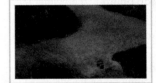

FIGURE 18.93

(Project 18G Juneau continues on the next page)

PowerPoint 2016, Windows 10, Microsoft Corporation

Mastering PowerPoint   Project 18G Juneau (continued)

1 Start PowerPoint and create a presentation using the **Integral** theme. Use the default color variant.

2 As the title of this presentation type **Juneau Highlights** and as the subtitle type **Kodiak West Travel** Save the presentation in your **AIO Chapter 18** folder as **Lastname_Firstname_18G_Juneau**

3 Insert a **New Slide** using the **Content with Caption** layout. In the title placeholder, type **The View from Above**

4 In the content placeholder on the right side of the slide, from your student data files, insert the picture **p18G_Aerial_View**. Format the picture with the **Beveled Matte, White** picture style.

5 In the text placeholder on the left, type **View a glacial ice field from above by plane or helicopter. If you are more adventurous, try glacier trekking in Juneau where you can land on a glacier and climb an ice wall.**

6 Insert a **New Slide** using the **Two Content** layout. In the title placeholder, type **On Land and Sea**

7 In the content placeholder on the left, type the following text, increasing and decreasing the list level as shown below. In this presentation theme, the first level bullet points do not include a bullet symbol.

> **On the water**
> > **Whale watching**
> > **Kayaking**
> **Mount Roberts tramway**
> > **Spectacular views of Juneau**
> > **Recreational hiking trails**

8 In the content placeholder on the right, from your student data files, insert the picture **p18G_Whale**. Apply the **Rotated, White** picture style.

9 Insert a new slide with the **Picture with Caption** layout. In the title placeholder, type **Mendenhall Glacier** and then in the picture placeholder, from your student data files, insert the picture **p18G_Falls**.

10 In the text placeholder, type **Walk to Mendenhall Glacier from the Visitor Center to get a close-up view of Nugget Falls.**

11 In the **Notes** pane, type **Mendenhall Glacier is the most famous glacier in Juneau and in some years is visited by over 400,000 people.**

12 Insert a **Header & Footer** on the **Notes and Handouts**. Include the **Date and time** updated automatically, the **Page number**, and a **Footer**— using your own name—with the text **Lastname_ Firstname_18G_Juneau** and apply to all the slides.

13 Display the **Document Properties**. As the **Tags** type **Juneau** As the **Subject** type your course and section number. Be sure your name is indicated as the author.

14 **Save** your presentation, and then view the slide show from the beginning. As directed by your instructor, create and submit a paper printout or an electronic image of your presentation that looks like a printed document; or, submit your completed PowerPoint file. **Close** PowerPoint.

> **END | You have completed Project 18G**

Mastering PowerPoint   Project 18H Refuge

In the following Mastering PowerPoint project, you will edit a presentation regarding a wildlife refuge where Kodiak West Travel conducts tours. Your completed presentation will look similar to Figure 18.94.

PROJECT FILES

For Project 18H, you will need the following files:

p18H_Refuge
p18H_Excursions

You will save your presentation as:

Lastname_Firstname_18H_Refuge

PROJECT RESULTS

FIGURE 18.94

PowerPoint 2016, Windows 10, Microsoft Corporation

(Project 18H Refuge continues on the next page)

Mastering PowerPoint Project 18H Refuge (continued)

1 Start PowerPoint, and then from your student data files, open the file **p18H_Refuge**. In your **AIO Chapter 18** folder, **Save** the file as **Lastname_Firstname_18H_Refuge**

2 Change the **Slide Size** to **Widescreen (16:9)**.

3 Display the presentation **Outline**. In the **Outline**, on **Slide 2**, increase the list level of the third and the fifth bullet points. Click at the end of the last bullet point after the word *roads*, and then type **or facilities**

4 Return the presentation to **Normal view**, and then display **Slide 4**. Display the **Reuse Slides** pane. Browse to open from your student data files, **p18H_Excursions**. Make sure the **Keep source formatting** check box is *cleared*. With **Slide 4** in your presentation displayed, insert the last two slides from the **Reuse Slides** pane.

5 Display **Slide 1**, and then change the layout to **Title Slide**.

6 Select the subtitle—*Experience Alaska with Kodiak West Travel*. Change the **Font** to **Arial**, and the **Font Size** to **28**. Change the **Font Color** to **Black, Text 1**. **Center** the title and the subtitle.

7 Display **Slide 5**, and then select the paragraph in the content placeholder. Apply **Bold** and **Italic**, and then change the **Font Size** to **16**.

8 **Center** the paragraph text, and then change the **Line Spacing** to **1.5**. **Center** the slide title.

9 In **Slide Sorter** view, delete **Slide 3**. Move **Slide 5** to position it after **Slide 2**.

10 Move **Slide 4** to the end of the presentation.

11 In **Normal** view, display **Slide 1**. Apply the **Split** transition and change the **Effect Options** to **Horizontal Out**. Change the **Duration** to **1.75** and apply the transition to all of the slides in the presentation. View the slide show from the beginning.

12 **Insert** a **Header & Footer** on the **Notes and Handouts**. Include the **Date and time** updated automatically, the **Page number**, and a **Footer** with the text **Lastname_Firstname_18H_Refuge**

13 Display the **Document Properties**. As the **Tags** type **refuge, tours** As the **Subject** type your course and section number. Be sure your name is indicated as the author.

14 **Save** your presentation, create and submit a paper printout or an electronic image of your presentation that looks like a printed document; or, submit your completed PowerPoint file as directed by your instructor. **Close** PowerPoint.

END | You have completed Project 18H

Mastering PowerPoint | Project 18I Coasters

In the following Mastering PowerPoint project, you will format a presentation describing new roller coasters being constructed at several Sensation Park Entertainment Group amusement parks. Your completed presentation will look similar to Figure 18.95.

PROJECT FILES

For Project 18I, you will need the following file:

p18I_Coasters

You will save your presentation as:

Lastname_Firstname_18I_Coasters

PROJECT RESULTS

FIGURE 18.95

(Project 18I Coasters continues on the next page)

Mastering PowerPoint   Project 18I Coasters (continued)

1 Start PowerPoint. From your student data files, locate and open **p18I_Coasters**. In your **AIO Chapter 18** folder, **Save** the file as **Lastname_Firstname_18I_Coasters**

2 On **Slide 2**, remove the bullet symbol from the paragraph, and then **Center** the paragraph.

3 With the content placeholder selected, display the **Shape Styles** gallery, and then apply the **Subtle Effect – Blue-Gray, Accent 5** style. Apply the **Art Deco** beveled shape effect to the placeholder.

4 On **Slide 3**, apply **Numbering** to the first-level bullet points—*Intensity, Hang Time,* and *Last Chance.* Change all of the second-level bullets to **Star Bullets**, and then change the bullet color to **Aqua, Accent 1, Lighter 40%**—in the fifth column, the fourth color.

5 On **Slide 3**, select the title. Using the **Eyedropper**, select the light yellow color of the stripe on the roller coaster car at the right side of the picture and change the font color of the title. On **Slides 1** and **2**, apply the same light yellow color to the slide title on each slide.

6 Display **Slide 3**, and then apply an **Aqua, 5 pt glow, Accent color 2** picture effect to the picture.

7 Display **Slide 4**. Insert an **Online Picture** by searching for **roller coaster** and then insert a picture of people riding a roller coaster. **Crop** the picture by dragging the crop handles so that it's roughly square in shape.

8 Align the upper left corner of the picture with the top left corner of the slide, and then change the **Height** to **4.5** Modify the **Picture Effect** by applying a **50 Point Soft Edges** effect.

9 Duplicate the picture, and then use the **Align to Slide** option to align the pictures with the left edge of the slide and to distribute the pictures vertically.

10 Insert a **Text Box** aligned with the **horizontal ruler at 0 inches** and with the **lower half of the vertical ruler at 2.5 inches**. In the text box, type **Starting Summer 2019!** Change the **Font Size** to **28**. Change the **Shape Fill** to the last color in the last column—**Blue, Accent 6, Darker 50%**.

11 Select the title and the text box, and then, using the **Align Selected Objects** option, apply **Align Right** alignment. View the slide show from the beginning.

12 **Insert** a **Header & Footer** on the **Notes and Handouts**. Include the **Date and time updated automatically**, the **Page number**, and a **Footer** with the text **Lastname_Firstname_18I_Coasters**

13 Display the document properties. As the **Tags** type **coasters** and as the **Subject** type your course and section. Be sure your name displays as author, and then **Save** your file.

14 As directed by your instructor, create and submit a paper printout or an electronic image of your presentation that looks like a printed document; or, submit your completed PowerPoint file. **Close** PowerPoint.

END | You have completed Project 18I

Mastering PowerPoint Project 18J Northern Lights

In the following Mastering PowerPoint project, you will edit an existing presentation that describes the Northern Lights and ideal viewing areas. Your completed presentation will look similar to Figure 18.96.

Apply 18A, 18B, and 18C skills from these Objectives:

1 Create a New Presentation
2 Edit a Presentation in Normal View
3 Add Pictures to a Presentation
4 Print and View a Presentation
5 Edit an Existing Presentation
6 Format a Presentation
7 Use Slide Sorter View
8 Apply Slide Transitions
9 Format Numbered and Bulleted Lists
10 Insert Online Pictures
11 Insert Text Boxes and Shapes
12 Format Objects

PROJECT FILES

For Project 18J, you will need the following files:

p18J_Northern_Lights
p18J_Lights
p18J_Slides

You will save your presentation as:

Lastname_Firstname_18J_Northern_Lights

PROJECT RESULTS

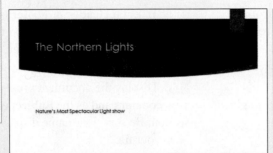

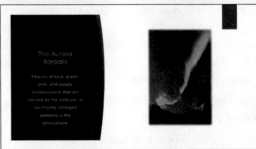

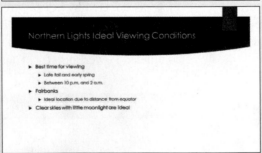

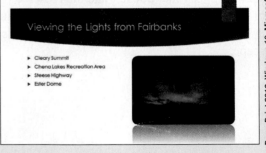

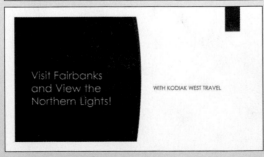

FIGURE 18.96

PowerPoint 2016, Windows 10, Microsoft Corporation

(Project 18J Northern Lights continues on the next page)

1 Start PowerPoint, and then from your student data files, open the file **p18J_Northern_Lights**. In your **AIO Chapter 18** folder, **Save** the file as **Lastname_Firstname_18J_Northern_Lights**

2 Replace all occurrences of the text **North** with **Northern** and then change the layout of **Slide 1** to **Title Slide**.

3 Apply the **Ion Boardroom** theme, with the default purple variant option.

4 Change the **Slide Size** to **Widescreen (16:9)**.

5 Display **Slide 2**, open the **Reuse Slides** pane, and then from your student data files browse for and open the presentation **p18J_Slides**. If necessary, clear the Keep source formatting check box, and then insert the last two slides from the **p18J_Slides** file.

6 Display **Slide 2**. In either the slide pane or in the slide outline, click at the end of the first bullet point after the word *time*. Add the words **for viewing** and then in the same slide, increase the list level of the second and third bullet points. Change the bullets to Arrow bullets.

7 With **Slide 2** still displayed, select the title and change the **Font Size** to **32**. In the **Notes** pane, type the following notes: **The lights reach their peak in September and March.**

8 Display **Slide 3**. Select the paragraph of text, and then change the **Font Color** to **Purple, Accent 6, Lighter 60%**—in the last column, the third color**.** Change the **Font Size** to **16**, and then apply **Bold**. Remove the bullet.

9 Change the paragraph **Line Spacing** to **1.5**, and then **Center** the paragraph and the slide title.

10 With **Slide 3** still displayed, format the picture with the **Soft Edge Rectangle** picture style and the **Marker** artistic effect.

11 Display **Slide 4**. In the content placeholder on the right, from your student data files, insert the picture **p18J_Lights**. Change the **Height** to **3.0**. Modify the **Picture Effect** by applying a **10 Point Soft Edges** effect.

12 Move **Slide 3** between **Slides 1** and **2**.

13 Display **Slide 4**. Insert a **New Slide** with the **Section Header** layout. In the title placeholder type **Visit Fairbanks and View the Northern Lights!** In the text placeholder type **With Kodiak West Travel**

14 Apply the **Uncover** transition and change the **Effect Options** to **From Top**. Change the **Timing** by increasing the **Duration** to **01.25**. Apply the transition effect to all of the slides. View the slide show from the beginning.

15 **Insert** a **Header & Footer** on the **Notes and Handouts**. Include the **Date and time** updated automatically, the **Page number**, and a **Footer**, using your own name, with the text **Lastname_Firstname_18J_Northern_Lights**

16 Display the **Document Properties**. As the **Tags** type **northern lights, Fairbanks** As the **Subject** type your course and section number. Be sure your name is indicated as the author.

17 **Save** your presentation, create and submit a paper printout or an electronic image of your presentation that looks like a printed document; or, submit your completed PowerPoint file as directed by your instructor. **Close** PowerPoint.

END | You have completed Project 18J

GO! Fix It	Project 18K Rain Forest	MyITLab
GO! Make It	Project 18L Eagles	MyITLab
GO! Solve It	Project 18M Packrafting	MyITLab
GO! Solve It	Project 18N Packing	MyITLab

GO! Think	Project 18O Bears	MyITLab
GO! Think	Project 18P Sitka	MyITLab
You and GO!	Project 18Q Travel	MyITLab
GO! Collaborative Team Project	Project 18R Bell Orchid Hotels	MyITLab

Build From Scratch

Build From Scratch

Build From Scratch

Introduction to Computers, Windows 10, and Office 2016 Features

1 Unit

Lars Zahner /shutterstock

In this unit, you will learn what a computer is and look at the development of modern computers. You will use Microsoft Windows to create a personal dashboard to connect you to the things that matter to you. You will use the taskbar and desktop features to get your work done with ease, and you will use File Explorer to navigate the Windows folder structure, create a folder, and save files. You will examine features in Microsoft Office 2016 that are common across Office applications. In this unit, you will also learn how to set up a free Microsoft account.

Job Focus

Throughout this text, the projects will relate to various jobs in a large organization. One organization, among others, is the **Oro Jade Hotel Group**, headquartered in Boston, and which owns and operates resorts and business-oriented hotels around the world. Resort properties in the United States are located in popular destinations, including Honolulu, Orlando, San Diego, and Santa Barbara. The resorts offer deluxe accommodations and a wide array of dining options. Other Oro Jade hotels are located in major international business centers and offer the latest technology in their meeting facilities. Oro Jade offers extensive educational opportunities for employees. The company plans to open new properties and update existing properties over the next decade.

A Guest Relations Officer's primary role is to provide customer service, providing hotel guests with exceptional service to ensure that their experience will be worth remembering. The Guest Relations Officer ensures that guests are happy from the moment that they arrive at the hotel until they leave.

Case Project Tasks Performed by an Interior Designer Using Windows and Office 2016

In this Unit Case Project, you will use Windows and Office 2016 to complete tasks that you might encounter working as an Interior Designer for Oro Jade Hotel Group. You will work with computer files and create a simple memo. Your file will look similar to Figure 1.1.

PROJECT FILES

For Unit 1 Case Project, you will need the following file:

U1_Furniture_Memo

You will save your files as:

Lastname_Firstname_U1_Furniture_Memo
Lastname_Firstname_U1_Furniture_Memo_PDF
Lastname_Firstname_U1_Snip
Lastname_Firstname_U1_ZIP

PROJECT RESULTS

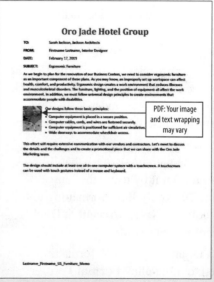

FIGURE 1.1

PowerPoint 2016, Windows 10, Microsoft Corporation

(Unit 1 Case Project continues on the next page)

Case Project — Tasks Performed by an Interior Designer Using Windows and Office 2016 (continued)

1 Start Word. On the left, click **Open Other Documents**, click **Browse**, and then in the **Open** dialog box, navigate to the student data files that accompany this Project.

2 Open the file **U1_Furniture_Memo**. Click the **File tab**. On the left, click **Save As**, click **Browse**, and then in the **Save As** dialog box, navigate to your storage location. Create a new folder named **All in One Unit 1** and then open the folder. In the **File name** box, using your own name, save the document as **Lastname_Firstname_U1_Furniture_Memo**

3 Be sure the rulers and formatting marks display. In the paragraph that begins *FROM:* select the text **Laura Mabry Hernandez** and type your name.

4 Click to place the insertion point at the beginning of the paragraph that begins *Our designs follow*.

5 On the **Insert tab**, in the **Illustrations group**, click **Online Pictures**. In the **Bing Image Search** box, search for and then insert an image of your choice that relates to **ergonomic chair**

6 With the image selected, on the **Picture Tools Format tab**, in the **Size group**, click in the **Shape Height** box, type **1"** and press Enter. With the image selected, click the **Layout Options** button, and then under **With Text Wrapping**, in the first row, click the first layout—**Square**.

7 At the top of the document, select the title **Oro Jade Hotel Group** and the paragraph mark that follows it. **Center** the text and format it by using the font **Cambria** and font size **26**. Apply **Bold** formatting to the text. Change the text color to **Green, Accent 6, Darker 50%**—in the last column, the last color.

8 Select the text **TO:** and apply **Bold** formatting. With *TO:* still selected, double-click **Format Painter**. Use the **Format Painter** to copy the formatting to *FROM:*, *DATE:*, and *SUBJECT:*. On the ribbon, click **Format Painter** to turn the command off.

9 Select the third bullet point text **Computer cables, cords, and wires are fastened securely**. On the **Home tab**, in the **Clipboard group**, click **Cut**.

10 Click to position the insertion point to the left of the second bullet text *Computer equipment is positioned for sufficient air circulation*, right-click, and then on the shortcut menu, under **Paste Options**, click the first button—**Keep Source Formatting**.

11 Move the insertion point to the end of the last bullet point, press Enter, and add a new bullet: **Wide doorways to accommodate wheelchair access.**

12 Press Ctrl + Home. At the bottom of the screen, click the **Proofing** icon to open the **Spelling** pane. Check and correct document spelling.

13 Press Ctrl + End to move the insertion point to the end of the document, and then press Enter to insert a blank paragraph. In your own words, add a paragraph explaining why the company might include all-in-one touchscreen computers in the design.

14 On the **Insert tab**, in the **Header & Footer group**, click **Footer**. At the bottom of the list, click **Edit Footer**. On the ribbon, on the **Header & Footer Tools Design tab**, in the **Insert group**, click **Document Info**, and then click **File Name** to insert the name of your file in the footer. Click **Close Header and Footer**.

15 Click the **File tab** to display **Backstage** view. On the right, at the bottom of the **Properties** list, click **Show All Properties**. On the list of **Properties**, in the **Tags** box, type **ergonomics, design** In the **Subject** box, type your course name and section number. Under **Related People**, be sure that your name displays as the author. If necessary, right-click the author name, click **Edit Property**, type your name, click outside of the **Edit person** dialog box, and then click **OK**.

16 On the left, click **Print** to view the Print Preview, and then on the left, click **Save**. Click the **File tab** again to display **Backstage** view, click **Export**, click **Create PDF/XPS Document**, and then click the **Create PDF/XPS** button. Publish the PDF in your **All in One Unit 1** folder as **Lastname_Firstname_U1_Furniture_PDF**

17 Close Word and close all open windows.

18 With the Windows 10 desktop displayed, in the lower left corner, click in the search box, type **get started** and then at the top of the search results, click **Get Started Trusted Windows Store** app.

19 **Maximize** the window, and then on the left, click **Office**. In the displayed results, click **Office apps in Windows 10**.

20 Start the **Snipping Tool**, create a **Window Snip**, click anywhere in the window to capture the snip, and then in your **All in One Unit 1** folder, save the image as a JPEG with the file name **Lastname_Firstname_U1_Snip** Close the **Snipping Tool**. Close the **Get Started** window.

21 Open **File Explorer** to your **All in One Unit 1** folder. Select and compress your three files. Name the compressed file **Lastname_Firstname_U1_ZIP**

22 Submit your files to your instructor as directed.

The Internet, Cloud Computer, and Digital Awareness

Mock Hotel / Alamy Stock Photo

In this unit, you will explore some of the tools and information that the Internet makes available to you. You will use your browser to search for information and to manage content on the web. You will use cloud computing tools to store information, manage and process data, and collaborate on projects. You will use your Microsoft account for free email and online and, you will use OneNote to gather, store, and share information. You will also explore Skype, Gmail, and LinkedIn.

Job Focus

A **Brand Manager** leads the marketing team in promoting the Oro Jade brand. The **Development Director** focuses on the development of hotel properties in his or her region. The **Feasibility Manager** is responsible for research and analysis to evaluate hotel markets and determine the potential development or franchise opportunities with the feasibility team.

Case Project Cloud Computing and a OneNote Notebook Created by a Director of Sales for Oro Jade Hotel Group

In this Unit Case Project, you will use Google Chrome to search the Internet, use Gmail and Calendar, store files on OneDrive, and use Twitter. You will also create a OneNote notebook to store information related to the upcoming bridal show that will be held at the hotel. This is an important event for the hotel, because brides attending the show will also be looking for venues at which to hold their weddings and receptions. Your completed screenshots and notebook will look similar to Figure 2.1.

PROJECT FILES

For Unit 2 Case Project, you will need the following files:

U2_Vendor_Form
U2_Special_Activities
U2_Saturday_Schedule
U2_Cake_Flyer

You will save your files as:

Lastname_Firstname_U2_Screens
Lastname_Firstname_U2_Bridal_PDF

PROJECT RESULTS

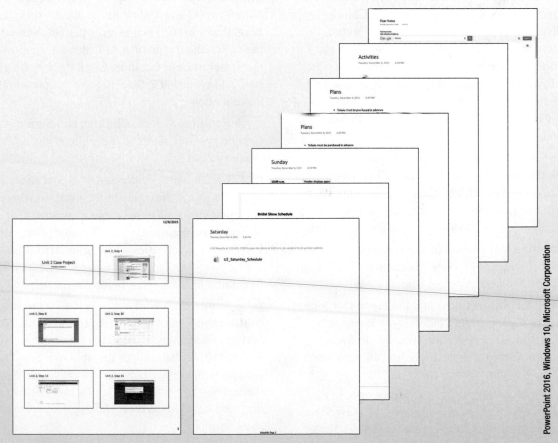

PowerPoint 2016, Windows 10, Microsoft Corporation

FIGURE 2.1

(Unit 2 Case Project continues on the next page)

Case Project **Cloud Computing and a OneNote Notebook Created by a Director of Sales for Oro Jade Hotel Group** (continued)

1 On your storage device, create a new folder named **All in One Unit 2**

2 Open **Google Chrome**. Click in the **Search** text box, type **wedding cakes** and then press Enter. On the navigation bar, click **Images**. Display the Search tools, and limit the *Size* to **Medium** and the *Type* to **Line drawing**.

3 Display a new tab. Click in the **address bar**, and type **foodsafety.gov** Point to the *Keep Food Safe* link and right-click. From the shortcut menu, click **Open link in a new tab** to open the Keep Food Safe page on its own tab. Click the **Keep Food Safe tab** to make it active.

4 Start **PowerPoint 2016**. On the right, click **Blank Presentation**. Click the **Click to add title** box, and type **Unit 2 Case Project** Click the **Click to add subtitle** box, and type your **Firstname Lastname**. On the **Home tab**, in the **Slides group**, click the upper portion of the **New Slide** button to add a new slide in the presentation. Click the **Insert tab**. In the **Images group**, click **Screenshot**, and then click **Screen Clipping**. When the Chrome window displays, hold down the left mouse button, and then drag to select the entire screen. Release the mouse button to place the screen shot in the slide. Click the **Click to add title** box, and type **Unit 2, Step 4** Save the presentation in your **All in One Unit 2** folder as **Lastname_Firstname_U2_Screens** Leave the PowerPoint presentation open.

5 Return to Google Chrome, and display a new tab. Right-click the new tab, and then click **Close other tabs**. On the right, click **Gmail**, and then **sign in** using your Google account and password to display your Gmail window.

6 In the upper left portion of the **Gmail** window, click **COMPOSE** to display the **New Message** box. Click in the **To** box and type **goseries.aio@gmail.com**

7 Click in the **Subject** box, and then type **Oro Jade Bridal Show** In the message window, type **Susan** and press Enter two times. Type a short message to Susan inviting her to the bridal show, including an appropriate closing. *Do not send the email*.

8 Return to PowerPoint. On the **Home tab**, in the **Slides group**, click the upper portion of the **New Slide** button to add a new slide in the presentation. Click the

Insert tab. In the **Images group**, click **Screenshot**, and then click the image of the Gmail window to place the screen shot in the slide. Click the **Click to add title** box, and type **Unit 2, Step 8** Save the presentation, and leave it open.

9 Return to Google Chrome. Close the message window without sending. Display your **Google Calendar** in the **Month** view, and add the following events to this month:

> Vendor Information Night on the second Wednesday, 7:00pm–8:00pm in the Ranchero Room
> Luncheon Committee meets on the first Tuesday, will repeat every week for 3 weeks, 1:00pm–2:30pm in the Board Room
> Fashion Show Setup Committee meets on the third Thursday, 1:00pm–3:00pm in Facilities conference room

10 Return to PowerPoint. On the **Home tab**, in the **Slides group**, click the upper portion of the **New Slide** button to add a new slide in the presentation. Click the **Insert tab**. In the **Images group**, click **Screenshot**, and then click the image of your Calendar window to place the screen shot in the slide. Click the **Click to add title** box, and type **Unit 2, Step 10** Save the presentation, and leave it open.

11 Return to Google Chrome, and **Sign out** of your Google account. Click in the address bar, and type **onedrive.com** and sign in using your Microsoft account.

12 Create a new folder named **Bridal Show** and open the folder. Navigate to the location where your student data files for this project are stored, and then upload two documents—**U2_Vendor_Form** and **U2_Special_Activities**—into your **Bridal Show** folder. Using your own name, rename each file with **Lastname Firstname** in front of, or before to the original file name.

13 Return to PowerPoint. On the **Home tab**, in the **Slides group**, click the upper portion of the **New Slide** button to add a new slide in the presentation. Click the **Insert tab**. In the **Images group**, click **Screenshot**, and then click the image of your OneDrive window to place the screen shot in the slide. Click the **Click to add title** box, and type **Unit 2, Step 13** Save the presentation, and leave it open.

(Unit 2 Case Project continues on the next page)

Case Project | Cloud Computing and a OneNote Notebook Created by a Director of Sales for Oro Jade Hotel Group (continued)

14 **Sign out** of OneDrive. Navigate to **twitter.com** and **sign in** to Twitter. Display the **Compose new tweet** text box, and then type a tweet to invite local companies to participate in the upcoming bridal show as vendors. *Do not click Tweet.*

15 Return to PowerPoint. On the **Home tab**, in the **Slides group**, click the upper portion of the **New Slide** button to add a new slide in the presentation. Click the **Insert tab**. In the **Images group**, click **Screenshot**, and then click the image of Google Chrome window to place the screen shot in the slide. Click the **Click to add title** box, and type **Unit 2, Step 15** Save the presentation, and close **Lastname_Firstname_U2_Screens**. Print the presentation as handouts, six to a page, horizontal as directed by your instructor. Close PowerPoint.

16 **Close** the **Compose new tweet** box, and **Log out** of your Twitter account. **Close** Google Chrome.

17 Open **OneNote**. **Close** any open notebooks. Create a new notebook stored on your computer. As the notebook **Name**, use your own name and type **Lastname_Firstname_U2_Bridal_Show** Under the **Create Notebook** button, click **Create in a different folder**. Navigate to your **All in One Unit 2** folder, and then click **Create**.

18 Rename *New Section 1* as **Luncheon** Click the **Create a New Section tab**. Name the new section **Program** Add two additional new sections named **Schedule** and **Special Events**

19 Click the **Schedule tab** to make the section active. Name the first page **Saturday** Create a new page in the section, and name it **Sunday**

20 In the **page tabs list**, click the **Saturday** page tab. Click below the date and time, and type **Call Security at 212-555-1700 to open the doors at 6:00 a.m. for vendors to set up their exhibits.** Select the text in the container, and then, on the mini toolbar, click **Styles** and click **Heading 4**.

21 On the **Saturday** page, click below the note related to security and time. Click the **Insert tab**, and then in the **Files group**, click **File Printout**. From your student files, insert **U2_Saturday_Schedule**, and then wait a few moments for the Inserting Documents indicator to complete.

22 In the **page tabs list**, click the **Sunday** page tab. Click below the date and time, and then type **10:00 a.m.** press [Tab], type **Vendor displays open** and then press [Enter]. Type **11:00 a.m. and 1:00 p.m.** Press [Tab], type **Bridal fashion shows** and then Press [Enter]. Type **2:00 p.m.** Press [Tab], type **Workshops begin** and then press [Enter]. Type **4:00 p.m.** Press [Tab], and then type **Show closes** Select all the text in the first column, and then on the mini toolbar, click **Bold.**

23 Click the **Luncheon** section tab. In the **Page Title** box, type **Plans** to title the first page of this section. Click below the date and time to display a note container. Type **Tickets must be purchased in advance** and press [Enter]. Type **Final count is due to catering on Thursday** Select the two lines you typed, and then on the mini toolbar, click **Bullets**.

24 Insert a new page using the **Simple To Do List** page template. Replace the existing title with **Task List**

25 In the **Special Events** section, in the **Page Title** box, type **Activities** to title the first page of this section. Click below the date and time and insert file **U2_Cake_Flyer** as an attachment.

26 Add a page and name it **Flyer Notes** Click below the date and time, and then type two formatting suggestions for making the Cake Flyer more effective: **Add more color** and **Add websites of bakeries**

27 From the taskbar, start **Google Chrome**, navigate to **google.com** and perform a search for **bakery**

28 Return to OneNote. On the **Insert tab**, in the **Images group**, click **Screen Clipping** Holding down the left mouse button, drag to select the entire Google search screen. Release the mouse button to display the webpage in your notebook.

29 Rearrange your notebook so that the **Luncheon** section displays between the **Schedule** and **Special Events** section. Export your notebook as a PDF with the name **Lastname_Firstname_U2_Bridal_PDF** Print as directed by your instructor.

30 **Close** OneNote. **Close** your browser. Submit your files as directed by your instructor.

Computer Hardware and Microsoft Word

In this unit, you will examine the hardware components of a computer system and also learn about troubleshooting and maintaining a computer. Then you will use Microsoft Word to create documents with special formatting and elements such as pictures, SmartArt, and tables. You also will use Word tools to create a research paper, including citations, footnotes, and a bibliography using the MLA (Modern Language Association) format. You will also create a resume and cover letter.

Job Focus

A **Site Manager** at Oro Jade Hotels coordinates and supervises the day-to-day operations of the hotel. The **Health & Safety Director** implements safety and risk management processes to provide a safe experience for guests and staff. The Oro Jade Hotel Group employs **interns** for short-term assignments—usually a summer or a semester—to give college students a chance to practice the skills they are learning in school and to learn from experts in the field. A **Human Resources Assistant** is an entry-level position with many duties such as handling incoming applications and confirming previous experience and references. A **Trainer** implements training for employees throughout the hotel.

Case Project Documents Created by a Marketing Manager for Oro Jade Hotel Group

In this Unit Case Project, you will create and modify Word documents that you might encounter while working as a Marketing Manager for Oro Jade Hotel Group. You will modify a company newsletter, which explains the various printers available throughout the hotel and the company's efforts to reduce printing and improve sustainability. Then you will create a flyer to promote an upcoming event for college students. Your completed documents will look similar to Figure 3.1.

PROJECT FILES

For Unit 3 Case Project, you will need the following files:

U3_Company_Newsletter
U3_Workshop_Text

You will save your files as:

Lastname_Firstname_U3_Company_Newsletter
Lastname_Firstname_U3_Workshop_Flyer

PROJECT RESULTS

Oro Jade Connection

January Newsletter

COMPANY ANNOUNCEMENTS

Blood Drive

Mark your calendars! Our spring blood drive will take place on March 23 from 10 a.m. until 4 p.m. in Meeting Rooms A, B, and C. All employees that give blood at this event will be eligible to win two free vacation days to be used before the end of April. We have a hefty goal based on last year's donations.

Year	Donors
2018	144
2017	101
2016	132

Monthly Roundtable

Roundtable discussions are held on the third Thursday of each month at 11:30 a.m. in Meeting Room C.

The topics are determined the month prior by those in attendance; they are posted on the break room bulletin board. Roundtables are open to all employees.

Technology Upgrades

Be sure to review the software/hardware update schedule that was emailed last week. You should plan to back up your files before your system is scheduled for upgrade.

June 14 Annual Company Picnic

Save the date of June 14 for the annual company picnic. Information regarding food, activities, and guests will be included in the next issue of *The Oro Jade Connection*.

OTHER NEWS

Oro Jade Goes Green

Oro Jade takes pride in our green initiatives. One area where we can all pitch in is by reducing our printing costs. All employees are encouraged to reduce printing by using electronic communication and documents whenever possible.

For those times when printing is necessary, the following printers are available in each hotel:

✓ Laser printer – front offices for business documents, letters
✓ Color laser printer – Business Center
✓ Color plotter – Marketing department for marketing materials, reports, flyers
✓ Thermal printer – front desk receipts

Southwest Regional Travel and Tourism

Enjoy this annual publication featuring original content revolving around the travel and tourism in the southwest region of the United States. This is a must-have for hotels in this region.[1]

Attention: College Juniors and Seniors

The Oro Jade Group employs interns from local colleges and universities in all of our hotels. Positions are available in most hotel departments and fill up quickly. Students are encouraged to apply early. More information is available on our website or by calling Human Resources.

[1] Past issues can be read online or downloaded as a pdf.

Lastname_Firstname_U3_Company_Newsletter

Travel and Tourism as a Career

The Oro Jade Hotel Group, in conjunction with three local colleges, is a presenting the *Becoming a Travel and Tourism Professional* series at the San Antonio hotel. The event includes panel discussions, instructional workshops, and portfolio reviews to assist aspiring Travel and Tourism Professionals.

The series will be presented over six weeks, on Tuesday evenings from 7 p.m. to 9 p.m. beginning on May 14. The workshops will be held in the Conference Center and include the following topics:

• Exploring the Travel Industry, May 14
• Choosing a College Major, May 21
• Applying for an Internship, May 28
• Preparing Your Resume, June 4
• Dress for Success, June 11
• Professional Resources, June 18

Advance registration is recommended through the Student Activities office at the student's school. Admission is free for students and $10 per session for the public.

For additional information or to register, visit your Student Activities office.

Monday-Thursday	8 a.m. to 8 p.m.
Friday	8 a.m. to 4 p.m.
Saturday	9 a.m. to 1 p.m.

Lastname_Firstname_U3_Workshop_Flyer

FIGURE 3.1

PowerPoint 2016, Windows 10, Microsoft Corporation

(Unit 3 Case Project continues on the next page)

Case Project Documents Created by a Marketing Manager for Oro Jade Hotel Group (continued)

1 Start Word. On the left, click **Open Other Documents**, click **Browse**, and then in the **Open** dialog box, navigate to the student data files that accompany this Project.

2 Open the file **U3_Company_Newsletter**. Click the **File tab**. On the left, click **Save As**, click **Browse**, and then in the **Save As** dialog box, navigate to your storage location. Create a new folder named **All in One Unit 3** and then open the folder. In the **File name** box, using your own name, save the document as **Lastname_Firstname_U3_Company_Newsletter**

3 Add the file name to the footer. Be sure the rulers and formatting marks display.

4 Change the top, bottom, left, and right margins to **1"**. Select the entire document, and then change the **Line Spacing** to **1.15**.

5 Select the title *Oro Jade Connection* and the paragraph mark that follows it. Format the text using the **Fill – Blue, Accent 1, Shadow** text effect.

6 Select the text beginning with *Company Announcements* and ending with the blank paragraph at the end of the document, and then change the format to two columns. Set the alignment to **Justify**.

7 Insert a **column break** before the heading *Other News*.

8 In the blank paragraph above the heading *Monthly Roundtable*, insert a **2x3** table, and then type the following text into the table:

2018	144
2017	101
2016	132

9 Under the heading *Oro Jade Goes Green*, format the four paragraphs beginning with *Laser Printer* and ending with *front desk receipts* as a **bulleted list** using the check mark bullet style.

10 In the paragraph that begins *Enjoy this annual*, immediately following the period after the last sentence that ends *region*, insert a footnote and type **Past issues can be read online or downloaded as a pdf.** Modify the font size of the **Footnote Text style** to **8 pt.** and apply it to your footnote.

11 Insert a new first row in the table. In the new row type **Year** press [Tab], and then type **Donors**

12 Select the three cells in the table that contain the number of donors and apply **Align Right** alignment.

13 Select the entire table and **AutoFit** the contents. **Center** the table within the first column of the newsletter.

14 Select the headings *Company Announcements* and *Other News* and set **Spacing Before** to **6 pt**.

15 Add a **Box** page border to the document using the default settings.

16 Press [Ctrl] + [End] to position the insertion point in the blank paragraph at the end of the second column. On the Insert tab, in the Illustrations group, click **Insert a SmartArt Graphic**, and then in the **Relationship group**, click **Converging Arrows**. Type **Oro Jade** in the left arrow and **Goes Green** in the right arrow. Change the height of the **SmartArt** graphic to **1.2** so that the newsletter fits on one page.

17 Display the **Document properties**; be sure your name displays as the **Author**. As the **Subject**, add your course name and section number. As the **Title** type **January Newsletter**

18 On the left, click **Print** and examine your document in Print Preview. On the left, click **Save**. Click the **File tab**. On the left, click **Close** to close the newsletter but leave Word open.

19 Click the **File tab**. On the left, click **New**, and then click **Blank document**. Save the document in your **All in One Unit 3** folder as **Lastname_Firstname_U3_Workshop_Flyer**

20 Type **Travel and Tourism as a Career** and press [Enter]. Select the title, and then in the **Text Effects** gallery, apply the **Fill – Orange, Accent 2, Outline - Accent 2** effect. **Center** the title, and change the **Font Size** to **36 pt**.

21 Click in the blank paragraph below the title. Insert the file **U3_Workshop_Text**.

22 Select the list of six workshop topics, and then format the selected text as a bulleted list.

23 Position the insertion point to the left of the paragraph that begins *The series*. Search for and then insert a clip art image of your choice that relates to **luggage** Set the height of your inserted image to **2"** and apply **Square** text wrapping.

(Unit 3 Case Project continues on the next page)

Case Project   Documents Created by a Marketing Manager for Oro Jade Hotel Group (continued)

24 Press Ctrl + End to move to the end of the document, and then type **For additional information or to register, visit your Student Activities office.** Press Enter one time.

25 Display the **Tabs** dialog box. Set a **Left** tab stop at **1.5"** and a **Right** tab stop with a **dot leader** at **5"** As you type the following text, be sure to press Tab to begin each line and press Tab between the days and the times. Press Enter at the end of each line.

Monday-Thursday	8 a.m. to 8 p.m.
Friday	8 a.m. to 4 p.m.
Saturday	9 a.m. to 1 p.m.

26 Add the file name to the footer. Display the document properties. Be sure your name displays as the author. As the **Subject**, type your course and section number. As the **Tags**, type **student workshop**

27 On the left, click **Print** and examine the Print Preview. Then on the left, click **Save**. **Close** Word.

28 Submit your two Word files as directed by your instructor.

System Software and Microsoft Excel

CHAPTER 3	Concepts: System Software
CHAPTER 15	Applications: Creating a Worksheet and Charting Data
CHAPTER 16	Functions, Tables, Large Workbooks, and Pie Charts

ariadna de raadt /Shutterstock

In this unit, you will learn about the system software—operating systems and utility software—that make computers run smoothly and securely. You will use Microsoft Excel to enter, format, and analyze data. You will use functions and formulas and create charts and tables. Finally, you will apply formatting to enhance and organize your data.

Job Focus

The **IT Technical Support Officer's** responsibilities include supporting users of Oro Jade Hotel Group's computer systems, maintaining and securing systems, and managing user access to the systems. The **Marketing Coordinator** for gift shops markets products by developing and implementing marketing campaigns, tracking sales data, maintaining databases, and creating reports. The **Purchasing Agent** for the gift shops seeks reliable vendors or suppliers and manages inventory. The **Chef** has overall responsibility for all of the food that comes out of the kitchen as well as the kitchen operations. **Restaurant managers** are responsible for managing all of a restaurant's daily operations.

Case Project Excel Workbooks Created by a Day Spa Manager

In this Unit Case Project, you will work with multiple worksheets and enter formulas and functions to calculate totals and other statistics that you might encounter as a Day Spa Manager for Oro Jade Hotel Group. You will also format cells; insert charts and sparklines; and create, sort, and filter an Excel table. Finally, you will compare backup solutions for spa records. Your completed worksheets will look similar to Figure 4.1.

PROJECT FILES

For Unit 4 Case Project, you will need the following file:

U4_Day_Spa

You will save your file as:

Lastname_Firstname_U4_Day_Spa

PROJECT RESULTS

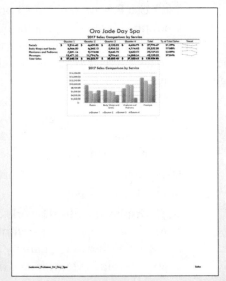

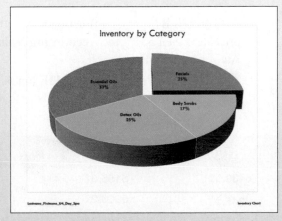

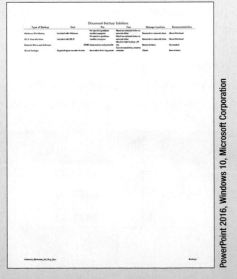

FIGURE 4.1

PowerPoint 2016, Windows 10, Microsoft Corporation

(Unit 4 Case Project continues on the next page)

Case Project | Excel Workbooks Created by a Day Spa Manager (continued)

1 Start Excel. From your student files, open the file **U4_Day_Spa**. In the location where you are storing your projects, create a new folder named **All in One Unit 4** and then **Save** the workbook as **Lastname_Firstname_U4_Day_Spa**

2 On **Sheet1**, in cell **A2**, type **2017 Sales Comparison by Service** and then change the **Theme** to **Droplet**.

3 In cell **B3**, type **Quarter 1** and then use the fill handle to enter *Quarter 2*, *Quarter 3*, and *Quarter 4* in the range **C3:E3**. In cell **F3**, type **Total** In cell **G3**, type **% of Total Sales** and in cell **H3**, type **Trend**

4 In the range **A4:A7**, type the following row titles:

Facials
Body Wraps and Scrubs
Massages
Total Sales

5 Widen **column A** to **160 pixels**. Widen **columns B:H** to **105 pixels**. **Merge & Center** the title across the range **A1:H1**, apply the **Title** cell style, and then change the font size to **26**. **Merge & Center** the subtitle across the range **A2:H2**, and then apply the **Heading 1** cell style. **Center** the column titles in **row 3**, and then apply the **Heading 3** cell style. Apply the **Heading 4** cell style to the range **A4:A7**.

6 In the range **B4:E6**, enter the sales values for each quarter as shown in the table at the bottom of this page.

7 Use **Quick Analysis** to **Sum** the **Quarter 1** sales, and then copy the formula across for the remaining quarters. By using **Quick Analysis**, **Sum** the sales for *Facials*, and then copy the formula down through cell **F7**. Apply **Accounting Number Format** to the first row of sales figures and to the total row, and **Comma Style** to the remaining sales figures. Format the totals in **row 7** with the **Total** cell style.

8 Insert a new **row 6** with the row title **Manicures and Pedicures** and the following sales figures for each quarter:

7691.16 and **9774.38** and **9648.75** and **2622.73** Fill the formula in cell **F5** down to cell **F6** to sum the new row, and then remove the bold formatting from the range **F4:F7**.

9 In cell **G4**, using absolute cell references, construct a formula to calculate the **% of Total Sales** for *Facials* by dividing the total for *Facials* sales by the total sales for all quarters. Fill the formula down for the remaining services. To the range **G4:G7**, apply **Percent Style** with two decimal places, and then **Center** the percentages.

10 In the range **H4:H7**, insert **Line** sparklines that compare the quarterly data. Do *not* include the totals in the sparkline range. Show the **Markers**, and apply the first style in the third row—**Sparkline Style Accent 1 (no dark or light)**.

11 Use **Recommended Charts** to insert a **Clustered Column** chart to compare the quarterly sales of each service, with the services—not the quarters—on the **Category** axis. Do *not* include the totals in the data range.

12 Position the upper right corner of the chart in the upper right corner of cell **F10**. Apply **Style 14** to the chart. Change the chart title to **2017 Sales Comparison by Service** and then change the title font size to **14**.

13 Center the worksheet **Horizontally** and scale the **Width** to fit to **1 page**.

14 Display the **Sheet2** worksheet. Scale the **Width** to fit on **1 page**, centered **Horizontally**. In cell **B9**, enter a function to sum the **Quantity in Stock** data, and then apply **Comma Style** with zero decimal places to the result.

15 In cell **B11**, enter a function to calculate the average price, and then apply the **Accounting Number Format**. Autofit **column B**.

16 In cell **B4**, enter a **COUNTIF** function to determine how many different types of **Facials** products are in

	QUARTER 1	QUARTER 2	QUARTER 3	QUARTER 4
Facials	9516.40	6439.50	5155.82	6684.75
Body Wraps and Scrubs	6966.30	6245.13	5906.22	4114.63
Massages	13471.32	11794.76	9794.61	14098.34

Return to Step 7.

(Unit 4 Case Project continues on the next page)

Case Project | Excel Workbooks Created by a Day Spa Manager (continued)

stock. By using the same technique, in **B5:B7**, enter a **COUNTIF** function to determine the number of types in each of the other categories.

17 In cell **G14**, enter an **IF** function to determine the items that must be ordered. If the **Quantity in Stock** is less than **65** the **Value_if_true** is **Order** Otherwise, the **Value_if_false** is **OK** Fill the formula down through all the rows.

18 Apply **Conditional Formatting** to the **Stock Level** column so that cells that contain the text *Order* are formatted with **Bold Italic** with a font color of **Green, Accent 2, Darker 25%**. Apply **Gradient Fill Green Data Bars** to the **Quantity in Stock** column.

19 Move the range **A4:B7** to the range beginning in cell **D4**. In cell **C6**, type **Categories** and then merge cells **C4:C7**, and rotate the text **30** degrees. Change the font size to **18 pt**, apply **Bold**, and **Align Right**.

20 Format the range **A13:G37** as a table with headers, and apply **Table Style Light 9**. Insert a Total row, filter by **Category** for **Body Scrubs**, and then **Sum** the **Quantity in Stock** column. Record the result in cell **B10**, and apply **Comma Style** with zero decimal places.

21 Clear the filter. Sort the table on the **Item #** column from **Smallest to Largest**, and then remove the Total row.

22 Using the range **D4:E7**, insert a **3-D pie** chart on a new sheet named **Inventory Chart** As the chart title type **Inventory by Category** Change the font size to **28 pt** and change the font color to **Blue-Gray, Text 2**—in the fourth

column, the first color. Remove the **Legend**. Format the **Data Labels** so that they are centered and display only the **Category Name** and **Percentage**. With the data labels selected, apply **Bold** and change the font size to **14**. Explode the **Facials** section by **15%**.

23 Display **Sheet3**. **Merge & Center** the title across the range **A1:F1** and apply the **Title** cell style. To the range **A2:F2**, apply the **Heading 2** style and then **Center** the text. Apply the **Heading 4** style to the text in the range **A3:A6**.

24 In your own words, complete the sheet comparing different methods to back up spa records. Adjust column widths and wrap text as necessary. Scale the sheet to fit on **1 page**, and center the sheet **Horizontally**.

25 Rename **Sheet1** as **Sales** rename **Sheet2** as **Inventory** and rename **Sheet3** as **Backups** Move the **Inventory Chart** sheet to the right of the **Inventory** worksheet.

26 Display the document properties, and then, as the **Tags**, type **sales, inventory** As the **Subject**, type your course name and section number. Be sure your name displays as the **Author**.

27 On each sheet, insert a footer to display the file name in the left section and the sheet name in the right section.

28 **Save** your workbook, and then print or submit electronically as directed.

Networks, Security and Privacy, Microsoft PowerPoint, and Microsoft Access

| CHAPTER **4** | Concepts: Networks, Security, and Privacy | CHAPTER **17** | Applications: Introduction to Microsoft Access | CHAPTER **18** | Applications: Getting Started with Microsoft PowerPoint |

Andresr /Shutterstock

In this unit, you will learn about different kinds of computer networks. You will also explore some of the most common security threats and how you can protect yourself from them. You will use Microsoft PowerPoint to develop your presentation skills and enhance your communications. Finally, you will use Microsoft Access to organize data so that information can be retrieved and managed efficiently.

Job Focus

A **Convention Planner** at **Oro Jade Hotel Group** is responsible for organizing and coordinating all aspects of conventions that are held at each hotel. The **Recreation Supervisor** promotes a fun, relaxing, and safe atmosphere for guests. A **Fitness Center Attendant** is responsible for fitness operations including supervising the floor, operations of equipment and safety, and ensuring a clean workout environment. The **Oro Jade Area Marketing** Managers promote the hotel property within the community to attract local events. They also act as a go-between for the hotel staff and many of the corporate functions. The **Oro Jade Area Sales Assistant** is responsible for assisting the Sales team by booking and servicing groups and meeting space while providing exceptional customer service to guests.

Case Project PowerPoint Presentation and Database Created by a Sales Operations Manager for Oro Jade Hotel Group

In this Unit Case Project, you will modify a PowerPoint presentation for Oro Jade Hotel Group, regarding computer security. You will also create a new table in the Career Resources database and append data from Excel into it. You will use the table to create a form and a report. You will use the database to answer questions about the resources by creating, editing, and formatting queries. Your completed presentation and database will look similar to Figure 5.1.

PROJECT FILES

For Unit 5 Case Project, you will need the following files:

U5_Computer_Security (PowerPoint presentation)
U5_Picture1 (JPG image)
U5_Career_Resources (Access database)
U5_Interns (Excel spreadsheet)

You will save your files as:

Lastname_Firstname_U5_Computer_Security (PowerPoint presentation)
Lastname_Firstname_U5_Career_Resources (Access database)

PROJECT RESULTS

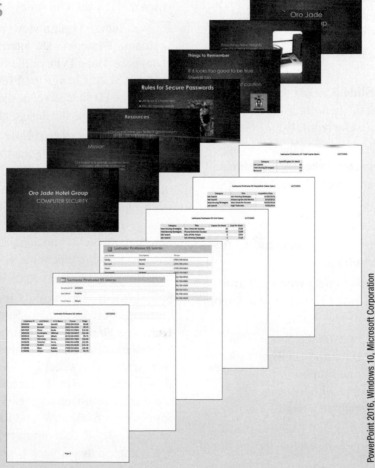

FIGURE 5.1

PowerPoint 2016, Windows 10, Microsoft Corporation

(Unit 5 Case Project continues on the next page)

Case Project | **PowerPoint Presentation and Database Created by a Sales Operations Manager for Oro Jade Hotel Group** (continued)

1 ▸ Start PowerPoint. From your student data files, open the file **U5_Computer_Security**. Create a new folder named **All in One Unit 5** and then **Save** the presentation as **Lastname_Firstname_U5_Computer_Security**

2 ▸ Apply the **Ion** design theme to all slides in the presentation.

3 ▸ On **Slide 2**, remove the bullet symbol from the paragraph and **Center** the text.

4 ▸ On **Slide 3**, apply the picture style **Reflected Rounded Rectangle** to the picture.

5 ▸ On **Slide 4**, change the bullet style to **Hollow Square Bullets**.

6 ▸ Change the slide layout of **Slide 5** to **Two Content**. In the right placeholder, insert the **U5_Picture1** picture.

7 ▸ In the left placeholder, add a bullet point **Don't use names of people or pets** Using the Internet or your textbook, add two additional rules for secure passwords.

8 ▸ In **Slide Sorter** view. Move **Slide 3** into the **Slide 6** position.

9 ▸ In **Normal** view, on **Slide 5**, select the three pictures, and **Align** them at the bottom. With the three pictures selected, **Distribute Horizontally**.

10 ▸ In the **Notes** pane on **Slide 6**, add the following speaker note: **With the increase in cyber security threats, we face new challenges every day.**

11 ▸ Delete **Slide 7** from the presentation.

12 ▸ To the title *Oro Jade Hotel Group* on **"Slide 7"**, apply the **Shape Fill** color, in the third column, the first color—**Dark Teal, Background 2.**

13 ▸ Apply the **Fade** transition effect with the **Through Black** option to all slides in the presentation at a duration of **1.5**.

14 ▸ **Insert** a **Header & Footer** on the **Notes and Handouts**. Include the **Date and time** updated automatically, the **Page number**, and a **Footer**, using your own name, with the text **Lastname_Firstname_U5_Computer_Security**

15 ▸ Display the Properties area, and add your name, your course name, and section number, and the keywords **computer security**

16 ▸ View your presentation from the beginning and correct any errors.

17 ▸ **Save** and **Close** the presentation. Submit as directed by your instructor.

18 ▸ Start **Access**. From your student files, open the **U5_Career_Resources** database; if necessary, enable the content. Save the database in your **All in One Unit 5** folder as **Lastname_Firstname_U5_Career_Resources** Enable the content if necessary.

19 ▸ Open the two tables to become familiar with the data, view the relationship between the two tables, and then close all the database objects.

20 ▸ **Create** a new table in **Datasheet** view. Change the field name of the **ID** field to **Employee ID** Using the **Short Text** data type, name the next three fields as **Last Name** and **First Name** and **Phone** Name the fifth field **Wage** and use the **Currency** data type.

21 ▸ Switch to **Design** view; name the table **Lastname_Firstname_U5_Interns** In **Design** view, change the **Data Type** of the field **Employee ID** field to **Short Text**. Change the **Field Size** to **7** Be sure that **Employee ID** field is set as the **Primary Key**. Close the table and save the design changes.

22 ▸ From the **External Data tab**, import an **Excel** spreadsheet. **Navigate** to the location of your student files, and then select the Excel file **U5_Interns**. **Append** a copy of the records to your **Lastname_Firstname_U5_Interns** table. Open your **Lastname_Firstname_U5_Interns** table to display the data that was imported from Excel. Select all the fields and apply **Best Fit**. **Save** the table. Create a paper or electronic printout as directed, and then hold this file until you complete the project.

23 ▸ With the **Lastname_Firstname_U5_Interns** table open, create a **Form**. **Save** the form as **Lastname_Firstname_U5_Interns_Form** Using **Form** view, display the fifth record, and then click the **Record Selector bar** on the left to select only this record. Display the **Print** dialog box, and in the lower left corner, click **Setup**. Click the **Columns tab**, change the **Width** to **7.5** so that the form prints on one page, and then click **OK**. Print or create an electronic printout of this record and hold the file until you complete this project. **Close** the form.

(Unit 5 Case Project continues on the next page)

Case Project | PowerPoint Presentation and Database Created by a Sales Operations Manager for Oro Jade Hotel Group (continued)

24 With the **Lastname Firstname U5 Interns** table open, create a **Report**. Delete the **Employee ID** and **Wage** fields from the report. At the bottom of the report, select and then delete the page number control. At the top of the form in the blue title, delete the date and time. Click the title of the report, and then drag the right orange border to the right if necessary to display the title on one line. **Save** the report as **Lastname_Firstname_U5_Phone_List** Display the **Print** dialog box and change the column width to **7.5**. Create a paper or electronic printout as directed. Hold this file until you complete this project. **Close** the report and the table. **Close** the **navigation pane**.

25 **Create** a query in **Query Design** view using the **Career Titles** table to answer the question, *In alphabetical order by Category, what are the Titles, the number of Copies On Hand, and the Cost Per Book for titles that cost $100 or more?* Display the fields in the order listed in the question. Four records meet the criteria. Apply **Best Fit** to the columns in the query results. **Save** the query as **Lastname_Firstname_U5_Cost_Query** and create a paper or electronic printout as directed. **Close** the query.

26 Display the **navigation pane**, open the **Acquisition Dates** query, and then display the query in **Query Design**

view. Save a copy of the query object as **Lastname_Firstname_U5_Acquisition_Dates_Query** Modify the query to answer the question *By category, which titles were acquired—shown in reverse chronological order by Acquisition Date—after 1/15/2014?* Display the fields in the order listed in the question. Four records meet the criteria. Apply **Best Fit** to the columns in the query results. Create a paper or electronic printout as directed. Hold this file until you complete the project. **Close** the query, saving changes.

27 **Create** a query in **Query Design** view. Use the **Career Titles** table and the **Sum** aggregate function to answer the question *For each category, how many copies are on hand displayed in descending sort order?* Apply **Best Fit** to the columns in the query results. **Save** the query as **Lastname_Firstname_U5_Total_Copies_Query** and then create a paper or electronic copy as directed. **Close** the query and hold the file.

28 **Close** any open database objects. **Close** the database and then **Exit** Access. Submit your database and the six paper or electronic printouts—table, single record form, report, and three queries—that are the results of this project.

Appendix

IC3 GS5 Standard	GO! All in One Concept or Activity
Computing Fundamentals	
Section 1.01 Mobile Devices	
(a) Understand cellular phone concepts	1.01, 1.10, 4.05
(b) Be familiar with cellular-enabled tablets	1.08, 4.05, 4.06
(c) Be familiar with smartphones	1.01, 1.10, 3.08, 4.05
(d) Understand the use of hard wired phones	6.19
(e) Know how to configure and use voice mail	6.19
(f) Use of instant messaging	6.19
(g) Know how to configure notifications	6.01
Section 1.02 Hardware	
(a) Types of devices	1.07, 1.08, 1.12, 1.13, 4.02, 4.03
(i) Server	1.12, 1.13, 4.02, 4.03
(ii) Laptop	1.08
(iii) Desktop	1.07
(b) Know the impact of memory and storage on usage	1.05, 2.06, 2.09, 2.20, 2.21, 5.11
(c) Know how to connect to different peripherals	2.03, 2.04, 2.09, 2.11, 2.13, 2.14, 2.16, 4.04
(i) Camera	2.04, 2.09
(ii) Audio	2.14
(iii) Microphone	2.11
(iv) Printer	2.16
(v) USB devices	2.04
(vi) External display	2.13
(d) Understand the use of Ethernet ports	2.17, 4.04, 4.06
(e) Connect a device wireless network (Wi-Fi)	4.06, 5.02
(f) Understand power management and power settings	3.03, 5.03
(g) Understand driver concepts as well as their device compatibility	3.03, 4.03, 5.04
(i) Know what drivers do	3.03, 5.04
(ii) Know if specific drivers are compatible with a personal device	3.03, 4.03, 5.04
(h) Know platform implications and considerations	1.09, 3.03, 3.08
(i) For Example Mac, PC, Linux, iOS, Android, Firmware	1.09, 3.03
(i) Know platform compatibility	3.18, 4.06, 5.11
(i) Media compatibility issues (Why won't my video play?)	5.11
(ii) Device limitations (a device might only have Wi-Fi or only have wired capabilities)	3.18, 4.06
(j) Know the difference between cellular, Wi-Fi, and wired networks	3.18, 3.19, 4.04, 4.06

IC3 GS5 Standard	GO! All in One Concept or Activity
(k) Understand concepts regarding connecting to the Internet	2.17, 4.06, 4.07
(i) Modem	2.17
(ii) Bandwidth, speed	4.06
(iii) Have a basic understanding of what a router is	4.07
(iv) Wired	4.06
(v) Wireless	4.06
(l) Understand common hardware configurations	2.07
(m) Implications for document usage	2.10, 3.18, 3.19
(n) Understand the pros and cons of touch screens vs. non-touch screen devices	2.08
Section 1.03 Computer Software Architecture	
(a) Understand operating system versioning and update awareness	3.05, 3.06
(b) Know concepts surrounding applications vs. operating system vs. global settings	3.03, 3.05, 3.06, 6.01
(c) Have a general understanding of operating systems and software settings	3.05, 3.06
(i) Know basic desktop customization	IT SIM - System Software, 10.04
(ii) Know window management (minimize, maximize, resizing windows)	10.08
(d) Set software preferences	6.01, 9.17
(e) Users and profiles	4.16
(f) Know file structures and file/folder management	1.10, 3.10, 3.11, 3.12, 3.13, 3.14, 3.15
(i) Moving/renaming files	3.12
(ii) File permissions	3.14
(iii) File extensions	3.13
(iv) Managing electronic media (eBooks, songs, videos)	1.10, 3.18
(v) Zipping/compression	3.15
(g) Document Management	2.10, 3.18, 3.19
(i) Scanning documents	2.01
(ii) Taking pictures	3.18, 3.19
(h) Menu navigation	10.07, 10.08
(i) Radio buttons	11.04
(ii) Check boxes	11.02, 11.10
(iii) Drop-down menus	11.04, 11.15
(iv) Multi-select	10.29
(i) Searching for files	3.16, 3.17
(j) Rights and permissions (administrative rights)	3.09, 4.09, 4.16
(k) Define an IP address	4.01

IC3 GS5 Standard	GO! All in One Concept or Activity
(l) Know how to install, uninstall, update, repair software	5.13, 5.14
(i) From the Internet	5.13, 5.14
(ii) Using local media (DVD-ROM, etc.)	5.13
(m) Troubleshooting	4.10, 5.01, 5.02, 5.06
(i) Know basic problem-solving techniques	5.01
(ii) Know how to determine problems involving hardware vs. software	5.01, 5.06
(iii) Know proper terminology to be able to describe the problem	5.01, 5.06
(iv) Know how to find an IP address on a personal computer	4.10, 5.02
(v) Know how to determine a connection speed	5.02
Section 1.04 Backup and Restore	
(a) Understand backing up concepts	5.07, 5.08, 5.09, 5.10
(b) Know how to back up and restore	5.07, 5.08, 5.09, 5.10
(c) Know how to complete a full system restore on a personal device	5.05, 5.10
Section 1.05 File Sharing	
(a) Understand file transfer options and characteristics	3.15, 3.19
(i) Know how to attach files to email	3.19
(ii) Know how to get links to online stored files	3.19, 9.05, 9.12
(iii) Understand the difference between publicly shared vs. shared links vs. shared folders	3.19
(b) Understand needs for file compression/zipping in sharing	3.15, 6.08
Section 1.06 Cloud Computing	
(a) Understand "cloud" concepts	3.19, 6.14
(i) Understand cloud storage vs. cloud access concepts	3.19, 6.14
(ii) Understand sharing and collaboration via the cloud	3.19, 6.14
(b) Know the benefits of using cloud storage	3.19, 6.14
(c) Access and utilization of the cloud	3.19, 6.14
(i) Understand account management on the cloud	3.19
(ii) Know how to upload content to the cloud	3.19, 9.05, 9.10
(iii) Know how to download content from the cloud	3.19
(iv) Know how to sync files between devices using the cloud	3.18, 3.19
(d) Web apps vs. local apps	6.14
(i) Understand Software as a Service (SAAS) concepts	6.14
(ii) Know what Learning Management Systems (LMS) do	6.18
(e) Understand web app types	3.18, 3.19, 6.14
(i) Online storage apps (Google Drive, Dropbox, OneDrive, iCloud storage)	3.18, 3.20, 9.05, 9.10
(ii) Online office apps (Google apps, Office 365)	3.18, 3.21, 6.14

IC3 GS5 Standard	GO! All in One Concept or Activity
(iii) Database Driven CRM apps (Salesforce, Oracle, Attask)	6.18
(iv) Browser vs. tablet vs. smartphone vs. desktop apps	6.14, 6.16
Section 1.07 Security	
(a) Know credential management best practices	4.16
(i) Usernames	4.16
(ii) Passwords	4.16
1) Understand the components of a good password	4.16
(b) Know basic account setting management	4.16
(c) Know the basic threats to security of computers, data, and identity	4.13, 4.14, 5.15
(i) Viruses	5.15
(ii) Trojans	5.15
(iii) Malware	5.15
(iv) Social engineering	4.14
(d) Understand the implications of monitoring software (surveillance)	5.15
(e) Connecting to secured vs. unsecured network (wired and wireless)	4.12
(i) Know the ramifications	4.12
(ii) Understand the risks	4.12
(iii) Know the difference between public vs. private computing (using a public computer)	5.16
1) Browser histories	5.16
2) Cache/cookies	5.16
3) Logging out of online and OS accounts	5.16
(f) Know the use of and importance of anti-virus software	5.17
(i) Understand how to prevent virus issues	5.17
(ii) Understand how to maintain and update anti-virus software	5.17
(g) Know the use of firewalls and basic settings	4.11, 5.17
(h) Know eCommerce interactions and best practices	4.17
(i) Recognize the use of a secure connection, networks, (https:)	4.17
(ii) Know how to be a savvy ecommerce consumer	4.17
(i) Understand what Virtual Private Networks (VPNs) are	4.05

Key Applications	
Section 2.01 Common Features	
(a) Know copy, cut, and paste keyboard equivalents	11.17
(b) Understand the difference between plain text and HTML (text with markup)	Online Supplemental
(c) Know how to use spell check	11.03, 13.20
(d) Know how to use reviewing features	Online Supplemental
(e) Know the find/replace feature	13.17
(f) Be able to select text or cells	11.02
(g) Be able to redo and undo	11.05
(h) Be able to drag and drop	13.18
(i) Know the read-only view	11.09
(j) Understand what a protected mode means	11.09
(k) Be able to use the zoom feature	11.14
Section 2.02 Word Processing	
(a) Perform basic formatting skills	11.02, 11.04, 11.05, 11.07, 11.12, 11.15, 11.16, 12.03
(b) Adjust margins, page sizes, and page orientation	11.14
(c) Alter text and font styles	11.15, 12.03, 13.02, 13.03, 13.09, 14.04, 14.24, 14.25
(d) Create and save files	11.06
(e) Know page layout concepts	11.05, 12.18, 13.05, 13.08, 13.09, 13.10, 13.12, 14.02, 14.26
(i) Page numbering	14.02
(ii) Columns	14.15
(iii) Margin	12.17
(iv) Alignment, text in paragraphs and tables	11.05, 12.18, 13.05, 13.08, 13.09, 13.10, 13.12, 14.02, 14.26
(v) Tabs and rulers	11.02, 12.25, 12.26
(vi) Orientation	11.14
(vii) Spacing	12.19, 14.01
(f) Know how to print a word processing document	11.08, 12.16
(g) Use and configure print views	Online Supplemental
(h) Use reviewing options within a word processing document	Online Supplemental
(i) Turn on and off change tracking features	Online Supplemental
(ii) Accept or reject proposed changes	Online Supplemental
(i) Be able to use tables	13.01, 13.02, 13.19
(j) Understand which file types are compatible and/or editable with woXrd processors	Online Supplemental
(i) Example include Pdf, Pub, Doc, Docx, Txt, etc.	14.13
(k) Use word processing templates to increase productivity	13.13, 14.13

IC3 GS5 Standard	GO! All in One Concept or Activity
Section 2.03 Spreadsheets	
(a) Understand common spreadsheet terms	15.01, 15.04, 16.11, 16.21
(i) Cell	15.01
(ii) Column	15.01
(iii) Row	15.01
(iv) Range	15.01
(v) Worksheet	15.01
(vi) Workbook	15.01
(vii) Navigation	15.01, 16.11, 16.21
(b) Be able to insert/delete rows and columns	15.25
(c) Be able to modify cell sizes	Online Supplemental
(d) Be able to filter and sort data	15.06, 15.20, 16.15, 16.16
(e) Understand functions, formulas, and operators	15.06, 15.07, 15.20, 15.22, 16.03
(i) Understand their purpose and how they are used	15.06, 15.07, 15.20, 15.22, 16.03
(ii) Recognize syntax	15.06,16.03
(iii) Be able to create simple formulas	15.20, 16.03
(f) Be able to enter data in a spreadsheet	15.01, 15.03, 15.05, 15.06, 15.07, 15.19, 15.23
(g) Use and create spreadsheet charts	15.11, 16.37
(i) Recognize charts	15.11, 16.37
(ii) Read and interpret charts	15.11, 16.37
(iii) Create simple charts	15.12, 16.37
(h) Create spreadsheet tables	16.14
(i) Recognize tables	16.14
(ii) Use and manipulate tables	16.14
(iii) Create simple tables	16.14
(i) Manipulate data within a spreadsheet	15.08, 16.24
(i) Merge and unmerge cells	15.08
(ii) Cut, copy, and paste data	16.24
(j) Format data within spreadsheets	15.09, 15.13, 15.14, 15.24,
(i) Modify borders, fill color, text color, alignment, data type	15.04, 15.14, 15.17, 15.24, 15.26, 15.27
(k) Understand compatible spreadsheet file types	Online Supplemental
(i) Examples include Csv, Xlsx, Tab delimited, etc.	Online Supplemental
(l) Be able to use spreadsheet templates to increase productivity	Online Supplemental
(m) Understand how a spreadsheet can be used as a simple database	16.15

IC3 GS5 Standard	GO! All in One Concept or Activity
Section 2.04 Databases	
(a) Understand what data is	17.01
(b) Understand how websites utilize databases	17.01
(c) Know basic concepts of a relational database	17.01, 17.14, 17.15, 17.28, 17.30, 17.32, 17.33, 17.37, 17.39, 17.40, 17.41, 17.42, 17.43, 17.44, 17.47, 17.50
(i) Field	17.01
(ii) Table	17.01
(iii) Data	17.01
(iv) Query	17.14, 17.28, 17.30, 17.32, 17.33, 17.37, 17.39, 17.40, 17.41, 17.42, 17.43, 17.44, 17.47, 17.50
(v) Form	17.15
(d) Know what metadata is	17.01
Section 2.05 Presentations	
(a) Understand file types compatible with presentation software	18.12, 18.13, 18.15, 18.16, 18.19
(i) Sharing (presentation, handout, outlines, video)	18.13, 18.15, 18.16, 18.19
(ii) Publishing (pptx, pdf, jpg, show, png)	18.15
(b) Understand how to connect to external/extended monitors to display presentation	18.12
(i) Cables	Tech to GO! Video: Connect to an External Monitor or Projector to Display Presentations
(ii) Audio	Tech to GO! Video: Connect to an External Monitor or Projector to Display Presentations
(c) Be able to use presentation views and modes	18.11, 18.12, 18.33
(d) Know how to add animations, effects, and slide transitions	18.31, 18.32
(e) Know how to create and organize slides	18.04, 18.08, 18.38, 18.39
(i) Slide management	18.04
(ii) Inserting and managing media files	18.08, 18.38, 18.39
(f) Know how to design slides	18.01, 18.03, 18.22
(i) Be able to use templates	18.03, 18.22
(g) Identify presentation software options	18.01, 18.04, 18.18, 18.20, 18.27, 18.28, 18.29, 18.30
(i) Presentations	18.01, 18.18, 18.20
(ii) Add slides	18.04, 18.18
(iii) Delete slides	18.20, 18.28
(iv) Revise slide order	18.20, 18.28, 18.29, 18.30
(v) Layout	18.04, 18.27

IC3 GS5 Standard	GO! All in One Concept or Activity
Section 2.06 App Culture	
(a) Understand how to obtain apps	6.15, 6.16
(i) Web apps	6.16
(ii) App stores	6.16
(b) Identify different app genres	6.01, 6.05, 6.09. 6.10, 6.11, 6.12, 6.13
(i) Productivity	6.01
(ii) Reference	6.05
(iii) Content	6.12, 6.13
(iv) Creation	6.09, 6.10
(v) Social media	6.16
(vi) Music	6.11, 6.13
(vii) Health	6.05
(c) Understand strengths and limits of apps and applications	6.16
(i) Applications may only run on certain devices	6.16
Section 2.07 Graphic Modification	
(a) Be able to import and insert images into documents	18.38, 18.39
(b) Understand how to crop images	18.42, 18.43

IC3 GS5 Standard	GO! All in One Concept or Activity
Living Online	
Section 3.01 Internet (Navigation)	
(a) Understand what the Internet is	1.04, 4.04, 4.10, 5.15, 6.17, 7.02, 7.03, 7.07, 8.01, 8.02, 8.03, 8.04, 8.05, 8.06
(i) Understand how the Internet works	1.04, 4.04, 4.10, 7.02, 7.03, 7.07
1) Network topologies	4.04, 7.02
2) DNS, IP addresses	4.10, 7.07
3) Domain types (.gov, .edu, .com, .us, .uk, etc.)	7.07
4) Bandwidth	7.03
5) Understand data sizes (bits vs. bytes vs. megabytes, etc.)	1.04, 7.03
(ii) Be familiar with media literacy	8.01, 8.02, 8.03
1) Know how to search the Internet	8.01, 9.03
a) Advance searches (keyword, hashtag)	8.01, 9.03
2) Research fluency	8.03
a) Validity of resources	8.03, 9.03
(iii) Understand browser functionality	5.15, 7.04, 7.05, 7.06, 7.07
1) HTML/CSS	7.04
2) Cookies	5.15, 7.05
3) Cache	5.15, 7.05
4) Breadcrumbs	7.07
5) Plugins	7.06
6) Widget	7.06
7) Add-ons	7.06
8) In-browser apps	7.06
9) Popups	7.05
10) Different browsers	7.04
11) Browser navigation (URLs, scroll bars, etc.)	7.07, 9.01
12) New window, tabs	7.04, 9.01
13) Bookmarks, favorites, synchronize bookmark	7.04. 9.02
(iv) Know about IP rights/usage	8.04
(v) Know about licensing rules/laws	6.17, 8.04
1) Of intellectual property	8.04
2) Software programs.	6.17
(vi) Know about copyrights	8.05
(vii) Know about censorship and filtering	8.06
(viii) Know plagiarism rules/laws	8.05
(ix) Fair use	8.05

IC3 GS5 Standard	GO! All in One Concept or Activity
Section 3.02 Common Functionality	
(a) Understand how to use common website navigation conventions	9.01, 9.02, 9.03
(i) Click / delayed / double click	9.03
(ii) Mouse over	9.03, 9.04
(iii) Drag and drop	9.02
(iv) Basic web navigation principles	9.01
Section 3.03 Email clients	
(a) Identify email applications	7.10
(i) Desktop application platform (ie. Outlook)	7.10
(ii) Web-based platform (Gmail, Yahoo!)	7.10
(b) Understand email etiquette	5.16, 7.10, 9.04
(i) Reply vs. reply all, forward	7.10, 9.04
(ii) Cc vs. Bcc	7.10, 9.04
(iii) Signature	7.10, 9.20
(iv) Header	9.04
(v) SPAM	5.16, 7.10
(vi) Junk mail	7.10
(c) Understand email history and management	7.10
(i) Spam / junk email	7.10
(ii) Archiving	7.10
(iii) Trash	7.10
(iv) Folders	7.10, 9.06
(d) Understand email attachments	7.10, 9.05
(i) Size limits	7.10
(e) Understand contact management	7.10, 9.04
(i) Address books	7.10
Section 3.04 Calendaring	
(a) Know how to create events and appointments	9.08
(i) Recurring	9.08
(ii) Details (location, time zone, notes)	9.08
(b) Know how to share calendars	9.09
(i) Invitations	9.09
(c) Know how to view multiple calendars	9.09
(d) Understand how to subscribe to calendars	9.09
Section 3.05 Social Media	
(a) Understand what a digital identity is (identity on social media)	7.12
(i) Know what social networks are and how they are used (FB, LinkedIn, etc.)	7.12, 9.19
(ii) Know other types of networks (YouTube, Instagram, etc.)	7.14

IC3 GS5 Standard	GO! *All in One* Concept or Activity
(b) Recognize the difference of internal (school/business) vs. open media sites	7.12
(i) Neo vs. Facebook	7.12
(c) Know what blogs, wikis, and forums are and how they are used	7.11, 7.15, 7.17
(d) Know what cyber bullying is	4.13, 8.09
Section 3.06 Communications	
(a) Know the best tool for the various situations and scenarios	6.19, 7.08, 7.09, 7.10, 8.12, 8.14
(i) Email	7.10, 8.12
(ii) SMS	6.19, 8.12
(iii) Instant message	7.08, 8.12
(iv) VoIP	7.09, 8.12
(v) Phone calls	8.12
(vi) Web ex	8.14
(vii) Conference calls	8.14
(b) Know how to use SMS texting	6.19, 8.12
(i) Etiquette	6.19, 8.12
(ii) Know what it is and how it can be used as a tool	6.19, 8.12
(iii) Know when to use and not use	6.19, 8.12
(iv) Determine when it is appropriate to use it	6.19, 8.12
(c) Know how to use chat platforms	7.08, 9.07, 9.14
(d) Understand options for and how to use distant/remote/ individual learning technologies	8.13
(i) Know basic remote workforce tools	8.13
Section 3.07 Online Conferencing	
(a) Understand and identify online conference offerings	7.11, 8.14
(i) VoIP conferencing (Skype)	7.11, 8.14
(ii) Video conferencing (Google hangouts, Skype, FaceTime)	7.11, 8.14
(iii) Phone conferencing	8.14, 9.15
(iv) Screen sharing	8.14
Section 3.08 Streaming	
(a) Understand what streaming is and how it works with devices	7.14
(i) Video streaming	7.14
(ii) Live streaming	7.14
(iii) Audio streaming	7.14
Section 3.09 Digital Principles/Ethics/Skills/Citizenship	
(a) Understand the necessity of coping with change in technology	8.14
(i) Audience awareness	8.14

IC3 GS5 Standard	GO! All in One Concept or Activity
(b) Understand Digital Wellness basics	8.08
(i) Screen time	8.08
(ii) Ergonomic best practices	1.14, 8.08
(c) Understand an online identity management	7.12, 8.09
(i) Branding	7.12
(ii) Managing profiles	7.12, 8.09
1) Gaming	8.09
2) Facebook	7.12
3) Twitter	7.12, 9.22
4) LinkedIn	7.12, 9.19, 9.20
5) etc...	7.12
(d) Know the difference between personal vs. professional identity	7.12, 8.09

Glossary

.png An image file format, commonly pronounced *PING*, that stands for Portable Network Graphic; this is an image file type that can be transferred over the Internet.

.txt file A simple file consisting of lines of text with no formatting that almost any computer can open and display.

3D The shortened term for three-dimensional, which refers to an image that appears to have all three spatial dimensions—length, width, and depth.

802.11 standards The standards that define the way data is transmitted over a Wi-Fi network.

AAC (advanced audio coding) A codec used to compress audio files that creates files that are somewhat higher quality than MP3 files.

Absolute cell reference A cell reference that refers to cells by their fixed position in a worksheet; an absolute cell reference remains the same when the formula is copied.

Acceptable use policy (AUP) A policy that computer and network users in a business or school must follow that forces users to practice safe computing.

Accounting Number Format The Excel number format that applies a thousand comma separator where appropriate, inserts a fixed U.S. dollar sign aligned at the left edge of the cell, applies two decimal places, and leaves a small amount of space at the right edge of the cell to accommodate a parenthesis for negative numbers.

Accounting software Business software that tracks business finances such as expenses, invoicing, payroll, and inventory management, and generates reports and graphs to help you make business decisions.

Action Center A vertical panel that displays on the right side of your screen when you click the icon in the notifications area of the taskbar; the upper portion displays notifications you have elected to receive such as mail and social network updates and the lower portion displays buttons for frequently used system commands.

Active cell The cell, surrounded by a border, ready to receive data or be affected by the next Excel command.

Ad hoc network A network created when two wireless devices connect to each other directly.

Adapter card A small circuit board that plugs directly into an expansion slot on the motherboard and enables you to connect additional peripheral devices to a computer. Also called expansion card.

Add-on A browser extension created for a specific browser to add features to it.

Address bar (File Explorer) The area at the top of a File Explorer window that displays your current location in the folder structure as a series of links separated by arrows.

Address bar The area at the top of the browser window in which you can type a URL to visit a website.

Administrator account A user account that should be used only when necessary, for such tasks as configuring and troubleshooting the system, and that should be protected by a strong password.

Aggregate functions Calculations such as Min, Max, Avg, and Sum that are performed on a group of records.

Airplane mode A setting that disables or turns off all network adapters on a device.

Algorithm A procedure for solving a problem.

Alignment The placement of paragraph text relative to the left and right margins.

Alignment guide A green vertical or horizontal line that displays when you are moving or sizing an object to assist you with object placement.

All apps A command that displays all the apps installed on your computer in alphabetical order on the Start menu.

All-in-one computer A compact desktop computer with the system unit integrated into the monitor.

All-in-one printer A multifunction device that has a built-in printer and scanner, and that may also have fax capabilities.

Alt text Another name for alternative text.

Alternative text Text added to a picture or object that helps people using a screen reader understand what the object is.

American Psychological Association (APA) One of two commonly used style guides for formatting research papers.

AMOLED (active matrix OLED) screen A screen type found in mobile devices that has a sharper display with a wider viewing angle than an LCD and is ideal for watching movies and sports.

Analog output device An output device such as a telephone, television, or CRT monitor that translates the digital electronic pulses back into audio and video signals.

Analytical Engine A mechanical computer designed, but never built, in the early nineteenth century by mathematician Charles Babbage that could be programmed using punched cards.

Analytics The process of detecting patterns in data.

AND condition A compound criteria used to display records that match all parts of the specified criteria.

Android An embedded version of Linux that runs on many smartphones and tablets.

Antispyware software A program that prevents adware and spyware software from installing itself on a computer.

Antivirus software A program that protects a computer from computer viruses.

App The shortened version of the term *application*, and which typically refers to a smaller application designed for a single purpose.

App bar A term used to describe a horizontal or vertical array of command icons in a Windows app.

Append To add on to the end of an object; for example, to add records to the end of an existing table.

Application A set of instructions that a computer uses to accomplish a task; also called a program.

Application developer An individual who writes computer applications.

Application programming interface (API) The feature of an operating system that enables an application to request services from the operating system, such as a request to print or save a file.

Application software Programs that direct the computer to carry out specific tasks, for example, word processing, playing a game, or computing numbers on a worksheet.

Apps for Office A collection of downloadable apps that enable you to create and view information within Office programs, and that combine cloud services and web technologies within the user interface of Office.

Arguments The values that an Excel function uses to perform calculations or operations.

Arithmetic logic unit (ALU) The part of the CPU that performs arithmetic (addition and subtraction) and logic (AND, OR, and NOT) calculations.

Arithmetic operators The symbols +, −, *, /, %, and ^ used to denote addition, subtraction (or negation), multiplication, division, percentage, and exponentiation in an Excel formula.

ARPANET A U.S. Department of Defense ARPA project that later became the Internet. A communications system designed to have multiple pathways through which information could travel so that losing one part of the system—for example, in a nuclear strike—would not cripple the whole system.

Artificial intelligence The branch of science concerned with making computers behave like humans.

Artistic effects Formats applied to images that make pictures resemble sketches or paintings.

Ascending order A sorting order that arranges text alphabetically (A to Z) and numbers from the lowest number to the highest number.

ASCII (American Standard Code for Information Interchange) An 8-bit binary code set with 256 characters.

Aspect ratio The ratio of the width of a display to the height of the display.

Asynchronous communication Communication that does not require the participants to be online at the same time.

Auto Fill An Excel feature that generates and extends values into adjacent cells based on the values of selected cells.

AutoCalculate A feature that displays three calculations in the status bar by default—Average, Count, and Sum—when you select a range of numerical data.

AutoComplete A feature that speeds your typing and lessens the likelihood of errors; if the first few characters you type in a cell match an existing entry in the column, Excel fills in the remaining characters for you.

AutoCorrect A feature that corrects common typing and spelling errors as you type, for example, changing *teh* to *the*.

AutoFit An Excel feature that adjusts the width of a column to fit the cell content of the widest cell in the column.

AutoNumber data type A data type that describes a unique sequential or random number assigned by Access as each record is entered and that is useful for data that has no distinct field that can be considered unique.

AutoSum A button that provides quick access to the SUM function.

Avatar A virtual body used to interact with others in virtual worlds and games.

AVERAGE function An Excel function that adds a group of values, and then divides the result by the number of values in the group.

Backing up Making copies of important files.

Backlit A device that includes an internal light source.

Backstage tabs The area along the left side of Backstage view with tabs to display screens with related groups of commands.

Backstage view A centralized space for file management tasks; for example, opening, saving, printing, publishing, or sharing a file. A navigation pane displays along the left side with tabs that group file-related tasks together.

Backup utility A program that makes copies of important files.

Backward compatibility The ability to run some older programs on a newer system.

Badge An icon that displays on the Lock screen for lock screen apps that you have selected.

Bandwidth The speed or data transfer rate of a network.

Barcode scanner An input device that scans barcodes such as those found on merchandise and library books.

Bcc An abbreviation for blind carbon copy (or blind courtesy copy), and is used to send a copy of the message to one or more recipients who would be interested in the message and whose name is not visible to other recipients of the message.

Best Fit An Access command that adjusts the width of a column to accommodate the column's longest entry.

Between ... And operator A comparison operator that looks for values within a range.

Bevel A shape effect that uses shading and shadows to make the edges of a shape appear to be curved or angled.

Bibliography A list of cited works in a report or research paper; also referred to as Works Cited, Sources, or References, depending upon the report style.

Binary code A system that represents digital data as a series of 0s and 1s that can be understood by a computer.

Binary number system (base 2) A number system that has only two digits—0 and 1.

Bing Microsoft's search engine, which powers Cortana.

Biometric scanner An input device that measures human characteristics such as fingerprints and eye retinas.

BIOS (basic input output system) A program, stored on a chip on the motherboard, that starts the computer.

Bit (binary digit) The smallest unit of digital data.

BitLocker A Windows feature that encrypts an entire drive.

Bitmapped graphics Images composed of tiny squares or dots that correspond to one pixel.

Black slide A slide that displays after the last slide in a presentation, indicating that the presentation is over.

BlackBerry OS A mobile operating system that runs on smartphones from BlackBerry.

Blank desktop database A database that has no data and has no database tools—you must create the data and tools as you need them; the database is stored on your computer or other storage device.

Blog (weblog) An online journal.

Blogosphere All the blogs on the web and the connections among them.

Bluetooth A short-range wireless technology that connects many types of peripheral devices.

Blu-ray disc An optical disc with about five times the capacity of a DVD; the single-layer disc capacity is 25 GB, and double-layer disc capacity is 50 GB.

Body The text of a letter.

Bookmark A command that identifies a word, section, or place in a document so that you can find it quickly without scrolling.

Bookmarks The term used to describe saved links to commonly visited webpages that allow for efficient web browsing.

Boolean search A search that uses logical operators—AND, OR, and NOT—to link the words you are searching for.

Boot The process of turning on a computer that has been completely shut down and during which the BIOS program will run.

Booting the computer The process of turning on a computer when the computer has been completely shut down and during which the BIOS program will run.

Bot A computer that is part of a botnet, controlled by a master, and used to launch various types of attacks.

Botnet A network of computer zombies or bots that is controlled by a master and that can be used to send out spam and viruses or to launch a denial-of-service attack.

Braille embosser A special printer that translates text to Braille.

Breadcrumb trail A list of links that you have followed through the structure of the website, which enables you to see the path you have taken and to quickly go back in that path by clicking the appropriate page name.

Brightness The relative lightness of a picture.

Broadband Internet access that exceeds 10 Mbps as defined by the FCC.

Browser hijacker A form of spyware that changes your home page and redirects you to other websites.

Browsing The term used to describe the process of using your computer to view webpages.

Browsing window In Internet Explorer 10, the area of the screen in which the webpage displays.

Buffer An area of memory that temporarily holds data and instructions.

Bug A flaw in software programming.

Bulleted list A list of items with each item introduced by a symbol such as a small circle or check mark, and which is useful when the items in the list can be displayed in any order.

Bullets Text symbols such as small circles or check marks that precede each item in a bulleted list.

Burst mode A feature found on some digital cameras that enables you to take several pictures in a burst by holding down the shutter button.

Bus topology A local area network topology in which the nodes are all connected using a single cable; the data travels back and forth along the cable, which is terminated at both ends.

Byte Consists of 8 bits and is used to represent a single character in modern computer systems.

Cable Internet access A broadband Internet service offered by a cable TV provider that uses the same wires to carry both TV and Internet signals.

Cable modem A special type of digital modem that connects to the cable system instead of a telephone line to provide fast Internet access.

Cache memory Fast memory that stores frequently accessed information close to the processor.

Calculated field A field that stores the value of a mathematical operation.

Can comment A Gmail sharing setting applied when the recipient can view and comment on the document, but cannot edit the document.

Can edit A Gmail sharing setting applied when the recipient can view, comment on, and edit the document.

Can view A Gmail sharing setting applied when the recipient can view the document, but cannot comment on or edit the document.

Capacitive screen A touchscreen that senses the conductive properties of an object such as a finger or a specially designed conductive stylus.

CAPTCHA (Completely Automated Public Turing Test to Tell Computers and Humans Apart) A series of letters and numbers that are distorted in some way.

Caption A property setting that displays a name for a field in a table, query, form, or report different from the one listed as the field name.

Card reader A device that provides a slot to insert a memory card into a computer so that the data on the card can be read. Used to transfer data, such as photos and music, between a card and a computer or printer.

Cascade Delete Related Records A cascade option that enables you to delete a record in a table and also delete all of the related records in related tables.

Cascade options Relationship options that enable you to update records in related tables when referential integrity is enforced.

Cascade Update Related Fields A cascade option that enables you to change the data in the primary key field in the table on the *one* side of the relationship and update that change to any fields storing that same data in related tables.

Category axis The area along the bottom of a chart that identifies the categories of data; also referred to as the x-axis.

Category labels The labels that display along the bottom of a chart to identify the categories of data; Excel uses the row titles as the category names.

Cc An abbreviation for *courtesy copy* or *carbon copy*, and is used to send a copy of the email to one or more recipients who are interested in the message but not the primary recipient.

CD (compact disc) The oldest type of optical disc in use today, with a storage capacity of about 700 MB.

Cell The intersection of a column and a row.

Cell address Another name for a cell reference.

Cell content Anything typed into a cell.

Cell reference The identification of a specific cell by its intersecting column letter and row number.

Cell style A defined set of formatting characteristics, such as font, font size, font color, cell borders, and cell shading.

Cellular network A network that uses cell towers to transmit voice and data over large distances.

Censorship Blocking access to content on the Internet or restricting what can be posted or published.

Center alignment The alignment of text or objects that is centered horizontally between the left and right margin.

Central processing unit (CPU) A complex integrated circuit that contains processing circuitry that enables it to behave as the brain of the computer, control all functions performed by other components, and process all the commands it receives. Also referred to as a *microprocessor*.

Chart The graphic representation of data in a worksheet; data presented as a chart is usually easier to understand than a table of numbers.

Chart area The entire chart and all of its elements.

Chart Elements button A button that enables you to add, remove, or change chart elements such as the title, legend, gridlines, and data labels.

Chart Filters button A button that enables you to change which data displays in the chart.

Chart layout The combination of chart elements that can be displayed in a chart such as a title, legend, labels for the columns, and the table of charted cells.

Chart style The overall visual look of a chart in terms of its graphic effects, colors, and backgrounds; for example, you can have flat or beveled columns, colors that are solid or transparent, and backgrounds that are dark or light.

Chart Styles button A button that enables you to set a style and color scheme for your chart.

Chart Styles gallery A group of predesigned chart styles that you can apply to an Excel chart.

Chart types Various chart formats used in a way that is meaningful to the reader; common examples are column charts, pie charts, and line charts.

Chat A synchronous form of online communication among multiple people at the same time in a chat room.

Check Accessibility A command that checks the document for content that people with disabilities might find difficult to read.

Check Compatibility A command that searches your document for features that may not be supported by older versions of Office.

Chrome A free web browser application developed by Google.

Chromebook A laptop that runs Google's Chrome operating system and Chrome web browser to provide a web-based environment for using applications; however, some apps may run offline as well.

Ciphertext Plain text that has been encrypted.

Citation A note inserted into the text of a research paper that refers the reader to a source in the bibliography.

Click The action of pressing the left mouse button.

Clickjacking A social network attack in which clicking a link enables malware to post unwanted links on your page.

Client A computer that connects to, or requests services from, another computer called a server.

Client for Microsoft Networks A Windows feature that enables a computer to remotely access files and printers on a Microsoft network.

Client-server network A network that has at least one server at its center. Users log in to the network instead of their local computers and are granted access to resources based on that login.

Client-side program A program in which the coding is within a webpage, downloaded to the client computer, and compiled and executed by a browser or plug-in.

Clip A single media file such as art, sound, animation, or a movie.

Clipboard A temporary storage area for information that you have copied or moved from one place and plan to use somewhere else.

Clock speed The speed at which the processor executes the machine cycle, measured in gigahertz (GHz)—billions of cycles per second.

Cloud Another term for the Internet.

Cloud computing Applications and services that are accessed over the Internet, rather than accessing applications that are installed on your local computer.

Cloud service provider (CSP) A company that provides cloud (Internet-based) computing services.

Cloud storage Storage space on an Internet site that may also display as a drive on your computer.

Cluster A group of sectors where files are stored on a disk.

CMOS (complementary metal oxide semiconductor) A chip on the motherboard where the BIOS settings are stored. It is volatile memory that uses a small battery to provide it with power to keep the data in memory even when the computer is turned off.

Codec Short for compression/decompression; an algorithm used to reduce the size of media files.

Collaborate To work with others as a team in an intellectual endeavor to complete a shared task or to achieve a shared goal.

Column A vertical group of cells in a worksheet.

Column break indicator A dotted line containing the words *Column Break* that displays at the bottom of the column.

Column chart A chart in which the data is arranged in columns and that is useful for showing data changes over a period of time or for illustrating comparisons among items.

Column heading The letter that displays at the top of a vertical group of cells in a worksheet; beginning with the first letter of the alphabet, a unique letter or combination of letters identifies each column.

Comma Style The Excel number format that inserts thousand comma separators where appropriate and applies two decimal places; Comma Style also leaves space at the right to accommodate a parenthesis when negative numbers are present.

Command-line interface An operating system interface that requires the user to type all commands.

Commands Instructions to a computer program that cause an action to be carried out.

Common field A field included in two or more tables that stores the same data.

Communication device A device that serves as both input and output device and enables you to connect to other devices on a network or to the Internet.

Compact system camera (CSC) An advanced point-and-shoot camera that has interchangeable lenses, some manual controls, a 10x to 26x optical zoom lens, and the ability to capture HD video. Also called a mirrorless camera or superzoom.

Comparison operators Symbols that are used to evaluate data in the field to determine if it is the same (=), greater than (>), less than (<), or in between a range of values as specified by the criteria.

Complimentary closing A parting farewell in a business letter.

Compound criteria Multiple conditions in a query or filter.

Compressed file A file that has been reduced in size and that takes up less storage space and can be transferred to other computers faster than uncompressed files.

Compressed Folder Tools File Explorer tools, available on the ribbon, to assist you in extracting compressed files.

Computer A programmable machine that converts raw data into useful information.

Computer fraud A scheme perpetrated over the Internet or by email that tricks a victim into voluntarily and knowingly giving money or property to a person.

Computer network Two or more computers that share resources.

Computer virus A program that replicates itself and infects computers; a virus needs a host file on which to travel.

Computer zombie A computer that is part of a botnet, controlled by a master, and used to launch various types of attacks.

Conditional format A format that changes the appearance of a cell— for example, by adding cell shading or font color—based on a condition; if the condition is true, the cell is formatted based on that condition, and if the condition is false, the cell is not formatted.

Connections The people with whom you have some level of online relationship using LinkedIn.

Constant value Numbers, text, dates, or times of day that you type into a cell.

Content app An app for Office that integrates web-based features as content within the body of a document.

Context menus Menus that display commands and options relevant to the selected text or object; also called *shortcut menus*.

Context sensitive A command associated with the currently selected or active object; often activated by right-clicking a screen item.

Context-sensitive commands Commands that display on a shortcut menu that relate to the object or text that you right-clicked.

Contextual tab A context-sensitive menu that displays commands and options relevant to the active object.

Contextual tabs Tabs that are added to the ribbon automatically when a specific object, such as a picture, is selected, and that contain commands relevant to the selected object.

Contiguous slides Slides that are adjacent to each other in a presentation.

Contrast The difference between the darkest and lightest area of a picture.

Control Panel An area of Windows 10 where you can manipulate some of the Windows 10 basic system settings—a carryover from previous versions of Windows.

Control unit The part of the CPU that manages the movement of data through the CPU.

Convergence The integration of technology on multifunction devices, such as smartphones.

Conversation A Gmail message that gets sent back and forth many times as you and your recipient exchange thoughts about a topic.

Convertible notebook A type of notebook computer that has a screen that can swivel to fold into what resembles a notepad or tablet.

Cookie A small text file placed on your computer when you visit a website that is used to identify you when you return to the site.

Copy A command that duplicates a selection and places it on the Clipboard.

Copyright Legal protection for literary and artistic works.

Cortana Microsoft's intelligent personal assistant that is part of the Windows 10 operating system.

COUNT function A statistical function that counts the number of cells in a range that contains numbers.

COUNTIF function A statistical function that counts the number of cells within a range that meet the given condition and that has two arguments—the range of cells to check and the criteria.

Cover letter A document that you send with your resume to provide additional information about your skills and experience.

Creative Commons A nonprofit organization that provides free legal tools to change the creator copyright terms from "All Rights Reserved" to "Some Rights Reserved".

Criteria Conditions in a query that identify the specific records you are looking for.

Crop A command that removes unwanted or unnecessary areas of a picture.

Crop handles Handles used to define unwanted areas of a picture.

Crop pointer The pointer used to crop areas of a picture.

Crosshair pointer The pointer used to draw a shape.

Crosstab query A query that uses an aggregate function for data that can be grouped by two types of information and displays the data in a compact, spreadsheet-like format with column headings and row headings.

Crowdfunding Project funding from multiple small investors rather than few large investors.

Crowdsourcing Trusting collective opinion of a crowd of people—referred to as *the wisdom of the crowd*—rather than that of an expert.

Currency data type An Access data type that describes monetary values and numeric data that can be used in mathematical calculations involving values with one to four decimal places.

Custom web app A database that you can publish and share with others over the Internet.

Customer Relations Management system (CRM) A database system for maintaining customer information and connections.

Cut A command that removes a selection and places it on the Clipboard.

Cybercrime Criminal activity on the Internet.

Cyberterrorism An unlawful attack against computers or networks that is done to intimidate a government or its people for a political or social agenda.

Dashboard A descriptive term for the Windows 10 Start menu because it provides a one-screen view of links to information and programs that matter most to the signed-in user.

Data All the files—documents, spreadsheets, pictures, songs, and so on—that you create and store during the day-to-day use of your computer.

Data bar A cell format consisting of a shaded bar that provides a visual cue to the reader about the value of a cell relative to other cells; the length of the bar represents the value in the cell—a longer bar represents a higher value and a shorter bar represents a lower value.

Data breach A situation in which sensitive data is stolen or viewed by someone who is not authorized to do so.

Data bus Wires on the motherboard over which data flows between the components of the computer.

Data management The process of managing your files and folders in an organized manner so that you can find information when you need it.

Data marker A column, bar, area, dot, pie slice, or other symbol in a chart that represents a single data point; related data points form a data series.

Data point A value that originates in a worksheet cell and that is represented in a chart by a data marker.

Data series Related data points represented by data markers; each data series has a unique color or pattern represented in the chart legend.

Data source A document that contains a list of variable information, such as names and addresses, that is merged with a main document to create customized form letters or labels.

Data type Classification identifying the kind of data that can be stored in a field, such as numbers, text, or dates.

Database An organized collection of facts about people, events, things, or ideas related to a specific topic or purpose.

Database management system (DBMS) Database software that controls how related collections of data are stored, organized, retrieved, and secured; also known as a DBMS.

Database management system (DBMS) Software that controls how related collections of data are stored, organized, retrieved, and secured.

Database template A preformatted database that contains prebuilt tables, queries, forms, and reports that perform a specific task, such as tracking events.

Datasheet view The Access view that displays data organized in columns and rows similar to an Excel worksheet.

Date & Time A command with which you can automatically insert the current date and time into a document in a variety of formats.

Dateline The first line in a business letter that contains the current date and which is positioned just below the letterhead if a letterhead is used.

DBMS An acronym for database management system.

Default The term that refers to the current selection or setting that is automatically used by a computer program unless you specify otherwise.

Denial-of-service attack (DoS) An attack that is perpetrated by sending out so much traffic that it cripples a server or network.

Descending order A sorting order that arranges text in reverse alphabetical order (Z to A) and numbers from the highest number to the lowest number.

Deselect The action of canceling the selection of an object or block of text by clicking outside of the selection.

Design grid The lower area of the query window that displays the design of the query.

Design view An Access view that displays the detailed structure of a table, query, form, or report. For forms and reports, may be the view in which some tasks must be performed, and only the controls, and not the data, display in this view.

Desktop The main Windows 10 screen that serves as a starting point and surface for your work, like the top of an actual desk.

Desktop app A computer program that is installed on the hard drive of a personal computer and that requires a computer operating system like Microsoft Windows or Apple OSX to run.

Desktop application A computer program that is installed on your PC and requires a computer operating system such as Microsoft Windows; also known as a *desktop app*.

Desktop background Displays the colors and graphics of your desktop; you can change the desktop background to look the way you want.

Desktop computer A personal computer designed to sit on your desk.

Desktop operating system An operating system that runs on a personal computer.

Desktop publishing program Software used to create newsletters, product catalogs, advertising brochures, and other documents that require unusual design and layout not normally provided by a word processor.

Desktop shortcuts Desktop icons that link to any item accessible on your computer or on a network, such as a program, file, folder, disk drive, printer, or another computer.

Destination table The table to which you import or append data.

Detail sheets The worksheets that contain the details of the information summarized on a summary sheet.

Details pane Displays the most common properties associated with the selected file.

Details view A view in File Explorer that displays a list of files or folders and their most common properties.

Device driver Software that acts as a translator, which enhances the capabilities of the operating system by enabling it to communicate with hardware.

Dialog box A small window that displays options for completing a task.

Dialog Box Launcher A small icon that displays to the right of some group names on the ribbon and that opens a related dialog box or pane providing additional options and commands related to that group.

Digital device A device that represents audio or video data as a series of 0s and 1s.

Digital footprint All the information that someone could find out about you by searching the web, including social network sites.

Digital rights management (DRM) A technology that is applied to digital media files such as music, eBooks, and videos to impose restrictions on the use of these files.

Digital single lens reflex (DSLR) The most expensive and versatile type of digital camera. A high-end digital camera that enables you to change the lens, attach a hot shoe flash, manually adjust focus and exposure, and look through the viewfinder to frame your shot.

Digital video camera A camera designed to record digital video that is easily uploaded to your computer, where it can be edited, stored, and shared.

DIMM (dual in-line memory module) The form of RAM found in most desktop computers.

Disk cleanup utility A program that looks for files that can be safely deleted to free up disk space, enabling you to have more space to store your files and to help keep your system running efficiently.

Disk defragmenter A utility that rearranges the fragmented files on a disk.

Disk formatting The process that prepares a disk to hold files and which consists of two steps: low-level formatting and high-level formatting.

Disk-checking utility A program that monitors the health of the file system on a disk.

Display adapter The card that provides the data signal and connection for a monitor or projector. Also called a video card.

Displayed value The data that displays in a cell.

Distributed computing The distribution of the processing of a task across a group of computers.

Distribution A version of Linux that includes the operating system, various utilities, and software applications such as browsers, games, entertainment software, and an office suite.

Distro Short for distribution.

DLP (digital light-processing) projector A digital projector that has hundreds of thousands of tiny swiveling mirrors that create an image.

DNS (Domain Name System) The directory system on the Internet that allows you to use a friendly name like google.com instead of an IP address like 173.194.43.2 to contact a website.

Document management The ability to save, share, search, and audit electronic documents throughout their life cycle.

Document management system (DMS) Software that businesses use to save, share, search, and audit electronic documents throughout their life cycle.

Document properties Details about a file that describe or identify it, including the title, author name, subject, and keywords that identify the document's topic or contents; also known as *metadata*.

Domain A network composed of a group of clients and servers under the control of one central security database on a special server called the domain controller.

Domain controller A special server that contains the central security database of a domain network.

Domain name An organization's unique name on the Internet, which consists of a chosen name combined with a top-level domain such as .com, .org, or .gov.

Donationware A form of freeware where the developers accept donations, either for themselves or for a nonprofit organization.

Dot leader A series of dots preceding a tab that guides the eye across the line.

Double-click The action of pressing the left mouse button twice in rapid succession while holding the mouse still.

Download The action of transferring or copying a file from another location—such as a cloud storage location or from an Internet site—to your computer.

Downloads folder A folder that holds items that you have downloaded from the Internet.

Drag The action of moving something from one location on the screen to another while holding down the left mouse button; the action of dragging includes releasing the mouse button at the desired time or location.

Drag-and-drop A technique by which you can move, by dragging, selected text from one location in a document to another.

Drawing objects Graphic objects, such as shapes, diagrams, lines, or circles.

Drive An area of storage that is formatted with a file system compatible with your operating system and is identified by a drive letter.

Drive bay Part of the system unit that holds the storage devices.

Drive controller A component located on the motherboard that provides a drive interface that connects disk drives to the processor.

Drive imaging The process of creating a mirror image of an entire hard disk.

Drone An aircraft piloted by remote control or onboard computers. Also known as an *unmanned aircraft system* (UAS).

DSL (digital subscriber line) Telephone lines designed to carry digital signals and therefore are much faster than ordinary telephone lines; a broadband Internet service.

DVD (digital video disc/digital versatile disc) An optical disc that can hold approximately 4.7 GB of information in a single-layer (SL) disc. Double-layer (DL) discs have a second layer to store data and can hold about 8.5 GB.

DVI (digital visual interface) port The standard digital video port found on video cards.

Dvorak Simplified Keyboard An alternate keyboard designed to put the most commonly used letters where they are more easily accessed to increase efficiency and reduce fatigue.

Dye-sublimation printer A printer that uses heat to turn solid dye into a gas that is transferred to special paper.

E-book A book in a digital format that can be read on a screen.

E-commerce Conducting business on the web.

eCycling Recycling electronics.

Edit The process of making changes to text or graphics in an Office file.

Editing The process of modifying a presentation by adding and deleting slides or by changing the contents of individual slides.

EIDE (enhanced integrated drive electronics) An older—legacy—drive interface that may still be found on older computers.

E-ink An e-reader technology that creates a screen that is easy on the eyes and most like the experience of reading a printed book.

Ellipsis A set of three dots indicating incompleteness; an ellipsis following a command name indicates that a dialog box will display if you click the command.

Em dash A punctuation symbol used to indicate an explanation or emphasis.

Email A method of exchanging messages via the Internet in which the message resides in the recipient's mailbox until he or she signs in to read it.

Email header The first part of an email message generated by the email provider.

Email string (Email thread) The history of the email messages created through multiple responses and answers to an originating message in a thread.

Embed code A code that creates a link to a video, picture, or other type of rich media content.

Embedded computer A specialized computer found in ordinary devices, such as gasoline pumps, supermarket checkouts, traffic lights, and home appliances.

Embedded operating system A specialized operating system that runs on GPS devices, ATMs, smartphones, and other devices.

Emoji A small image that represents facial expressions, common objects, and people and animals.

Emoticon An image that represents facial expressions. An emoticon should be used only in informal electronic communication to convey feelings.

Enclosures Additional documents included with a business letter.

Encrypting File System (EFS) A Windows feature that enables you to encrypt individual files.

Encryption The conversion of unencrypted, plain text into code called ciphertext.

Endnote In a research paper, a note placed at the end of a document or chapter.

End-user license agreement (EULA) The contract between the software user and the software publisher.

Energy Star A rating system that awards devices that use an average of 20 percent to 30 percent less energy than comparable devices.

Enhanced ScreenTip A ScreenTip that displays more descriptive text than a normal ScreenTip.

ENIAC (Electronic Numerical Integrator and Computer) The first working, digital, general-purpose computer; built at the University of Pennsylvania between 1943 and 1946.

Enterprise fund A municipal government fund that reports income and expenditures related to municipal services for which a fee is charged in exchange for goods or services.

Enterprise network A large network that has multiple local area networks located in the same location.

Enterprise server A large multiuser computer that can perform millions of transactions in a day.

E-reader A special class of tablet specifically to read books, magazines, and other publications.

Ergonomic keyboard A full-sized keyboard with a curved shape that positions the wrists in a more natural position to reduce strain.

Ergonomics The study of the relationship between workers and their workspaces.

Ethernet Standards that define the way data is transmitted over a local area network.

Ethernet adapter A wired network adapter.

Ethernet card A wired network adapter with a port that resembles a telephone jack.

E-waste (electronic waste) Old computers, cell phones, TVs, VCRs, and other electronic devices that are discarded.

Excel pointer An Excel window element with which you can display the location of the pointer.

Excel table A series of rows and columns that contains related data that is managed independently from the data in other rows and columns in the worksheet.

Expand Formula Bar button An Excel window element with which you can increase the height of the Formula Bar to display lengthy cell content.

Expand horizontal scroll bar button An Excel window element with which you can increase the width of the horizontal scroll bar.

Expansion card A small circuit board that plugs directly into an expansion slot on the motherboard and that enables you to connect additional peripheral devices to a computer. Also called adapter card.

Expansion slot A component located on the motherboard that enables you to connect an adapter card to a computer.

Explode The action of pulling out one or more pie slices from a pie chart for emphasis.

Export The process of copying data from one file into another file, such as an Access table into an Excel spreadsheet.

Expression A formula that will perform the calculation.

Extension Software that extends the functionality of a web browser.

External drive A drive that may be attached as a peripheral device using a USB or FireWire connection.

Extract The action of decompressing—pulling out—files from a compressed form.

Eyedropper A tool that captures the exact color from an object on your screen and then applies it to any shape, picture, or text.

Facebook The largest social network site on the web.

FaceTime An application built into OS X and iOS that enables you to make video calls to other FaceTime users.

Fair use The use, without the permission of the rights holder, of brief selections of copyright material for purposes such as commentary and criticism, news reporting, teaching, and research.

FAT file system The file system used on some external disks or those running older versions of Windows.

Fax device (or facsimile) A communication device that scans a document and converts it into a digital format that can be transmitted over telephone lines to a receiving fax device, which then prints or displays the document.

Fiber-to-the-home (FTTH) A broadband Internet service that carries signals on fiber-optic cable and is the fastest type of broadband Internet connection.

Field A single piece of information that is stored in every record; represented by a column in a database table.

Field list A list of field names in a table.

Field properties Characteristics of a field that control how the field displays and how data can be entered in the field; vary for different data types.

Fields In a mail merge, the column headings in the data source.

File A collection of information that is stored on a computer under a single name, for example, a text document, a picture, or a program.

File compression The process of making files smaller to conserve disk space and make them easier to transfer.

File Explorer A window that displays the contents of the current location and contains helpful parts so that you can navigate within the file organizing structure of Windows.

File Explorer window A window that displays the contents of the current location and contains helpful parts so that you can navigate within the file organizing structure of Windows.

File extension A set of characters at the end of a file name that helps the operating system determine what kind of information is in a file and what program should open it.

File fragmentation A process that occurs as files are broken into small pieces that are stored in nonadjacent or noncontiguous clusters on the disk.

File History A Windows utility that creates copies of your files on an external or network drive.

File list Displays the contents of the current folder or location; if you type text into the Search box, only the folders and files that match your search will display here—including files in subfolders.

File management The process of opening, closing, saving, naming, deleting, and organizing digital files.

File name extension A set of characters at the end of a file name that helps Windows 10 understand what kind of information is in a file and what program should open it.

File name The property of a file that identifies it and describes the contents of the file.

File Printout A OneNote feature that inserts information from a file as a printed copy in the page; this feature is useful because text in the printout can be searched just like any content in OneNote.

File properties Information about a file such as its author, the date the file was last changed, and any descriptive tags.

File system A system that keeps track of what files are saved and where they are stored on the disk.

FileVault An OS X feature, which, when turned on, encrypts the contents of your hard disk.

Fill The inside color of an object.

Fill color The inside color of text or of an object.

Fill handle The small square in the lower right corner of a selected cell.

Filter The process of displaying only a portion of the data based on matching a specific value to show only the data that meets the criteria that you specify.

Filtered list A display of files that is limited based on specified criteria.

Finance software A program that tracks your personal bank accounts, monitors your investments, helps you create and stick to a budget, and files your income taxes.

Find and Replace A command that searches the cells in a worksheet—or in a selected range—for matches and then replaces each match with a replacement value of your choice.

Finder In Mac OS X, the program used to find and organize files, folders, and apps; similar to File Explorer in Windows.

Firewall A device or software that blocks unauthorized access to a network.

FireWire A standard port type that is hot-swappable and can connect up to 63 devices per port. It also allows for peer-to-peer communication between devices, such as two video cameras, without the use of a computer. Also known as IEEE 1394.

Firmware Software stored on a flash ROM (read-only memory) chip in a piece of hardware that provides instructions for how the device communicates with the other computer hardware.

First principle of good database design A principle of good database design stating that data is organized in tables so that there is no redundant data.

Flame A message that expresses an opinion without holding back any emotion and that may be seen as being confrontational and argumentative.

Flash drive A small, portable, solid-state drive that can hold up to 128 GB of information.

Flash Fill Recognizes a pattern in your data, and then automatically fills in values when you enter examples of the output that you want. Use it to split data from two or more cells or to combine data from two cells.

Flash memory Nonvolatile storage used in solid-state storage devices such as solid state drives (SSDs), flash drives, and memory cards.

Flat database A simple database file that is not related or linked to any other collection of data.

Flickr The largest image-sharing site on the web.

Flip A command that creates a reverse image of a picture or object.

Floating object A graphic that can be moved independently of the surrounding text characters.

Folder A container in which you store files.

Folder structure The hierarchy of folders in Windows 10.

Following A term used to describe the accounts to which you are subscribing or seeing tweets from when using Twitter.

Font A set of characters with the same design and shape.

Font styles Formatting emphasis such as bold, italic, and underline.

Footer Text that displays at the bottom of every slide or that prints at the bottom of a sheet of slide handouts or notes pages. The bottom section of a webpage that typically contains the name of the entity that publishes the website, copyright information, and basic navigation links.

Footnote In a research paper, a note placed at the bottom of the page.

Foreign key The field that is included in the related table so the field can be joined with the primary key in another table for the purpose of creating a relationship.

Form An Access object you can use to enter new records into a table, edit or delete existing records in a table, or display existing records.

Form view The Access view in which you can view records, but you cannot change the layout or design of the form.

Format Changing the appearance of cells and worksheet elements to make a worksheet attractive and easy to read.

Formatting The process of establishing the overall appearance of text, graphics, and pages in an Office file—for example, in a Word document.

Formatting marks Characters that display on the screen, but do not print, indicating where the Enter key, the Spacebar, and the Tab key were pressed; also called *nonprinting characters*.

Formula Bar An element in the Excel window that displays the value or formula contained in the active cell; here you can also enter or edit values or formulas.

Formula An equation that performs mathematical calculations on values in a worksheet.

Forum A conversation much like chat but not in real time. Also known as a discussion board or message board.

Forward An email response used to send an email message to someone else.

Free-form snip When using Snipping Tool, the type of snip that lets you draw an irregular line, such as a circle, around an area of the screen.

Freemium Software offered for free that requires in-app purchases for additional content.

Freeware Software you can use at no cost for an unlimited period of time.

Freeze Panes A command that enables you to select one or more rows or columns and freeze (lock) them into place; the locked rows and columns become separate panes.

Full-screen snip When using Snipping Tool, the type of snip that captures the entire screen.

Function A predefined formula—a formula that Excel has already built for you—that performs calculations by using specific values in a particular order or structure.

Gallery An Office feature that displays a list of potential results instead of just the command name.

Game console A home entertainment system that connects to a television or monitor to display a game.

Game controller A device used to interact with a video game.

Genealogy program Software to create family trees and slideshows of your photos, view timelines and maps, and search through millions of historical records on the Internet.

General format The default format that Excel applies to numbers; this format has no specific characteristics—whatever you type in the cell will display, with the exception that trailing zeros to the right of a decimal point will not display.

General fund The term used to describe money set aside for the normal operating activities of a government entity such as a city.

Geocaching An electronic scavenger hunt where players (geocachers) hide geocaches and post GPS coordinates on the Internet for other geocachers to find.

Get Started A feature in Windows 10 to learn about all the things that Windows 10 can do for you.

Gmail Google's free web-based email service.

Goal Seek A feature that finds the input needed in one cell to arrive at the desired result in another cell.

Google doodle A modified Google search engine home page logo created to observe a special event, season, or holiday.

Google Drive Free storage available for anyone with a Google account; it can be used to store any type of file.

GPS (global positioning system) A system of at least 24 satellites that transmit signals that can be picked up by a receiver on the ground and used to determine the receiver's current location, time, and velocity through triangulation of the signals.

Gradient fill A fill effect in which one color fades into another.

Graphical user interface (GUI) The system by which you interact with your computer and which uses graphics such as an image of a file folder or wastebasket that you click to activate the item represented.

Graphical user interface The system by which you interact with your computer and which uses graphics such as an image of a file folder or wastebasket that you click to activate the item represented.

Graphics Pictures, charts, or drawing objects.

Graphics processing unit (GPU) A processor on a video card that can contain multiple cores.

Green computing The efficient and eco-friendly use of computers and other electronics.

Grid computing Distributed computing using a few computers in one location.

Groups On the Office ribbon, the sets of related commands that you might need for a specific type of task.

Guest account A user account for users who need temporary access to a system. This account is turned off by default.

GUI The acronym for a graphical user interface, pronounced *GOO-ee*.

Hacking The act of gaining unauthorized access to a computer system or network.

Hacktivism Hacking to make a political statement.

Hamburger Another name for the hamburger menu.

Hamburger menu An icon made up of three lines that evoke a hamburger on a bun.

Hanging indent An indent style in which the first line of a paragraph extends to the left of the remaining lines and that is commonly used for bibliographic entries.

Hangouts A hangout is a private space where contacts can post status updates, chat, or initiate a video call using their Google accounts.

Hard disk drive The primary storage device located inside your computer and where most of your files and programs are typically stored; usually labeled as drive C.

Hard drive The principal mass-storage device in a computer that stores data magnetically on metal platters.

Hardware The physical components of a computer.

Hashtag A word or phrase preceded by a # symbol that is used to organize and make tweets searchable.

HDMI A digital port that can transmit both audio and video signals. It is the standard connection for high-definition TVs, video game consoles, and other media devices.

Header A reserved area for text or graphics that displays at the top of each page in a document.

Headphones Output devices that convert digital signals into sound; available in several different sizes and styles, ranging from tiny earbuds that fit inside your ear to full-size headphones that completely cover your outer ear.

Headset Headphones that also include a microphone.

Heat sink A part of the cooling system of a computer, mounted above the CPU and composed of metal or ceramic to draw heat away from the processor.

HFS+ file system The OS X file system.

Hierarchy An arrangement where items are ranked and where each level is lower in rank than the item above it.

Hits Another term for search results.

HoloLens A see-through holographic computer developed by Microsoft.

Home folder In OS X, a folder that is created on a Mac computer for each user and which contains subfolders to store Documents, Downloads, Movies, Music, and Pictures.

Home page On your own computer, the webpage you have selected—or that is set by default—to display on your computer when you start your browser. When visiting a website, the starting point for the remainder of the pages on that site.

Homegroup The computers on a home network running Windows 7 or later.

Hotfix A software update that addresses individual problems as they are discovered.

HTML (Hypertext Markup Language) The authoring language that defines the structure of a webpage.

http The protocol prefix for HyperText Transfer Protocol.

Hub A feature in Microsoft Edge where you can save favorite websites and create reading lists.

Hyperlinks Links that connect pieces of information on the Internet.

Hypertext Text that contains links to other text and allows you to navigate through pieces of information by using the links, known as hyperlinks, that connect them.

HyperText Transfer Protocol The set of communication rules used by your computer to connect to servers on the Web.

ICANN (Internet Corporation for Assigned Names and Numbers) The organization that coordinates the Internet naming system.

iCloud Apple's cloud storage that is integrated into its Mac and iOS operating systems.

Icons Small images that represent commands, files, or other windows.

Identity theft Theft that occurs when someone uses your name, Social Security number, or bank or credit card number fraudulently.

IEEE 1394 A standard port type that is hot-swappable and can connect up to 63 devices per port. It also allows for peer-to-peer communication between devices, such as two video cameras, without the use of a computer. Also known as FireWire.

IF function A function that uses a logical test to check whether a condition is met, and then returns one value if true, and another value if false.

Image editor A sophisticated graphic program to edit and create images and save them in a variety of file formats.

Image stabilization A feature found on some digital cameras that accounts for camera shake and results in sharper images.

Import The process of copying data from another file, such as a Word table or an Excel workbook, into a separate file, such as an Access database.

In-app purchases A common way to monetize a mobile app. The app itself is free to download and install, but additional features, levels, or other content can be purchased for small, one-time payments or via subscriptions.

Incremental backup A backup that includes only those files that have changed.

Index Contains information about the files located on your computer.

Info tab The tab in Backstage view that displays information about the current file.

Information Data that is accurate, timely, and organized in a useful manner.

Information processing cycle (IPC) The process a computer uses to convert data into information. The four steps of the IPC are input, processing, storage, and output.

Infrastructure as a Service (IaaS) Part of cloud computing; the use of Internet-based servers.

Infrastructure wireless network A wireless network in which devices connect through a wireless access point.

Inkjet printer A printer that sprays droplets of ink onto paper.

Inline object An object or graphic inserted in a document that acts like a character in a sentence.

Innermost sort field When sorting on multiple fields in Datasheet view, the field that will be used for the second level of sorting.

Input The process of entering raw data into a system.

Input device A device to enter data into the computer system so that it can be processed.

Insertion point A blinking vertical line that indicates where text or graphics will be inserted.

Inside address The name and address of the person receiving the letter and positioned below the date line.

Inspect Document A command that searches your document for hidden data or personal information that you might not want to share publicly.

Instant messaging (IM) The real-time communication between two or more participants over the Internet.

Instruction cycle The four-part process used by the CPU to process each instruction: fetch, decode, execute, store. Also called a machine cycle.

Integrated circuit A chip that contains a large number of tiny transistors that are fabricated into a semiconducting material called silicon.

Intellectual property (IP) Creations of the mind, such as inventions; literary and artistic works; designs; and symbols, names, and images used in commerce.

Interactive media Computer interaction that responds to your actions; for example, by presenting text, graphics, animation, video, audio, or games. Also referred to as rich media.

Interactive whiteboard A large interactive display with a touch-sensitive surface commonly used in classrooms and businesses.

Internal drive A drive located inside the system unit in an internal drive bay that is not accessible from the outside.

Internet A global network of computer networks.

Internet backbone The high-speed connection points between networks that make up the Internet.

Internet of Things (IoT) The connection of the physical world to the Internet. Objects are tagged and can be located, monitored, and controlled using small embedded electronics.

Internet of Things A growing network of physical objects that will have sensors connected to the Internet.

Internet Protocol (IP) The protocol responsible for addressing and routing packets to their destination.

Internet service providers (ISPs) Companies that offer Internet access.

Intranet A private network that runs on web technologies.

iOS A mobile operating system that is a scaled-down version of OS X and that uses direct manipulation and multi-gesture touch such as swipe, tap, and pinch to control it.

iOS device An iPod, iPhone, or iPad.

IoT The common acronym for the Internet of Things.

IP (Internet protocol) address A unique numeric address assigned to each node on a network.

IP address A set of four numbers, separated by periods, which uniquely identifies devices on a network.

Is Not Null A criteria that searches for fields that are not empty.

Is Null A criteria that searches for fields that are empty.

Join line In the Relationships window, the line connecting two tables that visually indicates the common fields and the type of relationship.

Joystick An input device that is mounted on a base and consists of a stick, buttons, and sometimes a trigger. Typically used as a game controller, especially in flight-simulator games, it can also be used for such tasks as controlling robotic machinery in a factory.

JPEG An acronym for Joint Photographic Experts Group, and which is a common file type used by digital cameras and computers to store digital pictures; JPEG is popular because it can store a high-quality picture in a relatively small file.

Jump list A list that displays when you right-click a button on the taskbar, and which displays locations (in the upper portion) and tasks (in the lower portion) from a program's taskbar button.

Justified alignment An arrangement of text in which the text aligns evenly on both the left and right margins.

Keyboard An input device that uses switches and circuits to translate keystrokes into a signal a computer understands, and the primary input device for entering text into a computer.

Keyboard shortcut A combination of two or more keyboard keys, used to perform a task that would otherwise require a mouse.

Keychain An OS X feature that stores various passwords and passphrases in one place and makes them accessible through a master password.

Keylogger A program or hardware device that captures what is typed on a keyboard.

Keypad A small alternative keyboard that does not contain all the alphabet keys.

KeyTip The letter that displays on a command in the ribbon and that indicates the key you can press to activate the command when keyboard control of the ribbon is activated.

Keywords Custom file properties in the form of words that you associate with a document to give an indication of the document's content; used to help find and organize files. Also called *tags*.

Label Another name for a text value, and which usually provides information about number values. A storage system used to organize Gmail messages into categories; more than one label can be applied to a message.

Landscape orientation A page orientation in which the paper is wider than it is tall.

Laptop A portable personal computer. Also referred to as a *notebook*.

Laser printer A printer that uses a laser beam to draw an image on a drum. The image is electrostatically charged and attracts a dry ink called toner. The drum is then rolled over paper, and the toner is deposited on the paper. Finally, the paper is heated and pressure is applied, bonding the ink to the paper.

Layout The arrangement of elements, such as title and subtitle text, lists, pictures, tables, charts, shapes, and movies, on a slide.

Layout Options A button that displays when an object is selected and that has commands to choose how the object interacts with surrounding text.

Layout view The Access view in which you can make changes to a form or report while the data from the underlying data source displays.

LCD (liquid crystal display) Two layers of glass glued together with a layer of liquid crystals between them. Electricity passed through the individual crystals causes them to pass or block light to create an image. Found on most desktop and notebook computers.

LCD projector A digital projector that passes light through a prism, which divides the light into three beams—red, green, and blue—that are then passed through an LCD screen.

Leader character Characters that form a solid, dotted, or dashed line that fills the space preceding a tab stop.

Learning Management System (LMS) An application used in both schools and corporate training environments to deliver educational materials, track student interactions, and assess student performance.

LED (light-emitting diode) An electronic component that emits light when an electrical current is passed through it.

Left alignment The cell format in which characters align at the left edge of the cell; this is the default for text entries and is an example of formatting information stored in a cell.

Legend A chart element that identifies the patterns or colors that are assigned to the categories in the chart.

Lettered column headings The area along the top edge of a worksheet that identifies each column with a unique letter or combination of letters.

Letterhead The personal or company information that displays at the top of a letter.

Line break indicator A nonprinting character in the shape of a bent arrow that indicates a manual line break.

Line spacing The distance between lines of text in a paragraph.

Link A connection to data in another file.

LinkedIn A professional social networking site where you can find past and present colleagues and classmates, connect with appropriate people when seeking a new job or business opportunity, or get answers from industry experts.

Linux An open source operating system distribution that contains the Linux kernel and bundled utilities and applications.

List level An outline level in a presentation represented by a bullet symbol and identified in a slide by the indentation and the size of the text.

Live Layout A feature that reflows text as you move or size an object so that you can view the placement of surrounding text.

Live Preview A technology that shows the result of applying an editing or formatting change as you point to possible results—*before* you actually apply it.

Live tiles Tiles on the Windows 10 Start menu that are constantly updated with fresh information relevant to the signed-in user; for example, the number of new email messages, new sports scores of interest, or new updates to social networks such as Facebook or Twitter.

Local area network (LAN) A network that has all connected devices or nodes located in the same physical location.

Location Any disk drive, folder, or other place in which you can store files and folders.

Location services Feature of computers and mobile devices that determines your location by using GPS or wireless networks.

Lock screen The first screen that displays after turning on a Windows 10 device and that displays the time, day, and date, and one or more icons representing the status of the device's Internet connection, battery status on a tablet or laptop, and any lock screen apps that are installed such as email notifications.

Lock screen apps Apps that display on a Windows 10 lock screen and that show quick status and notifications, even if the screen is locked.

Logic bomb An attack by malware that occurs when certain conditions are met.

Logical functions A group of functions that test for specific conditions and that typically use conditional tests to determine whether specified conditions are true or false.

Logical operators Operators that combine criteria using AND and OR. With two criteria, AND requires that both conditions be met and OR requires that either condition be met for the record to display in the query results.

Logical test Any value or expression that can be evaluated as being true or false.

Lossless compression A compression algorithm that looks for the redundancy in a file and creates an encoded file by removing the redundant information; when the file is decompressed, all the information from the original file is restored.

Mac computer A personal computer manufactured by Apple that runs the OS X operating system.

Machine cycle The four-part process used by the CPU to process each instruction: fetch, decode, execute, store. Also called the instruction cycle.

Machinima The art of creating videos using screens captured from video games.

Magnetic strip reader An input device that can read information encoded in the magnetic strip on plastic cards, such as drivers' licenses, gift cards, library cards, credit cards, and hotel door keys.

Mail app An app for Office that displays next to an Outlook item.

Mail merge A feature that joins a main document and a data source to create customized letters or labels.

Main document In a mail merge, the document that contains the text or formatting that remains constant.

Mainframe A large multiuser computer that can perform millions of transactions in a day.

Malicious script A social network attack in which copying and pasting some text into the address bar executes code that creates pages and events or sends spam out to your friends.

Malware Malicious software; a program that is designed to be harmful or malicious.

Manual column break An artificial end to a column to balance columns or to provide space for the insertion of other objects.

Manual line break A break that moves text to the right of the insertion point to a new line while keeping the text in the same paragraph.

Manual page break The action of forcing a page to end and placing subsequent text at the top of the next page.

Margins The space between the text and the top, bottom, left, and right edges of the paper.

Massively multiplayer online role-playing games (MMORPG) An online game that allows you to interact with people in real time using an avatar—a virtual body.

MAX function An Excel function that determines the largest value in a selected range of values.

Maximize The command to display a window in full-screen view.

Media Graphics, video, animation, and sound.

Media management software Programs that organize and play multimedia files such as music, videos, and podcasts.

MEDIAN function An Excel function that finds the middle value that has as many values above it in the group as are below it; it differs from AVERAGE in that the result is not affected as much by a single value that is greatly different from the others.

Memory Temporary storage that is used by a computer to hold instructions and data.

Memory board A small circuit board that contains memory chips.

Memory card A storage medium that uses flash memory to store data in a small, flat design.

Menu A list of commands within a category.

Menu bar A group of menus.

Menu icon Another name for the hamburger menu.

Merge & Center A command that joins selected cells in an Excel worksheet into one larger cell and centers the contents in the merged cell.

Message Bar The area directly below the ribbon that displays information such as security alerts when there is potentially unsafe, active content in an Office document that you open.

Metadata Details about a file that describe or identify it, including the title, author name, subject, and keywords that identify the document's topic or contents; also known as *document properties*.

Metasearch engine A search engine that searches other search engines.

Metropolitan area network (MAN) A network that covers a single geographic area.

Microblogging A social form of blogging in which posts are typically limited to a relatively small number of characters and users post updates frequently.

Microphone An input device that converts sound into digital signals. It is used to chat in real time or as part of voice-recognition applications used in video games and for dictating text.

Microprocessor A complex integrated circuit that contains processing circuitry that enables it to behave as the brain of the computer, control all functions performed by other components, and process all the commands it receives. Also referred to as the *central processing unit*, or *CPU*.

Microsoft account A single login account for Microsoft systems and services.

Microsoft Edge The default web browser included with Windows 10.

Microsoft Windows The most common desktop operating system.

MIN function An Excel function that determines the smallest value in a selected range of values.

Mini toolbar A small toolbar containing frequently used formatting commands that displays as a result of selecting text or objects.

Mission-critical information Information that, if lost, will result in the failure of business operations.

Mobile application (mobile app) A program that extends the functionality of a mobile device.

Mobile browser A web browser used on small-screen devices, such as tablets, e-readers, and smartphones.

Mobile device A portable computer for business and entertainment; mobile devices come in many different shapes and sizes such as smartphones, tablets, and other specialized devices.

Mobile device platform The hardware and software environment for smaller-screen devices such as tablets and smartphones.

Mobile Internet access A broadband Internet service that uses cellular 3G (third generation) and 4G (fourth generation) network standards. The signals are transmitted by a series of cellular towers.

Mobile operating system An embedded operating system that runs on mobile devices such as smartphones and tablets and is more full-featured than other embedded operating systems.

Mobile payment system Using a mobile device rather than cash or credit cards to pay for items.

Modem A communication device that modulates digital data into an analog signal that can be transmitted over a phone line and, on the receiving end, demodulates the analog signal back into digital data.

Modern Language Association (MLA) One of two commonly used style guides for formatting research papers.

Modifier key A keyboard key, such as Ctrl, Alt, and Shift, that you press in conjunction with other keys.

Moore's Law An observation made by Gordon Moore in 1965 that the number of transistors that can be placed on an integrated circuit had doubled roughly every two years.

Motherboard The main circuit board of a computer that houses the processor (CPU) and contains drive controllers and interfaces, expansion slots, data buses, ports and connectors, the BIOS, and memory. A motherboard may also include integrated peripherals, such as video, sound,

and network adapters. It provides the way for devices to attach to your computer.

Mouse An input device that may include one or more buttons and a scroll wheel and works by moving across a smooth surface to signal movement of the pointer.

Mouse over A term used to describe hovering your mouse pointer over text or an image on a webpage.

Mouse pointer Any symbol that displays on your screen in response to moving your mouse.

MP3 (MPEG-1 Audio Layer 3) A codec to compress audio files, allowing them to maintain excellent quality while being reasonably small.

MRU Acronym for *most recently used*, which refers to the state of some commands that retain the characteristic most recently applied; for example, the Font Color button retains the most recently used color until a new color is chosen.

Multi-core processor A CPU that consists of two or more processors that are integrated on a single chip.

Multimedia Content that integrates text and media—graphics, video, animation, and sound.

Multimedia Messaging Service (MMS) A service used to send electronic messages that include multimedia such as images or videos to mobile devices.

Multitasking The ability to do more than one task at a time.

Multiuser computer A system that allows multiple, simultaneous users to connect to it, allowing for centralized resources and security.

Municipal Wi-Fi Free wireless Internet service offered in some cities and towns.

My Drive Google Drive location that stores files that you create using Google applications.

Name Box An element of the Excel window that displays the name of the selected cell, table, chart, or object.

Nameplate The banner on the front page of a newsletter that identifies the publication.

Navigate The process of moving within a worksheet or workbook.

Navigation area An area at the bottom of the Access window that indicates the number of records in the table and contains controls in the form of arrows that you click to move among the records.

Navigation bar A set of buttons or images in a row or column that display on every webpage to link the user to sections on the website.

Navigation pane The area on the left side of a folder window in File Explorer that displays the Quick Access area and an expandable list of drives and folders.

Near field communication (NFC) A method that enables devices to share data with each other by touching them together or bringing them within a few centimeters of each other.

Netbook A lightweight, inexpensive notebook computer designed primarily for Internet access, with built-in wireless capabilities, a small screen, and limited computing power and storage.

Netiquette Short for *Internet etiquette*, the code for acceptable behavior and manners while on the Internet.

Network adapter A communication device that establishes a connection with a network; may be onboard, an expansion card, or a USB device, and may be wired or wireless.

Network administrator The person responsible for managing the hardware and software on a network.

Network and Sharing Center A Windows 10 feature in the Control Panel where you can view your basic network information.

Network operating system (NOS) A multiuser operating system that controls the software and hardware that runs on a network. It enables multiple client devices to communicate with the server and each other, share resources, run applications, and send messages.

Network resource Software, hardware, or files shared among computers on a network.

Newsletter A periodical that communicates news and information to a specific group.

No Paragraph Space Style The built-in paragraph style—available from the Paragraph Spacing command—that inserts *no* extra space before or after a paragraph and uses line spacing of 1.

Noise-cancelling headphones An audio output device that reduces the effect of ambient noise; especially useful in noisy environments, such as airplanes.

Noncontiguous slides Slides that are not adjacent to each other in a presentation.

Nonprinting characters Characters that display on the screen, but do not print, indicating where the Enter key, the Spacebar, and the Tab key were pressed; also called *formatting marks*.

Nonvolatile memory A memory chip that needs no power to retain information.

Normal template The template that serves as a basis for all Word documents.

Normal view A screen view that maximizes the number of cells visible on your screen and keeps the column letters and row numbers close to the columns and rows. The primary editing view in PowerPoint where you write and design your presentations.

Normalization The process of applying design rules and principles to ensure that your database performs as expected.

Note In a research paper, information that expands on the topic, but that does not fit well in the document text.

Note container A box in OneNote for text, pictures, video clips, and other types of notes.

Notebook A portable personal computer. Also referred to as a *laptop*. In OneNote, a collection of files organized by major divisions and stored in a common folder.

Notepad A basic text-editing program included with Windows 10 that you can use to create simple documents.

Notes Typed text, handwritten text if you have a tablet PC, pictures and graphics—including images and text that you capture from webpages—audio and video recordings, and documents from other applications such as Word or Excel, that can be included in a OneNote notebook.

Notes page A printout that contains the slide image on the top half of the page and notes that you have created on the Notes pane in the lower half of the page.

Notes pane An area of the Normal view window that displays below the Slide pane with space to type notes regarding the active slide.

NOW function An Excel function that retrieves the date and time from your computer's calendar and clock and inserts the information into the selected cell.

NTFS file system The file system used on hard disks in Windows.

Number data type An Access data type that represents a quantity, how much or how many, and may be used in calculations.

Number format A specific way in which Excel displays numbers in a cell.

Number values Constant values consisting of only numbers.

Numbered list A list of items preceded by numbers, which indicate sequence or rank of the items. Sometimes called ordered lists.Wizard A feature in Microsoft Office that walks you step by step through a process. **Artistic effects** Formats applied to images that make pictures resemble sketches or paintings.

Numbered row headings The area along the left edge of a worksheet that identifies each row with a unique number.

Object A text box, picture, table, or shape that you can select and then move and resize.

Object anchor The symbol that indicates to which paragraph an object is attached.

Object tab In the object window, a tab that identifies the object and which enables you to make an open object active.

Object window An area of the Access window that displays open objects, such as tables, queries, forms, or reports; by default, each object displays on its own tab.

Objects The basic parts of a database that you create to store your data and to work with your data; for example, tables, queries, forms, and reports.

Office 365 A version of Microsoft Office to which you subscribe for an annual fee.

Office application suite A group of applications that work together to manage and create different types of documents and include features that allow multiple users to collaborate.

Office Presentation Service A Word feature to present your Word document to others who can watch in a web browser.

Office Store A public marketplace that Microsoft hosts and regulates on Office.com.

OLED (organic light-emitting diode) A monitor composed of extremely thin panels of organic molecules sandwiched between two electrodes.

Omnibox Another name for the Address bar in Google Chrome, because it serves as both an address and a search bar.

One-click Row/Column Insertion A Word table feature with which you can insert a new row or column by pointing to the desired location and then clicking.

OneDrive A free file storage and file sharing service provided by Microsoft when you sign up for a free Microsoft account.

OneNote A Microsoft application with which you can create a digital notebook that gives you a single location where you can gather and organize information in the form of notes.

One-to-many relationship A relationship between two tables where one record in the first table corresponds to many records in the second table—the most common type of relationship in Access.

Open dialog box A dialog box from which you can navigate to, and then open on your screen, an existing file that was created in that same program.

Open source Software that has its source code published and made available to the public, enabling anyone to copy, modify, and redistribute it without paying fees.

Open source software license A license that grants ownership of the copy to the end user. The end user has the right to modify and redistribute the software under the same license.

Operating system (OS) A computer program that manages all the other programs on your computer, stores files in an organized manner, enables you to use software programs, and coordinates the use of computer hardware such as the keyboard and mouse.

Operators The symbols with which you can specify the type of calculation you want to perform in an Excel formula.

Optical disc A form of removable storage that stores digital data by using a laser.

Optical mouse An input device that detects motion by bouncing light from a red LED (light-emitting diode) off the surface below it.

Optical network terminal (ONT) The device that connects a fiber-optic network to the Internet.

Optical scanner An input device that converts photos or documents into digital files.

Option button In a dialog box, a round button that enables you to make one choice among two or more options.

Options dialog box A dialog box within each Office application where you can select program settings and other options and preferences.

OR condition A compound criteria used to display records that match at least one of the specified criteria.

OS X The desktop operating system that runs on Apple Mac computers.

Outermost sort field When sorting on multiple fields in Datasheet view, the field that will be used for the first level of sorting.

Outline view A PowerPoint view that displays the presentation outline to the left of the Slide pane.

Output The display of processed data.

Output device A device, for example, a printer or monitor, that returns processed information to the user.

Page A subdivision of a section where notes are inserted.

Page break indicator A dotted line with the text *Page Break* that indicates where a manual page break was inserted.

Page tabs list A list on the right side of the OneNote notebook that displays the name of each page in the active section.

Page template In OneNote, a file that serves as a pattern for creating a new page; ensures a uniform page layout and design.

Page Width A view that zooms the document so that the width of the page matches the width of the window. Find this command on the View tab, in the Zoom group.

Paging The process of transferring files from the virtual memory file on the hard disk to RAM and back.

Paging file A virtual memory file on the hard disk used as a temporary storage space for instructions that the operating system can access as you do your work. Also known as the swap file.

Paint program Software to create bitmapped graphics, which are images composed of tiny squares or dots that correspond to one pixel.

Pane A portion of a worksheet window bounded by and separated from other portions by vertical and horizontal bars.

Paragraph symbol The symbol ¶ that represents the end of a paragraph.

Parallel processing The process of using multiple processors, or multi-core processors, to divide processing tasks.

Parameter A value that can be changed.

Parameter query A query that prompts you for criteria before running the query.

Parent folder In the file organizing structure of File Explorer, the location where the folder you are viewing is saved—one level up in the hierarchy.

Parenthetical references References that include the last name of the author or authors, and the page number in the referenced source.

Password manager A program used to store passwords; some of these programs can also generate passwords.

Paste The action of placing cell contents that have been copied or moved to the Clipboard into another location.

Paste area The target destination for data that has been cut or copied using the Office Clipboard.

Paste Options gallery A gallery of buttons that provides a Live Preview of all the Paste options available in the current context.

Patch A software update that addresses individual problems as they are discovered.

Patent Legal protection for inventions.

Path A sequence of folders (directories) that leads to a specific file or folder.

Payload The action or attack by a computer virus or malware.

PC Reset A backup and recovery tool that returns your PC to the condition it was in the day you purchased it.

PDF The acronym for *Portable Document Format*, which is a file format that creates an image that preserves the look of your file, but that cannot be easily changed; a popular format for sending documents electronically, because the document will display on most computers.

PDF Reflow The ability to import PDF files into Word so that you can transform a PDF back into a fully editable Word document.

Peer-to-peer network (P2P) A network that does not require a network operating system, in which each computer is considered equal; each device can share its resources with every other device, and there is no centralized authority.

Pen A pen-shaped stylus that you tap on a computer screen.

Peripheral devices The components that serve the input, output, and storage functions of a computer.

Per-seat license A license that assigns a product key to individual users in an organization.

Personal area network (PAN) A small network that consists of devices connected by Bluetooth.

Personal computer (PC) A small microprocessor-based computer designed to be used by one person at a time.

Personal folder A folder created for each user account on a Windows 10 computer, labeled with the account holder's name, and which contains the subfolders *Documents, Pictures, Music*.

Personal information manager (PIM) A program to manage email, calendar, and tasks that is often part of an office suite.

Petaflops A measure of computer performance obtainable by today's supercomputers.

Pharming Redirects you to a phony website to trick you into revealing information, such as usernames and passwords for your accounts.

Phishing Email messages and instant messages that appear to be from those you do business with, designed to trick you into revealing information, such as usernames and passwords for your accounts.

Photo editing software A program that enables you to create a professional finished photo or image.

Photo printer A printer that prints high-quality photos on special photo paper.

Picture effects Effects that enhance a picture, such as a shadow, glow, reflection, or 3-D rotation.

Picture element A point of light measured in dots per square inch on a screen; 64 pixels equals 8.43 characters, which is the average number of characters that will fit in a cell in an Excel worksheet using the default font.

Picture styles Frames, shapes, shadows, borders, and other special effects that can be added to an image to create an overall visual style for the image.

Pie chart A chart that shows the relationship of each part to a whole.

Piggybacking Using an open wireless network to access the Internet without permission.

PIN Acronym for personal identification number; in Windows 10 Settings, you can create a PIN to use in place of a password.

Pipelining A process used by a single processor to process multiple instructions simultaneously; as soon as the first instruction has moved from the fetch to the decode stage, the processor fetches the next instruction.

Pixel The term that is the shortened version of *picture element* and which represents a single point on a display screen. Each pixel contains three colors: red, green, and blue (RGB).

Placeholder A box on a slide with dotted or dashed borders that holds title and body text or other content such as charts, tables, and pictures.

Placeholder text Nonprinting text that holds a place in a document where you can type.

Plasma screen monitor A large display type that works by passing an electric current through gas sealed in thousands of cells inside the screen. The current excites the gas, which in turn excites the phosphors that coat the screen to pass light through an image.

Platform An underlying computer system on which application programs can run.

Platform-as-a-Service (PaaS) In cloud computing, an online programming environment in which to develop, deploy, and manage custom web applications.

Platform-neutral An application that can run on all modern personal computing systems.

Plug and Play (PnP) An operating system feature that you can use to easily add new hardware to a computer system. When you plug in a new piece of hardware, the operating system detects it and helps you set it up.

Plug-in A third-party browser extension, such as Adobe Reader.

Podcast A digital media file of a prerecorded radio- or TV-like show that is distributed over the web to be downloaded and listened to or watched on a computer or portable media player.

Podcast client A Program used to search for and play podcasts.

Point and click method The technique of constructing a formula by pointing to and then clicking cells; this method is convenient when the referenced cells are not adjacent to one another.

Point to The action of moving the mouse pointer over a specific area.

Point-and-shoot The easiest, least expensive type of digital camera.

Pointer Any symbol that displays on your screen in response to moving your mouse and with which you can select objects and commands.

Pointing device A mouse, touchpad, or other device that controls the pointer position on the screen.

Pointing device An input device, such as a mouse or touchpad, that enables you to interact with objects by moving a pointer on the computer screen.

Points A measurement of the size of a font; there are 72 points in an inch.

Populate The action of filling a database table with records.

Pop-up blocker A browser feature that prevents webpages from opening a new window.

Port A connection point that is used to attach peripheral devices to the motherboard.

Portable apps Programs that can run from a flash drive.

Portable Document Format A file format that creates an image that preserves the look of your file, but that cannot be easily changed; a popular format for sending documents electronically, because the document will display on most computers; also called a *PDF*.

Portrait orientation A page orientation in which the paper is taller than it is wide.

Presentation application A program to create electronic presentations made up of slides that contain text, graphics, video, audio, or any combination of these.

Presenter view A view that shows the full-screen slide show on one monitor or projection screen while enabling the presenter to view a preview of the next slide, notes, and a timer on another monitor.

Primary key A required field that uniquely identifies a record in a table; for example, a Student ID number at a college.

Print buffer An area of memory that holds documents until they can be sent to the printer.

Print Preview A view of a document as it will appear when you print it.

Print queue The list of documents in the print buffer waiting to be printed.

Print Titles An Excel command that enables you to specify rows and columns to repeat on each printed page.

Processing The manipulation, calculation, or organization of data to create useful information.

Processor The brain of a computer housed inside the system unit on the motherboard. Also known as the CPU.

Product key A code supplied with a software license that you must enter when you install the software that helps a software publisher verify that the software was legally purchased.

Productivity program General-purpose application software that helps you work more efficiently and effectively on both personal and business-related documents.

Program A set of instructions that a computer uses to accomplish a task; also called an application.

Progress bar In a dialog box or taskbar button, a bar that indicates visually the progress of a task such as a download or file transfer.

Project management software An application to help you to complete projects, keep within your budget, stay on schedule, and collaborate with others.

Property Sheet A list of characteristics—properties—for fields or controls on a form or report in which you can make precise changes to each property associated with the field or control.

Proprietary software license Grants a license to use one or more copies of software, but ownership of those copies remains with the software publisher.

Protected View A security feature in Office 2016 that protects your computer from malicious files by opening them in a restricted environment until you enable them; you might encounter this feature if you open a file from an email or download files from the Internet.

Protocol A set of rules for communication between devices that determines how data is formatted, transmitted, received, and acknowledged.

Protocol prefix The letters that represent a set of communication rules used by a computer to connect to another computer.

pt The abbreviation for *point*; for example, when referring to a font size.

Public domain Works not restricted by copyright.

QR code A digital code that can be scanned to learn more information.

Query A database object that retrieves specific data from one or more database objects—either tables or other queries—and then, in a single datasheet, displays only the data you specify.

Quick access The navigation pane area in File Explorer where you can pin folders you use frequently and that also adds folders you are accessing frequently.

Quick Access Toolbar (File Explorer) The small row of buttons in the upper left corner of a File Explorer window from which you can perform frequently used commands.

Quick Access Toolbar In an Office program window, the small row of buttons in the upper left corner of the screen from which you can perform frequently used commands.

Quick Analysis Tool A tool that displays in the lower right corner of a selected range, with which you can analyze your data by using Excel tools such as charts, color-coding, and formulas.

QWERTY The first alphabetic keys on the upper left of the keyboard.

RAM (random access memory) A volatile form of memory that stores the operating systems, programs, and data the computer is currently using.

Range Two or more selected cells on a worksheet that are adjacent or nonadjacent; because the range is treated as a single unit, you can make the same changes or combination of changes to more than one cell at a time.

Range finder An Excel feature that outlines cells in color to indicate which cells are used in a formula; useful for verifying which cells are referenced in a formula.

Read Mode A view in Word that optimizes the Word screen for the times when you are reading Word documents on the screen and not creating or editing them.

Reading view A view in PowerPoint that displays a presentation in a manner similar to a slide show but in which the taskbar, title bar, and status bar remain available in the presentation window.

Read-only A property assigned to a file that prevents the file from being modified or deleted; it indicates that you cannot save any changes to the displayed document unless you first save it with a new name.

Recently added On the Start menu, a section that displays apps that you have recently downloaded and installed.

Recolor A feature that enables you to change all colors in the picture to shades of a single color.

Recommended Charts An Excel feature that displays a customized set of charts that, according to Excel's calculations, will best fit your data based on the range of data that you select.

Record All of the categories of data pertaining to one person, place, event, thing, or idea; represented by a row in a database table.

Record selector bar The bar at the left edge of a record when it is displayed in a form, and which is used to select an entire record.

Record selector box The small box at the left of a record in Datasheet view that, when clicked, selects the entire record.

Rectangular snip When using Snipping Tool, the type of snip that lets you draw a precise box by dragging the mouse pointer around an area of the screen to form a rectangle.

Recycle Bin A folder that stores anything that you delete from your computer, and from which anything stored there can be retrieved until the contents are permanently deleted by activating the Empty Recycle Bin command.

Redundant In a database, information that is duplicated in a manner that indicates poor database design.

Referential integrity A set of rules that Access uses to ensure that the data between related tables is valid.

Relational database A sophisticated type of database that has multiple collections of data within the file that are related to one another.

Relationship An association that you establish between two tables based on common fields.

Relative cell reference In a formula, the address of a cell based on the relative position of the cell that contains the formula and the cell referred to.

Removable storage device A portable device on which you can store files, such as a USB flash drive, a flash memory card, or an external hard drive, commonly used to transfer information from one computer to another.

Reply An email response that is sent back to the original sender.

Reply All An email response that is sent to all the addressees of the original message and the original sender.

Report A database object that summarizes the fields and records from a table or query in an easy-to-read format suitable for printing.

Resistive screen A touchscreen that can sense pressure and can be used with a finger or an ordinary stylus.

Resolution The number of horizontal by vertical pixels on a display screen or image; for example, 1280 × 1024 or 1920 × 1080.

Resources A term used to refer collectively to the parts of your computer such as the central processing unit (CPU), memory, and any attached devices such as a printer.

Restore Down A command to restore a window to its previous size before it was maximized.

Retail software A type of software for which the user pays a fee to use the software for an unlimited period of time.

Retweet The process of sharing another user's tweet, giving them credit for the original tweet.

RFID (radio frequency identification) A digital technology that uses RFID tags to provide information and is used in inventory tracking, electronic toll collection, and contactless credit card transactions.

RFID scanner An input device that can read the information in an RFID tag, such as those found on credit cards and passports.

RFID tag A digital tag that contains a tiny antenna for receiving and sending a radio-frequency signal.

RGB A color model in which the colors red, green, and blue are added together to form another color.

Ribbon The area at the top of a folder window in File Explorer that groups common tasks such as copying and moving, creating new folders, emailing and zipping items, and changing views on related tabs.

Rich media Computer interaction that responds to your actions; for example, by presenting text, graphics, animation, video, audio, or games. Also referred to as interactive media.

Right alignment An arrangement of text in which the text aligns at the right margin, leaving the left margin uneven.

Right-click The action of clicking the right mouse button one time.

Ring topology A local area network topology in which the devices are connected to a single cable; the ends of the cable are connected in a circle and the data travels around the circle in one direction.

ROM (read-only memory) A nonvolatile form of memory that does not need power to keep its data.

Rootkit A set of programs that enables someone to gain control over a computer system while hiding the fact that the computer has been compromised.

Rotation handle A symbol with which you can rotate a graphic to any angle; displays above the top center sizing handle.

Rounding A procedure in which you determine which digit at the right of the number will be the last digit displayed and then increase it by one if the next digit to its right is 5, 6, 7, 8, or 9.

Router A device that connects two or more networks together.

Row A horizontal group of cells in a worksheet.

Row heading The numbers along the left side of an Excel worksheet that designate the row numbers.

RSS (Really Simple Syndication) A format used for distributing web feeds that change frequently.

Ruler guides Dotted red vertical and horizontal lines that display in the rulers indicating the pointer's position.

Run The process in which Access looks at the records in the table(s) included in the query design, finds the records that match the specified criteria, and then displays the records in a datasheet; only the fields included in the query design display.

Safe Mode A special diagnostic mode for troubleshooting the system that loads Windows without most device drivers.

Salutation The greeting line of a business letter.

Sans serif font A font design with no lines or extensions on the ends of characters.

SATA (serial ATA) The standard internal drive interface used to connect drives to the motherboard.

Satellite Internet access A broadband Internet service that uses communications satellites positioned in the southern sky.

Scale A command that resizes a picture to a percentage of its size.

Scale to Fit Excel commands that enable you to stretch or shrink the width, height, or both, of printed output to fit a maximum number of pages.

Scaling The process of shrinking the width and/or height of printed output to fit a maximum number of pages.

Scanner An input device that increases the speed and accuracy of data entry and converts information into a digital format that can be saved, copied, and manipulated.

Screen capture software Tools that enable you to create a video of what happens on your computer screen.

Screen clipping A copy of what you are seeing on your screen, a webpage, or a document is then sent to the active notebook page.

Screen reader Software that enables visually impaired users to read text on a computer screen to understand the content of pictures.

Screensaver A moving image that appears on a computer screen when the computer has been idle for a specified period of time.

Screenshot An image of an active window on your computer that you can paste into a document. Another name for a screen capture.

ScreenTip A small box that displays useful information when you perform various mouse actions such as pointing to screen elements or dragging.

Scroll arrow An arrow at the top, bottom, left, or right, of a scroll bar that when clicked, moves the window in small increments.

Scroll bar A bar that displays on the bottom or right side of a window when the contents of a window are not completely visible; used to move the window up, down, left, or right to bring the contents into view.

Scroll box The box in a vertical or horizontal scroll bar that you drag to reposition the document on the screen.

Search engine optimization (SEO) The methods used to make a website easier to find by both people and software that indexes the web and to increase the webpage ranking in search engine results.

Search engine A computer program that searches for specific words and returns a list of documents in which the search term was found.

Search provider A website that provides search capabilities on the web.

Search utility A program with which you can search an entire disk or any indexed network storage device for a file.

Second principle of good database design A principle stating that appropriate database techniques are used to ensure the accuracy and consistency of data as it is entered into the table.

Section A portion of a document that can be formatted differently from the rest of the document. The primary division of a notebook identifying a main topic and containing related pages of notes.

Section break A double dotted line that indicates the end of one section and the beginning of another section.

Section header A type of slide layout that changes the look and flow of a presentation by providing text placeholders that do not contain bullet points.

Section tab A tab that identifies a primary division of the active notebook.

Sector A wedge-shaped section of a disk where data is stored.

Secure Sockets Layer (SSL) A protocol that encrypts information before it is sent across the Internet.

Security suite A package of security software that includes a combination of security features.

Select To specify, by highlighting, a block of data or text on the screen with the intent of performing some action on the selection.

Selecting Highlighting, by dragging with your mouse, areas of text or data or graphics, so that the selection can be edited, formatted, copied, or moved.

Select All box A box in the upper left corner of the worksheet grid that, when clicked, selects all the cells in a worksheet.

Select query A type of Access query that retrieves (selects) data from one or more tables or queries, displaying the selected data in a datasheet; also known as a simple select query.

Series A group of things that come one after another in succession; for example, January, February, March, and so on.

Serif font A font design that includes small line extensions on the ends of the letters to guide the eye in reading from left to right.

Server A multiuser computer system that provides services, such as Internet access, email, or file and print services, to client systems.

Server virtualization Running multiple versions of server software on the same computer.

Service pack A large, planned software update that addresses multiple problems, or adds multiple features, and includes previous patches and hotfixes.

Service set identifier (SSID) A wireless network name.

Shape A slide object such as a line, arrow, box, callout, or banner.

Shapes Lines, arrows, stars, banners, ovals, rectangles, and other basic shapes with which you can illustrate an idea, a process, or a workflow.

Share button Opens the Share pane from which you can save your file to the cloud—your OneDrive—and then share it with others so you can collaborate.

Shared with Me Google Drive location that stores files that others have shared with you.

SharePoint A Microsoft technology that enables employees in an organization to access information across organizational and geographic boundaries.

Shareware Software offered in trial form or for a limited period that enables you to try it out before purchasing a license.

Sheet tab scrolling buttons Buttons to the left of the sheet tabs used to display Excel sheet tabs that are not in view; used when there are more sheet tabs than will display in the space provided.

Sheet tabs The labels along the lower border of the Excel window that identify each worksheet.

Short Message Service (SMS) A service used to send brief electronic text messages to mobile devices.

Short Text data type An Access data type that describes text, a combination of text and numbers, or numbers that are not used in calculations, such as the Postal Code.

Shortcut menu A menu that displays commands and options relevant to the selected text or object; also called a *context menu*.

Show Formulas A command that displays the formula in each cell instead of the resulting value.

Shut down Turning off your computer in a manner that closes all open programs and files, closes your network connections, stops the hard disk, and discontinues the use of electrical power.

Shutter lag The time between pressing the shutter button and the camera snapping the picture.

Signature line A block of text that is automatically put at the end of an email message.

Simple select query Another name for a select query.

Single spacing The common name for line spacing in which there is *no* extra space before or after a paragraph and uses line spacing of 1.

Site license A contract with a software publisher that enables an organization to install copies of a program on a specified number of computers.

Sitemap A page that displays all of the pages in a website in one place.

Sizing handles Small squares or circles that indicate a picture or object is selected.

Skype A Microsoft product with which you can make voice calls, make video calls, transfer files, or send messages—including instant messages and text messages—over the Internet.

Sleep Turning off your computer in a manner that automatically saves your work, stops the fan, and uses a small amount of electrical power to maintain your work in memory.

Slide A presentation page that can contain text, pictures, tables, charts, and other multimedia or graphic objects.

Slide handout Printed images of slides on a sheet of paper.

Slide pane A PowerPoint screen element that displays a large image of the active slide.

Slide Sorter view A presentation view that displays thumbnails of all of the slides in a presentation.

Slide transitions Motion effects that occur in Slide Show view when you move from one slide to the next during a presentation.

Small caps A font effect that changes lowercase letters to uppercase letters, but with the height of lowercase letters.

Smart appliance An appliance that plugs into the smart grid and can monitor signals from the power company. When the electric grid system is stressed, the appliance can react by reducing power consumption.

SmartArt A designer-quality visual representation of your information that you can create by choosing from among many different layouts to effectively communicate your message or ideas.

Smart grid A network for delivering electricity to consumers that includes communication technology to manage electricity distribution efficiently.

Smart guides Dashed lines that display on your slide when you are moving an object to assist you with alignment.

Smart home A building that uses automation to control lighting, heating and cooling, security, entertainment, and appliances.

Smartphone A small computer that combines a cellular phone with such features as Internet and email access, a digital camera, GPS and mapping tools, the ability to edit documents, and access to mobile apps.

Snap Assist The ability to drag windows to the edges or corners of your screen, and then having Task View display thumbnails of other open windows so that you can select what other windows you want to snap into place.

Snip The image captured using Snipping Tool.

Snipping Tool A program included with Windows 10 with which you can capture an image of all or part of a computer screen, and then annotate, save, copy, or share the image via email.

Social bookmarking site A website that enables you to save and share your bookmarks or favorites online.

Social media marketing (SMM) The practice of using social media sites to sell products and services.

Social media Websites that enable you to create user-generated content, connect, network, and share.

Social media sharing site A website that enables anyone to create and share media.

Social networks Online communities that combine many of the features of other online tools.

Social news site Different from traditional media news sites in that at least some of the content is submitted by users.

Social review site A website that enables you to review hotels, movies, games, books, and other products and services.

SODIMM (small outline dual in-line memory module) The type of RAM used by most notebook computers.

Software A set of instructions that tells the hardware how to perform a certain task.

Software developer A person who designs and writes computer programs.

Software license A contract distributed with a program that gives you the right to install and use the program on one or more computers.

Software-as-a-Service (SaaS) A form of cloud computing that delivers applications over the Internet.

Solid-state storage A nonmechanical storage format that stores data by using flash memory on a chip.

Sort The process of arranging data in a specific order based on the value in each field.

Sorting The process of arranging data in a specific order based on the value in a field.

Sound card Provides audio connections for both input devices—microphones and synthesizers—and output devices—speakers and headphones.

Sound file Digitized data in the form of recorded live sounds or music, which are saved in one of several standardized sound formats.

Source file When importing a file, refers to the file being imported.

Spamming Sending mass, unsolicited email messages.

Sparkline A tiny chart in the background of a cell that gives a visual trend summary alongside your data; makes a pattern more obvious.

Speakers Output devices that convert digital signals from a computer or media player into sound.

Speech recognition Technology that enables you to control a device without a keyboard by using voice commands.

Spider A program sent out by a search engine to crawl the web and gather information.

Spin box A small box with an upward- and downward-pointing arrow that lets you move rapidly through a set of values by clicking.

Split Splits the window into multiple resizable panes that contain views of your worksheet. This is useful to view multiple distant parts of your worksheet at one time.

Split button A button that has two parts—a button and an arrow; clicking the main part of the button performs a command and clicking the arrow opens a menu with choices.

Sponsored links Paid advertisements shown as links, typically for products and services related to your search term. Sponsored links are the way that search sites like Bing, Google, and others earn revenue.

Spooling program A program that monitors the print requests in the buffer and the busy state of the printer.

Spotlight A search tool in OS X.

Spreadsheet Another name for a worksheet.

Spreadsheet application A program that creates electronic worksheets composed of rows and columns.

Spyware A form of malware that secretly gathers personal information about you.

Standard account A user account created for normal use, which has limited access to change system and security settings.

Standards Specifications that have been defined by an industry organization, which ensure that equipment that is made by different companies will be able to work together.

Star topology A local area network topology in which every node on the network is attached to a central device such as a switch or wireless access point.

Start menu The menu that displays when you click the Start button, which consists of a list of installed programs on the left and a customizable group of app tiles on the right.

Statistical functions Excel functions, including the AVERAGE, MEDIAN, MIN, and MAX functions, which are useful to analyze a group of measurements.

Status bar The area along the lower edge of the Excel window that displays, on the left side, the current cell mode, page number, and worksheet information; on the right side, when numerical data is selected, common calculations such as Sum and Average display.

Storage Saving digital information for archiving or later access.

Storage area network (SAN) A network between the data storage devices and the servers on a network that makes the data accessible to all servers in the SAN; normal users are not part of the SAN but are able to access the information through the local area network servers.

Store-and-forward technology An email server holds messages until the client requests them.

Streaming media Accessing video or audio clips almost immediately after you click a link on a webpage without waiting for the entire file to download.

Streaming video Accessing video clips almost immediately after you click a video link on a webpage without waiting for the entire file to download.

Structure In Access, the underlying design of a table, including field names, data types, descriptions, and field properties.

Style A group of formatting commands, such as font, font size, font color, paragraph alignment, and line spacing that can be applied to a paragraph with one command. Combinations of formatting options that look attractive together. A special pen-like input tool that enables you to write directly on a touch screen.

Style guide A manual that contains standards for the design and writing of documents.

Style set A collection of character and paragraph formatting that is stored and named.

Subdatasheet A format for displaying related records when you click the plus sign (+) next to a record in a table on the *one* side of the relationship.

Subfolder A folder within another folder.

Subject line Part of an email message used to give the recipient some idea of the content of the email. The optional line following the inside address in a business letter that states the purpose of the letter.

subnotebook A notebook computer that is thin and light and that has high-end processing and video capabilities.

Subset A portion of the total records available.

SUM function A predefined formula that adds all the numbers in a selected range of cells.

Summary sheet A worksheet where totals from other worksheets are displayed and summarized.

Supercomputer A very expensive computer system that is used to perform complex mathematical calculations, such as those used in weather forecasting and medical research.

Suppress A Word feature that hides header and footer information, including the page number, on the first page of a document.

Surfing The process of navigating the Internet either for a particular item or for anything that is of interest, and quickly moving from one item to another.

Surround sound A technique used in movies and video games that makes it sound as if the audio surrounds the listener.

Swap file A virtual memory file on the hard disk used as a temporary storage space for instructions that the operating system can access as you do your work. Also known as the paging file.

Switch Hardware that connects multiple devices on a local area network and uses address information to send data packets only to the port to which the appropriate device is connected.

Switch Row/Column A charting command to swap the data over the axis—data being charted on the vertical axis will move to the horizontal axis and vice versa.

Sync To update files that are located in two or more locations

Synchronization The process of updating computer files that are in two or more locations according to specific rules—also called *syncing*.

Synchronous online communication Communication that happens in real time, with two or more people online at the same time.

Syncing The process of updating computer files that are in two or more locations according to specific rules—also called *synchronization*.

Synonyms Words with the same or similar meaning.

System image backup A backup and recovery tool that creates a full system image backup from which you can restore your entire PC.

System requirements The minimum hardware and software specifications required to run a software application.

System resources The processor and memory on your computer.

System restore A Windows tool that enables you to return the system to a previous state saved as a restore point.

System software The programs that provide the infrastructure and hardware control necessary for the computer and its peripheral devices.

System tray Another name for the notification area on the taskbar.

System unit The case that encloses and protects the power supply, motherboard, processor (CPU), and memory of a computer.

Tab stop A specific location on a line of text, marked on the Word ruler, to which you can move the insertion point by pressing the Tab key, and which is used to align and indent text.

Table A format for information that organizes and presents text and data in columns and rows; the foundation of a database.

Table area The upper area of the query window that displays field lists for the tables that are used in a query.

Tablet computer A handheld, mobile device somewhere between a computer and a smartphone.

Tabs (ribbon) On the Office ribbon, the name of each task-oriented activity area.

Tagging Labeling images or files with keywords to make them easier to organize, search for, and share.

Tags Custom file properties in the form of words that you associate with a document to give an indication of the document's content; used to help find and organize files. Also called *keywords*.

Task Manager A utility that displays the processes running on a Windows computer.

Task pane app An app for Office that works side-by-side with an Office document by displaying a separate pane on the right side of the window.

Taskbar The area of the desktop that contains program buttons, and buttons for all open programs; by default, it is located at the bottom of the desktop, but you can move it.

Tax preparation software A program that enables you to complete your income tax returns on your computer or online.

TCP/IP protocol stack A suite of protocols that define many types of data movement, including the transfer files and webpages, sending and receiving email, and network configuration.

Tell Me A search feature for Microsoft Office commands that you activate by typing what you are looking for in the Tell Me box.

Tell me more A prompt within a ScreenTip that opens the Office online Help system with explanations about how to perform the command referenced in the ScreenTip.

Template A preformatted document that you can use as a starting point and then change to suit your needs.

Text alignment The horizontal placement of text within a placeholder.

Text box A movable resizable container for text or graphics.

Text effects Decorative formats, such as shadowed or mirrored text, text glow, 3-D effects, and colors that make text stand out.

Text messaging Sending brief electronic messages between mobile devices using Short Message Service (SMS).

Text string A sequence of characters.

Text values Constant values consisting of only text, and which usually provide information about number values; also referred to as labels.

Text wrapping The manner in which text displays around an object.

Theme A predesigned combination of colors, fonts, and effects that looks good together and is applied to an entire document by a single selection.

Thermal printer A printer that creates an image by heating specially coated heat-sensitive paper, which changes color where the heat is applied.

Thesaurus A research tool that provides a list of synonyms.

This PC An area on the navigation pane that provides navigation to your internal storage and attached storage devices including optical media such as a DVD drive.

Thread A conversation in a discussion board or forum.

Three-dimensional (3D) printer A printer that can create objects such as prototypes and models.

Three-dimensional spreadsheet A spreadsheet that has multiple worksheets that are linked together.

Thumbnail A reduced image of a graphic.

Thumbnails Miniature images of presentation slides.

Thunderbolt A port that carriers both PCIe and DisplayPort video signals on the same cable, so it can be used to connect many different types of peripherals to a computer. Thunderbolt combines two 10 Gbps channels and can connect up to six devices using one connection.

Tiles Square and rectangular boxes on the Windows 10 Start menu from which you can access apps, websites, programs, and tools for using the computer by simply clicking or tapping them.

Time bomb A logic bomb that is triggered by a specific date or time.

Time Machine The backup utility in OS X.

Timeline The real-time stream of tweets that display in the center of the Twitter window.

Title bar The bar across the top of the window that displays the program name.

Title slide A slide layout—most commonly the first slide in a presentation—that provides an introduction to the presentation topic.

Toggle button A button that can be turned on by clicking it once, and then turned off by clicking it again.

Toggle key A keyboard key, such as CapsLock or NumLock, that turns a feature on or off when pressed.

Toolbar In a folder window, a row of buttons with which you can perform common tasks, such as changing the view of your files and folders.

Top-level domain (TLD) The suffix that follows the domain name in a URL that indicates the type of website you are visiting.

Topology The physical layout of a local area network.

Touchpad An input device that detects your finger moving across the touch-sensitive surface.

Touchscreen An input device that can accept input from a finger or stylus.

Track A concentric circle created on a disk during low-level disk formatting.

Trademark Logos or symbols that represent a brand.

Transistor A tiny electric switch used in second-generation computers.

Transmission Control Protocol (TCP) The protocol responsible for assuring that data packets are transmitted reliably.

Triangulation A mathematical principle used by GPS to determine the position of the receiving device in three dimensions.

Trimmed content The history of the Gmail conversation, sometimes referred to as the email string or the email thread.

Triple-click The action of clicking the left mouse button three times in rapid succession.

Trojan horse A program that appears to be a legitimate program but that is actually malicious.

Truncated Data that is cut off or shortened because the field or column is not wide enough to display all of the data or the field size is too small to contain all of the data.

Trust Center An area of Access where you can view the security and privacy settings for your Access installation.

Trusted Documents A security feature in Office that remembers which files you have already enabled; you might encounter this feature if you open a file from an email or download files from the Internet.

Tumblr A microblogging site where posts are limited to a relatively small number of characters and users post updates frequently.

Turing machine A machine that can perform mathematical computations.

Turing test Measures a machine's ability to display intelligent behavior.

Tweet A short message posted in Twitter, limited to 140 characters and spaces.

Twitter A microblogging platform used for social networking, which allows registered users to post and send messages to other registered users.

Two-in-one notebook A portable computer that converts to a tablet by detaching the screen from the keyboard.

Ubiquitous computing (ubicomp) Sometimes called invisible computing, technology that recedes into the background and becomes part of the user's environment.

Ultrabook A small Windows notebook computer with high-end processing and video capabilities built into a lightweight system.

Underlying formula The formula entered in a cell and visible only on the Formula Bar.

Underlying value The data that displays in the Formula Bar.

Unicode An extended ASCII set that has become the standard on the Internet and includes codes for most of the world's written languages, mathematical systems, and special characters. It has codes for over 100,000 characters.

Uniform resource locator An address that uniquely identifies a location on the Internet.

Universal apps Windows apps that use a common code base to deliver the app to any Windows device.

Universal design Design principles that help create environments that accommodate people with disabilities, but also benefit those without.

Unix A pioneering operating system that was developed at AT&T's Bell Laboratories in 1969.

Unmanned aircraft system (UAS) An aircraft piloted by remote control or onboard computers. Also known as a drone.

Unzip Extracting files.

Upload Google Drive location that stores files that you have uploaded to Drive.

URL (uniform resource locator) The address of a website.

USB (Universal Serial Bus) A standard port type used to connect many kinds of devices, including printers, mice, keyboards, digital cameras, cell phones, and external drives. Up to 127 devices can share a single USB port.

User account A collection of information that tells Windows 10 what files and folders the account holder can access, what changes the account holder can make to the computer system, and what the account holder's personal preferences are.

User Account Control (UAC) A Windows feature that will notify you before changes are made to your computer.

User folder A personal folder with subfolders inside it that Windows creates automatically for each username.

User interface The part of the operating system that you see and with which you interact.

User-generated content Web content created by ordinary users.

Utility software Software that helps maintain, repair, and protect the computer; it may be included with the operating system or supplied by another organization.

Vacuum tube A tube that resembles an incandescent light bulb that was used in first-generation computers.

Value Another name for a constant value.

Value axis A numerical scale on the left side of a chart that shows the range of numbers for the data points; also referred to as the Y-axis.

Variant A variation on the presentation theme style and color.

Vector graphic program An application used to create math-based vector graphics.

Video card The card that provides the data signal and connection for a monitor or projector. Also called a display adapter.

Video editor A program that enables you to modify digitized videos.

Video game simulation A system that replicates realistic environments and scenarios.

Video game system A computer system that is designed primarily to play games.

Viral video An online video that becomes extremely popular because of recommendations and social sharing.

Virtual desktop An additional desktop display to organize and quickly access groups of windows.

Virtual memory A technique that uses a portion of the computer's hard disk as an extension of RAM.

Virtual private network (VPN) Creates a private network through the public network—the Internet—enabling remote users to access a local area network securely without needing dedicated lines.

Virtual reality An artificial world that consists of images and sounds created by a computer and that is affected by the actions of a person who is experiencing it.

Virus hoax An email message that does not contain a virus but that tricks you into behavior that can be harmful, such as searching for and deleting files that the computer actually needs.

Voice recognition Technology that enables you to use a device without a keyboard by using voice commands.

Voice-recognition software A program that enables you to control a computer verbally and dictate text.

VoIP (voice over IP) Calls transmitted over the Internet instead of over traditional telephone lines or cellular towers.

Volatile A term used to describe an Excel function that is subject to change each time the workbook is reopened; for example, the NOW function updates itself to the current date and time each time the workbook is opened.

Volatile memory Memory that loses information when the power is turned off.

Volume license A software license that allows multiple installations of software in an organization using the same product key.

VRAM (video RAM) The memory found on a display adapter.

Wallpaper Another term for the desktop background.

Wardriving Driving around and locating open wireless access points.

Watermark A text or graphic element that displays behind document text.

Wearable tech Computing devices that are worn on the body, such as wearable computers, virtual reality headsets, and smartwatches.

Web 2.0 tools The tools that allow users to create content.

Web apps Applications that run in a browser.

Web browser A program that interprets HTML to display webpages as you browse the Internet.

Webcam A specialized video camera that provides visual input for online communication.

Webpage Information on the web, written in HTML, and viewable in a web browser.

Website One or more webpages that all are located in the same place.

What-if analysis The process of changing the values in cells to see how those changes affect the outcome of formulas in a worksheet.

Wide area network (WAN) A network that spans multiple locations and connects multiple local area networks over dedicated lines by using routers.

Widget A small program in a webpage that can be run by the person viewing the page.

Wi-Fi hotspot A wireless access point available in many public locations, such as airports, schools, hotels, and restaurants, either free or for a fee.

Wi-Fi Protected Setup (WPS) A way to set up a secure wireless network by using a button, personal identification number, or USB key to automatically configure devices to connect to a network.

Wiki A website that enables you to edit content, even if it was written by someone else.

Wikipedia The most well-known wiki, a massive free encyclopedia that can be written by anyone.

Wildcard character In a query, a character that represents one or more unknown characters in criteria; an asterisk (*) represents one or more unknown characters, and a question mark (?) represents a single unknown character.

Window snip When using Snipping Tool, the type of snip that captures the entire displayed window.

Windows 10 An operating system developed by Microsoft Corporation designed to work with mobile computing devices of all types and also with traditional PCs.

Windows apps An app that runs on all Windows device families—including PCs, Windows phones, Windows tablets, and the Xbox gaming system.

Windows Defender Protection built into Windows 10 that helps prevent viruses, spyware, and malicious or unwanted software from being installed on your PC without your knowledge.

Windows Firewall Protection built into Windows 10 that can prevent hackers or malicious software from gaining access to your computer through a network or the Internet.

Windows Journal A desktop app that comes with Windows 10 with which you can type or handwrite—on a touchscreen—notes and then store them or email them.

Windows Phone An embedded version of Windows based on Windows Embedded CE that runs on mobile devices.

Windows Store The program where you can find and download Windows apps.

Wireless access point (WAP) A device that enables wireless devices to join a network.

Wireless adapter A network adapter used to connect to Wi-Fi networks.

Wireless encryption A system that adds security to a wireless network by encrypting transmitted data.

Wireless LAN (WLAN) A network that uses Wi-Fi to transmit data.

Wireless network adapter A network adapter used to connect to Wi-Fi networks.

Word processor An application to create, edit, and format text documents. The documents can also contain images.

WordArt An Office feature in Word, Excel, and PowerPoint that enables you to change normal text into decorative stylized text.

Wordwrap The feature that moves text from the right edge of a paragraph to the beginning of the next line as necessary to fit within the margins.

Work access A Windows 10 feature with which you can connect to your work or school system based on established policies.

Workbook An Excel file that contains one or more worksheets.

Workgroup Computers in a peer-to-peer network.

Works Cited In the MLA style, a list of cited works placed at the end of a research paper or report.

Worksheet The primary document that you use in Excel to work with and store data, and which is formatted as a pattern of uniformly spaced horizontal and vertical lines.

Worksheet grid area A part of the Excel window that displays the columns and rows that intersect to form the worksheet's cells.

Workstation A high-end desktop computer or one that is attached to a network in a business setting.

World Wide Web The hypertext system of information on the Internet that enables you to navigate through pieces of information by using hyperlinks that connect them.

Worm A form of self-replicating malware that does not need a host to travel; worms travel over networks and spread over the network connections without any human intervention.

Writer's identification The name and title of the author of a letter, placed near the bottom of the letter under the complimentary closing—also referred to as the *writer's signature block*.

Writer's signature block The name and title of the author of a letter, placed near the bottom of the letter, under the complimentary closing—also referred to as the *writer's identification*.

X-axis Another name for the horizontal (category) axis.

XML Paper Specification A Microsoft file format that creates an image of your document and that opens in the XPS viewer.

XPS The acronym for XML Paper Specification—a Microsoft file format that creates an image of your document and that opens in the XPS viewer.

Y-axis Another name for the vertical (value) axis.

YouTube The largest online video hosting site in the world.

Zip Compressing files.

Zoom The action of increasing or decreasing the size of the viewing area on the screen.

Index